INTERNATIONAL SALES LAW

A Global Challenge

This book brings together the top international sales law scholars from twenty-three countries to review the Convention on Contracts for International Sale of Goods (CISG) and its role in the unification of global sales law at present and into the future. The book covers three general research methodologies: (1) doctrinal or descriptive, (2) theoretical, and (3) practical. In the area of doctrinal–descriptive analysis, the substance of CISG rules is reviewed and alternative interpretations of those rules are analyzed. A comparative analysis is given of how numerous countries have accepted, interpreted, and applied the CISG. Theoretical insights are offered into the problems of uniform laws, the CISG's role in bridging the gap between the common and civil legal traditions, and the debate over the proper role of good faith in CISG jurisprudence. The practitioner perspective argues that the CISG should be viewed as a tool for furthering the interests of business clients.

The book includes a review of the case law relating to the interpretation and application of the provisions of the CISG; analyzes how the CISG has been recognized and implemented by national courts, as well as arbitral tribunals; offers insights into the problems of uniformity of application of an international sales convention; compares the CISG with the English Sale of Goods Act and places the CISG in the context of other texts of UNCITRAL; and analyzes the CISG from the practitioner's perspective, including how to use the CISG proactively.

Larry A. DiMatteo is the Huber Hurst Professor of Contract Law and Legal Studies at the Warrington College of Business Administration and Affiliate Professor at the Levin College of Law at the University of Florida. He is the author or editor of more than seventy scholarly publications including *International Sales Law: A Critical Analysis of the CISG* (2005) and *Commercial Contract Law: Transatlantic Perspectives* (2013). Professor DiMatteo obtained his J.D. from Cornell Law School, LL.M. from Harvard Law School, and Ph.D. in Business and Commercial Law from Monash University.

International Sales Law

A GLOBAL CHALLENGE

Edited by

Larry A. DiMatteo

Warrington College of Business Administration,
University of Florida

CAMBRIDGE
UNIVERSITY PRESS

CAMBRIDGE
UNIVERSITY PRESS

32 Avenue of the Americas, New York, NY 10013-2473, USA

Cambridge University Press is part of the University of Cambridge.

It furthers the University's mission by disseminating knowledge in the pursuit of
education, learning, and research at the highest international levels of excellence.

www.cambridge.org
Information on this title: www.cambridge.org/9781107020382

© Cambridge University Press 2014

First published 2014

Printed in the United States of America

A catalog record for this publication is available from the British Library.

Library of Congress Cataloging in Publication Data
International sales law : a global challenge / Larry A. DiMatteo, Warrington College of Business
Administration, University of Florida.
    pages cm
Includes bibliographical references and index.
ISBN 978-1-107-02038-2 (hardback)
1. Export sales contracts.   2. United Nations Convention on Contracts for the International Sale of
Goods (1980)   I. DiMatteo, Larry A., editor of compilation.
K1030.I585   2014
343.08'7–dc23   2013030074

ISBN 978-1-107-02038-2 Hardback

"Founding Father"

John Honnold
(1916–2011)

> "The only way to create a genuine and effective international legal system is to explore and appreciate the world's diverse views on challenging topics."
> *Harry Flechtner*

"The Great Scholar"

Peter Schlechtriem
(1933–2007)

> "Nonetheless, you had the firm impression that he had rather preferred to sit in his office and write one of his books or articles."
> *Ulrich Magnus*

"The Great Disseminator"

Al Kritzer
(1928–2010)

> "Al poured his heart and his soul, and his money, into building systems and networks which enabled us to share knowledge and insight. Now, with Al gone, it is up to us to ensure that we all continue to share."
> *Camilla Andersen*

"Society" of Scholars

In referencing Honnold, Schlechtriem, and Kritzer, Harry Flechtner notes that "I have often thought that the spirit and personalities of these wonderful people formed a distinctive culture around the CISG that partook of their character. I have often noticed what a remarkable group of scholars that have been attracted to the Convention as a major focus of their careers – thinkers who are not just bright and energetic, but truly friendly and other-centered."

Brief Contents

Contents

PART II: INTERPRETATION AND USE OF THE CISG

PART IV: REMEDIES AND DAMAGES

List of Contributors

Yehuda Adar Dr. Adar teaches at the University of Haifa in Israel. He works in the areas of contract law, private law theory, legal remedies, consumer law, and comparative law. He is the author of a book entitled *Contract Law: The Remedies – Towards Codification of the Civil Law* (2009) (in Hebrew), as well as many journal articles. His articles analyze the role of remedies in relational contract theory, remedies in mixed-jurisdiction countries, contributory negligence, mitigation, and punitive damages. He has also analyzed the new Israeli Civil Code and the possibility of unifying contract and tort remedies. Dr. Adar is a Lecturer in Private Law, Faculty of Law, at the University of Haifa. He earned his LL.B., LL.M., and LL.S. at Hebrew University.

Javier Solana Álvarez Mr. Álvarez graduated from Universidad Carlos III de Madrid in Law and Business Administration and was awarded the Premio Extraordinario Fin de Carrera for the highest grades among the students in the class of 2010. In 2009, he was awarded an Honorable Mention as Best Individual Oralist at the 16th Willem C. Vis International Commercial Arbitration Moot representing Universidad Carlos III de Madrid. He coached the team for the three following years. In 2011, Mr. Álvarez was awarded the "la Caixa" Fellowship to obtain a LL.M. at Harvard Law School. His main fields of research include arbitration, international sales of goods, and regulation of financial contracts.

Camilla Baasch Andersen Camilla Baasch Andersen is a Professor at University of Western Australia. She was previously a Senior Lecturer at the University of Leicester in the United Kingdom, a lecturer at the Centre for Commercial Law Studies at Queen Mary, University of London, and before that she was a PhD research and teaching Fellow at the University of Copenhagen in her native Denmark. She has lectured externally for several universities, including SOAS in London (UK), University of Essex (UK), University of Turku (Finland), and Victoria University (Melbourne, Australia). She has worked with the CISG Advisory Council and has served as the National Reporter for the United Kingdom for the International Academy of Comparative Law. Dr. Andersen was the founding coeditor of *The Journal of Comparative Law* and is a Fellow at the Institute of International Commercial Law at Pace Law School. She has written extensively on the CISG, including the recent *Practitioners Guide to the CISG* (with Mazzotta and Zeller, 2010) and numerous articles on uniformity of international law, the methodology of the CISG, and the examination and notification provisions of the CISG. She was also coeditor of *Sharing International Commercial Law across National Boundaries* (with

Ulrich Schroeter, 2008) which was written in honor of her mentor, Professor Albert H Kritzer.

Petra Butler Petra Butler is an Associate Professor at Victoria Wellington University in New Zealand. Previously, she has worked at the universities of Göttingen and Speyer (Germany) and was a clerk at the South African Constitutional Court. She won a Holgate Fellowship from Grey College, Durham University. Her publications include "Commentary on Articles 53 to 60 CISG" in *Commentary on the CISG* (Mistelis and Kroell, eds.), *UN Law on International Sales* (coauthored with Peter Schlechtriem, Springer, 2009); "New Zealand" in *The Law of Human Rights*, 2nd ed. (Clayton and Tomlinson, eds., Oxford, 2009); and "New Zealand and the CISG" in *The CISG and Its Impact on National Legal Systems* (Ferrari, ed., 2008).

Luca G. Castellani Mr. Castellani is a legal officer in the Secretariat of the United Nations Commission on International Trade Law (UNCITRAL), where he is tasked, inter alia, with the promotion of the adoption and uniform interpretation of UNCITRAL texts relating to sale of goods and electronic commerce. He joined the Office of Legal Affairs of the Secretariat at the United Nations in New York in 2001 and the UNCITRAL Secretariat in Vienna, Austria, in 2004; and he served as legal advisor to the United Nations Mission in Ethiopia and Eritrea (UNMEE) in Addis Ababa, Ethiopia, in 2008. He has published in the fields of international trade law and comparative law, focusing, in particular, on trade law reform in Africa, on aspects relating to the promotion of the CISG, and on electronic communications.

Martin Davies Martin Davies is the Admiralty Law Institute Professor of Maritime Law and Director of the Maritime Law Center at the Tulane University Law School. He previously taught at the University of Melbourne, Australia, where he was Harrison Moore Professor of Law. He serves on the editorial boards of *Lloyd's Maritime and Commercial Law Quarterly* and the *Melbourne Journal of International Law*. Professor Davies is the author of seven books and more than fifty articles and book chapters.

Larry A. DiMatteo Professor DiMatteo is the Huber Hurst Professor of Contract Law and Legal Studies at the Warrington College of Business Administration at the University of Florida, as well as an Affiliated Professor of Law at the Levin College of Law and at the Center for European Studies, both at the University of Florida. He holds a J.D. from Cornell University, a LL.M. from Harvard Law School, and a Ph.D. from Monash University (Australia). He is the author of numerous books and articles on contract law, international sales law, and legal theory. His most recent books include *International Contracting: Law and Practice*, 3rd ed. (Wolters Kluwer, 2013) and *Commercial Contract Law: Transatlantic Perspectives* (DiMatteo, Zhou, and Saintier, eds., Cambridge University Press, 2013). He was the 2011–2012 University of Florida Teacher-Scholar of the Year and was awarded a 2012 Fulbright Professorship.

Milena Djordjević Milena Djordjević is an Assistant Professor in the University of Belgrade, Faculty of Law, where she teaches International Commercial Law, International Commercial Arbitration, EU Trade Policy, and Legal English. She holds a LL.B. (U. Belgrade), LL.M. (U. Pittsburgh), and Dr. iur. (U. Belgrade). She also has coached the Belgrade Moot team for the Willem C. Vis International Commercial Arbitration

Moot for the past eleven years. Previously, she served as Legal Consultant at the USAID/ WTO Accession Project for former Yugoslavia, was a national delegate at the GTZ Open Regional Fund's project for the promotion of the CISG and arbitration in Southeast Europe, and a visiting professor at University of Pittsburgh. She is also an arbitrator at the arbitration courts attached to chambers of commerce in Serbia and Montenegro and does consulting work for domestic companies, institutions, and international organizations. Ms. Djordjević has published extensively on the CISG, arbitration, WTO law, and EU trade law, and she is one of the contributors to the latest commentary on the CISG edited by Stefan Kröll, Loukas Mistelis, and Pilar Perales Viscasillas. Ms. Djordjević's publications also include a monograph – *Commercial and Economic Law of Serbia* – coauthored with Professor Mirko Vasiljević and published by Kluwer Law International.

Sieg Eiselen Professor Eiselen is a Professor in Private Law at the University of South Africa. He is the secretary for the CISG Advisory Council. He has written more than forty articles in the areas of contract law, unjust enrichment, international trade law, e-commerce, and private international law. His CISG work includes: co-author of Volumes 4 and 5 with Albert Kritzer in Kritzer et al., *International Contract Manual: Guide to the Practical Application of the United Nations Convention on the International Sale of Goods* (2008); "The Purpose, Scope and Underlying Principles of the UNECIC" in Andersen and Schroeter, *Festschrift for Albert Kritzer* (2008); various chapters in Felemegas, *An International Approach to the Interpretation of the United Nations Convention on Contracts for the International Sale of Goods (1980) as Uniform Sales Law* (Cambridge University Press, 2007). Professor Eiselen's CISG research has focused on such areas as e-commerce and the CISG, remedies and damages, modification, anticipatory breach, and the charging of interest.

Hossam A. El-Saghir Professor El-Saghir is a Professor of Commercial Law in the Faculty of Law at Helwan University and obtained an LL.B in Law (1971) from Ain Shams University, Egypt. He obtained Higher Diplomas in Public Law (1973), Islamic Law (1974), and Private Law (1979), and a Ph.D. in Commercial Law (1987) from Cairo University. He also obtained a Master of Laws (LL.M) in Intellectual Property from Turin University, Italy, in 2003. From 1987 he taught commercial and intellectual property law in Ain Shams, Asiout, Menofia, Cairo, and Helwan Universities (Egypt). He was a visiting professor at Saint Louis University (1990–1991) and Pace University (1996–1997 and 1999) in the United States. He is the founding Director of the Middle East Center for International Commercial Law established with the cooperation of Pace University in 1998. He is also the founding Director of the Regional Institute for Intellectual Property established with the cooperation of the World Intellectual Property Organization (WIPO) in 2006 at Helwan University. The government has appointed him a member of several committees responsible for drafting commercial legislations including the Egyptian Intellectual Property Law. He has represented the WIPO as an intellectual property expert in several missions to provide advice to Arab countries, in addition to representing the WIPO at many conferences, workshops, and symposiums. He is a member of the International Association for the Advancement of Teaching and Research in Intellectual Property (ATRIP). He has written in the fields of commercial and intellectual property law including "Fundamental Breach of Contract: Remarks on the Manner in which the Principles of European Contract Law May Be Used to Interpret or Supplement Art. 25

of the CISG," in *An International Approach to the Interpretation of the United Nations Convention on Contracts for the International Sale of Goods (1980) as Uniform Sales Law*, (Felemegas, ed., Cambridge University Press, 2006) and "The Interpretation of the CISG in the Arab World," in *CISG Methodology* (Janssen and Meyer, eds., Sellier, 2009), as well as "Intellectual Property" in the *International Encyclopedia of Laws* series (Kluwer Law International, 2009). He practices law before the Court of Cassation, the Higher Administrative Court, and the Constitutional Court, and he was a Presidential appointment to the Board of Directors of the National Authority for Quality Assurance and Accreditation in Education.

Robert W. Emerson Professor Emerson is the Huber Hurst Professor of Business Law and Legal Studies at the University of Florida's Warrington College of Business. He is an expert on United States and international franchise law, and has written numerous books and articles and testified before the U.S. Congress and served as an invited speaker for the International Distribution Institute. A lecturer on comparative franchise law at numerous universities in the United States and Europe, Professor Emerson is an eleven-time winner of University of Florida teaching awards and seven-time winner of Academy of Legal Studies in Business awards for best paper. His most recent published articles include "Can Franchisee Associations Serve as a Substitute for Franchisee Protection Laws?," "Franchise Contract Interpretation: A Two-Standard Approach," "Franchise Encroachment," "Franchise Goodwill: 'Take a Sad Song and Make It Better,'" "Franchising and the Parol Evidence Rule," and "The French Huissier as a Model for U.S. Civil Procedure Reform." Professor Emerson is the sole North American member of the Conseil Scientifique of the International Association of Judicial Officers (Union Internationale des Huissiers de Justice – UIHJ) and was a reporter for the UIHJ's triennial World Congress (Cape Town, 2012).

Wolfgang Faber Professor Faber teaches in the Department of Private Law at the University of Salzburg, Austria. He was a Member of the Working Group on the "Transfer of Movables" within the Study Group on a European Civil Code, and he led the preparation of Book VIII of the Draft Common Frame of Reference (DCFR). His work was published in Christian von Bar and Eric Clive (eds.), *Principles, Definitions and Model Rules of European Private Law: Draft Common Frame of Reference (DCFR) Full Edition*, Volume 6 (2009), and in Brigitta Lurger and Wolfgang Faber, *Principles of European Law – Acquisition and Loss of Ownership of Goods (PEL Acq. Own.)* (2011). Professor Faber has also written a number of monographs on warranty law and contractual liability and articles on such subjects as consumer law, bank guarantees, personal injury, transferring ownership in movables, proprietary security rights in movables, warranty law, and the DCFR. He was a coeditor of a six-volume set entitled *National Reports on the Transfer of Movables in Europe* (2008–11) and *Rules for the Transfer of Movables: A Candidate for European Harmonization or National Reforms?* (Faber and Lurger, eds., 2008).

Edoardo Ferrante Professor Ferrante is affiliated with the Law School at the University at Torino, Italy, as an Assistant Professor in the Faculty of Law at the University of Turin, and has been a Fellow, researcher, and host at the Centre for European Private Law at the University of Münster, Germany. He has written numerous articles on and provided commentary on the EU Directive on guarantees in the sale of consumer goods, Unfair Contract Terms Directive, rules for insurance contracts, impossibility of performance, reforming the BGB, and the possibilities for a European contract law. Professor Ferrante has also written extensively on the comparative law of Germany and Italy. His CISG scholarship includes articles on the "Battle of Forms" and a general commentary on the CISG, as well as "Contractual Disclosure and Remedies under the Unfair Contract Terms Directive," in Howells, Janssen, and Schulze, eds., *Information Rights and Obligations*.

Harry M. Flechtner Professor Flechtner is a Professor of Law at the University of Pittsburgh, School of Law, where he joined the faculty in 1984. He teaches courses in Contracts and Commercial Transaction in Goods (domestic and international sales and leases) as well as a seminar on International Sales Law, and he has for many years coached the team from the University of Pittsburgh in the Willem C. Vis International Arbitration Moot. He is a five-time winner of the University of Pittsburgh School of Law's Excellence-in-Teaching Award and a recipient of the Chancellor's Teaching Award from the University of Pittsburgh. He teaches abroad frequently, including as a Visiting Professor at the University of Salzburg (Austria) in spring 2012 under a Fulbright Teaching and Research grant. Professor Flechtner has published extensively on international and domestic commercial law, with particular emphasis on international sales law; his publications include the fourth edition (2009) of *John Honnold's Uniform Law for International Sales under the 1980 United Nations Convention*, which Professor Flechtner edited and updated, and *Drafting Contracts under the CISG* (with Brand and Walter, eds., Oxford, 2008.). He speaks frequently in the United States and abroad on commercial law topics, and he has been cited by the Solicitor General of the United States as "one of the leading academic authorities on the [United Nations Sales] Convention." Professor Flechtner serves as a National Correspondent for the United States at the United Nations Commission on International Trade Law (UNCITRAL); he was one of the original group of experts who created the UNCITRAL Digest of Case Law on the CISG, and he served as coordinator for the team of nine international legal academics that produced a ten-year update of the Digest. He is a graduate of Harvard College; he received his J.D. from Harvard Law School and a M.A. in literature from Harvard University.

Morton M. Fogt Professor Fogt is professor in civil and international law in the Department of Law, School of Business and Social Science, at Aarhus University in Denmark. At Aarhus University, Professor Fogt teaches an Aarhus Summer University course on CISG and a semester course on Private International Law in English and gives Danish lectures on contract law, the law of obligation, and property law. He has held permanent positions at the University in Kiel, Germany, and at the Baltic Universities in Vilnius, Riga, and Tartu. Professor Fogt is a guest professor at the University of Kiel, Tarty, and Louvain la Neuve where he teaches the CISG. In addition, Professor Fogt is a temporary member of St. John's College, Oxford, and is attached to the Institute of European and Comparative Law, Oxford University. During the Danish Presidency of The European Union in 2012, Professor Fogt was Chair of the EU Council Working Party on Civil Law Matters and the negotiations on the European Commission Proposal for a Common European Sales Law (CESL) from 2011. His many writings in English, German, French, and Danish include publications in the area of application and scope of the CISG, mixed contracts, stipulation and interpretation of freight prepaid delivery clauses, reform of Part II of the CISG, timely objection and avoidance of contract in case of goods with rapid obsolescence under the CISG, Nordic law on suretyship and the protection of private sureties, European perspectives on producers' liability, and direct producers' liability for nonconformity, the civil law consequence of corruption in international trade and private international law.

Claire M. Germain Professor Germain is the Associate Dean for Legal Information and Clarence J. TeSelle Professor of Law in the Frederic G. Levin College of Law at the University of Florida. She is the Edward Cornell Law Librarian and Professor of Law, Emerita, at the Cornell Law School where she also was the Director of Dual Degree Programs, Paris and Berlin, 2002–11. She has served as president of the American Association of Law Libraries. Professor Germain is currently the Chair of the Law Libraries Section of the International Federation of Library Associations (IFLA). In 2007, Germain was honored with the Chevalier de la Légion d'Honneur (Knight, Legion of Honor) medal, France's highest honor, for her efforts in bridging American and French legal cultures. She is the author of the award-winning *Germain's Transnational Law Research* and numerous articles, notably on French statutory interpretation and the French criminal jury. Professor Germain teaches a course on French Law and publishes and teaches in the areas of French law, comparative law, and international legal research.

Helena Haapio Helena Haapio, LL.M., MQ (Master of Laws, Master of Quality), works as an International Contract Counsel with Lexpert Ltd. (www.lexpert.com), based in Helsinki, Finland. She helps her clients become more successful by applying a proactive approach to law; one that helps them achieve better business results and avoid legal trouble. After completing legal studies at the University of Turku and Cambridge University, Ms. Haapio served as in-house counsel for a major manufacturing company in Finland, Norway, Sweden, and the United States. Nominated Finland's "Export Educator of the Year," she regularly conducts training workshops. She is the coauthor of *Proactive Law for Managers* (Gower, 2011) and *A Short Guide to Contract Risk* (Gower, 2013), and she acts as an arbitrator in cross-border contract disputes. Ms. Haapio's current research focuses on ways to improve the usability of commercial contracts. Her goal is to fundamentally change the way contracts and the law are perceived and taught, allowing businesses to use the law to create new value and innovate in areas often neglected.

André Janssen Dr. Janssen is a senior research Fellow at the Centre for European Private Law and the Centre of International Trade Law at the University of Münster. He is an editor of the *European Review of Private Law*. He previously acted as the country reporter for German law within the Study Group on a European Civil Code, Principles of European Private Law: Commercial Agency, Distribution, Franchise. Dr. Janssen has written more than one hundred books, book chapters, and articles on European private and business law, comparative law, and international sales law. He recently coedited a book entitled *CISG Methodology* in 2009 with Dr. Olaf Meyer. His CISG work includes research on the relationship between the CISG and consumer protection laws, inspection and notice of nonconformity, battle of forms, general conditions, general principles of the CISG, and the application of the CISG in Dutch courts.

Sörren Kiene Sörren Kiene is currently a lawyer at the law firm of BRANDI Rechtsanwälte where he practices in the areas of commercial law and international business law. Previously, he was a Research Assistant at the Centre for European Private Law and the Institute for International Business Law at the University of Münster, Germany. In 2007, Dr. Kiene held a guest lectureship at Beijing University of Political Science and Law. He has published on such topics as the role of general principles in the CISG, defects in title and the duty to give notice, the right of avoidance in the CISG compared with German law, and principles of EC contract law.

Tadas Klimas Professor Klimas is the former dean of a law school in Lithuania and former Chief Legal Counsel to the Speaker of the Lithuanian Parliament. He is the author of *Comparative Contract Law: A Transystemic Approach with an Emphasis on the Continental Law* (2006). He has been awarded the title of Cavalier of the Lithuanian Order of Merit by presidential decree. He is also a former Special Agent of the FBI and is the recipient of one of the United States's top honors: the National Intelligence Medal of Achievement, which was presented to him by the DCI and the Secretary of Defense, Robert Gates. Professor Klimas has taught law in the United States, Lithuania, Viet Nam, Brazil, and Spain.

Stefan Kröll Stefan Kröll is a lawyer in Cologne (Köln) and an Honorary Professor at the Bucerius Law School (Hamburg). He is a German national correspondent to UNCITRAL for arbitration and international commercial law and has been retained by UNCITRAL as one of three experts drafting the Digest on the MAL. Professor Kröll is a Visiting Reader at the School of International Arbitration, CCLS – Queen Mary University, London, and a member of the board of editors or advisory board of several international journals including the *IHR* (*Internationales Handelsrecht – International Commercial Law*). He is the author of several books and more than fifty articles and book chapters in the areas of national and international business law. These include his book *Comparative International Commercial Arbitration* (with Lew and Mistelis, 2003) and a commentary on the *The UN-Convention on the International Sale of Goods* CISG: (coedited with Loukas Mistelis and Pilar Perales Viscasillas). Professor Kröll is a member of the Academic Council of the Institute for Transnational Arbitration at the Center for American and International Law (Dallas) and since 2012 has been a director of the Vis-Moot Court.

Sonja A. Kruisinga Professor Kruisinga is an Associate Professor in Commercial Law at the Molengraaff Institute for Private Law of Utrecht University in the Netherlands, where she teaches International Commercial Law and Company Law. She has written a monograph entitled *Non-conformity in the 1980 United Nations Convention on Contracts for the International Sale of Goods: A Uniform Concept?* (2004). She was a visiting researcher at Columbia Law School in 2006. Kruisinga has also researched in the areas of the impact of uniform law (CISG, UNIDROIT Principles, Draft Common Frame of Reference) on Dutch law, INCOTERMS, letters of comfort, and letters of credit. She also has written on the draft EU Regulation on a Common European Sales Law, standard terms and the CISG, and the application of CISG in Dutch courts.

Kaon Lai Kaon Lai is currently serving as the Assistant Law Clerk to Hon. Sandra B. Sciortino, J.S.C., in Orange County, New York. She was a Research Assistant at the Pace Institute of International Commercial Law from 2010 to 2012.

Ole Lando Professor Lando is Professor Emeritus; he received his dr. jur. from Copenhagen University and Dr., *honoris causa*, from Stockholm School of Economics,

University of Osnabrück, University of Fribourg, and University of Würzburg. He was professor of comparative law at the Copenhagen Business School (CBS) from 1963 to 1992. Professor Lando was Chairman of the Commission on European Contract Law that drafted the Principles of European Contract Law (PECL) published in 2000 and 2003. He was also a member of the Working Group for the preparation of the Unidroit Principles of International Commercial Contracts. Professor Lando has published many books and articles on comparative law and private international law. In 2001, he was awarded the German Alexander von Humboldt Research Award for Foreign Humanists; in 2008, the Nordic Lawyers Prize; and in 2010, the A. S. Ørsted Prize Medal in Gold.

Li Wei Li Wei is Professor of Law at China University of Political Science and Law in Beijing, China. His research focuses on the CISG, WTO, and international trade law. He is the author of *Comments and Interpretation of CISG* (in Chinese, 2009), "Study on Some Cases on the Formation of the Contracts for International Sale of Goods: Comparison of the CISG, UCC and PRC Contract Law" in the *Journal of Comparative Law*, and a chapter entitled "The Interpretation of the CISG in China" in *CISG Methodology* (Janssen and Meyer, eds., 2009). Professor Li has also published "The Contribution of CISG to the Uniform Application of International Business Law – Marking the 20th Anniversary of CISG Entry into Force," 15 *Journal of International Economic Law* (2008); and "On China's Withdrawing Its Reservation to Article 1b CISG," 5 *The Jurist* (2012).

Corinne Widmer Lüchinger Corinne Widmer Lüchinger is a Professor of Private Law, Comparative Law, and Private International Law at the University of Basel in Switzerland, as well as a lecturer at the University of Zurich. She is the author of numerous publications on contract and tort law, private international law, international sales law (CISG), and comparative law. Her most recent book is entitled *A Civil Lawyer's Introduction to Anglo-American Law: Torts*, published in 2008. She has written on Articles 30 through 34 of the CISG in *Schlechtriem and Schwenzer Commentary on the Convention on the International Sale of Goods*, with a particular focus on the interplay between the place of delivery under Article 31 CISG and jurisdictional rules on the place of performance, as well as on the CISG in legal practice.

Ulrich Magnus Professor Magnus was formerly a Professor of Law at the University of Hamburg; Chair for Civil Law, Private International Law and Comparative Law. He has written twenty books and almost 200 articles in these fields. He was previously a Judge at the Court of Appeal of Hamburg; Executive Vice-Director of the European Centre for Tort and Insurance Law in Vienna; Germany's National Correspondent at UNCITRAL; Director and Co-speaker of the International Max-Planck-Research School for Maritime Affairs; Member of the German Council for Private International Law, Member of the European Group on Tort Law and of the European Acquis Group; editor of two book series and the legal periodical *Internationalales Handelsrecht* (*IHR*). His many books, chapters, and articles on the CISG include a commentary on the CISG in German, CISG and INCOTERMS, CISG interpretive methodology, incorporating standard terms under the CISG, right to compensation and interest, battle of forms, delayed performance, principle of good faith, avoidance, impact of the CISG on European legislation, nonconformity, *force majeure* and the CISG, and open price term, among others.

Virginia G. Maurer Professor Maurer is a Professor of Business Law and Legal Studies, the Darden Restaurants Professor of Management, and Chair of the Poe Center for Business Ethics at the University of Florida's Warrington College of Business. She is the Director of the Elizabeth B. and William F. Poe, Sr., Center for Business Ethics Education and Research. Professor Maurer is a past president of the Academy of Legal Studies in Business and former editor-in-chief of the *American Business Law Journal*. She provided an early overview of the CISG soon after it went into force. She is also a coauthor of *International Sales Law: A Critical Analysis of CISG Jurisprudence* (Cambridge University Press, 2005).

Francesco G. Mazzotta Francesco Mazzotta received his J.D. at the University of Naples (Italy) and a J.D. at the University of Pittsburgh, School of Law, and is admitted to the bar in New York and Italy. He is currently a Judicial Law Clerk to Justice J. Michael Eakin, Supreme Court of Pennsylvania. Mr. Mazzotta is also a Fellow at the Institute of International Commercial Law at the Pace University School of Law. He has written numerous articles, chapters, and commentaries on the CISG in such areas as the preservation of goods, restitution, the impact of the United Nations's electronic communications convention on the CISG, the writing requirement for arbitration agreements and the CISG, avoidance, and right to interest.

Olaf Meyer Dr. Meyer has more than ten years of research and teaching experience in international commercial law. He is currently in residence at the Centre of European Law and Politics (ZERP) at the University of Bremen, where he chairs a major research project on corruption in international contracts. His main research areas include comparative law, international contracts, uniform commercial law, and arbitration. He coedited a book in 2009 with Dr. André Janssen entitled *CISG Methodology*. He has written on the CISG in practice and CISG interpretation, as well as articles on the Principles of European Contract Law and the UNIDROIT Principles.

Marie Stefanini Newman Professor Newman has been the Director of the Pace Law Library since 1999. She teaches a course in Advanced Legal Research. For many years, she served as database manager for Pace's Institute of International Commercial Law and directed the work involved in producing the Institute's award-winning database devoted to the CISG (cisgw3). Professor Newman's article on quality control procedures for legal databases on the Internet won a *Law Library Journal* Article of the Year Award. Professor Newman is the editor of a book entitled *Remedies for Non-Performance: Perspectives from CISG, UNIDROIT Principles and PECL*.

Ann M. Olazábal Professor Olazábal is Professor of Business Law and Ethics and Vice Dean for Undergraduate Business Education at the University of Miami School of Business Administration, where she teaches business ethics, contract law, and international commercial transactions to undergraduates, graduates, and executives. Professor Olazábal is a former editor-in-chief of the *American Business Law Journal* and the recipient of numerous teaching and research awards. Her comprehensive work cataloging recent U.S. case law under the CISG was published in the American Bar Association's *The Business Lawyer* (2012).

Vladimir Pavić Professor Pavić is an Associate Professor in the University of Belgrade Faculty of Law. He teaches and specializes in Private International Law, International

Commercial Arbitration, International Business Law, Foreign Direct Investment, and Competition Law and publishes extensively in these areas. He is currently a vice president of the Permanent Court of Arbitration attached to the Serbian Chamber of Commerce. Professor Pavić is a listed arbitrator at the permanent arbitration centers in Serbia, Croatia, Macedonia, and Montenegro and has acted as arbitrator, counsel, and expert witness in a number of international commercial arbitrations and litigations. He is listed in the *Global Arbitration Review 2013 Who's Who in International Commercial Arbitration*.

Pilar Perales Viscasillas Professor Perales Viscasillas is a Commercial Law Professor at University Carlos III of Madrid and formerly was the Chair of Commercial Law at the University of La Rioja. She has authored or coauthored a number of books on the CISG, commercial law, and comparative law. They include *Formation of Contracts in CISG, International Commercial Law, The Uniform Law*, and *Arbitrability and Arbitration Agreements in Corporations*. Professor Perales Viscasillas is a member of the CISG Advisory Council, a Spanish Representative to UNCITRAL in the Working Group on International Commercial Arbitration, a member of the Chartered Institute of Arbitrators, and an associate member of the General Commission for the Codification of Commercial Law in Spain. Her many CISG articles research such areas as the principle of good faith, unilateral contracts or contracts by silence, formation, determination of interest rates, battle of forms, and the interrelationship between the CISG and the UNIDROIT Principles.

Sylvaine Poillot-Peruzzetto Professor Poillot-Peruzzetto teaches at Université des Sciences Sociales de Toulouse where she is a Professor of Private Law and Vice-President in Chargée des relations Internationales. She is the author of a book and numerous articles on such subjects as international law, European law, and company law. In 2005, she created the Masters of International and Comparative Law Program at Toulouse 1. In 2007, she created an English-language version of the master's program. She previously served as Director of the Master droit international européen et comparé, Director of the DESS Juriste International, and creator and Director of the Laboratoire de droit at the University de Toulouse.

Burghard Piltz Burghard Piltz is a Senior Partner in the law firm of BRANDI with more than 65 professionals and offices in Bielefeld, Detmold, Gütersloh, Hannover, Minden, Paderborn, and Leipzig, as well as in Paris and Beijing. Professor Piltz specializes in commercial and international business law, particularly international sales and related transactions. He previously was a lecturer at the University of Hamburg and he still teaches at the University of Bielefeld. His many positions in service to the academy and the practice of law include being Chairman of the Committee for European Contract Law of the German Federal Chamber of Lawyers, as well as being the copublisher of *Internationales Handelsrecht, European Journal of Commercial Contract Law*, and *Nederlands Tijdschrift voor Handelsrecht*. He is currently the President of the Arbitration Centre established by the German–Argentinean Chamber of Commerce in Buenos Aires and is a member of the Task Force on International Sales established by the International Chamber of Commerce (ICC). Professor Piltz is also Conseiller du Président of the Union Internationale des Avocats (UIA). His recent publications include *Internationales Kaufrecht*, 2nd ed. (C. H. Beck, Munich, 2008) and commentaries on Articles 30–34 of the

CISG – Commentary (C. H. Beck, Munich, 2011). He is the author of more than one hundred publications.

Jan Ramberg Professor Ramberg is an Emeritus Professor at Stockholm University, where he previously served as the Dean of the Faculty of Law and specialized in the research of commercial and maritime law. He was the first Rector of Riga Graduate School of Law. He is an international arbitration court judge and was a member of the International Arbitration Court of London. Professor Ramberg is known for his work in the area of international commercial transactions and the law of carriage of goods. He served as Vice President of the International Chamber of Commerce's Commission on Commercial Law and Practice and as Chairman of the working groups, which in 1980, 1990, and 2000 prepared *INCOTERMS* revisions. His *ICC Guide to INCOTERMS* is the foremost authority on international trade terms. In addition, Professor Ramberg previously served as Chair of the CISG Advisory Council, President of the Maritime Law Association of Sweden, member of the editorial board of *Lloyd's Maritime and Commercial Law Quarterly*, and President of the Board of the Scandinavian Maritime Law Institute. He is an honorary vice president of the Comité Maritime International and an honorary member of FIATA. His research has been published in English, French, Spanish, Russian, Chinese, Arabic, German, Italian, Ukrainian, and Finnish, and, of course, Swedish.

Vikki Rogers Vikki Rogers is the Director of the Institute of International Commercial Law at Pace University Law School and an Adjunct Law Professor at Pace and Fordham Law Schools where she teaches international sales law and a practicum on international arbitration. Ms. Rogers is responsible for maintaining the award-winning online CISG Database and is an editor of the UNCITRAL CISG Digest. The Institute's database of legal information on the CISG is recognized as the world's most comprehensive source for CISG case law, arbitral law, and scholarly works. She also represents the Institute as an NGO observer in Working Groups II and III at UNCITRAL, and is an expert advisor at UNCITRAL for Working Group III on ODR. She developed and manages the online Certificate Program on International Commercial Law and International Alternative Dispute Resolution offered by the Institute.

Ulrich G. Schroeter Ulrich G. Schroeter is Professor of Law at the University of Mannheim (Germany), where he holds the Chair for Private Law, International Corporate Law, and European Business Law and is also Director of the Institute for Corporate Law (IURUM). He previously served as Acting Professor at the University of Münster and as Assistant Professor at Albert-Ludwigs-University Freiburg (Germany). His research interests include international corporate law; international commercial law and contract law, in particular the Vienna Sales Convention of 1980 (CISG); international, European, and German financial markets law; German and European private and business law; and the law of international arbitration. He is a contributor to the *Schlechtriem and Schwenzer Commentary on the Convention on the International Sale of Goods (CISG)* (3rd edition, Oxford, 2010) in which he, inter alia, authored the sections on formation of contract (Articles 14–24 CISG), fundamental breach of contract (Article 25 CISG), and modification of contracts (Article 29 CISG). In addition, he served as rapporteur to the CISG Advisory Council (CISG-AC) for its Opinion on Declarations under Articles 95 and 96 CISG.

Ingeborg Schwenzer Professor Schwenzer is a Chaired Professor for Private and Comparative Law at the University of Basel where she is Director of the Global Sales Law Project and was previously the Dean of the Faculty of Law. Professor Schwenzer is an Associate Member of the International Academy of Comparative Law. She is the editor and principal author of the *Schlechtriem and Schwenzer Commentary on the UN Convention on the International Sale of Goods*, published in German, English, Spanish, and Chinese. Her other books include *International Sales Law* (with Christiana Fountoulakis) in 2007 and *International Commerce and Arbitration* in 2008. Professor Schwenzer is the Chair of the CISG Advisory Council. She has published widely in the areas of comparative law, international commercial law and arbitration, and the law of obligations, and is regularly called upon to act as counsel, expert witness, and arbitrator in these fields. Professor Schwenzer has written numerous articles on the CISG covering areas such as nonconformity, examination and notice, avoidance, Articles 35–43, remedies and damages, principle of uniformity, excuse (*force majeure* and hardship), countertrade, and contract formation, as well as problems of regional and global unification of sales law.

Jan M. Smits Professor Smits is Professor of European Private Law at Maastricht University and Academic Director of the Maastricht European Private Law Institute. He is also Research Professor of Comparative Legal Studies at the University of Helsinki. Previously, he was the Distinguished Professor of European Private Law and Comparative Law at Tilburg University. His research interests include European private law, comparative law, and legal theory, as well as the harmonization of law. He has written extensively on European private law including on issues relating to the harmonization of European law and comparative law. Professor Smits has published more than 150 books, book chapters, and articles. His authored or edited books include *Elgar Encyclopedia of Comparative Law* (2nd edition, 2012), *The Mind and Method of the Legal Academic* (2012), *The Need for a European Contract Law: Empirical and Legal Perspectives* (2005), and *The Making of European Private Law: Toward a Ius Commune Europaeum as a Mixed Legal System* (2002).

Lisa Spagnolo Lisa Spagnolo lectures at the Faculty of Law at Monash University in Melbourne, Australia. She previously practiced in the law of insolvency, banking, derivatives, stand-still agreements, and financial restructuring at Minter Ellison, one of Australia's leading law firms. Her papers on the CISG have been published in the *Journal of Private International Law*, *Melbourne Journal of International Law*, and the *Temple International & Comparative Law Journal*. She acts as an articles editor for the *Vindobona Journal of International Commercial Law and Arbitration*, is a member of the Roundtable on Consumer Law and the Australian Consumer Research Network, and has acted as an expert advisor to the International Section of the New York State Bar Association. She is presently Rapporteur for the CISG Advisory Council for an Opinion on Article 6, and she participated in the UNCITRAL Expert Group Meeting held in Seoul, Korea. Ms. Spagnolo also coedits a volume that presents papers of the annual MAA CISG Schlechtriem Conference.

Aneta Spaic Professor Spaic is an assistant professor on the Law Faculty and Faculty of Political Science at the University of Montenegro, where she teaches Introduction to Law, International Commercial Law, and Media Law. She was appointed as the national correspondent by the government of Montenegro to UNCITRAL in 2010. Professor Spaic has taught the Law of International Business Transactions at the Washington and Lee Law School. In 2010, she visited Washington College of Law, American University, where she completed work on her monograph, *Mediation in Commercial Disputes*. She is also the author of a monograph entitled *Legal Aspects of Mitigating Risks in Project Finance*, as well as a number of articles in the areas of commercial law and legal doctrine.

Matthias Spilker Matthias Spilker is a lawyer at the international law firm Bird & Bird, LLP, in the field of Commercial Law in Frankfurt (Main). He was a research assistant at the Institute for International Business Law and the Centre for European Private Law at the University of Münster. He completed his Master of Laws at the University of the West of England (Bristol) and his PhD and diploma iuris at the University of Münster. He was also a research Fellow at the Université Jean Moulin (Lyon III) and is a member of the bar association in Frankfurt (Main), as well as the Vereinigung Henri Capitant Deutschland e.V. (Association Henry Capitant – Germany).

Marco Torsello Marco Torsello is Professor of Comparative Private Law at the University of Verona School of Law. He was previously tenured Research Professor at the University of Bologna School of Law, and he served as a visiting professor at numerous universities, including Columbia Law School, NYU School of Law, Fordham Law School, University of Pittsburgh School of Law, and University of Paris Ouest Nanterre La Defense. Professor Torsello has published in the areas of comparative law and uniform law, with a focus on several aspects of the CISG, including preliminary agreements, remedies, and the application of the CISG in Italy and other domestic legal systems. In recent years, he provided a chapter on "Preliminary Agreements and CISG Contracts" in *Drafting Contracts under the CISG* (Oxford, 2008) and an entry on "Remedies for Breach of Contract" in the *Elgar Encyclopedia of Comparative Law* (Cheltenham/Northampton, 2012). Professor Torsello is also the coauthor with Aldo Frignani of a book on International Contracts (*Il contratto internazionale Diritto comparato e prassi commerciale*, 2010).

Bruno Zeller Professor Zeller is a Professor of International Law at the University of Western Australia. In 2008, he was appointed as an arbitrator by the Maritime Law Association of Australia and New Zealand. Professor Zeller is the author or coauthor of a number of recent books on the CISG. They include *CISG and the Unification of International Trade Law, Damages under the Convention on Contracts for the International Sale of Goods* (Oxford University Press, 2007), and, most recently, *A Practitioner's Guide to the CISG* (Juris, 2010). He is also the author of more than three dozen chapters and articles on the CISG. His articles on the CISG cover such areas as CISG and China, principle of good faith, CISG Article 7, nonconformity of goods, *Nachfrist* notice, CISG and cyberspace, interpretation, CISG and parole evidence, fundamental breach, damages, CISG and equitable estoppel, mitigation, and excuse. Professor Zeller is a Fellow of the Australian Institute for Commercial Arbitration and the Panel of Arbitrators (MLAANZ); and Associate, The Institute for Logistics and Supply Chain Management; a Visiting Professor at the Institut fur Anwaltsrecht, Humboldt University, Berlin; and a Visiting Professor at Stetson Law School, Florida

Qi "George" Zhou Professor Zhou is an Associate Professor at the University of Leeds. He previously was a Lecturer at the University of Sheffield, School of Law, in the United

Kingdom. Previously, he was a practicing attorney in the People's Republic of China. His research interests are in the areas of contract law, commercial law, and regulation, as well as law and economics. Dr. Zhou is a member of the Standing Committee of the UK Chinese Law Association, an assistant editor of the *Journal of International Trade Law and Policy*, and a member of the Institute of Commercial Law Study. He has researched such areas as efficient breach, remedies and unconscionable contracts, misrepresentation, and unilateral mistake. Most recently, Dr. Zhou talked on "The Interaction between Contract Law Reform and Economic Development in China from 1978 to 2010," at the Institute for Global Law and Policy at Harvard University.

Preface

On 11–12 November 2011, a group of internationally recognized scholars – from more than two dozen countries and six continents – convened at the University of Florida. Papers were presented by scholars representing the civil, common, Islamic, mixed, and socialist market legal systems. The countries represented at the conference included Argentina, Australia, Austria, Canada, Colombia, Denmark, Egypt, Finland, France, Germany, Israel, Italy, Mexico, Montenegro, The Netherlands, the People's Republic of China, Saudi Arabia, Serbia, Slovak Republic, South Africa, Sweden, Switzerland, the United Kingdom, and the United States. Between those in attendance at the conference and the full complement of contributors to this book, the total country representation reached thirty with subsequent contributions coming from Lithuania, New Zealand, and Spain.

The title of the conference was "The Global Challenge of International Sales Law." Within this umbrella, the United Nations Convention on Contracts for the International Sale of Goods (CISG) was analyzed from numerous perspectives. The diversity of the subject areas and scholars allowed for a better understanding of the issues still confronting the CISG and its application. The scholars and practitioners that wrote papers for this book provided original research that has resulted in numerous insights not thoroughly explored previously. This book's goal is to provide this scholarship to a broader audience encompassing scholars, practitioners, judges, arbitrators, and students.

The purposes of the conference were three-fold. First, the conference sought to advance CISG scholarship. In this regard, the conference structure was constructed from a preformed table of contents. In this way, the conversion of the papers presented to book form was undertaken within a holistic framework. The papers were grouped into six parts: "Introductory Materials"; a review of the case law relating to the interpretation and application of the "Substantive Provisions of the CISG"; a series of "Country Analyses" analyzing how the CISG has been recognized and implemented by the judicial and arbitral courts of a given nation; "Insights" into the problems of uniformity of application of an international sales convention and whether the CISG can act as a bridge between the common and civil law systems; "CISG in Context," which compares the CISG with a competing system of rules represented by the English Sale of Goods Act, the CISG in the context of other texts of the United Nations Commission on International Trade Law (UNCITRAL), and the substantive area of precontractual liability as it relates to the CISG; and finally, a "Practitioner's Perspective," which covers the decision of legal counsel to exclude, ignore, or use the CISG, as well as how to use the CISG proactively.

In the end, this book uses three general research methodologies: (1) doctrinal or descriptive, (2) theoretical, and (3) practical. In the area of doctrinal–descriptive analysis, the substance of CISG rules is reviewed and alternative interpretations of those rules are analyzed. A comparative analysis is given of how numerous countries have accepted, interpreted, and applied the CISG. Theoretical insights are offered into the problems of uniform laws, the civil–common law divide and the CISG's role in bridging the gap between the two legal traditions, and the debate over the proper role of good faith in CISG jurisprudence. The view of the practitioner perspective argues that the CISG should be viewed as an opportunity to further the interests of business clients.

A few additional notes are required. There is a preconceived connection between Parts III–IV and V–VI. The substantive provisions reviewed in Parts III–IV are then used as a template for the country analyses found in Parts V–VI. Parts V–VI apply the substantive topics covered in Parts III–IV and analyzes them in relationship to particular countries' CISG case law. Second, the countries selected for analysis are a diverse sampling of countries and legal systems. This diversity includes Western Europe, where the deep jurisprudence, literature, and commentaries provide the anchor for understanding the CISG and its civilian nature. These countries include Austria, France, Germany, Italy, The Netherlands, Spain, and Switzerland. Separate chapters analyze the use of the CISG at the regional level: Baltic countries, the Nordic countries, and Southeastern Europe. Continental reports are provided under the titles of the United States and Canada and Central and South America. Asia is represented by a report on the People's Republic of China. Finally, reports are provided for Australia and New Zealand. An important analysis of the application of the CISG within an Islamic legal system is given through a country analysis of Egypt. Finally, another report analyzes the CISG and the Israeli legal system.

The conference and book provided a forum for CISG scholars to gather and discuss the CISG's role in the world at present and into the future. The conference also honored three visionaries without whom the CISG would never have come into existence and would not have achieved a high level of success – John Honnold, Peter Schlectriem, and Albert Kritzer.

I would like to thank the sponsors that provided the funding and support for making such a large undertaking possible. The major financial support was provided by the University of Florida Center for International Business Research and Education and the Warrington College of Business Administration. Additional financial support was provided by the University of Florida's Levin College of Law, University of Florida's Center for European Studies, and the University of Florida's Office of Research. The conference was also sponsored and promoted by the United Nations Commission on International Trade Law and Pace University's Institute for International Commercial Law.

Tributes

In Memory of John Honnold

On January 21, 2011, John Honnold, the William A. Schnader Professor of Commercial Law Emeritus at the University of Pennsylvania Law School, died at the age of ninety-five. All interested in the CISG know his name and have benefited from his scholarship. Some of you, like me, had the privilege and honor of meeting him personally. I had the extraordinary luck of meeting him several times during my days as a junior academic. John's insights into international commercial law, his passion for promoting and understanding the topic, his unique role in shaping the area in the second half of the twentieth century and the resulting authority with which he spoke on the topic, his obvious desire to understand the views of others, his understanding and appreciation of those views, and the sweetness of personality that allowed him to encourage their expression – all these combined to make him one of the biggest influences on my career. I know there are many others who would say the same.

All who met John knew immediately that they were in the presence of a great man. John's professional life encompassed four or five careers that would, separately, be proud accomplishments for the most talented and ambitious. After receiving his B.A. from the University of Illinois, where he met his future wife and lifelong helpmate and colleague Annemarie, John attended Harvard Law School. He graduated with honors and served as editor of the *Harvard Law Review*. He hinted at the international bent of his future by honeymooning with Annemarie in Europe on the eve of the outbreak of the Second World War. When he returned to the States, John began the first (and shortest) of his careers – working on Wall Street (at a modest salary), living in Brooklyn, and beginning a family with Annemarie. Their family eventually came to include three children – Carol, Heidi, and Edward.

John soon began his next career, which took him to public service and Washington, D.C., to work for the Securities Exchange Commission and, during World War II, as Chief of the Court Review Branch in the Chief Counsel's Office of Price Administration. Then, in 1946, John joined the law faculty at the University of Pennsylvania, where he taught and authored casebooks on constitutional and commercial law. It was from this position that John took a key role in one of the most significant law reform projects in U.S. commercial law history – the development and enactment of the Uniform Commercial Code. In 1958, John entered the arena of international commercial law when he taught the subject, under a Fulbright grant, at the University of Paris Law School. As a result of his talent and passion, he was soon representing the United States at the Hague Diplomatic Conference on International Law.

But John was not finished with public service – and this time the public service was of a particularly courageous kind. In 1965, John served as chief counsel of the Lawyers' Committee for Civil Rights in Mississippi, and he became a Director and a member of the Executive Committee of the Board of the American Friends Service Committee. His dedication to social justice was not just a public cause; it was a personal commitment. John and Annemarie resigned from the swim club where they lived because of its racially discriminatory policies. During the "red scare" days he joined other academics in signing an open letter against the proposed Subversive Activities Control Act of 1948, and as a delegate to the 1968 Democratic Party National Convention he publicly criticized the tactics of the Chicago police in quelling street demonstrations. But the call of international service grew increasingly strong for John. After teaching at the Salzburg Seminar in American Studies, he began to focus professionally on international commercial arbitration.

In 1969, in the most significant development for those interested in uniform international commercial law, John was appointed Director of the International Trade Law Division of the Office of Legal Affairs of the U.N. Secretariat, which made him the Secretary of the then-fledgling UNCITRAL. He oversaw the work of UNCITRAL as secretary from 1969 to 1974, guiding the critical early efforts that led to the creation of the CISG. When he left UNCITRAL to rejoin the University of Pennsylvania Law Faculty in 1974 (succeeded as UNCITRAL's Secretary by Willem Vis) he remained actively involved in drafting the treaty text. In 1980, he led the U.S. delegation (and played a crucial role) at the diplomatic conference in Vienna, where the text of the CISG was finalized and approved for signature and ratification by states.

Thereafter, John worked tirelessly to elucidate the significance and meaning of the CISG. Two milestones of particular note followed quickly. In 1981, John published his seminal commentary on the CISG: *Uniform Law for International Sales under the 1980 U.N. Convention*. This work, now in its fourth edition (which this author is extremely honored to have taken over editing and updating), quickly became one of the most authoritative and cited works on the CISG – a distinction due (no doubt) to John's unique knowledge of and insights into the creation of the CISG, to his understanding of its global commercial and political significance, to his appreciation of the extraordinary challenges it presents to those who must apply it, and to his insightful analysis of the operation of its provisions. In December 1986, the United States ratified the CISG – a ratification that, along with simultaneous ratifications by Italy and the People's Republic of China, brought the number of contracting states to eleven, surpassing the number required to bring the CISG into force; the CISG became effective in the United States and the other original contracting states on January 1, 1988.

Throughout this period, John lectured and published prolifically on the CISG. He continued to build a remarkable record of achievement as a member of the Penn Law faculty by issuing new editions of his influential casebooks on sales and on security interests. He reinforced and added to his distinguished reputation as a classroom teacher, and he built Penn's program for foreign law graduates.

It was during this period that I had my first contact with John. It occurred at a Pittsburgh conference on the CISG in December 1987. The conference was organized by my colleague, dear friend, and the other main influence on my own career, Professor

Ronald Brand – another great man and a recipient, like John, of the prestigious Leonard
J. Theberge Award for Private International Law. At that time, I was strictly a domestic
commercial law specialist, teaching contracts, sales, and bankruptcy law. I had barely
heard of the CISG, but Ron talked me into participating in the conference that he was
organizing. I remember reading the CISG for the first time as I prepared my paper
for the conference. I found the text mildly interesting, but John's keynote conference
address, with its profound opening and closing remarks,[1] opened up a whole new world
of thought for me.

John continued his distinguished work even after he became an emeritus professor in
1984; he still taught at Penn, spoke around the world on the CISG, and published important commentaries on international sales law from a perspective that only he could bring.
And I continued to have opportunities for personal contact with him in connection with
conferences on the CISG. Once, while I was in Philadelphia to moderate an all-star CISG
workshop at which John was one of the featured participants, I had the honor of staying
in his home and meeting his wife Annemarie. John and I grew to have a friendship –
a respectful friendship between a junior academic and a great senior scholar and mentor,
but it included a personal dimension. For example, I dabble in performing folk music,
and I found out during one of our meetings that John's broad-ranging musical interests
encompassed the folk genre. In fact, he revealed that he was a longtime collector and
sometime performer of folk songs. I was so bold as to record a couple of my performances
and send them to him. From his response I learned how a consummate diplomat can
express puzzlement in the most polite, friendly, and encouraging fashion!

It was through our personal contact that I gained insight into the special nature of
John's achievements and the light they shed on his work with the CISG. Of course,
the formal record of John's extraordinary career bespeaks a great man. Among the many
special honors it brought him were a Guggenheim Fellowship, a visiting appointment as
the Arthur Goodhart Professor in the Science of Law at Cambridge University, and the
Theberge Award. But the nature of John's greatness, I believe, derived almost as much
from his personality as from his powerful intellect and astonishing drive.

Anyone who ever met him will testify that John was one of the sweetest, most soft-
spoken, and most thoughtful people imaginable. In the end, this sweetness and gentleness
of personality gave John his special greatness; it made possible his lifetime of breakthrough
achievements, including his crucial role in bringing the CISG into existence, making
it understood, and making it successful. He was a genuinely extraordinary man because
he combined a marvelous intellect and drive with a profound and powerful passion for
understanding the views of others. John was a good listener – one who conveyed the vivid
impression that he was truly interested in, even inspired by, your ideas. He conveyed
that impression because it was true. From the moment I met John in 1987 it was clear
to me that he was a genuine student in the best sense of the word, passionate to acquire
knowledge by seeing things through the eyes of others.

I can imagine how John's listening skills and powers of empathy and sympathy were
tested as he worked to get the CISG project off to a good start, and as he helped shepherd
it through the drafting and approval processes. Of course an achievement such as the

---

[1] See John Honnold, "The Sales Convention: Background, Status, Application," 8 J.L. & Com. 1 (1988);
John Honnold, "The Sales Convention in Action – Uniform International Words: Uniform Application?"
8 J.L. & Com. 207 (1988).

CISG – a complex substantive law covering a critically important area and requiring worldwide acceptance – is possible only through the efforts of many talented people. Its success has required many to hear and truly understand the views of a diverse international community, and to bring that diverse community into agreement. The CISG project has had the extraordinary good fortune to attract a number of remarkable people, in addition to John, who were capable of taking on this challenge; people such as Peter Schlechtriem and Albert H. Kritzer who, like John, have now passed on and are being honored in this book. I have often thought that the spirits and personalities of these wonderful people formed a distinctive culture around the CISG that partook of their character. I have often noticed what a remarkable group of scholars have been attracted to the CISG as a major focus of their careers – thinkers who are not just bright and energetic, but truly friendly and other-centered. And I have often recognized how undeservedly lucky I am to have stumbled into becoming a part of that group.

I smile to think of John as an invisible presence wherever people gather to discuss the CISG. I have often sensed his tolerant and inquisitive spirit pushing me to understand the law from a broader and more humane perspective. I have been far less true than I should have been to his example of always respecting, and always seeking to understand and profit from, the wisdom of others. I recognize that even my chapter for this book is combative and challenging in a way that is not fully in keeping with John's spirit. He was a strong and effective advocate for his own positions, but he never lost sight of the fact that even he did not have a monopoly on wisdom, and that the only way to create a genuine and effective international legal system is to explore and appreciate the world's diverse views on challenging topics. I know I would be better at what I do if I more often remembered and emulated that attitude, which was such a notable aspect of John's work and character. It would be a fitting memorial to John Honnold – and yet another breakthrough achievement to be added to John's long list – if we all agreed to follow more closely his inspiring example of curiosity about and openness to the ideas of others.

Harry M. Flechtner,[2]
Pittsburgh

In Memory of Peter Schlechtriem

I want to say some words in the memory of Peter Schlechtriem. He lived from 1933 to 2007. For many years he was *the* globally leading scholar on the CISG, the UN Convention on Contracts for the International Sale of Goods. Everybody concerned with the CISG knows his name from his numerous and leading publications in the field of international sales law; his book *UN Law on International Sales* is used in CISG courses all over the world; many of us have met him personally.

I met Peter Schlechtriem for the first time forty years ago, in 1971, in Heidelberg. It was in the Institut für ausländisches und Internationales Privat- und Wirtschaftsrecht (Institute for Foreign and International Private and Commercial Law) at the University Place in the center of Heidelberg. He had become the successor of my doctoral supervisor

---

[2] I wish to thank John Honnold's son, Mr. Edward Honnold, for supplying much of the biographical information included herein.

at that law faculty and for reasons that will become evident a little later I must mention that my doctoral supervisor, Professor Dr. Eduard Wahl, was a pupil and close collaborator of Ernst Rabel, the famous comparatist, founder of modern comparative law, and creator and driving force behind the uniform international sales law movement, which led to the CISG. I visited Peter Schlechtriem in his new office only a few days after his arrival in Heidelberg and met a young, sportive looking man with elastic and energetic movements, a warm voice, and very bright eyes. He was the model of a young, modern professor, open-minded and international in his thinking. Remember, these were the years shortly after the students' revolt against the old, politically conservative patriarchs and he fully represented the new type of professor that I and my fellow students sought.

His way was indeed colorful and closely tied to the German history of the twentieth century. He was born on March 2, 1933, a fatal year for Germany with the rise of the Nazi dictatorship. He was born in the town of Jena, which after the Second World War became part of the socialist German Democratic Republic, or East Germany, and exposed Schlechtriem to a second dictatorial regime. He finished school there but immediately after school he left his hometown and the socialist part of the then-divided Germany. He went to Hamburg – in the "capitalistic" West – where he studied first shipbuilding and then political science and sociology and finally law. In 1956, he moved to Freiburg, where he finished his law studies, wrote his dissertation, and became an assistant of Professor Dr. Ernst von Caemmerer, another pupil and former collaborator of Ernst Rabel. In 1964–65, Schlechtriem studied at Chicago Law School and was awarded a Master of Comparative Law. There he met Professor Max Rheinstein, yet another close collaborator of Rabel. From 1968 to 1990, Schlechtriem served as assistant professor at Chicago Law School. Back in Freiburg, he completed his *habilitation* with a comprehensive comparative law study in 1970 and was offered a chair at both the University of Heidelberg and the University of Erlangen. He accepted the position at Heidelberg. Rabel's thinking and method – practiced by Rabel's students – had very much influenced Schlechtriem's scientific ideas and convictions. In his work he used and perfected Rabel's functional comparative method and the idea that the purpose of a legal norm is the key to its understanding. Moreover, he was passionate about the need for a uniform sales law and, in particular, the CISG, which became a lifelong subject of his scientific work. Scientifically, Schlechtriem became an important part of Rabel's progeny. He remained true to the long and prestigious tradition of German legal science.

The reason for my visit to his new office in Heidelberg in 1971 was to obtain a position as one of his assistants. When I asked him, he said: "I am very sorry but I have already made the contracts with my collaborators." As was his custom, he had things carefully arranged in advance. I was very disappointed but fittingly I found a position at the Max-Planck-Institute in Hamburg, which had previously been founded by Rabel in Berlin before the Nazis expelled him because of his Jewish heritage. With respect to my first meeting with Peter Schlechtriem, one could not think of a better start to a long-standing scientific and friendly relationship. I did not see Schlechtriem again until 1985, after I had become a professor at the University in Hamburg where I worked in the same field as Peter, namely on the CISG. He had meanwhile moved to Freiburg where he succeeded his mentor von Caemmerer and had become more and more involved with the CISG. In 1980, he was a member of the German delegation to the Vienna Conference that adopted the CISG. He subsequently wrote about the conference and contributed to the first comprehensive commentary on the new uniform sales law. He had heard that I collected court decisions on the Hague Uniform Sales Law (the predecessor of the CISG) and we agreed to work together to publish these decisions. In the beginnings of the electronic communications era this was no easy task; nonetheless, the work was well received.

In the following years, Schlechtriem became one of the leading German scholars in various areas of the law. His publications on the law of obligations strongly influenced German legislation and educated generations of students. His international experience, interest in other legal systems, comparative approach to law study, wise judgment, and organizational talents expanded his influence far beyond Germany. He was asked and gave advice when Estonia reformed its law of obligations, when UNIDROIT prepared the 2004 version of its Principles, and when the Draft Common Frame of Reference of the EU was in the making. For seven years, he served as president of the German Society of Comparative Law. When the CISG entered into force in Germany in 1991, Schlechtriem edited and authored the first great commentary on the subject; a little later the work was translated into English, which he saw as the language of international commerce and law. Today, the commentary is the most authoritative and influential source for the international application of the CISG. Now the editorship is in the hands of Ingeborg Schwenzer, his former pupil and collaborator, and so the tradition begun with Rabel continues.

Schlechtriem was also one of the founders and the first chairman of the CISG Advisory Council, an association of CISG experts who publish opinions on specific CISG problems and issues. The idea behind the Council is to support the uniform interpretation and application of the CISG.

Among the many honors he received were honorary doctorates from the University of Basel and the University of Tartu in Estonia, as well as an appointment as a Fellow of St. Catherine's College in Oxford. In 2003, on his seventieth birthday, he received a Festschrift of almost one thousand pages and he gave a grand reception in appreciation at Freiburg's finest hotel and restaurant. A broad staircase led to the entrance of the reception rooms. Schlechtriem stood at the top of the stairs at the entrance and greeted every guest by name and welcomed each very warmly. Nonetheless, you had the firm impression that he would rather have been sitting in his office writing a book or an article. He was not much interested in parties and small talk and even less in celebrating his own achievements.

The last time I saw him was at a CISG conference in Pittsburgh in November 2005. He gave an impressive speech on the CISG as *lingua franca* of international commercial law. In private talks at the conference he was as friendly and interested as ever. He kept secret that he was already fatally ill. His last publication was a contribution to the *Festschrift* for Albert H. Kritzer. Peter's article dealt with the conflict between merger and form clauses with oral modifications under the CISG. The *Festschrift* was published on the occasion of Kritzer's eightieth birthday on April 21, 2008. Peter had submitted his article far in advance in order to see it completed before his death. He died on April 23, 2007, at the age of seventy-four. His combination of intellect and character was a rarity, and for this he will not be forgotten.

Ulrich Magnus,
Hamburg

In Memory of Albert H. Kritzer

The last time I gave a speech about Albert H. Kritzer he was in the room. I was standing with my good friend and colleague Ulrich Schroeter on the stage of the Vienna Concert Hall, and we were bursting with joy! It was 2008, and we were presenting the *Festschrift* in honor of Al's eightieth birthday, and we had managed to solicit great contributions that took Al completely by surprise. It was an occasion of pure unadulterated exuberance – the unquestioned high point of my career – an "Oscar-style" achievement speech, an accolade (and a song) for Al in front of thousands. I thought writing my speech would be daunting, but it was a breeze, thrown together in the back of a taxi and driven by pure pleasure.

In stark contrast, I thought writing this tribute would be easy – but it has been grueling. Not only was he not in the room when my tribute was given (although the room was named "Alberts"!), but Albert will never be in the room with me again – I have lost my "other father," whom I have not been able to say a proper goodbye to before now. As a result, I am unable to provide an objective insight into Albert H. Kritzer – I offer you my subjective take on the man, the scholar, and my friend. I will explain my relationship to Al first, then list his accomplishments, and then try to surmise some of the wisdom I have been able to glean from my experiences with him.

My Other Father...

"Other father?" You may ask, "What does that mean?" You would have to have known Al to truly understand, but I will do my best to explain. I was "adopted" by Al at the age of 26. Moreover, my parents – who are both still alive and well and had taken excellent care of me until I left home some years before – were somewhat surprised at the time, and – frankly – so was I, as I felt I was taking great care of myself. I first met Al at the Vis Moot in the spring of 1997, where he judged my contribution to the Essay Competition. Subsequently, Al decided that he would adopt me, and he announced his intentions in a formal email – and so it was. I was not the first to be subject to this rather eccentric practice of "adopting" grown-ups – I have an older adopted CISG "sister," Pilar Perales Viscasillas, who has been nurtured far more successfully than I. In both of us, Al saw potential that he wanted to unlock, and once he decided to nurture he dedicated himself to the task with fervor. I must admit that at first I found it somewhat awkward (especially the good-natured squabbling with Al about who would lead me down the aisle at my wedding, eventually resolved by my refusal to marry at all, much to my partner's delight!). But Al soon became a welcome and invaluable part of my family's life. He visited us, and my parents, often, and arranged visits to New York; he spoiled my children as extravagantly as any grandfather would; and we spent holidays together and shared many wonderful moments. Professionally, Al guarded me and guided me; often subtly, as required when trying to help a pig-headed, anti-authoritarian like myself, and sometimes without the desired result. But Al never ceased to express his love and support for me, even when we both knew I could have reacted better to a given situation or task. He would send emails – out of the blue – simply saying "I am proud of you and I love you," and he once sent me a crystal Steuben heart to remind me of his support. Initially, this was very overwhelming, but, today, I really miss his caring ways and generosity of spirit. I can unequivocally state that I would not be where I am today if it were not for Al's love and support, which made my journey not only more enjoyable, but for his advice and interference, made the journey possible.

Biography of Albert H. Kritzer

Al was a native of New York, born in April 1928. He was educated at the College of William and Mary, and went on to gain distinction at Cornell Law School in 1951. Before his final graduation, he took time to travel through Europe and already showed signs of greatness, not only because he was driven by the need to expand his horizons, but because of the way he did it. I will explain how he did it when I address the subject of "thinking big." After graduating Cornell, he was called to the New York Bar, where he remained a member for almost 70 years and was reconized for his accomplishments. After Cornell, he went to work as a Judge Advocate in the U.S. Air Force; he told many exciting stories from that time, especially about his experiences in Japan. Upon returning to New York, he joined the law firm of Donovan, Leisure, Newton and Irvine and married the love of his life, Jacqueline, with whom he was to father four beautiful daughters of great character and intellect.

· In 1966, he joined the legal section of General Electric (GE), which sparked his interest in writing an international contract manual (ICM). Al realized that standard form contracting would make GE's negotiating and contacting much more streamlined and simple, so he formalized an approach to GE's contracts and developed a manual that would act as a flexible standard form contract – with built-in contract checklists to facilitate negotiation of customized modifications of the contract when needed. In this area, Al was ahead of his time; for example, the ICC had not yet begun its work on model contract forms. Having seen how his manual worked within GE, he realized its wider potential, generalized the approach, and brought the initial volumes of the ICM into publication. Kluwer now publishes the manual, with contributions from leading contract scholars, in seven volumes – its success is immense, and the royalties funded many of Al's subsequent projects.

After the tragic loss of his youngest daughter in a car accident, Al often said that he took stock of his life and decided to start giving back. His life changed pace, literally, when he moved to Pace University School of Law in 1991 at the age of 63. He spent the next nineteen years there, working for a dollar a year, creating the Institute for International Commercial Law and some of the most impressive and cutting-edge information-sharing mechanisms for dealing with uniform international commercial law, most notably, the preeminent CISG database in the world.

Al is best known for his pioneering establishment and ongoing building of the CISGW3 database, realizing early on that the key to a successful international private law, such as the CISG, would require access to information and the dissemination of knowledge. He not only saw the potential in the Internet for fulfilling this vital role, he realized it, ensuring (and often personally funding) translations of cases and soliciting permission for free access to articles and even books. It was no surprise that in 2002 the Association of Law Librarians awarded the CISGW3 Database its Best Website Award. The database remains an outstanding example of how scholarship and case law can be shared across national and cultural boundaries.

Al was also a key player in the creation of the Willem C. Vis Moot Competition, which he saw as an opportunity to spread knowledge of the CISG and to educate the coming generations of legal professionals. He attended the Vis whenever possible (but famously never acted as an arbitrator because he did not wish to judge students) and he strongly influenced the creation of the Vis Moot Alumni Association (MAA). He did this in his typical way of encouraging and prompting others to make good things happen without taking much deserved credit for his actions. Again, in 2000, Al helped spearhead the creation of the CISG Advisory Council. He saw the need to create a council of experts to guide the application of the CISG. He refused a leadership role, handing the reigns to his good friend Peter Schlechtriem, but he continued to sit on the council and occasionally funded its activities.

Al often stated that scholars had designed the CISG, but that it now belonged to those who had to apply it, the judges and the council. But what he failed to see was how instrumental one academic – himself – was in advancing the cause of uniform law – enabling practitioners to access information on the CISG and advancing educational efforts, such as the creation of the Vis Competition and CISG Advisory Council. In many ways, he adopted the CISG and guided it and guarded it, in much the same way he adopted me and Pilar – but I doubt he saw the extent of his personal and professional impact and importance.

Three Lessons Subtly Taught by Al

Al's accomplishments are truly impressive. But the worth of the man is in more than just a list of accomplishments – it is in the judgment of him found in the memories of those left behind, which is a sum of choices made, means applied to ends, and moments we choose to recall. In Danish legends, Viking burials are said to have included the recalling of an Icelandic saga: "Fae doe, fraende doe, en ting ved jeg som aldrig doe: dommen over doed mands minde," which, loosely translated, means "Enemies die, allies die, one thing I know doth never die: our judgment of our memories of dead men."

I have chosen to outline three of the main characteristics of Al Kritzer, and to pepper them with anecdotes from his life, to help explain why he should be remembered so fondly, what made him special, and what we could all learn from the life he lived. There are undoubtedly more than those three to be had, but for now I offer these three: "sharing," "thinking big," and "loving."

Sharing!

Sharing was Al's favorite thing to do, and his exceptional form of generosity motivated others to want to share and work for the betterment of others. It for this reason that Ulrich Schroeter and I named the *Festschrift* in Al's honor: *Sharing International Commercial Law*. But the ease with which that entire 2008 *Festschrift* project was produced and delivered speaks volumes about the kind of dedication and enthusiasm Al sparked. Incredibly busy scholars dropped what they were doing to contribute – because this was an accolade that was worth contributing to. Sharing something with Al, or on his behalf, was an honor and a joy for many of us.

Al was indeed a great sharer – he shared his wisdom, joy, and experiences, as well as being generous with time, money, insight, and gifts. What kind of a man would spend his private funds financing ideas like the CISG database, financing case translations, and establishing the CISG Advisory Council? What kind of person would work about eighty hours a week for one dollar a year? The answer is that only a special, caring, and thoughtful person would undertake such Herculean efforts. When I hear the expression "putting your money where your mouth is" I invariably think of Al, who never sought credit for his many acts of generosity, but financed efforts because he believed in their efficacy and worth for the greater good.

Moreover, sparked by a wealth of generosity and enthusiasm, he had a knack for teasing commitments from others and establishing a stable network of people to share information, insight, and commitments to a cause. Al would fly across the globe to investigate opportunities and dig for needed sources. Al could motivate people to find their own inner generosity and enthusiasm in contributing to his undertakings. Al poured his heart and his soul, and his money, into building systems and networks that allowed for the international sharing of knowledge and ideas. Now, with Al gone, it is for us to follow his example to ensure that what he started continues to grow and nurture future generations of scholars, jurists, students, and lawyers.

Think Big!

Those of us who knew him would often get a kind of vertigo from the rate and intensity of the ideas that streamed out of Al. Peter Schlechtriem used to talk of the boxes in his own garage, accumulated over almost 20 years, all labeled "Al's Ideas," many of which had been realized and many of which would never be taken up again. But Al's mind was sharp as a honed blade and always on the prowl for a good idea, and he was never afraid to air his thoughts.

Thinking big for Al wasn't an impetuous state; he took as much time as needed to intellectually vet his big ideas, to fine-tune them, and to finally determine their feasibility. I invite you to imagine a young Albert, still a law student about to graduate, traveling through Europe on a shoestring budget. He was driven by a need to expand his horizons, to meet people from other countries, and to gain insight into how others think and how their countries function. He wrote letters to leaders of states, asking them to meet with him so he could learn more about their politics, their views, and their culture. He often spoke of an intriguing meeting with President Josip Tito of the former Yugoslavia. Where most would be too timid to ask, Al would charge ahead. Sometimes like the proverbial bull in the china shop, he often did not get what he wanted, but sometimes he did!

I have at home a letter from the Danish Ministry of Royal Affairs, politely declining his request for Her Royal Majesty Queen Margaret to present me with my Vis Essay Competition Prize. The fact that he thought of asking the Queen makes me smile to this day. Al was never shy about asking for things from important people, especially when it was on the behalf of someone else. Thinking big means not holding back; it means pursuing an idea until it is achieved or the pursuit is exhausted.

Loving!

The final characteristic I have chosen to describe is love, and I do apologize for the built-in sentimentality of doing so, but Al was a man defined by love. I am not referring to a schmaltzy kind of love, but I refer to the kind of love that fuels our personalities and our energy for life and work. First of all, Al had a profound love for what he did, a love for ideas, a love for seeing and realizing potential, a love for curiosity, and a love for the complexities of law and society. These loves sparked an intense dedication in him and those inspired by him. His work was its own reward. He also had a great love for life – a love for the arts, for good food, and for travel. He had a love for humanity and a love of silly hats and a love for plain old fun! These loves sparked a pure joy in him, which made you want to be in his company and share experiences and moments with him.

The sharing and loving aspects of his character made him a very energetic and joyful individual. His love of his work fueled him to continue on past the point that would exhaust the rest of us, and his love of fun balanced it out so it never wore him down. His energy levels were extraordinary. Al was unique in that the abundance of energy he possessed allowed him to live life to the fullest even past the age of eighty. Al also inspired love in others, love for the work at hand, in sharing his enthusiasm, and love of life. He was the kind of man who made you want to be a better person. Al frowned on negativity and constantly steered me away from negative responses and toward more positive trains of thought.

A Final Goodbye: Learning to Lose

Most of us have experienced the tragic loss of a loved one – and those who have not will one day. Al was eighty-two when he died, and he had lived a full, rich life, and wanting him back is simply too selfish a thought. But it is a very natural reaction to losing such an important person in one's life. The finality of death can often make us frustrated and bitter at the things that are so nonnegotiable; the missed opportunities and regrets of not doing more when the person was alive. I keep trying to be the person that Al saw in me. I will leave this memorial tribute the way Al would have liked – with a positive spin.

I am much more grateful for my fourteen years as Al's adopted daughter than I am sad at having lost him.

Goodbye, Albert. I miss you very much.

Camilla Andersen,
Western Australia

Part I   *History of and Researching the CISG*

1   Global Challenge of International Sales Law

Larry A. DiMatteo

I. Introduction

The genesis for this book was an interest in looking at the world's most successful substantive international commercial law convention – the United Nations Convention on Contracts for the International Sale of Goods (CISG) – from various national and methodological perspectives. Success here is measured by the overwhelming reception of the CISG by countries throughout the world. By late 2013, Brazil (4 March 2013) and Bahrain (25 September 2013) became the seventy-ninth and eighth countries to adopt the CISG.[1] Thus, the CISG, along with the New York Convention,[2] can be seen as the two most successful international private law conventions in history. The former deals with the substantive area of sales of goods; the latter is a procedural law requiring signatory countries to enforce the arbitral awards of other countries to the Convention. At the current rate of adoption, there is little doubt that the CISG will in the near future reach one hundred adoptions.

The ordinary measure of importance of a convention is by the number of countries adopting, acceding, or ratifying the convention. Many international conventions or model laws are impressive in name, but are of little significance in practice. Numerous worthy, and not so worthy, conventions have failed to reach the minimum number of signatories to become effective, and others have entered into law, but have not obtained the critical mass of participating countries to have much of an effect in the real world. The CISG has clearly reached both thresholds of importance – entering into force and a critical mass of adoptions. But, unlike the New York Convention, private parties have the ability to opt out of the CISG, thus presenting a third threshold of effectiveness – the CISG importance in practice. This issue was the thematic genesis for this book.

The CISG has reached the level of acceptance in which it can be declared the face of international sales law. However, the "global challenge" is whether practicing lawyers will educate themselves in the substantive provisions of the CISG and recognize the

---

[1] Brazil acceded to the United Nations Convention on Contracts for the International Sale of Goods (CISG) on March 4, 2013, becoming the 79th State Party to the Convention. The Convention will enter into force in Brazil on April 1, 2014. See Journal of the United Nations, No. 2013/43 (March 5, 2013), available at http://www.un.org/Docs/journal/En/20130305e.pdf.

[2] United Nations Convention on Recognition and Enforcement of Foreign Arbitral Awards (10 June 1958), 330 U.N.T.S. 38. As of this writing, there are approximately 140 signatory countries to the New York Convention. See William Park, *Arbitration of International Business Disputes*, 2nd ed. (Oxford: Oxford University Press, 2012), 461–8.

benefits of a uniform international sales law, whether parties and trade associations will begin to embrace it as a preferred choice of law, and whether courts and arbitral tribunals will recognize it as applicable law and as evidence of international customary law.

This book examines these issues from the perspectives of the scholar and the practitioner. It reviews the strengths and shortcomings of the CISG, as well as the crucial issue of the uniformity of its application. A uniform text often masks chaotic, nonuniform interpretations and applications of the text. In fact, disunity in application is a contradiction to the harmonizing goal of uniform law. Divergent applications create a jurisprudence that acts as an obstacle instead of serving the intended purpose of diminishing variant national laws as an obstacle to internatonal trade. A chaotic CISG jurisprudence creates the type of uncertainty represented by the private international law regime that it seeks to replace. Currently, we are at a crucial time in the life of the CISG: Will it reach the level of uniformity of application that will allow it to be recongized as a truly uniform international law?

The two fundamental questions noted earlier are what this book addresses. First, will the CISG eventually be accepted at the grassroots level of legal and business practice, so that its degree of importance at the transactional level becomes closer to the degree of importance it has reached at the level of national adoptions? Second, will a significant or minimal level of uniformity of application allow the CISG to become all it can be – a truly uniform international sales law that solves the problem of uncertainty caused by private international law?

Fortunately, the accessible cases and arbitral case law are of enough density to make the second question primarily a descriptive undertaking. Thus, the book, through its analysis of the substantive provisions of the CISG and its broad menu of country analyses, offers a solid foundation to assess whether it is being uniformly interpreted and applied. A tentative assessment here on the second question is that, after a period of numerous divergent interpretations and a slew of homeward-biased decisions, the trend has been toward a convergence in the CISG jurisprudence toward greater uniformity of application. In those areas where such convergence has not resulted in a uniform interpretation, there has been a greater recognition in the case law around majority and minority views or a number of minority views.

This bifurcation between majority and minority views is a second-order means to greater uniformity of application. Instead of total chaos, legal practitioners will be able to better assess how the CISG is interpreted in the different national court systems. In many ways, these interpretive groupings of case law replicate what happens at the national or domestic law level. The American Uniform Commercial Code (UCC) is applied by fifty-three independent court systems.[3] It was inevitable, despite the presence of a common legal tradition, that the different court systems would interpret identical UCC provisions differently. However, the number of such divergent interpretations is low, and where they occur, the different interpretations are well known. A savvy transactional lawyer may simply choose the state law that has the preferred interpretation. This would seem to be a rarity, however, as the differences are primarily in degree, rather than in kind. The mainstream scholarly and lawyerly view of the UCC is that it is a "uniform" commercial law.

---

[3] The UCC has been adopted, except for Article 2 (Sale of Goods) in Louisiana, in the fifty American states, Puerto Rico, U.S. Virgin Islands, and the District of Columbia.

Another element that has reduced the number of divergent interpretations of the UCC, over time, is the use of case law from other states as persuasive precedent. The need to use foreign case law is much discussed in CISG scholarship. Whether the use of foreign case law is a required element of CISG interpretive methodology is beside the point. Article 7's mandate – that the interpretation of the CISG should take into account its international character and the need to promote uniformity in its application – is unobtainable without reviewing well-reasoned cases from other jurisdictions. Just as in UCC jurisprudence, nothing requires the courts applying the CISG to look to other legal systems for cases that can be used as persuasive precedent, but uniformity of application is greatly enhanced by doing so. In the civilian legal tradition, the lack of the notion of binding precedent provides another example of the potential for a less-than-uniform "uniform law." Judges in the civilian tradition are trained to go directly to their countries' codes to find the applicable solution to a case in dispute. Thus, the seeds of divergent interpretations within the same national legal systems are constantly present. Yet few scholars and judges would argue against the view that there exists a relatively uniform national law in civil law countries. In Germany and some other civilian countries, the scholarly legal commentary serves as the glue that binds together a relatively uniform private law.

The history of CISG jurisprudence is not so different than what is found in the early development of the American UCC[4] and the national private law systems in countries of the civil law tradition. The first step in the process of applying a new uniform law involves cases of first impression that are often seminal in nature. At the same time, with no preexisting jurisprudence,[5] this is the period when there is the greatest opportunity for divergent interpretations. The second step is the accumulation of a critical mass of jurisprudence that can then be analyzed to determine the majority and minority views of given interpretations of the uniform law. It is also a time to ascertain trends and anomalies in the case law. The hopeful third step is a more universal recognition of variant interpretations and the coalescing of courts and arbitral tribunals around the best-reasoned interpretation given the underlying principles of the law. This process of coalescing requires that some of the initial positions taken in a national court system would need to be modified to bring its law into conformity with the "best-reasoned interpretation." An example of this phenomenon is found in the German case law relating to the reasonable time to give notice of nonconformity of goods under CISG Article 39. The early German case law favored a homeward trend interpretation of the notice requirement. The courts interpreted the reasonable time period of Article 39 very restrictively. In one case, a period of eight days from delivery of the goods was construed as being a belated notice. The more recent German case law on the subject has taken a much more liberal view of the time allowed to give notice.

It is the third step of the process of formulating a more uniform jurisprudence that the CISG has hopefully reached. It is a stage in which it can be said that a relative or acceptable level of uniformity of application is near. Through scholarship, as represented

---

[4] See Larry A. DiMatteo, "The Curious Case of Transborder Sales Law: A Comparative Analysis of the CESL, CISG, and UCC," in *CISG and Regional Private Law Unification* (ed. Ulrich Magnus), (Sellier European Publishers, 2012).

[5] Although in the case of the CISG, the Hague Sales Conventions are considered predecessors to the CISG. Some national courts applied those Conventions by analogy to their initial interpretations of the CISG.

by this book, as well as better education on the CISG in law schools and at the bar, it is likely that uniformity of application will continue to improve. It may take another generation of lawyers before the threshold of acceptability of the CISG and a uniformity of application will be universally recognized. The trend toward better-reasoned CISG case decisions provides the hope that CISG jurisprudence is on the right track. However, it must be recognized that absolute uniformity is unreachable for any transborder law being applied by independent court systems. Further, the CISG, just as in the UCC or BGB, is infused with the principles of reasonableness, trade usage, and good faith that are forever changing to reflect changes in society. The dynamism found in the business world and international trade will continue to present cases of first instance likely to lead to variant interpretations as CISG rules are applied to novel fact patterns. Over time, the novelty will be embraced by CISG jurisprudence and the poorly reasoned decisions will be worked out of the CISG canon and relative uniformity of application will be reached again and again.

II. Blueprint for a Conference and a Book

From the very beginning stages of planning for the conference and this book the focus was on a targeted, communal research effort. Simply stated, the menu of topics or table of contents was set before scholars were invited to contribute. The task then was to find the best scholars to fit the preselected topics. At the same time, it was a goal of the organizer to make sure that a great amount of diversity was represented in the pool of authors. The diversity goal was reached at a spectacular level. The author pool includes scholars from numerous common and civil law legal systems, mixed common–civil law systems, Islamic legal systems, and a socialist market system. The authors came from six continents and some twenty-two countries. This diversity of scholars ensures that the different perspectives of the CISG have been represented in this book.

Also, from the beginning, the book was planned to serve multiple audiences – scholar, student, jurist, and practitioner. This multifaceted purpose is reflected in the different parts of the book. Part I provides context in reviewing the history and evolution of the CISG. The use of the CISG in national courts is examined, as well as divergences between theory and practice and the unevenness of CISG case law in the interpretation of the numerous CISG provisions. It also provides material of interest to all audiences – sources of CISG law, research methodologies, and problems of translation. Part II examines the area of the interpretation of the CISG and the related issue of the problem of divergent interpretations. The meta-principle of good faith is analyzed as a critical component of CISG interpretive methodology. Part II also examines the use of the CISG in arbitration and as soft law.

Part III examines three key substantive, and heavily litigated, areas of the CISG: contract formation, including the battle of the forms scenario; the inspection and notice requirements relating to the nonconformity of goods; and the determination of fundamental breach. A note of thanks is owed to Morton Fogt for covering the numerous CISG provisions dealing with the formation of contracts. Part IV extends the substantive analysis to the area of remedies, damages, and excuse. A special note of appreciation is owed to Ulrich Magnus for his sweeping analysis of damages, price reduction, avoidance, mitigation, and preservation of goods. A discussion of the usefulness of the excuse provided in Article 79 (impediment) is provided, and the issues of legal costs as reimbursable damages are studied as well.

Parts V and VI analyze the CISG at the nation-state level. The authors were asked to review the substantive issues discussed in Parts III and IV from the perspective of their national legal systems. These country analyses serve two purposes – to present knowledge of CISG law as interpreted within each national court system and to find divergent interpretations within and across national legal systems. The country analyses also provide a longitudinal perspective as to how the CISG has evolved within certain national court systems. Part V focuses on the CISG in Europe with country reports on Austria, France, Germany, Italy, Spain, Switzerland, and The Netherlands. Due to the scarcity of case law (Southeastern Europe, Baltic States, Belarus, and the Ukraine) or a communal approach to the CISG (Nordic countries), a number of the reports are regional in nature. Part VI explores the CISG's application elsewhere in the world, including Australia, Egypt, Israel, New Zealand, and People's Republic of China. Again, due to the scarcity of cases, two of the reports were regionalized – North America, as well as Central and South America.

Parts VII and VIII crosses the theoretical–practical divide with the former providing some theoretical insights and the latter reviewing issues relating to the use of the CISG in practice. These parts show that the areas of theoretical insight and legal practice are not mutually exclusive. Part VII examines the potential use of the CISG to bridge the gap between the common and civil laws. Alternatively stated, the CISG was constructed to bridge differences between the two major legal systems. Part VII also looks at the problem of interpreting and applying uniform laws, as well as the issues of precontractual liability and the enforceability of precontractual agreements. These three chapters should be required reading for all international transactional lawyers. Part VIII is entitled "Practitioner's Perspective" and covers a number of disparate, but important, issues relating to the CISG and the practice of law. The issues examined include the potential for professional liability (malpractice) for ignoring or avoiding the CISG, a review of complimentary texts (convention) that can be used in conjunction with the CISG, a comparison of the CISG with the English Sale of Goods Act, the use of soft law alongside of the CISG, and the active implementation of the CISG in legal practice.

III. Conclusion

The goal of this book was to bring a diverse group of top-flight CISG scholars together to analyze the CISG's current place in international business transactions. They used various research methodologies, including doctrinal, comparative, empirical, theoretical, and practice-oriented. The organization of the book allows for breadth in coverage and in-depth analysis of key issues. Ultimately, the quality of this undertaking rests on the quality of the research of the contributing authors. The assembled pool of top-flight CISG scholars have provided outstanding, original scholarship, which combined makes a significant contribution to the CISG literature.

2 History of the CISG and Its Present Status

Vikki Rogers and Kaon Lai

I. Introduction

The United Nations Convention on Contracts for the International Sale of Goods (CISG) is a remarkable historical achievement and success for the unification of international private law. It is the progeny of centuries of custom and trade practice, as well as comparative legal scholarship. The CISG reflects the modern willingness[1] of countries to incorporate into their national laws a uniform sales law for international transactions.[2] The list of contracting states currently includes eighty countries and is growing. The Pace CISG database disseminates approximately 3,000 cases and arbitral awards on the CISG and in excess of 10,000 articles have been written on the CISG. Several countries have used the CISG as the basis for modernizing their domestic contract and sales laws.

This chapter will describe the historical building blocks that led to the creation of the CISG and provide an introduction to its structure. It will then discuss the current status of the CISG, specifically identifying (1) the number of contracting states and the representation of contracting states within regions; (2) the impact of the CISG on the interpretation and modernization of domestic sales law codes and the development of other private international commercial law agreements; and (3) the current global efforts toward promoting awareness and use of the CISG.

II. Movement toward Uniform International Sales Law

The root of international sale of goods law harmonization is traceable to the twelfth century's *lex mercatoria*, an "autonomous, practical body of commercial law created

---

[1] See Camilla B. Andersen, *Uniform Application of the International Sales Law: Understanding Uniformity, the Global Jurisconsultorium and Examination* (The Netherlands: Kluwer Law International, 2007), 5 ("Modern unification of laws is a political *voluntary* process whereby different jurisdictions elect to share a set of rules – not where it is imposed upon them, as opposed to historical uniformity (like Roman law, common law, or other colonial laws)" (citations omitted)).

[2] See id., 4–5 ("Uniform law is a new form of lawmaking, with a different *origin* and a different *focus*, and it usually arises in a transnational context – or at least in a trans-jurisdictional context (the United States, for instance, being multi-jurisdictional as far as state law is concerned), applies uniform laws within the national boundaries") (citations omitted).

not by legal scholars but by merchant court[s]."[3] Used throughout Europe during the medieval period, it allowed merchants to settle disputes based on customary business usage.[4] Over time, the law for merchants slowly evolved and found its way into national laws.[5] The expansion of international trade created a need to unify substantive law of sales in order for merchants to operate within increasingly complex legal systems.[6] In the latter half of the nineteenth century, an internationalist movement developed in Europe, which sought to create a *uniform ius commune* based on domestic laws.[7] The internationalist movement led to the formation of L'Institut de droit international (Institute of International Law) in Belgium and the International Law Association in Brussels in 1873.[8]

The determination to remove barriers to international trade led to a push for greater predictability regarding applicable law for international sales.[9] Ernst Rabel, an Austrian scholar and academic, became an influential force in the unification and harmonization of the law of sales. In 1917, he founded the Institute of Comparative Law at the University of Munich.[10] In 1926, the Kaiser Wilhelm Foundation for the Advancement of Science established two larger comparative law institutes, one in the area of foreign and international public law and the other in foreign and international private law.[11] Ernst Rabel became the director of the Kaiser Wilhelm – now Max Planck[12] – Institute for Foreign and International Private Law in Berlin.[13] Along with these institutes, the *Journal of Foreign and International Private Law (Rabel's Journal)* was established.[14] One of the studies undertaken by the Institute was the comparative study of the law of the sale of goods. In 1926, the League of Nations in Rome founded an intergovernmental organization, the Institut international pour l'unification du droit privé (International Institute for the

---

[3] Franco Ferrari, "International Business, Law Merchant, and Law School Curricula," 6 *Yale J. of L. & the Humanities* 95, 96 (1994).

[4] Gabrielle S. Brussel, "The 1980 United Nations Convention on Contracts for the International Sale of Goods: A Legislative Study of the North-South Debates," 6 *New York Int'l L. Rev.* 53, 56 (1993); Klaus P. Berger, "The CENTRAL: List of Principles, Rules and Standards of the Lex Mercatoria, Transnational Law in Commercial Legal Practice," 1 *Central Practice and Study Guides* 127–31 (1999) (describing the different sets of rules and principles of the *lex mercatoria* that were used by the community of merchants).

[5] Harold J. Berman and Colin Kaufman, "The Law of International Commercial Transactions (Lex Mercatoria)," 19 *Harvard Int'l L. J.* 221, 227 (1978).

[6] Brussel, "1980 United Nations Convention," 57.

[7] Allison E. Butler, *A Practical Guide to the CISG: Negotiations through Litigation* (Aspen Publishers, 2006), 7.

[8] Sieg Eiselen, "Adoption of the Vienna Convention for the International Sale of Goods (the CISG) in South Africa," 116 *So. African L. J.* 323, 332 (1999).

[9] Kurt H. Nadelmann, "The Uniform Law on the International Sale of Goods: A Conflict of Laws Imbroglio," 74 *Yale L. J.* 449, 449–50 (1965).

[10] Max Rheinstein, "In Memory of Ernst Rabel," 5 *American J. of Comparative L.* 185, 190 (1956).

[11] Id.

[12] "In the course of World War II, the Institute which Rabel had founded was evacuated from Berlin to Tübingen, and its library suffered severe losses. After the War, the Institute was reorganized under the energetic directorship of Professor Hans Dölle. Under the name Max Planck Institute of Foreign and Private International Law, it [was] ready to move from its constrained emergency quarters in Tübingen to a spacious new building in Hamburg, the city which has traditionally been Germany's window toward the world." Id., 194.

[13] Curriculum vitae of Prof. Dr. Ernst Rabel, available at http://www.globalsaleslaw.org/index.cfm?pageID=649.

[14] Rheinstein, "In Memory," 191.

Unification of Private Law) (UNIDROIT).[15] This institute was an important initiative toward sales unification.[16] UNIDROIT's stated purpose is:

> [T]o examine ways of harmonising and coordinating the private law of States and of groups of States, and to prepare gradually for the adoption by the various States of uniform rules of private law. To this end the Institute shall: (a) prepare drafts of laws and conventions with the object of establishing uniform internal law; (b) prepare drafts of agreements with a view to facilitating international relations in the field of private law; (c) undertake studies in comparative private law; (d) take an interest in projects already undertaken in any of these fields by other institutions with which it may maintain relations as necessary; (e) organise conferences and publish works which the Institute considers worthy of wide circulation.[17]

In 1928, Rabel, as a member of UNIDROIT's board of directors, suggested that its first project focus on the unification of the law relating to international sale of goods.[18] Rabel submitted a provisional report concerning the unification of sales as well as the "Blue Report"[19] in 1929.[20] In 1930, UNIDROIT set up a committee, with Rabel as one of its members, to work on the uniform law of sales project.[21] Other members came from four major legal systems: the Anglo-American, Latin, Germanic, and Scandinavian systems.[22] The committee met eleven times between 1930 and 1934[23] and in 1935 produced a preliminary draft,[24] which was "considerably influenced by the comparative studies on the law of sales which Rabel and his colleagues at the Berlin Institute for International and Foreign Private Law had undertaken."[25] Subsequently, member states of the League of Nations debated and commented on the draft, and in 1939, a second draft was completed.[26] World War II halted negotiations on the draft,[27] but Rabel published his

[15] "Following the demise of the League [of Nations], [UNIDROIT] was re-established as an independent intergovernmental organization on the basis of a multilateral agreement, the UNIDROIT Statute, on 15 March 1940." *Commentary on the UNIDROIT Principles of International Commercial Contracts (PICC)* (ed. S. Vogenauer and J. Kleinheisterkamp) (New York: Oxford University Press, 2009), 6.

[16] Butler, *A Practical Guide*, 7.

[17] Article 1 of the Statute of UNIDROIT, as amended on March 26, 1993, available at www.unidroit.org/mm/statute-e.pdf.

[18] Peter Schlechtriem and Ingeborg Schwenzer, *Commentary on the UN Convention on the International Sale of Goods (CISG)*, 2nd ed. (Oxford, 2005), 1.

[19] *Rapport sur le droit comparé de vente par le "Institut für ausländisches und internationales Privatrecht" de Berlin* (Rome: Pallotta, 1929).

[20] Schlechtriem and Schwenzer, *Commentary*, 2.

[21] Peter Huber and Alastair Mullis, *The CISG: A New Textbook for Students and Practitioners* (Sellier European Law Publishers, 2007), 2.

[22] Gary K. Nakata, "*Filanto S.P.A. v. Chilewich Int'l Corp.*: Sounds of Silence Bellow Forth Under the CISG's International Battle of the Forms," 7 *Transnational Lawyer* 141, 145 (1994).

[23] Huber and Mullis, *The CISG*, 2.

[24] John O. Honnold, *Uniform Law for International Sales under the 1980 United Nations Convention*, 4th ed. (ed. Harry M. Flechtner) (The Netherlands: Kluwer Law International, 2009), 5.

[25] Huber and Mullis, *The CISG*, 2.

[26] Peter Winship, "The Scope of the Vienna Convention on International Sales Contracts," in *International Sales: The United Nations Convention on Contracts for the International Sale of Goods* (ed. N. M. Galston and H. Smit) (1984), 4.

[27] E. Allan Farnsworth, "Formation of International Sales Contracts: Three Attempts at Unification," 110 *U. of Pennsylvania L. Rev.* 305, 306 (1962).

epochal treatise *Das Recht des Warenkaufs* on the law of sale of goods in 1936 (Volume 1) and 1957 (Volume 2).[28]

The project on the law of sale of goods resumed in the 1950s. In 1951, UNIDROIT held a conference of twenty-one states at The Hague.[29] Revised drafts were sent to governments for comments in 1956 and 1963 while work also commenced on a uniform law for the formation of sales contracts.[30] A diplomatic conference of twenty-eight states met at The Hague in April of 1964 to work on both drafts.[31] Shortly thereafter, the Uniform Law for the International Sale of Goods (ULIS) and the Uniform Law on the Formation of Contract for the International Sale of Goods (ULF) were finalized.[32] ULIS and ULF came into force in 1972 with ratification by five States[33] but ultimately, only nine States[34] ratified the Conventions.

The ULIS and ULF were criticized for the abstractness of several key legal concepts and the failure to address the needs of the developing countries, Eastern Europe, and the United States.[35] Another effort at sales law unification began in 1966 when the General Assembly of the United Nations established the United Nations Commission on International Trade Law (UNCITRAL), a permanent committee initially consisting of twenty-nine States.[36] In 1968, with the general mandate to promote "progressive harmonization and unification of the law of international trade,"[37] the commission created a Working Group consisting of fourteen states[38] to "prepare [draft legislation] that would facilitate acceptance by countries of different legal, social, and economic systems."[39] Taking into consideration earlier failures at unification, UNCITRAL carefully weighed its approach to its unification project. John Honnold has stated that:

> [W]hen UNCITRAL met to organize its works on the unification of the law for international trade, it was agreed at the outset that priority should be given to sales of goods,

---

[28] Huber and Mullis, *The CISG*, 2.

[29] Honnold, *Uniform Law for International Sales*, 4th ed., 5.

[30] Id.

[31] Id., 6.

[32] John O. Honnold, *Documentary History of the Uniform Law for International Sales: The Studies, Deliberations, and Decisions that Led to the 1980 United Nations CISG with Introductions and Explanations* (The Netherlands: Kluwer Law and Taxation Publishers, 1989), 1.

[33] Winship, "Scope of the Vienna CISG," 12 n. 25.

[34] ULIS and ULF entered into force in Belgium on August 18, 1972; Gambia on September 5, 1974; Germany on April 16, 1974; Israel on August 18, 1972 (ULIS) and November 20, 1980 (ULF); Italy on August 23, 1972; Luxembourg on August 6, 1979; the Netherlands on August 18, 1972; San Marino on August 18, 1972; Great Britain (with reservation requiring parties to opt-in) on August 18, 1972.

[35] Winship, "Scope of the Vienna Convention," 11–12.

[36] UNCITRAL's membership expanded to thirty-six states in 1973; Africa was represented by nine states, Asia by seven states, Eastern Europe by five states, Latin America by six states, Western Europe and others (including Australia, Canada, the United States, and New Zealand) by nine states. Schlechtriem and Schwenzer, "Commentary," 2–3. For the U.N.'s determination of the need for a uniform sales law, see UNCITRAL Web site at http://www.uncitral.org/uncitral/en/about/origin.html (recognizing that the disparity in domestic laws governing international trade created obstacles to the flow of trade).

[37] UNCITRAL Web site.

[38] Although the Working Group represented less than half of the full commission's membership, the states nevertheless reflected UNCITRAL's worldwide representation. These states included: Brazil, France, Ghana, Hungary, India, Iran, Japan, Kenya, Mexico, Norway, Tunisia, Union of Soviet Socialist Republics, the United Kingdom of Great Britain and Northern Ireland, and the United States of America.

[39] John O. Honnold, *Uniform Law for International Sales under the 1980 United Nations Convention*, 3rd ed. (The Hague: Kluwer Law International, 1999), 8.

negotiable instruments for international payments, and arbitration. In considering what to do about international sales, the first question was: Should UNCITRAL promote a wider adoption of the 1964 Hague Sales Conventions as it did with respect to the 1958 Convention on the Recognition and Enforcement of Foreign Arbitral Awards? Or should it prepare a new Convention? This led to a more specific question: Would it be possible to obtain a wide spread adoption of the 1964 Conventions? On this question further information was needed. So the Commission authorized the Secretary General to ask Governments whether they intended to adhere to these Conventions, and to give their reasons.[40]

In deciding whether The Hague Conventions would be adopted, the text of the conventions, along with a commentary by Professor André Tunc, an influential member of the ULIS drafting committee,[41] were sent to all governments with an invitation to comment on the conventions as well as their positions on ratification.[42] During this consultation period, it was determined that major trading nations would not ratify The Hague Conventions, even if they were revised, because states were concerned that these conventions "reflected the legal traditions and economic realities of continental Western Europe."[43] Although it was decided that it was necessary to draft a new convention.[44] The Hague Conventions nevertheless marked a significant achievement in the development of a uniform international sales law, and would provide the framework for the drafting of the CISG.[45]

III. Development of the CISG

There were three phases in the development of the CISG.[46] Between 1970 and 1977, under the leadership of Chairman Jorge Barrera Graf, the Working Group held nine sessions.[47] The first session was held on January 5, 1970 with all Working Group members represented, except for Tunisia, along with various observer states, as well as intergovernmental and international nongovernmental organizations.[48] In 1976, the Working Group completed and unanimously passed a draft Convention on the International Sale of Goods (Sales Draft), which set forth the rights and obligations of sellers and buyers under sales contracts.[49] The following year, the Working Group Draft on Formation of the Sales Contract (Formation Draft) was also completed.[50] Starting the second phase of

---

[40] John O. Honnold, *On the Road to Unification of the Law of Sales* (The Netherlands: Kluwer Law and Taxation Publishers, 1983), 6.

[41] E. Allan Farnsworth, "Developing International Trade Law," 9 *California Western Int'l L. J.* 461, 462 (1971).

[42] Honnold, *Uniform Law for International Sales*, 3rd ed., 8.

[43] Claire M. Germain, "The United Nations CISG on Contracts for the International Sale of Goods: Guide to Research and Literature," 24 *Int'l J. of Legal Information* 48, 50 (1996).

[44] Franco Ferrari, "Specific Topics of the CISG in the Light of Judicial Application and Scholarly Writing," 15 *J. of L. & Commerce* 1, 7–8 (1995).

[45] Trevor Perea, "*Treibacher Industrie, A.G. v. Allegheny Technologies, Inc.*: A Perspective on the Lackluster Implementation of the CISG by American Courts," 20 *Pace Int'l L. Rev.* 191, 196 (2008).

[46] Honnold, *Documentary History*, 2–3.

[47] Id., 3.

[48] Id., 15.

[49] Id., 3.

[50] Id.

the CISG's development, UNCITRAL convened in Vienna from May to June 1977 to review, finalize, and unanimously approve the Sales Draft.[51] In New York, from May to June of 1978, the full commission reviewed the Formation Draft and formed a drafting group of ten states to integrate the Sales Draft and Formation Draft.[52] In June 1978, the commission completed the integration work and unanimously approved the 1978 UNCITRAL Draft Convention on Contracts for the International Sale of Goods (New York Draft).[53]

A UN-authorized diplomatic conference[54] for the purpose of voting on the New York Draft[55] was convened in Vienna from March 10 to April 11, 1980, with sixty-two states and eight international organizations in attendance.[56] In this third phase of the CISG's development, two committees were formed to work on different sections of the New York Draft: the First Committee focused on the substantive provisions (Parts I-III, Articles 1–88), while the Second Committee worked on the final provisions governing CISG entry into force and related matters (Part IV, Articles 89–101).[57] The Second Committee also prepared a protocol to the 1974 Convention on the Limitation Period in the International Sale of Goods, modifying its provisions on sphere of applicability, to make the 1974 Limitation Convention conform to the New York Draft.[58] The texts prepared by the First and Second Committees were then voted on, article by article, in plenary session.[59] Honnold observed:

> Nearly all the provisions in the UNCITRAL Draft Convention of 1978 were approved in substance . . . The degree of approval resulted from the fact that representatives from each region of the world had participated in preparing the draft. In addition, most delegates realized that the eighty-eight articles of the uniform sales law (Parts I-III) were closely related to each other [and] major changes in individual articles could affect the integrity of the structure. As the Conference progressed with its article-to-article discussion it became evident that the time for review of the draft as a whole would be limited, as compared with the repeated reviews that occurred during the decade of work [proceeding the Conference].[60]

Although each article required approval by a two-thirds majority, of the eighty-eight substantive articles found in Parts I-III, seventy-four were approved unanimously and eight received only one or two negative votes.[61] Except in two instances, the remaining articles received approval with large majorities, and the outstanding two articles were also approved with no dissent after ad hoc working groups resolved the disagreements.[62]

---

[51] Id., 318.
[52] Id., 364.
[53] Schlechtriem and Schwenzer, *Commentary*, 2.
[54] See generally Honnold, *Documentary History*.
[55] Heidi Stanton, "How to Be or Not to Be: The United Nations Convention on Contracts for the International Sale of Goods, Article 6," 4 *Cardozo J. Int'l & Comp. L.* 423, 426 (1996).
[56] Honnold, *Uniform Law for International Sales*, 4th ed., 10.
[57] Honnold, *Documentary History*, 3–4.
[58] Honnold, *Uniform Law for International Sales*, 4th ed., 12.
[59] Id.
[60] Id., 10–11.
[61] Id., 12.
[62] Id.

After the plenary vote, the entire CISG was submitted to a roll call vote and approved unanimously.[63]

The CISG was adopted on April 11, 1980.[64] Eleven states, representing "every geographical region and every major legal, social, and economic system"[65] signed the CISG immediately.[66] By September 30, 1981, a total of eighteen states signed the CISG.[67] By December 11, 1986, eleven states deposited instruments of adherence with the Secretary General, satisfying the requirements of Article 99, which provides that the CISG will come into force "on the first day of the month following the expiration of twelve months after the date of deposit of the tenth instrument of ratification, acceptance, approval or accession, including an instrument which contains a declaration made under Article 92."[68] The CISG entered into force on January 1, 1988.[69]

While the CISG contains elements found in the ULIS and ULF, there are major differences between these conventions. The CISG is a self-executing treaty "where legal rules arising from the treaty are open for immediate application by national judges and all living persons in contracting states are entitled to assert their rights or demand the fulfillment of another person's duty by referring directly to the legal rules of the treaty."[70] On the other hand, The Hague Conventions were "drawn up as an annex to an international treaty and had to be brought into force."[71] ULIS has a vertical structure and addressed remedies related directly to each obligation, while the CISG adopts a horizontal structure – first providing rules for sellers' obligations followed by buyers' remedies, and then setting out buyers' obligations followed by sellers' remedies.[72] The CISG, unlike the ULIS and ULF, regulates the formation of the sales contract between two foreign parties and provides the substantive law governing international sales in one document.[73] Another difference is that the CISG reconciles "different legal traditions" and involved more countries in the drafting process, as shown in Table 2.1.[74] Finally, compared to The Hague Conventions, the CISG contains more open-ended legal concepts in order to allow it to gain wider acceptance of the participating countries.[75]

---

[63] Franco Ferrari, *The Sphere of Application of Vienna Sales Convention* (The Netherlands: Kluwer Law International, 1995), 4.

[64] Honnold, *Uniform Law for International Sales*, 4th ed., 3.

[65] Germain, "United Nations Convention on Contracts," 51.

[66] The eleven states were: Argentina, China, Egypt, France, Hungary, Italy, Lesotho, Syrian Arab Republic, the United States, Yugoslavia, and Zambia. Honnold, *Uniform Law for International Sales*, 4th ed., 3.

[67] The eighteen signatory states are: Austria, Chile, China, Denmark, Finland, France, Germany, Ghana, Hungary, Italy, Lesotho, The Netherlands, Norway, Poland, Singapore, Sweden, the United States, and Venezuela. Three additional states also signed the CISG but they no longer exist: the former German Democratic Republic, the former Czechoslovakia, and the former Yugoslavia.

[68] CISG, Article 99, "United Nations Convention on Contracts for the International Sale of Goods (1980)," 52 *Federal Register* 6262, 6264–80 (March 2, 1987).

[69] Honnold, *Uniform Law for International Sales*, 4th ed., 3.

[70] Ferrari, *The Sphere of Application*, 4–5.

[71] Schlechtriem and Schwenzer, *Commentary*, 3.

[72] Id., 4.

[73] Kathryn S. Cohen, "Achieving a Uniform Law Governing International Sales: Conforming the Damage Provisions of the United Nations Convention on Contracts for the International Sale of Goods and the Uniform Commercial Code," 26 *U. of Pennsylvania J. of Int'l Economic L.* 601, 606 (2005).

[74] Id., 605–6.

[75] Schlechtriem and Schwenzer, *Commentary*, 4.

Table 2.1. *Country Membership According to Economic Development Stage and Political System*[76]

Events	Country Economic Region		
	Developed	Developing	Socialist Bloc
Hague Conference	78.6%	10.7%	10.7%
UNCITRAL	25.0%	61.0%	14.0%
Working Group	33–41%	41–50%	14–21%
CISG Participation	35.5%	46.8%	17.7%

IV. Structure of the CISG

The CISG has been translated into six official languages (Arabic, Chinese, English, French, Russian, and Spanish) and dozens of unofficial languages.[77] The text of the treaty is divided into four parts. The first three parts provide the general rules and principles governing sales transactions: Part I, Articles 1–13 (sphere of application, rules of interpretation, and form requirements), Part II, Articles 14–24 (contract formation), Part III, Articles 25–88 (obligations of seller and buyer, remedies for breach, passing of risk, anticipatory breach and instalment contracts, damages, interest and exemptions), and Part IV (states' ratification, acceptance, approval, or accession to the CISG and applicability – Articles 91 and 100; CISG's relationship with other international agreements – Article 90 and 99; State declarations and Reservations – Articles 92, 94–98; applicability to territorial units – Article 93; denunciation – Article 101).

V. Contracting States

Since its entry into force, eighty countries have adopted the CISG,[78] reflecting a global consensus on legal principles related to the international sale of goods. Statistically, this means an average of 2.6 ratifications or accessions per year; this pace of adoption makes the CISG the second most adopted treaty in the field of international trade law, after the New York Convention.[79] However, two major trading nations have not adopted the CISG: India and the United Kingdom. Interestingly, India and the United Kingdom are consistently within the top ten users of the Pace CISG Database. Maps 2.1, 2.2, 2.3, 2.4, and 2.5 show the CISG contracting states by region.[80]

---

[76] Brussel, "1980 United Nations Convention," 61.

[77] Unofficial language versions include Czech, Danish, Dutch, Finnish, German, Italian, Japanese, Norwegian, Persian, Polish, Portuguese, Serbian, and Swedish.

[78] For a "Table of Contracting States" see http://www.cisg.law.pace.edu/cisg/countries/cntries.html.

[79] Luca G. Castellani, "Promoting the Adoption of the United Nations Convention on Contracts for the International Sale of Goods (CISG)," 13 *Vindobona J. of Int'l Commercial L. & Arbitration* 244 (2009) (citations omitted). Based on the number of ratifications and/or accessions to the CISG since 2009, the yearly average is slightly lower at 2.48 per year.

[80] Transcontinental countries have been listed within both regions of which they are a part solely for purposes of calculating regional representation.

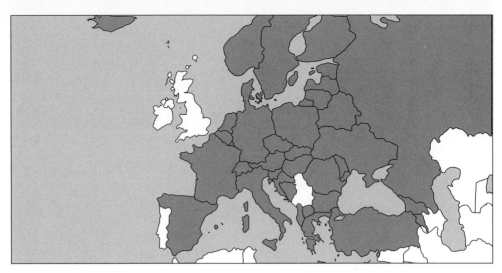

Map 2.1. Europe (39 contracting states out of 48 European UN member states or 81.25%).

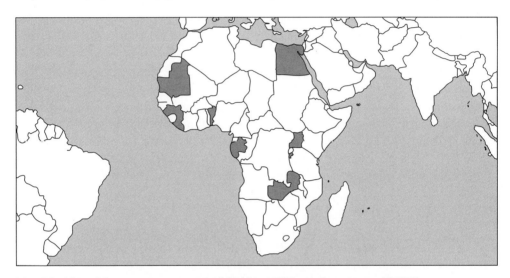

Map 2.2. Africa (10 contracting states out of 54 African UN member states or 18.52%).

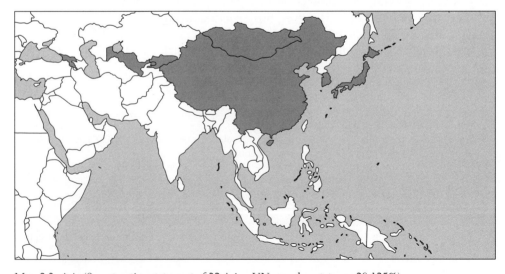

Map 2.3. Asia (9 contracting states out of 32 Asian UN member states or 28.125%).

Map 2.4. South America (8 contracting states out of 12 South American UN member states or 66.67%).

The majority of European countries have adopted the CISG and the European Commission has recently issued a proposal for a Common European Sales Law.[81] The formation rules of the CESL were influenced by the CISG.[82]

Despite the presence and involvement of African countries in the development of the CISG, it has been adopted by less than one-fifth of African countries. However, the Organization for the Harmonisation of Business Law in Africa (OHADA) published a Draft Uniform Act on Contract Law that is modeled on the UNIDROIT Principles of International Commercial Contracts. Considering the limited number of contracting states, including non-OHADA members, further work must be done in the region to promote the adoption of the CISG.

With the relatively recent adoption of the CISG by Japan, along with previous adoptions by the People's Republic of China and South Korea, a major regional trading block within Asia is under the auspices of the CISG. However, as the map demonstrates, southeastern and western states within Asia have not adopted the CISG. This is partly due to the lack of influence Asian culture and Islamic law had in the development of

---

[81] European Commission's Proposal for a Regulation of the European Parliament and of the Council on a Common European Sales Law, 2011/0284 (COD) (October 11, 2011). See also European Parliament's Report on Policy Options for Progress Towards a European Contract Law for Consumers and Businesses, A7–0164/2011 (April 18, 2011).

[82] See generally *Common European Sales Law (CESL): Commentary* (ed. Reiner Schulze) (Baden-Baden, Germany: Nomos; Munich: C.H. Beck; and Hart Publishing, 2012). For a critical review of the CESL in relationship to the CISG, see Larry A. DiMatteo, "The Curious Case of Transborder Sales Law: A Comparative Analysis of CESL, CISG, and the UCC," in *CISG vs. Regional Sales Law Unification* (ed. Ulrich Magnus) (Sellier, 2012), 25. The development of a European Contract Law follows the extensive work that has already been completed by the Principles of European Contract Law, published in three parts from 1995 to 2003. In its relevant parts, the principles largely adhere to the same conclusions established within the CISG. See *Principles of European Contract Law Parts I and II* (ed. O. Lando and H. Beale) (The Hague: Kluwer Law International, 2000).

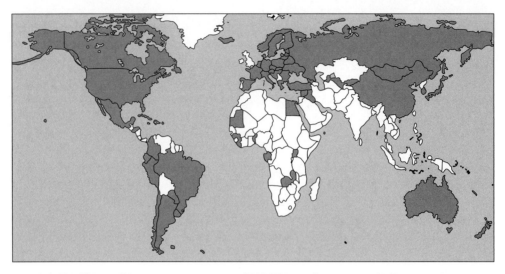

Map 2.5. World Map (80 contracting states out of 193 UN member states = 41%).

the CISG.[83] Partly given this consideration, an academic initiative is underway to the harmonize contract rules via the drafting of the Principles of Asian Contract Law.

It is further worth noting that the China International Economic and Trade Arbitration Commission (CIETAC) has been one of the most transparent arbitration associations in the world regarding the dissemination of its CISG arbitral awards. The Pace CISG Database includes over three hundred CIETAC awards (translated into English). Since most international sales contracts contain arbitration clauses, the reporting of CISG arbitration awards is essential to the creation of a "global jurisconsultorium" (see discussion *infra*) as well as uniform application of the CISG.

It is noteworthy that Brazil has just acceded to the Convention, becoming the seventy-ninth contracting state. Well before the accession by Brazil, academics and practitioners have been laying the foundation to educate Brazilian lawyers about the CISG via the creation of a Brazilian CISG Database, an essay competition to encourage scholarly writing on the CISG and a translation program to translate CISG decisions into Portuguese.[84]

In its totality, the world map (Map 2.5) shows that the CISG is a remarkable achievement in having been adopted across many distinct and varying legal cultures. But it is also clear that there are gaps in representation that need to be closed.

VI. Impact of the CISG on National Law Reform

The CISG's modern rules have gone far to help international trade to escape from what Ernst Rabel called the "awesome relics of the dead past that populate in amazing multitude the older codifications of sales law."[85]

---

[83] Gary F. Bell, "New Challenges for the Uniformisation of Laws: How the CISG is Challenged by 'Asian Values' and Islamic Law," in *Towards Uniformity: The 2nd Annual MAA Schlechtriem CISG Conference* (ed. I. Schwenzer and L. Spagnolo) (The Hague: Eleven International Publishing, 2011), 11.
[84] See http://www.cisg-brasil.net.
[85] Honnold, *On the Road to Unification*, 12.

Whether or not foreseen at the time of creation, history will determine if the CISG's greatest contribution was providing a set of uniform rules for international sales contracts or if its greatest impact was establishing a model for international, regional, and domestic law reforms. Professor Hiroo Sono refers to this latter process "as uniformity or harmonization through 'assimilation.'"[86] Professor Sono states that:

> Assimilation is most conspicuous in legislation influenced by the CISG, e.g., China, Germany, the Scandinavian countries (other than Denmark), former socialist states such as Russia and Estonia. This process of "legislative assimilation" is occurring also in Japan, which acceded to the CISG in 2008.

> On the other hand, there is a more discreet and indirect way in which assimilation is achieved. That is by interpretation of existing domestic laws in light of the CISG, and thereby transforming understanding of existing laws. This process of "interpretative assimilation" can also be observed in Japan even prior to its accession to the CISG.[87]

Professor Peter Schlechtriem on the legislative assimilation of the CISG in the former socialist states:

> [The influence of the CISG] is most obvious in the former socialist states, which, in the process of transforming and restructuring their societies and economic systems to accommodate democratic and market-oriented Western-style systems, also reformed and re-codified their legal systems. The CISG model was one of those considered, compared, and weighed, especially in countries that had implemented it already – or were to implement it – as their international sales law, and the Estonian Law of Obligations Act is a noteworthy example. Since 10 of these former socialist states have become members of the European Union and had to implement the European *acquis* – i.e., the legal rules of the EU enacted as regulations, directives, etc. – they also had to implement the Directive on the Sale of Consumer Goods, thereby initiating another "channel of influence" of the CISG.[88]

The legislative assimilation is not restricted to the development of modern domestic sales laws. As noted previously, the CISG has had an impact on regional agreements on the sale of goods.[89] Moreover, its specific provisions have had an impact on the content of related international agreements:

> Article 7 of the CISG offers several safeguards to prevent a "re-nationalization" of international uniform law by, firstly, stating directives for its interpretation and, secondly, providing for gap-filling. These, too, have become almost standard clauses for international instruments – e.g., in Art. 7 of the Limitation Convention . . . , Art. 6 (1) of the 1983 (Geneva) draft Convention on Agency in the International Sale of Goods, Art. 4 (1) of the UNIDROIT Convention on International Factoring of 1988 (Ottawa), Art. 6 (1) of the UNIDROIT Convention on International Financial Leasing of 1988 (Ottawa), Art. 7 (1) of the 2001 UN Convention on the Assignment of Receivables in International

---

[86] Hiroo Sono, "The Diversity of Favor Contractus: The Impact of the CISG on Japan's Civil Code and Its Reform," in Schwenzer and Spagnolo, *Towards Uniformity*.

[87] Id.

[88] Peter Schlechtriem, "Basic Structures and General Concepts of the CISG as Models for a Harmonization of the Law of Obligations," *Juridica Int'l* 27–36 (2005).

[89] See Michael J. Bonell, "The CISG, European Contract Law and the Development of a World Contract Law," 56 *American J. of Comparative L.* 1 (2008).

Trade, and Art. 5 of the Convention on International Interests in Mobile Equipment (Cape Town Convention) of 2001.[90]

Regarding interpretative assimilation, Petra Butler has analyzed the impact of the CISG on the interpretation of domestic contract law in common law jurisdictions, noting, by way of example:

> In New Zealand a comparatively greater shift has occurred in regard to the use of pre- and post-contractual conduct as an aid to contractual interpretation . . . Sitting in New Zealand's highest Court, McGrath J recently noted in *Vector Gas Ltd v. Bay of Plenty Energy Ltd* that "[o]ver the past 40 years the common law has increasingly come to recognize that the meaning of a contractual text is clarified by the circumstances in which it was written and what they indicate about its purpose" (it is not quite clear though whether his Honour is only referring to New Zealand or also to English law). An impact of the CISG can be felt in regard to the question of the extent to which pre- and post-contractual conduct can be taken into account when interpreting a contract.[91]

> [The Canadian case of] *Brown & Root Services Corp v. Aerotech Herman Nelson Inc.* concerned a contract for the sale of portable heaters between a Manitoba vendor and a Texas buyer. Even though the CISG would have applied to the contract the Court failed to recognise its applicability and resolved all of the issues with exclusive reference to Manitoba statutory law, common law and domestic cases. However, the defendant relied on Articles 38 and 40 to enhance its position in that the claimant took too long to assert a fundamental breach or repudiation of the contract. The Court accepted the principle stipulated by Articles 38 and 40 but rejected the argument on the facts.[92]

These examples illustrate the broad impact the CISG has had on domestic and international sales law development. As domestic and regional contract laws continue to modernize, it is clear the CISG will remain an influential template.

VII. Global Efforts to Promote the Adoption and Use of the CISG

The widespread adoption of the CISG, along with its influence on the development of international, regional, and domestic law, is a reflection of the international efforts aimed at promoting the CISG. For example, in 2004, UNCITRAL created a Technical Assistance and Coordination Unit within the secretariat to promote UNCITRAL texts. One of the efforts of this unit was to sponsor several conferences around the world celebrating the twenty-fifth anniversary of the CISG.[93] Since then, the majority of conferences promoting awareness of the CISG bear UNCITRAL sponsorship. UNCITRAL has also developed the CLOUT[94] database that provides abstracts of cases as well as arbitral awards and is translated into the official UN languages: "The purpose of the system is to promote international awareness of the legal texts formulated by the Commission

---

[90] Schlechtriem, "Basic Structures," 27–36.

[91] Petra Butler, "The Use of the CISG in Domestic Law," 3 *Annals of the Faculty of Law in Belgrade-Belgrade L. Rev. Year LIX* 7, 18–19 (2011).

[92] Id., 25.

[93] Castellani, "Promoting the Adoption," 244.

[94] Case Law on UNCITRAL Texts (CLOUT), information available at http://www.uncitral.org/uncitral/en/ case_law.html.

and to facilitate uniform interpretation and application of those texts."[95] Moreover, UNCITRAL publishes a CISG Digest of Case Law reporting on CISG decisions from around the world.[96]

Academic institutions from around the world report domestic CISG developments online, including case law and scholarly commentaries. This "autonomous network" of CISG databases not only provides accessibility and awareness, but also has been a critical tool in mitigating "homeward trend" bias. Franco Ferrari defines the concept as follows:

> According to those CISG commentators who have not only referred to the homeward trend, but who have also attempted to define it, the homeward trend is akin to the natural tendency of those interpreting the CISG to project the domestic law in which the interpreter was trained (and with which he or she is likely most familiar) onto the international provisions of the Convention. It is, in other words, the tendency to think that the words we see in the text of the CISG are merely trying, in their awkward way, to state the domestic rule we know so well.[97]

The opposite of "homeward trend" is reasoning based on a "global juris-consultorium."[98] The autonomous network of CISG databases provides a platform for global jurisconsultorium reasoning:

> The foundation of the Autonomous Network of CISG Websites is collegiality. The Internet is a very inexpensive and effective way for us to cooperate in this manner.

> This is a uniform law network. The world's uniform international sales law belongs to each country and to all countries. To help one another, we share experience and lessons learned. Each national or regional website provider designs its site to best serve traders and counsel of its home market; together we serve the world market. The network is synergetic – the whole is greater than the sum of its parts.[99]

As a member of the network, the Pace CISG Database is one of the most comprehensive databases on international sales law materials, accumulating domestic law materials into one global reporting database. The database currently contains more than 2,900 cases and arbitral awards, 9,469 bibliography entries in thirty-one languages, and 1,440 full-text CISG articles. To promote the concept of the global jurisconsultorium, the Pace Institute of International Commercial Law created the Queen Mary Case Translation Programme: "The Queen Mary Case Translation Programme is a public service open to the academic and practising legal communities and provides high quality professional translations into English of foreign case law (including arbitral awards) relating to the

[95] Id.

[96] UNCITRAL CISG Digest of Case Law, information available at http://www.cnudmi.org/uncitral/en/case-law/digests/cisg.html.

[97] Franco Ferrari, "Homeward Trend and Lex Forism Despite Uniform Sales Law," 13 *Vindobona J. of Int'l Commercial L. & Arbitration* 15, 22 (2009).

[98] The term was originally proposed in Vikki Rogers and Albert Kritzer, "A Uniform Sales Law Terminology," in *Festschrift für Peter Schlechtriem zum 70 Gerburtstag* (ed. I. Schwenzer and G. Hager) (Tübingen: J.B.C. Mohr/Paul Siebeck, 2003), available at http://CISGw3.law.pace.edu/CISG/Biblio/rogers2.html. See Andersen, *Uniform Application*, 13 (global jurisconsultorium as "cross-border consultation in deciding issues of uniform law").

[99] The Autonomous Network of CISG Websites, Pace CISG Database, available at http://www.cisg.law.pace.edu/network.html.

CISG and UNIDROIT Principles."[100] To date, almost 2,000 cases have been translated into English via the Translation Programme. Professor Kritzer stated that:

> To comply with the mandate recited in article 7(1) CISG, courts *must* have due regard to the "international character" of the CISG "and to the need to promote uniformity in its application," and scholars *must* be equipped to assist judges struggling to comprehend the ramifications and applications of this uniform international sales law.[101]

Twenty years ago, the Pace Institute of International Commercial Law established the Willem C. Vis International Arbitration Moot (Moot).

> [In order to a]chieve the universal acceptance and common use of the Sales Convention as the law applicable to contracts for the international sale of goods, it is suggested that UNCITRAL establish the International Trade Law Moot Arbitration Programme and annually conduct a global competition open to teams representing locally accredited educational institutions with a nexus to international trade. Such teams would be comprised of matriculating students from any graduate level business school or school of international affairs and any law school.

> An UNCITRAL moot arbitration competition based on a problem stemming from transactions for the international sale of goods and open to teams from schools of business, international affairs and law would stimulate and captivate the interest of persons on the campus. The preparation of the briefs for submission to the Moot arbitration Board would enlist an expansive spectrum of competent persons to ponder and comment on Sales Convention issues present in real world transactions as framed by the problem. The Moot Arbitration Programme would also engage the interest of jurists, practicing lawyers, arbitrators, academicians and others invited to serve as moot arbitrators.[102]

Indeed, the Moot has engaged the interest of the international commercial law and arbitration community. The Moot now attracts teams from over 300 schools (more than one thousand students) from about sixty countries, along with hundreds of practitioners and academics who review written memoranda and serve as arbitrators during the oral arguments. Student participants enter the competition knowledgeable in their own domestic contract law, and leave with a firm understanding of international sales law and international arbitration.

VIII. Conclusion

The long history of the CISG produced a credible legal instrument influencing both international trade law and the modernization of domestic and regional sales laws. The further collection and dissemination of CISG materials will expand its influence in the future.

---

[100] The Queen Mary Translation Programme, available at http://www.cisg.law.pace.edu/cisg/text/queenmary .html.

[101] Id.

[102] Uniform Commercial Law in the Twenty-First Century: Proceedings of the Congress of the United Nations Commission on International Trade Law, Remarks of Michael Sher, 94–103, 101, New York, May 18–22, 1992, available at A/CH.9/Ser.D/1; UN Sales No. E.94.V.14.

3   The CISG: Divergences between Success–Scarcity and Theory–Practice

*Olaf Meyer**

I. The CISG: A Success Story

The two Hague Conventions on the sale of goods that preceded the CISG fell far short of the expectations placed upon them. So the expectations for the CISG were hopeful, but not very realistic.[1] However, more than thirty years later, the creators of the CISG would have reason to be satisfied with its development. This success can be viewed from several different perspectives. It has been adopted by eighty nations, and the number is growing. The widespread adoption of the CISG has been called "a success story beyond imagination."[2] It has also stimulated a prodigious amount of research on international sales and contract law. The CISG provides a wealth of highly interesting questions of interpretation, which have challenged international and comparativist scholars for a long time and are now being debated by authors from all over the world. The deep and broad literature on the CISG provides a rich knowledge base for future harmonization efforts.[3]

The best measure of the success of the CISG is the number of court decisions and arbitral awards that have used it. Its practical significance is represented in more than 2,800 published judicial and arbitral decisions, which are listed on the Pace Law School Database.[4] The CISG now enjoys a solid footing in practice.[5] New decisions appear so regularly that the central question has become how to ensure its uniform application.[6]

* The author wishes to express his sincere thanks to Jason Dinse for his very helpful comments and suggestions on an earlier draft.

[1] Twenty-nine states adopted the Convention on the Limitation Period in the International Sale of Goods (1974), but produced only twelve decisions; Geneva Convention on Agency in the International Sale of Goods (1983) never came into force; United Nations Convention on the Assignment of Receivables (2001) was ratified by only one country.

[2] Stefan Kröll, Loukas Mistelis, and Maria del Pilar Perales Viscasillas, eds., "Introduction to the CISG," para. 22 in *UN Convention on Contracts for the International Sale of Goods* (Munich: Beck, 2011) (hereafter referred to as *UN Convention*).

[3] See http://www.cisg.law.pace.edu/cisg/biblio/biblio.html.

[4] See http://www.cisg.law.pace.edu/cisg/text/casecit.html.

[5] See "Introduction to the CISG," in *UN Convention*, paras. 39–45.

[6] Cf. *CISG Methodology* (ed. André Janssen and Olaf Meyer) (Munich: Sellier European Law Publishers, 2009); Camilla Baasch Andersen, *Uniform Application of the International Sales Law: Understanding Uniformity, the Global Jurisconsultorium and Examination and Notification Provisions of the CISG* (Alphen aan den Rijn: Kluwer Law International, 2007); Sonja Kruisinga, *(Non-)Conformity in the 1980 UN Convention on Contracts for the International Sale of Goods: A Uniform Concept?* (Antwerp: Intersentia, 2004).

However, the dispersion of cases among the provisions has been uneven. At one end of the spectrum, there are some highly disputed provisions, such as Articles 39 and 78, which have generated a great many of cases. Other provisions have rarely been interpreted and applied. Does this uneven distribution of cases necessitate a different evaluation of the success of the CISG? Not all areas of the sales or contract law, whether domestic or international, generate an equal number of cases, as some legal questions are more susceptible to being contested than others. Nonetheless, it is perhaps interesting and worthwhile to take a closer look at the least utilized of the CISG provisions to determine whether the underutilization is due to poor drafting, or whether other explanations can be found.

II. Measuring Success by the Numbers

The 2,872 cases listed in the Pace CISG Database is an inflated number because the only criterion for inclusion is that a case makes any reference to the CISG.[7] No further special criteria, such as that a case needs to apply a substantive provision or rule of the CISG, is required. Nonetheless, because not all cases, especially arbitral decision, are reported, the database acts as a representative sample of all CISG cases. Amongst the most cited CISG provisions is Article 53, the basic rule of the buyer's obligation to pay the contract price (551 citations in the database). Its counterpart, Article 30, the basic obligations of the seller to deliver goods or documents, was cited only 171 times, perhaps an indicator that sellers bring more cases than buyers. One reason for this imbalance is the high thresholds, under Articles 38 and 39, which buyers must overcome to preserve their rights arising from the seller's defective performance. As a result, Article 39 CISG is likewise and not surprisingly among the most widely contested provisions of the CISG (563 citations).

The most cited provisions are in the area of remedies and damages, including Article 78, relating to recovering interest (797 decisions), and Article 74, the CISG's basic damages provision (855 citations). The damage remedy clearly dominates in practice over the other rights available to the parties for a breach of contract.

The informative value of the empirical accounting just presented is dubious without being more thoroughly scrutinized. For example, citation counts may be affected by the quality of the drafting of respective provisions. A well-written, well-formulated rule will not generate as many disputes over its application irrespective of the area of the law. It has been stated that the fact that the CISG contains numerous vague terms likely accounts for a portion of CISG contract disputes.[8]

Moreover, the databases do not differentiate whether a provision was a basis for a decision or was simply mentioned as *obiter dictum*. For instance, a party might wrongly rely

---

[7] See http://www.cisg.law.pace.edu/cisg/text/casecit.html (as of October 5, 2011). The UNILEX database (www.unilex.info) lists 891 entries regarding the CISG. The Clout database, maintained by UNCITRAL (http://www.uncitral.org/uncitral/en/case_law.html?lf=899&lng=en), lists a total of 648 decisions. Cases citing only Article 1 are not counted in determining the most cited CISG provisions since "almost every CISG case is in a certain sense an Article 1 case." In his commentary, Loukas Mistelis tallied known Article 1 cases and found 731 of such cases. Loukas Mistelis, in *UN Convention*, Article 1, para. 24.

[8] Cf. Filip de Ly, "Opting Out: Some Observations," in *Quo Vadis CISG?* (Franco Ferrari ed., Bruylant: Brussels 2005), 37f.; Ulrich Magnus, "Germany," in *The CISG and Its Impact in National Legal Systems* (ed. Franco Ferrari) (Munich: Sellier, 2008), 146f.

upon a certain provision, which ultimately does not factor into the court's decision. Furthermore, the fact that many provisions regulate several different issues is not adequately taken into consideration through the undifferentiated references in the databases. This applies, for example, to the two paragraphs in CISG Article 7, as well as to the various limitations to the scope of the CISG found in Articles 2 and 4. Some articles, such as Article 31 CISG (149 cases) and Article 58 CISG (130 cases), are quoted not because of their substantive significance, but rather to deal with jurisdictional issues particular to the forum court.[9]

III. "Quiet" Areas of the CISG

This part explores the uneven nature of CISG case law. It also analyzes some seemingly important CISG provisions that have had limited impact in the case law. Finally, it offers reasons for the uneven nature of CISG case law. It examines the jurisdictional scope of the CISG, exclusion and partial derogation under Article 6, and the divergence in the depth of scholarly literature with the relative depth of the case law relating to given provisions of the CISG.

A. *Theoretical Issues and Practical Significance*

This section explores the twin areas of CISG jurisdiction under CISG Article 1, as well as the exclusion of product liability under Article 5.

1. Indirect Application of the CISG by Noncontracting States: Article 1(1)(b)

CISG Article 1 acts as the gateway to CISG jurisdiction. Article 1 provides two avenues for CISG jurisdiction – either both parties to the contract have their places of business in different contracting states (Article 1(1)(a)) or the rules of private international law lead to the application of the law of a contracting state (Article 1(1)(b)). Article 1(1)(a) jurisdiction is the easiest to determine because the court does not need to apply conflict of law rules. Article 1(1)(b) was controversial from the beginning both because it expanded the reach of the CISG and because it allowed countries to opt out of its application, adding unneeded complexity to the determination of jurisdiction.[10] However, with the growth in the number of contracting states, Article 1(1)(a) jurisdiction has expanded and correspondingly, Article 1(1)(b) has diminished in importance.[11] Nonetheless, Article 1(1)(b) serves as an internal choice of law rule for the law of the contracting state, when the conflict of law rules of the forum court of a noncontracting state direct the court to the contracting state.[12]

---

[9] Cf. Ronald A. Brand, "CISG Article 31: When Substantive Law Rules Affect Jurisdictional Results," 25 *J. of L. & Commerce* 181ff. (2005/6); Ulrich Magnus, "Das UN-Kaufrecht und die Erfüllungsortzuständigkeit in der neuen EuGVO," *Internationales Handelsrecht* (2002), 45ff.

[10] Cf. Ulrich Magnus in Wiener UN-Kaufrecht (*Staudinger Kommentar zum Bürgerlichen Gesetzbuch* (Munich: Sellier, 2005), Article 1, para. 94 (hereafter referred to as *Staudinger*).

[11] Loukas Mistelis in *UN Convention*, Article 1, para. 47; Paul Volken, "Das Wiener Übereinkommen über den internationalen Warenkauf: Anwendungsvoraussetzungen und Anwendungsbereich," in *Einheitliches Kaufrecht und Nationales Obligationenrecht* (ed. Peter Schlechtriem) (Baden-Baden: Nomos, 1987), 96.

[12] Loukas Mistelis in *UN Convention*, Article 1, para. 54; *Staudinger*, Article 1, para. 95; cf. Peter Huber and Alastair Mullis, *The CISG* (Munich: Sellier, 2007), 55f.

Given the existence of Article 1(1)(b), one would expect more CISG cases from noncontracting states. For example, the United Kingdom, a major trading nation, has not yet produced a single substantive decision regarding the CISG. English courts are bound to the European conflict of laws rules, which regularly subject the sales contract to the law of the country where the seller has its place of business.[13] Accordingly, in principle, every English import contract with a party from a CISG contracting state, barring an express opting out, would come under the jurisdiction of the CISG. This is even more remarkable as higher English courts have called on the CISG as persuasive authority when dealing with the development of domestic contract law.[14] One explanation is offered by Qi Zhou in Chapter 41 of this book. He argues that the English Sale of Goods Act is not only a popular choice of law for English traders, but is a popular choice internationally. Hence, if the parties have chosen English law (as is common practice, especially in the commodities trade[15]), the question of applicability of the CISG does not arise. Another reason is that the English judicial system is notoriously expensive[16] and, thus, commercial disputes are often settled out of court.

2. Domestic Product Liability Law under CISG Article 5

Article 5, which excludes from the CISG's scope any liability of the seller for death or personal injury caused by the goods, is among the least cited provisions of the CISG. There have been only two judicial decisions that casually mention Article 5.[17] There are numerous decisions regarding the general relationship between the CISG and national tort law; however, the core subject matter of Article 5 remains unexplored. This practical insignificance is even more surprising given the controversial issue of whether Article 5 excludes a buyer's claim for indemnification against the seller when the buyer is held to be liable to his or her customers for personal harm caused by the goods.[18] The question of whether national product liability standards or the narrow liability regime of the CISG will be applied is of crucial importance.

---

[13] Articles 4(1) and 19(1)(2) Rome I Regulation.

[14] *Proforce Recruit Ltd v. Rugby Group Ltd.*, UK Court of Appeal, 2006 EWCA Civ 69, Feb. 17, 2006, available at http://cisgw3.law.pace.edu/cases/060217uk.html; cf. Michael Joachim Bonell, "The UNIDROIT Principles and CISG: Sources of Inspiration for English Courts?," *Uniform L. Rev.* 305ff. (2006). For an example of a passing reference from Brazil, cf. Rio Grande do Sul Appellate Court, Apelação Cível no. 70025609579, May 20, 2009, available at http://cisgw3.law.pace.edu/cases/090520b5.html.

[15] Cf. regarding the rivalry between the CISG with English law Michael Bridge, "The Bifocal World of International Sales," in *Making Commercial Law: Essays in Honour of Roy Goode* (ed. Ross Cranston) (Oxford: Clarendon, 1997), 277ff.; Alastair Mullis, "Twenty-Five Years On: The United Kingdom, Damages and the Vienna Sales Convention," 71 *RabelsZ* (2007), 35ff.

[16] Gavin Lightman, "The Civil Justice System and Legal Profession: The Challenges Ahead," 22 *Civil Justice Q.* 235, 239 (2003). ("It is sufficient to say that increasingly informed advisors wisely recommend prospective litigants . . . in order to make savings in terms of cost, where it is practical, to sue on the Continent.")

[17] Commercial Court Zurich, HG 920670, April 26, 1995, available at http://cisgw3.law.pace.edu/cases/950426s1.html; *TeeVee Tunes, Inc. et al. v. Gerhard Schubert GmbH*, Federal District Court [New York], 00 Civ. 5189 (RCC), August 23, 2006, available at http://cisgw3.law.pace.edu/cases/060823u1.html.

[18] Cf. *UN Convention*, Article 5, para. 11ff; Ingeborg Schwenzer and Pascal Hachem in *Commentary on the UN Convention on the International Sale of Goods (CISG)*, 3rd ed. (ed. Peter Schlechtriem and Ingeborg Schwenzer) (Oxford University Press, 2010), Article 5, para. 8ff.

Article 5 only indicates when the CISG is not applicable, and, therefore, it is not strictly necessary to cite the provision when a court directly applies domestic product liability law. A German court held that the CISG applied to a claim for indemnification resulting from a demand for damages from a third party, without recognizing Article 5.[19] However, the main reason for the lacking case law in this area is probably due to the peculiarities of product liability law in general. In legal systems in which product liability has developed into its own specific area, product liability insurance is common and most such claims are settled out of court. This reason is supported by the fact that there are also relatively few judicial decisions relating to the European Product Liability Directive.[20]

B. *Derogation by the Parties*

Another explanation for the absence of case law regarding certain provisions of the CISG is that the provisions are excluded in the contract. Article 6 CISG allows the parties to exclude part or all the CISG. So far, the primary attention of researchers has focused on the complete exclusion of the CISG. Their decision to opt out of the CISG is likely due to the parties', and their lawyers', unfamiliarity with its rules.[21] Opting out entirely removes the uncertainty of learning a new law. Professor Ulrich Schroeter, in Chapter 40 of this book, provides an in-depth analysis of opting out of the CISG under Article 6.

The partial derogation of CISG provisions, under Article 6, is the more interesting issue for this chapter. The drafters of the CISG were aware that international commerce is a complex and fast-moving matter and that the parties should be given the flexibility to deal with new developments. The rules of the CISG were thus designed as default rules that apply only to the extent that the parties do not provide for a different rule.[22] Not surprisingly, then, the subject of drafting contracts under the CISG has received increased attention in recent years.[23]

Modification or specification of a CISG rule accommodates the needs of the parties. At several points, the CISG offers the opportunity to provide for increased legal certainty through contractual clarification. For instance, in order to prevent the uncertainty of a judicial determination of the "reasonableness" criterion in Article 39(1), parties can establish a certain period of time for giving notice of nonconforming goods. In recent years, in some countries, courts have recognized a rule of thumb of approximately one month for inspection of goods and giving notice of nonconformity.[24] However, this requirement depends in each case upon the judge's evaluation of a multitude of factors. The result is regularly an all-or-nothing decision. The parties can take precaution by

---

[19] Appellate Court Düsseldorf, 17 U 73/93, July 2, 1993, available at http://cisgw3.law.pace.edu/cases/930702g1.html.

[20] Cf. Report from the Commission on the Application of Directive 85/374 on Liability for Defective Products (COM/2000/0893 final). ("The number of product liability cases seems to be relatively low. 90% of these claims are settled out of court.")

[21] See Chapter 40 of this book.

[22] "Introduction," in *UN Convention*, para. 18, recognizes the principle of party autonomy as a central theme of the CISG.

[23] Cf., e.g., *Drafting Contracts under the CISG* (ed. Harry M. Flechtner, Ronald A. Brand, and Mark S. Walter) (Oxford University Press, 2008).

[24] Huber and Mullis, *The CISG*, 161; *UN Convention*, Article 39, para. 86; Ingeborg Schwenzer, "The 'Noble Month': The Story behind the Scenery," 7 *European J. of L. Reform* 353ff. (2006).

including a clause detailing the requirements for inspection and notice.[25] In many cases, the standard terms and conditions already contain a precise time period for giving notice.[26] Concrete terms could also be used to clarify the concept of "fundamental breach" (CISG Article 25) by providing a measure or criterion for breach or exemption for liability (Article 79(1)) through a detailed *force majeure* clause.[27] Contract clauses modifying Article 74, such as liability limitations or contractual penalties, are standard in international contracts.[28]

Unlike modifying a CISG rule or providing standards for its application, the parties may agree to exclude a CISG rule. Such adaptation through contractual agreement is not problematic for CISG Part III. However, in order to be effective, an agreement to change the rules on contract formation (Part II) should be agreed to in a preliminary agreement, a framework agreement, or an offer composed with modified conditions.[29] In this way, parties could, for example, exclude the modified acceptance rule in Article 19 or the delayed acceptance rule in Article 21. In practice, the customization of CISG rules is rare. The reasons for the lack of revising or excluding specific CISG rules are two-fold. First, the benefit of default rules is lower transaction costs that are incurred by negotiating and drafting highly custom contracts. Second, the party profiting from such a variation or cancellation must regularly give a concession in return for the exclusion of the rule.[30] The parties' willingness to apply the rules of the CISG as they stand may also be understood as proof that the Convention contains a fair and equitable set of rules that is acceptable to both buyers and sellers alike.

The situation is different in trades where preformulated standard conditions or established trade usages exist, which play an important role in CISG interpretive methodology. The drafters were naturally aware that some provisions of the CISG would be eclipsed by other sets of rules, usages, and customs. Here, two common instruments for the unification of international trade law collide, that is, an international convention on the one side and privately established law on the other side.[31] The latter offers the advantage of greater flexibility, as the private texts can be revised by the trade or publishing organization in regular intervals to accommodate new developments. For example, the 2010 revision

---

[25] Cf., e.g., Ticino Appellate Court Lugano, 12.19.00036, June 8, 1999, available at http://cisgw3.law.pace.edu/cases/990608s1.html: 8 days.
[26] *UN Convention*, Article 39, para. 16.
[27] International Chamber of Commerce (ICC) (model clauses on hardship and force majeure); cf. Christoph Bruner, *Force Majeure and Hardship under General Contract Principles: Exemptions for On-Performance in International Arbitration* (Austin: Wolters Kluwer, 2009); Ingeborg Schwenzer, "Force Majeure and Hardship in International Sales Contracts," 39 *Victoria U. of Wellington L. Rev.* 709ff. (2009).
[28] Alexander Komarov, "Limitation of Domestic and International Contract Damages," in *Contract Damages* (ed. Djakhongir Saidov and Ralph Cunnington) (Oxford: Hart Publishing, 2008), 257ff.
[29] Cf. Maria del Pilar Perales Viscasillas, "CISG Articles 14 through 24," in Flechtner et al., *Drafting Contracts*, 295ff.; Michael Joachim Bonell in *Commentary on the International Sales Law* (ed. Cesare Massimo Bianca and Michael Joachim Bonell) (Milan: Giuffrè, 1987), Article 6, cmt. 2.4.
[30] For example, the seller would agree to the exclusion of Article 39 notice only in exchange for concessions on other aspects of the contract or if the change is due inequality of bargaining power; cf. *UN Convention*, Article 39, para. 15.
[31] Cf. John O. Honnold, "Uniform Law and Uniform Trade Terms: Two Approaches to a Common Goal," in *Transnational Law of International Commercial Transactions* (ed. Norbert Horn and Clive Schmitthoff) (Deventer: Kluwer, 1982), 161ff.; Ingeborg Schwenzer and Pascal Hachem, "The CISG: Successes and Pitfalls," 57 *American J. of Comparative L.* 476f. (2009). Regarding the unification of law through private law-making, see Klaus-Peter Berger, *The Creeping Codification of the New Lex Mercatoria*, 2nd ed. (Austin: Wolters Kluwer, 2010), 40ff.

of INCOTERMS included several adaptations related to modern container shipping.[32] In contrast, a convention routinely leads to petrification of the law, as modifications are only possible through the agreement of all contracting states. The inclusion of an INCOTERMS trade term into a contract has priority over the default rules of the CISG. Furthermore, the mere inclusion of a combination of letters (FOB, CIF, DES) without express reference to the INCOTERMS could likely have the same result – a court or arbitral tribunal could use INCOTERMS as evidence of trade usage, under CISG Article 9(2).[33]

The rules provided under Article 31 (seller's obligation to deliver the goods) and Articles 66–69 (passing of risk) are substantively related to the rules provided by INCOTERMS.[34] The Pace Database lists 149 decisions referencing Article 31, although a good portion of those are merely *obiter dicta*. Article 31 CISG is to be understood as an assisting provision, applied in the event that the parties failed to fix a place of delivery. Despite the predominant use of INCOTERMS, Article 31 retains some real material significance, for example to determine the place of performance of a party's restitution obligation under Article 81(2) after successful avoidance.[35]

Courts are also rarely faced with problems of interpreting Articles 66–99. It is true that all of these provisions are referenced in judicial decisions, but here contractual stipulations by the parties play a much greater role.[36] This is also an area in which the regulation of loss is primarily controlled by transit insurance.

C. *Divergence between Scholarship and Practice*

Some CISG provisions, though not heavily referenced in the case law, have attracted substantial academic research. These are examples of the divergence of research and practice in certain areas. What scholars find interesting does not always equate with practical significance. Of course, provisions enjoying immensely common application, such as those governing the obligation to give notice of nonconformity under Article 38 or the obligation to pay interest under Article 78, have also been thoroughly dealt with in the literature, but other provisions have awakened a disproportionately excessive amount of interest in the research community.

1. The Price Paradox

The first example that comes to mind here is the well-known paradox created by CISG Articles 14 and 55 regarding the relationship between concluding a contract and

---

[32] Cf. Burghard Piltz, "Incoterms 2010," 11 *Internationales Handelsrecht* 1ff. (2011).

[33] Cf. Burghard Piltz, *Internationales Kaufrecht*, 2nd ed. (Munich: Beck, 2008), paras. 4–10; Corinne Widmer in Schlechtriem and Schwenzer, *Commentary*, Article 30, para 3.

[34] Cf. regarding the differences between the CISG and the Incoterms, Jan Ramberg, "To What Extent Do Incoterms 2000 Vary Articles 67(2), 68 and 69?," 25 *J. of L. & Commerce* 219ff. (2005/6); id., "CISG and INCOTERMS 2000," in *Sharing International Commercial Law across National Boundaries* (ed. Camilla Andersen and Ulrich Schroeter) (London: Wildy, Simmons & Hill, 2008), 394ff.; Burghard Piltz, "Incoterms und UN-Kaufrecht," in *Transport- und Vertriebsrecht* 2000 (ed. Karl-Heinz Thume) (Bielefeld: Luchterhand, 1999), 20ff.

[35] Austrian Supreme Court, 1 Ob 74/99k, June 29, 2000, available at http://cisgw3.law.pace.edu/cases/990629a3.html.

[36] Cf., e.g., UNCITRAL *Digest of Case Law on the United Nations Convention on Contracts for the International Sale of Goods* (2012) (hereafter referred to as *UNCITRAL Digest*), Article 68 CISG.

determining the price. Article 14(1)(2) CISG requires that a proposal must expressly or implicitly fix or make provision for determining quantity and price. Article 55 contains a rule for determining the contract price according to objective criteria, if the parties fail to agree on a price term. Article 55 implies in the absence of a legally effective offer, a contract price is then, nevertheless, to be determined according to objective criteria. This question has been dealt with thoroughly in the literature, and there is a wide spectrum of opinions as to how to resolve this contradiction.[37] Interestingly, this legal flaw was fully debated at the consultations prior to the adoption of the CISG. However, no diplomatic compromise could be reached and, in the end, the contradiction failed to be rectified.[38]

Despite this obvious conflict within the CISG, this issue has caused few problems in practice.[39] There have been more cases referencing Article 14 than Article 55, which can be attributed to the former article's wider scope of regulation. However, the necessity of stipulating a price to form a contract has rarely been disputed in the case law. The few cases on this point overwhelmingly involve situations in which contractual consent was in dispute. This is not a question to be analyzed under Article 55 CISG but, rather, to be decided solely according to Articles 14 and the other provisions of CISG Part II.

Article 55 CISG maintains a small sphere of application in the area of open price contracts, as the parties have agreed to a sales contract. It is understood that a good will be exchanged for payment of money.[40] Article 55 CISG already presupposes an agreement to exchange performances and, thus, does not aid in the determination of whether a contract had been formed. It is equally not applicable when the parties have agreed to negotiate the price term at a later time, as here the contract is not yet complete.[41] A price can be determined by the circumstances, such as being stated in the seller's catalogue; it can also be determined by way of practice recognized under Article 9(1). Thus, it seems that nearly every problem can be solved though a sensible interpretation of the parties' representations made during the negotiations.[42] If the parties assume inconsistent price terms and this conflict cannot be resolved by an objective interpretation of their statements under Article 8(1), then there is a failure of agreement and the contract is not yet concluded according to Articles 18 and 19. An objective determination of the price term under Article 55 only arises in the few remaining cases, in which the judge is convinced that the parties surely wanted an exchange of performance without in some way making a price term a part of the contract.

---

[37] Cf. Loukas Mistelis, "Article 55 CISG: The Unknown Factor," 25 *J. of L. & Commerce* 285ff. (2005–6); Ulrich Magnus, "Unbestimmter Preis und UN-Kaufrecht," *Praxis des Internationalen Privat- und Verfahrensrechts* (1996), 145ff.

[38] See Mohs in Schlechtriem and Schwenzer, *Commentary*, Article 55, para. 2.

[39] See Peter Schlechtriem, "Uniform Sales Law: The Experience with the Uniform Sales Laws in the Federal Republic of Germany," *Juridisk Tidskrift* 19 (1991/2).

[40] Schwenzer and Hachem in Schlechtriem and Schwenzer, *Commentary*, Article 1, para. 8; Huber and Mullis, *CISG*, 43.

[41] Arbitration proceeding, 309/1993, March 3, 1995, available at http://cisgw3.law.pace.edu/cases/950303r1.html (the arbitral tribunal did not decide that Article 14 should preempt Article 55 but, rather, that a contract does not yet materialize, as long as both of the parties assume that the price term is still negotiable).

[42] Cf., e.g., Austrian Supreme Court, 2 Ob 547/93, November 10, 1994, available at http://cisgw3.law.pace.edu/cases/941110a3.html (held that, based on the facts of the case, a default price "between 35 DM and 65 DM" was sufficiently definite according to Article 14).

That this problem has nevertheless attracted so much attention in the legal literature despite its practical insignificance is attributable to the question's popularity in comparative law. The various legal systems have differing views on whether a *pretium certum*, a definite price, is indispensible to a legally effective contract.[43] Since this difference in conception amounts to a fundamental question of contract law, no consensus could be reached in the drafting of the CISG. However, the fundamental diversity existing in contract theory has had little effect on international sales transactions. The drafters of the CISG left it to practitioners to find an adequate solution, and the judicial decisions generally exhibit a good understanding of whether or not the parties had reached an agreement.

2. Battle of the Forms

The battle of forms scenario is a highly debated and critiqued area in national contract laws. Given the ubiquitous use of standard forms in sales transactions and the difficulty in reaching consensus on how to treat contracts based on the exchange of forms with conflicting terms, the topic has been the subject of a tremendous amount of scholarly studies. True, colliding terms about something like the scope of liability can easily attain great significance in a lawsuit.[44] Still, this appears to be more a problem of contract drafting and less of a practical problem of law. Despite the apparent significance, most battle of the forms situations rarely involve questions of validity, but rather questions of contract interpretation to be determined under Article 8.[45]

The two dominant theories for resolving the battle of the forms scenario rest upon a standardized interpretation of the behavior of the parties. According to the "mirror image" rule codified in Article 19(1) and (2), an acceptance that contains additional terms or terms materially different from those of the offer constitutes a rejection of the offer and acts as a counteroffer. The offspring of the mirror image rule is the "last shot" rule, under which the original offeror is held to have implicitly accepted the terms of the counteroffer by performance, so, for example, a seller is deemed to have accepted a buyer's counteroffer by shipping the goods without objection. Thus, the last shot principle concedes the terms to the party who sends the last counteroffer.[46]

A counterpoise to the "last-shot" rule is the "knock-out" rule, which assumes a different interpretation of the parties' behavior. Under this theory, it is assumed that if the parties undertook performance on the contract they must have attached little importance to inconsistent standard terms. The knock-out rule corresponds with the general experience that such "boilerplate" terms are routinely ignored until a dispute

---

[43] Article 1591 of the French Code Civile, the price of a sale must be determined and stated by the parties. Additionally, at least at the time the CISG was promulgated, such a requirement was still found in many socialist legal systems; cf. Gyula Eörsi in Bianca and Bonell, *Commentary*, Article 55, cmt. 121; Ewoud Hondius, "CISG and a European Civil Code," 71 *RabelsZ* 101f. (2007). See also Jan Kleinheisterkamp in *Commentary on the UNIDROIT Principles of International Commercial Contracts (PICC)* (ed. Stefan Vogenauer and Jan Kleinheisterkamp) (Oxford University Press, 2009), Article 5.1.7, para. 4.

[44] Cf. Documentation in the *UNCITRAL Digest*, Article 19, cmt. 6.

[45] Ulrich Schroeter in Schlechtriem and Schwenzer, *Commentary*, Article 19, para. 34.

[46] Franco Ferrari, in *UN Convention*, Article 19, para. 15; Maria del Pilar Perales Viscasillas, "'Battle of the Forms' under the 1980 United Nations Convention on Contracts for the International Sale of Goods: A Comparison with Section 2–207 UCC and the UNIDROIT Principles," 10 *Pace Int'l L. Rev.* 97ff. (1998).

arises.[47] A party who begins performance despite the existing divergence is not expressing an unconditional acceptance of the other party's standard terms, but it is instead more likely that both parties understand the contract to have been concluded on the basis of the consistent terms (and possibly any other nonconflicting, reasonable terms in one of the exchanged forms). Under the knock-out rule, the conflicting terms do not become part of the contract and, if necessary, any remaining gap will be filled by the default rules of the CISG. However, the knock-out rule is at odds with the broad definition of materiality found in Article 19(3), which prevents the recognition of a contract formation based upon the exchanged forms. It is rationalized that the parties implicitly derogated, under Article 6, based on the assumption that the parties rejected the application of the "mirror-image" rule of Article 19(1) by performing despite the conflicting terms.[48]

Applying Article 19 rigidly is ill suited to effectively resolve a conflict concerning questions of interpretation. Instead, courts retain discretion to carve out decisions that are fair to the interests present in the specific case.[49] For example, it is yet unclear whether the knock-out rule can be retained when a contracting party includes a "defence clause" against the validity of the other party's boilerplate terms in his or her own set of standard terms or even as an individual term in the contract.[50]

D. Compromise and Dispute

Provisions that were imprecisely formulated as the result of compromises during the drafting process represent another potential source of legal disputes. The CISG contains numerous "compromise provisions." This is due to the drafters' goal of creating an instrument that would be acceptable to varying legal traditions and political systems. The experience of the Hague Conventions, rejected by many states as Eurocentric, was still fresh in the minds of the drafters. Some of the compromises were of a technical nature, such as those intended to help bridge the divide between the civil and common law legal systems,[51] while other compromises were politically motivated and intended to mitigate the opposing interests among the Western, socialist, and developing countries.[52]

---

[47] Larry A. DiMatteo et al., *International Sales Law: A Critical Analysis* (Cambridge University Press 2005), 66.

[48] Ulrich Schroeter in Schlechtriem and Schwenzer, *Commentary*, Article 19, para. 41; Huber and Mullis, *CISG*, 94; John O. Honnold, *Uniform Law for International Sales Law under the 1980 United Nations Convention*, 4th ed. (Austin: Wolters Kluwer, 2009), cmt. 170.4.

[49] Cf. German Supreme Court, VIII ZR 304/00, January 9, 2002, available at http://cisgw3.law.pace.edu/cases/020109g1.html; here, the Supreme Court expressly left open which of the positions it would adopt, as according to its interpretation in concreto, both would lead to the same result. For criticism, see Maria del Pilar Perales Viscasillas, "Battle of the Forms and the Burden of Proof: An Analysis of BGH 9 January 2002," 6 *Vindobona J. of Int'l Commercial L. & Arbitration* (2002), 217ff.

[50] Cf. Article 2.1.22 UNIDROIT Principles of International Commercial Contracts. The provision generally follows the knock-out doctrine, unless one party clearly indicates in advance or later and without undue delay informs the other party that it does not intend to be bound by such a contract. The Principles do not give a more precise explanation of what is required for a "clear indication," although the official commentary suggests that a mere "boilerplate" term in the standard terms will, as a rule, be insufficient. An almost identical rule is also found in Article 2:209(2)(a) Principles of European Contract Law and Article II-4:209(2)(a) DCFR.

[51] See Chapter 38 of this book.

[52] Cf. Sara G. Zwart, "The New International Law of Sales: A Marriage between Socialist, Third World, Common, and Civil Law Principles," 13 *No. Carolina J. of Int'l L. & Commercial Regulation* 109ff. (1988).

1. Revocability of an Offer

The revocability of offers (CISG Article 16) is an area where various national legal systems have taken opposing positions. An offer remains freely revocable under common law as long as the offeree has not provided consideration, as one-sided obligations are not generally enforceable. In contrast, continental European legal systems are more protective of the offeree's reliance in the continued existence of the offer and regularly hold the offeror bound for a certain period of time.[53] Article 16 attempts to accommodate this divergence with a rule-exception provision. According to paragraph 1, an offer is generally freely revocable, but paragraph 2 sets out two exceptions to the general rule of revocability. The provision is far from unambiguous, and there is indeed much debate in the literature about how the exceptions should be applied. The interpretation of paragraph 2 has been susceptible to the influence of varying national perceptions.[54] However, the revocability of an offer has not generated much dispute in practice, with the Pace Database containing only fourteen decisions and none of them dealing with this specific problem of interpretation.

2. Specific Performance

The different view of the right to specific performance between the civil law (ordinary remedy) and the common law (extraordinary remedy) resulted in the drafting of CISG Article 28, which defers recognition of this remedy to domestic law. Article 28 is not intended to protect the contracting parties, but rather to protect the courts' discretionary powers over the granting of remedies.[55] Therefore, Article 28 is not subject to the principle of party autonomy and the parties cannot opt out of its application.[56] Of the nine reported decisions referring to Article 28, only one originated in a common-law court, and there the plaintiff was granted specific performance as special circumstances existed, in which case the domestic law would have also granted such relief.[57]

Despite its relative insignificance in CISG case law, the right to specific performance plays an important role in the CISG's remedial scheme. For example, even in a country that regularly grants specific performance, Article 77's duty to mitigate may in some situations require a party claiming breach to choose a remedy that is less onerous on the breaching party.[58] The nonbreaching party may be required to obtain substituted performance to mitigate damages, thus rendering the right to specific performance moot. More importantly, in practice, damages is the preferred remedy, as a cover purchase with

---

[53] Konrad Zweigert and Hein Kötz, *An Introduction to Comparative Law*, 3rd ed. (Oxford: Clarendon, 1998), 356ff.

[54] Henry Mather, "Firm Offers under the UCC and the CISG," 105 *Dickinson (Penn State) L. Rev.* 44ff. (2000); Ulrich Schroeter in Schlechtriem and Schwenzer, *Commentary*, Article 16, para. 10.

[55] Bruno Zeller, *CISG and the Unification of International Trade Law* (Oxford: Routledge-Cavendish, 2007), 59f.; Marco Torsello, "Remedies for Breach of Contract," in Ferrari, *Quo Vadis CISG?*, 68.

[56] Huber and Mullis, *CISG*, 190; Ingeborg Schwenzer and Markus Müller-Chen in Schlechtriem and Schwenzer, *Commentary*, Article 28, para. 24.

[57] *Magellan International v. Salzgitter Handel*, Federal District Court [Illinois], 99 C 5153, December 7, 1999, available at http://cisgw3.law.pace.edu/cases/991207u1.html (interests of the buyer were not sufficiently served by a cover purchase).

[58] Ingeborg Schwenzer and Markus Müller-Chen in Schlechtriem and Schwenzer, *Commentary*, Article 46, para. 14; Zeller, *CISG and Unification*, 63.

a subsequent claim for damages is much more sensible in most breach situations. Most businesspersons would not want to incur the delay and uncertainty of receiving goods from the breaching seller when they could get substitute materials elsewhere and then sue for any additional expenses. The circumstances that would persuade a party to request specific performance would exist only in exceptional situations, which would likely warrant specific performance under the common law.[59] This analysis is supported by the high number of judicial decisions regarding Article 74 (damages) and the small number of Article 28 cases.[60]

3. Compromises and the Developing Countries

An explicit goal in the creation of the CISG was to integrate developing nations into the international sales law system. One example of this is found in CISG Article 72(2), which establishes the obligation to give reasonable notice of intent to avoid the contract in cases of anticipatory breach. In practice, Article 72, specifically the obligation to give notice, has produced little case law.[61] Late notice is rare given modern methods of communication.[62] The more important issue is whether notice of avoidance is still required, when, under the circumstances, it constitutes a mere formality.

Two other compromise provisions have come before the courts more often. Article 9(2) makes it a condition for the objective application that a usage "in international trade is widely known to, and regularly observed by, parties to contracts of the type involved in the particular trade concerned." The requirement of "known in international trade" stemmed from the developing countries' concern that their traders, as newcomers to international commerce, were not informed on the content of industry trade usage and customs, and had no influence in their development.[63]

Even more interesting, however, is CISG Article 44, which moderates the complete loss of rights for failure to give timely notice of nonconformity. Under Article 44, if a buyer fails to give timely notice of nonconformity, but has a reasonable excuse for failure to give the required notice, the buyer retains his or her right to reduce the price and a limited right to claim damages. The complete revocation of rights under Article 39 was seen as too draconian by the developing countries in light of the fact that the duty to give notice is unknown in numerous legal systems.[64] Because many claims fail under the strict requirements of Articles 38 and 39, Article 44 is a defense of last resort for buyers failing to give proper notice. Despite the fact that the Pace Database lists sixty-nine cases referring to Article 44, the granting of relief under Article 44 has rarely been given. The

---

[59] Andrea K. Björklund in *UN Convention*, Article 28, para. 2; Zeller, *CISG and Unification*.

[60] Zeller, *CISG and Unification*, 62f.; cf. also Ulrich Magnus, "Beyond the Digest: Part III," in *The UNCI-TRAL Draft Digest and Beyond* (ed. Franco Ferrari, Harry Flechtner, and Ronald A. Brand) (Munich: Sellier European Law Publishers, 2004), 326 (stating: "The provision is a good example of one of those theoretically interesting attempts to deal with irreconcilable conceptual problems which in practice prove unimportant. But since the provision does no harm it seems unnecessary to change it. Equally unnecessary appears extended discussion of it.").

[61] See CIETAC Arbitration proceeding, December 31, 1996, available at http://cisgw3.law.pace.edu/cases/961231c2.html (decision on Article 72(2)).

[62] Fritz Enderlein, *Internationales Kaufrecht* (ed. Fritz Enderlein, Dietrich Maskow, and Heinz Strohbach) (Berlin: Haufe, 1991), Article 72, para. 5; *Staudinger*, Article 72, para. 22.

[63] *Staudinger*, Article 9, para. 16.

[64] U.N. Conf. on CISG, *Official Records* 320, 322 (1981).

UNCITRAL Digest shows only two arbitral awards in favor of a buyer who had failed to give the required notice.[65] It appears that the practical significance of this exception is extremely slight, and the courts have placed the threshold for its application at a high level.[66]

E. *Part II Formation and Scarcity of Case Law*

Looking purely at the numbers, a group of provisions in Part II of the CISG is remarkable for having few citations. This is especially true of the formation rules found in Articles 17, 20, 21, and 22. Article 17, according to which an offer is terminated when the offeror receives a rejection, has produced no substantive decisions regarding its application.[67] Article 20 (time for acceptance) appears in only one case; its inclusion is by way of a passing reference. When read more precisely, however, this judgment merely refers again to "Articles 14–24 CISG" for the premise that, under the CISG, sales contracts are concluded through offer and acceptance.[68] Regarding Article 21, five cases appear in the Pace Database regarding the consequences of late acceptance, only three of which can be verified.[69] Finally, the database returns two decisions appropriately referencing Article 22.[70]

Part II (contract formation) is strongly influenced by continental European law. The low rate of citation for the aforementioned formation rules is likely due to their technical nature. For example, in the absence of the rules found in Articles 17, 22, and 23, it is unlikely that a court decision would be rendered any differently. Article 20 deals merely with a codified rule of interpretation, subject to the reservation that the offeror explicitly or implicitly provided a different method for calculating the time period for acceptance. Article 21, however, which in certain cases gives effect to a late acceptance, provides a truly original rule favoring the validity of international contracts. It is an expression of the general principle of *favor contractus* (presumption of the effectiveness of international contracts) enshrined in the CISG.[71]

---

[65] Cf. *UNCITRAL Digest*, Article 44, para. 6. According to Kröll, the low number of successful references to Article 44 CISG can also be due to the fact that almost all of the published decisions on this issue originate in courts from Western countries, which are perhaps totally unfamiliar with the problems of buyers in developing countries; see *UN Convention*, Article 44, para. 6.

[66] DiMatteo et al., *International Sales*, 92f.

[67] District Court Oldenburg, 12 O 2943/94, February 28, 1996, available at http://cisgw3.law.pace.edu/cases/960228g1.html (referenced the Article only once in wholesale as "Articles 14–19" [sic], whereas the revocation of an offer played absolutely no role in the underlying facts); *Chateau des Charmes Wines Ltd v. Sabaté USA, Inc. et al.*, Superior Court of Justice, Ontario, 03-CV-261424CM3, October 28, 2005, available at http://cisgw3.law.pace.edu/cases/051028c4.html (same).

[68] Appellate Court Graz, 4 R 224/98p, February 24, 1999, available at http://cisgw3.law.pace.edu/cases/990224a3.html.

[69] ICC Arbitration Case No. 7844 of 1994, available at http://cisgw3.law.pace.edu/cases/947844i1.html; District Court Hamburg, 419 O 48/01, December 21, 2001, available at http://cisgw3.law.pace.edu/cases/011221g1.html; Appellate Court Dresden, 10 U 0269/10, November 30, 2010, available at: http://cisgw3.law.pace.edu/cases/101130g2.html.

[70] *Pratt & Whitney v. Malev*, Metropolitan Court Budapest, 3 G 50.289/1991/32, January 10, 1992, available at http://cisgw3.law.pace.edu/cases/920110h1.html; Munich Appellate Court, 23 U 4446/99, December 3, 1999, available at: http://cisgw3.law.pace.edu/cases/991203g1.html.

[71] Bertram Keller, "Favor Contractus in the CISG," in Andersen and Schroeter, *Sharing International Commercial Law across National Boundaries*, 252.

In any case, modern business practice often experiences difficulties with rigid offer and acceptance rules. Because of this, the formation rules of the CISG do not represent progressive advancement, bringing the rules, at times, into conflict with actual practice. The scholarly literature is currently focused on whether the CISG contract formation model fits the complex conclusion of contracts in practice, often consisting of protracted negotiations and preliminary and partial agreements.[72]

A similar decisional vacuum exists regarding Article 70. The provision establishes that the buyer's right to avoid the contract in cases of a seller's fundamental breach survives, even when the breach occurs after the risk passed to the buyer and the goods cannot be returned under Article 82(1). The Pace Database does not contain a single reported case referencing Article 70.[73] Three CISG Articles – 17, 20, and 70 – are still awaiting their inaugural deployment in a judicial decision.

IV. Conclusion

Regardless of the reasons behind the absence of certain CISG provisions in case law, the CISG should be evaluated as a whole. The fact that references to an article are not found in judicial decisions does not necessarily mean that the provision is of no importance. It remains a part of the system as a whole, and may remain important to the integrity of that system.

This chapter's brief examination of the "quieter domains" of the CISG has shown that the drafters tried to create a balanced document. This approach required that the delegations reach compromises, with the resulting formulations often seen as less than ideal. With the experience of the past twenty years, interpreters of the CISG view these provisions differently. As a result, there have been attempts to develop the CISG further and work out some of its flaws in other rule-drafting projects, such as the UNIDROIT Principles of International Commerial Contracts and the Draft Common Frame of Reference, as well as the proposed Common European Sales Law.[74] The chapter has shown that some theoretical questions often do not result in practical problems. Thus, the goal of reaching agreement over certain conceptual differences between scholars and practitioners from different legal systems may be less important and, at the same time, easier to achieve.

---

[72] Peter Schlechtriem and Petra Butler, *UN Law on International Sales* (Berlin: Springer, 2009), para. 69; cf. Marco Torsello, "Preliminary Agreements and CISG Contracts," in Flechtner et al., *Drafting Contracts*, 191ff.

[73] *Conservas La Costeña v. Lanín, Compromex* Arbitration proceeding, M/21/95, April 29, 1996, available at http://cisgw3.law.pace.edu/cases/960429m1.html (Article 70 may have been applicable to the facts, but the court did not discuss its applicability).

[74] Michael Joachim Bonell, "The Unidroit Principles of International Commercial Contracts and CISG: Alternatives or Complementary Instruments?," *Uniform L. Rev.* 26ff. (1996); Sonja Kruisinga, "The Impact of Uniform Law on National Law: Limits and Possibilities – CISG and Its Incidence in Dutch Law," 13 *Electronic J. of Comparative L.* 5ff. (2009).

4   CISG Sources and Researching the CISG

Marie Stefanini Newman

I. Introduction

The United Nations Convention on Contracts for the International Sale of Goods[1] (CISG) has been adopted by a growing number of countries with currently seventy-nine contracting states.[2] The CISG is a uniform law, and like other uniform laws, it was "created with the deliberate aim of establishing shared law between multiple jurisdictions."[3] A shared sales law aims to reduce "transaction costs for commercial parties," to help resolve disputes, and to "facilitate negotiating and drafting sales contracts."[4] One of the important reasons for the success of the CISG has been the development of high-quality online resources.

After providing a brief history of the CISG, this chapter discusses the difficulties of researching the CISG and the use of that research to advance Article 7(1)'s mandate of uniform application. The chapter goes on to describe the unique features of the Internet that have led to its critical role in promoting the CISG, and suggests a methodology for approaching CISG research. Finally, it compares and contrasts the materials available through several major databases, all of which are available without charge, and concludes with a brief look at three commercial databases. It is important to note that some of the most valuable materials on the CISG are found offline in treatises and other scholarly commentary.[5] In recognition of their value, some of these print sources have been digitized and made available online.

---

[1] United Nations Convention on Contracts for the International Sale of Goods, April 11, 1980, S. Treaty Doc. 98–9 (1983), 19 I.L.M. 668 (1980), available at http://www.uncitral.org/uncitral/en/uncitral_texts/sale_goods/1980CISG.html.

[2] UNCITRAL, http://www.uncitral.org/uncitral/en/uncitral_texts/sale_goods/1980CISG_status.html (last accessed August 5, 2013). Three major trading states recently ratified the CISG – Japan in 2008, Turkey in 2010, and Brazil in 2013. Id.

[3] Camilla Andersen, "The Global Jurisconsultorium of the CISG Revisited," 13 *Vindobona J. of Int'l Commercial L. & Arbitration* 43, 44 (2009).

[4] Ingeborg Schwenzer and Pascal Hachem, "The CISG: Successes and Pitfalls," 57 *American J. of Comparative L.* 457, 478 (2009) (footnotes omitted).

[5] See, e.g., Peter Schlechtriem and Ingeborg Schwenzer, *Commentary on the UN Convention on the International Sale of Goods (CISG)*, 3rd ed. (ed. I. Schwenzer) (Oxford: Oxford University Press, 2010); John O. Honnold, *Uniform Law for International Sales under the 1980 United Nations Convention*, 4th ed. (ed. H.M. Flechtner) (Austin: Wolters Kluwer, 2009); and *Convention on Contracts for the International Sale of Goods (CISG)* (ed. S. Kröll) (Munich: C.H. Beck, 2011).

II. Brief History of the CISG

The history of the CISG has been extensively documented elsewhere,[6] but the unini-
tiated will benefit from a brief overview[7] of the origins and development of the CISG.
In the late 1920s, "scholars, lawyers, and traders . . . began to explore the possibility of
creating a uniform law to govern international trade."[8] From 1926 until 1939, several
draft uniform sales laws were discussed under the guidance of the International Institute
for the Unification of Private Law [UNIDROIT] and the Hague Conference on Private
International Law. Efforts at unification of international sales law came to a halt with the
beginning of World War II, and did not resume until January 1951, when the Dutch government convened a diplomatic conference at The Hague:[9] "The conference established
a special commission to make further progress in the unification process."[10] During the
1950s and early 1960s, several drafts were circulated, resulting in two documents that
proved important to the development of international sales law – the Uniform Law on
the Formation of Contracts for the International Sale of Goods [ULF][11] and the Uniform
Law on the International Sale of Goods [ULIS].[12] Although these conventions, which
were finalized at The Hague in 1964, were ultimately adopted by only nine countries
and were not considered a success, they were the "basis for the 'new' Uniform Sales Law
drawn up by . . . UNCITRAL, and they influenced not only the basic structures and key
concepts [found] in the . . . [CISG, which was] eventually concluded in 1980, but also
many of its detailed solutions."[13]

One reason that ULF and ULIS did not win general acceptance was that major
trading countries such as the United States and France did not ratify them. In addition,
"socialist and developing nations perceived [them] as favoring sellers from industrialized
Western economies and thus stayed away . . . as well."[14] In 1966, the United Nations
Commission on International Trade Law [UNCITRAL] was established to continue work
on an international sale of goods convention. "The drafting and negotiation process, for

---

[6] See, e.g., Kazuaki Sono, "The Vienna Sales Convention: History and Perspective," in *International Sale
of Goods: Dubrovnik Lectures* (ed. P. Šarčević and P. Volken) (New York: Oceana, 1986), 1–17; Honnold,
Uniform Law, 5–12; Schlechtriem and Schwenzer, *Commentary*, 1–3. The definitive collection of "studies,
deliberations and decisions that led" to the CISG is John O. Honnold, *Documentary History of the Uniform
Law for International Sales* (Deventer: Kluwer Law and Taxation, 1989).

[7] This overview of the CISG's history is derived from Schwenzer and Hachem, *CISG*, 459–60, and from
Tom McNamara, "The U.N. Sale of Goods Convention: Finally Coming of Age?," *Colorado Lawyer*,
February 2003, at 11.

[8] McNamara, "U.N. Sale of Goods Convention," 12.

[9] Schwenzer and Hachem, *CISG*, 459.

[10] Id.

[11] Convention Relating to a Uniform Law on the International Sale of Goods, July 1, 1964, 834 U.N.T.S.
107, available at http://www.cisg.law.pace.edu/cisg/text/ulis.html (last updated May 27, 1998).

[12] Convention Relating to a Uniform Law on the Formation of Contracts for the International Sale of Goods,
July 1, 1964, 834 U.N.T.S. 107, available at http://www.cisg.law.pace.edu/cisg/text/ulf.html (last updated
January 1996).

[13] Schlectriem and Schwenzer, *Commentary*, 1–2. Commentators have noted other positive effects. "ULIS
and ULF have achieved considerable importance in the practice of German, Benelux, and Italian courts.
When developing domestic sale of goods laws, national reformers and legislatures have increasingly used
ULIS and ULF as an example and model." Id.

[14] Schwenzer and Hachem, *CISG*, 460 (citing Peter Schlectriem, *Uniform Sales Law: The UN-Convention
on Contracts for the International Sale of Goods* 16, 17 (1986)).

what ultimately became the CISG, was quite inclusive."[15] A draft dealing with contract formation and substantive sales law was circulated to members of the United Nations in 1978, and the UNCITRAL Secretariat issued a Commentary on the draft.[16] In 1980, representatives of sixty-two nations gathered in Vienna to deliberate.[17] The representatives came from a variety of different legal systems, and included "[a]cademics, corporations, traders, diplomats, and lawyers."[18] Ultimately, forty-two countries voted in favor of the CISG, and after ratification by the required ten countries, it entered into force on January 1, 1988. Reflecting its international character, the CISG was published in six official languages: Arabic, Chinese, French, English, Russian, and Spanish.[19]

III. Challenges in Researching the CISG and Its Uniform Application

The CISG has generated a significant amount of commentary.[20] In fact, it has been suggested that "[m]ore has been written on this uniform law than on any law since the Code of Hammurabi."[21] It has also generated a large and growing body of case law from courts and arbitral tribunals:[22] "With such an abundance of material, the challenge is not its availability but mining it in an efficient manner."[23] In addition, cases and commentaries may be written in foreign languages with no translations available. These hurdles to research on the CISG have largely been eliminated thanks to free online sources on the CISG. However, perceptions about the difficulty of performing international law research persist, creating disincentives to select the CISG as applicable law.[24]

---

[15] McNamara, "U.N. Sale of Goods Convention," 12.

[16] "Upon completion of the 1978 Draft, the Secretariat prepared a Commentary on it that summarized the thinking that led to this text . . . The Secretariat Commentary which accompanied it was prepared pursuant to United Nations General Assembly Resolution 33/93 . . . Ziegel, "Report to the Uniform Law Conference of Canada on *Convention on Contracts for the International Sale of Goods*" (July 1980), at p. 5) . . . This Commentary is the closest counterpart to an Official Commentary on this Convention." "Summary of UNCITRAL Legislative History of the CISG," *CISG Database,* http://cisgw3.law.pace.edu/cisg/linkd. html (last updated January 7, 1999). Unfortunately, there is no commentary on the 1980 Convention. Honnold, *Documentary History,* 404.

[17] Schwenzer and Hachem, *CISG,* 460.

[18] McNamara, "U.N. Sale of Goods Convention," 12.

[19] The official texts are available at the UNCITRAL Web site, http://www.uncitral.org/uncitral/en/uncitral_ texts/sale_goods/1980CISG.html (last accessed August 5, 2013), and at the Pace University School of Law Albert H. Kritzer CISG Database, http://www.cisg.law.pace.edu/cisg/text/text.html (last updated June 21, 2013) (hereafter referred to as CISG Database). Deviations among the texts have led to problems of interpretation because "no matter how much care was taken in casting the CISG into its six official language versions, there were bound to be differences in the meanings conveyed." Harry M. Flechtner, "The Several Texts of the CISG in a Decentralized System: Observations on Translations, Reservations and Other Challenges to the Uniformity Principle in Article 7(1)," 17 *J. of L. & Commerce* 187, 190 (1997–8).

[20] As of August 5, 2013, the CISG Database listed 10,049 texts in its bibliography on the CISG; http://www. cisg.law.pace.edu/.

[21] Albert H. Kritzer, foreword to *A Practitioner's Guide to the CISG* (ed. Camilla Baasch Andersen, Francesco G. Mazzotta, and Bruno Zeller) (Huntington, NY: Juris, 2010), vii.

[22] As of July 17, 2013, the CISG Database listed 2,872 cases from fifty-three jurisdictions and arbitral tribunals; http://www.cisg.law.pace.edu/.

[23] Kritzer, foreword, ix.

[24] Even when known by practicing lawyers, "there still seems to be a tendency to recommend the exclusion of the Convention." Schwenzer and Hachem, *CISG,* 463. There are four reasons why parties opt out of the

A. *Moving from "Homeward Trend" to Uniform Application*

Reliance on domestic law for purposes of interpreting the CISG contradicts the intent of CISG Article 7(1), which states that: "In the interpretation of this Convention, regard is to be had to its international character and to the need to promote uniformity in its application." Despite this mandate, some misguided practitioners and judges have too quickly resorted to domestic law when applying the CISG. Professor John Honnold coined the term "homeward trend" for the practice of choosing domestic law concepts and rules over unfamiliar CISG rules:

> The Convention . . . will often be applied by tribunals (judges or arbitrators) who will be intimately familiar only with their own domestic law. These tribunals, regardless of their merit, will be subject to a natural tendency to read the international rules in light of the ideas that have been imbedded at the core of their intellectual formation. The mind sees what the mind has means of seeing.[25]

Although uniformity in international sales transactions leads to predictability in contracts and facilitates international transactions, it has proven to be somewhat elusive in the application of the CISG:

> [U]niformity does not follow automatically from a proclamation of uniform rules . . . [U]niform words do not always ensure uniform results, especially where a Convention is in effect throughout countries with completely differing social, economic, and cultural backgrounds, and perhaps most significantly, different legal systems. Differences in interpretation and application will arise.[26]

There is another difficulty in achieving uniform interpretation, namely, that there is no central appellate court, tribunal, or other body whose function it is to ensure uniformity of application:

> Before the CISG entered into force, the Convention was debated at a conference in Freiburg, Germany in 1987, where Professor John O. Honnold – in anticipation of the problems of uniformity that would arise – stated that he presumed most countries would condition their ratification of the Convention on the establishment of an International Sales Law Centre to monitor the international practice of the convention, as proposed by Professor Rajski of Poland. Such a centre was never created.[27]

In order to fill this need, the CISG Advisory Council (CISG-AC) was founded in 2001 "as a private initiative to respond to the emerging need to address some controversial,

---

CISG when drafting contracts governing international sales of goods: lawyers are not particularly familiar with the CISG and prefer the predictability of their domestic law; "whenever the position of a party in the market allows that party to retain its own domestic law in a contract, it prefers to do so"; some parties think that their domestic law is more advantageous to them; and although there are six official languages for the CISG, inevitably there are inconsistencies among the versions which can lead to problems in application and interpretation. Id., 463–4.

[25] Honnold, *Documentary History*, 1.

[26] Camilla Baasch Andersen, "Furthering the Uniform Application of the CISG: Sources of Law on the Internet," 10 *Pace International L. Rev.* 403, 404 (1998) (citing John O. Honnold, "The 1980 Sales Convention: Can Uniform Words Give Us Uniform Results?," 2 *Juridisk Tidskrift vid Stockholms Universitet* 3–14 (1990–1).

[27] Andersen, "Furthering the Uniform Application," 410 (footnote omitted).

unresolved issues relating to the CISG which merit interpretative guidance."[28] Its ultimate goal is the uniform interpretation of the CISG. Scholars representing different legal traditions "issue opinions relating to the interpretation and application of the Convention on request or on its own initiative."[29] Such requests may come from "international organizations, professional associations and adjudication bodies."[30] So far, the CISG-AC has issued twelve opinions, which are available on its own website[31] and on the Pace CISG Database.

Uniformity in interpreting the CISG is impossible; a more realistic goal is "for the provisions of the Convention to be applied similarly, if not identically, throughout the Signatory States."[32] This places a responsibility on the researcher to locate and take into consideration "similar cases from international practice."[33] Some commentators have argued that the failure to consider relevant case law from foreign jurisdictions may "give rise to . . . malpractice."[34] The term "jurisconsultorium" has been applied to the process of comparing case law (and scholarly commentary) from varying jurisdictions to determine how the law has already been applied, thus enhancing uniformity of application.[35]

B. *Internet to the Rescue*

The Internet has provided a mechanism for promoting uniform application of the CISG by making available to the international community the primary and secondary sources needed for thorough research. The Internet has played a critical role in creating a common legal culture for the CISG.[36] According to Professor Albert H. Kritzer, the founder of the CISG Database at the Pace University School of Law, "the birth of the CISG coincided with the birth of the Information Age. That has led to an explosion of

---

[28] Loukas Mistelis, "CISG-AC Publishes First Opinions," http://www.cisg.law.pace.edu/cisg/CISG-AC.html (last updated March 26, 2008). The CISG Advisory Council was founded by the Institute of International Commercial Law at Pace University School of Law and the Centre for Commercial Law Studies, Queen Mary, University of London.

[29] Id.

[30] Id.

[31] http://www.cisgac.com/default.php?sid=128 (last accessed August 5, 2013).

[32] Andersen, "Furthering the Uniform Application," 404.

[33] Id., 405. "[W]hen taking [CISG] cases out of their domestic context, they have no real value on a precedential scale in any event, so it will be the commercial reasoning which speaks for itself . . ." Andersen et al., *A Practitioner's Guide*, xxi. The use of foreign law by judges in the United States to inform their decisions is highly controversial. Nonbinding authorities, including law reviews, scholarly treatises, and judgments of courts from other U.S. jurisdictions, are widely consulted. See Martha Minow, "The Controversial Status of International and Comparative Law in the United States," 52 *Harvard International L.J. Online* 1, 18–19 (2010), http://www.harvardilj.org/2010/08/online_52_minow/. ("[C]onsultation of nonbinding sources can be instructive and clarifying though never binding." Id., 19.) See also Gary F. Bell, "Uniformity through Persuasive International Authorities: Does Stare Decisis Really Hinder the Uniform Interpretation of the CISG?," in *Sharing International Commercial Law across National Boundaries: Festschrift for Albert H Kritzer on the Occasion of His Eightieth Birthday* (ed. C.B. Andersen and U.G. Schroeter) (London: Wildy, Simmonds & Hill, 2008), 47 (concluding that the common-law doctrine of stare decisis need not stand in the way of uniformity in international sales law).

[34] Andersen et al., *A Practitioner's Guide*, 87.

[35] Vikki Rogers and Albert H. Kritzer, "A Uniform International Sales Law Terminology," in *Festschrift für Peter Schlechtriem zum 70. Geburtstag* 227–8 (ed. I. Schwenzer and G. Hager) (Tübingen: Mohr Siebeck, 2003).

[36] Shani Salama, "Pragmatic Responses to Interpretive Impediments: Article 7 of the CISG, an Inter-American Application," 38 *University of Miami Inter-American L. Rev.* 225, 236 (2006). "A common

material on the Internet on this law."[37] Internet-based sources provide research material that "conforms with the transnational character" of the CISG, the global reach of the Web, the nature of the new *lex mercatoria*,[38] and the "quick and continuous updating and dynamic evolution" of information.[39]

IV. Methodology for CISG Research

Every attorney in the United States is familiar with online databases such as Lexis and Westlaw. Attorneys also still rely on printed annotated codes, which include the text of the statute, as well as supplementary material to aid in its interpretation. Supplementary materials typically include related case law, legislative history, administrative regulations, and secondary authorities[40] such as law review articles and practice materials.

When approaching a CISG issue, the best place to begin is with the text of the relevant CISG Article, along with the *travaux préparatoires*,[41] the Secretariat's official commentary, scholarly commentary, and cases and arbitral awards.[42] Professor Claire Germain recommends that CISG researchers also consider:

[I]nternational trade usages and practices (*e.g.*, Article 9 of the Convention, UNIDROIT principles of international commercial contracts[43] which might supplement the CISG

legal culture refers to a common socioeconomic and political structure, combined with a common general legal framework, which plays a significant role in how legal rules are understood and applied." Id., 236.

[37] Kritzer, foreword, vii.

[38] New Lex Mercatoria (NLM) is a synonym for transnational commercial law. NLM includes the CISG, but is broader in scope, also encompassing "general transnational commercial law principles such as 'good faith,' [etc.]." Klaus Peter Berger, "The TransLex Principles: An Online Research Tool for the Vis Moot and International Arbitration," in *International Arbitration and International Commercial Law – Synergy, Convergence and Evolution: Liber Amicorum Eric Bergsten* (ed. S. Kröll) (Alphen aan den Rijn: Wolters Kluwer Law & Business, 2011), 34.

[39] Id., 44, discussing specifically the Transnational Law Database of the Center for Transnational Law (CENTRAL), at the University of Cologne, http://www.central-.uni-koeln.de.

[40] Some codes, such as McKinney's Consolidated Laws of New York Annotated, also include commentaries written expressly for the publication by expert practitioners. William H. Manz, *Gibson's New York Legal Research Guide*, 3rd ed. (Buffalo: William S. Hein, 2004), 76.

[41] *Travaux préparatoires* may be useful to understand the "common intentions and agreed definitions" of the drafters as long as "all the parties had become familiar with the documents or material by the time the treaty was signed." Young Loan Arbitration, 59 I.L.R. 495, 545 (Arb. Trib. for the Agreement on Ger. External Debts 1980). They are not, however, the equivalent of legislative history, a term used in the United States for the "chronology of events and the publications generated during the legislative process . . . A *legislative* history is the record of the events that transpire, the dates of those events, and the publications generated." Elyse H. Fox, *The Legal Research Dictionary: From Advance Sheets to Pocket Parts*, 2nd ed. (Chapel Hill: Legal Information Services, 2006), 59. See generally Jonathan Pratter, "À la Recherche des Travaux Préparatoires: An Approach to Researching the Drafting History of International Agreements," GlobaLex (November/December 2012), http://www.nyulawglobal.org/globalex/Travaux_Preparatoires1.htm.

[42] "The importance of CISG precedents does not solely apply to court judgments. Arbitral awards are also, indeed especially, significant due to their internationality and 'stateless' context. '[A]n arbitral award could have more influence on a specific solution than a decision of a supreme court of a country whose judges are not accustomed to dealing with international issues in general, and the CISG in particular.'" Camilla Baasch Andersen, "The Uniform International Sales Law and the Global Jurisconsultorium," 24 J. of L. & Commerce 159, 170 (2005) (quoting Franco Ferrari, "CISG Case Law: A New Challenge for Interpreters?," 17 J. of L. & Commerce 245, 260 (1999)).

[43] The UNIDROIT Principles of International Commercial Contracts, which were prepared under the aegis of UNIDROIT, were first published in 1994. "[T]hey attempt to set forth the principles that the drafters

when a CISG provision requires further interpretation); . . . *lex mercatoria*, the law used by merchants since the middle ages and created by standard commercial practices and arbitral decisions; and . . . previous UNIDROIT international sales conventions (i.e., ULIS or UFL [sic]).[44]

In most research situations, consulting the "four pillars of CISG research"[45] – text, *travaux*, commentary, and cases and arbitral awards – should suffice.[46] There are a number of online research guides on the CISG[47] that can be reviewed before the researcher accesses the major databases. The CISG is an area of law for which online sources are far more complete than what is available in print. Fortunately for the researcher, a number of valuable online resources have been developed to make research on the CISG "highly practicable."[48]

V. Leading Online Resources for CISG Research

This part reviews the major online databases dedicated to providing access to primary and secondary sources on the CISG.

A. *UNCITRAL*

The UNCITRAL database is the product of the organization responsible for the drafting of the CISG. The scope of the UNCITRAL database goes beyond the CISG.

---

thought applied generally to international contracts. The drafters hoped that they would be a source that adjudicators could turn to when resolving disputes." *Research Handbook in International Economic Law* 279 (ed. A.T. Guzman and A.O. Sykes) (Cheltenham: Edward Elgar, 2007). Like the Principles of European Contract Law (PECL), which were drawn up under the aegis of the European Union and first issued in 1995, the UNIDROIT Principles postdate the CISG and do not carry any legal force. "They might, however, be useful as they provide an accurate, although partial, picture of what the current trends are in international transactions . . . Thus, they could be used to support a solution already existing under the CISG, but should not be used to add features to the CISG." Andersen et al., *A Practitioner's Guide*, 90. Both sets of Principles could also be used to establish "general principles" on which the CISG is based, as set out in Article 7(2) of the CISG. Salama, "Pragmatic Responses," 243. These general principles include such concepts as good faith, reasonableness, freedom of contract, and party autonomy. Cesare Massimo Bianca and Michael Joachim Bonell, *Commentary on the International Sales Law: The 1980 Vienna Sales Convention* (Milan: Giuffrè, 1987), 80–2.

[44] Claire M. Germain, "The United Nations Convention on Contracts for the International Sale of Goods: Guide to Research and Literature," 24 *Int'l J. of Legal Information* 48, 52 (1996).

[45] Vikki M. Rogers, "American Society of International Law, Teaching International Law Interest Group Conference: Employing Web 2.0 in International Law Teaching and Scholarship" (May 6, 2011).

[46] See Albert H. Kritzer, "Guide to the Pace Database on the CISG and International Commercial Law," *CISG Database*, http://www.cisg.law.pace.edu/cisg/guide.html (last updated June 30, 2005).

[47] See, e.g., Jonathan Pratter, "Guide to Researching the CISG," http://tarltonguides.law.utexas.edu/CISG (last updated November 20, 2012); Duncan Alford, "A Guide on the Harmonization of International Commercial Law," GlobaLex, http://www.nyulawglobal.org/globalex/Harmonization_international_commercial_law.htm (last accessed August 5, 2013) (focusing not only on the CISG, but also on international commercial law generally); Jean M. Wenger, "International Economic Law," *ASIL Guide to Electronic Resources for International Law*, http://www.asil.org/iell.cfm (last updated October 25, 2010) (including links to resources broader in scope than the CISG). Note that in some cases, CISG is included as a subtopic of research guides on international commercial arbitration. See, e.g., Julienne Grant, "International Commercial Arbitration Research," http://lawlibguides.luc.edu/content.php?pid=116835&sid=1007854 (last updated June 21, 2013).

[48] Honnold, *Uniform Law*, 133.

Available in the six official languages of the United Nations, the database covers numerous instruments relating to the harmonization of international trade.[49] The database offers texts and explanations of international agreements within its purview, as well as *travaux préparatoires*, working group documents, and a regularly updated bibliography of commentaries on subjects related to UNCITRAL's work.

For the CISG researcher, however, the most important component of the UNCITRAL database is the CLOUT (Case Law on UNCITRAL Texts) system,[50] which provides abstracts of cases and arbitral decisions that have construed the conventions for which UNCITRAL is responsible, including the CISG. The purpose of CLOUT is:

> [T]o promote international awareness of . . . legal texts elaborated or adopted by the Commission, to enable judges, arbitrators, lawyers, parties to commercial transactions and other interested persons to take decisions and awards relating to those texts into account in dealing with matters within their responsibilities and to promote the uniform interpretation and application of those texts.[51]

The system relies on national correspondents who "monitor and collect court decisions and arbitral awards, and prepare abstracts of those considered relevant in one of the official languages of the United Nations."[52] The abstracts are translated by the Secretariat into the other official languages and are "published [in print and online] at irregular intervals."[53] The full text of the decisions is archived by the Secretariat, and made available to individuals upon request. The abstracts can be searched by fields,[54] and indicate the Articles of the CISG discussed in the case. The CLOUT abstracts have been incorporated into the Pace CISG Database.[55]

Another aid to locating relevant cases provided by UNCITRAL is its "Digest of Case Law on the United Nations Sales Convention,"[56] also available through the Pace CISG Database. The Digest is organized by chapters, which group articles of the CISG under broad topics: "Each chapter contains a synopsis of the relevant case law, highlighting common views and reporting any divergent approach. The Digest is meant to reflect the evolution of case law"[57] in order to further the goal of uniformity and predictability in

---

[49] According to the UNCITRAL Web site, UNCITRAL is "a subsidiary body of the General Assembly of the United Nations with the general mandate to further the progressive harmonization and unification of the law of international trade. UNCITRAL has since prepared a wide range of conventions, model laws and other instruments dealing with the substantive law that governs trade transactions," http://www.uncitral. org/uncitral/en/about/origin_faq.html (last accessed August 5, 2013).

[50] See http://www.uncitral.org/uncitral/en/case_law.html (last accessed August 5, 2013).

[51] U.N. Comm'n on Int'l Trade, Case Law on UNCITRAL Texts (CLOUT) User Guide, at 2, U.N. Doc. A/CN.9/SER.C/GUIDE/1/Rev.2 (June 2, 2010).

[52] Id.

[53] Id.

[54] The fields include country, UNCITRAL text, court, parties, case number, CLOUT number, and date of decision.

[55] See, e.g., http://cisgw3.law.pace.edu/cases/000712i3.html (last updated December 5, 2005). Note that while there were 1,238 cases and arbitral decisions in the CLOUT system as of August 5, 2013, there were 2,872 cases in the CISG Database on the same date.

[56] See http://www.uncitral.org/uncitral/en/case_law/digests.html (last accessed August 5, 2013).

[57] U.N. Comm'n on Int'l Trade Law, Introduction to the Digest of Case Law on the United Nations Sales Convention, at x, U.N. Doc. A/CN.9/562, June 9, 2004.

international sales law.[58] UNCITRAL also produces an index and thesaurus,[59] which "assist users of CLOUT in identifying cases relevant to a given issue by listing cases under the provision or sub-issue with which they deal."[60] These classification numbers have also been incorporated into the case law presentations of the Pace CISG Database.

B. *CISG Database, Pace University School of Law*

The premier database for research on the CISG is maintained by the Institute of International Commercial Law[61] at Pace University School of Law (Database). This "extraordinary"[62] database is designed to be a self-contained virtual library, where the researcher can find what he or she needs in order to complete a research project on the CISG. The database provides the official text of the CISG in all its official languages as well as several unofficial texts, extensive *travaux préparatoires*, a large collection of commentaries available in full text, and cases and arbitral awards from around the world. It also includes lists of signatories, reservations, and declarations;[63] guides and articles written by and for practitioners;[64] CISG-AC opinions; CISG drafting tips;[65] and a copious collection of links to other relevant websites.[66]

The CISG Database was officially launched in 1996 by Albert H. Kritzer, who

> [w]as among the first members of the legal community to understand that the Internet would transform the way legal information is disseminated. The CISG database has leveled the playing field for the world trading and academic communities. In addition, it has laid the groundwork for a uniform application of the CISG by courts of the signatory nations.[67]

---

[58] See Franco Ferrari, "Remarks on the UNCITRAL Digest's Comments on Article 6 CISG," 25 *J. of L. & Commerce* 13 (2005) (asserting that the Digest is "helpful as it organizes all decisions under different headings," but poses a risk to users because "certain statements drafted in one language [are] being wrongly translated into another." Id., 13). Furthermore, the Digest neither criticizes nor supports decisions, and is selective in which cases it chooses to include. See also Joseph Lookofsky, "Digesting CISG Case Law: How Much Regard Should We Have?," 8 *Vindobona J. of Int'l Commercial L. & Arbitration* 181 (2004) (The Digest lacks critical information; it "cannot help us distinguish the . . . precedents which are persuasive from those which are not." Id., 194).

[59] See http://www.uncitral.org/uncitral/en/case_law/thesauri.html (last visited January 5, 2013).

[60] Id.

[61] For more information about the Institute, see Marie Stefanini Newman, "Albert Kritzer: Pioneer of Open Access to International Private Law," in *Sharing International Commercial Law across National Boundaries: Festschrift for Albert H Kritzer on the Occasion of His Eightieth Birthday* (ed. C.B. Andersen and U.G. Schroeter) (London: Wildy, Simmonds & Hill, 2008), 363 n. 8.

[62] Honnold, *Uniform Law*, 132.

[63] A reservation is "a formal declaration by a state becoming party to a treaty, specifying a certain condition on which its acceptance of the treaty is based." James R. Fox, *Dictionary of International and Comparative Law*, 3rd ed. (Dobbs Ferry: Oceana, 2003), 281. Under CISG Article 98, only reservations explicitly authorized by the Convention are permitted. For a complete and provocative discussion of reservations and their effect on the CISG, see Flechtner, "The Several Texts of the CISG," 193–7 (1998).

[64] See http://www.cisg.law.pace.edu/cisg/guides.html (last updated May 25, 2010); http://www.cisg.law.pace.edu/cisg/biblio/butler6.html (last updated May 26, 2010).

[65] See http://www.cisg.law.pace.edu/cisg/contracts.html (last updated July 26, 2005).

[66] See http://www.cisg.law.pace.edu/cisg/links.html (last updated November 9, 2011). The value of the CISG Database was recognized when it was awarded the 2002 Web site award in the noncommercial category by the International Association of Law Libraries.

[67] Newman, "Albert Kritzer," 362 (footnote omitted).

Professor Kritzer was the guiding force behind the creation and development of the database. The many sources and features of the database include:

- A broad variety of treatises and law review articles are also available on the database. Other resources, such as the commentaries on each article of the CISG and case commentaries, were commissioned for the CISG Database by Professor Kritzer.[68] These original works were written by some of the foremost authorities on the CISG, and reflect a high level of scholarship.[69]
- The database is regularly updated to incorporate new cases, awards, and commentaries. Professor Kritzer also insisted that the CISG Database be user friendly so that researchers whose first language is not English would be able to use it without undue difficulty. Making the CISG Database searchable has been an ongoing goal; keyword, Boolean, and advanced search features are available.
- The CISG Database includes an "annotated text" of the CISG, which is one of its most useful features. For each article of the CISG, the annotated presentations make available links to introductions to the article, to its *travaux*, to cases that have construed the article, to scholarly commentaries about the article, and to comparisons between the article and relevant provisions of the UNIDROIT Principles and the Principles of European Contract Law.[70]
- The database also offers the text and related cases of the CISG's antecedents, the ULIS and the ULF, "which are available for comparative purposes and help to elucidate the genesis of the CISG."[71] Because some articles of the CISG are very similar to articles of ULIS and ULF,[72] the two antecedents can be "mined" to aid in the interpretation of the CISG.[73] Researchers can also take advantage of the "match-ups" of each article of the CISG with articles from ULIS and ULF. The match-ups make it easy to see to what extent the language of the earlier conventions was incorporated into the CISG.
- The database provides an organized and coherent presentation of an extensive collection of *travaux préparatoires*, which includes materials distributed to the 1980 Vienna Diplomatic Conference delegates before the meeting, proceedings of the 1980 Diplomatic Conference, and an article-by-article chronology of Diplomatic Conference proceedings so that the researcher can see how each article of the CISG evolved.
- The database includes an extensive bibliography, which "benefits from the 'bibliography *rapporteurs*,' individuals in countries around the world who provide information about relevant articles and texts published in their countries."[74] Almost 1,600 of the entries are available in full text.

---

[68] Born-digital information is "created in digital form rather than converted from analog to digital." Amy Friedlander, "Summary of Findings," in *Council on Library & Info. Res. & Library of Congress, Building a National Strategy for Digital Preservation: Issues in Digital Media Archiving* 2 (2002), available at http://www.clir.org/pubs/reports/pub106/pub106.pdf.

[69] See, e.g., Article 7 with commentaries by Professors Robert Hillman, Ulrich Magnus, and John Felemegas, http://www.cisg.law.pace.edu/cisg/text/e-text-07.html#schol (last updated January 4, 2012).

[70] For a brief discussion of the UNIDROIT Principles and the PECL and their research value, see note 43.

[71] Newman, "Albert Kritzer," 366–7. For more information about ULIS and ULF, see text accompanying notes 11–14.

[72] Honnold, *Documentary History*, 6.

[73] "Antecedents to the CISG," *CISG Database*, http://www.cisg.law.pace.edu/cisg/text/antecedents.html (last updated March 1996).

[74] Newman, "Albert Kritzer," 367 n. 29.

- The publishing of case law is "the best spur to further convergence of decision making."[75] This promotes uniformity in application. The case presentations include case abstracts, case history, and links to scholarly commentary. The presentations of cases and arbitral awards[76] benefit from the contributions of individuals around the world who translate cases into English[77] under the auspices of the Case Translation Programme, a partnership between the Institute of International Commercial Law and Queen Mary College of the University of London.[78] These translations are unique to the CISG Database.
- The CISG Database is further enriched by the content provided by members of the Autonomous Network of CISG Websites.[79] The Autonomous Network, one of Professor Kritzer's most inspired ideas,[80] is a "worldwide collection of Internet websites dedicated to the CISG and organized on a national basis. Each of the respective participating jurisdictions is charged with collecting all the CISG case law in the jurisdiction and publishing the decisions through the network."[81] The "major benefit flowing from the Autonomous Network is the increased volume of case law that is now available on the database."[82] However, the members of the Network not only provide cases; they also provide unofficial translations of the Convention and entries for the bibliography, and are instrumental in advocating for the adoption of the CISG.

The case law component of the database has resulted in a growing number of soundly argued cases in which courts have referenced cases and scholarly commentaries from other jurisdictions.[83] As one commentator has noted, the database has led to "international cross-referencing of sources, as scholars include more languages and international cases in their comments on the CISG."[84]

C. UNIDROIT and UNILEX

UNIDROIT offers the UNILEX database,[85] which describes itself as an "intelligent database" and "a collection of international caselaw and bibliography on two of the

---

[75] Arthur W. Rovine, "Introduction: Convergence in International Arbitration," in *Contemporary Issues in International Arbitration and Mediation: The Fordham Papers 2009* (ed. A.W. Rovine) (Leiden: Martinus Nijhoff, 2010), xx.

[76] The database includes hundreds of arbitral awards from CIETAC, the China International Economic and Trade Arbitration Commission, all translated into English.

[77] One commentator has pointed out, in relation to statutes, that "[t]he hegemony of English is such that there are few if any large-scale examples of free-access translations of legislation into languages other than English for primarily foreign consumption." Graham Greenleaf, "Free Access to Legal Information, LIIs, and the Free Access to Law Movement," in *The IALL International Handbook of Legal Information Management* (ed. R.A. Danner and J. Winterton) (Burlington, VT: Ashgate, 2011), 216–17.

[78] See Newman, "Albert Kritzer," 371, and The Queen Mary Case Translation Programme, *CISG Database*, http://www.cisg.law.pace.edu/cisg/text/queenmary.html (last updated February 23, 2012).

[79] http://cisgw3.law.pace.edu/network.html (last updated August 22, 2011).

[80] As of this writing, there are twenty-six members of the Autonomous Network representing six continents. See Newman, "Albert Kritzer," 368–71.

[81] McNamara, "U.N. Sale of Goods Convention," 22; Newman, "Albert Kritzer," 369–70.

[82] Newman, "Albert Kritzer," 370 (describing the history and success of the Autonomous Network).

[83] Andersen, "The Global Jurisconsultorium," 50 (discussing a number of CISG cases that considered foreign decisions).

[84] Id., 63.

[85] http://www.unilex.info/dynasite.cfm?dssid=2375&dsmid=14276 (last accessed August 5, 2013). UNILEX is also in the process of establishing the UNILAW database, http://ulr.unidroit.org/program.cfm?

most important international instruments for the regulation of international commercial transactions" – the CISG and the UNIDROIT Principles of International Commercial Contracts. The database is compiled and maintained under the editorial direction of Michael Joachim Bonell, one of the leading authorities on international sales law.

In addition to the text of the CISG and information about its status, UNILEX provides detailed abstracts of selected cases and arbitral decisions, and, whenever possible, the full text. The Pace CISG Database links to all available UNILEX abstracts within its case law presentations. Cases can be searched by date, country, arbitral tribunal, CISG article number, and subject. The extensive bibliography can be searched by author, CISG article, and area, such as "Damages" and "Passing of Risk." The difference between the approaches of the CISG Database and the UNILEX database has been articulated as follows:

> [The Pace CISG Database] has templates for keyword, Boolean and advanced searching as well as open queries; UNILEX uses a more conceptual approach to access articles and other documents on the CISG. The integration of textual commentary with the norms of transnational legal instruments provides a robust and ideal platform for research which the codex format cannot easily match as a tool of discovery for documents related inter-textually.[86]

UNIDROIT has also introduced the UNILAW database, which is "intended to permit ready access by governments, judges, arbitrators, practising lawyers and scholars to up-to-date information regarding uniform law conventions and other instruments."[87] However, it offers very little specifically relating to the CISG, and is best viewed as a work in progress.

D. *TransLex*

The premise underlying the TransLex database,[88] a product of the Center for Transnational Law at the University of Cologne, is that sources of law beyond the CISG might sometimes be needed because the CISG is limited in scope to the conclusion of contracts, obligations of buyers and sellers, and remedies for breach of contract. Often practitioners and scholars need to consult "black letter text, materials and sources of general transnational commercial law principles."[89] The goal of TransLex is to

> [r]eproduce in a list all those rules and principles . . . as black letter law which have been accepted in international arbitral and contract practice together with comprehensive comparative references. The list unifies the various sources that have fostered the evolution of a transnational commercial legal system into one single, open-ended set of rules and principles.[90]

---

menu=about&file=convention&pid=1&lang=en (last accessed August 5, 2013), which will offer materials on a variety of uniform law instruments.

[86] Marylin J. Raisch, "Shaping Electronic Collections in Foreign, Comparative and International Law," in *The IALL International Handbook of Legal Information Management* (ed. R.A. Danner and J. Winterton) (Burlington, VT: Ashgate, 2011), 267.

[87] http://ulr.unidroit.org/program.cfm?menu=about&file=convention&pid=1&lang=en   (last   accessed August 5, 2013).

[88] http://www.trans-lex.org.

[89] Berger, "The TransLex Principles," 34.

[90] Id., 37.

TransLex is composed of four sections, each of which is separately searchable: the TransLex Principles, which "contain[s] more than 120 principles and rules of transnational law,"[91] and gives "access to many full-text references such as domestic statutes, legal doctrine, uniform law instruments, court decisions and arbitral awards"; the TransLex-Bibliography, "a selected collection of bibliographic references on transnational law organized in alphabetical order," with some documents available in full text through the website; TransLex-Materials, "a collection of domestic statutes, international conventions, model laws, restatements and other soft-law instruments"; and TransLex-Links, "a selected collection of links to sites relevant for . . . doing research in transnational law and international business law." The entire database can be searched as well. Several filters are available to make the search more precise; the researcher can filter by type of document and by language, in addition to limiting the search to a particular section of the database. TransLex's scope – transnational commercial law – is very broad, and the CISG is but one of the many topics it covers. Nevertheless, TransLex may be useful in filling in the gaps where the CISG does not extend, and in helping to interpret the CISG.

E. *Commercial Databases*

In addition to the free resources on the CISG, there are several commercial, fee-based databases that offer some useful materials to the researcher who has access to them.[92] However, as will become obvious, no commercial database begins to rival the depth and breadth of the materials offered by the free databases discussed above.

1. Lexis and Westlaw

Lexis and Westlaw are the leading commercial legal databases marketed to attorneys in the United States. Both contain federal and state primary authorities, as well as extensive proprietary secondary authorities. Neither is known for deep holdings of foreign and international law materials. The same is even more true of Bloomberg Law (BLaw), the latest entrant to this market, which is still adding content and functionality. There are a number of lower-cost[93] and free[94] legal databases, but they offer even less access to foreign and international law than the two large commercial databases.

---

[91] "How to Use," *TransLex Database*, http://www.trans-lex.org/how-to-use-the-site-id3 (last accessed August 5, 2013).

[92] In addition to the commercial databases discussed in this section, there are other databases worth mentioning. Researchers will find the text of the CISG on HeinOnline, which also contains a collection of law review articles on international law, international arbitration materials (mainly historical in nature), and materials from and on the United Nations, including the *UNCITRAL Digest*, the *UNCITRAL Yearbook*, and the Records of the 1980 Diplomatic Conference, http://home.heinonline.org/. The CALI Web site offers four interactive lessons that might be helpful to the researcher: CISG Basics: Scope and General Provisions; CISG Basics: Formation; CISG Basics: Performance; and Private International Law Research, http://www.cali.org/category/cali-topics/2l-3l-upper-level-lesson-topics/international-law. SSRN, a searchable international database of scholarly working papers and forthcoming articles, http://www.ssrn.com/, offers access to materials that might not be otherwise available.

[93] Examples include Loislaw, http://www.loislaw.com/, which offers extensive secondary authority, and Fastcase, http://www.fastcase.com/, which focuses on primary authority.

[94] Examples include FindLaw, http://www.findlaw.com/, which is owned by Thomson Reuters, but includes none of its proprietary content, and Lexis Web, http://www.lexisweb.com, which offers access to free content from Web sites vetted by Lexis.

Lexis and Westlaw have not created databases dedicated to the law governing international sale of goods,[95] although both offer the text of the CISG and searchable databases
of law review articles on international law topics. Westlaw offers an arbitration database
containing decisions,[96] treatises, law review articles, and texts, but the focus is on international commercial arbitration, and not specifically on sources that refer to the CISG.
Westlaw also offers commentary on the CISG through its online version of *Guide to the
International Sale of Goods Convention*, which is a practitioner-oriented work. It does
include case abstracts and legal summaries on the convention. Lexis offers even less
relevant content than Westlaw. It has an international arbitration database, but otherwise
there is nothing relevant to the CISG.

2. Kluwer Arbitration

A product of Kluwer Law International, this database is highly valued by students who
are preparing for the Vis International Commercial Arbitration Moot because it synthe-
sizes all of the primary authorities on international commercial arbitration along with
some of the leading commentaries. It is equally valued by practitioners who appreciate the
well-organized, comprehensive, and high-quality content. Kluwer Arbitration includes
court and arbitral decisions, legislation, treatises, journal articles, as well as lists of arbitrators, practice tools,[97] and a blog devoted to international commercial arbitration –
Kluwer Arbitration Blog.[98] Like other commercial databases, Kluwer Arbitration offers
a great deal of functionality, including basic and advanced search; the latter allows the
researcher to craft very specific queries, resulting in precise search results. There are no
materials specifically on international sales of goods, but the CISG, which is discussed
in cases, arbitral awards, and commentary, can be searched effectively thanks to Kluwer
Arbitration's powerful search engine.

VI. Conclusion

As this chapter has demonstrated, the Internet offers a wealth of primary and secondary
authorities on the CISG. These materials are freely accessible; moreover, they are well-
organized and full-featured databases that offer sophisticated search functionality. The
online resources discussed in this chapter have led to increased knowledge about the
CISG and greater willingness on the part of attorneys to use the CISG when drafting
international sales contracts for their clients. They have also encouraged judges and
arbitrators to consider and to cite foreign cases and commentaries when interpreting and
applying the CISG. The CISG databases provide the means that allow courts and arbitral
tribunals to render decisions that respect the CISG's "international character" and the
"need to promote uniformity in its application."[99]

---

[95] Professor Kritzer believed that if such a database were available as part of Lexis or Westlaw, it would foster
the use of the CISG by attorneys in the United States.
[96] The scope of the database is very limited, e.g., no CIETAC awards are included. See note 76 and
accompanying text.
[97] See, e.g., customizable "Smart Charts" that introduce arbitrators to practice in various arbitral tribunals.
[98] See http://kluwerarbitrationblog.com/about/ (last accessed August 5, 2013).
[99] CISG Art. 7(1).

5   Reducing Legal Babelism

CISG Translation Issues

Claire M. Germain

I. Introduction

The CISG has been celebrated as the *lingua franca* for drafting international contracts.[1] *Lingua franca* is the universal language developed and used by merchants around the Mediterranean from the fourteenth until the nineteenth century.[2] The reason for the use of the expression in the CISG context is to demonstrate the drafters' intent to create a universal, neutral, and uniform language in order to avoid the problems inherent in international conventions that have members from a variety of countries with a multitude of different languages. The CISG has remarkably facilitated commercial transactions across boundaries and different legal systems. This chapter discusses the remaining difficulties caused by signatories' use of different languages in interpreting and applying the CISG. The obvious problem is that words in the CISG are sometimes interpreted differently when translated into different languages. The chapter also proposes some solutions to minimize the problems of translation.

Language and translation issues in CISG come up in a variety of types due to its multilingual inception and drafting, as well as the worldwide development of CISG case law and legal scholarship. The first set of issues relates to the peculiar problems associated with the CISG being enunciated in six official languages. Although equally authentic, the several language versions contain significant differences, as do translations from one of the official languages to nonofficial languages. Despite the CISG drafters' aim of creating a neutral, independent legal language, sometimes the same word has different meanings in different languages.[3] The second set of issues deals with the interpretation of the CISG. The problems of statutory interpretation are multifold when an international convention such as the CISG is applied in countries with different legal systems, cultures, legal traditions, and usages. The third set of issues consists of contract problems among the parties involving translated documents, or documents written in a language not understood by one of the parties or by the forum court of a dispute.

---

[1] Peter Schlechtriem, "25 Years of the CISG: An International 'Lingua Franca' for Drafting Uniform Laws, Legal Principles, Domestic Legislation and Transnational Contracts," in *Drafting Contracts under the CISG* (ed. Harry M. Flechtner, Ronald A. Brand, and Mark S. Walter) (New York: Oxford, 2007), 167, 168.

[2] "*Lingua franca*," in *Encyclopedia Britannica* (2011), http://www.britannica.com/EBchecked/topic/342377/lingua-franca.

[3] Ingeborg Schwenzer and Pascal Hachem, "The CISG: Successes and Pitfalls," 57 *American J. of Comparative L.* 457, 461 (2009).

II. Drafting Issues: Six Official Languages

Drafting and translating a multilingual convention is a complex process. The CISG was adopted in the six official languages of the United Nations – Arabic, Chinese, English, French, Russian, and Spanish[4] – and further translated into additional languages. These other translations have no binding effect and can only assist courts in the respective countries where one of the official languages is not spoken.[5] For instance, the four German-speaking countries – Austria, Germany, former East Germany, and Switzerland – jointly produced a semiofficial German translation of the CISG in 1983.[6] There is a rich literature exploring the interrelationship between translation, legal drafting, and the role of "jurilinguists," particularly in bilingual cultures such as Canada, the European Union, and in the international context in general.[7]

Much care has been taken by UNCITRAL in the drafting and translating of the CISG.[8] However, the first issue asks if there is a difference in meaning between two of the official language versions, how does a court determine which language version should govern? The UN Vienna Convention on the Law of Treaties states that, in case of discrepancies in an international text, recourse should be made to the rules of interpretation of treaties,[9] and if it fails, to the "meaning which best reconciles the texts, having regard to the object and purpose of the Treaty."[10] Some commentators, such as Professor Peter Schlechtriem and Professor Ingeborg Schwenzer, argue that the preliminary work on the CISG was done in English and French, and that it is reasonable to give priority to these two language versions.[11] Schwenzer goes further by stating that, in practice, the majority view gives priority to the English version.[12] Professor Ole Lando also favors English as the working

---

[4] See United Nations Commission on International Trade Law, "Witness Clause to the Convention," in *UNCITRAL Digest of Case Law on the United Nations Convention on the International Sale of Goods* 453 (2012 ed.), available at www.uncitral.org/pdf/english/clout/CISG-DIGEST-2012-e.pdf, which explains that textual discrepancies are possible given the nature of language and that they are subject to the rules of interpretation of the Convention on the Law of Treaties. See also *Vienna Convention on the Law of Treaties*, Article 33, May 23, 1969, 1155 U.N.T.S. 331.

[5] *Commentary on the UN Convention on the International Sale of Goods*, 3rd ed. (ed. Peter Schlechtriem and Ingeborg Schwenzer) (New York: Oxford, 2010), 25.

[6] Id.; see also Peter Schlechtriem, *Uniform Sales Law: The UN-Convention on Contracts for the International Sale of Goods* 114 (Manz: Vienna 1986), available at http://www.cisg.law.pace.edu/cisg/biblio/schlechtriem.html.

[7] See Mala Tabory, *Multilingualism in International Law and Institutions* (Alphen aan den Rijn: Sijthoff & Noordhoff, 1980). See also Jean-Claude Gémar, "L'interprétation du texte juridique ou le dilemme du traducteur," in *Interprétation des textes juridiques rédigés dans plus d'une langue* (ed. Rodolfo Sacco) (Torino: L'Harmattan, 2002), 103–41. The EC Commission's Directorate General for Translation has an extensive Web site with useful information and resources to help in translation. Olivier Moréteau, "Le prototype, clé de l'interprétation uniforme: la standardisation des notions floues en droit du commerce international," in Sacco, *Interprétation des textes*, 183–202; O. Moréteau and D. Lamèthe, "L'interprétation des textes juridiques rédigés dans plus d'une langue," *Revue Internationale de Droit Comparé* 327 (2006); *Jurilinguistique: entre langues et droits; Jurilinguistics: Between Law and Language* (ed. Jean-Claude Gémar and Nicholas Kasirer) (Brussels: Bruylant, 2005), 407.

[8] See the thoughtful description of the process in Luca Castellani, "International Trade Law and Language: The UNCITRAL Experience" (2006) (unpublished draft, on file with author).

[9] *Vienna Convention*, Art. 31–2.

[10] United Nations Commission, "Witness Clause," 453 (citing *Vienna Convention*, Art. 33(4)).

[11] Schlechtriem makes the argument for using the English (and French) text to resolve discrepancies in different languages. Schlechtreim and Schwenzer, *Commentary*, 21, 940.

[12] Id.

language of the drafters, although he notes that a court in some countries will rely on a translation rather than the authentic version.[13] In the end, these arguments state that when there are conflicts in translations of the text, the English and, occasionally, the French versions are used because they best express the intentions of the drafters of the CISG – French and English being the languages of the negotiations, English being the drafting language.[14]

Not surprisingly, a commentary in French speaks against the notion that in case of doubt the English text should prevail, supposedly because of the "uncertainties" of the legal Anglo-American language.[15] An ancillary argument given is that most contributors to the drafting process were people who were not fluent in English, that it is safer to rely on the concordance of texts in several official languages, and that French and Spanish could often serve as starting points.[16] Clearly, this is a minority position.

III. Drafting Issues: Choice of Words and Neutral Language

The drafters of the CISG came from different legal traditions, mostly from civil and common law countries. They therefore aimed to avoid domestic legal terms and concepts, and sought to use an independent legal language.[17] CISG drafters chose what was intended to create a neutral, international language detached from domestic legal concepts.[18] For instance, to explain the passing of risk, the CISG uses the words "[goods] handed over" rather than the "title or property" passing to the buyer.[19]

To avoid tradition-laced concepts, such as hardship or *force majeure*, CISG's Article 79 uses "impediment without control" or *"empêchement independant de sa volonté."* The CISG solution started a drafting trend, and was influential on the terminology used in other international documents. The UNIDROIT Principles use the phrase events "beyond control" and *"événement qui lui échappe."* The PECL uses "impediment beyond its control" and *"événement qui échappe à son contrôle."* It is a fair statement that the CISG has succeeded in creating common concepts and legal language unique

---

[13] Ole Lando, preface to *CISG Methodology* (ed. André Janssen and Olaf Meyer) (Munich: Sellier, 2009), 3; Frank Diedrich, "Maintaining Uniformity in International Uniform Law via Autonomous Interpretation: Software Contracts and the CISG," 8 *Pace Int'l L. Rev.* 317, 318 (1996) (posits that the French and English are the preferable versions). Compare Camille Baasch Andersen, *Uniform Application of the International Sales Law* (The Netherlands: Kluwer, 2007), 89 (objects to the notion of the English version being the best, as being politically incorrect and Eurocentric).

[14] Schlechtreim and Schwenzer, *Commentary*, 130.

[15] Karl H. Neumayer and Catherine Ming, *Convention de Vienne sur les contrats de ventei de marchandises. Commentaire* (ed. Francois Dessemontet) (Lausanne: CEDIDAC, 1993), 100.

[16] Id.

[17] Schwenzer and Hachem, *CISG*, 457, 461 n. 27.

[18] "When drafting the single provisions these experts had to find sufficiently neutral language on which they could reach a common understanding." Michael Joachim Bonell, Article 7, in *Bianca-Bonell Commentary on the International Sales Law* (Giuffrè: Milan 1987), 65, 74. See also United Nations Commission, "Witness Clause," ix. ("The drafters of the Convention took special care in avoiding the use of legal concepts typical of a given legal tradition.") They succeeded to a large extent, favoring "non-legal earthy words to refer to physical acts." Bruno Zeller, "Four-Corners: The Methodology for Interpretation and Application of the UN Convention on Contracts for the International Sale of Goods," *Pace Law School Albert H. Kritzer CISG Database*, n. 187 (May 2003), http://www.cisg.law.pace.edu/cisg/biblio/4corners.html.

[19] Id.

to international sales law.[20] This common vocabulary is not linked to national legal systems.[21] An example would be the French and English versions of Article 79 noted earlier.[22]

As Professor Bruno Zeller aptly puts it, "[D]omestic legislation needs to consider the choice and clarity of words. International legislation, in addition, needs to consider the effects of translation on the meaning of words as most conventions unfortunately are not . . . written in [a single] language."[23] He cites, as an example, the issue of mixed sales dealt with in CISG Article 3(1). Article 3(1) states that a transaction is not a sale of goods if the buyer supplies a "substantial" part of the materials. The German "*wesentlich*" and the French "*part essentielle*" are a better match to each other than they are to the English adjective "substantial." These imperfect matches will lead to ambiguities, which can only be avoided by reviewing the text in different languages.[24]

Professor Eric Bergsten notes that much has been written about the problems of translation, but less has been written about drafting in one language with the expectation that the text will be translated.[25] Professor Bernard Audit notes the need to use a simple language in such international instruments. The terms should refer to material events without using words with a legal connotation. Thus, terms such as the French "*délivrance*" and "*force majeure*" were avoided.[26] The French concept of delivery associates the delivery and the conformity, including warranty against hidden defects ("*garantie contre les vices cachés*"). It is nearly impossible to translate this concept, which provides instances where the goods are determined to not have been delivered when the buyer is in possession of the goods.[27]

As well as being simple and nonlegal in nature, words in a multijurisdictional private law instrument have to be comprehensive and functional enough to overcome technical divergences in domestic legal systems. For instance, the word "avoidance" in CISG Article 26, "*résolution*" in the French text, covers the German concepts of *Rücktritt, Wandelung, Kündigung, Irrtumsanfechtung,* as well as termination, cancellation, rescission, and the French concept of "redhibitory defects."[28] From a French perspective, the notion of fundamental breach in CISG Article 25 is problematic because it seems to be somewhere between the French *contraventions essentielles et non essentielles.* In English law it is akin to the distinction between conditions and warranties. The contract can only be voided because of a violation of a condition. This approach is similar in regard to that of Article 1184 of the French Civil Code.[29]

---

[20] Castellani, "International Trade Law," 7–8 (citing Bruno Zeller, "International Trade Law: Problems of Language and Concepts?," 23 *J. L. & Commerce* 39, 43 (2003).
[21] Castellani, "International Trade Law," 6 (citing Moréteau, "Le prototype," 183–202).
[22] See United Nations Commission, "Witness Clause," 252.
[23] Zeller, "International Trade Law."
[24] Id.
[25] Eric Bergsten, "Methodological Problems in the Drafting of the CISG," in Janssen and Meyer, *CISG Methodology,* 18.
[26] Bernard Audit, *La vente internationale de marchandises* (Paris: LGDJ, 1990), 48 n. 1.
[27] Id., 80 n. 1.
[28] Horatia Muir Watt, "Book Review," 87 *Revue Critique de Droit International Privé* 818 (1998); Peter Schlechtriem, ed., *Commentary on the UN Convention on the International Sales of Goods,* 2nd ed. (English trans. Geoffrey Thomas) (Oxford: Clarendon, 1998).
[29] Audit, *La vente internationale,* 119 n. 2.

Differences in official translations, at times, have led to different meanings in the official texts. An example of this phenomenon is seen when comparing the English and French wordings of Articles 71 and 72.[30] Article 71(1) allows a party to temporarily suspend performance if "it becomes apparent that the other party will not perform a substantial part of his obligations."[31] Article 72(1) allows a party to avoid the contract if "it is clear" that the other side will commit a fundamental breach."[32] The English version of these two articles uses two different words: "substantial" and "fundamental." The use of two different words implies two different standards were intended by the drafters of the CISG with a higher one for the permanent avoidance of a contract. But this may not be the case, because the French version of the CISG uses the same word for both articles, *"essentielle."* Article 71 requires the nonperformance of *"une partie essentielle de ses obligations"* and Article 72 requires the threat of a *"contravention essentielle au contrat."*

Although the translations were done carefully, when one looks at the different language versions synoptically,[33] one notes that some words are translated differently. An illustration is provided by Article 3(2) where the French version refers to a *"part essentielle"* (essential part) and the English version refers to a "substantial part." The unofficial German text refers to a *"wesentlicher Teil,"* which corresponds to the French version, and would be translated as "essential part."[34] It is instructive to go back to the legislative history, where it appears that ULIS contained both "substantial and essential," but the English version removed "essential" and the French version removed "substantial."[35]

Bergsten mentions one small discrepancy that was knowingly included with regard to the Chinese translation, but overall, he celebrates the high congruence of the English and French CISG texts, and also the Russian text.[36] He has less confidence in the Spanish, and even less in the Arabic and Chinese. Some of the language versions have been officially rectified, which requires a formal procedure to amend the text called *procès-verbal*.[37] He also mentions the special problem of more than one state sharing the same language, such as with German.[38] The Chinese and Russian versions differ markedly from the

---

[30] Harry M. Fletcher, "The Several Texts of the CISG in a Decentralized System: Observations on Translations, Reservations and other Challenges to the Uniformity Principle in Article 7(1)," 17 *J. of L. and Commerce* 187 (1998), available at http://www.cisg.law.pace.edu/cisg/text/flechtnerauthentic.html.

[31] United Nations Convention on Contracts for the International Sale of Goods Art. 71(1), April 11, 1980, 52 Fed. Reg. 6262, 6264–6280 (1987) (CISG). ("A party may suspend the performance of his obligations if, after the conclusion of the contract, it becomes apparent that the other party will not perform a substantial part of his obligations.")

[32] Id. at Article 72(1). ("If prior to the date for performance of the contract it is clear that one of the parties will commit a fundamental breach of contract, the other party may declare the contract avoided.")

[33] For a nice synoptic display of CISG convention articles and other texts, see Heinz Albert Friehe and Winfried Huck, "Uniform Sales Law (CISG): Synopsis of Selected Texts" (2011), http://web.law-and-business. de/cisg7/index2.php?lang=2, which is in ten languages: five authentic texts (Chinese, English, French, Russian, and Spanish) and five translations (Dutch, German, Italian, Japanese, and Swedish).

[34] Schlechtreim and Schwenzer, *Commentary*, 25 n. 62.

[35] Id., 62. See also Zeller, "Four-Corners," n. 131. Generally on the problems raised by the different languages versions under CISG, see Bergsten, "Methodological Problems," 18–21.

[36] Bergsten, "Methodological Problems," 19–20.

[37] For more information on the *procès-verbal* of correction, see UN Office of Legal Affairs (OLA) Treaty Section, Summary of Practice of the Secretary-General as Depositary of Multilateral Treaties, at paras. 48–62, U.N. Doc. ST/LEG/7/Rev. 1, U.N. Sales No. Sales No. E. 94. V. 15, available at http://untreaty. un.org/ola-internet/Assistance/Summary.htm.

[38] Bergsten, "Methodological Problems," 21.

English and French ones.[39] There is also some criticism of the German translation.[40] Andersen mentions some issues with the Norwegian text, an unofficial translation, which was incorporated into domestic Norwegian law, creating its own problems because it sets itself apart.[41]

The discrepancies observed and debated here do not seem to have created particular practical problems for courts and arbitral tribunals. This is probably due to the excellent work of UNCITRAL translators in the preparation of the texts, and the various methods available and used for comparing wording among the various versions.

IV. Interpretation and Homeward Trend

A substantial number of CISG cases, especially in the earlier case law, suffer from a homeward trend bias where courts apply domestic rules of interpretation in applying the CISG.[42] Differences in language and other domestic peculiarities sometimes make it difficult for outsiders to even "hear" the message of foreign precedent.[43] The issue of language and translation arises in the interpretation of CISG Articles 7 and 8. Article 7(1) aims for an autonomous interpretation of the CISG[44] "free from preconceptions of domestic law."[45] The guiding principles focus on the international character of the CISG, the goal of promoting uniformity, and the promotion of good faith in international trade. The CISG allows the use of domestic law only as a last resort.

Professor John Honnold noted the difference between uniform words and uniform meaning.[46] The uniform interpretation of text meaning is best achieved through autonomous interpretations detached from the traditional concepts, principles, rules, and terms of domestic legal systems.[47] Identical words in the CISG and domestic law may be *faux-amis* and have different meanings.[48] CISG is filled with undefined terms, such as "good faith." CISG Article 7(1) lists good faith as a general principle, but fails to provide a definition or criteria for applying the principle.[49]

To expect a single interpretation of each provision of the CISG is unrealistic.[50] It is difficult enough in domestic law, and unthinkable with a text in multiple languages and where no court of final appeal can give a uniform interpretation.[51] The aim of uniformity of application can only be attained if the national courts and arbitral tribunals interpret

[39] Schlechtreim and Schwenzer, *Commentary*, 123 n. 22.
[40] Id.
[41] Andersen, *Uniform Application*, 88 n. 272.
[42] The expression "homeward trend" is attributed to John Honnold. He mentions it in *Documentary History of the Uniform Law for International Sales* 1 (Deventer: Kluwer, 1989). See Franco Ferrari, "Homeward Trend: What, Why, and Why Not," in Janssen and Meyer, *CISG Methodology*, 171.
[43] Joseph Lookofsky, *Understanding the CISG: A Compact Guide to the 1980 United Nations Convention on Contracts for International Sale of Goods* (Frederick, MD: Kluwer, 2008), 35.
[44] Schlechtreim and Schwenzer, *Commentary*, 122.
[45] Id.
[46] John Honnold, "The Sales Convention in Action: Uniform International Words: Uniform Application," 8 J. of L. & Commerce 207–12 (1988).
[47] Schlechtreim and Schwenzer, *Commentary*, 115. Id.
[48] Id., 118.
[49] Bruno Zeller, "The Observance of Good Faith in International Trade," in Janssen and Meyer, *CISG Methodology*, 133, 134–5.
[50] Bergsten, "Methodological Problems," 29.
[51] Id., 30.

the CISG in a uniform way.[52] To achieve this goal, they have to look at the decisions of other courts and scholarly commentary to develop common interpretations.[53]

Several methods of interpretation are well documented in the scholarly literature, including use of scholarly commentary, legislative history,[54] interpretive methods found in public international law, comparative law, and uniform law principles espoused in soft law instruments.[55] UNCITRAL has played a fundamental role in starting a comprehensive way to gather and disseminate international case law (*jurisprudence*) and scholarly writings (*doctrine*), which in many countries have a higher authority than cases.[56]

Useful information may be gathered from the experience of officially bilingual countries such as Canada.[57] Three methods of interpretation of bilingual legislation often occur in decisions of the Canada Supreme Court and Federal Court: unilingual, if there are no discrepancies in translation but the meaning is ambiguous; bilingual, if one version helps define the meaning of a term better than the other one; and when the two versions lead to divergent meanings, legislative objectives should be used as a guide to a meaning that best achieves those objectives.[58]

Finally, even when translations lead to the same meaning, similar terms can be interpreted differently. For instance, the notion of "reasonable time" has a consistent meaning across languages. So, even when the CISG is found textually uniform, the text may be applied differently. Reasonably timely notice of nonconformity under CISG Article 39, as an example of an open-textured rule, has been interpreted by different courts to range from four days being untimely to four months being timely.[59]

V. Solutions to Deal with Language and Translation Issues

It is obvious that the stated goal of the uniform interpretation of the CISG presupposes the accessibility and availability of foreign legal materials, both case law and scholarly writings and commentaries. Thanks to the remarkably successful efforts of several groups, notably Professor Albert Kritzer at the Pace Law School, and others, in developing easily accessible databases, the CISG is one of the most fully documented international conventions.

UNCITRAL's mandate is to promote uniform interpretation and application of international trade conventions and uniform laws through the collection and dissemination

---

[52] Schlechtreim and Schwenzer, *Commentary*, 124.

[53] Professor Honnold notes that "traditional barriers to the use of scholarly writing in legal development broke down long" in the United States and other common law countries, and civil law countries have always relied on scholarly writings. Honnold, "The Sales Convention in Action," 207.

[54] Id., 208.

[55] See Schlechtreim and Schwenzer, *Commentary*, 130, for a good discussion.

[56] Id., 211 n. 10.

[57] Marie Lajoie, "L'interprétation judiciaire des textes législatifs bilingues," 24 no. 1 *Meta: Translators' J.* 115–24 (1979), available at http://www.erudit.org/revue/meta/1979/v24/n1/003376ar.html?vue=resume.

[58] Article 8 of the Law on Official Languages. Id., 117.

[59] Schlechtreim and Schwenzer, *Commentary*, 127, 629–33; Camilla Baasch Andersen, "The Global Jurisconsultorium of the CISG Revisited," 13 *Vindobona J. of Int'l Commercial L. & Arbitration* 43, 45 (2009); Camilla Baasch Andersen, "The Uniform International Sales Law and the Global Jurisconsultorium," 24 *J. of L. and Commerce* 159 (2005); Camilla Baasch Andersen, "Reasonable Time in Article 39(1) of the CISG: Is Article 39(1) Truly a Uniform Provision," in *1998 Review of the CISG* 63 (ed. Pace University) (Kluwer, 1998), available at http://www.cisg.law.pace.edu/cisg/biblio/andersen.html.

of information.[60] Since 1983, UNCITRAL has worked on a method to disseminate court decisions and arbitral awards interpreting the CISG,[61] resulting in CLOUT (Case Law on UNCITRAL Texts) abstracts in 1988.[62] National correspondents monitor cases in their respective countries, create an abstract of each case, and send it together with the full opinion to the UNCITRAL Secretariat, which adds them to the database.[63] The second edition of the CLOUT Digest was released in 2012. The case digest is authoritative, each chapter "highlighting common views and reporting divergent approaches,"[64] but does not allow for critical commentary.[65] The unofficial CISG Advisory Council, which held its inaugural conference in 2003, is composed of scholars who prepare opinions on suggested interpretations of CISG provisions.[66] The UNILEX database is a collection of international case law and bibliography on the CISG, as well as the UNIDROIT Principles of International Commercial Contracts.[67]

A. *International Sales Law Thesauri and Case Translations*

The development of international sales law thesauri is essential in promoting accessibility and uniformity of interpretation. Two of them are of particular note, the UNCITRAL and the Pace thesauri.

In 1995, the United Nations Commission on International Trade Law commissioned Professor John O. Honnold to develop a classification system of the provisions of the CISG.[68] UNCITRAL refers to this classification on its database as a thesaurus, but the UNCITRAL Thesaurus is more aptly described as a classified index.[69] This outline classifies decisions under the CISG. It includes a detailed breakdown of the subjects addressed in each provision of the CISG, which makes it very useful for searching for particular words or concepts in the outline.[70]

---

[60] UNCITRAL should be active, inter alia, in "promoting ways and means of ensuring a uniform interpretation and application of international conventions and uniform laws in the field of the law of international trade [and] collecting and disseminating information on national legislation and modern legal developments, including case law, in the field of the law of international trade": General Assembly resolution 2205 (XXI) of December 17, 1966, available on UNCITRAL's website at www.uncitral.org.

[61] Rep. of the U.N. Comm. on Int'l Trade Law on the Work of Its Sixteenth Session, May 24–June 3, 1983, U.N. Doc. A/38/17; GAOR, 38th Sess., Supp. No. 17 (1983).

[62] 7 Report of the United Nations Commission on International Trade Law on the Work of Its Twenty-First Session, New York, April 11–20, 1988, United Nations document A/43/17, paragraphs 98–109. CLOUT reports are published as United Nations documents A/CN.9/SER.C/ABSTRACTS/1 to A/CN.9/SER.C/ABSTRACTS/112 (latest document available at the date of this UNCITRAL DIGEST revision). The 112 CLOUT reports are also available on UNCITRAL's Web site at www.uncitral.org/clout/showSearchDocument.do?lf=898&lng=en.

[63] United Nations Commission, "Witness Clause," x.

[64] Id.

[65] For an evaluation of the usefulness and weaknesses of the *UNCITRAL Digest*, see Franco Ferrari, "Remarks on the UNCITRAL DIGEST's Comments on Article 6 CISG," 25 *J. L. & Commerce* 13–37 (2005–6), http://www.uncitral.org/pdf/english/CISG25/Ferrari.pdf.

[66] See http://www.cisgac.com.

[67] See http://www.unilex.info.

[68] See http://www.cisg.law.pace.edu/cisg/text/uncitral.html.

[69] See http://www.uncitral.org/uncitral/en/case_law/thesauri.html.

[70] Personal communication from Professor Vikki Rogers to author (December 16, 2011) (on file with author).

The Pace CISG Database provides a truer form of a thesaurus because it includes a controlled vocabulary.[71] As an example, all information on termination of contract is placed under "avoidance of contract." Alternative terms, phrases, and expressions used in legal systems around the world are cross-referenced to the controlled vocabulary. The Global Sales Law Thesaurus provides a uniform international sales law indexing language. The thesaurus includes terminology from the UCC, but directs the user to parallel legal concepts in international sales law.

The Pace CISG Thesaurus, on the other hand, is a controlled indexing vocabulary, created in accordance with the ISO Standards for monolingual thesauri (ISO 2788). It establishes equivalence relationships, hierarchical relationships, and associative relationships (preferred terms, broader and narrower terms, and related terms). It is thus a uniform terminology that will used to index CISG materials. The intent is to share freely the thesaurus so that other databases will be able employ the same controlled vocabulary to index their CISG collections.[72]

The CISG Database also provides English translations of foreign cases using the Queen Mary Case Translation program. This allows for a fuller dissemination of foreign cases, which may be used by courts in interpreting the CISG.[73] The Pace website includes a list of cases translated, arranged by country, as well as a chart of court hierarchies in different countries.[74]

B. *Reading Foreign Decisions: French Cour de cassation*

The role of higher courts is not the same in the different national legal systems. This can be misleading if one reads a foreign decision with a domestic perspective.[75] For example, the highest court in France for civil and commercial cases is the Cour de cassation. Its decisions are brief, sketchy, and often less than a page in length. They do not include policy reasoning or citations to court cases or scholarly writings, and have been the subject of misunderstandings by common law scholars. One misunderstanding lies in the fact that the Cour de cassation is not a "supreme court" in the common law sense,[76] as it does not review the facts on appeal, but only whether the law was correctly applied to the facts as found by the lower court. The Cour de cassation reviews the law applied in the lower court, either confirms or "quashes" (*casse*) the decision, and then remands the case to another lower court for a decision.[77] The *Cour* decides which issues are matters

---

[71] Vikki M. Rogers and Albert H. Kritzer, "A Uniform International Sales Law Terminology," SISU on Behalf of CISG Database, Pace Institute of International Commercial Law (March 23, 2004), available at http://www.jus.uio.no/sisu/a_uniform_international_sales_terminology.vikki_rogers.and.albert_kritzer/. See also Andersen, "The Uniform International Sales Law."

[72] Id.

[73] The Queen Mary Case Translation Programme, *Pace Law School Albert H. Kritzer CISG Database*, http://cisgw3.law.pace.edu/cisg/text/queenmary.html.

[74] CISG Database Country Case Schedule, *Pace Law School Albert H. Kritzer CISG Database*, http://www.cisg.law.pace.edu/cisg/text/casecit.html.

[75] Sofie Geeroms, "Comparative Law and Legal Translation: Why the Terms Cassation, Revision and Appeal Should Not Be Translated," 50 *American J. of Comparative L.* 201, 202 (2002).

[76] Id. See also Sofie Geeroms, *Foreign Law in Civil Litigation: A Comparative and Functional Analysis* (New York: Oxford University Press, 2004).

[77] *Principles of French Law* (ed. John Bell, Sophie Boyron, and Simon Whittaker) (New York: Oxford University Press, 1998), 3.

of law, and which ones are matters of facts left to the "sovereign power of assessment" of the *juges du fonds* (lower court judges who judge the facts).[78] A long-standing tradition has left the interpretation of contracts and the measure and quantification of damages to the lower courts. A 2000 Cour de cassation decision left the issue of "reasonable time" for a buyer to give notice of lack of conformity of goods pursuant to CISG Article 39(1) to the lower court judge.[79] This decision was subject to criticism.[80]

The lack of reasoned opinions by the Cour de cassation masks the several commentaries that are available for important decisions, including the recommendations of the reporting judge (*Conseiller rapporteur*), the recommendations of the *Avocat Général* (judge representing the public interest), and commentaries prepared by scholars in the specialized law reviews. These various commentaries provide the likely reasons for the decision with citations to relevant cases and scholarly writings. Nonetheless, several French commentators have argued that French Cour de cassation decisions should contain a better explanation of the Court's policy reasoning.[81]

C. *Role of Foreign Decisions and Scholarly Writings*

There is consensus that case law is to be considered a major source for the interpretation of the CISG: "A consistent body of case law is progressively being built under the CISG."[82] Several trends have appeared. Civil law countries are becoming increasingly sensitive to foreign case law, and common law courts have begun to use scholarly writings as a source of interpretation.[83] Doctrinal writings are influential not only in describing the state of affairs of a particular issue, but also in taking positions on critical issues in order to provide guidance to courts in the creation of an international common law of sales.[84]

However, the debate is ongoing as to how much weight courts should give to foreign decisions and scholarly commentary in applying the CISG. There is general agreement that well-reasoned foreign decisions should have persuasive authority.[85] Of course, this presupposes that the foreign cases can be read or translated by lawyers and judges. As noted previously, the development of databases and translations of cases have provided much greater access to foreign case laws. The reading of foreign decisions needs to be done with the awareness of the context and the procedural and remedial aspects of the

---

[78] Id.

[79] Claude Witz, *Un arrêt regrettable: le délai de dénonciation des défauts prévu par la Convention de Vienne laissé à l'appréciation souveraine des juges du fond*, 2000 Recueil Dalloz, 788.

[80] Id.

[81] Adolphe Touffait and André Tunc, "Pour une motivation plus explicite des décisions de justice, notamment de celles de la Cour de cassation," 72 *Rev. Trim. Dt. Civ.* 487 (1974). See also Intervention de M. Christian Charruault, président de la première chambre civile de la Cour de cassation, Cour de Cassation, April 2010, available at http://www.courdecassation.fr/colloques_activites_formation_4/2010_3159/christian_charruault_15853.html.

[82] Schlechtreim and Schwenzer, *Commentary*, 128, citing other authors who think that it is the most important source.

[83] Id., 129.

[84] Anna Veneziano, "Uniform Interpretations: What Is Being Done? Unofficial Efforts and Their Impact," in *The 1980 Uniform Sales Law: Old Issues Revisited in the Light of Recent Experiences*, Verona Conference 2003 (ed. Franco Ferrari) (Milan: Giuffrè, 2003), 326, n. 6. She cites to one French decision: CA Grenoble, October 23, 1996, which cites to a German decision. Id., 328, n. 13.

[85] Id., 125, citing Lookofsky, *Understanding the CISG*.

decision.[86] Finally, foreign case precedent must be analyzed critically in order to prevent the perpetuation of faulty reasoning in such cases.[87]

VI. Language Risk

When the parties to a contract use different languages (which may result in the contract being written in different languages), the issue of which party is allocated the risk of differences in the respective languages is raised.[88] According to CISG Article 8, regarding the interpretation of statements made by and other conduct of the parties, the party making the statement bears the risk of defective formulation. The parties should specify the language of the contract for purposes of resolving disputes over divergent interpretations due to language differences. This is especially important for the interpretation of standard terms and conditions.[89] The language of the contract is almost always the language of the negotiations. To be effective, a reference by one party to its standard terms must be sufficient to put a reasonable person in the place of the other party in a position to understand the reference and to gain knowledge or an understanding of the standard terms.

In one case, the seller's standard contract terms were not in the language of the contract, and the court held that the terms did not become part of the contract because of the seller's failure to provide a translation of the terms. Another court stated that standard contract terms written in a language different from that of the contract do not bind the other party.[90] An early German court decision ruled that a case-by-case approach must be employed in determining the effectiveness of a notice written in a language other than the language in which the contract was made.[91] The reasonableness of the language used is to be determined from the perspective of a reasonable person, looking at the usages and practices observed in international trade. The mere fact that a notice was in a language that was neither that of the contract nor that of the addressee did not necessarily prevent the notice from being effective if it was an acceptable language from the perspective of trade usages and practices. Furthermore, the court noted that the recipient of the notice might reasonably have been expected to request a clarification explanations or a translation.

The Tribunale di Rovereto held that standard terms have to be drafted "either in the language of the contract, or in that of the opposing party or a language that the opposing

---

[86] Silvia Ferreri, "Remarks Concerning the Implementation of the CISG by the Courts (the Seller's Performance and Article 35)," 25 *J. of L. and Commerce* 223, 229 (2005–6), available at http://www.cisg.law.pace.edu/cisg/biblio/ferreri.html.

[87] Schlechtreim and Schwenzer, *Commentary*, 126–7 (citing an Australian decision that cites the Cour de cassation decision, itself inconsistent with another decision). For a review of the main obstacles in finding and evaluating foreign decisions, see also Fabio Liguori, "UNILEX: A Means to Promote Uniformity in the Application of CISG," 4 *Zeitschrift für Europäisches Privatrecht* 600 (1996).

[88] Id., 166.

[89] Id., 166, 173. See also Ulrich Magnus, "Incorporation of Standard Contract Terms under the CISG," in *Sharing International Commercial Law across National Boundaries: Festschrift for Albert H. Kritzer on the Occasion of His Eightieth Birthday* (ed. Camilla B. Andersen and Ulrich G. Schroeter) (Wildy, Simmonds & Hill, 2008), 303, 324.

[90] United Nations Commission, "Witness Clause," 58, citing 84 Rechtbank Koophandel Hasselt, Belgium, June 2, 1999, available at www.law.kuleuven.ac.be/int/tradelaw/WK/1999–06–02.htm.

[91] Id., citing CLOUT case No. 132 (Oberlandesgericht Hamm, Germany, February 8, 1995).

party knows" to be a part of the contract.[92] Another court ruled that the other contracting party had to be sufficiently notified for the standard terms to be incorporated into the contract either in the language of negotiations or in the party's native language."[93] Yet another court[94] held that if a party accepts statements relating to the contract in a language different from the one used for the contract, it is bound by the contents, and it is the receiving party's responsibility to determine the meaning of the contents.

In the end, language and translation issues have not become major problems in the application of the CISG, based on a review of the reported cases. A survey of the Pace and French CISG databases, using the key words "translation," "*traduction,*" "language," "*langage,*" found only a handful of cases in which language issues were mentioned.[95]

VII. Conclusion

The CISG has been adopted by a large number of countries. It has generated a vast scholarly literature. And, to a surprising degree, it has reached a reasonable level of uniformity in its application.[96] The CISG can be credited for the decline of legal babelism that beset the private international law rules it was created to replace.[97] There has been serious progress toward the convergence of legal systems, and the CISG has had positive influence on the reforming of a number of national contract-sales legal systems. The most effective way to prevent the homeward trend is to educate the current and future generations of law students and lawyers about foreign legal systems and comparative law, and also to increase the ability of lawyers to read and understand foreign languages.

---

[92] Id., citing Tribunale di Rovereto, Italy, November 21, 2007, Unilex.

[93] Id., citing Landgericht Memmingen, Germany, September 13, 2000, available at http://cisgw3.law.pace .edu/cases/000913g1.htm.

[94] Id., citing 88 CLOUT case No. 409 (Landgericht Kassel, Germany, February 15, 1996), also Unilex.

[95] See, e.g., CISG France Cour d'Appel de Paris, 5eme Chamber Section A, Sept. 10, 2003, Societe H.H....GMBH & Co. v. SARL MG. available at http://www.cisg-france.org/decisions/100903v.htm (French Court of Appeals held that the German "*Auftragsbestätigung*" could be translated as "*confirmation de commande*" despite it being in a language that the party did not understand); Cour d'appel de Versailles, douzième chambre section 2, 13 Octobre 2005 (documents were written in a foreign language without any translation, such that the Court could not interpret it); Société E. contre Société T.D. SARL B, available at http://www.cisg-france.org/decisions/131005a.htm; Cour d'appel de Grenoble, chambre commerciale, 13 Septembre 1995. Monsieur C..., R... contre Société française de f... international F...F..." S.F.F." (SA), available at http://www.cisgfrance.org/decisions/130995v.htm (Court held that the date listed on the translation was an obvious material error).

[96] Bergsten, "Methodological Problems," 31.

[97] Claude Witz talks about the "recul du babélisme juridique" in "Les vingt-cinq ans de law Convention des Nations Unies sur les contrats de vente internationale de merchandises: Bilans et perspectives" ["The 25th anniversary of the CISG: Evaluations and perspectives"], 123 *Journal du Droit Int'l* 5, 25 (2006). The Babel reference is also attributable to John Honnold, in *Documentary History,* 1 ("Babel of diverse legal systems").

6 The CISG in National Courts

Camilla Baasch Andersen

> The UN Sales Convention was created primarily by academics. However, it today belongs to the practicing attorney and his clients and to the jurists and arbitrators.[1]
> Albert H. Kritzer

I. Breadth of CISG Applications

As Albert H. Kritzer so piercingly pointed out in the quote above, the CISG now no longer belongs to the scholars and nongovernmental organizations that drafted it (and its predecessors), but control of its fate lies in the hands of those who apply and use it – the practitioners, lawyers, judges, and arbitrators. The national courts play a crucial role in the application, misapplication, and nonapplication of the CISG. The CISG has now been adopted in 79 countries,[2] including Brazil where it will soon enter into effect.[3] However, parties opt out of it and, at times, it is ignored by judges and lawyers in many of the contracting states. On the other hand, the CISG is used in unexpected ways outside its ordinary sphere of application (national courts).

A. *Nonapplication of the CISG*

In commercial practice, approval of the CISG is mixed; many practitioners are distrustful of an international sales law with which they are unfamiliar and that possesses concepts foreign to their domestic legal systems. Many practitioners encourage clients to opt out of the CISG for the more familiar territory of domestic law, such as the American Uniform Commercial Code (UCC), United Kingdom Sales of Goods Act, and German Handelsgesetzbuch (HGB), or will simply opt out of the CISG in drafting contracts without consulting their clients. Both of these scenarios raise the possibility of legal malpractice when a lawyer has failed to become knowledgeable of the content of the CISG before electing to opt out.[4] A claim of unfamiliarity is no excuse for a lawyer's lack of due diligence in understanding applicable law. Another troubling scenario is those

---

[1] Albert H. Kritzer, foreword to Camilla Baasch Andersen, *Uniform Application of the International Sales Law* (Kluwer, 2007), xiii.

[2] As of March 5, 2013, UNCITRAL reports that seventy-nine states have adopted the CISG. See http://www.uncitral.org/uncitral/en/uncitral_texts/sale_goods/1980CISG_status.html.

[3] Brazil ratified the CISG on March 3, 2013, and it will enter into force there on April 1, 2014, see http://www.unis.unvienna.org/unis/pressrels/2013/unisl182.html.

[4] See Chapter 40 of this book.

instances where the CISG applies to a dispute between parties and is disregarded either by the attorneys or the courts, or both. A more prevalent occurrence is where national courts prematurely resort to domestic law in interpreting the CISG (homeward trend bias). Some of these cases are discussed in the section entitled "Blatant Disregard."

B. *National Application outside the Scope of the CISG*

The CISG has become more than just a shared law in the states that have adopted it; it is being used as a benchmark for international sales law and practice in different contexts – as a blueprint for new laws, as a contract checklist for negotiating contracts, and as a benchmark for good commercial practice. For example, in the modernization and revisions of existing sales laws, the CISG has influenced the drafting of statutory revisions in a number of contracting states. In the recent revisions of the German Commercial Code of 1869 (*Handelsgesetzbuch*) and Chinese Contract Law, the CISG was relied on heavily as a model law. For some emerging states, the CISG has been incorporated into their commercial codes as the countries' domestic and international sales law.[5]

Moreover, the CISG has been used in contracting states beyond its scope of application. One such example is a case decided by the Danish Eastern High Court (Østre Landsret) concerning the leasing of a steam plant, which is outside the scope of the CISG.[6] However, the court applied the CISG to the sale of the purely moveable tangible goods ("*de rene løsørekøb*") ancillary to the leasing agreement. The substantive issues relating to the lease were settled according to Danish law as dictated by the Rome Convention. But in establishing the proper forum under the criteria found in the Brussels Convention (EC Convention on Jurisdiction and the Enforcement of Decisions in Civil and Commercial Matters), the court relied on the principle that the place of payment is the seller's place of business as provided in CISG Article 57(1). The court, in essence, used the CISG as support for the argument that there is a general international rule for the place of payment.

Other courts have gone even further by recognizing the CISG as an expression of customary international law.[7] One such example is found in a 1989 decision of the Iran–U.S. Claims Tribunal.[8] The case involved a reduction in monetary relief sought by the seller for the buyer's nonpayment of the contract price. The relief sought was reduced to proceeds of the sale, less completion and modification expenses and reselling costs. After ruling on this matter under the applicable law (which was not the CISG), the tribunal stated: "Moreover [seller's] right to sell undelivered equipment in mitigation of its damages is consistent with *recognized international law of commercial contracts*. The conditions of Article 88 of the [CISG] are all satisfied in this case – there was

---

[5] See Peter Schlechtriem, "25 Years of the CISG: An International Lingua Franca for Drafting Uniform Laws, Legal Principles, Domestic Legislation and Transnational Contracts" in *Drafting Contracts under the CISG* (ed. Brandt, Flechtner, and Walter) (CELI series, Oxford University Press, 2008).

[6] Denmark, December 4, 2000, Appellate Court Copenhagen, available at http://cisgw3.law.pace.edu/cases/001204d1.html.

[7] See, e.g., ICC Arbitration Case No. 6149 of 1990, available at http://cisgw3.law.pace.edu/cases/906149i1.html; ICC Arbitration Case No. 7331 of 1994, available at http://cisgw3.law.pace.edu/cases/947331i1.html.

[8] See Iran/U.S. Claims Tribunal, award of 28.07.1989, available at http://cisgw3.law.pace.edu/cases/890728i2.html.

unreasonable delay by the buyer in paying the price and the seller gave reasonable notice of its intention to sell."

Two decisions of the English Court of Appeals referenced the CISG despite the fact that the United Kingdom has not adopted the CISG.[9] In both cases, the judges used CISG Article 8 as a source of inspiration for interpreting the reasonableness of a contracting party's conduct.[10] Both cases involved domestic sales transactions. In the *ProForce* case, the Court stated:

> In addition, careful consideration may have to be given to the aims to be achieved by contractual interpretation and the precise extent to which the law requires an objective interpretation . . . It may be appropriate to consider a number of international instruments applying to contracts. The UN Convention on Contracts for the International Sale of Goods (1980) provides that a party's intention is in certain circumstances relevant, and in determining that intention regard is to be had to all relevant circumstances, including preliminary negotiations.

The same wording is used in the *Square Mile* case. According to these decisions, the CISG is now an appropriate source of sound commercial practice in the interpretation of contracts between two English parties. Given the complicated history of the UK and the CISG, this is an encouraging development.[11]

II. CISG Case Law: Uniform Law in National Courts

This part notes that a solid body of case law represents "mainstream" CISG jurisprudence. Although overlooked and disregarded in some jurisdictions, the CISG is applied regularly in German courts, as well as numerous Western European countries. It has also been commonly applied in CIETAC arbitration in China, as well as by arbitration tribunals in the Russian Federation. The volume of cases applying the CISG has grown exponentially.

---

[9] For a review of the complicated history between the UK and the CISG, see Andersen, "National Report of the United Kingdom," in *The CISG and Its Impact on National Legal Systems* (ed. Franco Ferrari) (Selliers European Law Publishers, 2008), 303–11; Michael Bridge, "Uniformity and Diversity in the Law of International Sale," 15 *Pace Int'l L. Rev.* 55 (2003); Michael Bridge, "The Bifocal World of International Sales: Vienna and Non-Vienna," in *Making Commercial Law* (ed. Cranston) (Oxford University Press, 1997), 277–96; Moss, "Why the United Kingdom Has Not Ratified the CISG," *J. of L. & Commerce* 483 (2005); Nicholas, "The Vienna Convention on International Sales Law," 105 *Law Quarterly Rev.* 201–43 (1989); Mullis, "Twenty-Five Years On: The United Kingdom, Damages and the Vienna Sales Convention," 71 *Rabels Zeitschrift für ausländisches und internationals Privatrecht* (*RabelsZ*) 35–51 (2007); Williams, "Forecasting the Potential Impact of the Vienna Sales Convention on International Sales Law in the United Kingdom," in *Pace Review of the Convention on Contracts for the International Sale of Goods* (CISG) (Kluwer Law International, 2000–1); Takahashi, "Right to Terminate (Avoid) International Sales of Commodities," *Journal of Business Law* 102 (2003); Lee, "The UN Convention on Contracts for the International Sale of Goods: OK for the UK?," *J. of Business Law* 131–48 (1993); Bruno Zeller, "Commodity Sales and the CISG," in *Sharing International Commercial Law across National Boundaries* (ed. C. Andersen and U. Schroeter) (Wildy & Sons, 2008), 627–40. See also Wheatley, "Why I Oppose the Winds of Change," *The Times*, March 27, 1990, and reply, Roy Goode, "Why Compromise Makes Sense," *The Times*, May 22, 1990.

[10] *ProForce Recruit Ltd v. Rugby Group Ltd.*, available at http://cisgw3.law.pace.edu/cases/060217uk.html; *The Square Mile Partnership Ltd v Fitzmaurice McCall Ltd.*, available at http://cisgw3.law.pace.edu/cases/061218uk.html.

[11] For a commentary on these decisions, see Bonell, "The UNIDROIT Principles and CISG: Sources of Inspiration for English Courts?," *Uniform L. Rev.* 305 (2006).

The Pace Law School CISG Database – W3CISG – lists nearly 3,000 CISG cases. Scholarly works, such as the UNCITRAL Digest and Opinions of the CISG Advisory Council, complement this large body of case law.

The sharing of a uniform law instrument across boundaries of legal cultures, languages, and jurisprudential systems creates a considerable challenge for national courts to apply the law in a uniform manner. Some national courts are acutely aware of their obligation to develop uniform international approaches; others have been more concerned with the compatibility of the CISG with their own domestic laws. Still other courts are blissfully unaware of the transnational precedents they are creating. The context and method with which the CISG is being applied raises important questions: (1) What level of uniform application should be expected in the context of an instrument like the CISG? (2) Given the mass of case law, has the CISG attained a sufficient measure of uniform application?

A. *Understanding Uniformity*

It stands to reason that uniformity in law cannot be defined by a dictionary definition of "uniformity," as laws are never applied in "always the same" way. One definition of uniformity as it relates to uniform laws states that: "We can define 'uniformity' as the varying degree of similar effects on a legal phenomenon across boundaries of different jurisdictions resulting from the application of deliberate efforts to create specific shared rules in some form."[12] This definition highlights the need to distinguish between textual uniformity and uniform application, as well as the need to determine basic interpretive rules that encourage autonomous interpretations of the CISG.

Modern uniform law is a relatively new form of law making, with a different *origin* and a different *focus* from those of conventional domestic law making.[13] It is a *voluntary* process whereby different jurisdictions elect to share a set of rules. This process is to be contrasted with mandated legal uniformity imposed by Roman law[14] and the common law.[15] Transborder uniform laws are laws created with the deliberate aim of establishing shared law across multiple jurisdictions. Agreeing to a uniform text is the beginning of the process; it is in the uniform application of the text that a uniform law achieves its intended purpose. It is only when a uniform law has been applied cross-jurisdictionally on the intended legal phenomenon and creates the intended degree of similarity that the label "uniform" can be affixed.

B. *Textual Uniformity versus Applied Uniformity*

Applied uniformity is the true goal of international law unification. Peter Schlechtriem distinguished between "unity achieved at a verbal level" (substantive legal rules) and the "uniform understanding–interpretation" of law (commentary and application of the

[12] Camilla Baasch Andersen, "Defining Uniformity in Law," 12 *Uniform Law Review* 5 (2007).
[13] See Niklas Luhmann, who defines the process of law in globalization as a process of law where "functional criteria increasingly replace geographic ones, with nation-states' traditional law-generating organs diminishing in importance in determining legal significance, regulation and evolution." In *Das Recht der Gesellschaft* (trans. Vivian Curran) (1993).
[14] See Cicero, *De Republica*, 3.22.33: "[T]here shall not be one law at Rome, another at Athens, one now, another hereafter, but one everlasting and unalterable law shall govern all nations for all time."
[15] De Cruz argues that James the First, King of England and Scotland, introduced uniformity to England and Scotland when proposing to unify them under a single legal system in the early sixteenth century; see Peter De Cruz, *Comparative Law in a Changing World* (Cavendish Publishing, 1999), 23.

rules).[16] This is the distinction between *textual uniformity*[17] and *applied uniformity*. Textual uniformity, like applied uniformity, is not an absolute. The textual uniformity of legal instruments can vary immensely depending on the quality of translations and the style of promulgated text (model laws versus conventions). Language is not a precise science. Harry Flechtner labels the limitation of language as "textual non-uniformity."[18] Such differences may, naturally, have an effect on the way scholars and practitioners working in these different languages interpret and use provisions of the CISG, so the degree of *textual uniformity* directly affects the degree of actual uniformity.

Although it is true that textual uniformity has profound effects on applied uniformity, even the most diligently created piece of textually uniform legislation will not achieve uniformity of application. As pointed out by Honnold, "uniform words do not create uniform results."[19] Textual uniformity is the means to the end of actual uniformity, but it is in the decisions of differing national courts where true uniformity is measured.

C. *The CISG and Uniformity*

The CISG finds its basis for uniformity in its preamble, and in CISG Article 7(1), which provides: "In the interpretation of this Convention, regard is to be had to its international character and to the need to promote uniformity in its application." The question at issue is "how uniform is uniform?" A detailed analysis of the CISG, its *travaux préparatoires* (including the Secretariat's Commentary and antecedent laws ULF and ULIS), and current practice indicates that different provisions aspire to different degrees of applied uniformity as some CISG articles are drafted in more flexible terms than others. However, given the genesis of the CISG, and the professed aim of its drafters to create a level playing field in commercial law and remove barriers to international trade, a reasonable level of applied uniformity is needed to serve those purposes.[20] The greatest threat to uniformity of application is national courts' inappropriate reliance on domestic law and domestic legal tradition in applying the CISG.

III. The CISG and Nonuniformity

There are two basic instances where there is cause for concern regarding the uniform application of the CISG in national courts, and both create a pattern of misapplication

---

[16] See Peter Schlechtriem, introduction to *Commentary on the UN Convention on the International Sale of Goods* (ed. Peter Schlechtriem and Ingeborg Schwenzer) (Oxford University Press, 2005), 6.

[17] This term also accords with the way in which Harry Flechtner talks of "textual non-uniformity" when comparing the different texts of the six official languages of the CISG and their meanings, but Flechtner uses it to indicate the level of similarity between the texts in question. By inference, if they did have the same meanings linguistically then these texts would (together) represent a textual uniformity. An instrument with only one official text will thus, by definition, always represent a single *textual uniformity*. See Harry Flechtner, "The Several Texts of the CISG in a Decentralized System: Observations on Translations, Reservations and other Challenges to the Uniformity Principle in Article 7(1)," 17 *J. of L. & Commerce* 187 (1998), available at http://cisgw3.law.pace.edu/cisg/biblio/flecht1.html.

[18] Id.

[19] See John Honnold, "Uniform Words and Uniform Application: The 1980 Sales Convention and International Juridicial Practice," in *Einheitliches Kaufrecht und Nationales Obligationenrecht* (ed. Peter Schlechtriem) (Nomos, 1987), 146–7.

[20] See Camilla Baasch Andersen, *Uniform Application of the International Sales Law* (Kluwer 2007), chapter 2.

within the sphere that encourages forum shopping; the inadvertent "homeward trend" of interpretation and the blatant disregard for the uniform characteristics of the CISG.

A. *Inadvertent "Homeward Trend"*

Some CISG rules are open to various interpretations. In these cases, inadvertent homeward trend analysis may be used to select from feasible, variant interpretations.[21] The inadvertent application of domestic law traditions and perceptions to the interpretation of a CISG provision leads to specific, predictable patterns, which are clearly nonuniform. CISG Article 39's "reasonable time" requirement to give notice of nonconformity is an example of this phenomenon. Courts have interpreted the reasonable time requirement to range from no more than four days to up to four months or longer.[22] This wide variation of time periods is best explained by the identity of the national court making the interpretation. For example, French courts, where domestic law is more buyer-friendly, have allowed for longer periods to give notice, while Germany courts have applied stricter time periods. German domestic law is more seller-friendly, requiring shorter periods of time for notice giving. Article 39 is one of the most disputed areas of the CISG because failure to comply with the notice requirement, with few exceptions,[23] deprives the buyer of remedies for nonconformity of goods. In the interpretation of key provisions such as the inspection and notice requirements of CISG Articles 38 and 39,[24] with regard to this particular issue, the determination of "reasonable time," the domestic variations observed in the case law are unacceptable.[25] The various interpretations are so predictable as to encourage forum shopping by one of the contracting parties.

A similar problem is created surrounding the principle of "good faith." CISG Article 7 prescribes a duty to promote "the observance of good faith in international trade." However, it has been hotly debated whether this reference to good faith in the interpretation of CISG rules is sufficient grounds for imposing on parties a general duty to act in good faith. Jurisdictions such as France, Italy, Austria, and Germany – where general principles of good faith have long been embraced – support a broad application of the good faith principle in the interpretation of contracts and in judging party conduct.[26] But

---

[21] See Franco Ferrari, "Have the Dragons of Uniform Sales Law Been Tamed?," in *Sharing International Commercial Law across National Boundaries: Festschrift for Albert H. Kritzer on the Occasion of His Eightieth Birthday* (ed. Andersen and Schroeter) (Wildy & Hill, 2008), 134–67 (problem of homeward trend bias).

[22] See CISG Advisory Opinion No. 2, available at http://www.cisg.law.pace.edu/cisg/CISG-AC-op2.html; Camilla Baasch Andersen, "Reasonable Time in the CISG," in *1998 Rev. of the CISG* (ed. Pace) (Kluwer, 1998), 63.

[23] Exceptions are found in Article 40 (for the seller in bad faith or quasi-bad faith) and Article 44 (for the buyer who has a reasonable excuse). For more on these exceptions, see Camilla Baasch Andersen, "Exceptions to the Notification Rule: Are They Uniformly Interpreted?," 9 *Vindobona L. J.* 17 (2005).

[24] For more on the civil law versus common law approach to solving the problem of reasonable time, see Camilla Baasch Andersen, "Noblesse Oblige . . . ? Revisiting the 'Noble Month' and the Expectations and Accomplishments It Has Prompted," in *Festschrift for Ingeborg Schwenzer: Private Law National – Global – Comparative*, Vol. 1 (ed. Muller-Chen and Buchler) (Bern: Stämpfli Verlag, 2011), 33–50; see "Differing Mentalities: Each to His Own?"

[25] Andersen, "Reasonable Time in the CISG," 63; Daniel Girsberger, "The Time Limits of Article 39 CISG," 25 *J. of L. & Commerce* 241 (2005–6).

[26] Cases where courts and tribunals infer a general good faith obligation include: Cour d'Appel Grenoble, No. 93/3275 (February 22, 1995), *J. du Droit Int'l* [J.D.I.] 632 (1995), Hungarian Chamber of Commerce

in other jurisdictions, where the good faith is not recognized or is limited in scope, such a broad use of the principle would be considered to be inappropriate.[27] Although these divergences in applying the good faith principle seem to be a major threat to uniformity, in practice, the use of good faith in most cases has not changed the result based on more specified CISG rules. Often, the good faith principle is used more as a rationale for a rule application than actually as the means of determining the case outcome.

B. *Blatant Disregard*

A more extreme case of homeward trend in interpretation is seen in selected cases from the United States. In these cases, the courts have analogized that a CISG rule was the same as the domestic rule. The courts then proceeded to use the case law relating to the domestic rule in the interpretation of the CISG. Professors Joseph Lookofsky and Harry Flechtner soundly criticized *Raw Materials Inc. v. Manfred Forberich GmbH*[28] as the worst-reasoned CISG case of the past twenty-five years.[29] In *Raw Materials*, the judge acknowledged the application of CISG Article 79 as applicable law, but then proceeded to use domestic UCC case law and commentary in making its determination of whether a contractual excuse should be given. This is an appalling noninternational and nonuniform application of shared international law, in direct violation of the interpretational rule of Article 7. Unfortunately, the case does not stand alone – earlier U.S. case law[30] noted that: "Case law interpreting analogous provisions of Article 2 of the Uniform Commercial Code may also inform the court where the language of the relevant CISG provisions tracks that of the UCC."[31] This type of faulty reasoning is largely due to an absence of awareness of the uniform nature of the CISG.[32] How can courts be influenced to move away from homeward trends in interpretation and embrace a more uniform and shared approach to the application of the CISG?

IV. Global Jurisconsultorium of the CISG

Over the last decade, the notion that shared global law needs shared global doctrine and jurisprudence has gained support in domestic courts and in international

---

and Industry Court of Arbitration, Arbitral Award, No. VB/94124 (November 17, 1995), pt. IV, P 6, Italy 25 (February 2004), District Court Padova SO. M. AGRI s.a.s di Ardina Alessandro & C. v. Erzeugerorganisation Marchfeldgemüse GmbH & Co. KG, Germany, November 12, 2001, Appellate Court Hamm 13 U 102/01, Austria (February 6, 1996), Supreme Court (Propane case), Case No. 10 Ob 518/95.

[27] Natalie Hofmann, "Interpretation Rules and Good Faith as Obstacles to the UK's Ratification of the CISG and to the Harmonization of Contract Law in Europe," 22 *Pace Int'l L. Rev.* 145 (2010).

[28] *Raw Materials Inc. v. Manfred Forberich GmbH* 2004, WL 1535839 (N.D. Ill. 2004).

[29] Joseph Lookofsky and Harry Flechtner, "Nominating Manfred Forberich: The Worst CISG Decision in 25 Years?," 9 *Vindobona J. of Int'l Commercial L. & Arbitration* 199 (2005).

[30] See, e.g., *Orbisphere Corp. v. United States*, 726 F.Supp. 1344, 1355 (Ct. Int'l Trade 1989).

[31] *Chicago Prime Packers, Inc. v. Northam Food Trading Co.* (D.C. Ill. 2004), n. 11 (CISG internationally and uniformly, but makes parallel cites to the UCC); *Delchi Carrier S.p.A. v. Rotorex Corp.*, 71 F.3d 1024 (2nd Cir. 1995). See Harry Flechtner, "The CISG in American Courts: The Evolution (and Devolution) of the Methodology of Interpretation," in *Quo Vadis CISG* (ed. Franco Ferrari) (Selliers European Publishers, 2005).

[32] See some of the points made by James Bailey in "Facing the Truth: Seeing the Convention on Contracts for the International Sale of Goods as an Obstacle to a Uniform Law of International Sales," 32 *Cornell Int'l L.J.* 273, 282 (1999).

CISG scholarship. Collectively, these contributions can be described as a *global jurisconsultorium*.[33] It can be defined as a process of consultation that takes place across borders and legal systems with the aim of producing autonomous uniform interpretations and applications of uniform law.

A. *The "Legal" Arguments*

Jurisconsultorium or shared interpretational sphere is based on jurists from around the globe consulting with one another, either in scholarly contexts or by referring to each other's decisions and opinions. This jurisconsultorium can be divided into two major groups: the *scholarly jurisconsultorium* (the sphere of cooperation and consultation between transnational scholars) and the *practical jurisconsultorium* (the sphere in which transnational shared case law is used to resolve disputes before domestic courts). An example of the latter group can be found in the United States, where shared doctrines and precedents relating to the Uniform Commercial Code (UCC) are throughout the country. The English Commonwealth system has developed a shared body of persuasive precedents, used to decide cases in a wide range of jurisdictions.

Article 7(1) provides the legal basis for a duty to aim for a uniform, transnational interpretation of the CISG. Professor Lookofsky argues that "Article 7(1) commands national courts also to have (some measure of) 'regard' to the international view."[34] This is a logical conclusion based on the wording of Article 7(1) CISG and its requirement of "regard" for internationality and uniformity. However, it does not support a duty for uniform application – merely a uniform *interpretation*. Uniformity of interpretation does not guarantee uniformity of application.

In the words of John Honnold: "tribunals construing an international convention will appreciate that they are colleagues of a world-wide body of jurists with a common goal."[35] The judges and legal counsel who apply an international uniform convention must recognize that they are sharing it with colleagues in other jurisdictions, and that the development of its jurisprudence is a communal effort requiring an approach different from the one that they use when applying domestic law. The jurisconsultorium requires that the sources be shared.

The principle of comity supports a shared interpretive approach when a uniform or transjurisdictional law is the applicable law. The legal basis of this principle is the duty to understand that shared international laws are unique, and the sources of such laws are as diverse as the legal systems that share them. This duty requires the interpreter to refer to and consider foreign sources and to take relevant foreign decisions into account. This view of a shared interpretive approach has been supported by numerous CISG experts,

[33] In the context of the CISG, this term was first employed by Rogers and Kritzer: "A global Jurisconsultorium on uniform international sales law is the proper setting for the analysis of foreign jurisprudence on terminology of international sales"; see Vikki Rogers and Albert Kritzer, "A Uniform International Sales Law Terminology," in *Festschrift für Peter Schlechtriem zum 70. Geburtstag* (ed. Schwenzer and Hager) (Tubingen: Mohr/Siebeck, 2003), 223; Andersen, *Uniform Application of the International Sales Law* (global jurisconsultorium); Camilla Baasch Andersen, "The Uniform International Sales Law and the Global Jurisconsultorium," 24 *J. of L. & Commerce* 159 (2005).
[34] Joseph Lookofsky, *Understanding the CISG* (Kluwer, 2008), 34, 35.
[35] John Honnold, "Uniform Laws for International Trade: Early 'Care and Feeding' for Uniform Growth," 1 *International Trade and Business Law Journal* (2005), 1.

including Professors Schlechtriem,[36] DiMatteo,[37] Ferrari,[38] Zeller,[39] Flechtner,[40] and –
last but not least – Honnold himself.

B. *The "Policy" Arguments*

The notion of a global jurisconsultorium is not unique to the CISG. It is also apparent
in the decision of the House of Lords in *Fothergill v. Monarch Airlines* – concerning
the interpretation of the *Warsaw Convention on the Liability of Air Carriers* (1929) –
where the Lords stated that uniform international aviation law is unique and must be
treated uniquely.[41] The U.S. Supreme Court decided in the *Air France v. Saks* case –
a case concerning the meaning of the term "accident" in the Warsaw Convention –
that judicial decisions from other countries interpreting a treaty term are "entitled to
considerable weight."[42] This premise was restated by the U.S. Supreme Court in the *El
Al* case,[43] which restated the propriety of using foreign case law in applying international
conventions.

International commercial law is especially dependent on the efforts of a global jurisconsultorium. First, the harmonization of commercial law gives immediate economic benefits to the community of states by reducing barriers to international trade. Second, there is
no one body charged with the task of monitoring international commercial laws. Despite
suggestions dating back to 1911, there is no international commercial court competent
enough to monitor the application of shared global instruments such as the CISG.[44]
So, in the application of uniform international commercial law, courts should treat
such laws as a unique phenomenon, and not follow the path of domestic law. Using a
jurisconsultorium – whether practical or scholarly – can help to ensure a common

---

[36] See Peter Schlechtriem, "Uniform Sales Law: The Experience with Uniform Sales Laws in the Federal
Republic of Germany," 2 *Juridisk Tidskrift* (1991–2), available at http://cisgw3.law.pace.edu/cisg/biblio/
schlech2.html (critique of case law in other jurisdictions, as well as help from scholars and comparative
law centers, smooth out divergent interpretations of uniform law).

[37] See Larry A. DiMatteo, "The CISG and the Presumption of Enforceability: Unintended Contractual
Liability in International Business Dealings," 22 *Yale Int. L. J.* 111 (1997); Larry A. DiMatteo et al., "The
Interpretive Turn in International Sales Law: An Analysis of Fifteen Years of CISG Jurisprudence," 24
Northwestern J. of Int'l L. & Business 299 (2004).

[38] Franco Ferrari, "CISG Case Law: A New Challenge for Interpreters?," 17 *J. of L. & Commerce* 246 (1999)
("As many legal writers have pointed out, this means, above all, that one should not read the Convention
through the lenses of domestic law, but rather in an autonomous manner").

[39] Bruno Zeller, "Traversing International Waters: With the Growth of International Trade, Lawyers Must
Become Familiar with the Terms of the Convention on Contracts for the International Sale of Goods,"
78(9) *Law Institute Journal* (2004) 52.

[40] Harry Flechtner, "The Several Texts of the CISG in a Decentralized System: Observations on Translations,
Reservations and Other Challenges to the Uniformity Principle in Article 7(1)," 17 *J. of L. & Commerce*
187 (1998), available at http://cisgw3.law.pace.edu/cisg/biblio/flecht1.html.

[41] *Fothergill v. Monarch Airlines* [1980] 2 All E.R. 696.

[42] *Air France v. Saks*, 470 U.S. 392, 404 (1985).

[43] *El Al Israel Airlines, Ltd. v. Tsui Yuan Tseng*, 525 U.S. 155, 176 (1999).

[44] See Hans Wehberg, *Ein Internationaler Gerichtshof für Privatklagen* (Liebheit & Thiesen, 1911), 23;
Louis Sohn, "Uniform Laws Require Uniform Application: Proposals for an International Tribunal to
Interpret Uniform Legal Texts," in *Uniform Commercial Law in the Twenty-First Century: Proceedings of
the Congress of the United Nations Commission on International Trade Law, 18–22 May 1992* (UN doc
E.94.V.14), 50–4; Filip De Ly, "Uniform Interpretation: What Is Being Done? Official Efforts," in *The
1980 Uniform Sales Law* (ed. Franco Ferrari) (Selliers, 2003), 346.

approach to similar problems, and to ensure the shared development of uniform law.

Moreover, it is directly in the interest of legal counsel and their clients to "shop" for precedents and scholarship as widely as possible. If courts share common commercial values, as assumed in international commercial law,[45] and also share one uniform legal text, then it would be appropriate for judges to use transnational sources and determine their persuasive weight. As Professor Koch states: "Only a fool would refuse to seek guidance in the work of other judges confronted with similar problems."[46]

C. *Global Jurisconsultorium: The CISG in National Courts*

The past decade or so has witnessed a growing number of soundly argued cases from a number of jurisdictions that have referenced cases from other jurisdictions as persuasive or inspirational precedents. An Italian court, in *Sport d'Hiver di Genevieve Culet v. Ets. Louys et Fils*, cited German and Swiss case law in applying CISG Articles 38 and 39 CISG.[47] A French court followed a German decision on CISG Article 57 to determine that the place of payment was the seller's place of business.[48] Eventually, jurisconsultorium-focused cases became more abundant.[49] Here, it is sufficient to make two observations. First, numerically and statistically these cases are the exception rather than the rule (1.1% of reported CISG cases). Second, Italian courts have produced a proportionately high level of well-reasoned decisions.

The Italian courts have been the most successful in applying the practical jurisconsultorium. First, most of the early jurisconsultorium cases came from Italian courts, which were the first to consistently reference foreign case law. Second, some of the most comprehensive examples of the use of international CISG sources and precedents are found in Italian cases. The acclaimed *Vigevano* case, *Rheinland Versicherungen v. Atlarex*, cited American, Austrian, Dutch, French, German, Italian, and Swiss CISG cases as well as arbitral awards.[50] The Italian cases indicate that well-reasoned cases, using the jurisconsultorium, are more of a production of education than of judicial method. Italian judges are relatively young when they take office, and when they do so they bring their modern understanding of the role of uniform laws and shared sources to the bench.[51]

---

[45] This view has prevailed since 1974 when Otto Kahn-Freund, the noted comparativist, first stated that commercial law is comparatively culture-free; see Otto Kahn Freund, "On Uses and Misuses of Comparative Law," 37 *Modern L. Rev.* 1 (1974).

[46] Charles Koch, "Envisioning a Global Legal Culture," 25 *Michigan J. of Int'l L.* 51 (2003).

[47] District Court of Cuneo (*Sport d'Hiver di Genevieve Culet v. Ets. Louys et Fils*), Italy, January 31, 1996, available at http://cisgw3.law.pace.edu/cases/960131i3.html. Ten years ago, in Franco Ferrari, "Remarks on the Autonomy and the Uniform Application of the CISG on the Occasion of Its Tenth Anniversary," in *International Contract Advisor* (Kluwer, 1998), the decision from Cuneo was the only one of 300 cases reported by Michael Will to comply with the duty to look to foreign case law.

[48] CA Grenoble (*Scea. Gaec des Beauches B. Bruno v. Société Teso Ten Elsen GmbH & Co KG*), France, October 23, 1996, available at http://cisgw3.law.pace.edu/cases/961023f1.html.

[49] See Andersen, "The Uniform International Sales Law and the Global Jurisconsultorium."

[50] District Court Vigevano (*Rheinland Versicherungen v. Atlarex*), Italy, July 12, 2000, available at: http://cisgw3.law.pace.edu/cases/000712i3.html. (Although criticized by Sant 'Elia for not containing references to commentaries at the aforementioned link, it should be remembered that Italian civil procedure prohibits references to such academic work in cases).

[51] As an interesting aside, according to Professor Franco Ferrari, the judges in all the reported Italian jurisconsultorium cases are his recently graduated students from law school. This is heartening news for the crusading academic trying to make a difference in a practical world of law.

This certainly accords with Roy Goode's point that legal development in this field is dependent on a reeducation of the judiciary.[52]

The way Italian courts are applying foreign precedents is also very interesting, and shows the progress of the jurisconsultorium. In the first reported case, a lengthy justification is provided for why foreign cases should be consulted, and reference is made to a duty to look at foreign precedents under Article 7(1) CISG. In *Tessile v. Ixela*, the court stated that a foreign case "although not binding, is however to be taken into consideration as required by Article 7(1)."[53] However, in more recent cases, foreign cases have been elevated alongside Italian precedents. The 2008 case *Mitias v. Solidea* cited a range of decisions from Switzerland, Austria, Germany, France, and the Netherlands on a variety of issues connected with the conformity of goods, notification, and remedies under the CISG.[54] In this case, Italian and foreign cases are intermingled and referred to as "the jurisprudence." The *Mitias* case illustrates decision making at its best – a court embracing the international character of the CISG and interpreting it as part of a global jurisconsultorium.

The developments and improvements in the use of the global jurisconsultorium are not limited to Italian courts. Since 2005, more CISG cases referring to foreign precedents have been reported. Most importantly, there is a wider variety of countries contributing to the body of reported jurisconsultorium cases. Examples can now be found in Australia, the United States, France, Germany, Italy, Serbia, Poland, Spain, and Switzerland. In 2005, The Netherlands Supreme Court, in the *Gran Canaria Tomatoes* case, referred to the UNCITRAL Digest and commentary of foreign case law.[55]

In 2007,[56] the Supreme Court of Poland cited an Austrian Supreme Court decision in its analysis of the right to withhold performance under CISG Article 71. The Court stated that its view was "shared by some Contracting States' courts. For example, the Austrian Supreme Court." The Polish court did not feel it necessary to justify why the views of other contracting states' courts were relevant. The *Sport d'Hiver di Genevieve Culet v. Ets. Louys et Fils*, *Rheinland Versicherungen v. Atlarex*, and *Gran Canaria Tomatoes* cases show a natural recourse to international precedents. This is a hopeful indication of the wider acceptability of using cases from foreign jurisdictions as persuasive sources to inform legal reasoning.

Nevertheless, despite the positive evidence of the rise in the number of CISG jurisconsultorium cases, overall, such cases are few. The statistical figures from 2005 indicated that fewer than 1.1% of reported CISG cases used the jurisconsultorium, while the

---

[52] See Roy Goode, "Reflections on the Harmonization of Commercial Law," in *Commercial and Consumer Law: National and International Dimensions* (ed. Cranston and Goode) (Oxford University Press, 1993), 24–7. ("It is primarily by the spreading of awareness of foreign legal systems among our students that we can hope to accelerate the process of harmonization and to produce practitioners and judges of the future prepared to look beyond the horizon of their own legal system.")

[53] District Court Pavia (*Tessile v. Ixela*), December 29, 1999, available at http://cisgw3.law.pace.edu/cases/991229i3.html.

[54] District Court of Forli (*Mitias v. Solidea S.r.l.*), December 11, 2008, available at http://cisgw3.law.pace.edu/cases/081211i3.html.

[55] Supreme Court (*B.V.B.A. Vergo Kwekerijen v. Defendant*), January 28, 2005, available at http://cisgw3.law.pace.edu/cases/050128n1.html.

[56] Supreme Court of Poland (Shoe Leather Case), May 11, 2007, available at http://cisgw3.law.pace.edu/cases/070511p1.html.

proportion today is about 1.5%.[57] This confirms the position that judicial resort to the jurisconsultorium is the exception rather than the rule.

V. Criteria for Judging CISG Case Law

Harry Flechtner makes the point that those in pursuit of uniformity should beware not to pursue it at any price. The principal goal is sound judgment, and we must establish a set of criteria for determining the persuasive weight of a foreign precedent.[58] According to Flechtner, these criteria should include the authority of the court rendering the decision; the extent of agreement on the issue among other courts and tribunals; the level of experience the court has with international trade law; and the extent to which the foreign precedent complies with the guidelines of internationality, good faith, and uniformity. Given that the primary goals of UNCITRAL are "modernity," "flexibility," "clarity," and "fairness," such criteria are necessary to distinguish well-reasoned from poorly reasoned decisions. However, criteria aside, a court should not hesitate to consider foreign cases. As long as courts search foreign case law for *inspirational* guidance, and in the interests of rendering of autonomous interpretations, they are acting properly in avoiding homeward trend bias.

Sir Basil Markesinis, speaking generally on the use of foreign decisions, drew a biblical parallel, saying that the task of the comparative lawyer is to "probe everything and keep the best,"[59] to find cases that can lend inspiration to a given problem.[60] This kind of general freedom to explore case law, find analogous foreign decisions, and apply them in the interests of justice is the best overall framework for interpreting the CISG.[61]

Filip De Ly very cleverly distinguishes between *foreign law* and *uniform law* in his discussion of precedents, and makes the point that "uniform law is the law of the land" where it is applied through Article 1(1)(a) versus a CISG state applying its own international sales law via Article 1(1)(b).[62] Professor De Ly's distinction is correct, but courts are likely to consider foreign judicial interpretations of uniform law to be foreign law. However, if emphasis is placed on the notion of this case law being *shared*, it may even further accentuate the need to consider it at the level of the domestic court.

[57] For the present chapter, thirty-two cases from national courts and three from arbitral tribunals utilizing the jurisconsultorium have been identified, among the 2,294 cases reported on the CISG database at www.cisg.law.pace.edu.

[58] Harry Flechtner, "Recovering Attorneys' Fees as Damages under the U.N. Sales Convention: A Case Study on the New International Commercial Practice and the Role of Case Law in CISG Jurisprudence, with Comments on *Zapata Hermanos Sucesores, S.A. v Hearthside Baking Co.*," 22 *Northwestern J. of Int'l L. & Bus.* 121 (2002), available at http://cisgw3.law.pace.edu/cisg/biblio/flechtner4.html#iv.

[59] St. Paul, "Letter to the Christians in Thessalonia."

[60] See Basil Markesinis, "Judicial Mentality: Mental Disposition or Outlook as a Factor Impeding Recourse to Foreign Law, Centenary Lecture of the Society of Comparative Legislation," 80 *Tulane L. Rev.* 1325 (2006).

[61] Juergen Schwartze suggested another way to screen precedents – similarly broad and based on individual applicability – by reference to the "reasoning which the decisions . . . bring to bear on the problem at hand." Juergen Schwartze, "The Role of the European Court of Justice (ECJ) in the Interpretation of Uniform Law Among the Member States of the European Communities (EC)," in *International Uniform Law in Practice/Le droit uniforme international dans la pratique* (Acts and Proceedings of the 3rd Congress on Private Law held by the International Institute for the Unification of Private Law, Rome, September 7–10, 1987) (ed. UNIDROIT) (Oceana Publishing, 1988), 193.

[62] See De Ly, "Uniform Interpretation: What Is Being Done?," 357.

VI. Future of the Jurisconsultorium

On the whole – and concluding on an optimistic note – the CISG seems to be enjoying
an international perspective in most domestic courts today. It can only be hoped that we
are approaching an era where the notion of the CISG as a shared global law is more fully
embraced. If this understanding develops, it will contribute to the autonomous uniform
interpretation of the CISG.

Part II *Interpretation and Use of the CISG*

7 Interpretive Methodologies in the Interpretation of the CISG

*Larry A. DiMatteo and André Janssen**

I. Introduction

Nowadays, writing about the interpretation of the United Nations Convention on Contracts for the International Sale of Goods (CISG) requires justification due to the impressive number of publications in numerous languages dedicated to this issue. This chapter will review numerous interpretive methodologies used in common and civil law countries. Despite some differences, there is a great deal of commonality in the interpretive methodologies of the two legal systems. Most of the differences are more of a difference in emphasis than in kind. The goal of this chapter is to provide a menu of interpretive methodologies that can be used in interpreting the CISG.

Despite the in-depth jurisprudence and scholarship relating to the interpretation of the CISG, a number of interpretive issues remain unresolved. A closer look at the scholarly literature on the CISG shows a surprising disconnect between the recognized interpretative aims and principles under Article 7(1) (*Auslegungsziele* or *Auslegungsprinzipien*)[1] and the variety of methods of interpretation (*Auslegungsmethode*) used in the application of those principles.[2] Because the CISG is silent about methods of interpretation, it appears that the majority of the authors analyze the application of these general principles in a similar way.[3] It is remarkable that although there are several outstanding

---

* The authors would like to acknowledge and thank the Nederlands Tijdschrift voor Handelsrecht for permission to use the material found in a longer version of this chapter, previously published as: L. DiMatteo and A. Janssen, "Interpretive Uncertainty: Methodological Solutions for Interpreting the CISG," 2 Nederlands Tijdschrift voor 52 (2012).
[1] Perales Viscasillas, "Article 7 CISG," in *UN Convention on Contracts for the International Sale of Goods (CISG)* (ed. Kröll, Mistelis, and Perales Viscasillas) (Munich: C.H. Beck, 2011); Schwenzer and Hachem, "Article 7 CISG," in *Commentary on the UN Convention on the International Sale of Goods (CISG)*, 3rd ed. (ed. Peter Schlechtriem and Ingeborg Schwenzer) (Oxford: Oxford University Press, 2010) (guidelines for the interpretation of the Convention).
[2] See, e.g., Gebauer, "Uniform Law, General Principles and Autonomous Interpretation," 5 *Uniform L. Rev.* 683, 685 (2000); Gruber, *Methoden des internationalen Einheitsrechts* (Tubingen: Mohr Siebeck, 2004), 119; Schwenzer and Hachem, "Article 7 CISG."
[3] It is "common understanding" that the CISG does not govern the methods of interpretation. See, e.g., Ferrari, "Uniform Interpretation of the 1980 Uniform Sales Law," 24 *Ga. J. Int'l & Comp. L.* 183, 200 (1994) ("choice is not one of interpretative technique or method, but rather one of policy"); Gebauer, "Uniform Law," 685 ("[CISG] does not appear to answer any methodological question"); Huber and Mullis, *The CISG* 9 (Munich: Sellier, 2007) ("guidelines"); Ulrich Magnus, "Tracing Methodology in the CISG: Dogmatic Foundations," in *CISG Methodology* (ed. André Janssen and Olaf Meyer) (Munich: Sellier, 2009), 40 ("Taken seriously Art. 7(1) CISG formulates aims rather than a precise method of interpretation").

contributions on the methods of interpretation at the national law level[4] and at the European level,[5] there is scant literature on the methodological aspects for interpreting the CISG. A consensus on CISG interpretive methodologies would support the interpretative aims of Article 7(1) and the functioning of the CISG as a whole.[6] In addition, the national courts have failed to develop autonomous interpretive methodologies for interpreting and applying the CISG. Instead, they predominantly apply national interpretative methods to the CISG.[7]

This chapter focuses on methodological issues relating to the interpretation of the CISG. The authors come from civil and common law backgrounds, so a degree of "methodological homeward trend" is likely to creep into the analysis.[8] This chapter is not focused on the interpretative aims of the CISG, as enunciated in Articles 7(1) (international character, promotion of uniformity, good faith), 7(2) (general principles), 8 (party intent, reasonable person standard), and 9 (trade usage). The focus here is the development, or lack of development, of CISG interpretive methodologies.

The first part of the chapter will review "traditional" civil law methods used in the interpretation of statutes: (1) literal interpretation, (2) systemic interpretation, (3) historical interpretation, and (4) teleological or purposive interpretation. In addition, the relative 'weight' of these four methods and their appropriateness in interpreting the CISG will be analyzed. The second part will focus on further methodological tools for interpreting the CISG, including analogical reasoning, comparative law analysis, economic analysis, contextualism, use of scholarly commentary, reasoning from soft law, good faith interpretation, and interpretation from party-generated rules.

II. Traditional National Methods for Interpreting the CISG

This part examines the notion of common interpretive methodologies across national legal systems and the combining of them into a methodological blend to be used in the interpretation of the CISG.

A. Need for a "Blend" of Different National Methodologies

CISG Article 7(1) requires an autonomous interpretation of CISG rules. From this it follows that the applied method of interpretation within the sphere of application of the

---

[4] See Bydlinski, *Juristische Methodenlehre und Rechtsbegriff*, 2nd ed. (Vienna: Springer, 1991) (Austria); Bennion, *Statutory Interpretation: A Code*, 4th ed. (London: Butterworth, 2002) (England); Gény, *Méthode d'interprétation et sources en droit privé positif*, 2 vols., 2nd ed. (Paris: F. Pichon et Durand-Auzias, 1919) (France); Larenz, *Methodenlehre der Rechtswissenschaft*, 6th ed. (Berlin: Springer, 1991) (Germany); Wiarda, *Drie typen van rechtsvinding* (Deventer: Tjeenk Willink, 1999) (Netherlands); Kramer, *Juristische Methodenlehre*, 2nd ed. (Berne: Stämpfli, 2002) (Switzerland); Dickerson, *The Interpretation and Application of Statutes* (Boston: Little, Brown, 1975) (United States); Eskridge, *Dynamic Statutory Interpretation* (Cambridge, MA: Harvard University Press, 1994) (United States); Hager, *Rechtsmethoden in Europa* (Tubingen: Mohr Siebeck, 2009) (comparative law perspective); Henninger, *Europäisches Privatrecht und Method* (Tubingen: Mohr Siebeck, 2009) (same).

[5] See, e.g., Langenbucher, "Europäische Methodenlehre," in *Europarechtliche Bezüge des Privatrechts*, 2nd ed. (Baden-Baden: Nomos, 2008), 3.

[6] Ulrich Magnus, "Tracing Methodology," in Janssen and Meyer, *CISG Methodology*, 59 ("a uniform method of interpretation is indispensable in order to achieve and further the unification purpose of the Convention").

[7] See Gruber, *Methoden*, 61.

[8] See Janssen and Meyer, foreword to *CISG Methodology* (methodological homeward trend).

CISG must be autonomous, too.[9] Thus, an immediate, direct resort to national interpretive methodology would be inappropriate. As the CISG remains silent on *how* to reach autonomous interpretations,[10] the question arises as to which methods of interpretations are appropriate to interpreting the CISG. Even though it is accepted that direct recourse by a judge to his or her own national methodology is prohibited, it is, however, acknowledged that the *sum* of the national methodologies are useable as an *Erkenntnisquelle* or "source of insight" and as an "aid to orientation" (*Orientierungshilfe*).[11] The rationale for resorting to commonly used national methodologies is that they are international in nature because, taken as a whole, they all follow similar logical rules of reasoning.[12] Assuming a "methodological minimum common understanding" among national laws, there is good reason to make use of this understanding in interpreting the CISG. However, it would be inappropriate for a court to use a single or idiosyncratic national methodology. The use of traditional national methodologies for interpreting the CISG derives from the principle of the *Natur der Sache* or "nature of things."[13] In the words of Professor Filip De Ly: "Uniform interpretation creates a new methodology in which different interpretation techniques from different legal traditions are being blended."[14] But what should such a "blend" of different national methodologies look like? What ingredients can be taken from national legal systems to create a useful international methodology for the interpretation of the CISG?

B. *National Methodologies: A Summary*

This section provides a brief summary of traditional national interpretive methodologies with a focus on civil law countries.[15] The ancient roots of legal interpretive methodology – at least in continental Europe – can be found in Roman law.[16] The reception of Roman law allowed for its interpretative rules to play an important role in the development of national methodologies. The Roman jurists developed "the fine art of law finding" as the interpretation of statutes under Roman law contained grammatical and systemic elements.[17] However, the Romans never established a fully developed methodology to interpret legal statutes as are found in today's Western legal systems.[18]

---

[9] Ferrari, "Article 7," in *Kommentar zum Einheitlichen UN-Kaufrecht*, 5th ed. (ed. Schlechtriem and Schwenzer) (Munich: C.H. Beck, 2008); Gruber, "Legislative Intention and the CISG," in Janssen and Meyer, *CISG Methodology*, 95.

[10] See Hager, *Rechtsmethoden*, 84.

[11] Gruber, *Methoden*, 67. See also Schwenzer and Hachem, "Article 7," in Schwenzer, *UN Convention* (the national methods to be used for interpretation "may . . . help in interpreting the Convention, unless they conflict with the maxims of Article 7(1)").

[12] Schwenzer and Hachem, "Article 7" ("their methods no longer fundamentally differ from each other"); van Alstine, "Dynamic Treaty Interpretation," 146 *U. Pa. L. Rev.* 687, 740 (1998) ("substantial agreement").

[13] Hager, *Rechtsmethoden*, 84.

[14] De Ly, "Uniform Interpretation: What Is Being Done? Official Efforts," in *The 1980 Uniform Sales Law: Old Issues Revisited in the Light of Recent Experiences* (ed. Franco Ferrari) (Milan: Sellier, 2003), 344.

[15] See generally Hager, *Rechtsmethoden*; Henninger, *Europäisches Privatrecht*, 45; Torsello, *Common Features of Uniform Commercial Law Convention: A Comparative Study Beyond the 1980 Uniform Sales Law* (Munich: Sellier, 2004), 157; Linhart, *Internationales Einheitsrecht und einheitliche Auslegung* (Tubingen: Mohr Siebeck, 2005), 33.

[16] See Zimmermann, "*Europa und das römische Erbe*," 202 *Archiv für die Civilistische Praxis* 243, 303 (2002).

[17] Hager, *Rechtsmethoden*, 12.

[18] Lundmark and Suelmann, "Der Umgang mit Gesetzen im europäischen Vergleich," 52 *Zeitschrift für Rechtsvergleichung* 173, 184 (2011); S. Vogenauer, *Die Auslegung von Gesetzen in England und auf dem Kontinent*, Vol. 1 (Tubingen: Mohr Siebeck, 2001), 433.

The foundation for the modern interpretative methodology in Germany was laid down by Friedrich Carl von Savigny in the early to mid-nineteenth century. Von Savigny developed the so-called *Viererkanonlehre*,[19] which remains the most influential and leading methodology used in Germany to interpret statutes. It is because of the *Viererkanonlehre* that the *Bürgerliches Gesetzbuch* refrained from incorporating rules of statutory interpretation. The widely accepted traditional methodologies are grammatical or textual, historical, systemic, and teleological.[20] Teleological interpretation can be divided into subjective-teleological and objective-teleological interpretation methodologies.[21] Subjective-teleological interpretation is based on the uncovering of legislative intent at the time of drafting and to a certain extent overlaps with the historical interpretation method. The more widely used approach in Germany is the objective-teleological method, which looks at the intention of the article or statute in question and, lastly, at the intention of the whole legal system or a subpart, such as the law of obligations. The comparative law approach is sometimes seen as a "fifth interpretative method" for interpreting German law – as proposed by Konrad Zweigert[22] and other scholars.[23] However, it has so far not been accepted as an appropriate mainstream interpretive methodology.[24] In addition, other nations of the German legal tradition, such as Austria (ABGB §§6, 7) and Switzerland (ZGB Article 1),[25] also use the four aforementioned interpretative methods[26] Further, comparable methods can be found in countries from the non-German, Roman legal tradition, such as Italy in Article 12 of the Disposizioni sulla legge in generale of the Codice civile of 1942[27] and Spain in Articles 3 and 5 of the Código civil of 1889.[28] Even in countries, such as France, that do not expressly recognize a specific interpretative methodology, the four traditional methods are an important part of legal reasoning, but are often shrouded in different terminology.[29]

Larger differences in interpretive methodologies exist between the civil and common law systems. However, despite these differences, differences in terminology and approaches often mask the fact that the methodologies generally lead to the same or at least similar results. Unlike in the civil law's statutory system, the common law of contracts is primarily the product of case law. Nonetheless, the starting point in English interpretation is similar to that of the continental European methodology – an

---

[19] Von Savigny, *System des heutigen Römischen Rechts*, Vol. 1 (Berlin: Veit und Comp., 1840), 212.

[20] Henninger, *Europäisches Privatrecht*, 54; Larenz, *Methodenlehre der Rechtswissenschaft*, 6th ed. (Berlin: Springer, 1991), 320.

[21] Hager, "Zur Auslegung des UN-Kaufrechts: Grundsätze und Methoden," in *Festschrift für Huber zum 70 Geburtstag* (Tubingen: Mohr Siebeck, 2006), 319, 322; Gruber, *Methoden*, 183.

[22] Zweigert, "Rechtsvergleichung als universelle Interpretationsmethode," 15 *Rabelszeitung* 1, 8 (1949–50).

[23] See, e.g., Häberle, "Grundrechtsgeltung und Grundrechtsinterpretation im Verfassungsstaat: zugleich zur Rechtsvergleichung als "fünfter" Auslegungsmethode," *Juristenzeitung* 913, 916 (1989).

[24] See Janssen and Schulze, "Legal Cultures and Legal Transplants in Germany," 19 *European Rev. Private L.* 224, 246 (2011).

[25] See Henninger, *Europäisches Privatrecht*, 76, 100 (Austria and Switzerland). In Dutch law (1992 *Nieuw Burgerlijk Wetboek*), the four interpretative methods (*spraakgebruik, systeem, wetsgeschiedenis,* and *ratio*) are accepted and applied. Id., 176.

[26] In Switzerland, the comparative law approach is more commonly used as a fifth interpretative method. Also, some civil codes contain specific provisions on interpretation, such as those of Austria, Italy, and Spain. See S. Vogenauer, "Statutory Interpretation," in *Elgar Encyclopedia of Comparative Law* (ed. Smits) (Cheltenham: Edward Elgar, 2006), 677, 682.

[27] See Henninger, *Europäisches Privatrecht*, 168.

[28] Id., 149.

[29] Hager, "Zur Auslegung," 322. See also Henninger, *Europäisches Privatrecht*, 113 (Scandinavian countries).

examination of the wording of the statute. Interpretation based on ordinary meaning is captured by the common law's "plain meaning rule."[30] However, some consideration is given to the context in which an ambiguous term was written or applied.[31] Ultimately, the literal rule combines the grammatical and the systemic interpretative methodologies found in civil law countries.[32] Beginning in the middle of the last century, the purposive approach gained more weight among English judges.[33] Even though the plain meaning rule is still the most commonly used interpretative tool, English courts now attach more importance to the purpose of a term or statute. The purposive approach is similar to the continental method of teleological interpretation. For many years, consideration of the *travaux préparatoires* in the interpretation of statutes was largely ignored in English common law. Recourse to legislative history was forbidden by the "exclusionary rule."[34] However, this changed in 1993 with the House of Lords decision in *Pepper v. Hart.*[35] In principle, England now accepts the possibility of an historical interpretation of statutes. In some respects, an opposite development, especially with regard to the use of legislative history and purposive interpretation, can be observed in the United States. Both methods have been allowed and used for more than one hundred years by American judges,[36] though, since the late 1980s, both have been applied with more reluctance due to the rise of "new textualism," an approach that focuses on the text of the statute and ignores evidence based on a study of legislative history or legislative purpose.[37] Therefore, one methodological difference between common and civil laws is that civil law countries rely much more on historical and teleological interpretation than common law courts, which still remain loyal to plain meaning interpretation.[38]

The differences between national methodologies are also reflected in the use of different terminology (such as teleological, dynamic, or purposive interpretation). Often, the differences in terminology mask the similarities between the two systems. Most of the traditional methodologies exist in some form in both systems. In practice, the differences are often found in the relative weight given to the different methodologies. However, the four interpretative elements – wording, system, history, and purpose or teleos – can be observed in every national methodology.[39] It is a rational extension to use these methodologies to interpret the CISG.

[30] Hager, "Zur Auslegung 323; Lundmark and Suelmann, "Der Umgang mit Gesetzen," 188.

[31] See Hager, "Zur Auslegung," 323; Ingman, *The English Legal Process*, 13th ed. (Oxford: Oxford University Press, 2010), 8.10.2.4. ("The statute must be read as a whole.")

[32] Hager, "Zur Auslegung," 323.

[33] See Lundmark and Suelmann, "Der Umgang mit Gesetzen," 189.

[34] Hager, "Zur Auslegung," 323; Lundmark and Suelmann, "Der Umgang mit Gesetzen," 189.

[35] *Pepper v. Hart* [1993] A.C. 593. See also Gruber, "Legislative Intention," in Janssen and Meyer, *CISG Methodology*, 93. ("Therefore, the previously assumed gap between the Civil Law methods of interpretation and the methods used in England seems to have somewhat decreased or even, as some say, almost diminished.")

[36] Gruber, "Legislative Intention," 94; Manning, "Textualism as a Nondelegation Doctrine," 97 *Colum. L. Rev.* 673, 674 (1997).

[37] Gruber, "Legislative Intention," 94; A. Scalia, *A Matter of Interpretation: Federal Courts and the Law* (Princeton: Princeton University Press, 1997).

[38] See also S. Eiselen, "Literal Interpretation," in Janssen and Meyer, *CISG Methodology*, 63; Magnus, "Tracing Methodology," 53.

[39] See Vogenauer, "Statutory Interpretation," 683 ("such differences [between civil and common law systems] exist but that they primarily concern the terminology and the classifications used in scholarly writings, rather than the substance of statutory interpretation").

The starting point for interpreting the CISG and rendering autonomous interpretations would be some sort of blend of these traditional methodologies.[40] Subsequent sections of this chapter will take a closer look at each of these methodologies before suggesting the right mixture of the four different methods in the quest for the appropriate interpretative blend to apply to the CISG. The last part of the chapter will explore more controversial or nontraditional interpretive methodologies that may be appropriate to add to the interpretive menu.

The CISG embraces the modern trend in the legal interpretation of contracts by adopting liberal evidentiary rules. It borrows from the interpretive methodologies of the civil and common law systems. However, in vital ways, the CISG interpretive methodology is more akin to the one found in the civil law system. The CISG's liberal evidence rules, along with its recognition of the subjective theory of contracts and the importance of contextual evidence, is similar to the civil law's "agreement-in-fact" model. This model of contract interpretation seeks to discover the true understanding of the parties as opposed to a purely objective meaning. The agreement-in-fact model of the CISG is aligned with civil law and, to a lesser extent, the American Uniform Commercial Code (UCC). In this model, the external manifestations of the promising party are only a part of the interpretive process. The external manifestations of the parties need to be placed in their proper contexts in order to determine the agreement-in-fact. This model logically leads to the conclusion that, to understand the written words of a contract, an analysis of the contextual background of the contract is required. The same can be said of statutory interpretation. Thus, under the CISG interpretive methodology, the plain meaning of the statutory language is only the starting point and invites the use of other interpretive methodologies.

III. Textual Interpretation

Interpretation always begins at the level of text – by determining the "ordinary meaning" of words.[41] However, ordinary meaning is not identical to the dictionary or plain meaning approach found in the common law. An ordinary meaning can be defined as the meaning that is normally used and understood in the "CISG Community."[42] For example, does the meaning of "writing" in CISG Article 13 also include electronic communication or is this a gap under Article 7(2) CISG?[43] As is true with all international treaties, the text of the CISG is an "outcome of extended discussions and often a well-balanced compromise where each single word counts"[44] and attaching meaning to each word is

---

[40] See Hager, "Zur Auslegung," 323; Hager, *Rechtsmethoden*, 84; Huber and Mullis, *The CISG* 9 (Munich: Sellier, 2007) ("the following matters may be relevant when interpreting the Convention: the wording of the provision; the drafting and negotiating history, in particular the 'Travaux Préparatoires'; the purpose of the provision and the underlying policy; the position of the provision within the framework of the Convention [systemic approach]"); Perales Viscasillas, "Article 7 CISG," ("scholars are in agreement as to the way [method] in which interpretation is to be done: a wide interpretation of the CISG that is to be complemented by a literal, teleological, systemic and historical interpretations"); Schwenzer and Hachem, "Article 7."

[41] See Eiselen, "Literal Interpretation," 61.

[42] See Magnus, "Tracing Methodology," 53.

[43] See Perales Viscasillas, "Article 13," *supra* note 1; Schlechtriem and Schmidt-Kessel, "Article 13," in Schwenzer, *UN Convention*.

[44] Magnus, "Tracing Methodology," 53.

the challenge of the interpretive undertaking.[45] The literal interpretation of the CISG is complicated due to the fact that there are six different official language versions of the CISG (English, French, Russian, Arabic, Spanish, and Chinese). Each version is to be given the same weight in the interpretation of the CISG. In practice, it is not plausible to think a national judge could or would consider all the language versions. There has evolved an implicit recognition of English as the "official" language of interpretation, given that English was the main working language of the drafting committee. Therefore, when there are discrepancies between the different language versions, it is reasonable to defer to the English text in determining the meaning of the CISG.[46] Another problem is the common use of nonofficial language translations, such as German or Dutch. So, in Germany, for example, the nonbinding language version (German) is regarded as a "de facto official language." This is regrettable, as divergences can arise between the nonbinding and the official versions of the CISG. This could be avoided by comparing the nonbinding language interpretation with an interpretation given using an official language version.[47] However, a translation problem persists that is best approached by researching the variant meanings caused by translation and using other interpretive methodologies to determine the most appropriate CISG interpretation.

IV. Systemic Interpretation: Intraconventional and Interconventional

The primary textual method of interpretation is generally coupled with systemic interpretation.[48] The value of the systemic method varies depending on the context.[49] There are two kinds of systemic interpretation applicable to the CISG. The traditional or "intraconventional" systemic interpretation deduces meaning from the positioning of a provision within a statute.[50] For example, the positioning of Article 78 in a separate section of its own shows that the exemption provision of Article 79 does not apply to Article 78.[51] The other, albeit less frequently discussed, version of systemic interpretation considers the particularities of the CISG being a part of a growing international body of uniform law.[52] "Interconventional" systemic interpretation recognizes that uniform

---

[45] Ferrari, "Article 7," in Schlechtreim and Schwenzer, *UN-Kaufrecht*; Magnus, "Tracing Methodology," 53; Perales Viscasillas, "Article 7" ("primary method for the interpretation of the CISG").

[46] Hager, "Zur Auslegung," 324; Hager, *Rechtsmethoden*, 84; Magnus, "Tracing Methodology," 53; Melis, "Article 7," in *Kommentar zu UN-Kaufrecht*, 2nd ed. (ed. Honsell) (Heidelberg: Springer, 2010). See also *Swiss Supreme Court*, November 13, 2003, CISG-online 840 (considering primarily the English version and secondly the French text in regard to the German nonbinding translation of the CISG). Contra, Perales Viscasillas, "Article 7" ("no prima facie preference for the English version").

[47] See, e.g., Switzerland, *Swiss Supreme Court*, November 13, 2003, CISG-online 840 or from Germany, *Appellate Court Cologne*, August 26, 1994, CISG-online 132.

[48] Ferrari, "Article 7," in Schlechtreim and Schwenzer, *UN-Kaufrecht*; Hager, "Zur Auslegung," 324; Hager, *Rechtsmethoden*, 84; Melis in Honsell, *Kommentar*; Perales Viscasillas, "Article 7."

[49] Hager, "Zur Auslegung," 324; Hager, *Rechtsmethoden*, 84.

[50] Magnus, "Tracing Methodology," 54.

[51] Id. (the debtor cannot rely on Article 79 CISG in order to claim an exemption from the obligation to pay interest); Bacher, "Article 78," in Schlechtreim and Schwenzer, *UN-Kaufrecht*. For further examples of a systemic interpretation, see Hager, "Zur Auslegung," 324; Hager, *Rechtsmethoden*, 84 (use of Article 36(2) for the interpretation of Article 66).

[52] See, e.g., the Limitation Convention, the Convention on the Contract for the International Carriage of Goods by Road (CMR), the Montreal Convention, the Ottawa Conventions on International Financial Leasing and International Factoring.

law conventions often share many common terms and underlying general principles.[53] Therefore, a settled meaning under one convention may provide guidance in interpreting another convention. The rationale for interconventional interpretation is that basic terms of uniform law, such as "contract," "breach of contract," or "damages," should have the same meaning across uniform law conventions.[54] It is important to note that there is a difference between conventions and soft law. The use of soft law as an interpretive methodology for the CISG will be discussed later in this chapter.

V. Historic Interpretation

It is widely accepted that a historic interpretation on the basis of the legal history of the CISG is a viable interpretive methodology.[55] However, the historic interpretative methodology generally is utilized only after the textual and systemic methodologies fail to provide a clear meaning.[56] The common reasons for the reluctance to apply historic interpretation are that draftsmen cannot foresee future fact scenarios and developments, legal history is not always clear and is subject to multiple interpretations, and the longer the CISG is interpreted, the less relevant becomes the legislative history.[57]

Despite the foregoing, historic interpretation remains an accepted method of interpretation in the field of international sales law. While countries of the German legal tradition recognize an obligation to research legislative history, others countries refer to legislative history in various degrees or not at all.[58] Historic interpretation is especially useful in cases where the wording of the provision is in question and the system in which it is situated does not give enough guidance to reach a final conclusion. For instance, the *travaux préparatoires* are used frequently when interpreting open terms, such as the terms of "short period" and "reasonable time" in CISG Articles 38(1) and 39(1). It follows from the drafting history of both articles that these provisions were intended as a compromise between two views.[59] In particular, the drafters sought to avoid the strict requirements found in countries of the German legal tradition. Thus, it was primarily their aim "to convince the German courts to abandon their rigid time limits and slowly move towards the other legal systems that had not previously stipulated any [fixed] notice

---

[53] Ferrari, "Article 7"; Magnus, "Konventionsübergreifende Interpretation internationaler Staatsverträge privatrechtlichen Inhalts," in *Aufbruch nach Europa: 75 Jahre Max-Planck-Institut* (ed. Basedow et al.) (Tubingen: Mohr Siebeck, 2001), 571.

[54] Magnus, "Tracing Methodology," 54.

[55] There is a general agreement that the legislative history can and should be used for the interpretation of the CISG. See, e.g., Ferrari, "Article 7"; Gruber, "Legislative Intention," 91; Hager, *Rechtsmethoden*, 85; Magnus, "Tracing Methodology," 56; van Alstine, "Dynamic Treaty Interpretation," 146 *U. Pa. L. Rev.* 687 (1998).

[56] Magnus, "Tracing Methodology," 56; Perales Viscasillas, "Article 7"; Schwenzer and Hachem, "Article 7."

[57] Perales Viscasillas, "Article 7"; Schwenzer and Hachem, "Article 7."

[58] See Janssen, *Die Untersuchungs- und Rügepflichten im deutschen, niederländischen und internationalen Kaufrecht: Eine rechtsvergleichende Darstellung der Gemeinsamkeiten und Unterschiede* (Baden Baden: Nomos, 2001) (comparative analysis).

[59] See Kröll, "Article 38" and "Article 39," in Kröll et al., *UN Convention*; Reitz, "A History of Cutoff Rules as a Form of Caveat Emptor: Part I – The 1980 U.N. Convention on the International Sale of Goods," 36 *Am. J. Comp. L.* 437 (1988).

requirements."[60] The goal was achieved because the German courts looked to CISG legislative history, leading to significantly different interpretations of the requirements found in Articles 38 and 39 as compared with the corresponding German provisions in the German Commercial Code.[61]

VI. Teleological Interpretation

The final "traditional" method is referred to as the teleological, dynamic, or purposive interpretation.[62] Even though this method of interpretation is generally accepted in common and civil law countries to interpret their domestic statutes, it is the most "obscure" of the interpretive tools. On the one hand, teleological interpretation is indispensable for the development of the CISG.[63] As in all commercial and civil codes, the drafters of the CISG could not foresee every future legal and technical development. Thus, some issues fall within the scope of the CISG but textual analysis, supplemented by systemic and historical analyses, does not provide a conclusive answer. Under such conditions, the teleological or purposive method seeks an answer through an analysis of the spirit and purpose of the CISG. This approach provides the flexibility needed to address novel cases produced by transactional or technical changes. The clarity of thought possessed by lawmakers is unlikely to be fully captured by the statutory text. Statutes and codes will inevitably have gaps, yet the applicable statute, in the civil law tradition, is seen as providing answers to every issue that comes within its scope.

Teleological interpretation is the vaguest "canon" of the traditional interpretative methods and provides considerable discretion to judges. In an international law instrument a particular danger emerges – that the teleological method could lead to *homeward trend* interpretations.[64] More specifically, national courts may assume that the purposes of CISG rules are similar to the purposes of the rules found in their domestic laws. This increases the chances of divergent interpretations. The teleological interpretation is indispensable in finding a solution to some interpretive problems, however, when applied to international sales law it should be used with caution.[65] Judges using the teleological approach must focus on the general goals and purposes of the CISG, especially those enunciated in Article 7(1).[66] For example, one of the underlying goals of the CISG is to minimize transaction costs and to allocate the remaining costs to the most efficient avoider.[67] Such transaction costs are generally higher in international than in domestic transactions. The fundamental breach rule, found in Article 25, is a reflection of the goal

---

[60] See Schwenzer, "The Noble Month (Articles 38, 39 CISG) The Story behind the Scenery," 8 *European J. L. Reform* 353, 358 (2006).

[61] See §377 *Handelsgesetzbuch* (HGB); Gruber, "Legislative Intention," 106. See also Hager, *Rechtsmethoden*, 85 (Article 68 CISG) (historic interpretation); Magnus, "Tracing Methodology," 56 (Article 28) (same).

[62] See Barak, *Purposive Interpretation in Law* (Princeton: Princeton University Press, 2005).

[63] Melis in Honsell, *Kommentar*; Perales Viscasillas, "Article 7"; Piltz, *Internationales Kaufrecht*, 2nd ed. (Munich: C.H. Beck, 2008), §2–185.

[64] See Ferrari, "Homeward Trend: What, Why and Why Not," in Janssen and Meyer, *CISG Methodology*, 171.

[65] See also Melis in Honsell, *Kommentar*; Piltz, *Internationales Kaufrecht*, §2–185.

[66] Magnus, "Tracing Methodology," 57.

[67] See Cenini and Parisi, "An Economic Analysis of the CISG," in Janssen and Meyer, *CISG Methodology*, 151 (economic analysis of the CISG).

of reducing transaction costs in international sales. A teleological interpretation of the fundamental breach rule limits the cases in which breaches are considered fundamental, in order to avoid transportation costs and the wasting of nonconforming goods caused by avoidance.[68]

VII. Relative Weight of the Different Interpretative Methods

A question remains as to how these methods of interpretation are to be used in conjunction with each other. There is no generally recognized ordering rule that ranks the interpretative methods. This may be for the best, as the CISG is a broad enough code to justify a flexible system of interpretative methods or techniques.[69] The applicability of one interpretative method should not exclude another. In the search for the "right" interpretive outcome, all four methods should be applied when possible. However, the exception to a nonordering approach is that a textual analysis of the words of the CISG is always the starting point for its interpretation. The other interpretive methodologies work as "extenders" to flush out the "inner" meaning of CISG rules, especially when a court or arbitral tribunal is confronted by novel or hard cases. The three nontextual methods of interpretation provide the context for a better understanding of the CISG – the history and context of the process of its drafting (historical interpretation) and the context of a specific rule or article within the entire CISG (systemic interpretation). Teleological interpretation, because of the danger of homeward trend-biased interpretation, should be restricted to cases where the other three interpretative methods do not yield a clear outcome.

VIII. CISG Interpretive Methodology

This part will examine a number of methodologies, some inherent in CISG interpretive methodology, and others that are at least plausible as supplementary methodologies. The former types include analogical reasoning within the CISG and in the surrounding case law, as well as the development of underlying principles. Other methodologies reviewed include the use of scholarly commentary and soft law as aids in interpreting the CISG. Finally, a survey of a number of methods of interpretation are reviewed, including contextualism, comparative law, economic analysis of law, good faith interpretation, and party-generated rules of interpretation.

The earlier part of this article focused on the use and appropriateness of traditional interpretive methodologies and techniques as they apply to the CISG. However, it is useful now to restate expressed CISG interpretive methodology before reviewing other methodologies.[70] The CISG provides an interpretive methodology for interpreting and applying its substantive rules, including those dealing with the interpretation of intent. The spirit of this methodology is preventing recourse to domestic legal methodologies. This is implicit in the view that the CISG directs decision makers to develop *autonomous interpretations* of CISG provisions. It is only in this way that the CISG can rise above the inherent differences between national contract laws and legal systems. The next five

---

[68] See Articles 46(2) and 49(1)(b).
[69] Gebauer, "Uniform Law," 704; Magnus, "Tracing Methodology," 58.
[70] See generally Janssen and Meyer, *CISG Methodology*.

sections will consider core methodologies at least implicitly acknowledged as legitimate pieces of CISG interpretive methodology.

A. Creative Interpretation: Self-Generation of Underlying Principles

Ronald Dworkin famously rejected the "argument from vagueness" that holds that the vagueness of legal or statutory language means that there cannot be one, true interpretation of a statutory provision. A more nihilistic view of the argument from vagueness is that statutory language is open to many equally plausible interpretations. Dworkin rejects this argument based upon the role of underlying principles. He states that:

> [T]he impact of the statute on the law is determined by asking which interpretation, of the different interpretations admitted by the abstract meaning of the term, best advances the set of principles and policies that provide the best . . . justification for the statute at the time it was passed.[71]

Because of its use of neutral terminology, mandate of autonomous interpretations, and express embrace of traditional interpretive methodologies, CISG jurisprudence has moved to address the shortcomings stemming from the argument from vagueness. This interpretive challenge falls into two areas: (1) the recognition of underlying or implied principles to justify interpretations of the CISG, whether autonomous or not, and (2) the creation of implied default rules where an issue is within the scope of CISG coverage, but which the CISG fails to directly address.

An example of courts projecting general principles into the CISG or recognizing implicit default rules was demonstrated by a Finnish court's implication of a principle of loyalty. The Helsinki Court of Appeals recognized the importance of continuation of contract within the principle of loyalty. It reasoned that the so-called principle of loyalty has been recognized in scholarly writings. According to the principle, the parties to a contract have to act in favour of the common goal; they have to reasonably consider the interests of the other party.[72] In essence, each party owes a duty of loyalty to the other party to preserve the viability of the transaction. From such a duty, the court recognized an implied default rule of a duty to continue a sales relationship beyond the discrete individual sales transactions.

The case involved a buyer who purchased carpets for resale on an ad hoc basis. The seller abruptly ended its relationship with the buyer. The court held that on the basis of a two-year business transaction, the buyer's operations cannot be made dependent on the risk of an abrupt ending of the contractual relationship.[73] Therefore, the seller was restricted in its right to terminate its relationship with the buyer despite the fact that there was no agency or long-term supply contract in place. The court reasoned that the buyer had obtained de facto exclusive selling rights.[74] Such implied rights, based on good faith and trade usage, make the seller of multiple discrete transactions susceptible to damage claims under Article 74.[75] In essence, the court held that principles of reasonableness

---

[71] R. Dworkin, *A Matter of Principal* (Cambridge, MA: Harvard University Press, 1985), 129.

[72] Helsinki Court of Appeals (Finland 2000), available at cisgw3.law.pace.edu/cases/001026f5.html.

[73] Id., 12 of 14.

[74] Id.

[75] A party must pay damages "in the light of the facts and matters of which he knew or ought to have known, as a possible consequence of the breach of contract" (see Article 74 CISG).

and trade usage require an extended notice of termination where damages to a buyer are foreseeable, regardless of the fact that the discrete contract fails to require such notice.[76] The need for creative interpretation is made a necessity due to the open-ended nature of CISG rules.[77] Many of the CISG's rules are open ended in order to allow their applications to numerous contextual situations. For example, the CISG makes repeated use of the "reasonableness standard" in its gap-filling provisions. Open-ended rules derive their content from post-hoc application to real world transactions and practices.[78]

B. *Analogical Reasoning within the CISG*

The use of analogical reasoning within the CISG and between its articles is not expressly recognized in the CISG. However, a number of rationales support the argument that such reasoning is implied in the CISG. First, the role of general principles, either express or implied, underlies all CISG articles. Article 7 states that interpretive issues "are to be settled in conformity with the general principles on which [they are] based."[79] The role of the general principles that underlie the CISG implies that individual articles should be interpreted to conform to the spirit of those principles. It is not an illogical step to acknowledge that the individual articles should be interpreted with reference to each other, especially when one of them has been more fully interpreted and can act as a guide to the application of underlying principles to the article being interpreted. The case for analogical reasoning has been made by numerous scholars, including John Honnold,[80] Michael Bonell,[81] Phanesh Koneru,[82] and Mark Rosenberg.[83] Their arguments are straightforward – reasoning by analogy is an extremely useful interpretive methodology, especially when an issue in one article or provision is analogous to an issue found in another.[84]

Even though the CISG is not a comprehensive code in the civilian sense, it is code-like nonetheless. As such, analogical reasoning is intuitively needed to ensure that the articles

---

[76] DiMatteo et al., *International Sales Law: A Critical Analysis of the CISG* (New York: Cambridge University Press, 2005), 24–5 (French court held that the principle against abrupt discontinuance is applied through an inter-party business usage as permitted under Article 9 CISG); CLOUT Case No. 202 (*Court of Appeal of Grenoble*, France 1995).

[77] For an explanation of open-textured rules, see Collins, *Regulating Contracts* (Great Britain: Oxford University Press, 1999) 266–74.

[78] DiMatteo, *Critical Analysis*, 25–6. The cases reviewed were taken from abstracts, summaries, and commentaries provided mainly in "CISG Case Presentations" in the Pace Law School Web site at cisgw3.law.pace.edu/cases, the UNILEX database at unilex.info/case, and CLOUT abstracts at A/CN.9/SER.C/ABSTRACTS or at the UNCITRAL Web site at www.un.or.at/uncitral. UNCITRAL regularly releases abstracts of CISG court and arbitral decisions under the name CLOUT.

[79] Article 7(2) CISG.

[80] J. Honnold, *Uniform Law for International Sales* (Cambridge, MA: Kluwer Law International, 1991), 3.

[81] Bonell, "Introduction to Convention," in *Commentary on the International Sales Law* (ed. Bianca and Bonell) (Milan: Giuffrè, 1987), 79.

[82] Koneru, "The International Interpretation of the UN Convention on Contracts for the International Sale of Goods: An Approach Based on General Principles," 6 *Minnesota J. Global Trade L.* 105 (1997).

[83] Rosenberg, "The Vienna Convention: Uniformity Interpretation for Gap-Filling – An Analysis and Application," 20 *Australian Bus. L. Rev.* 442 (1992).

[84] DiMatteo, *Critical Analysis*, 21.

within the CISG do not conflict with one another, or, stated in Dworkinian terms, each part should be made to fit the whole.[85] The use of analogical or systemic interpretation of code or statute provisions is not as well developed under common law. Common law statutes are filled with cross-references to other sections within the statute and courts will look at the referenced sections in determining the meaning of a statutory provision. However, common law lacks the tradition of a grand civil code. Civil law tradition centers on going directly to the relevant code – civil or commercial – to get the answer to the issue of law in dispute, whereas common law judges often seek guidance from existing case law relating to the provision in question. The body of easily acceptable case law relating to the UCC is immense. So, instead of personally conducting an analogical analysis of code provisions, judges will generally go directly to the case law to find an existing decision that relates to the legal issue being disputed. If the case law provides a consensus as to the proper interpretation or meaning of the statutory provision, then the search for meaning is often terminated without any first-hand analysis of the code as a whole. Such a truncated analysis preempts the use of analogical reasoning within the code to see if a "better" meaning can be found.

If case law fails to provide an answer to the issue in question, then a return to the code to perform analogical reasoning would be the next logical approach. The judicial arbiter would attempt to answer the following question: do other provisions of the code or the code as a whole provide insight or guidance to determine a reasonable interpretation of the meaning of the provision in question? However, due to a lack of training in statutory interpretation,[86] lawyers and judges will often avoid such intracode analogical reasoning and determine the meaning through analogical reasoning from existing case law. It is possible that such intracode analogical reasoning was performed by the earlier case law. If so, it can be argued that even though the analogical reasoning was not performed first hand, it is found, covertly, in case law. This may be wishful thinking. In sum, despite the UCC being America's greatest and most successful attempt at a unifying code, it should be recognized that it is still a code embedded in a common law system. As such, the unification of commercial law began to diminish soon after the enactment of the UCC. UCC law is rarely a direct application of a UCC provision to a case. It involves a search for cases of mandatory or persuasive precedent to provide an interpretation.[87] The proof of this proposition is found in the variant meanings given by different state court systems to the same provisions of the CISG.

Given the lead role of the civil law countries in interpreting CISG provisions, the use of analogical reasoning within the CISG should be a matter of standard practice. The fact is that the use of various CISG articles to help interpret other articles has been uneven in practice. For example, in some cases, courts have recognized the right to avoidance without adequately determining if there was a fundamental breach. The

---

[85] Dworkin, *A Matter of Principal*.
[86] Justice Scalia has noted that "there are few law-school courses on the subject." Scalia, *A Matter of Interpretation*, 14.
[87] In the area of precedent, one state court has no obligation to follow the judicial decisions of another state's courts. In practice, however, American courts often cite cases from other states as persuasive precedent to support their decisions. For an historical analysis of *stare decisis*, see Cross, *Precedent in English Law*, 3rd ed. (Oxford: Oxford University Press, 1977).

CISG provides that the buyer[88] or seller[89] is allowed to avoid a contract if the other party's performance amounts to a fundamental breach.[90] In *Italdecor SAS v. Yiu Industries*,[91] the court determined there was a fundamental breach supporting the remedy of avoidance. Yet, the court never made reference to Article 25's discussion of fundamental breach.[92] To look directly at the avoidance provisions to determine fundamental breach based solely on the facts of the case is antithetical to analogical reasoning that would require reference to Article 25, which provides a definition and standards to be used in making the fundamental breach determination.[93] The failure to use analogical reasoning within the CISG, such as in using Article 25 in making an avoidance decision, is an abdication of the need to apply CISG and traditional interpretive methodologies.

C. Analogical Reasoning Using CISG Case Law

The use of foreign case law by analogy to interpret the CISG has been mixed and mostly nation-specific. Despite the fact that the Pace Institute of International Commercial Law's CISG Database provides easy access to more than 2,700 CISG cases, many national courts fail to use or cite foreign case law in interpreting the CISG. There are a number of plausible explanations, including the courts going "directly" to the CISG and applying CISG general principles in rendering an interpretation. In the alternative, the lack of foreign case law citation may be a reflection of the avoidance of CISG interpretive methodology in favor of nation-specific methods of legal reasoning.

It is not a controversial statement that the predominant force in shaping and interpreting the CISG has been the German court system. When other European national courts cite foreign case law, invariably at least one reference is to German case law. The problem is that the "international character" of the CISG can be questioned given the overwhelming amount of CISG jurisprudence that come from a half-dozen or so European civil law countries. Of the 2,718 reported cases, 1,364 came from eight European countries: Germany (477), the Netherlands (203), Switzerland (182), Belgium (142), Austria (128), France (100), Spain (83), and Italy (49). By contrast, common law countries yielded only 200 cases (United States, 151; Australia, 19; Canada, 16; New Zealand, 11; United Kingdom, 3).

The analogical use of foreign cases is a powerful interpretive device. Foreign case law on the whole often provides in-depth analysis of the issues before the court or arbitral panel. The application of foreign case law by analogy can provide a matrix of factors or rationales that may have gone unnoticed by the present court. It can provide evidence of consensus relating to the interpretation of CISG articles or it can offer a number of

---

[88] CISG, Article 49(1)(a).

[89] CISG, Article 64(1)(a). See also Article 72(1) ("prior to the date for performance it is clear that one of the parties will commit and fundamental breach"); Article 73(1) CISG (fundamental breach of installment); Article 73(2) ("in respect to any installment gives the other party good grounds to conclude that a fundamental breach will occur with respect to future installments, he may declare the [entire] contract avoided").

[90] CISG, Article 46(2).

[91] *Italdecor SAS v. Yiu Industries*, CA Milano, March 20, 1998, available at cisgw3.law.pace.edu/cisg/wais/db/cases2/980320i3.html1#ct.

[92] See Romito and Sant' Elia, "Case Comment, CISG: Italian Court and Homeward Trend," 14 *Pace Int'l L. Rev.* 179 (2002).

[93] CISG Article 25 provides a "substantial deprivation" standard with a limitation of lack of foreseeability.

divergent – reasonable and unreasonable – interpretations. In the latter situation, the case at bar offers the presiding court the opportunity to help harmonize the divergences by creating a compromise interpretation or to argue for the superiority of one of the divergent interpretations over another. Thus, the use of foreign case law serves two important purposes – it is a valuable resource for a court attempting to write a well-reasoned decision and it advances the core CISG principle of promoting uniformity in its application.

There has been a debate as to what the founding principle of promoting uniformity means in practice.[94] In order to accomplish a relative uniformity of application, despite the lack of a supranational appellate court system, common sense supports the idea that courts should look to prior decisions from other jurisdictions on the issue in question. Professors Ferrari and DiMatteo have debated the issue as to what the praxis of the uniformity principle should entail. Part of this is a pseudodebate caused by issues of semantics. DiMatteo asserted that "[t]he Convention envisioned the use of an *informal system of stare decisis* to help ensure uniformity of interpretation."[95] Ferrari responded that "the suggestion to create a *supranational stare decisis* . . . must be criticized, since it does not take into account the rigid hierarchical structure of various countries [sic] court systems."[96] DiMatteo responded that Ferrari did not use the full phrase coined; that this would be an "informal system" that was meant to imply the use of foreign case law as persuasive, not mandatory precedent. The power of the recognition of persuasive *stare decisis* is found in the United States. An example is the citation of Delaware corporate law by other states as persuasive precedent.

The recognition of well-reasoned foreign case law as persuasive is all the more important given the fact that the CISG "is applied through a nonunified court system."[97] The Ferrari–DiMatteo positions can be rectified by moving away from the terminology of *stare decisis* to more substantive propositions. The first proposition is that the hierarchy of court systems within countries should be recognized. Decisions by a country's highest court should have greater persuasive precedent than lower court decisions (despite the differences in the common and civil legal systems on this issue). It is expected that the highest courts provide better-reasoned decisions given the quality of the justices.

The second proposition is that poorly reasoned opinions, even if rendered by the highest national courts, should be largely ignored in favor of better reasoned opinions. Alternatively stated, poorly reasoned cases that avoid the use of CISG interpretive methodology and show homeward trend bias reasoning should be mostly ignored. The characteristics of better reasoned cases are those that avoid premature reliance on national legal concepts and traditions in interpreting the CISG. Such cases often look to foreign case decisions or scholarly commentary in guiding the interpretive process. Unfortunately, decisions of some courts are ignored because their legal tradition does not require the giving of reasoned opinions. For example, French court decisions are often misinterpreted or ignored by other court systems because of the lack of reasoned opinions, especially by its highest court – the Cour de cassation. A long-standing tradition has left the interpretation

---

[94] CISG, Article 7(1).

[95] DiMatteo, "The CISG and the Presumption of Enforceability: Unintended Contractual Liability in International Business Dealings," 22 *Yale J. Int'l L.* 111, 136 (1997) (emphasis added).

[96] Ferrari, "Ten Years of the U.N. Convention: CISG Case Law – A New Challenge for Interpreters?," 17 *J. L. & Commerce* 245 (1998) (emphasis added).

[97] DiMatteo, "Presumption of Enforceability," 136.

of contracts to the lower courts.[98] A 2000 Cour de cassation decision left the issue of "reasonable time" for a buyer to give notice of lack of conformity of goods pursuant to Article 39(1) CISG to the discretion of the lower court judge.[99] Another source of misunderstanding is the brevity of the decision of the Cour de cassation. But this is more a matter of style than substance. The judicial reasoning behind a decision can be found outside the formal court opinion. Commentaries include the recommendations of the reporting judge (*Conseiller rapporteur*), the recommendations of the *Avocat Général*, and commentaries prepared by scholars in the specialized law reviews. These various commentaries go into detail about relevant cases and scholarly writings that were the likely basis of the court's decision.[100]

D. *Secondary Legal Sources in Interpreting the CISG*

Support for the use of scholarly literature and opinions of the CISG Advisory Council can be found in public international law's foundational treaties, such as the Vienna Convention on the Law of Treaties (Law of Treaties)[101] and the Statute of the International Court of Justice (ICJ). Even though the Law of Treaties has been primarily used in public international law, as it is directed at country-to-country treaties, its rationales are equally applicable to the CISG.[102] In the area of interpretation, the Law of Treaties can be applied by analogy to the CISG. Its Article 26 states that obligations under the treaty should be "performed in good faith" and a "party may not invoke the provisions of its internal law as justification for its failure to perform a treaty." Articles 31 and 32 provide general rules of interpretation: (1) it shall be interpreted in good faith in accordance with the ordinary meaning to be given to the terms of the treaty in their context and in the light of its object and purpose and (2) recourse may be had to supplementary means of interpretation, including the preparatory work of the treaty, when its meaning is ambiguous or obscure or leads to a result that is manifestly absurd or unreasonable.

The ICJ statute provides a list of sources that could be used in the interpretation process. Article 38 states that sources of interpretation include international conventions, international custom, evidence of a general practice, the general principles of law recognized by civilized nations, judicial decisions, and the teachings of the most highly qualified publicists of the various nations. Once again, these treaties are not directly applicable to the CISG, but they do provide an interpretive methodology that could be applied to the CISG. This methodology includes methods expressly stated in the CISG, such as the importance of good faith in its interpretation and application. From there, an interpretive template can be constructed and would include use of general principles (in the light of its object and purpose), autonomous interpretations (ordinary meaning to be given to the terms in their context and in the light of its object and purpose), *travaux préparatoires* (preparatory work), purposive or consequence-based interpretation (leads

---

[98] Id.

[99] Witz, "Un arrêt regrettable: le délai de dénonciation des défauts prévu par la Convention de Vienne laissé à l'appréciation souveraine des juges du fond," *Recueil Dalloz* 788 (2000).

[100] The material in this paragraph was generously provided by Professor Claire Germain.

[101] Vienna Convention on the Law of Treaties, May 23, 1969 (entered into force on January 27, 1980); United Nations, *Treaty Series*, vol. 1155, at 331.

[102] See Magnus, "Tracing Methodology," 46–52.

to a result which is manifestly absurd or unreasonable), trade usage (international custom and general practice), foreign case law (judicial decisions), and secondary sources
(teachings of the most highly qualified publicists), as well as a disdain for homeward
trend analysis (party may not invoke the provisions of its internal law as justification for
its failure to perform a Treaty).

E. *Good-Faith Interpretation*

The German legal system provides an interpretive methodology based upon a single
meta-principle – the principle of good faith. Through the prism of good faith, a judge
may not only measure whether a party acted in bad faith in the performance of a
contract, but also determine a good-faith interpretation of a contract term and of contract
law rules. This approach, applied to the CISG, would simply ask: what is a good-faith
interpretation of a CISG term or rule? The *Treu und Glauben* doctrine is used primarily
to interpret a contract or the performance or enforcement of the contract by one of the
contracting parties. But such a tool can be used in the interpretation of the CISG or the
UCC, which are essentially template contracts that provide gap-filling terms for private
contracts. In fact, the good faith principle found in Article 7(1) of the CISG says exactly
that – in interpreting the CISG, regard is to be made to the "observance of good faith in
international trade." Many courts and arbitral panels have expanded this restrictive use
of good faith to imply good-faith obligations in international sales contracts. This is the
good-faith principle found in the UCC and the BGB which states that "every contract
or duty imposes an obligation of good faith in its performance and enforcement."[103]
Although interpreted as such, this is not the principle of good faith found in the CISG,
which is directed at statutory interpretation.

IX. Supplementary Methodologies

This part examines a number of supplemental methodologies – some generally accepted,
as well as others that are more controversial – that may be used in the interpretation of
the CISG. These include the use of soft law, contextualism, comparative, and economic
analysis of law.

A. *Use of Soft Law in the Interpretation of the CISG*

Much has been written on the use of other bodies of law as sources to be used in
the interpretation of the CISG.[104] The soft laws most often discussed in this regard
are the Unidroit Principles of International Commercial Contracts (Principles) and the
Principles of European Contract Law (PECL). The most recent example is the proposed

---

[103] UCC §2–304.

[104] See Janssen, "Die Einbeziehung von allgemeinen Geschäftsbedingungen in internationale Kaufverträge
und die Bedeutung der UNIDROIT und der Lando-Principles," 6 *Internationales Handelsrecht* 194 (2004);
Perales Viscasillas, "The Role of UNIDROIT Principles and the PECL," in Janssen and Meyer, *CISG
Methodology*, 287. See generally Gabriel, "The Advantages of Soft Law in International Commercial Law:
The Role of UNIDROIT, UNCITRAL and the Hague Conference," 34 *Brooklyn J. Int'l L.* 655 (2009);
Gopolan, "A Demandeur-centric Approach to Regime Design in Transnational Commercial Law," 39
Georgetown J. Int'l L. 327 (2008).

Common European Sales Law (CESL). Use of the Principles in the interpretation of the CISG is mostly found in arbitral decisions. In fact, a brief, unscientific review of 45 arbitral decisions shows that one in three cited the Principles in interpreting the CISG.[105] The rationale behind the use of the Principles is that many of its provisions are very similar to related articles of the CISG. The application of soft law to interpret similarly worded rules in the CISG, at first blush, seems like a reasonable interpretive methodology.

The more important question is the normative one of whether soft law should be used in the interpretation of the CISG. The somewhat counterintuitive answer is no. If the interpretation and application of the CISG is to be truly autonomous, referencing soft law is more an obstacle than a facilitator to autonomous interpretation. There is no practical reason to look outside the deep body of CISG case law and scholarly commentary.

B. *Contextualism: Internal–External Exchange*

A method of interpretation often discussed in Anglo-American legal literature is the notion of contextualism. The concept is part of the long-term debate over formalist[106] versus contextual means of interpretation.[107] Formalism is associated with a direct application of closed, fixed rules to the case at bar; a plain-meaning interpretation of the words of a contract; a four-corner analysis in which the contract (much as the formal rules of contract) provides answers to all possible issues of dispute or interpretation; and a hard parol evidence rule barring extrinsic evidence that contradicts the contract, even when such evidence would uncover the contracting parties' true intent. Contextualism is closely aligned with legal realism and holds that there is no such thing as plain meaning; the meaning of a word can only be determined by analyzing the background context behind its use. The strong version of this proposition was given by Arthur Corbin who, along with Samuel Williston, is considered the greatest American contract law scholar of the first half of the twentieth century.[108] Corbin asserted that "a word has no meaning apart from these [contextual] factors; much less does it have an objective meaning, one true meaning."[109]

Although contextual evidence plays an important role in American and English case law, it is more openly embraced in American jurisprudence. English interpretive jurisprudence continues to espouse the virtues of formalism while at the same time avoiding formalistic interpretation when contextual evidence shows that the plain meaning of the words being interpreted is not the meaning intended. Although often focused on the interpretation of contracts and not statutes or conventions, it is important to review contextual interpretation for the purpose of interpreting the CISG. Inductive interpretive

---

[105] DiMatteo, "Case Law Precedent and Legal Writing," in Janssen and Meyer, *CISG Methodology*, 113.

[106] See DiMatteo, "Reason and Context: A Dual Track Theory of Interpretation," 109 *Penn St. L. Rev.* 397 (2004); DiMatteo, "A Theory of Interpretation in the Realm of Idealism," 5 *DePaul Bus. & Commercial L. J.* 17 (2006).

[107] See Mitchell, *Interpretation of Contracts* (Great Britain: Routledge-Cavendish, 2007) (review of formal and contextual interpretive methodologies).

[108] Williston was the Chief Report and Corbin a Special Advisor for Restatement (First) of Contracts, which was issued by the American Law Institute in 1932.

[109] Corbin, "The Interpretation of Words and the Parol Evidence Rule," 50 *Cornell L.Q.* 161, 187 (1965).

methodology is necessary to give content to the CISG's many rules of reasonableness.[110] The use of reasonableness as a standard in numerous CISG rules requires the use of extrinsic evidence of reasonableness in giving content to the rule in its application to a particular case. The CISG's reasonableness standard directs the interpreter to the world of business – the law of the merchant embodied in trade usage, commercial practice, and business custom. Thus, any plausible interpretive methodology relating to the CISG must account for or incorporate the primary directive that the content of CISG rules is to be found outside of the CISG. The recognition of trade usage as providing guidance in interpreting the reasonableness standard in the CISG is an example of the use of contextualism in giving content to formal rules.[111]

C. *Use of Comparative Law in the Interpretation of the CISG*

It would seem that when a court determines the need to make use of the last-resort interpretive methodology of national law, a comparative analysis of various national laws on the issue is more appropriate.[112] A comparative law interpretive methodology makes especially good sense given the fact that the CISG is a mixture of civil and common law traditions.[113] A comparative approach is closely aligned to the "international character" of the CISG and its "need to promote uniformity in its application."[114] Comparative law analysis has historically involved two approaches – the common core[115] and the better rules approach. The common core approach searches for commonalities found within different legal systems.[116] Generally, many differences in legal systems, especially in the areas of contract and sales law, are differences in degree and not differences in kind. Often, the difference in degree is the product of the different legal terminology found in legal systems, as well as differences in emphasis.

The nuances captured by these references to differences in degree and not in kind will be difficult for someone outside the legal tradition being compared to understand. A comparative analysis, even by those knowledgeable of the laws being compared, may be affected by a subconscious subjective determination due to the comparativist inability to objectively detach from one's own legal tradition.[117] The CISG and its application reflect all these types of differences. In the area of legal terminology, the CISG provides national legal system-neutral concepts. Comparing CISG terminology to the common law, the CISG uses avoidance instead of cancellation or voiding, anticipatory breach instead of anticipatory repudiation, and impediment instead of impossibility or

---

[110] See CISG, Articles 8, 18(2), 25, 27, 33(c) 34, 35(b), 37, 38(1), 39, 43(1), 44, 46(2), 46(3), 47(1), 48(1), 48(2), 55, 60, 63(1), 64(2), 65(1), 65(2), 68, 75, 76(2), 77, 79(1), 79(4), 85, 86(1), 86(2), 87, 88(1).

[111] CISG, Article 7(2).

[112] See *Corocraft v. Pan Am*, 2 Lloyd's 459, 467 (1968) (Lord Denning's assertion of the importance of comparative law analysis in interpretation). See generally Zweigert and Kötz, *An Introduction to Comparative Law*, 3rd ed. (New York: Oxford University Press, 1998).

[113] Garro, "Reconciliation of Legal Traditions in the U.N. Convention on Contracts for the International Sale of Goods," 23 *Int'l Lawyer* 443 (1989).

[114] CISG, Article 7(1).

[115] *Formation of Contracts: A Study of the Common Core of Legal Systems* (ed. Schlesinger) (New York: Oceana, 1968).

[116] See Bussani and Mattei, "The Common Core Approach to European Private Law," 3 *Colum. J. European L.* 339 (1997).

[117] Von Nessen, *The Use of Comparative Law in Australia* (Sydney: Thomson Learning, 2006).

frustration. Differences in emphasis can be seen at work in the application of the duty of good faith in the interpretation and enforcement of CISG contracts. The concept is found across legal systems, but its role varies dramatically. Good faith is viewed as *the* meta-principle in most civil law countries, especially in Germany, that must be satisfied in rendering solutions to interpretive disputes. In contrast, good faith plays a much lesser role in the common law, especially in English law.

Finally, there are two types of rules that reflect actual differences between civil and common law – adoption and selection. Adoption relates to a number of CISG concepts and rules taken from one legal system that do not have a counterpart in another legal system. The civil concept of *Nachfrist* notice and price reduction remedy is not found in the common law. In this case, a resort to comparative national private law would be confined to the use and application of these concepts among different civil law countries. The idea of selection refers to cases where there are contrary or competing rules found in the different legal systems. In some of these cases, the CISG drafters simply made a choice between the two competing rules. One would assume that the drafters used the comparative law's better rules approach to select the best rule. An example would be the difference between the common law dispatch rule and the civil law receipt rule for the effectiveness of acceptances. An economic analysis argument could be made that the civil law rule is the better rule because it places the risk of faulty transmission on the party in the best position to ensure delivery of the acceptance. The better rules approach is revisited in a later section on the economic analysis of law. Once again, in the area of rule selection, recourse would be to a comparative analysis of the legal systems that employ that rule.

In interpreting the CISG, the resort directly to national law increases the likelihood of homeward trend bias. It takes much less intellectual effort to simply rely on the law that you know than to do a broader analysis. This has been the case in a number of U.S. cases where CISG interpretive methodology was ignored and UCC rules applied by analogy. The intellectual benefit of a comparative analysis in the context of the CISG is that it forces the evaluator to critically assess numerous nation-specific rules. Under a common core interpretive methodology, relative agreement across legal systems would provide powerful interpretive guidance when CISG interpretive methodology fails to bring clarity to an ambiguous rule or term, or fails to adequately fill a gap in the CISG.[118] However, a comparative analysis may uncover diametrically opposed rules. In this case, the better rules analysis would need to be undertaken in the selection of one of the rules or borrowing from a number of nation-specific rules to create a new rule that is deemed to be a better fit for the CISG. A better fit interpretive methodology would be guided by the general principles of the CISG. Which rule or rule creation best honors the international character of the CISG? Which rule would advance the promotion of uniformity? Which rule would be more acceptable to the various legal systems?

D. *Economic Interpretation of the CISG*

The economic analysis of law or law and economics (LAE) has been applied to many different areas of law in the United States, and to a lesser extent in Europe.[119] There is

---

[118] See, e.g., Ole Lando, "The Common Core of European Private Law and the Principles of European Contract Law," 21 *Hastings Int'l & Comp. L. Rev.* 809 (1988).

[119] The European Association of Law and Economics (EALE) is the institutional response to the increasing importance of the economic analysis of law in Europe. See Winkler, "Review, Some Realism and

also sizeable literature applying LAE to contract law. Most of that literature focuses on the crafting of efficient rules of contract law (default rules) and the writing of efficient contracts (incomplete contracts and contract design). More recently, LAE has been applied to the CISG mostly to assess the efficiency of its rules.[120] The application of LAE to interpretation is relatively sparse. Nonetheless, there is sufficient research in this area to support economic interpretations of the CISG.

In the interpretation of the CISG, instead of analyzing the efficiency of its rules, the focus here is on analyzing the relative efficiencies of different interpretations of a given CISG rule. One of the key tenets of LAE is reducing transaction costs (making contracting and interpretation more efficient). One way to lower transaction costs is through information sharing. Information sharing leads to truer mutual consent and leads to more efficient contracts and fewer misunderstandings, and lower back-end costs related to breach, litigation, and alternative dispute resolution. The importance of information sharing underlies the contextual rules, such as the reasonableness standard of the CISG. At some level, most rules or principles are incomplete or vague. This leads to problems of over- and underenforcement. Overenforcement occurs when contract law rules lead courts to enforce contracts that were never subjectively agreed to or to underenforce contracts by refusing to enforce agreements that were subjectively understood at the time of agreement. Allowing contextual information to be used in the interpretation of the CISG reduces the cases of over- or underenforcement.

Kronman and Posner argue that one way of reducing transaction costs is for contract law to offer default rules (standard terms), that reduce the need to negotiate.[121] In essence, the CISG, as well as the UCC, do just that. They provide a list of "gap-filling" terms that can be used to fill gaps in contracts. For this to be truly effective, interpretations of these rules should focus on the construction of the most efficient rules. Put simply, in interpreting CISG articles, the better interpretation between divergent or alternative possible interpretations is the one that produces the most efficient interpretive outcome. The question then becomes how one determines the more efficient of two divergent interpretations of a CISG rule. A device often used in the transaction cost analysis is that, unless expressly stated otherwise, risk should be allocated to the most efficient insurer, contractor, auctioneer, and so forth.[122] For example, the CISG's fundamental breach rule and the allocation of risk of defective goods are placed on the buyer because the buyer is the most efficient auctioneer. The buyer is in the best position to obtain value for the defective goods and to prevent waste. The maximizing of value and the prevention of waste act as surrogates for lower transaction costs.

Rationalism: Economic Analysis of Law in Germany," 6 *German L. J.* 1 (2005) (discusses the publication in German of American LAE classics); Montagné, "Law and Economics in France," in *Encyclopedia of Law and Economics* (ed. Bouckaert and De Geest) (Northampton, MA: Edward Elgar, 1999), 150. See generally Mattei, *Comparative Law and Economics* (Ann Arbor: Michigan University Press, 1997); Kirchner, "The Difficult Reception of Law and Economics in Germany," 11 *Int'l J.L. & Econ.* 277 (1991); Santos Pastor, "Law and Economics in Spain," 11 *Int'l J.L. & Econ.* 309 (1991); Ota, "Law and Economics in Japan: Hatching Stage," 11 *Int'l J.L. & Econ.* 301 (1991). See also Schäfer and Ott, *The Economic Analysis of Civil Law* (Northampton, MA: Edward Elgar, 2004).

[120] Cenini and Parisi, "An Economic Analysis of the CISG," in Janssen and Meyer, *CISG Methodology*, 151; DiMatteo and Ostas, "Comparative Efficiency in International Sales Law," 26 *Am. U. Int'l L. Rev* 371(2011).

[121] Kronman and Posner, *The Economics of Contract Law* (Boston: Little, Brown, 1979).

[122] See, e.g., Richard Posner and Andrew Rosenfield, "Impossibility and Related Doctrines in Contract Law: An Economic Analysis," 6 *J. Legal Studies* 83 (1977) ("superior risk taker").

X. Party-Generated Rules of Interpretation

There is an ongoing debate in American legal scholarship as to whether contracting parties should be able to expressly agree to the rules of interpretation to be applied to their contracts. Should the parties be able to contract out of CISG interpretive methodology? Should the parties be able to preempt the application of the traditional interpretive methodologies in the interpretation of CISG rules and in the interpretation of their contracts? One answer to these questions is that parties can avoid the uncertainty of judicial interpretation by writing better contracts. The diminution of interpretive uncertainty is obtainable by writing clear and more complete contracts. But as is often the case, clarity is in the eye of the interpreter and not the writer of the contract. And contracts can never be fully complete due to the bounded rationality of the negotiating parties, the loss in translation between business deals and legal contracts, and increasingly high transaction costs. Assuming a certain level of ambiguity and incompleteness, the parties' last recourse is to provide rules of interpretation in their contracts.

Professors Schwartz and Scott have argued that in business-to-business contracts, parties should be able to incorporate rules of interpretation in which their contracts are to be interpreted by third parties, such as judges and arbitrators. They further assert that businesspersons prefer formal, anticontextual methods of interpretation because they prize certainty and predictability.[123] Schwartz and Scott argue that the use of contextual evidence to uncover meaning is antithetical to the type of interpretation that parties to business contracts would want. Business contractors are willing to trade off an occasional misinterpretation for the certainty of formalistic interpretation. If taken to the extreme, the Schwartz–Scott thesis would support the existence of specialized rules of interpretation for business contracts. That is, even if parties do not incorporate rules of interpretation into their business contracts, the default rules of interpretation should be formalistic in nature and seek a direct interpretation of the words of the statute and of the contract, and only rarely resort to extrinsic evidence.

The issue for this chapter is whether contracting parties should have the power to place rules of interpretation into their contracts that would bind a future court in how it applies the CISG to the contract. In the case of an express contractual provision providing rules of interpretation, the core premise that contracts are exercises of private autonomy at first blush supports the enforcement of such rules of interpretation. But, as with any other term in a contract, the context of the bargaining process should also be assessed. Not all businesspersons are as sophisticated or possess the equality of bargaining power that the Schwartz–Scott thesis assumes. Also, just like any term in a contract, business or otherwise, contextual influences will still be relevant in a court's determination of the meaning of CISG rules as applied to the parties' rules of interpretation. Even if business parties intend to adopt formalistic rules of interpretation it would still "take a contextual . . . approach to determin[e] whether formalist principles apply" to a certain issue.[124] Furthermore, in the case of gaps in the contract, prohibiting the use of contextual evidence or CISG gap fillers becomes nonsensical. Finally, simply focusing on the incorporation of similar rules of interpretation in a series of contracts fails

[123] Schwartz and Scott, "Contract Theory and the Limits of Contract Law," 113 *Yale L. J.* 541, 544–8 (2003).
[124] Miller, "Contract Law, Party Sophistication and the New Formalism," 75 *Missouri L. Rev.* 493, 535–6 (2009).

to reflect the relational nature of transactions between repeat contractors. A better theory to explain the relationships between businesspersons is relational contract theory, which is contextual in nature.[125] Over a long-term contractual relationship, the formalism of such rules is unlikely to reflect the intent of the parties or the nature of the relationship.

XI. Conclusion

This chapter reviews the traditional methods used in the interpretation of statutes – textual, systemic, historical, and purposive. The move from formalism to contextualism in Anglo-American law is also examined, as well as economic interpretive methodology. These methods of interpretation are reviewed with the hope of providing insights into the interpretation of the CISG. More cynically, these methods can be seen as techniques of justification for a court or arbitrator's subjective interpretation of the CISG. In the words of Stephen Smith, "it is difficult to say when interpretation ends and creation begins."[126] This chapter, albeit mostly descriptive in nature, is based on a more positive view. It sees these traditional and nontraditional methods as tools for an appropriate interpretation of statutes in general and the CISG in particular. They are useful in checking subjective interpretations of the CISG. This is especially important for an international convention that uses nondomestic legal terminology in the hope that interpretations will be autonomous in nature. This does not mean domestic or traditional methods of interpretation are to be ignored, but that they should be used in the search for autonomous meanings. The various methods of statutory interpretation act not only as a check on subjectivity, but also as checks on themselves.

The methods of interpretation reviewed in this chapter have a place in the interpretation of the CISG. But, because of the nature of the CISG as an international instrument, certain methods are more useful than others. Ultimately, their usefulness comes within the domain of the arbiter of interpretation. It also depends on the particular article or provision of the CISG being subjected to interpretation. As a matter of best practice, it would seem that the more methods used in the interpretive process, the better the interpretive outcome. If all methods point to a certain interpretation, then judges and arbitrators can be more confident in their rulings and bolder in their exposition of the interpretation. In other instances, the methods might point in different interpretive directions. Hopefully, in such cases, the neutrality of the CISG language, being truthful to CISG's interpretive methodology, and the proper use of the other methods of interpretation will lead to the most reasonable autonomous interpretation.

---

[125] Macneil, "Relational Contract Theory: Challenges and Queries," 94 *Northwestern U. L. Rev.* 877, 881 (2000).

[126] Smith, *Contract Theory* (New York: Oxford University Press, 2004), 270.

8 Divergent Interpretations: Reasons and Solutions

Ingeborg Schwenzer

I. Introduction

In recent times much has been said and written about homeward trend reasoning by domestic courts when applying the CISG.[1] In general, this homeward trend is strongly criticized,[2] although a few select authors seem to support it by arguing it might prevent some parties from opting out of the CISG.[3] The background of this discussion begins with CISG Article 7. It is this article that lays down the basic methods on interpretation of the CISG. Article 7 contains two rules that are simple in principle: first, Article 7(1) seeks to secure an autonomous interpretation of the provisions of the CISG and its general principles,[4] that is, an interpretation free from preconceptions of domestic laws,[5]

---

[1] See, e.g., Petra Butler, "The Use of the CISG in Domestic Law," 59 *Belgrade L. Rev.* 7 et seq. (2011); Larry DiMatteo et al., "The Interpretive Turn in International Sales Law: An Analysis of Fifteen Years of CISG Jurisprudence," 24 *Nw. J. Int'l L. & Bus.* 299 et seq. (2004); Franco Ferrari, "Homeward Trend: What, Why and Why Not," *Internationales Handelsrecht*, 8 et seq. (2009), and in *CISG Methodology* (ed. A. Janssen and O. Meyer) (Munich: Sellier, 2009), 171 et seq.; Franco Ferrari, "The CISG and Its Impact on National Legal Systems: General Report," in *The CISG and Its Impact on National Legal Systems* (ed. F. Ferrari) (Munich: Sellier, 2008), 413 et seq.; Harry M. Flechtner, "Article 79 of the United Nations Convention on the International Sale of Goods (CISG) as a Rorschach Test: The Homeward Trend and Exemption for Delivering Non-Conforming Goods," 19 *Pace Int'l L. Rev.* 29 et seq. (2007); Mathias Reimann, "The CISG in the United States: Why It Has Been Neglected and Why Europeans Should Care," 71 *RabelsZ* 115 et seq. (2007).

[2] DiMatteo et al., 24 *Nw. J. Int'l L. & Bus.* 299, 303 (2004); Ferrari, *Internationales Handelsrecht*, 8, 11 (2009); Ferrari, "The CISG and Its Impact," 458; Flechtner, 19 *Pace Int'l L. Rev.* 29, 31 (2007); Reimann, 71 *RabelsZ* 115, 124 (2007). See also Francesco G. Mazzotta, "Why Do Some of the American Courts Fail to Get It Right?," 3 *Loyola U. Chicago Int'l L. Rev.* 85, 89 (2005); Luke R. Nottage, "Who's Afraid of the Vienna Sales Convention (CISG)? A New Zealander's View from Australia and Japan," 36 *VUWLR* 815, 838 (2005).

[3] Gilles Cuniberti, "Is the CISG Benefiting Anybody?," 39 *Vanderbilt J. Transnat'l L.* 1511, 1540 et seq. (2006); Halverson Cross, "Parole Evidence under the CISG: The 'Homeward Trend' Reconsidered," 68 *Ohio St. L.J.* 133 et seq. (2007); Clayton P. Gillette and Robert E. Scott, "The Political Economy of International Sales Law," 25 *Int'l Rev. L. & Econ.* 446, 481 (2005); Steven D. Walt, "Novelty and the Risks of Uniform Sales Law," 39 *Virginia J. Int'l L.* 671, 687 et seq. (1999).

[4] Franco Ferrari in *Kommentar zum Einheitlichen UN-Kaufrecht*, 5th ed. (ed. P. Schlechtriem and I. Schwenzer) (Munich: C.H. Beck, 2008), CISG, Article 7, para. 5; Joseph M. Lookofsky, *Understanding the CISG*, 3rd ed. (Alphen aan den Rijn: Kluwer, 2008), 33 et seq.; Ulrich Magnus, "Tracing Methodology in the CISG: Dogmatic Foundations," in Janssen and Meyer, *CISG Methodology*, 33, 39 et seq.; Gudrun Schmid, *Einheitliche Anwendung von internationalem Einheitsrecht* (Baden-Baden: Nomos, 2004), 36.

[5] Ferrari in Schlechtriem and Schwenzer, *UN-Kaufrecht*, Article 7, para. 9; Harry M. Flechtner, "The Several Texts of the CISG in a Decentralized System: Observations on Translations, Reservations and Other Challenges to the Uniformity Principle in Article 7(1)," 17 *J.L. & Commerce* 187, 188 (1998);

by focusing on the international character of the CISG, the need to promote uniformity in its application, and the observance of good faith in international trade;[6] and second, Article 7(2) serves as a basis for gap filling.[7]

The CISG has been in force now for more than twenty-five years and has eighty member states,[8] potentially governing about 80% of world trade. However, it is still – or more and more it seems – extremely hard work to achieve even a basic level of uniformity in the application and interpretation of the CISG.[9] That uniformity is our collective goal has already been decided by the mere fact of its adoption by so many states. Thus, we should not debate the merits of uniformity but rather how it can best be achieved.

This chapter will first identify the main areas where problems with interpreting the CISG from a domestic view have so far arisen. It will then analyze the reasons for homeward trend and finally discuss remedies that could ensure a higher level of uniformity in the future.

II. Main Areas of the Homeward Trend

A. *General*

The homeward trend may take different forms;[10] the first is the nonapplication of the CISG where it should be applied; the second is interpreting the provisions of the CISG according to existing or merely presumed domestic counterparts; and the third, the undermining of the CISG by resorting to concurring domestic remedies.

There are a number of countries that are accused of being especially prone to homeward trend.[11] The largest general group is the common law countries, especially

---

John O. Honnold and Harry M. Flechtner, *Uniform Law for International Sales*, 4th ed. (Alphen aan den Rijn: Kluwer, 2009), Article, 7 para. 87; Christopher Niemann, *Einheitliche Anwendung UN-Kaufrechts in italienischer und deutscher Rechtsprechung und Lehre: Eine Untersuchung zur Einheitlichen Auslegung unbestimmter Rechtsbegriffe und interner Lückenfüllung im CISG* (Frankfurt a.M.: Peter Lang, 2007), 42; Wolfgang Witz in *International Einheitliches Kaufrecht* (ed. W. Witz, H. C. Salger, and M. Lorenz) (Heidelberg: Verlag für Recht und Wirtschaft, 2000), Article 7, para. 8. See also Ingeborg Schwenzer and Pascal Hachem, in *Commentary on the UN Convention on the International Sale of Goods (CISG)*, 3rd ed. (ed. P. Schlechtriem and I. Schwenzer) (Oxford: Oxford University Press, 2010), Article 7, para. 1 et seq.

[6] Magnus, "Tracing Methodology," 33, 42 et seq.; Bruno Zeller, "The Observance of Good Faith in International Trade," in Janssen and Meyer, *CISG Methodology*, 133, 135 et seq.; Schwenzer and Hachem in Schlechtriem and Schwenzer, *Commentary*, Article 7, para. 7; Witz in Witz et al., *International Einheitliches*, Article 7, para. 12.

[7] André Janssen and Sörren Claas Kiene, "The CISG and Its General Principles," in Janssen and Meyer, *CISG Methodology*, 621, 626 et seq.; Magnus, "Tracing Methodology," 33, 44 et seq.; Schwenzer and Hachem in Schlechtriem and Schwenzer, *Commentary*, Article 7, para. 27 et seq.; Witz in Witz et al., *International Einheitliches*, Article 7, para. 26.

[8] For a detailed list of the member states, see http://www.uncitral.org/uncitral/en/uncitral_texts/sale_goods/1980CISG_status.htm (last accessed October 25, 2013).

[9] Schwenzer and Hachem in Schlechtriem and Schwenzer, *Commentary*, Article 7, para. 10 et seq.; Lookofsky, *Understanding the CISG*, 33; Philip Hackney, "Is the United Nations Convention on the International Sale of Goods Achieving Uniformity?," 61 *Louisiana L. Rev.* 473, 474 (2001).

[10] See Flechtner, 17 *J.L. & Commerce* 187, 199 (1998); Honnold and Flechtner, *Uniform Law for International Sales*, Article 7, paras. 87, 92. See also Ferrari, *Internationales Handelsrecht*, 8, 14 (2009).

[11] For a general overview, see Ferrari, *Internationales Handelsrecht*, 8 (2009).

Australia,[12] New Zealand,[13] and the United States.[14] But French courts do not seem to do much better.[15] And, although there are German authors who emphasize the achievements of the German judiciary in the uniform interpretation of the CISG,[16] a closer examination of German decisions reveals that they, too, are much less international than would be expected.[17] Finally, the high praise of Italian courts[18] must, in the end, also be questioned. Although it is true that there are Italian decisions mentioning up to forty foreign cases,[19] the fact that in most cases this was just a formalistic exercise cannot be overlooked; for example, the conclusion that the CISG applies if both parties have their places of business in contracting states may simply be deducted from Article 1(1)(a) CISG. Relying on an abundant number of foreign decisions to support this result is superfluous.[20]

B. *Not Applying the CISG Where it Should be Applied*

As mentioned earlier, the first form of homeward trend consists of simply disregarding the applicability of the CISG.[21] Certainly, no numbers exist in how many cases courts did

---

[12] Lisa Spagnolo, "The Last Outpost: An Australian Pre-History of the Convention on Contracts for the International Sale of Goods (CISG)," 10 *Mel. J. Int'l L.* 1 et seq. (2009); Bruno Zeller, "The UN-Convention on Contracts for the International Sale of Goods (CISG): A Leap Forward Towards Unified International Sales Laws," 12 *Pace Int'l L. Rev.* 79, 80 (2000); Bruno Zeller, "The CISG in Australia: An Overview," in *Quo Vadis CISG?: Celebrating the 25th Anniversary of the United Nations Convention on the International Sale of Goods* (ed. F. Ferrari) (Brussels: Bruylant, 2005), 293, 294. Furthermore, see Lisa Spagnolo, "A Glimpse through the Kaleidoscope: Choices of Law and the CISG (Kaleidoscope Part I)," 13 *VJ Int'l Com. & Arb.* 135 (2009).

[13] Petra Butler, "New Zealand," in *The CISG and Its Impact on National Legal Systems* (ed. F. Ferrari) (Munich: Sellier, 2008), 251, 252. However, the Court of Appeal of New Zealand in a very recent case referred to German, Austrian, U.S., and French case law, expressly stating that domestic law must be avoided; see *RJ & AM Smallmon v. Transport Sales Limited and Grant Alan Miller* C A545/2010 [2011] NZ C A 340 (New Zealand Court of Appeal, July 22, 2011), CISG-online 2215. Therefore, this case suggests that New Zealand also acknowledges the need for a uniform interpretation of the CISG.

[14] Honnold and Flechtner, *Uniform Law for International Sales*, Article 7, para. 92; Harry M. Flechtner, "The CISG in U.S. Courts: The Evolution (and Devolution) of the Methodology of Interpretation," in Ferrari, *Quo Vadis CISG?*, 91, 92 et seq.; Alain A. Levasseur, "United States of America," in *The CISG and Its Impact on National Legal Systems*, 313, 314 et seq.; Mazzotta, 3 *Loyola U. Chicago Int'l L. Rev.* 85 et seq. (2005); Zeller, 12 *Pace Int'l L. Rev.* 79, 80 et seq. (2000).

[15] Below para. II. 2.

[16] Ulrich Magnus, "CISG in the German Federal Civil Court," in Ferrari, *Quo Vadis CISG?*, 211, 233, arguing that the "decisions [of the German Federal Civil Court] give good guidance and meet the necessary balance between certainty of law and justice in the case at hand . . . A good number of cases are now internationally accepted leading cases concerning the interpretation and application of the CISG."

[17] Camilla Baasch Andersen, "The Uniform International Sales Law and the Global Jurisconsultorium," 24 *J.L. & Commerce* 159, 176 (2005); Flechtner, 19 *Pace Int'l L. Rev.* 29, 47; Niemann, "Einheitliche Anwendung," 249.

[18] Franco Ferrari, "Applying the CISG in a Truly Uniform Manner: Tribunale di Vigevano (Italy)," 5 *Uniform L. Rev.* 203, 207 (2001), arguing that "the importance of the *Tribunale di Vigevano* decision is self-evident . . . [T]he court referred to some 40 foreign court decisions and arbitral awards. In other words, the court has . . . taken into account the need to have regard to foreign case law in order to promote uniformity."

[19] See, e.g., Tribunale di Vigevano, July 12, 2000, CISG-online 493.

[20] See also, Tribunale Forli, December 11, 2008, CISG-online 1788.

[21] For a very interesting survey about the CISG and its nonapplication in the United States, see Michael W. Gordon, "Some Thoughts on the Receptiveness of Contract Rules in the CISG and UNIDROIT Principles

not apply the CISG despite it being applicable and not excluded by the parties. But it is likely to be in the thousands. In Australia, the CISG formally entered into force as early as April 1, 1989,[22] and yet to this day, there are only eleven Australian cases that apply the CISG beyond the mere decision whether the CISG is applicable or not.[23] This may in part, or even to a great extent, be attributed to the fact that many Australian parties automatically exclude the CISG in their contracts.[24] But this fact alone – even if it is true – cannot explain the whole picture. The CISG has been in force in Australia now for more than twenty years and Australia's top five trading partners are all CISG member states; there certainly must have been more than these eleven cases litigated before Australian courts where the CISG applied. It seems very likely that in many cases neither the parties, nor their counsel, nor the judges ever realized that they were pleading and deciding the case under the wrong law.[25] A similar picture is found in New Zealand, where the CISG entered into force on October 1, 1995.[26] One of its first true CISG cases

---

as Reflected in one State's (Florida) Experience of (1) Law School Faculty, (2) Members of the Bar with an International Practice, and (3) Judges," 46 *Am. J. Comp. L.* 361, 369 et seq. (1998). See also Albert H. Kritzer, "The Convention on Contracts for the International Sale of Goods: Scope, Interpretation and Resources," *Rev. CISG* 147, 163 (1995); Reimann, 71 *RabelsZ* 115, 120 et seq. (2007).

[22] The CISG first appeared in Australian statute books in 1986 (NSW) and 1987 (Vic). It was similarly inserted into the legislation of other states of Australia at about the same time. Under Australia's constitution, trade is a state matter and thus it was necessary for the CISG be introduced at a state level. However, the state legislation contained a provision stating that the law would not become operative until the date CISG entered into force at a federal level.

[23] See *Castel Electronics Pty Ltd. v. Toshiba Singapore Pte Ltd.* [2011] FCAFC 55 (April 20, 2011, Federal Court of Australia), CISG-online 2219; *Castel Electronics Pty Ltd. v. Toshiba Singapore Pte Ltd.* [2010] FCA 1028 (Federal Court of Australia, September 28, 2010), CISG-online 2158; *Delphic Wholesalers (Aust) Pty Ltd. v. Agrilex Co. Limited* [2010] VSC 328 (Supreme Court of Victoria, August 6, 2010) CISG-online 2127; *Vetreria Etrusca Srl v. Kingston Estate Wines Pty Ltd.* [2008] SASC 75 (Supreme Court of South Australia, March 14, 2008), CISG-online 1891; *Italian Imported Foods Pty Ltd. v. Pucci SRL* [2006] NSWSC 1060 (Supreme Court of New South Wales, October 13, 2006), CISG-online 1494; *Summit Chemicals Pty Ltd. v. Vetrotex Espana SA* [2004] WASCA 109 (May 27, 2004), CISG-online 860; *Playcorp Pty Ltd v. Taiyo Kogyo Ltd.* [2003] VSC 108 (Supreme Court of Victoria, April 24, 2003), CISG-online 808; *Ginza Pte Ltd. v. Vista Corp. Pty Ltd.* [2003] WASC 11 (Supreme Court of Western Australia, January 17, 2003), CISG-online 807; *Downs Investments Pty Ltd. v. Perwaja Steel SDN BHD* [2002] 2 Qd R 462 (Queensland Court of Appeal, October 12, 2001), CISG-online 955; *Perry Engineering Pty Ltd. v. Bernold AG* [2001] SASC 15 (Supreme Court of South Australia, February 1, 2001), CISG-online 806; *Roder Zelt- und Hallenkonstruktionen GmbH v. Rosedown Park Pty Ltd.* (1995) 57 FCR 216 (Federal Court of Australia, April 28, 1995), CISG-online 218. See also Spagnolo, 10 *Mel. J. Int'l L.* 1, 4 (2009) (discussion of the respective cases).

[24] Spagnolo, 10 *Mel. J. Int'l L.* 1, 4 (2009). For a detailed analysis why parties and lawyers tend to opt out of the CISG, see Lisa Spagnolo, "Green Eggs and Ham: The CISG, Path Dependence, and the Behavioural Economics of Lawyers' Choices of Law in International Sales Contracts," 6 *J. Priv. Int'l L.* 417 et seq. (2010); Spagnolo, 13 *VJ Int'l & Com. Arb.* 135 et seq. (2009). See also Lisa Spagnolo, "Rats in the Kaleidoscope: Rationality, Irrationality, and the Economics and Psychology of Opting in and Opting out of the CISG (Kaleidoscope Part II)," 13 *VJ Int'l Arb. & Com.* 157 et seq. (2009), for an economical analysis of the problem.

[25] See, e.g., *Italian Imported Foods Pty Ltd. v. Pucci SRL* [2006] NSWSC 1060 (Supreme Court of New South Wales, October 13, 2006), CISG-online 1494; Spagnolo, 10 *Mel. Int. L.J.* 1, 31 (2009). See also Bruno Zeller, "*Downs Investment Pty Ltd. v. Perwaja Steel SDN BHD* [2000] QSC 421 (November 17, 2000)," 5 *VJ Int'l Com. & Arb.* 124 (2001); Bruno Zeller, "*Downs Investments Pty Ltd. (in liq) v. Perwaja Steel SDN BHD* [2002] 2 Qd R 462," 9 *VJ Int'l Com. & Arb.* 43 (2005).

[26] See Butler, "New Zealand," 251, 254 et seq., arguing that "in all the cases the CISG provisions are used to back up a court's interpretation of domestic law." Butler further notes that the New Zealand courts

appeared in 2011 and is still pending before the Court of Appeal.[27] However, the Court of Appeal of New Zealand applied the CISG in a very recent case.[28] Furthermore, there are quite a few CISG cases litigated and decided outside Australia and New Zealand involving Australian and New Zealand parties.[29] Notably, there are many such CISG awards delivered under auspices of CIETAC, the China International Economic, and Trade Arbitration Commission.[30]

Another prominent example of circumventing the application of the CISG can be found in France.[31] In contrast to decisions from many other countries,[32] the Cour de cassation[33] held that pleading a case in court under French law amounted to a subsequent implicit exclusion of the CISG irrespective of whether the parties were aware or not that the CISG applied to their contract.[34]

C. Interpreting CISG Provisions in Light of Domestic Law

There are innumerable examples of national courts equating CISG concepts and provisions with familiar domestic ones, not realizing and probably not being interested in the

mentioned the CISG in only seven cases; see 251, 254 et seq. for further references. Furthermore, see *Hideo Yoshimoto v. Canterbury Golf International Ltd.* [2001] 1 NZLR 523, CISG-online 1080.

[27] *International Housewares (NZ) Limited v. SEB S.A.* (High Court Auckland, March 31, 2003), CISG-online 833.

[28] *RJ & AM Smallmon v. Transport Sales Limited and Grant Alan Miller* C A545/2010 [2011] NZ C A 340 (New Zealand Court of Appeal, July 22, 2011), CISG-online 2215. For a discussion of the case see Butler, 49 *Belgrade L. Rev.* 7, 22 (2011).

[29] See, e.g., Guangdong Province Higher Court, January 11, 2005, CISG-online 1610; CIETAC China International Economic and Trade Arbitration Commission, January 19, 2004, CISG-online 1804; CIETAC China International Economic and Trade Arbitration Commission, April 8, 1999, CISG-online 1114; *Helen Kaminski Pty. Ltd. v. Marketing Australian Products, Inc.* d/b/a Fiona Waterstreet Hats U.S. Dist. LEXIS 10630 (1997) (S.D. NY 1997), CISG-online 297.

[30] For a detailed list of the cases, see the CISG-online database on http://www.globalsaleslaw.org/index.cfm?pageID=29 (last accessed October 25, 2013).

[31] Filip De Ly, "Opting Out: Some Observations on the Occasion of the CISG's 25th Anniversary" in Ferrari, *Quo Vadis CISG?*, 25, 32; Claude Witz, "France," in Ferrari, *The CISG and Its Impact*, 129, 137. See also Vincent Heuzé, *La vente internationale de marchandises: Droit uniforme* (Paris: L.G.D.J., 2000), para. 95 et seq.

[32] For Italian decisions, see, e.g., Tribunale di Vigevano, July 12, 2000, CISG-online 493; Tribunale di Padova, February 25, 2004, CISG-online 819, holding that the reference in the pleadings to the nonuniform domestic rule of a contracting state alone is not, by itself, sufficient to exclude the applicability of the CISG. Several German courts held that the parties' referring to German substantive law in the choice of law clause also includes the CISG and therefore does not lead to an opting out of the CISG, see Oberlandesgericht Stuttgart, March 31, 2008, CISG-online 1658; Landgericht Bamberg, October 23, 2006, CISG-online 1400; Oberlandesgericht Rostock, October 10, 2001, CISG-online 671. For a U.S. decision, see *American Mint LLC, Goede Beteiligungsgesellschaft, and Michael Goede v. GOSoftware, Inc.* 2006 WL 42090 (M.D. PA 2006), CISG-online 1175. For a Russian decision, see Tribunal of International Commercial Arbitration at the Russian Federation Chamber of Commerce and Industry, November 5, 2004, CISG-online 1360. See also Schwenzer and Hachem in Schlechtriem and Schwenzer, *Commentary*, Article 6, para. 19; Ferrari, *Internationales Handelsrecht* 8, 21 (2009).

[33] Cour de Cassation, October 25, 2005, CISG-online 1226; Cour de Cassation, June 26, 2001, CISG-online 598.

[34] For a detailed discussion about this matter, see Claude Witz, "Vente internationale: l'office du juge face au pouvoir des plaideurs d'écarter le droit uniforme et jeu combiné," in *Convention de Bruxelles et de la Convention de Vienne, Dalloz* 3607 et seq. (2001); Günter Hager, "Zur Auslegung des UN-Kaufrechts: Grundsätze und Methoden," in *Festschrift für Ulrich Huber zum siebzigsten Geburtstag* (ed. T. Baums et al.) (Tübingen: Mohr Siebeck, 2006), 319, 326; Ferrari, *Internationales Handelsrecht*, 8, 21 (2009).

fact that they are – at least sometimes – totally different. This chapter highlights some of the most striking examples.

Many American courts seem to be convinced that it is perfectly normal to interpret the CISG according to UCC case law.[35] In a recent case, a U.S. District Court, unfortunately without further reflection, noted that "case law is relatively sparse" even though this is not true, and consequently relied on the UCC while interpreting the CISG.[36] Also, in 2008, two additional District Court decisions[37] relied on the UCC "to clarify the CISG" claiming that there was "virtually no American case law on the CISG," relying on a statement in the 1995 *Delchi Carrier* decision[38] and ignoring the already abundant U.S. case law on the CISG.[39] Not only did the District Court fail to research foreign decisions, it ignored the considerable case law from other U.S. courts.[40]

Similar attitudes, however, can be found around the globe.[41] For example, Australian courts have interpreted the CISG through comparisons with domestic legislation.[42] In Europe, the Austrian Supreme Court, in order to justify the result that a notice of nonconformity to become effective under Article 27 CISG has to be properly dispatched, refers only to a commentary on the Austrian Commercial Code.[43]

[35] Cases where the CISG was interpreted according to specific provisions of the UCC. See, e.g., *Hilaturas Miel, S.L. v. Republic of Iraq* 573 F. Supp. 2d 781 (S.D. NY 2008), CISG-online 1777; *Macromex Srl. v. Globex International Inc.* 2008 WL 1752530 (S.D. NY 2008), CISG-online 1653; *TeeVee Toons, Inc. (d/b/a TVT Records) & Steve Gottlieb, Inc. (d/b/a Biobox) v. Gerhard Schubert GmbH* 2006 WL 2463537 (S.D. NY 2006), CISG-online 1272; *Chicago Prime Packers, Inc. v. Northam Food Trading Co.* 408 F. 3d 894 (7th Cir. 2005), CISG-online 1026; *Genpharm Inc. v. Pliva-Lachema A.S., Pliva d.d.* 361 F. Supp. 2d 49 (E.D. NY 2005), CISG-online 1006; *Raw Materials Inc. v. Manfred Forberich GmbH & Co., KG* 2004 WL 1535839 (N.D. IL 2004), CISG-online 925; *Chicago Prime Packers, Inc. v. Northam Food Trading Co.* 320 F. Supp. 2d 702 (N.D. IL 2004), CISG-online 851; *Ajax Tool Works, Inc. v. Can-Eng Manufacturing Ltd.* 2003 U.S. Dist. LEXIS 1306 (N.D. IL 2003), CISG-online 772; *Schmitz-Werke GmbH & Co. v. Rockland Industries, Inc.*; Rockland International FSC, Inc. 37 Fed. Appx. 687 (4th Cir. 2005), CISG-online 625. For further references, see the CISG-online database at http://www.cisg-online.ch (last accessed October 25, 2013). See also Honnold and Flechtner, *Uniform Law for International Sales*, Article 7, para. 92; Levasseur, "United States of America," 313, 315 et seq.

[36] *Hanwha Corporation v. Cedar Petrochemicals Inc.* 09 Civ. 10559 (AKH) (S.D.N.Y. 2011), CISG-online 2178.

[37] *Hilaturas Miel, S.L. v. Republic of Iraq* 573 F. Supp. 2d 781 (S.D. NY 2008), CISG-online 1777; *Macromex Srl. v. Globex International Inc.* 2008 WL 1752530 (S.D. NY 2008), CISG-online 1653.

[38] *Delchi Carrier, SpA v. Rotorex Corp.* 10 F. 3d 1024 (2nd Cir. 1995), CISG-online 140.

[39] According to the entries in the CISG-online database, in 2011, there were more than 120 cases decided by U.S. courts that are dealing with the CISG. All cases are freely available at http://www.cisg-online.ch (last accessed October 25, 2013) and http://www.cisg.law.pace.edu (last accessed October 25, 2013).

[40] For a suggestion of how the homeward trend could be overcome in the United States, see James E. Bailey, "Facing the Truth: Seeing the Convention on Contracts for the International Sale of Goods as an Obstacle to Uniform Law of International Sales," 32 *Cornell Int'l L.J.* 273, 313 et seq. (1999).

[41] Hossam El-Saghir, "The Interpretation of the CISG in the Arab World," in Janssen and Meyer, *CISG Methodology*, 355, 366. See also Cairo Chamber of Commerce and Industry, October 3, 1995, CISG-online 1289, where the arbitrator applied Egyptian law to interpret CISG. For China, see Shiyuan Han, "China," in Ferrari, *The CISG and Its Impact*, 71, 78 et seq., stating that "many courts did not distinguish where the CISG was applied and where domestic law was applied, but enumerated articles both of the CISG and domestic laws." See also Wei Li, "The Interpretation of the CISG in China," in Janssen and Meyer, *CISG Methodology*, 343, 344 et seq. For Argentina, see Nood Taquela, "Argentina," in Ferrari, *The CISG and Its Impact*, 3, 5, arguing that "Argentine courts are not conscious enough of the mandate to interpret the CISG in the light of the international character and in general do not take into account the need to promote uniformity."

[42] Spagnolo, 10 *Mel. J. Int'l L.* 141, 177 (2009).

[43] Oberster Gerichtshof, May 24, 2005, CISG-online 1046.

Although the German courts are widely praised as interpreting the CISG in a truly international manner and not falling back on purely domestic law,[44] many rely solely on German Commentaries on the CISG and German case law.[45] The same holds true for Austrian and Swiss courts.[46] Thus, the quality and internationality of the commentaries used by the courts largely determine the quality of the judicial decisions. The following sections review the areas that are especially prone to be interpreted from a domestic perspective and serve to illustrate the extent of the problem.

1. Examination and Notice Requirements: CISG Articles 38 and 39

In domestic sales laws, there is a great variety of views concerning the question of whether a buyer has to inspect the goods and give notice to the seller of a nonconformity thereby discovered.[47] Most domestic sales laws do not recognize any such obligations of the buyer.[48] Even in those countries whose domestic sales laws do contain such provisions, their function and interpretation varies greatly from very rigid requirements to

---

[44] Ulrich Magnus, "Germany," in Ferrari, *The CISG and Its Impact*, 143, 156; Ulrich Magnus, "CISG in the German Federal Civil Court," in Ferrari, *Quo Vadis CISG?*, 211, 233 et seq.; Martin Karollus, "Judicial Interpretation and Application of the CISG in Germany 1988–1994," *Rev. CISG* 51, 52 (1995).

[45] An analysis of the fourteen most recent German cases published on the CISG-online database shows that none of the German courts made reference to either foreign case law or scholarly materials from outside of the Germanic legal system, see, e.g., Oberlandesgericht Düsseldorf, March 23, 2011, CISG-online 2218; Oberlandesgericht Hamm, November 30, 2010, CISG-online 2217; Oberlandesgericht Jena, November 10, 2010, CISG-online 2216; Landgericht Bielefeld, November 9, 2010, CISG-online 2204. Only Oberlandesgericht Stuttgart, March 31, 2008, CISG-online 1658, made reference to a Dutch decision.

[46] For Switzerland, see, e.g., Schweizerisches Bundesgericht, December 20, 2006, CISG-online 1426; Schweizerisches Bundesgericht, June 12, 2006, CISG-online 1516; Schweizerisches Bundesgericht, April 5, 2005, CISG-online 1012. For Austria, see, e.g., Oberster Gerichtshof, December 19, 2007, CISG-online 1628; Oberster Gerichtshof, November 30, 2006, CISG-online 1417; Oberster Gerichtshof, September 12, 2006, CISG-online 1364; Oberster Gerichtshof, January 25, 2006, CISG-online 1223.

[47] CISG-AC, "Opinion No. 2, Examination of the Goods and Notice of Non-Conformity: Articles 38 and 39," (June 7, 2004, Rapporteur: Eric Bergsten), available at http://www.cisgac.com/default.php?ipkCat=128&ifkCat=144&sid=144 (last accessed October 25, 2013), Comments 2.1. et seq.; Ingeborg Schwenzer and Pascal Hachem, "The CISG: Successes and Pitfalls," 57 *Am. J. Comp. L.* 457, 469 (2009); Ingeborg Schwenzer, "National Preconceptions That Endanger Uniformity," 19 *Pace Int'l L. Rev.* 103, 105 et seq. (2007); Ingeborg Schwenzer, "Buyer's Remedies in the Case of Non-conforming Goods: Some Problems in a Core Area of the CISG," in *Proceedings of the 101st Annual Meeting: The Future of International Law* (ed. American Society of International Law) (Washington, DC: ASIL, 2007), 416, 417 et seq.; Ingeborg Schwenzer, "The Noble Month (Articles 38, 39 CISG): The Story behind the Scenery," 7 *EJLR* 353, 354 et seq. (2005); Schwenzer in Schlechtriem and Schwenzer, *Commentary*, Article 39, para. 4.

[48] Among the exceptions are the domestic sales laws of Germany, Austria, and Switzerland, which all know an express duty of the buyer to examine the goods and to give notice of any lack of conformity, see §§377, 378 German Handelsgesetzbuch (HGB), §377 Austrian Unternehmensgesetzbuch (UGB), and Article 201 Swiss Code of Obligations (OR). For further exceptions see, e.g., U.S., §2-607(3)(a) UCC; Italy, Article 1667(2) Italian Codice Civile (CC); The Netherlands, Article 7:23.1 Dutch Burgerlijk Wetboek (BW), and Portugal, Article 471 Codigo de Commercio (Ccom); see also Schwenzer and Hachem, 57 *Am. J. Comp. L.* 457, 469 (2009); Schwenzer, 19 *Pace Int'l L. Rev.* 103, 106 et seq. (2007); Schwenzer in Schlechtriem and Schwenzer, *Commentary*, Article 39, para. 4; Schwenzer, 7 *EJLR* 353, 354 (2005).

more flexible ones[49] designed to prevent fraud.[50] Thus, it does not come as a great surprise that diverging domestic preconceptions have heavily influenced the interpretation of these CISG provisions.[51]

Many if not most decisions, especially in common law countries, do not mention the fact of when or even if the buyer had given notice of nonconformity of the goods.[52] In most cases, neither the parties, nor the counsels, nor the courts recognized the issue of the requirement of timely notice. If the issue of timely notice is discussed, generous timeframes are usually allowed.[53] Sometimes, notice given several weeks or months after delivery of the goods has been deemed to be appropriate.[54] However, interestingly, CISG Article 39 was recently relied on by a U.S. District Court[55] in a manner for which it was not designed. It was applied by analogy to a case of an alleged late delivery of goods – Article 39 CISG only relates to nonconformity and its Paragraph 2 is interpreted as a statute of limitation. The CISG, however, does not deal with the prescription of actions.[56] There is a separate U.N. Limitation Convention to which the United States is also a party.[57]

[49] See, Germany, §377 HGB (strict examination of the goods and notice of nonconformity requirements); Peter Schlechtriem, *Schuldrecht Besonderer Teil*, 6th ed. (Tübingen: J.C.B. Moor, 2003), para. 70; Barbara Grunewald, in *Münchener Kommentar zum Handelsgesetzbuch*, 2nd ed. (ed. K. Schmidt) (Munich: C.H. Beck, 2007), §377, para. 3. See also Honnold and Flechtner, *Uniform Law*, Articles 39, 40, and 44, para. 258; Schwenzer and Hachem, 57 *Am. J. Comp. L.* 457, 469 (2009); Schwenzer in Schlechtriem and Schwenzer, *Commentary*, Article 39, para. 4; Schwenzer, 7 *EJLR* 353, 354 (2005); Schwenzer in Schlechtriem and Schwenzer, *UN-Kaufrecht*, Article 39, para. 4.

[50] For the meaning of "reasonable time" under the UCC, see James J. White and Robert S. Summers, *Uniform Commercial Code*, 6th ed. (St. Paul: West, 2010), 419 et seq.

[51] See Harry M. Flechtner, "Funky Mussels, a Stolen Car, and Decrepit Used Shoes: Non-Conforming Goods and Notice Thereof under the United Nations Sales Convention," 26 *Boston U. Int'l L.J.* 1, 15 et seq. (2008).

[52] For Australia, see Spagnolo, 10 *Mel. J. Int'l L.* (2009) 141, 197 et seq. referring to *Italian Imported Foods Pty Ltd. v. Pucci SRL* [2006] NSWSC 1060 (Supreme Court of New South Wales, October 13, 2006), CISG-online 1494. For the United States, see, e.g., *BP Oil International v. Empresa Estatal Petroleos de Ecuador* 332 F. 3d 333 (5th Cir. 2003), CISG-online 730. Although some recent U.S. decisions do in fact mention Article 39 CISG and the requirement of timely notice of the nonconformity of the goods, they do not elaborate on the reasonableness, see, e.g., *TeeVee Toons, Inc. (d/b/a TVT Records) and Steve Gottlieb, Inc. (d/b/a Biobox) v. Gerhard Schubert GmbH* 2006 WL 2463537 (S.D. NY 2006), CISG-online 1272; *Chicago Prime Packers, Inc. v. Northam Food Trading Co.* 320 F. Supp. 2d 702 (N.D. IL 2004), CISG-online 851. Furthermore, see Schwenzer, 19 *Pace Int'l L. Rev.* 103, 118 (2007); Schwenzer in Schlechtriem and Schwenzer, *Commentary*, Article 39, para. 4.

[53] *Shuttle Packaging Systems, L. L.C. v. Jacob Tsonakis, INA S. A. and INA Plastics Corporation* 2001 U.S. Dist. LEXIS 21630 (W. D. MI 2001), CISG-online 773 stating that "it will not be practicable to require notification in a matter of a few weeks."

[54] See, e.g., *TeeVee Toons, Inc. (d/b/a TVT Records) and Steve Gottlieb, Inc. (d/b/a Biobox) v. Gerhard Schubert GmbH* 2006 WL 2463537 (S.D. NY 2006), CISG-online 1272 ("two months"). See also Schwenzer, "Buyer's Remedies in the Case of Non-conforming Goods," 416, 419; Schwenzer, 19 *Pace Int'l L. Rev.* 103, 118 (2007); Schwenzer, 7 *EJLR* 353, 363 (2005).

[55] *Sky Cast, Inc. v. Global Direct Distribution LLC* 2008 WL 754734 (E.D. KY 2008), CISG-online 1652.

[56] Honnold and Flechtner, *Uniform Law*, Articles 39, 40, and 44, para. 254.2; Ulrich Magnus in *J. von Staudingers Kommentar zum Bürgerlichen Gesetzbuch mit Einführungsgesetz und Nebengesetzen, Wiener UN-Kaufrecht (CISG)*, 15th ed. (Berlin: De Gruyter, 2005), Article 4, para. 38 (hereafter referred to as *Staudinger*); Schwenzer and Hachem in Schlechtreim and Schwenzer, *Commentary*, Article 4, para. 50.

[57] United Nations Convention on the Limitation Period in the International Sale of Goods (New York, June 14, 1974), available at http://www.uncitral.org/pdf/english/texts/sales/limit/limit_conv_E_Ebook.pdf (last accessed October 25, 2013). See also Honnold and Flechtner, *Uniform Law*, Articles 39, 40, 44, para. 261.1; Schwenzer in Schlechtriem and Schwenzer, *Commentary*, Article 39, para. 28.

At the other end of the spectrum are the decisions from the Germanic legal systems. Since the German, Austrian, and Swiss domestic sales laws are known for very rigid notice obligations,[58] parties and courts thoroughly investigate the question of whether timely notice of any nonconformity was given. When the CISG first came into force, German courts merely relied on the interpretation of the respective domestic provisions, consequently allowing buyers only a few days for inspection of the goods and giving notice.[59] Over time, the German courts,[60] as well as the Swiss Supreme Court,[61] were convinced by comparative scholarly writings[62] that this was not in line with an international interpretation of the CISG.[63] In general, case law from both countries now allows the buyer one month for giving notice.[64] However, the Austrian Supreme Court still favors an overall period of a fortnight to inspect and notify.[65] It was inspired to do so

[58] See Germany, §377 HGB; Switzerland, Article 201 OR. Austria changed the provision regarding the timely notice of nonconformity of the goods (§377 HGB) from "*unverzüglich*" (without delay) to "*binnen angemessener Frist*" (within reasonable time) in order to adjust the domestic law to the CISG, see §377 UGB. See also CISG-AC "Opinion No. 2," Comment 5.1; Flechtner, 26 *Boston U. Int'l L.J.* 1, 16 (2008).

[59] See, e.g., Landgericht Stuttgart, August 31, 1989, CISG-online 11; Oberlandesgericht Düsseldorf, January 8, 1993, CISG-online 76; Oberlandesgericht Düsseldorf, March 12, 1993, CISG-online 82; Oberlandesgericht Saarbrücken, January 13, 1993, CISG-online 83; Oberlandesgericht Düsseldorf, February 10, 1994, CISG-online 116; Oberlandesgericht München, February 8, 1995, CISG-online 142. See also Honnold and Flechtner, *Uniform Law*, Articles 38, 39, and 44, para., 257.1; Niemann, "Einheitliche Anwendung," 161.

[60] Bundesgerichtshof, November 3, 1999, CISG online 475, referring to Bundesgerichtshof, March 8, 1995, CISG-online 144.

[61] Schweizerisches Bundesgericht, October 10, 2005, CISG-online 1353.

[62] Honnold and Flechtner, *Uniform Law*, Articles 38, 39, and 44, para. 257.1; Schwenzer, 19 *Pace Int'l L. Rev.* 103, 115 et seq. (2007); Schwenzer, 7 *EJLR* 353, 361 (2005). See, e.g., Camilla Baasch Andersen, "Reasonable Time in Article 39(1) of the CISG: Is Article 39(1) Truly a Uniform Provision?," available at http://www.cisg.law.pace.edu/cisg/biblio/andersen.html (last accessed October 25, 2013); DiMatteo et al., 24 *Nw. J. Int'l L. & Bus.* 299, 364 (2004).

[63] German scholarly writings and case law have been met with criticism; see Claude Witz, *Les premières applications du droit uniforme de la vente internationale (Convention des Nations Unies du 11 avril 1980)* 90 et seq. (Paris: L.G.D.J., 1995); Lookofsky, "Understanding the CISG," 87; Claude Witz, "A Raw Nerve in Disputes Relating to the Vienna Sales Convention: The Reasonable Time for the Buyer to Give Notice of a Lack of Conformity," 11 *ICC Ct. Bull.* 15, 20 (2000). See also Schwenzer in Schlechtriem and Schwenzer, *UN-Kaufrecht*, Article 39, para. 17.

[64] In a very recent decision, a German court acknowledged that the relevant scholarly writings advocate a one-month period. However, the court left the issue open because two and a half months passed prior to the notification which was in any case too long, see Oberlandesgericht Hamm, November 30, 2011, CISG-online 2217 ("Die angemessene Rügefrist nach Article 39 CISG beträgt nach der einschlägigen Kommentar-Literatur hingegen 1 Monat.") For further decisions, see, e.g., Oberlandesgericht Koblenz, October 19, 2006, CISG-online 1407; Landgericht Bamberg, October 23, 2006, CISG-online 1400; Landgericht Hamburg, September 6, 2004, CISG-online 1085. But, see Oberlandesgericht Köln, May 19, 2008, CISG-online 1700, and Landgericht Tübingen, June 18, 2003, CISG-online 784, wrongly assuming a standard period of two weeks. Furthermore, see Oberlandesgericht Düsseldorf, January 23, 2004, CISG-online 918, where the court did not make reference to any standard period at all. For Switzerland, see, e.g., Schweizerisches Bundesgericht, November 13, 2003, CISG-online 840; Obergericht Luzern, May 12, 2003, CISG-online 846; Handelsgericht St. Gallen, February 11, 2003, CISG-online 960; Obergericht Luzern, January 8, 1997, CISG-online 228. See also Flechtner, 26 Boston U. Int'l L.J. 1, 17 (2008); Schwenzer in Schlechtriem and Schwenzer, *UN-Kaufrecht*, Article 39, para. 17.

[65] See Oberster Gerichtshof, January 14, 2002, CISG-online 643; Oberster Gerichtshof, August 27, 1999, CISG-online 485; Oberster Gerichtshof, October 15, 1998, CISG-online 380. See also Magnus in

exclusively by Austrian scholars who negatively commented on the shift by the German Supreme Court toward more internationality.[66] Consequently, Articles 38 and 39 are an area where national preconceptions heavily influence the interpretation of the CISG.

2. Other Areas of Divergent Interpretation

Other areas of domestically influenced divergent interpretations of the CISG include the major areas of damages (Article 74 CISG)[67] and exemption (Article 79 CISG),[68] as well as the special problem of the common law parol evidence rule.[69]

D. *Narrowing the Scope of the CISG*

Another facet of the homeward trend can be seen in endeavors to narrow the scope of the CISG, be it by applying concurrent domestic law remedies or by relying on rules that are defined as concerning issues of validity or as being procedural in nature.

Staudinger, Article 39, para. 49; Burghard Piltz, *Internationales Kaufrecht*, 2nd ed. (Munich: C.H. Beck, 2008), paras. 5–65; Schwenzer, 19 *Pace Int'l L. Rev.* 103, 116 (2007).

[66] Martin Karollus, "UN-KR: Anwendungsbereich, Holzhandelsusancen, Mängelrüge," *JBl* 318, 321 et seq. (1999); Ernst Kramer, "Rechtzeitige Untersuchung und Mängelanzeige bei Sachmängeln nach Article 38 und 39 UN-Kaufrecht: Eine Zwischenbilanz," in *Beiträge zum Unternehmensrecht: Festschrift für Hans-Georg Koppensteiner zum 65. Geburtstag* (ed. E. Kramer et al.) (Vienna: Orac, 2001), 617, 627 et seq.; Magnus in *Staudinger*, Article 39, para. 49. See also Schwenzer, 19 *Pace Int'l L. Rev.* 103, 116 (2007); Schwenzer, 7 *EJLR* 353, 361 (2005).

[67] CISG-AC, "Opinion No. 6, Calculation of Damages under CISG Article 74" (Spring 2006, Rapporteur: John Gotanda), available at http://www.cisgac.com/default.php?ipkCat=128&ifkCat=148&sid=148 (last accessed October 25, 2013), Comments 2.5. and 9.5.; Susanne V. Cook, "The U.N. Convention on Contracts for the International Sale of Goods: A Mandate to Abandon Legal Ethnocentricity," 16 *J.L. & Commerce* 257 et seq. (1997); DiMatteo et al., 24 *Nw. J. Int'l L. & Bus.* 299, 420 (2004); Ferrari, *Internationales Handelsrecht*, 8, 14 (2009). See also Schwenzer in Schlechtriem and Schwenzer, *Commentary*, Article 74, para. 1.

[68] CISG-AC, "Opinion No. 7, Exemption of Liability for Damages under Article 79 of the CISG" (October 12, 2007, Rapporteur: Alejandro Garro), available at http://www.cisgac.com/default.php?ipkCat=128&ifkCat=148&sid=169 (last accessed June 6, 2013), Comment 26; Flechtner, "Article 79," 1, 29, 31; Honnold and Flechtner, *Uniform Law*, Article 79, para. 427; Joseph M. Lookofsky and Harry M. Flechtner, "Nominating Manfred Forberich: The Worst CISG Decision in 25 Years?," 9 *VJ Int'l Com. & Arb.* 199, 202 et seq. (2005). See also Schwenzer in Schlechtriem and Schwenzer, *Commentary*, Article 79, para. 1.

[69] CISG-AC, "Opinion No. 3, Parol Evidence Rule, Plain Meaning Rule, Contractual Merger Clause and the CISG," (October 23, 2004, Rapporteur: Richard Hyland), available at http://www.cisgac.com/default.php?ipkCat=128&ifkCat=145&sid=145 (last accessed October 25, 2013), Comment 1.2.; Rod N. Andreason, "MCC-Marble Ceramic Center: The Parol Evidence Rule and Other Domestic Law under the Convention on Contracts for the International Sale of Goods," 24 *BYU L. Rev.* 351, 353 et seq. (1999); Flechtner, 17 *J.L. & Commerce* 187, 201 (1998); Harry M. Flechtner, "More U.S. Decisions on the U.N. Sales Convention: Scope, Parol Evidence, 'Validity' and Reduction of Price Under Article 50," 50 *J.L. & Commerce* 153, 156 (1995); Lookofsky, *Understanding the CISG*, 42 et seq.; Marlyse McQuillen, "The Development of a Federal CISG Common Law in the U.S. Courts: Patterns of Interpretation and Citation," 61 *U. Miami L. Rev.* 509, 520 (2007); Paolo Torzilli, "The Aftermath of MCC-Marble: Is This the Death Knell for the Parol Evidence Rule?," 4 *St. John's L. Rev.* 843, 855 (2000). See also Schmidt-Kessel in Schlechtriem and Schwenzer, *Commentary*, Article 8, para. 33.

1. Concurring Domestic Law Remedies

A special form of homeward trend is the application of concurrent domestic law remedies.[70] The CISG and its uniform interpretation can be severely undermined in this way, too.[71] Again, American courts,[72] with the support of at least some U.S. scholars,[73] seem to be especially prone to this form of a homeward trend. The main device to circumvent the CISG seems to be negligent misrepresentation.[74] As negligent misrepresentation is conceived as sounding in tort it is not regarded as being excluded by the CISG – which allegedly only deals with the contractual obligations of the parties.[75] However, the mere fact that there is hardly any case in which a buyer complaining about nonconformity of the goods under a sales contract is not simultaneously relying on negligent misrepresentation shows how the two fields overlap. Allowing concurring domestic remedies undermines the CISG in a core area, namely, seller's liability for nonconformity of the goods. Unification is thus highly endangered. The best answer to this question is the one

[70] See the seminal article about this issue by Peter Schlechtriem, "The Borderland of Tort and Contract: Opening a New Frontier?," 21 *Cornell Int'l L.J.* 467 et seq. (1988). See also Franco Ferrari, "The Interaction between the United Nations Convention for the International Sale of Goods and Domestic Remedies," 71 *RabelsZ* 52, 70 et seq. (2007); Helen E. Hartnell, "Rousing the Sleeping Dog: The Validity Exception to the Convention on Contracts for the International Sale of Goods," 18 *Yale J. Int'l L.* 1, 72 (1993); Peter Huber, "Some Introductory Remarks on the CISG," *Internationales Handelsrecht* 228, 231 (2006); Joseph M. Lookofsky, "In Dubio pro Conventione? Some Thoughts about Opt-Outs, Computer Programs and Preemption under the 1980 Vienna Sales Convention (CISG)," 13 *Duke J. Comp. & Int'l L.* 263, 283 (2003); Joseph M. Lookofsky, "Loose Ends and Contorts in International Sales: Problems in the Harmonization of Private Law Rules," 39 *Am. J. Comp. L.* 403 et seq. (1991); Schwenzer and Hachem, 57 *Am. J. Comp. L.* 457, 470 (2009); Schwenzer, "Buyer's Remedies in the Case of Non-conforming Goods: Some Problems in a Core Area of the CISG," 416, 419.

[71] Hager, "Zur Auslegung des UN-Kaufrechts," 319, 320; Flechtner, "The CISG in U.S. Courts," 91, 97; Monica Kilian, "CISG and the Problem with Common Law Jurisdictions," 10 *Transnat'l L. & Pol'y* 217, 228 (2001); Lookofsky, 13 *Duke J. Comp. & Int'l L.* 263, 266 (2003); Schwenzer and Hachem, 57 *Am. J. Comp. L.* 457, 471 (2009); Schwenzer, "Buyer's Remedies in the Case of Non-conforming Goods: Some Problems in a Core Area of the CISG," 416, 421; Spagnolo, 10 *Mel. J. Int'l L.* 1, 6 (2009).

[72] *Usinor Industeel v. Leeco Steel Products, Inc.* 209 F. Supp. 2d 880 (N.D. IL 2002), CISG-online 1326; *Chicago Prime Packers, Inc. v. Northam Food Trading Co.* 320 F. Supp. 2d 702 (N.D. IL 2004), CISG-online 851; *Ajax Tool Works, Inc. v. Can-Eng Manufacturing Ltd.* 2003 U.S. Dist. LEXIS 1306 (N.D. IL 2003), CISG-online 772.

[73] Cuniberti, 39 *Vanderbilt J. Transnat'l L.* 1511, 1546 (2006); Gillette and Scott, 25 *Int'l Rev. L. & Econ.* 446, 447 (2005). See also the non-U.S. American scholars Peter Huber and Alastair Mullis, *The CISG: A New Textbook for Students and Practitioners* (Munich: Sellier, 2007), 26; Lookofsky, *Understanding the CISG*, 23.

[74] See *Sky Cast, Inc. v. Global Direct Distribution LLC* 2008 WL 754734 (E.D. KY 2008), CISG-online 1652; *Miami Valley Paper, LLC v. Lebbing Engineering & Consulting GmbH* 2006 WL 2924779 (S.D. OH 2006), CISG-online 1326; *Geneva Pharmaceuticals Tech. Corp. v. Barr Labs. Inc.* 201 F. Supp. 2d 236 (S.D. NY 2002), CISG-online 653. See also Honnold and Flechtner, *Uniform Law*, Article 5, para. 73; Lookofsky, *Understanding the CISG*, 25; Schwenzer in Schlechtriem and Schwenzer, *Commentary*, Article 35, para. 48; Schwenzer and Hachem, 57 *Am. J. Comp. L.* 457, 471 (2009); Schwenzer, "Buyer's Remedies in the Case of Non-conforming Goods: Some Problems in a Core Area of the CISG," 416, 420. For a basic description of the concept of negligent misrepresentation under the U.S.-American law, see Joseph M. Perillo, *Calamari and Perillo on Contracts*, 6th ed. (St. Paul: Thomson West, 2007), 336 et seq.

[75] *Viva Vino Import Corp. v. Franese Vini S.r.l.* 2000 U.S. Dist. LEXIS 12347 (E.D. PA 2000), CISG-online 675; Lookofsky, *Understanding the CISG*, 25. For further details, see Schwenzer and Hachem, 57 *Am. J. Comp. L.* 457, 471 (2009); Schwenzer, "Buyer's Remedies in the Case of Non-conforming Goods: Some Problems in a Core Area of the CISG," 416, 419.

already given by the late John Honnold,[76] that the CISG displaces any domestic rules – whether based in contract or tort – if the facts that invoke such rules are the same facts that invoke the CISG.[77] In 2009, this position was acknowledged by a U.S. District Court.[78] This is a promising move in the right direction.

2. Issues of Validity

A further field open to homeward trend is the question of validity.[79] According to CISG Article 4(2)(a), the CISG is not concerned with the validity of the contract and any of its clauses. There are numerous examples of court decisions relying on domestic concepts of validity, not realizing that the very term "validity" has to be interpreted autonomously.[80] This may very well yield bizarre results. Thus, a U.S. District Court[81] has recently discussed a clause disclaiming liability for nonconformity pursuant to CISG Article 35(2) by using UCC Section 2–316(2). The court highlighted the word "merchantability" without having regard to the fact that this is not a concept under the CISG.[82]

3. The Substantive–Procedural Divide

Finally, drawing the line between so called "substantive" and "procedural" law issues often leads to familiar domestic law.[83] Procedural questions are not dealt with by the CISG.[84] Thus, it is questionable whether such issues as burden and standard of proof

---

[76] Honnold and Flechtner, *Uniform Law*, Article 35, para. 240.

[77] Schlechtriem, 21 *Cornell Int'l L.J.* 467, 475 (1988); Ferrari, 71 *RabelsZ* 52, 75 (2007); Schwenzer and Hachem, 57 *Am. J. Comp. L.* 457, 471 (2009); Schwenzer, "Buyer's Remedies in the Case of Non-conforming Goods: Some Problems in a Core Area of the CISG," 416, 421. See also Joseph M. Lookofsky, "CISG Case Commentary on Concurrent Remedies in *Pamesa v. Mendelson*," available at http://www.cisg. law.pace.edu/cisg/biblio/lookofsky19.html (last accessed October 25, 2013) (discussing an Israeli case).

[78] *Electrocraft Arkansas, Inc. v. Electric Motors, Ltd. et al.*, 2009 U.S. Dist. LEXIS 120183 (E.D. AR 2009), CISG-online 2045.

[79] For a detailed analysis of the problem, see Patrick C. Leyens, "CISG and Mistake: Uniform Law vs. Domestic Law, the Interpretative Challenge of Mistake and the Validity Loophole," *Rev. CISG* 3, 14 et seq. (2003–4). See also Ferrari, 71 *RabelsZ* 52, 59 et seq. (2007); Ferrari in Schlechtriem and Schwenzer, *Commentary*, Article 4, para. 16; Lookofsky, *Understanding the CISG*, 23; Schwenzer and Hachem in Schlechtriem and Schwenzer, *Commentary*, Article 4, para. 24; Schwenzer and Hachem, 57 *Am. J. Comp. L.* 457, 472 (2009).

[80] See, e.g., *Norfolk Southern Railway Company v. Power Source Supply, Inc.* 2008 U.S. Dist. LEXIS 56942 (W.D. PA 2008), CISG-online 1776; *Barbara Berry, S.A. de C.V. v. Ken M. Spooner Farms, Inc.* 2007 WL 4039341 (9th Cir. 2007), CISG-online 1603; *Geneva Pharmaceuticals Tech. Corp. v. Barr Labs. Inc.*, 201 F. Supp. 2d 236 (S.D. NY 2002), CISG-online 653. See also Flechtner, 50 *J.L. & Commerce* 153, 165 (1995); Ferrari in Schlechtriem and Schwenzer, *Commentary*, Article 4, para. 16; Schwenzer and Hachem, 57 *Am. J. Comp. L.* 457, 472 (2009). Contra, Lookofsky, *Understanding the CISG*, 22.

[81] *Norfolk Southern Railway Company v. Power Source Supply, Inc.* 2008 U.S. Dist. LEXIS 56942 (W.D. PA 2008), CISG-online 1776.

[82] See Honnold and Flechtner, *Uniform Law*, Article 35, para. 225.

[83] Id., Article 4, para. 70.1; Stefan Kröll, "Selected Problems Concerning the CISG's Scope of Application," 25 *J.L. & Commerce* 39, 47 (2005); Schwenzer and Hachem, in Schlechtriem and Schwenzer, *Commentary*, Article 4, para. 24.

[84] Honnold and Flechtner, *Uniform Law*, Article 4, para. 70.1; Schwenzer and Hachem in Schlechtriem and Schwenzer, *Commentary*, Article 4, para. 24; Kurt Siehr in *Kommentar zum UN-Kaufrecht*, Article 4, para. 29 (ed. Honsell) (Berlin: Springer, 1997).

(which may often decide the outcome of a case) need to be decided autonomously.[85] Similarly, compensation for legal costs has also been given considerable attention.[86]

Although the view that national conceptions of drawing the line between procedural and substantive law cannot be decisive in applying the CISG has become more and more accepted, there are still those who advocate the necessity of relying on this distinction.[87] The modern trend that regards such a distinction as being outdated and unproductive[88] is too often discarded by some courts. Leaving questions such as burden and standard of proof to domestic law is nothing more than a clear expression of homeward trend.

III. Reasons for the Homeward Trend

Why are courts prone to fall back on their own domestic law? What are the reasons that impede the uniform interpretation of the CISG called for in its Article 7(1)?

A. *Lack of Knowledge*

The first and probably the most important reason for the deplorable application of the CISG by national courts seems to be sheer lack of knowledge.[89] Although the CISG itself should by now be commonly known to exist, the degree of familiarity with the CISG is still very low. This seems to be reinforced by prejudices being nourished especially

---

[85] This is a highly debated issue; see CISG-AC, "Opinion No. 6," Comment 2. For scholars in favor of the CISG governing the burden of proof in a standard sense, see, e.g., Wilhelm-Albrecht Achilles, *Kommentar zum UN-Kaufrechtsübereinkommen (CISG)* (Berlin: Hermann Luchterhand, 2000), Article 4, para. 15; Bernard Audit, *La vente internationale de marchandises, Convention des Nations-Unies du 11 avril 1980* (Paris: L.G.D.J., 1990), 100; Heuzé, *La vente internationale de marchandises*, 260; Kröll, 25 *J.L. & Commerce* 39, 47 (2005); Magnus in *Staudinger*, Article 4, para. 63; Karl H. Neumayer and Catherine Ming in *Convention de Vienne sur les contrats de vente internationale de marchandises* (ed. F. Dessemontet) (Lausanne: CEDIDAC, 1993), Commentaire, Article 4, para. 13; Ferrari in Schlechtriem and Schwenzer, *Commentary*, Article 4, para. 8; Schwenzer and Hachem in Schlechtriem and Schwenzer, *Commentary*, Article 4, paras. 25 et seq.; Anna Veneziano, "Mancanza di conformità delle merci ed onere della prova nella vendita internazionale: un esempio di interpretazione autonoma del diritto uniforme alla luce dei precedenti stranieri," *Dir. com. int.* 509, 515 (2001). See also Oberlandesgericht Köln, January 14, 2008, CISG-online 1730; Schweizerisches Bundesgericht, November 13, 2003, CISG-online 840. But see Honnold and Flechtner, *Uniform Law*, Article 4, para. 70.1.

[86] Harry M. Flechtner, "Recovering Attorneys' Fees as Damages under the U.N. Sales Convention: A Case Study on the New International Commercial Practice and the Role of Case Law in CISG Jurisprudence, with Comments on *Zapata Hermanos Sucesores, S.A. v. Hearthside Baking Co.*," 22 *Nw. J. Int'l L. & Bus.* 121, 127 (2002); Troy Keily, "How Does the Cookie Crumble? Legal Costs under a Uniform Interpretation of the United Nations Convention on Contracts for the International Sale of Goods," 1 *Nordic J. of Commercial L.* 1, 2 (2003); Joseph M. Lookofsky and Harry M. Flechtner, "Zapata Retold: Attorneys' Fees Are (Still) Not Governed by the CISG," 26 *J.L. & Commerce* 1, 2 et seq. (2006); Joseph M. Lookofsky and Harry M. Flechtner, "Viva Zapata! American Procedure and CISG Substance in a U.S. Circuit Court of Appeal," 7 *VJ Int'l Com. & Arb.* 93, 94 (2003); Ingeborg Schwenzer, "Rechtsverfolgungskosten als Schaden?," in *Mélanges en l'honneur de Pierre Tercier* (ed. P. Gauch et al.) (Zurich: Schulthess, 2008), 417, 422 et seq.

[87] Chiara Giovannucci Orlandi, "Procedural Law Issues and Law Conventions," 5 *Uniform L. Rev.* 23, 25 (2000).

[88] See CISG-AC, "Opinion No. 6," Comment 5.2.

[89] Andersen, 24 *J.L. & Commerce* 159, 177 (2005). For a detailed analysis of the reasons for the lack of familiarity with the CISG, see Spagnolo, 13 *VJ Int'l Com. & Arb.* 135, 137 (2009); Spagnolo, 13 *VJ Int'l Com. & Arb.* 157 (2009).

by U.S. scholars. There are numerous articles in American law journals that blame the CISG for being unpredictable, imprecise, and not suited for the needs of (American) international trade; in short, being clearly inferior to the Uniform Commercial Code.[90]

However, it is not only a lack of knowledge of the CISG that is a problem; it is even worse, a lack of knowledge that there can ever be another dogmatic solution to a legal problem than the one that a person has learned and practiced for a long time. Can many common law lawyers imagine a legal system without the doctrine of consideration? How difficult is it for a German lawyer to acknowledge that special abstract rules for legal acts, apart from those for contracts, may be unnecessary and simply stem from historical whimsicalities? Will a French lawyer easily find a substitute concept for that of *cause*? Thus, simply speaking, for many lawyers, counsels, and judges, there is no alternative legal world other than the one they already know. Having this in mind it is perfectly understandable why – if the CISG is applied at all – this is mostly done through domestic lenses. Many of those applying the CISG just do not possess alternative perspectives.

B. *Language Barriers*

A truly international application and interpretation is frustrated by language barriers. This applies despite the fact that nowadays many CISG court decisions and arbitral awards are translated into English and are freely accessible via websites around the globe.[91] More and more scholarly articles are published in English and also made available on websites.[92] The reasons why these materials still are not widely utilized differ for the English-speaking legal community on the one side and the rest of the world on the other.

Although, at least for international transactional lawyers, English has become the *lingua franca*, this does not hold true for many if not most domestic judges in French, Germanic, and Ibero-American legal systems. Even if English as a language may be widely spoken in these societies – at least in academic circles – the command of legal English is still very low. Only very recently are some law classes taught in English. With more classes taught in law schools in English this picture may hopefully change in a couple of years. Furthermore, in many countries, judges are working under severe time constraints. When dealing with their daily domestic cases they consult only one – if at all – of certain handbooks and commentaries. They exclusively rely on one domestic database that is provided by the justice administration. Expecting these judges to consider foreign decisions and to access foreign databases for the few, if any, CISG cases they are

---

[90] Kathryn S. Cohen, "Achieving a Uniform Law Governing International Sales: Conforming the Damages Provisions of the United Nations Convention on Contracts for the International Sale of Goods and the Uniform Commercial Code," 26 *U. Pa. J. Int'l Econ. L.* 601, 610 (2005); Cuniberti, 39 *Vanderbilt J. Transnat'l L.* 1511, 1549 (2006); Gillette and Scott, 25 *Int'l Rev. L. & Econ.* 446, 479 (2005), suggesting a "competition for laws," where the CISG "ultimately will lose out in competition with alternative legal regimes." See also Paul B. Stephan, "The Futility of Unification and Harmonization in International Commercial Law," 39 *Va. J. Int'l L.* 743, 779 (1999).

[91] See the database of the Pace Law School, available at http://www.cisg.law.pace.edu (last accessed October 25, 2013). Furthermore, see http://www.cisg-online.ch and http://www.unilex.info (both last accessed October 25, 2013).

[92] See the extensive online collection of scholarly writings (currently more than 1,400 texts) at the Pace database, available at http://www.cisg.law.pace.edu/cisg/biblio/bib2.html (last accessed October 25, 2013).

confronted with is asking too much of them. They just do not have the necessary time to do so, let alone to learn doing it on the job.

For English-speaking lawyers, the picture is different. They may not rely on the excuse of not being able to access relevant materials in their own language. Many common law lawyers are very happy with the common law and just do not want to have it substituted by any set of rules with which they are not familiar. This seems to be especially the case for parties, lawyers, and judges in Australia and New Zealand. Furthermore, many common law lawyers are not accustomed to consulting case law outside their own jurisdiction. And – one may add – even if they did so they might not understand, for example, a translated decision of the Supreme Court of France because they are not familiar with the peculiarities of French judicial decisions.

C. *Relevant Cases Are Arbitrated*

The number of international sales law cases being litigated in domestic courts should not be overestimated. Having a closer look at the facts of the cases being decided by domestic courts reveals the relative insignificance of these cases, at least from a global trade perspective.[93] A random look at fifty recent cases from all over the world reveals the following picture. The parties involved in these cases are typically small- to medium-sized businesses. In a majority of cases the goods sold are agricultural products – fruits,[94] trees,[95] cherries,[96] potatoes,[97] rice,[98] watermelons,[99] and poppy seeds,[100] as well as other food-stuffs such as beer,[101] crabs,[102] and shrimps.[103] A second group comprises textile products, including yarn,[104] leather,[105] shoes,[106] and the like, as well as small- and medium-sized machinery such as heating equipment,[107] motor vehicle parts,[108] or locomotives.[109]

---

[93] For a detailed analysis about the commonness of application of the CISG in international commercial arbitration, see Loukas Mistelis, "CISG and Arbitration," in Janssen and Meyer, *CISG Methodology*, 375, 388.

[94] Handelsgericht des Kantons Aargau, November 26, 2008, CISG-online 1739.

[95] Landgericht Bamberg, October 23, 2006, CISG-online 1400.

[96] *Hannaford (trading as Torrens Valley Orchards) v. Australian Farmlink Pty Ltd.*, [2008] FCA 1591 (October 24, 2008), CISG-online 1743.

[97] Cour de Cassation, September 16, 2008, CISG-online 1821; Rechtbank Maastricht, July 9, 2008, CISG-online 1748; Oberlandesgericht Köln, August 14, 2006, CISG-online 1405.

[98] *The Rice Corporation v. Grain Board of Iraq*, 2008 U.S. Dist. LEXIS 40204 (E.D. CA 2008), CISG-online 1770.

[99] Rechtbank Breda, January 16, 2009, CISG-online 1789.

[100] Oberster Gerichtshof, May 8, 2008, CISG-online 1784.

[101] Oberlandesgericht Brandenburg, November 18, 2008, CISG-online 1734.

[102] Rechtbank Rotterdam, November 5, 2008, CISG-online 1817.

[103] Oberlandesgericht Rostock, September 25, 2002, CISG-online 671.

[104] Oberlandesgericht Düsseldorf, April 21, 2004, CISG-online 913.

[105] Corta Suprema Chile, September 22, 2008, CISG-online 1787.

[106] Tribunale di Forli, December 11, 2008, CISG-online 1788.

[107] *Brown & Root Services Corp. v. Aerotech Herman Nelson Inc.* 2002 MBQB 229 [Court of Queen's Bench of Manitoba], CISG-online 1327.

[108] *Valeo Sistemas Electricos S.A. de C.V. v. CIF Licensing, LLC d/b/a GE Licensing v. Stmicroelectronic* 2008 U.S. Dist. LEXIS 53058 (D. DE 2008), CISG-online 1775.

[109] *Norfolk Southern Railway Company v. Power Source Supply, Inc.* 2008 U.S. Dist. LEXIS 56942 (W.D. PA 2008), CISG-online 1776.

Most notable are the respective amounts in controversy. The vast majority of these cases involved amounts well under one hundred thousand dollars;[110] in only one of the cases the claim amounted to more than one million dollars.[111]

The reason why only more or less marginal cases are treated by domestic courts, thus keeping the overall number and possible experiences with CISG cases relatively low, is self-evident; sophisticated parties with contract values well above one million USD regularly submit their disputes to arbitration and not to domestic courts. Additionally, only sophisticated parties have the money necessary to employ sophisticated lawyers knowledgeable in international trade. This is a vicious circle from which escape hardly seems possible.

IV. Homeward Trend: How Can it be Changed?

The reasons given for homeward trend decisions inherently show ways to overcome such reasoning.

A. *Comparative Research*

First, there must be a quest for truly comparative research in the field of the law of sales in general.[112] This has to be emphasized despite the fact that the literature on the CISG is abundant. The international sales law bibliography counts more than 8,000 references.[113] However, a closer look reveals that many – too many – publications circle around questions of the scope of applicability, gap filling, uniform interpretation, and methodology, in general often culminating in the lamentation that uniformity has not been achieved or is again jeopardized.

Thorough comparative research of genuine sales law issues is lacking to a great extent. More research is needed that applies the functional approach and embraces more than just one or two legal systems and comparing them to the CISG. Since the times of Rabel's seminal work on *Das Recht des Warenkaufs*,[114] the two-volume book on sale of goods that established the basis for all sales law unification more than fifty years ago, for a long time there has been no such endeavor of that magnitude until the *Global Sales and Contract Law*.[115] The requirement established by Article 7(1) CISG that solutions are to be found that are acceptable in different legal systems with different legal traditions

---

[110] One of the rare cases where the amount in dispute exceeded 100,000 USD is Schweizerisches Bundesgericht, December 16, 2008, CISG-online 1800.

[111] Appellationsgericht Basel-Stadt, September 26, 2008, CISG-online 1732.

[112] The challenge of producing a comprehensive work on sales law encompassing all legal systems and taking into account present-day problems has been resumed by the Global Sales Law Project and was published in 2012, Ingeborg Schwenzer, Pascal Hachem, and Christopher Kee, *Global Sales and Contract Law* (Oxford: Oxford University Press, 2012), see also http://www.globalsaleslaw.org (last accessed October 25, 2013).

[113] This bibliography contains most of the references to scholarly writing related to the CISG and is available at http://www.cisg.law.pace.edu/cisg/biblio/biblio.html (last accessed October 25, 2013).

[114] Ernst Rabel, *Das Recht des Warenkaufs: eine Rechtsvergleichende Darstellung* (Berlin: De Gruyter, 1956/73).

[115] Ingeborg Schwenzer, Pascal Hachem, and Christopher Kee, *Global Sales and Contract Law*.

requires carving out common ground in the field of international trade law.[116] This has recently become particularly visible with regard to the general understanding of the law of damages where the principles underlying this area of the law have moved to the center of academic debate around the world and new solutions to new challenges have been developed.[117] Furthermore, in order to solve the respective issues under the CISG, detailed research is needed on the substantive–procedure divide in the different legal systems involved; questions of validity of unfair contract terms should be decided under the CISG once a clear overview of the different approaches by domestic legal systems in controlling contract terms has been established. The argument that it was not the intention of the drafters of the CISG to cover certain issues is a threat to uniform application and dooms the CISG to insignificance.

B. *Language*

The next step must be to address the problem of language barriers. Although this basic comparative research has to be carried out in English in order to be accessible to the entire CISG community, there must be more translations into other languages. The best way to do this seems to be via comprehensive commentaries that discuss relevant CISG provisions from a comparative perspective, thus enabling the domestic practitioner to understand how to reconcile his or her domestic perspective with the uniform solution.[118] Only a few commentaries currently available on the market are living up to these high standards. For example, most of the various German commentaries more or less content themselves with references to other German sources. The same applies to the existing French and U.S. commentaries.

C. *CISG as Genuine Contract Law*

The CISG has yet to arrive at the core of contract law. Although it has been pointed out that some textbooks on contract law in the United States refer to the CISG in one way or the other,[119] it is obvious that there are not many leading contract scholars in their respective countries who are dedicated to the CISG. In many countries, the CISG is left to lecturers or scholars engaged in other specialized (and often optional) subjects such as International Business Transactions or Conflicts of Laws. Frequently these academics are excellent scholars but the relative importance of the subjects they teach does not provide them with the profiles they deserve. On the other side, when teaching contracts, many eminent scholars focus on the hardcore dogmatic domestic issues such as contract formation, consideration, and mistake, and do not ever even touch on the domestic law of remedies.

---

[116] Schwenzer and Hachem, in Schlechtriem and Schwenzer, *Commentary*, Article 7, para. 24.
[117] For further references, see Ingeborg Schwenzer and Pascal Hachem, "The Scope of the CISG Provisions on Damages," in *Contract Damages: Domestic and International Perspectives* (ed. D. Saidov and R. Cunnington) (Oxford: Hart, 2008), 91.
[118] See Schlechtriem and Schwenzer, *Commentary*; Schlechtriem and Schwenzer, *Comentario sobre la convencion de las naciones unidas sobre los contratos de compraventa internacional de mercaderias* (ed. I. Schwenzer and E. Munoz) (Cizur Menor: Thomson Reuters, 2011). Translations into Mandarin, Turkish, Russian, Portuguese and French are currently prepared.
[119] Reimann, 71 *RabelsZ* 115, 120 (2007).

D. *CISG in Education and Legal Practice*

This leads us directly to the role of the CISG in legal education. Whether a substantive number of students study the CISG exclusively depends on whether it is part of a final exam – if such a final exam exists at all.[120] Setting the CISG as a subject for a bar exam has proven to be very effective. At this stage of their careers, young lawyers are better able to acknowledge the considerable advantages of the CISG over their domestic sales law, and are close enough to real world practice such that they will not forget those advantages in their law practice. Bar associations must be persuaded to support the dissemination of knowledge of the CISG in this way. Still, it will certainly take quite a while before genuine familiarity with the CISG is achieved in young lawyers in a significant number of countries.

Thus, it is important to make the CISG a subject of continuing education of lawyers. Much dread among practitioners could be removed by teaching them contract drafting and litigating under the CISG. Furthermore, they should be told that not considering the CISG in advising a client either in contracting or in litigating might lead to a case of professional liability. If nothing else, at least the threat of liability might spur some further interest in the CISG.

V. Conclusion

Homeward trend decisions are a phenomenon that has to be taken seriously in jeopardizing uniformity in international sales law. Although some countries are more prone to homeward trend bias than others, it can be found among all member states of the CISG. The reasons for the homeward trend include lack of knowledge, language barriers, and the fact that disputes involving large damage claims often are resolved in private arbitration. Overcoming homeward trend necessitates genuine comparative research with corresponding translations in different languages and, most of all, the CISG needs to be taken seriously by contract scholars and taught in law schools and in continuing legal education. While overcoming the homeward trend in applying and interpreting the CISG is an important and necessary step towards unification of international sales law, harmonization of contract law stays incomplete if it is not enhanced further. This is why Switzerland called upon UNCITRAL in 2012 to embark upon the question of whether future work in the area of globally harmonizing general contract law is desirable and feasible.[121]

---

[120] Corinne Widmer and Pascal Hachem, "Switzerland," in *The CISG and Its Impact on National Legal Systems* (ed. F. Ferrari) (Munich: Sellier, 2008), 281, 288.

[121] United Nations Commission on International Trade Law, "Possible future work in the area of international contract law: Proposal by Switzerland on possible future work by UNCITRAL in the area of international contract law," 45th session, New York, June 25 – July 6, 2012, A/CN.9/758 (May 8, 2012), available at www.uncitral.org/uncitral/commission/sessions/45th.html (last accessed October 25, 2013)).

9   Good Faith Principle: *Vexata Quaestio*

Francesco G. Mazzotta

I. Introduction

This contribution deals with the concept of good faith as understood in common and civil law jurisdictions and its meaning within the United Nations Convention on Contracts for the International Sale of Goods (CISG). The chapter will consider the concept as understood in the United States and, to a lesser extent, in the United Kingdom. The chapter will also analyze the role of good faith analysis in civil law systems, such as Italy and Germany. Against this background, the chapter reviews the legislative history of CISG Article 7 and its current application by the courts in the United States, Italy, and Germany. The analysis will show that "good faith" escapes any meaningful definition. Finally, definitional problems aside, it is important to maintain the distinction between "good faith" and "equity."

II. Domestic Meanings of Good Faith

This part briefly reviews the role of the principle of good faith in the legal systems of the United States, United Kingdom, Italy, and Germany.

A. *United States*

In 1766, Lord Mansfield referred to good faith as "[t]he governing principle . . . applicable to all contracts and dealings." However, the principle never took root in England. The recognition of the doctrine of good faith in common law countries was mostly inspired by legal developments in the United States. It can be traced to Professor Karl Llewellyn, Chief Reporter for the Uniform Commercial Code (UCC):

> Llewellyn, who had taught at Leipzig, was inspired not by Mansfield, but by the *Treu and Glauben* provision of the German Civil Code. Although the common law doctrine of a few states – notably, New York and California – mentioned good faith before the adoption of the UCC, it was not until good faith was included in the Code that the doctrine reached national prominence.

> Over fifty Code sections specifically mention good faith. Section 1–203 of the UCC provides for a general obligation of good faith. It states that "[e]very contract or duty within this Act imposes an obligation of good faith in its performance or enforcement." Section 1–201(19) contains the Code's general definition of good faith. It describes good faith as "honesty in fact in the conduct or transaction concerned." Some of the

Code's substantive articles, however, contain variant definitions. Article 2 (sale of goods) provides that in the case of a merchant good faith means not only "honesty in fact," but also "the observance of reasonable standards of fair dealing in the trade."[1]

It should be noted, however, that the meaning of "good faith," although substantially similar throughout the United States, it is not necessarily identical. For example, consider the following comparison between New York and Pennsylvania. Section 1–201 of the New York UCC reads as follows: "'Good faith' means honesty in fact in the conduct or transaction concerned."[2] The Official Comment, in relevant part, reads as follows:

> "Good faith," whenever it is used in the Code, means at least what is here stated. In certain Articles, by specific provision, additional requirements are made applicable. See, e.g., §§ 2–103(1)(b), 7–404. To illustrate, in the Article on Sales, § 2–103, good faith is expressly defined as including in the case of a merchant observance of reasonable commercial standards of fair dealing in the trade, so that throughout that Article wherever a merchant appears in the case an inquiry into his observance of such standards is necessary to determine his good faith.[3]

The Official Comment to the Section to 1–203 (general obligation of good faith in all UCC contracts) states:

> This section sets forth a basic principle running throughout this Act. The principle involved is that in commercial transactions good faith is required in the performance and enforcement of all agreements or duties. Particular applications of this general principle appear in specific provisions of the Act such as the option to accelerate at will (§ 1–208), the right to cure a defective delivery of goods (§ 2–508), the duty of a merchant buyer who has rejected goods to effect salvage operations (§ 2–603), substituted performance (§ 2–614), and failure of presupposed conditions (§ 2–615). The concept, however, is broader than any of these illustrations and applies generally, as stated in this section, to the performance or enforcement of every contract or duty within this Act. It is further implemented by § 1–205 on course of dealing and usage of trade. This section does not support an independent cause of action for failure to perform or enforce in good faith. Rather, this section means that a failure to perform or enforce, in good faith, a specific duty or obligation under the contract, constitutes a breach of that contract or make unavailable, under the particular circumstances, a remedial right or power. This distinction makes it clear that the doctrine of good faith merely directs a court towards interpreting contracts within the commercial context in which they are created, performed, and enforced, and does not create a separate duty of fairness and reasonableness which can be independently breached.[4]

---

[1] E. Allan Farnsworth, "Duties of Good Faith and Fair Dealing under the Unidroit Principles, Relevant International Conventions, and National Laws," 51–2, available at http://tldb.unikoeln.de/php/pub_show_document.php?pubdocid=122100. See also John O. Honnold, *Uniform Law for International Sales under the 1980 United Nations Convention* 199–24, 4th ed. (The Netherlands: Kluwer Law International, 2009); Robert S. Summers, "The Conceptualisation of Good Faith in American Contract Law: A General Account," in *Good Faith in European Contract Law* (ed. R. Zimmermann and S. Whittaker) (New York: Cambridge University Press, 2008), 119.

[2] New York UCC §1–201 (McKinney 2001).

[3] Id., at Official Comment; see also UCC §1–203, Official Comment (good faith as applied to merchants).

[4] See UCC §1–203, Official Comment. Several decisions emphasize that, under New York law, "a duty of good faith is implied in every contract [not just UCC contracts]." See, e.g., *Medinol Ltd. v. Boston Scientific Corp.*, 346 F. Supp. 2d 575, 618 (S.D. N.Y. 2004) (although it "does not give rise to an independent cause of action"); *Gain Traders, Inc. v. Citibank N.A.*, 960 F. Supp. 784, 792 (S.D. N.Y. 1997).

As noted above, in New York, there are two definitions of good faith – a narrower, subjective version found in Section 1–203 ("honesty in fact") and a broader, subjective–objective version found in Section 2–103 ("honesty in fact"; "observance of reasonable commercial standards"). The commercial reasonableness standard of Section 2–103 looks to the objectivity provided by the ever-changing standards and practices found in the complex world of business to determine if a party has acted in good faith: "The Code leaves many definitions open-ended in recognition of the multiplicity of situations the terms must conform to, and to give courts the ability to blend their understanding of certain aspects of commercial transactions with the realities of a constantly evolving market place."[5]

In Pennsylvania, good faith is defined as "honesty in fact and the observance of reasonable commercial standards of fair dealing."[6] The Comment to Section 1201, in relevant part reads as follows:

> Former Section 1–201(19) defined "good faith" simply as honesty in fact; the definition contained no element of commercial reasonableness. Initially, that definition applied throughout the Code with only one exception. Former Section 2–103(1)(b) provided that, in that Article, "'good faith' in the case of a merchant means honesty in fact and the observance of reasonable commercial standards of fair dealing in the trade." Over time, however, amendments to the Uniform Commercial Code brought the Article 2 merchant concept of good faith (subjective honesty and objective commercial reasonableness) into other Articles. First, Article 2A explicitly incorporated the Article 2 standard.[7] Then, other Articles broadened the applicability of that standard [by adopting the two elements of honesty in fact and commercial reasonableness] for all parties rather than just for merchants.[8] Finally, Articles 2 and 2A were amended so as to apply the standard to non-merchants as well as merchants.[9] Only revised Article 5 defines "good faith" solely in terms of subjective honesty.

> Thus, the definition of "good faith" in this section merely confirms what has been the case for a number of years as Articles of the UCC have been amended or revised – the obligation of "good faith," [is defined] as including both the subjective element of honesty in fact and the objective element of the observance of reasonable commercial standards of fair dealing (other than Article 5).[10]

The next definitional issue is the meaning of "fair dealing"? How does fair dealing relate to "reasonable commercial standards"?

> As noted above, the definition of "good faith" in this section requires not only honesty in fact but also "observance of reasonable commercial standards of fair dealing." Although "fair dealing" is a broad term that must be defined in context, it is clear that it is concerned with the fairness of conduct rather than the care with which an act is performed. This is an entirely different concept than whether a party exercised ordinary care in conducting a transaction. Both concepts are to be determined in the light

---

[5] Roslyn K. Myers, West's McKinney's Forms Uniform Commercial Code, §1–203.
[6] 13 Pa. C.S.A. §1201 (2008).
[7] See Section 2A-103(7).
[8] See, e.g., Sections 3-103(a)(4) (negotiable instruments), 4A-105(a)(6) (bank transfers), 7-102(a)(6) (documents of title), 8-102(a)(10) (investment securities), and 9-102(a)(43) (secured transactions).
[9] See Sections 2-103(1)(j), 2A-103(1)(m).
[10] *13 Pa. C.S.A.* §1201, cmt. 20.

of reasonable commercial standards, but those standards in each case are directed to different aspects of commercial conduct. See e.g., Sections 3–103(a)(9) and 4–104(c) and Comment 4 to Section 3–103.[11]

It should be noted that former Section 1–203, now Section 1304, which reads as follows: "Every contract or duty within this title imposes an obligation of good faith in its performance and enforcement."[12]

However, what makes "good faith" even more unfit for a definition is the courts' reliance, in some instances, upon the *Restatement (Second) of Contracts*. American *Restatements of Law* in the American legal tradition is not law – it is not statutory law or part of the common law; it does not even act as a description of the common law of contracts in each state.[13]

> Instead, a Restatement represents an attempt by the American Law Institute, a private organisation of scholars, judges and practitioners, to formulate with some precision the leading rules and principles in major fields of American Law, "in the aggregate," so to speak, as if the United States consisted of only one, rather than fifty, state jurisdictions. Where the actual legal rules and principles in the various states are in conflict, or are not well developed, the Restatements frequently purport to formulate rules and principles that represent "the better view."[14]

Good faith, as defined by the UCC, is not identical to the definition provided in the Restatement. Section 205 of the *Restatement Second*, in relevant part, provides as follows:

a. *Meanings of "good faith."* Good faith is defined in Uniform Commercial Code § 1–201(19) as "honesty in fact in the conduct or transaction concerned." In the case of a merchant, Uniform Commercial Code § 2–103(1)(b) provides that good faith means "honesty in fact and the observance of reasonable commercial standards of fair dealing in the trade." The phrase "good faith" is used in a variety of contexts, and its meaning varies somewhat with the context. Good faith performance or enforcement of a contract emphasizes faithfulness to an agreed common purpose and consistency with the justified expectations of the other party; it excludes a variety of types of conduct characterized as involving "bad faith" because they violate community standards of decency, fairness or reasonableness. The appropriate remedy for a breach of the duty of good faith also varies with the circumstances.

b. *Good faith purchase.* In many situations, a good faith purchaser of property for value can acquire better rights in the property than his transferor had.[15] In this context, "good faith" focuses on the honesty of the purchaser, as distinguished from his care or negligence. Particularly in the law of negotiable instruments, inquiry may be limited to "good faith" under what has been called "the rule of the pure heart and the empty head." When diligence or inquiry is a condition of the purchaser's right, it is said that good faith is not enough. This focus on honesty is appropriate to cases of good faith purchase; it is less so in cases of good faith performance.

---

[11] Id.

[12] Id., at §1304.

[13] Summers, "The Conceptualisation of Good Faith," 120.

[14] Id.

[15] See, e.g., UCC §342.

c. *Good faith in negotiation*. Bad faith in negotiation, although not within the scope of this Section, may be subject to sanctions. Particular forms of bad faith in bargaining are the subjects of rules as to capacity to contract, mutual assent and consideration and of rules as to invalidating causes such as fraud and duress.[16] Moreover, remedies for bad faith in the absence of agreement are found in the law of torts or restitution.[17] In cases of negotiation for modification of an existing contractual relationship, the rule stated in this Section may overlap with more specific rules requiring negotiation in good faith.[18]

d. *Good faith performance*. Subterfuges and evasions violate the obligation of good faith in performance even though the actor believes his conduct to be justified. But the obligation goes further: bad faith may be overt or may consist of inaction, and fair dealing may require more than honesty. [T]he following types are among those which have been recognized in judicial decisions: evasion of the spirit of the bargain, lack of diligence and slacking off, willful rendering of imperfect performance, abuse of a power to specify terms, and interference with or failure to cooperate in the other party's performance.

e. *Good faith in enforcement*. The obligation of good faith and fair dealing extends to the assertion, settlement and litigation of contract claims and defenses.[19] The obligation is violated by dishonest conduct such as conjuring up a pretended dispute, asserting an interpretation contrary to one's own understanding, or falsification of facts. It also extends to dealing, which is candid but unfair, such as taking advantage of the necessitous circumstances of the other party to extort a modification of a contract for the sale of goods without legitimate commercial reason.[20] Other types of violation have been recognized in judicial decisions: harassing demands for assurances of performance, rejection of performance for unstated reasons, willful failure to mitigate damages, and abuse of a power to determine compliance or to terminate the contract.[21]

B. *United Kingdom*

There is not a general concept of good faith in English law.[22] Good faith is required in particular situations only.[23] For example, "the tort of breach of confidence protects

---

[16] See, e.g., §§90 and 208.

[17] For examples of a statutory duty to bargain in good faith, see, e.g., National Labor Relations Act §8(d) and the Federal Truth in Lending Act.

[18] See §§73 and 89; Uniform Commercial Code §2-209 and Comment.

[19] See, e.g., §§73 and 89.

[20] See Uniform Commercial Code §2-209, Comment 2.

[21] Restatement (Second) of Contracts §205 (1981). There are a number of conceptualizations of good faith in American scholarly writings: (1) Professor Robert S. Summers (excluder analysis), (2) writings of Professor Steven J. Burton, and (3) writings of Professor E. Allan Farnsworth. For details about these conceptualizations, see Summers, "The Conceptualisation of Good Faith," 125–34; For a statutory duty of good faith in termination, see the federal Automobile Dealer's Day in Court Act, 15 U.S.C. §§1221–25 (1976).

[22] See generally Simon Whittaker and Reinhard Zimmermann, "Good Faith in European Contract Law: Surveying the Legal Landscape," in Zimmermann and Whittaker, *Good Faith*, 39–48.

[23] Barry Nicholas, "The United Kingdom and the Vienna Sales Convention: Another Case of Splendid Isolation?," available at http://www.cisg.law.pace.edu/cisg/biblio/nicholas3.html. See also Nathalie

confidential information acquired by the parties during their negotiations from exploitation after the breakdown of negotiations."[24] Another example is "found in the observance of fairness and equality in the tendering process leading to the award of a major construction contract."[25] One instance in which English law imposes a general duty of good faith is in connection with agency,[26] consumer contracts,[27] and insurance contracts (positive disclosure is required).[28]

English law does not recognize precontractual liability or "*culpa in contrahendo*."[29] It does not recognize that the negotiation of a contract by itself creates any sort of relational duty. English law takes the view that both parties are at risk until a contract is actually formed. Therefore, there is nothing wrong in a party that is conducting negotiations to arbitrarily break them off, even if it has brought the other party to the brink of the contract. There is also nothing wrong in a party conducting negotiations and failing to disclose that it is negotiating with multiple parties.[30]

C. *Italy*

There are four provisions of the Italian Civil Code that create a general duty of good faith.[31] First, Article 1175 requires debtors and creditors to act fairly in relationship to each other. Parties are allowed to advance their self-interests even if that might negatively affect the other party. However, they are precluded from harming the other party more than is necessary to reasonably look after their own interests. This duty not to harm relates only to the conduct that affects a legally recognized interest of the affected party.

Hofmann, "Interpretation Rules and Good Faith as Obstacles to the UK's Ratification of the CISG and to the Harmonization of Contract Law in Europe," 22 *Pace Int'l L. Rev.* 145, 162–5 (2010).

[24] John Felemegas, "The United Nations Convention on Contracts for the International Sale of Goods: Article 7 and Uniform Interpretation," *Pace Review of the Convention on Contracts for the International Sale of Goods (CISG)* (The Netherlands: Kluwer Law International, 2000–1), 115, 234, and accompanying text, available at http://www.cisg.law.pace.edu/cisg/biblio/felemegas.html.

[25] Id., at 235 and accompanying text.

[26] Id., text accompanying n. 250.

[27] Nicholas, "The United Kingdom and the Vienna Sales Convention."

[28] Roy Goode, "The Concept of 'Good Faith' in English Law," available at http://www.cisg.law.pace.edu/cisg/biblio/goode1.html.

[29] Similarly, *culpa in contrahendo* is not recognized in the United States. Professor Farnsworth noted, however, "[w]e do have a variety of other concepts that often serve as a substitute for good faith in precontractual relations (i.e., unjust enrichment, misrepresentation, and breach of a specific promise made during negotiations)." Farnsworth, "The Concept of 'Good Faith' in American Law." See also E. Allan Farnsworth, "Precontractual Liability and Preliminary Agreements: Fair Dealing and Failed Negotiations," 87 *Colum. L. Rev.* 217 (1987). Regarding the precontractual liability in general and under the CISG, see, e.g., Albert H. Kritzer, "Pre-Contract Formation," available at http://www.cisg.law.pace.edu/cisg/biblio/kritzer1.html.

[30] Goode, "The Concept of 'Good Faith' in English Law."

[31] Good faith is mentioned in several articles of the Italian Civil Code, in addition to the instances discussed here. See, e.g., Articles 534, 535, 936, 937, 938, 1147, 1153, 1155, 1159, 1162, 1358, 1415, 1416, 1445, and 1460. For a brief analysis of the concept of good faith under Italian law, see, e.g., Ivana Musio, "Breve analisi comparata sulla clausola generale della buona fede" (June 2010), 5–13, available at http://www.comparazionedirittocivile.it/prova/files/ncr_musio_buonafede.pdf; Nicola W. Palmieri, "Good Faith Disclosures during Precontractual Negotiations," 24 *Seton Hall L. Rev.* 70, 201–9 (1993). See generally *Commentario Breve al Codice Civile and Complemento Giurisprudenziale* (ed. G. Cian and A. Trabucchi) (Padova, 2008).

Article 1337 covers the negotiation and formation of contracts. Typical situations falling within the purview of Article 1337 include the unjustified breaking off of negotiations, failure to cooperate, and failure to disclose. However, because Article 1337 creates a general legal duty of good faith in the precontractual context, it might be relied upon in numerous scenarios.[32] A violation of Section 1337, in itself, does not render a contract void.[33] Article 1366 requires the good faith interpretation of contracts. The parties' intent is to be objectively determined to prevent giving effect to unilateral understandings or interpretations inconsistent with what a reasonable person would have understood. Good faith interpretation is used only if contractual provisions remain ambiguous as to the parties' intent and after the court has exhausted the other interpretive tools provided for in the code.

Finally, Article 1375 recognizes a duty of good faith in the performance of contracts. Parties are required to make reasonable efforts, not unduly costly or inconvenient, to preserve the other party's interest in the contract. This obligation is in addition to any other contractual obligation or extracontractual duty by which the party is already bound. There is a deep Italian case law in which the courts have actively applied the concept of good faith.[34]

In 2009, the Italian Supreme Court, in a case dealing with a unilateral termination of a dealership contract, noted that, pursuant to Articles 1175 and 1375 of the Civil Code, parties must conduct themselves in good faith – from the formation to performance and its interpretation. The court also noted that good faith is an expression of the general principle of social solidarity recognized under the Italian Constitution. Because of its constitutional underpinnings, good faith operates to impose autonomous duties on the parties to preserve the contract and not to unnecessarily harm the interests of the other party, regardless of any contractual provision.[35] Accordingly, the Supreme Court held that courts may modify contracts to assure a proper balance between the parties' interests.

D. *Germany*

In the German Civil Code (BGB),

> the observance of *Treu und Glauben mit Rücksicht auf die Verkehrssitte*,[[36]] – embodied in such general provisions as §§ 157, 242 BGB, but repeated throughout the code in more specific contexts – has become a legal principle of such pervasive influence that it is sometimes claimed the codified provisions could be dispensed with; the whole system of private law (or, more modestly, certain parts of it such as unjust enrichment) might be taken as a mere embodiment of the principle and could, in theory, be administered by reference to "*Treu und Glauben*" only. These are, of course, exaggerations, not taken seriously by the majority of legal writers, by the courts or by the legislator, but they are

---

[32] See also Italian Civil Code, Articles 1338, 1341, and 1342.

[33] Unless, for example, the matter falls within the scope of Articles 1439 of the Italian Civil Code.

[34] See, e.g., Cass., sez. III, November 10, 2010, n. 22819; Cass., sez. III, March 3, 2010, n. 22353; Cass., sez. III, September 18, 2009, n. 20106; Cass., sez. I, September 11, 2008, n. 23393; Cass., sez. I, July 13, 2007, n. 15669; Cass., sez. III, February 15, 2007, n. 3462.

[35] Some commentators noted that this definition of good faith is broader than the definition previously embraced by the Supreme Court. See, e.g., Giovanni D'Amico, "Il Commento," in *I Contratti*, 1/2010, 14 n. 8, available at http://www.casaregi.unige.it/insegnamenti/documents/materiali.pdf.

[36] See generally Whittaker and Zimmermann, *Good Faith*, 18–32.

worth mentioning at the outset, if only because of the arguments by which they are usually rebutted: The certainty of law and its application would be abandoned entirely if each case, each individual solution had to be based on such uncertain principles.".[37]

III. Good Faith in the CISG

This part examines the evolution and adoption of the good faith principle in CISG Article 7. It then reviews CISG case law on the interpretation and application of good faith and concludes with an analysis of its proper role in CISG jurisprudence.

A. *CISG Article 7(1)*

The legislative history behind the limited scope of good faith in CISG Article 7(1) is not very helpful.[38] A number of versions and proposals were hotly debated.[39] The compromise reached was not a knock out for the common law delegations but certainly a major victory,[40] though not for long. As the subsequent practice in the application of the Convention shows, good faith became much more than a tool for the interpretation of the Convention.[41] A clear indication that good faith would play a bigger role than anticipated could be perceived in the Secretariat Commentary: "The principle of good faith is, however, broader than these examples and applies to all aspects of the interpretation and *application* of the provisions of this Convention."[42]

---

[37] Peter Schlechtriem, "Good Faith in German Law and in the International Uniform Law," available at http://www.cisg.law.pace.edu/cisg/biblio/schlechtriem16.html.

[38] Bruno Zeller, "Four-Corners: The Methodology for Interpretation and Application of the UN Convention on Contracts for the International Sale of Goods" (2003), available at http://www.cisg.law.pace.edu/cisg/biblio/4corners.html.

[39] For an historical account of the provision, see, e.g., Honnold, *Uniform Law*, 119–24; Lisa Spagnolo, "Opening Pandora's Box: Good Faith and Precontractual Liability in the CISG," 21 *Temple Int'l & Comp. L.J.* 161 (2008), also available at http://www.cisg.law.pace.edu/cisg/biblio/spagnolo.html; Benedict C. Sheely, "Good Faith in the CISG: Interpretation Problems in Article 7" (2004), available at http://law.bepress.com/expresso/339; Disa Sim, "The Scope and Application of Good Faith in the Vienna Convention on Contracts for the International Sale of Goods" (2001), available at http://www.cisg.law.pace.edu/cisg/biblio/sim1.html; Schlechtriem, "Good Faith"; Alejandro M. Garro, "Reconciliation of Legal Traditions in the U.N. Convention on Contracts for the International Sale of Goods," 23 *Int'l Law.* 443 (1989), available at http://www.cisg.law.pace.edu/cisg/biblio/garro1.html; Michael J. Bonell, "Commentary on Article 7," in *Commentary on the International Sales Law* (ed. C. M. Bianca and M. J. Bonell) (Milan: Giuffrè, 1987), 65, available at http://www.cisg.law.pace.edu/cisg/biblio/bonell-bb7.html; Peter Schlechtriem, *Uniform Sales Law: The U.N. Convention on Contracts for the International Sale of Goods* (Vienna: Manz, 1986), available at http://www.cisg.law.pace.edu/cisg/biblio/schlechtriem-07.html; See also the CISG Database at Pace University at http://www.cisg.law.pace.edu/cisg/text/link7.html.

[40] They must have thought that appeasing the civil law jurisdictions by agreeing to relegate "good faith" to the interpretation of the Convention only would have done "little harm." See James Bailey, "Facing the Truth: Seeing the Convention on Contracts for the International Sale of Goods as an Obstacle to a Uniform Law of International Sales," 32 *Cornell Int'l L. J.* 273, 295 (1999), available at http://www.cisg.law.pace.edu/cisg/biblio/bailey.html.

[41] See, e.g., Michael P. Van Alstine, "Dynamic Treaty Interpretation," 146 *U. Pa. L. Rev.* 687, 777–82 (1998), available at http://www.cisg.law.pace.edu/cisg/biblio/alstine2.html.

[42] The examples listed in the Secretariat Commentary include Articles 7(1), 16(2)(b), 21(2), 29(2), 37, 38, 40, 49(2), 64(2), 82, and 85–8. Secretariat Commentary on Article 7, available at http://www.cisg.law.pace.edu/cisg/text/secomm/secomm-07.html.

CISG Article 7(1) reads as follows: "In the interpretation of this Convention, regard is to be had to its international character and to the need to promote uniformity in its application and the observance of good faith in international trade." The 2008 UNCITRAL Digest of case law on the CISG comments on "good faith" as follows:

> Although good faith is expressly referred to only in article 7(1), relating to the Convention's interpretation, there are numerous rules in the Convention that reflect the good faith principle. The following provisions are among those that manifest the principle:
>
> - Article 16(2)(b), which makes an offer irrevocable if it was reasonable for the offeree to rely upon the offer being held open and the offeree has acted in reliance on the offer;
> - Article 21(2), which deals with a late acceptance that was sent in such circumstances that, had its transmission been normal, it would have reached the offeror in due time;
> - Article 29(2), which in certain circumstances precludes a party from invoking a contractual provision that requires modifications or terminations of the contract to be in writing;
> - Articles 37 and 46, on the right of a seller to cure non-conformities in the goods;
> - Article 40, which precludes a seller from relying on the buyer's failure to give notice of non-conformity in accordance with articles 38 and 39 if the lack of conformity relates to facts of which the seller knew or could not have been unaware and which he did not disclose to the buyer;
> - Article 47(2), article 64(2), and article 82, on the loss of the right to declare the contract avoided;
> - Articles 85 to 88, which impose on the parties obligations to preserve the goods.[43]

B. CISG Case Law

Regarding case law dealing with "good faith," one general comment is applicable to the cases surveyed: decisions and awards dealing with "good faith" rarely, if ever, examine the concept in a meaningful way.

1. United States

In comparison with the civil code countries, good faith plays a much smaller role in United States contract law. However, unlike the United Kingdom, it is recognized as a general principle that attaches to all contracts. These are not American CISG decisions specifically dealing with "good faith," although it has been mentioned in several decisions. While the principle of good faith is found in Article 2 of the UCC, it is unclear whether American courts will be able to make autonomous interpretations of the good faith principle in the CISG.[44]

---

[43] *UNCITRAL Digest of Case Law on the United Nations Convention on the International Sale of Goods* (New York, 2008), "Article 7," available at http://www.cisg.law.pace.edu/cisg/text/digest-art-07.html#g.

[44] See, e.g., *Dingxi Longhai Dairy, Ltd. v. Becwood Technology Group L.L.C.*, 635 F.3d 1106 (8th Cir. 2011):

> It is undisputed that the contract was governed by the United Nations Convention on Contracts for the International Sale of Goods ("CISG"), the "international analogue" to Article 2 of the Uniform Commercial Code (UCC). *Chicago Prime Packers, Inc. v. Northam Food Trading Co.*, 408 F.3d 894, 898 (7th Cir. 2005). In applying the Convention, we look to the language of its provisions and the "general principles on which it is based." CISG Art. 7(2). "Caselaw interpreting analogous provisions

2. Italy

The Tribunale di Padova (February 25, 2004) faced the issue of the granting of additional time under CISG Article 59. It reasoned that the use of supplemental time periods "cannot be carried out arbitrarily, since the seller must follow the due diligence criteria," as implied from the reference to the "reasonable duration" of the supplemental period.[45] The Tribunal further notes that: "the conduct of the contracting parties must respect the principle of the good faith, . . . since it is one of the general principles on which [CISG] is based."[46] In essence, the good faith principle "must not only influence the entire regulation of the international sale, but also supplies an essential standard for the interpretation of the rules set forth in the [CISG]."[47] The Tribunal goes on to state that:

> One must conclude that it would be *contrary to the principle of good faith to file a claim* in court [just a] few days after the expiration of the deadline [seeking] the payment of the price, *without having demanded of the buyer adequate explanations for the delay or having conceded him a period for providing performance* [cure]. Conversely, the conduct of the seller cannot be regarded as unfair, where the seller brings a claim before the judge after having wait[ed] at least six months for payment of the price, without the buyer having communicated any excuse in the meantime.[48]

Italian decisions have been lauded because of their use of foreign case decisions in order to comply the CISG's mandate to interpret its provisions with regard to the CISG's international character and the need to promote uniformity. However, the decision of the Padova court goes outside the CISG text in implying the existence of positive good faith obligations on the contracting parties. CISG Article 59, for example, expressly exempts a seller from having to make a formal request for payment of an agreed price when the date is fixed by or determinable under the contract. Additionally, there is nothing in the CISG suggesting a seller should wait before taking a buyer to court. Similarly, there is no requirement that a seller request the reason for nonpayment prior to bringing suit. It is this kind of willingness to expand the reach of the "good faith" concept that concerns practitioners and (some) commentators.

---

of Article 2 . . . may also inform a court where the language of the relevant CISG provisions tracks that of the UCC." *Delchi Carrier SpA v. Rotorex Corp.*, 71 F.3d 1024, 1028 (2d Cir. 1995). Id. at 1107.

[45] Trib., February 25, 2004, n. 40552, available at http://cisgw3.law.pace.edu/cases/040225i3.html (trans. G. Micheli, ed. J. Gulino). See also n. 48, infra. Cf. LG Aachen [Germany], May 14, 1993, in Recht der internationalen Wirtschaft (1993), 760.

[46] The Tribunal cites: Hof Beroep Gent [Belgium], May 15, 2002, available at http://www.law.kuleuven.ac .be/ipr/eng/cases/2002–05–15.html; German Federal Supreme Court, January 9, 2002, in Internationales Handelsrecht 2002, 19; German Federal Supreme Court, October 31, 2001, in Internationales Handelsrecht 2002, 14; Corte d'Appello Milano, December 11, 1998, in Rivista di diritto internazionale privato e processuale, 1999, 112; German Federal Supreme Court, November 25, 1998, in Recht der internationalen Wirtschaft (1999), 385; Arbitral award Dulces Luisi v. Seoul International, November 30, 1998 given by Comission para la Protecion del Comercio Exterior de Mexico, in Diario Oficial del January 29, 1999, 69.

[47] Tribunal references, German Arbitral award of the Hamburg Court of Arbitration, March 21, 1996, in Recht der internationalen Wirtschaft (1996), 766.

[48] Trib., February 25, 2004, n. 40552, available at http://cisgw3.law.pace.edu/cases/040225i3.html (trans. G. Micheli, ed. J. Gulino) (emphasis added).

3. Germany

The German Federal Supreme Court (Bundesgerichtshof or BGH) rendered a decision on October 31, 2001 relating to the incorporation of standard terms.[49] The court appropriately noted that CISG Article 8 required the Court to determine whether the general terms and conditions incorporated in the offer had been a subject of the negotiations, existing practices between the parties, or international customs.[50] The Court then reasoned whether a "reasonable person of the same kind as the other party" would have understood that the offeror intended the standard terms to be incorporated into the contract:[51]

> It is unanimously required that the recipient of a contract offer that is supposed to be based on general terms and conditions have the possibility to become aware of them in a reasonable manner . . . An effective inclusion of general terms and conditions thus first requires that the intention of the offeror that he wants to include his terms and conditions into the contract be apparent to the recipient of the offer. In addition, . . . the Uniform Sales Law requires the user of general terms and conditions to transmit the text or make it available in another way.

The court then notes that national legal regulation of standard terms may apply under CISG Article 4(a) (validity) and that such regulation may vary depending on the national law. Therefore, the court reasons,

> The [other party] of the user of the clause can often not foresee to what clause . . . he agrees in a specific case because significant differences exist between the particular national clauses. It is true that, in many cases, there will be the possibility to make inquiries into the content of the general terms and conditions. This can, however, lead to delays in the conclusion of the contract, in which neither party can have an interest. For the user of the clauses, however, it is easily possible to attach to his offer the general terms and conditions, which generally favor him. It would, therefore, contradict the principle of good faith in international trade as well as the general obligations of cooperation and information of the parties . . . to impose on the other party an obligation to inquire concerning the clauses that have not been transmitted and to burden him with the risks and disadvantages of the unknown general terms and conditions of the other party.[52]

In 2009, a German Court of Appeals (Oberlandesgericht or OLG) in Celle again took up the issue of standard terms incorporation. It noted that "effective incorporation" is to be determined under the contract formation rules of CISG Articles 14 and 18. Following the logic of the above German Federal Supreme Court decision, the existence of standard terms in the offer is not sufficient for their incorporation into the subsequent contract:

> According to Article 8 CISG, the recipient of a contract offer, which is supposed to be based on standard terms and conditions, must have the possibility to become aware of them in a reasonable manner . . . [T]he effective inclusion of standard terms and

---

[49] BGH October 31, 2001, VIII ZR 60/01, available at http://cisgw3.law.pace.edu/cases/011031g1.html (trans. and ed. William M. Barron and Birgit Kurtz).

[50] See CISG, Article 8(3).

[51] See CISG, Article 8(2).

[52] BGH October 31, 2001, VIII ZR 60/01, available at http://cisgw3.law.pace.edu/cases/011031g1.html (trans. and ed. William M. Barron and Birgit Kurtz).

conditions [under the CISG] requires not only that the offeror's intention that he wants to include his standard terms and conditions into the contract [but that that intention] be apparent to the recipient.

The court references German domestic sales law that permits inclusion if the standard terms are made available to the other party or the other party was aware of their existence. However, it does not require "the recipient's positive knowledge of [their] content." The court then referred to the good faith principle of CISG Article 7(1):

> [I]t would violate the principle of good faith in international trade as stated under Article 7(1) CISG and the parties' general duties of cooperation and information, if the recipient of standard terms and conditions was obliged to enquire about the content of the standard terms and conditions which had not been transmitted, thus laying upon him the risk and disadvantage of unknown standard terms being introduced by the other side.[53]

The Hamburg Court of Appeals had previously discussed the role of good faith in relationship to the application of CISG rules. The court invoked the good faith principle in modifying the express declaration of avoidance as an absolute requirement:

> [A]n explicit declaration of avoidance was not necessary because, before Buyer made the cover purchase, the Seller had seriously and finally refused to perform under the sales contract. Although the CISG does not make an exception from the requirement of a declaration of avoidance, the rule of the "observance of good faith in international trade" leads to the result that a declaration of avoidance is not necessary, if it is certain that the other party will not perform its obligations in a case.

In that case, the buyer continued to demand contract performance and threatened to demand damages. The seller failed to respond and reiterate its intent to perform on the contract. The seller's lack of performance was due to problems between the seller and its supplier. The seller gave no indication that it would find substituted goods to honor its contract with the buyer. The seller did express the willingness to pay compensation in the event that the negotiations with its supplier failed and it would not be able to provide the goods in a timely matter. The buyer had continuously emphasized the importance of timely delivery. The court reasoned because of all these factors and the high level of uncertainty in the seller's ability of willingness to provide the goods, the "Seller did not need the protection by a declaration of avoidance since it did not itself try to [fulfill] the contract."[54] The lesson of this review of German cases is that German courts give good faith a large role when evaluating parties' rights and obligations under the CISG.

C. Analysis

CISG Article 7 at first glance appears to limit the application of the good faith concept to the interpretation of the CISG. This was the intent. The wording and practice in the application of the CISG, however, has strayed from this intent. The CISG has not been and will not be interpreted by courts and tribunals in abstract but as applied to actual

---

[53] OLG Celle, July 24, 2009, 13 W 48/09, available at http://cisgw3.law.pace.edu/cases/090724g1.html (trans. Veit Konrad).

[54] OLG Hamburg, February 28, 1997, 1 U 167/95, available at http://cisgw3.law.pace.edu/cases/970228g1.html (trans. Linus Meyer).

situations. Therefore, despite the limiting wording of Article 7(1), the good faith concept has been applied, *de facto*, to the conduct of contracting parties.[55]

A review of the decisions and awards shows how difficult it is to separate the interpretation of the CISG from the interpretation of contracts. Professor Eörsi provides another example of the application of the good faith principle in relation to a relative straightforward CISG rule – acceptance is effective when received at the other party's place of business:

> Under Article 24, a declaration of acceptance "reaches" the addressee when "it is . . . delivered . . . to his place of business or mailing address . . . " If a party knows that the other party who has a place of business is away from his home for a considerable period of time, and he nevertheless sends the declaration to the mailing address, he may violate the requirement of good faith.[56]

Professor Eörsi argues that the use of the good faith principle in the interpretation of CISG rules inherently results in the application of the principle to the interpretation of contracts: "[I]interpretation of the two [CISG and contracts] cannot be separated since the Convention is necessarily interpreted by the parties also; after all, the Convention constitutes the law of the parties insofar as they do not make use of Article 6 on freedom of contract."[57]

As shown in this chapter, courts and tribunals from many jurisdictions apply the good faith concept in the interpretation of the CISG "as applied" to the contracting parties. This conclusion is supported by direct and indirect references in the CISG to the good faith concept as well as to closely related concepts, such as reasonableness,[58] *venire contra factum proprium*,[59] and estoppel.[60]

Thus, despite the compromise to limit the use of good faith through the language of Article 7(1), good faith has been applied well beyond the interpretation of the CISG. The *vexata questio* is to what extent does good faith affect the parties' legal relationship? As noted earlier, good faith in the CISG has been used as: (1) an aid to interpreting the CISG itself, (2) a general principle to assist in gap filling, (3) a direct, positive obligation imposed upon parties, (4) a collective term denoting derivative general principles for gap filling, (5) a product of international usages or practices established by the parties, and (6) an independent source of rights and obligations that may contradict or extend CISG rules.[61]

---

[55] See, e.g., Ulrich Magnus, "Remarks on Good Faith: The United Nations Convention on Contracts for the International Sale of Goods and the International Institute for the Unification of Private Law, Principles of International Commercial Contracts," 10 *Pace Int'l L. Rev.* 89 (1998); Bonell, "Commentary on Article 7," para. 2.4.1; Schlechtriem, "Good Faith in German Law."

[56] Gyula Eörsi, "General Provisions," in *International Sales: The United Nations Convention on Contracts for the International Sale of Goods* (ed. N. M. Galston and H. Smit) (New York: Matthew Bender, 1984), §2.03.

[57] Id.

[58] See CISG Articles 8(2), 16(b), 18(2), 34, 38(3), 39(1), 48(1), and 48(2).

[59] See OLG München, September 15, 2004, 7 U 2959/04 (Ger.), available at http://cisgw3.law.pace.edu/cases/040915g2.html; Internationales Schiedsgericht der Bundeskammer der gewerblichen Wirtschaft [Vienna Arbitration proceeding], June 15, 1994, SCH-4318, available at http://cisgw3.law.pace.edu/cases/940615a4.html.

[60] OLG Karlsruhe, June 25, 1997, 1 U 280/96 (Ger.), available at http://cisgw3.law.pace.edu/cases/970625g1.html.

[61] Spagnolo, "Opening Pandora's Box," 273.

It is undisputed that good faith is an aid to interpreting the CISG. Additionally, the use of good faith as a general principle to assist in gap filling, as a collective term denoting derivative general principles for gap filling, and as a product of international usages or practices established by the parties are good fits and within the scope of Article 7(1). However, the use of good faith as a direct, positive obligation imposed on parties and as an independent source of rights and obligations that may contradict or extend CISG rules, are problematic in that they are outside the mandate of Article 7(1).

Some scholars have criticized the expansive use of the good faith concept as outside the scope of the CISG.[62] Nonetheless, the majority of scholars and a majority of the reported (civil law) cases have embraced it as a sort of implied condition to the exercise of rights and duties under the CISG,[63] as imposing a direct, positive obligation upon the parties,[64] or, more broadly, as an independent source of rights and obligations that may contradict or extend the CISG.[65] Such expansive use of good faith makes it *de facto* impossible to foresee to what extent courts and tribunals are willing to rewrite or rebalance a contract. A possible consequence may be that practitioners will more likely opt out of the CISG.[66]

Moreover, if the good faith principle is abused in being viewed "as a 'super-tool' to override the rules and policies of the Convention whenever one regards the solution to a particular case or problem as inadequate,"[67] then the overall integrity and uniformity of application of the CISG will be endangered. The unlimited use of good faith also raises the concerns expressed by other commentators about the risks of purely subjective notions informed by personal, political, or religious convictions.[68]

Because good faith, or a lack thereof, depends on the circumstances of the cases, before rewriting the contract under the perceived authority of Article 7, a court or tribunal should carefully consider Articles 8 and 9.[69] It is clear that good faith is not defined nor can it be, at least for purposes of the CISG.[70] It would be improper for us to

---

[62] See, e.g., Camilla Baasch Andersen, "General Principles of the CISG – Generally Impenetrable," in *Sharing International Commercial Law across National Boundaries: Festschrift for Albert H. Kritzer on the Occasion of his Eightieth Birthday* (ed. C. B. Andersen and U. G. Schroeter) (London: Wildy, Simmonds & Hill, 2008), 13, available at http://cisgw3.law.pace.edu/cisg/biblio/andersen6.html.

[63] OLG München, February 8, 1995, n. 7 U 1720/94 (Ger.), available at http://cisgw3.law.pace.edu/cases/950208g1.html.

[64] Cour d'appel [CA] [Court of Appeals] Grenoble, February 22, 1995, n. 93/3275 (Fr.), available at http://cisgw3.law.pace.edu/cases/950222f1.html.

[65] See, e.g., Troy Kelly, "Good Faith and the Vienna Convention on Contracts for the International Sale of Goods (CISG)," 3 *Vindobona J. Int'l Com. & Arb.* 15 (1999), available at http://www.cisg.law.pace.edu/cisg/biblio/keily.html.

[66] Apparently, it is one of the reasons the United Kingdom has been reluctant to ratify the CISG. See Hofmann, "Interpretation Rules and Good Faith."

[67] Peter Huber, "Some Introductory Remarks on the CISG," in *Internationales Handelsrecht* (Sellier European Law Publishers, 2006), 228, available at http://www.cisg.law.pace.edu/cisg/biblio/huber.html.

[68] See Schlechtriem, "Good Faith in German Law," 20.

[69] See Hof Arnhem [Hof = Gerechtshof = District Appeal Court] Arnhem, August 25, 1995, n. 94/305 (Neth.), available at http://cisgw3.law.pace.edu/cases/950822n1.html. See also Sergio M. Carbone, "L'attualita' dei criteri interpretativi adottati nella CVIM," paper presented at La Convenzione di Vienna del 1980 sui contratti di vendita internazionale: la prassi contrattuale, l'interpretazione giurisprudenziale e l'analisi dottrinale, Milan, Camera Arbitrale, October 7–8, 2011; Bruno Zeller, "The UN Convention on Contracts for the International Sale of Goods (CISG): A Leap Forward towards Unified International Sales Law," 12 *Pace Int'l L. Rev.* 79 (2000), available at http://cisgw3.law.pace.edu/cisg/biblio/zeller3.html.

[70] See Schlechtriem, "Good Faith in German Law," 4–5.

try to define the indefinable.[71] Good faith is a general principle underlying the CISG,[72] but that does not mean that it has more weight than other principles. Nor does it rise to the level of imposing specific duties of good faith autonomously enforceable or as an implied condition to the exercise of rights and duties under the CISG.

IV. Conclusion

Good faith is an elusive and easily stretchable concept that can be adapted to cover unlimited situations. It is the "Scarlet Pimpernel" of the CISG.[73] It is a factual determination that must be done under the circumstances of the case and cannot be easily generalized. Situations where good faith or lack thereof requires a court's intervention are not the problem; the problem arises when, deliberately or unconsciously, good faith is used to rewrite the contractual relationship to be more just or equitable.

---

[71] See, e.g., Paul J. Powers, "Defining the Undefinable: Good Faith and the United Nations Convention on the Contracts for the International Sale of Goods," 18 *J.L. & Commerce* 333 (1999), available at http://www.cisg.law.pace.edu/cisg/biblio/powers.html. See also James Gordley, "Good Faith in the Medieval *Ius Commune*," in Zimmermann and Whittaker, *Good Faith*, 116–17; Franco Ferrari, "Uniform Interpretation of the 1980 Uniform Sales Law," 24 *Georgia J. Int'l & Comp. Law* (1994–5), available at http://www.cisg.law.pace.edu/cisg/biblio/franco.html.

[72] See, e.g., Ferrari, "Uniform Interpretation." See also *UNCITRAL Digest*, Article 7.

[73] Bruno Zeller, "Good Faith, The Scarlet Pimpernel of the CISG," available at http://www.cisg.law.pace.edu/cisg/biblio/zeller2.html.

10 The CISG and International Arbitration

André Janssen and Matthias Spilker

I. Introduction

The United Nations Convention on Contracts for the International Sale of Goods (CISG) has established itself as a major force in international commercial law. Its reach has been diminished in practice as contracting parties routinely opt out of its application.[1] Nonetheless, eighty countries have adopted the CISG and the number is sure to grow. Parties to a contract, particularly one of an international nature, frequently contract to have their disputes resolved by arbitration, thereby removing the jurisdiction from national courts.[2] International arbitration dominates international business disputes where the CISG may have its greatest impact.

The crucial question becomes: How and how often do arbitral tribunals use the CISG? Surprisingly, a review of the literature confirms Urs Peter Gruber's conclusion that the relationship between the CISG and international arbitration "has not been really discovered as a subject of discussion."[3] This chapter will explore the relationship between the CISG and international arbitration. The CISG, at first blush, seems like the type of international law instrument that would be an ideal resource for arbitration panels deciding international sales and contract disputes. Yet there is little evidence whether this relationship is as strong as one would hypothesize. This chapter will, therefore, review the current evidence and assess the role of the CISG in the context of international arbitration. More specifically, it will examine the obstacles that have prevented a fuller embrace of the CISG in arbitration proceedings. Finally, a short assessment will be offered regarding the future role of the CISG in arbitration.

II. A Short Look at International Arbitration

Before the scope of possible harmonies and disharmonies between the CISG and international arbitration is reviewed, a brief review of international arbitration law is provided in this part.

---

[1] See Justus Meyer, "UN-Kaufrecht in der deutschen Anwaltspraxis," 69 *Rabels Zeitschrift für Internationales Privatrecht* 457 et seq. (2005); Chapter 40.

[2] Klaus Peter Berger, *The Creeping Codification of the New Lex Mercatoria*, 2nd ed. (Alphen aan den Rijn: Kluwer Law International, 2010), 88 (more than 90% of all major international commercial disputes are resolved through arbitration).

[3] Urs P. Gruber, "The Convention on the International Sale of Goods (CISG) in Arbitration," 1 *Int'l Business L.J.* 15, 20 (2009).

A. *International Arbitration and Its Popularity*

International arbitration is an optional means of dispute resolution that, due to its flexibility and adaptability, is able to respond to new developments in international business and through its carefully crafted rules provide a fair process in resolving disputes. Compared with court litigation, arbitration is a private method of dispute resolution.[4] The parties agree to submit any dispute or differences between them to arbitration.[5] It is chosen by the parties as an effective way of resolving their dispute without recourse to national courts.[6] However, similar to a court, the arbitral tribunal is entrusted to make a binding decision that, in contrast to a court decision, is always final.[7] Furthermore, unlike judicial decisions, arbitration awards are more easily enforced internationally due to regional and worldwide treaties and conventions relating to the recognition and enforcement of foreign arbitral awards,[8] in particular The Convention on the Recognition and Enforcement of Foreign Arbitral Awards or "New York Convention."[9] Presently, there are 149 member states to the New York Convention.[10] To summarize, arbitration can be characterized as a hybrid or alternative legal system available by private agreement by parties seeking private proceedings, and culminating with internationally binding and enforceable awards.

What makes actors of international business seek arbitration? In spite of some weaknesses, arbitration displays various advantages over litigation.[11] One major advantage, especially for multinational corporations, is the confidential nature of arbitral proceedings and awards. The level of confidentiality differs from arbitration board to arbitration board, although the decision on confidentiality issues normally remains with the parties.[12]

---

[4] See Julian D.M. Lew, Loukas A. Mistelis, and Stefan M. Kröll, *Comparative International Commercial Arbitration* (The Hague: Kluwer Law International, 2003), 1. Their working definition of international arbitration is: "International arbitration is a specially established mechanism for the final and binding determination of disputes, concerning a contractual or other relationship with an international element, by independent arbitrators, in accordance with procedures, structures and substantive legal or non-legal standards chosen directly or indirectly by the parties."

[5] See, e.g., Option 1 Article 7(1) or Option 2 Article 7 UNCITRAL Model Law on International Commercial Arbitration 1985 with amendments as adopted in 2006; Nigel Blackaby, Constantine Partasides, Alan Redfern, and Martin Hunter, *Redfern and Hunter on International Arbitration*, 5th ed. (Oxford: Oxford University Press, 2009), 5.

[6] *Redfern and Hunter on International Arbitration*, 1; David St. John Sutton, Judith Gill, and Matthew Gearing, *Russel on Arbitration*, 23rd ed. (London: Sweet & Maxwell, 2007), 8 (parties select tribunal); Martin Domke, Larry Edmonson, and Gabriel M. Wilner, *Domke on Commercial Arbitration*, 3rd ed. (St. Paul: Thomson/West, 2003), 1 (same).

[7] Lew et al., *Comparative International Commercial Arbitration*, 4 et. seq.; *Redfern and Hunter on International Arbitration*, 10.

[8] *Redfern and Hunter on International Arbitration*, 7.

[9] See also Rainer Hausmann, "Schiedsvereinbarungen," in *Internationales Vertragsrecht*, 7th ed. (ed. C. Reithmann and D. Martiny) (Cologne: Verlag Dr. Otto Schmidt, 2010), 2018, 2025; Rolf A. Schütze, *Schiedsgericht und Schiedsverfahren*, 5th ed. (Munich: C.H. Beck, 2012), 15.

[10] See http://www.uncitral.org/uncitral/en/uncitral_texts/arbitration/NYConvention_status.html.

[11] For the advantages and disadvantages of arbitration in comparison to national courts, see Hausmann, "Schiedsvereinbarungen"; Schütze, *Schiedsgericht*, 13 et seq.; Herbert Stumpf, "Vor- und Nachteile des Verfahrens vor Schiedsgerichten gegenüber Verfahren vor ordentlichen Gerichten," in *Festschrift für Arthur Bülow zum 80. Geburtstag* (ed. K.-H. Bockstiegel and O. Glossner) (Cologne: C. Heymann, 1981), 271 et seq.

[12] See, e.g., Article 34 International Arbitration Rules of the American Arbitration Association; Sections 42, 43 DIS (Deutsches Institut für Schiedsgerichtsbarkeit)-Arbitration Rules (Schiedsgerichtsordnung).

Furthermore, the distrust that often arises in an unknown, foreign jurisdiction can be eliminated when the parties choose arbitration based on a widely accepted body of arbitration rules.[13] The parties choose the composition of the arbitral tribunal and the place of arbitration.[14] Despite the perception that arbitration is an inexpensive means of dispute resolution,[15] this is not always the case.[16] What can be said is that unlike litigation, the parties have more control over the costs of the proceeding. Equally, the parties control the arbitral procedures. They are able to choose an appropriate procedural law or leave the decision to the tribunal's discretion.[17]

B. *International Arbitration Rules*

Apart from regional and international agreements relating to the recognition and enforcement of foreign arbitration awards, arbitration is governed by arbitration rules with detailed provisions concerning the procedure and other essential issues. An example is the UNCITRAL Arbitration Rules 1976 (revised 2010), which are widely accepted and used by arbitration institutions all over the world. In 1985, UNCITRAL realized the need for uniformity in the area of arbitration and introduced the UNCITRAL Model Law on International Commercial Arbitration, subsequently amended in 2006. The Model Law's goal is to provide greater uniformity over the various existing and conflicting arbitration rules and national arbitration laws. Numerous countries have adopted the Model Law in the years following its publication. This chapter will reference both mentioned sets of rules, as well some rules of well-known arbitration institutions, such as the rules published by the International Chamber of Commerce (ICC).

III. The CISG and Arbitration

There are a number of indications and areas of law favoring a harmonic relationship between the CISG and international arbitration. Several of these will be noted here and will be followed by brief consideration of the reasons for this harmony.

A. *Statistical Evidence*

The frequency at which arbitral tribunals apply the CISG can only be ascertained through statistical investigations. Loukas Mistelis,[18] using the PACE CISG Database,

---

[13] See Hausmann, "Schiedsvereinbarungen," 2018, 2025; Schütze, *Schiedsgericht*, 13 et seq.

[14] See, e.g., Articles 7 and 18 UNCITRAL Arbitration Rules (as revised in 2010).

[15] See Mitchell L. Marinello, "Protecting the Natural Cost Advantages of Arbitration," available at http://apps.americanbar.org/litigation/litigationnews/practice_areas/corporate_naturalcost.html (2010). See also Hausmann, "Schiedsvereinbarungen," 2018, 2025; Lew et al., *Comparative International Commercial Arbitration*, 9; Schütze, *Schiedsgericht*, 15.

[16] Some arbitration institutions with the parties' consent publish the cost of the arbitral awards. In an award rendered in 2001 by the Arbitration Institute of the Stockholm Chamber of Commerce (SCC Case 117/1999, available at http://www.jfarmesto.com/documentos/Commentary%20to%20a%20Separate%20Arbitral%20Award-SCC%20Case%20117–1999.pdf), the arbitration costs were 182,000.00 EUR. The amount in dispute was 990,500 EUR. Hence, the costs were nearly 20% of the value in dispute.

[17] Lew et al., *Comparative International Commercial Arbitration*, 5.

[18] Loukas A. Mistelis, "CISG and Arbitration," in *CISG Methodology* (ed. A. Janssen and O. Meyer) (Munich: Sellier European Law Publishers, 2009), 375, 386 et seq. See also Ugo Draetta, "La Convenzione delle

undertook the most detailed investigation of this kind in 2008. His survey showed that, toward the end of 2008, over a quarter of the 2,000 decisions contained in the database were made by an arbitral tribunal. By August 2013, 818 of the 2,872 documented cases in the PACE database were arbitral awards. According to Mistelis's survey, the application of the CISG was determinative in 57% of arbitral cases; in 22% of cases, the law was determined by conflict of law rules; in 11% of cases, the law was determined by choice of law; and in 2% of cases, the law was determined by general principles of law. In 8% of the cases, no reason was given as to why the CISG was applied.[19]

However, considering the arbitral institutions' confidentiality policy, it is very likely that the real number of arbitration cases involving the CISG is markedly higher. Based on the PACE database, Mistelis estimates that fewer than 5% of arbitration awards are published.[20] On that basis he concludes that the CISG was applied in 4,250 to 5,000 arbitration cases by the end of 2008.[21] If he is correct, then arbitral tribunals have decided 70 to 80% of CISG-related cases.[22] At the least, one can conclude that there are several thousands of nonpublished international arbitration cases in which the CISG was applied.[23]

B. *Application of the CISG by Arbitral Tribunals: Choice of Law*

The determination of the applicable law in an arbitral proceeding is primarily made by the parties' choice law, such as selecting a domestic law by opting out of the CISG as provided in Article 6 CISG. In addition, arbitration laws and rules provide guidance as to deciding applicable law[24] by recognizing the preeminence of party autonomy. There are three scenarios in determining whether the CISG is applicable law: the parties expressly choose the CISG ("direct choice"), the parties choose the law of a contracting state ("indirect choice"), or the parties exclude the CISG ("opt out").

1. Direct Choice

With regard to national courts, it is debatable whether EU-private international law in the form of the Rome I Regulation[25] allows the parties to directly choose nonnational

Nazioni Unite del 1980 sui contratti di vendita internazionale di beni mobili e l'arbitrato," 25 *Diritto Del Commercio Internazionale* 633 (634 et seq.) (2011); Nils Schmidt-Ahrendts, "CISG and Arbitration," 49 *Belgrade L. Rev.* 211 (213 et seq.) (2011).
[19] See Mistelis, "CISG and Arbitration," 375, 388 et seq.
[20] Loukas A. Mistelis in *UN Convention on Contracts for the International Sale of Goods (CISG)* (ed. S. M. Kröll, L. A. Mistelis, and P. P. Viscasillas) (Munich: C.H. Beck, Hart & Nomos, 2011), Article 1 CISG, para. 18.
[21] Mistelis, "CISG and Arbitration," 375, 387.
[22] Mistelis, "CISG and Arbitration," Article 1 CISG, para. 18.
[23] However, one has to take into account that national court decisions on the CISG are not always published and this fact impacts any statistical analysis.
[24] See, e.g., Article 28(1) UNCITRAL Model Law on International Commercial Arbitration 1985 (with amendments as adopted in 2006), Article 59(a) WIPO Arbitration Rules and Article 21(1) and (2) ICC Arbitration and ADR Rules.
[25] Regulation (EC) No 593/2008 of the European Parliament and the Council of June 17, 2008, on the law applicable to contractual obligations (Rome I), published in the Office Journal of the European Union 2008 L 177/6. The regulation came into force on December 17, 2009, replacing the "Rome Convention"

law or only the law of a state.[26] Although this problem has been discussed in cases where the parties directly chose the CISG, it does not arise in relation to arbitration because Article 1(2) of the Rome I Regulation does not apply to arbitration proceedings[27] and in general, arbitration procedures are more flexible. Arbitration laws and rules – for example Article 28(1) UNCITRAL Model Law on International Commercial Arbitration 1985 and 2006,[28] Article 59(a) WIPO Arbitration Rules,[29] and Article 21(1)-(2) ICC Arbitration and ADR Rules[30] – give priority to the parties' agreement as to choice of law. As a result, these regulations offer a wider range of choice by expressly allowing the parties to choose the "rules of law" they consider appropriate to their agreements.[31]

2. Indirect Choice and Opting Out

There are few differences between litigation and arbitration when the CISG is applied through an indirect choice of law by the parties or not applied when they opt out of its application. In arbitration proceedings, if the parties to an international sales contract were to choose the law of a contracting state to the CISG as the law governing, the arbitration tribunal would apply the CISG as an integral part of this state's law in the same way as a domestic court.[32]

---

in most of the EU member states (Article 24.1 Rome I) and in the UK the "Contract (Applicable Law) Act 1990."

[26] See Article 3(1) Rome I Regulation. For a good overview, see Jan van Hein in *Europäisches Zivilprozess- und Kollisionsrecht EuZRP/EuIPR* (ed. Th. Rauscher) (Munich: Sellier European Law Publishers, 2011), Article 3 Rome I Regulation, para. 62 et seq.; Dieter Martiny in *Münchener Kommentar zum Bürgerlichen Gesetzbuch*, 5th ed. (ed. F. J. Säcker and R. Rixecker) (Munich: C.H. Beck, 2009), Article 3 Rome I Regulation, para. 28 et seq., 31.

[27] See, e.g., Jan van Hein in *Europäisches Zivilprozess- und Kollisionsrecht EuZRP/EuIPR*, Article 1 Rome I Regulation, para. 38 et seq. As to the opposite opinion, see Peter Mankowski, "Rom I und Schiedsverfahren," 57 *Recht der Internationalen Wirtschaft* 30 et seq. (2011).

[28] Article 28(1) UNCITRAL Model Law on International Commercial Arbitration 1985 and 2006: "The arbitral tribunal shall decide the dispute in accordance with such rules of law as are chosen by the parties as applicable to the substance of the dispute."

[29] Article 59(a) WIPO Arbitration Rules: "The Tribunal shall decide the substance of the dispute in accordance with the law or rules of law chosen by the parties."

[30] Article 21(1) ICC Arbitration and ADR Rules: "The parties shall be free to agree upon the rules of law to be applied by the arbitral tribunal to the merits of the dispute," and Article 21(2) ICC Arbitration and ADR Rules: "The arbitral tribunal shall take account of the provisions of the contract."

[31] In the light of such provisions it is questionable whether the parties can also agree to apply the CISG in arbitration proceedings (so-called opt in) to contracts not covered by the CISG (e.g., where the contract deals with a subject other than the sale of goods). Generally speaking, this would appear to be permitted by both the literal meaning of these rules and the flexible character of arbitration based on party autonomy. However, when choosing the CISG directly, the parties cannot opt out of mandatory national rules (e.g., provisions regarding consumer protection). See Ingeborg Schwenzer and Pascal Hachem in *Commentary on the UN Convention on the International Sale of Goods (CISG)*, 3rd ed. (ed. P. Schlechtriem and I. Schwenzer) (Munich: C.H. Beck, 2010), Article 6 CISG, para. 3; Peter Schlechtriem and Petra Butler, *UN Law on International Sales: The UN Convention on the International Sale of Goods* (Heidelberg: Springer, 2009), 21 et seq. See also Gruber, "The Convention on the International Sale of Goods," 15, 26.

[32] This is illustrated in ICC Arbitration Case No. 6653, March 26, 1993 (Steel bars case), available at http://cisgw3.law.pace.edu/cases/936653i1.html. The written contract, concluded in 1988, contained a clause stipulating that French law was to apply. The CISG took effect in France in January 1988. The tribunal held that the sales contract was governed by the CISG because the parties had chosen French law, which incorporated the CISG by the time the contract was concluded.

If the CISG is applicable but the parties decide in favor of a certain national law or other rules and exclude the CISG, then the arbitration tribunal, as well as national courts, will respect such exclusion.[33] However, courts will, at times, not honor a choice law that is unrelated to the transaction as applicable conflict of laws rules provide that. In contrast, arbitration tribunals will always honor the parties' choice of law.

C. *Application of the CISG in the Absence of a Choice of Law: Direct Method*

The relationship between the CISG and international arbitration is also proven harmonic when the parties refrain from determining the law applicable to their contract and the arbitration tribunal applies the direct method (or *voie directe*) to determine the applicable law.[34] One has to consider that unlike national courts, arbitral tribunals are not bound by a state's private international law rules or by the CISG.[35] Instead, arbitral tribunals are bound by the applicable arbitration rules in determining the applicable substantial law for the arbitration proceedings.[36] If the parties fail to choose the applicable law, the arbitration tribunal's application of the CISG only arises from the tribunal's own regulations. In doing so, the different regulations generally stipulate two different approaches: the indirect and the direct method of application.[37] According to the indirect method of application, the arbitration tribunal determines the applicable law by means of "the law determined by the conflict of laws rules which it considers applicable."[38] Modern arbitration laws and rules, however, do allow for a direct choice of rules and standards without the need to apply conflict of laws rules.[39] A particularly clear example

---

[33] See Arbitration Tribunal of the Russian Federation Chamber of Commerce and Industry, October 22, 1998, Case No. 196/1997, available at http://cisgw3.law.pace.edu/cases/981022r1.html. In that arbitration, the parties did not agree on a choice of law, but both referred to provisions of the Russian Civil Code during the arbitration proceedings. The tribunal (corresponding to decisions of many national courts in similar cases) held that such a reference did not necessarily mean that the parties intended to exclude the CISG. In any event, it applied the CISG and used the Civil Code of the Russian Federation as a subsidiary statute.

[34] See Ingeborg Schwenzer and Simon Manner, "The Claim is Time-Barred: The Proper Limitation Regime for International Sales Contracts in International Commercial Arbitration," 23 *Arbitration Int'l* 293, 306 et seq. (2007); Benjamin Hayward, "New Dog, Old Tricks: Solving a Conflict of Laws Problem in CISG Arbitrations," 26 *Journal of Int'l Arbitration* 405, 412 et seq. (2009); Lew et al., *Comparative International Commercial Arbitration*, 434 et seq.; Mistelis, "CISG and Arbitration," 375, 385 et seq.

[35] See also Peter Huber and Alastair Mullis, *The CISG: A New Textbook for Students and Practitioners* (Munich: Sellier European Law Publishers, 2007), 67; Schmidt-Ahrendts, "CISG and Arbitration," 211, 214 et seq.

[36] Such rules often allow arbitral tribunals to apply conflict of law rules in order to determine the applicable law. Under certain circumstances, such as according to article 28 UNCITRAL Model Law on International Commercial Arbitration, arbitral tribunals are obliged to use conflict of law rules. Other rules, such as Article 17(1) ICC Rules of Arbitration, in some cases, allow the arbitral tribunal to determine the applicable law by itself without restriction.

[37] This chapter does not consider the use of the CISG by the arbitration tribunals as *lex mercatoria* or international trade usage. As to these problems, see André Janssen and Matthias Spilker, "The Application of the CISG in the World of International Commercial Arbitration," 77 *Rabels Zeitschrift für Internationales Privatrecht* 132, 146 et seq. (2013).

[38] See, e.g., Article 28(2) of the UNCITRAL Model Law on International Commercial Arbitration.

[39] Examples of authorization to choose law *voie directe* include the following laws: Swiss Article 187(1) Bundesgesetz über das Internationale Privatrecht (IPR, Federal Statute on International Private Law); Article 834(1) of the Italian codice di procedura civile (CPC, Civil Procedure Law); Section 1051(2) of the German Zivilprozessordnung (ZPO, Code of Civil Procedure).

of such a direct method of application is provided in the Rules of Arbitration of the London Court of International Arbitration. Article 22.3 stipulates that:

> [T]he Arbitral Tribunal shall decide the parties' dispute in accordance with the law(s) or rules of law chosen by the parties as applicable to the merits of their dispute. If and to the extent that the Arbitral Tribunal determines that the parties have made no such choice, the Arbitral Tribunal shall apply the law(s) or rules of law, which it considers appropriate.

By virtue of this provision, the arbitral tribunal is endowed with the widest possible discretion to act. The ICC Arbitration and ADR Rules take a similar approach. According to its Article 21(1), if there is no choice of law by the parties, an arbitral tribunal "shall apply the rules of law which it determines to be appropriate."[40] Other arbitration rules contain comparable provisions.[41]

Applying the rules of law that the tribunal deems appropriate "gives the tribunal broad discretion for its decision."[42] At the same time, even a tribunal capable of applying the CISG *voie directe* has to substantiate its choice to a certain extent,[43] although this is not always the case in practice.[44] Tribunals that are entitled to choose the substantial law by such a *voie directe* tend to apply the CISG in two ways. In the majority of cases, they apply the CISG because it is convenient in terms of material scope. In such cases, they verify (like a national court) whether the requirements for the applicability under Articles 1 CISG et seq. have been satisfied (despite the fact that they are not bound by the CISG).[45] In some cases, the CISG tribunals note that the CISG is applicable because both parties were based in contracting states without directly applying Article 1 CISG,[46] or they apply the CISG without explanation.[47]

---

[40] The ICC Arbitration Rules were revised in 2011, effective January 1, 2012. The old version contained this provision in Article 17(1). The same wording is used in the World Intellectual Property Organisation (WIPO) Rules (Article 59(a)) and in the International Arbitration Rules of the International Centre for Dispute Resolution of the American Arbitration Association (AAA/ICDR; in Article 28(1)).

[41] See, e.g., Article 34.1 ACICA Rules, which states: "The Arbitral Tribunal shall apply the law designated by the parties as applicable to the substance of the dispute. Failing such designation by the parties, the Arbitral Tribunal shall apply the rules of law which it considers applicable."

[42] As the ICC stated in a case worth reading: ICC Arbitration Case No. 10274 of 1999 (Poultry feed case), available at http://cisgw3.law.pace.edu/cases/990274i1.html.

[43] Beda Wortmann, "Choice of Law by Arbitrators: The Applicable Conflict of Laws Systems," 14 *Arbitration Int'l* 97, 101 (1998); Hayward, "New Dog, Old Tricks," 405, 412 et seq.; Hong-Lin Yu, "Choice of Law for Arbitrators," 4 *Int'l Arbitration L. Rev.* 152 (2001).

[44] See ICC Arbitration Case No. 10274 of 1999 (Poultry feed case), available at http://cisgw3.law.pace.edu/cases/990274i1.html. See also *International Commercial Arbitration* (ed. W. M. Reisman, W. L. Craig, W. Park, and J. Paulsson) (New York: Foundation Press, 1997), 708 (may choose, but must follow a legal system).

[45] Many ICC cases serve as examples: ICC Arbitration Case No. 9448 of July 1999 (Roller bearing case), abstract available at http://cisgw3.law.pace.edu/cases/999448i1.html; ICC Arbitration Case No. 9978 of March 1999 (Penalty clause case), available at http://cisgw3.law.pace.edu/cases/999978i1.html; ICC Arbitration Case No. 10274 of 1999 (Poultry feed case), available at http://cisgw3.law.pace.edu/cases/990274i1.html.

[46] See, e.g., China, July 26, 2002, CIETAC Arbitration proceeding (Green beans case), available at http://cisgw3.law.pace.edu/cases/020726c1.html. See further ICC Award 7531/1994, January 1, 1994, available at CISG-online Case No. 565 http://www.globalsaleslaw.org/index.cfm?pageID=29&action=search.

[47] Iran/U.S. Claims Tribunal, July 28, 1989 (*Watkins–Johnson v. Islamic Republic of Iran*), available at http://cisgw3.law.pace.edu/cases/890728i2.html.

In a case concerning the international law of sales, arbitration panels have significant freedom in selecting the law to be applied. The tribunal is simply entitled to choose the CISG as a rule of law whenever it considers the CISG to be the appropriate law. It can apply the CISG even if it is not directly or indirectly applicable under the facts of the case. And an arbitral tribunal can choose to apply only parts of the CISG.

D. *Some Observations*

This study has shown up to now the relationship between the CISG and international arbitration. It is noticeable from Mistelis's survey that the CISG is very often applied (57%) by the choice of arbitral tribunals. It appears that whenever parties relinquish the decision on the appropriate law to the arbitrators, they tend to apply the CISG. But if these two elements, CISG and international arbitration, can be brought together effortlessly, and if this happens so frequently in practice, what are the underlying reasons?

1. Party Autonomy and Transnational Spirit

The CISG and international commercial arbitration have, as far as the structure is concerned, several features in common.[48] First, as well as arbitration, the CISG is based upon private autonomy or, more precisely, party autonomy. As a contract law code, the CISG's dominant theme is party autonomy, acting mostly as a series of default rules to fill in gaps in contracts and to assist in the interpretation of contracts. Likewise, international arbitration is voluntarily entered into by the parties' agreement.[49] Secondly, according to Article 1 CISG, the CISG applies to contracts for sale of goods between parties whose places of business are in different countries, that is, the CISG, as a whole, is designed for cross-border sales. International commercial arbitration is by definition focused on the transnational transactions. Both the CISG and international arbitration possess a transnational spirit.

2. Practical Reasons

It is in the nature of things that national courts would rather apply national laws. Even if national courts are concerned with international issues, they are accustomed to applying national law. Arbitral tribunals, however, are not as focused on national law and are accustomed to applying hard and soft international sources of law. There is a bulk of arbitration institutions that for the most part deal with international disputes. For these arbitral tribunals, being concerned with various systems of law and applying them is part of their daily business. They regularly apply both different national legal systems and transnational laws, and as such there is a greater tendency to apply the CISG.[50] Furthermore, unlike the vast majority of national laws, the CISG is easily accessible to the parties as well as to the arbitrators. There are official UN versions of the CISG in

---

[48] See on this also Ugo Draetta, "La Convenzione delle Nazioni Unite del 1980 sui contratti di vendita internazionale di beni mobili e l'arbitrato," 25 *Diritto Del Commercio Internazionale* 633, 634 (2011).

[49] Note, however, the CISG is an opt-out instrument, while international arbitration is "opt in" (agreement of the parties).

[50] See also Larry A. DiMatteo et al., *International Sales Law: A Critical Analysis of CISG Jurisprudence* (New York: Cambridge University Press, 2005), 13.

Arabic, Chinese, English, French, Russian, and Spanish, and also many other officially translated language versions. In addition, the various CISG databases, such as the PACE Law School CISG Database, provide constantly updated information, which can be easily accessed by parties all over the world.

3. The CISG as a "Neutral Law"

Another reason for the application of the CISG by arbitrators is that arbitration professionals view it as a practical and highly regarded source of international private law. The status of the CISG is enhanced due to the fact that it is viewed a "neutral law."[51] Parties going to arbitration quite often choose a neutral place for the arbitration to take place; an arbitration institution's prestige is largely based on the perception of its neutrality.[52] In a similar manner, parties and arbitrators tend to prefer neutral laws such as the CISG in arbitration. From a practical and objective perspective, the CISG's status seems not only to be neutral and impartial, its substantive content is viewed as taking a balanced approach to buyers' and sellers' rights and obligations. The CISG represents a compromise legal instrument that balances the interests of legal traditions – in particular the common and civil law systems, as well as the interests of the industrial and developing countries.[53] For these reasons, the CISG is seen as neutral, balanced international law or set of rules, making it a popular source of law in international arbitration.

E. *Indirect Method of Application: Absence of a Choice of Law*

This chapter has concentrated until now on indicating and describing the fundamental common features, that is, a harmony between the CISG and international arbitration, and has given reasons for such. The next part examines the interaction between the CISG and international arbitration in greater detail to seek out possible complications.

1. Initial Situation Provided by Arbitration Rules

In contrast to the aspects described here, the relationship between the CISG and international arbitration is not unproblematic in cases in which the parties have made no effective choice of law and the applicable arbitration rules only provide for an indirect method of application. In cases where the tribunal is bound to apply conflict of laws rules due to the applicable arbitration rules and thereby comes to the application of a contracting state's law (indirect method of application), it will – like a domestic court – apply *eo ipso* the CISG on the basis of Article 1(1)(b) CISG.[54] For example, Article 28(2) of the UNCITRAL Model Law on International Commercial Arbitration provides that, in absence of a choice of national law by the parties, an arbitral tribunal "shall apply the law determined by the conflict of laws rules which it considers applicable."[55] Traditionally,

---

[51] Schlechtriem and Butler, *UN Law on International Sales*, 16; Schmidt-Ahrendts, "CISG and Arbitration."
[52] Lew et al., *Comparative International Commercial Arbitration*, 7.
[53] Ulrich Magnus, "The Vienna Sales Convention (CISG) between Civil and Common Law: Best of All Worlds?," 3 *J. of Civil L. Studies* 67 et seq. (2010); DiMatteo et al., *International Sales Law*, 15.
[54] All additional requirements (sales contract, transnationality) must of course be satisfied, too.
[55] See also England, Arbitration Act, Section 46; Article 16 Vienna Rules.

arbitral tribunals have used the conflict of laws rules of the seat of arbitration, but nowadays, a cumulative approach is preferred.[56]

2. Significance of Article 95 CISG

Arbitral tribunals could encounter problems if these conflict of laws rules lead to the application of the law of CISG member states, such as China and the United States, which have declared a reservation to Article 1(1)(b) CISG (only one party is a member to the CISG). In this case, a national tribunal can only apply the CISG if the requirements of Article 1(1)(a) CISG (both parties are from CISG member states) are satisfied.[57] The question here does not concern where the tribunal is based but whether a tribunal, recognizing that the application of the conflict of laws rules will lead to the application of a member state's law, has to respect a country's reservation from Article 1(1)(b) CISG.

There are few published decisions regarding this problem. In an award decided by the China International Economic and Trade Arbitration Commission (CIETAC) in 2004,[58] the parties (a Japanese seller and a Chinese buyer) agreed on a sales contract, which did not contain a choice-of-law clause. The contract was concluded in China and the place of performance was in China. At the time, Japan was not a member to the CISG. The tribunal viewed the parties' references to Chinese law as evidence that the parties had chosen Chinese law to govern the contract. However, as China had made a reservation under Article 95 CISG, Article 1(1)(b) CISG jurisdiction was not available. The tribunal selected Chinese domestic contract law, and not the CISG, as the applicable law.

Although the reasoning of the award was insufficiently documented, it is easy to see how the tribunal reached its decision. Where an arbitral tribunal determines the law applicable to an international sales contract on the basis of the rules relating to conflict of laws and these rules lead to the application of a CISG member state's law, it must apply this law correctly and thus in its entirety.[59] For example, suppose that a dispute arises between two parties to an international sales contract and one of the parties is based in the United States, a contracting state to the CISG, which has made a reservation under Article 95 CISG. In this case, even if the conflict of laws rules refer to U.S. law, the CISG could not be applied because it does not form part of the national legal system. The Article 95 CISG reservation removes the jurisdiction of the CISG over these types of cases. To hold otherwise would, on the one hand, contradict arbitration laws and rules that oblige tribunals to correctly apply conflict of laws rules. On the other hand, if an arbitrator were to ignore the United States' rejection of Article 1(1)(b) CISG jurisdiction, then it would effectively incorporate the CISG contrary to what U.S. law actually dictates. Finally, in arbitration practice, the exclusion of the CISG pursuant to Article 1(1)(b)

---

[56] See Lew et al., *Comparative International Commercial Arbitration*, paras. 17–51; Schwenzer and Hachem in *Commentary on the UN Convention*, Introduction to Articles 1–6 CISG, para. 13.

[57] See the U.S. example: November 22, 2002, U.S. District Court, Southern District of Florida, Unilex No. 01-7541, available at http://www.unilex.info/dynasite.cfm?dssid=2376&dsmid= 13356.

[58] China, December 24, 2004, CIETAC Arbitration proceeding (Medical equipment case), available at http://www.cisg.law.pace.edu/cisg/wais/db/cases2/041224c1.html.

[59] See also Georgios C. Petrochilos, "Arbitration Conflict of Laws Rules and the 1980 International Sales Convention," 52 *Revue Hellenique de Droit Int'l* 191 et seq. (1999), available at http://www.cisg.law.pace .edu/cisg/biblio/ petrochilos.html, 5.

CISG is recognized because panels expressly take into consideration whether or not the respective CISG member state has made a reservation under Article 95 CISG.[60]

3. Article 1(1)(a) CISG as a Conflict-of-Laws Rule

Article 28(2) UNCITRAL Model Law on International Commercial Arbitration and several other associations' rules oblige arbitral tribunals to apply conflict of laws rules. Therefore, it is likely that they will make use of Article 1(1)(a) CISG as the appropriate conflict of laws rule.[61] The first point to note is that this situation differs from that in which a tribunal is granted complete freedom under its arbitration rules to choose directly the applicable law and is not obliged to refer to conflict of laws rules. The following example illustrates this point.

In an ICC case[62] decided in 1992, a legal dispute arose between an Austrian seller and a Yugoslavian buyer (whose states were both contracting parties to the CISG). At that time, the applicable Article 13.3 of the ICC Rules of Conciliation and Arbitration[63] provided that, in the absence of an indication of the law applicable to the main issue, the arbitral panel could apply the law designated by the conflict of laws rule it deemed appropriate. Accordingly, the arbitral tribunal applied the CISG with recourse to Article 1(1)(a) CISG. Admittedly, although the wording of Article 13.3 of the ICC Rules of Conciliation and Arbitration implied that an ICC tribunal was bound to apply a conflict of laws rules first, some commentators argued that Article 13.3 allowed a tribunal to choose the applicable law directly.[64] In a comparable case from 1997 involving a contract between a Romanian seller and an Italian buyer that did not contain a choice-of-law clause, the ICC tribunal reached a similar decision because both parties were from CISG member countries.[65] However, just as in the first case, it is not entirely clear whether the arbitrator applied the CISG directly and merely referred to Article 1(1)(a) CISG to support its reasoning or whether he applied this provision as a rule of private international law.

In order to be considered as a rule of private international law, a legal provision must offer abstract solutions to a conflict of laws. Article 1(1)(a) CISG, however, is specific and not applicable in the abstract to numerous fact scenarios. Therefore, technically speaking, it is not a rule of private international law. Nevertheless, Article 1(1)(a) CISG should be regarded as expressing as a conflict of laws rule in terms of arbitration rules and

[60] See ICC Arbitration Case No. 7645 of March 1995 (Crude metal case), available at http://www.cisg .law.pace.edu/cisg/wais/db/cases2/957645i1.html#cx; Serbia, January 28, 2009, Foreign Trade Arbitral Tribunal attached to the Serbian Chamber of Commerce (Medicaments case), available at http://cisgw3 .law.pace.edu/cases/090128sb.html (CISG can only be applied via Article 1(1)(b) CISG).

[61] Concerning this problem, see also Gruber, "The Convention on the International Sale of Goods," 15, 27.

[62] ICC Arbitration Case No. 7153 of 1992 (Hotel materials case), available at http://cisgw3.law.pace.edu/ cases/927153i1.html.

[63] ICC Rules of Conciliation and Arbitration (1975), replaced by ICC Rules of Arbitration, as of January 1, 1998.

[64] See Dominique Hascher, "Commentary on ICC Case 7153 of 1992," 14 *J.L. & Commerce* 220, 221 (1995). This assumption is at least questionable. An ICC tribunal held that the mere entry into force of the ICC Arbitration Rules in 1998 meant that the court was no longer bound to make use of conflict of law rules. ICC Arbitration Case No. 9887 of August 1999 (Chemicals case), available at: http://cisgw3.law .pace.edu/ cases/999887i1.html.

[65] ICC Arbitration Case No. 8962 of September 1997 (Glass commodities case), available at http://cisgw3 .law.pace.edu/cases/978962i1.html.

laws in cases involving an indirect method of application.[66] First, this provision offers a solution to a conflict of laws. When there is a sales contract between parties from CISG member states, Article 1(1)(a) CISG rules that the contract is to be governed by the CISG rather than a national sales law. In this respect, the CISG settles a conflict of laws matter. Second, a different view could, under certain circumstances, prevent an arbitral tribunal from applying the CISG in a "typical" CISG case. This is because, hypothetically, the rules of arbitration require the tribunal to apply conflict of laws rules in determining the applicable law. When both parties have their places of business in different CISG member states, many conflict of laws rules, such as the Rome I Regulation, would lead to the application of a domestic law. In such a case it would be easy to apply the CISG on the basis of Article 1(1)(b) CISG as part of one of the member states' laws. However, the situation would be different if one of the states in which a party has its place of business has made a reservation under Article 1(1)(b) CISG. If the conflict of laws rules were to result in the application of the domestic law of a reservation state, there would be a dogmatic hindrance for the tribunal to apply the CISG. The tribunal, in that case, cannot apply the CISG directly because the arbitration rules provide in this case that the conflict of laws rules must be applied first and we had assumed that Article 1(1)(a) CISG is not a conflict of laws rule. If conflict of laws rules point to the laws of the states that have declared a reservation under Article 95 CISG, the arbitral tribunal has to respect such a reservation and cannot apply Article 1(1)(b) CISG still. The tribunal might apply Article 1(1)(a) CISG, but that would contradict conflict of laws rules.

This result of not applying the CISG due to an Article 95 CISG reservation is unsatisfactory for several reasons. First, every national court of these two states would even be under an obligation to apply the CISG by means of Article 1(1)(a) CISG, as both are CISG member states. Second, the CISG would be the appropriate law in terms of its substance and status but it would not be applicable. Finally, this result would negate the benefits of arbitral tribunals over national courts (i.e., in the sense that they offer more remedies, more options, and greater flexibility). In order to ensure that the CISG is applied in those cases where tribunals are bound to use conflict of laws rules in determining the applicable law and the CISG appears the most appropriate, Article 1(1)(a) CISG would have to be deemed a conflict of laws rule.

IV. Formalities: The CISG versus International Arbitration

This part reviews the differences in the role of formalities in the enforcement of arbitration agreements under the CISG and arbitration rules. It will provide three potential solutions to the issue of whether the CISG or the pertinent arbitration rules control the enforceability of arbitration agreements relating to international sales contracts.

A. *Conflict*

Another obstacle to the use of the CISG in international arbitration is differences in formal requirements. Before an arbitral tribunal can deal with an international commercial dispute and determine the applicable law, it must first determine that it has jurisdiction.

---

[66] See Hascher, "Commentary on ICC Case 7153 of 1992"; Gruber, "The Convention on the International Sale of Goods," 15, 27.

The arbitration agreement constitutes the essential basis for jurisdiction. In terms of its legal status, the private agreement to use arbitration is the law that controls the method dispute resolution.[67] The UNCITRAL Model Law on International Commercial Arbitration,[68] along with many other bodies of arbitration rules, such as Section 5 of the United Kingdom Arbitration Act 1996 and Section 1031(1) of the German Code of Civil Procedure, as well as the New York Convention,[69] require an arbitration agreement in a written form. This formal requirement applies regardless of whether the arbitration agreement or contract has been concluded orally, by conduct of the parties, or by other means.[70] The arbitration agreement has to at least be *evidenced* in writing.[71] In principle, the parties' signature is not required and it is not necessary that the arbitration agreement be contained in the same document as the sales contract itself.

As a rule, the CISG does not require a sales contract to be concluded or evidenced in writing nor does it stipulate any other formal requirements. This lack of formality requirements is subject to a reservation under Articles 12 and 96 CISG.[72] So, on the one hand, sales contracts governed by the CISG are exempt any formality requirements. On the other hand, arbitration rules require arbitration agreements to be made in writing. For that reason, arbitral tribunals have to cope with divergent rules. Arbitration clauses are often contained in sales contracts and if the latter are governed by the CISG then it can be assumed that the CISG encompasses the arbitration agreements. A necessary consequence of this is that the CISG suspends the formal requirements for arbitration agreements. For example, two parties from different CISG countries enter into a contract by telephone. During this conversation, they agree that disputes will be settled by arbitration. Assuming that the applicable arbitration rules require a written arbitration agreement (see, e.g., Section 1031(1) German Code of Civil Procedure) and the CISG is applicable, is this agreement to arbitrate valid and enforceable even if it does not comply with applicable arbitration rules requiring a written form? An explanatory note by the UNCITRAL Secretariat on the Model Law on International Commercial Arbitration refers to the newly introduced Option 2 of Article 7,[73] according to which informal arbitration agreements are effective. The rationale behind Option 2 is that "in a number of situations, the drafting of a written document was impossible or impractical."[74]

---

[67] See Option 1 Article 7(1) or Option 2 Article 7 UNCITRAL Model Law on International Commercial Arbitration; UK Arbitration Act 1996 s. 6(1).

[68] See Option 1 Article 7(2)-(6) UNCITRAL Model Law on International Commercial Arbitration. Option 2 of Article 7, which was introduced in 2006, now implies the possibility of an informal arbitration agreement.

[69] See Article II (2) New York Convention on the Recognition and Enforcement of Foreign Arbitral Awards.

[70] See Option 1 Article 7(3) UNCITRAL Model Law on International Commercial Arbitration.

[71] See, e.g., Section 5(2) UK Arbitration Act 1996; Section 1031(1) and (2) of the German Zivilprozessordnung (Code of Civil Procedure).

[72] Article 96 CISG allows states to opt out of Article 11 CISG "no writing required" provision. The states that have made an Article 96 CISG reservation are Argentina, Belarus, Chile, China, Hungary, Latvia, Lithuania, Paraguay, Russian Federation, and Ukraine. See DiMatteo et al., *International Sales Law*, 38. Numerous national sales laws rejected the writing requirement before the CISG was created. See UK Sale of Goods Act 1979, Section 4; Germany Bürgerliches Gesetzbuch (German Civil Code), Section 433 et seq. In contrast, the American UCC §2.201(2) requires a written form for sales of goods exceeding $500.

[73] Option 2 of Article 7 of UNCITRAL Model Law is worded as follows: An "arbitration agreement is an agreement by the parties to submit to arbitration all or certain disputes which have arisen or which may arise between them in respect of a defined legal relationship, whether contractual or not."

[74] Explanatory Note by the UNCITRAL secretariat on the 1985 Model Law on International Commercial Arbitration as amended in 2006, 28.

B. *Solution*

There are three different views regarding the problem of the applicability of Article 11 CISG to arbitration agreements. The first view asserts that Article 11 CISG and the CISG in general govern related arbitration agreements.[75] The express reference to the "settlements of disputes" in Articles 19(3) and 81(1) CISG supports the argument that agreements to arbitrate fall within the scope of the CISG. Consequently, Article 11 CISG applies to dispute resolution clauses as arbitration agreements with the consequence that a valid agreement to arbitrate need not be in a written form.

A different view advocates that the CISG is not applicable to arbitration agreements.[76] If one follows this view, the contract would be subject to the CISG, yet the CISG would not preempt the formal requirements relating to the agreement to arbitrate found in arbitration rules. This argument is premised on the principle of separability of the arbitration agreement from the main contract. This perception is derived from Article 16(1) of the UNCITRAL Model Law on International Commercial Arbitration[77] and is reflected in the arbitration laws of many jurisdictions.[78] According to the principle of separability, an arbitration provision is a separate agreement[79] that is distinct from the main contract. Further, it is argued that the CISG governs only the substance of a contract and not the procedural aspects of applying the CISG. Thus, according to this view, the CISG is not intended to govern arbitration agreements.[80]

A third view is a hybrid of these two views. It also asserts that the formation of the arbitration agreement is subject to the CISG, however, Article 11 CISG is not applicable to arbitration agreements.[81] The rationale of the first view – Articles 19(3) and 81(1) CISG's use of "settlements of disputes" language – makes the CISG applicable. However,

---

[75] See, e.g., Pilar Perales Viscasillas in *UN-Convention on the International Sales of Goods (CISG)* (ed. S.M. Kröll, L.A. Mistelis, and P.P. Viscasillas) (Munich: C.H. Beck, Hart & Nomos, 2011), Article 11 CISG, para. 13 et seq. (UN-Convention); Pilar Perales Viscasillas and David Ramos Muñoz, "CISG & Arbitration," 10 *Spain Arbitration Rev.* 63, 70 et seq. (2011); Burghard Piltz, *Internationales Kaufrecht*, 2nd ed. (Munich: C.H. Beck, 2008), 69 et seq.; Janet Walker, "Agreeing to Disagree: Can We Just Have Words? CISG Article 11 and the Model Law Writing Requirement," 25 *J. L. & Commerce* 153, 163 (2005/6).

[76] See, e.g., Stefan M. Kröll, "Selected Problems Concerning the CISG's Scope of Application," 25 *J.L. & Commerce* 39, 43 et seq. (2005–6); Peter Schlechtriem and Martin Schmidt-Kessel in *Commentary on the UN Convention*, Article 11 CISG, para. 8; Germany, *District Court Duisburg*, April 17, 1996 (textiles), CISG-Online 186, available at http://www.globalsaleslaw.org/index.cfm?pageID=29&action=search; Switzerland, Supreme Court, July 11, 2000 (construction materials), CISG-Online 627, available at http://www.globalsaleslaw.org/index.cfm?pageID=29&action=search.

[77] Article 16(1) UNCITRAL Model Law on International Commercial Arbitration states: "The arbitral tribunal may rule on its own jurisdiction, including any objections with respect to the existence or validity of the arbitration agreement. For that purpose, an arbitration clause, which forms part of a contract, shall be treated as an agreement independent of the other terms of the contract. A decision by the arbitral tribunal that the contract is null and void shall not entail ipso jure the invalidity of the arbitration clause."

[78] See Germany Zivilprozessordnung (Code of Civil Procedure), Section 1040(1).

[79] Kröll, "Selected Problems," 44; Lew et al., *Comparative International Commercial Arbitration*, 102.

[80] Kröll, "Selected Problems," 44; Schlechtriem and Butler, *UN Law on International Sales*, 42 et seq.

[81] See, e.g., Robert Koch, "The CISG as the Law Applicable to Arbitration Agreements?," in *Sharing International Commercial Law across National Boundaries: Festschrift for Albert H. Kritzer on the Occasion of His Eightieth Birthday* (ed. C.B. Andersen and U.G. Schroeder) (London: Wildy, Simmonds & Hill, 2008), 267, 282 et seq.; Mistelis, "CISG and Arbitration," 375, 393 et seq.; Schlechtriem and Schmidt-Kessel in *Commentary on the UN Convention*, Article 11 CISG, para. 7. Opposing opinion Burghard Piltz, *Internationales Kaufrecht*, 2nd ed. (Munich: C.H. Beck, 2008), 70 et seq.

due to the drafting history, the wording of Article 11 CISG, and its systematic structure, Article 11 CISG is not applicable to the arbitration agreement.[82]

Although the two latter views – despite varying reasoning – exclude the application of Article 11 CISG to arbitration agreements, the former allows for the informal conclusion of arbitration agreements to the extent they are concluded under a CISG contract. The view that Article 11 CISG is applicable to arbitration agreements is the least convincing. In particular, it does not sufficiently acknowledge the separability of the international sales contract from the arbitration agreement. Furthermore, according to Article 90 CISG, this view would actually have to give precedence to the formal requirement of Article II of the New York Convention. In practice, this view does not involve a simplification of the formal requirement. In cases involving CISG sales contracts with oral arbitration agreements, awards resulting from such agreements would not be enforceable under Article II of the New York Convention.[83] Thus, to ensure the enforceability of a future arbitration award, the parties need to fulfill the formalities required in arbitration rules.

V. Divergent Interpretations: National Courts and Arbitral Tribunals

A danger to the relationship between international arbitration and the CISG is the problem of divergent interpretations of the CISG by national courts and arbitration tribunals. Inconsistency in the application of law makes it a less reliable source of law for arbitration. In order to cast light on diverging approaches in CISG interpretive methodology, examples will be taken from the use by the national courts and arbitral tribunals of the Principles of European Contract Law (PECL) and the UNIDROIT Principles of International Commercial Contracts (PICC) in the application of the CISG. An issue in which this has been the case relates to the determination of interest rates under Article 78 CISG.[84]

The application of both of these sets of rules in the framework of the CISG is at the center of debate in the legal literature.[85] The opinions on their role in the interpretation of the CISG are diverse – they vary from a perception of insignificance, to one of persuasive authority, to their application as international trade usages pursuant to Article 9(2) CISG, and to PECL and PICC serving central instruments of soft law applicable as "general principles upon which the CISG is based."[86] National courts have been less receptive in using PICC and PECL in the interpretation of the CISG. Indeed, there are

---

[82] See, esp., Koch, "The CISG as the Law Applicable to Arbitration Agreements?," 267, 270 et seq.

[83] Several scholars view Article 11 CISG as a "more favourable provision," with the consequence that New York Convention Article II is not applicable. See Pilar Perales Viscasillas in *UN-Convention*, Article 11 CISG, para. 13 et seq.; Perales Viscasillas and Ramos Muñoz, "CISG & Arbitration," 63, 70 et seq.; Walker, "Agreeing to Disagree," 153, 163 et seq.

[84] With regard to the application of the PICC in the context of arbitration tribunals, see Klaus P. Berger, "International Arbitration Practice and the UNIDROIT Principles of International Commercial Contracts," 46 *American J. of Comparative L.* 129 et seq. (1998); Fabio Bortolotti, "The UNIDROIT Principles and the Arbitral Tribunals," 5 *Uniform L. Rev.* 141 et seq. (2000).

[85] See, e.g., Fabian Burkart, *Interpretatives Zusammenwirken von CISG und UNIDROIT-Principles* (Baden-Baden: Nomos, 2000), 1 et seq.; Pilar Perales Viscasillas, "The Role of the UNIDROIT Principles and the PECL in the Interpretation and Gap-Filling of CISG," in *CISG Methodology*, 287 et seq.

[86] See Perales Viscasillas, "The Role of the UNIDROIT Principles," 287, 296 et seq.

only a handful decisions in which national courts have used soft law instruments in the context of the CISG.[87] In comparison, the number of decisions from arbitral tribunals in which the PICC or PECL have been referred to is considerably larger.[88] The UNILEX database, which only contains decisions that refer to the PICC (and not to the PECL), does contain, in spite of the lower number of published awards, a total of 28 arbitral awards (as of August 2013) in which the PICC is referred to and applied in the context of the CISG.

Article 78 CISG, the assessing of interest as damages, is one of the most controversial provisions of the entire CISG.[89] National courts and the prevailing views in literature view the determination of interest rates as an "external gap" with the consequence that to the extent that no trade usage exists, Article 7(2) CISG refers to the national law applicable by virtue of private international law.[90]

However, a number of arbitral tribunals[91] have seen the determination of interest rates as an "internal gap" under Article 7(2) CISG (first alternative).[92] In these cases the tribunals have equated the aforementioned soft law instruments with the CISG's underlying "general principles" and applied the solution provided in the Principles'

---

[87] Only five decisions in the UNILEX database can be found using PECL or PICC in relationship to the CISG. See www.unilex.info.

[88] See Perales Viscasillas, "The Role of the UNIDROIT Principles," 287, 288: "The use of the UNIDROIT Principles of International Commercial Contracts and the Principles of European Contract Law (PECL) in the interpretation and gap-filling of the CISG is beginning to be seen in practice particularly in international commercial arbitration." Again, the number of arbitral cases is larger given the unreported arbitration awards.

[89] Article 78 CISG states: "If a party fails to pay the price or any other sum that is in arrears, the other party is entitled to interest on it, without prejudice to any claim for damages recoverable under Article 74."

[90] See, e.g., Belgium, April 24, 2006, Appellate Court Antwerp (*GmbH Lothringer Gunther Grosshandels- gesellschaft für Bauelemente und Holzwerkstoffe v. NV Fepco International*), available at http://cisgw3.law .pace.edu/cases/060424b1.html; Germany, 3 April 2006, Appellate Court Köln (Strawberry plants case), available at http://cisgw3.law.pace.edu/cases/060403g1.html; Germany, July 22, 2004, Appellate Court Düsseldorf (Shoes case), available at http://cisgw3.law.pace.edu/cases/040722g1.html. There are also arbi- tral decisions following this approach. See, e.g., ICC Ct. Bull. 2000, 107 et seq.; ICC Ct. Bull. 1995, 64, 66). See also Ulrich Magnus, in *Kommentar zum UN-Kaufrecht*, 2nd ed. (ed. H. Honsell) (Heidelberg: Springer, 2010), Article 78 CISG, para. 13; Huber and Mullis, *The CISG*, 358 et seq.; Franco Ferrari, in *Internationales Vertragsrecht*, 2nd ed. (ed. F. Ferrari, E.M. Kieninger, and P. Mankowski) (Munich: C.H. Beck, 2012), Article 78 CISG, para. 18. The problem is that there is no uniform approach for selecting a national law to be applied to an interest claim, as well as a lack of unanimity concerning whether procedural or substantive law governs the issue of the appropriate rate. Thus courts have resolved interest issues in different ways – by applying the law of the creditor's place of business, the law of the debtor's place of business, the law of the country of the currency of payment, and the law of the country in which payment is to be made. See John Y. Gotanda in *UN-Convention*, Article 78 CISG, para. 21 et seq.

[91] See, e.g., *ICC Arbitral Award*, Case No. 8128/1995 (Chemical fertilizer case), available at http://cisgw3 .law.pace.edu/cases/958128i1.html; *Arbitral Award*, Austria June 15, 1994, Vienna Arbitration proceeding SCH-4366 (Rolled metal sheets case), available at http://cisgw3.law.pace.edu/cases/940615a3.html; ICC Arbitration Award, Case No. 8769 of December 1996 (Electrical appliances case), available at http:// cisgw3.law.pace.edu/cases/968769i1.html.

[92] For different approaches to determining the rate of interest, see, e.g., Klaus Bacher in *Commentary on the UN Convention*, Article 78 CISG, para. 26; Franco Ferrari, Harry Flechtner, and Ronald A. Brand, *The Draft UNCITRAL Digest and Beyond: Cases, Analysis and Unresolved Issues in the U.N. Sales Convention* (Munich: Sellier European Law Publishers, 2003), Article 78 CISG, para. 7 et seq.

Article 7.4.9 PICC[93] and PECL's Article 9:508 PECL[94] of using the average short-term credit rate for the currency of the place where payment is due.[95]

The reason that soft law instruments are more widely used by arbitral tribunals for the interpretation and gap-filling of the CISG may be due to the freedom granted to arbitrators to use different sources of law. Furthermore, the increased awareness and understanding of the PICC and PECL among arbitrators, who frequently decide international cases, is much higher than for national judges. National judges are trained and generally apply national (hard) law. Furthermore, national judges tend toward the application of codified legal rules rather than principles drafted primarily by academics. On the basis of present data it appears that arbitral tribunals more frequently than national courts, for the reasons noted in this chapter, use the PICC and PECL to interpret and fill gaps in the CISG.

VI. Specific Performance in International Arbitration

Another difficulty in the relationship between the CISG and arbitration is the use of the remedy of specific performance. In principle, the CISG assumes that the buyer and the seller can claim specific performance in the event of a breach of contract.[96] However, Article 28 CISG limits this remedy in stating: "If, in accordance with the provisions of this Convention, one party is entitled to require performance of any obligation by the other party, a court is not bound to enter a judgment for specific performance unless the court would do so under its own law in respect of similar contracts of sale not governed

---

[93] Article 7.4.9 PICC states:

> If a party does not pay a sum of money when it falls due the aggrieved party is entitled to interest upon that sum from the time when payment is due to the time of payment whether or not the non-payment is excused.
>
> The rate of interest shall be the average bank short-term lending rate to prime borrowers prevailing for the currency of payment at the place for payment, or where no such rate exists at that place, then the same rate in the State of the currency of payment. In the absence of such a rate at either place the rate of interest shall be the appropriate rate fixed by the law of the State of the currency of payment.
>
> The aggrieved party is entitled to additional damages if the non-payment caused it a greater harm.

[94] Article 9:508 PECL states:

> If payment of a sum of money is delayed, the aggrieved party is entitled to interest on that sum from the time when payment is due to the time of payment at the average commercial bank short-term lending rate to prime borrowers prevailing for the contractual currency of payment at the place where payment is due.
>
> The aggrieved party may in addition recover damages for any further loss so far as these are recoverable under this Section.

[95] See, e.g., *ICC Arbitral Award*, Case No. 8128/1995 (Chemical fertilizer case), available at http://cisgw3 .law.pace.edu/cases/958128i1.html; *Arbitral Award*, Austria June 15, 1994 Vienna Arbitration proceeding SCH-4366 (Rolled metal sheets case), available at http://cisgw3.law.pace.edu/cases/940615a3.html; *ICC Arbitral Award*, Case No. 8769 of December 1996 (Electrical appliances case), available at http:// cisgw3.law.pace.edu/cases/968769i1.html. Some national courts have also adopted this approach. See, e.g., Supreme Economic Court of the Republic of Belarus, May 20, 2003 (*Holimplex Inc. v. State Farm-Combine Sozh*, available at http://cisgw3.law.pace.edu/cases/030520b6.html). See generally, Klaus P. Berger, "International Arbitral Practice and the UNIDROIT Principles of International Commercial Contracts," 46 *American J. of Comparative L.* 129, 137 (1998); Lu Song, "Award of Interest in Arbitration under Article 78 CISG," 12 *Uniform L. Rev.* 79 et seq. (2007).

[96] See Articles 46 and 62 CISG.

by this Convention." This provision reflects a compromise between civil law countries, which tend to grant specific performance routinely, and common law countries, which consider specific performance as an extraordinary remedy.[97]

At first glance, the answer to the question of whether Article 28 CISG is applicable to arbitral tribunals seems to be a straightforward one. In contrast to other provisions, for instance Articles 45(3) and 61(3) CISG, Article 28 CISG expressly refers to "court," but not to "arbitral tribunal." The path toward application of Article 28 CISG by arbitral tribunals therefore already appears to be blocked by its wording. However, reasons for the different treatment of specific performance by national courts and arbitral tribunals cannot be ascertained. The primary aim of Article 28 CISG (the avoidance of a conflict with national court systems) also affects arbitral tribunals, which serve as substitutes for domestic courts.[98] The CISG's Secretariat's commentary states that: "Although the buyer has a right to assistance of a court or arbitral tribunal to enforce the seller's obligation to perform the contract, [Article 28 CISG] limits that right to a certain degree."[99] Accordingly, Article 28 CISG is applied analogously to arbitral tribunals.[100]

The wording of Article 28 CISG refers to "its own law" in referencing Article 28 CISG application by national courts. "Its own law" refers to the domestic substantive law of the forum state, excluding the conflict of laws, thus the *lex fori* and not the *lex causae*.[101] The problem with international arbitration is the arbitration tribunal does not possess "its own law" nor a real *lex fori*. The question is now: What happens in the event a party brings an action for specific performance before an arbitral tribunal? In following as close as possible the legal status before a national court, the arbitral tribunal's "own law" is to be understood as the substantive law of the state to whose *lex arbitri*[102] the arbitral tribunal is subject to, which generally means the law of the place of arbitration.[103] Thus, whether

---

[97] See Andrea Björklund, in *UN-Convention*, Article 28 CISG, para. 1; Beate Gsell in *Kommentar zum UN-Kaufrecht*, 2nd ed. (ed. H. Honsell) (Heidelberg: Springer, 2010), Article 28 CISG, para. 9; Huber and Mullis, *The CISG*, 186; Markus Müller-Chen in *Commentary on the UN Convention*, Article 28 CISG, para. 1; Perales Viscasillas and Ramos Muñoz, "CISG & Arbitration," 63, 64.

[98] For more detail on this aspect, see Gsell in *UN-Kaufrecht*, Article 28 CISG, para. 9. Secretariat Commentary on 1978 Draft, Article 42 (now Article 46 CISG), para. 9.

[99] Id.

[100] See also Björklund, in *UN-Convention*, Article 28 CISG, para. 18; Markus Müller-Chen, in *Commentary on the UN Convention*, Article 28 CISG, para. 8; Perales Viscasillas and Ramos Muñoz, "CISG & Arbitration," 63, 64.

[101] Björklund, in *UN-Convention*, Article 28 CISG, para. 16; John M. Catalano, "More Fiction Than Fact: The Perceived Differences in the Application of Specific Performance under the United Nations Convention on Contracts for the International Sale of Goods," 71 *Tulane. L. Rev.* 1807, 1819 (1997); Huber and Mullis, *The CISG*, 187; Gsell in *UN-Kaufrecht*, Article 28 CISG, para. 1; Amy H. Kastely, "The Right to Require Performance in International Sales: Towards an International Interpretation of the Vienna Convention," 63 *Washington. L. Rev.* 607, 637 et seq. (1988); Müller-Chen, in *Commentary on the UN Convention*, Article 28 CISG, para. 9; Steve Walt, "For Specific Performance under the United Nations Sales Convention," 26 *Texas Int'l L.J.* 211, 219 (1991).

[102] Müller-Chen in *Commentary on the UN Convention*, Article 28 CISG, para. 9, n. 26 (describes the *lex arbitri* as follows: "the law according to which the validity of the arbitration convention, the arbitrability, the composition of the arbitration tribunal, the principal rules of the proceedings, the support by State courts, and the appealability are determined").

[103] See Björklund in *UN-Convention*, Article 28 CISG, para. 18; Huber and Mullis, *The CISG*, 187; Gsell in *UN-Kaufrecht*, Article 28 CISG, para. 12; Müller-Chen in *Commentary on the UN Convention*, Article 28 CISG, para. 8; Perales Viscasillas and Ramos Muñoz, "CISG & Arbitration," 63, 64.

an arbitral tribunal has the ability to order specific performance will depend on the *lex arbitri* and will vary depending on the jurisdiction.[104]

VII. Concluding Remarks

The CISG and international arbitration both possess the same or at least very similar fundamental values. The CISG is often applied in arbitration either by choice of law (direct method) or in the absence of a choice of law through conflict of laws rules. Because of the similarity of values, arbitration tribunals are well equipped to apply an international law instrument like the CISG. However, the application of the CISG in international arbitration is not without problems. In particular, the indirect method of application in cases without a choice of law, the clash of formality requirements of international arbitration, and the lack of formality in CISG rules, as well as whether the remedy of specific performance should be given, are examples of disharmonies between the two institutions. Moreover, the danger of differentiated interpretation and gap-filling by national courts and arbitral tribunals, and whether there will be a convergence of these interpretations, is a matter that will have to be observed in the future. Nevertheless, in spite of these problems, the CISG and international arbitration will remain symbiotic in nature.

---

[104] See also Björklund in *UN-Convention*, Article 28 CISG, para. 18; Henry D. Gabriel, in *Drafting Contracts under the CISG* (ed. H. M. Flechtner, R. A. Brand, and M. A. Walter) (New York: Oxford University Press, 2007), 530.

11 The CISG as Soft Law and Choice of Law: Gōjū Ryū?[1]

Lisa Spagnolo

I. Introduction

It goes without saying that the CISG is hard law. Yet, in many ways, it mimics soft law in its operation and impact. This is largely due to its emphasis on party autonomy, by allowing parties to modify its provisions or exclude its application altogether. However, whether parties actually exercise their autonomy is determined by broader factors concerning choice of law. In the context of adjudication, CISG is applied as hard law. However, in this chapter it is argued that the CISG behaves like soft law in many senses. Consequently, this chapter argues that an approach that takes into account the effect on party choices of law in selecting from otherwise equally valid doctrinal interpretations may help mold the CISG in a manner more conducive to its underlying aims. In other words, by recognizing the CISG's "quasi-soft" or "optional" nature, scholars can focus attention on the effect of interpretation on choices of law in practice.

Soft law depends for its effectiveness entirely on its acceptability to potential users, primarily in terms of its economic value. In other words, its effectiveness depends on its desirability as a choice of law. Likewise, if factors affecting choices of law are taken into account in interpreting the CISG, then such an approach will make it a more desirable choice of law. This may increase the frequency with which the CISG is applied and its comparative efficiency vis-à-vis other choices of law. This, in turn, will enhance its impact and arguably improve the efficiency of international trade.

Section II considers the characteristics of hard and soft laws. Section III highlights the various hard and soft law aspects of the CISG in the adjudicatory context, and Section IV discusses the nature of the CISG as soft law and Section V analyzes the usefulness of acknowledging this aspect of its nature. Examples of how this might influence interpretation are given in Section VI. Finally, the limits to the soft law conceptualization of the CISG are emphasized in Section VII and some conclusions are provided in Section VIII.

II. Characteristics of Hard and Soft Law

It is useful to first consider the classic differences between what is meant by hard and soft law. In the area of contractual relations, most national systems normally allow their

[1] "Goju-Ryu" in Japanese literally means "hard/soft" and is one of the four original Okinawan styles of Karate.

subjects ample freedom in conducting their private transactions. Naturally, this autonomy is not unfettered, and thus some private transactions will be deemed devoid of legal effect or otherwise affected by domestic hard laws aimed at upholding certain public policies. An example of government intervention into the private sphere of contract law is laws prohibiting trade in human body parts, but hard law may also restrict such things as choice of law; for example, Brazilian law deems the *lex loci contractus* as the governing law, and this rule is widely construed as a prohibition on private choices of law.[2]

For international law, hard law qualities can be discerned, but often with less ease. International rules generally do "not work without the constant help, co-operation and support of national legal systems."[3] International laws become hard when they are incorporated into national law, or alternatively, take effect within each sovereign jurisdiction by virtue of that State's constitutional machinery. In some cases, a "hard legal order" of institutional structures is established to ensure compliance, such as the International Court of Justice (ICJ) or WTO dispute panels and Appellate Body. However, unless an international adjudicatory mechanism has been created to enforce the law in question, international law depends completely on national legal systems for its implementation and enforcement. Thus, in a sense, even hard international law falls short of the "hardness" achieved by domestic law.[4]

Although international law often relies on the states for its effect, it is nonetheless hard[5] because, provided states fulfil their treaty obligations, the law in question will bind the parties at which it is aimed. Increasingly, however, many rules at the international level are soft laws, described as "a body of standards, commitments, joint statements, or declarations of policy or intention"[6] created by multilateral bodies, which then promote use of the rules. Antonio Cassesse describes soft law as the provenance of "international organizations or other collective bodies"; dealing with "new concerns . . . to which previously the international community was not sensitive or . . . alert"; and instituting nonlegally binding obligations on matters regarding which it is "hard for States to reach full convergence of views."[7] He concludes that soft law may gradually "turn into law proper," or provide a catalyst for change, but emphasizes that soft law *per se* is "no real law at all."[8]

There are, of course, many domestic nonbinding standards, codes of practice, and guidelines or soft law. The first two of Cassesse's characteristics of soft law can also be equally true of hard law; it can also deal with new concerns, and is created by international organizations. It follows that the defining feature of soft law is the third characteristic,

---

[2] "Article 9 Lei de Introdução ao Código Civil Brasileiro 1942," in Introductory Law to the Brazilian Civil Code, Decreto-Lei No 4657/1942 (contracts not containing arbitration clauses).

[3] Antonio Cassesse, *International Law*, 2nd ed. (Oxford: Oxford University Press, 2005), 9.

[4] R. R. Baxter, "International Law in 'Her Infinite Variety,'" 29 *Int'l & Comparative L. Quarterly* 549, 554 (1980); Kenneth W. Abbott and Duncan Snidal, "Hard and Soft Law in International Governance," 54 *Int'l Organization* 421, 426 (2000).

[5] See Cassesse, *International Law*, 12 (describing "proper" international law as opposed to "soft laws"); Abbott and Snidal, "Hard and Soft Law," 426. See generally Harold H. Koh, "Why Do Nations Obey International Law?," 106 *Yale L.J.* 2599 (1997) (broad description of the processes and repeated interactions).

[6] Cassesse, *International Law*, 196.

[7] Id., 196.

[8] Id., 196, 507–8.

that is, its nonbinding nature, that, in and of itself, it has no legal effect.[9] Charles Lipson argues this distinction is not traditional, but arises from the definition of treaties codified in Article 26 of the Vienna Convention on the Law of Treaties, which states every treaty is "binding upon the parties."[10]

A far more accurate delineation between hard and soft law involves a sliding scale based on three characteristics: legally binding nature of obligations, precision, and delegation of authority for interpretation and implementation.[11] The combination of the binding nature of the rules, the degree to which they fix consequences or allow them to be determined *ex post*, and the existence of centralized enforcement processes all indicate whether a law is hard or soft.[12] Combinations of these qualities of binding obligations, precision, and delegation in varying strengths indicate relative hardness on a sliding scale rather than as a binary choice.[13] Using these criteria, it is unclear where the CISG sits on this sliding scale – the CISG has a hard, legally binding nature, but lacks a central judicial structure. It involves a high degree of delegation to states regarding implementation and enforcement.

The rate of soft law creation is on the rise for a number of reasons. Unlike hard law, soft law is cheaper to create due to its informal status.[14] It has no requirement of participation by state officials and carries no lengthy ratification process. The informal nature of the process lends the development of soft law much flexibility, which is highly advantageous in terms of ease and speed of negotiation and drafting of such instruments.[15] The political environment of hard law negotiations often results in instruments of limited scope to ensure agreement, and leads to compromise on substantive content by the use of vague provisions.[16] By contrast, soft law can focus on "elegant solutions rather than forced

---

[9] See also Anthony Aust, "The Theory and Practice of Informal International Instruments," 35 *Int'l & Comparative L. Quarterly* 784, 794 (1986); Chris Brummer, "Why Soft Law Dominates International Finance – And Not Trade?," 13 *J. of Int'l Economic L.* 623, 623, 628 (2011); Janet Koven Levit, "A Bottom-Up Approach to International Lawmaking: The Tale of Three Trade Finance Instruments," 30 *Yale J. of Int'l L.* 125, 190 (2005).

[10] And further "must be performed by them in good faith." Charles Lipson, "Why Are Some International Agreements Informal?," 45 *International Organization* 495, 502 (1991). See also Baxter, "International Law in 'Her Infinite Variety,'" 556; Article 26 Vienna Convention on the Law of Treaties, opened for signature on May 23, 1969, UN Doc. A/CONF. 39/27, 115 UNTS 331 (entered into force on January 27, 1980).

[11] Abbott and Snidal, "Hard and Soft Law," 421 (citing earlier work by Abbott, Keohane, Moravcsik, Slaughter, and Snidal).

[12] Id., at 427. See similarly Lipson, "Why Are Some International Agreements Informal?," 498–9 (referring to the level of "informality" of international agreements as determined by the governmental level at which the agreement is made; the visibility of agreement by the head of state as opposed to bureaucratic delegate, and by its form (written, oral)).

[13] Cassese, *International Law*, at 194; Abbott and Snidal, "Hard and Soft Law," 421–4.

[14] Abbott and Snidal, "Hard and Soft Law," 434; Brummer, "Why Soft Law Dominates International Finance," 631.

[15] Aust, "The Theory and Practice of Informal International Instruments," 789 (referring to the advantages of speed, flexibility and confidentiality collectively as "convenience"); Lipson, "Why Are Some International Agreements Informal?," 500; Brummer, "Why Soft Law Dominates International Finance," 631; Abbott and Snidal, "Hard and Soft Law," 434.

[16] Clayton P. Gillette and Robert E. Scott, "The Political Economy of International Sales Law," 25 *Int'l Rev. L. & Economics* 446, 458–9, 448–9, 457, 462, 465–6, 468–9, 473–5 (2005); Steven Walt, "The CISG's Expansion Bias: A Comment on Franco Ferrari," 25 *Int'l Rev. L. & Economics* 342, 347 (2005). See generally Alan Schwartz and Robert E. Scott, "Contract Theory and the Limits of Contract Law,"

consensus."[17] Their nonbinding nature makes soft laws an attractive alternative. Essentially, participants are able to learn the consequences of the new rules over time, thus avoiding unpleasant surprises, and can work to resolve originally unforseen problems.[18] For hard law, the involvement of state negotiators naturally introduces concerns regarding intrusion on national sovereignty,[19] a problem unlikely to prevent agreement on soft law by nongovernment representatives.

The flexibility afforded by the soft law process also makes it easier to adopt amendments after promulgation.[20] By contrast, changes to hard law are, at best, extremely difficult to achieve. Future amending protocol is rarely adopted by all state parties to the original treaty, resulting in a degree of fragmentation.[21] Ease of amendment allows soft law to be more dynamic and to keep pace with developments, whereas hard law is more likely to fall behind current practice.[22] Soft law can foster norms within skilled collegial "networks,"[23] and those norms may then eventually "percolate" to become recognized formal law.[24]

The positive features of soft law are also the bases of its disadvantages. Chief among them is something that derives from its flexibility and nonbinding quality; it affords parties "a cheap exit from commitments."[25] It thus lacks, in a game theory sense, the "assurance" value of a credible commitment to hard law by which states signal their cooperation with other states in reaching the same mutually beneficial coordination point.[26] Hard law has an independent legitimacy that creates a stronger "compliance

---

113 *Yale Law J.* 541 (2003). Contra Abbott and Snidal, "Hard and Soft Law," *passim* (noting "precision" as one of the defining characteristics of "hard law").

[17] Robert A. Pate, "The Future of Harmonization: Soft Law Instruments and the Principled Advance of International Lawmaking," 13 (August 2009), available at http://works.bepress.com/robert_pate/1.

[18] Lipson, "Why Are Some International Agreements Informal?," 500; Abbott and Snidal, "Hard and Soft Law," 423, 441; Brummer, "Why Soft Law Dominates International Finance," 633.

[19] Aust, "The Theory and Practice of Informal International Instruments," 789; Pate, "The Future of Harmonization," 11–12 (describing the reason for the United States making a declaration pursuant to Article 95 CISG as a desire to preserve the operation of the UCC so far as possible); Brummer, "Why Soft Law Dominates International Finance," 631; Abbott and Snidal, "Hard and Soft Law," 423, 436, 441.

[20] Aust, "The Theory and Practice of Informal International Instruments," 791; Lipson, "Why Are Some International Agreements Informal?," 500; Brummer, "Why Soft Law Dominates International Finance," 631; Abbott and Snidal, "Hard and Soft Law," 423, 436.

[21] See, e.g., UNCITRAL Model Law on International Commercial Arbitration 1985, GA Res. 40/72, UN Doc. A/40/17, annex I, December 11, 1985, which was adopted by legislation in many nations. The Model Law was subsequently amended in 2006: GA Res. 61/33, December 4, 2006. At the time of writing, the amended Model Law had been enacted in only twelve of the member states to the original 1985 version (or provinces thereof). See UN Status Page, available at http://www.uncitral.org/uncitral/en/uncitral_texts/ arbitration/1985Model_arbitration_status.html.

[22] See also Levit, "A Bottom-Up Approach," 171; Brummer, "Why Soft Law Dominates International Finance," 631.

[23] Anne-Marie Slaughter, "Governing the Global Economy through Government Networks," in *The Role of Law in International Politics: Essays in International Relations and International Law* (ed. M. Byers) (Oxford: Oxford University Press, 2000), 202; Charles K. Whitehead, "What's Your Sign? International Norms, Signals, and Compliance," 27 *Michigan J. of Int'l L.* 695, 703 (2006); Brummer, "Why Soft Law Dominates International Finance," 634.

[24] Levit, "A Bottom-Up Approach," 172, 180–2 (noting that the process of norm generation can be either top-down percolation or bottom-up).

[25] Brummer, "Why Soft Law Dominates International Finance," 630. See also Lipson, "Why Are Some International Agreements Informal?," 501, 518.

[26] Whitehead, "What's Your Sign?," 712; Abbott and Snidal, "Hard and Soft Law," 426. See also Baxter, "International Law in 'Her Infinite Variety,'" 555, *passim* (perception of mutual advantage); Lipson, "Why

pull."[27] Political or economic forces motivate the creation of soft rather than hard law,[28] and these same forces determine whether it will have practical effect in the absence of any legally binding quality. In some instances, avoidance of negative reputational effects can provide informal law with similar or greater coercive effect in practice as hard law.[29]

There are numerous international examples of soft law in the area of contracts, such as the Principles of European Contract Law (PECL) and the UNIDROIT Principles of International Commercial Contracts (UNIDROIT Principles).[30] Other, more targeted soft laws, such as the International Chamber of Commerce's (ICC) Uniform Customs and Practices for Documentary Credit Transactions (UCP) and Incoterms, have been universally recognized as international customary law.[31] There are also a host of international arbitral rules that are applied to the resolution of contractual disputes, including ICC Arbitration Rules and UNCITRAL Arbitration Rules.[32] A more abstract example of soft law is the traditional notion of the *lex mercatoria*.[33] In each case, broadly speaking, the soft law in question has no binding legal effect, unless the parties themselves have validly agreed to apply the rules, or alternatively, the forum court or arbitral tribunal uses such soft law in resolving the dispute.[34] On the basis of the sliding scale definition

---

Are Some International Agreements Informal?," 508–11 (referring to the "shadow of the future" as an influence on the strength of the signal of commitment), and 513.

[27] Abbott and Snidal, "Hard and Soft Law," 428 (citing Thomas Franck 1990).

[28] Lipson, "Why Are Some International Agreements Informal?," 518 (arguing that soft law allows governments to enter international agreements "quickly and quietly"); id., 630.

[29] Whitehead, "What's Your Sign?," 707–12; Koh, "Why Do Nations Obey International Law?," 2642.

[30] Commission on European Contract Law, Principles of European Contract Law, Parts I & II (1999) & Part III (2003), available at http://www.cisg.law.pace.edu/cisg/text/textef.html (PECL); International Institute for the Unification of Private Law (UNIDROIT), *UNIDROIT Principles of International Commercial Contracts 2004* (Rome: UNIDROIT, 2004). The DCFR could also be utilized in this manner. See *Principles, Definitions and Model Rules of European Private Law: Draft Common Frame of Reference (DCFR)* (ed. Christian von Bar and Eric Clive) (Munich: Sellier, 2009).

[31] *International Chamber of Commerce (ICC), Incoterms 2010* (Paris: ICC, 2010); ICC, *Uniform Customs and Practice for Documentary Credits (UCP) 600* (Paris: ICC, 2007). See also, Levit, "A Bottom-Up Approach," 172–4 (noting their impact and the fact that they do not fit within technical definitions of laws, but are considered soft law nonetheless). Thus it seems surprising that a recent survey found Incoterms and UCP to have been used at least "sometimes" by only 62% and 57% of 67 corporate counsel respondents surveyed; see School of International Arbitration at Queen Mary, University of London, *International Arbitration Survey: Choices in International Arbitration* (2010), available at http://www.arbitrationonline.org/docs/2010_InternationalArbitrationSurveyReport.pdf, at 15.

[32] ICC, *ICC Rules of Arbitration* (Paris: ICC, 2011), available at http://www.iccwbo.org/uploadedFiles/Court/Arbitration/other/2012_Arbitration%20and%20ADR%20Rules%20ENGLISH.pdf; UNCITRAL, *UNCITRAL Arbitration Rules* (Vienna: UNCITRAL, 2011), available at http://www.uncitral.org/pdf/english/texts/arbitration/arb-rules-revised/arb-rules-revised-2010-e.pdf.

[33] See Berthold Goldman, "The Applicable Law: General Principles of Law – The Lex Mercatoria" in *Contemporary Problems in International Arbitration* (ed. J.D.M. Lew) (Dordrecht: Martinus Nijhoff, 1986), 113, 116 ("*lex mercatoria* is, at the least, *a set of general principles and customary rules spontaneously referred to or elaborated in the framework of international trade, without reference to a particular national system of law*"); Harold J. Berman and Colin Kaufman, "The Law of International Commercial Transactions (Lex Mercatoria)," 19 *Harvard Int'l L.J.* 221, 272–3 (1978) (describing *lex mercatoria* as "an international body of law, founded on commercial understandings and contract practices of an international community composed principally of mercantile, shipping, insurance and banking enterprises of all countries"); Levit, "A Bottom-Up Approach," 186; Ole Lando, "The Lex Mercatoria in International Commercial Arbitration," 34 *Int'l & Comparative L. Quarterly* 747 (1985).

[34] See also Christopher Kee and Edgardo Muñoz, "In Defence of the CISG," 14 *Deakin L. Rev.* 99, 118 (2009).

adopted earlier, they remain soft law, despite the fact that their pervasive use in practice may mean that individual parties have little choice but to use them.[35]

Harder to categorize is supranational religious law. For example, since it finds its source in the *Quran*, the *Sunna*, and other religious texts, Islamic law can be described as supranational rather than international law.[36] The extent to which the forum applies a contractual law reflecting Islamic principles essentially determines whether or not Islamic law has legal effect in the particular case. Nonetheless, the binding legal effect derives from the fact that a state law has been influenced by Islamic law, in much the same way as state laws might have been influenced by other soft law, such as the influence of UNIDROIT Principles on Chinese contract law. The parties could choose to apply Islamic law to govern the contract, subject to restrictions on choice of anational law,[37] but this in effect is the same as a choice of soft law. Ultimately, it seems Islamic law should therefore arguably be seen as international soft law.

In the examples considered here, soft law provides a set of contractual terms from which the parties may choose. Parties may prefer to simply incorporate preexisting terms rather than expend time to negotiate and draft their own custom terms. Soft law operates in much the same way as "boilerplate" contractual terms. It provides an efficient and convenient shortcut for contracting. Yet, one might ask, if the CISG provides parties with a set of default rules, is the CISG, in effect, really all that different from the types of soft law mentioned above?

A. *When Soft Is Not So Soft*

As indicated by the sliding scale approach, the soft–hard law divide is not a crisp one. Some soft laws are in reality "harder" than they might first appear. For example, international financial law is, on an institutional assessment of the manner in which it is

---

[35] An example of this is the use of SWIFT standard protocols for electronic interbank transfers, which are invariably required by transferring banks. See Society for Worldwide Financial Telecommunication, available at http://www.swift.com. See also Whitehead, "What's Your Sign?," 707–12.

[36] Gary F. Bell, "New Challenges for the Uniformisation of Laws: How the CISG is Challenged by 'Asian Values' and Islamic Law," in *Towards Uniformity: The 2nd Annual MAA Schlechtriem CISG Conference* (ed. I. Schwenzer and L. Spagnolo) (The Hague: Eleven International Publishing, 2011), 11, 22.

[37] Indeed, English courts have rejected a choice of Shari'a law on the basis that it was not a valid choice of law pursuant to Article 3(1) Rome Convention on the Law Applicable to Contractual Obligations, 1980 OJ (L 266), June 19, 1980, 19 ILM. 1492 (1980): *Shamil Bank of Bahrain v. Beximco Pharm. Ltd* [2004] EWCA Civ. 19 (Court of Appeal); Gary B. Born, International Commercial Arbitration (Kluwer: Dordrecht 2009) 2227, n. 559. By contrast, French law now specifically allows arbitrators of international disputes to apply anational "rules of law" chosen by parties to govern their contract: Article 1496 Code de Procédure Civile (New French Code of Civil Procedure) (October 1, 2011). As a matter of choice of law rules, the Rome I Regulation permits only choices of "law" (national law), but allows anational rules to be incorporated as contractual terms: Regulation (EC) No 593/2008 of the European Parliament and of the Council of June 17, 2008, on the Law Applicable to Contractual Obligations [2008] OJ L 177/6, Recital [13], Article 3. See also Symeon C. Symeonides, "Party Autonomy in Rome I and II from a Comparative Perspective," in *Convergence and Divergence in Private International Law – Liber Amicorum Kurt Siehr* (ed. Katharina Boele-Woelki et al.) (The Hague: Eleven International Publishing, 2010), 513, 539–40; Helmut Heiss, "Party Autonomy," in *Rome I Regulation: The Law Applicable to Contractual Obligations in Europe* (ed. F. Ferrari and S. Leible) (Munich: Sellier, 2009), 1, 2. See Tribunale di Padova-Sez. Este, Italy, January 11, 2005, available at http://cisgw3.law.pace.edu/cases/050111i3.html (CISG was incorporated into the contractual terms rather than a valid choice of law).

enforced, harder than its soft-law quality suggests.[38] Soft law commitments are in some cases commonly observed and can have a strong "compliance pull."[39]

So too, it must be acknowledged that soft law takes on a harder edge for contractual relations. The "cheap exit" disadvantage of soft law mentioned earlier is really only relevant to states, not individual persons or entities. Provided the parties have agreed to apply the soft law to their contractual relations, then absent any prohibition on such a choice of law,[40] most legal regimes will effectively enforce that choice due to the primacy of party autonomy in contract law. Thus, despite the fact that it is soft law, the rules in question will legally bind the parties.

Despite lacking legal force, soft law can have greater operational effect than hard law due to political or economic forces. Institutional and behavioral influences can step into the legal void. For example, if a soft law provides a cheap, accessible, and desirable set of default rules that can therefore be used conveniently and efficiently, it may become a habitual choice for contractual parties. Major market players (such as banks) may incorporate references to soft law in their standardized contract forms. Once a certain level of popularity is reached, such a choice may no longer in truth be a choice at all, as it would be highly inefficient, or perhaps commercially unacceptable to make an alternative choice in most transactions. Market forces may increase the economic value and popularity of soft law by virtue of "network effects."[41]

The ICC's Incoterms and UCP exemplify the economic value and network effects of soft law, because they overwhelmingly dominate choice of terms of each type in international trade.[42] The impact of soft law is often dependent on the political and economic power of the institutions that create and support its use, such as the international financial rules created by the Financial Stability Board, the Basel Committee on Banking Supervision, and the International Organization of Securities Commissions, bodies dominated by powerful central banks, regulatory agencies, and finance ministries.[43] Market forces have shaped the disciplinary effect of these technically nonbinding rules. For example, a bank's failure to adopt the Basel Committee's capital standards acts as a reputational signal to the market regarding its solvency and capitalization.[44] Clearly, soft laws can be ubiquitous, and can rival or surpass hard law in importance and practical impact.

On the other hand, where a soft law is not widely accepted by major institutional players or by most parties in the market, then the difference in impact between soft and hard law becomes apparent. For example, the CISG enjoys a good degree of operational effectiveness in part because it applies as a default law. Conversely, the UNIDROIT Principles and PECL only become applicable when chosen by the parties as governing

---

[38] Levit, "A Bottom-Up Approach," 189; Brummer, "Why Soft Law Dominates International Finance," 624.

[39] Brummer, "Why Soft Law Dominates International Finance," 624.

[40] See *supra* note 37.

[41] See also Lisa Spagnolo, "Green Eggs and Ham: The CISG, Path Dependence, and the Behavioural Economics of Lawyers' Choices of Law in International Sales Contracts," 6 *J. of Private Int'l L.* 417 (2010) (behavioral economics and psychological influences on choice of law).

[42] Sir Roy Goode, Herbert Kronke, Ewan McKendrick, and Jeffrey Wool, *Transnational Commercial Law: Text, Cases and Materials* (Oxford: Oxford University Press, 2007), 358 (discussing the "[n]ear universal adoption" of the UCP). But see evidence on UCP usage, School of International Arbitration at Queen Mary, *International Arbitration Survey* (finding UCP to have been used at least "sometimes" by only 57% of 67 corporate counsel respondents surveyed).

[43] Brummer, "Why Soft Law Dominates International Finance," 627.

[44] Id., at 638.

law.[45] Consequently, the UNIDROIT Principles and PECL are far less utilized than the CISG,[46] despite their "broader and less compromising" nature.[47] In sum, it can be observed that, while hardness certainly assures some degree of impact, often its ultimate impact depends not so much upon its hard or soft characterization, but on its acceptance, perceived utility, and frequent use by those with economic influence in the relevant market for law. These observations hold important implications for the CISG, as discussed in the following sections.

B. *When Hard Is Not So Hard*

The list of treaties or conventions that never entered into force is a long one. The list is also long for conventions that entered into force, but made little impact. This can be due to a number of factors, including a low number of adopting nations or numerous reservations to the convention, which was the case for the Uniform Law on the International Sale of Goods (ULIS).[48] Other factors relate to applicability and enforceability. In the former case, courts may narrowly construe a convention to limit its applicability. In the latter case, there may be no effective enforcement mechanism to ensure compliance to treaty obligations. These factors reduce the effectiveness and thwart the purposes of hard law conventions. Another quality may likewise reduce the impact of hard law, but in a manner entirely consistent with its original purpose. A case in point is the CISG. One of

[45] An exception to the nonparty choice model of soft laws is when the forum allows their application as a guide to international contractual principles or evidence of international commercial usages (international customary law). See *infra* note 59.

[46] Institute of European and Comparative Law, Oxford University, and Clifford Chance LLP, *Civil Justice and Choice of Contract Law: A Business Survey* (2008) (reporting that 10% of respondent businesses occasionally or almost never used PECL; 17% of respondent businesses often or occasionally using UNIDROIT Principles; yet more than 31% had had the CISG apply; 29% were in contracting states and never or only occasionally opted out; a further 2% were in noncontracting states but usually or occasionally opted in; and, additionally, presumably a small fraction of the 46% who indicated they usually opt out and the 20% who "don't know" would sometimes be subject to the CISG) (Questions 25–27 spread sheet on file with the author; email correspondence with author October 2009). See summary, Stefan Vogenauer, "Oxford Civil Justice Survey – Civil Justice Systems in Europe: Implications for Choice of Forum and Choice of Contract Law A Business Survey," Final Results, available at http://denning.law.ox.ac.uk/iecl/pdfs/Oxford%20Civil%20Justice%20Survey%20-%20Summary%20of%20Results,%20Final.pdf, and subsequent publication: *Civil Justice Systems in Europe: Implications for Choice of Forum and Choice of Contract Law*, Studies of the Oxford Institute of European and Comparative Law (ed. Stefan Vogenauer and Chris Hodges) (Oxford: Hart Publishing, 2014 (forthcoming)). Contra School of International Arbitration at Queen Mary, *International Arbitration Survey*, at 15 (reporting that 53% of corporate counsel surveyed indicated they had "sometimes" used the CISG compared with 62% stating they had "sometimes" used UNIDROIT Principles/Incoterms). However, this surprising result can probably be explained by the inclusion within a single category of both UNIDROIT Principles and the very widely used Incoterms. Indeed, respondents indicated that Incoterms were used more frequently than UNIDROIT Principles: at 15.

[47] Lars Meyer, "Soft Law for Solid Contracts? A Comparative Analysis of the Value of the UNIDROIT Principles of International Commercial Contracts and the Principle of European Contract Law to the Process of Contract Law Harmonization," 34 *Denver J of Law & Policy* 119, 132 (2006).

[48] See, e.g., *Convention Relating to a Uniform Law on the International Sale of Goods*, opened for signature July 1, 1964, 834 UNTS 107 (entered into force August 18, 1972) ("ULIS") http://www.unidroit.org/english/implement/i-main.htm. ULIS contained a number of reservations. For example, pursuant to the reservation permitted by ULIS Article V, contracting states could ensure the convention had little effect as there would be no obligation to apply it unless parties agreed to opt in.

its central tenets is party autonomy. Hence, CISG Article 6 allows the parties to agree to modifications of CISG provisions or to partially or entirely exclude its application. Thus, the impact of the CISG to a large extent depends on the preferences of parties engaged in international trade.

Contracting parties may select the law of a member state to apply to their contract, resulting in the application of the CISG as governing law of the contract, or, more problematically, may directly choose the CISG, provided this can be validly done under forum choice of law rules.[49] Presumably, parties might prefer to select the CISG rather than expend time and effort negotiating and then drafting terms, or selecting a law unfamiliar to one or both parties.[50] It may also serve as a neutral law ideal for situations where the parties are unable to easily agree on a choice of law.[51] The very fact that parties may voluntarily make their contract subject to the CISG in circumstances where it would not otherwise apply demonstrates one way in which a hard law such as the CISG can actually be used as soft law.[52] Just like soft law, the CISG can provide an efficient and convenient shortcut for contracting.

III. CISG in Adjudication as Hard and Soft Law

As was stated at the outset of this chapter, the CISG is undoubtedly hard law. The rights and obligations created by its provisions legally bind the buyer and seller when it is applied to the contract. It applies automatically to contracts where the prerequisites for its application are satisfied and the parties have not agreed to opt out. Yet, in the context of its application by a court or tribunal, there are a number of ways in which its respective hardness or softness can be considered. The extent to which the CISG is binding will vary depending on the adjudicatory setting and the circumstances underpinning its relevance to the proceedings.

A. *When the CISG Is Hard Law*

Although the CISG creates obligations for the parties, its impact upon adjudicators is a different matter. The crucial question in relation to the hard–soft characterization is whether the adjudicator must apply the CISG, or whether, instead, the adjudicator has discretion to apply it. However, in the case of the CISG, the binding duty to apply it as hard law derives from the nature of the CISG as a treaty, creating an obligation in international law to apply it within member states where its applicability

---

[49] See discussion regarding choice of law in the various authorities referred to *supra* note 37.

[50] See School of International Arbitration at Queen Mary, *International Arbitration Survey, infra* note 80.

[51] Larry A. DiMatteo et al., *International Sales Law: A Critical Analysis of CISG Jurisprudence* (New York: Cambridge University Press, 2005), 14, n. 48 (referring to the CISG's potential as a "compromise choice of law for parties from different national legal systems"); C. Widmer and P. Hachem, "Switzerland," in *The CISG and Its Impact on National Legal Systems* (ed. F. Ferrari) (Munich: Sellier, 2008), 281, 286 (from a survey of 153 Swiss lawyers in 2008, finding that 26% thought the CISG made choice-of-law negotiations easier).

[52] DiMatteo et al., *International Sales Law*, 13–14. See also Tribunale di Padova-Sez. Este, Italy, January 11, 2005 (CISG incorporated into contractual terms rather than a valid choice of law).

prerequisites have been satisfied.[53] The CISG is not a foreign law in such courts, so domestic law cannot be relied on by the court as a default law for matters covered by the CISG.[54] In such circumstances, a court in a member state has no residual discretion to apply domestic law that has been displaced by the CISG.[55] Under such circumstances, the CISG is hard law.

This situation is markedly different for a court sitting in a nonmember state, or an arbitral tribunal. For courts in nonmember states, application of the CISG may be nondiscretionary, but that turns entirely on the choice of law rules of the forum. Application of the CISG in such circumstances amounts to an application of foreign law and, therefore, is subject to the procedural rules regarding proof.[56] Arbitral tribunals are not subject to the same duties as courts in member states, and thus the obligation to apply the CISG, or, alternatively, the discretion to apply a different law will depend entirely on the arbitration agreement and the procedural rules applicable to the arbitration.[57]

B. When the CISG Is More Soft Than Hard

The potential soft law application of the CISG is now considered. Even where a court or arbitral tribunal has determined – perhaps by virtue of failure to satisfy the CISG's own applicability prerequisites, or due to the forum's choice of law rules – that the CISG is not applicable as a matter of law, the adjudicator may still decide to look to it as evidence of *lex mercatoria*, evidence of usages of international sales law, or customary international commercial law.[58] This has occurred in a number of cases,[59] particularly in China where the propensity for CISG application is heightened.[60] In these cases, regardless of one's views as to the legitimacy of the CISG as evidence of such usages, it can be said that the CISG is being applied not as hard or binding law, but as soft law. Like the *lex mercatoria*,

---

[53] See Lisa Spagnolo, *"Iura Novit Curia* and the CISG: Resolution of the Faux Procedural Black Hole," in Schwenzer and Spagnolo, *Towards Uniformity*, 181, 190. For member states, the CISG becomes hard law either by its adoption by the forum state, or through its subsequent incorporation or transformation into domestic law. Id., 190–6.

[54] Id., 196.

[55] Id., 196–8 (arguing that forum procedural laws that some might argue provide such discretion such as waiver rules are likewise displaced).

[56] Id., 198–9. Normally, forum domestic law applies as a default in absence of such proof.

[57] Id., 199–203.

[58] DiMatteo et al., *International Sales Law*, 14; Larry A. DiMatteo, "Resolving International Contract Disputes," 53 *Dispute Resolution J.* 75, 79 (1998).

[59] The CISG was referred to as evidencing international commercial practices and usages in the following cases: *Watkins-Johnson Co. v. Islamic Republic of Iran*, Iran-U.S. Claims Tribunal, July 28, 1989, at [95], [99], available at http://cisgw3.law.pace.edu/cases/890728i2.html; ICC Award No. 7331/1994, available at http://cisgw3.law.pace.edu/cases/947331i1.html; ICC Award No. 8502/1996, available at http://cisgw3.law.pace.edu/cases/968502i1.html; ICC Award No. 8817/1997, available at http://cisgw3.law.pace.edu/cases/978817i1.html; ICC Award No. 8908/1998, available at http://cisgw3.law.pace.edu/cases/988908i1.html (normative text); ICC Award No. 9474/1999, available at http://cisgw3.law.pace.edu/cases/999474i1.html; *South Sydney District Rugby League Football Club Ltd v. News Ltd* (2000) 177 ALR 611, Federal Court of Australia, November 3, 2000, available at http://cisgw3.law.pace.edu/cases/001103a3.html; Audiencia Provincial de Barcelona, Spain, February 4, 1997, available at http://cisgw3.law.pace.edu/cases/970204s4.html.

[60] See, e.g., China International Economic and Trade Arbitration Commission (CIETAC), June 30, 1999, available at http://cisgw3.law.pace.edu/cases/990630c1.html.

when used in this way, the CISG's value is as persuasive authority as to the norms of international sales, and not as binding law.[61]

An arbitral tribunal may sometimes determine that parties have not made a choice of law, and often will thereby be free to apply the "appropriate law." For example, this would be the case under Article 28 of the UNCITRAL Model Law.[62] The tribunal might consider the CISG, PECL, UNIDROIT Principles, or any number of domestic laws as appropriate law to be applied, or by way of *dépeçage* apply different laws to different issues in dispute.[63] Given the wide discretion available to the arbitrator, the CISG can be utilized as a soft law.

When the parties select the CISG to govern their contract "directly," as opposed to having it "indirectly" apply as part of the law of a member state, then their choice becomes contingent on the choice of law rules of the forum. These might prohibit the choice of anational rules. For example, in the EU, the Rome I Regulation disallows such a choice of anational "rules" rather than national "law," but instead treats such a choice as an incorporation of the CISG as part of the contractual terms.[64] Conceptually, the CISG in such circumstances applies in a softer fashion than if it were applied as law *per se*. It is true that, subject to any mandatory rules of the forum, this effectively binds the parties, but this is no different than any choice of soft law.

C. When the CISG Is More Hard Than Soft

The applicability of the CISG as the default governing law pursuant to CISG Article 1(1) is an important point of difference between it and soft laws, such as UNIDROIT Principles or PECL, which can only apply by agreement or where a tribunal considers them "appropriate law."[65] When drafting the CISG, the decision in favor of an opt-out scheme was contested,[66] but ultimately, this step in favor of a hard law approach has proven important in ensuring the success of the CISG in terms of the frequency of its application in practice.[67] More nuanced is the situation where the parties choose to opt

---

[61] Ole Lando, "The Lex Mercatoria and International Commercial Arbitration," 34 *Int'l & Comparative L. Quarterly* 747, 754 (1985) (lex mercatoria generally); Peter J. Mazzacano, "Harmonizing Values, Not Laws: The CISG and the Benefits of a Neo-Realist Perspective," *Nordic J. of Commercial L.* 1, 17 (2008).

[62] Article 28(2) UNCITRAL Model Law on International Commercial Arbitration 1985, as amended in 2006, GA Res A/40/72, UN Doc A/40/17 annex I (December 11, 1985) & GA Res A/RES/61/33, UN Doc A/61/17 annex I (December 4, 2006) (UNCITRAL Model Law) (failing designation by the parties, "the arbitral tribunal shall apply the law determined by the conflict of laws rules which it considers applicable").

[63] DiMatteo et al., *International Sales Law*, 18; DiMatteo, "Resolving International Contract Disputes," 75, 79 ("The CISG, along with the UNIDROIT Principles [and European Principles], provide arbitrators a suitable framework for deciding international contract disputes by the application of the general principles that underlie [these] documents").

[64] This can be more complicated in situations where an Article 95 CISG declaration has been made. See Spagnolo, *supra* note 53, at 196.

[65] See authorities regarding indirect choice of law, *supra* note 37.

[66] A similar proposal was rejected during the drafting of the CISG: 1980 Diplomatic Conference, *Summary Records of Meetings of the Second Committee*, UN Doc A/CONF.97/C.2/SR.1 [40] et seq; UN Doc A/CONF.97/C.2/SR.2 [6], available at http://www.cisg.law.pace.edu/cisg/2dcommittee/articles/meeting1.html.

[67] The need to exclude the CISG's application and thus ensure a more widespread application of the CISG has arguably led to its much greater use by comparison with opt-in schemes such as PECL or UNIDROIT Principles. See *supra* note 46, at 15

in despite the fact the CISG would not apply on its own terms. The forum may be bound by this choice, but in a manner similar to an agreed choice of soft law.

IV. How CISG Article 6 Transforms Hard law to Soft Law

The discussion in the previous section demonstrates that the CISG can be used as soft law where it would not otherwise be applicable as hard law, either due to the choices made by parties or decisions of the adjudicator. Conversely, in this section it is argued that the CISG operates like a soft law, even when it applies as hard law. Irrespective of any initial hardness in applicability, the paramount status of party autonomy in CISG Article 6 makes it appear somewhat soft. The availability of exclusion under Article 6 renders a technically hard law into a quasi-soft law, at least in terms of its practical or operational effect.

A. *Legal Effect of Exclusion*

Where parties choose a soft law such as UNIDROIT Principles, then, as noted earlier, the validity of their choice is determined by the applicable choice of law rules. In other words, provided the choice of soft law is supported by the adjudicator as a hard law substitute, the choice becomes legally binding – albeit by virtue of the hard law machinery in the form of choice of law rules. At least for the individual parties involved, this means soft law is effectively converted to hard law.

In reverse, it could be argued that a contractual exclusion of the CISG converts it from hard to soft law. This arguably removes the hardness of the CISG because it no longer legally binds the parties involved. Exclusion by parties cannot alter the legal effect of the treaty in binding the member state concerned, nor alter the primary applicability of the CISG to those individual circumstances to which it applies. In fact, unlike true soft law, the hard machinery that supports the removal of the binding effect of the CISG is located within the CISG. Article 6 CISG is what gives effect to the parties' choice. Without Article 6, the parties would have no autonomy to exercise in favor of exclusion of the CISG. Because Article 6 might be said to facilitate the capacity of parties to "convert" the CISG from a legally binding hard law to an inapplicable set of rules, it would follow that the CISG remains hard law in every sense until Article 6 is satisfied.[68]

---

[68] Spagnolo, *supra* note 53, at 205–6, 220. See, e.g., Appellate Court (OLG) Oldenburg, Germany, December 20, 2007, available at http://cisgw3.law.pace.edu/cases/071220g1.html; *Golden Valley Grape Juice and Wine, LLC v. Centrisys Corp.*, 2010 U.S. Dist. LEXIS 11884 (E.D. Cal.), January 22, 2010, available at http://cisgw3.law.pace.edu/cases/100121u1.html (Golden Valley case); *Easom Automation Systems, Inc. v. Thyssenkrupp Fabco, Corp.*, 2007WL2875256, U.S. District Court (E.D. Mich.), September 28, 2007, CISG online 1601, available at http://www.cisg-online.ch/cisg/urteile/1601.pdf; Lisa Spagnolo, "The Last Outpost: Automatic CISG Opt Outs, Misapplications and the Costs of Ignoring the Vienna Sales Convention for Australian Lawyers," 10 *Melbourne J. Int'l L.* 141, at 205 (2009) (CISG should determine the matter, at least until the point at which exclusion is established under its formation provisions); I. Schwenzer and P. Hachem in *Commentary on the UN Convention on the International Sale of Goods (CISG)*, 3rd ed. (ed. P. Schlechtriem and I. Schwenzer) (Oxford: Oxford University Press, 2010), Article 6, at 104, 105 (formation and interpretation of exclusion clauses subject to CISG rules); M. Schmidt-Kessel in Schlechtriem and Schwenzer, *Commentary*, Article 8, at 177, [61] (incorporation of choice of law clauses including exclusions of CISG within the sphere of CISG formation provisions). Contra, P. Schlechtriem in *Commentary on the UN Convention on the International Sale of Goods (CISG)*, 2nd ed.

Thus, the CISG differs markedly from soft law, because it applies as a preliminary matter to every case falling within its sphere of applicability, irrespective of what the parties desire. The CISG certainly remains as hard law unless and until a determination is made that it has been effectively excluded under Article 6. Hence, at least within member state courts where it applies *ipso iure*, any "conversion" is necessarily delayed until after a preliminary determination of the applicability of the CISG and whether the parties had properly opted out. It is only after this point that the legal effect of the CISG can be considered to have been "softened."

However, "softening" may not be an accurate description of what occurs on an effective exclusion of the CISG via Article 6. It is also true of most domestic sales laws and contract law more broadly that, except for mandatory rules, parties can elect to modify or derogate from the rules by agreement on express terms to the contrary. The wide exception to this approach is in the field of consumer contracts where most rules are immutable. However, where businesses agree in their B2B contract on a right or obligation diverging from the rule in the applicable domestic sales or contract law, does this render the law in question soft rather than hard? Surely, the relevant law is still hard law, and the fact that it permits derogation does not alter its fundamental nature as such. Contractual terms are, within limits, normally paramount, yet it is the default law that sets those limits and that facilitates the paramount status of contract terms, and the election between different sets of default rules. The same can be said of the CISG and Article 6.

In conclusion, although it might be said that the CISG no longer has binding effect in relation to the parties' obligations once an effective exclusion is found to exist, strictly speaking, the term "soft law" is not entirely appropriate to describe the legal effect of the CISG thereafter, since its nonapplicability is really no different to the inapplicability of any hard law that allows election between laws.

B. *Operational and Practical Effect of Exclusion*

It is possible to speak of the CISG as soft law in relation to its practical effect rather than its legally binding nature. It could be argued that the CISG has a similar practical effect to true soft laws. When the CISG is applied as evidence of usages or a tribunal applies it as the "appropriate law" under procedural rules, there are obvious parallels with soft law instruments. Additionally, while the CISG is an opt-out and soft laws are opt-in schemes, both, at their core, have party autonomy as the controlling factor over applicability. To this extent, the CISG bears a striking softness in regard to its *practical effect*. On the "sliding scale" approach discussed earlier, the CISG has a hard law nature, but involves a high degree of "delegation." Arguably, the broad autonomy to exclude shifts the CISG to the softer end of the scale in a realist, practical sense.

There is an obvious counterargument to this proposition. Although it is true that parties can control applicability in both cases (subject to choice of law rules), in terms of how many contracts are governed by the CISG, its practical effect is broadened by its default application where that autonomy is not exercised. Indeed, some have contended

(ed. P. Schlechtriem and I. Schwenzer) (Oxford: Oxford University Press, 2005), Article 6, at 85–9, [7]–[10] (stating that rules of private international law determine the issue).

that this is the main source of the CISG's applicability.[69] In any event, as noted earlier, as a result of it being an opt-out instrument, the CISG is certainly more broadly known than the UNIDROIT Principles or PECL.

Nonetheless, it is undeniable that to a large degree, the CISG's practical effect is determined by the choices made by parties to either exclude or opt in. It is in regard to these situations that the CISG can most accurately be described as a quasi-soft law, not in terms of strict legal effect, but in practical or operative effect.

V. When and Why the Quasi-Softness of the CISG Is Relevant

When does the softness of the CISG become relevant? The answer to this is rather simple. The CISG was created to improve the efficiency of global trade.[70] If widespread use of the CISG enhances efficiency in world trade, then its broader use is a desirable norm. This proposition assumes that there are a proportion of contracts excluding the CISG in which the CISG is either equally efficient to or more efficient than the substituted law. Given the cognitive issues and behavioral pressures influencing choices of law, as well as other rational and strategic reasons driving such choices, it is likely that a portion of choices of law are less-than-optimal selections.[71]

If the CISG is construed or interpreted in a manner that makes it a more desirable choice of law, logically it will be less likely to be excluded by parties seeking to lower transaction costs by selection of an efficient governing law.[72] Provided this can be done within the CISG interpretive framework, it is argued that a preference for interpretations likely to improve the CISG's acceptability among parties that presently exclude it would extend the practical effect of the CISG and thus advance its aims.

Although there are many nonsubstantive reasons for exclusion, such as unfamiliarity, information costs, and bargaining strength, as well as institutional reasons,[73] it is nonetheless true that a proportion of exclusion decisions are based on an evaluation of the CISG's substantive qualities – the nature of its rules by comparison with alternative choices. One survey showed that the analysis of comparative substantive qualities plays a part in decisions to exclude (or use) the CISG in 22–37% of cases in some jurisdictions. The survey also noted that the substantive evaluation of the CISG as a primary reason for exclusion (or choice) of the CISG is likely to increase relative to each of the

---

[69] Gilles Cuniberti, "Is the CISG Benefiting Anybody?," 39 *Vanderbilt J. of Transnational L.* 1511, 1529 (2006).

[70] See, e.g., id., *passim*; Gillette and Scott, "The Political Economy of International Sales Law"; Walt, "The CISG's Expansion Bias"; Marta Cenini and Francesco Parisi, "An Economic Analysis of the CISG," in *CISG Methodology* (ed. A. Janssen and O. Meyer) (Munich: Sellier, 2009), 151, 152; Lisa Spagnolo, *CISG Exclusion and Legal Efficiency*, (Alphen aan den Rijn, Kluwer, (2014), Chapters 3–7.

[71] See Spagnolo, "Green Eggs and Ham.".See also the findings of the School of International Arbitration at Queen Mary, *International Arbitration Survey*, 11–12 (reporting that 58% of the 67 respondent corporate counsels surveyed indicated that familiarity with the particular law was a powerful influence on choice of law). Similarly, the survey reported that if parties "cannot adopt their own national law as the governing law, they will seek alternations that have a similarity with their law . . . or a law from the same broad legal tradition"): 11, 13. Furthermore, when asked why they chose their preferred law, respondents they referred to "familiarity" in addition to "certainty," 13.

[72] The nuances of the decision-making process are analyzed in the author's forthcoming work, Spagnolo, *CISG Exclusion and Legal Efficiency*, Chapter 5, §V.

[73] Id. See Spagnolo, "Green Eggs and Ham."

other factors just mentioned.[74] Indeed, from anecdotal accounts, this already seems to be occurring in Germany following reform of the German Law of Obligations.[75] This is because as familiarity grows, the predominant reasons for choice of or exclusion of CISG will change, even as the overall number of exclusions decrease.

It is in this regard that the relevance of the softness of the CISG becomes apparent. It focuses attention on its acceptability in terms of conscious decisions to exclude or apply. It highlights the importance of ensuring interpretations of the CISG that will enhance its desirability as a choice of law. Thus, the idea of the CISG as quasi-soft can be useful as an additional interpretive tool.

Under what circumstances should this concept be considered in the interpretation of the CISG? How can the desirability of one interpretation be measured against the relative desirability of an alternative interpretation? It is proposed that the underlying aim of the CISG is to improve the economic efficiency of trade.[76] Majoritarianism in default laws is an important indicator of their efficiency, because rules favored by a majority of parties result in lower costs being expended overall by parties contracting to avoid default rules they dislike.[77] Interpretations, which are likely in the majority of cases to make the CISG a more efficient choice, should be encouraged. Such interpretations are consistent with the purpose of the CISG to promote efficiency in trade. Notably, the efficiency of the CISG increases as the number of contracting parties using it increases.

Interpretations likely to appeal to a greater number of those engaging in international sales will promote more widespread use of the CISG, which in turn will improve its functional status as a preferred choice of law. Naturally, "its goals of relative uniformity of international sales law are enhanced by its application to greater numbers of cases . . . [because this] provides additional incentive to business people and their lawyers to become knowledgeable of its substance."[78] Thus the quasi-soft law nature of the CISG carries implications for the extent to which practical uniformity is achieved. It mandates the consideration of economic arguments in the interpretation of such rules.

The importance of greater (not universal) uniformity is to improve the efficiency of international trade. The acceptability of the CISG is crucial to this goal of efficiency. As mentioned earlier, the more often a law is chosen generally, the more efficient that choice becomes simply by virtue of its pervasiveness. A frequently chosen law lowers information costs. Parties are more likely to be able to efficiently compare rights and obligations

---

[74] See Spagnolo, *CISG Exclusion and Legal Efficiency*, chapter 6, section IV, and chapter 7, section III (concluding that in the United States 22%, Germany 24%, and China 37% of respondents to various surveys based their decisions primarily upon substantive comparisons of legal rules).

[75] A number of German speakers at the Global Challenges of International Sales Law Conference related the heightened incidence of nonexclusion in Germany due to these reforms, which left the CISG more advantageous as a choice of law for sellers than German domestic rules had previously been.

[76] This aim is evident not only from the Preamble CISG, but from the legislative history. See Spagnolo, *CISG Exclusion and Legal Efficiency*, chapters 2 and 3.

[77] See, e.g., Charles J. Goetz and Robert E. Scott, "The Mitigation Principle: Toward a General Theory of Contractual Obligation," 69 *Virginia L. Rev.* 967, 971 (1983) (pursuant to majoritarianism, default rules are efficient if they give parties "what they wanted"; default rules "should mimic the agreements contracting parties would reach were they costless to bargain out each detail of the transaction"); Schwartz and Scott, "Contract Theory and the Limits of Contract Law," 596, 597 (same); Gillette and Scott, "The Political Economy of International Sales Law," 447 (same).

[78] DiMatteo et al., *International Sales Law*, 14.

arising from such a choice at the negotiation, performance, and dispute stages of the contract. Negotiation costs are reduced due to the parties' comfort in choosing a familiar law.

Therefore, frequency of choice impacts efficiency in much the same way as boilerplate contract terms – additional economic value attaches to such a choice of law simply by virtue of network effects.[79] This is consistent with evidence that parties strongly prefer choices of law with which they are familiar. This is one of the reasons why parties frequently choose English or New York law.[80]

The nature of the CISG as a quasi-soft law as outlined earlier has a role to play in linking interpretation to the goal of uniformity. It highlights the importance of market forces in choice of law, and their ramifications for interpretation in ensuring that substantive rules carry broad appeal. Consequently, it is argued here that in order to promote frequency of choice and efficiency, majoritarianism is an appropriate guiding norm in cases of interpretive deadlock between interpretations that are equally valid on doctrinal grounds. However, a law can be more efficient where it does the exact opposite. Some laws are efficient precisely because they do *not* appeal to the majority, such as penalty default rules, which encourage efficient behavior by penalizing parties who do not act in a particular manner.[81] Such rules do exist within the CISG.[82] Thus, the overall efficiency of a body of law is dependent on the proper balance between majoritarian and penalty default rules. The next section provides examples of majoritarian interpretation of rules found in the CISG.[83]

VI. Examples

The following sections illustrate some practical interpretive examples based on the analysis provided in the previous part of this chapter.

A. *Commodities and Majoritarianism*

The practical application of a majoritarian approach to interpretation need not take the form of a choice between two competing views about default law. It can instead involve the adoption of a range of views, which allow for the adaption of a single rule to different contextual applications. CISG Article 25 on fundamental breach is an example of such a rule. Normally, the burden of proving fundamental breach is set at a high threshold, restricting the availability of avoidance of the contract in presumption of a

---

[79] See Spagnolo, "Green Eggs and Ham," 453–4; Spagnolo, *CISG Exclusion and Legal Efficiency*, chapter 3.

[80] School of International Arbitration at Queen Mary, *International Arbitration Survey* (finding familiarity a powerful influence in choice of law), and Vogenauer, "Oxford Civil Justice Survey," *infra* note 96 (on frequency of English and New York choices of law).

[81] Ian Ayres and Robert Gertner, "Filling Gaps in Incomplete Contracts: An Economic Theory of Default Rules," 99 *Yale L.J.* 87, 101–4 (1989); Michael Whincop and Mary Keyes, "Putting the 'Private' Back into Private International Law: Default Rules and the Proper Law of the Contract," 21 *Melbourne U. L. Rev.* 515, 524 (1997).

[82] See Spagnolo, *CISG Exclusion and Legal Efficiency*, chapter 4.

[83] See id., chapters 3 and 4 (for full discussion of efficiency of rules in CISG).

favor contractus designed to preserve the contractual relationship and to make available remedies less drastic and costly than termination, such as damages, price reduction, and repair. Parties can indicate in their contract what particular breaches they consider to be fundamental. Another example of deal preservation and minimization of remedies or damages rules in the CISG is the seller's right to cure found in CISG Articles 34 and 48(1).[84]

However, in the case of commodities, the industry norm is for relatively easy availability of termination for breach. Documentary irregularities frequently give rise to the right to terminate commodity transactions. The "perfect tender rule" in English law enabling the rejection of goods or documents that do not strictly conform arguably upholds the expectations within the commodity trade regarding availability of termination for breach.[85]

While the general approach of the CISG in preserving contracts and restricting the availability of avoidance might succeed in reflecting majoritarian preferences for international sales, the approach would be unsuited to commodity sales where multiple onselling of the documents occurs before physical delivery of the goods.[86] However, in apparent recognition of this, the CISG Advisory Council has acknowledged that the interpretation of fundamental breach must operate differently in relation to commodities, where string trading and large price fluctuations prevail.[87] Thus, a breach is far more likely to be fundamental if it occurs in relation to a commodity sale.[88] In particular, delivery of unclean documents must be considered to substantially deprive the buyer of what it was entitled to expect, because the almost universal expectation of onselling means delivery of clean documents is an essential requirement of the bargain struck between

[84] On Article 34, see CISG Advisory Council, CISG-AC "Opinion No. 11: Issues Raised by Documents under the CISG Focusing on the Buyer's Payment Duty," August 3, 2012, Rapporteur: Martin Davies, available at http://www.cisgac.com/default.php?ipkCat=213&sid=213.

[85] See Sale of Goods Act 1979 (UK), Section 35; *Cehave NV v. Bremer Handelsgesellschaft mbH (the Hansa Nord)* [1976] QB 44 (UK) (Court of Appeal), July 16, 1975; *Hansson v. Hamel & Horley Ltd* [1922] 2 AC 36 (UK) (House of Lords), March 16, 1922; P. S. Atiyah, *The Sale of Goods*, 8th ed. (London: Pitman Publishing, 1990), 488; Michael G. Bridge, "A Law for International Sales," 37 *Hong Kong L.J.* 17, 28 (2007); Michael G. Bridge," Uniformity and Diversity in the Law of International Sale," 15 *Pace Int'l L. Rev.* 55, 65, 69 (2003). However, not all commodity traders favor such harsh rights of rejection. See G. H. Treitel in *Benjamin's Sale of Goods*, 6th ed. (ed. A. G. Guest) (London: Sweet & Maxwell, 2002), [18–231] 1142.

[86] Noting that the CISG applies to such transactions trading "commercial paper": CISG Advisory Council, CISG-AC "Opinion No. 5: The Buyer's Right to Avoid the Contract in Case of Non-Conforming Goods or Documents," May 7, 2005, Rapporteur: Ingeborg Schwenzer, *Commentary* [4.12], available at http://www.cisgac.com/default.php?ipkCat=128&ifkCat=147&sid=147.

[87] Id., §4.12, §4.17, *Commentary* [2.2], notes 18–22 (stating delivery of "clean" documents is "of the essence" in documentary sales generally, referring in this regard to Incoterms 2000, cl. B8, and dealing specifically with the perfect tender rule).

[88] CISG-AC "Opinion No. 5," Commentary [4.17]; Peter Schlechtriem, "Interpretation, Gap Filling and Further Development of the UN Sales Convention," 16 *Pace Int'l L. Rev.* 279, §5(bb) (2004); Ingeborg Schwenzer, "The Danger of Domestic Pre-Conceived Views with Respect to the Uniform Interpretation of the CISG: The Question of Avoidance in the Case of Non-Conforming Goods and Documents," *Victoria U. Wellington L. Rev.* 795, 806–7 (2004–5). Contra, Bridge, "A Law for International Sales," 19, 22. For an example of the court's willingness to view time as essential given the circumstances, see, e.g., Oberlandesgericht [Court of Appeal](OLG) Hamburg, Germany, February 28, 1997, available at http://cisgw3.law.pace.edu/cases/970228g1.html (holding time was foreseeably of "special interest" to the buyer, as denoted by the Incoterm CIF, so delay amounted to fundamental breach).

commodities traders.[89] Thus the threshold for termination within the CISG in this context is not discernibly different from the "perfect tender rule" in English law,[90] as failure to deliver clean documents on time amounts to fundamental breach.[91]

Deal preservation through the ability for the seller to cure is unlikely to be available for a documentary breach. CISG Article 34, which obliges the seller to hand over the documents, only mentions cure in relation to *early* delivery of documents, and even then, makes it a precondition of cure that it not cause unreasonable expense or inconvenience.[92] Not only does such a position denying documentary cure conform with the preferences of parties within the commodities sector, such an interpretation is completely consistent with this proviso – that cure would be unreasonable and highly inconvenient in the context of string trading.[93] In terms of the present discussion, this approach demonstrates an interpretative methodology that examines the likely perception of the CISG as a desirable choice of law within a particular sector. By placing the interpretation of fundamental breach in context, this approach provides a majoritarian interpretation of Article 25. The majoritarian interpretation allows for two ways of interpreting Article 25 – the first being a general approach, and the second, an exceptional approach sensitive to the context of a particular business sector.

One justification for this interpretive view is found in CISG Article 9(2), which allows usages in international trade to be taken into account in the interpretation of contracts.[94] Certainly, the norm within commodities trade is for documentary irregularities to give rise to a right to terminate, as such irregularities would preclude the vital function of the document in string trading. However, it can also be justified by taking into account what a reasonable commodities trader might have understood pursuant to Article 8(2), or recognition of the background commodities market and/or past trade practices observed by the parties through Article 8(3).[95]

---

[89] See Schwenzer, "The Danger of Domestic Pre-Conceived Views," 806–7 (arguing delivery of clean and timely documents is always of the essence in commodity trade); Peter Huber, "CISG: The Structure of Remedies," 71 *Rabels Zeitschrift für ausländisches und internationales Privatrecht* 13, 32 (2007) (arguing documentary obligations are "at least as strict as current English law"). See also Alastair C. L. Mullis, "Termination for Breach of Contract in C.I.F. Contracts under the Vienna Convention and English Law: Is There a Substantial Difference?," in *Contemporary Issues in Commercial Law: Essays in Honour of Professor A. G. Guest* (ed. E. Lomnicka and C. G. J. Morse) (London: Sweet & Maxwell, 1997) (stating more equivocally that it is at least arguable that for documents disclosing a slight defect . . . or late delivery . . . the CISG might allow avoidance"), 137, notes 149–53 and accompanying text.

[90] CISG-AC, "Opinion No. 5," Commentary [4.17]; Huber, "CISG: The Structure of Remedies," 32; Peter Schlechtriem, "Subsequent Performance and Delivery Deadlines – Avoidance of CISG Sales Contracts Due to Non-Conformity of Goods," 18 *Pace Int'l L. Rev.* 83, 87, 92–5 (2006) (on a different basis).

[91] CISG-AC, "Opinion No. 5," §7, *Commentary* [4.17]. See also *UNIDROIT Principles 2004*, Art 7.3.1, Comment 3(b).

[92] See also ICC, Incoterms 2010, cls. A8 and B8.

[93] See CISG-AC, "Opinion No. 5," *Commentary* [4.17]; Schwenzer, "The Danger of Domestic Pre-Conceived Views," 806–7 (arguing ability to cure defective documents inapplicable to commodity sales); Huber, "CISG: The Structure of Remedies," 32. Contra, Bridge, "A Law for International Sales," 30, 31 (arguing the right to cure would interfere with the need for "clean documents" in commodity trade).

[94] Schlechtriem, "Interpretation, Gap Filling and Further Development of the UN Sales Convention," at §5(bb) (arguing variable stringency on the requirement of fundamental breach depending on usage pursuant to Article 9(2)).

[95] Ibid., at §2(c); CISG-AC, "Opinion No. 5," Commentary [4.17]; Lachmi Singh and Benjamin Leisinger, "A Law for International Sale of Goods: A Reply to Michael Bridge," 20 *Pace Int'l L. Rev.* 161, 175 (2008).

The flexibility of the fundamental breach determination allows for its application in different contexts. However, the parties can avoid the uncertainty of judicial or arbitral interpretations by incorporating express terms in their contract, making "time of the essence" or specifying the types of breaches that should be considered as fundamental for the purposes of Article 25. The preferable course to increase use of the CISG is through a majoritarian default rule that "fits" strong preexisting sector norms. The "substantiality" metric of Article 25, along with Articles 8 and 9, provide the interpretive flexibility for sector-specific majoritarian determinations of fundamental breach.

In the case of Article 25, dual interpretations – one general, one sector-specific – ensure that a greater number of parties will consider the CISG an efficient choice of law, though choices of law in commodities trade are largely institutionally entrenched.[96] However, for present purposes, the approach is just one example of how consideration of the CISG's quasi-soft nature might usefully inform its interpretation.[97]

B. *Good Faith and Precontractual Liability*

The notion that CISG contracts may be adjusted or effectively rewritten on the basis of good faith has been rightly rejected by some commentators on the basis that practitioners would perceive the CISG to be an "unpredictable" choice of law.[98] Although such a pervasive use of good faith might be doctrinally feasible,[99] its use must be treated with caution if the CISG is to gain wider acceptance within common law countries.

---

[96] It is wise to temper expectations of any rapid changes to current majority choices of English (and in some cases, New York) law entrenched within standard form commodity trade contracts promulgated by commodity trade associations. See Bridge, "Uniformity and Diversity," 69 (stating "every commodities sale form and oil company's standard terms that I have seen expressly excludes the operation of the CISG"); Mullis, "Termination for Breach of Contract," 386, *passim*; Schlechtriem, "Interpretation, Gap Filling and Further Development of the UN Sales Convention," at §I.1; Filip De Ly, "Opting Out: Some Observations on the Occasion of the CISG's 25th Anniversary," in *Quo Vadis CISG? Celebrating the 25th Anniversary of the United Nations Convention on Contracts for the International Sale of Goods* 25, 28, 40 (ed. F. Ferrari) (Munich: Sellier, 2005). Outside the sphere of commodities trade, in contracts more generally, English, New York, and Swiss law are preferred choices for parties (other than the law of their home jurisdiction). In the absence of an exclusion clause this will often result in the CISG applying, except for English law. See Vogenauer, "Oxford Civil Justice Survey," 15, 16, Questions 17.4 and 18 (Swiss law was the most preferred by businesses other than their own law (29%), followed by English law (23%), although paradoxically they perceived that others preferred English law (59%), then Swiss law (13%) followed by U.S. law (11%)); School of International Arbitration at Queen Mary, *International Arbitration Survey*, 11 (reporting corporate counsel respondents, other than their own law, preferred English law (40%), New York Law (17%), or Swiss law (8%)); Andrea J. Menaker and Nicole Thornton, "Reflections on the New International Arbitration Global Survey, Kluwer Arbitration Blog," October 22, 2010, available at http://kluwerarbitrationblog.com/blog/2010/10/22.

[97] See, e.g., Clayton P. Gillette and Franco Ferrari, "Warranties and 'Lemons' under CISG Article 35(2)(a)," *Internationales Handelsrecht* 2 (2010) (the use of law and economics in analysis of Article 35 and Article 74); Nils Schmidt-Ahrendts, "Disgorgement of Profits under the CISG," in *State of Play: The 3rd Annual MAA Schlechtriem CISG Conference* (ed. I. Schwenzer and L. Spagnolo) (The Hague: Eleven International Publishing, 2012) (same).

[98] Francesco Mazzotta, "The Vexata Quaestio: Good Faith – What Is It?," presented at Global Challenges of International Sales Law Conference, November 11, 2011. See *infra*, Chapter 12.

[99] See, e.g., CISG-AC, "Opinion No. 7, Exemption of Liability for Damages under Article 79 of the CISG," Rapporteur: Alejandro M. Garro, Commentary [40] (arguing potential for "adaption" pursuant to Article 79(5)).

In the area of precontractual liability, again, it is possible to discern the theoretical feasibility of a certain degree of precontractual liability under the CISG for breaking off negotiations and "breaching" precontractual agreements, however, the lack of any concrete provisions upon which to base *purely* precontractual liability means that such doctrinal justifications through either Article 7, Article 6, or a combination of both must be rejected, as stretching the CISG in this manner would significantly increase uncertainty.[100] But this does not prevent liability in all precontractual scenarios. If no contract is formed, the party breaking off negotiations might be liable pursuant to the applicable domestic law, such as *culpa in contrahendo*. Alternatively, if the CISG requirements of revocability are not satisfied, the aggrieved party can accept the offer and pursue remedies under the CISG for failure to perform.[101] In the latter case, again, an argument can be made that to ensure the certainty and effectiveness of the CISG, domestic remedies relating to the same event should be displaced.[102] The important point for present purposes is that the choice between competing interpretations must be assessed in light of whether it clarifies CISG's rules and their relationship with the residual law, or whether the interpretation substitutes a more comprehensive but more unpredictable solution such that the CISG becomes a less desirable choice of law.

C. *Formation and Nonconformity*

There are numerous examples in which economic effects of interpretations can be taken into account in determining whether a contract has been formed. Some courts and commentators have utilized relevant incentive and cost issues to support interpretative choices in this area. René Franz Henschel notes that decisions of the German Supreme Court have referred to economic grounds.[103] In relation to CISG Articles 14–19 on formation, transmission of general standard terms was preferred rather than a duty on the offeree to enquire because, inter alia, the latter interpretation would lead to delays in the conclusion of contracts.[104] In the New Zealand Mussels case, the German Supreme Court decided the issue of which party should bear responsibility for conformity with relevant statutory regulations, in relation to Article 35.[105] The court decided that a foreign seller is not obligated to determine the conformity of the goods to the regulations and standards of the buyer's country, unless certain circumstances exist that would give the seller insight into those regulations or standards. This ruling selects the party

---

[100] Lisa Spagnolo, "Opening Pandora's Box: Good Faith and Precontractual Liability in the CISG," 21 *Temple Int'l & Comparative L.J.* 261 (2007) (for an analysis of the various views and appropriate solutions); Spagnolo, *CISG Exclusion and Legal Efficiency*, Chapter 9.

[101] Id.; Marco Torsello, at Global Challenges of International Sales Law Conference, November 12, 2011 (similar conclusion). See *infra*, Chapter 39.

[102] This aspect is discussed at greater length in Spagnolo, *CISG Exclusion and Legal Efficiency*.

[103] René Franz Henschel, "The Use of Law and Economics Arguments in Cases Governed by CISG," in Schwenzer and Spagnolo, *Towards Uniformity*, 29.

[104] Bundesgerichtshof [Federal Supreme Court], Germany, October 31, 2001, available at http://cisgw3.law.pace.edu/cases/011031g1.html.

[105] See Bundesgerichtshof [Federal Supreme Court], Germany, March 8, 1995, available at http://cisgw3.law.pace.edu/cases/950308g3.html.

with the cheapest means of accessing the relevant rules,[106] thus utilizing the least-cost avoider principle to locate the most efficient of the competing alternative interpretations. Similarly, the position that the buyer bears the burden of proof that it conformed to the notice periods for the delivery of nonconforming goods is justifiable as the most efficient rule, as generally, information regarding inspection and reasons for the time taken to give notice are within the buyer's sphere of influence; the overall burden of proving proper notice is less costly when placed primarily upon the buyer.

VII. Limitations of the Concept of the CISG as Soft Law

There are some important provisos to the argument that the CISG can be seen as a soft or quasi-soft law. The first is an acknowledgement that this conception, though useful for the purposes of determining an interpretation that might best promote the CISG's desirability and efficiency, should not be confused with its legal effect within contracting state courts. The CISG remains hard law in such a setting, and the court will be obliged to impose it unless parties have successfully opted out.

The second proviso relates to the setting in which interpretation is done. Scholars have found law and economics arguments useful in justifying their views, and this has occurred to a limited degree within CISG scholarship.[107] However, law and economics arguments are sometimes criticized as being inadmissible in legal argument, even though, arguably, they underpin many legal policies, and are frequently inseparable from legal arguments.[108]

This concern need not present an insurmountable hurdle to the use of such arguments in court in the case of the CISG. It has been often observed that CISG Article 7 encourages the use of scholarship in interpretation of the CISG as a tool in achieving a uniform and international interpretation. Apart from jurisdictions in which reference to academic works within judicial reasoning is prohibited,[109] use of law and economics arguments can therefore be indirectly used in application of the CISG by reference to academic works that take economic policy into consideration. Reference by courts to the CISG's *traveaux preparatoires* also reveal that economic policy considerations were taken into account in the drafting and negotiation of the CISG.[110]

VIII. Conclusion

The operational softness of the CISG reminds us of the fragility of its existence as a practical force for improving efficiency in international sales transactions. While the

---

[106] See also Henschel, "The Use of Law and Economics Arguments," 39; Gillette and Ferrari, "Warranties and 'Lemons,'" 6 (stating that this approach is consistent with placing quality warranties upon sellers only when sellers enjoy an informational advantage).

[107] Id., 37.

[108] Id., 44.

[109] See, e.g., judgments rendered by Italian courts cannot cite scholars: Giuseppe F. Ferrari and Antonio Gambaro, "The Italian Constitutional Court and Comparative Law: A Premise," 1 *Comparative L. Rev.* 1, 3–4, available at http://www.comparativelawreview.com/ojs/index.php/CoLR/article/viewFile/3/7, citing Article 118 Civil Procedure Code, implementing provisions and customary practice since the eighteenth century). Naturally, this inability to cite scholarly works does not prevent the latter from *influencing* court decisions.

[110] Though in a limited and usually nonspecific manner: Spagnolo, *CISG Exclusion and Legal Efficiency*, Chapters 2 and 3.

CISG is applicable law *ipso jure*, it remains applicable only when parties have not chosen to opt out; conversely, in cases where it does not apply *ipso jure*, it will be applied only where adjudicators find it of value as evidence of international commercial usages or principles, or parties consider it as a desirable and efficient choice of law. The CISG is hard in legal nature, but it behaves like soft law in an operational sense, since it too depends on the preferences of those who engage in trade for its practical impact in achieving uniformity and efficiency, despite its status as a convention. It is therefore submitted that, irrespective of the doctrinal attraction of a particular interpretation, where there are two reasonable competing interpretations of the CISG the best interpretation is that which better promotes acceptability and efficiency.

The fact that there is a "soft side" to the CISG does not mean that soft law instruments and market forces will solely drive the future harmonization of commercial law.[111] The dominant advantage of the CISG over other harmonization instruments has been the hard law foundation upon which it stands. The application of the CISG in cases where parties have not selected any choice of law has helped create of a large body of case law. It is hoped that over time this will increase base-level familiarity with the CISG, ultimately making it even more popular in the future. As envisaged by its drafters, the fact that the CISG is an opt-out system has made a difference to its practical impact compared with opt-in schemes.[112]

It is also important to note the ease with which parties can and do exclude the application of the CISG. This softer quality reminds us of the value of linking interpretation more closely with its original underlying and fundamental aim – the promotion of efficiency in trade. As demonstrated, it is the acceptance of a law by potential users due to its perceived economic value, not its hardness, that determines whether and to what extent it will be effective in achieving its ends. In other words, the CISG's relevance depends on economic and market forces, not its legal form. This justifies reference to the relative economic efficiency of various interpretations of CISG rules and consideration of how contemplated interpretations impact the frequency of the use of the CISG as a choice of law.

A hard law that is never applied in practice fails to achieve its harmonizing purpose. Similarly, a hard law that is applied in practice but without consideration of its underlying policies is doomed to stray from its original aims. Ironically, an interpretation that recognizes the quasi-soft nature of the CISG, and which is therefore sensitive to the economic impact likely to flow from alternative interpretations, can ensure that the CISG not only continues to be applied in a practical sense, but also remains capable of achieving its original purpose.

---

[111] See Herbert Kronke, "International Uniform Commercial Law Conventions: Advantages, Disadvantages, Criteria for Choice," 5 *Uniform L. Rev.* 13, 20 (2000) (stating it would be a "misconception to envisage a future of harmonization and unification of commercial law solely driven by the market operators and loosely framed by soft law instruments").

[112] See School of International Arbitration at Queen Mary, *International Arbitration Survey, supra* note 46.

Part III *Interpreting the CISG's Substantive Provisions*

12 Contract Formation under the CISG: The Need for a Reform

Morten M. Fogt

I. Introduction

This chapter will analyze the rules of contract found in Part II of the CISG, as well as the modern practice of contract formation in international commerce. Modern contract practices in international sales transactions often do not fit the pattern of identifiable offers and acceptances that are the basis of CISG formation rules. Frequently, there are numerous communications between the parties that taken as a whole make up their agreement.

The CISG is in many ways a very modern set of rules in that Part I rejects the requirement of written contracts and provides flexible general principles of contract law.[1] However, the rules of formation found in Part II stay true to the traditional contract formation and do not address the alternative means of contract formation in modern international commerce. Furthermore, Part II does not regulate all issues of contract formation, such as the validity of contract terms. The existence of internal and external gaps in the formation rules requires courts and arbitral tribunals to seek solutions both inside and outside of Part II. The lack of comprehensiveness in CISG formation rules raises a number of questions: (1) Does the traditional contract formation regime of the CISG function satisfactorily in international commerce? (2) How should the fragmental and noncomprehensive character of Part II be managed? (3) How can issues relating to alternative means of contract formation, not dealt with expressly in the CISG, be regulated under Part II? (4) How should distinctions between contract formation, interpretation, and contract validity (not governed by the CISG) be drawn? (5) Should CISG Part II be reformed and, if so, what issues should a revision address? These are some of the questions that will be addressed in this chapter.

II. Case Study: *Hanwha Corporation v. Cedar Petrochemicals, Inc.*

Hanwha Corporation v. Cedar Petrochemicals, Inc. (*Hanwha v. Cedar*) illustrates the traditional modes of contract formation and, on the other hand, variations from these modes of formation and current methods found in international commerce.[2] Hanwha,

---

[1] See on the freedom of form Article 11 CISG. The provisions of CISG Part I that bear on contract formation include Articles 7(1) (good faith), Article 8 CISG (interpretation), and Article 9 (practices between the parties and international trade usages). Article 18(3) is *lex specialis* with the general provision stated in Articles 8(3).

[2] *Hanwha Corporation, Plaintiff v. Cedar Petrochemicals, Inc.*, Case No. 09 Civ. 10559 (S.D.N.Y. 2011), available at http://www.unilex.info/case.cfm?id=1583 and http://cisgw3.law.pace.edu/cases/110118u1.html.

a Korean buyer (buyer), and Cedar, an American petrochemical trader (seller), entered into twenty transactions over a six-year period. In each of the twenty transactions, the parties formed contracts under the same procedure. First, buyer would submit a "bid" to seller for a given petrochemical at a given quantity and price. Seller would accept buyer's bid, forming what the parties describe as a "firm bid," or an agreement regarding product, quantity, and price. Following formation of the firm bid, seller would transmit a package of contract documents to buyer, which were meant to incorporate and finalize the contract terms. The buyer would do one of three things – he would countersign and return the contract sheet, accepting seller's terms; modify the contract sheet, and then sign and return it for seller's consideration; or not sign at all. On three occasions, buyer modified the contract sheets by adding a different choice of law to govern the contract. Whenever buyer modified the contract sheets and sent them back to seller, seller did not object to the changes – including buyer's choice of law provision – but also failed to countersign the modified contract. On all twenty occasions, on completion of this process, Cedar and Hanwha both performed their obligations under their contracts.

The dispute relates to the parties' attempt to form a twenty-first contract. The buyer submitted a bid for the purchase of 1,000 metric tons of the petrochemical toluene at $640 per metric ton, the market rate at the time. The seller accepted the bid, thus creating a firm bid for the purchase and sale of the toluene. The "bid" was addressed to a specific addressee and contained the necessary terms in conformity with the requirements of CISG Article 14(1). In conformity to the acceptance rule of CISG Article 18, the acceptance of the "bid" by seller indicated assent and mirrored the terms of the offer. Consequently, under CISG rules a contract was concluded at the time the acceptance of the "bid" under CISG Articles 23 and 24. But did the buyer and seller intend to be bound by their "bid" (buyer's offer) and the seller's "acceptance"? Based on the facts of the published text of the decision it seems doubtful whether a common intention was given. First, the use of the word "bid" instead of "agreement" or "contract" indicates that the parties or at least one of the parties still were in the phase of consideration and negotiations. Second, the expression "firm bid" could more reasonably point to the fact that a "firm offer" (compare U.S. UCC Art. 2–205) or a "binding offer" had been made in which case the parties merely have derogated from CISG Article 16(1) but not concluded a sales contract.

The seller followed up its acceptance of the bid by sending the buyer, via e-mail, a signed contract sheet and a document setting forth seller's usual standard terms and conditions including a choice of law term. The buyer did not immediately respond to the contract documents but engaged with seller in preparing a bill of lading and nominated a vessel for the ocean carriage. Neither the "bid" by buyer nor the "acceptance" of seller contained the standard terms. Based on prior practice, the terms of the contract were sent afterwards. Such established practice, under CISG Article 9(1), has the potential of a binding effect. If, according to CISG Article 8, both parties had a *de facto* intention to be bound in their first exchange of communications ("bid" and "firm bid"), the contract would be concluded at this earlier point in time. Subsequently, the documents sent by Cedar came under the CISG formation rules *ex post* after the contract formation and would raise the question of a possible contract modification. Since buyer did not immediately react to what amounted to a confirmation and did engage in a common preparation of the contract performance, an expectation and reliance of seller were created that perhaps could lead to a contract being concluded on the terms of the confirmation (firm bid) under the CISG rules. However, if there was no intent to be bound at that stage, the "signed contract sheet and the document setting seller's usual standard terms and conditions" could be regarded as either an offer (CISG Article 14) or a modified acceptance (counteroffer) under CISG Article 19(1). Under this latter scenario, the communications leading to the "firm bid" were merely an exchange of information creating a basis for further negotiations.

The later scenario of continued negotiations, however, contradicts the presumption of a common intent to enter into a contract based on an objective (reasonable man) interpretation (Article 8(2)). Presuming that a common intention could not be established or that the traditional offer and acceptance model of the CISG was derogated from, the issue becomes whether the modified acceptance nonetheless created a contract. This depends on whether it materially altered the offer pursuant to Articles 19(2) and 19(3).

Additional facts in the case provide a tentative answer. Approximately a week after seller had sent the contract documents for the toluene sale to buyer, the buyer returned them in a modified form. The buyer's contract sheet crossed out the bid's (offer) choice of law clause selecting New York law and its Uniform Commercial Code as governing law, leaving only the provision that Incoterms 2000 were to govern the contract. Buyer also provided a new set of "standard" terms and conditions; in relevant part, the buyer's new set of conditions provided that Singapore law would govern the contract.

The case presents the issue of the legal consequence of a party's silence or inactivity after receipt of confirming documents that contain conflicting standard terms. Part II of the CISG, unfortunately, does not provide specific rules dealing directly with the incorporation of standard terms into contracts. CISG Article 18(1) simply states that "silence or inactivity does not in itself amount to acceptance." It does not expressly settle the question of the incorporation of standard terms. Article 19 provides a limited rule, in the context of the battle of the forms, allowing a purported acceptance to incorporate additional, nonmaterial terms.

Seller refused to accept buyer's terms, and sent buyer an e-mail conditioning contract formation on buyer's acceptance of seller's original terms. The e-mail asked buyer to sign and return an unaltered version of the contract documents. In the meantime, the parties agreed on the details of the letter of credit for the transaction. Buyer provided an acceptable letter of credit on June 10, 2009. However, the next day, June 11, 2009, seller advised buyer that due to its failure to sign the unaltered version of its offer, no contract had been concluded between the parties, and that seller retained the right to sell the toluene to another party. The price of toluene as of that date, June 11, 2009, had risen from $640 per metric ton to $790.50.

Hanwha v. Cedar illustrates how a relatively simple framework of offer-acceptance rules can become convoluted in application when faced by the complexity of modern transactions, involving numerous communications and exchanges of forms. The serial battle of the forms outlined above ended with the seller's "rejection" being the "last shot" in the cycle. At this stage, there was a *dissens* between the parties concerning the contract terms and standard forms but simultaneously a common intention of the parties, based upon their conduct. If the parties had proceeded with the ongoing performance, as they had done twenty previous times, a contract would have been formed due to the subsequent conduct of both parties under Article 8(3), but the content of the contract would have been in dispute. In the present case, it turned out differently. Seller did not deliver according to the alleged contract and buyer sued for breach of contract.

The case sets out a dilemma between the traditional model of offer and acceptance and alternative means of contract formation, including possible derogation of the CISG offer and acceptance rules – silence on the part of the buyer (first, one week after receipt of additional terms, and second, after receipt of the last email request) and parallel conduct of both parties in preparing for performance on the contract, all of which were embedded in an established practice between the parties in a longstanding business relationship. The U.S. court held that the question of contract formation was to be decided by the CISG, that, with reference to the course of dealing between the parties, there was no opting out of the CISG as neither of the parties' standard terms were incorporated into the alleged contract and, moreover, there was no conclusion of the twenty-first contract.

This case demonstrated the complexity of transactions, and indicates that the CISG formation rules may be ill-equipped to render uniform, predictable, and just decisions in certain cases. A more detailed review of the CISG contract formation regime will follow. The focus will thereby be on the overall functioning in practice of the contract formation regime in Part II of the CISG.

A. *The CISG as a Dynamic Instrument of Unification*

The late Professor Schlechtriem wrote in his introductory note to his CISG commentary that:

> Codifications and Conventions age from the moment the draftsman lays down his pen and often become buried under layers of case law and scholarly exegeses. It is unnecessary to remind the reader of this in regard to a text drafted only in 1980. But the basic structure of the CISG [is] much older, and in its detailed solutions the Convention has sometimes laid down rules based on knowledge and legal experience which today may seem somewhat antiquated, if not outdated. A more important example is the emphasis on offer and acceptance as the sole tools of contracting, which not only neglects other forms of reaching consensus, but also can offer only the inadequate rules of Article 19 for the problem of the battle of forms.[3]

To overcome the unavoidable problem of obsolescence, the CISG must be interpreted autonomously and through its "reasonableness standards" dynamically in order to respond to novel changes in sale of goods transactions. The CISG must – like other formal instruments of commercial law – be seen as a "living law" capable of a further development.[4] The dynamic nature of the CISG is seen in its mandate for international (autonomous) interpretations pursuant to CISG Article 7(1). However, a dynamic interpretation lies in the borderland between interpretation and law-making. It has rightly been stated that the "fabrication of law is not within the mandate of the CISG."[5] Nonetheless, some scholars and courts have been creative in their interpretation and extension of CISG provisions, in particular with regard to CISG contract formation in Part II.

---

[3] Peter Schlechtriem in *Commentary on the UN Convention on the International Sale of Goods (CISG)*, 2nd English ed. (ed. P. Schlechtriem and I. Schwenzer) (Oxford, 2005), 8–9.

[4] See the contributions in *Uniformity and Harmonization of International Commercial Law: Interaction or Deharmonization?* (ed. Morten M. Fogt) (The Hague: Kluwer Law International, 2012).

[5] Bruno Zeller, "The Black Hole: Where Are the Four Corners of the CISG?," 7 *Int'l Trade & Bus. L. Ann.* 251, 257 (2002).

The maxim *a verbis legis non est recedendum* ("You may not vary the words of a statute") is not an absolute, especially when a law contains conflicting provisions or when the law needs to be extended to a change in practice. A situation of conflicting provisions is CISG Article 14's specificity of price requirement and CISG Article 55's open price term. The foundational question is whether an offer with an open-price term constitutes a valid offer despite the clear wording of Article 14(1). Theoretically, a failure to specify a price term, as required under Article 14(1), could be rectified by the open price term provision of Article 55.[6] Without using the rationale of the parties implicitly opting out of the Article 14(1) requirement, the wording of one of the provisions must be neglected. A preference should be given to the default rule of Article 55 CISG as *lex specialis*. An example of the need for a dynamic interpretation of a narrowly worded provision is the obsolescence of CISG Article 13's definition of the written form ("writing includes telegram and telex"). First, various electronic means of communication have been interpreted to be writings. Second, CISG Article 24's notice of "reaching the addressee" requires a determination as to when electronic communications reach the receiving party.[7] Thus, Articles 13 and 24 require dynamic interpretation to respond to technological changes.[8]

A more complex question arises in situations where CISG Part II covers an area, but fails to provide an express rule. This is not unexpected given that Part II provides a mere nine substantive rules (CISG Articles 23 and 24 are merely definitional in nature). It is supported, however, from the general provisions of Part I.[9] A weak and less convincing interpretation of the formation rules of Part II is that it is a set of exhaustive rules leaving no gaps. The stronger and persuasive interpretation is that contract formation is governed but not for all issues settled by Part II.[10] The CISG formation rules therefore have a number of internal gaps or *lagunae*. In such cases, the interpreter turns to the gap-filling provision of CISG Article 7(2). The use of general principles allows the interpreter to build a bridge over the failing express rule or rules to regulate alternative means of contract formation. The combination of these provisions of Part I and II CISG are the means by which autonomous and dynamic interpretations can be made.[11]

---

[6] See Article 55: "Where a contract has been validly concluded but does not expressly or implicitly fix or make provision for determining the price." See generally John O. Honnold, *Uniform Law for International Sales*, 3rd ed. (The Hague, 1999), 154–5 (legislative history of the two provisions).

[7] Compare here CISG Advisory Council Opinion No. 1 Electronic Communications under CISG, available at http://www.cisgac.com.

[8] The question of whether to include new electronic means of communication under the definition of the "written form" (Article 13) is a question of interpretation and not a gap-filling question under Article 7(2). However, for an alternative argument, see J. Lookofsky, *Understanding the CISG*, 4th ed. (The Netherlands, 2012), 35–6.

[9] See Articles 7(1), 8, and 9; see also note 1.

[10] See the arguments by Morten M. Fogt, "Konkludente Vertragsannahme und grenzüberschreitendes kaufmännisches Bestätigungsschreiben nach CISG," 27 *Praxis des Internationalen Privat- und Verfahrensrechts (IPRax)* 361 et seq. (2007). For a detailed discussion of the mechanism of gap-filling according to Article 7(2), see Morten M. Fogt, "Private International Law in the Process of Harmonization of International Commercial Law: The 'Ugly Duckling'?," in Fogt, *Uniformity and Harmonization*, 57 et seq., 91–8.

[11] Cf. Honnold, *Uniform Law*, §21, 17 ("How can one establish the general principles on which the Convention is based? How diligently should a tribunal look for such principles before it turns, via rules of private international law, to a rule of domestic law?").

B. *The CISG's Principles of Contract Law*

Two overarching principles of contract law are freedom of contract and *pacta sunt servanda*, and these principles find unequal treatment in the CISG. CISG Article 6 recognizes freedom of contract as the premier principle of contract law.[12] If the CISG applies, Article 6 gives the contracting parties the freedom, except for the application of national form requirements under Articles 12 and 96, to derogate or vary from the CISG rules.[13] In fact, the parties may opt out of the CISG and choose the *lex contractus*, which in most legal systems will provide the same degree of freedom of contract.[14] The fact that the CISG only applies to commercial transactions[15] allowed the drafters to codify an extensive freedom of contract regime. An implied limitation on contractual freedom under the CISG is the general principle of good faith. Freedom of contract does not mean that parties are free to act in bad faith, not to cooperate in the performance of the contract, or to abuse contractual rights. This limitation will exist independently of whether it is based on good faith as an underlying principle of the CISG or on the *lex contractus* governing validity issues.

The principle of *pacta sunt servanda* is not expressly codified in the CISG.[16] However, the binding effect of a contract is self-evident. The main remedy provisions in CISG Part III provide for no fault liability for breach of contract, except for the narrow exemption provided in CISG Article 79. CISG Articles 45(1) and 61(1) make clear that the remedies are available in the case of the other party's failure "to perform any of his obligations under the contract or this Convention."

III. The CISG's Traditional Contract Formation Regime

The "meeting of the minds" model of mutual consent confirmation posited on offer-acceptance rules was prevalent across legal systems at the beginning of the twentieth century. The acceptance had to *mirror* the offer in order for a contract to be formed. Because the traditional "offer" and "acceptance" model was part of the common core of

---

[12] Cf. Article 1.1 UPICC, Article 1:102 (1) PECL, Article II 1:102 of the European Draft Common Frame of Reference (DCFR) and Article 1 of the European Commission Proposal for a Common European Sales Law, COM (2011) 635/4, October 12, 2011 (CESL). See also Articles 30, 35(1), and 53 ("required by the contract").

[13] There are few provisions in the CISG that, depending on the domestic law applicable, may have a mandatory character, such as the form reservation in Article 96 and rules on civil procedure applicable under Article 28.

[14] See Honnold, *Uniform Law*, para. 82, at 84.

[15] Article 2(a) excludes consumer protection laws from CISG transactions, unless they apply to the commercial seller who "neither knew or ought to have known" it was faced with a consumer. Domestic consumer protection rules that are qualified as validity provisions control under CISG Article 4 (validity). Mandatory and in particular international mandatory consumer protection rules, such as EU law, can under the European Private International Law regime demand application and should in such consumer cases be given preference over the commercial regime of the CISG; see Morten M. Fogt, "Private International Law Issues by Opt-out and Opt-in Instruments of Harmonization: A Comparison between CISG and CESL," in *Liber Amicorum Ole Lando* (ed. M. J. Bonell et al.) (2012), 117 et seq., 129–32. But see Franco Ferrari in *Kommentar zum Einheitlichen UN-Kaufrecht (CISG)*, 5th ed. (ed. Peter Schlechtriem and Ingeborg Schwenzer) (Munich, 2008), Article 2, Randnote (Rn.) 25–6 and *obiter dictum* by Austrian Supreme Court (February 11, 1997), Case No. 10 ob. 1506/95, available at http://www.unilex.info/case.cfm?id=283.

[16] The principle of *pacta sunt servanda*; see, e.g., Article 1.3 UPICC.

most legal systems, it was a natural basis for harmonization of international contract law.[17] However, in the drafting of the Hague Convention on a Uniform Law on the Formation of Contracts for the International Sale of Goods from 1964 (ULF) and the UNCITRAL CISG draft in 1978, and as adopted in 1980, the common core or traditional model remained unchanged. The 1935 draft for an international sales law was divided into two sections; one concerning the offer (*L'offre*) and another addressing the acceptance (*L'acceptation*). CISG Part II (Articles 14–23) mimics the ten articles of the 1935 draft for an international sales law.[18] This first draft, however, contrary to the adopted text of the Part II CISG, did give effect to silence on the part of the offeree based on an established practice between the parties and included a provision on the incorporation of standard terms.[19] The contract formation rules of the CISG merely reflect the model found in most national contract acts or codes of the nineteenth and twentieth centuries[20] – a contract is formed by indication of assent in an acceptance to a definite offer. Fortunately, the general provisions of CISG Part I can supplement and, thus, mitigate some of the drawbacks of the traditional formation rules of Part II.

CISG Part II is nevertheless innovative in the sense that some peculiar national doctrines and concepts were avoided. The common law doctrine of "consideration"[21] and the Romanic concept of a "cause" or "causa" are not incorporated into the CISG. These core concepts were also avoided in the drafting of the Principles of European Contract Law (PECL) and the UNIDROIT Principles of International Commercial Contracts (UPICC).[22] As Professor Ole Lando states in a recent essay on a possible future global commercial code:

> In fact, the English and American courts have had problems with the doctrine of consideration and have tempered it by relying on commercial usages, estoppel and "invented consideration" to avoid some of the hardship which the doctrine creates. For these reasons the PECL and UPICC follow the continental rule, which does not require consideration. Chinese law appears to be to the same effect.

> The functions which French law and other Romanist legal systems have attributed to the legal cause by invalidating contracts due to absence of legal basis, illegality or immorality, absent or insufficient quid pro quo, etc., are better taken care of by specific rules governing these matters. One may conclude that cause is an unclear concept with several incoherent roles. It is unknown in German law, the Nordic laws and the Common Law. I have not found traces of it in Chinese Contract Law. The UPICC and PECL do without it.[23]

---

[17] See the comparative work of Ernst Rabel: Ernst Rabel, *Recht des Warenkaufes, Eine rechtsvergleichende Darstellung*, 1. Band (Berlin, 1936), 71 et seq. See also *Formation of Contract: A Study of the Common Core of Legal Systems*, 2 vols. (ed. Rudolph B. Schlesinger) (New York: Oceana, 1968).

[18] French version of draft in Rabel, *Recht des Warenkaufes*, 116.

[19] See Articles 9–10, 1935 Draft, *supra* n. 17.

[20] See Ole Lando, "Tradition versus Harmonization in the Recent Reforms of Contract Law," in *The Xiamen Academy of International Law, Collected Courses 2010* (The Netherlands, 2010), 83–15, 107.

[21] See Michael Bridge, *The International Sale of Goods, Law and Practice*, 2nd ed. (Oxford, 2007), 550: "Consideration is not merely formally absent from the CISG; it is also deprived of any secondary effect on promises to keep offers open and on contractual variation." See also id., at 557–8.

[22] Cf. Lando, "Tradition versus Harmonization," 107.

[23] Cf. id., 109 and 111.

The CISG's drafters also ignored the Nordic countries' "promise theory" of contract formation. The Nordic promise theory (*løfteprincip*) recognizes the binding nature of reasonable reliance on promises of businesspersons to ensure certainty and predictability. Businesspersons are expected to act in good faith in upholding their promises. In contrast to the Roman-influenced concept of a contractual obligation, which can only be created by a contractual agreement, under Nordic law the promise in itself creates the obligation.[24] Consequently, an offer is legally binding. Although practical and in principle convincing, the Nordic doctrine of the promise theory[25] is not represented in the CISG.[26] In the Nordic countries, this lack of the promise theory has been given as one of the reasons for the Nordic countries' reservation to CISG Part II, which now has been withdrawn by Sweden, Finland, and Denmark.[27]

A. Contract Formation: The Offer

Contract formation under the CISG is a combination of the traditional provisions of CISG Part II with the general principles of CISG Part I. This combination anchors CISG contract formation in the traditional approach and yet provides pragmatic flexibility for nontraditional modes of contract formation. A U.S. Court in *Geneva Pharmaceuticals Technology Corp. v. Barr Laboratories, Inc.*[28] states:

> The CISG, intended to ensure the observance of good faith in international trade, CISG Article 7(1), embodies a liberal approach to contract formation and interpretation, and a strong preference for enforcing obligations and representations customarily relied upon by others in the industry . . . A contract may be proven by a document, oral representations, conduct, or some combination of the three. CISG Article 11. The usages and practices of the parties or the industry are automatically incorporated into any agreement governed by the Convention, unless expressly excluded by the parties. CISG Article 9.

> While embodying a liberal approach, the CISG does not vitiate the need to prove concepts familiar to the common law, including offer, acceptance, validity and performance.[29]

---

[24] See Ernst Rabel, *supra* note 17, at 70: "Zur Entstehung einer Schuldverpflichtung gehört in den meisten Rechten grundsätzlich ein Vertrag. Eine Ausnahme macht die *skandinavische Löfte-Theorie*. Danach entsteht die Obligation der Parteien nicht durch ihre Willensübereinstimmung, sondern dadurch, daß jeder in seiner Vertragserklärung eine Verpflichtung übernimmt: Der Verkäufer zu liefern, der Käufer zu bezahlen."

[25] See Rabel, *Recht des Warenkaufes*, 71: "Die vom römischen Recht beeinflußten Rechtsvorstellungen der meisten Länder werden wohl hier den Ausschlag geben müssen."

[26] A reflection of the Nordic "promise theory" may be seen in the PECL Article 2: 107: "A promise which is intended to be legally binding without acceptance is binding." Lando, "Tradition versus Harmonization," 111.

[27] National proposals to withdraw the Article 92 CISG reservation to CISG Part II were presented and adopted in 2011–12. The withdrawal of the Nordic Article 92 reservations took effect on December 1, 2012, for Sweden and Finland, and on February 1, 2013, for Denmark. For these Nordic countries (including Iceland, which did not make an Article 92 reservation in the first place), the CISG will now apply to contract of the sale of goods with other non-Nordic CISG states according to Article 1(1)(a) but not according to the Article 94 neighboring reservation to inter-Nordic sales.

[28] *Geneva Pharmaceuticals Technology Corp. v. Barr Laboratories, Inc., et al.*, Case No. 98CIV861 (RWS), 99CIV3607 (RWS), F. Supp. (Second Series) 201, 236 (S.D.N.Y. 2002), available at http://www.unilex .info/case.cfm?id=739 (Geneva Pharmaceuticals).

[29] Id.

The general conditions for contract formation under the CISG are based on the principle of *consensus*. Consensus under the CISG requires a common intention to contract and the parties to agree on the essential elements of a sales contract. These essential elements must be found either in an offer and a corresponding acceptance or though alternative means of contract formation. An important limitation is that the CISG only regulates the apparent consensus of the contracting parties,[30] whereas hidden defects in the consensus such as cases of mistake, fraud, duress or threat, unfairness, and contracts against the law or public policy are excluded from its scope.

1. Common Intention to Be Bound by a Contract (*animus contrahendi*)

The intention to be bound by a contract (*animus contrahendi*) is a general requirement under domestic laws and international contract law instruments. In principle, there must be an intention to be bound to the specific contract of sale and agreement on material, concrete terms and conditions. In the vast majority of international sale transactions governed by the CISG, there is some lack of express agreement on the terms of the contract, especially when standard forms are used. The contracting parties mostly agree on fundamental aspects of the transaction, such as description of the goods, quantity, and price. Other terms are to be determined later or left unaddressed and, thus, to be filled by established practice, usages, or default rules (CISG provisions).

2. Criteria for Distinguishing the Elements of a Contract

The terms of a contract can be divided based on different characteristics. First, the essential elements (*essentialia negotii* or *essentialia contractus*) must be agreed to by the parties to make a binding and enforceable contract. Second, the additional elements (*accidentalia negotii*) can be, but need not be, addressed in order to form a binding contract. Moreover, the *naturalia negotii* can be used to indicate the legal nature of the specific contract in question and characterize the rights and obligations stemming from the contract.[31] If this terminology is employed the distinction results in the following: The *naturalia negotii* indicates the type of a contract and inherent rights and obligations of parties that were intended. The *essentialia negotii* (negotiated essential consensus) or *essentialia contractus* (contractual essential consensus) will be *sine qua non* for the formation of the contract. The *accidentalia negotii* can be regulated by the applicable default rules.

3. CISG *essentialia negotii*

The essential elements (*essentialia negotii* or *contractus*) of an offer or a sales contract are not specified in Article 4 ULF, which only states that an offer must be "sufficiently definite to permit the conclusion of the contract by acceptance and indicates the intention

---

[30] German doctrine makes a linguistic distinction by which the CISG only covers the objective consent (*äußerer Konsens*) and possible defects in subjective consent are excluded and left to the domestic law. See Peter Schlechtriem and U. Schroeter, in Schlechtriem and Schwenzer, *Commentary*, Rn. 1–2, pp. 253–4.

[31] The use of the Latin terms may differ, but for a similar use, see P. Cvetkovic, "The Characteristics of an Offer and Acceptance in CISG and PECL," 14 *Pace Int'l L. Rev.* 121, 123 (2002).

of the offeror to be bound."[32] In its critical analysis of the ULF, the UNCITRAL Secretary in its report 1976 proposed an alternative text that in three new sections defines the *essentialia contractus* to be an agreement on "at least the kind and quantity of the goods and that a price is to be paid."[33] The comparative problem of the requirement of a definite price – *pretium certum* – that some legal systems have taken over from Roman law was strongly debated in the drafting of the CISG, ending without the achievement of consensus.[34]

According to the wording of the CISG, the essential requirements of an offer are stated in CISG Article 14(1) – specification of the goods, quantity, and price.[35] Article 14(1) has in case law been interpreted as providing the *essentialia contractus* of a CISG sales contract.[36] The Austrian Federal Supreme Court stated:

> Der Vorschlag muß daher seinem Inhalt nach ausreichend bestimmt sein. Dies ist dann der Fall, wenn der Vorschlag die Ware bezeichnet und die Menge der zu liefernden Ware sowie den Preis ausdrücklich oder stillschweigend festsetzt bzw deren Festsetzung ermöglicht. Diesem Erfordernis ist dann entsprochen, wenn die essentialia negotii im Anbot ausdrücklich festgelegt werden, doch erlaubt Abs 1 Satz 2 dieser Bestimmung auch eine "stillschweigende Festsetzung." Damit sind Anhaltspunkte gemeint, die eine Auslegung ermöglichen, die zu einem bestimmten Preis, einer bestimmten Ware oder (und) ihrer Menge führt ... *Der Vertrag ist daher mit zumindest bestimmbarer Menge und bestimmbaren Preisen zustande gekommen.*[37]

An alternative interpretation argues that prices are not an essential element of the contract. An open price term does not prevent the formation of a contract under the CISG – thus reducing the *essentialia negotii* under the CISG to goods and quantity.[38] The price is presumed according to CISG Article 55 as long as the parties "have impliedly made reference to the price generally charged."

---

[32] Article 4(1) ULF does not refer to a "proposal" but to "the communication . . . with the object of concluding a contract of sale."

[33] Report of the Working Group on the International Sale of Goods on the Work of Its Eighth Session (New York, January 4–14, 1977) (A/CN.9/128, from February 3, 1977), Appendix I, Article 4, Proposed alternative text; published in John O. Honnold, *Documentary History of the Uniform Law for International Sales* (The Hague 1989), 254 et seq., see text at p. 260.

[34] See, e.g., the considerations by the Working Group Doc. A(14), IX YB, A/CN.9/142, at 73–4. For details on the legislative history on the "definite price" issue, see G. Eörsi in *Commentary on the International Sales Law* (ed. C. M. Bianca and M. J. Bonell) (Milan 1987), Article 14, at 133–4.

[35] The definition of "material" terms in CISG Article 19(3) does not have any bearing on the issue of the *essentialia negotii* and refers to an acceptance and not an offer.

[36] See Ulrich Magnus, *Staudinger Kommentar zum Bürgerlichen Gesetzbuch, Wiener UN-Kaufrecht (CISG)*, 2nd ed. (Berlin, 2005), Article 14, Rn. 3, 16–17: "Auch in den Fällen, in denen Angebot und Annahme nicht als selbständige Erklärungen identifizierbar sind, kommt ein Vertrag grundsätzlich nur zustande, wenn die essentialia, die Article 14 Abs. 1 Satz 2 nennt, hinreichend bestimmt sind"; T. Dornis in *Kommentar zum UN-Kaufrech*, 2nd ed. (ed. H. Honsell) (Berlin/Heidelberg, 2010), Article 14, Rn. 1, at 96. Cf. K. Steensgaard, *Standardbetingelser i internationale kontrakter* (Copenhagen 2010): 82 et seq., at 86–7, who will limit Article 14(1) CISG to the minimum requirement of an offer only and find it difficult to view the provision as indication of the *essentialia negotii* of a CISG contract; perhaps similar to Eörsi in Bianca and Bonnell, *Commentary*, Article 55, para 2.2.2, at 407: "Article 14 is concerned with offers and Article 55 with contracts. Once a contract has been concluded, the offer becomes irrelevant."

[37] Austrian Federal Supreme Court, Oberster Gerichtshof (OGH) (November 10, 1994), Case No. 2 Ob 547/93, available at http://www.unilex.info/case.cfm?id=110, emphasis by author.

[38] This interpretation is in line with Article 2.1.2 UPICC (2010), Article 2:201 PECL, Article II. 4.201 DCFR, and Article 31 CESL, *supra* note 12.

The requirement of a definite price (*pretium certum*) was intensively debated during the Vienna Conference 1980 resulting in seemingly conflicting provisions in Articles 14 (need for indication of price) and 55 (implying a price into an open price term). The best resolution of this conflict is to ignore the principle of *pretium certum* and enforce a contract where the parties intended to be bound. Two exceptions to enforcement of a contract without a price term would be in cases where agreement on the price was made a condition to the formation of the contract and in the rare situation where a market price cannot be determined.[39] A strong argument can be made that the interpreter should determine a market price based under Article 55 when there was intent to be bound. Article 55 will only salvage a contract when there are objective criteria for determining a reasonable price. The first criterion is to determine a price generally charged for such goods and under comparative circumstances in the trade concerned. Other criteria include the price used in previous sales by the parties or third parties, a seller's normal overheads, a seller's or producer's average costs allocated to material, personnel, and production of similar or identical goods, and ordinary profit in the trade concerned. In order to rebut this presumption *in dubio pro contractus*, a party must show that it is impossible to determine a market price.[40]

4. Nonformalistic Definition of Offer and Counteroffer

A CISG offer must be "addressed to one or more specific persons" (offer *ad personam*),[41] be "sufficiently definite" (*essentialia negotii*), and indicate "the intention of the offeror to be bound in case of acceptance" (*animus contrahendi*). The requirement of a definite price (*pretium certum*) should be reduced to an *accidentalia negotii*. The concepts of offer and counteroffer in the CISG formation regime are nonformalistic.

a. *Offer by a specific offeror to a specific addressee*

The identity of the contracting parties must be evident in the offer. Even though CISG Article 14(1) only notes the specification of the offeree, the identity of the person making the offer must also be known. This follows tacitly from Article 14(1) and other provisions of CISG Part II.[42] In most cases the identity of the offeror will be clear from the facts of the case or can be determined by interpretation according to CISG Article 8 or by a practice established between the parties under CISG Article 9(1). Doubts about the identity of the offeror may, however, arise in international sales involving multinational companies with many branches and agents with authority to represent one or more companies.[43] Contractual identity may also be confused where there is a

---

[39] See Supreme Court of the Republic of Hungary (September 25, 1992) (which held that a price for engines to airplanes did not have a market price and, therefore, a contract was not concluded). See also A. Vida, "Unwirksamkeit der Offerte wegen Unbestimmtheit nach UN-Kaufrecht," 15 *IPRax* 1995, 261 et seq.; P. Amato, "U.N. Convention on Contracts for the International Sale of Goods: The Open Price Term and Uniform Application: An Early Interpretation by Hungarian Court," 13 *J. L. & Commerce* 118 (1993).

[40] See CISG Articles 55 and 76 (references to market price).

[41] In contrast to an *invitatio ad offerendum*, see Article 14(2).

[42] Several provisions of CISG Part II presuppose a specific person as "offeror," see Articles 17, 18(2), 19(2), 21–2, and Article 20(2) ("place of business of the offeror").

[43] See, e.g., Austrian Supreme Court (Oberste Gerichtshof, OGH) (June 18, 1997), Case No. 3 Ob 512/96, available at http://www.unilex.info/case.cfm?id=284.

long supply chain of trading parties.[44] Often, there are multiple parties involved in a particular international sale of goods, and the legal role of the participants is not always clear. Moreover, as a consequence of the traditional model of offer and acceptance, a negotiation of the parties will in many cases lead to a constant "shift of roles" as initial offeror and offeree to subsequent counter offeror and counter offeree and vice versa.

The Swiss Supreme Court was faced with a case involving a chain of sales contracts concluded between multiple parties (Swiss seller, Italian supplier or producer, subsequent Swiss buyer of wine).[45] In the case, a Swiss buyer A (initial offeror) with place of business in Zürich renegotiated with a Swiss seller B (initial offeree), also in Switzerland, a contract of sale of wine in gift packs of three pieces. The contract gave A the right to return parts of the wine because the business idea did not result in expected returns. Under previous contracts, B bought the wine from an Italian supplier, C, who purchased the goods from an Italian producer, D. The supplier D had previously made delivery directly to A in Switzerland. New renegotiation between A and B resulted in a price reduction and an agreement that B (seller) should deliver only one type of Italian wine in a gift pack of six pieces. Buyer A accepted a new offer from an employee of B under the renegotiated terms and agreed to take delivery of a large quantity of specified wine. B, however, forwarded A's acceptance to D with the request that D deliver to A directly and demand payment from A directly. D delivered the ordered quantity of wine and A took delivery; the latter, then, rejected the request of payment from D. The question arose whether B or D was the offeror and contracting party to the sale transaction with A. In the proceeding before the Swiss Federal Supreme Court, D disputed the authority of the employee of B and claimed that the delivery of wine direct to A was an offer that A tacitly accepted by conduct.

Under domestic Swiss law, the court held that A and B had concluded a contract despite any lack of authority by B's employee. Under Swiss law, the court made reference to the doctrine of the binding effect of nonreaction to a letter of confirmation (A's acceptance of B's offer), as well as to the principle of good faith (*Treu und Glauben*).[46] However, the international sale under which the Italian supplier D claimed payment of the purchase price from the Swiss buyer A was governed by the CISG. A key factor, under a CISG analysis, is the common intention of the parties. The initial offer of A was addressed specifically to B, and D was considered by A a third party performing a sales contract on behalf of the seller B. In addition, a possible intention of seller B to transfer a contract or a contract proposal to its supplier D and the likewise intention of D to assume the obligation of performance and gain the rights under such the contract or proposal were not communicated to A. Therefore, this intention of B and D was not shared with A, which is a requisite for the subjective intention under CISG Article 8(1), nor would a reasonable person in A's position expect D as a contracting party under Article 8(2).

---

[44] See Peter Schlechtriem and U. Schröder in Schlechtriem and Schwenzer, *Commentary*, Article 14, Rn. 4, at 278–9.

[45] Swiss Federal Supreme Court, Bundesgericht (BG) (August 4, 2003), Case No. 4C.103/2003, available at http://www.unilex.info/case.cfm?id=954.

[46] Id., at para. 3.4: "Demnach wäre die B . . . SA unter Berücksichtigung des Umstands, dass sie mit der Beklagten bereits früher einen Kaufvertrag über Weine abgeschlossen hatte, *nach Treu und Glauben* gehalten gewesen, der Beklagten die eventuelle Ablehnung der Bestellung innert kurzer Frist mitzuteilen. Aus dem Umstand, dass die B . . . SA sich in der Folge nicht vernehmen liess, durfte die Beklagte daher nach dem Vertrauensprinzip darauf schliessen, die B . . . SA sei mit der Bestellung einverstanden gewesen."

The requirement of a common intention of the parties, under Article 8, was not satisfied. Hence, the only fact that could amount to an implied offer from D would be the delivery itself. Given these circumstances, the Swiss Federal Supreme Court rightly held that this was not enough:

> Aus der Lieferung des Weins musste die Beklagte nicht schliessen, die Klägerin wolle mit ihr einen Kaufvertrag abschliessen. Vielmehr musste die Beklagte auf Grund der Tatsache, dass sie den gelieferten Wein bei der B . . . bestellt hatte und die Klägerin für diese bereits die bei ihr bestellten 3er-Geschenkkartons geliefert hatte, annehmen die Klägerin handle auch in diesem Fall als Erfüllungsgehilfin der B . . . Damit musste die Beklagte die Weinlieferung als Erfüllungshandlung der B . . . und nicht als Antrag der Klägerin zu einem Vertragsschluss verstehen. Die Entgegennahme des Weins konnte demnach keine Annahme eines Vertragsangebots darstellen.

b. *Specification of the offeree*

CISG Article 14(1) requires that an offer in principle is a "private offer" to one or more specific persons. Article 14(2) does allow an offer to be addressed to an indefinite group of persons if the intent to be bound is clearly indicated by the offeror. A cautious seller will know to make use of the freedom of contract provided for in CISG Article 6. For example, seller could condition the public offer by stating it is only good for as long as stock is available. It is only by way of exception and in case of a clear indication that a "public offer" is binding under the CISG. In the lack of such a clear intent, an offer to an indefinite group of persons is an invitation to make an offer (*invitatio ad offerendum*) according to Article 14(2).

c. *Sufficiently definite offer: Requirements of CISG* essentialia negotii

The *essentialia negotii* for a sales contract should be deduced from a narrow interpretation of Article 14(1) to include an indication of the goods and an express or implicit fixing of the quantity. A tacit indication of the goods by the offeror is suitable for purposes of CISG Article 8.[47] Moreover, a definite price should not be part of the essential elements even though the majority view seems to be that an offer must indicate a price expressly or implicitly.[48] In determining whether an offer is sufficiently definite, existing practice established between the parties and international trade usage according to CISG Article 9 should be considered. Also, framework agreements between the parties may provide the means to imply a sufficient definition of the goods and quantity. It is important to note that the offer need not expressly fix a quantity, but can provide the means to determine a quantity at a later time by one of the parties or by a third party. This follows from the wide latitude, which Article 14(1), Sentence 2, allows for determining the quantity (and price) – the offer "expressly or *implicitly* fixes or makes provision for determining" price or quantity.

Determinability of the goods at a later date after the conclusion of the contract should not be regarded as sufficient, as this would not allow the contracting parties to estimate or predict their obligations and rights under the contract.[49] An indication of the goods

---

[47] See Magnus, *Staudinger*, Article 14, Rn. 20, at 199.

[48] See in case law *inter alia Golden Valley Grape Juice and Wine, LLC v. Centriys Corporation v. Centriys Corporation v. Separator Technology Solutions Pty Ltd*, Case No. CV F 09–1424 LJO GSA (E.D. Cal. 2010), available at http://www.unilex.info/case.cfm?id=1510 (Golden Valley).

[49] Article 14(1), Sentence 2, applies to the "quantity and price" only, not to the goods. See Austrian Federal Supreme Court, Oberster Gerichtshof (OGH) (November 10, 1994) ("Zusammenfassend ist daher

can be made specifically (*species* of goods) and generically (*genus* of goods), provided that the goods are indicated by nature and type. The further specification of details can be made subsequently, which does not prevent the formation of the contract.[50] CISG Article 65 recognizes the parties' ability to determine the specifications of the goods subsequent to contract formation. The contract may require the buyer "to specify the form, measurement or other features of the goods," and, failing to do so, the seller may provide the specifications. Article 65(2) requires seller to send proposed specifications to buyer and fix a reasonable time for buyer to amend the specifications. Upon the expiration of the time to change the specifications, buyer is bound by seller's specifications.[51] A specification under Article 65 does not require acceptance, but if the Article 65 specification is combined with a statement of different terms of the contract, inter alia time for delivery, this will amount to an amendment of the contract under CISG Article 29 and necessitate acceptance.[52]

As noted earlier, the CISG gives some flexibility regarding the offer's fixing of the quantity of the goods. The offeror's ability to "implicitly fix" the quantity of goods has been the issue in numerous cases, including the sale of tomato tins and truck loads,[53] specification of 700–800 tons of propane gas,[54] and for the delivery of textiles.[55] In particular, weight has been attached to specifications of quantities well known to the parties or by commercial practice. A failure to agree to a fixed quantity may still be fixed by subsequent conduct under CISG Article 8(3). The key issue becomes whether the parties intended to be bound. The Federal Supreme Court of Austria concluded that the parties intended to be bound in the Chinchilla furs case.[56] Without such

eine stillschweigende Festlegung und eine bloß die Festsetzung ermöglichte Vereinbarung sowohl zur Umschreibung von Warenmenge als auch des Preises zulässig"). Cf. Peter Schlechtriem in Schlechtriem and Schwenzer, *Commentary*, Article 14, Rn. 5, at 191 ("The minimum elements do not have to be fixed by express indication or by indication capable of being interpreted; it is sufficient if 'provision' is made 'for determining' them, that is to say, if they are determinable").

[50] Honnold, *Uniform Law*, §137(2), 150 ("this does not make a contract too indefinite").

[51] Article 65(2) is one of the CISG provisions in Part III that expressly provides for a binding effect of silence, see also Article 48(3) and in Part II Article 19(2) and Article 21(2).

[52] See, e.g., Oberlandesgericht (OLG) Munich (February 8, 1995), Case No. 7 U 1720/94, available at http://www.unilex.info/case.cfm?id=118, at para. III 2 c) bb). "Die von der Beklagten mit Schreiben vom (April 14, 1992) (Anl. K 9) vorgenommene noch notwendige Spezifikation der Fahrzeuge (Article 65) sowie die Angabe der Lieferzeit 'ca. Juli/August/September/Oktober 1992' beinhaltet eine gem. 29 CISG zulässige Vertragsergänzung, die der Annahme durch die Klägerin bedurfte (Article 18 ff.). Soweit die Klägerin in dem maßgeblichen Schreiben vom 10.04.1992 – gegenbestätigend – die Lieferzeit abgeändert hat, stellt dies eine Ablehnung des Angebots der Beklagten und ein Gegenangebot dar, welches von dem Angebot der Beklagten wesentlich abweicht. Insoweit bedurfte es der Annahme durch die Beklagte (Art. 19 CISG)."

[53] OLG Hamburg (July 4, 1997), Case No. 1 U 143/95 and 410 O 21/95, available at http://www.unilex.info/case.cfm?id=438 (not unpublished): "Die Klägerin schlägt darin vor, der Beklagten *20 LKW-Ladungen Tomatenmark* bis Ende Mai 1994 zu liefern. Dabei sind die Beteiligten ganz offensichtlich von ihnen bekannten branchenüblichen Mengen betreffend Doseninhalt und Ladefähigkeit eines LKW ausgegangen."

[54] Austrian Federal Supreme Court, Oberster Gerichtshof (OGH) (February 6, 1996), Case No. 10 Ob 518/95, available at http://www.unilex.info/case.cfm?id=202: "Lieferung von 700–800 Tonnen Flüssiggas zu einem Preis von US-$ 376,- prompt."

[55] Bezirksgericht St. Gallen, Switzerland (July 3, 1997), Case No. 3PZ 97/18, available at http://www.unilex.info/case.cfm?id=306, where the buyer despite a later disagreement on the quantity requested a bill for delivered goods by stating: "Bitte lassen Sie das Material in Rechnung stellen."

[56] Austrian Federal Supreme Court, Oberster Gerichtshof (OGH) (November 11, 1994) ("Dabei ist vor allem das spätere Verhalten des Beklagten zu berücksichtigen, der die übersandten Felle bis auf einen

additional evidence of intent, a quantity term stating a large quantity of Chinchilla furs (*einer größeren Menge von Chinchilla-Fellen*) would not have been sufficiently definite.

In some long-term relationships, such as supply contracts involving multiple install-ments, the quantity term will initially be left open. It will be filled subsequently based upon the buyers' requirements (demand) or the sellers' production (output). The ques-tion then arises whether the parties are bound by such a contract and at what point in time the contract is deemed to be concluded. Professor John Honnold, supported by the *traveau préparatoire*, has rightly argued that such "Requirements" and "Output Contracts" are enforceable under the CISG: "Article 14(1) should not be construed to nullify these important transactions on the ground that the quantity will not be fixed until the buyer's requirements or the seller's output become known."[57]

CISG case law has accepted that either party can determine the exact quantity at a later stage,[58] and that quantity can be determined based on a customer's needs. The latter was the case in a decision of the French Cour de Cassation involving a framework agreement (*un accord de collaboration*) between a Swiss seller and a French buyer of cranks for trucks over a period of eight years.[59] The goods were clearly identified, but the quantity was stated to be an annual amount dependent on the requirements of the final customer:

> Les quantités à livrer sont déterminées à l'article 2 Volumes de livraison ainsi qu'il suit:
> Au moins 20.000 unités sur un laps de temps de 8 années appelées suivant les besoins de RVI.
> Estimations prévisionnelles:
> 1991 environ 3.000 unités (sur toute l'année);
> 1992 environ 4.000 unités;
> 1993 environ 5.000 unités;
> 1994 environ 6.000 unités;
> 1995 environ 6.000 unités.

The Cour d'appel de Colmar held this to be a sufficient determination of the quantity with the following pragmatic argument:[60] These terms should be read as a minimum quantity of 20,000 goods to be delivered over an eight-year period. The reference to the needs of the final customer does not relate to the volume but constitutes a simple repartition of the quantity. The French Cour de cassation confirmed that a binding

---

geringen Teil weiterverkaufte, ohne Vorbehalte über die Menge der übersandten Waren zu machen. Es muß daher auf Grund des späteren Verhaltens der Parteien davon ausgegangen werden, daß auch die Bestellung einer 'größeren Menge von Fellen' als hinreichend bestimmt anzusehen ist").

[57] Honnold, *Uniform Law*, para. 137.3, at 150.

[58] Commercial Court of Zürich (Handelsgericht des Kanton Zürich) (July 10, 1996), Case No. HG 940513, available at http://www.unilex.info/case.cfm?id=381.

[59] French Cour de Cassation (June 30, 2004), Case No. Y 01–15.964, available at http://www.unilex.info/case.cfm?id=981.

[60] Cour d'appel de Colmar (June 12, 2001), available at http://www.unilex.info/case.cfm?id=814 ("Si les mots ont un sens, la lecture – et non pas l'interprétation qui ne se justifie qu'en cas d'omission, d'imprécision ou de contradiction apparente – des termes 'au moins 20.000 unités' ne renvoie pas à un ordre 'approximatif' de grandeur, comme le soutient la société B . . . France, mais bien à un nombre minimal de 20.000 carters à livrer sur une durée de 8 ans. La référence aux 'besoins de RVI' ne se rapporte pas au volume des 'livraisons' mais constitue un simple critère de répartition").

contract had been concluded and interpreted the parties' statements and conduct, using the principles of Article 8 and the good faith principle, as follows:

> Attendu que l'arrêt retient, d'une part, que dans le contrat litigieux les parties sont désignées comme "fabricant" et "acheteur" et d'autre part qu'y sont déterminées précisément la marchandise à fournir, les quantités à livrer, la méthode de détermination du prix et les modalités de paiement; qu'interprétant les éléments de preuve qui lui étaient soumis au regard des principes définis à l'article 8 CVIM et notamment de celui selon lequel les contrats doivent s'interpréter de bonne foi, la cour d'appel a pu en déduire que l'accord comportait des obligations réciproques de livrer et d'acheter une marchandise déterminée, à un prix convenu de sorte qu'il constituait une vente.

d. *Intention of the offeror to be bound* (animus contrahendi)

Difficult, but important, distinctions need to be drawn between nonbinding inquiries, exchange of information, negotiations, and contractually binding statements (intention of the offeror and offeree to be bound or *animus contrahendi*). The demarcation line is determined by the existence of or the lack of an intention to be bound.

The requirement of a general intent to be bound is found in CISG Articles 14, 18, and 19 CISG. It is, however, left to the general rules on interpretation in CISG Article 8 to determine whether a contract is concluded.[61] The intention must relate to the CISG *essentialia negotii* in order to form a binding contract. Under Article 8(3), such intent is determined with due regard to all relevant circumstances and, as stated by UNCITRAL in the commets to the 1978 UNCTRAL Draft, by the CISG rule of interpretation of the parties statement and conduct in CISG Article 8:[62]

> "In order for the proposal for concluding a contract to constitute an offer it must indicate the intention of the offeror to be bound in case of acceptance." Since there are no particular words, which must be used to indicate such an intention, it may sometimes require a careful examination of the "offer" in order to determine whether such an intention existed. This is particularly true if one party claims that a contract was concluded during negotiations, which were carried on over an extended period of time, and no single communication was labeled by the parties as an "offer" or as an "acceptance." Whether there is the requisite intention to be bound in case of acceptance will be established in accordance with the rules of interpretation contained in [CISG Article 8].[63]

e. *Revocability of offer and the precontractual relationship*

Professor John Honnold discussed the issue of the effect of a "fixed time for acceptance" set by the offeror according to CISG Article 16(2)(a): "It is not easy to assess the outcome of this dispute, which may well appear to be a tempest in a teapot." Honnold, thereby, refers to the question of whether a "fixed time for acceptance" placed in an offer sets the time period for acceptance under CISG Article 18(2) or in addition creates a presumption of irrevocability of the offer under Article 16(2)(a). The most plausible answer is that a

---

[61] See I. Schwenzer. and F. Mohs, "Old Habits Die Hard: Traditional Contract Formation in a Modern World," 6 *Internationales Handelsrecht (IHR)* 240 (2006) (must indicate the intention to buy or sell the goods).

[62] See, e.g., German Court of Appeal decision (Landgericht Kiel) (July 27, 2004), Case No. 16 O 83/04, unpublished; see commentary by Morten M. Fogt, "Konkludente Vertragsannahme," 361 et seq.

[63] UNCITRAL Commentary on the 1978 Draft Convention, Article 12 (CISG Article 14).

"fixed time of acceptance" in the offer does both. However, there are only a few cases interpreting Article 16(2)(b).[64] This is surprising when one considers that Article 16(2) was a product of compromise. One explanation is that business persons in fact regard an offer with a fixed time for acceptance as irrevocable within the fixed period. Another explanation is that an offer is generally regarded in practice as freely revocable. In both scenarios no dispute on the interpretation of Article 16(2)(a) and (b) would arise. The first explanation is a more plausible one.

B. *Realistic Concept of Acceptance*

The CISG provides a realistic concept of acceptance, which focuses on the indication of assent. The acceptance under the CISG has a nonformalistic definition, much like the offer. Case law on the CISG Article 18(3) has stated that: "conduct is adequate acceptance ... Pursuant to the CISG, acceptance does not require a signature or formalistic adoption of the offered terms."[65] The indication of assent (*animus contrahendi*) of the offeree can follow from a formal acceptance or any conduct at the time of the conclusion of the contract or subsequently.[66]

The legal questions raised by CISG Article 19, however, are of practical importance to modern international commerce. The provision encompasses the traditional distinction between an acceptance that mirrors the offer and an acceptance that alters the offer and prevents the formation of the contract. On the other hand, Article 19 provides for a limited rule on the binding effect of modified acceptances in cases of nonmaterial deviations from the offer coupled with a nonresponse on the part of the offeror. However, Article 19 creates more questions than answers: (1) How are alternative forms of contract formation dealt with under the CISG? (2) What is the effect of silence or passivity in business relations? (3) What is the legal effect of confirmation letters? (4) For the determination of the content, how and when are standard terms incorporated into a contract? (5) What is the legal effect of purported offers and acceptance containing conflicting standard terms (battle of the forms), which in many cases will entail material different terms? All these questions are covered within the scope of the CISG, and more specifically, Part II on formation of contract. These questions remain unsettled or are at least not expressly settled by CISG provisions.

In an Article 19 scenario involving additional or conflicting terms, a number of matters need to be clarified: (1) the definition of material and nonmaterial terms; (2) the scope of the rule on the binding effect of a modified acceptance; (3) the related question of acceptance by silence, such as a failure to react against a commercial letter of confirmation; and (4) the general issue of the incorporation of standard forms. In the battle of the forms scenario, a number of views have been offered, including that the battle of the forms is not governed by the CISG or that it is governed but not settled by the CISG. In the latter view, the battle of the forms is either resolvable by applying the general principles of the CISG or, if not resolvable, then to be decided through private international law of the forum. Most U.S. courts apply "the last short" rule under the

---

[64] See partially Geneva Pharmaceuticals, *supra* note 28 (Article 16(2)(b) and reliance principle compared with common law promissory estoppel doctrine).

[65] Golden Valley, *supra* note 48, at para. C 2.

[66] See Articles 8(3) and 18(1) and (3).

CISG;[67] German courts have generally applied the "the knock out" rule,[68] reasoning that the parties intended a derogation under Article 6;[69] and in some jurisdictions, such as France and the Nordic states, the result is uncertain.[70] Some courts have used the Unidroit Principles of International Commercial Contracts to fill in the gaps of the CISG.[71]

C. *Validity: External* Lagunae

CISG Article 11 governs formal "validity" or formalities. The validity of substantive terms comes in three forms: the binding effect of an offer (promise); defects of consent; and the illegality, immorality, unfairness, or unreasonableness of contract terms.[72] The CISG governs the first form of substantive validity by providing rules for an offer in order to be binding. On the contrary, the CISG is not concerned with the other forms of substantive validity that make a contract or a contract term voidable or void *ab initio* due to defects of consent, unfairness or unreasonableness, and illegality and immorality.

The question of an "apparent or objective" consent (*äußere Konsens*) between the parties is regulated by Part II. But the CISG does not provide any regulation relating to defects in apparent or objective consent and states in Article 4 that validity is a question for domestic law. Thus, defects in consent due to duress, fraud, exploitation, and mistake are outside the scope of the CISG. However, if a mistake is made concerning matters for which the CISG provides a remedy, the CISG applies. An example is a mistake concerning the characteristics or conformity of the goods, which under some domestic laws is a ground for invalidity.[73]

---

[67] See *Norfolk Southern Railway Company v. Power Source Supplz, Inc.*, Case No. 07–140-JJf, 2008 U.S. Dist. LEXIS 56942 (W.D. Pa. 2008), available at http://cisgw3.law.pace.edu/cases/080725u1.html ("This battle of the forms must be resolved by reference to CISG Article 19" and coming as the result of a counteroffer as the "last shot"). Cf. P. O. Viscasillas, "Battle of Forms, Modification of Contract, Commercial Letters of Confirmation: Comparison of the United Nations Convention on the Contracts for the International Sale of Goods (CISG) with the Principles of European Contract Law (PECL)," 14 *Pace Int'l L. J.* 153, 156–8 (2002); "Battle of the Forms" under the 1980 United Nations Convention on Contracts for the Sale of Goods: A Comparison with Section 2–207 UCC and the Unidroit Principles," 10 *Pace Int'l L. J.* 97 (1998). For the "knock out" rule still, however, cautious, see John O. Honnold, *Uniform Law for International Sales under the 1980 United Nations Convention*, 4th rev. ed. (ed. Harry Flechtner) (Alphen aan den Rijn, 2009), 254.

[68] See BGH (January 9, 2002), available at www.unilex.

[69] Schlechtriem and Schröeter in Schlechtriem and Schwenzer, *Kommentar zum Einheitlichen UN-Kaufrecht*, 352, Rn. 25.

[70] Cf. F. C. Dutilleul and P. Delebecque, *Contracts civils et commerciaux*, 8th ed. (Paris: Dalloz, 2007), 120, n. 116.

[71] See, e.g., Hof's-Hertogenbosch (October 16, 2002) Nederlands Internationaal Privaatrecht (NIPR) 2003, no. 92 (2003), available at http://www.unilex.info/case.cfm?id=960 (incorporation of general business terms); Cour de Cassation, Belgium, (June 19, 2009) in the case of *Lourraine Tubes v. Scaform International BV*, Case No. C.07.0289.N, available at http://www.unilex.info/case.cfm?id=1457 (hardship).

[72] Cf. U. Drobnig in *International Sales of Goods, Dubrovnik Lectures* (ed. Sarcevic and Volken) (1986), 313; Zeller, "The Black Hole," 259.

[73] See Oberster Gerichtshof Austria (April 13, 2000), Case No. 2 Ob 100/00, available at http://www.unilex.info/case.cfm?id=687: "Art 45 UN-K regle die Ansprüche des Käufers gegen den Verkäufer umfassend und abschließend. Der Rückgriff auf nationale Vorschriften sei ausgeschlossen. Über die im Übereinkommen geregelten Ansprüche hinausgehende, im nationalen Recht vorgesehene Ansprüche könnten nicht geltend gemacht werden. Dies gelte trotz Article 4(a) UN-K auch für die Irrtumsanfechtung."

Invalidity based on unfairness or unreasonableness is relevant in a commercial setting where the rights of one party are limited too much, such as excessive limitations in standard forms,[74] "sold as is clauses,"[75] or where the remedies provided for one party are overly one-sided (e.g., excessive penalty clauses). Despite the position of validity as an external gap in the CISG, account should be taken to the fundamental rights of the parties under the CISG. The Federal Supreme Court of Austria has rightly held that the question of validity – even when this is referred to domestic law – should be measured against the values and fundamental rights of the CISG (*Grundwertungen des CISG*).[76]

The question of illegality and immorality generally involves a violation of national public law[77] and criminal law. For example, if one of the parties to a CISG contract is responsible for an act of corruption in connection with a contract of sale, the civil law treats the act of corruption as a breach of contract (most likely a fundamental breach under Article 25) or states that a contract influenced by corruption is invalid and unenforceable.[78]

IV. General Principles of Part II

This part provides a brief history of the negotiation and drafting of Part II. It concludes with a summary or template of the underlying principles that should be liberally applied in the interpretation of the formation rules found in Part II.

A. *Brief Legislative History of Part II*

In 1969, UNCITRAL established a Working Group on the International Sale of Goods (Working Group). Representatives from fourteen countries were given the task of

---

[74] See, e.g., the decision of the French Cour de Cassation in the case Société DIG v. Société Sup, available at http://www.unilex.info/case.cfm?id=1372, where the court reversed a decision of the Cour d'appel Paris (February 25, 2005, Case No. 03/21335, available at http://www.unilex.info/case.cfm?id=1095) that the seller's liability exemption clause according to the CISG were valid between professional parties: "Attendu qu'en statuant ainsi, alors que la Convention de Vienne régit exclusivement la formation du contrat de vente et les droits et obligations qu'un tel contrat fait naître entre le vendeur et l'acheteur mais ne concerne pas la validité du contrat ni d'aucune de ses clauses, la cour d'appel a violé le texte susvisé."

[75] See *Barbara Berry, S.A. de C.V. v. Ken M. Spooner Farms, Inc.* (W.D. Wash. 2006), Case No. C05–5538FDB, available at http://www.unilex.info/case.cfm?id=1105.

[76] Oberster Gerichtshof Austria (September 7, 2000), Case No. 8 Ob 22/00v, available at http://www.unilex.info/case.cfm?id=473 ("Diese Regelung widerspricht auch nicht den Grundwertungen des UN-Kaufrechts; nur diesen Grundwertungen widersprechende nationale Bestimmungen könnten als unzulässig angesehen werden. Zu den jedenfalls zu wahrenden Grundwertungen des UN-Kaufrechts zählt u.a. das Recht zur Aufhebung des Vertrages, das der vertragstreuen Partei als ultima ratio grundsätzlich erhalten bleiben muss, soweit die Gegenpartei die Ware auch nicht nach einer angemessen verlängerten Frist liefert oder die Ware trotz einer Nacherfüllung im Wesentlichen unbrauchbar bleibt. Wird auch dieses Aufhebungsrecht eingeschränkt, so muss der vertragstreuen Partei in jedem Fall ein Anspruch auf Ersatz des durch den Erfüllungsmangel entstandenen Schadens verbleiben").

[77] See, e.g., German Federal Supreme Court (Bundesgerichtshof, BGH) (July 23, 1997), Case No. VIII ZR 134/96, available at http://www.unilex.info/case.cfm?id=259 (contract violating national unfair competition law).

[78] Cf. Morten M. Fogt, "Korruptionens civilretlige virkning komparativt – Om status efter Oil-for-Food, det internationale privat-, straffe- og offentligretlige lovvalg samt Europa Rådets Civil Law Convention on Corruption, Del I og II," 5 (4) *Erhvervsjuridisk Tidsskrift* 271 (2010); id., "Del III," 6 (1) *Erhvervsjuridisk Tidsskrift* 1 (2011).

preparing a draft of uniform sales law rules that would be acceptable "by countries of different legal, social and economical systems."[79] The initial draft was based on the 1964 ULF, culminating in the 1976 Sales Draft Convention. At the Working Group's seventh session (January 1976), the group requested the UNCITRAL Secretary to prepare a critical analysis of the ULF and the 1972 UNIDROIT draft law on the validity of contracts of international sale (LUV). In a 1977 report, the UNCITRAL Secretary came to two fundamental limitations of the coverage of the new uniform rules on the formation of contract. First, a suggestion not to codify every aspect of contract formation and that the new rules should be based on the ULF and limited to the areas of offer and acceptance. Second, a proposal should not include any provision on validity based on the 1972 LUV. The reasons for these two limitations are explained as follows:

> Fortunately, it is not necessary to codify every aspect of the subject in a text of uniform law since there is more agreement on the practical result in various situations than there is on the theory by which that solution is attained or justified. Therefore, it may be enough to prepare a text, which offers solutions to practical problems caused by such differences in the law in various systems.

> For this reason, it is suggested that the draft convention on formation of contract to be prepared by the Working Group might follow the plan of ULF in regard to its coverage. Such a draft convention would be largely limited to offer and acceptance. These matters are ones in which the differences between the various legal systems are such that practical problems are caused in international trade. Nevertheless, they are subjects in which it appears possible to formulate a generally acceptable text.

> It is also suggested that the draft convention to be prepared not include any provisions in respect of validity of contract based on the [1972] LUV . . . all available evidence suggests that these problems of validity are relatively rare events in respect of contracts for the international sale of goods.[80]

This very brief account of part of the legislative history of CISG Part II shows that the focus was not on a broad harmonization of the "law on contract formation" but on a limited and fragmented legal regime on contract formation. Contract formation in the CISG has more the character of an annex to the more important sales law rules of the CISG. A review of the legislative history of the CISG indicates that another reason for the limitation of coverage on contract formation was a lack of time. The Working Group noted the following when adopting the agenda for the work on Part II:

> In the discussion of the adoption of agenda, the Working Group noted the views of the Commission at its ninth session [1976] that "the Working Group should restrict its work to the preparation of rules on the formation of contracts for the international sale of goods so as to complete its task in the shortest possible time, but that the Working Group had discretion as to whether to include some rules in respect of the validity of such contracts."[81]

---

[79] Cf. Honnold, *Documentary History*, 2.

[80] Report of the Secretary General: formation and validity of contracts for the international sale of goods (A/CN.9/128, annex II, from February 3, 1977), paras. 16–18 in Honnold, *Documentary History*, 256.

[81] Report of the Working Group on the International Sale of Goods on the work of its eighth session (New York, January 4–14, 1977) (A/CN.9/128 (February 3, 1977), para. 8 in Honnold, *Documentary History*, 275.

From the Working Group's eighth session (January 1977) to its ninth session (September 1977), the work on the draft on the Formation of a Sale Contract was completed and subsequently combined with the Sales Draft Convention from 1976 into the UNCITRAL 1978 Draft that provided the foundational document for the 1980 Vienna Conference.

B. *General Principles*

Due to the fragmented nature of Part II, supplementation of its core rules is needed to make its formation rules fully functional and responsive to international sales transactions. First, important parts of contract formation are excluded from the scope of the CISG, including alternative means of contract formation and contract validity. Both are important parts of determining whether a contract comes into existence. One area of contract formation, the traditional offer–acceptance model, is regulated under Part II, although alternative means of contract formation are bypassed in the text of the CISG. Issues of contract validity are excluded expressly according to CISG Article 4. In sum, the rules of traditional contract formation are settled in Part II, alternative means of contract formation are governed but not settled (internal *lagunae*), and issues of validity are not governed (external *lagunae*). Such a framework represents an arbitrary fragmentation of the area of contract formation.

A way to remedy the noncomprehensive character of the CISG's formation rules is to employ a liberal interpretation methodology and to develop (implied) general principles on which the CISG is based. The gap-filling provision of CISG Article 7(2) provides the means for a liberal interpretive methodology based on implied general principles. In trying to establish underlying principles on contract formation, CISG Parts I and III should be used to help fill in the gaps in Part II.

The following is a nonexhaustive list of general underlying principles of the CISG that relate to contract formation. Some of the principles are general and some specific; some are found in express statements in the CISG, some are tacit and implied. Some of the principles are disputed and some remain uncertain regarding existence and content:

- Freedom of contract or party autonomy (Articles 6, 30, 35(1), and 53).
- Freedom of form (Article 11 and 29, unless reservation in Article 96).
- Binding effect of a contract – *pacta sunt servanda* (implicitly found in Articles 45, 61, and 79).
- Principle of consensus between the parties – a common *animus contrahendi* (Articles 14 and 18–19).
- The principle that a contract can be concluded by conclusive conduct (in German "*konkludentes Verhalten,*" Article 18(1) and 18(3)).
- The *favor contractus* principle in that the CISG limits the possible grounds and applies strict conditions for avoidance (Articles 25, 49, 64, 72, 73; the "cure" provisions Articles 34, 37, and 48; and the "*Nachfrist*" provisions, Articles 47, 63).
- Intention of the parties as common or shared intention (Article 8(1) – subjective interpretation).
- Reasonable businessperson standard (Article 8(2) – objective interpretation).
- Receipt theory – increases party awareness that a contract has been concluded and contractual rights and obligations have been created (Article 24 and in Part III inter alia Articles 48(4), 65(2), and 79(4)).

- Importance of statements and conduct before, at, and subsequent to the conclusion of a contract as an indication of parties' intent (Article 8).
- Binding effect of practices established between the parties under gentle conditions (Article 9(1)).
- Binding effect of international trade usage under strict conditions (Article 9(2)).
- CISG *essentialia negotii* limited to an indication of goods and quantity (Article 14(1)).
- CISG *accidentalia negotii* (including the indication of price and exemplified by other contract elements in Article 19(3) and CISG default rules).
- CISG *naturalia negotii* – the reasonable reliance and expectation principles (Articles 16(2)(b), 19(2), 21(2), and some provisions in Part III).[82]
- CISG *naturalia negotii* in the sense of *venire contra factum proprium* (Articles 16(1)(b) and 29(2)).
- CISG *naturalia negotii* – the duty of cooperation calling for exchange reasonable communications and exchanges of information to provide notice and avoid ambiguity, doubts, and mistakes[83] (Part II and numerous provisions of Part III support of reliance and expectation principles).[84]
- CISG *naturalia negotii* recognition of the principle of reasonableness (Part I, Article 8(2); Part II, Articles 16(2)(b) and 18(2); and numerous provisions of Part III).[85]
- Principle of good faith and fair dealing as the overall CISG *naturalia negotii* (Articles 7(1), 29(2), 40, and 80).

The application and interpretation of these principles determine the scope and limits of Part II and when recourse to domestic law is permitted. If the principles are narrowly construed as they apply to Part II, then uniformity of law is restricted and the divergences between national laws will continue to be barriers to international sales transactions. As an example, the rule on reasonable reliance espoused in Article 16(2)(b) could be interpreted as supporting a general reliance principle. On the other hand, as applied in *Geneva Pharmaceuticals Technology Corp. v. Barr Laboratories, Inc., et al.*,[86] the scope of the rule in Article 16(2)(b) is fairly limited and allows for the application of domestic principles, such as estoppel: "The question of whether it preempts a separate claim for promissory estoppel presents a closer question. Breach of contract and promissory estoppel are two sides of the same coin, and that coin is a cause of action for breach of contract." In that case, an American buyer utilized promissory estoppel to prove that a promise on which it relied should be recognized as binding on the promisor. The court reasoned that: "[I]f the CISG had contemplated a similar 'reliance' principle . . . this promissory estoppel claim would be preempted. The defendants have presented no argument that the CISG does so, and therefore this particular promissory estoppel claim is not preempted."[87] However, because Article 16(2)(b) appears to employ a modified version of promissory estoppel, the CISG and not domestic law should govern a claim

---

[82] See Articles 35(2)(b), 48(2), and 65(2).
[83] Cf. Honnold, *Uniform Law*, Article 14, para 134, n. 2 ("The Convention's numerous provisions calling for communications to enable a party to know where the other stands suggest a 'general principle' that a party may not take advantage of ambiguity when an inquiry could readily remove the doubt").
[84] See Articles 32(2)–(3), 48(2), 60(a), and Article 65(2).
[85] See Articles 33(c), 34, 35(2)(b), 37, 39, 40, 43, 46(2)–(3), 47–49, 60, and 63.
[86] Geneva Pharmaceuticals, *supra* note 28.
[87] Id.

of promissory estoppel made to avoid the need to prove the existence of a "firm offer." Such a claim under the CISG would not require a finding of foreseeability or detriment, as required under American common law.

If principles are too broadly construed and/or purported underlying principles are developed on a weak or absent legal basis in the CISG, then uniformity of law may be pushed too far with a possible effect of deharmonization in practice. There are, thus, likewise reasons to warn against an excessive development of underlying (implied) principles of the CISG:

> My doubt does not concern the basis or most of the achieved results in general but rather the danger of overworking the tool of Article 7, section 2 CISG with a possible deharmonization effect within an instrument of unification and harmonization of Commercial Law. The outcome of this academic laboratory of "underlying principles of the CISG" which, admittedly, I gladly join can be pushed too far, yielding a result that is less predictable, certain, and that lacks the legitimacy of the contracting states. The latter concern is not crucial, but the needs of international business for legal predictability and certainty surely are. Here, I see perhaps the most critical danger for the process of unification and harmonization of International Commercial Law. Excess limiting of unification instruments beyond their original scope and wording can run counter to the expectations of the contracting states and, even more dangerously, come as a surprise to businessmen and their legal counsel. Such uncertainty can turn into major disadvantages for international commerce.[88]

In sum, for the gap-filling within the scope of the convention, the provision of Article 7(2) CISG demands and allows the search for "general principles on which it is based," but Article 7(2) does not mandate the development of underlying principles of the convention based on general principles of the law of the CISG contracting states or all legal systems.

V. Conclusion: Reforming CISG Part II

The fragmented nature of Part II has created numerous external and internal "gaps." Until these gaps are filled though liberal interpretation, analogies, and implied underlying principles, the more uncertainty and national discrepancies will appear in the case law. The line between dynamic interpretation and new law-making is unclear, but for the CISG to provide uniform formation rules, the scope of Part II will have to be interpreted as broadly as possible. This review of Part II has shown a number of things. First, the traditional contract formation regime of the CISG only satisfactorily covers a portion of international sales transactions. Because of its failure to expressly deal with alternative means of contract formation, its application to these other means of formation has been uneven and nonuniform. The fact that contract formation and interpretation are governed by the CISG and contract validity is not has led to problems of interpretation that can only be corrected by reforming Part II.

The CISG's formation rules fail to provide coverage on numerous contract formation issues that are of practical importance to international sales transactions. Part II should be reformed to expand its scope into areas such as alternative means of contract formation

---

[88] Morten M. Fogt, "Private International Law in the Process of Harmonization of International Commercial Law: The 'Ugly Duckling'?," in Fogt, *Uniformity and Harmonization*, 57 et seq., 95.

and contract validity. This invitation has been made and addressed to the UNCITRAL some years ago and is today even more urgent.[89] Part II is the weakest part of the CISG, falling far short of being a clear, comprehensive, and functional legal regime. *Hanwha Corporation v. Cedar Petrochemicals, Inc.*,[90] and many similar cases, could have been prevented or more easily resolved if Part II were clearer and more comprehensive.

---

[89] See Morten M. Fogt, "The Stipulation and Interpretation of Freight Prepaid Delivery Clauses under the CISG: Preliminary Considerations for Reform of Part II of the CISG and a Limited Withdrawal of Scandinavian Declarations," *European Legal Forum* 61 (2003).

[90] Hanwha Corporation, *supra* note 2.

13 The CISG and the Battle of the Forms

Bruno Zeller

I. Introduction

Much has been written in relation to the battle of the forms, not only in relation to the CISG, but also in domestic laws. However, the CISG's mandate that in interpreting contracts "due consideration" shall be given "to all relevant circumstances"[1] makes it clear that "parol evidence regarding the negotiations to the extent they reveal the parties' subjective intent" is admissible evidence.[2] The hope is that with the freer admittance of extrinsic evidence, the battle of forms scenario would be less problematic. For example, the scenario where the standard terms are introduced during the negotiation stage, but none of the terms were ever expressly accepted, becomes important given Article 8(1)'s requirement that courts should consider subjective intent in the interpretation of contracts. The court in *MCC-Marble Ceramic Center v. Ceramica Nuova D'Agostino* (*MCC Marble*) correctly noted that this does not mean the written contract is less meaningful:

> This is not to say that parties to an international contract for the sale of goods cannot depend on written contracts or that parol evidence regarding subjective contractual intent need always prevent a party relying on a written agreement from securing summary judgment. In most cases, therefore, article 8(2) of the CISG will apply, and objective evidence will provide the basis for the court's decision.[3]

In common law, the objective approach is predominantly used and the parol evidence rule, barring the admission of extrinsic evidence that contradicts the written contract, is still the law. The CISG, on the other hand, allows the use of objective evidence, but allows as well the admission of evidence of the subjective intent of the parties. Article 8 recognizes negotiations, any practice that the parties have established between themselves, usages, and any subsequent conduct of the parties as probative evidence of intent.[4] This approach best enables courts and arbitral tribunals to arrive at sound decisions – given that often the parties use standard form contracts without an agreement of which standard terms are applicable to their contracts.

---

[1] CISG, Article 8(3).
[2] *MCC-Marble Ceramic Center v. Ceramica Nuova D'Agostino*, United States Court of Appeals, Eleventh Circuit. 144 F.3d 1384 (1998), available at http://cisgw3.law.pace.edu/cases/980629u1.html.
[3] Id.
[4] CISG, Article 8(3).

The problem is which of the standard forms tendered by both parties during the negotiation stage are considered to be part of the eventual contract. The appeals court in Koblenz expressed succinctly that "the contract is more important to the parties than the diverging clauses."[5] The court noted:

> [I]t seems more necessary than before to take into consideration the reality of business dealings. In this respect, experience shows that the contractual partners normally do not want to have the conclusion of the contract fail due to a missing agreement on colliding standard terms. Thus the collision problem is often intentionally left open. Only if difficulties arise during the performance, do the parties return to the point in order to strengthen their own legal position. Therefore, simple and qualified defense clauses in standard terms also serve the purpose to possibly deliver arguments in those cases.[6]

Despite being a German domestic case, the observations of the court are also valid in relation to the CISG and standard term contracts. It is for this reason that special attention must be directed to the formation of contracts governed by the CISG without losing sight of the overarching purpose of a contract, namely, to regulate business activities.

In its simple form, the solution is obvious and does not create undue problems; an offer is followed by a counter offer, which can be accepted by both parties as the governing contractual document. However, in many cases the resolution of what constitutes an acceptance is complicated and hence rules governing the formation of contracts are needed to provide an answer.

II. Formation of Contracts

At the outset it must be noted that the CISG does not provide any specific rules in relation to the treatment of standard form contracts. The incorporation of standard terms is a matter to be determined under the offer–acceptance rules of Part II of the CISG in conjunction with Article 8. The incorporation of standard terms as part of the formation of contracts comes within the scope of the CISG and "contrary to some courts' decisions, the incorporating of standard terms is not an issue of validity" delegated to domestic national law.[7]

The subjective intent approach of Article 8(1) has led some courts to interpret the use of a foreign language as meaning that there is no such intent to be obligated to terms provided in that language. In the German Knitware case, the court held that since "the [buyer] did not state that it had included an Italian translation of its Terms for Purchasing, the language in this case was not German [and therefore,] the General Terms of Business written in German did not become part of the contract."[8] Another German court, in the Vacuum cleaners case, further elaborated on this point by stating:

[5] Peter Schlechtriem, "Battle of the Forms in International Contract Law Evaluation of Approaches in German law, UNIDROIT Principles, European Principles, CISG, UCC Approaches under Consideration," available at http://www.cisg.law.pace.edu/cisg/biblio/schlechtriem5.html.
[6] OLG Koblenz WM 1984, 1347 et seq.
[7] Camilla Anderson, Francesco Mazzotta, and Bruno Zeller, *A Practitioner's Guide to the CISG* (Juris, 2010), 199.
[8] Germany, October 6, 1995, Lower Court Kehl (Knitware case), available at http://cisgw3.law.pace.edu/cases/951006g1.html.

[S]tandard terms in the German language may apply to a foreigner if German is the language of both the contract and the negotiations. For the present dispute, this means that Dutch would have to have been the language of the contract and the negotiations – as expounded above, this language was not Dutch, but German. The standard terms are therefore not incorporated under German law.[9]

These decisions ought to be the exception rather than the rule. Only in cases where it is proven that one party ought to have known that the other party is not in a position to understand the other's language should nonincorporation be justified. Otherwise, the party receiving a foreign language contract has to use due diligence (such as translation into native language) before signing the contract. The U.S. court in *MCC Marble* held that:

> [W]e find it nothing short of astounding that an individual purportedly experienced in commercial matters, would sign a contract in a foreign language and expect not to be bound simply because he could not comprehend its terms. We find nothing in the CISG that might counsel this type of reckless behavior and nothing that signals any retreat from the proposition [under domestic law] that parties who sign contracts will be bound by them regardless of whether they have read them or understood them.[10]

In sum, terms written in a foreign language are valid and applicable unless it can be shown differently under Article 8. In the end, it is the application of Articles 14 and 18 that decide whether a contract has been concluded and which standard terms, if any, were validly incorporated into the contract. The German Federal Supreme Court confirmed this view by noting:

> According to the general view, the inclusion of general terms and conditions into a contract that is governed by the CISG is subject to the provisions regarding the conclusion of a contract (CISG Articles 14 and 18); recourse to the national law that is applicable based on a conflict of laws analysis is generally not available. The CISG does not, however, contain special rules regarding the inclusion of standard terms and conditions into a contract. This was not deemed necessary because the Convention already contains rules regarding the interpretation of contracts.[11]

It follows that an examination of Articles 14, 18, and 19 in conjunction with Articles 8 and 9 is the means to a solution. Key factors include whether standard terms are tendered correctly and at what stage of the negotiation process this occurs. Furthermore, the question of how the terms are made available will need to be resolved with the assistance of Article 8.

A. *CISG Article 14*

Article 14 notes that a proposal for concluding a contract, once accepted, binds the offeror. Often, the offeror simply accepts the offer, or he or she makes a counteroffer. The first situation is of no interest to this chapter, as the only question is whether the

---

[9] Germany, September 2, 1998, Appellate Court Celle (Vacuum cleaners case), available at http://cisgw3. law.pace.edu/cases/980902g1.html.

[10] *MCC-Marble Ceramic Center v. Ceramica Nuova D'Agostino.*

[11] Germany, October 31, 2001 Supreme Court (Machinery case), available at http://cisgw3.law.pace.edu/ cases/011031g1.html.

stated terms form part of the contract. However, a battle of the forms scenario is created when both parties indicate that their standard terms are applicable.

To resolve this question, an initial analysis starts with Article 14. According to the German Supreme Court,[12] two requirements need to be fulfilled: "Firstly the offeror intention to incorporate its standard terms must be apparent to the recipient; this will generally require a clear and understandable reference to those standard terms. Second the offeror must transmit the text of the standard terms to the recipient or make it available otherwise."[13]

Article 14 does indicate that a proposal addressed to a specific person can only be considered an offer if it is "sufficiently definite and indicates the intention of the offer."[14] The definition of what is "sufficiently definite" requires the naming of the goods (description) and making provisions for determining the price and the quantity.[15] Article 14 does indicate that an offer must make the intentions of the offeror clear, including his or her intentions as to the terms to be incorporated into the contract. The German Supreme Court was asked whether standard terms attached to the confirmation of the offer were validly communicated. The court noted:

> An effective inclusion of general terms and conditions thus first requires the intention of the offeror that he wants to include his terms and conditions into the contract be apparent to the recipient of the offer. In addition, as the Court of Appeals correctly assumed, the Uniform Sales Law requires the user of general terms and conditions to transmit the text or make it available in another way.[16]

Therefore, the terms need to be made available to the offeree and a mere reference to the terms might not be sufficient. But how does one define "making the terms available?" The responses have ranged from the need to actually include the terms in the contract to simply referring to a party's website where the terms are readily available. Article 8 assists in answering this question. Article 8(2) mandates that "the reasonable person" test is applied. The statements and conduct of the parties are interpreted from a position of whether "the other party knew or could not have been unaware what the intent was."

A reasonable businessperson would understand the other party's statement to "please consult webpage for terms" as something that ought to be investigated. In such a case, the risk has passed to the receiving party, who would be bound by the standard terms. In sum, any indication especially in writing that standard terms will apply suffices to alert the other party to exercise due diligence. The party attempting to incorporate its standard terms needs to show that the other party knew or ought to have known its intent to incorporate the standard terms into the contract. Because the battle of the forms is characterized by an exchange of terms, would-be acceptances are, in reality, counteroffers governed by Article 18. Once an offer is made, the question becomes whether there is an acceptance under Article 19.

---

[12] Id.

[13] Peter Huber, "Standard Terms under the CISG," 13 13 *Vindobona Journal of International Commercial Law & Arbitration* (1/2009) 123, 127.

[14] CISG, Article 14(1) CISG.

[15] Id.

[16] Germany, October 31, 2001, Supreme Court (Machinery case), available at http://cisgw3.law.pace.edu/cases/011031g1.html.

B. *CISG Article 19*

Article 19, by implication, reflects the mirror image rule, in which a reply to an offer containing "additions, limitations or any other modifications is a rejection of the offer and constitutes a counteroffer."[17] Article 19 relies on the traditional concept that there has to be a meeting of the minds before a valid contract can be formed. In effect, "adopting the common law mirror image rule the CISG's approach to contract formation . . . allows the offeror to be master of the offer."[18] In practice, the mirror image rule will often lead a court or tribunal to the last-shot rule, where the terms of the counteroffer prevail if there is a subsequent acceptance, generally by conduct, by the other party. The German Supreme Court stated that:

> [T]he partial contradiction of the referenced general terms and conditions of [buyer 1] and [seller 1] did not lead to the failure of the contract within the meaning of Articles 19(1) and 19(3) CISG because of the lack of a consensus. [The] appraisal, that the parties have indicated by the execution of the contract that they did not consider the lack of an agreement between the mutual conditions of contract as essential within the meaning of Article 19 CISG, cannot be legally challenged and is expressly accepted by the appeal.[19]

Article 19(2) though indicates that the mirror image rule is not fixed, as there are exemptions, namely, additions that do not materially alter the offer. An acceptance therefore can contain additions or modifications that are not considered to be material and therefore do not convert the acceptance into a counteroffer. Furthermore, Article 19(3) lists the terms that materially alter an offer. The construction of Article 19(3) makes it clear that the list is not an exhaustive one. Therefore, the facts of each case must be examined in order to decide what terms are to be considered as material terms. For example, courts have found that changing the time of delivery[20] or shipping terms does not materially alter the offer.[21] However, most standard terms are likely to be considered as material given the breadth of Article 19(3)'s definition, therefore, standard form contracts cannot be considered to be exceptions pursuant to Article 19(2).

If the terms are materially different, does that mean there is no contract to be enforced? Most of the rulings on the battle of the forms conclude that a contract was formed due to the parties' subsequent performances.[22] Karollus argues correctly that "in the absence of evidence that clearly shows at least one party did not want a contract without particular terms, the formation of the contract should be indisputable."[23] However, care must be

---

[17] CISG, Article 19(1).

[18] Henry Gabriel, "A Primer on the United Nations Convention on the International Sale of Goods: From the Perspective of the Uniform Commercial Code," 7 *Indiana Int'l & Comparative L. Rev.* 279–310 (1997), 281.

[19] Germany, January 9, 2002, Supreme Court (Powdered milk case), available at http://cisgw3.law.pace.edu/cases/020109g1.html.

[20] China, June 10, 2002, CIETAC Arbitration Proceeding (Rapeseed dregs case), available at http://cisgw3.law.pace.edu/cases/020610c1.html.

[21] Germany, April 27, 1999, Appellate Court Naumburg (Automobile case), available at http://cisgw3.law.pace.edu/cases/990427g1.html.

[22] See, as an example, Germany, January 9, 2002, Supreme Court (Powdered milk case), available at http://cisgw3.law.pace.edu/cases/020109g1.html.

[23] M. Karollus, "Judicial Interpretation and Application of the CISG in Germany 1988–1994," *Cornell Review of the Convention on Contracts for the International Sale of Goods* 51 (1995), 62.

taken, as contracts can be modified or terminated at a later stage by a mere agreement of the parties pursuant to Article 29. A U.S. Court of Appeal correctly noted the difference between modification pursuant to Articles 19 and 29:

> Nothing in the Convention suggests that the failure to object to a party's unilateral attempt to alter materially the terms of an otherwise valid agreement is an "agreement" within the terms of Article 29. The court took into account the various circumstances recommended in Article 8(3) to determine the parties' intent, but concluded that there was no evidence or conduct that indicated the party had agreed to the modifications added to the invoice.[24]

If it has been established that only a counteroffer exists, then a court or tribunal needs to determine if a contract has been formed pursuant to Article 18.

C. CISG Article 18

It has been pointed out previously that in an exchange of the forms, standard terms must be communicated before an acceptance of those can be recognized. The Regional court in Trier noted:

> The provisions of Article 14 et seq. CISG do not allow the mere reference to existing standard terms to lead to their binding incorporation into a contract. It is in no way sufficient that the [seller]'s standard terms were only ever mentioned on the invoices, since at the time the invoices are sent the contracts are already concluded.[25]

It is obvious that if either party objects to the inclusion of the other's boilerplate, the relationship never progresses past the negotiation stage. When an offer has been followed by a counteroffer and no clear acceptance of the counteroffer can be found, the parties' subsequent performance must be investigated.

Assent as such is not defined in the CISG, but Article 8 may be consulted for assistance.[26] Under Article 8, performance may by implication be construed as consenting to be bound by the counteroffer. The initial argument that performance is tantamount to acceptance is confirmed in Article 18(1), which states that "a statement made by or other conduct of the offeree indicating assent to an offer is an acceptance." Furthermore, Article 18(3) indicates that "the offeree may indicate assent by performing an act such as dispatching the goods or payment... [and] the acceptance is effective at the moment the act is performed." In *Golden Valley Grape Juice and Wine, LLC v. Centrisys Corporation*,[27] a U.S. court noted that:

> Pursuant to the CISG, acceptance does not require a signature or formalistic adoption of the offered terms. Pursuant to Article 18(3), "the offeree may indicate assent by performing an act, such as one relating to the dispatch of the goods or payment of the

---

[24] *Chateau des Charmes Wines Ltd. v. Sabaté USA, Sabaté S.A,* ___ 328 F.3d 528, 531 (9th Cir) available at http://cisgw3.law.pace.edu/cases/030505u1.html.

[25] Germany, January 8, 2004, District Court Trier (Synthetic window parts case), available at http://cisgw3.law.pace.edu/cases/040108g1.html.

[26] Andersen et al., *A Practitioner's Guide to the CISG,* 175.

[27] *Golden Valley Grape Juice and Wine, LLC v. Centrisys Corporation et al.* (E.D.Cal, No. CV F 09–1424 LJO GSA, January 22, 2010 (9th Cir. 2010, unreported), available at http://cisgw3.law.pace.edu/cases/100121u1.html.

price, without notice to the offeror, the acceptance is effective at the moment the act is performed." The evidence establishes that at the time STS sent its sales quote to Centrisys, it contemporaneously sent its General Conditions as part of the attachments. By adopting the terms of the sales quote, Centrisys accepted the terms upon which the centrifuge had been offered, including the General Conditions. Thus, Centrisys accepted the General Conditions.[28]

If no clear acceptance can be found, nevertheless the parties engage in a transaction, then "the principle of party autonomy, which enables the parties to form the procedure of contract conclusion and to deviate from Article 19" controls.[29] If no agreement pursuant to Article 18 is reached, no contract is formed and hence the question of the battle of the forms does not arise. It is argued that the issue of the battle of the forms is in effect restricted to situations where there is an exchange of different sets of standard terms, creating several counteroffers.

Under this scenario, under Articles 18(1) and 18(3), performance creates the acceptance and thus "permits the coming together by conduct independent of the declarations of offer and acceptance as well as the waiver of present conditions of their validity."[30] If the argument is advanced that the counteroffer was never really accepted, then no contract would come into existence under the mirror image rule. The stronger argument is that both parties accepted the performances, hence, by implication and pursuant to the principle of party autonomy, and Article 8, a contract must be presumed. Because the formation of contracts and the incorporation of standard terms are within the scope of the CISG, a solution to the issue of the existence of additional terms in a would-be acceptance must be found within the CISG. The best solution is one that recognizes performance as tantamount to acceptance. This argument is supported by a case decided by the Lower Court in Kehl:

> Assuming that [seller] had sent its General Terms of Business to the [buyer], this would have constituted a counter-offer in the sense of CISG Article 19(1). However, based on the realization of the contract, both parties were in agreement about the *essentialia negotii*, and it must be assumed that they waived the validity of their conflicting Terms of Business or that they derogated from the application of Article 19, taking advantage of their autonomy pursuant to Article 6. In this case, the contract would have been entered into in accordance with the terms of the CISG.[31]

It follows that the courts are obliged to "reconstruct" the contract instead of dismiss cases based upon Article 19(3). The task therefore is what clauses or terms are applicable to the contract. Peter Schlechtriem correctly points out that in the reconstruction of a contract, no differentiation should be made between substantial and unsubstantial terms.[32] The rationale for this approach is that the differentiation between Articles 19(2) and (3) needs to be explained as only Subsection 2 affects the mirror image rule and the validity of the offer and acceptance. Also, Article 8(3) is required to interpret the

---

[28] Id. at slip op 5.
[29] Schlechtriem, "Battle of the Forms."
[30] Id.
[31] Lower Court Kehl (Knitware case).
[32] Schlechtriem, "Battle of the Forms."

meaning of the parties' intentions, which will embrace both minor and major terms, hence a distinction is not very practicable.[33]

III. Battle of the Forms

Where there is an offer, counteroffer, and acceptance by performance, the battle of the forms never eventuates, as only one set of standard terms is present. The problem becomes complicated if many forms containing different terms are exchanged. However, the basic principle as noted earlier remains the same. The court or tribunal starts from the premise that a valid contract is in existence, as the contract has been executed either partially or fully. What is left is to decide is which terms form the contract. Where there are multiple forms, it is obvious that each party has not accepted the other party's terms but nevertheless has opted to perform the contract. Courts and tribunals have several tools at their disposal to construct the terms of the contract.

The first option is simply to see whether the CISG can supply the answer by applying contract theory within the four corners of the CISG. However, the "pure" contract theory approach contains elements of the "last-shot rule" and the "knock-out rule" under Article 8. The next two sections examine the arguments in favor of and against these two rules.

A. *Last-Shot Approach*

As noted previously, the first step is to examine the offer. The question the court needs to address is whether the standard terms were brought to the attention of the offeree. More specifically, were they made available in a form whereby both parties knew or should have known that the standard terms were included in the offer? If the answer is negative, that is, the parties were not aware of this fact, then the acceptance needs to be examined and the question will need to be addressed by the court. If performance follows the counteroffer, then the issue is twofold: First, is there a contract? And second, which terms apply to the contract?

Once the court or tribunal is satisfied that a contract exists, the last-shot rule recognizes the terms of the counteroffer as being the ones governing the contract. The last-shot rule is a clinical determination of the terms of the contract, is noted by its simplicity, and arguably is based on the application of the plain reading of Article 19. The court of appeal in Saarbrucken noted that:

> [Buyer] did, however, implicitly accept [seller]'s standard conditions of sale under Articles 8(2), 18(1) first sentence, 19(1) CISG, as it accepted the first delivery of [seller], which was made in accordance with the confirmation of order, and subsequently placed further orders with [seller]. Each confirmation of such order made reference to the standard conditions of sale on the front page and were printed on the reverse side.[34]

Arguably, the last-shot approach is dictated in this case as the buyer, through repeated orders, affirmed his assent, real or otherwise, and therefore the seller could not have been left in doubt as to the acceptance of the terms contained in the confirmation notices.

[33] Id.
[34] Germany, January 13, 1993, Appellate Court Saarbrücken (Doors case), available at http://cisgw3.law. pace.edu/cases/930113g1.html.

It can also be argued that the last-shot approach relies heavily on the timing and mode of performance.

The last-shot approach relies heavily on a determination of when the contact has been concluded or performance started. The time of the acceptance is an important determination, as the parties are likely to continue their communications (negotiations) past the time of acceptance. Once a contract is concluded, then Article 8 will guide the court to establish the terms of the contract through the conduct of the parties. In *Filanto v. Chilewich*,[35] the court put it succinctly by stating that the:

> [The buyer's] Agreement, as noted above, specifically referred to the incorporation by reference of the arbitration provision in the Russian Contract; although Filanto, in its August 7 letter, did purport to "have to respect" only a small part of the Russian Contract, Filanto in that very letter noted that it was returning the March 13 Memorandum Agreement "signed for acceptance." In light of Filanto's knowledge that Chilewich had already performed its part of the bargain by furnishing it the Letter of Credit, Filanto's characterization of this action as a rejection and a counteroffer is almost frivolous.[36]

The court relied heavily on Article 8(3) in determining that the applicable terms were those of the second communication:

> The Sale of Goods Convention specifically directs that "in determining the intent of a party . . . due consideration is to be given to . . . any subsequent conduct of the parties," Sale of Goods Convention Article 8(3). In this case, as the letter post-dates the partial performance of the contract, it is particularly strong evidence that Filanto recognized itself to be bound by all the terms of the Russian Contract.[37]

In sum, courts and tribunals applying the last-shot rule rely heavily on the conduct of the parties pursuant to Article 8. The conduct of a party will determine which standard terms are incorporated into the contract. The conduct (performance) prevents a party claiming that they did not accept what was in effect a counteroffer. Once performance of the contract has been detected by a court it can be equated to an acceptance of the other party's terms: "The last shot-doctrine thus provides for outcomes that may be predictable for the courts and tribunals, but are merely coincidental for the parties."[38] It is important to note that the majority of courts and commentators apply the last-shot approach but there are a growing number of courts that have adopted the knock-out approach,[39] arguing that it better reflects the intentions of the parties.

B. *Knock-Out Approach*

The knock-out approach takes a pragmatic view. Courts and tribunals start from the traditional point of view that negotiations culminate into agreements, which are then executed. However, in many sales transactions the terms of the contract can be found

---

[35] *Filanto v. Chilewich*, ___U.S. District Court, Southern District of New York, 789 F.Supp. 1229, available at http://cisgw3.law.pace.edu/cases/920414u1.html.

[36] Id., 1240.

[37] Id.

[38] Ingeborg Schwenzer and F. Mohs, "Old Habits Die Hard: Traditional Contract Formation in a Modern World," *Internationales Handelsrecht* 239, 244 (2006).

[39] K.A. Stemp, "A Comparative Analysis of the 'Battle of the Forms,'" 15 *Transnational Law & Contemporary Problems* 243, 262 (2005).

"scattered" throughout the negotiations and communications between the parties. When these communications produce varying terms, the courts need to determine which of the terms are included in the contract. Two approaches of knocking out terms can be applied. The first holds that the contract is valid, but the standard terms are disregarded and replaced by the gap-filling provisions of the CISG. The problem with this approach is that the intent of the parties is not taken into consideration. Both parties introduced their standard terms into the negotiations, which is a clear indication that they did not want the default rules of the CISG to be applied in the areas covered by the standard terms.

A better approach is to apply the additional terms (counteroffer) that do not favor one party over the other. The German Federal Court recognized this problem and noted that "under the point of view of good faith and fair dealing (Article 7(1) CISG), the seller should not have assumed that the question whether certain provisions of the opposing terms and conditions contradicted its own could be answered in isolation for individual clauses with the consequence that the individual provisions that were beneficial to it would apply."[40] The real question becomes which standard terms of the parties ought to be made part of the "reconstructed" contract. The German Supreme Court stated that:

> The question to what extent colliding general terms and conditions become an integral part of a contract where the CISG applies, is answered in different ways in the legal literature. According to the (probably) prevailing opinion, partially diverging general terms and conditions become an integral part of a contract (only) insofar as they do not contradict each other; the statutory provisions apply to the rest. Whether there is such a contradiction that impedes the integration, cannot be determined only by an interpretation of the wording of individual clauses, but only upon the full appraisal of all relevant provisions.[41]

The point is that the standard terms that are similar in both parties' forms should be part of the contract. All the conflicting terms, on the other hand, where by implication no consensus has been achieved, are simply "knocked out," or cancelled.

Like the last-shot rule, it can be argued that the court artificially constructs the contract where it in reality should have deemed the contract invalid because the last counteroffer was not expressly accepted. As already indicated, the CISG under Article 8 has recognized that many contracts are a culmination of negotiations. Therefore, the intent and behavior of parties are taken into consideration when constructing the contract. The knock-out rule simply puts the courts into the shoes of the parties. Using the principles of party intent and good faith, the court finds an agreement by eliminating conflicting terms that are not a product of mutual consent.

The knock-out rule follows the fact that "business people rarely read the 'boiler-plate' language on purchase forms and that both parties rely on the existence of a contract despite the [existence of conflicting] forms."[42] Additional support comes from the UNIDROIT Principles of International Commercial Contracts (Article 2.1.22), as well as the Principles of European Contract Law (Article 2:209), which have adopted the knock-out rule.

---

[40] Germany, January 9, 2002, Supreme Court (Powdered milk case), available at http://cisgw3.law.pace.edu/cases/020109g1.html.

[41] Id.

[42] Gabriel, "A Primer on the United Nations Convention on the International Sale of Goods," 284.

IV. Conclusion

This chapter has shown that the basic problem of the battle of the forms scenario is the need to resolve a disagreement as to which standard terms are applicable to the contract. It is not whether a contract exists or not. If no contract has been formed, the battle of the forms scenario fails to come into existence. The term "battle of the forms" only truly applies in cases where the parties have partially or fully performed and performance is grounds for "acceptance." In order to resolve the question of which terms are applicable, two approaches are used – the last-shot rule and the knock-out rule.

The last-shot rule follows the path of the offer to the acceptance, which, in battle of the forms cases, is the performance of the contract. This approach relies heavily on the mirror image rule in general and particularly on CISG Article 19. However, it neglects the fact that contractual parties did not have a true meeting of the minds on the terms being incorporated into the contract. Furthermore, given that there may be a series of communications, it may not always be clear what should be considered the "first shot" and what is to be considered the "second shot" communication. The court in *Miami Valley Paper, LLC v. Lebbing Engineering & Consulting GmbH*[43] noted this issue:

> First, both parties admit that a contract was formed, and indeed the Court believes this to be the case. However, there remains a dispute of fact as to when the contract was formed, and as to the terms of the contract. As noted, [buyer] sets forth two different dates for when the contract was formed. [Seller] refutes the dates set forth by the [buyer], and instead argues that the contract was formed in mid-July 2003. Both parties set forth persuasive arguments in favor of their respective positions, and this Court believes such arguments cannot be resolved short of trial.[44]

The pragmatic solution to the battle of the forms is the realization that a contract is the culmination of the negotiations of the parties and finding mutual consent is essential. Arguably, if there is no meeting of the minds, the mirror image rule cannot be adopted pursuant to CISG Article 19. The fact that the parties have performed the contractual obligations is sufficient proof that they intended to form a contract. Courts, by using the knock-out rule, place themselves into the shoes of both parties and "construct" a meeting of the minds contract by eliminating conflicting standard terms and replacing them by the rules found in the CISG. The contract only contains terms on which the parties have no disagreement. Schlechtriem put it succinctly by noting:

> The knowledge or – practically more important – the possibility of knowing certain – usual – clauses of the other side can also become important for the interpretation of a party's conduct. Where such interpretation of one party's conduct is not possible – or the necessary circumstances for their support cannot be proven – one should stick to the basic rule that colliding terms of business remain unrecognized for the contents of the contract and will be replaced by statutory rules.[45]

The spirit of the CISG suggests that the knock-out rule is the appropriate rule that ought to be used. The preamble of the CISG notes clearly that the "development of international

---

[43] *Miami Valley Paper, LLC v. Lebbing Engineering & Consulting GmbH*, ___ No. 1:05-CV-00702, 2006 WL 2924779, available at http://cisgw3.law.pace.edu/cases/090326u1.html.
[44] Id., slip op 7.
[45] Schlechtriem, "Battle of the Forms."

trade on the bases of equality and mutual benefit is an important element... in the removal of legal barriers" and, therefore, requires a dispute resolution outcome that equates as closely as possible to the wishes of the contracting parties. The battle of the forms is of real relevance only when performance is the means of acceptance. The knock-out rule delivers contractual terms that conform to the meeting of the minds, and where there is substantial divergence, the role of the CISG as gap-filler is to be applied.

14 Conformity of Goods: Inspection and Notice

Harry M. Flechtner

I. Introduction

The CISG provisions governing the quality, quantity, description, and packaging of the goods that the seller is obligated to deliver (Article 35), as well as the buyer's obligation to give the seller notice when the delivered goods do not conform (Articles 38–39), are among the most important and contentious in the CISG. A review of the last ten years of decisions that is the basis of this chapter was undertaken as part of a project to update the UNCITRAL CISG Case Law Digest.[1]

II. Conformity of Goods: CISG Article 35

Article 35 addresses issues concerning the quality of goods – issues that are critical for any sales law regime. It provides the standards that determine whether the goods delivered conform to the quality and features (as well as the quantity and packaging) that the buyer is entitled to expect. Article 35(1) focuses on obligations created expressly, or at least affirmatively, by the parties' contract; Article 35(2) addresses implied obligations – that is, obligations that arise automatically "[e]xcept where the parties agree otherwise." The latter type of obligations include the need for the goods to be fit for their ordinary purposes (35(2)(a)); to be fit for particular purposes that the buyer conveyed to the seller by the time the contract was concluded (unless the buyer did not reasonably rely on the seller's skill and judgment) (35(2)(b)); to "possess the qualities of goods which the seller has held out to the buyer as a sample or model" (35(2)(c)); and to be "contained or packaged in the manner usual for such goods or, where there is no such manner, in a manner adequate to preserve and protect the goods" (35(2)(d)). Finally, Article 35(3) relieves a seller of liability for a lack of conformity to the implied obligations of Article 35(2) "if at the time of the conclusion of the contract the buyer knew or could not have been unaware of such lack of conformity."

The last ten years have brought many interesting decisions, surveyed in the updated UNCITRAL Digest, that construe Article 35. Decisions applying Article 35(1) have

---

[1] The National Correspondents to UNCITRAL accepted the updated Digest in July 2011; it is now available online at http://www.uncitral.org/pdf/english/clout/CISG-digest-2012-e.pdf and in hard copy as a special edition of the *Journal of Law & Commerce*, 30 *J.L. & Com.* 1 (special issue, 2012). The author had the good fortune of acting as the coordinator for the Digest that included contributions from distinguished scholars, including Sieg Eiselen, Alejandro Garro, Ulrich Magnus, Pilar Perales Viscasillas, Vikki Rogers, Hiroo Sono, and Claude Witz.

held that a "lack of conformity" under that provision exists where the seller delivers less than the required quantity of goods[2] and where the goods are accompanied by false documents relating to their origin;[3] they have also held that, in proper circumstances, a lack of conformity under Article 35 can constitute a fundamental breach of contract (as defined in CISG Article 25) that justifies the buyer avoiding the contract under Article 49 (1) of the CISG.[4] Several decisions have also emphasized that the CISG's general rules for determining the content of the parties' agreement – including Articles 8 (party intent) and 9 (usages and practices) – determine whether the contract requires goods of a particular quantity, quality, description, or packaging.[5]

The CISG rules for determining the content of the contract also apply in determining whether the parties have agreed to contract out of the implied quality obligations in Article 35(2).[6] The question whether the parties have excluded the standards of Article 35(2) by "agree[ing] otherwise," however, has produced (it appears) one of the more striking and important splits in interpretative approaches to the CISG. A number of decisions have held or included language indicating that the existence of an express contractual provision addressing the quality of the goods excludes the standards of Article 35(2). In other words, these decisions indicate that the existence of such an express contractual provision constitutes an "agreement otherwise," by implication, to opt out of the standards of Article 35(2). They treat the standards of Article 35(2) as "default rules" meant to apply only in the absence of an agreement by the parties on the subject of the required quality of the goods. Thus where a contractual provision required the seller to deliver "ADOS type carpets," the Czech Supreme Court held that Article 35(2)(b) did not apply because the parties had agreed on the quality requirements for the carpet:

> [T]he parties have, in the purchase agreement . . . agreed on delivering ADOS carpets for the price of SKK 590 per square meter. Thereby, according to Article 35(1) CISG, the quality of the goods was agreed upon. Carpets of such quality were delivered to the [seller]. Article 35(2) of CISG is not applicable in this case since the seller is not liable for any lack of conformity provided that the purchaser has determined the particular type of goods or parameters that goods should have.[7]

Another court declared that the standards of Article 35(2) apply "only . . . if the parties have not themselves expressly or impliedly stipulated the required performance conforming

[2] Bundesgericht, Switzerland, July 7, 2004, CLOUT case No. 894, available at http://cisgw3.law.pace.edu/cases/040707s1.html. Partial deliveries, however, were held not to violate Article 35(1) where the contract permitted them and the buyer accepted them without complaint. See Hof van Beroep Antwerpen, Belgium, April 24, 2006 (*GmbH Lothringer Gunther Grosshandelsgesellschaft für Bauelemente und Holzwerkstoffe v. NV Fepco International*), available in Unilex.

[3] Foreign Trade Court of Arbitration attached to the Serbian Chamber of Commerce, Serbia, January 23, 2008, available at http://cisgw3.law.pace.edu/cases/080123sb.html.

[4] Oberlandesgericht Koblenz, Germany, December 14, 2006, CLOUT case No. 724, available at http://cisgw3.law.pace.edu/cases/061214g1.html.

[5] Polimeles Protodikio Athinon, Greece, 2009 (docket no. 4505/2009), available at http://cisgw3.law.pace.edu/cases/094505gr.html; Audiencia Provincial Madrid, Spain, March 22, 2007; Oberster Gerichtshof, Austria, February 27, 2003, CLOUT case Nos. 477 and 536, available at http://cisgw3.law.pace.edu/cases/030227a3.html.

[6] U.S. District Court, Southern District of New York, United States, August 23, 2006 (*TeeVee Toons, Inc. v. Gerhard Schubert GmbH*), available at http://cisgw3.law.pace.edu/cases/060823u1.html.

[7] Supreme Court, Czech Republic, March 29, 2006, available at http://cisgw3.law.pace.edu/cases/060329cz.html.

to their contract, or when such duty to perform in the sense of Article 35(1) has not been sufficiently specified."[8] Other decisions have also included *dicta* suggesting that express contractual quality standards exclude the implied quality standards in Article 35(2).[9] Some opinions, however, appear to indicate that express contractual provisions addressing the quality of the goods do not automatically exclude the implied quality standards in CISG Article 35(2); in other words, these cases indicate that express quality provisions

---

[8] Landgericht Aschaffenburg, Germany, April 20, 2006, available at http://cisgw3.law.pace.edu/cases/060420g1.html, citing P. Schlechtriem and I. Schwenzer, *Kommentar zum Einheitlichen UN-Kaufrecht – CISG*, 4th ed. (2004), 35, para. 12.

[9] *See* Tribunale di Forli, Italy, February 16, 2009, available at http://cisgw3.law.pace.edu/cases/090216i3.html ("If the parties did not negotiate specific qualities or did not expressly and clearly specify them and it is not possible to ascertain the requisite quality by referring to usages or practice established between the parties (according to Article 9 of the CISG), reference has to be made to Article 35(2) [in order to determine the characteristics the goods must possess]"); *Polimeles Protodikio Athinon*, Greece, Decision 4505/2009, available at http://cisgw3.law.pace.edu/cases/094505gr.html ("If [the parties have not agreed on the quality of the goods and no usages or practices relating to quality are applicable under CISG Article 9], then the conformity of the goods to the contract shall be judged based on the above criteria set out in the provisions of CISG Article 35(2)"); Tribunale di Forli, Italy, December 11, 2008, available at http://cisgw3.law.pace.edu/cases/081211i3.html; Oberlandesgericht Koblenz, Germany, November 21, 2007, available at http://cisgw3.law.pace.edu/cases/071121g1.html ("A seller *inter alia* has to deliver goods which are of the quality required by the contract according to Article 35(1) CISG. If the parties have not agreed on a certain quality, the goods do conform with the contract if they are fit for the purposes for which goods of the same description would ordinarily be used (Article 35(2)(a) CISG)"); Kantonsgericht Zug, Switzerland, August 30, 2007, available at http://cisgw3.law.pace.edu/cases/070830s1.html ("The goods are not in conformity if they lack the characteristics agreed upon by the parties or – in the absence of a particular agreement between the parties – if they do not comply with the relevant objective minimum standard [stated in Article 35(2)]," citing Magnus, *Kommentar zum UN-Kaufrecht*, 1997, Article 35, para. 10 et seq.); Landgericht Coburg, Germany, December 12, 2006, available at http://cisgw3.law.pace.edu/cases/061212g1.htm ("If the parties – as in the case at hand – accept the determination of the kind and quantity but have not stipulated particular agreements concerning the characteristics of the goods, . . . Art. 35(2) CISG prescribes which requirements goods have to meet to conform to the contract"); Oberster Gerichtshof, Austria, January 25, 2006, CLOUT case No. 752, available at http://cisgw3.law.pace.edu/cases/060125a3.html ("[I]t is in accordance with jurisprudence that if there is no provision on a certain quality of goods in an international contract of sale, the required quality will be determined by the objective minimum standards under Article 35(2) CISG"); Tribunal of International Commercial Arbitration at the Russian Federation Chamber of Commerce and Industry, Russian Federation, February 2, 2004, available at http://cisgw3.law.pace.edu/cases/040202r1.html ("In the absence of contractual provisions relating to the quality and purposes of purchased goods, by virtue of art. 35 of the CISG, goods do not conform with the contract if they are not fit for the purposes for which the goods of the same description are ordinarily used"); Kantonsgericht Schaffhausen, Switzerland, January 27, 2004, CLOUT case No. 892 ("If there is no contractual agreement, the CISG sets forth an objective minimum standard for certain cases, such as the suitability for the normal usage, the suitability for a certain use, the conformity with a sample in case of a sale on approval or sample and a usual or adequate package for the requirements of the package of the goods (Art. 35(2) CISG; so called objective conformity)."). See also Ingeborg Schwenzer, "Article 35" ¶ 12, in *Schlechtriem & Schwenzer Commentary on the UN Convention on the International Sale of Goods (CISG)* (Ingeborg Schwenzer, ed.) (3rd ed. 2010), 575 ("Article 35(2), which sets out a series of objective criteria to be used in order to determine the conformity of the goods, applies in so far as the contract does not contain any, or contains only insufficient, details of the requirements to be satisfied by the goods for the purposes of Article 35(1)"); Sanna Kuoppala, "The Application and Interpretation of the CISG in Finnish Case Law 1997–2005," Licentiate thesis, University of Turku, Faculty of Law, April 2009, chapter 9 (Helsinki Court of Appeal, S 01/269 (May 31, 2004) §9.4.4.4, available at http://www.cisg.law.pace.edu/cisg/biblio/kuoppala2.html, commenting on Hovioikeus/hovrätt Helsinki, Finland, May 31, 2004, available at http://cisgw3.law.pace.edu/cases/040531f5.html ("However, recourse to the second paragraph of Article 35 is needed only if the contract does not contain any details or contains only insufficient details of the requirements to be satisfied by the goods for the purposes of Article 35(1)").

do not by themselves constitute an agreement to exclude the implied standards of Article 35(2).[10] These latter decisions appear to treat the implied Article 35(2) standards as, in nature, cumulative with, rather than excluded by, express contractual quality standards. I have addressed this issue elsewhere,[11] arguing for an approach similar to that of the latter cases – that is, treating the obligations of Article 35(2) as cumulative with express contractual quality standards and not as mere default rules, except to the extent the Article 35(2) standards contradict the express contractual terms, or the facts indicate that the parties' contractual quality provisions were intended to be a complete and exclusive regime defining the seller's obligations concerning the quality of the goods.

Other Article 35(2) issues addressed in relatively recent decisions include whether the obligations in CISG Article 35(2)(a) (goods must be fit for ordinary purposes)[12] and Article 35(2)(b) (goods must be fit for particular purposes conveyed to the seller before the contract was formed)[13] equate to specified domestic law requirements; specific

[10] See Arbitration Institute of the Stockholm Chamber of Commerce, Sweden, June 5, 1998, CLOUT case No. 237, available at http://cisgw3.law.pace.edu/cases/980605s5.html (an agreement as to the general quality of goods did not derogate from Article 35(2) if the agreement contained only positive terms concerning the qualities that the goods would possess, and not negative terms relieving the seller of responsibilities). See also China International Economic and Trade Arbitration Commission [CIETAC], People's Republic of China, April 13, 2008, available at http://cisgw3.law.pace.edu/cases/080418c1.html (finding that the seller had an obligation under Article 35(1) to deliver goods conforming to the technical requirements of the contract as well as an obligation under Article 35(2)(a) to deliver goods fit for their ordinary purposes, both of which the seller violated); Ad Hoc Arbitral Tribunal, Denmark, November 10, 2000 (*Construction Acton Vale Lteé (Canada) v. KVM Industrimaskiner A/S*), CLOUT case No. 999 (buyer of machine provided seller with specifications that products produced by the machine would have to meet, and seller "guaranteed" that the machine would function, but seller was also bound by the implied obligations in Articles 35(2)(a) and (b)).

[11] Harry M. Flechtner, "Excluding CISG Article 35(2) Quality Obligations: The 'Default Rule' View vs. the 'Cumulation' View," in *International Arbitration and International Commercial Law: Synergy, Convergence and Evolution: Festschrift for Liber Amicorum Eric Bergsten on the Occasion of His Eightieth Birthday* (ed. S. Kroll, L. A. Mistelis, P. Perales, and V. Rogers) (2011), 571ff.

[12] See U.S. District Court, Western District of Pennsylvania, United States, July 25, 2008 (*Norfolk Southern Railway Company v. Power Source Supply, Inc.*), available at http://cisgw3.law.pace.edu/cases/080725u1.html (equating Article 35(2)(a) with the implied warranty of merchantability under U.S. domestic law); Supreme Court of Victoria, Australia, April 24, 2003 (*Playcorp Pty. Ltd. v. Taiyo Kogyo Limited*), available at http://cisgw3.law.pace.edu/cases/030424a2.html (equating Article 35(2)(a) with sellers' obligations under Australian domestic law); Supreme Court of Western Australia, Australia, January 17, 2003 (*Ginza Pty. Ltd. v. Vista Corporation Pty Ltd*), available at http://cisgw3.law.pace.edu/cases/030117a2.html (equating Article 35(2)(a) with sellers' obligations under Australian domestic law); China International Economic and Trade Arbitration Commission, People's Republic of China, July 18, 2002, available at http://cisgw3.law.pace.edu/cases/020718c1.html (equating Article 35(2)(a) with sellers' obligations under Chinese domestic law).

[13] See U.S. District Court, Southern District of Ohio, United States, April 3, 2009 (*Miami Valley Paper, LLC v. Lebbing Engineering & Consulting GmbH*), available at http://cisgw3.law.pace.edu/cases/090326u1.html (equating Article 35(2)(b) with the "implied warranty of fitness for particular purposes" under U.S. domestic sales law); U.S. District Court, Western District of Pennsylvania, United States, July 25, 2008 (*Norfolk Southern Railway Company v. Power Source Supply, Inc.*), available at http://cisgw3.law.pace.edu/cases/080725u1.html (equating Article 35(2)(b) with the "implied warranty of fitness for particular purposes" under U.S. domestic sales law); CLOUT case No. 532 (Supreme Court of British Columbia, Canada, August 21, 2003) (equating Article 35(2)(b) to the "statutory warranty of fitness" under Canadian domestic sales law); Supreme Court of Victoria, Australia, April 24, 2003 (*Playcorp Pty. Ltd. v Taiyo Kogyo Limited*), available at http://cisgw3.law.pace.edu/cases/030424a2.html (equating Article 35(2)(b) with sellers' obligations under Australian domestic law); Supreme Court of Western Australia, Australia,

circumstances that constitute violations or nonviolations of Articles 35(2)(a),[14] 35(2)(b),[15] 35(2)(c),[16] and 35(2)(d)[17]; whether Article 35(2)(a) requires goods of "average" quality,

January 17, 2003 (*Ginza Pty Ltd. v. Vista Corporation Pty. Ltd*), available at http://cisgw3.law.pace.edu/cases/030117a2.html (equating Article 35(2)(b) with sellers' obligations under Australian domestic law).

[14] See Oberlandesgerich München, Germany, November 17, 2006, available at http://cisgw3.law.pace.edu/cases/061117g1.html (Article 35(2)(a) held violated where a dust ventilator diffused dust rather than removing it, and contained components that caused the ventilator to shut down prematurely); U.S. District Court, Southern District of New York, United States, August 23, 2006 (*TeeVee Toons, Inc. v. Gerhard Schubert GmbH*), available at http://cisgw3.law.pace.edu/cases/060823u1.html (Article 35(2)(a) violated where machinery failed to produce the intended product rapidly or reliably); Bundesgericht, Switzerland, October 10, 2005, English abstract available in Unilex (Article 35(2)(a) violated where "pocket ash trays" came equipped with excessively sharp and dangerous blades); Hovioikeus/hovrätt Helsinki, Finland, May 31, 2004 (*Crudex Chemicals Oy v. Landmark Chemicals S.A.*), available at http://cisgw3.law.pace.edu/cases/040531f5.html (Article 35(2)(a) violated where the seller delivered colored phenol that was not fit for all the ordinary purposes of the contractually required "colourless phenol"); Court of Arbitration of the International Chamber of Commerce, 2002 (Arbitral award No. 10377), *Yearbook Commercial Arbitration*, vol. 31, p. 72 (2006) (Article 35(2)(a) violated where machinery for the production of textiles failed to produce a product of consistent weight). But see Landgericht Coburg, Germany, December 12, 2006, available at http://cisgw3.law.pace.edu/cases/061212g1.html (Article 35(2)(a) not violated where plants that the seller delivered were generally fit to prosper, but not fit for the local climate where the buyer placed them).

[15] See U.S. District Court, Southern District of New York, United States, August 23, 2006 (*TeeVee Toons, Inc. v. Gerhard Schubert GmbH*), available at http://cisgw3.law.pace.edu/cases/060823u1.html (Article 35(2)(b) violated where machinery that the buyer had purchased to mass produce buyer's environmentally friendly packaging for cassettes malfunctioned and did not produce the packaging "rapidly or reliably"); Handelsgericht Aargau, Switzerland, November 5, 2002, CLOUT case No. 882 (Article 35(2)(b) violated where inflatable arches used for advertising were not suitably safe). But see Supreme Court of British Columbia, Canada, August 21, 2003, CLOUT case No. 532 (Article 35(2)(b) not violated where the goods were made to work properly within a year after delivery).

[16] See Cour d'appel Versailles, France, October 13, 2005, available at http://cisgw3.law.pace.edu/cases/051013f1.html (Article 35(2)(c) violated where the seller provided the buyer a sample of a toy intended for young children and included a designation indicating it was safe for young children, but the delivered goods did not meet safety regulations); U.S. District Court, Southern District of New York, United States, August 23, 2006 (*TeeVee Toons, Inc. v. Gerhard Schubert GmbH*), available at http://cisgw3.law.pace.edu/cases/060823u1.html (Article 35(2)(c) violated where the seller held out to the buyer a properly functioning model of machinery but delivered goods that malfunctioned and failed to produce products reliably or rapidly). It has also been held that Article 35(2)(c) requires the seller to provide goods in conformity with a sample or model even if the buyer rather than the seller provided the sample or model: Rechtbank van Koophandel, Belgium, September 14, 2005, available at http://cisgw3.law.pace.edu/cases/050914b1.html (buyer provided a model document to the seller/printer and ordered printed media in conformity); Landgericht Aschaffenburg, Germany, April 20, 2006, available at http://cisgw3.law.pace.edu/cases/060420g1.html (buyer specified the required seam slippage strength of material for use in mattresses by providing the seller a sample produced by another manufacturer). But see Rechtbank van Koophandel Hasselt, Belgium, April 19, 2006 (*Brugen Deuren BVBA v. Top Deuren VOF*), available at http://cisgw3.law.pace.edu/cases/060419b1.html (Article 35(2)(c) not violated where the seller provided a sample of the wood to be used to fabricate doors but the sample was too small to indicate that the wood in the completed doors would be evenly colored).

[17] See Oberlandesgericht Saarbrücken, Germany, January 17, 2007, available at http://cisgw3.law.pace.edu/cases/070117g1.html (Article 35(2)(d) violated where marble panels were damaged during transport because of improper packaging; seller's previous deliveries to the buyer, some of which involved different kinds of goods and during which the goods had not been damaged, did not give rise to an implied agreement concerning the packaging of the goods and did not supplant the requirements of Article 35(2)(c)); Oberlandesgericht Koblenz, Germany, December 14, 2006, CLOUT case No. 724 (although the buyer bore risk of loss while bottles were being transported by truck, the seller's breach of its obligations under Article 35(2)(c) to package the goods adequately meant that the seller was responsible for damage that occurred during transport).

"marketable" quality, or "reasonable" quality,[18] or goods that are resaleable;[19] whether the seller was obliged to deliver goods that comply with public law standards in the buyer's jurisdiction;[20] and the circumstances in which, for purposes of Article 35(2)(b), a buyer is deemed to have conveyed to the seller a particular purpose for the goods,[21] and to have reasonably relied on the seller's skill and judgment.[22]

Article 35 does not expressly address the question of which party bears the burden of proving whether or not delivered goods conform to the contract under Article 35. Decisions on the issue have taken a number of different, sometimes incompatible,

---

[18] Landgericht Coburg, Germany, December 12, 2006, available at http://cisgw3.law.pace.edu/cases/061212g1.html (goods that meet the expectation of the average user); Supreme Court of Western Australia, Australia, January 17, 2003 (*Ginza Pty. Ltd. v. Vista Corporation Pty. Ltd.*), available at http://cisgw3.law.pace.edu/cases/030117a2.html (merchantability standard); Netherlands Arbitration Institute, the Netherlands, October 15, 2002 (Arbitral award, No. 2319), available in Unilex (reasonable quality rather than average or merchantable quality).

[19] Bundesgerichtshof, Germany, March 2, 2005, CLOUT case No. 774. See also China International Economic and Trade Arbitration Commission, People's Republic of China, June 3, 2003, available at http://cisgw3.law.pace.edu/cases/030603c1.html (the fact that the goods were not resalable, even at a discounted price, established a violation of Article 35(2)(a)); Rechtbank van Koophandel Mechelen, Belgium, January 18, 2002, English abstract available in Unilex (Article 35(2)(a) required that goods be fit for resale).

[20] See Bundesgerichtshof, Germany, March 8, 1995, CLOUT case No. 123, available at http://cisgw3.law.pace.edu/cases/950308g3.html. See also High Court of New Zealand, July 30, 2010, available at http://cisgw3.law.pace.edu/cases/100730n6.html; Rechtsbank Rotterdam, the Netherlands, October 15, 2008 (*Eyroflam S.A. v. P.C.C. Rotterdam B.V.*), abstract published in European Journal of Commercial Contract Law; Oberster Gerichtshof, Austria, April 19, 2007, available at http://cisgw3.law.pace.edu/cases/070419a3.html; Oberster Gerichtshof, Austria, January 25, 2006, CLOUT case no. 752; Cour d'appel Versailles, France, October 13, 2005, available at http://cisgw3.law.pace.edu/cases/051013f1.html; Bundesgerichtshof, Germany, March 2, 2005, CLOUT case no. 774, available at http://cisgw3.law.pace.edu/cases/050302g1.html. According to another decision, the fact that the seller had previously advertised and sold the good in the buyer's jurisdiction could have constituted "special circumstances" that would, under the approach in the mussels case, oblige the seller to comply with regulations of the buyer's jurisdiction; in the particular case, however, the seller had made it clear to the buyer that the buyer was responsible for assuring regulatory compliance. High Court of New Zealand, July 30, 2010, available at http://cisgw3.law.pace.edu/cases/100730n6.html.

[21] Landgericht Coburg, Germany, December 12, 2006, available at http://cisgw3.law.pace.edu/cases/061212g1.html (where the seller agreed to deliver plants to a particular place, the buyer had conveyed to the seller the particular purpose of using the plants at that place, although the seller was not liable under Article 35(2)(b) because the buyer had not reasonably relied on the seller's skill and judgment); Cour d'appel Lyon, France December 18, 2003, CLOUT case No. 492 (where the buyer's order described its requirements for the goods, the seller was obligated to meet those requirements under Article 35(2)(b)); Landgericht München, Germany, February 27, 2002, available at http://cisgw3.law.pace.edu/cases/020227g1.html (where it was "crystal clear" that the buyer intended to use the goods – large, heavy, and expensive globes – as long term advertising furniture for its offices, it was implied under Article 35(2)(b) that the goods would have an operational lifetime of at least three years). But where the contract did not indicate the specific purpose for which the goods would be used, Article 35(2)(b) did not apply. Chambre Arbitrale de Paris, France, 2007, available at http://cisgw3.law.pace.edu/cases/079926f1.html. And where the buyer revealed its particular purpose only to the seller's traveling sales agent, the requirements of Article 35(2)(b) were deemed not satisfied. Audiencia Provincial Barcelona, Spain, January 28, 2004, CLOUT case No. 555.

[22] High Court of New Zealand, New Zealand, July 30, 2010, available at http://cisgw3.law.pace.edu/cases/100730n6.html (a buyer was deemed not to have reasonably relied on the seller's skill and judgment where the buyer itself was an experienced importer of the goods); Landgericht Coburg, Germany, December 12, 2006, available at http://cisgw3.law.pace.edu/cases/061212g1.html (a buyer was deemed not to have relied on the seller's skill and judgment where the buyer possessed skill and knowledge concerning the goods that was equal to or greater than that of the seller).

positions.[23] Some decisions base their analysis on burden of proof principles taken from applicable domestic law;[24] others use the general principles of the CISG itself, pursuant to Article 7(2), to derive burden of proof rules;[25] many, however, fail to specify the source of the burden of proof rules they apply in a given case. Some decisions have allocated to the seller the burden of proving that the goods conformed,[26] but others have required the buyer to bear the burden of proving that the goods lacked conformity;[27] some have indicated that the result depends on which party is seeking a remedy,[28] or on whether the buyer has accepted and retained the goods for a period of time before complaining.[29] The decisions are trending toward the position articulated in a leading CISG commentary:

> The prevailing view is that the burden [of proving conformity or lack of conformity] shifts from the seller to the buyer in conjunction with the delivery of goods ... In general, a buyer who has taken delivery of the goods without any complaints or reservation as to their conformity has to prove that the goods were non-conforming at the time the risk passed.[30]

---

[23] *See* High Court, New Zealand, New Zealand, July 30, 2010 (*RJ & AM Smallmon v. Transport Sales Limited and Grant Alan Miller*), available at http://cisgw3.law.pace.edu/cases/100730n6.html (finding "a conflict in the authorities on the Convention" over which party has the burden of proof with respect to conformity of the goods).

[24] U.S. Court of Appeals for the Seventh Circuit, United States, May 23, 2005 (*Chicago Prime Packers, Inc. v. Northam Food Trading Co.*), available at http://cisgw3.law.pace.edu/cases/050523u1.html; Oberlandesgericht Köln, Germany, January 12, 2007, available at http://cisgw3.law.pace.edu/cases/070112g1.html; Chambre Arbitrale de Paris, France, 2007 (Arbitral award No. 9926), available at http://cisgw3.law.pace.edu/cases/079926f1.html.

[25] Tribunal Cantonal Valais, Switzerland, April 27, 2007, CLOUT case No. 934, available at http://cisgw3.law.pace.edu/cases/070427s1.html; Oberlandesgericht Karlsruhe, Germany, February 8, 2006, CLOUT case No. 721; Bundesgericht, Switzerland, July 7, 2004, CLOUT case No. 894, available at http://cisgw3.law.pace.edu/cases/040707s1.html; Bundesgericht, Switzerland, November 13, 2003, CLOUT case No. 885.

[26] E.g., Oberlandesgericht Köln, Germany, January 12, 2007, available at http://cisgw3.law.pace.edu/cases/070112g1.html; High People's Court of Shadong Province, People's Republic of China, June 27, 2005 (*Norway Royal Supreme Seafoods v. China Rizhao Jixiang Ocean Food Co. and China Rizhao Shanfu Food Co.*), available at http://cisgw3.law.pace.edu/cases/050627c1.html.

[27] E.g., U.S. District Court, Western District of Washington, United States, April 3, 2009 (*Barbara Berry S.A. de C.V. v. Ken M Spooner Farms, Inc.*), available at http://cisgw3.law.pace.edu/cases/090403u1.html; Juzgado de Primera Instancia e Instrucción, no. 5 de La Laguna, Spain, October 23, 2007, English abstract available in Unilex; Arbitral Institute of the Stockholm Chamber of Commerce, Sweden, April 5, 2007, English abstract available in Unilex; Cour d'appel de Rouen, France, December 19, 2006 (*Société Agrico v. Société SIAC*), available at http://cisgw3.law.pace.edu/cases/061219f1.html, affirmed by Cour de Cassation, France, September 16, 2008, CLOUT case No. 1028.

[28] E.g., Bundesgericht, Switzerland, November 13, 2003, CLOUT case No. 885.

[29] E.g., Hovioikeus/hovrätt Helsinki, Finland, May 31, 2004 (*Crudex Chemicals Oy v. Landmark Chemicals S.A.*), available at http://cisgw3.law.pace.edu/cases/040531f5.html; Bundesgericht, Switzerland, July 7, 2004, CLOUT case No. 894, available at http://cisgw3.law.pace.edu/cases/040707s1.html; Landgericht Saarbrücken, Germany, June 1, 2004, CLOUT case No. 590, available at http://cisgw3.law.pace.edu/cases/040601g1.html; Appelationshof Bern, Switzerland, February 11, 2004, available at http://cisgw3.law.pace.edu/cases/040211s1.html.

[30] Stefan Kröll, "Article 35" ¶ 175, in *UN Convention on Contracts for the International Sale of Goods (CISG)* (Stefan Kröll, Loukas Mistelis & Pilar Perales Viscasillas, eds.) (2011), 534-5. Accord, Ingeborg Schwenzer, "Article 35" ¶ 53, in Schwenzer, Commentary at 592-3 ("Once the buyer has physically taken over the goods (Article 60(b)), he generally has to prove their non-conformity at the time of passing of risk ... In exceptional cases, however, the buyer is relieved of his general burden of proof by shift of the burden of proof based on uniform law. If the buyer rejects the goods or notifies the seller of their nonconformity

Note that this approach means that the buyer bears the burden of proving that the goods lacked conformity whenever there may be a question about the timeliness of the buyer's notice of lack of conformity under CISG Article 39. In sum, the buyer must immediately complain upon taking delivery of the goods in order to prevent the burden of proof from shifting from the seller on the issue of the conformity of the goods. The burden of proof question will be examined in greater depth later in the chapter.

III. Notice of Lack of Conformity: CISG Article 39

The core of the provisions governing the buyer's obligation to give notice of delivered goods' nonconformity rests in Article 39. This provision imposes on the buyer an obligation to give the seller notice specifying the nature of a claimed lack of conformity within a reasonable time after the buyer discovered or ought to have discovered the nonconformity (Article 39(1)), or at any rate within two years from the date on which the goods were "handed over to the buyer" (provided this two-year period is not "inconsistent with a contractual period of guarantee") (Article 39(2)). Failure to meet this notice obligation, if not "excused" under Articles 40 or 44, carries a very severe sanction – the buyer "loses the right to rely" on the lack of conformity; in other words, the buyer is stripped of all remedies for the lack of conformity.

Decisions over the past ten years have raised a number of interesting issues concerning Article 39. Several cases focus on the scope of the Article 39 obligation. In what situations is the buyer required to give Article 39 notice? For example, it was held some time ago that the notice obligation applies not only when the goods (allegedly) do not comply with standards created by the CISG itself (Article 35(2)), but also when the buyer claims breach of a contractual warranty, even if the contract provision does not expressly impose a notice requirement.[31] That result is surely correct, given that Article 35(1) incorporates contractual quality provisions into the obligations imposed by the CISG. Article 39 only applies, however, when the buyer claims a "lack of conformity" in delivered goods. A Stockholm arbitration panel reasoned that not all contractual provisions relating to the quality of the goods create obligations that go to "conformity" within the meaning of the CISG, and therefore breach of such provisions may not require the Article 39 notice. For example, a German case involved a seller's agreement to reimburse the buyer's costs in servicing goods that were resold to the buyer's customers to the extent that the defect rate in the delivered goods exceeded five percent. The court held that this contractual obligation "does not amount to a warranty agreement in the classical sense, to which Articles 38 and 39 CISG would be applicable"; the buyer's failure to examine the goods and give notice as required by Article 39, therefore, did not relieve the seller of its obligations under this clause.[32]

Article 39 has been held to require a second notice where a buyer provides a notice of nonconformity, but allows the seller to attempt a repair of the goods, which subsequently

immediately at the time of taking over, the seller has to prove the goods were in conformity with the contract at the time of passing of risk").

[31] Arbitration Institute of the Stockholm Chamber of Commerce, Sweden, June 5, 1998, CLOUT case No. 237, available at http://cisgw3.law.pace.edu/cases/980605s5.html.

[32] Oberlandesgericht Düsseldorf, Germany, May 28, 2004, CLOUT case No. 591, available at http://cisgw3 .law.pace.edu/cases/040528g1.html.

fails.[33] In other cases, courts have held that Article 39 requires notice where the claimed lack of conformity consisted of a failure to supply proper instruction manuals[34] or to deliver required documentation.[35] Further, it has long been established that delivery of an improper quantity of goods,[36] including delivery of too many goods,[37] constitutes a lack of conformity that triggers the Article 39 notice obligation.

Other Article 39 issues arising in relatively recent cases include whether the buyer's notice obligations can be satisfied cumulatively by multiple communications,[38] whether the seller has an obligation to make inquiries after receiving inadequate notice,[39] to whom notice must be given in order to satisfy Article 39,[40] the purposes of Article 39

---

[33] Hof van Beroep Ghent, Belgium, November 14, 2008 (*Volmari Werner v. Isocab NV*), available at http://cisgw3.law.pace.edu/cases/081114b1.html.

[34] Landgericht Darmstadt, Germany, May 9, 2000. CLOUT case No. 343, available at http://cisgw3.law.pace.edu/cases/000509g1.html.

[35] Gerechtshof Arnhem, the Netherlands, June 17, 1997, available in Unilex at http://www.unilex.info/case.cfm?pid=1&do=case&id=317&step=Abstract.

[36] Landgericht Köln, Germany, December 5, 2006, available at http://cisgw3.law.pace.edu/cases/061205g1.html; Landgericht Saarbrücken, Germany, October 26, 2004, available at http://cisgw3.law.pace.edu/cases/041026g1.html; Landgericht München, Germany, February 20, 2002, available at http://cisgw3.law.pace.edu/cases/020220g1.html; Oberlandesgericht Düsseldorf, Germany, January 8, 1993, CLOUT case No. 48, available at http://cisgw3.law.pace.edu/cases/930108g1.html; Oberlandesgericht Koblenz, Germany, January 31, 1997, CLOUT case No. 282, available at http://cisgw3.law.pace.edu/cases/970131g1.html; Landgericht Landshut, Germany, April 5, 1995, English abstract available in Unilex at http://www.unilex.info/case.cfm?pid=1&do=case&id=121&step=Abstract.

[37] Oberlandesgericht Rostock, Germany, September 25, 2002, available at http://cisgw3.law.pace.edu/cases/020925g1.html.

[38] Retten i København, Denmark, October 19, 2007, CLOUT case No. 992 (in determining the propriety of a buyer's written notice of a pony's lack of conformity, a court took into account the fact that the buyer had, before a "final diagnosis" of the pony's condition was made, "continuously advised the seller" of the pony's worsening condition); Hoviokeus/hovrätt Turku, Finland, May 24, 2005, available at http://cisgw3.law.pace.edu/cases/050524f5.html (notice by telephone that the buyer had received complaints about the goods from its customers, later followed by emails detailing laboratory test results); Cour d'appel, Versailles, France, January 29, 1998, CLOUT case No. 225, English translation available at http://cisgw3.law.pace.edu/cases/980129f1.html. See also Cour d'appel Versailles, France, October 13, 2005, available at http://cisgw3.law.pace.edu/cases/051013f1.html, where the court took into account a series of communications from the buyer to the seller and its representative in determining that the seller was made aware of the lack of conformity.

[39] Landgericht Bamberg, Germany, October 23, 2006, available at http://cisgw3.law.pace.edu/cases/061023g1.html.

[40] Hoge Raad, the Netherlands, February 4, 2005 (*Isocab France S.A. v. Indus Projektbouw B.V.*), available in Unilex at http://www.unilex.info/case.cfm?pid=1&do=case&id=1049&step=Abstract (notice given to a member of the seller's corporate group was found sufficient where the entity that received the notice shared responsibility for the sale with the seller); Landgericht Köln, Germany November 30, 1999, CLOUT case No. 364 (notice given to an agent of the seller would satisfy Article 39, although the question of the recipient's agency status and authority were matters beyond the scope of the CISG to be determined under applicable domestic law); Landgericht Bochum, Germany, January 24, 1996, CLOUT case No. 411, available in Unilex at http://www.unilex.info/case.cfm?pid=1&do=case&id=194&step=Abstract (notice given to an employee of the seller who was not authorized to receive such communications but who promised to transmit the information to the seller was found to be insufficient when the employee in fact did not inform the seller; the court noted that, when notice is not given to the seller personally, the buyer must ensure that the seller actually receives the notice). Compare, Landgericht Stuttgart, Germany, August 31, 1989, CLOUT case No. 4, available at http://cisgw3.law.pace.edu/cases/890831g1.html (holding that the buyer had not satisfied the requirements of Article 39 because it did not prove, inter alia, that the person to whom the buyer faxed notice had "reception competency in regard to the faxes"). Another decision avoided determining whether notice sent to the seller's agent met the requirements of Article

notice,[41] whether the buyer's notice must indicate that the seller is in breach,[42] and how Article 39 applies in the case of latent defects not reasonably discoverable during an initial examination.[43] Some recent decisions suggest that, although Article 39 imposes

39 because the alleged notice was insufficient on other grounds. Amtsgericht Freiburg, Germany, July 6, 2007, available at http://cisgw3.law.pace.edu/cases/070706g1.html.

[41] Landgericht Stuttgart, Germany, October 15, 2009, available at http://cisgw3.law.pace.edu/cases/091015g1.html ("to take the necessary measures, such as to send a representative to the buyer to examine the goods, to secure the necessary evidence for potential disputes regarding conformity of the goods, to offer exchange, additional delivery or cure the defect, or to have recourse against a supplier"); Rechtbank Breda, the Netherlands, January 16, 2009, available at http://cisgw3.law.pace.edu/cases/090116n1.html) (to clarify whether seller has breached and to assist the seller in defending itself against invalid claims); Judicial Board of Szeged, Hungary, December 5, 2008, available at http://cisgw3.law.pace.edu/cases/081205h1.html (to clarify whether the seller has breached and to arrange for repair or replacement of the goods at minimal cost); Arrondissementsrechtbank Zutphen, the Netherlands, February 27, 2008 (*Frutas Caminito Sociedad Cooperativa Valenciana. v. Groente-En Fruithandel Heemskerk BV*), available at http://cisgw3.law.pace.edu/cases/080227n2.html (to permit the seller to inspect the goods and to gather evidence); Kantonsgericht Zug, Switzerland, August 30, 2007, CLOUT case No. 938, available at http://cisgw3.law.pace.edu/cases/070830s1.html ("to put the seller in a position to understand the asserted lack of conformity and to take the necessary steps to gather any required evidence for possible future legal proceedings about the question of conformity, to initiate either a substitute delivery or a repair of the goods, and finally to take recourse against its own supplier"); Oberlandesgericht Koblenz, Germany, December 14, 2006, CLOUT case No. 724, available at http://cisgw3.law.pace.edu/cases/061214g1.html (to give the seller the information needed to determine how to proceed with respect to the buyer's claim and to clarify whether a breach has occurred); Oberster Gerichtshof, Austria, November 30, 2006, available at http://cisgw3.law.pace.edu/cases/061130a3.html (to minimize disputes over whether the condition of the goods had changed after delivery and "to enable the parties to take appropriate measures"); Gerechtshof's-Hertogenbosch, the Netherlands, September 19, 2006, CLOUT case No. 939 (to clarify whether seller has breached and, in the case of an installment contract, to clarify whether the buyer can expect the seller to make further deliveries); Landgericht Aschaffenburg, Germany, April 20, 2006, available at http://cisgw3.law.pace.edu/cases/060420g1.html (to facilitate seller's cure of defects); Hoge Raad, the Netherlands, February 4, 2005, English abstract available in Unilex (to give the seller "a fair opportunity to remedy the defects and in general gather evidence on the alleged lack of conformity"); U.S. District Court, Northern District of Illinois, United States, May 21, 2004 (*Chicago Prime Packers, Inc. v. Northam Food Trading Co.*), available at http://cisgw3.law.pace.edu/cases/040521u1.html (to avoid controversies over the condition of the goods at the time of transfer); U.S. Bankruptcy Court, District of Oregon, United States, March 29, 2004 (*In re Siskiyou Evergreen, Inc.*), CLOUT case No. 694, available at http://cisgw3.law.pace.edu/cases/040329u2.html ("European cases construing the Convention have required the notice to describe the claimed non-conformity with enough detail to allow the seller to identify and correct the problem without further investigation. A more practical interpretation would hold that the notice must be given in time, and in sufficient detail, to allow the seller to cure the defect in a manner allowing the buyer the benefit of his bargain."); Audiencia Provincial de la Coruña, Spain, June 21, 2002, CLOUT case No. 486, available at http://cisgw3.law.pace.edu/cases/020621s4.html (to enable the seller to prepare to defend itself against the allegations of lack of conformity and to allow the seller to take measures against the spread of a virus allegedly infecting the goods (fish eggs)); Bundesgericht, Switzerland, May 28, 2002, available at http://cisgw3.law.pace.edu/cases/020528s1.html (to clarify whether seller has breached (dicta – transaction governed by domestic law)).

[42] Compare Hoge Raad, the Netherlands, February 20, 1998, English abstract available in Unilex (so long as the notice precisely describes defects in the goods reported by the buyer's customer, the notice need not claim that such defects constitute a breach by the seller, and may even express doubts that the customer's complaints were justified) with Oberlandesgericht Karlsruhe, Germany, February 8, 2006, CLOUT case No. 721, available at http://cisgw3.law.pace.edu/cases/060208g1.html (the notice must "contest the conformity of the goods" and demonstrate the buyer's "intention to object").

[43] Tribunale di Busto Arsizio, Italy, December 13, 2001, available in *Rivista di Diritto Internazionale Privato e Processuale*, 2003, 150–5, English summary available in Unilex (buyer's Article 39 notice concerning latent defects need only convey the information reasonably available to the buyer at the time of the notice, to be supplemented by information in later notices). To the same effect, see Cour d'appel Versailles,

on the buyer the obligation to give notice, the seller also bears responsibility under the provision for inquiring and communicating about a lack of conformity in the goods it had delivered.[44] It was also held that notice sent to the seller by the buyer's customer satisfied the requirements of Article 39 where the seller accepted the customer complaints as notice of lack of conformity in its delivery to the buyer (seller questioned the buyer about the defect and made a request to examine goods in the buyer's control).[45]

The most important (but not necessarily the most interesting) Article 39 issue is a longstanding one: determining if a buyer has given notice within a "reasonable time" as required by Article 39(1). The CISG case law is deep in this area, but remains unsettled and decisions continue to exhibit a range of results. A German court held that notice given eight days after delivery, where the buyer alleged that seller delivered an insufficient quantity, was too late,[46] whereas a Chinese arbitration decision held that notice of quality defects in goods that was given nine months after delivery was timely.[47] Despite the significant disparity in these time periods, such decisions are not necessarily inconsistent, as all agree that the "reasonable time" for giving Article 39 notice is a flexible standard that varies with the circumstances,[48] including the obviousness of the lack of conformity;[49] the nature of the

France, January 29, 1998, CLOUT case No. 225; Hoge Raad, the Netherlands, February 20, 1998, English summary available in Unilex.

[44] Landgericht Bamberg, Germany, October 23, 2006, available at http://cisgw3.law.pace.edu/cases/061023g1.html (if the buyer's notice left the seller unclear concerning the nature or extent of the claimed lack of conformity, "the seller can be expected to inquire of the buyer"); Bundesgericht, Switzerland, November 13, 2003, CLOUT case No. 885, available at http://cisgw3.law.pace.edu/cases/031113s1.html ("in the age of technology, the seller can be expected to ask questions if he desires more precise instructions from the buyer").

[45] Hof van Beroep Antwerpen, Belgium, February 14, 2002 (*NV Carta Mundi v. Index Syndicate Ltd.*), available at http://cisgw3.law.pace.edu/cases/020214b1.html.

[46] Landgericht Tübingen, Germany, June 18, 2003, available at http://cisgw3.law.pace.edu/cases/030618g1.html.

[47] China International Economic & Trade Arbitration Commission, People's Republic of China, June 3, 2003, available at http://cisgw3.law.pace.edu/cases/030603c1.html.

[48] See, e.g., United States District Court, Southern District of Ohio, United States, March 26, 2009 (*Miami Valley Paper, LLC v. Lebbing Engineering & Consulting GmbH*), available at http://cisgw3.law.pace.edu/cases/090326u1.html; Rechtbank Breda, the Netherlands, January 16, 2009, available at http://cisgw3.law.pace.edu/cases/090116n1.html; Tribunale di Forlì, Italy, February 16, 2009, English translation available at http://cisgw3.law.pace.edu/cases/090216i3.html; Tribunale di Forlì, Italy, December 11, 2008, available at http://cisgw3.law.pace.edu/cases/081211i3.html; Kantonsgericht Zug, Switzerland, August 30, 2007, CLOUT case No. 938, available at http://cisgw3.law.pace.edu/cases/070830s1.html; Tribunal Cantonal Valais, Switzerland, April 27, 2007, CLOUT case No. 934, available at http://cisgw3.law.pace.edu/cases/070427s1.html; Oberlandesgericht Koblenz, Germany, October 19, 2006, CLOUT case No. 723, English translation available at http://cisgw3.law.pace.edu/cases/061019g2.html; Tribunale Civile di Cuneo, Italy, January 31, 1996, Unilex; Landgericht Hamburg, Germany, September 6, 2004, available at (http://cisgw3.law.pace.edu/cases/040906g1.html); Kantonsgericht Schaffhausen, Switzerland, January 27, 2004, CLOUT case No. 892, available at http://cisgw3.law.pace.edu/cases/040127s1.html; Landgericht Tübingen, Germany, June 18, 2003, available at http://cisgw3.law.pace.edu/cases/030618g1.html; Single-Member Court of First Instance of Thessalonika, Greece, 2003 (docket No. 14953/2003), available at http://cisgw3.law.pace.edu/cases/030001gr.html; Tribunale Rimini, Italy, November 26, 2002, CLOUT case No. 608, available at http://cisgw3.law.pace.edu/cases/021126i3.html.

[49] Arrondissementsrechtbank Zutphen, the Netherlands, February 27, 2008 (*Frutas Caminito Sociedad Cooperativa Valenciana. v. Groente-En Fruithandel Heemskerk BV*), available at http://cisgw3.law.pace.edu/cases/080227n2.html; Audiencia Provincial de Pontevedra, Spain, December 19, 2007, CLOUT case No. 849, available at http://cisgw3.law.pace.edu/cases/071219s4.html; Tribunal Cantonal Valais,

goods[50] (e.g., perishable[51] or seasonal,[52] as opposed to durable and nonseasonal,[53] or complex in nature[54]); and the buyer's plans for the goods.[55] Although German courts developed a reputation for being strict in determining the reasonableness of the time a buyer has taken to give notice, more recently, Austrian courts appear to have taken the lead in this rather dubious category: the Oberster Gerichtshof, the highest Austrian court with jurisdiction over CISG cases, has declared that a buyer must generally give notice within two weeks from delivery (a week to examine the goods and discover the lack of conformity, followed by notice within an additional week) – although the facts of the particular case may lengthen or shorten this period.[56]

One issue where there is consensus in the reported decisions, even though Article 39 does not expressly address the matter, is that the buyer bears the burden of proving that

Switzerland, April 27, 2007, CLOUT case No. 934, available at http://cisgw3.law.pace.edu/cases/070427s1. html ("the extent of the non-conformity"); U.S. District Court, Northern District of Illinois, United States, May 21, 2004 (*Chicago Prime Packers, Inc. v. Northam Food Trading Co.*), available at http://cisgw3.law. pace.edu/cases/040521u1.html; Hof van Beroep Gent, Belgium, May 12, 2003 (*S. GmbH v. A. bvba*), available at http://cisgw3.law.pace.edu/cases/030512b1.html.

[50] Tribunal Cantonal Valais, Switzerland, April 27, 2007, CLOUT case No. 934, available at http://cisgw3. law.pace.edu/cases/070427s1.html; Single-Member Court of First Instance of Thessalonika, Greece, 2003 (docket No. 14953/2003), available at http://cisgw3.law.pace.edu/cases/030001gr.html; Tribunale Rimini, Italy, November 26, 2002, CLOUT case No. 608, available at http://cisgw3.law.pace.edu/cases/021126i3. html.

[51] Rechtbank Arnhem, the Netherlands, February 11, 2009, available in Unilex; Rechtbank Breda, the Netherlands, January 16, 2009, available at http://cisgw3.law.pace.edu/cases/090116n1.html; Arrondissementsrechtbank Zutphen, the Netherlands, February 27, 2008 (*Frutas Caminito Sociedad Cooperativa Valenciana. v. Groente-En Fruithandel Heemskerk BV*), available at http://cisgw3.law.pace.edu/cases/ 080227n2.html; Audiencia Provincial de Pontevedra, Spain, December 19, 2007, CLOUT case No. 849, available at http://cisgw3.law.pace.edu/cases/071219s4.html (perishable goods intended for human consumption); Hof van Beroep Ghent, Belgium, April 16, 2007, available at http://cisgw3.law.pace.edu/ cases/070416b1.html (frozen meat for human consumption); Gerechtshof's-Hertogenbosch, the Netherlands, January 2, 2007, CLOUT case No. 828 (live trees); Oberlandesgericht Koblenz, Germany, October 19, 2006, CLOUT case No. 723, available at http://cisgw3.law.pace.edu/cases/061019g2.html; Oberlandesgericht Köln, Germany, August 14, 2006, CLOUT case No. 825, available at http://cisgw3.law. pace.edu/cases/060814g1.html; Rechtbank van Koophandel Veurne, Belgium, March 19, 2003 (*CVBA L. v. E.G. BV*), available at http://cisgw3.law.pace.edu/cases/030319b1.html (fresh vegetables); Single-Member Court of First Instance of Thessalonika, Greece, 2003 (docket No. 14953/2003), available at http://cisgw3.law.pace.edu/cases/030001gr.html ("consumables"); Tribunale Rimini, Italy, November 26, 2002, CLOUT case No. 608, available at http://cisgw3.law.pace.edu/cases/021126i3.html.

[52] Oberlandesgericht Koblenz, Germany, October 19, 2006, CLOUT case No. 723, available at http://cisgw3. law.pace.edu/cases/061019g2.html; Hof van Beroep Gent, Belgium, May 12, 2003 (*S. GmbH v. A. bvba*), available at http://cisgw3.law.pace.edu/cases/030512b1.html;

[53] District Court in Komarno, Slovak Republic February 24, 2009, available at http://cisgw3.law.pace.edu/ cases/090224k1.html (because the goods – new potatoes – were not subject to rapid deterioration, the buyer had a longer time in which to give notice); Obergericht Zug, Switzerland, December 19, 2006, available at http://cisgw3.law.pace.edu/cases/061219s1.html; Landgericht München, Germany, February 27, 2002, available at http://cisgw3.law.pace.edu/cases/020227g1.html (video screen apparatus).

[54] Obergericht Luzern, Switzerland, July 29, 2002, available at http://cisgw3.law.pace.edu/cases/020729s1. html.

[55] Gerechtshof Arnem, the Netherlands, July 18, 2006, CLOUT case No. 941.

[56] Oberster Gerichtshof, Austria, April 2, 2009, available at http://cisgw3.law.pace.edu/cases/090402a3.html; Oberster Gerichtshof, Austria, January 14, 2002, CLOUT case No. 541, available at http://cisgw3.law. pace.edu/cases/020114a3.html; Oberster Gerichtshof, Austria, August 27, 1999, CLOUT case No. 423, English abstract also available in Unilex.

it complied with the notice obligations under Article 39.[57] Some decisions have described the buyer's burden in considerable detail.[58] There is, however, some disagreement in the reported cases over the source of the principles that place the burden on the buyer. Some decisions reach the result by applying domestic burden of proof principles;[59] a greater number of decisions have used the CISG's general principles, pursuant to Article 7(2), to place the burden of proof on the buyer. Not surprisingly, some decisions do not specify any source for determining the allocation of the burden of proof.

IV. Inspection of Goods: CISG Article 38

Article 38(1) requires a buyer to examine (or to cause to be examined) delivered goods "within as short a period as is practicable in the circumstances." The remaining two subparts of Article 38 relax somewhat this demanding standard. A contract for sale (or the default rule that applies if the issue is not addressed by the parties' agreement) often provides that technical "delivery" (for risk of loss purposes) takes place at the start of the goods' journey to the buyer, if the goods are transported by "carriage" (via a third party carrier). In such instances, Article 38(2) provides that the buyer may defer examining the goods "until after the goods have arrived at their destination." And where the goods are "redirected in transit or re-dispatched by the buyer without a reasonable opportunity for examination by him," Article 38(3) permits the buyer to defer examination "until the

[57] E.g., Landgericht Stuttgart, Germany, October 15, 2009, available at http://cisgw3.law.pace.edu/cases/091015g1.html; District Court in Komarno, Slovak Republic, March 12, 2009, available at http://cisgw3.law.pace.edu/cases/090312k1.html; Rechtbank Breda, the Netherlands, January 16, 2009, available at http://cisgw3.law.pace.edu/cases/090116n1.html; Polimeles Protodikio Athinon, Greece, 2009 (docket No. 4505/2009), available at http://cisgw3.law.pace.edu/cases/094505gr.html; Handelsgericht Aargau, Switzerland, November 26, 2008, available at http://cisgw3.law.pace.edu/cases/081126s1.html; Tribunal Cantonal Valais, Switzerland, April 27, 2007, CLOUT case No. 934, English translation available at http://cisgw3.law.pace.edu/cases/070427s1.html; Oberlandesgericht Köln, Germany, January 12, 2007, available at http://cisgw3.law.pace.edu/cases/070112g1.html; Obergericht Zug, Switzerland, December 19, 2006, English translation available at http://cisgw3.law.pace.edu/cases/061219s1.html; Kantonsgericht Appenzell-Ausserhoden, Switzerland, March 9, 2006, CLOUT case No. 909, available at http://cisgw3.law.pace.edu/cases/060309s1.html; Rechtbank van Koophandel Kortrijk, Belgium, June 4, 2004 (*Steinbock-Bjonustan EHF v. N.V. Duma*), available at http://cisgw3.law.pace.edu/cases/040604b1.html; U.S. District Court, Northern District of Illinois, United States, May 21, 2004 (*Chicago Prime Packers, Inc. v. Northam Food Trading Co.*), available at http://cisgw3.law.pace.edu/cases/040521u1.html; Appelationshof Bern, Switzerland, February 11, 2004, available at http://cisgw3.law.pace.edu/cases/040211s1.html, reasoning upheld in Bundesgericht, Switzerland, July 7, 2004, CLOUT case No. 894, available at http://cisgw3.law.pace.edu/cases/040707s1.html; Landgericht Bielefeld, Germany, August 15, 2003, available at http://cisgw3.law.pace.edu/cases/030815g1.html; Tribunale Rimini, Italy, November 26, 2002 (*Al Palazzo S.r.l v. Bernardaud di Limoges S.A.*), CLOUT case No. 608, available at http://cisgw3.law.pace.edu/cases/021126i3.html; Kantonsgericht Schaffhausen, Switzerland, February 25, 2002, available at http://cisgw3.law.pace.edu/cases/020225s1.html.

[58] For example, one recent decision explained that, to carry its burden, a buyer must prove when the nonconformity was discovered, the time and exact addressee of the notice of nonconformity, and the way in which the nonconformity was described in the notice; the court held that the buyer's general statement that it had notified the seller that many deliveries were nonconforming was not sufficient because the statement failed to identify the specific deliveries and nonconformities covered. Handelsgericht Aargau, Switzerland, November 26, 2008, available at http://cisgw3.law.pace.edu/cases/081126s1.html.

[59] District Court in Komarno, Slovak Republic, March 12, 2009, available at http://cisgw3.law.pace.edu/cases/090312k1.html; Pretura di Torino, Italy, January 30, 1997, English abstract available in Unilex, available at http://www.cisg.law.pace.edu/cisg/wais/db/cases2/970130i3.html.

goods have arrived at their new destination," provided that at the time the contract was concluded the seller knew or ought to have known of the "possibility" of redirection or redispatch.

A. *Relationship between Article 38 Inspection and Article 39 Notice*

The close connection between the buyer's duty to examine delivered goods under Article 38 and the buyer's duty to give notice of a claimed lack of conformity in delivered goods has long been recognized. Article 39 requires a buyer to give the seller notice within a reasonable time from when the buyer "discovered or *ought to have discovered*" a lack of conformity; thus, in the case of a lack of conformity that ought to have been discovered during the Article 38 examination, the reasonable time for the buyer to give Article 39 notice will begin to run from the time that the Article 38 examination should have been conducted, whether or not it was actually conducted at that time.[60] A buyer who fails to conduct an examination that is timely and adequate under Article 38 runs the risk of failing to give timely notice of defects that should have been (but were not) discovered, and thereby losing "the right to rely" on the lack of conformity pursuant to Article 39. Article 38 does not specify a sanction for failure to comply with the duty to examine. As noted earlier, however, the failure to conduct a proper Article 38 examination may lead to the loss of the buyer's right to make a claim for a lack of conformity under Article 39. Thus, Article 39 indirectly provides a very significant penalty for failure to meet Article 38 obligations. Indeed, it has been almost universally held – including in an opinion by the CISG Advisory Council – that there is no other independent sanction for failure to comply with Article 38.[61]

B. *Purpose of Article 38*

Several recent decisions addressed the purpose of the Article 38 examination, suggesting that the procedure is designed to prevent disputes over whether the goods changed condition after delivery.[62] A prompt inspection allows the buyer "to prepare for a notification and to rectify asymmetric levels of information between buyer and seller,"[63] and generally to permit the buyer to determine expeditiously if the goods conform to the contract and

---

[60] See, e.g., UNCITRAL Digest of case law on the United Nations Convention on Contracts for the International Sale of Goods (2008 Revision), available at http://www.uncitral.org/uncitral/en/case_law/digests/cisg2008.html, Article 38, para. 2 and Article 39, para. 18; CISG Advisory Council Opinion No. 2, June 7, 2004, para. 4.1, available at http://www.cisg.law.pace.edu/cisg/CISG-AC-op2.html.

[61] CISG Advisory Council, "Opinion No. 2," June 7, 2004, para. 4.1, available at http://www.cisg.law.pace.edu/cisg/CISG-AC-op2.html.

[62] Oberlandesgericht Köln, Germany, August 31, 2006, available at http://cisgw3.law.pace.edu/cases/060831g1.html; U.S. District Court, Northern District of Illinois, United States, May 21, 2004 (*Chicago Prime Packers, Inc. v. Northam Food Trading Co.*), available at http://cisgw3.law.pace.edu/cases/040521u1.html. Compare Oberlandesgericht Schleswig, Germany, August 22, 2002, available at http://cisgw3.law.pace.edu/cases/020822g2.html (livestock had to be examined immediately after delivery because of the possibility of rapid change in their condition).

[63] Appelationshof Bern, Switzerland, February 11, 2004, available at http://cisgw3.law.pace.edu/cases/040211s1.html, reasoning upheld in CLOUT case No. 894 (Bundesgericht, Switzerland, July 7, 2004) (see full text of the decision).

to take "appropriate measures."[64] Courts have recognized a number of factors in determining the reasonableness of the buyer's inspection. One decision stated that the extent of the required examination is dictated by the nature and features of the goods, their proposed use, the capabilities and situation of the buyer, and the circumstances present at the place of examination; the court added that the required examination "can vary between a mere visual check and an in-depth inspection by expert personnel."[65] Another decision suggested limits to the scope of the buyer's obligation to examine, holding that the buyer need not examine electrical equipment to determine if it included basic electrical safety features.[66] Two decisions addressed the role of Article 38 in discovering latent defects: one apparently suggests that Article 38 requires a repeated or continuous examination process designed to discover even latent nonconformities that would not reveal themselves until long after delivery;[67] the other decision, in contrast, implies that the required Article 38 examination is a single discrete event that should occur soon after delivery, and that Article 38 does not play a role with respect to defects reasonably not discovered during that initial inspection.[68]

C. "Short a Period as Is Practicable"

A significant number of recent decisions have addressed the time for the buyer to conduct the Article 38 examination. According to Article 38(1), examination is required within "as short a period as is practicable in the circumstances." This standard is, of course, a flexible one. One court declared that "[t]he actual examination may take from a couple of hours up to several months."[69] Other decisions have emphasized the strict time period for examination imposed by Article 38. One decision held that, although the buyer received deliveries while it was still examining an earlier shipment, this did not postpone the buyer's obligation to examine the later deliveries in a timely fashion; the court explained that "[i]n the international context, diligence is the first

---

[64] Oberlandesgericht Köln, Germany, August 31, 2006, available at http://cisgw3.law.pace.edu/cases/060831g1.html; Appelationshof Bern, Switzerland, February 11, 2004, available at http://cisgw3.law.pace.edu/cases/040211s1.html, reasoning upheld in Bundesgericht, Switzerland, July 7, 2004, CLOUT case No. 894. English translation available at http://cisgw3.law.pace.edu/cases/040707s1.html; Oberlandesgericht Innsbruck, Austria, April 26, 2002, CLOUT case No. 538, available at http://cisgw3.law.pace.edu/cases/040707s1.html.

[65] Appelationshof Bern, Switzerland, February 11, 2004, English translation available at http://cisgw3.law.pace.edu/cases/040211s1.html, reasoning upheld in CLOUT case No. 894 (Bundesgericht, Switzerland, July 7, 2004).

[66] Landgericht München, Germany, February 27, 2002, available at http://cisgw3.law.pace.edu/cases/020227g1.html.

[67] Gerechtshof–Hertogenbosch, the Netherlands, October 11, 2005, CLOUT case No. 944 (reasonable time for giving Article 39 notice regarding defects that ought to have been discovered during a "simple examination" when the goods were delivered to the buyer began to run from the time of the simple examination; reasonable time for giving Article 39 notice regarding defects that could not be discovered until a "more thorough" examination when the goods arrived at the premises of the buyer's customer began to run from the time of the more thorough examination).

[68] Landgericht Saarbrücken, Germany, June 1, 2004, available at http://cisgw3.law.pace.edu/cases/040601g1.html ("the reasonable period of time commences for hidden defects without further examination periods, as soon as the buyer discovers the lack of conformity").

[69] Appelationshof Bern, Switzerland, February 11, 2004, available at http://cisgw3.law.pace.edu/cases/040211s1.html, reasoning upheld by Bundesgericht, Switzerland, July 7, 2004, CLOUT case No. 894, available at http://cisgw3.law.pace.edu/cases/040707s1.html.

duty of all involved."[70] A significant number of decisions issued over the last ten years have attempted to establish a general presumptive deadline for the buyer's Article 38 examination, subject to enlargement (or shortening) depending on the facts of the individual case. Recent decisions have suggested presumptive periods ranging from three or four days,[71] to two weeks,[72] to two to three weeks,[73] to a month[74] following delivery. Other relatively recent decisions have indicated that perishable and generic goods must be examined immediately on delivery or, at the latest, within the next few days.[75]

As noted above, Articles 38(2) and 38(3) extend the time for the buyer's examination in certain circumstances. Decisions over the last ten years have held that the requirements for delayed examination under Article 38(3) were not met where the goods were in the possession of the buyer for an extended period, thus affording the buyer an opportunity to examine them before they were redispatched.[76] In the "used shoes" case,[77] the court held that a buyer that had agreed to delivery "FOB Mombassa Kenya" was not entitled to defer examining the goods until after they had arrived at the buyer's home country of

[70] Hof van Beroep Ghent, Belgium, April 16, 2007, available at http://cisgw3.law.pace.edu/cases/070416b1.html.

[71] Oberlandesgericht Karlsruhe, Germany, June 25, 1997, CLOUT case No. 230. See also U.S. District Court, Northern District of Illinois, United States, May 21, 2004 (*Chicago Prime Packers, Inc. v. Northam Food Trading Co.*), available at http://cisgw3.law.pace.edu/cases/040521u1.html (citing with approval decisions that, as a general rule, require examination within three to four days of delivery, as well as decisions requiring examination immediately upon delivery). Compare Handelsgericht St. Gallen, Switzerland, February 11, 2003, available at http://cisgw3.law.pace.edu/cases/030211s1.html ("within a few working days").

[72] Obergericht des Kantons Appenzell Ausserhoden, Switzerland, August 18, 2008, English abstract available in UNILEX (examination period of two weeks is reasonable where the buyer's customers discovered the defects); Obergericht Zug, Switzerland, December 19, 2006, available at http://cisgw3.law.pace.edu/cases/061219s1.html (as a basic rule for examination of nonperishable goods not subject to major price fluctuations, two weeks (but not less than one week or five working days) after delivery).

[73] Appelationshof Bern, Switzerland, February 11, 2004, available at http://cisgw3.law.pace.edu/cases/040211s1.html, reasoning upheld in Bundesgericht, Switzerland, July 7, 2004, CLOUT case No. 894, available at http://cisgw3.law.pace.edu/cases/040707s1.html ("In the absence of further circumstances justifying either a shorter or longer period and in the absence of particular practices or usages, the period granted for examination of non-perishable goods should be set as 2–3 weeks"; although also indicating "[a]s a rough yardstick, which needs adjustment in either direction according to the circumstances of each case, a period for examination of one week – five working days – can apply").

[74] Kantonsgericht Schaffhausen, Switzerland, February 25, 2002, available at http://cisgw3.law.pace.edu/cases/020225s1.html.

[75] Audiencia Provincial de Pontevedra, Spain, December 19, 2007, CLOUT case No. 849, available at http://cisgw3.law.pace.edu/cases/071219s4.html; Oberlandesgericht Köln, Germany, August 31, 2006, available at http://cisgw3.law.pace.edu/cases/060831g1.html.

[76] Oberlandesgericht Dresden, Germany, November 8, 2007, available at http://cisgw3.law.pace.edu/cases/071108g1.html (buyer had reasonable opportunity to examine goods during three months they were in buyer's possession before being redispatched; Article 38(3) was, therefore, inapplicable); Rechtbank van Koophandel Hasselt, Belgium, January 6, 2004, available at http://cisgw3.law.pace.edu/cases/040106b1.html (six weeks was reasonable time to examine the goods, but whether the buyer had reasonable opportunity to examine them before redispatch depends on whether examination would require removing packaging, or seals or other proof of authenticity, necessary for transport to its customer; because buyer failed to prove that removal of such items was required, buyer could not invoke Article 38(3)).

[77] Landgericht Frankfurt, Germany, April 11, 2005, available at http://cisgw3.law.pace.edu/cases/050411g1.html. For further discussion of this decision see Harry M. Flechtner, "Funky Mussels, a Stolen Car, and Decrepit Used Shoes: Non-Conforming Goods and Notice Thereof under the United Nations Sales Convention ("CISG")," 26 *B.U. Int'l L.J.* 1 (2008), draft (University of Pittsburgh Legal Studies Research Paper No. 2008–21), available at http://ssrn.com/abstract=1144182; http://www.cisg.law.pace.edu/cisg/biblio/flechtner8.html#iii.

Uganda. The court reasoned that by agreeing to the "F.O.B. Mombassa" term, the buyer obligated itself to examine the goods in Kenya even if examination there would entail extra expense and even if such examination would trigger an obligation to pay Kenyan customs duties (in addition to the Ugandan duties).

A number of decisions indicate that the buyer bears the burden of proving that it conducted an adequate Article 38 examination of the goods, and that an alleged lack of conformity was a latent defect not reasonably discoverable during such an examination.[78] This burden has little direct significance in its own right, as the only "sanction" for failing to examine goods properly is that the buyer's reasonable time for giving notice of nonconformity under Article 39(1) may run before the buyer is aware of a lack of conformity.[79] Placing on the buyer the burden of proving that it conducted an adequate Article 38 examination, however, creates an additional indirect obstacle to proof that a buyer gave timely Article 39(1) notice.

V. Burden of Proof Governing Conformity of Goods and Notice of Lack of Conformity: A Systemic View

As noted in the discussion of individual provisions, a substantial number of cases decided over the last ten years have addressed the question of who bears the burden of proof under the CISG provisions governing conformity of goods and the buyer's obligation to give proper notice of a lack of conformity. Although a variety of positions have been taken on the question, there appears to be an emerging consensus in the case law (supported by prominent commentators) that under Article 35 the buyer bears the burden of proving that the seller delivered nonconforming goods, unless the buyer objected almost immediately after it received the goods.[80] Furthermore, there is a clear extant consensus that the buyer bears the burden of proving that it gave the seller sufficient and timely notice as required by Article 39.[81] Thus, under these approaches, whenever the timeliness of the buyer's notice of lack of conformity is in dispute, unless the buyer has not objected immediately after it received the goods, the buyer will bear the burden of proving both that the goods lacked conformity and that the buyer's notice satisfied the CISG's requirements.

There is disagreement in the case law,[82] and in scholarly commentary,[83] over the source of the burden of proof principles that apply when the CISG governs a transaction.

---

[78] Polimeles Protodikio Athinon, Greece, 2009 (docket No. 4505/2009), available at http://cisgw3.law.pace .edu/cases/094505gr.html; Oberlandesgericht Köln, Germany, January 12, 2007, available at http://cisgw3. law.pace.edu/cases/070112g1.html; Appelationshof Bern, Switzerland, February 11, 2004, available at http://cisgw3.law.pace.edu/cases/040211s1.html, reasoning upheld in Bundesgericht, Switzerland, July 7, 2004, CLOUT case No. 894, available at http://cisgw3.law.pace.edu/cases/040707s1.html; Landgericht Saarbrücken, Germany, June 1, 2004, CLOUT case No. 590, available at http://cisgw3.law.pace.edu/cases/ 040601g1.html; U.S. District Court, Northern District of Illinois, United States, May 21, 2004 (*Chicago Prime Packers, Inc. v. Northam Food Trading Co.*), available at http://cisgw3.law.pace.edu/cases/040521u1. html.

[79] See notes 60–1 and the text accompanying. Accord, Stefan Kröll, "Article 38" ¶ 146, in Kröll, Mistelis & Perales Viscasillas Commentary at 592.

[80] See notes 23–30 and accompanying text.

[81] See notes 57–9 and accompanying text.

[82] See notes 24–5 and accompanying text.

[83] For a clear and helpful account of this controversy, see Franco Ferrari, "Burden of Proof under the CISG," in *Review of the Convention on Contracts for the International Sale of Goods (CISG) 2001* (ed. Pace International Law Review) (2002), 1, 2–3.

A few commentators (this author included) argue that allocation of the burden of proof is a matter beyond the scope of the CISG (except where the CISG addresses it expressly, as in Article 79(1)), and is therefore governed by domestic law.[84] The majority opinion among scholars, however, is that the CISG contains general burden of proof principles that, pursuant to Article 7(2), should be used to allocate the burden where the CISG does not do so expressly.[85] Resolving the question of the source for allocating the burden of proof is probably inconsequential for the point under discussion. This is because, whether its source is domestic law or general principles of the CISG, the burden of proof principle relating to CISG Articles 35, 39, and 38 is the so-called "rule and exception principle."[86] As explained by Professor Ferrari:

> On one hand, this means that a party has to prove the existence of the factual prerequisites contained in the legal provision from which it wants to derive beneficial legal consequences. On the other hand, this also means that a party claiming an exception has the burden of proving its prerequisites.[87]

---

[84] See Harry M. Flechtner, "Selected Issues Relating to the CISG's Scope of Application," 13 *Vindobona J. Int'l Commercial L. & Arbitration* 91, 102–6 (2009); Warren Khoo in *Commentary on the International Sales Law: The 1980 Vienna Sales Convention* (ed. C.M. Bianca and M.J. Bonell) (1987), Article 2, para. 3.2. For other commentators supporting this approach, see the authorities cited in Ferrari, "Burden of Proof," 3 and notes 14–16. As Professor Ferrari has noted, commentators supporting this position are not in agreement over which domestic law – the law of the forum or the law designated by application of principles of private international law – should be the source for burden of proof principles in CISG transactions. See Ferrari, "Burden of Proof," 3–4.

[85] See Stefan Kröll, "Article 35" ¶ 170, in Kröll, Mistelis & Perales Viscasillas Commentary at 532–3; Ingeborg Schwenzer, "Article 35" ¶ 50, in Schwenzer Commentary at 592; Ferrari, "Burden of Proof," 4; Ulrich Magnus, "General Principles of UN-Sales Law," available at http://www.cisg.law.pace.edu/cisg/biblio/magnus.html (originally published in 59 *Rabels Zeitschrift für ausländisches und internationales Privatrecht* 469 (1995)), text accompanying notes 86–91; Sonja Kruisinga, *(Non) conformity in the 1980 UN Convention on Contracts for the International Sale of Goods: A Uniform Concept?* (2004), 157–86. For other commentators supporting this approach, see the authorities cited in Ferrari, "Burden of Proof," 4 notes 14–23.

[86] See Flechtner, "Selected Issues," 107; Ferrari, "Burden of Proof," 5; Stefan Kröll, "Article 35" ¶ 178 and "Article 39" ¶ 124, in Kröll, Mistelis & Perales Viscasillas Commentary at 536 and 624; Ingeborg Schwenzer, "Article 35" ¶ 52, in Schwenzer, Commentary at 592; Bundesgerichtshof, Germany, June 30, 2004, available at http://cisgw3.law.pace.edu/cases/040630g1.html. Both Professor Ferrari and the Bundesgerichtshof, in the decision just cited, suggest that another burden of proof principle found among the general principles of the Convention (and thus under Article 7(2) applicable to fill the burden of proof "gap") is the *Beweisnähe* or "proof proximity" principle under relieves a party of an evidentiary burden it would normally bear if the facts at issue are, as described by Professor Ferrari, "exclusively in [the other] party's sphere of responsibility and . . . therefore are, at least theoretically, better known to that party." Ferrari, "Burden of Proof," 6–7. It is on this point – not on the question of whether the rule/exception burden of proof principle should apply under the CISG – where differences in views on the source of burden of proof principles under the CISG really matter. According to the view that *Beweisnähe* is a general principle of the CISG, all courts would have to apply that principle in litigation governed by the CISG. I have argued, on the other hand, that not only is there scant (if any) evidence of the principle in the provisions of the CISG, but also the principle makes little sense and would not work in a jurisdiction, like the United States, that depends on pretrial discovery to enable a party acquire information and evidence in the possession of the other party. Flechtner, "Selected Issues," 105. This point in fact illustrates how burden of proof rules are often a product of and are "embedded" in particular procedural systems, which in turn demonstrates why the drafters of the CISG did not in general intend to address burden of proof questions. Id. That is why I believe the CISG should not be distorted to reach an issue – burden of proof – that it was never meant to cover.

[87] Ferrari, "Burden of Proof," 5.

Under the rule and exception principle, the seller rather than the buyer should bear the burden of proof under Article 39 that the buyer failed to give notice that was adequate and timely. Although this position has been explicitly rejected in major commentaries,[88] Article 39 should be viewed as an exception to the general rule that sellers are liable to buyers for delivering nonconforming goods. In other words, the general rule of the CISG is that sellers are liable for delivering nonconforming goods, and the buyer – the beneficiary of this general rule, and the party who will invoke it when claiming remedies for nonconforming goods – has the burden of proving such lack of conformity. But the general rule is subject to the exception that sellers are liable for delivering nonconforming goods *except where the buyer has failed to meet the notice requirements of Article 39*. It is sellers, not buyers, who are the beneficiaries of and who invoke the exception provided in Article 39. Thus, it is sellers, not buyers, who, under the rule and exception principle, should bear the burden of proving that the required notice was not given.

Placing the burden of proof on sellers with respect to Article 39 notice will have little impact on the actual production and presentation of evidence. Sellers will present evidence of the time and content of the notice they received, or evidence (testimony, backed up by a lack of anything in the seller's records) that they had not received any notice. If buyers claim that they sent notice even though the seller did not receive it, or that their notice was delayed in transmission, the buyers would be invoking Article 27, which provides that properly dispatched notice is effective even if delayed or lost in transmission, and would have the burden to prove their entitlement to this rule.

The real impact of allocating to sellers the burden of proving that the buyer failed to give the required notice is that this approach reframes the Article 39 issue in a way that more accurately captures the proper function of the provision. If the buyer bears the burden of proving that the goods the seller delivered were nonconforming and that the buyer gave proper notice of the lack of conformity, the questions will always be: "Why didn't the buyer give notice earlier?" and "Why didn't the buyer describe the lack of conformity more fully?" Placing the burden of proof on the buyer amounts to a presumption that the buyer has not given adequate notice – a presumption that the buyer must overcome. In other words, under this approach, when in doubt, the presumption is that the buyer failed to meet its notice obligations, and thus, even if the buyer can meet its burden of proving that the goods were nonconforming, the seller escapes liability for its breach – without having to show that the inadequacies in the buyer's notice caused the seller any harm.

Placing the burden on the seller to prove buyer's failure to give adequate notice, in contrast, amounts to a presumption that the buyer has fulfilled its notice requirements, and invites the following question: "Please explain, seller, why, even if the buyer is able to prove that the goods were nonconforming, the buyer's notice should deprive the buyer of any remedies for the lack of conformity?" This way of framing the issue requires the seller to come forward with reasons why a delay in notice, or the notice's lack of details about the nonconformity, should insulate the seller from liability for a breach that the buyer can prove. In other words, placing the burden of proof under Article 39 on the

---

[88] See, e.g., Stefan Kröll, "Article 39" ¶ 124, in Kröll, Mistelis & Perales Viscasillas, Commentary at 624 ("An orderly notice constitutes a requirement of the buyer's claims for non-conforming goods. It is not, as the reference to the loss of the buyer's right seems to indicate, a restriction of the seller's liability for which the seller would bear the burden of proof").

seller requires the seller to show that inadequacies in the buyer's notice had (or probably had) some actual negative impact, or else the seller cannot claim immunity from the consequences of a breach that the buyer can prove actually occurred.

This way of framing the Article 39 issue is preferable to the current approach, which places the burden on the buyer to prove that it gave proper notice under Article 39, and thus treats notice as part of the buyer's prima facie case, equivalent to the requirement that the buyer must prove a breach by the seller.[89] The current approach elevates the buyer's secondary, instrumental duty to give notice of lack of conformity into a role and an importance equal to the seller's primary obligation to deliver conforming goods.[90] The inflation of the significance of the buyer's obligation to give notice – treating it on par with the seller's basic sales obligation of delivering conforming goods – leads to unjust results.

In the "used shoes" case,[91] goods delivered to the Ugandan buyer were indisputably nonconforming; indeed, the goods were so far below the "class one" and "class two" standards required under the contract that Ugandan authorities recommended that the buyer destroy the goods because of their "bad and unhygienic condition," which rendered them "unfit for usage." The buyer not only derived no benefit from the goods, the buyer incurred additional costs to dispose of them. When the buyer sought a refund of the purchase price, however, a German court – which found the goods were nonconforming and that the lack of conformity constituted a fundamental breach of contract – held that the buyer had lost its right to rely on the lack of conformity because it had not examined the goods at Mombassa Kenya, the place of delivery designated by the F.O.B. term in the contract. It did not matter to the court that the buyer would have had to pay for an employee to travel to Mombassa, in order to examine the goods, or that such examination might have triggered liability for Kenyan customs duties. And it did not matter that there was no evidence that the delay in the buyer's notice of lack of conformity – which the buyer gave a little more than three weeks after the seller transferred the bill of lading to the buyer following the goods' arrival in Mombassa (but only one day after the goods were delivered to the buyer in Uganda) – had caused the seller any prejudice. This is, in my view, "a truly stunning injustice."[92] This is only a correct decision if the buyer's obligation to give notice is the fundamental duty posited by the current prevailing approach to Article 39: then the notice obligation is equal or superior in importance to the seller's more basic obligation to deliver conforming goods. Of course, the seller was in breach by delivering goods that were worth less than nothing. Nonetheless, the court decision irrationally posits that by waiting a little over three weeks to give notice, the buyer's default was at least as serious even if the delay caused the seller no harm. The buyer's neglect of its notice obligations, in the court's view, meant it deserved to lose

---

[89] See id. ("An orderly notice constitutes a requirement of the buyer's claims for non-conforming goods. It is not, as the reference to the loss of the buyer's right seems to indicate, a restriction of the seller's liability for which the seller would bear the burden of proof.")

[90] Harry M. Flechtner, "Buyer's Obligation to Give Notice of Lack of Conformity (Articles 38, 39, 40 and 44)," in *The Draft UNCITRAL Digest and Beyond: Cases, Analysis and Unresolved Issues in the U.N. Sales Convention* (Papers of the Pittsburgh Conference Organized by the Center for International Legal Education) (ed. Franco Ferrari, Harry Flechtner, and Ronald Brand) (2004), 377, 385–6.

[91] Landgericht Frankfurt, Germany, April 11, 2005, CLOUT case No. 775, available at http://cisgw3.law. pace.edu/cases/050411g1.html. For a more extended discussion of this decision, see Flechtner, *Funky Mussels*, at 1 ff.

[92] Flechtner, *Funky Mussels*, at 24.

the entire purchase price – and more.[93] This extreme valorization of the buyer's notice obligation is both unjust and a distortion of the system of party rights and obligations established by the CISG.

There is other evidence in the case law of the improperly elevated importance accorded the Article 39 notice requirement. The updated UNCITRAL CISG Digest shows a surprising disparity in the number of newer decisions that addressed notice of lack of conformity as opposed to lack of conformity itself. In the case law reviewed for the Digest, there were approximately 25% more new Article 39 decisions than there were Article 35 decisions, even though the latter provision deals with a far more basic, significant, and complex obligation than that in Article 39. One reason for this is the severe sanction imposed if a buyer fails to meet its Article 39 notice obligations – loss of all remedies for a lack of conformity – except in the extremely rare event the buyer can claim, under Article 44, a "reasonable excuse" for its failure to give proper notice (in which case some of the buyer's remedies are retained). The severe consequences imposed by Article 39 for a buyer's failure to provide the required notice gives a seller who has been accused of delivering nonconforming goods a strong incentive to challenge the sufficiency of the buyer's notice, even where the seller's argument is a weak one.[94] The strict notice standard, promoted by the misallocation of the burden of proof under Article 39, encourages such behavior.

Another factor that has contributed to the overemphasis on Article 39 in CISG litigation is that judges or arbitrators who are skeptical of a buyer's claim that delivered goods were nonconforming may choose to avoid the factually complex, difficult, and messy determination that the goods were in fact conforming. Instead, they simply find that that buyer loses because its notice was too late or not specific enough. This resolution also means that the decision maker need not suggest that the buyer's claim misrepresented the quality of the delivered goods.[95] Decisions that take an overly strict approach to the timing or content requirements of Article 39 in order to take the "easy way out," unfortunately, create precedent applicable in cases where the seller clearly did deliver nonconforming goods.[96] Nonetheless, decision makers are particularly tempted to use inadequate Article 39 notice as a pretext for dismissing the buyer's claim where there actually has been some delay in the buyer's notice. The decision maker may see the delay in giving notice as raising suspicions about the buyer's claim of lack of conformity. Asking why the buyer delayed complaining if the goods were indeed nonconforming is a perfectly legitimate inquiry for purposes of determining lack of conformity under Article 35. But if the buyer can overcome suspicions raised by a delay in its notice and carry its burden of proving that the goods were nonconforming, it should not be denied its rights under the CISG. In particular, suspicions about the buyer's claim that the goods lacked conformity should play no part in determining whether notice of lack of conformity was given within a reasonable time as required by Article 39. It makes no sense for a decision

[93] This author finds it difficult to reconcile Article 40 with the view that the Article 39 notice obligation creates such a fundamental buyer duty that failure to satisfy the notice requirement should deprive the buyer of its right to complain about a lack of conformity even if the deficiencies in the buyer's notice did not cause the seller any prejudice. Why would breach of the fundamental notice duty be excused, as it is under Article 40, just because the seller knew about the lack of conformity?

[94] See Flechtner, "Buyer's Obligation to Give Notice," 378–9.

[95] Id., 382–5.

[96] Id., 383.

maker to find that a buyer proved the goods were nonconforming, but that suspicions about its claim of nonconformity justify a finding that notice was late.

The approach to Article 39 advocated here – recognizing that Article 39 creates an exception to the usual rule that a breaching seller is liable for delivering nonconforming goods, and placing the burden of proof under Article 39 (under the "rule and exception principle") on the party claiming the benefit of that exception (seller) – would help correct the current distorted emphasis on and the resulting overly strict construction of Article 39. Unfortunately, the prevailing approach is unlikely to change, as it is deeply entrenched in the large group of existing decisions and is supported by prominent commentators. It remains a mystery why, absent a much clearer mandate in the text of Article 39, a breach by a seller of its core substantive obligation to deliver conforming goods – a breach that causes the buyer real and significant damage – should be completely excused by the buyer's failure to comply with a secondary, instrumental, procedural notice obligation, absent at least some proof by the seller that it has been prejudiced in some way by such noncompliance.

VI. Conclusion

This chapter, reviewing the decisions on Articles 35, 38, and 39 surveyed in the 2012 update of the UNCITRAL CISG Case Law Digest (which encompasses the last ten years of jurisprudence) I hope adds to the greater understanding of the CISG's definition of conformity of goods and of its requirement that the buyer notify the seller of a claimed lack of conformity. The cases of the last ten years address many challenging, important, and interesting issues; as a result, they provide rich material for lawyers litigating questions under those provisions, and for commentators analyzing them. Unfortunately, those decisions tend to confirm an exaggerated conception of the role and importance of the buyer's notice obligations under Article 39. This prevailing view encourages an overly strict interpretation of those obligations. It would be helpful in correcting this distortion to recognize that Article 39 creates an exception to the primary principle that the seller is liable for delivering nonconforming goods, and to accept the burden of proof consequences that flow from that recognition. Under the "rule and exception" approach, the seller should bear the burden of proving that the buyer failed to meet its Article 39 notice obligation. This would be a significant step in putting the interpretation of the CISG's notice rules on a track that is more "international," and that more effectively encourages good faith in international trade, as mandated by CISG Article 7(1).

15 Interpreting Fundamental Breach

Aneta Spaic

I. The CISG in Context

The *lex mercatoria*, the body of rules created by merchants during the Middle Ages, was widely recognized as the first unified international sales law.[1] However, in the twentieth century, as international trade expanded, the complexity of private international law rules began to be seen as a hindrance to such trade.[2] The application of national laws to international contracts created legal uncertainty because of the unpredictable conflicts of law provisions, especially in novel situations.[3] To help eliminate the uncertainty of conflicts between national laws, a search for a uniform text[4] began in the early twentieth century with its culmination in the UN Convention on Contracts for the International Sale of Goods (CISG).[5] However, provisions of international laws are not uniformly interpreted nor uniformly applied in different countries. Therefore, the successful unification of international sales law cannot be accomplished simply through the adoption and ratification of a uniform text. It is thus necessary for contracting states to uniformly apply these international sales law rules.[6] The basic methodology to achieve effective uniformity is through *autonomous interpretation* of CISG rules.[7]

---

[1] See Mirko Vasiljevic, *Trgovinsko pravo* (Belgrade, 2006), 9. The concept of uniformity was first introduced as a legal concept by Professor Ernst Rabel in 1929. This eventually led UNIDROIT to sponsor the enactment of two Hague Conventions on sales law in 1963, but these were largely unsuccessful. Uniformity in textual law was finally achieved in 1980 when the UN Convention on Contracts for the International Sale of Goods (CISG) entered into force in 1988.

[2] Mihailo Kanstantinovic, *Prethodne napomene, Obligacije i ugovori, Skica za Zakonik o obligacijama i ugovorima* (Belgrade 1996), 34 ("The existence of the different national laws, at the same time, preclude international commerce").

[3] See Jelena Perovic, *Bitna povreda ugovora, Medjunarodna prodaja robe* (Belgrade, 2004), 17.

[4] UNCITRAL defines uniformity as "that which removes barriers in international trade." CISG, Preamble.

[5] Vladimir Kapor, *Unifikacija pravila medjunarodnog robnog prometa* (Novi Sad, 1976), 11. "The basic instruments of unification of law of international sale of goods [include] model-laws, among them the most important is United Nations Convention on the Contracts for International Sale of Goods, general conditions on trade, practice established between contractual parties, international commercial customs, and the UNIDROIT Principles of International Commercial Contracts and Principles of European Contract Law."

[6] Sieg Eiselen, "Electronic Commerce and the UN Convention on Contracts for the International Sale of Goods (CISG) 1980," 6 *Edinburg L. Rev.* 21, 21–46 (1999).

[7] Camilla Baasch Andersen, "Furthering the Uniform Application of the CISG: Sources of Law on the Internet," 10 *Pace Int'l L. Rev.* 403 (1998). See also Camilla Baasch Andersen, *Uniform Application of the International Sales Law: Understanding Uniformity, the Global Jurisconsultorium and Examination and Notification Provisions of the CISG* (Kluwer Law International, 2007), 242.

The most relevant, and at the same time the most controversial, method of obtaining uniformity of interpretation is the use of foreign case law. Often uniformity in application[8] is possible through the use of traditional methods of legal interpretation, such as the use of legal doctrine, *travaux préparatoires*, and plain meaning interpretation. However, given its international dimension, reviewing foreign CISG case law offers the best option for ensuring uniformity of application. Thus, its terms, concepts, and principles must be interpreted autonomously from traditional, nation-biased meanings. Instead, the terms of the CISG should be first interpreted based on its general principles and from within its "four corners," generally through analogized interpretation of a rule from interpretations of other rules found in the CISG.[9] Domestic laws interpreting the same terms or rules must be ignored.[10] This chapter will argue that substantive uniformity of interpretation can be achieved through the use of interpretative aids, as well as the application of a uniform method of interpretation based on comparative analysis of case law, legal doctrine, *travaux préparatoires*, and plain meaning.[11] The importance of autonomous interpretation is due to the fact that the same legal concept may have different meanings in different national legal systems and that these differences are part of the *travaux préparatoires* of the CISG.[12]

II. Establishment of Precedents in International Law

In areas of law with international dimensions (private and public law), case law is becoming the more relevant and decisive legal source of interpretation. Unfortunately, case law is often not certain due to the diversity of methodological approaches, and resulting divergent interpretations, of various national courts. Before analyzing the utility of case law or precedent in the context of the CISG, a brief discussion on the varying roles of case law in the common and civil legal systems is in order. The different perceptions of common and civil law jurisdictions of CISG case law, as well as how these systems resolve conflicting CISG precedent, must be understood in order to achieve the desired goal of uniformity in interpretation and application. The common law system is based on

---

[8] John Felemegas, "The United Nations Convention on Contracts for the International Sale of Goods: Article 7 and Uniform Interpretation," 94, available at http://cisgw3.law.pace.edu/cisg/biblio/felemegas .html.

[9] Bruno Zeller, "Four-Corners: The Methodology for Interpretation and Application of the UN Convention on Contracts for the International Sale of Goods" (May 2003), available at http://www.cisg.law.pace.edu/ cisg/biblio/4corners.html.

[10] John Felemegas, "The United Nations Convention," 93. Also, traditional methods of interpreting law have been supplemented by new techniques that take into account the complex dynamics resulting from current globalization of both business and legal transactions. See Miroljub Simić, Srđan Đorđević, and Dejan Matić, "Uvod u pravo," Univerzitet u Kragujevcu Pravni fakultet (2009), 369. See also Slobodan Blagojević, "Uvod u pravo, Službeni," RCG 2003, 285.

[11] One way of ensuring greater uniformity would be through the establishment of an international appellate tribunal. John Honnold noted that the creation of an effective international tribunal among members of the global community would be a long and tenuous process.

[12] For example, the CISG concept of fundamental breach has different interpretations under common and civil laws. Despite the fact that the CISG concept of fundamental breach was created by combining elements of common law theory of warranty, as well as Swiss theory on tort liability, the CISG fundamental breach was intended as an international legal concept separate distinct from the two legal systems.

the doctrine of legal precedents.[13] Precedent in such a system relates to the mandatory authority of a decision of a higher court over lower courts (within the higher court's geographic jurisdiction) when deciding on the same or similar facts (*ratio legis*).[14]

In approaching uniformity in interpreting the CISG and creating a "supranational *stare decisis,*"[15] two main issues must be addressed in national legal systems. First, judges prefer to apply local court decisions – a phenomenon known as *"chauvinisme judiciaire"* – due to their uneasiness, inability, or lack of motivation in learning and interpreting foreign law.[16] Furthermore, when interpreting the CISG and deciding on a CISG case, a local judge would prefer to follow a local court decision interpreting CISG instead of a better-reasoned court decision rendered by a foreign court.[17]

This first issue is primarily an issue of education or a lack thereof. Legal academe must take a leading role in the training and education of law students on the CISG and the differences between national legal systems. Judges must also be educated and trained in the CISG as applicable law and be able to research CISG case law. Prior lack of access to foreign CISG decisions has been effectively addressed by the creation of three electronic databases – CISG Pace Law School's Database (http://www.cisg.law.pace.edu), UNCITRAL's CLOUT database (http://www.uncitral.org/uncitral/en/case-law.html), and UNIDROIT's UNILEX database (http://www.unilex.info).[18] Thus, the initial reluctance of national courts to adopt or use foreign court decisions interpreting the CISG due to perceived lack of access to these foreign decisions has been remedied.

The importance of these databases to better international understanding of the CISG can be seen in their increased usage rates. For example, elaborating on how often those databases are being used, Professor Kritzer, the founder of the Pace CISG Database, noted that by 1999, the database averaged 100,000 Internet hits per month. As of February 2007, the average was 50,000 hits per day. It is also notable that usage of the Database has come from "persons located in 160 countries or more." In 2011, the Database was receiving more than 100,000 hits per day.[19]

---

[13] Budimir Košutić, *Uvod u pravo, Službeni glasnik i Pravni fakultet* (Belgrade, 2007), 143 (*stare decisis et non quieta moveré* – "Maintain what has been decided and do not alter that which has been established").

[14] The part of the decision that is considered binding on lower courts is called *ratio decidendi* (English law) or the reason for decision, *holding* (American law).

[15] See Larry A. DiMatteo, "The CISG and the Presumption of Enforceability: Unintended Contractual Liability in International Business Dealings," 22 *Yale J. Int'l L.* 111, 133 (1997).

[16] For example, see the judgment of Lord Diplock in Fothergill (1981) A.C. 251 (Eng. H.L.); 3 W.L.R. 209, 225 (H.L. 1980).

[17] For example, in the interpretation of Article 31 of the *Geneva Convention on Bills of Exchange*, June 7, 1930, 143 *L.N.T.S.* 257, in cross-border cases, French courts chose to follow the French interpretation (*Hocke v. Schnubel*, (Cass. Comm.), March 4, 1963). See note by B. Goldman, *Journal du droit international* 807 (1964), while German courts have followed a different path, applying choice of law rules, as if different interpretations of a uniform act were equal to different substantive norms – BGH October 29, 1962: E. von Caemmerer, 2 *Internationale Rechtssprechung zum Genfer einheitliche Wechsel- und Scheckrecht* (Tübingen, 1967).

[18] See Michael Joachim Bonell, "Introduction to the Convention," in *Commentary on the International Sales Law: The 1980 Vienna Convention* (ed. Cesare Massimo Bianca and Michael Joachim Bonell) (Milan: Giuffre, 1987), 1–20, 3, available at http://cisg.law.pace.edu/cisg/biblio/bonell-bbintro.html and http://cisgw3.law.pace.edu/cisg/text/caseschedule.html.

[19] See http://www.cisg.law.pace.edu/cisg/Albert_Kritzer.html.

Second, scholars and practitioners have analyzed the dilemma of national courts on whether to apply bad precedent just to ensure that CISG is uniformly applied. Another important issue faced by national courts is the existence of conflicting interpretations among different contracting states. The forum court is thus faced with the dilemma of providing its own "autonomous interpretation" of the CISG, which may or may not be an adoption of one of the conflicting interpretations. The interpreter is faced with the decision of either interpreting the CISG "autonomously" or making a choice between the different "national" interpretations.

The voluntary use of decisions of other state courts in applying the American Uniform Commercial Code (UCC) provides an analogy for the use of foreign case decisions applying the CISG. Professor Flechtner noted that: "Article 7(1) of the CISG properly understood . . . requires a process or an approach not unlike the treatment of . . . interpretations of the CISG from outside one's own legal culture – an approach not unlike the treatment U.S. courts accord decisions of other U.S. jurisdictions when applying the Uniform Commercial Code."[20] Professor Kritzer explains that unlike the mandatory *stare decisis*, where decisions from a higher court in a given jurisdiction must be followed, while court decisions from another state interpreting the UCC are merely persuasive. Albert Kritzer explains the role of precedent in UCC cases as follows:

> We have fifty independent sales law jurisdictions. Forty-nine of our states have adopted fairly uniform versions of our Uniform Commercial Code (UCC). If I am pleading a UCC case before the courts of my state, New York, the only prior UCC decisions that have *stare decisis* is a UCC decision handed down by a higher New York court. Thus, UCC decisions handed down by the courts of the state of New Jersey or by the courts of the state of Montana, for example, are not *stare decisis* in the state of New York even though the New Jersey or Montana courts are dealing with precisely [the] same provision of the same statute.
>
> What happens is, if I am pleading a UCC case in New York and I have a New Jersey or Montana court ruling on the UCC that favors my client, I cite it in my brief so that the New York judge may consider it. If she agrees with the case, she will cite it to support her opinion. If she disagrees with the case, she will usually also cite it in her opinion and explain why she disagrees with it. This is a consideration of precedent but it is not a *stare decisis* consideration, as the New Jersey or Montana rulings are not, repeat not, *stare decisis* in New York.

On the other hand, in civil law, countries that do not provide a similar system of treatment or consideration of already existing decisions, the role and the significance of case law are of less importance. In some countries, such as Montenegro, the prevailing attitude toward legal precedents is that existing court decisions may be of *de facto* use, but not formally cited sources of law. Although Montenegro is a signatory to the CISG, there is only one national case decision involving the CISG. This is most likely due to the fact that judges are not trained to apply or interpret the CISG. Hence, they resort to domestic law concepts when interpreting a uniform international law such as the CISG.

---

[20] Harry M. Flechtner, "Several Texts of the CISG in a Decentralized System: Observations on Translations, Reservations and Other Challenges to the Uniformity Principle in Article 7(1)," 17 *J. of Law and Commerce* (1998) 187.

III. Fundamental Breach and Remedies under the CISG

This part briefly reviews the concept of fundamental breach by focusing on the roles of detriment and foreseeability in its determination. It then summarizes the CISG's remedial scheme and the role of fundamental breach in determining the relevant remedies to be applied.

A. *Concept of the Fundamental Breach*

The concept of fundamental breach in the drafting of the CISG was a product of common and civil law thinking.[21] Fundamental breach, a controversial and ambiguous concept, plays a substantial role in the remedial system of the CISG. The definition of fundamental breach of contract contains vague terms, such as "detriment," "substantially deprive," and "reasonable expectation." Article 25 of the CISG provides that a breach is fundamental if "it results in such detriment to the other party as substantially to deprive him of what he is entitled to expect under the contract, unless the party in breach did not foresee and a reasonable person of the same kind in the same circumstances would not have foreseen such result." The CISG's definition of fundamental breach, therefore, requires that the breach of contract cause a detriment that substantially deprives the contracting party of what is reasonably expected from the contract. Second, liability for that detriment is conditional, allowing the contracting party who committed the breach to prevent termination of the contract if he or she proves that such a result could not have reasonably been foreseen at the time of contract formation. The first part of the definition refers to the injured party and the second part refers to the breaching party.[22]

1. Detriment

The existence of fundamental breach of contract requires that the injured party suffered detriment that substantially deprives him or her of what is reasonably expected from the contract. The CISG fails to provide a definition or examples as to what constitutes detriment; it can be surmised that detriment assumes all (current and potential) negative consequences of the breach. It includes the actual injury, loss, damage (monetary harm), and damage caused by harming the activities of the injured party (interference with other activities).[23] The question remains as to what is considered to be

---

[21] Its origins in English law can be traced to the doctrine of "substantial violation [or substantial performance]." Because of the terminological correspondence between the English concept of fundamental breach and the CISG concept, the English doctrine has been falsely identified as the precursor of the CISG doctrine. The common law legal system concerning the obligations of the parties is divided into conditions and guarantees or warranties. Violation of the relevant provisions of the contract conditions authorizes the injured party to seek termination of the contract, and violation of the guarantees gives to the injured party the right to compensation and not termination of the contract. See M. Vasiljevic, *Trgovinsko pravo*. See Nebojsa Jovanovic, *The Relevant Differences in English and Serbian Contract Law* (Belgrade, 2008), 79.

[22] Andrew Babiak, "Defining Fundamental Breach under the United Nations Convention on Contracts for the International Sale of Goods," 6 *Temple Int'l & Comp. L.J.* 113, (1992), available at http://cisgw3.law.pace.edu/cisg/biblio/babiak.html.

[23] Frans J.A. van der Velden, "The Law of international Sales: The Hague Conventions 1964 and the UNCITRAL Uniform Sales Code 1980 – Some Main Items Compared," in *Hague-Zagreb Essays* (ed. Voskuil and Wade) (1983), 64–5 ("detriment need not be real and involve actual loss, nor does it necessarily refer to material disadvantage to the party suffering it, but means a legal detriment as distinguished from

"substantial" deprivation. The terminology of Article 25 indicates the criterion is not the degree of damage, but the importance of the underlying interests, the obligations under the contract, and the resulting consequences for the injured party. Therefore, the better interpretation of Article 25 provides that a substantial violation of the contract does not depend on the degree of damage, but whether the parties were deprived of what was reasonably expected. Substantial deprivation must be such that the injured party loses interest in fulfilling the contract, or such that the damaged party cannot be adequately compensated by the payment of damages, repairs, or a price reduction. This requirement of fundamental breach and how it is construed in the earlier discussion is consistent with the basic principle of the Vienna Convention that termination should be the remedy of last resort.[24]

2. Foreseeability

A limitation on the finding of fundamental breach is that the party who committed the breach could not have foreseen the consequences of breach. Foreseeability is determined from the perspective of a reasonable person of the same kind under the same circumstances who could not have foreseen such a result. When the breaching party could not have reasonably predicted the far-reaching consequences, he or she is exempt from liability. The phrase "reasonable person" is inherently ambiguous until defined by the facts of the case. Pursuant to CISG Article 8, when determining the element of "foreseeability," it is necessary to consider the subjective and objective elements relating to the breaching party's state of mind at the time of contract formation. Since evidence of subjective state of mind is often lacking or easily manipulated by a self-serving breaching party, the objective standard is the main approach used in making the foreseeability determination. Thus, if the party in breach was a merchant with special professional knowledge, the relevant inquiry involves examining what a similar expert would have foreseen in the same situation.[25]

B. *The CISG Remedial System*

The purpose and the role of the fundamental breach of contract can be best understood within the context of the remedial system of the CISG, especially in relationship with the remedies of termination and substitute delivery. Fundamental breach of contract is an essential condition for determining the right to terminate a contract or to demand delivery of replacement goods. The fundamental or nonfundamental breach divide provides the

---

a detriment in fact. It has also been defined as giving up something which one had the right to keep, or doing something which one had the right to do").

[24] See CISG, Article 8(3). Clemens Pauly, "The Concept of Fundamental Breach as an International Principle to Create Uniformity of Commercial Law," 19 *J.L. & Commerce* 234 (2000).

[25] Michael Will in Bianca and Bonell, *Commentary*, Article 25, p. 122. One can argue a party's specialized knowledge should not be considered in constructing the reasonable person. The reasonable person would not possess such knowledge. Jelena Perović, *Bitna povreda ugovora, Medjunarodna prodaja robe* (Belgrade, 2004), 115: "It is not acceptable to allow one person's breaching the contract, to hide behind the standard of the reasonable person." This is the mainstream view that the reasonable person is fabricated based on what the party actually knew or should have known. See Larry A. DiMatteo, "The Counterpoise of Contracts: The Reasonable Person Standard and the Subjectivity of Judgment," 48 *So. Carolina L. Rev* 297 (1997).

demarcation line between "hard," strict remedies – termination of contract and substitute delivery – and the use of "soft" remedies, such as compensation and the price reduction remedy.[26]

The nonbreaching party has the right to terminate the contract in the event that the failure of the other party constitutes a fundamental breach (CISG Articles 49 and 64); when the partial failure or lack of conformity is considered fundamental breach of contract (Article 51); if, prior to the date for performance of the contract, it is clear that one of the parties will commit a fundamental breach (Article 72); and if the failure of one party amounts to a fundamental breach of an installment or when a breach of an installment is grounds to conclude that a fundamental breach of contract is likely with respect to future installments (Articles 73(1) and (2)).

The CISG's is a unique system of remedies based on the distinction between fundamental and nonfundamental breach – specifying that termination can be resorted to only in cases of fundamental breach of contract. The key rationale of the system is contract preservation (derived from the principle *pacta sunt servanda*), which attempts to avoid contract termination. As a consequence of this underlying principle, termination will be granted only after exhaustion of other options.

IV. Analysis of CISG Case Law

Extant jurisprudence illustrates the different factors used by courts to determine the different types of breach of contract as well as factors that can be considered to determine whether or not the breach is fundamental for the purpose of the CISG.[27] Due to its practical importance within the CISG's remedial system and its vagueness, the concept of fundamental breach has generated much commentary by scholars and practitioners. However, these theorists have not agreed on the factors that are considered crucial in determining whether the harm was "sufficiently substantial" to constitute a fundamental breach of contract.[28] There is also no consensus as to determining the relevant moment in which the breaching party foresaw or should have foreseen the consequence of the breach.

This part examines seven approaches used in case law in making the determination as to whether a breach amounts to a fundamental breach: (1) strict performance approach, (2) economic loss approach, (3) frustration of purpose approach, (4) remedy-oriented approach, (5) anticipatory breach approach, (6) future performance approach, and (7) offer to cure approach.

A. *Strict Performance Approach*

This approach applies whenever contracting parties explicitly or implicitly agree that in case of breach of certain obligations specified in contract, the other party may terminate

---

[26] Andrew Babiak, "Defining Fundamental Breach," 126.

[27] Robert Koch, "The Concept of Fundamental Breach of Contract under the United Nations Convention on Contracts for the International Sale of Goods (CISG)," 13, available at http://cisgw3.law.pace.edu/cisg/biblio/koch.html.

[28] Existing case law has not determined what moment would be relevant for defining foreseeability. In the most publicized cases in which the court found the existence of fundamental breach, the particular interest of the injured party in the fulfillment of obligations clearly stemmed from elements of the contract.

the contract. Whether a fundamental obligation is a basis for fundamental breach can be determined by an express provision in the contract or from any existing business practices between the parties. In accordance with the principles of *pacta sunt servanda* and *bona fides*, courts often use the strict performance approach. However, the answer may not be obvious under this approach[29]

In the case of *Italdecor S.a.s. v. Yiu's Industries (H.K.) Ltd.*,[30] the court considered time of delivery as an essential term of the contract because of an express stipulation in the contract that delivery was to be made at an exact time. The Italian buyer and Hong Kong seller concluded a contract for the sale of knitted goods, with the following clause precisely defining the conditions for delivery and payment: "Delivery: 3rd December, 1990; Terms of payment: deposit: US $6,000.00; Balance: bank cheque." Before the delivery date, the buyer issued a bank cheque in the amount of the deposit, but the goods were not delivered. After the date for delivery had expired, the buyer canceled the purchase order. The seller replied on 14 December 1990, stating that it would deliver the goods but only after payment of the entire purchase price.

The court held that seller's failure to deliver the goods at the date fixed by the contract – as required by CISG Article 33(a), which states that the "seller must deliver goods if a date is fixed or determinable from the contract, on that date" – entitled the buyer to declare an avoidance of the contract under CISG Articles 45(1) and 49(1). It further held that the cancellation of the purchase order sent by the buyer was equivalent to a notice of avoidance required by CISG Article 26. The court reasoned that the concise text of the delivery clause and its fundamental importance to the buyer, who expected to receive the goods in time for the holiday season (which was made apparent to the seller), made it a fundamental element of contract performance. Therefore, the failure to deliver at the date fixed by the contract amounted to a fundamental breach by the seller.[31]

---

[29] See Spanish paprika case (Landgericht Ellwangen, August 21, 1995, 1 *KfH O* 32/95, available at http://cisgw3.law.pace.edu/cases/950821g2.html); *FCF S.A. v. Adriafil Commerciale S.r.l.t* (Case No. 4C.105/2000, Schweizerisches Bundesgericht Court of Switzerland, September 15, 2000, available at http://cisgw3.law.pace.edu/cisg/wais/db/cases2/000915s2.html); chemical fertilizer case (Arbitral Award No. 8128, the ICC Court of Arbitration, Basel (1995), available at http://cisgw3.law.pace.edu/cases/958128i1.html); *Foliopack AG v. Daniplast S.p.A.* (Case No. 77/89, the Pretura di Parma-Fidenza of Italy, November 24, 1989, available at http://cisgw3.law.pace.edu/cases/891124i3.html); *Italdecor S.a.s. v. Yiu's Industries (H.K.) Ltd.* (Case No. 790, the Corte di Appello di Milano of Italy, March 20, 1998, available at http://cisgw3.law.pace.edu/cases/980320i3.html).

[30] *Italdecor S.a.s. v. Yiu's Industries (H.K.) Ltd.*, Case No. 790, Corte di Appello di Milano of Italy, March 20, 1998, available at http://cisgw3.law.pace.edu/cases/980320i3.html.

[31] The same *ration decidendi* was followed in Foliopack AG v. Daniplast S.p.A., Case No. 77/89, Pretura di Parma–Firenza of Italy, November 11, 1989, available at http://cisgw3.law.pace.edu/cases/891124i3.html). The Italian court held that seller's delay in delivering the goods together and the fact that after two months from the conclusion of the contract the seller had delivered only one third of the goods amounted to a fundamental breach under CISG Article 49(1)(a). This case involved a Swiss buyer who ordered goods (plastic knapsacks, wallets, and bags) from an Italian seller, specifying that the goods shall be delivered within ten to fifteen days. After continued delays, the buyer cancelled the order and demanded refund of the price. The seller admitted that it had handed over the goods to the carrier only after receiving the notice of cancellation from the buyer and that, moreover, the delivery was partial. The buyer refused to accept the late and partial delivery and commenced an action claiming avoidance of the contract, along with a refund of the purchase price with interest and damages. The court held that the buyer was entitled to avoid the contract and to recover the full purchase price.

B. *Economic Loss Approach*

Despite the view noted previously that denies that the amount of the loss suffered is a determining factor in finding fundamental breach, the case law shows that in a significant number of cases the court focused on the degree of economic loss in reaching a decision. The courts determining fundamental breach and the right to terminate the contract consider the relative size of the nonconforming delivery or the amount of expenses needed to redress the consequences of the nonconformity or breach.[32]

In the pressure cooker case, a Portuguese seller and a French buyer entered into a contract for the sale of pressure cookers to be distributed in a French chain of supermarkets.[33] After delivery, some of the cookers had a defect that made their use dangerous. As a result, both the buyer and the distributor brought an action against the seller, claiming termination of contract and damages. The appellate court found the existence of fundamental breach because the number of the defective pressure cookers was substantial, amounting to almost one-third of the total sale.[34]

C. *Frustration of Purpose Approach*

In a significant number of cases,[35] the courts examined the purpose of the contract and whether that purpose had been frustrated. Applying this approach, courts start from the premise that the buyer asked for delivery of specific goods for specific and determined reasons. Thus, the buyer's inability to use the goods in a way stipulated by the contract constitutes a fundamental breach of contract. This approach is closest to the definition of the concept of fundamental breach as set out in CISG Article 25. Using this approach, courts ensure that the nonbreaching party is given the opportunity to get out of a contractual relationship when the purpose of maintaining the contract has ceased to exist. In that case, it is not relevant to assess whether the breach is full or partial nonperformance, whether there has been delay in delivery, or whether there was delivery of nonconforming

---

[32] This approach was applied in the frozen bacon case (Oberlandesgericht Hamm, September 22, 1992, 19 U 97/91 Landgericht Bielefeld, January 18, 1991, 15 O 201/90, available at http://cisgw3.law.pace.edu/cases/920922g1.html); sport clothing case (Landgericht Landshut, April 5, 1995, 54 O 644/94, available at http://cisgw3.law.pace.edu/cases/950405g1.html); *Delchi Carrier SpA v. Rotorex Corp.* (available at http://cisgw3.law.pace.edu/cases/940909u1.html); scaffold fitting case (Court of Arbitration of the International Chamber of Commerce, ICC Arbitration Case No.7531 of 1994, available at http://cisgw3.law.pace.edu/cases/947531i1.html); pressure cooker case (Case No. 2002/18702, Cour d'Appel de Paris of France, 4 July 2004, available at http://cisgw3.law.pace.edu/cases/040604f1.html), and T-13/05 case (Foreign Trade Arbitration Court attached to Serbian Chamber of Commerce, January 5, 2007).

[33] Pressure cooker case, Case No. 2002/18702, Cour d'Appel de Paris of France, April 4, 2004, available at http://cisgw3.law.pace.edu/cases/040604f1.html.

[34] In the T-13/05 case of the Foreign Trade Arbitration Court attached to Serbian Chamber of Commerce, January 5, 2007. The arbitrator rejected the plaintiff's request for substitute delivery of goods. The court held that the fact that eighteen percent of the goods were nonconforming did not amount to a fundamental breach. Vladimir Pavić and Milena Djordjević, *Primjena Bečke konvencije u arbitražnoj praksi Spoljnotrgovinske arbitraže pri Privrednoj komori Srbije* (Pravo i privreda, Belgrade, No. 5–8/2008), 580.

[35] *Medical Marketing International, Inc. v. Internazionale Medico ScientificaS.r.l.* (Civ. A. 90–0380, U.S. District Court, E.D., Louisiana, May 17, 1999, available at http://cisgw3.law.pace.edu/cases/990517u1.html); *Sacovini/M Marrazza v. Les fils de Henri Ramel* (Cour de Cassation, Ire chambre civile, January 23, 1996, available at http://cisgw3.law.pace.edu/cases/960123f1.html); machinery case (Tribunale di Busto Arsizio of Italy, December 13, 2001, available at http://cisgw3.law.pace.edu/cases/011213i3.html).

goods. If the purpose of the contract is no longer viable due to the breach, then the breach is fundamental. However, the nonbreaching party has to show that the consequences of the breach are of such a nature that the suffered damage essentially deprived him or her of what he or she reasonably expected from the contract.[36] This approach does not consider the remedial system of the CISG and the underlying principles of *pacta sunt servanda* and contract preservation.

In the designer clothes case, an Italian seller and a German buyer concluded a contract for the sale of high, quality seasonal women's clothes.[37] A large number of the clothes in the first delivery were of a bad fit and the clothing sizes deviated significantly from the customary scale. The buyer immediately complained about the nonconformity of the goods; at the same time, it informed the seller that it was no longer interested in further deliveries and requested a refund of the advance payment. The court found that the seller committed a fundamental breach of contract that entitled the buyer to avoid the contract. According to the court, although the remedy of avoidance should be the remedy of last resort, in the case at hand, avoidance was justified. The buyer had given timely notice of the nonconformity and provided an expert opinion confirming the seriousness of the defects. As to the objection raised by seller that the buyer had not expressly declared its intention to avoid the contract, the court held that under the CISG no such express declaration is required, it being sufficient that the buyer clearly indicates that it no longer wants to be bound by the contract. The notice of avoidance requirement was met by the buyer's fax stating that it placed the goods at the seller's disposal, that it wanted an immediate refund, and that it would not accept any further deliveries.[38]

D. *Remedy-Oriented Approach*

In cases involving delivery of nonconforming goods, the courts most frequently apply the remedy-oriented approach, following the remedial system of the CISG. This method determines whether it is reasonable for the buyer to retain the goods and to claim damages for the loss suffered. Under this approach, only if it is clear that the injured party cannot compensate the damage or successfully request a price reduction is it possible to resort to termination.[39] This approach applies only in case of nonconformity of goods, as in case of other type of injury this approach cannot be used.[40]

---

[36] Perović, *Bitna povreda ugovora*, 165.

[37] Designer clothes case, Case No. 16 U 77/01, Oberlandesgericht Köln of Germany (November 14, 2002), available at http://cisgw3.law.pace.edu/cases/021004g1.html.

[38] The primary consideration why the court found the existence of fundamental breach is the frustration of the purpose of the contract because the buyer was engaged in retail sales and the goods could not be resold due to the defects.

[39] For these statements of the court, see Oberlandesgericht Köln, Germany, October 14, 2002, available at http://cisgw3.law.pace.edu/cases/021014g1.html ("The buyer shall be authorized to request avoidance only as a last resort"); Landgericht Munich, Germany, February 27, 2002, available at http://cisgw3.law. pace.edu/cases/020227g1.html ("Since restitution as a result of the avoidance of a contract is – as is clearly illustrated by the case at hand – particularly burdensome in the international context, avoidance should only be a remedy of last resort"); Oberster Gerichtshof, Austria, September 7, 2000, available at http://www. cisg.at/8_2200v.htm (mentioning that the avoidance of the contract constitutes an "*ultima ratio*" remedy).

[40] This approach is also applied in the fabrics case (Case No. 6 119/93, the Oberlandesgericht Dusseldorf of Germany, February 10, 1994, available at http://cisgw3.law.pace.edu/cases/940210g2.html); saltwater isolation tank cases (Case No. HG920670, the HandelsgerichtZürich of Switzerland, April 26, 1995, available at http://cisgw3.law.pace.edu/cases/950426s1.html).

This approach was first used in the cobalt-sulfate case decided by the German Supreme Court.[41] A Dutch seller and a German buyer concluded several contracts for the sale of cobalt with specific technical qualities. The buyer declared the contracts avoided on the following grounds: the delivered cobalt was of a lower quality than that agreed to under the contracts, the cobalt was produced in South Africa and not in the UK as indicated in the contracts, and the seller had delivered nonconforming certificates of origin and quality. The seller denied the buyer's right to avoid and brought suit to recover the purchase price. The supreme court held that the buyer had not validly avoided the contracts and awarded the seller the full contract price.

According to the court, in the CISG remedial scheme, the remedy of avoidance for nonconformity of goods represents the last resort in respect to the other remedies available to the nonbreaching party. In the case at hand, the seller's delivery of nonconforming goods did not amount to a fundamental breach of contract. In determining whether the nonconformity is fundamental, it is decisive whether the buyer can make use of the goods or resell them in the ordinary course of business without unreasonable inconvenience. The fact that the buyer might be forced to resell the goods at a lower price is not to be considered in itself an unreasonable difficulty. The court denied the existence of a fundamental breach because the buyer should have proved unreasonable difficulties in trading the nonconforming goods.

The shoes case involved a contract for the sale of a stock of women's shoes.[42] The buyer did not pay part of the price, alleging that the seller had not delivered the goods within the agreed time and that the goods did not conform to the contract. The seller commenced legal action, claiming payment of the balance of the price. The court held that the nonconformity in the goods did not amount to a fundamental breach because the defects did not prevent the buyer from making reasonable use of the goods. The buyer had only alleged that the shoes had "defects" and that they had been made with a material different from that agreed upon by the parties. The buyer, however, failed to prove that the shoes could not be reasonably used otherwise because of these defects.

E. *Anticipatory Breach Approach*

Anticipatory breach approach is used in situations where, prior to the date of performance, one party reasonably believes that the other party will breach the contract in the future.[43] The CISG allows the nonbreaching party to anticipate the breach and leave the contractual relationship in order to minimize its damages.[44] In *Ostroznik Savo v.*

---

[41] Cobalt-sulfate case, Case No. VIII ZR 51/95, Bundesgerichtshof, April 3, 1996.

[42] See shoes case, Case No. 5 U 15/93, the Oberlandesgericht Frankfurt am Main of Germany, January 18, 1994, available at http://cisgw3.law.pace.edu/cases/940118g1.html.

[43] CISG, Article 72 provides:

> If prior to the date for performance of the contract it is clear that one of the parties will commit a fundamental breach of contract, the other party may declare the contract avoided.
>
> If time allows, the party intending to declare the contract avoided must give reasonable notice to the other party in order to permit him to provide adequate assurance of his performance.
>
> The requirements of the preceding paragraph do not apply if the other party has declared that he will not perform his obligations.

[44] This approach was also applied in *Roder Zelt- und Hallenkonstruktionen v. Rosedown Park Pty Ltd and Reginald R Eustace*, 1995 Fed. Ct. Rep., Australia, available at http://cisgw3.law.pace.edu/cases/950428a2.html.

La Faraona soc. coop. a r.l.,[45] the court ruled that the seller's failure to continue to supply the needed quality of goods constituted fundamental breach. Further, there was no need to fix an additional period for performance, as the parties had known from the outset that the seller would not have been in a position to deliver the goods for several months. Similar reasoning was applied in the iron-molybdenum case.[46] The Hamburg Court of Appeals found that the seller committed a fundamental breach when it asked for additional time or delivery beyond the stipulated time in the contract due to ongoing negotiations with its supplier. Such a declaration, the court held, constituted a fundamental breach because it created uncertainty for the buyer as to whether the goods would ever be delivered.

F. *Future Performance Approach*

The Future performance approach is used in contracts that require a series of deliveries. In such cases, the principle of fundamental breach when applied may lead to different results depending on the circumstances of the breach – failure to perform one obligation is not a fundamental breach relating to the contract as a whole or the breach of performance of one or more obligations (for example, nonconforming deliveries on one or more installments of an installment contract) is a fundamental breach of the entire contract.[47] Even though these scenarios relate to future performance, as does the anticipatory breach approach, the anticipatory breach approach relates to situations where fundamental breach of contract has not occurred yet. Under the future performance approach, at least, a substantial part of the obligation has already been breached.[48]

In the barley case,[49] the arbitration body ruled that the seller had the right to declare the contract avoided on the grounds of fundamental breaches in the buyer's payment on installment deliveries. The buyer alleged that the goods were nonconforming and refused to take further deliveries. After fixing an additional time for performance without results, the seller declared the contract avoided and claimed damages and interest. Interestingly, the court first held that the two separate contracts concluded by the parties were to be considered a unitary transaction and represented a contract for the delivery of goods in installments under CISG Article 73(2) CISG – the contracts had been executed on the same day; they provided for the delivery of the same kind of goods in installments, and were subject to similar terms. In the case of a contract for delivery of goods in installments, if one party's failure to perform with respect to any installment gives the other party reasonable grounds to conclude that a fundamental breach will occur with respect to future installments, the party may declare the entire contract avoided. The

[45] *Ostroznik Savo v. La Faraona soc. coop. a r.l.*, Tribunale di Padova – Sez. Este of Italy, January 11, 2005, available at http://cisgw3.law.pace.edu/cases/050111i3.html.
[46] *Roder Zelt- und Hallenkonstruktionen v.Rosedown Park Pty Ltd and Reginald R Eustace*, 1995 Fed. Ct. Rep. Australia, available at http://cisgw3.law.pace.edu/cases/950428a2.html.
[47] CISG, Article 73.
[48] This approach is also applied in the Marlboro case (Oberlandesgericht Frankfurt a.M., September 17, 1991, 5 U 164/90, available at http://cisgw3.law.pace.edu/cases/910917g1.html); Bonaventure jeans (*S.A.R.L. Bri Production Bonaventure v. Société Pan Africa Export*, Grenoble, Chambre Commercial, February 22, 1995, available at http://cisgw3.law.pace.edu/cases/950222f1.html).
[49] Barley case, Arbitral Award S2/97, Schiedsgericht der Börse für Landwirtschaftliche Produkte – Wien, December 10, 1997, available at http://www.unilex.info/case.cfm?pid=1&do=case&id=346&step=Abstract.

court held that if the first two installments were nonconforming, then that would amount to a fundamental breach of the entire contract. The nonconforming deliveries made it highly probable that such a breach would occur with respect to future installments, in the absence of contrary declarations or measures on the part of the seller. However, the arbitral court determined that the goods were not defective and ruled in favor of the seller.[50]

G. *Offer to Cure Approach*

Considering offers to cure the defect of goods is not explicitly provided as part of the definition of the concept of fundamental breach. However, the offer to cure approach can be applied in a limited number of cases where the following conditions are fulfilled: (1) the breaching party is able to cure without unreasonable delay and without causing the buyer unreasonable inconvenience or uncertainty, (2) a nonperforming party subsequently offers full performance, and (3) the cure of the defect would prevent the damaged party from being substantially deprived of what it expected under the contract.

In the acrylic blankets case, the court held that there is no fundamental breach when there is a serious offer to cure the defect.[51] In that case, the buyer refused payment of the purchase price on the grounds that the seller had broken an exclusive distribution agreement and had delivered defective goods. The Spanish manufacturer of the goods offered to make a substitute delivery against payment of the purchase price and was rejected. With regard to the alleged nonconformity of the goods, the court held that, even if proven, such a breach of contract would not be fundamental, because the seller's supplier had offered substituted delivery. The court reasoned that the buyer's right to avoid the contract under CISG Article 49(1)(a) generally prevailed over the seller's right to cure under CISG Article 48(1). However, referring to its underlying purposes, the court held that article 49(1)(a) only prevails if the delivery of nonconforming goods amounted to a fundamental breach. In determining fundamental breach, the court stated that regard must be had not only to the gravity of the breach, but also to the willingness of the seller to cure the defect. Where the seller is willing to make substitute delivery and such delivery would not cause the buyer unreasonable inconvenience even where the nonconformity is of "major significance" does not constitute a fundamental breach.

V. Hybrid Approach: A Proposal

Based on this chapter's analysis of the existing approaches to the determination of fundamental breach, an alternative or hybrid method – that combines the purpose of the

---

[50] Consequently, although the buyer could not rely on Article 73(2) CISG), the seller had the right to declare the two contracts avoided according to Article 64(1)(b) CISG because the buyer had breached its duty to take delivery of the goods, under CISG Article 60, and had expressly refused to accept any other future deliveries. The seller was awarded damages for lost profits.

[51] This approach is applied in: acrylic blankets case (OLG Koblenz, 2 U 31/96, January 31, 1997, available at http://cisgw3.law.pace.edu/cases/970131g1.html); *Marques Roque, Joaquim v. S.A.R.L. Holding Manin Riviegravere* (Cour d'appel de Grenoble, April 26, 1995, available at http://cisgw3.law.pace.edu/cases/950426f1.html); wall tiles case (LG Baden-Baden, August 14, 1991, 4 O 113/90, available at http://cisgw3.law.pace.edu/cases/910814g1.html); furniture case (OLG Oldenburg, February 1, 1995, available at http://cisgw3.law.pace.edu/cases/950201g1.html).

contract approach (whether the aggrieved party has been substantially deprived of what it expected out of the contract) and the remedy-oriented approach (whether the aggrieved party's interests can be protected through remedies short of avoidance) – is best. This hybrid approach includes the broadening of the frustration of purpose test because it most resembles the concept of fundamental breach as enunciated in CISG Article 25, where the breach "results in such detriment to the other party as substantially to deprive him of what he is entitled to expect under the contract."[52] This expansion should be coupled with the avoidance as last resort remedial scheme of the CISG. This approach requires a thorough examination of whether remedies other than avoidance, such as the payment of damages, would provide sufficient protection to the nonbreaching party.

A. *Methodology of the Hybrid Approach*

The new methodology that we propose consists of two phases. Accordingly, only when the conditions from both are cumulatively fulfilled should a court or arbitral tribunal find a fundamental breach and award the avoidance remedy. The first phase requires us to examine whether the purpose of the contract from the perspective of the nonbreaching party has been frustrated by the breach. The second phase examines whether the interests of the aggrieved party in five situations – difficulty in quantifying damages, loss of confidence in future party performance (installment contracts), anticipatory breach, cure fails to prevent frustration of contract, and Article 79 excuse is available – have been substantially damaged or affected as a consequence of the breach. If the two conditions are present, the court should grant the remedy of avoidance.

B. *Stage One: Purpose-Driven Test*

The first stage would consider whether the intended purpose of the contract had been frustrated by the breach. The first stage is purpose driven and, in essence, is a broader version of the frustration of purpose approach. It would not only be applicable to the delivery of nonconforming goods, but also to other cases of nonperformance enumerated in the CISG, such as late delivery or late payment, failure to deliver in full, defect in title, and missing or defective documents. Moreover, it would also apply to anticipated breaches of other obligations that as a whole "frustrate" the aggrieved party's purpose in entering into the contract.

C. *Stage Two: Interest-Driven Test*

The second stage of the hybrid approach examines whether the aggrieved party needs the remedy of avoidance or substitute delivery to be made whole, as opposed to the granting of damages or price reduction. If not, then the court should not declare a fundamental breach. The second stage considers the interests of the aggrieved party, thus, it is interest driven. Based on the analysis of case law and the text of the CISG, avoidance of the contract or request for the substantive delivery should be granted in the

---

[52] German contract law Professor Robert Koch proposed expansion of the remedy-oriented approach without full explanation (Koch, "The Concept of Fundamental Breach of Contract"). Given that his proposal has not been precisely formulated, we believe that our method will further strengthen and broaden it.

following situations. First, in cases where it is difficult to identify, quantify, and prove the damages caused to the nonbreaching party, such as where the court is unable to determine the market price for nonconforming goods or when the injured party has suffered or is likely to suffer damages for breach of business reputation. Second, in cases where the breach reasonably causes a party to lose confidence in the other party's ability to perform, which is often the case in installment contracts. Third, in cases where it is fairly clear that a party will commit a fundamental breach in the future. Fourth, when an offer to cure is not made or when it is impossible for cure to prevent the substantial frustration of the contract. Fifth, when a party is exempted from liability under CISG Article 79.[53]

D. *Application of Hybrid Approach*

The Supreme Court of Germany, in the shoes case,[54] applied the remedy-oriented approach, stating that the buyer did not have the right to avoid the contract despite the delivery of shoes of a different color than those specified in the contract. The rationale given by the court is that the nonconforming goods could have been resold. The application of the frustration of the purpose approach would bring us to a completely different result. The frustration of the purpose approach requires the court to examine whether the breach hindered the buyer's contractual expectations at the time of contract formation as to the disposition of the goods. The breach would have been deemed fundamental if the intent of the buyer was to be able to sell high-quality shoes of a certain color that were in high demand for that selling season.

The hybrid approach would prevent such divergent determinations. The hybrid approach requires an analysis of whether the intended use of the goods has been frustrated because of the breach of contract and an examination of whether an award of damages is a sufficient and adequate remedy for aggrieved party. Applying the hybrid approach to the shoes case would have resulted in a finding that the granting of damages was a sufficient remedy. The result would be different if evidence was provided that the breach resulted or would result in a loss of the goodwill and reputation.

E. *Advantages of Hybrid Approach*

It is clear that different approaches applied by the courts for determining fundamental breach are restricted in scope. For example, the anticipatory breach approach refers to future deliveries, whereas the remedy-oriented approach has been limited to cases of nonconformity of the goods. The hybrid approach combines an analysis of the intended purpose of the contract and the interests of the aggrieved party that is applicable to all situations involving future performance, as well as in the other scenarios discussed in this chapter.

Some further examples are provided here to show how a single hybrid approach would apply to the different fundamental breach scenarios and eliminate the myriad of existing

[53] Koch, "The Concept of Fundamental Breach of Contract." This scheme is a modified version of Koch's suggested approach.
[54] Shoes case, Case No. 5U 15/93, the Oberlandesgericht Frankfurt am Main of Germany, January 18, 1994, available at http://cisgw3.law.pace.edu/cases/020220g1.html.

approaches. In the fabric case,[55] the court applied the remedy-oriented approach focusing on whether the partial delivery of nonconforming goods could be used by the buyer and whether the aggrieved party could be compensated by an award of damages.[56] The hybrid approach would allow the aggrieved party to show that there has been substantial deprivation of what he or she was entitled to expect under the contract and that he or she cannot be adequately compensated by the award of damages or by a price reduction of the price. If the buyer is able to prove these elements, then he or she would be entitled to avoidance.

In *Foliopack v. Danipast*,[57] where the anticipatory breach approach was applied, the court held that there was a fundamental breach of contract. More precisely, in this case, the aggrieved party that was late in fulfilling its contractual obligations was given a time extension for delivery. Two months after payment of the price, however, the buyer was still waiting for two-thirds of the delivery. The court, in accordance with the CISG Article 73, held that the buyer was justified avoiding the contract. Application of the hybrid approach would have produced the same results, because this was a case of substantial deprivation and an offer to cure would not have alleviated the consequences of the delayed delivery. Because the interests of the aggrieved party were not fulfilled nor was there an offer by the breaching party to cure, application of the hybrid approach would have resulted in finding of a fundamental breach.

In sum, a hybrid approach would ensure a higher level of legal certainty in the determination of fundamental breach and the resulting right of avoidance. It is structured to require the parties to anticipate their inability to perform their essential obligations under the contract. The anticipating approach and approach of future performance also require the same response, but they cannot be used when the breach involves a nonconforming delivery. The hybrid approach focuses on two essential principles: contractual purpose and just compensation of the nonbreaching party. This approach incorporates a unified system of remedies provided by the CISG. Due to the different interpretations of fundamental breach of the contract by diverse courts and countries, international sales law has been plagued by legal uncertainty and insecurity. This makes it difficult for contracting parties to foresee whether an anticipated breach would be considered fundamental or whether a fundamental breach has occurred, triggering right of avoidance. In the absence of explicit contractual provisions that stipulate when fundamental breach arises (strict performance approach), the hybrid approach enables the aggrieved party to determine whether a fundamental breach has occurred and the remedies available in case of such breach. The hybrid approach thus contributes to the legal certainty and predictability of legal trade.

---

[55] Fabrics case, Case No. 6 U 119/93, the Oberlandesgericht Dusseldorf of Germany, February 10, 1994, http://cisgw3.law.pace.edu/cases/940210g2.html.

[56] In this case, the buyer stated that part of the delivered goods did not comply with the specifications of the contract, given that design had deviated from the agreed one. The buyer paid only for the part of the delivery that was in conformity with the terms of the contract. The seller filed a lawsuit and demanded full payment. The court decided in favor of the seller and held that the buyer did not have the right to terminate the contract due to the lack of conformity of the part of the delivered goods. The court further held that the buyer failed to prove that the nonconforming part of goods could not be used in the manner defined under contract.

[57] *Foliopack AG v. Daniplast S.p.A*, Case No. 77/89, the Pretura di Parma-Fidenza of Italy, November 24, 1989, available at http://cisgw3.law.pace.edu/cases/891124i3.html.

VI. Conclusion

This chapter reviewed the various approaches used by courts in making fundamental breach determination. Establishing a single approach for determining fundamental breach under CISG Article 25, instead of applying the numerous existing approaches for different types of breaches, would contribute to a greater uniformity in application in this important area of CISG coverage. The hybrid approach presented in this chapter would prevent the contradictory and inconsistent results currently found in CISG case law. This proposed approach would best define a vague concept in the CISG and help resolve the issue of when contract avoidance should be given.

Part IV Remedies and Damages

16 Remedies: Damages, Price Reduction, Avoidance, Mitigation, and Preservation

Ulrich Magnus

I. Introduction

The consequences of breaching a contract are seated at the center of contract law – without remedies there would effectively be no contract law. Remedies are the center of national contract and national sales law, as well as in the CISG. Consequences for breach are, at least partially, why parties perform on their contracts. Equally in the CISG, the regulation of these consequences constitutes a core issue. This chapter reviews those remedies under the CISG that are of most practical importance: damages, avoidance, and price reduction. The remedies of specific performance[1] and the right to suspend one's obligation[2] are treated elsewhere in this book.

The remedies of damages, avoidance, and price reduction can be affected by the conduct of the party entitled to them. Therefore, this chapter will analyze how such conduct may mitigate the remedy. Finally, the duty to preserve goods in one party's possession shall be examined. This special duty is not itself a remedy but can be regarded as a special case of mitigation. However, its violation may give rise to remedies. The goal of this chapter is to provide a survey over the requirements for obtaining remedies, satisfying the duties to mitigate damages and to preserve the goods, as well as to analyze the international practice with respect to them. It shall be asked where problems remain and how they can be solved.

At the outset, it can be stated that, under a broad perspective, the CISG's system of remedies works rather well. The CISG has removed many peculiarities of national laws, for instance the distinction between warranties and conditions in common law or the restrictions of damages under many civil law jurisdictions. Remaining problems under the CISG remedies scheme often lie in the nature of sales transactions and are inevitable. For instance, it is impossible to determine with mathematical precision when a party can unilaterally terminate a contract due to the other party's breach of that contract. It is clear that the slightest breach does not justify the termination of an international sales contract (unless the parties have so agreed).[3] Whatever solution is then chosen,

---

[1] CISG Article 46.

[2] CISG Article 71.

[3] That is even true for the perfect tender rule of §2–601 of the American Uniform Commercial Code (UCC) in which the buyer is entitled to reject the goods if "the goods or the tender of delivery fail in any respect to conform to the contract." Even here is it necessary to determine whether a very small deviation from the contracted standard amounts to a failure allowing rejection. Moreover, §2–612 UCC prescribes a different standard for installment contracts, namely where the breach "substantially impairs the value of

it is unavoidable that flexibility is required to make any remedial scheme work, which requires some vagueness – as to the seriousness of the breach irrespective of whether avoidance requires a serious breach or is only excluded where the breach is of minor or negligible importance. Without flexible terms, such as fundamental breach, it would be impossible to cover the breadth of breach of contract scenarios. Only through the analysis of international case law, on a case-by-case basis, can detailed subrules be recognized for specific situations, and to a remarkable extent this has already happened in the field of CISG remedies.

II. Elements Common to All CISG Remedies

Under the CISG, all remedies have certain basic elements in common: first, they presuppose a breach of a contractual duty. It does not matter whether the duty is specifically agreed by the parties or follows from the text of the CISG or from usages or is made by a judge. Though the breach of a duty is a necessary condition, it is as such not sufficient to entitle the innocent party to a specific remedy. The further requirements vary from remedy to remedy and are discussed in this chapter for each remedy separately.

Second, under the CISG, none of the remedies requires fault of the breaching party. Especially in the area of damages, this is in stark contrast to most civil law jurisdictions, which followed the Roman law tradition to require fault as a basis for claiming damages.[4] Under the CISG, in the common law tradition, a purely objective breach suffices. No subjective element such as intent or negligence is needed for determining breach or its consequences.

Third, despite its system of objective liability, in certain though rare circumstances, the CISG exempts a party from the consequences of its breach. Two different reasons can lead to an exemption from liability: first, if an impediment that hinders correct performance (within a party's sphere of risk) and is beyond the control of that party, then the party is relieved if the impediment was unforeseeable, unavoidable, and cannot be overcome without incurring undue expense (Article 79 CISG).[5] The courts have applied this exemption clause with utmost reluctance. A party is only excused in truly extraordinary circumstances.[6] The second ground of excuse is that the creditor itself caused the debtor's failure to perform (Article 80 CISG). Normally, such conduct is already an impediment in the sense of Article 79(1). Article 80 applies even when this conduct was foreseeable and when the debtor could overcome its consequences. This ground of exemption is warranted under the general principle of good faith (Article 7(1)) and of the broader maxim that no party should profit from its own wrongdoing, such as impeding the other party's performance.

---

that installment," but note the overall contract, then only that installment can be avoided and not future installments. This is closer to the CISG standard.

[4] An example is German law, which adapted its codified law of obligations in 2002 to a wide extent to conform with the CISG still, §280, para. 1 Civil Code (Bürgerliches Gesetzbuch [BGB]), requires fault as precondition for any claim of damages. However, the provision also states that in case of breach of contract the fault of the breaching party is presumed. The party in breach must rebut this presumption if it wants to avoid liability. The threshold for such rebuttal is relatively high, though not as high as in CISG Article 79.

[5] However, peculiarities apply with respect to Article 79 and the remedy of avoidance and price reduction; see later.

[6] See *infra* Part III C.

Fourth, the formal structure of the CISG distinguishes between the remedies of the buyer where the seller has breached the contract (Articles 45 et seq.) and the remedies of the seller in case of the buyer's breach (Articles 61 et seq.). However, the general requirements for damages and avoidance are identical irrespective who breaches the contract. Thus, due to this commonality of the requirements of buyer–seller remedies, most CISG remedies can be viewed as constituting general remedies, which apply to any breach of a CISG contract by either party. On the other hand, price reduction is only provided for where the seller breached the contract by delivering nonconforming goods.[7] It could be argued that this remedy should be available in other situations as well, even where the buyer did not fully perform its obligations so that the seller should be entitled to reduce its performance under the contract.[8] But price reduction is commonly construed as a buyers' remedy. It is difficult, although not entirely impossible, to imagine cases where the *seller* may reduce its performance because the buyer has not fully performed its obligations. However, to develop price reduction into a remedy of general application would overstretch the wording and aims of the CISG. Under the CISG, price reduction is considered a one-sided remedy that is only available to buyers.

Fifth, it must always be kept in mind that the CISG allows the parties to derogate from or vary the effect of any of its provisions (Article 6).[9] The parties are free to regulate remedies for breach of contract in a specific way or to provide for specific mitigation or preservation duties. For this reason, contracts have to be examined and interpreted first to determine if they contain specific provisions dealing with remedies, mitigation, and preservation. The validity of any such variation of CISG provisions depends, however, on the applicable national law.[10] Using CISG interpretive methodology, the application of domestic validity standards should use the CISG as the yardstick against which to measure any possible invalidity.

III. Damages

Under practical aspects, damages are the most relevant and most popular remedy. They are almost always available where a breach has occurred and the other party is almost never exempted from liability. The requirements the claimant must meet are limited in number and often reasonably easy to prove. Uncertainties and restrictions often linked to the remedies of avoidance and specific performance do not play a role in the assessment of damages. To make good the damage caused by a breach will in most cases satisfy the aggrieved party's interest. Moreover, the creditor can combine damages with any other remedy insofar as the other remedy leaves uncompensated losses unsettled.[11] It is the common understanding of the CISG's damages provisions that damages consist of a sum of money[12] and that creditors cannot claim restitution in kind.

---

[7] See CISG Article 50.

[8] See *infra* Part V.

[9] The only express exception is Article 12 CISG, which the parties cannot modify. They can also not derogate from the principle of good faith (CISG Article 7(1)).

[10] See Article 4 lit. b CISG.

[11] See CISG Article 45, para. 2, and Article 61, para. 2.

[12] See the text of CISG Article 74: "Damages for the breach of contract by one party consist of a sum equal to the loss"; see also Peter Schlechtriem and Petra Butler, *UN Law on International Sales: The UN Convention on the International Sale of Goods* (Springer: Berlin, Heidelberg 2009), para. 286; John

A. *The Concept*

The CISG's concept of damages is mainly modeled after the common law. Articles 74, 75, and 76 resemble the well-known formulations of the seminal English decision in *Hadley v. Baxendale*.[13] Despite this background, English decisions on contractual damages cannot simply be applied to interpret the CISG provisions on damages. This would run counter to the aim of uniform interpretation of the CISG. This is especially true considering that the foreseeability principle enunciated in *Hadley v. Baxendale* had its origin in Article 1150 of the French Civil Code.[14] That 1804 French Civil Code provision as formulated required that in order to recover losses, the losses must have been foreseeable at the time of conclusion of the contract. The underlying idea of this principle is evident and convincing: when concluding a contract, a party should be able to calculate and compare the risk linked with a breach of contract with the expected profit of the contract. For the CISG, however, autonomous interpretations must be found for its damages rules and the criteria by which they are to be applied. Decisions in English and French law of contractual damages may perhaps give some inspiring interpretative guidance, but by no means do they provide precedents.

B. *Requirements*

1. Breach of Obligation

The CISG provides a basis for a claim for damages in Article 45(1)(b) for the buyer and in Article 61(1)(b) for the seller. The CISG's regulation of damages is found in Articles 74 through 77. As mentioned previously, a breach of contract is an indispensable condition for liability in damages. It does not matter which duty has been breached ("*any* of his obligations under the contract or the Convention"),[15] including violations of additional duties that the parties have agreed on. In addition, breaches of the duties to return the goods after termination of the contract[16] or to preserve the goods[17] may result in damages. Only the breach of duties against the interests of the breaching party,[18] such as the buyer's "duty" to examine the goods and notify the seller of a nonconformity,[19] do not lead to damages (but to the loss of rights by the "breaching" party).

2. Damages

According to Article 74 CISG ("loss, including loss of profit"), the CISG neither provides for nominal or *de minimis* damages – where the aggrieved party suffered no loss

---

Gotanda in *UN Convention on Contracts for the International Sale of Goods (CISG)* (ed. S. Kröll, L. Mistelis, and P. Perales Viscasilllas) (Munich, Oxford: Beck, Hart, Nomos, 2011), Article 74, para. 37; Ulrich Magnus, "Wiener UN-Kaufrecht (CISG)," in *Julius von Staudingers Kommentar zum Bürgerlichen Gesetzbuch mit Einführungsgesetz und Nebengesetzen* (Munich: Sellier, 2005), Article 74, para. 24.

[13] (1854) 9 Exch. 341.

[14] *Hadley v. Baxendale* was inspired by comments in the U.S. textbook of Theodore Sedgwick, *A Treatise on the Measure of Damages*, 2nd ed. (New York: J.S. Voorhies, 1852), who in turn had relied on Article 1150 French Code civil (in its Louisiana version).

[15] See Articles 45(1) and 61(1) (emphasis added).

[16] See Article 81, para. 2.

[17] See Article 85 et seq.

[18] Apparently, only German law has a special legal term for such kinds of duty, namely "Obliegenheit."

[19] See Articles 38 and 39.

at all and damages are a symbolic sum for the violation of a right – nor for punitive or supracompensatory damages. It is the consensus view of international case law and legal writing that the "loss" in the sense of Article 74 can include immaterial or intangible loss, for instance, the loss of good will.[20]

The aim of compensating the damage caused by the breach does also not allow for stripping the gain that the debtor made by its breach. It is the creditor's actual loss that counts and sets the standard for compensation.

3. Duties of the Creditor

In general, damages for the delivery of nonconforming goods or of goods with title defects further require that the buyer fulfill its "duty" to examine the goods and give notice of defects. Without satisfying this precondition or fitting into one of the recognized exceptions to it,[21] no damages claim can be sustained. The creditor must further observe its duty (*Obliegenheit*) to mitigate any loss pursuant to CISG Article 77, to be discussed in Section VI. Failure to mitigate damages prevents the nonbreaching party from collecting the damages that would have been prevented by the mitigation.

C. *Exemption from Liability*

In rare situations, the party in breach is exempted from its liability to compensate for losses resulting from the breach (Article 79). The exemption does not enter automatically and is not to be recognized *ex officio*; the party in breach must invoke and prove it. Although not often granted, the CISG's exemption provision is always theoretically applicable. Because of Article 79(5) it has particular – theoretical – importance for damages claims and is, therefore, discussed here.

1. Impediment

The central prerequisite for exemption is an impediment beyond the debtor's control that it could not reasonably be expected to have taken into account at the time of the conclusion of contract or to have avoided or overcome it or its consequences. This is a high evidentiary threshold that a debtor rarely overcomes. In principle, impediments such as natural catastrophes, acts of war, terror attacks, strikes, or boycotts can result in an exemption; however, only if they were unforeseeable at the conclusion of the contract and if the contract did not expressly or implicitly allocate the risk to the debtor. The general possibility "that something can happen" does not make an event foreseeable. The debtor must have been able to foresee the event and its impact in the way in which it occurred. If, for example, a seller sells next year's crop and the crop is then partly destroyed by flooding, this is no excuse for nondelivery if such flooding is a relatively common occurrence. Only an extraordinary flood that destroyed the whole crop would be unforeseeable and exempt the seller from liability. A further issue is the question of how far the debtor is obliged to overcome the impediment or its

---

[20] See Bundesgericht (Swiss Federal Court [BG]) Schweizerische Zeitschrift für Internationales und Europäisches Recht (SZIER) 1999, 179; contra, see, e.g., Gotanda in *UN Convention*, Article 74, para. 39 (against compensation of immaterial losses) but see, id. at para. 63. (compensation for loss of good will).

[21] See CISG Article 40 or 44.

consequences.[22] In the given example, even if the flood was extraordinary, is the seller expected to buy at higher prices crops from other sources in order to overcome the impediment and its consequences? It is advocated here that such a duty exists, though narrow in scope. The CISG does not oblige the debtor to bear extra burdens where impediments beyond his or her control hinder performance. Only where it is easier for the debtor than for the creditor to overcome the impediment can it be reasonably expected. This expectation corresponds to the duty of cooperation and the commandment of good faith.[23] Where, in the example, the seller can easily find substitute crops at no higher price, then it should be obliged to buy and deliver the substituted goods.

2. Excuse Due to Third-Party Conduct

Where third parties outside the control of the debtor unforeseeably caused the non-performance of the debtor's contract, this may lead to an exemption from liability. For the debtor's own personnel and suppliers, the debtor regularly remains responsible.[24] It is, for instance, no excuse for a seller of vine wax that its supplier changed the mixture of the wax, without notice, so that the wax became dangerous and damaged the vine plants of a buyer of the wax.[25]

3. Hardship

It had been disputed whether Article 79 comprises also cases of hardship, cases where the sale has become an economic burden for one party, in particular because market prices have dramatically changed. In general, each party has to take into account economic risks when concluding a contract and bear the risks allocated to them. This is most evident in the commodities trade characterized by rapidly changing prices. The party disadvantaged by the fluctuation of prices is nevertheless bound by the contract. Only in extreme situations where the economic existence of the debtor is otherwise endangered may an exemption from liability – or, first, rather an adaptation of the contract – be granted. Thus far, the courts have not exempted a party because of economic hardship. An Italian court held that a thirty percent escalation in steel prices did not provide an excuse for a seller's nondelivery. The seller remains obliged to deliver at the agreed price.[26]

4. Exemption from Damages

According to the text of Article 79(5), the excuse applies to damages claims and does not prevent a party from exercising any other of its rights. Excuse, however, also extends

---

[22] See Yesim Atamer, *UN Convention*, supra note 12, Article 79, para. 55.

[23] See CISG Article 7(1); see also CISG Article 80, which recognizes a duty to cooperate; Thomas Neumann, *The Duty to Cooperate in International Sales Law* (Sellier, 2012).

[24] CISG Article 79(2) exempts the contract party from liability only when the party and the third party both meet the requirements of Article 79; see Atamer, *UN Convention*, Article 79, para. 62; Magnus, "Wiener UN-Kaufrecht," Article 79, para. 75.

[25] Bundesgerichtshof (German Federal Court [BGH]) NJW (Neue Juristische Wochenschrift) 1999, 2440.

[26] See Tribunale di Monza, January 14, 1993, Giurisprudenzia italiana 1994 I 145; see also Rechtbank van Koophandel t'Hasselt, May 2, 1995, Rechtskundig Weekblad (1995–6) no. 40, 1378 (price for raspberries had sharply dropped and the buyer unsuccessfully requested an adaptation of the price).

to the remedy of specific performance if performance has become temporarily suspended or rendered impossible. Avoidance and price reduction remain applicable despite the exemption.

5. Period of Exemption and Notice

Unlike other excuse doctrines, Article 79 excuse does not last longer than the period of the impediment. Where, for instance, a hurricane impedes timely delivery, the seller remains obliged to deliver as soon as possible after the hurricane. The buyer cannot request damages for the delay due to the hurricane, but may claim damages for any further delay caused by the seller. Article 79(4) obliges the debtor also to inform the creditor of the impediment and its effect on the debtor's ability to perform so that the creditor can undertake measures to avoid further loss. Failure to give notice is regarded as a breach, which in turn may lead to damages for any loss caused by the lack of notification, unless the failure to give notice is also excused (Article 79(4), sent. 2).

6. Limit of Damages under CISG Article 44

An entirely different limit of damages is encountered in situations covered by Article 44. Where the buyer has disregarded its notice duty under Articles 38, 39, or 43(1), it loses its remedial rights. Yet if the buyer has a reasonable excuse for the failure it remains entitled to damages, except for loss of profits. This provision, which the courts rarely apply, protects the indemnity interest of the buyer but not its expectation interest.

D. *Calculation of Damages*

1. Full Compensation

The general rule on assessing damages is Article 74. The provision prescribes that damages should provide compensation for the full extent of the nonbreaching party's losses (full compensation principle).[27] The aim of damages under the CISG is to put the aggrieved party, through the payment of damages, at the economic position it would have been in had the contract been correctly performed.[28] This also means that damages are not meant to enrich the aggrieved party; eventual benefits caused by the breach must

---

[27] Schlechtriem and Butler, *UN Law*, para. 299.

[28] UNCITRAL Secretariat Commentary, Article 70, para. 3 (of the draft): "the basic philosophy of the action for damages is to place the injured party in the same economic position he would have been in if the contract had been performed"; Victor Knapp, in *Commentary on the International Sales Law* (ed. Massimo Bianca and Joachim Michael Bonell) (Milan: Giuffré, 1987), Article 74, para. 3.1; John Honnold and Harry Flechtner, *Uniform Law for International Sales under the 1980 United Nations Convention*, 4th ed. (The Hague: Kluwer, 2009), para. 403; Ulrich Magnus in Festgabe für Professor Dr. Rolf Herber (Neuwied: Luchterhand 1999) 28; Peter Huber in *Kommentar zum Bürgerlichen Gesetzbuch*, vol. 3, 5th ed. (Munich: Beck, 2008), Article 74, para. 16; Magnus, "Wiener UN-Kaufrecht," Article 74, para. 16; Peter Mankowski in *Münchener Kommentar zum Handelsgesetzbuch*, vol. 6, 2nd ed. (Munich: Beck, 2007), Article 74, para. 8; Ingeborg Schwenzer in *Commentary on the UN Convention on the International Sale of Goods (CISG)*, 3rd ed. (ed. P. Schlechtriem and I. Schwenzer) (Oxford: Oxford University Press, 2010), Article 74, para. 3; see also Christoph Brunner, *UN-Kaufrecht – CISG* (Bern: Stämpfli, 2004), Article 74, para. 5.

be offset against the loss.[29] Such benefit would be, for instance, saved manufacturing costs where the buyer intended to finalize the nondelivered or nonconforming goods.[30] However, the fixed running costs of the creditor's business are not recoverable because these costs would fall due whether or not the contract was breached.[31]

2. Causation and Foreseeability

The loss is the negative consequence that the breach caused, however, limited to what the party in breach foresaw or ought to have foreseen when concluding the contract. Both causation and foreseeability attempt to limit damages in a fair and balanced way. However, both elements are not further defined in the CISG. Causation requires merely that the *conditio sine qua non*-formula is met: the loss would not have occurred but for the breach. If the breach is an omission, there must be a high probability that the loss would not have occurred if the omitted obligation had been fulfilled. The CISG does not recognize other restrictions on finding causation, such as the exclusion of indirect losses.

The primary limit to the payment of compensatory damages is the foreseeability of the loss requirement. Here, the debtor must bear such losses of which it knew, due to special information (generally provided by the creditor) or because it accepted the risk in the contract, as well as the "normal" losses that a reasonable person should have foreseen as the consequence of the breach ("reasonable person standard" found in Article 8, para. 2). For example, a seller contracted for copper who fails to deliver, but knows that copper prices are rising, must foresee and compensate the loss of the buyer who has to buy copper at higher prices from other sources.[32] In essence, the element of foreseeability, if properly interpreted, secures a fair allocation of risk between the contract parties.

For practical purposes, it often suffices to state that the loss is the diminution in market value of, or the costs for restoring, the position the aggrieved party would have been in had the contract been performed and the breach not occurred. Articles 75 and 76 CISG provide for special rules, which allow a kind of abstract calculation of damages. After avoidance of the contract the creditor may claim the difference either between the contract price and the price for a reasonable cover transaction or, without cover, between the contract price and the current market price as damages.

3. Proof and Certainty

Even if a loss was foreseeable, the creditor still must prove the extent of the loss. Although the CISG does not expressly say so and although the question of certainty may be regarded as part of procedural law (law of the *lex fori*), it is a common requirement

---

[29] See also CISG Advisory Council, "Opinion No. 6," (Reporter John Gotanda), available at CISG-online/cisg-ac.

[30] See *Delchi Carrier SpA v. Rotorex Corporation*, 71 F.3d 1024 (2d Cir., 1995) (Delchi Carrier); OLG Hamburg IHR 2001, 19 (21).

[31] Id.

[32] China International Economic and Trade Arbitration Commission (CIETAC), 12.1.1996, CLOUT No. 678.

in most legal systems that the loss and its extent must be reasonably certain, in particular with respect to lost profits.[33]

E. *Problems*

1. Unforeseeable Losses

There are not many cases where the courts held losses to be unforeseeable. An example is a German Federal Court decision that denied repair costs of 78,000 DM as unforeseeable, as the value of the goods was only 63,000 DM.[34] The court held that it was not to be expected that the seller would foresee repair costs that are out of proportion to the value of the bargain. In this case, the buyer also violated its duty to mitigate. Another German court, involving a Turkish seller and a German buyer of half-fabricated goods, held that the Turkish seller could not have foreseen that a delay in delivery would cause the buyer additional production costs due to buyer switching the place for completing the goods from Turkey to Germany because of time constraints. The German company was attempting to recover the higher costs of completing the goods in Germany.[35] The decision would have been different if the seller was informed of the buyer's plans when the contract was concluded.

2. Consequential Damages

"Normal" consequential damages are generally foreseeable. Collection of such damages is supported by the CISG's full compensation principle, and corresponds to the risk allocation envisioned by the CISG. Therefore, a buyer is, for instance, entitled to damages where a "floating center" (a basin filled with salt water so that a person can float on the water) leaks and damages the buyer's house.[36] If, as in this case, the nonconformity of the good is the ground for further damages, two restrictions must be taken into account. First, Article 5 excludes cases from the scope of the CISG where the good or its defect causes bodily harm to a person. In such cases, the national contract or tort law would be applied.[37] Second, in order to be entitled to compensation, the buyer must have fulfilled its duty to notify the seller of the defect, or failure to give notice was excused under Articles 40 or 44.

3. Loss of Business

CISG Article 74 provides expressly that lost profits are recoverable. As mentioned previously, the loss must be proved with sufficient certainty. It can also include the loss of further sales (volume sales), which would have been made had the breach not occurred.

---

[33] *Delchi Carrier.*

[34] BGH NJW 1997, 3311.

[35] Oberlandesgericht (Court of Appeal [OLG]) Bamberg Transportrecht-Internationales Handelsrecht (TranspR-IHR) 2000, 17.

[36] Handelsgericht Zürich SZIER 1996, 51 (the "floating centre" was evidently not used for private purposes).

[37] See Schlechtriem and Butler, *UN Law*, para. 39; contra, OLG Düsseldorf, July 2, 1993, Recht der Internationalen Wirtschaft (RIW) 1993, 845 (applying the CISG, though without any discussion of the problem).

The U.S. decision in *Delchi Carrier SpA v. Rotorex* dealt with such a situation. The buyer could not complete the manufacture of its air conditioners in the spring for the coming summer selling season because the seller had delivered 10,800 nonconforming compressors. With some delay, and after a short break of its production, the buyer was able to secure fitting compressors from another source. The court accepted that, although the buyer finally could produce the full number of air conditioners, it nevertheless lost sales due to the seller's breach – because of the postponed manufacture, the buyer could not fulfill orders to its customers during that time. The sale of air conditioners as a typical summer product meant the buyer could not later make good the lost volume of units that were not available for sale during the important selling period.[38] Under the circumstances in the *Delchi* case, compensation of lost volume was justified.

4. Wasted Expenditures

With compensation of "loss, including loss of profit," Article 74 protects the indemnity interest and the expectation interest of the creditor. International case law on the CISG acknowledges that the reliance interest also should be protected. A creditor is entitled to compensation of such expenditures as it reasonably incurred in reliance on the correct performance of the contract by the other party. If, for instance, the buyer purchased tooling uniquely fitted for its production process that proved to be defective, then it can claim the full costs of the tooling if the tooling cannot be used for other production purposes.[39]

5. Currency Loss

The CISG does not state in which currency the damages should be paid that a debtor owes as compensation or whether a loss in the value of currency falls under Article 74. Generally, the compensation sum is owed in the currency in which the loss was suffered. In most cases, in particular in cases of delayed payment of the price, this currency will be the contract currency. This is the currency on which the parties have explicitly or implicitly agreed or, absent such an agreement, an appropriate currency that would correspond to the parties' practices or to international usage, or in the last instance the currency at the seller's place of business.[40] It is a different question whether the debtor then *must* pay in this currency or is allowed to pay the value of the contract currency also in another currency. Again, this depends on the parties' express or implicit agreement on such right of substitution, on their practices, on international usage or, lastly, on the applicable law. The CISG itself does not provide such a right.[41]

A loss due to falling exchange rates can be a foreseeable recoverable loss, namely, when the creditor receives the compensation sum in a foreign currency. In that case it is foreseeable that the creditor has to exchange the money into the currency at his

[38] *Delchi Carrier.*
[39] Id.
[40] See KG January 24, 1994, RIW 1994, 683; Schlechtriem and Butler, *UN Law*, para. 211.
[41] Oberster Gerichtshof (Austrian Supreme Court [OGH]), October 22, 2001, Internationales Handelsrecht (IHR) 2002, 24.

or her place of business. Any exchange rate loss then falls under Article 74.[42] The internal loss of value of a currency (inflation) can also be a recoverable loss if the extent of that loss is unforeseeable (unexpectedly high) and can be proved with reasonable certainty.[43] Moreover, the applicable interest rate must not already cover the level of internal inflation.[44]

6. Litigation Costs

It has been held by U.S. courts that under the CISG, litigation costs are not recoverable.[45] The U.S. courts reference the so-called American rule according to which each party has to bear its own legal costs. The statement goes, however, too far; it is correct only insofar as provisions or rules of civil procedure regulate litigation costs. The rules of civil procedure in areas within their scope may exclude the CISG, except in the areas of the burden of proof and Article 11. However, the CISG provisions on damages remain applicable outside legal proceedings. In U.S. legal proceedings, the American rule may be justified because there are other mechanisms to compensate a successful claimant for litigation costs (in particular, contingency fees, high compensation awards, and punitive damages). Outside legal proceedings, no such means of compensation exist. Then to deny damages would contradict the full compensation principle of Article 74. Therefore, any litigation costs outside the coverage of the procedural rules can be recovered if reasonably foreseeable. That is generally the case where the kind of breach of contract and the conduct of the other party make it reasonable to require a lawyer, in particular, in

---

[42] Ulrich Magnus, "Währungsfragen im Einheitlichen Kaufrecht. Zugleich ein Beitrag zu seiner Lückenfüllung und Auslegung," 53 *Rabels Zeitschrift für ausländisches und internationales Privatrecht (RabelsZ)* 138 (1989); in the same sense Wilhelm Albrecht Achilles, "Kommentar zum UN-Kaufrechtsübereinkommen (CISG)," in *Gemeinschaftskommentar zum Handelsgesetzbuch mit UN-Kaufrecht*, 8th ed. (ed. J. Ensthaler) (Cologne: Heymann, 2011), Article 74, para. 11; Brunner, *UN-Kaufrecht*, Article 74, para. 45; Gotanda in *UN Convention*, Article 74, para. 52; Norbert Kranz, *Die Schadensersatzpflicht nach den Haager Einheitlichen Kaufgesetzen und dem Wiener UN-Kaufrecht* (1989), 150f.; Huber in *Kommentar zum Bürgerlichen Gesetzbuch*, Article 74, para. 50; Mankowski in *Münchener Kommentar*, Article 74, para. 40; Burghard Piltz, *Internationales Kaufrecht*, 2nd ed. (Munich: Beck, 2008) §5, para. 453; Burghard Piltz, *Neue Entwicklungen im UN-Kaufrecht*, Neue Juristische Wochenschrift (NJW) 1994, 1101, 1106; Bernd Scheifele, *Die Rechtsbehelfe des Verkäufers nach deutschem und UN-Kaufrecht* (Rheinfelden: Schäuble, 1986) 111; Schwenzer in Schlechtriem and Schwenzer, *Commentary*, Article 74, para. 41; Rolf Weber, "Vertragsverletzungsfolgen: Schadensersatz, Rückabwicklung, vertragliche Gestaltungsmöglichkeiten," in *Wiener Kaufrecht* (ed. E. Bucher) (Bern: Stämpfli, 1991), 165, 200–1; Wolfgang Witz, Hanns-Christian Salger, and Manuel Lorenz, *Internationales Einheitliches Kaufrecht* (Heidelberg: Recht und Wirtschaft, 2000), Article 74, para. 21.

[43] Rechtbank Roermond, May 6, 1993, in: UNILEX; Hof Arnhem Nederlands Internationaal Privaatrecht (NIPR) 1998 Nr 101; Handelsgericht Zürich SZIER 1998, 75.

[44] OLG Düsseldorf, January 14, 1994, Case Law on UNCITRAL Texts (CLOUT) Nr. 130.

[45] See *Zapata Hermanos Succesores, S.A. v. Heartside Baking Co. Inc.*, 313 F.3d 385 (7th Cir. 2002), reversing *Zapata Hermanos Successores S.A. v. Hearthside Baking Co.*, 2001 WL 1000927 (N.D. Ill., 2001); Harry Flechtner and Joseph Lookofsky, "Viva Zapata! American Procedure and CISG Substance in a U.S. Circuit Court of Appeal," *Vindobona J. Int'l Commercial Law & Arbitration* 93 (2003); Gotanda in *UN Convention*, Article 74, para. 69; Ulrich Magnus, Zeitschrift für Europäisches Privatrecht (ZEuP) 2006, 120–1; Peter Schlechtriem, Praxis des Internationalen Privat- und Verfahrensrechts (IPRax) 2002, 226; in the same sense as the second *Zapata* decision also *San Lucio, S.r.l. and San Lucio USA v. Import & Storage Services, LLC*, and others, April 15, 2009, IHR 2010, 64 (US District Court for the District of New Jersey); see also CISG Advisory Council, "Opinion No. 6," available at CISG-online/cisg-ac.

the pursuit of a claim in a foreign country.[46] For example, the creditor should be able to collect any legal costs, under Article 74, including those expended prior to the debtor's payment, even if incurred prelitigation.[47] Also, the costs of arbitration are recoverable unless there is a specific provision regulating them in the arbitration agreement or in the rules of the agreed arbitration court.[48]

7. Loss of Goodwill

In rare cases, the intangible loss of goodwill has been held to be recoverable under Article 74. The Swiss Federal Court stated that the buyer of nonconforming goods may claim compensation for loss of goodwill (loss of clients) "if the buyer appears to be a wholesaler in a sensitive market and has no possibility to provide its clients by own measures in time with conforming goods."[49] In the case at hand the seller had delivered meat with fifty percent of fat instead of the agreed upon thirty percent. If the wholesale buyer can prove that he had lost some of his sub-buyers, then the principle of full compensation requires that such losses are recoverable.

IV. Avoidance

Avoidance plays an almost equally important role as damages in the CISG remedial scheme. It is a remedy of particularly drastic and incisive effect; it releases the parties from their obligations and ends the maxim *pacta sunt servanda* for the individual contract. Only residual obligations, mainly of restitution or already incurred damages, remain in force.[50]

Contract law defines the borderline when a party is entitled to avoid a contract by unilateral declaration because the other party has committed, or is likely to commit, a breach of contract. An intuitive rule would probably free the aggrieved party from its contract where the breach of the other party has some weight, whereas a minor nonperformance may not provide a justification to cancel the contract that may have become burdensome for quite some other reason. For international sales transactions it has, in addition, to be taken into account that often considerable costs and efforts – higher than in internal sales – for transport, customs, and so forth, but also for the negotiation of the contract, are necessary and have been incurred. It is the respective party's interest that these costs and efforts should not be wasted. It is also in the public interest to have legal rules that safeguard the efficient use of resources and avoid any waste as far as possible.

---

[46] OLG Düsseldorf RIW 1996, 958; Handelsgericht Aargau SZIER 1999, 192; also AG Berlin-Tiergarten IPRax 1999, 172; AG Alsfeld NJW-RR 1996, 120 (though in the specific case rejecting the claim because it would have led to double costs); OLG Hamm, April 2, 2009, IHR 2010, 59 (63); LG Potsdam April 7, 2009, IHR 2009, 205.

[47] LG Flensburg IHR 2001, 202.

[48] Schiedsgericht der Handelskammer Hamburg (Arbitration Court of the Chamber of Commerce of Hamburg), NJW 1996, 3229.

[49] BG SZIER 1999, 179, 181: "wenn der Käufer erkennbar Zwischenhändler in einem empfindlichen Markt ist und zudem keine Möglichkeit hat, durch eigene Vorkehren seine Abnehmer anderweitig fristgerecht mit mangelfreier Ware zu versehen."

[50] See CISG Article 81(1) (contractual dispute resolution – jurisdiction or arbitration – clauses remain in force).

On the other hand, there must be a level of breach from which the aggrieved party is entitled to end the contract because its further continuation has become unacceptable.

A. *The Concept*

The CISG follows a modified concept of the common law rule that, unless the parties have not agreed otherwise, the right to terminate requires a serious breach of the contract where an ordinary party would have lost the interest in the contract. This breach must be either fundamental in nature or a complete nonperformance within an additional period of time set by the creditor.[51] This latter case can also be regarded as a specific, formalized form of fundamental breach. The CISG thus sets the threshold rather high for the avoidance of a contract. For this reason, courts have termed avoidance a remedy of last resort (*ultima ratio*) that is only available when the aggrieved party can no longer be expected to continue the contract.[52] The reason for this high threshold is to prevent the unnecessary waste of costs and efforts for the negotiation of the contract, transport of the goods, and other related costs.

B. *Requirements*

1. Breach of Contract

Like every CISG-remedy, avoidance presupposes a breach of contract in the same sense as already discussed with respect to damages. However, in contrast to damages and price reduction, a simple breach does not suffice. The breach must be of a specifically serious nature, namely, as mentioned above, a fundamental breach or the non-performance after an additional period for performance had been set (*Nachfrist*). The general rule, under the CISG, is that no fault of the party in breach is required.

2. Fundamental Breach

The core element of avoidance under the CISG is the fundamental breach.[53] Article 25 defines a breach as fundamental

> if it results in such detriment to the other party as substantially to deprive him of what he is entitled to expect under the contract, unless the party in breach did not foresee and a reasonable person of the same kind in the same circumstances would not have foreseen such a result.

Expressed in a simplified form, the fundamentality of a breach requires, first, that, under an objective perspective, the breach destroyed the aggrieved party's interest in the contract and, second, that the breaching party did foresee or should have foreseen such a result of

---

[51] See CISG Articles 49 and 64.

[52] BGH, April 3, 1996, BGHZ 132, 290; OGH, September 7, 2000, IHR 2001, 42; see also Tribunale di Busto Arsizio, Italy, December 13, 2001, Rivista di Diritto Internazionale Privato e Processuale, 2003, 150–5; OLG Hamburg, January 25, 2008, IHR 2008, 98; in the same sense also Cámara Nacional de Apelaciones en lo Comercial de Buenos Aires (Sala A), May 31, 2007, CISG-online No. 1517 (referring to the principle of performance and conservation of the contract).

[53] See thereto in more detail Chapter 15 in this book.

its breach. Although it is not the aggrieved party's subjective assessment of its detriment that is decisive, it is, however, clear that the contractual agreement sets the standard by which to measure the nonbreaching party's expectations under the contract.[54] The aggrieved party must then have been substantially deprived of his objectively determined expectations. Further, this must have been foreseeable by the party in breach. Article 25 does not fix the foreseeability determination at the time of the conclusion of the contract (Article 74). Nonetheless, the result of a breach should be foreseeable at that date in order to enable the parties to assess the risks they are undertaking.

The CISG's definition of "fundamental breach" contains a number of flexible and rather vague terms which can make it risky to rely on a fundamental breach as such. In hindsight, a court may decide that the breach was not substantial enough or could not have been reasonably foreseen as to allow avoidance. In such cases, the aggrieved party itself would be in fundamental breach for declaring the contract avoided. This risk can be minimized by express contract clauses listing fundamental breach events as well as by declaring avoidance in only cases of clear fundamental breach. Insofar, despite extended theoretical discussions on the definition of "fundamental breach," its precise contours can only be derived from existing international case law. Some of the problems of determining fundamental breach and applying the avoidance remedy are discussed in the following sections.

3. *Nachfrist* Procedure

A simpler and safer way to avoidance is the so-called *Nachfrist* procedure under Article 49(1)(b) in connection with Article 47(1) and, respectively, under Article 64(1)(b) in connection with Article 63(1).[55] This procedure is modeled after a similar principle in German law.[56] However, under the CISG, this way is not always available, as it requires the complete nonperformance of the debtor's duty – nondelivery by the seller,[57] as well as nonpayment and nonreceipt of the goods by the buyer.[58] The debtor's serious declaration not to perform within the additional period of time has the same effect as his or her nonperformance. Where the debtor has, however, performed, although incorrectly, this mechanism is not available. In such a case, the creditor can avoid the contract only if the incorrect performance in itself is a fundamental breach. The underlying idea is that the creditor should not be able to elevate a minor breach by mere *Nachfrist* to a fundamental breach that allows avoidance. This also shows that the drafters intentionally designed avoidance as a remedy of last resort.

If there is complete nonperformance of the debtor's principal sales duties, the creditor can "fix an additional period of time of reasonable length for performance"[59] and declare

[54] For a subjective perspective, see Schlechtriem and Butler, *UN Law*, para. 111 (agreement of the parties is decisive when they say that "rather the significance for the creditor is the key consideration").
[55] See to the *Nachfrist* procedure Larry A. DiMatteo, *Law of International Contracting*, 2nd ed. (Austin: Wolters Kluwer, 2009), 253 et seq.
[56] See §323 German Civil Code (BGB); see also Federal Court of Australia, May 20, 2009, [2009] FCA 522 = CLOUT case No. 956.
[57] See CISG Article 49(1)(b) ("in case of non-delivery").
[58] See CISG Article 64(1)(b) ("if the buyer does not . . . perform his obligation to pay the price or take delivery of the goods").
[59] CISG, Articles 47(1) and 63(1).

the contract avoided if the debtor does not perform during that period (Article 49(1)(b)). The contract then ends with the creditor's declaration of avoidance or the lapse of the additional period, whichever is the later. The reasonable length depends on the circumstances and takes into account how long a reasonable debtor would need to complete performance.

4. Part-Performance and Installment Contracts

Special avoidance rules apply in cases of part-performance and nonperformance in installment contracts. Under Article 51, the creditor can avoid the contract for the missing part, for instance for missing 50 units of the owed 100 units, if their nondelivery or their incorrect delivery constitutes a fundamental breach or is not delivered within a *Nachfrist* extension. The whole contract can only be avoided if the failure to correctly deliver performance is a fundamental breach of the whole contract. For example, if the delivered parts are unusable without the delivery of other goods, or a *Nachfrist* period has lapsed, then a fundamental breach of the entire contract has occurred.[60]

Almost the same rules apply to installment contracts where the parties must have agreed on delivery in at least two separate installments. In such a case, Article 73 is applicable. Under this provision, the creditor can avoid the contract for the single installment if the nonperformance or incorrect performance is a fundamental breach with respect to that installment; avoidance of the entire contract is possible, if the former installment(s) of the goods have become useless due to the missing or incorrect installment.

5. Avoidance for Anticipatory Breach

Still another rule applies where a party wants to avoid a contract before the date of performance because of its reasonable anticipation that the other party will in all likelihood commit a fundamental breach (Article 72). The party declaring an anticipatory breach risks liability if the declaration is not clearly supported by a high likelihood that a fundamental breach will occur. The mere suspicion that such a breach will happen does not suffice. There must be clear facts that show that it is almost certain that the breach will occur.[61] This has, for instance, been held to be the case where past deliveries were always significantly late and it is clear that this will also occur in future.[62] It is also the case where the bankruptcy of the debtor is expected and where it is obvious that the other party is no longer preparing to perform, especially where longer preparations are necessary for a timely and correct performance.

6. Duties of the Creditor

Parallel to the remedy of damages, where the breach concerns nonconforming goods, the buyer must always fulfill its duty to give notice of any defect in a timely manner if

---

[60] Article 51(1) refers to Articles 46 to 50 and thus includes Article 49 with its two alternatives of fundamental breach or *Nachfrist*. This must also apply to Article 51(2).

[61] OLG Düsseldorf April 24, 1997, CISG-online 385 [sicherer Schluss]; LG Berlin September 20, 1992, UNILEX.

[62] OGH JBl 1999, 54.

it wants to rely on the remedy of avoidance. Without correct notice, the buyer cannot avoid the contract unless the exceptions of Article 40 or 44 CISG apply. However, this limitation is only applicable where the seller violated its duty to deliver goods that conform to the contract and are free of third party rights and claims. It does not extend to the violation of other duties of the seller or to the duties of the buyer.

Further, the creditor must observe its mitigation duty, although Article 77 technically only regulates mitigation relating to damages claims. A neglect of this duty, for instance the speculative delay of the declaration of avoidance, may not exclude the creditor's right to avoid but may impact whether and what amount of damages are awarded.

7. Declaration of Avoidance

Avoidance does not occur automatically; the entitled party must declare it "by notice to the other party" (Article 26). According to Article 27, it suffices if the declaration is dispatched "by means appropriate in the circumstances" so that the other party would receive it in a timely fashion. If that is the case, the declaration becomes effective even if not received by the other party or not received in a timely or correct manner. Unless a form requirement under Articles 12 and 96 CISG applies, there is no specific formality for the declaration of avoidance except that it must be expressed – orally or in writing – in clear and unambiguous terms that the contract is terminated. A mere complaint of violations of contract duties does not suffice.[63] Further, the creditor must declare avoidance within a reasonable time after it knew or should have known that the ground for avoidance had occurred (Articles 49(2) and 64 (2)). Otherwise, the creditor loses the right to avoid the contract.

8. Exemption

Where the debtor is relieved from performance due to an unforeseeable and unavoidable impediment (Article 79), the creditor may nonetheless terminate the contract if the nonperformance constitutes a fundamental breach or if the debtor does not perform during an additional period of time, which the creditor can set despite the exemption of the debtor. Article 79(5) relieves the breaching party only from the duty to pay damages (and implicitly also from the duty to perform). Other remedies, in particular avoidance, remain available. The creditor should not be further bound by a contract that the other party cannot and does not, and is not obliged to, perform.[64]

9. Exclusion of Avoidance

In principle, the remedy of avoidance is further excluded in a specific case concerning only the buyer, namely when the buyer cannot return the received goods in substantially the same condition as they were received (Article 82(1)). If this return is impossible, the buyer loses the right of avoidance. The underlying consideration is that the buyer shall

---

[63] See, e.g., the formulation *"de maat is vol"* ("the glass is full") in connection with the request of repayment of the purchase price was held to be a sufficiently clear declaration of avoidance; see Rechtbank van Koophandel Kortrijk, June 4, 2004, available at CISG-online No. 945.

[64] As long as the exempting impediment lasts; see Article 79(3).

not profit from the avoided contract at the expense of the seller. However, Article 82(2) reduces the scope of this principle considerably. The provision saves the buyer's right of avoidance if any deterioration or destruction of the goods were not due to the buyer's act or conduct, examination of the goods, or normal use (including resale) provided that the buyer had not yet discovered or ought to have discovered the defect.[65] Additionally, the right of avoidance is not lost in cases where the buyer continued to use the bought good, for instance a machine, even after discovery of its defect, thereby, reducing the value of the good if such use avoided further damage, such as loss of profit.[66]

The CISG's solution, in principle to exclude the right of avoidance where the return of the unchanged goods is impossible, has been criticized as outmoded. Indeed, both the UNIDROIT Principles and the Principles of European Contract Law contain a more modern solution in cases where the goods cannot be returned in unchanged condition. The buyer does not lose the right of avoidance but has to compensate the seller for the loss in value.[67] However, both sets of principles provide for exceptions from this rule, thereby making their rules closer to the CISG solution and its many exceptions. Thus far, the results achieved under the CISG solution do not warrant a revision of CISG rules.

10. Combination with Other Remedies

The creditor can combine avoidance with a damages claim where the breach caused a loss.[68] A combination of avoidance and price reduction or of avoidance and a performance claim is, however, excluded. The purposes of these other remedies are inconsistent with the purpose of termination of the contract. The principle that inconsistent remedies cannot be requested at the same time is self-explanatory but also laid down in Articles 46(1) and 62.

C. *Problems*

1. Final Nonperformance or Refusal to Perform

Where a party finally does not perform all or most of its duties (for whatever reason) or where this party finally – and unjustifiably – refuses to perform its duties, this will generally rise to the level of a fundamental breach.[69] This is true both for nondelivery of

---

[65] See Michael Bridge in *UN Convention*, Article 82, para. 18.

[66] BG, May 18, 2009, IHR 2010, 27 et seq.; in the same sense already Appellationsgericht of the Kanton Basel-Stadt, September 26, 2008, IHR 2009, 164 et seq.

[67] See Article 7.3.6 UNIDROIT Principles, Article 9:309, Principles of European Contract Law. Both sets of principles allow a buyer to avoid a contract for fundamental breach although the buyer fully uses – and depreciates – the goods after discovery of their defects. In certain cases such conduct may violate the principle of good faith because the buyer shows that the goods are fully useable; for this reason avoidance should be excluded; see Bridge in *UN Convention*, Article 82, para. 24 et seq.

[68] See CISG Articles 45(2) and 61(2).

[69] Pretura circondariale di Parma, November 24, 1989, CLOUT case No. 90 (partial and very delayed delivery); OLG Celle, May 24, 1995, CLOUT case No. 136; China International Economic and Trade Arbitration Commission (CIETAC), June 4, 1999, CLOUT case No. 808 (buyer does not open valid letter of credit before delivery date); Juzgado de Primera Instancia, no. 3 de Badalona, May 25, 2006, CLOUT case No. 796; BG, July 17, 2007, CLOUT case No. 936 (refusal of delivery alleging buyer's lacking

the goods and nonpayment of the price. An exception may only apply where the missing part of performance is minor or relatively unimportant and only insubstantially impairs the other party's interest in the contract.

2. Delayed Performance

Merely delayed but executed performance in most cases is not considered a fundamental breach because the other party receives what it expected under the contract. Only where the parties have so agreed, or where it is clear from the circumstances, that time is of the essence – as for example in sales of seasonal goods – can delay amount to a fundamental breach. This is often the case in the commodity trade. Here, the quick row of transactions requires a clear and speedy ability to flip a contract to a series of buyers and sellers. According to agreement or usage, in these cases the creditor will therefore have the right to avoid the contract if the debtor does not perform in an extremely timely manner.

3. Delivery of Nonconforming Goods

Cases of delivery of nonconforming goods often pose problems.[70] The central question is whether the defects in the goods are a fundamental breach that deprives the buyer of what it reasonably expected under the contract. Where the goods are seriously defective and cannot be repaired, courts have generally found that this constitutes a fundamental breach. However, where goods are repairable (even by way of replacement), courts are rather reluctant to allow avoidance.[71] The reason for this is mainly the seller's right to cure found in Article 48. Under this provision, the seller may, even after the date for delivery, cure any failure to perform if possible without causing unreasonable delay and unreasonable inconvenience to the buyer. Although this right is subject to Article 49, it lasts only as long as the buyer has not avoided the contract. Courts have often denied a fundamental breach where the seller could easily repair the goods.[72] The same is true where the buyer can easily resell the defective goods – though with a rebate. Yet a buyer normally not trading in low-quality goods need not resell them; it can avoid the contract.[73]

On the other hand, where goods related to human health, such as food products and medical devices, are seriously defective and pose a health threat, the courts regularly allow avoidance even if the seller offers rapid response to cure by replacement or repair.[74] The reasons for the courts' attitude are the protection of health and the understandable

---

creditworthiness without justified reason); see also Huber in *Kommentar zum Bürgerlichen Gesetzbuch*, Article 49, para. 32; Magnus, "Wiener UN-Kaufrecht," Article 49, para. 13.

[70] See Huber in *Kommentar zum Bürgerlichen Gesetzbuch*, Article 49, para. 33.

[71] BG, October 28, 1998, CLOUT case No. 248 (delivery of frozen meat with higher fat and water content than agreed and therefore worth only three-quarters of the contracted quality = no fundamental breach because buyer could resell the meat at lower price and claim damages).

[72] Handelsgericht des Kantons Zürich, April 26, 1995, CLOUT case No. 196; Tribunal cantonal du Jura, July 26, 2007, CLOUT case No. 937 (no fundamental breach where easy and cheap repair can remedy the defect); Cour d'appel, Grenoble, April 26, 1995, CLOUT case No. 152; OLG Koblenz, January 31, 1997, CLOUT case No. 282.

[73] BG, May 18, 2009, IHR 2010, 27.

[74] See *Medical Marketing International, Inc. v. Internazionale Medico Scientifico Srl*, May 17, 1999, US Dist. Ct. (E. Dist. La.) (mammogram machines); Hof 's-Gravenhage, April 23, 2003, *Nederlands Jurisprudentie*

loss of trust in the seller's reliability. Because of the sensitivity of this area, the buyer shall not be required to give the seller a second chance to perform. Even the strong suspicion of a very serious defect, for instance a dioxin contamination, has supported the exercise of the right of avoidance.[75]

V. Price Reduction

Price reduction is a specific remedy for buyers. If the delivered goods do not conform to the contract, buyers are entitled to reduce the price (Article 50). The result of the breach is a readjustment of the contract to restore the balance of the contractual exchange at a lower level. The remedy is well known in civil law countries[76] but unfamiliar to common law jurisdictions, which regard it as more or less superfluous as in their view the awarding of damages serves to compensate for the reduced value of the goods in an adequate way. Under the CISG, price reduction has in some situations specific advantages in comparison with damages and even avoidance.[77] Moreover, it is practical insofar as the buyer can execute the right unilaterally by just withholding the reduced part of the price. Its separate existence is thus justified.

A. *Requirements*

1. Breach of Contract

Like the other CISG remedies, price reduction presupposes a breach of contract. However, neither certainty of the fundamentality of the breach nor fault of the breaching party is required. According to the text of Article 50, price reduction is only available if the seller has delivered nonconforming goods.[78] The provision thus covers all cases falling under Article 35 – defects concerning quality, quantity, description (*aliud*), or packaging.[79] Also, defects concerning documents are covered under Article 50.[80] The provision does not apply to other breaches of contract, such as delayed performance or breaches of additional duties; nor does it apply to violations of the buyer's duties.

2. Reduction of Value

It is a further requirement of Article 50 that the delivered goods have a lesser market value than they should have under the contract. For the determination of these values, it

---

2003 No. 713; Appellationsgericht of the Kanton Basel-Stadt, August 22, 2003, CLOUT case No. 887 (delivery of genetically modified soy in contrast to the explicit agreement = fundamental breach).

[75] BGH, March 2, 2005, IHR 2005, 158 (in that case, an export ban of the pork that was suspected to be contaminated was introduced, however, only after the risk had already passed to the buyer; nonetheless the buyer was not held to be obliged to pay the price).

[76] Price reduction has its origin in the Roman law's *actio quanti minoris*.

[77] They are discussed later.

[78] See CISG Article 50: "If the goods do not conform with the contract."

[79] For the latter see OLG Koblenz, December 14, 2006, CLOUT case No. 724 (seller's insufficient packaging of the sold bottles led to their partial cracking and partial unsterility during transport; the buyer was entitled to reduce the price to zero).

[80] CISG, Article 50, sent. 2 references Articles 37 and 48 (allow the seller the cure of defects in the documents); see also Article 34, sent. 2; Article 37; and Article 48; Magnus, "Wiener UN-Kaufrecht," at Article 48, para. 8.

does not matter how much the buyer paid. He or she may have paid either more or less than the market value. If there is no reduction in value because of the nonconformity of the goods, price reduction is not available. On the other hand, it is not necessary that the buyer suffer damage. Although the loss in value will regularly constitute damages, an actual loss is not a requirement under Article 50.

3. Declaration of Price Reduction

Like avoidance, price reduction needs a respective declaration or notice.[81] It does not enter automatically. However, no specific form is required (except where Articles 12 and 96 apply, requiring a written declaration). The refusal to pay has been regarded as implicit declaration of a price reduction to zero.[82] In contrast to avoidance, the CISG does not require the buyer to declare price reduction within a specified period of time. Even if avoidance is already excluded for time reasons (Article 49(2)), price reduction remains available. If, in exceptional cases, the buyer is entitled to reduce the price to zero because the goods have no value at all, this has the same effect as avoidance.[83]

4. Duties of the Buyer

The buyer can claim price reduction only when giving notice of the defect in timely and correct form or having dispensed of the notice requirements pursuant to Articles 40, 43(2), or 44.

Furthermore, Article 50, sentence 2 requires the buyer to accept the seller's cure or offer of cure if the seller meets the conditions for cure under Articles 37 and 48. This is in contrast to the remedy of avoidance where the buyer need not allow the seller a second chance if the latter's breach is fundamental.[84]

The duty of mitigation (Article 77) will rarely play a role. On the one hand, Article 77 applies directly only to damages claims. On the other hand, Article 50, sentence 2 is itself a specific expression of the general duty of mitigation and observance of good faith.[85] A creditor who claims a remedy for nonconformity but disallows the other party at the same time to remedy the nonconformity behaves in a contradictory manner and violates the dictates of the good faith principle, in particular the principle of *venire contra factum proprium*. Finally, even if Article 77 is applied by analogy to the remedy of price reduction, it is difficult to imagine cases where the buyer's conduct affected the amount of price reduction, for instance by increasing the difference in value between the delivered and the owed goods.

---

[81] See, e.g., OLG München, March 2, 1994, CLOUT case No. 83.

[82] OLG Koblenz, December 14, 2006, CLOUT case No. 724.

[83] *Ginza Pte. Ltd. v. Vista Corporation Pty. Ltd.* (Supreme Court of Western Australia, January 17, 2003) cisg.pace; OLG Koblenz, December 14, 2006, CLOUT case No. 724; OGH, May 23, 2005, CLOUT case No. 747; BGH, March 2, 2005, CLOUT case No. 774; OLG Köln, August 14, 2006, CLOUT case No. 825; Kantonsgericht of the Kanton Zug, August 30, 2007, CLOUT case No. 938. OLG Koblenz, December 14, 2006, CLOUT case No. 724.

[84] See Article 48(1), sent. 1, which entitles the seller to cure only: "Subject to article 49."

[85] Honnold and Flechtner, *Uniform Law*, para. 313.

5. Calculation of Price Reduction

The extent of the price reduction has to be calculated in a specific way; it is not just the lower value of the delivered goods that is the amount of reduction, as in case of damages. The aim of Article 50 is to maintain the proportion between the agreed price and the value conforming goods would have had on the market. In other words, the adjustment to a lower level of performance shall not affect whether it was originally a good bargain or a bad bargain. Therefore, price reduction has to be calculated as a proportion: the contract price is to be reduced in the proportion that exists between the value of the non-conforming delivered goods and the value that conforming goods would have. If the delivered goods have half of the value of the owed goods, then the contract price must also be halved. Where the delivered goods have no value at all, the price can be reduced to zero.

The relevant time for determining the respective values is the date of actual delivery at the place of delivery.[86] But where, for instance, the insufficient packaging of bottles made them completely useless (cracked or unsterile), their value was not the value at the time before transport[87] but after the bottles had reached their destination.[88]

6. Consequences

Price reduction maintains the contract; the contract must be fully performed on the adjusted lower level. The buyer must pay the reduced price; if the price is already paid in full, the seller may request repayment of the amount of reduction. This is the inherent consequence of Article 50.[89] It can be primarily based on the wording of Article 50, sentence 1 ("whether or not the price has already been paid"). Also, an analogy to Article 81(2) can be advanced.[90] Redress to the applicable national law of unjust enrichment is unnecessary.[91] In contrast to the remedy of avoidance, the buyer need not return the goods, even in a case where the price is reduced to zero.

The buyer can combine price reduction with a damages claim.[92] However, the damages claim may only cover losses not related to the reduced value of the goods.

---

[86] See Article 50, sent. 1 CISG; see also Canton of Ticino Pretore di Locarno Campagna, April 27, 1992, CLOUT case No. 56; OLG Graz, November 9, 1995, CLOUT case No. 175; Hof van Beroep Antwerpen, November 4, 1998, CLOUT case No. 1018.

[87] See Article 31(c) and 67(1), sent. 1; in principle the handing over of the goods to the first carrier is the place and date at which delivery is performed and risk passes.

[88] OLG Koblenz, December 14, 2006, CLOUT case No. 724.

[89] *In re: Siskiyou Evergreen. Inc., Debtor* (US Bankruptcy Ct. 2004) CLOUT case No. 29; see also International Commercial Tribunal at the Russian Federation Chamber of Commerce and Industry, Russia, March 1, 2005, available at cisg.pace; see also Commentary of the Secretariat to [then] Article 46, para. 5; further Achilles, "Kommentar zum UN-Kaufrechtsübereinkommen," Article 50, para. 8; Fritz Enderlein, Dietrich Maskow, and Heinz Strohbach,Internationales Kaufrecht (Berlin: Haufe 1991) Art 50 Bem 3; Matthias Hirner, *Der Rechtsbehelf der Minderung nach dem Un-Kaufrecht (CISG)* (Frankfurt: Lang, 2000) 411–12; Anton K. Schnyder and Ralf Michael Straub in *Kommentar zum UN-Kaufrecht* (ed. H. Honsell) (Heidelberg: Springer, 2010), Article 50, para. 50; Piltz, *Internationales Kaufrecht*, §5, para. 313; Marku Müller-Chen in Schlechtriem, and Schwenzer, Article 50, para. 16; contra, BG, July 7, 2004, IHR 2004, 252 [253].

[90] See Schlechtriem and Butler, *UN Law*, para. 204.

[91] See the two preceding notes; contra, BG, July 7, 2004, IHR 2004, 252 [253].

[92] See Articles 45(2) and 61(2).

A combination with performance (of the original contract) or avoidance is excluded because of the evident inconsistency of price reduction and these remedies.[93]

7. Exemption

Like avoidance and in contrast to damages, price reduction remains unaffected by an exemption of the seller under Article 79. Therefore, price reduction is still available where damages would be excluded due to Article 79(5). In a respective case, this is of considerable importance and advantage.[94]

B. *Problems*

1. Price Reduction and Title Defects

It is disputed whether Article 50 applies to cases of title defects under either Article 41 or 42. The practical importance of the question is limited but by no means excluded because there can be – admittedly rare – cases where neither avoidance nor damages are available[95] and the request for performance (Article 46(1)) is not fulfilled. Then, price reduction remains the only remedy.

The wording of Article 50 speaks more against than in favor of an interpretation that the provision covers title defects. The text uses the phrase "conform with the contract" and "conforming goods," which the CISG generally reserves for cases covered by Article 35. Title defects or "third party claims" are normally distinguished from quality defects.[96] On the other hand, Article 50, sentence 2 refers to Article 48, which allows the seller the cure of "any failure to perform." It is settled that Article 48 includes the cure of title defects as well.[97] Moreover, Article 44 explicitly allows price reduction under certain conditions in cases of Article 43 (notice requirement for title defects). This can be best interpreted to allow price reduction for title defects. At the Vienna Conference of 1980, the question was however not decided, but left to the courts.[98] With a view to the aim of Article 50 CISG it is evident that this provision intends to provide a practical and easy remedy where the goods have a reduced value as compared with what was agreed upon. For all practical purposes, there is no difference between defects concerning the conformity of the goods or concerning their legal status. Generally, the CISG treats the

---

[93] See also Articles 46(1) and 62 (where this principle is expressed with respect to performance).

[94] See also Ivo Bach in *UN Convention*, Article 50, para. 3.

[95] Avoidance may be time-barred due to Article 49(2) and damages may be excluded due to Article 79(5).

[96] See the heading of Section II of Ch. II of Part III of the Convention: "Conformity of the goods and third party claims."

[97] See, e.g., Achilles, "Kommentar zum UN-Kaufrechtsübereinkommen," Article 48, para. 2; Brunner, *UN-Kaufrecht – CISG*, Article 48, para. 2; Enderlein et al., (fn. 89) Article 48, para. 2; Gutknecht, *Das Nacherfüllungsrecht des Verkäufers bei Kauf- und Werklieferungsverträgen* (Frankfurt: Lang, 1996), 60 et seq.; Rolf Herber and Beate Czerwenka, *Internationales Kaufrecht* (Munich: Beck, 1991), Article 48, para. 2; Honnold and Flechtner, *Uniform Law*, para. 295; Magnus, "Wiener UN-Kaufrecht," Article 48, para. 8; Pier-Eiling, *Das Nacherfüllungsrecht des Verkäufers aus Art. 48 CISG.* (Berlin: Tenea, 2003), 67 (117–18: with respect to documents); Piltz, *Internationales Kaufrecht*, §4, Rn 63; Alexander Lüderitz & Dirk Schüssler-Langeheine in Hans Th. Soergel, Bürgerliches Gesetzbuch mit Einführungsgesetz und Nebengesetzen vol 13 (Stuttgart: Kohlhammer 13th ed. 2000) Article 48, Rn 2.

[98] See Official Records, 360 et seq.

both kinds of defects widely similarly. Moreover, their equal treatment under Article 50 is desirable.[99] The argument can be raised that the fixing of a realistic price reduction can be more difficult in the case of title defects than of conformity defects. If this assumption were true, the same difficulty would arise with respect to setting damages. In cases where the amount of the price reduction cannot be proved, then no reduction can be granted. In sum, it is the preferable view to also apply Article 50 to title defects under Articles 41 and 42.[100]

VI. Mitigation

A. *The Concept*

As in most legal systems, the CISG imposes on creditors a duty to reasonably mitigate any loss caused by the breach of the other party. Article 77 obliges creditors "to take such measures as are reasonable in the circumstances to mitigate the loss, including loss of profit, resulting from the breach." This duty or *Obliegenheit*[101] of minimizing a threatened or already existing loss is generally regarded as a more precise subrule of the general commandment of good faith, which the CISG alludes to in Article 7(1). Good faith requires that a creditor who, with reasonable effort, can avoid the consequences of the debtor's breach should do so and cannot expect to be compensated for the avoidable part of the loss.

The CISG addresses the complex issue of contributory negligence also in Article 80. This provision is not limited in its application to damages claims but extends to all kinds of breaches of contract. It prohibits a party to claim damages for breaches of the other party if and to the extent the breach was caused by its own acts or omissions. This may

---

[99] See Schlechtriem and Butler, *UN Law*, para. 202.

[100] International legal writing is split over this question: see, in favor, Schweizer Bundesrat, Botschaft betreffend das Wiener Übereinkommen über Verträge über den internationalen Warenkauf (Bundesgesetzblatt 1989 I 745 ss) 801 (for analogous application); Achilles, "Kommentar zum UN-Kaufrechtsübereinkommen," Article 50, para. 2; *Brunner, UN-Kaufrecht – CISG*, Article 50, para. 3; Alejandro M. Garro and Alberto Zuppi, Compraventa internacional de mercaderías (Buenos Aires: La Rocca 1990 171; Herber and Czerwenka, *Internationales Kaufrecht*, Article 50, para. 3; Roland Loewe, Internationales Kaufrecht (Wien: Manz 1989) 72; Magnus, "Wiener UN-Kaufrecht," Article 50, para. 10; Friedrich Niggemann in Hans Hoyer & Willibald Posch (eds), Das Einheitliche Wiener Kaufrecht (Wien: Orac 1992) 106; Gert Reinhart, *UN-Kaufrecht* (Heidelberg: C.F. Müller, 1991), Article 50, para. 2;Lüderitz & Schüssler-Langeheine in Soergel (fn. 97) Article 50, para. 2; Rudolf Welser in Peter Doralt (ed.), Das UNCITRAL-Kaufrecht im Vergleich zum österreichischen Recht (Wien: Manz 1985) 122f.; Michael Will in Bianca & Bonell (fn. 28) Article 50, para. 3. 4; Enderlein et al. (fn. 89), Article 50, para. 1; against application on title defects Commentary of the Secretariat, Article 39, para. 8;Bernard Audit, La vente international (Paris: LGDJ 1990) 133f.; Ingo Saenger in Heinz Georg Bamberger & Herbert Roth (eds.), Kommentar zum Bürgerlichen Gesetzbuch, vol. 3 (Munich: Beck 6th ed. 2007) Article 50, para. 2; Matthias Hirner, *Der Rechtsbehelf der Minderung nach dem Un-Kaufrecht (CISG)* (Frankfurt: Lang, 2000), 214–15; Honnold and Flechtner, *Uniform Law*, para. 313.1; Anton K. Schnyder and Ralf Michael Straub in Honsell, *Kommentar zum UN-Kaufrecht*, Article 50, para. 11; Martin Karollus, *UN-Kaufrecht* (Vienna: Springer, 1991), 158; Ivo Bach in *UN Convention*, Article 74, para. 12; Huber in *Kommentar zum Bürgerlichen Gesetzbuch*, Article 50, para. 8; Benicke in *Münchener Kommentar*, Article 50, para. 2; Piltz, *Internationales Kaufrecht*, §5, para. 304; Peter Schlechtriem in *Wiener Kaufrecht*, 132; Schlechtriem and Butler, *UN Law*, para. 202 ("desirable to allow a reduction in price for defects in regard to the legal status of the goods"); Markus Müller-Chen,in Schlechtriem & Schwenzer, Article 50, para. 2.

[101] See *supra* note 18 and accompanying text; see also Gotanda in *UN Convention*, Article 77, para. 5.

sound like the old *culpa* compensation, which excluded any damages in case of the creditor's fault. Yet, Article 80 has to be read and interpreted in connection with Article 77 in the sense that, where possible,[102] the damage must be proportionately allocated between the parties according to their respective part in the causation and nonavoidance of the loss.[103] The wording of Article 80 ("caused . . . by act or omission") could give the impression that only the contribution to causation is relevant. But, in fact, fault also has to be taken into account. The word "omission" in Article 80 implies that a duty must have been neglected in an imputable way. Article 77 makes it even clearer that the neglect of a duty ("fails to take such measures") is required.

B. *Mitigation Duties Only for Damages*

The wording of Article 77, and its positioning in the CISG's section on damages, as well as the intentions of its drafters,[104] make clear that the mitigation duty directly extends only to damages claims.[105] Avoidance and price reduction cannot be denied because the creditor neglected a duty to mitigate the consequences of the other party's breach. The creditor has no duty to avoid these remedies in the interest of the other party.

Indirectly, the mitigation duty plays a role with respect to avoidance and price reduction when these remedies are combined with a damages claim. Here, it has been held that the creditor is not allowed to wait for the declaration of avoidance – even within the reasonable time limit of Article 49(2) or price reduction if the extent of the loss is consequently increased, such as in the case of rapidly changing prices.[106]

Even though Article 77 does not directly apply to the remedy of avoidance and price reduction, it must be borne in mind that Article 80 and, more generally, Article 7 apply to the interpretation and application of these remedies. In special situations, for instance where the creditor intentionally delays the declaration of avoidance for speculative purposes, these provisions may hinder the creditor's ability to rely on its declaration of avoidance.

1. Measures of Mitigation

The measures to mitigate the ensued or threatened loss vary according to the circumstances of the case. Moreover, the creditor need apply only reasonable measures, which

---

[102] Apportionment in conjunction with avoidance is rare because termination generally ends the contract as a whole; apportionment remains possible for the remedies of damages and price reduction.

[103] See also Award No. Vb/97142 of the Arbitration Tribunal of the Hungarian Chamber of Industry and Commerce May 25, 1999, CLOUT Nr. 265 (division of damage).

[104] See Official Records, 396 et seq.; Honnold and Flechtner, *Uniform Law*, para. 419.3. The Vienna Conference rejected a proposal by the United States to expressly extend the mitigation duty to other remedies than damages.

[105] See Commentary of the Secretariat, Article 73, para. 3.

[106] Achilles, "Kommentar zum UN-Kaufrechtsübereinkommen," Article 77, para. 2; Brunner, *UN-Kaufrecht – CISG*, Article 77, para. 2; Jan, *Die Erfüllungsverweigerung im deutschen und UN-Kaufrecht* (Frankfurt/M: Lang, 1992), 164; Karollus, *UN-Kaufrecht*, 225; Mankowski, *Münchener Kommentar*, Article 77, para. 4f.; Schlechtriem, *UN-Kaufrecht*, 92; Schwenzer in Schlechtriem and Schwenzer, *Commentary*, Article 77, para. 5; Welser, in Doralt (fn. 100) 128; Wolfgang Witz, Hanns-Christian Salger, and Manuel Lorenz, *Internationales Einheitliches Kaufrecht* (Heidelberg: Recht und Wirtschaft, 2000), Article 77, para. 3; but see Reinhart, *UN-Kaufrecht*, Article 77, para. 4.

have the real chance to reduce the loss. Thus, it is rather apparent that a buyer must stop the use of goods when their further use would damage other goods of the buyer. In the already mentioned vine wax case, the German Federal Court held that the buyer of the dangerous vine wax was not entitled to damages for the loss of those vine plants, which he treated with the wax after having discovered that the wax was defective and damaged the plants.[107]

Also, where a repair of the nonconforming goods would avoid further damage, in particular to other goods, the buyer has to initiate the repair even though the seller may be obliged to repair under Article 46(3). The buyer cannot stand by and then expect compensation for the growing damage. On the contrary, the buyer violates Article 77 if it creates or authorizes repair costs that are out of proportion to the value of the goods.[108] It has been further held that a buyer of a unique machine must deconstruct it and resell its parts if they have sufficient value and the deconstruction can easily be performed.[109]

A special situation is a possible cover transaction to avoid further loss. It depends on the circumstances whether and when the creditor is obliged to undertake such a transaction.[110] Where the contract has been terminated, a cover transaction will often be necessary to avoid further loss. Particularly in volatile markets, the creditor will be regularly obliged to make a timely and adequate cover transaction or has else to bear the loss itself that such cover would have avoided.[111]

2. Consequences

A violation of Article 77 generally leads to an apportionment of the damages between the parties in accordance with their respective part in the causation and failure to avoid the loss.[112] Where the creditor's contribution clearly dominates, his or her damages claim may be fully excluded. Article 77 provides not only a defense for the liable debtor; it is the prevailing view that the court must take it into account *ex officio*.[113] Nonetheless, it is regularly the debtor who must prove the facts of a violation of the mitigation duty.

---

[107] BGH, March 24, 1999, NJW 1999, 2440.

[108] See BGH NJW 1997, 3311 (repair costs disproportionate to contract price unreasonable).

[109] Handelsgericht St. Gallen, December 3, 2002, IHR 2003, 181 (185).

[110] OLG Celle IHR 2001, 107 (buyer of nonconforming vacuum cleaners should have tried to make a cover purchase in the foreign country of purchase); Article 77 violated); OLG Braunschweig TranspR-IHR 2000, 4 (seller not obliged to resell deer meat before Christmas to third parties that the buyer had brought shortly before Christmas, but unjustifiably refused to take; deep-freezing of the meat and later resale at lower price sufficed); OLG Hamburg OLGR 1997, 149 (no violation of Article 77 where the seller resold chemicals with rapidly changing prices two weeks after the buyer had refused performance); OLG Düsseldorf January 14,1994, CLOUT Nr 130 (resale of goods that the buyer unjustifiably refused two months after termination of the contract adequate); OLG München February 8, 1995, CLOUT Nr 133.

[111] See, e.g., OLG Hamburg OLGR 1997, 149; Handelsgericht St. Gallen December 3, 2002, IHR 2003, 181 (185); see also OLG Braunschweig TranspR-IHR 2000, 4.

[112] See also Award No. Vb/97142 of the Arbitration Tribunal of the Hungarian Chamber of Industry and Commerce May 25, 1999, CLOUT Nr. 265; see also Gotanda in *UN Convention*, Article 77, para. 27.

[113] BGH WM 1999, 1466; see also Achilles, "Kommentar zum UN-Kaufrechtsübereinkommen," Article 77, para. 6; Brunner, *UN-Kaufrecht – CISG*, Article 77, para. 16; Herber and Czerwenka, *Internationales Kaufrecht*, Article 77, para. 8; Ulrich Huber, "Der UNCITAL-Entwurf eines Übereinkommens über internationale Warenkaufverträge," 43 *RabelsZ* 471 (1979); Mankowski, *Münchener Kommentar*, Article 77, para. 8; Schwenzer in Schlechtriem and Schwenzer, *Commentary*, Article 77, para. 12; Lüderitz & Dettmeier in Soergel (fn, 97) Article 77, para. 11; Rolf Weber, "Vertragsverletzungsfolgen," 165, 206; Wolfgang Witz et al., *Internationales Einheitliches Kaufrecht*, Article 77, para. 13; also in the same sense

VII. Preservation of the Goods

A. *The Concept*

Unlike numerous domestic laws, the CISG expressly regulates the parties' duties to preserve the goods in Articles 85 through 88. Each party is obligated to care for the goods of the other party as long as the goods are in its custody or under its control, although the other party is legally responsible for them, but factually unable to preserve the goods. The legal property title does not matter for this duty.

Articles 85 to 88 can be regarded as a special use of the mitigation duty and the general principle of good faith. These articles illustrate that under the CISG international sales contracts are not merely transactional exchanges, but contain a far-reaching duty to care for the interests of the other party and to cooperate in the other party's performance.[114] The party in control of the goods must care for them even if it is only in the interest of the other party.

B. *Requirements*

The CISG distinguishes the situation where the goods remain in the hands of the seller although the buyer has the obligation duty to take possession (Article 85) and when they are in the hands of the buyer although the seller is obligated retake possession (Article 86).

1. Seller's Duty of Preservation

Under Article 85, the preservation duty of the seller comes into existence when the buyer is in default either by failing to take possession of the goods or paying the price against the concurrent delivery of the goods. Of course, a rightful rejection equates to a seller's breach and means the seller remains the person responsible for the goods. For Article 85, the seller, on the other hand, must be in possession of the goods or in a position to dispose of them, for instance when the seller is entitled to give orders when they are on transport or stored in a warehouse.

2. Preservation Duty of the Buyer

According to Article 86, the buyer's duty of preservation comes into existence when the buyer has received the goods and is rightfully entitled and willing to reject them because the seller's breach allows for such rejection. This is the case where the buyer is entitled to avoid the contract (Articles 49, 51, 72, and 73), to request a substitute delivery (Article 46(2)), or to refuse a premature or excess delivery (Article 52).

---

to the Hague Uniform Sales Law: BGH NJW 1987, 290f.; contra, however – mere defense that must be invoked – Karollus, *UN-Kaufrecht*, 225; Schlechtriem and Butler, *UN Law*, (fn. 12) para. 316.

[114] See also Hiroo Sono in *UN Convention*, Introduction, Articles 85–8, para. 3.

3. Analogous Application

The underlying principle of CISG Articles 85 and 86 can be applied to analogous situations.[115] Where, for instance, the buyer is in possession of the goods to be substituted under Article 46(2), it should be obliged to care for their preservation as well.

4. Measures of Preservation

Whenever a party must care for the preservation of the goods, it has to take such steps as are reasonable in the circumstances. Articles 87 and 88 allow for the deposit in a warehouse or the sale of the goods, but also require the party to satisfy certain requirements and conditions before taking such measures. The cost of storage must not be unreasonable;[116] that means that in any event it must not exceed the value of the goods. Higher costs do not, however, exclude the right to deposit the goods elsewhere but the placing party will be liable for the excess costs.[117] A self-help sale – under Article 88(1) – is admissible only if the other party unreasonably delays in performing its duties, either to take the goods or pay their price or the costs of preservation.[118] Further, the self-help sale must be executed by appropriate means (so that a fair market price is reached) and the other party must be notified.[119] For an emergency sale, Article 88(2) requires the goods to be of a perishable nature or that their preservation would cause unreasonable expense. Again, the selling party must sell them in a reasonable manner and give notice only as far as possible.

The preservation measures mentioned in Articles 87 and 88 are only examples of possible steps to protect the goods. Depending on the circumstances the responsible party may be required to shelter, package, paint, cool or freeze,[120] control, safeguard the goods against theft, and so forth. The measure must, however, be reasonable, namely able to achieve the intended protection without incurring undue costs.

5. Consequences

The party who incurs costs for the preservation of the goods, under Articles 85 to 88, can recuperate its costs from the other party because it is acting on behalf of the interests

---

[115] See generally Commentary of the Secretariat, Article 66, para. 6; Hornung in *Kommentar zum einheitlichen UN-Kaufrecht – CISG*, 5th ed. (ed. P. Schlechtriem and I. Schwenzer) (Munich: Beck, 2008), Article 81, para. 3; Magnus, "Wiener UN-Kaufrecht," Article 85, para. 19, and Article 86, para. 23.

[116] See CISG Article 87.

[117] Achilles, "Kommentar zum UN-Kaufrechtsübereinkommen," Article 87, para. 1; Saenger in Bamberger & Roth (fn. 100) Article 87, Rn. 2; Brunner, *UN-Kaufrecht – CISG*, Article 87, para. 2; Armin Jentsch, *Die Erhaltungspflichten des Verkäufers und des Käufers im UN-Kaufrecht im Vergleich zum US-amerikanischen Uniform Commercial Code und zum deutschen Recht* (Frankfurt: Lang, 2002), 87; Karollus, *UN-Kaufrecht*, 97; Huber, *Münchener Kommentar*, Article 87, para. 6; Mankowski in *Münchener Kommentar*, Article 87, paras. 3, 5; Peter Schlechtriem, Internationales UN-Kaufrecht (Tübingen: Mohr Siebeck 4th ed. 2007) Rn 339; Klaus Bacher in Schlechtriem & Schwenzer, Article 87, para. 9; Magnus, "Wiener UN-Kaufrecht," Article 87, para. 4.

[118] See also Schiedsgericht der Hamburger freundschaftlichen Arbitrage (Arbitration Court of the Hamburg Amicable Arbitration) IHR 2001, 35.

[119] See CISG Article 88.

[120] See OLG Braunschweig TranspR-IHR 2000, 4 (deep freezing of meat).

of the other party.[121] The amount of those costs is limited to that what is reasonable in the circumstances. As security, the entitled party can retain the goods until reimbursement of the costs or sell the goods under Article 88(1), where the reimbursement is unreasonably delayed. In this latter case, the selling party is entitled to a portion of the proceeds of the sale to cover its expenses. Any surplus from the sale must be transferred to the other party.[122]

A party that neglects its duty of preservation becomes liable in damages to the other party for any loss that party suffers from this neglect. Even a failure to give notice of the planned sale, under Articles 88(1) or (2), makes the selling party liable in damages for the loss caused by that failure.

VIII. Concluding Remarks

The CISG's remedial machinery has been tested in practice for a quarter of a century; if one refers to the CISG's predecessor, the Hague Uniform Sales Law, with its almost identical set of remedies, the practical experience of applying these remedies is even longer. This experience, as of the present, has not shown the types of weaknesses that need urgent revision or replacement. It is also telling that international sets of contract law principles, such as the UNIDROIT Principles and the Principles of European Contract Law, as well as many national laws, have copied the remedies system of the CISG. The European Union used it to a considerable extent for its Consumer Sales Directive of 1999 and extensively for the 2011 Draft of a Common European Sales Law.

A reason for this wide acceptance is the long history of the development of the CISG. From the outset of the effort to develop an international sales law convention beginning in the late 1920s, intensive and broad comparison of law accompanied its preparation. Ernst Rabel, "the mastermind behind the scene," and his functional method of comparative law were very influential. The Rabel method entailed comparing as many legal systems as possible and selecting the best solutions or rules for the issues pertinent to international sale transactions.

Problems unavoidably remain. They stem a good deal from the CISG's use of indeterminate, flexible terms, such as the reasonableness standard, which play no little role in the remedy system. However, it is the price that every legal system has to pay when it regulates a broad field of law with a limited set of provisions. To cover the variety of possible factual situations and yet to allow for just solutions in individual cases requires, inevitably, the use of broad and flexible terms. Greater precision would handicap courts and arbitral tribunals in reaching a just solution for the case at hand.

The CISG approach is not principally different from the application of national statutory law. The courts' task is to interpret the CISG in a way that satisfies both the requirement of legal certainty and of justice in the individual case. However, legal certainty with respect to the CISG requires uniform international interpretation. In this regard, more progress could be requested or desired, in particular, that courts take better notice of CISG decisions from abroad.[123] However, given the results of the international case

---

[121] See CISG Articles 85 sent. 2, 86(1) sent. 2, and 88(3).

[122] See CISG Article 88(3).

[123] Citation to commentaries from a court's home country is an indirect reliance on international case law and literature, which are often used in writing such commentaries.

law concerning the CISG's remedies system, the outcome is by no means disappointing. The UNCITRAL's CISG Digest evidences that on many central questions, prevailing views have developed over the last two decades and have been followed by national courts from different countries.[124] Examples are, for instance, the overall restrictive use of the remedy of avoidance and the exemption from damages under Article 79. On the whole, the results of the international case law are remarkably uniform, given the wide variety of courts and legal cultures involved in the interpretation and application of the CISG. A certain degree of uncertainty is unavoidable and is due to the specific facts of each separate case.

[124] See *Medical Marketing International, Inc. v. Internazionale Medico Scientifico Srl* (E. D. La. 1999) (references and applies an exception formulated in a decision of the German BGH (March 8, 1995, NJW 1995, 2099)).

17 Litigation Costs as Reimbursable Damages

*Burghard Piltz**

I. Introduction

For more than 200 years, the so-called "American Rule" applicable in the United States provides that – independent of the outcome of judicial proceedings[1] – each party generally pays the costs and legal fees they incur as a consequence of the legal action.[2] The same principle is applicable in Japan.[3] However, in Germany, the legal situation is entirely different: Section 91 of the German Code of Civil Procedure (*Zivilprozessordnung* or ZPO) provides that at the conclusion of a judicial proceedings, the defeated party has to reimburse the other party for all costs, including those for their legal counsel, which were necessary for an adequate legal defence or in order to sufficiently assert legal rights (loser pays rule). The legal situation is similar in, for example, the Russian Federation.[4] Indeed, other legal systems contain, in principle, methods for costs to be decided according to the extent of success or defeat. However, such methods are different and are not as comprehensive as Section 91 of the ZPO.[5] On the whole, the reimbursement of costs awarded in cross-border proceedings in these countries does not suffice to cover those costs actually incurred for assertion of legal rights or for a legal defence. The rules regarding the reimbursement of costs as provided in the common rules of arbitration also display a high degree of variation.[6]

---

[*] This chapter is an updated version of the German text, which has been published in Büchler and Muller-Chen, *Private Law, Festschrift für Ingeborg Schwenzer zum 60. Geburtstag* (Bern: Stämpfli Verlag AG, 2011), 1387.

[1] Keith William Diener, "Recovering Attorneys' Fees under CISG: An Interpretation of Article 74," *Nordic J. of Commercial Law* (2008), available at http://www.njcl.fi/1_2008/article3.pdf, 1, 27.

[2] Ingeborg Schwenzer, "Rechtsverfolgungkosten als Schaden?," in *Mélanges en L'honneur de Pierre Tercier* (ed. P. Gauch, F. Werro, and P. Pichonnaz) (Zurich: Schulthess Verlag, 2008), 417, 419; Harry M. Flechtner, "Recovering Attorneys' Fees as Damages under the U.N. Sales Convention," 22 *Northwestern J. Int'l L. & Business* 121, 135 (2002), available at: http://www.cisg.law.pace.edu/cisg/biblio/flechtner4.html.

[3] Flechtner, "Recovering Attorneys' Fees," 35.

[4] Sergej Kopylov, "Marcus Antonius Hofmann, das Verfahren vor dem Wirtschaftsgericht (Arbitragegericht) der Russischen Föderation," 30 *Praxis des Internationalen Privat- und Verfahrensrechts* 268, 271 (2010).

[5] As is, for instance, the legal situation in Argentina, Denmark, France, Portugal, Switzerland, Spain, and the Czech Republic. See Thomas Försterling, "Fabienne Kutcher-Puis, Kosten des Zivilverfahrens in Frankreich – ein Überblick," 22 *Praxis des Internationalen Privat- und Verfahrensrechts* 245 (2002)).

[6] For more detail see Schwenzer, "Rechtsverfolgungkosten als Schaden?," 420, as well as Schiedsgericht der Handelskammer Hamburg, Rechtsprechung kaufmännischer Schiedsgerichte B 5 Nr. 21, 21.6.1996, 42 *Recht der Internationalen Wirtschaft* 771 (1996).

At present, UN Sales Law (CISG)[7] stipulates a party is liable to pay damages for any loss suffered by the other party that was a foreseeable consequence of a breach of contract.[8] There are no additional requirements, such as fault, in order to recover damages.[9] The CISG seeks to award full compensation for the injured party as a consequence of breach ("principle of complete reparation").[10] Under the full compensation principle, given the different national approaches regarding the reimbursement of litigation or arbitration costs and legal fees,[11] it is not implausible to recognize costs or fees as recoverable damages under applicable national laws and through the relevant provisions of the CISG.

II. Practice of Recovering Legal Costs as Damages

The next two sections briefly review the case law and legal literature dealing with the issue of the recoverability of a party's legal expenses as damages.

A. *Case Law*

Courts in Belgium,[12] Germany,[13] the Netherlands,[14] and Switzerland[15] have applied Article 74 CISG to award, without exception, the compensation of costs for asserting legal rights, including legal fees. The cases awarding costs, under CISG Article 61(1)(b),

---

[7] Currently, there are eighty countries that have adopted the CISG. A compilation of all contracting states is available at http://www.uncitral.org.

[8] See CISG Articles 45, 61, and 74.

[9] Ingeborg Schwenzer in *Kommentar zum Einheitlichen Un-Kaufrecht – CISG*, 5th ed. (ed. P. Schlechtriem and I. Schwenzer) (Munich: Beck-Verlag, 2008), Article 74, marginal note 12; Ulrich Magnus in *J. Von Staudingers, Kommentar Zum Bürgerlichen Gesetzbuch: Staudinger Bgb-Buch 2* (ed. J. von Staudinger) (Berlin: Sellier-de Gruyter, 2013) (hereafter referred to as *Staudinger*), Article 74 CISG marginal note 11; Bruno Zeller, *Damages under the Convention on Contracts for the International Sale of Goods* (New York: Oxford University Press, 2005), 63; Christoph Brunner, *Un-Kaufrecht – CISG* (Bern: Stämpfli Verlag, 2004), Article 61, marginal note 6; Marco Torsello, "Remedies for Breach of Contract under the 1980 Convention on Contracts for the International Sale of Goods (CISG)," in *Quo Vadis CISG* (ed. F. Ferrari) (Brussels: Sellier–de Gruyter, 2005), 42, 80.

[10] Schwenzer, supra note 9, Article 74, marginal note 3; Peter Mankowski in *Münchener Kommentar zum Handelsgesetzbuch: Hgb; Band 6: Viertes Buch*, 2nd ed. (Munich: Beck-Verlag, 2007), Article 74, marginal note 10; Magnus in *Staudinger*, Article 74, marginal note 19; Brunner, *Un-Kaufrecht – CISG*, Article 74, marginal note 1.

[11] *Supra* notes 1–6.

[12] Rechtbank van Koophandel te Hasselt, CISG-online no. 1107.

[13] Landgericht München, 10 *Internationales Handelsrecht* 150 (2010), CISG-online no. 1998; Landgericht Potsdam, 9 *Internationales Handelsrecht* 205 (2009), CISG-online no. 1979; Landgericht Hamburg, CISG-online no. 1999; Amtsgericht Freiburg, CISG-online no. 1596; Oberlandesgericht Köln, CISG-online no. 1218; Oberlandesgericht Düsseldorf, 5 *Internationales Handelsrecht* 29 (2005), CISG-online no. 916; Landgericht Berlin, CISG-online no. 785; Amtsgericht Viechtach, CISG-online no. 755; Amtsgericht Tiergarten, CISG-online no. 412; Oberlandesgericht Düsseldorf, 12 *Neue Juristische Wochenschrift-Rechtsprechungsreport* 822 (1997), CISG-online no. 201; Amtsgericht Augsburg, CISG-online no. 172; Landgericht Krefeld, CISG-online no. 101.

[14] Rechtbank Rotterdam, CISG-online no. 2098; Rechtbank Rotterdam, CISG-online no. 1815; Rechtbank Zutphen, *Nederlands Internationaal Privaatrecht* 126 (2001); Hof 's-Hertogenbosch, CISG-online no. 550.

[15] Kantonsgericht Zug, CISG-online no. 2024; Tribunal Cantonal Valais, 18 *Schweizerische Zeitschrift für Internationales und Europäisches Recht* 206 (2008), CISG-online no. 1532; Amtsgricht Willisau, CISG-online no. 961; Handelsgericht Aargau, 9 *Schweizerische Zeitschrift für Internationales und Europäisches Recht* 192 (1999), CISG-online no. 418.

involved a refusal or delay by the buyer to pay. With the exception of three Dutch decisions,[16] which are ambiguous in this regard, the cases allowed for the reimbursement of legal costs. Recovery of legal costs was considered as reimbursable damages under CISG Article 74. However, the reimbursement of the costs for court proceedings was not at issue in any of the cases; rather, the reimbursement of the costs for the legal counsel incurred prior to the court proceedings was sought in each case. An ICC arbitral award qualified "legal costs, arbitration" as "foreseeable according to Article 74."[17]

Various approaches to this subject have appeared in other legal systems. In Russia, a court held that legal costs were not recoverable under Article 74.[18] Two Chinese arbitration awards[19] allowed for the recovery of legal costs, but the decisions were unclear if the legal basis for the awards was CISG Article 74 or Article 46 of the CIETAC Rules.[20] An Argentinian court argued that prima facie legal costs are covered by Article 74, but as a procedural matter are excluded from the CISG's scope of application.[21] U.S. courts consistently held that legal costs do not fall within the scope of Article 74.[22] However, in one court decision,[23] which was overturned on appeal, the reimbursement of such costs was awarded due to an "extreme bad faith refusal to pay" (Zapata decision).[24] However, an attorney's fees can be awarded if there is a private agreement between the parties allowing such recovery, for instance provided by general terms and conditions forming part of a contract of sale.[25]

B. *Literature Review*

The Zapata decision has attracted the most attention.[26] The court reasoned that reimbursement of legal fees is a matter of procedural law and, therefore, does not fall within

---

[16] Rechtbank Rotterdam, CISG-online no. 2098; Rechtbank Rotterdam, CISG-online no. 1815; Hof's-Hertogenbosch, CISG-online no. 550.
[17] ICC Arbitration Case no. 7585 of 1992, CISG-online no. 105.
[18] Arbitration Court for the Moscow Region (August 24, 2000), CISG-Pace.
[19] China International Economic and Trade Arbitration Commission, CISG-online no. 1472, and China International Economic and Trade Arbitration Commission (December 18, 1996).
[20] See Sabine Stricker-Kellerer and Michael Moser, "Schiedsordnung der China International Economic and Trade Arbitration Commission," in *Institutionelle Schiedsgerichtsbarkeit* (ed. R. Schütze) (Cologne: Carl Heymanns Verlag, 2006), 447, 480.
[21] Cámara Nacional de Apelaciones en lo Comercial – Sala F, Buenos Aires, CISG-online no. 2132.
[22] CISG-online no. 851; CISG-online no. 772, 3 *Internationales Handelsrecht* 128 (2003), CISG-online no. 684; CISG-online 1836 (based on the same assumption).
[23] For extensive detail, see Diener, "Recovering Attorneys' Fees," 17; Harry Flechtner and Joseph Lookofsky, "Viva Zapata! American Procedure and CISG Substance in a U.S. Circuit Court of Appeal," 93 *Vindobona J. Of Int'l Commercial Law & Arbitration* 93 (2003).
[24] CISG-online no. 599.
[25] 2010 U.S. Dist. LEXIS 109893 (E.D. Pa. 2010).
[26] Cf., e.g., Diener, "Recovering Attorneys' Fees," 17; Peter Schlechtriem, "Verfahrenskosten als Schaden in Anwendung des UN-Kaufrechts," 6 *Internationales Handelsrecht* 49 (2006); Bruno Zeller, "Interpretation of Article 74 – Zapata Hermanos v Heartside Banking – Where Next?," *Nordic J. of Commercial Law* (2004), available at http://www.njcl.fi/1_2004/commentary1.pdf, 2; Troy Keily, "How Does the Cookie Crumble? Legal Costs under a Uniform Interpretation of the United Nations Conventions on Contracts for the International Sale of Goods," *Nordic J. of Commercial Law* (2003), available at http://www.njcl.fi/1_2003/commentary2.pdf, 2; John Felemegas, "An Interpretation of Article 74 by the U.S. Circuit Court of Appeals," 15 *Pace Int'l L. Rev.* 91 (2003), available at http://www.cisg.law.pace.edu/cisg/biblio/felemegas4.html); Flechtner, "Recovering Attorneys' Fees"; Peter Schlechtriem, "Anwaltskosten als Teil des ersatzfähigen Schadens," 22 *Praxis des Internationalen Privat- und Verfahrensrechts* 226 (2002).

the scope of the CISG; consequently, the awarding of such fees is determined by the *lex fori*.[27] However, in some instances a reimbursement pursuant to Article 74 CISG is granted insofar as the costs of asserting legal rights have incurred outside of the pending proceedings,[28] or if the rules of the *lex fori* are not sufficient to compensate all expenses incurred in the assertion of legal rights.[29]

A number of scholars argue that legal fees are not recoverable under Article 74. One rationale is that a winning plaintiff may plausibly recover legal fees as a direct consequence of the breach of contract, however, a winning defendant is unable to make such a causal connection. Such asymmetry violates the equal treatment of seller and buyer and can only be avoided if the reimbursement of legal fees incurred in connection to judicial proceedings is not a matter regulated by the CISG and is best entrusted to domestic law.[30] In principle, costs incurred in preparation of judicial proceedings,[31] as well as expenses not compensated under the procedure of the *lex fori*,[32] are subject to this rule also.

---

[27] Roeland I.V.F. Bertrams and Sonja A. Kruisinga, *Overeenkomsten in het Internationaal Privaatrecht en het Weens Koopverdrag*, 4th ed. (Deventer: Wolters-Kluwer, 2010), 248; Herbert Schönle and Thomas Koller in *Kommentar zum Un-Kaufrecht*, 2nd ed. (ed. H. Honsell) (Heidelberg: Springer-Verlag, 2010), Article 74, marginal note 32; Peter Huber in *Münchener Kommentar zum Bürgerlichen Gesetzbuch: Bgb Band 3*, 6th ed. (Munich: Beck-Verlag, 2012), Article 74, marginal note 43; Martin Brölsch, *Schadensersatz und Cisg* (Frankfurt: Peter Lang Verlag, 2007), 72; Ingo Saenger in Bamberger and Roth, *Kommentar BGB*, vol. 1, 3rd ed. (ed. H.G. Bamberger and H. Roth) (Munich: Beck-Verlag, 2012), Article 74, marginal note 8; Joseph Lookofsky and Harry Flechtner, "Zapata Retold: Attorneys' Fees Are (Still) Not Governed by the CISG," 25 *J. of Law & Commerce* 1, 9 (2006), available at http://www.cisg.law.pace.edu/cisg/biblio/lookofsky-flechtner.html; Magnus in *Staudinger*, Article 74, marginal note 52; Brunner, *Un-Kaufrecht – CISG*, Article 74, marginal note 31; Herbert Bernstein and Joseph Lookofsky, *Understanding the CISG in Europe*, 2nd ed. (The Hague: Wolters-Kluwer, 2003), 164; Flechtner and Lookofsky, "Viva Zapata!," 100; Flechtner, "Recovering Attorneys' Fees," 153, 155.

[28] John Gotanda in *Un-Convention on Contracts for the International Sale of Goods (CISG)* (ed. S. Kröll, L. Mistelis, and P. Perales Viscasillas) (Munich: Beck-Verlag, Hart-Publishing, Nomos, 2011), Article 74, marginal note 73; Huber in *Münchener Kommentar*, Article 74, marginal note 42; Bertrams and Kruisinga, *Overeenkomsten*; Brölsch, *Schadensersatz und Cisg*, 73; Saenger in Bamberger and Roth, *Kommentar BGB*, Article 74, marginal note 8; Mankowski in *Münchener Kommentar*, Article 74, marginal note 33; Magnus in *Staudinger*, Article 74, marginal note 52; Brunner, *Un-Kaufrecht – CISG*, Article 74, marginal note 31.

[29] Gotanda in *Un-Convention*; Mankowski in *Münchener Kommentar*, Article 74, marginal note 35; Magnus in *Staudinger*, Article 74, marginal note 52; Rolf Herber and Beate Czerwenka, *Internationales Kaufrecht* (Munich: Beck-Verlag, 1991), Article 74, marginal note 7.

[30] Gotanda in *Un-Convention*, marginal note 72; Markus Jäger, *Reimbursement for Attorneys's Fee* (The Hague: Eleven International Publishing, 2010), 162; Clayton P. Gillette and Steven D. Walt, *Sales Law: Domestic and International*, 2nd ed. (New York: Foundation Press, 2009), 407; Djakhongir Saidov, *The Law of Damages in International Sale* (Portland: Hart Publishing, 2008), 52; Schwenzer, "Rechtsverfolgungkosten als Schaden?," 423; Schwenzer in *Kommentar zum Einheitlichen Un-Kaufrecht*, Article 74, marginal note 29; Ingeborg Schwenzer and Pascal Hachem in *Contract Damages* (ed. D. Saidov and R. Cunnington) (Oxford: Hart Publishing, 2008), 104; Alastair Mullis, "Twenty-Five Years On: The United Kingdom, Damages and the Vienna Convention," 71 *Rabels Zeitschrift für Ausländisches und Internationales Privatrecht* 35, 45 (2007); Keily, "How Does the Cookie Crumble?," 21f.; CISG Advisory Council, Opinion No. 6, Calculation of Damages under CISG Article 74, para. 5.4, *Zeitschrift für Internatliones Handelsrecht* 250, 260 (2007).

[31] Jäger, *Reimbursement for Attorneys' Fee*, 162; Saidov, *The Law of Damages*; Schwenzer, "Rechtsverfolgungkosten als Schaden?," 425; Schwenzer in *Kommentar zum Einheitlichen Un-Kaufrecht*, Article 74, marginal note 30; Schwenzer and Hachem in *Contract Damages*, 105.

[32] Schwenzer in *Kommentar zum Einheitlichen Un-Kaufrecht*, Article 74, marginal note 29.

There are only a handful of opinions arguing that legal costs fall within the meaning of Article 74.[33] An alternative view considers Article 74 as a residual rule, which supplements national law to the extent that national law does not provide a sufficient reimbursement.[34] However, those authors who are in favor of acknowledging legal cost as losses covered by Article 74 CISG see the primary or at least an equal, competing approach in Article 74 CISG.

III. Interpreting the CISG on Recovering Legal Costs

In answering the question whether the litigation expenses are reimbursable under Article 74, the starting point is to review the CISG.[35] CISG's Article 4 delegation of issues of validity of contracts to national law is not applicable because legal costs come within the area of remedies, which are expressly within the scope of the CISG. Furthermore, the reimbursement of legal costs is not expressly excluded from the CISG's remedial scheme.[36] Because the costs of asserting legal rights or of legal defences are a type of financial loss, the "plain meaning" of Article 74 would hold that such foreseeable losses caused by a breach of contract qualify as reimbursable damages.[37] Thus, the broad scope of CISG damages and its failure to provide a specific exclusion should allow a party to collect reasonable legal costs.[38]

One counterargument is that the CISG is a body of substantive rules and the awarding of legal costs is a matter of procedural law.[39] However, the interpretation of the reimbursement of legal costs as a matter of procedural law is questionable.[40] First, the CISG's underlying principle of full compensation requires the payment of all foreseeable, provable losses that are caused by a seller's or buyer's breach of an obligation under the contract. Thus, the recovery of legal costs is supported by the substantive rules of the CISG. Second, the CISG in no place restricts itself to substantive rules of law.[41] In fact, the CISG contains rules of a procedural nature, such as Article 11's "no writing requirement" and the permissibility of witness testimony. In these areas, the CISG

---

[33] Schiedsgericht der Handelskammer Hamburg, 774; Keith William Diener, "Recovering Attorneys' Fees under CISG: An Interpretation of Article 74," *Nordic J. of Commercial Law* (2008), available at http://www.njcl.fi/1_2008/article3.pdf; Burghard Piltz, *Internationales Kaufrecht* (Munich: Beck-Verlag, 2008), marginal note 5–539; Zeller, *Damages under the Convention*, 162; Zeller, "Interpretation of Article 74," 9; Felemegas, "An Interpretation of Article 74," 91.

[34] *Supra* notes 28 and 29.

[35] Cf. Schwenzer, "Rechtsverfolgungkosten als Schaden?," 418; Mankowski in *Münchener Kommentar*, Article 74, marginal note 35.

[36] Schwenzer, "Rechtsverfolgungkosten als Schaden?," 423; CISG Advisory Council, Opinion No. 6, paras. 5.3 and 5.4; Flechtner, "Recovering Attorneys' Fees," 134.

[37] Schwenzer, "Rechtsverfolgungkosten als Schaden?," 423; Diener, "Recovering Attorneys' Fees," 55; CISG Advisory Council, Opinion No. 6, paras. 5.3 and 5.4; Schlechtriem, "Anwaltskosten als Teil des ersatzfähigen Schadens," 51; Keily, "How Does the Cookie Crumble?," 18; Flechtner, "Recovering Attorneys' Fees," 126. See also Piltz, *Internationales Kaufrecht*, marginal note 5–512 et seq.

[38] Likewise Schwenzer, "Rechtsverfolgungkosten als Schaden?," 423; CISG Advisory Council, Opinion No. 6, paras. 5.3 and 5.4; Zeller, "Interpretation of Article 74," 3 et seq.

[39] *Supra* note 27.

[40] Schwenzer, "Rechtsverfolgungkosten als Schaden?," 422; Zeller, supra note 26, 7.

[41] Cf. Diener, "Recovering Attorneys' Fees," 31 et seq.

preempts conflicting national procedural law.[42] Thirdly, the mainstream scholarly view has abandoned the substantive–procedural distinction.[43] The substantive law–procedural law distinction is not a functional test due to its generality and lack of generally acceptable criteria for applying the distinction.[44]

A further argument can be made that the underlying purpose of an international sales law is to reduce the legal obstacles to transborder trade related to divergences in national sales laws.[45] Given this mandate, when there is a dispute as to the scope of the CISG, that dispute should be resolved in favor of CISG coverage. The supranational nature of the CISG is founded on the basis of international law. Thus, conflicts between national laws and the CISG in areas of scope should be solved by a presumption in favor of the CISG's applicability. This precedence of the CISG can be seen with respect to the qualification of certain national provisions on validity that fall within the scope of the CISG. The issue of contract validity, when unclear, should result in the application of the CISG and not presumed to be within the scope CISG Article 4.[46] This argument is supported by the principle of autonomous interpretation manifested in CISG Article 7. A reasonable autonomous interpretation, free of homeward trend bias, would be that the payment of legal costs is a form of damages recoverable under Article 74.[47]

Another counterargument against the "plain-meaning understanding"[48] of CISG Article 74 is the asymmetrical nature of Article 74 if applied to recover legal costs. The

---

[42] Schlechtriem and Schmidt-Kessel in *Kommentar zum Einheitlichen Un-Kaufrecht – CISG*, 5th ed. (ed. P. Schlechtriem and I. Schwenzer) (Munich: Beck-Verlag, 2008), Article 11, marginal note 12.

[43] Cf., e.g., on the proof of the damage Saidov, *The Law of Damages*, 162, 168, and on jurisdiction agreements in the past, Peter Schlechtriem, *Internationales Un-Kaufrecht*, 1st ed. (Tübingen: Mohr-Siebeck, 1996), marginal note 58; Ulrich Magnus, "Das UN-Kaufrecht: Fragen und Problem seiner praktischen Bewährung," 5 *Zeitschrift für Europäisches Privatrecht* 823, 838 (1997); Peter Schlechtriem, *Internationales Un-Kaufrecht*, 4th ed. (Tübingen: Mohr-Siebeck, 2007), marginal note 58; Ferrari in Schlechtriem and Schwenzer, *Kommentar zum Einheitlichen Un-Kaufrecht*, Article 4, marginal notes 33 and 40.

[44] See also Jäger, *Reimbursement for Attorneys's Fee*, 160; Saidov, *The Law of Damages*, 52; Schwenzer in *Kommentar zum Einheitlichen Un-Kaufrecht*, Article 74, marginal note 28; Mankowski in *Münchener Kommentar*, Article 74, marginal note 35.

[45] Quinto Tribunal Colegiado en Materia Civil del Primer Circuito, decision of 20.05.2005 (293/2005), CISG-Pace, 5 *Zeitschrift für Internatliones Handelsrecht* 237, 239 (2003); Arbitration Court for the Moscow Region, decision of 11.02.2002, CISG-Pace; ICC Arbitration Case No. 7645 of 1995, 26 *Yearbook Commercial Arbitration* 130 (2001); Piltz, *Internationales Kaufrecht*, marginal note 2–125; Schlechtriem and Schmidt-Kessel, *Kommentar zum Einheitlichen Un-Kaufrecht*, Article 11, marginal note 12; Ulrich G. Schroeter, *Un-Kaufrecht und Europäisches Gemeinschaftsrecht* (Munich: Sellier, 2005), 83; Urs P. Gruber, *Methoden des Internationalen Einheitsrechts* (Tübingen: Mohr-Siebeck-Verlag, 2004), 229, 267; Felemegas, "An Interpretation of Article 74," 91; Schlechtriem, "Verfahrenskosten als Schaden in Anwendung des UN-Kaufrechts," 52 (doubting enforceability).

[46] Cf. Gillette and Walt, *Sales Law*, 170; Patrick C. Leyens, "CISG and Mistake: Uniform Law vs. Domestic Law, The Interpretative Challenge of Mistake and the Validity Loophole, Review of the Convention for the International Sale of Goods (CISG)," 3, 26, 36 (Pace Int'l L. Rev. ed., Sellier: Munich 2003–2004); Magnus in *Staudinger*, Article 4, marginal note 11; along the same lines, Ferrari in Schlechtriem and Schwenzer, *Kommentar zum Einheitlichen Un-Kaufrecht*, Article 4, marginal note 16; Anne-Kathrin Schluchter, *Die Gültigkeit von Kaufverträgen unter Dem Un-Kaufrecht* (Baden-Baden: Nomos Universitätsschriften Recht, 1996), 45.

[47] See also, Saidov, *The Law of Damages*, 52; Schwenzer, "Rechtsverfolgungkosten als Schaden?," 417, 422; CISG Advisory Council, Opinion No. 6, 259; Mankowski in *Münchener Kommentar*, Article 74, marginal note 35; Schlechtriem, "Verfahrenskosten als Schaden in Anwendung des UN-Kaufrechts," 51; Zeller, *Damages under the Convention on Contracts*, 149; Keily, "How Does the Cookie Crumble?," 12.

[48] *Supra* note 37.

principle of equal treatment of buyers and sellers is infringed on if legal expenses were deemed to be damages pursuant to Article 74[49] because, technically, only the party claiming a breach of contract is allowed to collect such damages. However, the CISG distinguishes between sellers and buyers. The principle of equal treatment of buyers and sellers is not clearly supported by the text of the CISG[50] and is rarely a principle that governs the conduct of the contracting parties usually.[51] The principle of equal treatment of buyers and sellers is further refuted given the primary obligations of the seller and buyer laid down in CISG Articles 30 et seq. and 53 et seq. The rules on the place of delivery (CISG Article 31) and on the place of payment (CISG Article 57) are examples where sellers and buyers are not treated equally. Thus it is implausible after reviewing the CISG as a whole to support the existence of an implied principle of equal treatment that would prevent the awarding of legal costs.

As discussed earlier, the CISG's rules on primary obligations do not support the denial of assessing legal costs as damages under a principle of equal treatment. Additionally, a review of the CISG remedial provisions[52] does not support the equal treatment argument. The catalogues of remedies found in CISG Articles 45 and 61 treat the seller who does not fulfil his or her obligations in the same manner as the buyer who is in breach of the contract. This applies irrespective of other differences with respect to the further arrangements concerning the remedies, in particular with regard to the remedy of damages. However, the aforementioned articles also prove that it is only the party in breach of the contract who is liable for damages toward the other party. The party in breach is exposed to the remedies of the other party and insofar is subject to a different system of rules than the nonbreaching party. The equal treatment structure of Articles 45 and 61 only applies when both parties claim a breach of contract. In the case of one-party breach, the CISG explicitly provides for different legal consequences. Only the party in breach of the contract is obliged to reimburse the other party in terms of "complete reparation."[53]

If, for instance, a party to the contract does not fulfil his obligations, causing the other party to incur expenses in order to enforce its rights out of court, such expenses are generally recoverable as damages.[54] Reimbursement of expenses arising extrajudicially,

---

[49] *Supra* note 30.

[50] In addition, the equal treatment of buyer and seller is not a general principle enunciated in CISG Article 7(2). Cf., e.g., André Janssen and Sören Kiene, "The CISG and Its General Principles," in *A CISG Methodology* (ed. A. Janssen and O. Meyer) (Munich: Sellier, 2009), 261 et seq.; Ferrari in Schlechtriem and Schwenzer, *Kommentar zum Einheitlichen Un-Kaufrecht*, Article 7, marginal note 48 et seq.; Schlechtriem, *Internationales Un-Kaufrecht*, marginal note 48 et seq.; Diener, "Recovering Attorneys' Fees," 50.

[51] Cf. Diener, "Recovering Attorneys' Fees," 50.

[52] Cf. Schwenzer, "Rechtsverfolgungkosten als Schaden?," 417, 423; CISG Advisory Council.

[53] See CISG Articles 45, 61, and 74; *supra* note 10.

[54] Schönle and T. Koller in Honsell, *Kommentar zum Un-Kaufrecht*, Article 74, marginal note 32; Schwenzer in *Kommentar zum Einheitlichen Un-Kaufrecht*, Article 74, marginal note 33; Huber in *Münchener Kommentar*, Article 74, marginal note 42; Bertrams and Kruisinga, *Overeenkomsten in het Internationaal Privaatrecht en het Weens Koopverdrag*, 248; Brölsch, *Schadensersatz und Cisg*, 72; Saenger in Bamberger and Roth, *Kommentar BGB*, Article 74, marginal note 8; Peter Huber in *The CISG* 279 (ed. P. Huber and A. Mullis) (Munich: Sellier, 2007); Mankowski in *Münchener Kommentar*, Article 74, marginal note 33; Brunner, *Un-Kaufrecht – CISG*, Article 74, marginal note 31; Magnus in *Staudinger*, Article 74, marginal note 51; Wolfgang Witz in *Internationales Einheitliches Kaufrecht* (ed. W. Witz, H. C. Salger, and M. Lorenz) (Heidelberg: Verlag Recht und Wirtschaft, 2000), Article 74, marginal note 39; Martin Karollus,

including ancillary legal expenses, is recoverable in most jurisdictions.[55] In consideration of the full compensation objective of Article 74,[56] the use of different standards for recovering judicial-related and extrajudicial legal costs is not justified. The party's role as claimant or defendant is of no significance for the application of UN Sales Law. Ultimately, the only standard for awarding legal costs of any kind, whether claimed by the plaintiff or defendant, should be whether the expenses, the reimbursement of which are sought, are a consequence of a breach of contract under Articles 45 and 61.

It should be noted that not all claims are for damages related to a breach of contract. For example, the buyer may seek negative declaratory action in contemplation of a seller's suit for payment.[57] If the buyer is unsuccessful because the claim for the purchase price rightly exists, then the prevailing defendant on the basis of Articles 61 and 74 should be able to claim reimbursement of the costs of the legal defence.[58] In this case, the prevailing defendant is entitled to damages because the plaintiff is in breach of the contract through the negation of the valid claim for the purchase price.[59] If, however, the declaratory action is decided in favor of the plaintiff, he or she is not entitled to damages pursuant to Article 74 due to a lack of a breach of contract by the defendant. A different outcome would arise if the seller were held in breach by making an unjustified demand for payment.[60]

This analysis shows that the defendant, as well as the plaintiff, is entitled to recover legal costs under Article 74. Thus, the statement that the award of costs of judicial proceedings as damages according to Article 74 favors the plaintiff[61] is not accurate as a generalization. It is correct to state that the party to a sales contact whose claims are not met as stipulated in the contract is privileged because of the remedies provided by Articles 45 and 61. However, this is the explicitly formulated objective of the CISG:[62] to restore the balance of the bargain (contract) after the occurrence of a breach.

The argument that the reimbursement of litigation or arbitration expenses is outside of the scope of the CISG[63] runs counter to the goal of unification of law upon which the CISG is premised. In the area of collecting legal costs, bringing the issue within the scope of the CISG avoids the various and complicated criteria for awarding such damages

---

Un-Kaufrecht (Vienna and New York: Springer, 1991), 213; Herber and Czerwenka, *Internationales Kaufrecht*, Article 74, marginal note 7.

[55] *Supra* notes 12–15.

[56] For more detail, see CISG Advisory Council, Opinion No. 6, para. 1.1, at 251.

[57] Such arrangements occur, for example, if the buyer wants to deny the seller the ability to select the court of the dispute in cases were various courts would have jurisdiction over the case.

[58] Cf. *supra* note 54.

[59] Günter Hager and Felix Maultzsch in *Einheitliches Un-Kaufrecht*, 5th ed. (ed. P. Schlechtriem and I. Schwenzer) (Munich: Beck-Verlag, 2008), Article 64, marginal note 5; Christoph Benicke in *Münchener Kommentar zum Handelsgestzbuch: Hgb, Band 6: Viertes Buch*, 2nd ed. (Munich: Beck-Verlag, 2007), Article 64, marginal note; Magnus in *Staudinger*, Article 64, marginal note 13.

[60] Cf., e.g., Bundesgerichtshof, 62 *Neue Juristische Wochenschrift* 1262, 1263 (2009) ("A contracting party which asks for something from the other party to which it is not obliged to by the contract or which exercises a right to alter a legal relationship which does not exist, violates its obligation of consideration pursuant to Section 241 (2) German Civil Code").

[61] Schwenzer, "Rechtsverfolgungskosten als Schaden?," 417, 423; Schwenzer in *Kommentar zum Einheitlichen Un-Kaufrecht*, Article 74, marginal note 30.

[62] *Supra* note 10.

[63] *Supra* notes 27 and 30.

found in the national legal systems[64] and purports a solid basis for the reimbursement of contingency fees or costs for party funding, issues that are generally not covered by the national procedural laws.

Even when applying the CISG generously, it is important to recognize that the mere incurring of costs is not sufficient to claim damages; the costs have to be causally related to a prior breach of contract. However, situations are conceivable where an unjustified claim can qualify as a violation of contractual obligations and constitute a breach of contract.[65] This particularly applies if a claim is clearly unsubstantiated, the amount claimed is deemed to be abundantly excessive, or the claim is an act of bad faith, such as where its primary purpose is exercising pressure on the other party.

IV. Remarks

The CISG's remedial provisions sanction every breach of contract by allowing damage claims that aim to fully compensate the nonbreaching party. This remedial objective supports recover of legal expenses. However, it is conceivable that a party cannot, despite favorable ruling, claim such costs as damages because the other party is not in breach of contract. This is often the case when the defendant is the winning party. This result is consistent with the CISG principle that damages are only justified when there is a breach of contract. However, because legal costs are monetary losses, and the purpose of the CISG is as a unifying law, legal costs should be recognized as recoverable damages under Article 74. Any prevailing party should be able to make a claim for reimbursement of legal costs.

---

[64] In such way, Section 91 of the German Code of Civil Procedure generally regulates the allocation of costs by means of the principle of instigation regardless of fault, Max Vollkommer in Zöller, *Zivilprozessordnung*, 28th ed. (ed. R. Geimer et al.) (Cologne: Verlag Dr. Otto Schmidt, 2010), §88, marginal note 11; Bundesgerichtshof, 59 *Neue Juristische Wochenschrift* 2490 no. 19 (2006).

[65] Cf., e.g., Bundesgerichtshof, 62 *Neue Juristische Wochenschrift* 1262, 1263 (2009); Magnus in *Staudinger*, Article 7, marginal note 47; Brunner, *Un-Kaufrecht – CISG*, Article 30, marginal note 7; Annette Kock, *Nebenpflichten im UN-Kaufrecht* (Regensburg: Roderer Verlag, 1995), 32; for criticism, see Schlechtriem, "Verfahrenskosten als Schaden in Anwendung des UN-Kaufrechts," 51.

18 Excuse of Impediment and Its Usefulness

Martin Davies

I. Introduction

The title of Joseph Heller's famous novel *Catch-22* is often used to describe any situation in which there are only two alternative choices, both of which lead to unpleasant outcomes. The real Catch-22 was tighter and more vicious: both alternatives led to the *same* unpleasant outcome, from which there was no escape. The novel is set during World War II and it follows the fortunes of Captain John Yossarian, a bomber pilot in a squadron that faced grave risks of death on every mission. Catch-22 made it impossible to get out of flying a mission: if a pilot was sane enough to realize the risks, he was not crazy enough to be grounded because of mental instability; if he was crazy enough not to realize the risks, he would go on flying without asking to be grounded.

> There was only one catch and that was Catch-22, which specified that a concern for one's safety in the face of dangers that were real and immediate was the process of a rational mind. Orr was crazy and could be grounded. All he had to do was ask; and as soon as he did, he would no longer be crazy and would have to fly more missions. Orr would be crazy to fly more missions and sane if he didn't, but if he were sane he had to fly them. If he flew them he was crazy and didn't have to; but if he didn't want to he was sane and had to.[1]

Article 79 of the CISG has much the same structure, which explains why it very seldom applies in cases where circumstances change drastically.[2] If a contracting party realizes that a change in circumstances might drastically affect the performance of the contract, he or she should have made provision in the contract by including a *force majeure* clause, a price escalation clause, or some other provision designed to mitigate the consequences if the foreseen circumstance came to pass. If some such provision is included in the contract, Article 79 should not apply, because Article 6 provides that the parties' own

[1] Joseph Heller, *Catch-22* (New York: Simon & Schuster, 1961), 54.

[2] UNCITRAL *Digest of Case Law on the United Nations Convention on the International Sale of Goods* (New York: United Nations, 2008), 253, Article 79, para. 7 ("Article 79 has been invoked with some frequency in litigation, but with limited success"); *Schlechtriem and Schwenzer in Commentary on the UN Convention on the International Sale of Goods* (CISG), 3rd ed. (ed. P. Schlechtriem and I. Schwenzer) (Oxford: Oxford University Press, 2010), 1063 ("The provision's drafting history, systematic placement and wording imply that such an exemption should be considered only under very narrow conditions").

agreement preempts the operation of the CISG.[3] If no special provision is included, Article 79 should still not apply in the event of a change of circumstances because the parties took the change of circumstances into account when making the contract.[4] In contrast, if a person fails to realize that a change in circumstances might drastically affect the performance of the contract, then Article 79 still should not apply, because such events are very commonly taken into account by reasonably prudent contracting parties, and Article 79 only provides relief against impediments to performance that "could not *reasonably* be expected to have [been] taken . . . into account at the time of the conclusion of the contract." If, for example, a seller is crazy enough not to realize that the market price of its product and the cost of raw materials might go up during the term of its contract, then it will go ahead and put itself in danger by agreeing to a long-term contract at a fixed price. In those circumstances, Article 79 should not apply to provide any relief, because such risks can and should have been taken into account when the contract was made. If the seller is sane enough to realize that the duration of contractual performance will be long enough that the market price and/or cost of materials might go up considerably, it will bargain for inclusion of a price escalation clause in the contract and Article 79 will have no work to do, or, alternatively, the seller will knowingly take the risk and Article 79 will still have no work to do because the risk was taken into account at the time of contracting.

The uselessness of Article 79 noted here is, of course, an exaggeration for rhetorical effect. There may be cases where something truly unexpected happens to interfere with contractual performance, in which case Article 79 should come into play. Nevertheless, for more routine impediments such as price rises, currency devaluations, predictable natural causes, and so forth, the operation of Article 79 is much more constrained because any party to a transnational sales contract should be expected to take into account a large number of possible adverse future events.[5] This was noted from the very beginning of the CISG's existence. The UNCITRAL Secretariat Commentary noted that:[6]

> All potential impediments to the performance of a contract are foreseeable to one degree or another. Such impediments as wars, storms, fires, government embargoes and the closing of international waterways have all occurred in the past and can be expected to occur again in the future. Frequently, the parties to the contract have envisaged the possibility of the impediment which did occur. Sometimes they have explicitly stated whether the occurrence of the impeding event would exonerate the non-performing

---

[3] However, in one case a court considered both the parties' own *force majeure* clause and Article 79: OLG Hamburg; 1 U 167/95; February 28, 1997, available at http://cisgw3.law.pace.edu/cases/970228g1.html. This seems to have been because the court concluded that the scope of the *force majeure* clause was no broader than Article 79: see id., para. 1(d), translation by Linus Meyer ("Therefore, the provision has the same effect as Article 79 CISG").

[4] Article 79 applies only to an impediment that "could not reasonably be expected to have [been] taken . . . into account at the time of the conclusion of the contract."

[5] Catherine Kassedjian, "Competing Approaches to Force Majeure and Hardship," 25 *International Rev. of L. & Economics* 415, 418 (2005) ("[A]ny party to a transnational sales contract is deemed to be a 'professional.' As such, she is expected to analyze the market, the situation in the country(ies) where the manufacturing of the goods takes place, where the delivery should occur, where the transport passes, and so on for each step in the performance of the contract. Such an analysis would require the party to foresee a large number of events, particularly in the unsettled world in which we are").

[6] UNCITRAL Secretariat, Commentary on the Draft Convention on Contracts for the International Sale of Goods, U.N. Doc. A/Conf. 97/5, 1978, at p. 55.

party from the consequences of the non-performance. In other cases it is clear from the context of the contract that one party has obligated himself to perform an act even though certain impediments might arise. In either of these two classes of cases, [CISG Article 6] assures the enforceability of such explicit or implicit contractual stipulations.

Most of the cases relating to Article 79 have understandably focused on the frustratingly enigmatic concept of "impediment,"[7] but the analysis in the pages that follow places more emphasis on the requirement that the party seeking relief could not reasonably have been expected to take the impediment into account when making the contract. The other two requirements of Article 79 – that the failure to perform be "due to" the impediment and that the party seeking relief could not have avoided or overcome the impediment or its consequences – are not dealt with in detail here, because the main argument is that the requirement that the impediment could not reasonably have been taken into account is the controlling feature of Article 79. Nevertheless, the inquiry begins, as it must, with the concept of "impediment" itself.

II. Impediment

The legislative history of Article 79 does not clearly indicate why the word "impediment" was chosen. At the 1964 Hague Conference that produced the Uniform Law on the International Sale of Goods (ULIS),[8] the CISG's predecessor, debate on the equivalent provision (ULIS Article 74) centered on the choice between two words: "obstacle" and "circumstances."[9] "Circumstances" was chosen at the insistence of a civil law group, led by the Federal Republic of Germany, which feared that use of the word "obstacle" might be interpreted to refer only to external events, rather than subjective matters such as the seller's due care, and might also bar excuse based on extreme and onerous changes in economic circumstances.[10] The word "circumstances" more likely includes a drastic change in costs or other economic conditions. Professor Honnold stated that UNCITRAL's use of the word "impediment" in what became Article 79 of the CISG was intended to revert to a word (like "obstacles") that implied an external, objective barrier to performance.[11] The UNCITRAL Working Group produced two alternatives, A and B, both intended to produce this result.[12] The Working Group largely adopted Alternative A but imported the concept of "impediment" from Alternative B[13] in producing the first draft of what would become Article 79.[14] After the draft emerged from the Working

---

[7] CISG-AC Opinion No. 7, *Exemption of Liability for Damages under Article 79 of the CISG* (Rapporteur: Alejandro Garro), para. 4 ("[T]he bulk of judicial decisions and arbitral awards touching on Article 79 focus, by and large, on the standards for exemption that may qualify as excuses under the guise of 'impediments'").

[8] Convention relating to a Uniform Law on the International Sale of Goods, 1964, 834 U.N.T.S. 107 (hereafter ULIS).

[9] John Honnold and Harry Flechtner, *Uniform Law for International Sales under the 1980 United Nations Convention*, 4th ed. (The Hague: Kluwer International, 2009), 617.

[10] Id.

[11] Id.

[12] John Honnold, *Documentary History of the Uniform Law for International Sales* (The Hague: Kluwer, 1989), 185.

[13] Hans Stoll in *Commentary on the UN Convention on the International Sale of Goods*, 2nd ed. (ed. Peter Schlechtriem, trans. Geoffrey Thomas) (Oxford: Clarendon, 1998), Article 79.

[14] *UNCITRAL Yearbook VIII: 1977* (1978); A/CN.9/SER.A/1977; E.78.V.7, pp. 56–7, paras. 432–57.

Group, debate focused on other features of the draft article; no delegate at any stage of the proceedings called for reconsideration of the use of the word "impediment." In any event, it seems clear that the use of the word "impediment" was not controversial.

Although there is no evidence in the *travaux préparatoires* to support the proposition, it seems likely that the word "impediment" was deliberately chosen for Article 79 with the intention of finding a concept that was not used in any country's domestic law, in the hope that a new jurisprudence would grow up to give shape to the new excuse principle. Commentators have repeatedly stressed the need to give Article 79 an "autonomous" interpretation, one that is not shaped by national law concepts such as frustration, force majeure, *eccesiva onerosità sopravvenuta*, or *Wegfall der Geschäftsgrundlage*.[15] As a purely textual matter, that is obviously correct. Predictably, however, it has not always happened. Professor Flechtner has written that Article 79 provides the "perfect environment for the homeward trend" biased interpretation because the Article's "non-specific and plastic norms" enable the interpreter to "project his or her subconscious assumptions and predilections" drawn from domestic law.[16] It will be argued in this chapter that not even those who advocate an autonomous reading of Article 79 have given sufficient attention to the words of the text, inappropriately reading the latter part of the Article as being synonymous with a foreseeability test.

Perhaps the most controversial issue is whether the word "impediment" in Article 79 includes hardship. The CISG Advisory Council has stated that it does (or should),[17] and Belgium's Hof van Cassatie so held in *Scaform International BV v. Lorraine Tubes S.A.S.*,[18] a decision that will be discussed further later. Purely as a matter of language, although the word "impediment" can be used to mean something that actually prevents or prohibits progress, it is more commonly used to mean something that merely impedes progress or makes it more difficult. The Latin word *impedimenta* referred to the baggage of an army, something that slowed but did not prevent its progress. Hardship is a matter of difficulty in performing, not actual prevention of performance. There seems to be good reason to accept that hardship can be an "impediment" for purposes of Article 79, particularly given the *imprimatur* the CISG Advisory Council has given to that idea.[19] Nevertheless, the more expansive interpretation of the word is radically undercut by the requirement that the "impediment" be such that the party seeking relief could not

---

[15] Ingeborg Schwenzer, "Force Majeure and Hardship in International Sales Contracts," 39 *Victoria University of Wellington L. Rev.* 709 (2009) (no gap in CISG, so no basis for consulting national law); Michael Bridge, "The Bifocal World of International Sales: Vienna and Non-Vienna," in *Making Commercial Law: Essays in Honour of Roy Goode* (ed. Ross Cranston) (Oxford: Oxford University Press, 1997), 288. Occasionally, courts echo that sentiment, regarding their domestic law as being displaced by the text of Article 79. See, e.g., LG Aachen, No. 43 O 136/92 (May 14, 1993) (Electronic hearing aids case), available at http://cisgw3.law.pace.edu/cases/930514g1.html; OLG Brandenberg, No. 6 U 53/07 (November 18, 2008) (Beer case), available at http://cisgw3.law.pace.edu/cases/081118g1.html; *Nuova Fucinati v. Fondmetall International*, Tribunale Civile di Monza (January 14, 1993), available at http://cisgw3.law.pace.edu/cases/930114i3.html.

[16] Harry M. Flechtner, "Article 79 of the United Nations Convention on Contracts for the International Sale of Goods (CISG) as Rorschach Test: The Homeward Trend and Exemption for Delivering Non-Conforming Goods," 19 *Pace International L.J.* 29, 32 (2007).

[17] CISG-AC Opinion No. 7, *Exemption of Liability for Damages under Article 79 of the CISG* (Rapporteur: Alejandro Garro), Opinion 3.1.

[18] Hof van Cassatie, No. C.07.0289N, June 19, 2009, available at http://cisgw3.law.pace.edu/cases/090619b1.html.

[19] See *supra* note 17.

reasonably be expected to have taken it into account at the time the contract was made. This is particularly true if the relevant hardship is the result of a market-wide change in conditions.

III. Change of Circumstances and Tacit Assumptions

Relief in the event of changed circumstances is typically justified by the idea that one or both of the contracting parties tacitly assumed that a particular set of circumstances would continue to exist, and that their promises were conditional on the continued existence of those circumstances.[20] Article 79 invites the court or arbitrator to inquire as to whether that tacit assumption was reasonable, or whether the party now seeking relief could reasonably have been expected to take the relevant change of circumstances into account. Unless this is to be an exercise in intuition, the court or arbitrator should presumably consider what similarly situated parties would assume and how they would act. A tacit assumption that any market will remain stable seems unreasonable on its face, depending on the length of time between contracting and the end of contractual performance.[21] The very existence of hedging, insurance, futures markets, and forward sales agreements suggests that at least some similarly situated parties do indeed routinely take into account the possibility of a change in prices.

The Belgian case *Scaform International BV v. Lorraine Tubes S.A.S.*[22] provides an illustration. A French seller agreed to sell steel tubes to a Dutch buyer for delivery in Belgium. After the contract was made but before delivery was due, the price of steel rose by 70%. The Hof van Cassatie described the price rise as "unforeseeable" and held that the seller was relieved of its obligation to deliver the tubes on the basis of the originally agreed terms. This result is startling and has already been much criticized.[23] Would any reasonable seller of steel products really regard a rise in the price of steel as unforeseeable? The price of raw materials fluctuates, sometimes widely. The price of a barrel of crude oil was 145.29 USD on July 4, 2008; by December 26, 2008, it was 37.71 USD.[24] Steel is no exception. The market price of steel is quite volatile. The CRU Steel Price Index measures the price of steel in specified markets, using the price of steel in April 1994 as the benchmark of 100. Between February 1, 2002, and May 24, 2002, the European steel prices index rose from 82.30 to 98.23, a rise of 19.35% in just four months.[25] That occurred just two years before the French seller in *Scaform* informed its buyer that the agreed price for the steel tubes would have to be changed because the price of steel had gone up. In sum, sudden changes in the price of steel in the European market were not unusual at the time of contract formation.

---

[20] James Gordley, "Impossibility and Changed and Unforeseen Circumstances," 52 *American J. of Comparative L.* 513 (2004) traces the history of this explanation.

[21] See, e.g., *Karl Wendt Farm Equipment Co. v. International Harvester Co.*, 931 F.2d 1112 (6th Cir. 1991).

[22] See *supra* note 18.

[23] See, e.g., Harry M. Flechtner, "The Exemption Provisions of the Sales Convention, Including Comments on the 'Hardship' Doctrine and the 19 June 2009 Decision of the Belgian Cassation Court," 59(3) *Belgrade L. Rev.* 84 (2010).

[24] "Crude Oil Price History: A Sampled History of Crude Oil Prices at the New York Mercantile Exchange from 2006 to the Present," available at http://www.nyse.tv/crude-oil-price-history.htm.

[25] The CRU European Steel Price Index can be viewed at www.cruonline.crugroup.com.

One response might be that although a change in the price of steel might be foresee-able, a change of the magnitude of 70% was not. (It should be noted, for what it is worth, that the CRU Steel Price Index shows a sharp rise of prices in 2004 but nothing like the 70% rise accepted by all parties in the *Scaform* case. The discussion here takes the court's findings as read, as it must.) This raises the question of whether it is sufficient that the *kind* of change in circumstances should have been taken into account, or whether it is necessary that the *exact* change in circumstances should have been taken into account. That issue was raised by the Norwegian delegation in Vienna, which argued for Article 79 to be amended so that it would refer to an impediment "of the kind which" the party seeking relief could not reasonably be expected to have taken into account. The delegation

> considered that it might be doubtful whether a party could foresee all the details of an impediment but he should be able to foresee the kind of impediment likely to arise. For example, he could reasonably be expected to foresee difficulties arising from general climatic conditions, but he could not anticipate the exact time and place of a particular thunderstorm.[26]

The proposed Norwegian amendment was not adopted, on the rather vague basis that: "It should be left to the courts to consider whether a particular concrete impediment should have been foreseeable or not."[27] But, importantly, Article 79 does not use the word "foreseeable." If there is indeed to be an autonomous CISG-specific interpretation without reference to national law concepts,[28] it might start by using the actual words in Article 79, rather than by assuming that they are equivalent to a concept of foreseeability used in national laws. The concept of foreseeability is explicitly used in CISG Articles 25 and 74; it is not used in Article 79. Ordinary principles of statutory interpretation suggest that therefore a different inquiry is called for, given that Article 79 uses different words. Article 79 asks whether an impediment should have been "taken . . . into account at the time of the conclusion of the contract." A price rise in raw materials of 70% might not be foreseeable, but any possible price rise can be *taken into account* in the same way. Any reasonable seller of steel products should take into account the possibility of a rise in steel prices. If it does, it can do one of three things: (1) it can bargain for a price escalation clause; (2) it can hedge against the possibility of a price increase by entering into a forward contract with its supplier, or by participating in a futures market, or by some other means of hedging the rise of a price increase; or (3) it can elect to take the risk of future price rises. If the French seller in *Scaform* had "taken into account" the possibility of a price rise by taking option (1) or (2), it would have been protected against the consequences of the rise in the price of steel, no matter what its magnitude. In fact, the court of first instance in the *Scaform* case noted that the seller *did* have a price escalation clause in its general conditions of contract, but it had not used those general conditions with this customer, the contracts being made by the seller accepting and returning the buyer's purchase order.[29] Thus, the *type* of impediment was not only

[26] *Summary Records of Meetings of the First Committee*, 27th meeting, Friday, March 28, 1980, A/CONF.97/C.1/L.191/Rev.1.
[27] Id.
[28] See *supra* note 15.
[29] Rechtbank van Koophandel Tongeren, No. A.R. A/04/01960, January 25, 2005, available at http://cisgw3.law.pace.edu/cases/050125b1.html.

foreseeable, it had been foreseen, and the seller could have taken it into account when making the contract simply by using its own general conditions of contract.

Timing is in itself an economic decision when dealing in fluctuating markets.[30] The French seller in *Scaform* sold steel tubes early at a low price and then apparently bought its raw materials late at a high price. The strategy of selling the product early and buying the raw materials late would show good returns in a falling market for raw materials, and the French seller presumably adopted it deliberately. Why, then, should it be given relief under Article 79 when its strategy turned out to be unwise? The consequence of the court's decision was that the Dutch buyer, which made what turned out to be a good bargain, was forced to buy steel tubes at a much higher price, either by renegotiating with the French seller, or by making a cover purchase from another provider. The Dutch buyer alleged that it had made fixed-price agreements with its downstream customers based on the price that it had agreed to with the French seller, but the Rechtbank van Koophandel Tongeren (the court of first instance) regarded the buyer's claim as unproven.[31] If the Dutch buyer had indeed made fixed-price downstream contracts, then the French seller's loss was actually passed on to the buyer, which was forced unwillingly into the same posture of having sold early at a low price but being forced by the court's decision to buy late at a high price. Even if the Dutch buyer had not contracted with its customers on the basis of the price that it had agreed to pay the French seller, it was still forced to pay more for its steel tubes. Relief for changed circumstances is a zero-sum game: the seller is relieved of a bad bargain only because the buyer is deprived of a good bargain. The same is true if the increase in market prices affects the finished product rather than the raw materials needed to make it – i.e., if the seller already has the finished product in its inventory or if the seller's production costs are otherwise stable, and if the seller has promised to sell the product to the buyer at an agreed price in the future, but before performance is due, the price of the product increases dramatically. In such a case, the seller's "loss" is its inability to make a larger profit in the higher market now prevailing. Again, if the seller were relieved of its obligation to sell at the agreed price, the buyer would have to make a cover purchase at a higher price, thereby depriving it of the good bargain it made on a forward contract.[32]

The analysis remains the same if the change in circumstances affects the buyer, rather than the seller, but with one small variation concerning mitigation and CISG Article 77. If the buyer's local currency devalues dramatically against the contract currency between the time of contracting and the time of performance, causing great hardship to the buyer, can it really be said that no reasonable buyer would have taken that possibility into account when making the contract? The existence of the Euro has eradicated currency fluctuation risks for international but intra-Eurozone sales, but the possibility of currency movement is an everyday risk in other international sales. The buyer can take it into account either by bargaining for a price modification clause or by hedging against future currency movements.[33] The difference between this situation and that of the buyer

---

[30] Victor P. Goldberg, "Excuse Doctrine: The Eisenberg Uncertainty Principle," 2 *J. of Legal Analysis* 359, 371 (2010).

[31] See *supra* note 29.

[32] See, e.g., the Sunflower seed case, Efetio Lamias, Case No. 63/2006, available at http://cisgw3.law.pace.edu/cases/060001gr.html, discussed below in the text accompanying notes 53 and 54.

[33] See, e.g., Arbitral Award No. 11/96 of the Bulgarian Chamber of Commerce and Industry, UNILEX Case No. 42, abstract available at http://www.unilex.info/case.cfm?pid=1&do=case&id=420&step=Abstract (no Article 79 relief for buyer affected by revaluation of currency of payment and change in market price).

forced to cover at a higher price is that the seller may still be able to make a cover sale at the original contract price to a different buyer if the currency fluctuation affects only the original buyer's country. For example, if a Mexican buyer would suffer great hardship as a result of a sudden devaluation of the Mexican peso against the American dollar, the American seller may still be able to sell its product at the original price to a buyer in a country other than Mexico with a stable exchange rate against the U.S. dollar. The duty to mitigate in Article 77 would require it to make reasonable efforts to do so. The seller's loss would then be confined to the additional transaction costs involved in finding the substitute buyer. It seems far better to use this analysis of buyer's breach and seller's duty to mitigate than to relieve the buyer from liability altogether under Article 79 because of the buyer's failure to take into account an everyday risk.

Similarly, there should be no relief to a buyer because the market price of the product has gone down drastically between the time of contracting and the time of performance. The buyer took this risk when making a forward contract.[34] If the buyer were to be granted relief under Article 79, the seller would be forced to make a cover sale at the new, low, market price. The zero-sum game would transfer the loss from the buyer to the seller, who made what turned out to be a good bargain.

IV. Foreseeability versus "Taken into Account"

As noted earlier, unlike other CISG articles, Article 79 does not use the language of foreseeability. Although consideration of changed circumstances often uses the language of foreseeability, the ultimate question under Article 79 should not be whether the impediment was foreseeable, but whether it was one that a reasonable person would have taken into account when making the contract. This is particularly true if we are to strive wherever possible for an autonomous interpretation of CISG provisions. This point may seem at first to be semantic quibbling; one can only take a possibility into account if one can foresee that it might happen. Nevertheless, there is a difference between foreseeing a possibility and taking it into account. Taking it into account involves considering what might be done to guard against the foreseen possibility and then deciding whether or not to take that action. That is why most of the events listed in a standard *force majeure* clause should fall *outside* the operation of Article 79, because it would be reasonable to expect that they could have been protected against by use of a standard *force majeure* clause. Inclusion of a *force majeure* clause is a simple and cost-free precaution that is unlikely to affect the bargained-for price because it may operate for the benefit of either of the parties, depending on what happens.[35] One can reasonably expect any foreseeable *force majeure* event to be taken into account when the contract is made, simply by including a *force majeure* clause. However, it should be noted that standard form *force majeure* clauses do not usually include major market changes in their list of *force majeure*

---

[34] See, e.g., *Vital Berry Marketing, N.V. v. Dira-Frost, N.V.*, Rechtbank van Koophandel, Hasselt, Case No. AR 1849/95, May 2nd, 1995, UNILEX Case 263, abstract available at http://www.unilex.info/case.cfm?pid=1&do=case&id=263&step=Abstract (Article 79 relief denied to buyer of frozen raspberries after significant drop in world market price).

[35] Larry A. DiMatteo, "Strategic Contracting: Contract Law as a Source of Competitive Advantage," 47 *American Business L.J.* 727, 761–2 (2010); Jennifer Bund, "Force Majeure Clauses: Drafting Advice for the CISG Practitioner," 17 *J. of L. & Commerce* 381 (1998).

events.[36] Such possible future "impediments" can be taken into account instead by using such provisions as express conditions, MAC (market adverse condition) clauses, expanded *force majeure* clauses, hardship clauses giving a right of cancellation in the event of a substantial market change, or price escalator and de-escalator clauses.[37]

The same should be true if the supposed *force majeure* event affects the seller's supplier rather than the seller itself. Article 79(2) relieves the seller from its obligation to its buyer only if the seller's supplier would be entitled to relief under Article 79(1). Any supplier that did not contractually protect against predictable *force majeure* risks should not be protected, and thus the seller should not be protected vis-à-vis the buyer.

This argument may sound (at least to common law ears) a little like the (supposed and now abandoned)[38] doctrine in *Paradine v. Jane*,[39] which refused relief even on the grounds of impossibility "because he [the promisor] might have provided against it by his contract."[40] Nevertheless, that is, in essence, what the structure of Article 79 calls for, a consideration of whether the party seeking relief might have "provided against" the relevant changed circumstances "by [its] contract."[41] For example, in *Société Romay, A.G. v. SARL Behr France*,[42] a French manufacturer of air conditioners for trucks contracted to buy "at least 20,000 units over a period of eight years" of polyurethane foam casings from a Swiss seller. The French buyer manufactured air conditioners exclusively for its downstream buyer, a truck manufacturer. Because of a sudden collapse in the demand for automobiles, the truck manufacturer radically changed the terms upon which it was prepared to buy air conditioners from the air conditioner manufacturer, imposing a price for the air conditioners that was 50% lower than the price of the polyurethane foam casings provided by the Swiss seller.[43] The French air conditioner manufacturer then informed its Swiss seller that it would no longer be using the polyurethane foam casings. The Swiss seller sued for breach of contract and the French buyer sought relief under Article 79, saying that the sudden drastic change in the price at which it could sell its product was an impediment preventing it from continued performance of the contract with the Swiss seller. The French Cour de Cassation affirmed the decision of the Cour

---

[36] Nathan Crystal and Francesca Giannoni-Crystal, "Contract Enforceability During Economic Crisis: Legal Principles and Drafting Solutions," 10 (3, Advances) *Global Jurist*, Article 3.

[37] Id. at 17–29.

[38] *Paradine* is always treated as a seminal case about impossibility, when in fact there was no impossibility of performance, merely hardship. A tenant had been expelled from the leased land by an invading prince, but was held to be obliged to continue paying rent. It was not *impossible* for him to continue paying, merely a hardship, given that he no longer enjoyed the benefit of the land. See William Herbert Page, "The Development of the Doctrine of Impossibility of Performance," 18 *Michigan L. Rev.* 589, 594–6 (1920); Richard Posner and Andrew Rosenfeld, "Impossibility and Related Doctrines in Contract Law: An Economic Analysis," 6 *J. of Legal Studies* 83, 97 (1977). The words quoted in the text accompanying note 40 were only tangentially related to what was being decided. Thus, the doctrine for which *Paradine* is usually cited was not the result of the decision in the case. The doctrine was abandoned in cases such as *Taylor v. Caldwell*, 3 B. & S. 826; 122 Eng. Rep. 309 (1863).

[39] *Paradine v. Jane*, Aleyn 26; 82 Eng. Rep. 897 (1647).

[40] Id., Aleyn at 27; 82 Eng. Rep at 897.

[41] See Gordley, *supra* note 20.

[42] Cour de Cassation (France), Judgment No. 1136 FS-P, June 30, 2004, available in English at http://cisgw3. law.pace.edu/cases/040630f1.html, available in French at http://www.cisg-france.org/decisions/300604v. htm.

[43] These facts appear in the decision of the Cour d'Appel Colmar, June 12, 2001, CLOUT Case No. 480, available at http://cisgw3.law.pace.edu/cases/010612f1.html.

d'Appel Colmar denying relief under Article 79: "[A]lors que, professionnelle rompue à la pratique des marchés internationaux, il lui appartenait de prévoir des mécanismes contractuels de garantie ou de révision,"[44] or, "As a professional who was familiar with the practices of international trade, it was for [the buyer] to provide contractual mechanisms of guarantee or revision of contract."[45]

Clearly, there may be events that are so unusual that one would not normally expect the parties to contemplate making contractual provision for their possible occurrence. It might be argued, for example, that events such as wars, strikes, droughts, and floods are sufficiently unusual that contracting parties would not routinely take them into account when making their contract. This is where the Article 79 catch-22 may be felt with full force because these events, although unusual, are very commonly included in the list of events in standard *force majeure* clauses.[46] For example, the ICC's Model Force Majeure Clause 2003 contains a very long and detailed list of events that are presumed to have prevented performance unless the contrary is proved.[47] If a reasonable contracting party contemplated including a *force majeure* clause of this kind in its contract, then almost no subsequent event affecting performance would trigger the operation of Article 79 (except market movement, which raises different issues already considered),[48] even if it constitutes an "impediment" for purposes of Article 79, because the party seeking relief could reasonably be expected to have taken that impediment into account when making the contract. If the contracting parties *do* include such a provision in their contract, then it will supersede the operation of Article 79 by virtue of Article 6. Thus, a claim under Article 79 cannot be sustained.

Furthermore, *force majeure* clauses are not the only way in which provision can be made for physical events such as bad weather or drought. If contractual provision for future events physically affecting performance can be made by some means, Article 79 should still not apply, even if the parties did not include such provision. For example, in *Agristo N.V. v. Macces Agri B.V.*,[49] the Arrondissementsrechtbank Maastricht held that

---

[44] See *supra* note 42, available at http://www.cisg-france.org/decisions/300604v.htm.

[45] See *supra* note 42, translation of Julia Hoffman, available at http://cisgw3.law.pace.edu/cases/040630f1.html.

[46] P.J.M. Declercq, "Modern Analysis of the Legal Effect of Force Majeure Clauses in Situations of Commercial Impracticability," 15 *J. of L. & Commerce* 213, 233 (1995).

[47] ICC Force Majeure Clause 2003/ICC Hardship Clause 2003 (International Chamber of Commerce Publication No. 650: Paris, 2003). The Force Majeure Clause covers the following: war; armed conflict or threat of it; hostilities; invasion; act of a foreign enemy; extensive military mobilization; civil war; riot; rebellion; military or usurped power; insurrection; civil commotion or disorder; mob violence; acts of civil disobedience; act of terrorism, sabotage or piracy; acts of authority, whether lawful or unlawful; compliance with any law or governmental order; curfew restrictions; expropriation; compulsory acquisition; seizure of words; requisition; nationalization; act of God; plague; epidemic; natural disaster such as but not limited to violent storm, cyclone, typhoon, hurricane, tornado, blizzard, earthquake, volcanic activity, landslide, tidal wave, tsunami, flood, damage or destruction by lightning, drought; explosion; fire; destruction of machines, equipment, factories, and of any kind of installation; prolonged breakdown of transport, telecommunication or electric current; general labor disturbance such as but not limited to boycott, strike and lock-out, go-slow, occupation of factories and premises.

[48] As noted in the text accompanying note 36, market movement is not typically included in standard force majeure clauses. It can, nevertheless, be dealt with by such provisions as price escalation or reduction clauses.

[49] Rb Maastricht, Case No. 120428/HA ZA 07–550, July 9, 2008, available at http://cisgw3.law.pace.edu/cases/080709n1.html.

a Belgian seller of potatoes was not entitled to relief under Article 79 when it delivered fewer potatoes than promised to its Dutch buyer because bad weather had prevented the seller from growing a crop of the usual, expected, size. The court first rejected the buyer's argument that the seller could have overcome the impediment of having grown fewer potatoes than expected by buying potatoes from other producers. The court held that the contract was for potatoes grown by the seller, not just potatoes.[50] Nevertheless, it was held that Article 79 did not relieve the seller of its obligation, even though the court described the impediment as being "*extreme* weather circumstances,"[51] because a "diligent grower" in the seller's position would not have made a forward contract to sell the whole of its expected potato harvest without taking into account that the amount harvested could be lower than expected due to bad weather conditions.[52] Similarly, in the Greek sunflower seed case,[53] a Bulgarian seller was unable to provide the agreed quantity of sunflower seeds to its Greek buyer because of prolonged drought, which led both to reduced production and also to a lowering of the level of the River Danube, which meant that there was no available river port from which the seeds could be shipped to the buyer, forcing the seller to use a more costly Black Sea port. The Lamia Court of Appeals held that Article 79 provided no relief to the seller because it could have proposed an alternative price for the goods if the need to transport the goods from a Black Sea port were to eventuate.[54] The zero-sum nature of relief for changed circumstances meant that the seller's "loss" was its inability to participate in the high-priced market for scarce sunflower seeds, whereas transferring the loss to the buyer by providing the seller with Article 79 relief would have required the buyer to cover at a higher price.[55]

V. Conclusion

If the Article 79 catch-22 were as wickedly perfect as Joseph Heller's original, there would be literally no cases in which Article 79 would apply. That is not the case. There have been some, although few, examples of its application.[56] Although the central working concept in Article 79 appears to be the requirement that there be an "impediment" to performance, the apparently secondary requirement that the party seeking relief could not reasonably have been expected to take that impediment into account when making the contract is, in practice, the principal obstacle to Article 79's application. Although that requirement is often discussed in terms of foreseeability, Article 79 in fact focuses on what could and should have been "taken into account." Foreseeability is obviously

---

[50] Id. at para. [3.8].
[51] Id. at para. [2.3], translation by Thorsten Tepasse, available at http://cisgw3.law.pace.edu/cases/080709n1.html.
[52] Id. at para. [3.10].
[53] Efetio Lamias, Case No. 63/2006, available at http://cisgw3.law.pace.edu/cases/060001gr.html.
[54] Id. at para. [2.2] of Editorial Remarks by Dionysios Flambouras.
[55] See *supra* note 32.
[56] The UNCITRAL Digest of Case Law on the United Nations Convention on the International Sale of Goods 253 (United Nations: New York, 2008), Article 79, para. 7, lists four examples of successful invocation of Article 79 (two each for seller and buyer) and fifteen examples of unsuccessful invocation. The decision in 2009 of the Hof van Cassatie in *Scaform International* (see *supra* note 18), makes at least one more example of successful invocation.

relevant to that inquiry, but it does not end the inquiry. Considering what a reasonable person would take into account when contracting involves considering how experienced traders contract around such problems. The prevalence of such contractual devices such as *force majeure* clauses, hedging contracts, price escalation (and de-escalation) clauses, and so on, explains why Article 79 has had very little work to do in practice.

Part V   *Country Analyses: Europe*

19 The CISG in Austria

Wolfgang Faber

I. Introduction

The mainstream view of Austrian academics and practitioners is that the CISG is opted out of by most contracting parties in Austria. Empirical data supports a somewhat more optimistic view.[1] For example, in one survey, when asked which law they chose when drafting international contracts of sale, 55% of the lawyers stated that they regularly exclude CISG explicitly. Only about 2% regularly make CISG applicable explicitly. About 38% follow different approaches depending on the circumstances (and about 8% do not mention the CISG). The reasons given for not applying CISG include: "lack of legal certainty" (58%), which included the lack of experience of the lawyer and presumed lack of experience of the courts, and that contracting out of CISG was preferred by the client (34%). In sum, the usual reason given is essentially that the client's "own" law is chosen because it is known better. However, despite the survey findings, Austrian courts have applied CISG in quite a remarkable number of cases. For the issues covered by this country analysis, thirty-eight cases decided by the Austrian Supreme Court (Oberster Gerichtshof, OGH), eighteen cases decided by lower courts,[2] and a handful of published arbitration cases have been reviewed.[3]

The Austrian legal system does not apply a doctrine of binding precedents. Yet Supreme Court decisions are usually followed by the Supreme Court itself in later cases, and by the lower courts. Similar to German courts, it is characteristic for the Austrian judiciary that decisions are often based on a broad analytic summary of views expressed in the academic literature. Also, decisions issued by German courts are often cited. The authorities quoted most frequently are the German CISG commentaries edited by

---

[1] See Justus Meyer, "UN-Kaufrecht in der österreichischen Anwaltspraxis," 63 *Österreichische Juristen-Zeitung* 792, at 795–7 (2008) (questionnaires sent to Austrian practicing lawyers).

[2] The availability of such a high number of CISG cases decided by lower courts is remarkable because, in contrast to Supreme Court cases which are always published in an official online database (the *RIS*, see note 3 below), decisions issued by lower courts usually remain unpublished in Austria. The fact that this is different regarding CISG cases clearly is an achievement of the specialized international databases CISG-online and the CISG database run by Pace Law School.

[3] This case law is almost completely accessible in CISG-online in the original (German) language, with English translations available at the Pace University CISG database. See also the official Austrian online database "Rechtsinformationssystem des Bundes (RIS)" (http://www.ris.bka.gv.at), subdatabase "Judikatur Justiz," (http://www.ris.bka.gv.at/Jus). Insert the reference number under "*Geschäftszahl*" and mark "*Entscheidungstexte (TE)*" to obtain the full text document, or enter a keyword under "*Suchworte.*" The most frequently used abbreviations for the CISG in these databases include: "UN-K," "UNK," "UN-Kaufrecht," or "UN-Kaufrechtsübereinkommen."

Peter Schlechtriem and Ingeborg Schwenzer,[4] and Ulrich Magnus' commentary as part of the Staudinger series.[5] The new CISG attracted interest shortly after its adoption,[6] but there is only one Austrian CISG textbook for students and practitioners,[7] and only one Austrian commentary on the CISG is available.[8] Austrian courts, practitioners, and academics therefore primarily consult German literature and case law, which is much more comprehensive.[9]

Some general observations regarding Austrian CISG case law can be made. Austrian courts, which operate with a codified civil law system, have had little difficulties in interpreting the provisions of the CISG in a systematic, coherent, and methodologically thorough way, notwithstanding the fact that some CISG concepts clearly deviate from domestic law. On the other hand, Austrian courts arguably have more difficulties in applying flexible (or indefinite) concepts such as "good faith," "fundamental breach," or "reasonable time," and appear to be reluctant to develop the law in these areas. The fact that the CISG widely makes use of such flexible concepts is often regarded as one of its major disadvantages,[10] and Austrian courts prefer tight and clear guidelines rather than being provided with an opportunity to develop "fair" solutions within a wide scope of discretion. However, once sufficient concretizations of such general principles are established, Austrian courts have no difficulty in applying them and developing them further. Austrian courts rarely revisit issues and have shown a reluctance to adjust them by taking into account developments in other countries. This reluctance, together with the fact that courts regularly seek guidance in German literature, results in a relatively high standard of predictability in Austrian court decisions.

---

[4] The most recent (German) edition is *Kommentar zum Einheitlichen UN-Kaufrecht*, 5th ed. (ed. P. Schlechtriem and I. Schwenzer) (Munich and Basel: C.H. Beck and Helbing Lichtenhahn, 2008), or *Commentary on the UN Convention on the International Sale of Goods* (CISG), 3rd ed. (ed. P. Schlechtriem and I. Schwenzer) (Munich: C.H. Beck, 2010) (English version).

[5] Ulrich Magnus in *J. von Staudingers Kommentar zum Bürgerlichen Gesetzbuch mit Einführungsgesetz und Nebengesetzen – Wiener Kaufrecht (CISG)* (Berlin: Sellier/de Gruyter, 2013) (hereafter referred to as *Staudinger*).

[6] See *Das UNCITRAL-Kaufrecht im Vergleich zum österreichischen Recht* (ed. P. Doralt) (Vienna: Manz Verlag, 1985); Georg Wilhelm, *UN-Kaufrecht – Einführung und Gesetzestext* (Vienna: Manz Verlag, 1993); Martin Karollus, "UN-Kaufrecht: Hinweise für die Vertragspraxis," 115 *Juristische Blätter* 23 (1993); later contributions include, e.g., Ernst A. Kramer, "Uniforme Interpretation von Einheitsprivatrecht – mit besonderer Berücksichtigung von Art 7 UNKR," 118 *Juristische Blätter* 137 (1996); Radivoje Petrikic, *Das Nacherfüllungsrecht im UN-Kaufrecht – Grundprobleme der Leistungsstörungen* (Vienna: Manz Verlag, 1999); Willibald Posch and Ulfried Terlitza, "Entscheidungen des österreichischen Obersten Gerichtshof zur UN-Kaufrechtskonvention (CISG)," 1 *Internationales Handelsrecht* 47 (2001); Ernst A. Kramer, "Rechtzeitige Untersuchung und Mängelrüge bei Sachmängeln nach Art 38 und 39 UN-Kaufrecht – Eine Zwischenbilanz," in *Beiträge zum Unternehmensrecht – Festschrift für Hans-Georg Koppensteiner zum 65. Geburtstag* (ed. E.A. Kramer and W. Schuhmacher) (Vienna: Orac Verlag, 2001), 617; Brigitta Lurger, "Die neue Rechtsprechungsentwicklung zum UN-Kaufrechtsübereinkommen," 124 *Juristische Blätter* 750 (2002).

[7] Martin Karollus, *UN-Kaufrecht – Eine systematische Darstellung für Studium und Praxis* (Vienna and New York: Springer-Verlag, 1991).

[8] Willibald Posch in *ABGB Praxiskommentar*, vol. 4, 3rd ed. (ed. M. Schwimann) (Vienna: LexisNexis ARD Orac, 2006), 1343–521.

[9] In addition to the references in notes 4 and 5, see, e.g., *Kommentar zum UN-Kaufrecht*, 2nd ed. (ed. H. Honsell) (Heidelberg: Springer, 2010), and the CISG commentary included in *Münchener Kommentar zum Handelsgesetzbuch – HGB*, vol. 6, 3rd ed. (Munich: C.H. Beck, 2013).

[10] See, e.g., Ferdinand Kerschner, *Zivilrecht VIII – Internationales Privatrecht*, 3rd ed. (Vienna: LexisNexis, 2010), 59, para. 13/3.

II. Principle of Good Faith

The principle of good faith, which is explicitly referred to as a criterion of interpretation in CISG Article 7(1), is one example where Austrian court practice has not contributed much to the development of CISG. The principle, for instance, is briefly referred to in the context of determining whether, under Article 77, a reasonable person would have reasonably be expected to take certain measures to mitigate loss.[11] These cases only reference the principle of good faith in general, but do not concretize standards that can be applied to Article 77. The same can be said in cases where Austrian courts apply the principle of good faith in determining whether a seller waived its right to invoke the buyer's failure to provide prompt and specific notification of nonconformity under Article 39.[12] Another instance concerns the determination of practices in the sense of Article 9, which are defined as "conduct that occurs with a certain frequency and during a certain period of time set by the parties, which the parties can then assume in good faith will be observed again in a similar instance. Examples are the disregard of notice deadlines, the allowance of certain cash discounts upon immediate payment, delivery tolerances, and so forth."[13] Another issue dealt with by an Austrian court is whether foreign-language standard terms have or have not been incorporated into a contract. It held that in a certain context, a party that has sent such standard terms and declared its intent that the standard terms govern the contract can, under the principle of good faith, expect the other party to reject the standard terms in the case it is not willing to accept them.[14]

III. Contract Formation

CISG contract formation rules have been the subject in a substantial number of cases. It is stated, for instance, that:

> [A]ccording to Article 14 CISG, a contract is concluded by two corresponding declarations of intent, that is, the offer of one party and the acceptance of the other party, and the contract of sale does not have to be in writing nor is it subject to any other form requirements (Article 11 CISG). The offer, which must be sufficiently definite in that it indicates the goods, the quantity and the price (the latter two must be at least determinable), is interpreted according to the offeror's intent where the offeree could not have been unaware of such intent.[15]

---

[11] See OGH, February 6, 1996, 10 Ob 518/95, CISG-online 224 = SZ 69/26 (propane case), English translation available at http://cisgw3.law.pace.edu/cases/960206a3.html; OGH, January 14, 2002, 7 Ob 301/01t, CISG-online 643 = JBl 2002, 592 (cooling system case), available at http://cisgw3.law.pace.edu/cases/020114a3.html. See also chapter VII.D.

[12] Cf. OGH, April 2, 2009, 8 Ob 125/08b, CISG-online 1889 = JBl 2009, 647 (boiler case), available at http://cisgw3.law.pace.edu/cases/090402a3.html (CISG contracted out implicitly); Internationales Schiedsgericht der Bundeskammer der gewerblichen Wirtschaft (Wien), June 15, 1994, SCH-4318, CISG-online 120 and 691 (metal sheet case).

[13] OGH, August 31, 2005, 7 Ob 175/05v, CISG-online 1093 (tantalum powder case), available at http://cisgw3.law.pace.edu/cases/050831a3.html (quote follows Pace translation).

[14] OLG Innsbruck, February 1, 2005, 1 R 253/04x, CISG-online 1130 (tantalum powder case), available at http://cisgw3.law.pace.edu/cases/050201a3.html.

[15] OGH, February 6, 1996, 10 Ob 518/95, CISG-online 224 = SZ 69/26 (propane case), available at http://cisgw3.law.pace.edu/cases/960206a3.html (quote follows Pace translation). See also OLG Graz, June 15, 2000, 4 R 80/00t, CISG-online 799 (ski-shoes case), available at http://cisgw3.law.pace.edu/cases/

Similarly, cases dealing with the offeree's declaration of acceptance summarize the prerequisites established in Article 18[16] or state that where there is a material modification of the terms, the response constitutes a counteroffer within the meaning of Article 19(1) and (3).[17] More specifically, the Austrian Supreme Court,[18] following Austrian legal doctrine, ruled that the "material" alteration standard does not establish a strict rule, but constitutes a rule of interpretation that is refutable in individual cases.[19] Accordingly, where the acceptance alters terms relating to the quantity of goods, this change may in certain cases still amount to a nonmaterial alteration in the sense of Article 19(2). The finding of a contract despite the change in the quantity term may be implied from the negotiations or from usages established between the parties. The Austrian Supreme Court held that because the alteration made by the offeree benefited the offeror, the response was an acceptance and not a counteroffer.[20]Another court held that where obtaining insurance has been made a condition of a contract of sale, no contract is established where the insurance company rejects the request for insurance.[21]

In another case, the Supreme Court held that where the buyer submits its offer to a special type of commercial agent who cannot, according to applicable domestic law, conclude contracts in its own name,[22] and the buyer is aware of this fact, the contract is concluded with the company represented by the agent.[23] Austrian courts have not been presented with a revocation of an offer under Article 16, which differs fundamentally from Austrian law where an offer is considered to be a binding promise.[24] Also, there is no Austrian case dealing with the problematic relationship between Articles 14 (offer) and 55 (open price term).

A. *Sufficient Determination or Determinability*

In its first CISG case, the Austrian Supreme Court had to determine whether the buyer's offer provided sufficient specification of the quantity of goods and price as required by Article 14.[25]

000615a3.html; OGH, March 9, 2000, 6 Ob 311/99z, CISG-online 573 = ZfRV 2000, 152 (roofing material case), available at http://cisgw3.law.pace.edu/cases/000309a3.html.

[16] OLG Graz, June 15, 2000, 4 R 80/00t, CISG-online 799 (ski-shoes case), available at http://cisgw3. law.pace.edu/cases/000615a3.html (impossible to establish which one of the two offerees had issued the declaration of acceptance).

[17] OGH, March 9, 2000, 6 Ob 311/99z, CISG-online 573 = ZfRV 2000, 152 (roofing material case), available at http://cisgw3.law.pace.edu/cases/000309a3.html.

[18] OGH, March 20, 1997, 2 Ob 58/97m, CISG-online 269 = JBl 1997, 592 (mono ammonium phosphate case), available at http://cisgw3.law.pace.edu/cases/970320a3.html.

[19] Court referred to Karollus, *UN-Kaufrecht*, 70; Franz Bydlinski, "Das allgemeine Vertragsrecht," in *Das UNCITRAL-Kaufrecht im Vergleich zum österreichischen Recht* (ed. P. Doralt) (Vienna: Manz Verlag, 1985), 57, at 72. See also Schroeter in Schlechtriem and Schwenzer, *Commentary*, Article 19, para. 8b.

[20] Offer defined quantity as "10,000 mt +/− 5%," while acceptance stated "10,000 mt +/− 10% subject to selection of the ship."

[21] OLG Graz, March 7, 2002, 2 R 23/02y, CISG-online 669 (pork case), available at http://cisgw3.law.pace. edu/cases/020307a3.html.

[22] *Selbständiger Handelsvertreter*, §84(1) of the German Commercial Code.

[23] OGH, June 18, 1997, 3 Ob 512/96, CISG-online 292 = JBl 1998, 255 (shoes case), available at http:// cisgw3.law.pace.edu/cases/970618a3.html.

[24] Cf. Bydlinski, "Das allgemeine Vertragsrecht," 66f.

[25] OGH, November 10, 1994, 2 Ob 547/93, CISG-online 117 = JBl 1995, 253 (with a gloss by Martin Karollus) (chinchilla furs case), available at http://cisgw3.law.pace.edu/cases/941110a3.html.

With reference to Articles 14(1) and 8, the court found that specification of quantity and price may be general in nature where the parties agree on *criteria that allow for an interpretation* that results in a definite price, type of goods, and quantity. This liberal interpretation of Article 14(1) requirements was derived from Article 8's reasonable person standard. On this basis, the Supreme Court held that ordering "a larger number of Chinchilla furs" would constitute a sufficient determination of the quantity of goods, taking into account the subsequent conduct of the parties, and in particular the fact that the buyer later sold most of delivered furs without raising any objection to the quantity of the goods delivered. The logic of the court formally complies with Articles 14 and 18, namely that the quantity of the goods due can be determined by way of interpretation. Such reasoning presupposes that it is possible to deduce from the term "a larger number" the number of 249 furs that were ultimately shipped by the seller. A more reasonable interpretation of the buyer's offer is that it granted the seller a right to unilaterally determine a certain quantity of goods within the scope of "larger number." Taking delivery of a quantity of 249 confirmed that this number was within the scope originally envisaged in the buyer's offer.[26]

Regarding the specification of price, the Supreme Court concluded that the parties' agreement on a price range between 35 and 65 German marks per item for furs of average to "above average" quality provides sufficient indication of price. As a result, the court upheld a lower court's calculation of a price of 50 German marks for furs of average quality. To hold otherwise would allow a buyer to take advantage of its own vague order.[27]

B. *Incorporation of Standard Terms*

Austrian courts hold that the question of whether standard terms and conditions used by one party are incorporated into the contract is to be solved under the CISG rules on the formation of contract (Articles 14–24).[28] Therefore, standard terms, in order to be applicable to a contract, must have become part of the offer, which is to be determined according to the offeror's intention assessed from the perspective of a reasonable person (Article 8). Inclusion of standard terms into the offer may be made by express or implied reference in the offeror's declaration, or can be implied from the negotiations or from a practice established between the parties (Article 9(1)). More specifically, the courts demand the satisfaction of two requirements for standard terms to become part of an offer: (1) their intended incorporation into the contract must be sufficiently *discernable* to the other party and (2) their incorporation must be *reasonable* from the other party's perspective (*zumutbar*), that is, the addressee must have the possibility to become aware of, and understand, the standard terms' content.[29]

---

[26] Cf. also gloss by Martin Karollus, 256.

[27] The buyer claimed that he had been able to sell the furs for an average price of only slightly more than ten German marks per item.

[28] Austrian courts have widely used German commentaries in this area, such as Schroeter in Schlechtriem and Schwenzer, *Commentary*, Article 14, paras. 32–76; Magnus in *Staudinger*, CISG Article 14, paras. 40–2.

[29] For these general principles, see OGH, December 17, 2003, 7 Ob 275/03x, CISG-online 828 = SZ 2003/175 (tantalum powder case), available at http://cisgw3.law.pace.edu/cases/031217a3.html. See also OGH, February 6, 1996, 10 Ob 518/95, CISG-online 224 = SZ 69/26 (propane case), available at http://

One case deserves particular mention, in which the Austrian Supreme Court discusses the second requirement mentioned here – the addressee's reasonable possibility to become aware of, and understand, the standard terms' content. In the case, the specific issue was whether the offeror's standard terms, written in a *foreign language*, could satisfy the second requirement and be incorporated into the contract.[30] In the case, an Austrian company order was in English, which was the language of the owner of the seller company, and made explicit reference to the buyer's standard terms, which were printed on the backside of the form. The standard terms, however, were in German. The seller did not know German, but another company, whose representative speaks German, negotiated the transaction. Also, the buyer had ordered several samples of tantalum powder prior to the transaction at issue. Each time the order was in English with an explicit reference to the German standard terms on its backside. The standard terms had never been objected in the previous orders or in the order in question.

The Supreme Court distinguished two groups of criteria for determining whether the addressee might be expected to have knowledge and understanding of the standard terms (which includes reasonable efforts for procuring a translation). First, the length, intensity, and economic importance of the *business relations* between the parties, and any practices that may have been established between them, are to be taken into account. The more intense and economically important the business relation, the more *can the offeror*, who has referred to its standard terms and repeatedly supplied them to the other party, *expect the addressee* to either procure a translation itself or ask the offeror to provide a translation.[31] Second, the *degree the language used is known* in the addressee's culture must be considered. The court noted "in the case of an internationally operating enterprise, the addressee must object to standard terms supplied in a world language without undue delay if this language is not understood, at least where knowledge of this world language is not unlikely." The Court held that German is a world language.[32] However, it appears doubtful whether German can really be regarded as a "universal language" or "world language" for the purposes of international trade, and it may also be

cisgw3.law.pace.edu/cases/960206a3.html; OGH, January 14, 2002, 7 Ob 301/01t, CISG-online 643 = JBl 2002, 592 (cooling system case), available at http://cisgw3.law.pace.edu/cases/020114a3.html; OGH, December 16, 2003, 4 Ob 147/03a, RdW 2004, 416 (spacers case); OLG Innsbruck, February 1, 2005, 1 R 253/04x, CISG-online 1130 (tantalum powder case), available at http://cisgw3.law.pace.edu/cases/050201a3.html; OLG Linz, September 24, 2007, 1 R 77/07k, CISG-online 1583 (laminated glass case), available at http://cisgw3.law.pace.edu/cases/070924a3.html (summarizing the named principles).

30 OGH, December 17, 2003, 7 Ob 275/03x, CISG-online 828 = SZ 2003/175 (tantalum powder case), available at http://cisgw3.law.pace.edu/cases/031217a3.html; confirmed by OGH, August 31, 2005, 7 Ob 175/05v, CISG-online 1093 (tantalum powder case), available at http://cisgw3.law.pace.edu/cases/050831a3.html; OLG Linz, August 8, 2005, 3 R 57/05f, CISG-online 1087 (spacers for insulation glass case), available at http://cisgw3.law.pace.edu/cases/050808a3.html; similar OLG Innsbruck, February 1, 2005, 1 R 253/04x, CISG-online 1130 (tantalum powder case), available at http://cisgw3.law.pace.edu/cases/050201a3.html.

31 The Supreme Court referred the case back to the lower court, which held that the standard terms were incorporated into the contract. See OLG Innsbruck, February 1, 2005, 1 R 253/04x, CISG-online 1130 (tantalum powder case), available at http://cisgw3.law.pace.edu/cases/050201a3.html; OGH, August 31, 2005, 7 Ob 175/05v, CISG-online 1093 (tantalum powder case), available at http://cisgw3.law.pace.edu/cases/050831a3.html.

32 OGH, December 17, 2003, 7 Ob 275/03x, CISG-online 828 = SZ 2003/175 (tantalum powder case), available at http://cisgw3.law.pace.edu/cases/031217a3.html; OLG Linz, August 8, 2005, 3 R 57/05f, CISG-online 1087 (spacers for insulation glass case), available at http://cisgw3.law.pace.edu/cases/050808a3.html (German is a world language).

questioned whether the "world language" criterion makes any substantial contribution in addition to the general principles outlined above.[33]

How do the criteria developed by the court fit the concepts of offer and acceptance under the CISG? Why should it matter whether *the offeror may expect* the addressee to act in a certain way (obtaining or asking for a translation)? Article 8(2) suggests that determining the content of the offer by asking how a reasonable *addressee* would understand it is a more appropriate approach. Also, the approach referring to the failure of the addressee to object to the standard terms (which is a *later* act or omission by the *other* party) is not well suited for determining whether the offeror's standard terms have become part of the offer. The criteria established by the court better fit as a test of how a reasonable offeror may understand the statement or conduct amounting to the addressee's *acceptance,* where the offeror's standard terms are not explicitly agreed or objected to in that acceptance. Where the addressee could be reasonably expected to understand the offeror's standard terms, they would be incorporated by the offeree's acceptance. Where, on the other hand, no such expectation is justified, any "acceptance" should not be regarded as incorporating the terms. In the latter case, however, placing this substantive test solely on the interpretation of acceptance would mean that the addressee's "acceptance" would only constitute a counteroffer in the sense of Article 19. Using the traditional approach applied by the court, on the other hand, standard terms that do not pass the substantive test described earlier do not become part of the offer, and any acceptance of the addressee will establish an enforceable contract. This result appears preferable from a policy point of view, as it helps to protect the interests of the addressee when entering into the contract while placing the risk of unintelligible standard terms on the person who intends to apply them. From the view of CISG interpretation it is preferable to phrase the Court's criteria for foreign-language standard terms by taking a reasonable addressee's perspective.[34]

This discussion illustrates the difficulties of incorporating substantive tests – which arguably are necessary in some instances to achieve appropriate results – into the formal scheme of offer and acceptance under the CISG. The appropriate means for doing so are the interpretation rules of Article 8 (standard of a reasonable addressee).

C. *Battle of the Forms*

As yet, the Austrian Supreme Court has not dealt with the problem of conflicting standard terms ("battle of forms") under the CISG. It is therefore an open question whether the Supreme Court would follow the so-called last-shot rule, under which the party that makes the last reference to its own standard terms will succeed in incorporating them into the contract, or the alternative knock-out rule,[35] under which conflicting standard

---

[33] Cf. critique by Schroeter in Schlechtriem and Schwenzer, *Commentary*, Article 14, paras. 65–6.

[34] The question could be phrased as whether a reasonable offeree can expect foreign-language standard terms to be legally accepted as a part of the offer. A reasonable person's expectation increases the greater the value of the transaction – because a reasonable person would be expected to undertake active steps to understand the terms – and if the standard terms are supplied in a commonly spoken language.

[35] Also known, in German, as the *Restgültigkeitstheorie* (meaning that the rest of the contract, i.e., to the extent no conflict as to content exists, remains valid) or *Teildissenslösung* (named by the idea that to the extent the parties' standard terms are incompatible, there is partial *dissensus*, while the parties agree on the rest of the contract).

terms are voided to the extent they are incompatible, and are substituted by the default rules provided by the CISG.

Martin Karollus[36] and an Austrian court of appeal – the Oberlandesgericht Linz[37] – have held that the last-shot rule follows the concept of Article 19(1) under which an "acceptance" containing modifications to the original offer constitutes a counteroffer. Consequently, the main issue for the court of appeal was whether the original offeror (buyer) accepted the counteroffer made by the original offeree (seller). The court concluded that such acceptance had been made because the buyer did not refer to its own standard terms in the later communication, whereas the seller referred to its terms in its subsequent correspondence.

However, the Austrian Supreme Court has shown a preference for the knock-out rule when dealing with non-CISG cases,[38] the German Supreme Court has adopted the knock-out approach in CISG cases,[39] and legal literature has developed approaches to bring the knock-out rule in line with the CISG system, for example, by assuming an implied contractual derogation from Article 19.[40] So, the likelihood is high that the Austrian Supreme Court will adopt the knock-out rule when confronted with a CISG battle of the forms case.

IV. Conformity of Goods: Inspection and Notice

CISG Articles 38 and 39 cover the buyer's duties to examine the goods and to notify the seller of any lack of conformity. They are the most litigated provisions of the CISG. Asserting that the buyer failed to comply with these duties is a standard defense for sellers in cases of the delivery of nonconforming goods. There is only one case where the parallel provision of Article 43 on the buyer's duty to notify the seller of any right or claim of a third party has played a significant role.[41]

A. CISG Articles 38 and 39

In this area, as in others, the courts have sought guidance in academic literature. For example, as to the *manner of examination* that must be performed by the buyer, it is stated that "primarily relevant for the type of examination are the agreements between the parties. In the absence of any such agreements, the required manner of examination can be gleaned from trade usage and practices." Where high quantities of goods are

---

[36] Karollus, *UN-Kaufrecht*, 70f. (Karollus does not favor the last-shot rule as to substance; battle-of-forms resolution in Article 19 is a "serious shortfall").
[37] OLG Linz, March 23, 2005, 6 R 200/04f, CISG-online 1376 = IHR 2007, 123 (conveyor band case), available at http://cisgw3.law.pace.edu/cases/050323a3.html.
[38] See, for instance, OGH, December 20, 1990, 7 Ob 590/90, JBl 1991, 120; OGH, September 13, 2001, 6 Ob 73/01f, RdW 2002, 149; OGH, April 24, 2003, 6 Ob 306/02x, JBl 2003, 856.
[39] BGH, January 9, 2002, VIII ZR 304/00, CISG-online 651 (powdered milk case), available at http://cisgw3.law.pace.edu/cases/020109g1.html.
[40] See, e.g., Schroeter in Schlechtriem and Schwenzer, *Commentary*, Article 19, paras. 31ff. (esp. paras. 38–51); Magnus in *Staudinger*, CISG Article 19, paras. 20–5.
[41] See OGH, September 12, 2006, 10 Ob 122/05x, CISG-online 1364 = IHR 2007, 39 (CD media case), available at http://cisgw3.law.pace.edu/cases/060912a3.html.

delivered, consulting experts may be required.[42] For determining the *short period* for the examination, reference is usually made to "the size of the buyer's enterprise, the kind of goods to be examined, their complexity or perishability or seasonal character, the quantity to be examined, the effort involved to do it, and so forth"[43] (note that "quantity to be examined" should be read as "the type of nonconformity that may occur").[44] Applicable contract terms regulating these issues are, of course, always to be considered.[45]

Regarding the computation of *reasonable time* for giving notice under Article 39(1), the courts have taken into account "the objective and subjective circumstances of each individual case . . . ; this entails the professional as well as personal situation of the buyer, the peculiarities of the goods, the size of the delivery or the kind of remedy chosen."[46] Such criteria, of course, leave open the question of what kind of standard to apply when there are no specific circumstances that would support a prolonging or shortening of the notice period. Courts therefore strive for establishing some kind of standard period for solving "normal" cases, and for providing a point of departure for others. First, lower courts contemplated a standard period of one month[47] or two months[48] to be appropriate. The Austrian Supreme Court sought guidance in German literature where it found two statements that fourteen days was considered a suitable standard period for effecting both inspection and notice.[49] In addition, the Supreme Court made reference to one German

---

[42] Cf. OGH, August 27, 1999, 1 Ob 223/99x, CISG-online 485 = ZfRV 2000, 31 (trekking shoes case), available at http://cisgw3.law.pace.edu/cases/990827a3.html.

[43] See (with the same wording) OGH, October 15, 1998, 2 Ob 191/98x, CISG-online 380 = JBl 1999, 318 (timber case), available at http://cisgw3.law.pace.edu/cases/981015a3.html; OGH, August 27, 1999, 1 Ob 223/99x, CISG-online 485 = ZfRV 2000, 31 (trekking shoes case), available at http://cisgw3.law.pace.edu/ cases/990827a3.html; OGH, January 14, 2002, 7 Ob 301/01t, CISG-online 643 = JBl 2002, 592 (cooling system case), available at http://cisgw3.law.pace.edu/cases/020114a3.html.

[44] This is an example for how a typing error can change "the law" in a country. In OGH, October 15, 1998, 2 Ob 191/98x (see note 43), the German word *Menge* (quantity) was written instead of the similar-sounding word *Mängel* (defects, nonconformities), which had been used in a CISG commentary from which the Supreme Court quoted: see Willibald Posch in *Praxiskommentar zum ABGB*, vol. 5, 2nd ed. (ed. M. Schwimann) (Vienna: Orac-Verlag, 1997), UN-Kaufrecht Article 38, para. 6 (Posch's text is identical in the current 3rd ed.).

[45] See, e.g., OGH, June 30, 1998, 1 Ob 273/97x, CISG-online 410 = JBl 1999, 252 (pineapples case), available at http://cisgw3.law.pace.edu/cases/980630a3.html, applying the "Common European Usages for the Domestic and International Sale of Eatable Fruits and Vegetables" (COFREUROP).

[46] See the cases quoted in *supra* note 43, which also state that the Article 39 period is less strict than the period available under the former Austrian law, §377 Commercial Code (HGB), under which notification after five days for Christmas trees or, in other cases, ten days had been considered to be too late; Ernst A. Kramer in *Kommentar zum Handelsgesetzbuch*, vol. 1, 3rd ed. (ed. M. Straube) (Vienna: Manz, 2003) §§377, 378, para. 42. This rule was changed in 2007 in order to adopt the standard applied under CISG Article 39. However, fourteen days is generally considered reasonable; cf. Ernst A. Kramer and Claudia K. Martini in *Wiener Kommentar zum Unternehmensgesetzbuch*, 15th installment of 4th ed. (ed. M. Straube) (Vienna: Manz, 2009), §§377, 378, paras. 41–4. See also OGH, April 25, 2001, 9 Ob 105/01h (mash case); OGH, August 31, 2010, 4 Ob 98/10f, JBl 2011, 49 (old wood parquet floor case).

[47] OLG Graz, March 11, 1998, 4 R 283/97p, CISG-online 670 (timber case), available at http://cisgw3.law. pace.edu/cases/980311a3.html.

[48] OLG Innsbruck, July 1, 1994, 4 R 161/94 (garden flowers case), available at http://cisgw3.law.pace.edu/ cases/940701a3.html.

[49] See Ulrich Magnus in *Staudinger*, 13th ed. (Berlin: Sellier/de Gruyter, 1994), CISG Article 39, para. 49. The second source quoted by the Supreme Court is stricter, discussing 3–4 days for the inspection period under Article 38 and 4–6 days for giving notice under Article 39; see Burghard Piltz, *UN-Kaufrecht – Wegweiser für die Praxis* (Bonn: Economica-Verlag, 1991), 52f., paras. 142, 145 (Supreme Court refers to this author as if he suggested a standard period of 14 days).

Supreme Court case where a period of one month was described as "very generous," and to one Austrian scholar who expressed the view that a period of one month would be too liberal.[50] On this basis, the Austrian Supreme Court held that a standard period of about fourteen days was an appropriate amount of time to effectuate an inspection and provide a notice of nonconformity.[51] This statement has been repeated by numerous further cases up to the present day,[52] completely ignoring foreign case law developments applying fundamentally more liberal standards, and attempts to consolidate these diverging views with a standard period of one month.[53]

On another level, a single fixed period cannot be a reasonable time in all circumstances. The Austrian Supreme Court[54] did recognize the need for flexibility in one case in which the buyer did not have the means to undertake detailed examinations to detect adulterations committed by adding sugar syrup to fruit mash, which is storable only for a short time, before processing the mash further. The Supreme Court upheld the lower courts' assessment that, in the particular case, only an external analysis could establish sufficient facts for an adequately concrete notification, and that extending the notice period to more than fourteen days in such a case was appropriate.

The standards as to the *specificity of the content* in a notice, under Article 39(1), are generally described as follows:

> Notice must be specific inasmuch as it specifies the lack of conformity. Sweeping statements and general complaints are in this respect not sufficient to meet the content requirements demanded for notice, so that the seller is put in a position to be able to reasonably react. According to prevailing opinion, it must nevertheless be sufficient if the seller is informed of the essential result of a proper inspection, so that the seller can form an idea of possible defects.[55]

---

[50] See BGH, March 8, 1995, VIII ZR 159/94, CISG-online 155 = NJW 1995, 2099 = JR 1996, 23 (New Zealand mussels case), available at http://cisgw3.law.pace.edu/cases/950308g3.html, and the case note by Martin Karollus in JR 1996, 27.

[51] OGH, October 15, 1998, 2 Ob 191/98x, CISG-online 380 = JBl 1999, 318 (timber case), available at http://cisgw3.law.pace.edu/cases/981015a3.html.

[52] See OGH, August 27, 1999, 1 Ob 223/99x, CISG-online 485 = ZfRV 2000, 31 (trekking shoes case), available at http://cisgw3.law.pace.edu/cases/990827a3.html; OGH, April 2, 2009, 8 Ob 125/08b, CISG-online 1889 = JBl 2009, 647 (boiler case), available at http://cisgw3.law.pace.edu/cases/090402a3.html; OGH, August 31, 2010, 4 Ob 98/10f, JBl 2011, 49 (old wood parquet floor case); OLG Innsbruck, April 26, 2002, 4 R 58/02i, CISG-online 1196 (tapping equipment case), available at http://cisgw3.law.pace.edu/cases/020426a3.html; OLG Linz, June 1, 2005, 1 R 68/05h, CISG-online 1088 (hydraulic crane case), available at http://cisgw3.law.pace.edu/cases/050601a3.html; HG Wien, May 3, 2007, 43 Cg 34/05f, CISG-online 1783 (poppy seed case), available at http://cisgw3.law.pace.edu/cases/070503a3.html. See also OGH, April 25, 2001, 9 Ob 105/01h (mash case), (applying a longer period based on specific circumstances).

[53] For a review of international case law, and for the suggestion of moving toward a compromise of about a one-month period, see Schwenzer in Schlechtriem and Schwenzer, *Commentary*, Article 39, para. 17; cf. also Stefan Kröll in *UN Convention on Contracts for the International Sale of Goods (CISG) – Commentary* (ed. S. Kröll, L. Mistelis, and P. Perales Viscasillas) (Munich: C.H. Beck, Hart & Nomos, 2011), Article 38, paras. 77–83, and Article 39, paras. 79–86 (suggesting, as starting points, one to two weeks for examination and about four weeks for giving notice). See, on the other hand, Ernst A. Kramer, "Rechtzeitige Untersuchung und Mängelrüge bei Sachmängeln nach Art 38 und 39 UN-Kaufrecht – Eine Zwischenbilanz," in *Beiträge zum Unternehmensrecht – Festschrift für Hans-Georg Koppensteiner zum 65. Geburtstag* (ed. E.A. Kramer and W. Schuhmacher) (Vienna: Orac Verlag, 2001), 617, esp. 627f. (defends the idea of a standard period of 14 days).

[54] OGH, April 25, 2001, 9 Ob 105/01h (mash case).

[55] See OGH, January 14, 2002, 7 Ob 301/01t, CISG-online 643 = JBl 2002, 592 (cooling system case), available at http://cisgw3.law.pace.edu/cases/020114a3.html; OGH, August 31, 2010, 4 Ob 98/10f, JBl 2011, 49

The content-related standards of a notice may be lower where a detailed inspection is prevented by the conduct of the seller. For example, where the seller's serious delay causes the buyer to assemble a machine immediately at the site of its customer, instead of first subjecting it to thorough examination and tests at the buyer's premises, a less detailed notice of nonconformity is justified.[56]

Some further aspects of notice of nonconformity found in Austrian case law include: (1) Notice must be given to the seller, so that it will generally not suffice to notify other companies operating within the supply chain or in an aftersales service network, unless the buyer can establish that these other companies are authorized by the seller to receive such notices in its name.[57] (2) There are no requirements as to form.[58] (3) It is on the buyer to prove that notice has been given timely and properly, and this also applies to proving that the defects noticed only at a later time could not have been discovered within a short time after delivery.[59] The buyer must only prove that the notice was sent in time; the risk that the notice gets lost during transmission is on the seller (Article 27).[60] (4) Where the buyer fails to comply with its duty of notification, its loss of rights and remedies under Article 39(1) only pertain to the particular delivery, but not to future installments under the contract.[61] (5) The seller, according to Article 40, was not entitled to rely on the buyer's failure to give due notice because the seller had actual knowledge of the nonconformity.[62]

An Austrian arbitration court held that the seller's defense of belated notification may be forfeited (*Verwirkung*) under the general principle of good faith and the principle of *venire contra factum proprium* (prohibition of contradictory conduct), pursuant to Article 7(2). The seller's defense is forfeited if the buyer reasonably relied on seller's (express or implied) assurance that it would not raise such a defense. In this case, the seller had created the impression of accepting the buyer's reclamations although they had been

---

(old wood parquet floor case); OGH, August 27, 1999, 1 Ob 223/99x, CISG-online 485 = ZfRV 2000, 31 (trekking shoes case), available at http://cisgw3.law.pace.edu/cases/990827a3.html (content-related standards of notice); OGH, May 8, 2008, 3 Ob 79/08a, CISG-online 1784 (poppy seed case), available at http://cisgw3.law.pace.edu/cases/080508a3.html (specified, but incorrect notice; seed contaminated with chamomile instead of caraway).

[56] OGH, January 14, 2002, 7 Ob 301/01t, CISG-online 643 = JBl 2002, 592 (cooling system case), available at http://cisgw3.law.pace.edu/cases/020114a3.html.

[57] See OLG Linz, January 23, 2006, 6 R 160/05z, CISG-online 1377 (auto case), available at http://cisgw3.law.pace.edu/cases/060123a3.html.

[58] See OGH, October 15, 1998, 2 Ob 191/98x, CISG-online 380 = JBl 1999, 318 (timber case), available at http://cisgw3.law.pace.edu/cases/981015a3.html; HG Wien, May 3, 2007, 43 Cg 34/05f, CISG-online 1783 (poppy seed case), available at http://cisgw3.law.pace.edu/cases/070503a3.html.

[59] OGH, August 27, 1999, 1 Ob 223/99x, CISG-online 485 = ZfRV 2000, 31 (trekking shoes case), available at http://cisgw3.law.pace.edu/cases/990827a3.html; OGH, March 21, 2000, 10 Ob 344/99g, CISG-online 641 = ZfRV 2000, 185 (wood case), available at http://cisgw3.law.pace.edu/cases/000321a3.html. See also Kröll in Kröll et al., *Commentary*, Article 39, para. 124; Schwenzer in Schlechtriem and Schwenzer, *Commentary*, Article 39, para. 40. For a different view, see Chapter 14 of this volume).

[60] OGH, May 24, 2005, 4 Ob 80/05a, CISG-online 1046 = RdW 2005, 539 (grinding stock case), available at http://cisgw3.law.pace.edu/cases/050524a3.html.

[61] Schiedsgericht der Börse für landwirtschaftliche Produkte in Wien, December 10, 1997, S 2/97, CISG-online 351 (barley case), available at http://cisgw3.law.pace.edu/cases/971210a3.html.

[62] OGH, November 30, 2006, 6 Ob 257/06x, CISG-online 1417 = IHR 2007, 74 (water-jet cutting machine case), available at http://cisgw3.law.pace.edu/cases/061130a3.html. See also OGH, April 22, 2010, 8 Ob 30/10k, IHR 2011, 38 (stair-panels case).

notified belatedly.[63] A similar, though not identical, approach is applied in a Supreme Court case where the seller is deemed to have impliedly waived its defense by taking back the nonconforming goods and stating its willingness to replace them.[64]

Finally, Austrian courts occasionally have dealt with Article 44 under which the buyer, notwithstanding its failure to comply with Articles 38 and 39, keeps the remedies of price reduction and damages (except for lost profits), if the buyer has a reasonable excuse for its failure. The Supreme Court clarified that Article 44 provides an exception only to Article 39(1), but not to the two-year limitation period found in Article 39(2).[65] The meaning of "reasonable excuse" is vaguely defined as those situations "where the buyer has refrained from giving notice on grounds which an average buyer in the ordinary course of business, acting in good faith, can be excused for, and if it acted with the kind of diligence which it could subjectively be expected to apply in the circumstances."[66] An excuse can also result from conduct of the seller, such as where the seller expresses that it is not interested in receiving a timely and proper notice.[67] In the latter situation, this approach can conflict with the waiver defense discussed in relationship to Article 40. Where the requirements of a full waiver of the seller's defense are fulfilled, the waiver approach should be applied[68] because the buyer then keeps the full range of remedies instead of the limited remedies allowed under Article 44.

B. *Two-Year Time Limit under Article 39(2)*

Some Austrian cases have dealt with the "long" time limit of two years for giving notice of a lack of conformity under Article 39(2). The Supreme Court clarified that this period "can be used only if the buyer could not have examined the goods earlier or if he could not have discovered the lack of conformity earlier in spite of an examination or if he could not have given notice earlier in spite of the discovery of the lack of conformity."[69] In accordance with the leading literature,[70] Austrian courts rule that Article 39(2) applies both to easily discernable and to hidden lacks of conformity, that

---

[63] Internationales Schiedsgericht der Bundeskammer der gewerblichen Wirtschaft (Wien), June 15, 1994, SCH-4318, CISG-online 120 and 691 = RIW 1995, 590 (metal sheet case).

[64] OGH, July 5, 2001, 6 Ob 117/01a, CISG-online 652 = ZfRV 2002, 25 (computer parts case), available at http://cisgw3.law.pace.edu/cases/010705a3.html. See also OGH, April 2, 2009, 8 Ob 125/08b, CISG-online 1889 = JBl 2009, 647 (boiler case), available at http://cisgw3.law.pace.edu/cases/090402a3.html (CISG had been implicitly contracted out); Schwenzer in Schlechtriem and Schwenzer, *Commentary*, Article 39, para. 33f.

[65] OGH, October 15, 1998, 2 Ob 191/98x, CISG-online 380 = JBl 1999, 318 (timber case), available at http://cisgw3.law.pace.edu/cases/981015a3.html; OLG Linz, September 24, 2007, 1 R 77/07k, CISG-online 1583 (laminated glass case), available at http://cisgw3.law.pace.edu/cases/070924a3.html.

[66] OGH, October 15, 1998, 2 Ob 191/98x, CISG-online 380 = JBl 1999, 318 (timber case), available at http://cisgw3.law.pace.edu/cases/981015a3.html; OGH, April 17, 2002, CISG-online 1020 (goods not named), available at http://cisgw3.law.pace.edu/cases/020417a3.html.

[67] Cf. OLG Graz, March 11, 1998, 4 R 283/97p, CISG-online 670 (timber case), available at http://cisgw3.law.pace.edu/cases/980311a3.html; OGH, October 15, 1998, 2 Ob 191/98x, CISG-online 380 = JBl 1999, 318 (timber case), available at http://cisgw3.law.pace.edu/cases/981015a3.html.

[68] Cf. Schwenzer in Schlechtriem and Schwenzer, *Commentary*, Article 44, para. 8.

[69] See OGH, May 19, 1999, 9 Ob 13/99y, CISG-online 484 = ZfRV 2000, 33 (goods not named), English translation available at http://cisgw3.law.pace.edu/cases/990519a3.html.

[70] Cf. Schwenzer in Schlechtriem and Schwenzer, *Commentary*, Article 39, paras. 22–3.

Article 39(2) is to be applied *ex officio*, and that it also applies to actions for a declaratory judgment.[71]

A special issue, primarily solved under Austrian civil procedure law, occurred in another case: The buyer had sued the seller before the two-year time limit had elapsed, but the allegation of facts it produced in the proceedings were incomplete, as became apparent later after more than two years had passed after delivery. The Supreme Court confirmed that, because the legal basis of the buyer's claim had already been argued in its action, the allegation could be supplemented. As phrased by the Court, the legal action filed by the buyer had the effect of interrupting the running of the time period, and the supplementing assertions had retroactive effect to the time of filing the action.[72] If the two-year period had elapsed before the first proper notice of nonconformity (which is not clarified in the case), this approach would be at conflict with the scholarly literature view that the time limit provided in Article 39(2) is an absolute one, meaning that it cannot be suspended or interrupted.[73]

V. *Nachfrist* Notice

There are a scarce few Austrian cases available on the issue of fixing an additional period of time for the other party to perform its obligations (*Nachfrist* notice). In the only case citing Article 47, the issue was settled by a contract clause.[74] Article 63 on the parallel issue in the case of the buyer's breach is briefly mentioned in two cases.[75] The small number of cases is not due to unfamiliarity of the concept because a similar concept is applied in domestic law. There are also no Austrian cases available on time extensions fixed by the breaching seller to cure its nonperformance under Article 48.

VI. Fundamental Breach

Given the importance of the concept of fundamental breach to the whole system of remedies under CISG, Austrian court practice is surprisingly poor in this area – in terms of quantity as well as quality. As far as can be seen, the Supreme Court touches the substance of Article 25 in only two cases. In one of them, it considers the seller's breach to be fundamental without giving any reasoning for that determination.[76] In the other, it deals with the criteria provided in Article 25, but hardly goes beyond what is already stated in the wording of Article 25. The Court counsels that it is primarily up to the parties to

---

[71] See OLG Linz, September 24, 2007, 1 R 77/07k, CISG-online 1583 (laminated glass case), available at http://cisgw3.law.pace.edu/cases/070924a3.html; see also Peter Huber, "Rügeversäumnis nach UN-Kaufrecht," 29 *Praxis des Internationalen Privat und Verfahrensrechts* 89 (2009).

[72] OGH, July 11, 2002, 6 Ob 147/02i.

[73] Cf. Schwenzer in Schlechtriem and Schwenzer, *Commentary*, Article 39, para. 23.

[74] OLG Graz, September 28, 2000, 4 R 55/00s, CISG-online 798 (computer telephone board case), available at http://cisgw3.law.pace.edu/cases/000928a3.html.

[75] OGH, September 11, 1997, 6 Ob 187/97m, CISG-online 340 = ZfRV 1997, 245 (carpets case), available at http://cisgw3.law.pace.edu/cases/970911a3.html (no period fixed); OGH, April 28, 2000, 1 Ob 292/99v, CISG-online 581 = SZ 73/75 (jewelry case), available at http://cisgw3.law.pace.edu/cases/000428a3.html (period of nine days). See also OLG Graz, January 24, 2002, 4 R 219/01k, CISG-online 801 (excavator case), available at http://cisgw3.law.pace.edu/cases/020124a3.html (Article 63 not explicitly mentioned).

[76] OGH, February 6, 1996, 10 Ob 518/95, CISG-online 224 = SZ 69/26 (propane case), available at http://cisgw3.law.pace.edu/cases/960206a3.html (failure to name loading port).

make clear in their contract what are its fundamental parts and obligations. This case also provides a marginal statement that a fundamental breach will be recognized where the other party's performance "actually cannot be used,"[77] but this is not enough to draw any conclusions as to the standards the Austrian courts would apply when being confronted with Article 25.

A lower court held that the seller who completely terminated the further technical development of the goods, needed to perform the contract, was in fundamental breach.[78] The Court of Appeal of Linz has provided the most detailed discussion of Article 25 in Austrian case law.[79] The case concerns a car that had been delivered with defects that could not be repaired for more than one year. The court held that the seller's breach was fundamental because the car was not of reliable quality. It based its finding on the fact that defects occurred repeatedly and suddenly, constituting a severe detriment to the buyer who needed the car for operating its business. The buyer could not be expected to resell a car with safety problems.[80] In addition, the court noted that the defects could not be cured, or at least that they went uncured for an unreasonably long time, and held that this would suffice to constitute a fundamental breach. The latter view is inconsistent with German case law and the majority view in German commentaries.[81]

In general, it appears that Austrian courts still have difficulties in dealing with the concept of fundamental breach under the CISG. The concept of fundamental breach, which is different than what is found in Austrian law, makes the courts feel uncomfortable when they have not yet established applicable criteria or standards for making the determination.

An arbitral tribunal ruled that if – as alleged by the buyer – the barley delivered by the seller was of nonconforming quality, then there would be a fundamental breach in the sense of Article 25, because then the buyer "would have been substantially deprived of what it was entitled to expect under the contract, i.e., barley of the agreed quality."[82] Under such reasoning, any breach of contract would be fundamental because the buyer always expects to receive conforming goods.

VII. Remedies, Damages, Mitigation, and Preservation

This part reviews the broad area of CISG remedies, including avoidance, damages, and price reduction, as well as the buyer's duties to mitigate damages and to preserve the nonconforming goods.

---

[77] OGH, June 21, 2005, 5 Ob 45/05m, CISG-online 1047 = IHR 2005, 195 (software case), available at http://cisgw3.law.pace.edu/cases/050621a3.html (Article 51(2); when partial non-performance justifies avoidance of the whole contract).

[78] OLG Graz, September 28, 2000, 4 R 55/00s, CISG-online 798 (computer telephone board case), available at http://cisgw3.law.pace.edu/cases/000928a3.html.

[79] For the following, see OLG Linz, January 23, 2006, 6 R 160/05z, CISG-online 1377 (auto case), available at http://cisgw3.law.pace.edu/cases/060123a3.html.

[80] See Schroeter in Schlechtriem and Schwenzer, *Commentary*, Article 25, paras. 46 and 52 (to what extent a buyer may be expected to sell on the goods, even at a severe loss).

[81] See BGH, April 3, 1996, VIII ZR 51/95, CISG-online 135 = BGHZ 132, 290 (cobalt sulphate case), available at http://cisgw3.law.pace.edu/cases/960403g1.html; Schroeter in Schlechtriem and Schwenzer, *Commentary*, Article 25, para. 50, with further references.

[82] Schiedsgericht der Börse für landwirtschaftliche Produkte in Wien, December 10, 1997, S 2/97, CISG-online 351 (barley case), available at http://cisgw3.law.pace.edu/cases/971210a3.html.

A. *Price Reduction*

Austrian case law on the remedy of price reduction is sparse, but interesting. There are three cases available; two of which deal with the specific issue of whether a price can be reduced to zero where the goods delivered are literally without any value. The first case, decided by the Supreme Court,[83] concerned coffee machines with such severe defects that they could not be resold and had no value at the time of delivery. The Supreme Court referred to the diverging opinions on the matter of "price reduction to zero" in the literature and opted for the predominant view that such reduction is possible, applying the calculation method provided in Article 50. It stated that Article 50 is in no way subsidiary to the remedy of avoidance in Article 49, and that reducing the price to zero without any restrictions as to time or an *ultima ratio* test is consistent with the CISG's remedial scheme. Rather, a buyer of goods without any value should not be worse off than a buyer of defective goods that still have some value.[84] In the present case, the seller had not demanded the defective goods to be returned. The Supreme Court noted that if such a return was claimed, the buyer's claim under Article 50 for recovery of the full price already paid *could* be dependent on the return of the goods to the seller.

A court of first instance also held that a price reduction to zero was compatible with CISG rules. However, in the particular case, the buyer's argument that the price should be reduced to zero "because there is no market for poppy seed of the delivered quality in Austria, and the market in Eastern Europe is of no interest for the buyer" was rejected because the buyer disregarded the possibility of reselling the goods to the Eastern Europe market or cleaning the contaminated seed and subsequently selling it in Austria.[85]

The third case concerned the interpretation of an agreement reached between the parties about the consequences of nonconformity on an earlier delivery. The parties had agreed on a price reduction of fifty percent and on delivery of the remaining number of items of (still nonconforming) stair panels. Later, the buyer's customer refused to pay the price. The buyer sought to recover the loss resulting from its customer's nonpayment as damages under Article 74. The Supreme Court began with an analysis of Article 45(2) and clarified that claims for damages raised in addition to another remedy are excluded to the extent that the aggrieved party's loss has already been covered by means of that other remedy. The court considered the fact that the seller had not succeeded in producing conforming panels over a considerable period of time, and that the parties, based on this fact, came to an agreement to reduce the price by fifty percent. The Supreme Court concluded that the issue had been settled between the parties and no further price reduction was justified. In the Court's opinion, the settlement covered all damage claims for foreseeable consequential losses, including remedies for nonconformity invoked by the buyer's customer. Ultimately, the agreement prevented the buyer from claiming further damages.[86]

---

[83] OGH, May 23, 2005, 3 Ob 193/04k, CISG-online 1041 = JBl 2005, 787 (coffee machines case), available at http://cisgw3.law.pace.edu/cases/050523a3.html.

[84] Cf. Schnyder and Straub in Honsell, *Kommentar zum UN-Kaufrecht*, Article 50, paras. 45f.

[85] HG Wien, May 3, 2007, 43 Cg 34/05f, CISG-online 1783 (poppy seed case), available at http://cisgw3.law.pace.edu/cases/070503a3.html (price was reduced by 10 percent).

[86] OGH, April 22, 2010, 8 Ob 30/10k, IHR 20011, 38 (stair-panels case).

B. *Avoidance of the Contract*

The CISG provisions on avoidance (Articles 49 and 64) are cited in a number of Austrian cases, but these cases make only small contributions, if any, to the interpretation and development of these rules. A number of courts noted that avoidance does not take effect *ipso facto* but requires a unilateral declaration by the entitled party.[87] A declaration addressed to a third party (e.g., another company in the seller's distribution network), of which the breaching party obtains knowledge indirectly and by coincidence, has been held insufficient.[88] A declaration of avoidance does not require any specific form.[89] The courts, however, have not yet developed a uniform view as to whether a declaration of avoidance should only be valid when made explicitly[90] or whether an implied declaration may also suffice. The Supreme Court left this issue open, but added that if implied declarations are accepted, they must meet high standards as to clarity of intent to avoid.[91] Where avoidance depends on the passing of an additional period for performance fixed under Articles 49(1)(b) or 64(1)(b), the standard view is that a party may declare an avoidance immediately after the expiration of the time extension. Courts have also recognized an anticipatory declaration of avoidance in the course of fixing the *Nachfrist* period.[92] On the other hand, avoidance can also be declared at the time the action is filed in court,[93] which is of practical relevance where the time limitations under Articles 49(2) and 64(2) do not apply.

In some cases, the courts particularly scrutinize whether a specific statement amounts to a declaration of avoidance.[94] For example, a seller declared that if the performance was not completed at the time the *Nachfrist* extension expires, "we will claim damages for non-performance or avoid the contract." The court rightly held that – due to the word "or" – avoidance had not yet been declared. However, because the buyer, in its reply, made reference to this statement and asked for a cancellation of the contract, the court held that no further declaration of avoidance was necessary.[95] In another case, the seller failed to fix a *Nachfrist* period, but declared the contract to be avoided immediately although the requirements of Article 64(1)(a) were not met. The contract was avoided

[87] See, e.g., OGH, February 6, 1996, 10 Ob 518/95, CISG-online 224 = SZ 69/26 (propane case), available at http://cisgw3.law.pace.edu/cases/960206a3.html (Article 49); OLG Graz, July 29, 2004, 5 R 93/04t, CISG-online 1627 (construction equipment case), available at http://cisgw3.law.pace.edu/cases/040729a3.html (Article 64).
[88] OLG Linz, January 23, 2006, 6 R 160/05z, CISG-online 1377 (auto case), available at http://cisgw3.law.pace.edu/cases/060123a3.html.
[89] OGH, April 28, 2000, 1 Ob 292/99v, CISG-online 581 = SZ 73/75 (jewelry case), available at http://cisgw3.law.pace.edu/cases/000428a3.html.
[90] In this direction: OLG Graz, July 29, 2004, 5 R 93/04t, CISG-online 1627 (construction equipment case), available at http://cisgw3.law.pace.edu/cases/040729a3.html.
[91] OGH, February 6, 1996, 10 Ob 518/95, CISG-online 224 = SZ 69/26 (propane case), available at http://cisgw3.law.pace.edu/cases/960206a3.html (no doubt may remain).
[92] OLG Graz, July 29, 2004, 5 R 93/04t, CISG-online 1627 (construction equipment case), available at http://cisgw3.law.pace.edu/cases/040729a3.html.
[93] OGH, April 28, 2000, 1 Ob 292/99v, CISG-online 581 = SZ 73/75 (jewelry case), available at http://cisgw3.law.pace.edu/cases/000428a3.html.
[94] See OLG Graz, January 24, 2002, 4 R 219/01k, CISG-online 801 (excavator case), available at http://cisgw3.law.pace.edu/cases/020124a3.html and the subsequent text.
[95] OLG Graz, July 29, 2004, 5 R 93/04t, CISG-online 1627 (construction equipment case), available at http://cisgw3.law.pace.edu/cases/040729a3.html.

nevertheless, because the court found that the buyer implicitly consented to the declared avoidance by sending back a portion of the goods.[96]

Where the right to avoid the contract is governed by contract terms agreed on by the parties, these terms control.[97] However, the right of avoidance cannot, in principle, be contracted out of completely. If the right to avoidance is limited the right to claim damages must be maintained.[98]

Article 82 also played a role in one case, where the buyer lost its right to avoid the contract by continuing to use a defective automobile after the defects had become apparent.[99] In another case, involving delivery of goods by installments, the right of avoidance was lost with regard to only the first installment, but not as to future installments.[100] Austrian courts have not ruled on how to determine reasonable time periods for *Nachfrist* extensions under Articles 49(2) and 64(2).[101]

C. *Damages*

The CISG provisions on damages, including Articles 45, 61, and 74, have been applied in a number of Austrian cases. The damage scheme, primarily based upon strict liability,[102] differs from the *culpa*-based principle found in domestic Austrian law. Nonetheless, Austrian courts have had little difficulty in applying CISG damage rules.

Many cases, especially those decided by the Supreme Court, broadly summarize principles established in academic writing, thereby introducing these principles into national jurisprudence. In one such case, the Supreme Court stated that the CISG is based on the principle of full compensation, protecting "not only the obligee's interest to not suffer any loss to his goods due to breach of contract (indemnity interest), but also and especially ... the interest of receiving the benefits of proper performance of the contract (expectation interest)." This includes the nonbreaching buyer's right, subject to the obligor's right to cure under Article 48, to undertake reasonable measures to procure a substituted performance equivalent to what it expected from the breached contract, and then invoice the obligor the costs as damages. Article 74 also protects the aggrieved party's interest that expenses caused by the contract do not become worthless (reliance interest). Expenses incurred because of the contract itself can be recoverable if it is determined that they would not have been incurred were it not for the obligee's reliance

---

[96] OGH, September 11, 1997, 6 Ob 187/97m, CISG-online 340 = ZfRV 1997, 245 (carpets case), available at http://cisgw3.law.pace.edu/cases/970911a3.html. See also OGH, June 29, 1999, 1 Ob 74/99k, CISG-online 483 = TranspR-IHR 1999, 48 with a gloss by Clemens Thiele (dividing wall panels case), available at http://cisgw3.law.pace.edu/cases/990629a3.html.

[97] Cf. Schiedsgericht der Börse für landwirtschaftliche Produkte in Wien, December 10, 1997, S 2/97, CISG-online 351 (barley case), available at http://cisgw3.law.pace.edu/cases/971210a3.html.

[98] *Obiter dictum* in OGH, September 7, 2000, 8 Ob 22/00v, CISG-online 642 = IHR 2001, 42 (tombstones case), available at http://cisgw3.law.pace.edu/cases/000907a3.html.

[99] OLG Linz, January 23, 2006, 6 R 160/05z, CISG-online 1377 (auto case), available at http://cisgw3.law.pace.edu/cases/060123a3.html.

[100] OGH, August 31, 2010, 4 Ob 98/10f, JBl 2011, 49 (old wood parquet floor case) (parquet assembled and destroyed upon removal).

[101] Article 49(2)(b) was touched in OGH, May 23, 2005, 3 Ob 193/04k, CISG-online 1041 = JBl 2005, 787 (coffee machines case), available at http://cisgw3.law.pace.edu/cases/050523a3.html.

[102] See, e.g., OGH, January 14, 2002, 7 Ob 301/01t, CISG-online 643 = JBl 2002, 592 (cooling system case), available at http://cisgw3.law.pace.edu/cases/020114a3.html; OLG Linz, January 23, 2006, 6 R 160/05z, CISG-online 1377 (auto case), available at http://cisgw3.law.pace.edu/cases/060123a3.html.

on contract performance. However, from the "viewpoint of a reasonable person under the same circumstances . . . , such expenses must have been appropriate and reasonable for the performance of the contract."[103] Where defective goods are delivered and the contract is not avoided, the buyer is entitled to claim as damages the differential between the value of goods as delivered versus the value of conforming goods.[104] Contractual arrangements always prevail.[105]

The Supreme Court also summarized main principles of the foreseeability test established in Article 74, under which damages may not exceed the loss that the party in breach foresaw or should have foreseen at the time of the conclusion of the contract. In particular, the Court stated that:

> [Article 74] does not require precise and detailed foreseeability of losses, and certainly not a numbered sum on the extent of loss. On the other hand, the invariably foreseeable possibility that a breach of contract will produce some type of loss is not sufficient. However, a (typical) loss due to non-performance is under prevailing opinion generally foreseeable. It is necessary that the obligor could recognize that a breach of contract would produce a loss essentially of the type and extent that actually occurred. Generally an objective standard is applied for foreseeability. The obligor must reckon with the consequences that a reasonable person in his situation . . . would have foreseen considering the particular circumstances of the case. Whether he actually did foresee this is as insignificant as whether there was fault. Yet, subjective risk evaluation cannot be completely ignored: if the obligor knows that a breach of contract would produce unusual or unusually high losses, then these consequences are imputable to him.[106]

The courts also noted that loss of profit, in the sense of the typical sales margin of a seller, is to be regarded as foreseeable by the buyer.[107]

A few cases deal with the provisions on the calculation of damages under Articles 75 and 76. Courts have held that Articles 75 and 76 apply only where the contract has been avoided.[108] However, a later case recognized an exception, which is now shared by many courts and authors in different countries, namely that avoidance is not required prior to a substitute transaction if the party in breach refuses to

---

[103] OGH, January 14, 2002, 7 Ob 301/01t, CISG-online 643 = JBl 2002, 592 (cooling system case), available at http://cisgw3.law.pace.edu/cases/020114a3.html.

[104] OLG Linz, January 23, 2006, 6 R 160/05z, CISG-online 1377 (auto case), available at http://cisgw3.law.pace.edu/cases/060123a3.html.

[105] Cf. OGH, January 14, 2002, 7 Ob 301/01t, CISG-online 643 = JBl 2002, 592 (cooling system case), available at http://cisgw3.law.pace.edu/cases/020114a3.html (exclusion of liability for consequential damages); Schiedsgericht der Börse für landwirtschaftliche Produkte in Wien, December 10, 1997, S 2/97, CISG-online 351 (barley case), available at http://cisgw3.law.pace.edu/cases/971210a3.html.

[106] OGH, January 14, 2002, 7 Ob 301/01t, CISG-online 643 = JBl 2002, 592 (cooling system case), available at http://cisgw3.law.pace.edu/cases/020114a3.html.

[107] OGH, April 28, 2000, 1 Ob 292/99v, CISG-online 581 = SZ 73/75 (jewelry case), available at http://cisgw3.law.pace.edu/cases/000428a3.html; OLG Graz, January 24, 2002, 4 R 219/01k, CISG-online 801 (excavator case), available at http://cisgw3.law.pace.edu/cases/020124a3.html. See also OGH, February 6, 1996, 10 Ob 518/95, CISG-online 224 = SZ 69/26 (propane case), available at http://cisgw3.law.pace.edu/cases/960206a3.html.

[108] OGH, February 6, 1996, 10 Ob 518/95, CISG-online 224 = SZ 69/26 (propane case), available at http://cisgw3.law.pace.edu/cases/960206a3.html; OLG Graz, January 24, 2002, 4 R 219/01k, CISG-online 801 (excavator case), available at http://cisgw3.law.pace.edu/cases/020124a3.html.

perform.[109] The method established in Article 75 is characterized as a "concrete" cal-culation by reference to the price agreed in a substitute transaction entered into by the aggrieved party.[110] Where, after collecting several offers, no better price can be achieved than in the substitute transaction, the substitute transaction was held to be made "in a reasonable manner" for the purposes of Article 75.[111] On the other hand, the method of calculating damages by reference to the market price (Article 76) is characterized as an "abstract" calculation.[112] In accordance with the prevailing opinion, Austrian courts hold that Article 76 can only be applied where no substitute transaction had been made.[113] However, neither Article 75 nor Article 76 prevent the aggrieved party, after avoidance of the contract, from calculating damages for nonperformance "concretely" according to the general rule of Article 74.[114]

Finally, a handful of specific issues relating to damages have been addressed by Austrian courts. The Court of Appeal in Vienna decided that costs incurred to have a lawyer make a formal demand for payment before filing an action at court were recoverable under Article 74, subject to national rules of civil procedure. In applying Austrian law (which requires recoverable costs to be both appropriate and necessary), by analogy, the court stated that asking a lawyer to send a reminder is certainly appropriate, but it would have been cheaper and more appropriate to hire an Austrian lawyer instead of a German lawyer.[115] In an *obiter dictum*, another court of appeal took a somewhat different approach and stated that the recovery of prejudicial costs – such as costs incurred by hiring a debt collecting agency – is exclusively governed by national rules of civil procedure.[116] An Austrian arbitration court, dealing with the controversial matter of whether the rate of interest payable under Article 78 is to be calculated by way of reference to domestic law or by way of gap-filling under CISG, took the latter approach and ruled that the principle of full compensation established in Article 74 allows fixing an interest rate that corresponds to ordinary commercial bank interest.[117] In another case, the Supreme

---

[109] OLG Graz, July 29, 2004, 5 R 93/04t, CISG-online 1627 (construction equipment case), available at http://cisgw3.law.pace.edu/cases/040729a3.html. The court cites Karollus, *UN-Kaufrecht*, 155f.; see also Schwenzer in Schlechtriem and Schwenzer, *Commentary*, Article 75, para. 5, and Article 76, para. 3.

[110] Cf. OGH, April 28, 2000, 1 Ob 292/99v, CISG-online 581 = SZ 73/75 (jewelry case), available at http://cisgw3.law.pace.edu/cases/000428a3.html; OLG Graz, January 24, 2002, 4 R 219/01k, CISG-online 801 (excavator case), available at http://cisgw3.law.pace.edu/cases/020124a3.html.

[111] OLG Graz, July 29, 2004, 5 R 93/04t, CISG-online 1627 (construction equipment case), available at http://cisgw3.law.pace.edu/cases/040729a3.html.

[112] OGH, April 28, 2000, 1 Ob 292/99v, CISG-online 581 = SZ 73/75 (jewelry case), available at http://cisgw3.law.pace.edu/cases/000428a3.html.

[113] OLG Graz, July 29, 2004, 5 R 93/04t, CISG-online 1627 (construction equipment case), available at http://cisgw3.law.pace.edu/cases/040729a3.html. Cf. also OGH, April 28, 2000, 1 Ob 292/99v, CISG-online 581 = SZ 73/75 (jewelry case), available at http://cisgw3.law.pace.edu/cases/000428a3.html.

[114] OGH, April 28, 2000, 1 Ob 292/99v, CISG-online 581 = SZ 73/75 (jewelry case), available at http://cisgw3.law.pace.edu/cases/000428a3.html.

[115] HG Wien, January 28, 1994, 1 R 408/93, WR 640. On the disputed matter of whether extrajudicial costs incurred in pursuing rights are recoverable under the CISG, see Schwenzer in Schlechtriem and Schwenzer, *Commentary*, Article 74, paras. 30 and 33; see also John Gotanda in Kröll et al., *Commentary*, Article 74, para. 73.

[116] LG Leoben, October 21, 1997, 1 R 189/97d (goods not named; seller sought to apply a provision of the German Civil Code but also referred to Article 74 CISG).

[117] Internationales Schiedsgericht der Bundeskammer der gewerblichen Wirtschaft (Wien), June 15, 1994, SCH-4366, CISG-online 121 and 691 (metal sheet case). On this issue, see Bacher in Schlechtriem and Schwenzer, *Commentary*, Article 78, paras. 26–43.

Court had to identify the place of performance of the buyer's obligation to pay damages. The Supreme Court, in ruling that damages for nonperformance of the obligation to pay the price are to be paid at the seller's place of business,[118] advanced two arguments. First, it stated that the place of performance of the secondary obligation shall be the place of performance of the primary obligation, which, in the present case, means that the rule in Article 57 applies (place of performance is seller's place of business). Second, the Supreme Court referred to an earlier case[119] where it had held that Article 57 could generally be applied by way of analogy to monetary obligations other than payment of the price. However, this leaves open the question of how the Supreme Court would decide where the two tests lead to diverging results. It is assumed here that the first test (primary obligation's place of performance) would be applied. This solution is also the one adopted by the two CISG commentaries consulted by the Austrian Supreme Court.[120]

D. *Mitigation of Loss*

Alleging that the aggrieved party failed to comply with its duty to mitigate the loss under Article 77 seems to be a standard excuse given by parties in breach when confronted with a claim for damages. Again, however, the development of this area by Austrian jurisprudence is not particularly rich.[121]

A typical statement to be found in case law is that a potential measure to mitigate loss is "reasonable" in the sense of Article 77, "if in good faith it could be expected under the circumstances. This is to be determined according to the actions of a reasonable person in the same circumstances."[122] This starting point obviously invites a more detailed discussion of the principle of good faith in general, and its use in concretizing the duty to mitigate damages. But such discussion has not taken place in Austrian CISG cases. This corresponds with the finding referred to earlier, namely that Austrian courts are reluctant

---

[118] OGH, March 29, 2004, 5 Ob 313/03w, CISG-online 926 (paint mist vacuuming machine case), abstract available at http://cisgw3.law.pace.edu/cases/040329a3.html.

[119] OGH, December 18, 2002, 3 Nd 509/02, CISG-online 1279, available at http://cisgw3.law.pace.edu/cases/021218a3.html.

[120] Cf. Magnus in *Staudinger*, CISG Article 74, para. 57; Schwenzer in Schlechtriem and Schwenzer, *Commentary*, Article 74, para. 61 (noting that applying Article 57 by way of analogy would mean a further extension of place of jurisdiction in favor of the plaintiff).

[121] Apart from the issues discussed in the text, a lower court stated that Article 77 applies the concept of *Obliegenheit* (i.e., a duty that, if breached, does not oblige the "debtor" to pay damages, but only causes the loss of own rights); see OLG Graz, January 24, 2002, 4 R 219/01k, CISG-online 801 (excavator case), available at http://cisgw3.law.pace.edu/cases/020124a3.html (the concept is explained by Schwenzer in Schlechtriem and Schwenzer, *Commentary*, Article 77, para. 2). Also, it has been stated that the second sentence of Article 77 adopts the ancient concept of *Culpakompensation* (contributory negligence leads to a complete loss of the right to damages); see OLG Graz, September 16, 2002, 2 R 62/02h, CISG-online 1198 (garments case), available at http://cisgw3.law.pace.edu/cases/020916a3.html. Critical: Helmut Koziol, "Rechtsfolgen der Verletzung einer Schadensminderungspflicht – Rückkehr der archaishen Culpakompensation," 6 *Zeitschrift für Europäisches Privatrecht* 593, 594f. (1998).

[122] See OGH, February 6, 1996, 10 Ob 518/95, CISG-online 224 = SZ 69/26 (propane case), available at http://cisgw3.law.pace.edu/cases/960206a3.html; OGH, January 14, 2002, 7 Ob 301/01t, CISG-online 643 = JBl 2002, 592 (cooling system case), available at http://cisgw3.law.pace.edu/cases/020114a3.html. The principle of good faith is also referred to in OLG Graz, January 24, 2002, 4 R 219/01k, CISG-online 801 (excavator case), available at http://cisgw3.law.pace.edu/cases/020124a3.html.

to make the decision of cases dependent on the application of flexible concepts to which they are not accustomed.

Part of the reason for the courts' lack of discussion on the duty to mitigate is their finding that the burden of proof is on the nonperforming party. The courts required it "to put forward detailed facts and the supporting evidence showing why the [other party] has breached its duty to mitigate damages, the possibilities of alternative conduct and which part of the damages would have been prevented by this alternative conduct."[123] Often, defenses put forward under Article 77 are unsubstantiated and consequently fail, without discussion, to meet the standards applied by the courts. In the cases where Austrian courts had to "substantively" apply Article 77, they have shown the ability to do so without difficulty. In one case, it was held that where a seller resells the goods (which the buyer neither paid for nor collected) for the same price as the seller paid to its supplier, there was no breach of a duty of mitigation.[124]

E. *Preservation of Goods*

CISG Articles 85 to 88 on the parties' obligations to preserve the goods have rarely been applied in Austrian case law. One case decided by a lower court dealt with a "self-help sale" of the goods by the seller under Article 88. The court stated that the seller's notice of its intention to sell was "reasonable" for the purposes of Article 88(1) if it leaves the other party enough time to prevent the sale. In accordance with Article 27, the court noted that "giving" the notice properly is sufficient (delay or arrival of the notice are not material). The party entitled to a sale under Article 88 may execute that sale itself.[125] In another case, the Supreme Court referred to Articles 85 and 86, and to the principle of a right of retention to construe, by way of analogy under Article 7(2), a right of the buyer to withhold performance (payment of the price) in the case of the delivery of nonconforming goods.[126]

VIII. Excuse in Case of Impediment

Article 79 on the breaching party's excuse in the case of an impediment beyond its control has played practically no role in Austrian case law so far.[127] In one case the court

---

[123] OGH, February 6, 1996, 10 Ob 518/95, CISG-online 224 = SZ 69/26 (propane case), available at http://cisgw3.law.pace.edu/cases/960206a3.html. Cf. also OLG Graz, January 24, 2002, 4 R 219/01k, CISG-online 801 (excavator case), available at http://cisgw3.law.pace.edu/cases/020124a3.html (responsibility of nonperforming buyer to demonstrate the seller's failure to enter into a *specific* substitute transaction); OGH, April 28, 2000, 1 Ob 292/99v, CISG-online 581 = SZ 73/75 (jewelry case), available at http://cisgw3.law.pace.edu/cases/000428a3.html (defense was completely unsubstantiated). On the issue of the burden of proof, see Gotanda in Kröll et al., *Commentary*, Article 77, paras. 11–14.

[124] OLG Graz, January 24, 2002, 4 R 219/01k, CISG-online 801 (excavator case), available at http://cisgw3.law.pace.edu/cases/020124a3.html. See also OLG Graz, September 16, 2002, 2 R 62/02h, CISG-online 1198 (garments case), available at http://cisgw3.law.pace.edu/cases/020916a3.html (sale under Article 88).

[125] OLG Graz, September 16, 2002, 2 R 62/02h, CISG-online 1198 (garments case), available at http://cisgw3.law.pace.edu/cases/020916a3.html.

[126] OGH, November 8, 2005, 4 Ob 179/05k, CISG-online 1156 = SZ 2005/162 (recycling machine case), available at http://cisgw3.law.pace.edu/cases/051108a3.html.

[127] Domestic law basically applies a fault-based system of liability for damages, cf. Sections 1295 and 1298 of the Austrian Civil Code (which, however, certainly is no reason for the lack of case law in this area). On the differences, see Karollus, *UN-Kaufrecht*, 205ff; Willibald Posch, "Pflichten des Käufers, Rechtsbehelfe

of appeal dealt with the question of whether the seller's supplier should be regarded as a "third person" for the purposes of Article 79(2); but the Supreme Court considered this question irrelevant and ruled that the seller is liable for nonconformity under a contractual guarantee contracted for by the parties.[128]

IX. Concluding Remarks

Regarding the future development of Austrian CISG case law, it is to be hoped that the courts will be more open to reviewing foreign case law in order to promote a uniform interpretation of the convention. Also, it is time for Austrian courts to overcome their traditional reluctance in applying the "flexible" concepts found in the CISG, such as "good faith" and "reasonableness," for a number of reasons. First, there are now a deep literature and rich foreign case law that have sufficiently concretized these concepts for purposes of practical application. Second, the Austrian courts have in fact demonstrated their ability to develop substantive criteria for applying standards and principles (such as in the case of concretizing the concepts of offer and acceptance for ruling when foreign-language standard terms are incorporated into a contract).

Relating to the general acceptance of CISG by Austrian lawyers and businesses, it is evident that the enormous amount of scholarly writings and case law has improved legal certainty in CISG matters considerably. Because much depends on getting accustomed to CISG concepts in legal education, CISG may indirectly benefit from the efforts to adopt a "Common European Sales Law" (CESL),[129] on which the CISG had a strong influence.[130] It is therefore submitted that, at least from the perspective of the present situation in Austria, the future relationship between the CISG and CESL (if ultimately adopted) will be synergistic in nature, because lawyers forced to get to know the latter will automatically improve their understanding of the former. When it comes to choosing the right instrument for future contracts, the CESL will have the advantage of being more comprehensive.[131] However, applying CESL will also create certain risks, which may, inversely, support opting into the CISG. First, given the large amount of case law and scholarship on the CISG, it provides greater certainty, at least initially, than the CESL. Second, there is a specific EU law risk in that issues of interpretation relating to the CESL will be subject to the jurisdiction of the European Court of Justice (ECJ) and the quality of the ECJ's judgments in contract law matters is rather poor.[132]

---

des Verkäufers, Gefahrenübergang und Schadenersatz," in *Das UNCITRAL-Kaufrecht im Vergleich zum österreichischen Recht* (ed. P. Doralt) (Vienna: Manz Verlag, 1985), 153, 174ff.

[128] OGH, April 21, 2004, 7 Ob 32/04p, CISG-online 1048 (omnibus case), available at http://cisgw3.law.pace.edu/cases/040421a3.html. Article 79 mentioned, but not applied: OGH, December 15, 1998, 1 Ob 289/98a (construction materials case), available at http://cisgw3.law.pace.edu/cases/981215a3.html (Article 79 briefly mentioned in summary of court of appeal's decision); OGH, June 29, 1999, 1 Ob 74/99k, CISG-online 483 = TranspR-IHR 1999, 48 (dividing wall panels case), available at http://cisgw3.law.pace.edu/cases/990629a3.html (Article 79 held to be irrelevant).

[129] See Commission's Proposal for a Regulation of the European Parliament and of the Council on a Common European Sales Law, COM(2011) 635 final (October 11, 2011).

[130] See Part IV (Articles 87 et seq.) of the CESL draft, *supra* note 129 (obligations and remedies).

[131] E.g., the CESL draft, *supra* note 129, includes rules on defects in consent (Articles 48–57) and on the effects of unfair contract terms (Articles 79–86).

[132] See, e.g., ECJ, June 16, 2011, joined cases C-65/09 (*Gebr. Weber GmbH v. Jürgen Wittmer*) and C-87/09 (*Ingrid Putz v. Medianess Electronics GmbH*), available at http://curia.europa.eu (ECJ foiled parts of the system of remedies for nonconformity in consumer sales contracts).

20 Baltic States, Belarus, and Ukraine

Tadas Klimas

I. History of the CISG in the Baltic States

The data provided by the foremost database on the CISG concerning Lithuania are bizarre. In the Pace Law School Institute of International Commercial Law's Albert H. Kritzer CISG Database, under "historical information" for Lithuania, it is asserted that: "The CISG had been in force in the Soviet Republic of Lithuania, effective 1 September 1991. However, when Lithuania became an independent State, it elected to adopt the Convention by accession rather than succession with an effective date of 1 February 1996."[1] As we will see in the following review both the date and the rationale given in the database are not only inaccurate, but inexplicable.

Although the Pace database claims that the CISG had been in force in the so-called Soviet Republic of Lithuania from September 1, 1991, this is simply not true. Lithuania was already independent by that date; indeed, Lithuania reestablished its independence on March 11, 1990. Even the date of the ratification of the CISG (as opposed to its effective date), May 23, 1990, in the Soviet Union was subsequent to Lithuania's March 11, 1990, reestablishment of independence. Thus, the Pace database's claim that the CISG had been in force in occupied Lithuania is quite strange and unsupported.

Secondly, the Pace database claims that Lithuania could have adopted the CISG by succession. Admittedly, this is a more subtle point, but the claim is also unsustainable. Lithuania was legally not a constituent part of the Soviet Union; Lithuania was an occupied territory, and as such it could not be a successor state. Indeed, the scholarly and diplomatic consensus is that all three Baltic States (Lithuania, Estonia, and Latvia), having been independent states prior to World War II, were illegally annexed by the Soviet Union during that conflict. Lithuania thus had the status of an *occupied territory*; as stated in the U.S. Embassy website: "The United States never recognized the forcible incorporation of Lithuania into the U.S.S.R. and views the present Government of Lithuania as a legal continuation of the interwar republic."[2] It is true, however, that Lithuania is

---

[1] Institute of International Commercial Law at Pace Law School, Albert H. Kritzer CISG Database (Pace), Lithuania, January 22, 1998, available at http://www.cisg.law.pace.edu/cisg/countries/cntries-Lithuania.html.

[2] Embassy of the United States to Lithuania, *History of U.S –Lithuania Relations*, available at http://vilnius.usembassy.gov/news/history-of-u.s–lithuanian-relations (accessed August 12, 2013); see also Robert A. Vitas, *The United States and Lithuania: The Stimson Doctrine of Non-Recognition* (New York: Praeger, 1990); James T. McHugh and James S. Pacy, *Diplomats without a Country: Baltic Diplomacy, International Law, and the Cold War* (New York: Praeger, 2001).

an anomaly in this regard; most countries that separated from the Soviet Union, such as the Ukraine, were not considered to be occupied territories, but constituent parts of the Soviet Union, and thus could adopt the CISG by succession.

Thus, in order for the CISG to come into effect in Lithuania, it had to be independently acceded to. Accordingly, on January 19, 1993, Lithuania's parliament voted to ratify the CISG.[3] Interestingly, the official UNCITRAL website identifies January 18, 1995, as the date of Lithuania's accession.[4] But this date again appears not to be supported by the evidence, as a translation of the CISG was published in the official record of the Republic of Lithuania on December 15, 1995, and the same official Lithuanian source describes it as coming into effect on February 1, 1996.[5]

In acceding to the CISG, Lithuania made an Article 96 Reservation opting out of the "no writing" requirement of CISG Article 11. Thus, the formality requirements found in Lithuanian national law applied to international sale of goods contracts covered by the CISG.[6] However, in response to an initiative of UNCITRAL, legislation was adopted in 2013 that removed the reservation.[7]

The Republic of Latvia reestablished its independence from Soviet occupation on August 21, 1991.[8] It does not consider itself as having formerly been the "Soviet Socialist Republic of Latvia."[9] The CISG came into force in Latvia in 1998. Just as in the case of Lithuania, it registered an Article 96 Declaration regarding contract formalities.[10] Also like Lithuania, it cannot be viewed as a successor state because Latvia established its independence prior to the CISG coming into force in the Soviet Union.[11]

[3] Dėl LR prisijungimo prie JTO 1980 m. bal. 11 d. Konvencijos dėl tarptautinio prekių pirkimo pardavimo sutarčių [Regarding the Accession of the Republic of Lithuania to the 1980 UN Convention on the International Sale of Goods] (I-51) (1993), English translation available at http://www3.lrs.lt/pls/inter3/dokpaieska.showdoc_l?p_id=93950.

[4] United Nations Commission on International Trade Law (hereinafter UNCITRAL), Status, available at http://www.uncitral.org/uncitral/en/uncitral_texts/sale_goods/1980CISG_status.html (accessed October 12, 2011).

[5] JTO 1980 m. Konvencija dėl Tarptautinio prekių pirkimo bei pardavimo sutarčių (Žin., 1995, Nr. 102–2283); UNCITRAL, Status, http://www.uncitral.org/uncitral/en/uncitral_texts/sale_goods/1980CISG_status.html (accessed October 12, 2011).

[6] Dėl LR prisijungimo prie JTO 1980 m. bal. 11 d. Konvencijos dėl tarptautinio prekių pirkimo pardavimo sutarčių [Regarding the Accession of the Republic of Lithuania to the 1980 UN Convention on the International Sale of Goods] (I-51) (1993), English transl. *available at* http://www3.lrs.lt/pls/inter3/dokpaieska.showdoc_l?p_id=93950.

[7] Letter of the Ministry of Justice of Lithuania, dated April 15, 2011, Nr. 111 7-R-3157, available at www.chamber.lt/LT/content/download/13426/456198/file/DOC.pdf (regarding the UNCITRAL initiative); LR Įstatymo projektas: Del LR Seimo nutarimo "Dėl LR prisijungimo prie Jungtinių tautų organizacijos 1980 m. balandžio 11 d. konvencijos dėl tarptautinio prekių pirkimo pardavimo sutarčių" 1 punkto pakeitimo (2013 m. balandžio 23 d. Nr. XII-235)."

[8] Latvian Institute, *Latvia in the 20th Century*, available at http://www.li.lv/index.php?option=com_content&task=view&id=27&Itemid=1096 (accessed October 13, 2011). (According to its Web site, the Latvian Institute was established by the government of Latvia.)

[9] See id. (all references are to "occupied Latvia").

[10] Albert H. Kritzer CISG Database (Pace), Latvia, January 22, 1998, available at http://www.cisg.law.pace.edu/cisg/countries/cntries-Latvia.html.

[11] Id.

The Republic of Estonia reestablished its independence from Soviet occupation on August 20, 1991.[12] The United States recognized the restoration of Estonia's independence on September 2, 1991.[13] The effective date of the CISG in Estonia is October 1, 1994.[14] Originally, Estonia ratified the CISG with an Article 96 reservation, which had the result of requiring formalities in regard to formation, but subsequently withdrew the reservation on March 9, 2004.[15]

II. CISG Jurisprudence in the Baltic States

CISG case law is scarce in the Baltic countries. Nonetheless, the cases that do exist provide insight in the problematic nature of the interpretation and application of the CISG in these countries, as well as in Belarus and the Ukraine.

A. *Contract Formation and Incorporating Standard Terms*

In *Compfitt Glas AS v. Snaige AB*,[16] the sole issue before the Appellate Court of Lithuania was whether a contract had been formed despite the fact that there was no formal, signed contract. There were, however, many other supporting documents signed by the parties, and the court decided that indeed a contract had been formed and attested to by the writings taken as a whole. As the goods had been tendered and the buyer had no defenses, the seller's complaint was satisfied in full against the Lithuanian buyer. This case illustrates that courts often are flexible in construing formality requirements, especially where an injustice would be done if the case is not judged on its merits. This is the same approach that most American courts would use in applying the statute of fraud (writing) requirements of the American Uniform Commercial Code (UCC).[17] Comment 1 to UCC Article 2–201 states that the formality requirement purpose is merely to "afford a basis for believing that the offered oral evidence rests on a real transaction." The existence of numerous documents noted in the *Compfitt Glas* case would likely satisfy the writing and signature requirements of the UCC.

In *Veka AG v. Omnetus UAB*,[18] a Lithuanian court addressed the issues of whether the standard terms of one party (Veka AG, a German firm) were incorporated in the contract. The problem was the choice of law provision in the standard terms conflicted with one in the main contract, as well as the standard terms of the other party. The court

---

[12] Estonia.eu: Official Gateway to Estonia, *Estonia's Return to Independence 1987–1991*, available at http://estonia.eu/about-estonia/country/estonias-return-to-independence-19871991.html (accessed October 13, 2011).

[13] U.S. Dept. of State, Office of the Historian, *A Guide to the United States' History of Recognition, Diplomatic, and Consular Relations, by Country, since 1776: Estonia*, available at http://history.state.gov/countries/estonia (accessed October 13, 2011).

[14] Albert H. Kritzer CISG Database (Pace), Estonia, September 7, 2004, http://www.cisg.law.pace.edu/cisg/countries/cntries-Estonia.html.

[15] Id.

[16] *Compfitt Glas AS v. Snaige AB*, Kauno apygardos teismas (Nr. 2–734–259/2010) (Kaunas regional court 2010).

[17] Uniform Commercial Code, Section 2–201.

[18] *Veka AG v. Omnetus UAB*, *Lietuvos apeliacinis teismas* (Nr. 2–567/2007) (Appellate Court of Lithuania 2007), rev'd on other grounds L.A.T. (Nr. 3K-3–196/2008) (Supreme Court of Lithuania 2008).

held that the standard terms are not as a matter of law to be considered inferior to the provisions of the main contract. However, an important fact was that the standard terms referred to here had been affixed physically to the contract at the time of its formation and therefore no issue of surprise or unfairness was presented.

B. *Right to Cover versus Duty to Cover*

A 2003 Estonian case, *Novia Handelsgesellschaft mbH v. AS Maseko*,[19] involved an Estonian buyer and a Turkish seller. The contract was for a certain amount of tomato sauce, to be shipped over a period of time. The Estonian buyer repudiated the contract after receiving and paying for several shipments. The seller in Turkey did not "cover" as provided under CISG Article 76 and sued for damages under CISG Article 74. The issue was raised as to whether a party must cover in order to obtain damages. The Tallinn Circuit Court held that Article 76 merely grants the party seeking damages the possibility of "cover," but this in no way restricts the party's right to seek damages under Section 74.

C. *No Latvian Cases*

Although there are no cases reported in English, there has been commentary on the use of the CISG in reforming Latvian law. Specifically, it appears there was an unsuccessful initiative to transplant a number of CISG provisions – including CISG Article 25 (fundamental breach), CISG Article 49(b) (*Nachfrist* notice or time extension for performance), and CISG Article 74 (foreseeability limitation on the collection of damages) – into Latvian law.[20]

In regard to limiting damages to those that are reasonably foreseeable, a commentator refers to this as being "revolutionary," and states that "[a]lthough such provisions may seem quite obvious to law specialists from other countries, thus far they have not been included in the Latvian Civil Code." Interestingly, these new or more modern concepts were criticized as leading to "overly broad judicial freedom [that] may lead to corruption, so less scope should exist for uncertainty created by concepts such as remoteness, hardship, and minor or fundamental breach."[21] This raises doubt as to whether Latvian courts are equipped to apply such concepts in cases where the CISG is the applicable law.

III. History of the CISG in Belarus and the Ukraine

Belarus became independent for the first time in its history on August 25, 1991.[22] According to the Pace database, Belarus is considered the successor country to the

---

[19] *Novia Handelsgesellschaft mbH v. AS Maseko*, Tallinn Circuit Court (No. 2–2/111/2004) (2004), available at http://cisgw3.law.pace.edu/cases/040219e3.html.

[20] Kalvis Torgans [Prof. U. of Latvia], "European Initiatives (PECL, DCFR) and Modernization of Latvian Civil Law," 14 *Juridica International* 137 (2008), available at http://www.juridicainternational.eu/public/pdf/ji_2008_1_137.pdf.

[21] Id.

[22] Central Intelligence Agency, World Factbook: Independence, available at https://www.cia.gov/library/publications/the-world-factbook/fields/2088.html (accessed October 13, 2011).

Byelorussian SSR, and as a member of the United Nations appears to have independently acceded to the CISG while part of the Soviet Union.[23] The effective date of the CISG in Belarus is given as November 1, 1990, predating its effective date in the Soviet Union thus confirming the hypothesis.[24]

The Pace database identifies February 1, 1991, as being the date the CISG became effective for the "Ukrainian SSR," and that "Ukraine is regarded as the successor to Ukrainian SSR's treaty obligations."[25] The Ukrainian SSR may have ratified the CISG independently,[26] although The Ukrainian SSR was a member of the United Nations, and an independent albeit anomolous accession would explain why the date given for the CISG's effective date in Ukraine is not the date on which the Ukraine declared independence, which was August 25, 1991.[27]

It is important to note – as in the People's Republic of China, the Netherlands, and Germany – the CISG greatly influenced the drafting of the 2003 Ukrainian Civil Code. The formation rules of the CISG were largely adopted as a whole.[28] It has also been asserted that the CISG has been referred to in interpreting the Civil Code.[29]

IV. CISG Jurisprudence in Belarus and the Ukraine

There are a number of CISG court decisions and about a dozen arbitral decisions in Belarus, but only two cases have been translated into English. There are three court cases in English translation concerning the CISG in Ukraine and more than a dozen arbitral decisions.

In the *Bird Factory* case,[30] a Belarus court failed to immediately enforce an arbitral award of another country in which the CISG was the applicable law. The court, instead, provided the defending party with a lengthy "grace period." The Belarus court stated that the CISG is inapplicable because the proceeding was one of execution of an award. This is antithetical to CISG Article 61, which specifically states that "no period of grace may be granted to the buyer [or seller] by a court or arbitral tribunal when the seller [or buyer] resorts to a remedy for breach of contract."[31]

---

[23] Albert H. Kritzer CISG Database (Pace), Belarus, January 22, 1998, http://www.cisg.law.pace.edu/cisg/countries/cntries-Belarus.html.

[24] Id. Compare with date given by the same database for Russia/Soviet Union at http://www.cisg.law.pace.edu/cisg/countries/cntries-RussianF.html. "September 1, 1991, is the date the CISG became effective in the USSR. The Russian Federation is regarded as successor to this treaty obligation.")

[25] Albert H. Kritzer CISG Database (Pace), January 22, 1998, Ukraine, available at http://www.cisg.law.pace.edu/cisg/countries/cntries-Ukraine.html.

[26] Teofil I. Kis, *Nationhood, Statehood and the International Status of the Ukrainian SSR* passim (University of Ottawa Press: Occasional Papers Ukrainian Studies).

[27] Central Intelligence Agency, World Factbook: Independence, available at https://www.cia.gov/library/publications/the-world-factbook/fields/2088.html (accessed October 13, 2011).

[28] Andrii Finogin, "Contract Formation: Can the CISG Fill the Gaps of the Ukrainian Civil Code?," 13 *Kyiv Student J. of International L.* 79, 83, available at http://jg.kiev.ua/pages/data/13/11.htm.

[29] Id. at 82.

[30] *Company "A" vs. Public Corp. "B,"* Cassational Board of the Supreme Economic Court (No. N1–5ux/06707K) (2006), available at http://cisgw3.law.pace.edu/cases/060731b5.html.

[31] See CISG Articles 45(3) and 61(3).

Another Belarus case involved a Russian buyer and a Belarus seller.[32] The Russian party failed to appear to defend against the claim. The arbitrator found that the CISG was applicable. The arbitrator found that the penalties provided in the contract for delay in payment were excessive. The arbitrator reduced the penalty as provided for under Belarus law, because the enforceability of penalties is not regulated under the CISG.

The Ukrainian arbitration court decision in the *Metal Production Goods* case is bizarre on two counts: one, it applied both Russian substantive law as well as the CISG, and two, it applied the CISG's Article 77 regarding mitigation of damages in a strange manner.[33] The Russian substantive law was applied to grant damages in the form of payment of the purchase price for goods that had been delivered; no explanation was given as to why the Russian law was applied instead of the CISG. The court then applied CISG Article 77, requiring the mitigation of damages, to prevent the seller from recovering a fine that it had incurred. The arbitrator found that the fine would not have been incurred if the seller had initiated arbitration proceedings within ninety days of the breach.[34]

In another Ukraine decision, the arbitrator in the so-called equipment case denied the foreign seller recovery of damages for delay of payment due to "non-conformity," citing CISG Article 80. Article 80, however, has another function, and it is hard to conclude otherwise than to find that the Article was misapplied.[35] In these cases, and others, the Ukrainian courts take an antirecovery position, limiting damages to something less than the full compensation required under the CISG.

In three other, unrelated, cases, the arbitrator applies both the CISG and the national civil code in a confusing manner, sometimes applying provisions of both and sometimes only the civil code, even though there is an applicable CISG provision.[36]

In a case involving a Czech buyer and a Ukraine seller, the arbitrator interpreted a contractual provision stating that the breaching party "shall compensate the other party's direct losses which were incurred as a consequence and are confirmed by the payment documents" to mean that the parties had agreed that lost profits were not to be recoverable, citing CISG Article 74. Again, this appears less to be a question of the interpretation of the CISG as it is of contractual interpretation. One wonders why the parties would have inserted such language. Were they really trying to restrict damages,

---

[32] Unknown parties, Economic Court of the City of Minsk (April 10, 2008), abstracted in UNCITRAL Case Law on UNCITRAL Texts, June 22, 2010 (A/CN.9/Ser.C/Abstracts/96), p. 7, Case 961 (April 10, 2008), available at http://daccess-dds-ny.un.org/doc/UNDOC/GEN/V10/546/26/PDF/V1054626.pdf? OpenElement.

[33] Unknown parties, Tribunal of International Commercial Arbitration at Ukraine Chamber of Commerce and Trade (1999), available at http://cisgw3.law.pace.edu/cases/990709u5.html.

[34] See also Unknown parties, Tribunal of International Commercial Arbitration at Ukraine Chamber of Commerce and Trade (2004) (similar ruling), available at http://cisgw3.law.pace.edu/cases/040112u5.html; Unknown parties, Tribunal of International Commercial Arbitration at Ukraine Chamber of Commerce and Trade (2004) (same), available at http://cisgw3.law.pace.edu/cases/040923u5.html.

[35] Unknown parties, Tribunal of International Commercial Arbitration at Ukraine Chamber of Commerce and Trade (2002), available at http://cisgw3.law.pace.edu/cases/020621u5.html.

[36] Unknown parties, Tribunal of International Commercial Arbitration at Ukraine Chamber of Commerce and Trade (2003), available at http://cisgw3.law.pace.edu/cases/031210u5.html; Unknown parties, Tribunal of International Commercial Arbitration at Ukraine Chamber of Commerce and Trade (2004), available at http://cisgw3.law.pace.edu/cases/041019u5.html; Unknown parties, Tribunal of International Commercial Arbitration at Ukraine Chamber of Commerce and Trade (2005), available at http://cisgw3.law.pace.edu/cases/050919u5.html.

or were they simply convinced that the only damages recoverable were those for which there was documentary evidence?[37]

The exact opposite result to that obtained in the previous case was reached in a 2005 arbitration decision, although the contractual provision describing damages is nearly identical. "According [to paragraph] 9.3 of the Contract . . . the party which has breached the contract shall compensate the other party's direct losses which were incurred as a consequence and are confirmed by the payment documents." Lost profits in this case were, however, awarded.[38]

V. Summary

The cases surveyed in this chapter have a great deal of commonality. They display the following characteristics: (1) Many merely state that the CISG is applicable, but there is no particular interpretation given, inasmuch as there are no real issues raised, only that of nonpayment. (2) Many of the case decisions produce the same outcome as would have been obtained had national law been applicable. (3) Very often buyers fail to adduce evidence to prove their claims. They often merely state the goods are nonconforming. (4) Often both local law and the CISG are applied, when the CISG should solely govern. (5) The few times that provisions of the CISG are applied, they are applied in a manner that appears to be at odds with the general understanding of the meaning of the applicable CISG provisions.

If indeed the idea that damages should be limited to those that are foreseeable, or the idea of fundamental nonperformance, is alien and even considered unnecessary, it is hardly to be expected that lawyers and judges in such territories would be equipped to bring such arguments to bear in CISG cases or even to recognize when such doctrines and rules should be applied. This may also explain why buyers in these territories fail to provide substantial evidence to support their claims of nonconformity. These difficulties are likely due to the unfinished reception of Western law, including the CISG, in the region. Lawyers and courts there find it difficult to apply law based upon on teleological or functional principles.[39] It may be some time still until Soviet legal theory is expunged from the law and role of private law is suitably developed in these countries. Western businesses may find it wise to avoid this problem by incorporating a choice of forum in their contracts that refers disputes to court systems better prepared to apply the CISG and Western legal theory.

---

[37] Unknown parties, Tribunal of International Commercial Arbitration at Ukraine Chamber of Commerce and Trade (2004), available at http://cisgw3.law.pace.edu/cases/041118u5.html.

[38] Unknown parties, Tribunal of International Commercial Arbitration at Ukraine Chamber of Commerce and Trade (No. 48, 2005), available at http://cisgw3.law.pace.edu/cases/050000u5.html.

[39] Tadas Klimas, *Comparative Contract Law* (Durham, NC: Carolina Academic Press, 2006), 5 (for an outline of the general problem); Zdeněk Kühn, "Worlds Apart: Western and Central European Judicial Culture at the Onset of the European Enlargement," 52 *Am. J. Comparative L.* 531 (2004).

21 French Perspective of the CISG

Sylvaine Poillot-Peruzzetto

I. Introduction

"Globalization . . . is the overreaching international system shaping the domestic politics and foreign relations of virtually every country, and we have to understand it as such."[1] The Vienna Convention on Contracts for the International Sale of Goods (CISG) came into force in France on January 1, 1988. It was preceded by two 1964 Hague Conventions, one dealing with the formation of international sales contracts and the other setting up a legal framework for the performance of international contracts. Traditionally, private international law is method used to select the national law applicable to a contract dispute, as well as the appropriate jurisdiction. The CISG has achieved a level of success well above that of the predecessor instruments. The key to the CISG's success is its flexibility of implementation and ability to supersede national legal traditions.

CISG's general principles instruct the interpreter to take into account its international character and to refrain from using national law in interpreting CISG rules. The judge has a general obligation to disregard national law and interpret and apply the CISG as an autonomous, uniform substantive law. With regard to substantive issues, the CISG governs three areas: (1) the conclusion (formation) of contracts, (2) the obligations of the seller including and the remedies of the buyer, and (3) the obligations of the buyer including and the remedies of the seller. The CISG, therefore, provides both a substantive "law of sales" and regulation of certain issues of the general law of contract.

Even though the CISG is regarded as French substantive law, its application may be excluded by agreement of the parties. This exclusion, under CISG Article 6, can be express or implied. For example, the Court of Cassation recognized an implied exclusion based on the fact that the parties referred to domestic French law in their pleadings and during the proceedings.[2] However, elsewhere, the Court of Cassation ruled that when the parties refer to both the CISG and French provisions in their pleadings, it should not be implied that they intended to exclude the application of the CISG.[3] In the end, the court held the CISG was inapplicable because the parties had chosen French law as the law governing a distributorship contract, which it determined was not covered by

---

[1] Thomas L. Friedman, *The Lexus and the Olive Tree: Understanding Globalization* (New York: Farrar Straus & Giroux, 1999), 7.
[2] CISG at Article 6.
[3] Cour de Cassation, First Civil division, October 25, 2005, no. 99–12.879.

the CISG; however, the CISG was applicable to the individual sales contracts executed under the distribution agreement.[4]

The application of the CISG can change the result of a case just because rules applicable differ, in certain instances, from French law and legal practice. Law practitioners in France would be well served by gaining a better understanding of the French courts' CISG decisions, so they can better advise their clients.

Through the analysis of case law that spans more than thirty-five years, it is now possible to see the influences of the CISG on the French domestic legal system. The goal of this chapter is not a complete study of the application of the CISG by the French courts, but to identify the differences and difficulties, which arise from its application and, therefore, highlight the nuances that legal professionals should be aware of when implementing the CISG.

The chapter will highlight the underlying practical utilities[5] of applying the CISG within the French legal system. Section II will review French CISG case law and commentary relating to the formation or conclusion of contracts. Section III analyzes the performance and breach provisions of the CISG as applied by French courts. Section IV examines the CISG's remedial scheme of damages, avoidance, and price reduction. Finally, Section V provides some concluding remarks.

II. Contract Formation

The two subjects that have been discussed in the French courts relating to contract formation under the CISG are the intent to be bound and agreement of terms (specification of quantity and price) requirements.

A. *Intention of the Parties*

The parties' intention to enter a binding contract is determined using the offer-acceptance rules found in Articles 14 to 18. The next section explores the scope of the offer-acceptance model of agreement. The subsequent section examines the difficulties the French courts have had in applying Article 18, which deals with the issue of acceptance by silence or inactivity.

1. Scope of the Intention Doctrine

The CISG's offer-acceptance rules are similar to those found in French law. First, an offer needs to be "sufficiently definite" to characterize the "intention of the offeror to be bound in case of acceptance."[6] Second, the acceptance should express an unconditional will to accept the offer, usually by "a statement or conduct indicating assent to the offer."[7]

---

[4] Court of Cassation, Commercial Division, November 3, 2009, no. 08–12.399.
[5] David G. Gerber, "Sculpting the Agenda of Comparative Law: Ernest Rabel and the Façade of Language," in *Rethinking the Masters of Comparative Law* (Hart Publishing, 2001), 197.
[6] CISG at Article14(1).
[7] Id. at Article 18(1).

The interpretation of parties' intentions is the subject of several doctrines. An opposition exists between two distinct sets of values known as the will theory of subjective intent and the theory of declaration based on an objective intent or reliance. CISG rules reflect a combination of these theories of consent, which are analogous to the Swiss "principle of confidence"[8] based on each party's expectations. CISG Articles 14(1) and 18 require a willful declaration by word or conduct by the parties to be bound to a contract. If a promise is ambiguous, under Article 8, the judge is to interpret the intent of the promisor from the point of view of the receiving party (promisee). This perspective is represented by the reasonable person standard found in Article 8(2).

In the first case brought before the Court of Cassation, the court discussed the nature of the applicable rules pertaining to the matter of an effective offer.[9] Claude Witz has argued has argued that Article 14 should be considered as a "complete rule which cannot be circumvented" by stricter conditions imposed by national law.[10] Nonetheless, the court failed to lay down a clear position on this issue. The Court of Cassation has had a difficult time in providing consistent interpretations on the matter of determining the intention of the parties. In the 2003 case of *Société H. H . . . GmbH & Co. v. SARL MG*,[11] a Court of Appeal determined that under CISG Article 9, despite the existence of a long-term, ongoing relationship, the seller could not use the evidence of party-fabricated common practices – including what constituted an acceptation – when the transaction in question dealt with a new kind of good. In contrast, the Court of Appeal of Grenoble ruled that even if silence or inactivity is usually insufficient to identify an acceptance, a long-term business relationship between the parties could override the general rule.[12] The case involved a longstanding supply relationship where the seller denied having received certain orders, leading to the buyer's claim of losses due to not receiving the goods and for damage to the company's brand image. Seller argued that no written contract was signed and also relied on the provisions of Article 18(1). The court held that the practice of previous years between the parties was sufficient proof to declare that the contract had been concluded, even without any express acceptance from the seller.

Legal counsel should inform its clients of decisions that lead to potential liability. This may include the incorporation of contract language, such as: "This offer shall be deemed to have been rejected unless we receive your notice of acceptance in writing on or before [certain date]."[13] This type of provision has the advantage of ruling out the possibility that silence could be interpreted as an acceptance. However, the parties could subsequently establish a practice in consistent with the provision. If the parties

[8] Bénédicte Fauvarque-Cosson, "La confiance légitime et l'estoppel," 11 *Electronic J. Comparative L.* 21 (2007), available at http://www.ejcl.org/113/Article113–8.pdf.
[9] *Fauba v. Fujitsu*, Cour of Cassation, First Civil Chamber (January 4, 1995), no. 92–16.993, available at http://cisgw3.law.pace.edu/cases/950104f1.html.
[10] Claude Witz, "The First Decision of France's Court of Cassation Applying the U.N. Convention on Contracts for the International Sale of Goods," 16 *J. of L. & Commerce* 345 (1997).
[11] *Société H. H. GmbH & Co. v. SARL MG*, Cour of Appeal of Paris (September 10, 2003), no. 2002/02304, available at http://cisgw3.law.pace.edu/cases/030910f1.html.
[12] *Calzados Magnanni v. Shoes General International*, Court of Appeal of Grenoble (October 21, 1999), no. 96J/00101, available at http://www.cisg.law.pace.edu/cases/991021f1.html.
[13] John P. McMahon, "Drafting CISG Contracts and Documents and Compliance Tips for Traders, Guide for Managers and Counsel" (2004), available at http://www.cisg.law.pace.edu/cisg/contracts.html.

develop a practice contrary to the provision, then they risk that the practice would win out over the conflicting express provision; or a finding of waiver or estoppel relating to the nonenforcement of the provision.

2. Acceptance by Silence

French judges have applied the same solution dictated by Article 18(1). They have generally held that silence does not in itself amount to acceptance.[14] In the case of *Hughes v. Sté Technocontact*, the Court of Cassation rendered a rather ambiguous decision. The case involved a buyer ordering additional items and requesting a change in some technical specifications. The seller responded by sending drawings with the requested modifications to the buyer. The buyer ultimately canceled the order, asserting confusion over the price and a lack of conformity of delivered goods. The court held again that silence does not, *in itself*, amount to acceptance, but under the circumstances of the case the buyer's silence could be interpreted as an acceptance. It reasoned that the long-term nature of the order, as well as the fact that modifications were ordered by the buyer, prevented the buyer from claiming lack of conformity under Article 49.

However, the court distinguished between two types of silence: (1) The silence referenced in Article 18(1), which is characterized by a situation where there was expression or conduct indicating acceptance,[15] and (2) circumstances where silence could be construed otherwise. This decision reflects longstanding judicial practice of holding professionals to a higher standard. The court expressly noted that the buyer, as a professional, could not invoke a lack of conformity due to its business knowledge and that the modification on the original drawings would have been obvious to even a "nonprofessional."

As noted earlier, the French legal system distinguishes between individuals acting for their own interest and those working in the capacity of a business professional. Professional buyers and sellers are assumed to know customs, usages, and the importance of trade context. The burden resting on them is therefore heavier than for ordinary individuals. It is because of the professional status of the buyer in the aforementioned case that the court determined that the buyer should have recognized that remaining silent was tantamount to an acceptance. A 2005 case expanded this rationale to cases involving nonprofessionals where there is a preexisting contractual relationship, coupled with a change order.

B. *Essential Terms of Contract*

The determination of the essential terms for the formation of a CISG contract is an issue with which French courts have struggled, because French doctrine about notions of fixing a price and quantity is totally different than that of the CISG.

---

[14] Court of Cassation (May 25, 1870) ("Attendu, en droit, que le silence de celui que l'on prétend obligé ne peut suffire, en l'absence de toute autre circonstance, pour faire preuve contre lui de l'obligation alléguée"); Eddy Lamazerolles, *Les Apports de la Convention de Vienne au droit interne de la vente* (Université de Poitiers, 2003), 30.

[15] Muriel Fabre-Magnan, *Droit des obligations*, vol. 1: *Contrat et engagement unilatéral* (Thémis Droit PUF, 2010), 255.

1. Price and Quantity

Article 14(1)[16] of the CISG identifies the stipulation of the price as required for a "sufficiently definite" offer. This clear mandate has been complicated because Article 55[17] allows for the implication of a price term. These articles serve to ensure the existence of the contract and to preclude the seller from unilaterally setting the price. The apparent contradiction between Articles 14 and 55 is a nuanced one. According to Article 14, an express or implicit setting of a price is required in order for a communication to qualify as an offer. This allows the offeror to search for potential buyers without fear of accidently entering into a contract. The failure to provide a determined price leads to the finding that a contract was never formed. Although harsh, this finding ensures the principal aim of Article 14, the protection of the offeror. Article 55 focuses on the buyer's obligations. It does not identify the validity of the contract but creates a legal framework that avoids a situation where the seller could fix the price by him- or herself. It provides a gap-filler by referencing the price generally charged at the time of the conclusion of the contract.

French contract law is based on two opposed postulates, which are the equality of the parties and protection of the weaker party. The French judge must balance these two opposing views of the contractual relationship.[18] French judges strictly enforce the price term requirement, under Article 1129 of the French Civil Code,[19] in initial contracts. The fixing of an actual price, however, need not be expressly stated as long as it can be objectively determined. Article 1174 of the Civil Code[20] strictly forbids the existence of any binding obligation relying on a prospective condition. More recently, the Court of Cassation in a series of decisions[21] recognized that Article 1129 was no longer applicable to the matter of "price" and that the indetermination of the price will not result in a null contract unless the fixing of a price is subject to abuse[22] or that a search for an objectively reasonable price proves unsuccessful.

It has been difficult for French jurists to accept the idea that a price can be set subsequent to the formation of a contract. This is because the requirement of a fixed price is firmly established in French law. The fixed price requirement can be traced to the first edition of the Civil Code, which declared that a meeting of the minds is required to create a binding contract. An obligation could not exist if the contract did not identify

---

[16] CISG at Article 14(1)

[17] Id. at Article 55

[18] Court of Cassation, Commercial Chamber (April 27, 1971); Court of Cassation, Commercial Chamber (November 1971); Court of Cassation, Commercial Chamber (October 11, 1978).

[19] Article 1129 of the French Civil Code states: "(1) An obligation must have for its object a thing determined at least as to its kind" and "(2) The quantity of the thing may be uncertain, provided it can be determined."

[20] Article 1174 of the French Civil Code: "An obligation is void where it was contracted subject to a protestative condition on the part of the one who binds himself."

[21] Court of Cassation (December 1, 1995), no. 91–15.578; Court of Cassation (December 1, 1995), no. 91–15.999; Court of Cassation (December 1, 1995), no. 91–19.653; Court of Cassation (December 1, 1995), no. 93–13.688.

[22] See Court of Cassation (November 29, 1994), Bull Civ., no. 348, D.1995, 122 (note by Aynès) (analysis of the notion of abuse).

the quantity of the goods and fix a determined price. The rationale for this rule excluded the hypothesis where a party could unilaterally fix the price. The nullity of the contract without an express, fixed price term was therefore justified.[23]

One school of thought holds that it is always possible to make reference to the "price generally charged" for such goods in a particular market.[24] However, it is doubtful in a worldwide context that one will be able to determine a precise market price, therefore, as a default, reference is made to the price generally paid in the seller's or buyer's country. In *Alain Veyron v. Ambrosio*,[25] a buyer did not pay for the delivered goods. It argued that the contract price was not determined and should therefore be fixed according to Article 55. The buyer tried to impose a market price, which was less than the market price at the time when the contract was concluded. The court noted that the buyer failed to challenge the "charged price" when taking delivery of the goods. The court held that the seller could have therefore reasonably interpreted this silence as an acceptance of the charged price. Under this interpretation, Article 55, which makes a direct reference to the market price, is applicable only if there is no express or implied agreement between the parties.

The extent to which the price has to be specified has caused some confusion due to the twin aims of the requirement – the protective and the qualifying aims.[26] Eddy Lamazerolles has argued that: "When a buyer does not agree to the price, the Court criticizes the behavior of the other party who abused his dominant position but not the contract in itself which usually has already been executed."[27] Article 1591 of the Civil Code[28] requires a sale of goods contract to contain a determined and stated price. The Court of Cassation interpreted Article 1591 to mean that the price should be able to be determined according to the provisions included in the contract.[29] In the alternative, a price may be implied by reference to official quotations of a specific market,[30] which do not rely on the discretion of a party to the contract.[31]

In sum, the requirement for the determination of the goods (kind and quantity) in French contract law is stricter than that of the CISG. The CISG provides greater flexibility because it states that a proposal for concluding a contract is sufficiently definite even if it provides "implicitly" for determining the goods and the price. Article 1129 indicates that even if the object of the contract is not fully determined at the time of the conclusion of the contract, the contract must contain explicit provisions that determine precisely the obligations of each party's obligations.[32]

---

[23] Id.

[24] Al Qudah Maen, "L'Exécution de Contrat de vente Internationale de Marchandises" (Université de Reims Champagne Ardenne, Faculté de Droit et de Sciences économiques, 2007), 333.

[25] *Alain Veyron v. Ambrosio*, Court of Appeal of Grenoble (April 26, 1995), no. 213, available at http://cisgw3.law.pace.edu/cases/950426f1.html.

[26] Lamazerolles, *Les Apports de la Convention de Vienne*.

[27] Id. at 43.

[28] Article 1591 of the French Civil Code: "The price of a sale must be determined and stated by the parties."

[29] Court of Cassation (January 7, 1925), D.H. 1925 at 57.

[30] Court of Cassation, first civil chamber, December 14, 2004, no. 01–17.063.

[31] Id.

[32] Fabre-Magnan, *Droit des obligations*, 360.

2. Battle of Forms: Strict Application of Article 19(1)

CISG Article 19(1) states that a reply to an offer containing "additions, limitations or other modifications of the offer" is considered as a counteroffer and, therefore, is a rejection of the initial offer. Article 19(2) limits this general prohibition against such terms to those that "materially alter the terms of the offer." In such cases, a contract is formed based on the terms of the acceptance, unless the offeror objects to the modifications in a timely manner.

French courts have broadly construed the notion of a material alteration based on Article 19(3)'s broad definition of "material" as including any term that modifies the price[33] or changes terms relating to the settlement of disputes,[34] or a reference to different general sales conditions.[35] In *Fujitsu Elektronik GmbH Company v. Fauba France Company (Fujitsu v. Fauba)*,[36] a buyer ordered electronic components from a seller at a fixed price, but the goods were to be delivered in installments on confirmation by the seller and subject to market fluctuations. A dispute arose when the buyer canceled an order that was already in transit. The Court of Cassation found the contract to be valid because the offer made by the buyer, which allowed price revisions (according to market fluctuations), was sufficiently definite. This was despite Article 19(3)'s statement that different terms in the reply relating to the price and the time of delivery should be "considered to alter the terms of the offer materially."

Claude Witz has questioned whether the presumption of Article 19(3) is rebuttable.[37] Unfortunately, this issue was not discussed in *Fujitsu v. Fauba*. Instead, the lower court took a traditional French law approach by attempting to determine what elements were "subjectively" essential to the parties at the time of the reply (acceptance). The lower court held, and subsequently confirmed by the Court of Cassation, that the delivery delay and the determination of the price did not essentially alter the terms of the offer.

The Court of Cassation in this case can be criticized, as it should have followed a more objective path in order to create a more autonomous interpretation free of French law's preference for subjective interpretation. However, the court did not follow national legal tradition, which would have eliminated the conflicting general conditions (knock-out rule).

French commentators have argued that the knock-out rule is the best approach to dealing with conflicting terms.[38] They reason that such an approach simply eliminates provisions that the parties did not expect to apply. The legal practitioner may want to consider advising its clients as a matter of business to routinely send a "Notice of

---

[33] Court of Appeal of Rennes (May 27, 2008), available at http://www.cisg.law.pace.edu/cases/080527f1.html (Brassiere cups case).

[34] *Les Verreries de Saint Gobain v. Martinswerk*, Court de Cassation, First Civil Chamber (July 16, 1998), no. 1309 P, available at http://www.cisg.law.pace.edu/cases/980716f1.html.

[35] *ISEA Industrie v. Lu*, Court of Appeal of Paris (December 13, 1995), no. 95–018179, available at http://www.cisg.law.pace.edu/cases/951213f1.html.

[36] *Fauba v. Fujitsu*, Cour of Cassation, First Civil Chamber (January 4, 1995), no. 92–16.993, available at http://cisgw3.law.pace.edu/cases/950104f1.html.

[37] Claude Witz, "The First Decision of France's Court of Cassation Applying the U.N Convention on Contracts for the International Sale of Goods," 16 *J. of L. & Commerce* 345 (1997).

[38] Bertrand Ancel and Horattia Muir Watt, "Le contentieux des ventes de marchandises intracommunautaires et le jeu combiné des Conventions de Bruxelles et de Vienne," *Revue critique de droit international privé, Recueil Dalloz* (1999), 122.

Objection" after receiving a purported acceptance with the other party's standard terms. It could simply state that the reply (state date of reply) "purports to be an acceptance, but contains additional and or different terms. We object to the discrepancy and regard your reply as a rejection of our offer and a counteroffer, which we reject."[39] An alternative response would be to state: "We (offeror) object to all the additional and different terms in your purported acceptance. Please confirm acceptance of our offer without the additional and different terms found in your reply." Both statements produce the same result of rejecting the counteroffer, however, the second statement is a bit more diplomatic.

III. Performance and Breach of Contract

CISG Article 35 requires the seller to deliver conforming goods. This provision has influenced the European Law. Directive 1999/44/EC of 1999,[40] which embraced the CISG's unitary notion of conformity.[41] French courts have barely attempted to define this obligation and still have difficulty applying Article 35. Article 35 allows for great flexibility in application. This flexibility is coupled with the fact that the CISG fails to define nonconformity. Such vagueness has made it difficult for French courts to understand the relationship between nonconformity of goods and fundamental breach.

A. *Fundamental Breach and Seller's Duty to Deliver Conforming Goods*

The notion of fundamental breach is one of the pillars of the CISG. Nevertheless, the CISG does not provide a general definition of fundamental breach.[42] The CISG also provides the seller the possibility of receiving an extension of the time for performance. The right to a time extension through *Nachfrist* notice is easier to understand, relative to fundamental breach, but it has proved to be more difficult in application.

1. Definition of Fundamental Breach

The lack of a clear definition of fundamental breach in the CISG has been the subject of criticism. Nonetheless, it does provide a counterweight to French law's favoritism toward buyers. French law's main purpose is to protect the weaker party. It has been criticized as being biased against freedom of contract in favor of social concerns. This theme in French law has led to a greater application of the CISG when a French company is involved because it incorporates common law pragmatism and its more conservative view of the role of protectionism in contract law.

The Appellate Court of Grenoble[43] defined fundamental breach as "a substantial deprivation of expectation which could be reasonably foreseen from one party of a

---

[39] McMahon, "Drafting CISG."

[40] Directive 1999/44/EC of the European Parliament and of the Council of 25 May 1999 on certain aspects of the sale of consumer goods and associated guarantees, at Article 2.

[41] Lise Koroma, "L'influence de la convention sur la vente internationale de marchandises sur les droits français et allemand," Université Paris Ouest, blog "Rapports droit interne et droit international ou européen."

[42] CISG, Article 25.

[43] *BRI Production Bonaventure v. Pan African Export*, Court of Appeal of Grenoble (February 22, 1995), no. 93/3275, available at http://www.cisg.law.pace.edu/cases/950222f1.html.

contract." In that case, a seller sold a certain quantity of clothes in which the contract specified that the pants bought were destined for the South American and African continents. The seller continually asked for proof of destination. Proof was made, but the buyer sent the goods to Spain. The seller then terminated the contract. The court invoked CISG Article 8(1) in concluding that the buyer had not respected the wishes of the seller and, therefore, the seller was entitled to declare the contract void. The Court invoked Article 73(2) in holding that the buyer's conduct constituted a fundamental breach of the entire installment contract. It also found the buyer's conduct "contrary to the principle of good faith in international trade laid down in Article 7 CISG."[44] It further held that the buyer's bringing of the claim as plaintiff constituted an abuse of process.

Under the French legal system, it is not possible for one party to avoid a contract without any judiciary intervention,[45] while the CISG tries to preserve the contract as much as possible. The avoidance of the contract will therefore rest on objective considerations and would be possible only in the presence of a fundamental breach of the contract.[46] French judges have succeeded to some extent at objectively analyzing the factual elements to determine whether or not there was a fundamental breach.[47]

One French court determined that even if the identification of defective goods was possible thanks to their reference number, a partial termination of the contract was not possible taking into account the number of defective items (almost one-third of the total order) coupled with the nature of the goods (pressure cookers).[48] In another case, a certain quantity of the ordered goods did not fit the previously agreed upon description of the products.[49] The court decided that the defect did not constitute a fundamental breach, as it was possible to repair the goods because the defect related to a specific component part. It ordered the seller to repair and furnish the new elements at its own expense.

2. CISG Nonconformity of Goods and French Law

Article 35 of the CISG lists several categories of requirements, which could be used by the parties to determine the conformity of the goods with the order.[50] For example, the goods must be fit for the purposes for which goods of the same description would ordinarily be used, possess the qualities of goods that the seller had held out to the buyer as a sample or model, and are contained or packaged in the manner usual for such goods or, where there is no such manner, in a manner adequate to prepare and protect the goods.[51]

---

[44] Id.

[45] Article 1184 French Civil Code: "A condition subsequent is always implied in synallagmatic contracts, for the case where one of the two parties does not carry out his undertaking. The party towards whom the undertaking has not been fulfilled has the choice either to compel the other to fulfil the agreement when it is possible, or to request its avoidance with damages."

[46] See CISG, Article 51.

[47] BRI Production Bonaventure v. Pan African Export, Court of Appeal of Grenoble (February 22, 1995), no. 93/3275, available at http://www.cisg.law.pace.edu/cases/950222f1.html.

[48] Court of Appeal of Paris (June 4, 2004), no. 2002/18702, available at http://www.cisg.law.pace.edu/cases/040604f1.html (pressure cookers case).

[49] Marques Roque Joachim v. Manin Rivière, Court of Appeal of Grenoble (April 26, 1995), no. RG 93/4879, available at http://www.cisg.law.pace.edu/cases/950426f2.html.

[50] CISG, Article 35.

[51] McMahon, "Drafting CISG."

French law places additional requirements in the determination of whether goods are conforming. In 2005, the Court of Appeal of Versailles ruled that goods ought to be in conformity with contract provisions. In addition, they have to be in conformity with requirements imposed by the national law of the receiving state. In this case, the buyer bought toys that were subsequently withdrawn from its marketing operation because of their nonconformity with security and labeling provisions required by the European Union. The seller argued that it was not obliged to search for the applicable security norms currently in force in the buyer's country, and it was simply obliged to comply with those applicable in its own country because both countries had implemented the harmonized norms arising out of a Community Directive. A reference to the European norm is indicated on the label of the plush toys by displaying the "CE" marking required by the directive; and is indicated by marketing the goods originating from outside of the community within the internal market. However, it was the seller's duty to verify the initial conformity of the products to standard EN-71.

In *Caito Roger v. Société Française de Factoring*,[52] the court found the goods to be nonconforming because of its packaging was not in accordance with the national requirements for labeling.[53] The Court of Appeal found that it was undeniable, given continuous business relationships between the parties, that the seller knew that the goods were destined for the French market and that this awareness obliged it to observe the marketing laws enforceable in France. The court decided that the failure to indicate the composition of the goods on the products' package rendered them nonconforming within the meaning of Article 35.

3. CISG Article 40

The merchantability of the goods has been used as a standard for identifying a fundamental breach. In the case *Sacovini/M Marrazza v. Les fils de Henri Ramel*,[54] the Court of Cassation ruled that a fundamental breach occurred as a result of the nonmerchantability of the wine on the French market. The seller added a certain quantity of sugar to the wine in breach of French wine laws. The court held that the manipulation changed the very nature of the wine to the extent that it amounted to a fundamental breach. The rationale was that even if the wine was still good for consumption or for resale, its composition was materially different than what the parties had agreed upon. One commentator noted that delivery of an adulterated product is a breach of "business loyalty."[55] The Court of Cassation succeeded in applying the regime of nonconformity stated in the CISG. It essentially noted that the CISG makes no distinction between nondelivery and delivery of goods with serious hidden defects for purposes of determining breach.[56]

---

[52] *Caito Roger v. Société Française de Factoring*, Court of Appeal of Grenoble (September 13, 1995), no. 48992, available at http://www.cisg.law.pace.edu/cases/950913f1.html.

[53] It has to be noted that this solution is legally justified because the parties were involved in a long-term business relationship, therefore, the seller could not argue about its ignorance of the destination of the goods.

[54] *Sacovini/M Marrazza v. Les fils de Henri Ramel*, Court of Cassation (January 23, 1996), no. 93–16.542, available at http://cisgw3.law.pace.edu/cases/960123f1.html.

[55] Dominique Bureau, "De la loi applicable à l'obligation de délivrance dans une vente internationale de marchandises," *Revue critique de droit international privé* 462 (1996).

[56] Claude Witz, "La Cour de cassation veille à l'application de la Convention des Nations unies sur les contrats de vente internationale de marchandises," 24 *Dalloz Sirey* 334 (1996).

CISG Article 40 provides an exception to the seller's right to a prompt inspection and notice of nonconformity. The *engine parts case*[57] involved a buyer of metallic parts. The parties agreed on a specific composition of metal. The contract obligated the seller to furnish a detailed laboratory test of the metal composition with the delivery of goods. Following the delivery of the third installment of the goods, a customer of the buyer discovered defects in the engine parts. Subsequent testing discovered inconsistencies in the metal. The Court of Appeal held that pursuant to Article 40, the seller had lost its right to rely on the buyer's duty to inspect (Article 38) and to give notice (Article 39). In the courts' opinion, the seller had purposely failed to provide the requested quality summary on the third delivery. Claude Witz notes that the Court of Cassation exhibited homeward trend bias. French law presumes that a professional seller could not be unaware of such quality defects. Such a presumption has no legal basis in the CISG.[58] However, the Court of Appeal decision was based on more than a presumption. It held that not only was the seller aware of the defect, but that it deliberately hid the defect from the buyer by not delivering the required laboratory tests. The court's approach required two findings – that the seller could not have been unaware of the defect and that it had purposely failed to inform the buyer of the defect.

In the *potato seedling case*,[59] the buyer bought potato plants grown from seed produced by the seller. The plants were found to be contaminated with a bacterial disease. The Court of Appeal dismissed the plaintiff's claim because the two-year notice period in Article 39(2) had expired. The court refused to apply Article 40, under which the two-year deadline can be set aside if the lack of conformity can be related "to facts of which the seller knew or could not have been unaware and which he did not disclose to the buyer." The Court of Cassation confirmed the Court of Appeal's position because, unlike in the engine parts case, there was no indication of bad faith on the part of the seller. The plants were furnished with a certificate showing negative test results for the bacterial disease. The court held that the seller had no obligation to inform the buyer that the crops of potatoes surrounding its growing area were contaminated with the disease.[60]

4. *Nachfrist* Notice

The aim of *Nachfrist* notice, which grants additional time for performance, is to allow a party another opportunity to perform its original obligation[61] and it allows the party granting the extension the ability to declare a fundamental breach and to avoid the contract at the time of the expiration of the *Nachfrist* extension period. The CISG does not require a party asking for the time extension or granting the extension to provide an explanation for the grant or request. Indeed, the *Nachfrist* notice is only an intermediary

---

[57] Court of cassation, first civil chamber (October 4, 2005), no. 02–15.981, available at http://cisgw3.law. pace.edu/cases/051004f1.html (engine parts case).

[58] Claude Witz, "Panorama," *Droit uniforme de la vente internationale de marchandises* (Dalloz, 2007), 530.

[59] Court of Cassation, Commercial Chamber (September 16, 2008), no. 07–11803, available at http://cisgw3. law.pace.edu/cases/051004f1.html (potato seedling case).

[60] Pauline Remy-Corlay, "Convention de Vienne: agreation, decheance de l'acheteur du droit de se prevaloir du defaut de conformite et connaisance du vice par le producteur," *Revue trimestrielle de droit civil* 272 (2006).

[61] Court of Appeal of Lyon (December 18, 2003), no. 2001/02620, available at http://www.cisg.law.pace. edu/cases/031218f1.html (coin change machines case).

step in the requirement to fulfill a party's obligation. The Court of Cassation requires additional content than what is required under the CISG. It requires that the *Nachfrist* notice set a reasonable and clear intent to pursue a legal process seeking remedies from the party granting the extension.

The duration of the extension period should be considered as reasonable on the basis of the usages accepted by the parties, the established practices between the parties, or relevant international trade usage.[62] Moreover, the court noted five weeks had passed since the conclusion of the contract and that the seller's granting the buyer an additional seven-day period was not sufficient because the original period for performance was unreasonable. The court factored into account the nature and the quantity of the goods sold, as well as the time needed for sorting items of that weight and size. The court further reasoned that the additional time extension does not need to be precise but only needs to be capable of being interpreted by the judge as reasonable.[63]

French case law seems to require that the content of the *Nachfrist* notice be reasonable before a party is allowed to avoid the contract. In the *brassiere cups case*, the court held that the cancellation of the orders by a buyer justified by a nonconformity of previous deliveries of goods was a reasonable statement of intent to avoid the contract in the future.[64] The buyer was, therefore, entitled to use it as a legal basis to justify its action seeking remedies. In another case, the court held that a buyer failed to provide sufficient proof of a delay in the delivery of goods, despite the incorporation of an "urgent clause" in the purchase orders. The buyer never made a demand for delivery or sent a *Nachfrist* notice stating its intent to seek remedies because of the delay in the delivery of the goods. The buyer is not required to grant an additional period; however, French courts place a burden on the buyer to provide some form of notice or risk being found guilty of wrongful termination of the contract. In essence, the buyer needs to have a viable reason for not granting an additional period to the seller. Under this type of reasoning, the *Nachfrist* extension can be seen as a seller's right.

In *Ego Fruits v. La Verja Begastri*,[65] the buyer was sent the August installment in exchange for a reduced price, but ultimately rejected the goods. However, the buyer still expected the originally scheduled September delivery. The seller refused to deliver the next installment, leading the buyer to buy substituted goods at a higher price. The Court of Appeal ruled that the seller had an obligation to grant an extended period of time for the buyer to accept the delivery. Seller's refusal to deliver was therefore an unfair termination of the contract. The seller failed to avail himself of this alternative basis for setting up a right to avoid contract. Alternatively stated, in order for the buyer's rejection to amount to a fundamental breach, seller should have granted a reasonable extension of time for the buyer to take delivery before avoiding the contract. Under this logic, every nonperformance requires the granting of a *Nachfrist* period. Even under

---

[62] CISG, Article 9.

[63] *Giustina International v. Perfect Circle Europe*, Court of Appeal of Versailles, (January 29, 1998), no. 1995–222, available at http://www.cisg.law.pace.edu/cases/980129f1.html.

[64] Court of Appeal of Rennes (May 27, 2008), available at http://www.cisg.law.pace.edu/cases/080527f1. html (brassiere cups case) (buyer cancelled orders because of manufacturing defects, then purchased replacement goods and sued for damages and interest).

[65] *Ego Fruits v. La Verja Begastri*, Court of Appeal of Grenoble (February 4, 1999), no. 97008146, available at http://www.cisg.law.pace.edu/cases/990204f1.html.

this broad interpretation of when a *Nachfrist* extension is required, however, a court that is confronted with a case of continuous nonperformance would be less strict about the need to grant a *Nachfrist* notice.

The court, in *Marques Roque Joachim v. Manin Rivière*,[66] expressly supported the characterization of *Nachfrist* notice as a right. In this case, the buyer purchased a warehouse partially to disassemble and then reassemble metal items in the warehouse. The buyer refused to pay the last portion of the total price on the grounds that the dismantled metal pieces were defective. The court ruled that several goods were not fit for the purpose of reassembly in the identical form. Because that defect related to only part of the warehouse and concerned metal elements, which could be repaired, it did not constitute a fundamental breach. The court found that it did not justify avoidance of the contract. The use of *Nachfrist* notice turned out to change the obligation of the seller who already failed to deliver goods in conformity with the original provisions of the contract. This obligation turned into a general obligation to use every possible means in order to restore the buyer into what he or she should have reasonably expected when entering the contract.

5. Buyer's Duties of Inspection and Notice

Under Article 38(1), buyers are obligated to inspect the goods "within as short a period as is practicable in the circumstances." Upon the discovery of non-conformities after a reasonable inspection, the buyer has a duty to give proper notice to the seller of the nature of the nonconformity within "a reasonable time."[67] The CISG sets up a maximum time limit of two years to claim nonconformity of goods from the date on which the goods were handed over to the buyer. The issues litigated include what constitutes a reasonable inspection and what is considered a reasonable period of time to give notice to the seller.

a. *Duty to inspect*

The duty of inspection finds no equivalent in French sales law, at least none as rigorous as the one found in Article 38. The requirement of prompt inspection makes it easier to determine which party is responsible for a possible defect.[68] The Court of Cassation has accepted common usage to recognize specific circumstances[69] to determine whether the time period should be considered as reasonable for the buyer to conduct a proper examination of the goods. There are two cases that constitute the law and the basis of the court's reasoning. The court uses this reasoning in *Paris Traction Levage SA v. Drahtseilerei*, in which a buyer of rift cables took delivery of the goods, and after making an inspection it repackaged the goods and sent the cables to its client. The buyer's customer noticed that the goods were defective and informed the buyer. The Commercial Court of Paris dismissed buyer's claim against the seller due to the delay between the reception

---

[66] *Marques Roque Joachim v. Manin Rivière*, Court of Appeal of Grenoble (April 26, 1995), no. 93/4879, available at http://www.cisg.law.pace.edu/cases/950426f2.html.

[67] CISG, Article 39.

[68] Lamazerolles, *Les Apports de la Convention de Vienne*, 43.

[69] Indeed, the Court of Cassation is supposed to give its opinion only on purely judicial matters. Factual determinations are a matter for the lower courts.

of the goods and the inspection of them. According to the Court,[70] the buyer should have carried out a proper inspection when the cables were repackaged on January 17, 1995. The notice of nonconformity was not given to seller until March 16, 1995. The court held that the buyer lost the right to rely on the lack of conformity of the goods under CISG Article 39. In *Schreiber v. Thermo Dynamique*,[71] the Court of Cassation confirmed that the buyer used reasonable efforts to inspect the goods within a reasonable period of time. This was because of the nature of the goods (heavy rolled sheet metal) and the difficulty in the inspection and detection of defects in such goods.

Professor Witz has criticized these decisions for a number of reasons. First, the Court of Cassation's policy to leave the determination of reasonable time to give notice to the lower courts is inconsistent with the international character of the CISG and Article 7's mandate of autonomous interpretations (not biased by domestic legal traditions). This criticism is supported by French CISG case law reliance on the concept of "short delay" found in Article 1648 of the French Civil Code.[72] It seems that an average time period of ten days is considered to be reasonable to set up a proper inspection of the goods.[73]

In sum, three criteria are often taken into account to determine if an inspection was unreasonably delayed: (1) the perishable character of the goods, (2) the nature of the goods, and (3) the obviousness of the defect.[74] Judges seem to have found a solution to balance Article 40, which, of course, has the main aim of protecting the buyer, but the obviousness of a defect protects the seller if not uncovered by an inspection. Also, delayed notice may be due to the defect resulting from the examination by the buyer.[75]

b. *Notice of nonconformity*

French judges have found it difficult to implement the CISG's notice requirement. Fifteen different legal notions[76] in French internal sales law are covered within CISG Article 39. The Court of Cassation mistakenly failed to realize that the failure to conduct a proper examination of the goods does not in itself prevent the buyer from suing the seller but only removes the option to argue a nonconformity.[77] The lower courts continue

---

[70] *Traction Levage SA v. Drahtseilerei*, Court of Appeal of Paris (November 6, 2001), no. 4607/2000, available at http://www.cisg.law.pace.edu/cases/011106f1.html.

[71] *Schreiber v. Thermo Dynamique*, Court of Cassation (May 26, 1999), no. 97–14315, available at http://www.cisg.law.pace.edu/cases/990526f1.html (purchase of rolled metal sheets delivered to multiple locations over a time period from October 28 to December 4, 1992; later, in December 1992, the buyer cancelled the contract).

[72] Claude Witz, "Vente internationale de marchandises: l'appréciation du délai raisonnable de dénonciation des défauts est laissée au pouvoir souverain a'appréciation des juges du fond," *Recueil Dalloz* (2000), 788.

[73] Eight days after delivery for the inspection of elevator cables and eleven days for laminated metal sheets were considered as reasonable time periods.

[74] Claude Witz, "Trois questions récurrentes de la vente internationale de marchandises au sein du même arrêt," *Recueil Dalloz* (2002), 2796.

[75] Id.

[76] Isabelle Cadet, "L'intérêt de la Convention de Vienne du 11 Avril 1980 pour les ventes francaises a l'étranger: la stratégie du risque dans la vente internationale de marchandises," in *Valoriser l'intégration du risque* (ed. Bernard Guillon) (Paris: L'Harmattan, 2011).

[77] *Société Novodec/Société Sigmakalon v. Soctiétés Mobacc et Sam 7*, Court of Cassation, First Civil Chamber (February 3, 2009), no. 07–21827, available at http://cisgw3.law.pace.edu/cases/090203f1.html (paint caps were specially ordered to be nonbreakable; nonetheless, the Court of Appeal rejected the plaintiff's claim on the grounds that it had failed to take action within two years, as required under CISG, Article 39(2)).

to show homeward biased reasoning interpreting the CISG through *lege fori*.[78] Witz has noted that the interpretation of Article 39 has been influenced by the Article 1648 of the French Civil Code,[79] which states that the action against the seller for nonconformity must be brought within a period of two years after the discovery of the defect.[80] The Court of Cassation overturned the decision of the Court of Appeal, based on a breach of the Article 39, stating that the two-year time deadline was "a time limit for a complaint of lack of conformity and not a time limit for action" (statute of limitations). The precise date of the handling of goods is the starting point for the two year delay for providing the notice of nonconformity of goods.[81]

The Court of Cassation has had the opportunity to refine its earlier rulings. The Court of Cassation strictly applied the Vienna Convention in the *floor tiles case*.[82] A buyer bought floor tiles from the seller. The seller guaranteed that the tiles would not freeze during the wintertime. A client of the buyer installed the tiles in 1997. During the winter of 2001–2002, the tiles started to crack. The buyer was declared liable. It then sued the seller for indemnification of the damages paid on the basis of the lack of conformity of goods. The court determined that due to the nature of the goods and the latent nature of the defect, the two-year period for giving notice did not commence until the defect became apparent.[83] The lower court interpreted CISG Article 39(2) to mean that the time to give notice expired two years after the handing over of the goods. This was not a decision influenced by homeward bias because Article 1648 of the French Civil Code uses a starting point for the action based on "redhibitory vices" at the time when the defect is discovered. The Court of Cassation properly interpreted the CISG and overturned the decision of the lower court. In cases involving the use of *Nachfrist* notice, the coin change machines case[84] held that the two-year period commences from the date of expiration of the additional period of time.

In *Pelliculest v. Morton International*,[85] the court dealt with the issue of the criteria related to "reasonableness" of the amount of time between the discovery of the defect and the notice of nonconformity. Two months after the indication of a defect, but not after the defect was confirmed through further testing, did the seller receive notice of nonconformity. The Court of Appeal held that the buyer had given notice of the defect within a reasonable time, just about two months after their discovery. The literature and

---

[78] *Sociétés Mobacc SARL et Sam 7 v. Société Novodec/Sociéte Sigmakaloné*, Court of Appeal of Amiens (September 27, 2007), no. 98/00063, available at http://www.unilex.info/case.cfm?pid=1&do=case&id=1459&step=FullText.

[79] Article 1648 of French Civil Code: "The action resulting from redhibitory vices must be brought by the buyer within a period of two years following the discovery of the vice." In the case provided for in Article 1642–1, the action must be brought, under pain of being time-barred, within the year following the date on which the seller may be discharged from patent defects.

[80] Claude Witz, "Un double éclairage sur le délai butoir de deux ans consacré par la Convention de Vienne," *Recueil Dalloz* (2009), 2907–10.

[81] CISG, Article 39.

[82] *Société Bati-Seul v. Société Ceramiche Marca Corona*, Court of Cassation, First Civil Chamber (April 8, 2009), no. 08–10.678, available at http://cisgw3.law.pace.edu/cases/090408f1.html.

[83] It must be said that: "Action resulting from lack of conformity lapses two years after delivery of the product" (Article L. 211–12 Consumer Code).

[84] Court of Cassation, Third Civil Chamber (February 13, 2007), no. 06–11.258, available at http://cisgw3.law.pace.edu/cases/070213f2.html (coin change machines case).

[85] *Pelliculest v. Morton International*, Court of Appeal of Colmar (October 24, 2000), available at http://www.cisg.law.pace.edu/cases/001024f1.html.

jurisprudence is split between those who believe a court should set a relatively fixed period of time to give notice and those that believe that reasonableness is context dependent so that the reasonableness of the notice period needs to be determined on a case-by-case basis.[86] The general policy adopted by the Court of Cassation is to allow lower courts to determine, according to the circumstances, what is a reasonable time period in a given case. Two criteria that are most often used in making this determination are perishability of the goods and obviousness of the defect. In sum, French courts have been very flexible in the determination of the reasonableness of when the notice of nonconformity should occur after the inspection of the goods. The study of the related case law demonstrates that courts have found a justified notification to the seller from a period of time going from thirty days after the delivery of goods to a period of six months.

The question of prescription of the right to take action has been discussed in the case law. The Court of Cassation indicated that the matter of the time barring of the right to take action is governed by the CISG, but not settled in it. Therefore, national private international law rules must be used to find the applicable prescription period. French international private law, based upon the Hague Convention of June 15, 1955 (Law Applicable to International Sales of Goods), holds that sales contracts are governed by the domestic law of the country in which the seller had its habitual residence at the time when it received the order. If the French law has been determined as the applicable law, the prescription period to take action would be ten years under Article L.110–4 of the French Commercial Code. The court was correct that the prescription period is to be determined by private international law. The court was wrong in stating that the limitation period is "governed" by the CISG. It is obvious that the CISG does not govern the prescription period, as UNCITRAL published an ancillary convention – United Nations Convention on the Limitation Period in the International Sale of Goods.

IV. Remedies

The part of the CISG that has proved to be most influential on a substantive level is the CISG's remedial scheme. The CISG does not adopt the cause-oriented approach of Roman heritage that is prevalent in civil law countries but rather follows the breach of contract approach of the common law tradition. The two main remedies available for fundamental breach are damages and avoidance of the contract, which will be discussed in the following sections.

A. Damages

The assessment of damages under the CISG integrates the concept of foreseeability (Article 74) with the nonbreaching party's duty to mitigate (Article 77).

1. Foreseeability

Article 74 adopts the principle of full compensation of the nonbreaching party. Thus, damages are broadly construed to include a sum of money equal to the loss resulting

---

[86] Claude Witz, "Défaut de conformité, délai raisonnable de dénonciation et prescription de l action en justice contre le vendeur," *Recueil Dalloz* (2002), 393.

from a breach of contract, which includes loss of profits that the other party might have reasonably expected at the time of the execution of the contract and damages that occurred as a consequence of the breach. The nature of damages allowed under the CISG is still unsettled in French case law. Lamazerolles argues that Article 1150 of the French Civil Code[87] has had a direct influence on the court's interpretation of the rule of foreseeability.[88]

The *ship sailing catamaran case*, of December 1, 2010, involved the sale of a ship. The seller failed to disclose that it had been damaged in a storm. An American court held the seller liable for compensatory damages and punitive damages, which are allowed under American tort law. The French court confirmed every aspect of the American decision but for the assessment of punitive damages, which are not authorized under Article 74. In addition, punitive damages are not recognized under the French Civil Code.

There is a tension in the France law of damages between the view of damages as serving the function of reparation, and the view that damages should place the injured party where it would have been if the other party had fully performed. No consensus seems to exist in France. This tension may explain the why the Court of Cassation incorrectly failed to reverse a lower court's awarding damages for "hurt feelings," yet the CISG does not permit nonpecuniary, noncompensatory damages.[89]

In another case,[90] the Court of Cassation failed to properly discuss the nature of damages. The buyer refused the late delivery of orange juice. The court granted damages based on the difference between the contract price and the price paid by the buyer for replacement goods. However, it failed to discuss the profits that would have been earned if it had accepted the late delivery. Indeed, the reduction of the original price granted by the seller has to be considered as a profit for the buyer so if its refusal of taking delivery was reasonably justified, then the court should have ordered the payment of the expected profit. The buyer should not have been required to provide evidence justifying its loss of gross margin. The collectable damages were simply the reasonably foreseeable lost profits as stated in Article 74.

Other cases have dealt with a number of damage-related issues. French courts often refuse to reimburse all of the costs suffered by the injured party because of the party's failure to satisfy its duty of mitigation.[91] Although Article 78 provides for payment of interest,[92] the CISG does not provide rules regarding from what date the interest is to be calculated or how the rate of interest is to be determined. In the *technical equipment case*,[93] the court ruled that the interest is to be calculated from the date of summons,

---

[87] Article 1150 French Civil Code: "A debtor is liable only for damages which were foreseen or which could have been foreseen at the time of the contract, where it is not through his own intentional breach that the obligation is not fulfilled."

[88] Lamazerolles, *Les Apports de la Convention de Vienne*, 347–8.

[89] *Sacovini/M Marrazza v. Les fils de Henri Ramel*, Court of Cassation (January 23, 1996), no. 93–16.542, available at http://cisgw3.law.pace.edu/cases/960123f1.html.

[90] *Ego Fruits v. La Verja Begastri*, Court of Appeal of Grenoble (February 4, 1999), no. 97008146, available at http://www.cisg.law.pace.edu/cases/990204f1.html.

[91] Court of Appeal of Rennes (May 27, 2008), available at http://www.cisg.law.pace.edu/cases/080527f1.html (brassiere cups case).

[92] Article 78 CISG: If a party fails to pay the price or any other sum that is in arrears, the other party is entitled to interest on it, without prejudice to any claim for damages recoverable under Article 74.

[93] Court of Appeal of Poitiers (October 26, 2004), available at http://cisgw3.law.pace.edu/cases/041026f1.html (technical equipment case).

not from the date on which the debt became enforceable. The court requires a positive action from the creditor who asks for recovery. In the *machinery case*,[94] the Court of Appeal ordered the buyer to pay the price with interest. The court applied the statutory rate of the domestic law of the buyer.

2. Prevention of Loss: Price Reduction, Mitigation, and Preservation

The CISG offers several mechanisms that aim to minimize waste and losses of the parties. Each party has the duty to protect the other from avoidable losses. There are three means that serve to diminish potential losses, including the price reduction remedy,[95] the duty of mitigation,[96] and the duty of preservation.[97]

Parties should be cautious when using the price reduction remedy. A Court of Appeal ruled that a granted request of an extraordinary discount on defective goods waived the buyer's right to rely on lack of conformity.[98] Mitigation is a traditional obligation under the common law and is defined by CISG Article 77 as follows:

> A party who relies on a breach of contract must take such measures as are reasonable in the circumstances to mitigate the loss, including loss of profit, resulting from the breach. If he fails to take such measures, the party in breach may claim a reduction in the damages in the amount by which the loss should have been mitigated.

The duty to mitigate damages aims to prevent the use of damages to punish the breaching party. It creates both an obligation for the buyer to take every reasonable means available to avoid more losses than necessary, such as to make a cover purchase, and for the seller to cure. French judges have understood Article 77 as an extension of the duty of good faith[99] and place a heavy burden on the party claiming damages to show it attempted to reduce the damages incurred. In the *brassiere cups case*,[100] the court ruled that the party claiming damages was not entitled to recover the difference between the contract price and the price of the replacement goods because of the excessive price paid for the replacement goods. Therefore, the court held that the cover purchase was not undertaken in a "reasonable manner."

The Court of Cassation has struggled to implement the buyer's duty to preserve rejected goods on behalf of the seller. In *Fauba v. Fujitsu*,[101] the seller shipped more goods than the quantity initially ordered. The Court of Appeal ordered the buyer to pay the total price of the shipment because he should have immediately sent the excess goods back to the seller, instead of requesting the seller to retrieve the goods. The buyer argued

---

[94] Court of Appeal of Grenoble (November 28, 2002), available at http://cisgw3.law.pace.edu/cases/021128f2.html (machinery case).

[95] CISG, Article 50.

[96] Id., Article 77.

[97] Id., Articles 85–88.

[98] Court of Appeal of Aix-en-Provence (July 1, 2005), no. 04–13.269, available at http://www.cisg.law.pace.edu/cases/050701f1.html (footwear case)

[99] *Société Romay AG v. SARL Behr France*, Court of Appeal of Colmar (June 12, 2001), no. 1998/00359, available at http://cisgw3.law.pace.edu/cases/010612f1.html.

[100] Court of Appeal of Rennes (May 27, 2008), available at http://www.cisg.law.pace.edu/cases/080527f1.html (brassiere cups case)

[101] *Fauba v. Fujitsu*, Cour of Cassation, First Civil Chamber (January 4, 1995), no. 92–16.993, available at http://cisgw3.law.pace.edu/cases/950104f1.html.

that it had the right to keep the goods from the seller until it was reimbursed for the costs it incurred to preserve the goods[102] The Court of Cassation avoided the question stating that Article 86 had no effect in this particular case because the "[buyer] never alleged having assumed such expenses for those goods which did not correspond to its purchase orders." The delivery of excess goods should be treated as delivery of nonconforming goods,[103] which is regulated by CISG Article 52(2). Article 52(2) allows the buyer the option to accept the excess goods or to reject them. However, the court failed to note the buyer remained obligated to satisfy the inspection and notice of nonconformity requirements of Articles 38 and 39 in regard to the excess goods.[104]

B. *Avoidance of Contract*

The finality of avoidance of contract is different than the concept found in French law. As a result, the courts' application of the avoidance remedy, as well as the excuse of "impediment," has been inconsistent.

1. Incomplete Understanding

French law considers the avoidance of a contract as the final solution against the debtor. On the contrary, the CISG has a different approach, which proceeds from the idea that avoidance of contract is a better mechanism to allow the parties to eliminate a legal element that no longer has any reason to exist.[105] Avoidance of the contract is not automatic in France.[106] It depends on the discretion of the judge as to what is considered a "fundamental breach." The CISG considers that a fundamental breach occurs when it results in the substantial loss of economic benefit for one of the parties. This view of fundamental breach (CISG) has helped French judges in applying the CISG,[107] but French judges still exhibit a tendency to favor French law's moral element,[108] along with the CISG's objective economic analysis. The French approach is that the avoidance might be justified if the breach has the consequence of making the contract useless. It does not matter whether the contract was fully or partially executed.

The French system is aligned with the CISG in that it analyzes the contract from the perspective of the purposes for the contract at the time of contract formation. Under this approach, a breach is considered fundamental as soon as the reasonable benefits of

---

[102] CISG, Article 86(1).
[103] Claude Witz, 16 *J. of L. & Commerce* 345 (1997); Claude Witz, "La determination du prix dans la Convention de Vienne du 11 avril 1980: clause de revision en function des tendances du marche et droit de retention de l'acheteur," *Recueil Dalloz* (1995), 289.
[104] Id.
[105] Lamazerolles, *Les Apports de la Convention de Vienne*, 326.
[106] Article 1184 French Civil Code: "A condition subsequent is always implied in synallagmatic contracts, for the case where one of the two parties does not carry out his undertaking. In that case, the contract is not avoided as of right. The party towards whom the undertaking has not been fulfilled has the choice either to compel the other to fulfill the agreement when it is possible, or to request its avoidance with damages. Avoidance must be applied for in court, and the defendant may be granted time according to circumstances."
[107] Claude Witz, "La Convention de Vienne sur la vente international de marchandises à l'épreuve de la jurisprudence naissante," *Recuiel Dalloz* (1995), 143.
[108] Lamazerolles, *Les Apports de la Convention de Vienne*, 327.

the contract expected by the parties have been eliminated.[109] French judges have done a fair job in applying the CISG concept of avoidance, and to some extent have freed themselves from more morally judgmental considerations.

In an early French case, *BRI Production "Bonaventure" v. Pan African Export*,[110] the influence of the national moralist approach is apparent. Nevertheless, a Court of Appeals made a convincing argument, based on the circumstances of the case, in voiding the contract. The case involved a seller in a contract that required or restricted resale of the goods to downstream buyers in South America and Africa. The seller continuously asked for proof of the destination of the goods. The seller became aware that the goods were actually sold in Spain. The seller then refused to pursue its business relationship with buyer.

The court invoked CISG Article 8(1) in concluding that the buyer had not respected the seller's request to "settle" the contract. The court held that the buyer's negative response to that request constituted a fundamental breach. Therefore, seller could declare the contract avoided. The reasoning was based on the crucial role that the "supremacy of the parties' will" plays in the French legal system. The bindingness of the contract is given the highest authority in French law. Whether the contract is still economically profitable (when one party fails to perform or comply) is technically irrelevant.

Anticipatory avoidance of a contract is allowed under the CISG. If there is strong objective evidence that the debtor will not honor its obligations, then there is no reason for the creditor to wait to avoid the contract. The French system follows a distinctively different approach. The principle of *debiteur* holds that the creditor's right to avoid or make a claim for damages must wait until the debtor fails to carry out its obligations.

Unfortunately, the CISG does not provide a clear definition or criteria for determining whether a fundamental breach relating to an installment or installments is sufficient to avoid the entire contract. The party is entitled to avoid the entire contract if the one party's failure gives "good grounds to conclude that a fundamental breach of contract will occur with respect to future installments." However, a temporary failure to execute an obligation does not amount to a reason to avoid the entire contract.[111] A French court recognized a category of cases where breach of a single installment will generally allow for avoidance of the entire contract – when the defects are of the type that could harm its users.[112]

A delay in taking delivery of goods is unlikely to be characterized as a fundamental breach permitting avoidance, unless a *Nachfrist* extension is granted and subsequently expires.[113] However, failure to pay the price is ordinarily considered a fundamental breach.[114]

---

[109] Id., 329.

[110] *BRI Production "Bonaventure" v. Pan African Export*, Court of Appeal of Grenoble (February 22, 1995), no. 93/3275, available at http://www.cisg.law.pace.edu/cases/950222f1.html.

[111] *Marques Roque Joachim v. Manin Rivière*, Court of Appeal of Grenoble (April 26, 1995), no. RG 93/4879, available at http://www.cisg.law.pace.edu/cases/950426f2.html (nonconformity of small quantity of ordered goods does not constitute a basis for avoidance).

[112] Court of Appeal of Paris (June 4, 2004), no. 2002/18702, available at http://www.cisg.law.pace.edu/cases/040604f1.html (pressure cookers case) (defective pressure cookers viewed as potentially dangerous).

[113] *Ego Fruits v. La Verja Begastri*, Court of Appeal of Grenoble (February 4, 1999), available at http://www.cisg.law.pace.edu/cases/990204f1.html (buyer not expected to understand that a few days' delay in taking delivery would constitute a fundamental breach; also, seller should have granted the buyer an additional period of time in which to take delivery).

[114] District Court of Strasbourg (December 22, 2006), available at http://cisgw3.law.pace.edu/cases/061222f1.html (cathode ray tube case).

French judges have managed to create a framework for dealing with the fundamental breach-avoidance issue. The questions asked include: (1) Is the avoidance of the contract justified by a fundamental breach? (2) Was the unilateral declaration of avoidance given within a reasonable time and made in a proper manner? (3) Is the replacement of goods possible in order to maintain the business relationship? French courts have held that written notice of avoidance is not required under CISG Article 26.[115] However, the legal practitioner should advise its clients to give written notice or confirmation of avoidance for evidentiary purposes.[116] A written notice of avoidance need not be detailed. It may simply provide the date of avoidance, be addressed to the proper party, reference the contract to be avoided, declare that the other party had committed a fundamental breach (including date of breach and a description of the breach), and state its intent to avoid the contract, while reserving all other rights and remedies.[117]

The avoidance of a sale under the CISG, as a consequence, requires the restitution of the goods against restitution of the price. French law offers the same solution. This is due to the view that the avoidance of a sale should result in placing the parties in the position they were in before the contract was signed.[118] The avoidance of contract is, therefore, retroactive.[119] Nevertheless, the French system has difficulty in dealing with the issue of interests. The restitution of interests that both parties might have enjoyed for a certain period of time is an issue dealt with in Article 84 of the CISG, which states that a total refund of any kind of interest a party might have enjoyed from the good or the money belonging to the other party is required.

The CISG follows a more pragmatic approach relating to restitution of interests. French commentators criticize the obligation of automatic restitution of interests. They assert that subjective elements could justify a party in keeping the benefits of using the goods or the money paid if the other party acted in bad faith. They also argue that both parties may have enjoyed benefits from each other's belongings,[120] thus eliminating the need for restitution. Finally, the courts should be allowed to justify as a reparation the harm or prejudice created by the avoidance. Catherine Guelfucci-Thibierge offers a strong argument that the restitution of interests has only one purpose and that is to objectively erase the effects that the void contract might have produced. Furthermore, restitution is a completely separate issue than the compensation or allocation of damages caused by the breach.[121]

The Court of Cassation adopted a strict application of the CISG's principle of restitution.[122] It ruled that the restitution of the price included the price paid but also

---

[115] Court of Appeal of Rennes (May 27, 2008), available at http://www.cisg.law.pace.edu/cases/080527f1.html (brassiere cups case).

[116] McMahon, "Drafting CISG."

[117] Id.

[118] *Les Verreries de Saint Gobain v. Martinswerk*, Court of Cassation, First Civil Chamber (July 16, 1998), no. 96–11.984, available at http://www.cisg.law.pace.edu/cases/980716f1.html; Court of Cassation, Third Civil Chamber (October 2, 2002), no. 01–02.924, available at http://www.legifrance.gouv.fr/affichJuriJudi .do?oldAction=rechJuriJudi&idTexte=JURITEXT000007444024&fastReqId=1342883343&fastPos=1.

[119] The French principle is *"quod nullum est nullum effectum producit"* ("What is void produces no effect").

[120] François Terré, *Les obligations* (Dalloz-Sirey, 2009).

[121] C. Guelfucci-Thibierge, *Nullité, restitutions, et responsabilités* (LGDJ, Bibliothéque de droit privé, 1993), 233.

[122] Court of Cassation, Commercial Chamber (May 11, 2010), no. 08–21266, available at http://www .globalsaleslaw.org/content/api/cisg/urteile/2184.pdf (vehicles case).

legal interest calculated from the day in which it had been settled and bank fees associated with security guarantees.[123] In another case,[124] the court filled a gap in the CISG as to how to determine where the restitution of the price ought to be paid. One argument asserts that because the price is portable in the CISG, the place of restitution should be determined under the CISG.[125] The court refused this approach and determined that the payment of restitution shall be reimbursed through the application of national private international law rules.

2. Misapplication of CISG Article 79

One case involved a sale of goods to a subcontractor of a French company. The buyer terminated the contract due to a collapse of the automobile market, which resulted in a reduction of the production costs of the goods by almost half of the contract price. The Court of Cassation refused to grant the buyer an excuse from contractual liability. The notion of *force majeure* in the CISG is actually the determination of the allocation of risks between the parties.[126] In French law, the *force majeure* excuse purpose has more to do with justification than forgiveness.[127]

The above case was founded on the belief that the absence of an obligation in the CISG to renegotiate the contract left the Court with no alternative than to reject the claim of excuse. The paradox of such a solution would be that any party that did not plan some supposedly foreseeable event in the initial contract would be liable until its termination by performance.[128]

Once again, the Court of Cassation fell into the trap of interpreting the CISG through its own national understandings and traditions. The decision of the Court is aligned with the well-known French tradition of strictly enforcing the duties and obligations of the "experienced professional acting in the international market." For example, the merchant should have included an express renegotiation clause in the contract. This obsolete solution has been modified in most French courts by the ordering of a renegotiation of the contract based on the general duty of good faith. In the end, the court misinterpreted the meaning of Article 79. The fact remains that the question of taking into account the changing circumstances is primarily a problem of risk allocation between the parties, and not a matter of good faith.[129]

Also, the court was incorrect in framing Article 79 as the *force majeure* Article. The concept of impediment was used to foster a more realistic approach to the difficulties encountered in the international sale of goods. Indeed, the strict conditions of *force majeure* are rarely met or even relevant to allowing one party to avoid the execution of

---

[123] *Schreiber v. Thermo Dynamique*, Court of Cassation (May 26, 1999), no. 97–14315, available at http://www.cisg.law.pace.edu/cases/990526f1.html.

[124] *Societé Productions v. Roberto Faggioni*, Court of Appeal of Paris (January 14, 1998) (seller repaid only a portion of the amount paid after discovering that the reason given for the cancellation was untrue).

[125] Bernard Audit, "Détermination de la loi applicable à la restitution du prix à la suite de la résolution d'une vente internationale de marchandises," *Recuiel Dalloz* (1998), 288–9.

[126] Pauline Remy-Corlay, *Internationales HandelsRecht* 147–51 (2005).

[127] Lamazerolles, *Les Apports de la Convention de Vienne*, 400.

[128] Remy-Corlay, *Internationales HandelsRecht* 147–51 (2005).

[129] Pauline Remy-Corlay, "Force majeure, imprevision et faute: la repartition des risques dans la Convention de Vienne," *Revue Trimestrielle Droit civil* 354 (2005).

the contract. Although *force majeure* is defined as an event irresistible and without a direct connection to the party claiming excuse, impediment is also independent of the will of the parties. Article 79 is a positive evolution of the appreciation of international business relationships in which the court should take into account the complexity of the business network and the volatile nature of markets. A practitioner may consider including a hardship clause in order to protect against the risks of sudden dramatic market or cost changes. Hopefully, courts will consider a liberal interpretation of the CISG's impediment provision, possibly by recognizing a usage relating to providing an excuse for "mere" hardship.

V. Conclusion

The CISG has had a wide-reaching impact on national and international sales laws. It often challenges established but archaic rules in the different national legal systems. On the whole, most judges have been able to apply CISG interpretive methodology (autonomous interpretations) in rendering correct interpretations of the CISG despite the existence of different approaches, rules, and concepts in their national legal traditions.

Most jurists, except for those who have been biased by their national traditions, see that the purpose of the CISG to unify sales law is the best step forward.[130] The success of the CISG in harmonizing international sales law is dependent on jurists' and lawyers' ability to decenter themselves from their own national systems. Business efficiency is enhanced when businesspersons and lawyers better understand the legal rules that apply to their contracts. The CISG contributes to this essential goal of creating a new common legal language, which allows people from different parts of the world to engage in transactions based on common legal concepts.

This chapter reviewed the major differences between the CISG and French law. The decisions of the different French courts have been mixed – often showing the need to advance the goal of harmonization through autonomous interpretations of the CISG, but also showing, at times, a bias toward French law versions of a given rule or concept. Professor Ingeborg Schwenzer sees the hope in greater harmonization of sales law in the next generation of lawyers and judges:

> At the end of the day, most criticism boils down to the reluctance of old dogs to learn new tricks. Yet, a new generation of lawyers is already waiting at the doorstep to take over business – a generation trained in the CISG and mindful of its advantages as well as a generation full of curiosity about the world beyond national law.[131]

At the present, it is important to realize that even when a court makes an incorrect interpretation of the CISG, as do courts applying national law, all is not lost. The true measure to be weighed is if they make an honest effort to apply CISG interpretive methodology. If so, then such incorrect interpretations will be worked out of the system in future cases.[132]

---

[130] Ingeborg Schwenzer and Pascal Hachem, "The CISG: Successes and Pitfalls," 57 *American J. Comparative L.* 457 (2009).

[131] Id.

[132] As Anna Gavalda states: "The important thing is not the place where we are, but the state of mind in which we are." Anna Gavalda, *Je voudrais que quelqu'un m'attende quelque part* (Editions J'ai Lu, 2001).

22 German Country Analysis: Good Faith, Formation, and Conformity of Goods

Stefan Kröll

I. Introduction: History of the CISG in Germany

The CISG became law in Germany on January 1, 1991. Since "replacing" its predecessors, the Hague Sales Conventions,[1] the CISG has been the source of a considerable body of case law and extensive discussion in the German legal literature. Most importantly, the CISG was the model for the revision of the national sales and contract laws in the German Civil Code (BGB).[2]

The German ratification and adoption of the CISG was the logical consequence of more than half a century of strong German contribution to the efforts to harmonize international sales law. Its roots can be traced to the work of German jurist Ernst Rabel (Director of the Kaiser Wilhelm Institute for Private International Law). His research culminated in the seminal work *"Das Recht des Warenkaufs"* in 1936,[3] leading to the "Rabel Draft" that resulted in the Hague Sales Conventions.[4] Given the considerable influence of German legal thinking, Germany was one of the few countries where the Hague Sales Conventions were adopted, and, more importantly, played a large role in practice and legal scholarship. The German Supreme Court made a number of decisions concerning the Hague Sales Conventions, which remain relevant for the application of the CISG. In particular, its decision on December 4, 1985,[5] concerning the exclusion of the Hague Sales Conventions, has been crucial for the development of the CISG in practice.

---

[1] Convention relating to a Uniform Law on the International Sale of Goods, with an Annex: The Uniform Law on the International Sale of Goods (ULIS), July 1, 1964, The Hague, available at http://www.unidroit. org/english/conventions/c-ulis.htm; Convention relating to a Uniform Law on the Formation of Contracts for the International Sale of Goods, with an Annex: The Uniform Law on the Formation of Contracts for the International Sale of Goods (ULF), July 1, 1964, The Hague, available at http://www.unidroit.org/ english/conventions/c-ulf.htm.

[2] For that and an overall evaluation of the CISG's role in Germany, see Ulrich Magnus, "Germany," in *The CISG and Its Impact on National Legal Systems* (ed. Franco Ferrari) (Munich: Sellier European Law Publishers, 2008).

[3] Ernst Rabel, *Das Recht des Warenkaufs*, vols. 1 (1936) and 2 (1958).

[4] For a more detailed account of the drafting history of the CISG, see Stefan Kröll, Loukas Mistelis, and Pilar Perales Viscasillas, "Introduction to the CISG," in *UN Convention on the International Sale of Goods* (ed. Stefan Kröll, Loukas Mistelis, and Pilar Perales Viscasillas) (Munich: C.H. Beck, 2011), paras. 3 et seq.

[5] Bundesgerichtshof, December 4, 1985, VIII ZR 17/85, BGHZ 96, 313.

In that decision, the German Supreme Court imposed strict requirements for the exclusion of harmonized sales law. While the court generally acknowledged that exclusion need not be explicit, it required proof of the parties' will to exclude the CISG. Therefore, the parties must have at least been aware that the CISG was applicable to their contract and in the light of this knowledge intended to exclude it as applicable law. A mere hypothetical will of the parties, in case they would have been aware of the CISG's applicability, is not considered to be sufficient. At the same time, the court considered choice of law clauses, which merely referred to the application of "German law," as generally not sufficient to exclude the CISG, as the latter is part of German law. As a consequence, as in many other jurisdictions, the CISG in Germany became "a trap for the unwary: those who think about it, escape; those who don't, get caught."[6]

Due to a mixture of a lack of familiarity with the CISG, established contract practices, and recommendations by the business associations, it was originally common practice for model contracts or general conditions to explicitly exclude the CISG.[7] With the new German sales and contract laws being modeled after the CISG,[8] practicing lawyers are much more familiar with the CISG's concepts, removing one of the biggest obstacles to its application. Moreover, the DIHT, one of the most influential business associations in Germany, now explicitly recommends the application of the CISG for use in export contracts.[9] That position is the prevailing view in the specialized legal literature, which favors the CISG's application.[10] Furthermore, the leading books on model contracts now recommend the application of the CISG to international sales transactions.[11]

German courts have generally complied with the guidelines set out in Article 7 in interpreting CISG provisions. On several occasions, the Supreme Court has reprimanded lower courts for relying on pre-CISG decisions deemed to be incompatible to rendering autonomous interpretations of the CISG. For example, in the Belgian meat case, dealing with questions on the conformity of the goods, the Supreme Court stated that:

---

[6]   Mathias Reiman, "The CISG in the United States: Why It Has Been Neglected and Why Europeans Should Care," 2007 *Rabels Zeitschrift für ausländisches und internationales Privatrecht* 115, 124; see also Franco Ferrari, "Zum vertraglichen Ausschluss des UN-Kaufrechts," 10 *Zeitschrift Für Europäisches Privatrecht* 737 (2002); Sven Regula and Bernd Kannowski, "Nochmals: UN-Kaufrecht oder BGB?, Erwägungen zur Rechtswahl aufgrund einer vergleichenden Betrachtung," 4 *Zeitschrift Für Internationales Handelsrecht (In the subsequent footnotes z.B. 19, 20 it is quoted only as Internationales Handelsrecht)* 45, 45 (2004).

[7]   A survey of current model contracts suggest that a number of leading business associations still exclude the CISG in their general conditions. Seven of the twelve model contracts of leading sector business associations available on the Internet still exclude the CISG.

[8]   In the official statement accompanying the proposal for the revision of the German law, it was explicitly mentioned that the law should be oriented on the principles of the CISG; see Bundestags-Drucksache 14/6040, p. 86. See Justus Meyer, "UN-Kaufrecht in der deutschen Anwaltspraxis," 69 *Rabels Zeitschrift für ausländisches und internationales Privatrecht* 457, 483 (2005).

[9]   DIHK, Die Schuldrechtsreform – Auswirkungen auf den Außenhandel 24 (2002).

[10]   Siehe dazu Robert Koch, Wider den formularmäßigen Ausschluss des UN-Kaufrechts, 53 Neue Juristische Wochenschrift 910 (2000); André Janssen, "Das Rückgriffsrecht des Letztverkäufers gemäß der Verbrauchsgüterkaufrichtlinie und das schwierige Verhältnis zum UN-Kaufrecht," 3 *The European Legal Forum* 181–4 (2003); Burghard Piltz, "Anmerkung zum Urteil des EuGH C-65/09 und C-87/09," 22 *Europäische Zeitschrift für Wirtschaftsrecht* 636–8 (2011).

[11]   See also Burghard Piltz, "Exportvertrag (*Maschine*)," in *Münchener Vertragshandbuch Band 4, Wirtschaftsrecht III* (Munich: C.H. Beck, 2007), 319–90; Franz-Jörg Semler, "Sales Agreement Pursuant to the United Nations Conventions on Contracts for International Sale of Goods," in id., 391–401.

[The Higher Regional Court] ignored the fact that these decisions were issued before the CISG went into effect in Germany and referred to §459 BGB (old version). The principles developed there cannot simply be applied to the case at hand, although the factual position – suspicion of foodstuffs in transborder trade being hazardous to health – is similar; that is so because, in interpreting the provisions of CISG, we must consider its international character and the necessity to promote its uniform application and the protection of goodwill in international trade (Article 7(1) CISG). The provisions of the CISG are, therefore, generally autonomous, *i.e.*, by themselves and within the overall context of the Convention, without recourse to the rules developed regarding the standards of the non-uniform national laws. Only insofar as can be assumed that national rules are also recognized internationally – where, however, caution is advised – can they be considered within the framework of the CISG.[12]

The Supreme Court followed its own advice by using only "precedents" rendered in comparable situations under the German national law with the required caution.[13]

II. Principle of Good Faith

The principle of good faith plays an enormous role in German domestic law. The source of good faith is found in Section 157 Civil Code (BGB) (interpretation of contracts) and Section 242 BGB (performance of contract). Section 242 BGB provides that: "An obligor has a duty to perform according to the requirements of good faith, taking customary practice into consideration." The bare wording of the provision only imposes good faith as a behavioral standard in the performance of the contract. Irrespective of this, in the domestic context, the principle of good faith has been a source of supporting additional duties from the preformation phase through to the postperformance and restitution phases.[14]

It is not surprising that German courts and scholars have also adopted an extensive interpretation of the good faith principle found in CISG Article 7(1). Despite Article 7(1)'s limited recognition of the use of good faith in the interpretation of the CISG, German courts have recognized good faith as a general principle that is applicable to the conduct of the parties throughout the life of a contract. Thus, the principle of good faith has been seen as an autonomous source of additional obligations in the context of Article 7(2), which states that issues within the scope of the CISG "are to be settled in conformity with the general principles on which it is based."[15] A 1997 German court decision[16] went as far as to state that the principle of good faith was a general principle that is to be applied even beyond the realm of gap filling.[17]

---

[12] Bundesgerichtshof, March 2, 2005, VIII ZR 67/04.

[13] See also Bundesgerichtshof, December 4, 1996, VIII ZR 306/95, 1997 *Neue Juristische Wochenschrift-Rechtsprechungsreport* 690, 9 Legal Materials CISG 3a (1997), CISG-Online No. 260, Clout No. 229.

[14] Werner Ebke and Bettina Steinhauer, "The Doctrine of Good Faith in German Contract Law," in *Good Faith and Fault in Contract Law* 171 (ed. Jack Beatson and Daniel Friedmann) (Oxford: Clarendon Press, 1995), 171; Steffen Keinath, *Der gute Glaube im UN-Kaufrecht* (Konstanz: Hartung-Gorre Verlag, 1997), 48.

[15] Franco Ferrari, "Article 7," in *Kommentar zum Einheitlichen UN-Kaufrecht – CISG*, 5th ed. (ed. Peter Schlechtriem and Ingeborg Schwenzer) (Munich: Beck-Verlag, 2008), para. 26; Eike Nikolai Najork, "Treu und Glauben im CISG," Dissertation, Bonn (2000), 5.

[16] Oberlandesgericht Hamburg, February 28, 1997, CISG-Online No. 261.

[17] That decision has, however, been heavily criticized as too far reaching. See Franco Ferrari in Schlechtriem and Schwenzer, *Kommentar zum Einheitlichen UN-Kaufrecht – CISG*, Article 7, para. 49.

In the context of Article 7(2), the good faith principle has been used primarily to recognize additional duties to inform or disclose information to the other party. For example, the German Supreme Court stipulated on the basis of good faith an implied "general obligations of cooperation and information of the parties."[18] Equally, it has deduced from the principle of good faith an obligation of a party to send a copy of its standard terms to the other party, if the sending party wants to rely on such terms.[19] Furthermore, the obligation to provide the standard terms either in the contract language or in the other party's language has been based on good faith.[20]

On a more general level, the German Supreme Court has also invoked good faith in the context of dealing with contradictory standard forms. In applying the "knock-out rule," the court has argued that it would be contrary to good faith to evaluate the application of individual clauses in isolation and allow the "cherry picking" of favorable clauses.[21]

A third area in which the principle of good faith has played a role is the loss of rights due to previous bad behavior. The Higher Regional Court in Munich held that it would be against the principle of good faith to allow a buyer to avoid a contract for nondelivery of goods two and a half years after its refusal to pick up the goods, because the buyer was the cause of the nondelivery in the first place.[22]

Last but not least, the good faith principle may also play a role in change of circumstance cases. Pursuant to section 313 BGB, codifying the previous jurisprudence based on the principle of good faith, the change of circumstances may in limited cases lead to an adaptation of the contract under the domestic law (*Wegfall der Geschäftsgrundlage*). There are indications in case law that German courts would at least consider an adjustment of the contract in cases where the CISG is applicable.[23]

In practice, given the vagueness of the principle of good faith,[24] courts base their decisions often on narrower and more specific good faith principles or concepts, such as the prohibition of contradictory behavior (*non venire contra factum proprium*).[25] The Higher Regional Court in Munich argued in this context that Article 7(1) opens the door for the consideration of national law concretions of the good faith principle.[26] Using the *non venire contra factum proprium* principle, as supported by the good faith principle, the court rejected a seller's argument that Articles 49(1)(a) and 76(1) require

---

[18] Bundesgerichtshof, October 31, 2001, VIII ZR 60/01; in that case, the duty was mentioned besides the duty of good faith, which could be interpreted as a reference to a separate duty. However, as no other justification for such duties was given but all references related to good faith, the duty can be understood as being based on good faith.

[19] Id.; Landgericht Neubrandenburg, August 2, 2005, 10 O 74/04, 2006 *Internationales Handelsrecht* 26, 28; for details, see below.

[20] Oberlandesgericht Düsseldorf, April 21, 2004, I-15 U 88/03, 2004 *Internationales Handelsrecht* 108, 112, 2005 *Internationales Handelsrecht* 24, 28, CISG-Online No. 915.

[21] Bundesgerichtshof, January 9, 2002, VIII ZR 304/00, CISG-Online No. 651.

[22] Oberlandesgericht München, February 8, 1995, 7 U 1720/94, CISG-Online No. 143, Clout No. 133.

[23] Oberlandesgericht Brandenburg, November 18, 2008, 6 U 53/07, 9 *Internationales Handelsrecht* 105 et seq. (3/2009), CISG-Online No. 1734; though the statement was only obiter it is very likely to be followed when the issue arises.

[24] See Ulrich Magnus, 59 *Rabels Zeitschrift für ausländisches und internationales Privatrecht* 469, 480 (1989) (critical analysis).

[25] Oberlandesgericht München, September 15, 2004, 7 U 2959/04, 2005 *Internationales Handelsrecht* 72 et seq., CISG-Online No. 1013, Clout No. 595.

[26] Id.

the buyer's express declaration of avoidance when the seller has definitely refused to fulfill its obligations under the contract.

III. Contract Formation

The provisions on contract formation in CISG Articles 14 to 24 are based on the offer-acceptance model of contract formation. The largely unanimous view underlying the jurisprudence of the German courts is that all other types of contract formation are also governed by the CISG.[27] These principles include the requirements of consent and agreement to subject matter and content of contract.[28] Thus the only requirement is that the parties reach an agreement on the relevant issues, in particular the goods and the price of the goods. The means of agreement may be by offer and acceptance or as the result of long-lasting negotiations without a set of distinct declarations of agreement.[29] Consequently, courts do not focus on a mechanical determination of offer and acceptance, but determine that at a certain point in time the parties have reached an agreement on the relevant issues.[30]

In determining whether, contrary to the allegations of one party, both parties reached an agreement, the courts rely on a number of factors, including the signature on the contractual document by the relevant party and performance of the contract without objection.[31] The rules on formation are also applied to other changes to a contract's content based on an agreement by the parties, such as modifications or joint termination.[32] In any case, parties can agree on different contract formation rules in accordance with CISG Article 6.[33]

In interpreting the relevant declarations made by the parties, either explicitly or implicitly through their conduct, the courts rely on the guidelines set out in CISG Article 8. A good example is a decision by the German Supreme Court dealing with subsequent amendments of a contract. In the case, after the formation of the contract, the buyer sent a facsimile asking for an increase in price in return for the seller paying "consulting and marketing fees" to a third company. The seller accepted. Nine months later, the buyer informed the seller that in the facsimile it had miscalculated the fees by one decimal, and therefore, the seller needed to pay the additional costs of the consulting and marketing fees, which the seller refused to do. The German Supreme Court reversed the lower courts' reasoning, stating that, according to Article 8(1), a party cannot hold the other party bound by the latter's calculation mistake (*offener Kalkulationsirrtum*).[34] It found the mistake to be apparent because several factors clearly indicated that the buyer with

---

[27] Oberlandesgericht München, March 8, 1995, 7 U 5460/94, 1996 *Neue Juristische Wochenschrift-Rechtsprechungsreport* 1532, 1533, CISG-Online No. 145.

[28] Id.

[29] See Burghard Piltz, *Internationales Kaufrecht*, 2nd ed. (Munich: C.H. Beck, 2008), paras. 3–12.

[30] See, e.g., Oberlandesgericht Zweibrücken, February 2, 2004, 7 U 4/03, CISG-Online No. 877, Clout No. 596.

[31] Oberlandesgericht München, March 8, 1995, 7 U 5460/94, 1996 *Neue Juristische Wochenschrift-Rechtsprechungsreport* 1532, 1533, CISG-Online No. 145.

[32] Oberlandesgericht Zweibrücken, February 2, 2004, 7 U 4/03, CISG-Online No. 877, Clout No. 596; cf. Bundesgerichtshof, November 27, 2007, X ZR 111/04, CISG-Online No. 1617.

[33] Peter Schlechtriem and Ulrich G. Schroeter, "Vor Artt. 14–24," in Schlechtriem and Schwenzer, *Kommentar zum Einheitlichen UN-Kaufrecht – CISG*, para. 23.

[34] Bundesgerichtshof, November 27, 2007, X ZR 111/04, CISG-Online No. 1617.

its request for an amendment of the contract merely wanted to artificially increase the price as part of its business strategy. As it did not want to change the financial balance of the deal it expected the seller to pay an equal amount in fees to the third party and not merely the lower amount mentioned in its request for amendment.

A. *Requirements for a Valid Offer*

In determining whether the declarations of a party merely constitute a nonbinding invitation or a binding offer, German courts have taken into account all attendant circumstances. These include, inter alia, the language the parties used for negotiations. The fact that this language is not the language of one party may limit the weight attached to the wording of that party's declarations. As a consequence, the use of the conditional does not exclude the finding that a party intended to be bound, in particular where the subsequent behavior, such as delivery of the goods, indicates the formation of a contract.[35]

Also, pro-forma invoices have been found to constitute valid offers provided they contain the necessary *essentialia* and are intended to be binding.[36] And even where pro-forma invoices merely serve the purpose of obtaining an import license, containing provisional descriptions of the goods and prices subject to later negotiation, they can be relevant in determining the content of a contract. German courts have held that in such cases invoices may, nevertheless, constitute the starting point for any interpretation to determine the content of the contract.[37]

An intention to be bound is regularly denied in cases of offers directed at an unlimited number of potential addressees.[38] Consequently, advertisements in newspapers, commercials, spam emails, or Internet presentations do not amount to offers.[39] Addressees must be specified, not merely specifiable. Exceptions to this rule include cases where the party making the declaration clearly intends to make an offer, such as by stating that the offer remains open "until supplies run out."[40]

Where parties have intended to enter into a binding contract, but deferred agreement on the price, German courts have not considered the specificity requirement (affixing a price) to constitute an obstacle to the valid formation of a contract. In such cases, courts have implicitly assumed that the parties derogated from the specificity requirement in Article 14 pursuant to Articles 6 or 9.[41] In the absence of the anticipated agreement, the courts have used Article 55, either directly or by interpreting the parties' agreement pursuant to Article 8 to fix a price. For example, a clause providing for the "price to

---

[35] Oberlandesgericht Hamburg, July 4, 1997, 1 U 143/95 and 410 O 21/95, Pace ("we can only propose you" "could be delivered").
[36] Oberlandesgericht Frankfurt, March 4, 1994, 10 U 80/93, 1996 *Neue Juristische Wochenschrift* 2770, CISG-Online No. 110, Clout No. 121.
[37] Oberlandesgericht Zweibrücken, February 2, 2004, 7 U 4/03, CISG-Online No. 877, Clout No. 596.
[38] Burghard Piltz, *Internationales Kaufrecht*, 2nd ed. (Munich: C.H. Beck, 2008), paras. 3–19.
[39] Id.
[40] Id., paras. 3–21.
[41] Landgericht Neubrandenburg, August 2, 2005, 10 O 74/04, 2006 *Internationales Handelsrecht* 26, 30, CISG-Online No. 1190; Piltz, *Internationales Kaufrecht*, paras. 3–27.

be agreed during season" in a sales contract for cherries was interpreted to provide for delivery at the market price at the seller's place of business.[42]

Equally, the mere reference to the seller's price lists in previous contracts was considered sufficient to assume an implicit agreement on the usual price for such goods as provided by the seller's list price.[43] On the other hand, a mere *invitatio ad offerendum* was found where an order, inter alia, contained goods that had unknown or undeterminable prices.[44] Because that part of the order did not constitute a valid offer, the court held that the whole order did not form a contract including those parts where a price had been fixed. Stricter requirements have been applied in the context of determining the contract partner. Declarations by agents, distributors, and independent subsidiaries have been interpreted in line with Article 8(2) based on the addressee's understanding.[45]

B. *Acceptance*

A party may perfect acceptance pursuant to the CISG either explicitly or implicitly by conduct. German courts have generally interpreted any conduct indicating assent to the offer as an acceptance.[46] The Higher Regional Court in Thüringen made clear that Article 8 does not touch upon the Article 18(1) rule that silence or inactivity does not in itself amount to acceptance. Rather, pursuant to Article 8(3), all relevant circumstances must be considered in determining whether silence was meant as an acceptance. The threshold is even higher if the acceptance in question concerns a subsequent inclusion of standard terms.[47]

German jurisprudence recognizes the importance of commercial confirmation letters and the failure of the addressees of such letters to respond. German courts generally accept that such letters have a significant evidentiary value in relation to the content of the agreement concluded orally between the parties.[48] Silence to such letters, under certain circumstances, results in the incorporation of its content into the contract or as a modification of a previously concluded contract. Article 18(1), by contrast, states that mere silence is not by itself an acceptance of an offer. German courts have recognized that this regulation in principle excludes the application of the German law doctrine on letters of confirmation.[49] Silence may, however, amount to acceptance where a usage to that effect is recognized under Article 9. Pursuant to the prevailing view, it is required

---

[42] Landgericht Neubrandenburg, 2.8.2005, 10 O 74/04, 2006 *Internationales Handelsrecht* 26, 30, CISG-Online No. 1190.

[43] Oberlandesgericht Rostock, October 10, 2001, 6 U 126/00, 2003 *Internationales Handelsrecht* 17, 18.

[44] Oberlandesgericht Frankfurt, March 4, 1994, 10 U 80/93, 1996 *Neue Juristische Wochenschrift* 2770, CISG-Online No. 110, Clout No. 121.

[45] Oberlandesgericht Frankfurt, August 30, 2000, 9 U 13/00, 2001 *Recht der internationalen Wirtschaft* 383 (conclusion of a contract with an independent subsidiary was denied because all the communication with the subsidiary could be understood by the German seller as referring to a contract with the Indian parent company).

[46] Landgericht Krefeld, November 24, 1992, 12 O 153/92, CISG-Online No. 62 (acceptance of shoes delivered by a seller which had sent an offer in reply to the buyer's order to a different seller).

[47] Oberlandesgericht Thüringen, November 10, 2010, 7 U 303/10, 11 *Internationales Handelsrecht* 79 (2/2011).

[48] Oberlandesgericht Köln, February 22, 1994, 22 U 202/93, 1994 *Recht der Internationalen Wirtschaft* 972.

[49] Id.

that such a usage is recognized in both parties' countries and that both parties knew the consequences of such a silence.[50] In some cases, courts have assumed the existence of a usage that has largely the same content as the German doctrine of *Schweigen auf ein kaufmännisches Bestätigungsschreiben*.[51] The mere existence of a comparable doctrine in the law of the other party has occasionally been considered sufficient to be recognized as a usage without further investigation.[52]

C. *Standard Terms*

It is commonly understood in Germany that the CISG's provisions on the formation of contract also govern the inclusion of standard terms.[53] The details concerning the exact requirements are, however, controversial. The prevailing view is based on a decision by the German Supreme Court of October 21, 2001, concerning the sale of a used machine.[54] The seller had stated in its order confirmation that the sale would be on the basis of its sale and delivery terms, which excluded any warranty for defects. These terms, however, were not attached to the faxed order confirmation and the buyer never asked for a copy of the terms.

The court first addressed the issue that the CISG, unlike the domestic German law on general terms and conditions,[55] does not contain special rules for the incorporation of such provisions. Pursuant to German law, the threat to contractual fairness inherent in normally one-sided conditions has resulted in control of their content and additional requirements for their inclusion into a contract. The court considered that to be unprob-lematic in light of the general principles of the CISG concerning the interpretation of the parties' declarations. It held that the relevant question in this respect was whether, on the basis of Article 8, the seller's general terms and conditions had become part of the contract. The court then reasoned that for this to happen "the recipient of a contract offer that is supposed to be based on general terms and conditions [must] have the possibility to become aware of them in a reasonable manner."

An effective inclusion of general terms and conditions first requires that the intention of the sender of the terms and conditions to incorporate them into the contract be apparent to the recipient. In addition, the Court of Appeals held that the user of general

---

[50] Oberlandesgericht Frankfurt, July 5, 1995, 9 U 81/94, CISG-Online No. 258, Clout No. 276; Oberlandesgericht Dresden, July 9, 1998, 7 U 720/98, CISG-Online No. 559.

[51] E.g., Oberlandesgericht Saarbrücken, February 14, 2001, 1 U 324/99–59; Landgericht Kiel, July 27, 2004, 16 O 83/04, 2007 *Praxis des Internationalen Privat- und Verfahrensrechts* 451.

[52] See Stefan Kröll and Rudolph Hennecke, "Kaufmännische Bestätigungsschreiben beim internationalen Warenkauf," *Rabels Zeitschrift für ausländisches und internationales Privatrecht* 478 (2003).

[53] Bundesgerichtshof, October 31, 2001, VIII ZR 60/01, 2002 *Internationales Handelsrecht* 142 et seq., CISG-Online No. 617; Oberlandesgericht München, January 14, 2009, 20 U 3863/08, 9 *Internationales Handelsrecht* 201 et seq. (5/2009), CISG-Online No. 2011; Landgericht Neubrandenburg, August 2, 2005, 10 O 74/04, CISG-Online No. 1190, 2006 *Internationales Handelsrecht* 26, 27; Oberlandesgericht Düsseldorf, April 21, 2004, I-15 U 88/03, 2004 *Internationales Handelsrecht* 108, 112, 2005 *Internationales Handelsrecht* 24, 28, CISG-Online No. 915; see also Piltz, *Internationales Kaufrecht*, paras. 3–8, 3–80.

[54] Bundesgerichtshof, October 31, 2001, VIII ZR 60/01; Landgericht Neubrandenburg, August 2, 2005, 10 O 74/04 (same), 2006 *Internationales Handelsrecht* 26, 27, CISG-Online No. 1190.

[55] Codified in §§305–10 of the Civil Code.

terms and conditions is required to "transmit the text or make it available in another way."[56]

The first requirement – an "obvious intention of the offeror" to have its general terms included – follows directly from Article 8's requirement that an offer be communicated to a specific addressee. By contrast, the second requirement, the need to transmit the general terms to the offeree, has given rise to considerable criticism. It deviates from the position adopted under German national law where the other party must ask for the general terms.[57] The court explained the duty of the incorporator of standard terms to provide the terms, under the CISG, was because in international transactions it is more difficult to foresee the content of such clauses, given the significant differences in the various jurisdictions. In addition, the court saw a greater need for controlling the inclusion of standard terms. It could not be guaranteed that their content would be controlled under domestic law pursuant to CISG Article 4. Given that the transmission of the standard terms does not unduly burden the user of the general terms, the court came to the conclusion that the potential delay resulting from the transmission requirement is justified. Other decisions have specified that the relevant time for making the standard terms available is the time of contract formation. Consequently, the fact that such terms are included in subsequent invoices is not sufficient.[58]

As critics have rightly pointed out,[59] the transmission obligation does not find any direct basis in the CISG. Irrespective of this, subsequent practice has followed the position of the Supreme Court.[60] The legal literature has emphasized that there should be exceptions to the duty to transmit standard terms. Those exceptions particularly concern cases of established business relationships characterized by repeated contractual exchanges. Although transmission of the standard terms may then be dispensable, an easily visible reference to them is not.[61]

Implicit in the duty to make the standard terms available to the other party is the requirement that the standard terms must be in the language of the contract or a language understood by the other party. As the Higher Regional Court in Düsseldorf held, if the contract language between the parties is English, a reference in German to standard terms also written in German cannot bring about the inclusion of those terms into the contract.[62] The court added that the burden of showing whether the receiving party is able to comprehend the standard terms is on the sending party. However, where

---

[56] Bundesgerichtshof, October 31, 2001, VIII ZR 60/01; Landgericht Coburg, December 12, 2006, 22 O 38/06, CISG-Online No. 1447 (same).

[57] Bundesgerichtshof, 1976 *Der Betrieb* 1616 seq.

[58] Oberlandesgericht München, January 14, 2009, 20 U 3863/08, 9 *Internationales Handelsrecht* 201 et seq. (5/2009), CISG-Online No. 2011; Landgericht Neubrandenburg, August 2, 2005, 10 O 74/04, 2006 *Internationales Handelsrecht* 26.

[59] See Schmidt-Kessel, 2002 *Neue Juristische Wochenschrift* 3444; see also Karollus, LM/H 3/2002, CISG No. 9.

[60] Landgericht Neubrandenburg, August 2, 2005, 10 O 74/04, 2006 *Internationales Handelsrecht* 26, 27 seq.; Oberlandesgericht Naumburg, February 13, 2013, 12 U 153/12, CISG-Online No. 2455 with a summary of the existing case law; see also Piltz, *Internationales Kaufrecht*, paras. 3–81 *et seq.* (mere reference to the standard conditions onlx sufficient if explicitly consented to).

[61] Landgericht Coburg, December 12, 2006, 22 O 38/06, CISG-Online No. 1447.

[62] Oberlandesgericht Düsseldorf, April 21, 2004, I-15 U 88/03, 2004 *Internationales Handelsrecht* 108, 112, 2005 *Internationales Handelsrecht* 24, 28, CISG-Online No. 915; see also Oberlandesgericht Thüringen, November 10, 2010, 7 U 303/10, 11 *Internationales Handelsrecht* 79 et seq. (2/2011).

jurisdiction over a CISG-governed dispute is determined according to Article 23 of the Brussels I Regulation, standard terms need not be drafted in the contract language.[63]

One German decision considered the material terms list provided in Article 19(3). It held that Article 19(3) only acts as an interpretive guideline to the effect that deviations in relation to one of the issues mentioned therein does not necessary constitute a material alteration. It held that the replacement of a term in a counteroffer stating that the goods had to be delivered "free construction side" (*frei Baustelle*), by a provision requiring that the buyer pay a certain amount for the transport of the goods, was a nonmaterial alteration under Article 19(2). Consequently, the buyer's failure to object to the provision resulted in the formation of the contract with the term included.[64]

IV. Battle of Forms

The correct treatment of the battle of forms under the CISG has given rise to considerable discussion in Germany. It is widely accepted that where the parties have started performing a contract has been formed, despite the existence of conflicting standard conditions in their respective forms. The underlying argument is that the parties, by executing the contract, indicated they did not consider the divergence between their general conditions to be "material within the meaning of Article 19."[65]

The issue remains whether the general conditions of one of the parties should become a part of the contract. There is a consensus that Article 19 favors the "last-shot doctrine," where the standard terms contained in the last communication (counteroffer) enter into the contract. Under this rule, the receiving party is deemed to accept the other party's standard terms if it begins performing without objecting to the terms. Irrespective of this interpretation, there is a substantial group of judges and scholars who prefer the knock-out rule, which is the prevailing solution in German law. It provides that as far as the different terms contradict each other, neither of them enters into the contract. The justifications given for this approach are anchored in Articles 8 and 9.[66]

The German Supreme Court in a 2002 case[67] showed a preference for the knock-out rule. In that case, both parties recorded the content of their oral agreement in written confirmations. These letters of confirmation, which were sent concurrently between the parties, each contained references to the standard terms of the respective party. The goods (powdered milk) were delivered to the buyer's customers, and when processed, developed a rancid taste. The case turned on which party's terms controlled. The court avoided any definitive statement on the appropriate approach, noting that both the last-shot and knock-out rules would lead to the same result. Irrespective of this argument, the judgment reveals a preference for the knock-out rule that the court considered to be the prevailing position.

In relation to the knock-out rule, the court held that in determining whether the clauses contradicted each other, not only the wording of the individual clause but all relevant provisions must be taken into consideration. In the end, the seller was prevented

---

[63] Oberlandesgericht Köln, May 24, 2006, 16 W 25/06, 2006 *Internationales Handelsrecht* 147, Clout No. 824.

[64] Oberlandesgericht Koblenz, October 4, 2002, 8 U 1909/01, 2003 *Internationales Handelsrecht* 66, 67.

[65] See Bundesgerichtshof, January 9, 2002, VIII ZR 304/00, CISG-Online No. 651 at II 1a.

[66] See Piltz, *Internationales Kaufrecht*, paras. 3–109.

[67] Bundesgerichtshof, January 9, 2002, VIII ZR 304/00, CISG-Online No. 651.

from relying on a particular clause in the buyer's general terms, which limited the seller's liability. The buyer's general terms were based on industry terms, which were internally balanced. Therefore, the seller could not benefit from the seller-friendly provisions in the buyer's general terms, which did not contradict the seller's own terms, and at the same time rely on existing contradictions in relation to the buyer-friendly terms. Despite the general preference for the knock-out rule, the last-shot doctrine is considered by a number of decisions as the appropriate interpretation of Article 19.[68]

V. Conformity of Goods: Inspection and Notice

There is abundant case law in Germany on the requirements relating to conformity of goods, as well as on the buyer's examination and notification requirements. In relation to the notice requirement, under domestic German law, much more stringent examination and notification duties exist. Pursuant to Section 377 of the German Commercial Code, the buyer has to examine the goods without undue delay and give notice of nonconformity. As a consequence, parties are aware of these buyer duties and the effect of noncompliance on the buyer's rights. In proceedings before German courts, sellers raise the "belated notice defense" as a matter of course. German courts are more inclined to entertain the defense than courts in jurisdictions without stringent notice requirements. German courts also recognize that, in principle, the seller may contractually exclude its liability for delivery of nonconforming goods. However, under German law, liability for intentional behavior cannot be disclaimed.[69]

A. *Conformity of the Goods*

In relation to the conformity of the goods, German courts have generally embraced the broad concept of nonconformity adopted by the CISG, which deviated from the narrower concept in German domestic law. Pursuant to the latter, a considerable deviation in the goods delivered from the goods contracted for may have been classified as the nondelivery of the goods contracted for and the delivery of a substitute. In international cases governed by the CISG, courts have, however, generally classified such deviations as a delivery of nonconforming goods and not as nondelivery of the goods contracted for.[70] Although the Supreme Court explicitly left the question open whether that also applies to blatant deviations, the prevailing view in the German literature assumes a delivery of nonconforming goods in such cases as well.

The German Supreme Court, in a number of landmark decisions, has addressed the impact of public law requirements on the conformity of goods. The question of government regulation often becomes an issue when the regulations differ between the seller's country and the buyer's country, and the goods do not comply with the regulations

---

[68] Oberlandesgericht Köln, May 24, 2006, 16 W 25/06, 2006 *Internationales Handelsrecht* 147, Clout No. 824; Oberlandesgericht Düsseldorf, April 21, 2004, I-15 U 88/03 (following the last-shot rule but denying inclusion for another reason), 2004 *Internationales Handelsrecht* 108, 112, 2005 *Internationales Handelsrecht* 24, 28, CISG-Online No. 915; Oberlandesgericht Köln, May 24, 2006, 16 W 25/06, 2006 *Internationales Handelsrecht* 147, Clout No. 824 (applied a two-step approach to determine the applicable terms).

[69] See, e.g., Oberlandesgericht Dresden, May 27, 2010, 10 U 450/09, 2011 *Internationales Handelsrecht* 187, CISG-Online No. 2182.

[70] Bundesgerichtshof, April 3, 1996, VII ZR 51/95, BGHZ 132, 290, CISG-Online No. 135.

of the buyer's country. The prevailing view, as enunciated in the New Zealand mussels case,[71] is that the public law provisions at the seller's place of business determine whether the goods are fit for their ordinary purpose in the sense of CISG Article 35(1)(a). The underlying rationale is that it is an undue burden for a seller to know the obscure regulations and standards at the buyer's place of business. The buyer is in a much better position to inform the seller about these provisions. Or he or she could unilaterally make the relevant standard for the contract by informing the seller about the use of the goods in the buyer's country and thereby making the "special purpose" standard under Article 35(2)(b) applicable. However, even in such a case, the buyer can only rely on the conformity requirements contained in the law of its home country if it was reasonable to rely on the seller's knowledge about such requirements.

The frozen meat case involved a situation in which, at the time of the passing of the risk, warnings and prohibitions of sale concerning Belgian meat had not yet been issued in the seller's country of origin.[72] The Supreme Court considered the suspicion that the meat was contaminated with dioxin to be sufficient to hold that the goods were the nonconforming. The fact that the public law prohibitions entered into force after the risk had passed was not considered relevant. Furthermore, unlike in the New Zealand mussels case, the goods in question were the reason for the issuance of the public law prohibition.

The allocation of the burden of proof for the nonconformity of the goods is governed by the CISG. The courts have generally imposed the burden of proving the nonconformity of the goods on the buyer.[73] By contrast, the applicable national law governs the question of what effect an admission of nonconformity has on the burden of proof. In the view of the German Supreme Court, the CISG does not deal with the question of acknowledgement, so its effects on the burden of proof are also outside the scope of application.[74]

B. *Examination and Notification Requirements*

It is common understanding in German jurisprudence that the specificity and "reasonable time" requirements of CISG Article 39 have to be answered on the basis of the particular circumstances of each case. There are a number of objective and subjective factors that courts take into account in making their determinations, such as the nature of the goods[75] and the experience, as well as the technical and financial abilities of the buyer.

In the early German CISG cases, the courts tended to adopt a fairly strict approach to both requirements. These decisions were likely influenced by the strict requirements found in German law and the Hague Sales Convention. Thus, the courts required a high level of specificity and examination and notice periods beyond several days to two weeks for nonperishable goods were often considered unreasonable.[76]

---

[71] See Stefan Kröll in Kröll et al., *UN Convention on the International Sale of Goods*, Article 35, para. 83.

[72] Bundesgerichtshof, March 2, 2005, VIII ZR 67/04.

[73] Bundesgerichtshof, January 9, 2002, VIII ZR 304/00, CISG-Online No. 651 at II 2a.

[74] Bundesgerichtshof, January 9, 2002, VIII ZR 304/00, CISG-Online No. 651 at II 2b.

[75] Landgericht München I, May 18, 2009, 28 O 20906/06, 10 *Internationales Handelsrecht* 150 (4/2010), CISG-Online No. 1998.

[76] See Oberlandesgericht Düsseldorf, February 10, 1994 (shirts), CISG-Online No. 116 (Pace); Oberlandesgericht Oldenburg, December 5, 2000 (tiller (subsoiler)), CISG-Online No. 618 (Pace); see I. Schwenzer,

The German Supreme Court, however, beginning with the tissue machine case, has advocated a more lenient approach to both the specificity and notice requirements.[77] The notice requirement is applied to any type of nonconformity recognized under Article 35.[78] It also applies to cases where a larger quantity is delivered than agreed upon.[79] The failure to give notice in such cases may result in an obligation to pay for the excess quantity pursuant to Article 52(2). The notice requirement also extends to goods delivered in replacement of nonconforming goods and other efforts of the seller to cure an existing lack of conformity.[80] In line with Article 6, German courts have generally given prevalence to contractual agreements regulating examination and notification duties.[81]

1. Specificity Requirement

German courts have interpreted the requirement of "notice" in a very literal sense. Consequently, as long as it is clear that the buyer wants to object to the lack of conformity, a mere notification of the specific nonconformity is sufficient.[82] Statements made by the buyer have to be interpreted according to the principles set out in Article 8. However, simply placing an order for new goods because the old ones have been damaged does not comply with the "notice" requirement. The seller must be able to deduce from the information provided that the damages leading to the new order are the result of a nonconformity of the goods, for example due to insufficient packaging.[83]

In cases where the buyer alleges to have informed the seller orally about the nonconformity of the goods, the buyer is obliged to prove the date of the telephone call, the person to whom the notice was conveyed, and the content of the notice.[84] Concerning the required "specificity" of the notice, again, German courts have started with comparably high requirements,[85] which have subsequently been lessened due to the decision of the German Supreme Court. Pursuant to the now prevailing view, it is necessary but

"The Noble Month (Articles 38, 39) – The Story behind the Scenery," 7 *European J. L. Reform* 353, 357 (2006) (criticism of these cases).

[77] Bundesgerichtshof, November 3, 1999, VIII ZR 287/98, CISG-Online No. 475.

[78] Oberlandesgericht München, February 8, 1995 (polypropylene plastic granulate), CISG-Online No. 142 (Pace); Oberlandesgericht Celle, March 10, 2004 (commercial vehicles).

[79] Oberlandesgericht Rostock, September 25, 2002 (frozen food), CISG-Online No. 672 (Pace).

[80] Franco Ferrari in *Internationales Vertragsrecht* (ed. Ferrari et al.) (Munich: C.H. Beck, 2007), Article 39, para. 4; Landgericht Oldenburg, November 9, 1994 (lorry platforms and belts), CISG-Online No. 114 (Pace).

[81] See, e.g., Landgericht Coburg, December 12, 2006 (plants), CISG-online No. 1447 (Pace); Oberlandesgericht München, March 11, 1998 (cashmere sweaters), CISG-Online No. 310 (Pace) – 14 days.

[82] Oberlandesgericht Karlsruhe, February 8, 2006 (Hungarian wheat), CISG-Online No. 1328 (Pace) (lack of conformity was mentioned in passing in one letter but not pursued in the following communications concerning the nonconformity); Landgericht München, February 8, 1995 (standard software), CISG-Online No. 203 (Pace) (buyer's request for assistance in solving a problem with the software was not considered to be sufficient).

[83] Saarländisches Oberlandesgericht, January 17, 2007 (natural stone marble panels), CISG-Online No. 1642 (Pace).

[84] Landgericht Frankfurt, July 13, 1994 (shoes), CISG-Online No. 118 (Pace); Landgericht Stuttgart, August 31, 1989 (shoes), CISG-Online No. 11 (Pace); Landgericht Kassel, June 22, 1995 (clothes), CISG-Online No. 370 (Pace).

[85] Bundesgerichtshof, December 4, 1996, VIII ZR 306/95, 1997 *Neue Juristische Wochenschrift-Rechtsprechungsreport* 690, 9 Legal Materials CISG 3a (1997), CISG-Online No. 260, Clout No. 229 (reference to missing documentation for printer "not considered to be sufficiently specific as it could mean

also sufficient that the notice enables the seller to take the steps necessary to cure the nonconformity.[86] Consequently, generic notices that merely express discontent with the quality of the goods or state their nonconformity without specifying at least the symptoms are not considered sufficiently precise. Formulations such as the goods are of a "poor workmanship,"[87] they "do not conform to the contractual specifications,"[88] or "cannot be used"[89] have been held insufficient. Such formulations do not put the seller into a position to decide what steps to be taken. The same was held to be the case in relation to missing documentation, where the notice did not specify whether the missing documentation related to the whole delivered system or only a component part.[90]

2. "Within a Reasonable Time" Requirement

As discussed earlier, what constitutes a "reasonable time" for notice depends on the individual facts of each case. The most important factor relates to the nature of the goods, so that for perishable goods such as flowers or livestock notice periods of several hours to a few days have been considered reasonable.

Notwithstanding the view that reasonable time for notice is heavily dependent on context, German courts have striven to provide for legal certainty to provide guidelines as to what constitutes a reasonable time for nonperishable goods. Still, there remains a number of highly criticized decisions imposing short notice periods. The District Court in Frankfurt has, for example, held, in a case concerning the sale of used shoes, that notice given within three weeks of delivery was not in compliance with Article 39(1).[91] The fact that the goods were not perishable and had to be transported to the buyer's place of business in Uganda after delivery was not considered sufficient either for deferring the examination until that time or for justifying a longer notice period, as the defects were easily discernable.

Irrespective of these strict interpretations of "reasonable period" to give notice, the prevailing view is based on the 1999 German Supreme Court's decision in the tissue machine case.[92] In that case, the seller had sold a grinding device to the buyer. It had to replace the first of three devices in a machine used by the buyer. A week after the first defective device was replaced, a second device broke down and had to be replaced by the buyer. On the following day, the replacement to the first device proved to be defective and was replaced by a device of a different producer. Shortly thereafter the manufacturer was informed by its customers that the tissue crepes produced during the

---

    in the context both the documentation for the printer as such or the whole unit delivered composed of the printer and other parts").

[86] Bundesgerichtshof, November 3, 1999, VIII ZR 287/98, CISG-Online No. 475.

[87] Landgericht München, July 3, 1989 (fashion textiles), CISG-Online No. 4 (Pace); cf. Landgericht Coburg, December 12, 2006 (plants), CISG-Online No. 1447 (Pace) (reference to "poor quality" in connection with plants not sufficient); Saarländisches Oberlandesgericht, January 13, 1993 (doors), CISG-Online No. 83 (Pace) ("miserable condition" not sufficient); Oberlandesgericht Frankfurt, January 18, 1994 (shoes), CISG-Online No. 123 (Pace) ("defective in all makings" not sufficient).

[88] Landgericht Saarbrücken, March 26, 1996 (furnishings for ice cream parlor), CISG-Online No. 391 (Pace).

[89] Oberlandesgericht Oldenburg, April 28, 2000 (furniture), CISG-Online No. 683 (Pace).

[90] Id.

[91] Landgericht Frankfurt a. M., April 11, 2005, 2–26 O 264/04, CISG-Online No. 1064.

[92] Bundesgerichtshof, November 3, 1999, VIII ZR 287/98, CISG-Online No. 475.

week in which the seller's devices had operated contained rusty stains. A subsequent examination revealed a hidden defect in the grinding device delivered by the seller.

The buyer complained about these defects by forwarding its customer's complaint within a few days after receipt. The expert reports were sent more than two months after delivery and seven weeks after the breakdown of the two grinding devices. In light of the time frame, the lower courts considered the notice belated and rejected the damage claim brought by the buyer's customer to whom the claim had been assigned. The Supreme Court overruled these decisions and held that the notice was given within a reasonable time. The court reasoned that even with the breakdown of the two devices, the deficiency of the first delivered grinding device was not immediately apparent. The buyer could not rule out the possibility that the problems were due to operating errors. Consequently, the court granted the buyer a period of one week to decide "as to what to do next and for the initiation of necessary measures." The court recognized that a period of one month to give notice would generally be considered a reasonable period pursuant to Article 39(1). Since that decision, the majority of German court decisions have applied what quickly became known as the "noble month" as a reasonable time for giving notice.[93]

The decision also established that the duty to examine, under Article 38, is not necessarily limited to a duty to be complied with once and forever immediately upon delivery of the goods. In cases of hidden defects, a further duty to examine is triggered once the first signs for defects have been discovered. Thus, in such cases, the notice period does not start once the hidden defects have actually become known to the buyer but when the buyer "ought to have known" if it had conducted a reasonable examination.

The "noble month" standard has also been applied to the notice requirement found in Article 43 for legal defects. In a case where the police seized the goods sold because they were stolen, the court found a period of two months to give notice of nonconformity was unreasonable because the significance of the incident was apparent even to a legally untrained person.[94] Additionally, the court held that the buyer needed to give the name and address of the third party alleging the existence of a right to meet the specificity requirement for the notice.

3. Waiver of the Right to Rely on the Belatedness of Notice

The strictness of the notice requirements is slightly mitigated by the fact that German courts also allow for implicit waivers of the right to rely on the belated or not sufficiently specific notice relating to the nonconformity of goods. In a case dealing with defective adhesive foil, which could not be removed without leaving stains, the German Supreme Court made clear that the mere fact that the seller negotiated about remedies for the nonconformity of the goods did not amount to an implicit waiver.[95] On the other hand, where negotiations relating to nonconformity are prolonged and the seller always creates the impression that it intends not to rely on a belated notice, this may amount to an implied waiver. In the case decided by the Supreme Court,[96] the seller had accepted

---

[93] See Schwenzer, "The Noble Month," 353, 357 seq.
[94] Bundesgerichtshof, January 11, 2006, VIII ZR 268/04, Clout No. 822.
[95] Bundesgerichtshof, December 25, 1998, VIII ZR 259/97.
[96] See also Bundesgerichtshof, June 20, 1997, VIII ZR 300/96.

that the goods were defective and had negotiated with the buyer about the amount of the damages for nearly fifteen months after receiving notice, without any indication that it wanted to reserve the right to rely on the belatedness of the notice.

In the stainless steel wire case, the seller had replied to an alleged belated notification of defects that he would credit the amount necessary if the goods already processed turned out to be nonconforming. Furthermore, he stated that if the remaining stock turned out to be defective as well, he would "also take responsibility for it and handle it properly." The Supreme Court considered that to be not only an acknowledgement of the timeliness of the notice of defects but at the same time a waiver of the defense of untimeliness for future claims.

4. Exclusions in Articles 40 and 44

Efforts by buyers to rely on the limitations of the seller's right to rely on a belated notice have rarely been successful. In particular, German courts have adopted a very restrictive attitude to the defense in Article 44. Concerning Article 40, the Supreme Court has dealt with the issue of who has to prove the seller's knowledge about the deficiency of the product.[97] In that case, the seller had delivered paprika powder, which had been irradiated contrary to what had been agreed between the parties. As the seller had itself obtained the powder from its supplier, it was not clear whether the irradiation had occurred at the seller's premises or at his supplier's premises. Although in principle the buyer bears the burden of proving the seller's knowledge about the nonconformity of the goods, the court, given the circumstances, alleviated the buyer's task under the principle of proof proximity. It required the seller to state first why he had no knowledge about the irradiation, which allegation could then be rebutted by the buyer.

VI. Conclusion

In applying the CISG, the German courts generally have striven to comply with the requirements of Article 7(1). However, German courts rarely reference foreign case law or legal literature. In the German legal tradition, courts rely more on the legal literature, especially legal commentaries, than on case law.[98] However, foreign case law and scholarship from other CISG states have an indirect bearing on the developments in Germany because the leading German commentaries and treatises, on which the courts rely, all follow a strong comparative and internationalist approach. Irrespective of the traditional domestic law focus, German courts, and in particular the Supreme Court, have attempted to avoid merely importing domestic law solutions when interpreting and applying the CISG. As a consequence, there are a number of decisions where the solution adopted in the context of the CISG deviates from the solution found in German law.

---

[97] Bundesgerichtshof, June 30, 2004, VIII ZR 321/03.
[98] See Bundesgerichtshof, June 30, 2004, VIII ZR 321/03.

23 German Country Analysis: Part II

Sörren Kiene

I. History of the CISG in Germany

The United Nations Convention on Contracts for the International Sale of Goods (CISG) entered into force in Germany on January 1, 1991. The history of the CISG in Germany has been one of mutual influences. The CISG has influenced the development of German contract law; in turn, the German courts have played an influential role in the initial interpretations of many CISG provisions. The importance of the CISG to German legal science is demonstrated inter alia by its influence on the 2002 Reform of the Law of Obligations in the German Civil Code (*Bürgerliches Gesetzbuch* or BGB) and, in particular, on the law of sales and breach of contract.[1] As with sales law in the Netherlands, China, and Scandinavia,[2] the reformed German Civil Code was consciously based on the CISG. For example, the law in the German Civil Code pertaining to breach of obligations opted for the core concept known as *Pflichtverletzung* (breach of obligation) on the basis of Articles 45(1) and 61(1).[3] On the other hand, the buyer's duties of examination and giving notice of non-conformity, under Articles 38 and 39, were originally based upon Section 377 of the German Commercial Code[4] (*Handelsgesetzbuch* or HGB) and, furthermore, the granting of an additional period of time (Article 47) finds inspiration in the German "*le Nachfrist allemande.*"[5]

The CISG has been extraordinarily relevant in international sales transactions. From the German perspective, all export transactions are on the basis of Article 1 (1)(b) in conjunction with the applicable private international law subject to the CISG unless the parties have effectively agreed on a different applicable law. In import transactions, about seventy-five percent of sales contracts are subject to the CISG, unless the parties agree otherwise. This applicability in import transactions is likely to increase as Article 1(1)(a) gains importance as more and more countries adopt the CISG. Turkey, a very important

---

[1] "The concept of UN Sales law ought to thus be considered in the reform of the law of obligations and can serve as a model in many other aspects of regulation," Federal Parliament (*Bundestags-Drucksache*) 14/6040, at 86.

[2] The Dutch *Burgerlijk Wetboek*, the Chinese reform of the law of contract and Scandinavian sales legislation have also been based on the CISG; see Sörren Claas Kiene, *Vertragsaufhebung und Rücktritt im UN-Kaufrecht und BGB* (Baden-Baden, Nomos Verlag, 2010), 23, for further references.

[3] See Bundesministerium der Justiz, Abschlussbericht zur Überarbeitung des Schuldrechts, 30.

[4] André Janssen, *Untersuchungs- und Rügepflichten im deutschen, niederländischen und internationalen Kaufrecht* (Baden-Baden: Nomos Verlag, 2001), 37.

[5] Peter Schlechtriem, "Rechtsvereinheitlichung in Europa und Schuldrechtsreform in Deutschland," 11 *Zeitschrift für Europäisches Privatrecht* 217, 235 (1993).

trade partner for Germany, acceded to the CISG on August 1, 2011. Also, the accession by Japan, effective from the August 1, 2009, is of considerable importance to Germany. Until 2008, Germany was the world's largest exporting nation, so it is thus not surprising that the greatest number of published court decisions still come from Germany. The Pace CISG Database contains 493 German court decisions.

Despite the importance of the CISG in German jurisprudence, it would be incorrect to assume that it has established itself completely in daily practice in Germany. There are still considerable reservations by the practicing attorneys as to its value. A 2004 study showed that only 8 percent of German attorneys who regularly advise on international sales contracts intended their contracts to be subject to the CISG;[6] in contrast, 42 percent often intentionally excluded the CISG in their contracts. The likely reason is the familiarity and confidence that law practitioners have in the German Civil and Commercial Codes.[7] That many disputes are anyhow solved on the basis of the CISG may thus ultimately be traced back to a failed choice of law.[8] However, the year 2002 proved to be a pivotal one because German sales law was revised to become much more similar to the CISG.[9] In light of the undisputed advantages of UN Sales law,[10] an exclusion of its application is no longer advocated, at least not publicly.[11] Further, there are a growing number of standard or sample contracts that expressly recommend the choice of the CISG for international sales contracts.[12] In sum, German legal practice shows that the CISG is gaining increasing acceptance as an instrument capable of achieving consensus and that offers appropriate solutions for problems arising in international sales contracts and that, furthermore, may be amended in accordance with the wishes of the parties.

II. Price Reduction Remedy

Although price reduction is an instrument of the legal systems of continental Europe, there are relatively few decisions of German courts interpreting this remedy. This may be

---

[6] See Justus Meyer, "UN-Kaufrecht in der deutschen Anwaltspraxis," 69 *Rabels Zeitschrift für ausländisches und internationales Privatrecht* 457, 483 (2005).

[7] Id., 474; Robert Koch, "Wider den formularmäßigen Ausschluss des UN-Kaufrechts," 53 *Neue Juristische Wochenschrift* 910, 910 (2000).

[8] Franco Ferrari, "Zum vertraglichen Ausschluss des UN-Kaufrechts," 10 *Zeitschrift für Europäisches Privatrecht* 737, 737 (2002); Sven Regula/Bernd Kannowski, "Nochmals: UN-Kaufrecht oder BGB?, Erwägungen zur Rechtswahl aufgrund einer vergleichenden Betrachtung," 4 *Internationales Handelsrecht* 45, 45 (2004).

[9] See Burghard Piltz, "Anmerkung zum Urteil des EuGH C-65/09 und C-87/09," 22 *Europäische Zeitschrift für Wirtschaftsrecht* 636–638 (2011); André Janssen, "Das Rückgriffsrecht des Letztverkäufers gemäß der Verbrauchsgüterkaufrichtlinie und das schwierige Verhältnis zum UN-Kaufrecht," 3 *The European Legal Forum* 181–184 (2003).

[10] See Burghard Piltz, "Anmerkung zum Urteil des EuGH C-65/09 und C-87/09" 22 *Europäische Zeitschrift für Wirtschaftsrecht* 636–638 (2011); ; André Janssen, "Das Rückgriffsrecht des Letztverkäufers gemäß der Verbrauchsgüterkaufrichtlinie und das schwierige Verhältnis zum UN-Kaufrecht," 3 *The European Legal Forum* 181–184 (2003).

[11] Most recently, Franz-Josef Schillo, "UN-Kaufrecht oder BGB?, Die Qual der Wahl beim internationalen Warenkauf, Vergleichende Hinweise zur Rechtswahl beim Abschluss von Verträgen," 3 *Internationales Handelsrecht*, 257 et seq. (2003).

[12] Burghard Piltz, "Export Contract (Exportvertrag Maschine)," in *Münchener Vertragshandbuch, Band 4, Wirtschaftsrecht III*, 7th ed. (Munich: C.H. Beck, 2011), 319–390; Franz-Jörg Semler, "Sales Agreement pursuant to the United Nations Convention on Contracts for the international Sale of Goods," in *Münchener Vertragshandbuch, Band 4, Wirtschaftsrecht III*, 391–400.

the result of two factors. First, the harm to the buyer's interest can generally be addressed by the awarding of damages.[13] Second, the buyer is often unable to prove either the non-conformity or his or her timely and substantiated notice to the seller under Article 39.[14] However, the remedy of price reduction is the better remedy when prices have fallen between conclusion of the contract and delivery[15] and when the seller's liability may be exempted under Article 79.[16] Furthermore, price reduction is especially attractive when the buyer has not given notice of the lack of conformity, but is excused under Article 44.[17] Another practical use of price reduction is when the deadline for declaration of avoidance under Article 49(2)(b) has expired.

A. *Declaration of Price Reduction*

German courts require the buyer to notify the seller of the declaration of price reduction.[18] Price reduction does not occur automatically. However, it is neither subject to formal requirements nor to a particular time limitation[19] and can either be claimed expressly or impliedly. The requirement of a declaration arises from the fact that the seller would otherwise be unaware of the buyer's selection of a remedy: The seller could not determine whether the buyer prefers damages or price reduction. Therefore, if the buyer makes no declaration whatsoever, the seller's claim for payment of full purchase price is not affected by a price reduction.[20]

B. *Calculation of Reduction Amount*

The extent of the reduction is the difference between the original purchase price and the depreciated purchase price. The depreciated purchase price is ascertained as follows: The actual value of the delivered goods at the time of delivery is multiplied by the contractual price. The sum of this calculation is then divided by the hypothetical value of goods if they were conforming to the contract at the time of delivery.[21] The buyer has the burden of proving the value of the delivered goods and the value of conforming goods.[22] However,

---

[13] Price reduction is not a claim to damages, but rather represents a particular form of contractual adaptation, see Markus Müller-Chen in *Kommentar zum Einheitlichen UN-Kaufrecht – CISG*, 5th ed. (ed. P. Schlechtriem and I. Schwenzer) (Munich: Beck-Verlag, 2008), Article 50, marginal note 1. However, in most cases with the claim for damages a similar – if not the same – result will be achieved.

[14] See e.g. LG München, May 18, 2009, 28 O 20906/06,CISG-online no. 1998; LG Coburg, December 12, 2006, 22 O 38/06,CISG-online no. 1447; LG Flensburg, March 24, 1999, 2 O 291/98, CISG-online no. 719.

[15] In such instance the amount of reduction is greater than the price calculated via a claim to damages, see Müller-Chen in Schlechtriem and Schwenzer, *Kommentar zum Einheitlichen*, Article 50, marginal note 18.

[16] See id.

[17] OLG Koblenz, December 14, 2006, 2 U 923/06, CISG-online no. 1408.

[18] LG Gießen, March 18, 2003, 8 O 57/01, CISG-online no. 951.

[19] OLG Düsseldorf, July 9, 2010, I-17 U 132/08, CISG-online no. 2171.

[20] OLG München, March 2, 1994, 7 U 4419/93, CISG-online no. 108.

[21] LG Aachen, April 3, 1990, 41 O 198/89, CISG-online no. 12. Cf. Section 441(3) of the BGB (determination of the value of the nonconforming and the conforming goods at the time of conclusion of the contract is decisive).

[22] Müller-Chen in Schlechtriem and Schwenzer, *Kommentar zum Einheitlichen*, Article 50, marginal note 15.

if the seller and the buyer agree on a specific reduction, the purchase price claimed is to be reduced accordingly.[23] If the seller and buyer agree that the buyer shall sell the nonconforming goods and shall "see what happens," such an agreement represents an understanding that the resale price corresponds to the reduced purchase price.[24] The contract price may be reduced to zero when the degree of the non-conformity is so high that the buyer is unable to effectuate a resell of the goods.[25] The same consequence, that is, a reduction to zero, also arises in the event that the goods are no longer marketable and cannot be resold because, for example, they pose a health risk.[26] In a case involving the delivery of nonconforming shoes, the seller demanded the purchase price from the buyer. As the wholesale price was already quite low and remedying the non-conformity repair would have caused considerable costs due to the hourly rates, the court reduced the value of the nonconforming goods to zero and denied the seller the claim to the payment of the purchase price.[27]

C. *Exclusion*

Article 50 sentence 2 prohibits the buyer from reducing the price if the seller remedies any failure to perform his obligations in accordance with Articles 37 or 48 or if the buyer refuses to accept performance by the seller as required by those Articles. If the buyer and the seller agree that the nonconforming goods are to be repaired at the seller's place of business, but the buyer refuses to surrender the goods, then the buyer loses the right to declare a price reduction.[28] The same applies if the buyer unreasonably rejects the seller's offer to remedy the non-conformity.[29]

D. *Relationship to Other Remedies*

According to German court decisions, price reduction does not lead to an exclusion of a claim of damages by the buyer. Claims for further damages, such as consequential losses, can be claimed in accordance with Article 45(1)(b).[30] In principle, a claim for loss of profit can also be claimed alongside price reduction.[31] However, the loss of profits,

---

[23] LG Oldenburg, February 15, 1995, 12 O 2028/93, CISG-online no. 197.

[24] OLG Köln, August 14, 2006, 16 U 57/05,CISG-online no. 1405.

[25] Id.

[26] BGH, March 2, 2005, VIII ZR 67/04, CISG-online no. 999. Cf. LG Stuttgart, February 4, 2002, 15 O 179/01, CISG-online no. 909 (here the court should have not drawn solely upon Article 50, but upon Article 51 (1) in conjunction with Article 50).

[27] AG Nordhorn, June 14, 1994, 3 C 75/94, CISG-online no. 259. The possibility of valuation of damages as provided by Section 287 Code of Civil Procedure (*Zivilprozessordnung* [ZPO]) is a peculiarity of German procedural law. In principle, the buyer must prove the value of the delivered goods and that the goods are free of any non-conformities. See also OLG Koblenz, December 14, 2006, 2 U 923/06, CISG-online no. 1408 (price reduction to zero).

[28] AG Cloppenburg, April 14, 1993, CISG-online no. 85.

[29] OLG Koblenz, January 31, 1997, 2 U 13/96, CISG-online no. 256.

[30] LG Stuttgart, June 4, 2002, 15 O 179/01, CISG-online no. 909.

[31] Id. (court rejected the buyer's claim for loss of profits from further tenders failed due to the lack of foreseeability under Article 74).

together with price reduction, can only be granted for the loss that has not already been compensated for by the reduction, that is, not for the non-conformity itself.[32]

III. Avoidance

Article 49 grants the buyer a right of avoidance in two situations: One is a fundamental breach of contract (Article 49(1)(a)). The other one pertains to the event of non-delivery, if the seller cannot deliver the goods within the additional period of time that has been fixed by the buyer in accordance with Article 47(1) (Article 49(1)(b)): Article 64 is the counterpart to the aforementioned article. It similarly stipulates that the seller may avoid the contract for fundamental breach or when the buyer does not fulfill his or her payment obligation within the additional period of time fixed by the seller. This differentiation between fundamental breach and the fixing of an additional period is very important because the expiration of the additional period in the event of the delivery of nonconforming goods does not allow a breach of contract which is not fundamental to become a fundamental one.[33]

A. *Right of Avoidance in Cases of Fundamental Breach (Non-delivery and Non-payment)*

Article 25 contains a definition of fundamental breach of contract. The recognition of a fundamental breach is a requirement for the avoidance under Articles 49(1)(a), 51(2), 64 (1)(a), 72(1), and 73(1) and (2). Furthermore, a claim under Article 46(2) for the delivery of substitute goods also requires a fundamental breach, as the nonconforming good would need to be shipped on or returned. Article 25's definition provides a high threshold for meeting the requirement of fundamental breach, especially since the nonbreaching party is protected by remedies that remain available in the event the breach is not deemed fundamental, such as a claim for damages on the basis of strict liability.

Late delivery of the goods by the seller may be deemed a fundamental breach of contract only if specific requirements are fulfilled. In principle, the mere delay does not give rise to a right of avoidance under Article 49(1)(a).[34] However, a right of avoidance may arise if it can be deduced from the contract that the buyer has a particular interest in the delivery taking place on a particular date.[35] Court decisions have held that exceeding the delivery date can only be a fundamental breach when "the buyer prefers not to receive delivery at all than receiving delayed delivery."[36] Therefore, the contract must set a fixed date for delivery, that is, the agreement to a particular date that, when not adhered to,

---

[32] OLG Schleswig, August 22, 2002, 11 U 40/01, CISG-online no. 710.

[33] For more details see Kiene, *Vertragsaufhebung und Rücktritt*, 180.

[34] OLG Düsseldorf, April 24, 1997, 6 U 87/96, CISG-online no. 385; OLG Hamburg, February 28, 1997, 1 U 167/95, CISG-online no. 261; OLG München, July 1, 2002, 17 U 2513/02, CISG-online no. 656; LG München, February 20, 2002, 10 O 5423/01, CISG-online no. 712.

[35] LG Halle, March 27, 1998, 14 O 458/97, CISG-online no. 521 ("if even without express agreement delivery date is clearly of exceptional importance"). See also AG Ludwigsburg, December 21, 1990, 4 C 549/90, CISG-online no. 17 (fundamental breach denied where the parties had agreed on a "fixed, no additional period" delivery, yet delivery took place two days after the agreed date).

[36] OLG Düsseldorf, April 24, 1997, 6 U 87/96, CISG-online no. 385; OLG Hamm, November 12, 2001, 13 U 102/01, CISG-online no. 1430.

determines the fate of the contract. However, it does not suffice to merely agree upon a set delivery time or the phrase "as soon as possible."[37] This is even applicable if the goods are subject to severe fluctuations in price.[38] It has been ruled that if the seller assures the delivery of car phones "as soon as possible" or "immediately after . . . payment has arrived," but does not, after receipt of payment deliver these as agreed ("dispatched by 3 July 2000 at the latest"), the buyer is entitled to avoid the contract due to a fundamental breach.[39] A German court held that the use of the "CIF" Incoterm represents an agreement on a set delivery date, which entitles the buyer to avoid the contract without first fixing an additional period.[40] However, this particular decision has been subject to criticism.[41] The fixed-date nature can also arise if seasonal goods are sold and not delivered on time.[42]

Non-payment by the buyer does not by itself amount to a fundamental breach of contract.[43] However, an exception exists if the buyer does not make payment and unjustifiably and finally backs out of the contract.[44] In the event of non-payment, the seller can in principle only exercise a right of avoidance after the expiration of a time extension provided under Article 63(1).[45] The seller may set the due date of the payment and the additional period at the same time, provided that a reasonable period for payment is granted.[46]

The breach of the obligation to take delivery does not typically amount to a fundamental breach. However, a German court held that a seller was justified in declaring avoidance where the buyer only accepted delivery of 83.4 tons of frozen bacon instead of the 200 tons purchased.[47] One can assume that a breach of the obligation to take delivery can amount to a fundamental breach if, for example, the seller has a particular interest in the timely clearing of his storage facilities.[48] In addition, a fundamental breach by

---

[37] OLG Hamm, November 12, 2001, 13 U 102/01, CISG-online no. 1430.

[38] Id. (prices had risen between order and delivery so one could not assume that "the buyer would rather desire no delivery than late delivery").

[39] OLG Düsseldorf, April 21, 2004, I-15 U 88/03, CISG-online no. 915.

[40] OLG Hamburg, February 28, 1997, 1 U 167/95, CISG-online no. 261.

[41] Peter Mankowski, "Kurzkommentar," 13 *Entscheidungen zum Wirtschaftsrecht* 791, 792 (1997).

[42] See OLG Düsseldorf, April 24, 1997, 6 U 87/96, CISG-online no. 385. Cf. OLG Hamm, November 12, 2001, 13 U 102/01, CISG-online no. 1430 (goods which are subject to considerable price variations may not be equated with seasonal goods). See also AG Oldenburg in Holstein, April 24, 1990, 5 C 73/89, CISG-online no. 20 (fixed period characteristic overlooked by court although seasonal goods were concerned; delivery term stated that textiles were to be delivered in "July, August and September" and buyer sought avoidance after delivery was made at the end of September; the court denied a right of avoidance because the buyer did not fix an additional period as required by Article 47(1) CISG, but failed to consider avoidance under Article 49(1)(a)).

[43] OLG Frankfurt a.M., March 24, 2009, 5 U 214/05, CISG-online no. 2165; OLG München, October 19, 2006, 23 U 2421/05, CISG-online no. 1394; OLG Düsseldorf, July 22, 2004, I-6 U 210/03, CISG-online no. 916.

[44] OLG Braunschweig, December 28, 1999, 2 U 27/99, CISG-online no. 510.

[45] OLG München, October 19, 2006, 23 U 2421/05, CISG-online no. 1394; OLG Frankfurt, March 24, 2009, 5 U 214/05, CISG-online no. 2165.

[46] OLG München, October 19, 2006, 23 U 2421/05, CISG-online no. 1394: nine days.

[47] OLG Hamm, September 22, 1992, 19 U 97/91, CISG-online no. 57 (doubt remains on the correctness of this decision as the court affirmed the fundamental nature of breach without providing any reasoning).

[48] Günter Hagen and Felix Maultzsch in *Kommentar zum Einheitlichen UN-Kaufrecht – CISG*, 5th ed. (ed. P. Schlechtriem and I. Schwenzer) (Munich: Beck-Verlag, 2008), Article 64, marginal note 6. See also OLG Brandenburg, November 18, 2008, 6 U 53/07, CISG-online no. 1734 (failure to accept an

the buyer is also present in the event he or she unequivocally refuses to perform his obligations under the contract.[49] However, strict requirements need to be fulfilled in such instances: A declaration by the buyer that he or she cannot take delivery at the moment is not sufficient for such an unequivocal refusal to perform and therefore no fundamental breach.[50]

B. *Fixing an Additional Period of Time*

Article 47 grants the buyer the right to fix an additional period of time of reasonable length for the seller to perform his or her obligations. The counterpart for the seller is to be found in Article 63. In the event that goods are delivered that do not conform with the contract, the fixing of an additional period is ultimately of no significance; it can only serve the purpose of granting the seller the opportunity to fulfill his contractual obligations. However, fixing an additional period is of particular relevance in the event of non-delivery insofar as the exceedance of the delivery date itself does not amount to a fundamental breach.[51] By fixing an additional time, the buyer can then, under Article 49(1)(a), exercise his or her right of avoidance upon the expiration of the time extension. Additionally, in the event that the buyer has lost his or her right to declare the contract avoided under Article 49(2), the buyer can – in some situations – obtain a renewed right of avoidance by fixing an additional period of time pursuant to Article 47(1).[52]

In sum, due to the fact that non-delivery and non-payment often do not by themselves amount to a fundamental breach, it is proper practice for the nonbreaching party to fix an additional period for performance in accordance with Article 47(1) or Article 63(1) in order to establish a right of avoidance under Article 49(1)(b) or Article 64(1)(b).

1. Determination of Additional Period and Request for Performance

Section 326(1) of the old BGB served as a model[53] for Article 49(1)(b) of the CISG.[54] There are, nevertheless, several differences between these two provisions. Under the CISG, the fixing of an additional period means that performance before a certain date or within a certain period is required. This means that in fixing the period one has to be able – in contrast to the domestic German Civil Code – to ascertain the last date thereof.[55] An effective period of time can therefore not be fixed if the buyer, to whom the goods were not delivered, uses phrases as "at once," "as soon as possible" or

---

incorrect amount of 7.5% in a long term beer delivery contract is not a fundamental breach; however, a 15% incorrect amount would be fundamental if buyer was main customer of seller and the facilities for the production of the goods cannot be operated economically due to the buyer's failure to accept).

[49] OLG Braunschweig, October 28, 1999, 2 U 27/99, CISG-online no. 510.

[50] OLG Düsseldorf, February 10, 1994, 6 U 119/93, CISG-online no. 115.

[51] See III.A. above.

[52] See OLG Koblenz, January 31, 1997, 2 U 31/96, CISG-online no. 256.

[53] Hans Georg Leser, "Vertragsaufhebung und Rückabwicklung unter dem UN-Kaufrecht," in *Einheitliches UN-Kaufrecht und nationales Obligationenrecht* (ed. P. Schlechtriem) (Baden-Baden: Nomos Verlag, 1987), 225, 231; Peter Schlechtriem, "Rechtsvereinheitlichung in Europa und Schuldrechtsreform in Deutschland," 1 *Zeitschrift für Europäisches Privatrecht*, 217, 235 (1993).

[54] Schlechtriem, "Rechtsvereinheitlichung in Europa," 217, 235.

[55] This can be deduced from the wording of Article 47, Abs. 1 CISG ("fix an additional period of time").

"immediately."[56] According to court decisions, the buyer cannot achieve avoidance of the contract by using such phraseology.[57]

The buyer may fix the additional period prior to the due date as long as the time extension begins on or after the due date set in the contract.[58] Even though it is acknowledged in court decisions that the buyer is not obliged to threaten the seller with declaring the contract avoided at the same time when fixing the additional period or that the words "additional period" are necessary,[59] the buyer should nevertheless refrain, where possible, from using language that is too polite. For example, a lower court held that a request stating "we kindly ask you for completion at the latest by 25 February 1993" was not considered to be an effective additional period within the context of Article 47(1).[60] However, this decision was overturned on appeal as the court of second instance decided that the request was sufficiently clear, thereby allowing the contract to be avoided.[61] In certain exceptional cases an additional period by the buyer may be unnecessary. If, for example, a seller requests an extension for performance and this is granted from the buyer with the indication that the adherence to the deadline is "very important" to him and that he will have to seek performance from a third party at the expense of the seller if the deadline is not observed, then the buyer need not formally fix an additional period of time.[62]

2. Reasonable Length of Time Extension

Whether the additional period fixed by the creditor is to be considered reasonable depends on the circumstances of the case. In this respect, court decisions provide little assistance. However, one can observe from court decisions that certain criteria have been used in making the reasonableness determination. Courts have found the following factors to be important: the buyer's interest in speedy delivery if this is apparent to the seller at the time of conclusion of the contract,[63] as well as the available modalities of transport.[64] An additional period of time that is too short is, in contrast to some views expressed in German literature,[65] not ineffective, but rather initiates a reasonable period.[66] In such cases it is sufficient for a right of avoidance if the additional period

---

[56] Müller-Chen in Schlechtriem and Schwenzer, *Kommentar zum Einheitlichen*, Article 47, marginal note 4.

[57] OLG Düsseldorf, April 24, 1997, 6 U 87/96, CISG-online no. 385 (buyer's demand for "immediate delivery" was insufficient; must reference a particular final date).

[58] OLG Brandenburg, November 18, 2008, 6 U 53/07, CISG-online no. 1734 (dissenting).

[59] LG Nürnberg, July 26, 1994, 5 HKO 10824/93, CISG-online no. 266.

[60] Id.

[61] OLG Nürnberg, September 20, 1995, 12 U 2919/94, CISG-online no. 267.

[62] OLG Hamburg, February 28, 1997, 1 U 167/95, CISG-online no. 261.

[63] OLG Naumburg, April 27, 1999, 9 U 146/98, CISG-online no. 512 (court failed to consider Article 19(3); court assumed effective conclusion of contract and considered the additional periods to be reasonable).

[64] OLG Celle, May 24, 1995, 20 U 76/94, CISG-online no. 152 (seller was dependent upon shipping timetable and capacity; court determined additional period of 11 days for shipping from Germany to Egypt to be unreasonably short).

[65] Anton K. Schneyder and Ralf M. Straub in *Kommentar zum UN-Kaufrecht* (ed. H. Honsell) (Berlin: Springer Verlag, 1997), Article 47 marginal no. 24.

[66] OLG Naumburg, April 27, 1999, 9 U 146/98, CISG-online no. 512; OLG Celle, 24 May 1995, 20 U 76/94, CISG-online no. 152; LG Ellwangen, August 21, 1995, 1 KfH O 32/95, CISG-online 279; OLG Karlsruhe, February 14, 2008, 9 U 46/07, CISG-online no. 1649.

fixed and the further time elapsing before the contract is actually declared avoided can be viewed jointly as "reasonable" within the context of Article 47(1).[67] The party that has set an additional period that is too short should therefore be advised to wait a reasonable amount of time before declaring avoidance of the contract.

C. *Right of Avoidance: Delivery of Nonconforming Goods*

German courts place a high threshold for the existence of a fundamental breach under Article 25.[68] In contrast to domestic German law, in which the breach of contract may only not be insignificant,[69] not every breach of contract entitles the buyer to avoidance in accordance with Article 49 (1)(b). Compared with decisions of Austrian courts, where the courts sometimes require a "factual uselessness,"[70] German court decisions have set slightly lower requirements for the granting of the remedy of avoidance, but recognize the CISG's preference for other remedies, such as price reduction or damages.[71] For this reason, German courts regularly examine whether the breach substantially affects the interest in performance and whether the interest of the buyer cannot alternatively be satisfied by a reduction in price or by damages.[72]

One factor in determining a fundamental breach is whether the nonconforming goods provided by the seller or goods not accepted by the buyer are resalable.[73] If the goods are not resalable, then that is a clear indication of fundamental breach.[74] It is thus to be ascertained whether a different method of processing or sale of the goods is possible and reasonable in the usual course of business without unreasonable efforts, even if such measures are combined with a reduction in price.[75] For example, the fact that cobalt sulfate originating from South Africa was only of "Feed Grade" quality other than the agreed-upon "English cobalt sulphate," and resulted in "unforeseeable difficulties" for the buyer due to trade embargos in place on South African goods, does not suffice.[76]

---

[67] LG Ellwangen, August 21, 1995, 1 KfH O 32/95, CISG-online 279; OLG Naumburg, April 27, 1999, 9 U 146/98, CISG-online no. 512.

[68] Dissenting OLG Hamburg, November 26, 1999, 1 U 31/99, CISG-online no. 515 (court found fundamental breach, but only stated that "the goods did not meet the contractually agreed quality requirements").

[69] In German law, the extent of the breach ("not insignificant") is principally always linked to an additional period. This contrasts to the CISG, where the breach of contract must either be fundamental or where avoidance can be declared – independent of the extent of the breach – in the event of non-delivery or non-payment after the additional period has expired.

[70] OGH, June 21, 2005, 5Ob45/05m, CISG-online no. 1047.

[71] BGH, April 3, 1996, VIII ZR 51/95, CISG-online no. 135.

[72] See OLG Köln, October 14, 2002, 16 U 77/01, CISG-online no. 709; BGH, April 3, 1996, VIII ZR 51/95, CISG-online no. 135. See also OLG Düsseldorf, July 9, 2010, I-17 U 132/08, CISG-online no. 2171; OLG Hamburg, January 25, 2008, 12 U 39/00, CISG-online no. 1681 (nonconforming goods must be practically useless for claiming a fundamental breach).

[73] OLG Köln, October 14, 2002, 16 U 77/01, CISG-online no. 709; LG Ellwangen, August 21, 1995, 1 KfH O 32/95, CISG-online 279.

[74] See also OLG Frankfurt a. M., January 18, 1994, 5 U 15/93, CISG-online no. 123 ("there is no fundamental breach in cases in which the buyer eventually can make some use of the nonconforming goods").

[75] BGH, April 3, 1996, VIII ZR 51/95, CISG-online no. 135; see also OLG Düsseldorf, July 9, 2010, I-17 U 132/08, CISG-online no. 2171.

[76] BGH, April 3, 1996, VIII ZR 51/95, CISG-online no. 135.

The lack of a possibility to process or sell in the usual course of business is to be substantiated by the buyer.[77] However, the requirements that are to be placed upon the possibility that the goods can be resold are not finally determined. The mere fact that the textiles ordered couldn't be used as intended due to incorrect colors does not amount to a fundamental breach.[78] However, according to a further decision the delivery of T-shirts that shrink by up to two sizes after being washed does amount to a fundamental breach because the buyer's customers would likely return such goods.[79] The general principle that can be deduced from the case law is that the goods still have to be suitable, somehow, for the contractual purpose behind their purchase.

The delivery of nonconforming shoes has been the subject of a number of cases. The fact that the nonconforming shoes are in some potential way still sellable does not prevent a finding of fundamental breach, when the shoes were purchased to be resold at a retail location, especially after the buyer made an unsuccessful attempt to sell the shoes despite their non-conformity.[80] The shoes are therefore not suitable for the purposes for which they would ordinarily be used (Article 35(2)(a)). Another case involved the delivery of shoes in which only a portion was visibly nonconforming. Customers who had purchased the shoes sought refunds. The court decided that the buyer was reasonable to fear that at least some of the shoes that had not yet been sold would also be of a poor quality. On this basis, the court approved the right to avoidance with regard to the whole contract in accordance with Articles 49(1)(a) and 51(2).[81] However, if one proceeds on the assumption that, in the event goods are intended for resale, a breach is not fundamental if further processing or resale is reasonably possible – albeit for a reduced price – without unreasonable efforts,[82] it is questionable whether a breach of contract that would have justified a twenty percent price reduction amounts to a fundamental breach.[83]

Where the delivery of machinery is concerned it is always especially difficult to assess whether the buyer's expectations under the contract have been substantially deprived. Mere insufficient performance does not generally lead to a fundamental breach, as the insufficiency can usually be compensated for with damages or a price reduction. However, a German court did accept a fundamental breach in a case in which a shredding machine had to be dismantled every twenty minutes in order for shredded material to be removed.[84] Furthermore, a fundamental breach is also present if a new machine is acquired to replace an old machine that only gives three layers of film coating to kitchen

---

[77] Id.; OLG Hamburg, December 14, 1995, 5 U 224/93, CISG-online no. 216 (buyer should have given due consideration to markets with no embargo).

[78] OLG Düsseldorf, February 10, 1994, 6 U 119/93, CISG-online no. 115 (buyer did not sufficiently show that material could not be resold).

[79] LG Landshut, April 5, 1995, 54 O 644/94, CISG-online no. 193.

[80] LG Berlin, September 15, 1994, 52 S 247/94, CISG-online no. 399.

[81] OLG Koblenz, November 21, 2007, 1 U 486/07, CISG-online no. 1733 (it is however questionable whether this decision is correct in light of the circumstance that almost half of the shoes had already been sold, of which only 20 percent had been returned). LG Heidelberg, July 3, 1992, O 42/92 KfH 1, CISG-online no. 38 (partial delivery of computer parts does not permit avoidance of the whole contract if the buyer can obtain the missing parts elsewhere).

[82] BGH, April 3, 1996, VIII ZR 51/95, CISG-online no. 135.

[83] OLG Oldenburg, July 6, 1994, 12 O 3010/93, CISG-online no. 274.

[84] AG Landsberg am Lech, June 21, 2006, 1 C 1025/06, CISG-online no. 1460.

furniture, yet the new machine also only actually gives three layers of film coating instead of the agreed four.[85]

According to the decisions of German courts, ascertaining a fundamental breach requires consideration of the seller's willingness to remedy non-conformities without "an unreasonable delay and burden to the buyer."[86] As such, the majority of court decisions consider that the breach is not fundamental if the non-conformity can be remedied under reasonable conditions.[87] Even a serious non-conformity does not amount to a fundamental breach when the seller is prepared to replace the good without unreasonable burden to the buyer.[88] However, it is not sufficient for a fundamental breach if the seller strongly disputes the non-conformity and refuses any repair or the delivery of substitute goods.[89]

In the event of an anticipatory breach, if the buyer invokes Article 72 and declares avoidance prior to the date of performance, it must be clear that the other party will commit a fundamental breach. German courts have strictly construed this provision. It has to be a high and manifest probability that must be obvious to all, but a probability that is close to certainty is not required.[90] According to Article 72(3), the requirement of reasonable notice under Article 72(2) is not necessary, if the other party has declared that he or she will not perform his or her obligations. Such a declaration requires that the debtor "seriously and expressly or unambiguously denies his obligations under the contract."[91]

D. *Right of Avoidance for Other Types of Breaches*

As the CISG does not distinguish between primary and ancillary obligations, the breach of an ancillary obligation can also amount to a fundamental breach and thus entitle the injured party to avoid the contract. Even the violation of an exclusivity agreement ancillary to the sale of goods may be considered as a fundamental breach of the primary (sales) contract. For example, if the seller agrees to manufacture shoes with the buyer's trademark solely for sale to the buyer, then the seller's display of the shoes for sale constitutes a fundamental breach in the event that adherence to the exclusivity agreement was fundamental to the buyer and the breach interferes with the contractual trust between the parties.[92] In contrast, nonadherence to an agreement to open a letter of credit is not a fundamental breach.[93]

---

[85] LG Heilbronn, September 15, 1997, 3 KfH O 653/93, CISG-online no. 562.

[86] OLG Köln, October 14, 2002, 16 U 77/01, CISG-online no. 709; OLG Koblenz, January 31, 1997, 2 U 31/96, CISG-online no. 256.

[87] LG München, November 29, 2005, 5 HKO 10734/02, CISG-online no. 1567; LG München, February 27, 2002, 5 HKO 3936/00, CISG-online no. 654; OLG Koblenz, January 31, 1997, 2 U 31/96, CISG-online no. 256; dissenting LG Berlin, September 15, 1994, 52 S 247/94, CISG-online no. 399.

[88] OLG Köln, October 14, 2002, 16 U 77/01, CISG-online no. 709.

[89] Dissenting LG Berlin, September 15, 1994, 52 S 247/94, CISG-online no. 399.

[90] LG Berlin, September 30, 1992, 99 O 123/92, CISG-online no. 70; see also LG Krefeld, April 28, 1993, 11 O 210/92, CISG-online no. 101.

[91] OLG Düsseldorf, July 22, 2004, I-6 U 210/03, CISG-online no. 916.

[92] OLG Frankfurt a.M., September 17, 1991, 5 U 164/90, CISG-online no. 28; see also LG Frankfurt a.M., September 16, 1991, 3/11 O 3/91, CISG-online no. 26 (breach of an exclusivity agreement).

[93] LG Kassel, September 21, 1995, 11 O 4261/94, CISG-online no. 192.

E. *Declaration of Avoidance*

The declaration of avoidance, which is always[94] required[95] for avoidance and which is not subject to formal requirements,[96] must express that the party concerned no longer wishes to be bound by the contract; the words "avoidance of contract" need not be used.[97] An implied declaration is also sufficient;[98] however, it must be sufficiently clear from the party's behavior that he or she no longer wishes to be bound by the contract.[99] The buyer's wording that the goods are "immediately and totally" at the seller's disposal and that he or she demands the immediate refund of the payment is thus sufficient.[100] The same applies to the offer to return the received goods,[101] even though in such cases it is not entirely clear whether the buyer seeks avoidance or delivery of substitute goods in accordance with Article 46(2).[102] However, making covering purchases[103] or requesting the seller to either take back the goods or grant a price reduction do not constitute an effective declaration of avoidance.[104] According to German case law, an exception to the requirement of a declaration has been recognized when the debtor unequivocally refuses to honor his obligations under the contract.[105]

From court decisions it can be noted that the courts have different considerations as to whether a party can declare avoidance by means of written pleadings to the court.[106] However, such an approach is ill advised due to the time constraints of Article 49(2), which will have already expired at the time the declaration reaches the other party.

1. Time Period

CISG Article 49(2) requires that the declaration of avoidance be made within a reasonable time.

In the case of late delivery, Article 49(2)(a) states that the buyer loses the right to declare the contract avoided unless it makes a declaration within a reasonable time after it has become aware of the delivery. Case law on the reasonableness of the time of notice

[94] OLG Hamburg, February 28, 1997, 1 U 167/95, CISG-online no. 261 (by way of exception it was decided that the notice of avoidance was unnecessary; this decision may, however, not be generalized, as the seller had refused to perform under the sales contract and had made an offer to pay "compensation" before the buyer made a cover purchase).
[95] LG Frankfurt a.M., September 16, 1991, 3/11 O 3/91, CISG-online no. 26; OLG Koblenz, January 31, 1997, 2 U 31/96, CISG-online no. 256 (threat of avoidance is not sufficient).
[96] OLG Düsseldorf, April 21, 2004, I-15 U 88/03, CISG-online no. 915 (notice of avoidance via fax).
[97] See OLG Frankfurt a.M., September 17, 1991, 5 U 164/90, CISG-online no. 28.
[98] LG München, March 20, 1995, 10 HKO 23750/94, CISG-online no. 164.
[99] LG Frankfurt a.M., September 16, 1991, 3/11 O 3/91, CISG-online no. 26; OLG Köln, October 14, 2002, 16 U 77/01, CISG-online no. 709; BGH, June 25, 1997, VIII ZR 300/96, CISG-online no. 277 ("place the goods at disposal").
[100] OLG Köln, October 14, 2002, 16 U 77/01, CISG-online no. 709.
[101] LG Berlin, September 15, 1994, 52 S 247/94, CISG-online no. 399; AG Charlottenburg, May 4, 1994, 7b C 34/94, CISG-online no. 386. Similarly, BGH, June 25, 1997, VIII ZR 300/96, CISG-online no. 277 ("the goods are at your disposal").
[102] See LG München, March 20, 1995, 10 HKO 23750/94, CISG-online no. 164 (delivery of substitute goods was not possible so placing the goods at disposal would have sufficed had the declaration been timely).
[103] OLG Bamberg, January 13, 1999, 3 U 83/98, CISG-online no. 516.
[104] AG Zweibrücken, October 14, 1992, 1 C 216/92, CISG-online no. 46.
[105] OLG Bamberg, January 13, 1999, 3 U 83/98, CISG-online no. 516.
[106] Cf. OLG Düsseldorf, November 18, 1993, 6 U 228/92, CISG-online no. 92.

is scarce. In one case, it was held that a declaration by the buyer given six weeks after the receipt of summer clothing was too late.[107] In making its decision, the court recognized that, due to the nature of the goods (seasonal clothing), a long delay would greatly reduce the possibilities for the seller to sell the goods elsewhere.[108]

Article 49(2)(b) also requires that notice must be given within a "reasonable period" for breaches other than late delivery. The purpose of this requirement is to enable the "seller within a short period of time to consider the further utilization of the goods."[109] With respect to the beginning of the avoidance period, Article 49(2)(b)(i) states it begins when the party "knew or ought to have known of the breach," thereby referring to the duty of examination under Article 38(1), so that the time period begins at the moment the buyer knew or ought to have known of the non-conformity after correct examination of the goods.[110] The avoidance period is therefore linked – as is the notification period – to the examination period. However, the "reasonable period" of Article 39(1) (notice of non-conformity) should not be equated with the "reasonable period" of Article 49(2)(b)(i) (notice of avoidance).[111] Such a perspective would contradict the underlying maxim of the CISG – avoidance of contract is only permitted as the *ultima ratio*.[112]

So, what is a reasonable period time to give notice of avoidance? Ultimately, the analysis of court decisions pertaining to Article 49(2)(b) results in the conclusion that the buyer may not take too much time. Periods of four[113] and five months[114] were considered untimely. In a purchase of an automobile, a notice of avoidance sent two months and eighteen days after knowledge of the breach was held to be late. The court noted that automobiles depreciate in value quickly and, thus, it was not reasonable to wait for such a length of time.[115] Clearly, the reasonableness period for notice of avoidance is dependent on the type of goods that are the subject of the dispute.[116] In a decision involving the delivery of acrylic blankets, the court deemed the declaration of avoidance, which occurred one and a half months after delivery, as not given within reasonable time,[117] whereas in the case of the delivery of nonconforming furniture an avoidance period of approximately five weeks was considered timely.[118] As in a further decision an

---

[107] AG Ludwigsburg, December 21, 1990, 4 C 549/90, CISG-online no. 17.

[108] Id.

[109] OLG Stuttgart, March 31, 2008, 6 U 220/07, CISG-online no. 1658.

[110] Kiene, *Vertragsaufhebung und Rücktritt*, 249.

[111] Dissenting LG Oldenburg, November 9, 1994, 12 O 674/93, CISG-online no. 114.

[112] It would be detrimental to the interests of the seller, in some cases, if the buyer was forced to give notice of non-conformity and avoidance at the same time. It may be in the interest of both the seller and the buyer if the non-conformity was remedied by repair. See also André Janssen and Sörren Claas Kiene, "The CISG and Its General Principles," in *CISG Methodology* (ed. A. Janssen and O. Meyer) (Munich: Sellier, 2009), 261, 284.

[113] OLG München, March 2, 1994, 7 U 4419/93, CISG-online no. 108; LG München, March 20, 1995, 10 HKO 23750/94, CISG-online no. 164.

[114] BGH, February 15, 1995, VIII ZR 18/94, CISG-online no. 149.

[115] OLG Stuttgart, March 31, 2008, 6 U 220/07, CISG-online no. 1658. The German court cited a Danish decision that involved delivery of perishable goods (Christmas trees), which required a much shorter period for a notice to be deemed reasonable. The Danish court decided that the declaration of avoidance made seven days after delivery was not timely; see Vestre Landsret, November 10, 1999, B-29–1998, CISG-online no. 704.

[116] See OLG Stuttgart, March 31, 2008, 6 U 220/07, CISG-online no. 1658.

[117] OLG Koblenz, January 31, 1997, 2 U 31/96, CISG-online no. 256.

[118] OLG Oldenburg, February 1, 1995, 11 U 64/94, CISG-online no. 253.

avoidance of the contract was deemed timely although the buyer made the declaration some three months after seizure of the vehicle by the police,[119] one can note that court decisions have not entirely developed coherent, clear criteria.

In one particular decision, which concerned the delivery of various luxury vehicles, the court recognized the avoidance declared by the seller roughly six months after expiration of the additional period of time for payment.[120] However, as the buyer had still not paid the purchase price when avoidance was declared, the court correctly did not address Article 64(2). The court instead concluded that "forfeiture" does not come into consideration "as the buyer could not expect that the seller would not make use of his rights despite the complete payment of the price still being outstanding."

2. Exclusion of Avoidance

According to Article 82(1), the buyer loses the right to declare the contract avoided or to require the seller to deliver substitute goods if it is impossible for him or her to make restitution of the goods substantially in the condition in which he or she received them. A number of possible reasons for impossibility of this kind come into consideration, for example, the subsequent processing of the goods[121] or resale[122] by the buyer. A change to, or loss of, the good after declaration of avoidance or after the right to claim the delivery of substitute goods does not affect the prior effective exercise of the right of avoidance.[123] Article 82(2)(b) allows the buyer to declare avoidance, despite considerable deterioration of the goods, when the goods or part of the goods have perished or deteriorated as a result of the examination provided for in Article 38. According to case law, Article 82(2)(b) is also applicable when the buyer processes the goods for the purpose of examination and in doing so they are improved.[124]

3. Legal Consequences

Effective avoidance of the contract results in the return of what has been paid or received under the contract (Article 81(2)). The place of performance for the return of the goods is determined by the inverse application of Article 31.[125] According to Article 84(2)(a), the buyer must account to the seller for all benefits he has derived from the goods. Article 84 also extends to a third party's benefits, for example, to the benefits of a furniture trader who sells the goods to his or her customers and ultimately, following the return of the goods by the customers, declares avoidance of the contract. If the furniture dealer is entitled to the benefits derived from use vis-à-vis his or her customer, he or she must account for them to the seller.[126] The basis of calculating the benefits derived from

---

[119] LG Freiburg, August 22, 2002, 8 O 75/02, CISG-online no. 711.

[120] OLG München, October 19, 2006, 23 U 2421/05, CISG-online no. 1394.

[121] OLG Koblenz, September 27, 1991, 2 U 1899/89, CISG-online no. 30.

[122] OLG Düsseldorf, February 10, 1994, 6 U 119/93, CISG-online no. 115.

[123] See BGH, June 25, 1997, VIII ZR 300/96, CISG-online no. 277; LG Krefeld, December 19, 1995, 12 O 160/93, CISG-online no. 397.

[124] BGH, June 25, 1997, VIII ZR 300/96, CISG-online no. 277.

[125] LG Gießen, March 18, 2003, 8 O 57/01, CISG-online no. 951; OLG Karlsruhe, December 19, 2002, 19 U 8/02, CISG-online no. 817; dissenting LG Krefeld, November 24, 1992, 12 O 153/92, CISG-online no. 62.

[126] OLG Oldenburg, July 6, 1994, 12 O 3010/93, CISG-online no. 274.

use is the principle of linear partial depreciation. The length of use is divided by the purchase price; the sum of this calculation is then multiplied by the actual time frame.[127]

Following avoidance by the buyer, the seller is also subject to the payment of the interest on the amount he has received; the calculation begins from the day on which the seller received the payment.[128] The interest rate is determined on the basis of the domestic law stipulated by private international law rules.[129]

IV. Damages

Under the CISG, each breach of an obligation gives rise – irrespective of fault[130] – to an obligation to pay damages. The creditor must prove the actual requirements of his claim for damages, namely breach of contract, causation and extent of damage.[131] In accordance with the principle of total reparation, the compensation encompasses economic loss and consequential damages as well as damages resulting from breach of interest in the performance of the contract.[132] If the buyer is a retailer, the buyer's loss, which results from the seller's nonperformance principally, consists of the difference between the purchase and sale price. The buyer's general expenses are not to be deducted from this amount, but merely such costs as would have arisen for the collection and sale of goods not actually delivered.[133] The losses encompassed as economic loss or consequential damages are, for example, transport, telephone, storage costs[134] and costs for complaint handling management[135] as well as losses caused by exchange rate fluctuations.[136] In addition, damages can be demanded for the costs incurred for undertaking measures to avoid or reduce the loss.[137] The damages are to be precisely calculated[138] within the scope of Article 74 and paid at the creditor's place of business.[139]

The obligation to pay damages is limited by Article 74's stipulation that damages may not exceed the loss that the party in breach foresaw or ought to have foreseen at the time of the conclusion of contract. The requirement of foreseeability is of particular relevance where consequential losses are concerned. If it was clear to the seller that the goods were to be resold, the buyer paying damages to his or her buyers can be foreseen, of course to the extent that the obligation to compensate does not exceed the typical scope.[140] Other foreseeable damages include losses related to changes in market rate,[141] and loss of profits

---

[127] Id.

[128] OLG Celle, May 24, 1995, 20 U 76/94, CISG-online no. 152.

[129] Id.

[130] OLG Zweibrücken, March 31, 1998, 8 O 1995/95, CISG-online no. 481; BGH, March 24, 1999, VIII ZR 121/98, CISG-online no. 396.

[131] OLG Zweibrücken, March 31, 1998, 8 O 1995/95, CISG-online no. 481.

[132] OLG Dresden, March 21, 2007, 9 U 1218/06 CISG-online no. 1626; LG Freiburg, August 22, 2002, 8 O 75/02, CISG-online no. 711 (transport costs may be awarded in this context).

[133] OLG Hamburg, November 26, 1999, 1 U 31/99, CISG-online no. 515.

[134] OLG Braunschweig, October 28, 1999, 2 U 27/99, CISG-online no. 510.

[135] OLG Celle, September 2, 1998, 3 U 246/97, CISG-online no. 506.

[136] OLG Düsseldorf, January 14, 1994, 17 U 146/93, CISG-online no. 119.

[137] OLG Köln, January 8, 1997, 27 U 58/96, CISG-online no. 217.

[138] OLG Celle, February 2, 1998, 3 U 246/97, CISG-online no. 506; OLG Hamburg, November 26, 1999, 1 U 31/99, CISG-online no. 515.

[139] OLG Düsseldorf, July 2, 1993, 17 U 73/93, CISG-online no. 74.

[140] OLG Köln, May 21, 1996, 22 U 4/96, CISG-online no. 254.

[141] Cf. LG Hamburg, September 26, 1990, 12 O 153/92, CISG-online no. 21.

(Article 74).[142] However, potential follow-up-orders lost by the buyer may – depending on the circumstances – not be foreseeable.[143]

If the contract has been effectively avoided and the buyer has bought replacement goods or when the seller resells goods following breach by the buyer, then Article 75 allows recovery for the difference between the contract price and the price for the substitute transaction.[144] Compensation for a third party's sales commission that arises in substitute transactions can be claimed under Article 74.[145] A cover transaction requires that the particular transaction satisfies the creditor's interest in seeking performance.[146] The creditor's interest in seeking performance is not satisfied if goods are sold for the purpose of disposal rather than trade,[147] as in such a case the sale cannot be compared with the avoided contract[148] and the calculation of damages under Article 76 would apply[149] instead of the burden of proving damages under Article 75.[150] However, the abstract calculation of damages according to Article 76[151] is not applicable if a market price cannot be determined.[152] Article 75 requires the contract to have been effectively avoided. According to court decisions, an exception to this requirement of an effective avoidance is when the debtor unequivocally refuses to fulfill his obligations. In such exceptional cases the buyer is – despite no avoidance having been declared – entitled to demand damages on the basis of Article 75 CISG.[153]

Article 75 stipulates that the cover transaction must be concluded within a reasonable time after avoidance; cover transactions made before the declaration of avoidance precludes further recovery under Article 75.[154] The type of goods and their market availability are factors used to determine the reasonableness of the time following avoidance in order to cover. As Article 75 – in contrast to its counterpart in Section 376(3) HGB – applies a "reasonable period" (and no "immediate" action as under Section 376(3) HGB is required), a two-week period for obtaining and considering offers is reasonable.[155] A period of three months has also been considered to be reasonable.[156] When applying Article 75, damages are to be paid in the currency in which the creditor has suffered the loss.[157]

---

[142] OLG München, March 5, 2008, 7 U 4969/06, CISG-online no. 1686. However; LG Darmstadt, May 9, 2000, 10 O 72/00, CISG-online no. 560 (a loss in sales is not to be equated with a loss of profit).

[143] LG Stuttgart, June 4, 2002, 15 O 179/01,CISG-online no. 909.

[144] LG Krefeld, April 28, 1993, 11 O 210/92, CISG-online no. 101.

[145] OLG Braunschweig, October 28, 1999, 2 U 27/99, CISG-online no. 510.

[146] OLG Hamburg, February 28, 1997, 1 U 167/95, CISG-online no. 261.

[147] OLG Hamm, September 22, 1992, 19 U 97/91, CISG-online no. 57.

[148] Id.

[149] Id.; OLG Hamburg, July 4, 1997, 1 U 143/95 and 410 O 21/95, CISG-online no. 1299 (calculation of damages under Article 76); see also OLG Braunschweig, October 28, 1999, 2 U 27/99, CISG-online no. 510.

[150] With regard to Article 75 CISG see LG Hamburg, October 23, 1995, 419 O 85/95, CISG-online no. 395.

[151] OLG Hamm, September 22, 1992, 19 U 97/91, CISG-online no. 57.

[152] OLG Celle, September 2, 1998, 3 U 246/97, CISG-online no. 506.

[153] OLG München, September 15, 2004, 7 U 2959/04, CISG-online no. 1013; OLG Frankfurt a. M., September 24, 2009, 5 U 21405, CISG-online no. 2165; OLG Düsseldorf, July 9, 2010, I-17 U 132/08, CISG-online no. 2171.

[154] OLG Düsseldorf, July 9, 2010, I-17 U 132/08, CISG-online no. 2171.

[155] OLG Hamburg, February 28, 1997, 1 U 167/95, CISG-online no. 261.

[156] OLG Düsseldorf, January 14, 1994, 17 U 146/93, CISG-online no. 119.

[157] OLG Hamburg, February 28, 1997, 1 U 167/95, CISG-online no. 261; dissenting LG Berlin, September 30, 1992, 99 O 123/92, CISG-online no. 70 (in the currency agreed for the purchase price).

Damages also encompass the out-of-court legal costs the seller has sustained in enforcing his claim to payment of the purchase price.[158] In contrast, following decisions from German courts the costs for debt-collecting agencies cannot be claimed if such services were requested prior to consulting an attorney.[159] The creditor thereby breaches his duty under Article 77 to mitigate loss,[160] which is to be examined *ex officio* by the court.[161]

V. Interest

Article 78 stipulates that the seller is entitled to claim interest on sums for which the other party is in arrears. This right to claim interest exists even without the specific requirements of a delayed payment according to national law; the sums only have to fall due for payment.[162] The CISG does not fix the rate of interest. German courts mainly refer to the statutory interest rate, which is applicable according to the national law that has been determined via private international law.[163] Some courts apply the rate of interest that is applicable at the creditor's place of business,[164] the debtor's place of business[165] or on the currency in which the purchase price is to be paid.[166] Under Article 78, the creditor can also seek damages under Article 74 for any interest-related damages that go beyond a claim under Article 78. It is therefore conceivable that, for example, the

---

[158] OLG Hamm, November 12, 2001, 13 U 102/01, CISG-online no. 1430; LG Coburg, December 12, 2006, 22 O 38/06, CISG-online no. 1447; OLG Düsseldorf, July 22, 2004, I-6 U 210/03, CISG-online no. 916; LG Berlin, March 21, 2003, 103 O 213/02, CISG-online no. 785; AG Freiburg, July 6, 2007, 4 C 4003/06 CISG-online no. 1596; LG Krefeld, April 28, 1993, 11 O 210/92, CISG-online no. 101; LG Berlin, September 30, 1992, 99 O 123/92, CISG-online no. 70; OLG Düsseldorf, July 11, 1996, 6 U 152/95, CISG-online no. 201; in the absence of a breach of contract not decided by AG Charlottenburg, May 4, 1994, 7b C 34/94, CISG-online no. 386. See also OLG Hamm, April 2, 2009, 28 U 107/08, CISG-online no. 1978. Sections 91 et seq. of the German Code of Civil Procedure make the losing party liable for the other party's legal expenses, which is why no reference to Article 74 is necessary.

[159] AG Berlin-Tiergarten, March 13, 1997, 2 C 22/97, CISG-online no. 412; LG Düsseldorf, August 25, 1994, 31 O 27/92, CISG-online no. 451; see also LG Frankfurt a. M., September 16, 1991, 3/11 O 3/91, CISG-online no. 26 (engaging a debt collection agency is appropriate only if the collection agency can take steps superior to those of the creditor); LG Berlin, October 6, 1992, 103 O 70/92, CISG-online no. 173 (costs of debt collection).

[160] LG Zwickau, March 19, 1999, 3 HKO 67/98, CISG-online no. 519; AG Berlin-Tiergarten, March 13, 1997, 2 C 22/97, CISG-online no. 412; LG Düsseldorf, August 25, 1994, 31 O 27/92, CISG-online no. 451.

[161] BGH, March 24, 1999, VIII ZR 121/98, CISG-online no. 396.

[162] LG Aachen, July 20, 1995, 41 O 111/95, CISG-online no. 169; LG Frankfurt a.M., September 16, 1991, 3/11 O 3/91, CISG-online no. 26. See also OLG Hamburg, January 25, 2008, 12 U 39/00, CISG-online no. 1681.

[163] LG Coburg, December 12, 2006, 22 O 38/06, CISG-online no. 1447; OLG Düsseldorf, July 22, 2004, I-6 U 210/03, CISG-online no. 916; OLG Karlsruhe, July 20, 2004, 17 U 136/03, CISG-online no. 858; LG Mönchengladbach, July 15, 2003, 7 O 221/02, CISG-online no. 813; OLG Köln, October 14, 2002, 16 U 77/01, CISG-online no. 709; OLG Karlsruhe, December 19, 2002, 19 U 8/02, CISG-online no. 817; OLG Rostock, October 10, 2001, 6 U 126/00, CISG-online no. 671; LG Stendal, October 12, 2000, 22 S 234/99, CISG-online no. 592; LG Darmstadt, May 9, 2000, 10 O 72/00, CISG-online no. 560. See also, LG Göttingen, September 20, 2002, 7 O 43/01, CISG-online no. 655; LG München, February 27, 2002, 5 HKO 3936/00, CISG-online no. 654.

[164] LG Heidelberg, November 2, 2005, 3 O 169/04, CISG-online no. 1416; LG Bamberg, April 13, 2005, 2 O 340/00, CISG-online no. 1402; LG Berlin, March 21, 2003, 103 O 213/02, CISG-online no. 785.

[165] LG Frankfurt a.M., September 16, 1991, 3/11 O 3/91, CISG-online no. 26.

[166] OLG Rostock, October 10, 2001, 6 U 126/00, CISG-online no. 671.

creditor can demand such interest he has to pay to draw on a bank credit.[167] However, Article 74 requires actual proof of the damages, which is not necessary under Article 78.[168]

VI. Mitigation and Preservation

Article 77 provides that the party who relies on a breach of contract has a duty to mitigate his loss. Mitigation of loss is considered *ex officio* and not, for instance, after a plea by a party.[169] The injured party cannot claim damages to the extent to which the damage could have been avoided through appropriate measures of prevention and mitigation. If the buyer recognizes the non-conformity of the goods, under some circumstances, he or she is required to cease using them.[170] In addition, the request to remedy the non-conformity should be made to the debtor before a third party is approached.[171] Article 77 is of particular importance with regard to the defense against subsequent losses. The duty of mitigation may require the injured party to conclude a cover transaction, particularly with respect to an already avoided contract.[172] However, if the contract has not yet been avoided, there is no obligation to conclude a cover transaction.[173] It has to be noted, though, that a cover transaction does not fall within the scope of appropriate measures covered by Article 74 if a price fluctuation was not foreseeable. In such cases, the objection cannot be raised against the buyer that following the avoidance of the contract he should have purchased the entire amount elsewhere.[174] The debtor possesses the burden of proving that the creditor failed to prevent or mitigate his losses.[175]

---

[167] LG München, February 20, 2002, 10 O 5423/01, CISG-online no. 712; AG Koblenz, November 12, 1996, 16 C 1056/96, CISG-online no. 400; AG Bottrop, June 25, 1996, 12 C 177/96, CISG-online no. 534.

[168] LG Darmstadt, May 9, 2000, 10 O 72/00, CISG-online no. 560; OLG Düsseldorf, April 24, 1997, 6 U 87/96, CISG-online no. 385; AG Bottrop, June 25, 1996, 12 C 177/96, CISG-online no. 534; AG Koblenz, November 12, 1996, 16 C 1056/96, CISG-online no. 400; OLG Hamm, February 8, 1995, 11 U 206/93, CISG-online no. 141; AG Alsfeld, May 12, 1995, 31 C 534/94, CISG-online no. 170; OLG Celle, May 24, 1995, 20 U 76/94, CISG-online no. 152; OLG Düsseldorf, January 14, 1994, 17 U 146/93, CISG-online no. 119 (court referred to German Code of Civil Procedure Section 287 to estimate the interest damage); LG Hamburg, September 26, 1990, 12 O 153/92, CISG-online no. 21 (estimation of damages under Article 78 in conjunction with Article 74).

[169] BGH, March 24, 1999, VIII ZR 121/98, CISG-online no. 396.

[170] Id.

[171] LG Darmstadt, May 9, 2000, 10 O 72/00, CISG-online no. 560.

[172] OLG Celle, September 2, 1998, 3 U 246/97, CISG-online no. 506 (first instance LG Göttingen, July 31, 1997, 3 O 198/96, CISG-online no. 564). See also LG Berlin, September 15, 1994, 52 S 247/94, CISG-online no. 399. Cf. also OLG Celle, September 2, 1998, 3 U 246/97, CISG-online no. 506 (buyer who has purchased goods from a seller abroad cannot limit its search for replacement goods to domestic suppliers).

[173] OLG Braunschweig, October 28, 1999, 2 U 27/99, CISG-online no. 510 (considering an exception if the time between performance and avoidance is so great that it is to be reasonably expected that the seller intends to seek performance or a secondary claim). See also OLG Düsseldorf, January 14, 1994, 17 U 146/93, CISG-online no. 119; OLG Düsseldorf, September 13, 1996, 17 U 18/96, CISG-online no. 407 (exception exists when the costs of repairs are considerably more expensive than the cost of a cover transaction); LG Bielefeld, January 18, 1991, 15 O 201/90, CISG-online no. 174. Cf. also OLG Hamm, September 22, 1992, 19 U 97/91, CISG-online no. 57.

[174] OLG Frankfurt a.M., March 24, 2009, 5 U 214/05, CISG-online no. 2165.

[175] OLG Celle, September 2, 1998, 3 U 246/97, CISG-online no. 506; AG München, June 23, 1995, 271 C 18968/94, CISG-online no. 368.

Articles 85 through 88 express the general principle that each party is obliged to cooperate with the other party. In contrast to Article 77, Articles 85 through 88 establish genuine legal obligations, which can lead to claims for damages if breached. If the other party refuses to take back the goods, the party who is bound to preserve the goods may sell them under Article 88(1).[176] According to Article 88(2), a duty to sell the goods may arise if they are, for example, subject to rapid deterioration, yet such a rapid deterioration in this context cannot arise if, for example, the goods can be frozen and thereby preserved.[177] An obligation to sell does not arise due to rapidly dropping market prices.[178]

VII. Excuse (Impediment)

According to Article 79, a party is not liable for a failure to perform any of his obligations if he or she proves that the failure was due to an impediment beyond his or her control and that he or she could not reasonably be expected to have taken it into account at the time of the conclusion of contract or to have avoided or overcome it or its consequences. Following case law on this matter, an objective test is applied in which the reasonable person standard is used to determine if the party claiming an excuse reasonably reacted to the impediment under the same circumstances.[179] Article 79 is only applicable to claims for damages (Article 79(5)); claims to performance are not affected.[180]

Within the scope of Article 79, impediments that prevent performance of an obligation are only objective circumstances that are beyond the debtor's control. The contrast is formed by personal, that is, subjective circumstances, which are particularly broad in scope, thus reducing the number of potential impediments that fall under Article 79.[181] German courts have recognized a number of subjective events that do not qualify as an impediment, including financial capabilities, the risk of timely procurement,[182] stockpiling and flawlessness of the goods, as well as the risks associated with personnel and organization.[183] For example, it was ruled that the fact that the vehicle sold was stolen and the seller could therefore not transfer ownership does not constitute an impediment. In this respect the seller carries the risk of procurement. Even if the seller – through repeated enquires with the police and vehicle registration office – maintains that he or she has done everything in order to adhere to the contractual obligations, he or she is precluded from claiming an impediment under Article 79.[184] On the basis of the seller's

---

[176] LG Köln, December 5, 2006, 85 O 200/05, CISG-online no. 1440.

[177] OLG Braunschweig, October 28, 1999, 2 U 27/99, CISG-online no. 510.

[178] Id.

[179] OLG Zweibrücken, March 31, 1998, 8 O 1995/95, CISG-online no. 481.

[180] BGH, November 27, 2007, X ZR 111/04, CISG-online no. 1617.

[181] OLG München, March 5, 2008, 7 U 4969/06, CISG-online no. 1686.

[182] This is at least applicable to generic goods, see BGH, March 24, 1999, VIII ZR 121/98, CISG-online no. 396; OLG Hamburg, February 28, 1997, 1 U 167/95, CISG-online no. 261; OLG Zweibrücken, February 2, 2004, 7 U 4/03, CISG-online no. 877; OLG Hamburg, July 4, 1997, 1 U 143/95 and 410 O 21/95, CISG-online no. 1299. See also OLG Hamburg, February 28, 1997, 1 U 167/95, CISG-online no. 261 (triplication of market price may be commercially reasonable in speculative transactions).

[183] With respect to this comprehensive list, see OLG München, March 5, 2008, 7 U 4969/06, CISG-online no. 1686, albeit in *obiter dictum*.

[184] OLG München, March 5, 2008, 7 U 4969/06, CISG-online no. 1686 (thereby taking into account that the circumstances surrounding the acquisition of the vehicle that was subject of the dispute should have raised doubts regarding the original seller's power of disposition). With regard to the obligation to transfer

procurement risk, he or she as a retailer cannot draw upon circumstances that have arisen within the supplier's sphere of control.[185] The same applies to the timely delivery by previous suppliers.[186]

Article 79 is applicable to all conceivable cases and forms of nonperformance that give rise to liability. The provision therefore especially applies in cases of delivery of nonconforming goods.[187] However, as the seller bears the risk of ensuring conformity, he or she will seldom be able to draw upon Article 79 CISG. Yet in a few cases it has been ruled that if a seller has ordered goods from a reliable supplier and the seller did not discover the non-conformity despite undertaking a careful examination, then the seller can be excused under Article 79.[188] However, these decisions have been subject to considerable criticism as the criteria give rise to the risk that the courts could understand Article 79 and its exemption from strict liability as a fault-based liability.[189]

Article 79(2) regulates the exemption from liability in the event that the nonperformance is due to nonperformance by a third party. The impediment in such cases must be beyond the control of either the debtor or the third party.[190] Under the CISG, it is the seller who bears the risk of procurement,[191] which is why typical suppliers are not considered to be third parties within the scope of Article 79(2).[192]

VIII. Concluding Remarks

In 1996, Louis and Patrick Del Duca admonished practicing lawyers to "Learn the CISG, whether you like it or not."[193] Every German lawyer involved with cross-border sales contracts must have a working knowledge of the CISG. In light of the indisputable advantages of UN sales law as opposed to the German BGB/HGB in some circumstances,

---

property, see also LG Freiburg, August 22, 2002, 8 O 75/02, CISG-online no. 711; OLG Dresden, March 21, 2007, 9 U 1218/06, CISG-online no. 1626.

[185] BGH, March 24, 1999, VIII ZR 121/98, CISG-online no. 396; LG Ellwangen, August 21, 1995, 1 KfH O 32/95, CISG-online 279. See also LG Hamburg, October 23, 1995, 419 O 85/95, CISG-online no. 395 (Article 79 excuse could arise if the seller concludes a cover transaction, but the supplier does not deliver on time); OLG Zweibrücken, March 31, 1998, 8 O 1995/95, CISG-online no. 481 (limited exception to the procurement obligation is to be made for production risks).

[186] BGH, March 24, 1999, VIII ZR 121/98, CISG-online Nr 481.

[187] BGH, January 9, 2002, VII ZR 304/00, CISG-online no. 651; LG Köln, November 16, 1995, 5 O 189/94, CISG-online no. 265; OLG Zweibrücken, March 31, 1998, 8 O 1995/95, CISG-online no. 481. Under Anglo-American law, a seller who has failed to deliver conforming goods is not entitled to claim an Article 79 excuse, see Barry Nicholas, "Prerequisites and extent of liability for breach of contract under the U.N. Convention," in *Einheitliches Kaufrecht und nationales Obligationenrecht* (ed. P. Schlechtriem) (Baden-Baden: Nomos Verlag, 1987), 283, 287.

[188] BGH, January 9, 2002, VII ZR 304/00, CISG-online no. 651; LG Köln, November 16, 1995, 5 O 189/94, CISG-online no. 265.

[189] See Elisabeth Sauthoff, *Die Annäherung der Schadensersatzhaftung für Lieferung mangelhafter Ware an das UN-Kaufrecht* (Berlin: Duncker & Humblot, 2007), 61.

[190] BGH, March 24, 1999, VIII ZR 121/98, CISG-online no. 396.

[191] Id.

[192] OLG Zweibrücken, March 31, 1998, 8 O 1995/95, CISG-online no. 481; OLG Hamburg, February 28, 1997, 1 U 167/95, CISG-online no. 261; Schiedsgericht der Handelskammer Hamburg, March 21, 1996, CISG-online no. 187.

[193] Louis F. Del Duca and Patrick Del Duca, "Practice Under the Convention on International Sale of Goods (CISG): A Primer for Attorneys and International Traders (Part II)," 29 *Uniform Commercial Code L. J.* 99, 157 (1996).

not knowing or taking advantage of these provisions may be grounds for malpractice. Furthermore, as in particular situations the exclusion of UN sales law in favor of the BGB/HGB can be viewed as a case of professional negligence on the part of the attorney, it is to be assumed that the importance of UN sales law will continue to grow, especially as UN sales law is now taught at every German university and in so doing the fear of the unknown is removed from the coming generation.

Moreover, in some cases the CISG leads to legal results that cannot be reached under the BGB or HGB, even if they were modified or deviated from by a contractual agreement. From the buyer's perspective one first has to emphasize the concept of strict liability, which is especially important if the seller's contractual partner is only an intermediate dealer. The BGB and HGB do not apply the concept of strict liability but stipulate a fault-based liability for damages. Under German law a seller is only liable for damages if he or she has deliberately or negligently breached his or her contractual obligations. An intermediate dealer – often encountered in today's global business environment – is not at fault if he or she sells nonconforming goods whose non-conformity could not have been discovered with the usual examination. Thus, in such situations, the buyer is on the basis of the BGB and HGB not entitled to damages. In this context it has to be noted that according to German law, strict liability clauses stipulated in general terms and conditions of the contract are void.[194]

Furthermore, a seller of goods ultimately be sold to a consumer, can, through choosing the CISG, avoid the so-called "recourse of the entrepreneur." Under the BGB and HGB, the buyer (who is liable vis-à-vis the consumer) can more easily take recourse against the seller. In such cases, German law places the seller at a disadvantage as it – in contrast to UN sales law – (1) provides that the buyer's legitimate expectations stipulate whether or not the goods are in conformity with the contract, (2) places for a given time period the burden of proof on the seller to show that the goods were conforming, and (3) can lead to a limitation period of up to five years.[195] All of these disadvantages are mandatory in their application and cannot be deviated from by contract.

Finally, it has to be noted that the CISG is an international treaty. In turn, this means that the provisions of UN sales law cannot be avoided by national laws and court orders based thereupon. For example, if a national court rules that on the basis of national insolvency law so-called "critical suppliers" of a buyer (who has applied for creditor protection) must fulfill their contracts with the buyer, may a supplier nevertheless exercise his right to a right of stoppage under Article 71? The answer is to be found by looking at the hierarchy of norms and the position of the CISG above national law. National rules that would, for example, undermine the right of stoppage under Article 71 are not, at least where the application of UN Sales law is concerned, applicable or to be followed. In one case, a German seller, who had already delivered the goods EXW (Incoterms 2000), was informed that the buyer was in severe financial difficulties and that the buyer had filed for creditor protection. As at that time the goods had not been handed over to the buyer by the carrier yet, the seller drew on Article 71(2), thereby preventing the handing over of the goods. In accordance with Article 71(3), the seller also immediately informed the buyer and exerted the right of stoppage. The buyer claimed that according

---

[194] Cf. BGH, 59 *Neue Juristische Wochenschrift* 47, 49 et. seq. (2006) with respect to defects in title.

[195] For more detail and with further reasoning, see Burghard Piltz, "Anmerkung zum Urteil des EuGH C-65/09 und C-87/09," 22 *Europäische Zeitschrift für Wirtschaftsrecht* 636 et seq. (2011).

to the court decision the seller was obliged to release the goods. In turn, the seller argued that the court decision neglected his Article 71 rights. The seller ultimately received a settlement of 70 percent of the purchase price and in return released the goods. As the legal arguments and basis imparted by UN sales law, it is clear that this result could not have been achieved on the basis of a national law, even if the parties had made further contractual agreements. Before one relinquishes the advantages of UN sales law in favor of the often more familiar national laws too hastily, one should therefore first give careful consideration and justification before making such a decision.

24 Italy

Edoardo Ferrante

I. Introduction: Issues of Methodology

Italy was part of the original group of countries to ratify the United Nations Convention on Contracts for the International Sale of Goods (CISG) – Italian Statute no. 765 of December 11, 1988 – and in accordance with CISG Article 99(1), it entered into force on January 1, 1988. Italy ratified the CISG without reservations, meaning the entire CISG was adopted into Italian law.

The early CISG case law dealt with the transition from the Hague Conventions to the CISG.[1] In *Nuova Fucinati vs. Fondmetall International*, the Tribunal of Monza[2] reviewed the applicability of the CISG under Article 1. The buyer's place of business was in Sweden, where the CISG entered into force after the contract proposal was made. The place of business of the seller was in Italy, where the CISG had already been in force. The parties agreed that the contract would be subject to Italian law. The tribunal decided that the CISG was not the applicable law. However, the tribunal failed to consider that the choice of law directed the tribunal to a CISG contracting state where the CISG has already entered into force at the time of the proposal. The *professio juris*, if admissible, is not an alternative to the rules on conflict of laws but is, rather, the criterion that determines the applicable law.[3] By this criterion the applicable law was

---

[1] Before adopting the CISG, Italy, pursuant to Article 99 (3) and (6), withdrew from predecessor Hague uniform laws dating back to July 1, 1964 – Uniform Law on the Formation of Contracts for the International Sales of Goods" (LUFC), the other relating to a Uniform Law on the International Sales of Goods (ULIS). Both Conventions were ratified by Italy with Statute no. 816 of June 21, 1971, and entered into force on January 1, 1972; only nine countries decided to ratify them and put them into force in their legal system (besides Italy, Belgium, Zambia, Israel, Luxemburg, the Netherlands, Germany, and San Marino), so that diplomatic negotiations were re-opened soon after their adoption: see Boschiero, "Le convenzioni internazionali in tema di vendita," in *21 Trattato di diritto privato* (ed. Rescigno) (Turin: Utet, 1987), 262; and Corte di Cassazione, October 24, 1988, no. 5739, *Foro italiano* I 2878 (1989), Giustizia civile I 1888 (1989), *Uniform L. Rev.* 857 (1989), available at http://www.unilex.info/case.cfm?id=2.

[2] *Tribunale di Monza*, January 14, 1993, *Giurisprudenza italiana* 149 (1994), Foro italiano I 916 (1994), Contratti 580 (1993), *Rivista di diritto internazionale privato e processuale* 367 (1994), available at http://cisgw3.law.pace.edu/cases/930114i3.html; see also Ferrari, "Diritto uniforme della vendita internazionale: questioni di applicabilità e diritto internazionale privato," *Rivista di diritto civile* II 669 (1995); and Maglio, "I criteri di applicazione della convenzione di Vienna sulla vendita internazionale: una sentenza italiana non persuasiva e l'insegnamento della giurisprudenza tedesca," *Contratto e impresa/Europa* 29 (1996).

[3] See Sendmeyer, "The Freedom of Choice in European Private International Law. An Analysis of Party Autonomy in the Rome I and Rome II Regulation," *Contratto e impresa/Europa* 792 (2009); Sacerdoti, "I criteri di applicazione della Convenzione di Vienna sulla vendita internazionale: diritto uniforme, diritto internazionale privato e autonomia dei contraenti," *Rivista trimestrale di diritto e procedura civile* 733

the CISG as the law of Italy. Nonetheless, the tribunal determined that the CISG did not qualify as "Italian law" and that when the parties chose "Italian law" they meant to exclude the CISG under CISG Article 6. In fact, the CISG is "Italian law" but in other cases, *professio juris*, although in favor of the law of a certain contracting State, could nevertheless be interpreted as an opt-out clause (CISG Article 8), especially if the choice of law provision is more specific by stating the choice as the "Italian civil code" or "Italian law exclusively"[4] rather than simply "Italian law."[5]

When the CISG was recognized as the applicable law of Italy, the early cases nevertheless tended to base their decisions on the Italian Civil Code or another national law.[6] Judges in the earlier decisions believed a well-reasoned case required referencing "traditional" Italian law, even if the applicability of the CISG was unquestioned. However, more recent cases have shown a trend away from such homeward-trend reasoning. Largely due to the expansion of EU law,[7] Italian judges have increasingly become receptive to transnational norms, principles, and values, as well as becoming more confident in using case law. Recent judgments have no longer felt the need to write *obiters* (dicta) based on the Italian civil code or other domestic provisions when the CISG is applicable law.[8]

There is a further interpretive methodological decision to be made. Italian judges often use Italian translations of the official text. Italian is not one of the official languages

---

(1990); Jayme in *Commentary on the International Sales Law* (ed. Bianca and Bonell) (Milan: Giuffré, 1987), 32.

[4] Florence Court of Arbitration, on April 19, 1994, *Diritto del commercio internazionale* 861 (1994), available at http://cisgw3.law.pace.edu/cases/940419i3.html.

[5] In this latter sense, though *obiter*, see Tribunale di Padova, January 11, 2005, *Rivista di diritto internazionale privato e processuale* 791 (2005), available at http://cisgw3.law.pace.edu/cases/050111i3.html (choice of regulations of the International Chamber of Commerce in Paris is not an implied exclusion of the CISG, given that ICC arbitration rules cannot be considered a "choice of law"). See Ferrari, *La vendita internazionale*, 2nd ed. (Padua: Cedam, 2006), 214 ("The parties' choice does not amount to an implied exclusion of the Convention").

[6] Pretura di Parma-Fidenza, November 24, 1989, in *Diritto del commercio internazionale* 441 (1995), available at http://cisgw3.law.pace.edu/cases/891124i3.html ("We focus our attention on the seller's partial performance. The seller's non-performance is a fundamental breach of contract according to Article 49 (1) (a)"); Tribunale di Padova, January 11, 2005; Corte di Cassazione, June 9, 1995, no. 6499, Giustizia civile I 2065 (1996), available at http://cisgw3.law.pace.edu/cases/950609i3.html ("The issues converge in this sense under either the criteria followed in the application of the rules of the Civil code or the criteria expounded in Article 3 of the CISG"); Pretura di Torino, January 30, 1997, *Giurisprudenza italiana* 982 (1998), available at http://CISGw3.law.pace.edu/cases/970130i3.html (The court, after claiming the applicability of the CISG, in dealing with the burden of proof, bases its arguments *tout court* on Article 2697 of Italian Civil Code). See also Bundesgerichtshof, January 9, 2002, *Neue Juristische Wochenschrift* 1651 (2002), *Recht der internationalen Wirtschaft* 396 (2002), *Wertpapier Mitteilungen* 1022 (2002), *Zeitschrift für Insolvenzpraxis* 672 (2002), available at http://cisgw3.law.pace.edu/cases/020109g1.html. See also Perales Viscasillas, "Battle of the Forms and the Burden of Proof: An Analysis of BGH 9 January 2002," *Vindobona J. for Int'l Commercial L. & Arbitration* 217 (2002).

[7] "Bin, Per un dialogo con il futuro legislatore dell'attuazione: ripensare l'intera disciplina della non conformità dei beni nella vendita alla luce della direttiva comunitaria," *Contratto e impresa/Europa* 403 (2000).

[8] Cf. Corte di Appello di Milano, December 11, 1998, *Rivista di diritto internazionale privato e processuale* 112 (1999), available at http://cisgw3.law.pace.edu/cases/981211i3.html. However, compare, Corte di Cassazione, December 14, 1999, no. 895, *Giustizia civile I* 2333 (2000), available at http://cisgw3.law.pace.edu/cases/991214i3.html.

of the CISG, therefore to refer to an informal translation of the text implies a violation of CISG Article 101(2). Use of unofficial texts also undermines the search for autonomous interpretations under CISG Article 7(1).[9] European jurists know the difficulties of "trans" or "meta" linguistics because of their need to apply EU law.[10] The interpretation of a text in a nonauthentic version is misleading. In practice, the English version has prevailed, being considered as the text *par excellence* of the CISG. There is therefore no reason to use versions other than the English one, even though they are official and better suited to native speakers. Conversely, the use of nonauthentic versions constitutes a violation of the CISG.

II. Sources of International Sales Law

Despite the revocation of the Hague Sales Conventions of 1964, the Hague Convention of June 15, 1955 "on the law applicable to the international sales of goods"[11] remains in force[12] and prevails over EC Regulation 593/2008 ("on the law applicable to contractual obligations"), in accordance with Article 25,[13] and the Rome Convention of June 19, 1980, as per Article 21 ("on the law applicable to contractual obligations").[14] It is quite strange that four judgments by the Italian Supreme Court in plenary session have made no comment on it, and have ruled on jurisdiction without even mentioning the Hague Convention of 1955.[15]

In any case, the normative framework summarized here raises a fundamental problem of international private law. In the Italian system, there are two conventions on sales that

[9] See Tribunale di Padova, January 11, 2005.
[10] See Marietta, "L'interpretazione dei trattati plurilingue nella prassi delle Comunità Europee," *Rivista di diritto europeo* 230 (1985).
[11] See Cassoni, "La compravendita nelle convenzioni e nel diritto internazionale privato italiano," *Rivista di diritto internazionale privato e processuale* 429 (1982).
[12] The second Hague Convention "on the applicable law to the contracts of international sale of goods" was adopted on October 31, 1985, but it never entered into force due to the fact that the minimum number for the deposit of ratifications (five, as per Article 21) was not been reached; the version of the Convention which is in force is therefore the one of 1955; see Boschiero, "Le convenzioni internazionali," 214 et seq. and 251 et seq.; Padovini, "La vendita internazionale dalle Convenzioni dell'Aja alle Convenzioni di Vienna," in *Rivista di diritto internazionale privato e processuale* 47 (1987); Luminoso, *La compravendita*, 7th ed. (Turin: Giappichelli, 2011), 498–500.
[13] In particular, there is no inconsistency with Reg. EC 593/2008 Article 25(2). See Frignani-Torsello, *Il contratto internazionale*, 2nd ed. (Padua: Cedam: Padova 2010), 438 n. 7.
[14] *A fortiori* the Hague Convention of 1955, which, for now, has not yet been replaced by the one of 1985, prevails over Statute no. 218 of the May 31, 1995 ("Reform of the Italian system of international private law"), where Article 57 refers to the Rome Convention of 1980 (Reg. EC 593/2008). The Rome Convention of June 19, 1980, ratified with Statute no. 975 of December 18, 1984, entered into force on April 1, 1991, was transposed into EU law with Reg. EC 593/2008, where Article 24(1), restricts, without excluding, its effectiveness; both the Rome Convention of 1980, though within the limits of Reg. EC 593/2008 Article 24(1), and this latter regulation is still applicable outside the subjective and objective sphere of the Hague Convention of 1955, Article 4(1)(a) and (c), Reg. EC 593/2008, but obviously under the condition that it is not excluded by the CISG.
[15] Corte di Cassazione, February 1, 1999, no. 6, available at http://cisgw3.law.pace.edu/cases/990201i3.html; id., December 14, 1999, no. 895; id., June 6, 2002, no. 8224, available at http://cisgw3.law.pace.edu/cases/020606i3.html; id., June 20, 2007, no. 14300, *Rivista di diritto internazionale privato e processuale* 511 (2008); cf. Tribunale di Pavia, December 29, 1999, *Corriere giuridico* 932 (2000), available at http://cisgw3.law.pace.edu/cases/991229i3.html.

are simultaneously in force:[16] the first, the Hague Convention of 1955, which provides conflict of laws rules; the other, the CISG, providing substantive sales rules. The question is, therefore, which of these two conventions should be primarily applicable.[17] The two laws may lead to the same result – the conflict of laws rules determine the applicable law to be the CISG if they refer to a contracting state of the CISG. A notable example is offered by the judgment of the Italian Supreme Court in plenary session in *Premier Steel Service vs. Oscam*:[18]

> For the international sales of goods . . . , the rules of international private law are established by the Hague Convention of 15th June 1955 . . . , which has an international nature (art. 7) and prevails over the Rome Convention of 19th June 1980 . . . , to which art. 57 of Statute no. 218/1995 refers (this prevalence can be deduced both from the final part of art. 57, and from art. 21 of the Rome Convention). The Hague Convention of 1955, in contrast with what was argued by the *resistente* [the party against whom a second-level appeal has been filed], cannot be considered as abrogated by the Vienna Convention of 11th April 1980 . . . , because this latter Convention contains substantive uniform rules, rather than international private law rules, given that the former provide substantive law whose purpose is to substitute domestic law, rather than to determine the law applicable to the contract of sale, which must be identified on the basis of the Hague Convention. According to art. 3 of this latter Convention, in default of a law declared applicable by the parties a sale shall be governed by Italian law, as it is the country in which the purchaser has his habitual residence . . . The *locus destinatae solutionis* . . . must therefore be determined on the basis of Italian law. Nonetheless, given that Italy has signed the above-mentioned Vienna Convention . . . , Italian law has been substituted by the provisions of that Convention (art. 1, paragraph 1, letter b).[19]

But such an undoubtedly complex interpretation would lead to the nonapplication a priori of CISG Article 1(1)(a), as if the article consisted only of 1(1)(b). If the applicability of the CISG originates from Article 1(1)(a), the CISG applies; it is *lex specialis* in relation to the provisions on the conflict of laws, which only govern the choice of applicable law indirectly. If the issue concerns international sales, the closer and more "specialized" source of law is the CISG, which contains uniform substantive provisions, rather than

---

[16] The framework of international conventions signed by Italy on the subject of sale is even more complicated, and includes, moreover, the two Hague Conventions of April 15, 1958; the New York Convention of June 14, 1974; and the Geneva Convention of 1983: but none of these conventions is actually into force, due to the lack of the necessary number of ratifications; for further information, see Boschiero, "Le convenzioni internazionali," 233 et seq. and 263 et seq.

[17] The problem is not be solved if the Hague Convention of 1955 was replaced by the Reg. EC 593/2008 or – but it is now very rare – the Rome Convention of 1980. See Boschiero, *Il coordinamento delle norme in materia di vendita internazionale* (Padua: Cedam, 1990).

[18] Corte di Cassazione, June 19, 2000, no. 448, *Giurisprudenza italiana* 233 (2001), Foro italiano I 527 (2001), Corriere giuridico 369 (2002), available at http://cisgw3.law.pace.edu/cases/000619i3.html.

[19] In the same direction Corte di Appello di Milano, March 20, 1998, *Rivista di diritto internazionale privato e processuale* 170 (1998), *diritto del commercio internazionale* 455 (1999), available at http://cisgw3.law. pace.edu/cases/980320i3.html; and the already mentioned Corte di Cassazione, February 1, 1999, no. 6; id., December 14, 1999, no. 895; id., June 6, 2002, no. 8224, which ignore the Hague Convention of 1955, but, however, permit the application of CISG through the filter of the provisions on the conflict of laws, rather than by virtue of its nature of *lex specialis* which directly regulates international sale (a peculiar opinion can be found in Corte di Cassazione, June 6, 2002, no. 8224, where, despite the fact that the contract *sub judice* has been qualified as a sale, the court does not apply either the Hague Convention of 1955, or the CISG; the motivation is too short to draw from it the exact principle of law applied to the case).

the Hague Convention of 1955, which merely provides criteria for the identification of applicable law.

After overcoming some initial uncertainties,[20] judges have definitively adopted this second solution. In 1999, the Tribunal of Pavia in *Tessile 21 v. Ixela*, balancing the relationship between the CISG and the Hague Convention of 1955, affirmed that "the reference to provisions of uniform substantive law (established by international conventions) prevails over the provisions on the conflict of laws due to their specific nature, must be preferred over the reference to international private law."[21] Therefore, in determining the applicable sales law, interpreters of Italian law will have to verify the applicability of the CISG first; then, if necessary, the applicability of the Hague Convention of 1955; and finally, if the latter is entirely or partially nonapplicable, Regulation EC 593/2008 (Rome Convention of 1980).[22]

Nevertheless, this hierarchy of sources must not be evaluated in a perfunctory way. Despite the trend in the private international legal system toward the preeminence of conventions establishing uniform law over conventions on the conflict of laws, it is important to note that it is the provisions on the conflict of laws that determine the applicability of substantive law. Thus, if the prerequisites of CISG Article 1(1)(a) are lacking, the applicable law is determined by conflict of laws rules (Hague Convention of 1955). The application of the Hague Convention, even though not prevailing, can lead to an exclusion of the application of the CISG.[23]

Conflict of laws rules are also relevant in relation to the CISG because of the noncomprehensive nature of the CISG. Besides numerous external gaps, CISG Article 4 delegates the issue of the validity of contract terms to national law. Due to its limited substantive sphere of application, the CISG necessarily competes with other "nonspecialized" sources, such as private international law and international conflict of laws conventions,

---

[20] See Treves, "Il labirinto della vendita internazionale," *Politica del diritto* 97 (1973); Lopez De Gonzalo, "Vendita internazionale," *Contratto e impresa* 267 (1988).

[21] Tribunale di Pavia, December 29, 1999; Tribunale di Vigevano, July 12, 2000, *Giurisprudenza italiana* 280 (2001), *Rivista di diritto internazionale privato e processuale* 143 (2001), available at http://cisgw3 .law.pace.edu/cases/000712i3.html; see also Ferrari, "Applying the CISG in a Truly Uniform Manner: Tribunale di Vigevano (Italy), 12 July 2000," *Uniform L. Rev.* 206 (2001); Ferrari, "Tribunale di Vigevano: Specific Aspects of the CISG Uniformly Dealt With," *J. of L. & Commerce* 225 (2001); Corte di Appello di Milano, January 23, 2001, *Rivista di diritto internazionale privato e processuale* 1008 (2001), available at http://www.unilex.info/case.cfm?id=768; Tribunale di Rimini, November 26, 2002, *Giurisprudenza italiana* 896 (2003), available at http://cisgw3.law.pace.edu/cases/021126i3.html; see also Ferrari, "International Sales Law and the Inevitability of Forum Shopping: A Comment on Tribunale di Rimini," *Vindobona J. of International Commercial L. and Arbitration* 1 (2004); Tribunale di Padova, February 25, 2004, *Giurisprudenza italiana* 1402 (2004), available at http://cisgw3.law.pace.edu/cases/040225i3. html; see Graffi, "L'interpretazione autonoma della Convenzione di Vienna: rilevanza del precedente straniero e disciplina delle lacune," *Giurisprudenza di merito* 867 (2004); Tribunale di Padova, March 31, 2004, *Giurisprudenza di merito* 1065 (2004), available at http://cisgw3.law.pace.edu/cases/040331i3.html; Tribunale di Padova, January 11, 2005; Tribunale di Rovereto, November 21, 2007, available at http:// www.unilex.info/case.cfm?id=1219; Tribunale di Forlì, December 9, 2008, available at http://cisgw3.law .pace.edu/cisg/text/081211i3italian.pdf and at http://cisgw3.law.pace.edu/cases/081211i3.html; id., February 16, 2009, available at http://www.unilex.info/case.cfm?id=1394 and at http://cisgw3.law.pace.edu/ cases/090216i3.html.

[22] See *supra* note 14, the above-mentioned Italian Statute no. 218/1995, in accordance with Articles 2(1) and 57, is in the background of the normative framework of international and EU law.

[23] The "interlocking puzzle" is clear in the judgment of Tribunale di Reggio Emilia, July 3, 2000, available at http://cisgw3.law.pace.edu/cases/000703i3.html.

as well as choices made by the contracting parties[24] or by the *lex mercatoria*.[25] Therefore, in Italy, as well as in many other countries, the CISG appears to be insufficient for complete harmonization and coordination, even supposing that these may be considered realistic aims.[26]

III. Problem of Scarcity

The CISG has been part of the Italian legal system since January 1, 1988. However, from a quantitative point of view, there are fewer than fifty Italian judgments and many of these are nonsubstantive law judgments dealing with issues of jurisdiction. On this point, it is possible only to formulate a number of hypotheses to explain the scarcity of cases. The normal practice in business-to-business contracts, with a particular focus on the setting of general terms and conditions for transnational business, excludes the application of the CISG pursuant to Article 6, and, instead, parties choose the domestic law of the drafting party.

The practice of opting out of the CISG has been expanded by decisions that hold that the opt out need not be by express verbal or written clause, but also may be implied by conduct, simultaneous or subsequent to the formation of the contract, showing tacit consent.[27] This expansion is a simple recognition[28] that the application of the CISG is dependent on the intentions of the parties toward exclusion.[29] However, some courts require the opt out be specific and expressed. The method of opting out is an external lacuna rather than an internal one, as opting out is permitted but not regulated by the CISG. Because it is an external gap, determination of whether the parties have properly opted out of the CISG is not bound by the general principles of CISG Article 7(2), but rather by the applicable law in accordance with conflict of laws rules. The "implied form" of opting out, even if consistent with the CISG interpretive methodology, may not be recognized under conflict of laws rules. Undoubtedly a concurrent factor may also be the general trend toward the exclusion of the CISG by commercial parties.

What is the reason for the widespread exclusion of the CISG by commercial entities? One factor may be the costs of learning a new law. These costs may be high because

---

[24] Nevertheless, freedom in its private international meaning is not unlimited, mainly as far as mandatory national provisions are concerned.

[25] See "Fundamental," in Italy, Bonell, *Le regole oggettive del commercio internazionale* (Milan: Giuffrè, 1976); Galgano, *La globalizzazione nello specchio del diritto* (Bologna: Il Mulino, 2005).

[26] Italian academics are doubtful in this respect, Mengoni, "L'Europa dei codici o un codice per l'Europa?," *Rivista critica del diritto privato* 515 (1992); contra Bonell, "La Convenzione di Vienna sulla vendita internazionale: origini, scelte e principi fondamentali," *Rivista di diritto internazionale privato e processuale* 715 (1990).

[27] In the same direction Tribunale di Vigevano, July 12, 2000; Tribunale di Rimini, November 26, 2002; Tribunale di Padova, February 25, 2004; id., March 31, 2004; id., 11 Gennaio 2005; Tribunale di Forlì, 9 Dicembre 2008; id., February 16, 2009 (all decisions mentioned *supra* note 21); and Patti, "Silenzio, inerzia e comportamento concludente nella Convenzione di Vienna sui contratti di vendita internazionale di beni mobili," *Rivista di diritto commerciale* I 135 (1991); similar questions are raised by the applicability of Article 11 CISG to the arbitration clause, which is not itself a subject dealt with by the convention. See André Janssen and Matthias Spilker, "CISG and International Arbitration," Chapter 10 in this book.

[28] See Tribunale di Padova, February 25, 2004.

[29] See Trib. Vigevano, July 12, 2000. Once the application of the CISG has been excluded, it is not a forgone conclusion that the rules on conflict of laws allow the free choice by the parties of the applicable law (this choice could not be implied through conduct).

Italian companies do not recruit specialized personnel with specific legal and language skills that would be needed to fully comprehend the CISG. A second factor is that Italy is a country of many small businesses that participate in the exporting and importing of goods. The task of learning a new law is more burdensome for them than for larger companies. Of course, escaping the costs of learning another law is only possible in cases where the Italian contracting party has sufficient bargaining power to insist on Italian law as the choice of law.

In business-to-business contracts, especially when the contracting companies are large and based in different countries, arbitration is the preferred means of dispute resolution.[30] Due to the importance of privacy, international arbitral awards are often unreported. Therefore the scarcity of court cases may be due to the fact that international sales disputes are often resolved through arbitration. Furthermore, the use of the CISG in arbitration proceedings is likely to be much higher than is known due to the fact that a large portion of awards are unreported.

Finally, the lack of Italian CISG court decisions is unlikely to be due to the lack of expertise on the part of lawyers and judges.[31] It is hard to believe that transactional lawyers in Italy remain unaware of the existence of the CISG. Italian academics have actively researched the CISG and published many articles and books on the subject. A more likely scenario is that Italian transactional lawyers are fully aware of the existence of the CISG, but remain somewhat ignorant of its substantive content[32] and, for this reason, simply decide to opt out of the application of the CISG.

IV. Toward Supranational *Stare Decisis*?

Despite the scarcity of Italian case law applying the CISG, the CISG decisions that have been rendered are of high quality. First of all there is a good use of autonomous interpretation, in accordance with the principles established by CISG Article 7.[33]

Italian court decisions have noticeably used foreign case law in rendering or supporting their decisions. If all courts followed this approach, there would be greater uniformity

---

[30] See Janssen and Spilker, "The Application of the CISG in the World of International Commercial Arbitration," *RabelsZ* (2011).

[31] Contra Torsello, "Italy," in *The CISG and its Impact on National Legal Systems* (ed. Ferrari) (Munich: Sellier, 2008), 187.

[32] Scholars dealing with such research are a small number, and there are few university courses on the subject and few lectures on international sale; on the contrary, in Germany, the topic plays a relevant role in the legal culture and practice. But see *Commentary on the International Sales Law* (ed. Bianca and Bonell) (Milan: Giuffré, 1987); Sannini, *L'applicazione della Convenzione di Vienna sulla vendita internazionale negli Stati Uniti* (Padua: Cedam, 2006); Ragno, *Convenzione di Vienna e Diritto europeo* (Padua: Cedam, 2008).

[33] See, e.g., Tribunale di Padova, February 25, 2004: "On the substantive side, it is necessary that the contract be a contract of sale, whose definition is not provided by [the CISG]. However, the lack of an express definition should not lead to turning to a national definition, e.g., as provided in Art. 1470 C.c. [Italian Civil Code]. On the other hand, as with most of the concepts used in the [CISG] (among which that of 'place of business,' 'domicile,' and 'goods' but not the concept of 'private international law' which instead corresponds to the private international law of the forum), the concept of 'sale' has to be identified autonomously, without referring to any domestic definition"; see also, Tribunale di Padova, January 11, 2005; Tribunale di Modena, December 9, 2005, available at http://www.cisg-online.ch/cisg/urteile/1398.pdf; Tribunale di Forlì, December 9, 2008.

of application and fewer instances of "forum shopping."[34] Italian courts have used well-reasoned foreign cases not as binding precedent, but as persuasive authority. Foreign case law, even though worthy of consideration, "is not binding." An almost fixed formula follows: "foreign case law . . . , which, *although not binding*, is however to be taken into consideration as required by CISG Article 7(1)."[35]

However, the expression "although not binding" is so lacking in authenticity as to raise doubts as to its substance. The Italian judges declared that they rejected the idea of a binding precedent in an international context, but, in practice, have openly embraced foreign case decisions and followed the principles established by foreign courts. If this is so, the expression "although not binding" should not be taken seriously. The key determinant in the use of foreign decisions is the degree of factual similarity between the foreign case and the case before the Italian court. Despite its negative connotation for the civilian authorities, the Italian CISG cases suggest that a supranational *stare decisis* is possible in the application of the CISG.[36]

The majority view, according to which foreign precedents have no binding force, regardless of the implications of Article 7(1), is based essentially on two arguments, one practical, the other technical. The former argument asserts that it is impractical to expect national judges to possess the knowledge and skills needed to study the case law from all CISG countries. The second argument against the notion of a supranational *stare decisis* asserts that such a system requires a supranational judicial system that would ensure the uniform application of the CISG.[37] These arguments are relatively weak. The amount of material to be collected and studied may be large, but it is hard to estimate if it is on average larger than the one needed to decide domestic cases. Furthermore, the current assortment of databases dedicated to CISG jurisprudence and scholarly commentary make foreign CISG cases easily accessible. An example has already been provided – the Italian CISG decisions had little difficulty in citing foreign cases.[38]

As to the second argument, is a supreme appellate body with a "nomophylactic" function ($\nu o\mu o\varphi\nu\lambda\alpha\kappa\iota\alpha$) really necessary to ensure uniformity of application of the CISG? Can supreme courts of the individual states act as surrogate (informal) appellate courts? If a domestic decision violates Article 7(1) by disregarding a foreign precedent – without distinguishing the foreign case as not being on point or as being an ill-reasoned

---

[34] Tribunale di Rimini, November 26, 2002 (does not hide the difficulties of the problem against "forum shopping"); Tribunale di Cuneo, January 31, 1996, *Diritto del commercio internazionale* 653 (1996), available at http://cisgw3.law.pace.edu/cases/960131i3.html. The decision is worth taking into account also for the absence of *obiter*, which are, on the contrary, more frequent in the other Italian judgments on the CISG.

[35] Tribunale di Pavia, December 29, 1999 (emphasis added); Tribunale di Vigevano, July 12, 2000; Tribunale di Rimini, November 26, 2002; Tribunale di Padova, February 25, 2004; Tribunale di Padova, January 10, 2006, Giurisprudenza italiana 1016 (2006), *Giurisprudenza di merito* 1408 (2006), *Rivista di diritto internazionale privato e processuale* 147 (2007), available at http://cisgw3.law.pace.edu/cases/060110i3. html; Tribunale di Forlì, February 16, 2009; contra, Tribunale di Padova, January 11, 2005.

[36] DiMatteo, "An International Contract Law Formula: The Informality of International Business Transactions Plus the Internationalization of Contract Law Equals Unexpected Contract Liability," 23 *Syracuse Journal of International Law and Commerce* 79 (1997); id., "Case Law Precedent and Legal Writing," in *CISG Methodology* 113 (ed. Janssen and Meyer) (Munich: Sellier, 2009), 113.

[37] See M. Torsello, "Il valore del precedente extrastatuale nell'applicazione del diritto interno: circolazione del formante giurisprudenziale e uso della giurisprudenza straniera nelle corti italiane," *Contratto e impresa/Europa* 19 (2009).

[38] Tribunale di Rimini, November 26, 2002.

decision – should a court of appeal or the national Supreme Court not rectify the lower court's different reasoning? The crucial point is the need to enhance the mandatory nature of Article 7(1) – with Article 2, paragraph 2, Statute no. 218/1995. The CISG is not simply a legislative policy, but a legal rule with a binding nature. Therefore, the disregard of foreign case law should be considered equivalent to any other violation of a mandatory provision of law and receive the same domestic procedural and substantive law treatment as any other domestic law.

If it is the word "binding" or the expression *stare decisis* that is the problem, it would probably be enough to use another expression without, however, changing the substance. Despite the labels, the courts should follow foreign precedents and consider Article 7 as a mandatory provision. The expression "although not binding" is therefore superfluous and misleading.

V. Interpreting the CISG

This section reviews Italian cases that have applied substantive provisions of the CISG, including the duty of good faith, contract formation, battle of the forms, and notice of nonconformity.

A. *Good Faith and the Prohibition of* Venire Contra Factum

The main danger in the application by national courts of an international substantive law is that they will be biased by their training and knowledge of their national law ("homeward trend"). In *So.m.agri v. Erzeugerorganisation Marchfeldgemüse*, the Tribunal of Padova decision was tainted by domestic law influences.[39] The Austrian seller of agricultural produce, after waiting for about six months for payment of the agreed price, filed an application against the Italian buyer, without previously sending him a warning or giving him a deadline for the performance (payment). The Tribunal held that the buyer was required to pay within the parameters established by CISG Articles 58[40] and 59. The court held that expiration of the time limit automatically implies that the buyer falls into arrears without requiring any formal notification.[41] Article 59 states that "the buyer must pay the price on the date fixed by or determinable from the contract . . . without the need for any request or compliance with any formality on the part of the seller." CISG Article 63(1) allows the seller to give the buyer a *Nachfrist* notice (time extension) for performance, but the seller is not required to unilaterally give such an extension. Nevertheless, the buyer may not know the exact moment from which the goods are at his or her disposal if the parties did not specify the time of performance. In such a situation, it would be against the principle of good faith to allow a seller to file a claim without indicating the expiration date for payment to the buyer. The Tribunal clearly stated that "the conduct of the contracting parties must be pursuant to the principle of good faith which – since it is one of the general principles on which [the CISG] is based . . . – must not only influence the entire regulation of the international sale . . . , but also supplies an essential standard for the interpretation of the rules set forth in the CISG."

---

[39] Tribunale di Padova, February 25, 2004.
[40] In the same direction Tribunale di Padova, March 31, 2004.
[41] See also id.

The Tribunal pointed out in *obiter* that because the Austrian seller filed approximately six months after the deadline and the Italian buyer had had every opportunity to make payment, the alleged violation of good faith for recklessness of remedy was inconsistent with the facts and was mentioned only as an example.[42] In addition, the decision is a result of a misinterpretation of CISG Article 7(1), which states that the principle of good faith is to be used in the interpretation of the CISG, rather than as a binding rule for the performance of the contract. The modification of good faith from a rule of interpretation to a rule of party conduct appears to be due to the strong role of good faith in many legal systems in continental Europe, including Germany and Italy, but finds only a weak basis in the Convention itself. The insertion of the principle of good faith by the Tribunal of Padova was the result of "homeward trend" influences.[43]

In *Scatolificio La Perla v. M. Frischdienst*, the Tribunal of Padova[44] invoked the prohibition of *venire contra factum proprium*, as a fundamental principle of the CISG. The German seller, in placing the goods at the Italian buyer's disposal, gave him extended payment terms of fifty days from the delivery date. Despite the specification of the payment date, the tribunal referred to the prohibition of *venire contra factum proprium*, a prohibition that is close to the continental principle of good faith. Again, the tribunal displayed "homeward trend" reasoning. The tribunal made a general reference to the "principles of the CISG" without specifying how the principle in question had a basis in the CISG.

B. *Formation of Contract and Battle of the Forms*

In *Takap v. Europlay*, decided by the Tribunal of Rovereto,[45] a dispute arose between the parties on a forum selection clause in favor of Dutch jurisdiction. The Italian seller obtained an order for payment from an Italian court. The Dutch buyer counter-claimed that the Dutch courts had jurisdiction pursuant to the forum selection clause pursuant to Article 23(b) of Regulation EC 44/2001. The question at issue was whether the clause was a term of the contract on which the parties had agreed.

The tribunal decided that the EC Regulation was applicable. Thus, it had to decide the validity and effectiveness of the forum selection clause pursuant to the regulation. However, it first needed to decide whether the parties had actually agreed to the clause, given that it had not been negotiated, but simply included in the form drafted by the buyer. This issue has been faced by every national legal system, and the CISG: how do standard terms and conditions become incorporated into a contract without having been individually negotiated or accepted (technically speaking) by the other party? The formation of contracts is within the scope of the CISG and, therefore, the CISG is the applicable law. Unfortunately, the CISG does not deal directly with the issue of the incorporation of standard terms, therefore, this represents an "internal gap"

---

[42] A reference to good faith appears also in Tribunale di Busto Arsizio, December 13, 2001, *Rivista di diritto internazionale privato e processuale* 150 (2003), available at http://cisgw3.law.pace.edu/cases/011213i3. html (*obiter*).

[43] Similarly, Tribunale di Rovereto, November 21, 2007; but here too the claim was not grounded on any provisions on good faith in its continental meaning.

[44] Tribunale di Padova, March 31, 2004.

[45] Tribunale di Rovereto, November 21, 2007.

to be filled through the application of general principles found in Article 7, as well as implied general principles.

In the case in question, the buyer claimed that he had sent the other party written offers, which expressly referred to the general conditions and terms found elsewhere in the document. The terms were immediately accessible to the offeree. The same cannot be said for the other standard clauses that were not accessible to the offeree. Such clauses need to be brought to the attention of the other party; the receiving party is not required to make efforts to become aware of them. No evidence of such incorporation was produced in court and, moreover, the seller proved that he had replied to the offers with letters of acceptance that included his own standard terms and conditions. If standard terms drafted by the buyer were neither knowable nor known to the seller, then the forum selection clause in favor of the Dutch courts was not valid.

If the forms of both parties fulfill the minimum "noticeability" requirement for incorporation, then a battle of the forms scenario arises. The tribunal discussed the battle of the forms in passing, but it was not an issue in the case because evidence was produced that the buyer's form had not been incorporated into the contract. In any case, the seller's form, embodied in the letter of confirmation subsequently countersigned by the buyer, would have prevailed over the buyer's form. In fact, under Article 19(3), the seller's form materially altered the offer, which made it a rejection of the offer (counteroffer). The subsequent acceptance by the original offeror (signing the confirmation) bound the buyer to a contract based upon the seller's form (confirmation). Therefore, in the end, this was not a battle of the forms case. Despite the unnecessary discussion of Article 19,[46] the tribunal provided a well-reasoned decision by properly applying the rules and principles of the CISG.

The issue in *Euroflash v. Arconvert* (Tribunal of Rovereto)[47] was the enforceability of a forum selection clause found in the Italian seller's form. The question was whether the French buyer had agreed to the incorporation of the clause into the agreement. The clause was located at the bottom of the seller's order confirmation, which was sent in response to the buyer's offer. Thus the buyer was given notice of the clause's existence, but there was no evidence that he had specifically accepted the term. Furthermore, there was no commercial usage that implied that the buyer's conduct amounted to an acceptance.

In the tribunal's view the acceptance was not compliant with the offer and therefore amounted to a counteroffer, which required acceptance by the original offeror. Given that there was no usage between the parties that permitted acceptance through conduct, the forum selection clause was not enforceable and could not establish jurisdiction in favor of Italian courts, which was in itself excluded by Regulation EC 44/2001.

The decision seems peculiar in three respects. First of all, the opinion according to which general terms and conditions require actual acceptance fails to make a distinction between unilateral clauses and negotiated clauses contrary to the rules found in CISG Article 14 et seq. and Article 1326 et seq. of the Italian Civil Code. Secondly, the tribunal should have drawn the conclusion that not only the forum selection clause, but the whole

---

[46] See E. Ferrante, "'Battle of Forms' and the 1980 United Nations Convention on Contracts for the International Sale of Goods (CISG): A Note on the BGH (German Supreme Court) Decision of 9 January 2002," VIII-4 *Uniform L. Rev.* 977–8 (2003).

[47] Tribunale di Rovereto, August 24, 2006, available at http://www.unilex.info/case.cfm?id=1147.

agreement was void, which can be deduced from CISG Articles 19(1) and (3), and Article 1326, paragraph 5 of the Italian Civil Code (mirror image rule). Finally, it is clear that the solution adopted – according to which the forum selection clause was voided due to a lack of consent, while the contract itself remained valid – is inconsistent with CISG Article 19(3) and the Italian Civil Code. In any case, regardless of the positive or negative remarks, the decision is not the result of "homeward trend."

C. *Notice of Lack of Conformity*

One of the more disputed issues in the CISG is the determination of "reasonable time" to give notice of nonconformity under CISG Article 39(1).[48] A preliminary remark needs to be made; although the CISG relies on the concept of reasonable time,[49] Italian Civil Code Article 1495, paragraph 1, fixes a time limit of eight days. In *Sport D'Hiver v. Ets Louys et Fils,*[50] the Tribunal of Cuneo noted that the requirement of reasonableness had "to be measured on the basis of a case-by-case approach." It held that a delay of twenty-three days in giving notice of lack of conformity of the goods sold (clothes) was untimely and that the buyer had lost his right to make a claim of nonconformity. Besides the observance of foreign case law, two implicit criteria of evaluation emerge from this decision. First, the measure of reasonableness should depend on the facts, rather than on systematic needs or by analogy. Second, the measure could consist of an extension of the time limits fixed by the Italian civil code – a period longer than eight days can indeed be reasonable. However, we should not lose sight of balance: eight days as well as twenty-three can be a reasonable time but, evidently, somewhere in between would be more desirable.

Less relevant than it appears is the case *C. & M. v. Bakintzopoulos,* where the Pretura of Turin, in deciding on notice that had been given seven months after the delivery of the goods (cotton fabrics), held that reasonable time had expired and that the buyer had lost his right to rely on it.[51] Similarly, in *Rheinland Versicherungen v. Atlarex,* the Tribunal of Vigevano, after emphasizing the need to consider the nature of the goods sold, excluded the reasonableness of notice given four months after the delivery of the goods (rubber sheeting).[52]

The smaller degree of relevance of these latter cases depends on the fact that, in both, notice was given quite a long time after delivery, so that it was clear from the beginning and *prima facie* that the buyer had lost his right to rely on the lack of conformity.

---

[48] See A. Janssen, "La durata dei termini d'ispezione e di denuncia di non-conformità dei beni nella Convenzione di Vienna: la giurisprudenza dei giudici nazionali a confronto," *Contratto e impresa/Europa* 1321 (2003).

[49] The formula of reasonable time has been expressly qualified as a "general clause" by Pretura di Torino, January 30, 1997.

[50] Tribunale di Cuneo, January 31, 1996.

[51] Pretura di Torino, January 30, 1997.

[52] Tribunale di Vigevano, July 12, 2000. To limit our analysis to the reasonable time of notice, either what has been said about the relevance of contractual freedom – here there was no agreement between the parties on fixing the time limits – or what has been said as to the *dies a quo* in case of the lack of conformity originates from a hidden defect – the judge believes that the nature of the defect had not been proved – or the long digression on the burden of proof, were not part of the *ratio decidendi,* given that the buyer had lost his right to rely on the lack of conformity.

The same remarks can be made for *Officine Maraldi v. Intesa BCI*, recently decided by the Tribunal of Forlì,[53] where the notice was more than thirteen months after delivery, despite the nonperishable nature of the goods (petrol tanks), clearly leading to the loss of the right to rely on the lack of conformity.

In *Expoplast v. Reg Mac*,[54] the Tribunal of Busto Arsizio focused on the discovery of the defect (*dies a quo*) and the requirement of specificity. Article 39(1) requires the notice of nonconformity "specify the nature of the lack of conformity." The exact fixing of the *dies a quo* was said to depend on the external or patent nature of the lack of conformity. If an examination is necessary to discover the nonconformity, the time for the notice does not begin with the delivery, but only after inspection. The issue of a timely or reasonable inspection is heavily debated in Italian case law due to the very short time limit to give notice of nonconformity fixed for domestic sales by Article 1495, paragraph 1, of the Italian civil code discussed earlier. This is because the Civil Code does not fix a time for *dies a quo* (inspection).

The tribunal's decision is free from homeward trend bias. Regarding the issue of the requirements for specificity of notice, it mediates between two opposing concerns – the need to avoid placing an undue burden on the buyer of nonconforming goods and the right of the seller to receive quality notice to give him or her an opportunity to cure the nonconformity, send substituted goods, or minimize his or her damages. The nature of the goods plays a vital role in determining the reasonableness of the notice. Inspecting large quantities of clothes,[55] fabrics,[56] rubber sheeting,[57] or complicated machinery impacts the determination as to the timeliness of the notice and degree of specificity. The tribunal espoused a "trade-off" approach to the reasonableness (time and specificity) determination: "the burden of proof on the timely notice of the lack of conformity as it appears is on the buyer, but he is not required to prove also the *specific cause of it*." Notice is itself an extrinsic act, so it does not require an explanation of the reasons on which the alleged lack of conformity is based; we should bear in mind that notice amounts neither to an application, nor implies that the buyer is already able to identify a violation due to the other party's fault.

In *Al Palazzo v. Bernardaud*, the Tribunal of Rimini[58] referenced the previous decisions but, nonetheless, specified that the buyer only needs to give notice within a reasonable time in order not to lose the right to rely on the lack of conformity, whereas the requirement to examine the goods within as short a period as is practicable is merely secondary and accessory. If this is true and notice is given within a reasonable time, what might be the consequences of a late examination? From the point of practicality, if the notice is timely, then it follows that the examination is to be considered timely as well. However, the timeliness of the notice is likely to be narrowly construed if the lack of conformity is immediately noticeable without any examination.

The Tribunal made clear the importance of trade usage and practices developed between the parties. It notes that the parties' agreement, the circumstances of the case, and the nature of the goods are all important factors in ruling on the reasonableness of

---

[53] Tribunale di Forlì, February 16, 2009.
[54] Tribunale di Busto Arsizio, December 13, 2001.
[55] Tribunale di Cuneo, January 31, 1996.
[56] Pretura di Torino, January 30, 1997.
[57] Tribunale di Vigevano, July 12, 2000.
[58] Tribunale di Rimini, November 26, 2002.

the specificity and timing of the notice. However, these factors may be overridden by an existing trade usage recognized under CISG Article 9 and previous conduct of mutual tolerance allowing for notice beyond a reasonable time.

Finally, in *Mitias v. Solidea*, the Tribunal of Forlì[59] distinguished between complaints and formal notices of nonconformity. It determined that, under certain circumstances, the former satisfies the requirements relating to the latter. If the seller, as a consequence of the buyer's complaints, offers a remedy to amend the lack of conformity, the complaints should be considered timely notice, as the seller's admissions would be equivalent to attesting to the reasonableness of the time period of notice. Although the rationale of the decision was correct, unfortunately the tribunal failed to recognize CISG Article 40 – "The seller is not entitled to rely on the provisions of Article 38 (inspection) and 39 (notice) if the lack of conformity relates to the facts of which he knew or could not have been unaware" – which directly deals with this issue and fully resolves the question.[60]

VI. Concluding Remarks

In Italy the CISG plays an important role, which goes far beyond its sphere of application. It has gradually increased its cultural and paradigmatic value, as it has become more widely recognized as a legitimate source of law.[61] The CISG is now seen as a tool to aid in the interpretation of other international conventions, as well as EU law. In particular, Italian case law has made use of the CISG to clarify the meaning of particular provisions of the Brussels Convention of 1968[62] and Regulation EC 44/2001.[63] A number of Italian cases have relied on CISG Article 31 in the interpretation of the convention and the regulation.[64] To limit our analysis to the most recent judgments, deciding on the basis of this regulation rather than of the convention, the controversial issue

[59] Tribunale di Forlì, December 9, 2008.

[60] The decision by Tribunale di Forlì, id., is also remarkable as it confirms that within the system of values of the CISG, the remedy of avoidance should be considered an *extrema ratio*, because it implies the break of the relationship; despite the fact that Article 1455 C.c. uses the expression "of non scarce importance," which appears to be something less severe than the fundamental breach. However, Tribunale di Padova, January 11, 2005, claimed that there is a "correspondence of meanings" between the two formulas, which promotes a harmonic interpretation of the CISG together with domestic law.

[61] In European law – and consequently in Italian law – the CISG has repeatedly operated as a "tool box" even *de jure condendo*; it is well known that a large part of the *Acquis communautaire*, at least in contract law, has been built on the model of the CISG; some CISG rules have been transposed into EU law, such as EU Directive 1999/44/EC on certain aspects of the sale of consumer goods and associated guarantees, as well as proposed "Common European Sales Law," COM(2011) 635 final (at http://ec.europa.eu/justice/contract/files/common_sales_law/regulation_sales_law_en.pdf.).

[62] See Article 5, no. 1 ("on the jurisdiction and enforcement of judgments in civil and commercial matters"), ratified by italian Statute no. 804 of April 21, 1971.

[63] See Article 5, no. 1 ("on jurisdiction and the recognition and enforcement of judgments in civil and commercial matters"). The regulation transposed the provisions of the Brussels Convention and replaced it "among the member-States." See Reg. EC 44/2001 Article 68(1).

[64] See Tribunale di Rovereto, August 28, 2004, available at http://cisgw3.law.pace.edu/cases/040828i3.html (CISG could support the interpretation of Article 5, no. 1, Brussels Convention of 1968); Corte di Cassazione, January 3, 2007, no. 7, *Rivista di diritto internazionale privato e processuale* 1105 (2007), available at http://www.unilex.info/case.cfm?id=1164; id., September 27, 2006, no. 20887, *Giustizia civile I* 1393 (2007), available at http://www.unilex.info/case.cfm?id=1153; Tribunale di Padova, January 10, 2006; Corte di Cassazione, October 5, 2009, no. 21191, available at http://www.unilex.info/case.cfm?id=1502.

concerns the operative requirements of the special jurisdiction provided for under Reg. EC 44/2001 Article 5, especially (1)(b): given that we are dealing with sales, the exception to the general jurisdiction established by Reg. EC 44/2001 Article 2(1) is possible when the judge has jurisdiction in "the place . . . , situated in a member-State, where the goods have been or should have been delivered," that is to say, the place where the obligation has or should have been performed (*forum destinatae solutionis*). If the contract does not say anything on this point – which is rather common – we must adopt some criteria to clearly identify the legal place of delivery (also in the case in which delivery has not taken place and represents the controversial issue). In doing this, the judges, despite some dissenting opinions,[65] rely on CISG Article 31, which incorporates detailed and comprehensive provisions.[66]

In these cases, the CISG is used as a tool for interpretation. Provisions are interpreted according to the meaning suggested by one or more CISG rules, which are respected as a "cultural paradigm" rather than for the fact that they are applicable to the case *sub judice*.

The view of the CISG as a model law is so strong that Italian case law has used CISG provisions to interpret domestic law. The Italian Constitutional Court compared Civil Code Article 1510(2) (sale and transport of goods) with provisions in the CISG. It noted that the Civil Code provision was compatible with CISG Articles 31 and 67 to which "the seller is discharged from the obligation to deliver when he hands the goods to the carrier."[67] The court, in essence, was using common, internationally recognized values and principles to ensure the conformity of the Italian Civil Code with the constitution. In so doing, the court was pursuing a line of reason diametrically opposed to "homeward trend" reasoning. Instead, it pursued a "CISG-trend" analysis in the interpretation of domestic law.

---

[65] Tribunale di Rovereto, August 28, 2004, available at http://www.unilex.info/case.cfm?id=982 and at http://cisgw3.law.pace.edu/cases/040828i3.html, in accordance with which the CISG could support the interpretation of art. 5, no. 1, Brussels Convention of 1968, which had the same nature of international treaty – also to the effects of Article 31 Vienna Convention of 1969 (on the interpretation of treaties) – but it could not do the same for Reg. EC 44/2001 Article 5, no. 1, which has transposed it into EU law; it would neither be persuasive to adopt a text of uniform law to fill with meaning another one on conflict of laws. The two arguments are recalled (by the same judge) in Tribunale di Rovereto, August 24, 2006, but they remained a minority opinion, although they seem to be partially confirmed by the recent judgment of Corte di Cassazione, October 5,2009, no. 21191.

[66] Corte di Cassazione, January 3, 2007, no. 7, *Rivista di diritto internazionale privato e processuale* 1105 (2007), available at http://www.unilex.info/case.cfm?id=1164; id., September 27, 2006, no. 20887, *Giustizia civile I* 1393 (2007), available at http://www.unilex.info/case.cfm?id=1153; Tribunale di Padova, January 10, 2006; Tribunale di Verona, December 21, 2006, available at http://www.unilex.info/case.cfm?id=1176; in another sense, recently, Corte di Cassazione, October 5, 2009, no. 21191.

[67] Corte Costituzionale, November 19, 1992, no. 465, *Giurisprudenza costituzionale* 4191 (1992); Foro italiano I 3201 (1992); Giustizia civile I 313 (1993); *Diritto del commercio internazionale* 446 (1995), available at http://cisgw3.law.pace.edu/cases/921119i3.html.

25 The Nordic Countries

Jan Ramberg

I. Introduction: Article 92 and the Nordic Countries

Denmark, Finland, Norway, and Sweden made reservations under Article 92, which allows the opting out of Part II of the CISG (contract formation). Iceland, however, did not opt out of Part II when ratifying the CISG in 2000. The rationale for opting out was to avoid a "two-track" system for the formation of contracts domestically and internationally between the Nordic countries. However, the success of the CISG through its adoption by eighty countries and counting, and the rarity of countries making an Article 92 reservation, provides a powerful rationale for the withdrawal of the Article 92 declarations. The ability of other countries to have domestic and international sales laws makes the Article 92 reservations difficult to defend. There may, in the view of some traditionalists, be substantive reasons for avoiding the formation rules of the CISG, such as the principle under the Scandinavian Contracts Acts that an offer in writing is binding and valid for acceptance under a reasonable time even if the parties have failed to agree on a fixed time for acceptance.[1] However, the disadvantages of opting out of Part II CISG outweigh the differences in a few substantive rules. First, applicable law decides to what extent the Article 92 reservation is effective. If the law of a CISG state not having excluded Part II is chosen, then the formation rules according to Part II become applicable according to Article 1(1)(b) (private international law rules direct court to law of CISG country). A further problem arises when a CISG state has made an Article 95 reservation whereby Article 1(1)(b) jurisdiction is withdrawn. In such cases, the domestic law on formation of contracts of that state may become applicable.

As noted above, the Article 92 reservations made by the Scandinavian states has resulted in some unexpected uncertainty among the contracting parties. In order to avoid confusion, the International Chamber of Commerce request the national committees of the Article 92 reservation states to approach their respective Departments of Justice to withdraw their reservations. As a result, Denmark, Finland, and Sweden have withdre their Article 92 reservations in 2012.[2]

The scarcity of CISG cases from Scandinavian countries is due to a number of reasons. As noted above, the decision to opt out of Part II of the CISG likely reduced

---

[1] J. Ramberg, *The New Swedish Sales Law*, Centro di studi e ricerche di diritto comparato e straniero publ. 28 (Rome, 1997), 3, 4; J. Lookofsky, "CISG Case Law in Scandinavia," in *CISG Part II Conference, Stockholm, September 4–5, 2008*, Stockholm Centre of Commercial Law publ. 11 (Stockholm, 2009), 55.

[2] Lookofsky, "CISG Case Law in Scandinavia," 57.

the number of contract disputes covered by the CISG. In addition, most international contract disputes are resolved by arbitration.[3] Many of these arbitration decisions are not reported. Even when the dispute is litigated, some national reporting systems are inadequate. Traditionally, in Sweden, for example, only decisions by the Supreme Court are reported and so far there are no reported CISG cases at that level. A further difficulty follows from the choice made in Norway to incorporate the CISG into its domestic Sale of Goods Act, which makes it difficult particularly for parties from other countries to extricate the CISG rules applicable to a CISG contract.[4] The incorporation method used by Norway explains why Norway has not yet withdrawn its Article 92 reservation. Most of the Scandinavian CISG cases have dealt with the issues of nonconformity, notice of nonconformity, fundamental breach, and avoidance.

II. Nonconformity and Notice of Nonconformity

This section examines the relationship between the buyer's duty to inspect and to provide reasonable notice of nonconformity, as well as the determination of whether the notice of nonconformity was given in a timely fashion.

A. *Duty to Inspect and Notice of Nonconformity*

A Finnish court recognized a trade usage under CISG Article 9 to override the plain meaning interpretation of a contract provision relating to inspection rights.[5] A Finnish seller sold steel plates FOB Tallinn to a buyer in the United Arab Emirates. The buyer had the right to defer examination until the arrival of the goods at the destination. The steel plates had to conform to certain quality requirements. The court held that it followed from trade usage that the seller must be given an opportunity to be present when the buyer examined the plates. Since the seller was not given such an opportunity, the buyer was unable to make a claim for nonconformity.

A case at the Maritime and Commercial Court of Copenhagen concerned the sale of frozen mackerel.[6] Shortly after delivery, the buyer received numerous complaints from its customers. After some delay the authorities declared the mackerel unfit for human consumption. The buyer avoided the contract but lost the possibility to claim nonconformity because it had not performed an adequate inspection under CISG Article 38(2) as it had failed to thaw a sample of the mackerel to inspect. If this had been done, notice could have been given within a reasonable time according to Article 39(1). In a Finnish case, complaints by the buyer's customers were again deemed the basis for a reasonably timely notice. In a case before the Turku Court of Appeal of December 11, 1997, a Spanish seller had sold canned food to a Finnish buyer. Notice of nonconformity was considered timely when made subsequent to the buyer's customers' complaints. The buyer was awarded a ten percent price reduction and damages for loss of goodwill.

---

[3] Id., 48–54.
[4] Ramberg, *The New Swedish Sales Law*, 3–4.
[5] UNILEX Case No. 490 (Helsinki Court of Appeal), January 29, 1998.
[6] CLOUT Case No. 997, January 31, 2002.

B. *Timely Notice of Nonconformity*

The Supreme Court of Denmark heard a case involving a Danish seller of chrome-plated steel tubes for use by the German buyer in the manufacture of furniture.[7] The parties agreed that some of the tubes could be delivered in raw steel. But after the first delivery, the buyer placed no further orders. Instead of paying the seller, the buyer made a set off equal to the amount of the payment. It was decided that the buyer had given notice too late and the fact that the seller was aware of the nonconformity did not trigger the application of Article 40.

In another Danish case, an Italian seller sold petroleum check valves to a Danish buyer.[8] Cracks occurred in the valves caused by a chemical additive (MTBE) mixed with the petrol. The buyer claimed that the valves should be resistant to MTBE under CISG Article 35(2)(a). The court agreed with the buyer as it was shown that MTBE is a commonly used additive. The buyer was considered to have given proper notice according to Article 39 but no reference was made to Article 38. The seller was held liable to pay for the buyer's foreseeable loss related to replacing the valves.

A decision by the Copenhagen District Court involved a Belgium seller of a pony to a buyer in Sweden.[9] The court had jurisdiction because the pony was to be delivered in Denmark. The CISG was found applicable, as the pony was not only for personal use but was to be used for riding lessons satisfying the "commercial" goods requirement of CISG Article 2(a). Buyer's presale examination did not show any problems with the pony and the seller guaranteed it to be "fully fit." Soon after delivery the pony became lame. After timely notice the buyer avoided the sale and recovered damages under CISG Article 74. The Supreme Court of Finland also weighed in on the distinction between personal goods (not covered by the CISG under Article 2(a)) and the sale of commercial goods.[10] The case involved the sale of a log house from a Finnish seller to a German buyer. However, because the buyer agreed to become the sales agent in Germany for the Finnish seller, the court held that the log house was not only for personal use but also for professional or commercial use and therefore applied the CISG to the dispute.

The contract in a Finnish case provided for a fixed time for notice – within "one month after occurrence."[11] The buyer maintained that this was too harsh. Considering the practice established between the parties the court decided that notice had to be given as provided for in the contract, which the buyer failed to do. Nevertheless, the seller could not claim that the buyer had lost its right of action, as the seller had discussed with the buyer compensation for the nonconformity within the reasonable time of notice. However, the buyer had no right to avoid the contract, because notice of avoidance was not given within a reasonable time as required under CISG Article 49(2). The court further decided that the buyer could not claim damages exceeding the sum fixed in the contract. This matter was decided with the application of Finnish law and not by the CISG (Article 4). The rate of interest was also decided on the basis of Finnish law.

Another Finnish case dealt with the allocation of responsibility for conforming to government regulations of the goods in question. As a general rule, the seller is not

[7] CLOUT Case No. 996, April 4, 2004.
[8] CLOUT Case No. 994 (Vestre Landsret), December 21, 2004.
[9] CLOUT Case No. 992, October 19, 2007.
[10] CLOUT Case No. 843, October 14, 2005.
[11] UNILEX Case No. 939 (Turku Court of Appeal), April 12, 2002.

expected to know the regulations and standards of the buyer's country. This can change if the seller through trade usage or prior dealings knew of the regulations and standards. The case in question concerned a contract between a Spanish seller and a Finnish buyer of paprika powder for use in spice mixes.[12] The seller had imported the powder from suppliers and the buyer sold the spice mix to customers, but had to withdraw the mix from the market due to an EU Directive requiring labeling of irradiated products. As a result, the buyer had to pay compensation to its customers. The contract only provided that the powder should be treated with steam. The court considered that, although the directive came into force during the contract period and not before, the seller should have been aware of the requirement not to irradiate the powder in addition to the treatment with steam. The seller was, in fact, unaware that its suppliers had performed radiation treatment. The powder was deemed to be nonconforming under CISG Article 35 (2)(a). The key fact was that the regulation stemmed from an EU Directive and not a unique national law. Owing to the difficulties in examining the powder, the buyer was considered to have given timely notice.

C. *Prescription Period: Notice of Nonconformity*

A Swedish arbitral panel addressed the issue of the tolling or stopping the CISG's two-year prescription period for claiming nonconformity of goods.[13] A manufacturer in the United States sold a press to a joint venture in the People's Republic of China. The seller substituted a different component than the one specified in the design documents given to the buyer. No information was given to the buyer about the replacement. When the disassembled press was delivered to the buyer for reassembly the lock plate was installed improperly. The improperly installed plate significantly damaged the press. The damage did not become apparent until four years after the delivery of the press. The arbitral tribunal held that the seller was aware of the possibility that the lock plate would fail if not properly installed. Therefore, the seller according to CISG Article 40 was not entitled to rely on the two-year time limit of CISG Article 39. It follows from the reasoning of the majority of the tribunal that Article 40 was considered a general principle applying to contractual obligations by virtue of CISG Article 7(2). This may be interpreted as a departure from Article 6, which permits an exclusion of Article 40. However, such an exclusion may be considered a failure to observe good faith and fair dealing.[14]

III. Avoidance and Fundamental Breach

This section examines the determination of when a nonconformity amounts to fundamental breach. It also examines the context when the parties may exercise the remedy of avoidance. The Supreme Court of Denmark decided a case involving a Danish seller of imported Japanese motorcycles and a German buyer.[15] The German buyer bought the

---

[12] Decision of May 5, 2005, Turku Court of Appeal.

[13] CLOUT Case No. 237 (Arbitration Institute of the Stockholm Chamber of Commerce), June 6, 1998.

[14] J. Ramberg and J. Herre, *Internationella Köplagen (CISG)* (Stockholm, 2009), 280–3; A. Garro, "The Buyer's 'Safety Valve' under Article 40: What Is the Seller Supposed to Know and When?," *J. of Law and Commerce* 253 et seq. (2005), and C. Baasch Andersen, "Exceptions to the Notification Rule – Are They Uniformly Interpreted?," 9 *Vindobona J. of Int'l Commercial Law & Arbitration* 117 (2005).

[15] CLOUT Case No. 993, November 10, 2007.

motorcycles for resale to German buyers. Due to a currency fluctuation to the detriment of the buyer, the parties attempted to renegotiate the contract price. The buyer was not satisfied with the proposed change and therefore did not pay and withdrew a guarantee for payment. The seller avoided the contract and the Supreme Court confirmed that there was a right of avoidance. The majority of the Supreme Court reduced the damages accorded to the seller by the lower courts, because the loss was deemed to be excessive as the cover sales had not been prudently made.

A Finnish court rejected the ability of a trade usage to determine if there was a fundamental breach for purposes of claiming avoidance.[16] The case concerned the sale of animal food from a Finnish seller to a German buyer. A trade usage required a delivery to be within eight weeks for it to be considered a reasonable delivery. The seller did not deliver the animal food until fourteen weeks had passed. The court held that such a delay is not considered a substantial detriment required for a fundamental breach under CISG Article 25 and, therefore, the buyer was not entitled to avoid the contract under CISG Article 49(1)(a).

An arbitral tribunal allowed a buyer to withdraw its avoidance and replace it by demanding cure of the non-conformity. The buyer obtained compensation for its costs, which exceeded the 15 percent of the contract price specified in the contract. The arbitrator determined that the validity of the limitation provision was an issue for Danish law under CISG Article 4. Under Danish law, the arbitrator ruled that such a provision in a standard form contract was unenforceable.

A case before the Helsinki Court of Appeal dealt with the interrelationship between nonconformity and the seller's right to cure.[17] The case concerned a sale of skin care products between a Swiss seller and a Finnish buyer. There were two orders, the second order coming almost one year after the first. Nonetheless, the products were deemed to be nonconforming under CISG Article 35. The seller's request for a right to cure was rejected because the nonconformity constituted a fundamental breach and the buyer would suffer unreasonable inconvenience if it were forced to wait for the cure.

[16] CLOUT Case No. 797 (Turku Court of Appeal), February 18, 1997.
[17] See UNILEX Case No. 491, June 30, 1998.

26 The CISG in Southeastern Europe

*Milena Djordjević and Vladimir Pavić**

I. Introduction

Before engaging in an analysis of the application of the United Nations Convention on Contracts for the International Sale of Goods (CISG) in the Balkans, or, more appropriately, Southeastern Europe, it would be prudent to define what Southeastern Europe encompasses. In geographic terms, "the Balkans" encompass the countries that lie within the boundaries of the Balkan Peninsula – an area of Southeastern Europe surrounded by three seas: the Adriatic Sea to the west, the Mediterranean Sea (including the Ionian and Aegean seas) to the south, and the Black Sea to the east; its northern boundary is marked by the Danube, Sava, and Kupa rivers. Countries whose borders lie entirely within the Balkan Peninsula are Albania, Bosnia and Herzegovina, Bulgaria, Greece, FYR Macedonia,[1] and Montenegro. Countries that have a significant portion of their land located within the Peninsula are Croatia and Serbia. Countries that have only a small portion of their land located within the Peninsula are Romania, Slovenia, and Turkey. This chapter will refer to all these countries as the part of Southeastern Europe within the boundaries of the Balkan Peninsula.

Although all of the abovementioned countries are signatories to the CISG,[2] not all of them will be covered in this chapter. Namely, Albania and Turkey have only recently acceded to the CISG and, according to relevant international databases on CISG cases,[3]

* The authors express their gratitude to Professor Gašo Knežević, the President of the Serbian Foreign Trade Court of Arbitration, for providing access to the court's archives and for his assistance in conducting this research. Special gratitude goes to our colleagues Marko Jovanović, Uroš Živković, and Sonja Srećković for their thorough editing of this chapter.

[1] The term "Macedonian" will be used in this chapter to designate parties and laws originating from the FYR Macedonia.

[2] The Socialist Federative Republic of Yugoslavia (SFRY) signed the CISG on April 11, 1980, and ratified it on December 27, 1984. The Law on Ratification of the CISG was published in the Official Gazette of the SFRY, MU 10/84 of December 31, 1984. The instrument of ratification was deposited with the Secretary General of the United Nations on March 27, 1985. Consequently, the CISG has been in force in the former Yugoslav republics (Bosnia and Herzegovina, Croatia, Macedonia, Montenegro, Serbia, and Slovenia), now independent states, from the date it entered into force, January 1, 1988. The CISG entered into force in other Southeastern European countries as follows: Bulgaria on August 1, 1991, Romania on June 1, 1992, and Greece on February 1, 1999. Albania and Turkey more recently ratified the CISG. The CISG entered into force in Albania on June 1, 2010, and in Turkey on August 1, 2011. See http://www.uncitral.org/uncitral/en/uncitral_texts/sale_goods/1980CISG_status.html (accessed September 5, 2011).

[3] See www.unilex.info; www.cisg.law.pace.edu; www.cisg-online.ch (accessed December 15, 2011). It should be noted that there are CISG cases that exist but are not accessible through the major international CISG databases. For example, there are likely dozens of CISG cases existing in Serbian courts'

419

there are no available CISG cases in these countries.[4] Fortunately, the Pace Institute's joint efforts with Queen Mary University on translating the CISG cases into English[5] have made more cases from these jurisdictions available to the global community. The Pace CISG Database lists 111 judgments and arbitral awards – 12 from Bulgaria, 9 from Croatia, 13 from Greece, 1 from Montenegro, 1 from Romania, 70 from Serbia, and 5 from Slovenia.[6] This chapter also makes use of more than 100 unpublished arbitral awards issued by the Serbian Foreign Trade Court of Arbitration at the Serbian Chamber of Commerce (Serbian FTCA). Two arbitral cases from Macedonia were provided by the Deutsche Gesellschaft für Technische Zusammenarbeit (GTZ) GmbH (German technical cooperation or GTZ).[7]

In total, this chapter is based upon a review of 200 cases, which dealt with a wide variety of sales contracts and issues of law. The subjects covered in this review include interpretation of the CISG; formation, modification, and interpretation of international sales contracts; nonconformity of goods; avoidance; damages; exemption from liability; and preservation of goods.

II. Interpretation of the CISG and Contracts

The correct application of the CISG often depends on courts and arbitral tribunals properly applying the interpretive methodology found in CISG Article 7. Furthermore, in order for the CISG to be properly applied in contract interpretation, apart from the terms of the contract, proper regard is given to the overall communications and practices between the parties, as well as the context of the transaction (surrounding circumstances). For the purposes of contract interpretation, a judge or an arbitrator should resort to the rules contained in Article 8 on contractual intent and to business practices and relevant usages, as required by Article 9.

A. *Autonomous Interpretation*

Article 7 of the CISG requires reading the CISG through an international lens even when expressions employed by the CISG are textually the same as expressions which

---

archives. See Vladimir Pavić and Milena Djordjević, "Application of the CISG before the Foreign Trade Court of Arbitration at the Serbian Chamber of Commerce: Looking Back at the Latest 100 Cases," 28 *J. of L. & Commerce* 1, 3–5 (2009) (hereafter referred to as CISG in Serbia).

[4] This is likely to change soon because of the reported increase of frequency with which large law firms in Albania insert the CISG as the choice of law in their contracts. See Fabian von Schlabrendorff, "A Report on a GTZ Project, Undertaken with the Support of UNCITRAL, on Implementation of the United Nations Convention on the International Sale of Goods and of the System of International Commercial Arbitration in Southeast Europe," 28 (2011), available at http://www.uncitral.org/pdf/english/whats_new/2011_02/GTZ_UNCITRAL_Southeast_Europe.pdf (GTZ Report).

[5] See The Queen Mary Case Translation Program, available at http://www.cisg.law.pace.edu/cisg/text/queenmary.html

[6] See Electronic Library on International Commercial Law and the CISG, available at http://www.cisg.law.pace.edu/cisg/text/casecit.htm (accessed December 15, 2011).

[7] According to the country reports on the CISG, prepared under the GTZ-UNCITRAL Project on Implementation of the CISG and of the System of International Commercial Arbitration in Southeast Europe, in June 2008, there are no cases available where the CISG was applied by Albanian and Bosnian courts or in arbitration tribunals. On the other hand, the Macedonian report prepared by Professor Arsen Janevski provides information regarding two arbitral cases in Macedonia where the CISG was applied. On the basis of all individual country reports (Albania, Bosnia and Herzegovina, Croatia, Macedonia, Montenegro, and Serbia) submitted to the GTZ, a joint report was prepared and published in 2011. See GTZ Report at 28.

have a specific meaning within a particular legal system. The rationale of Article 7(1) is to ensure the autonomous interpretation of CISG rules, free of the concepts and meanings of similar rules, in particular, domestic laws. This mandate for autonomous interpretation has been repeatedly confirmed by doctrine[8] and case law.[9] Unfortunately, there have been numerous cases worldwide and in Southeastern Europe that have not applied the CISG's interpretive methodology.[10] Instead, they cited parallel domestic law provisions along with citing the CISG.[11] Fortunately, there are numerous well-reasoned decisions that have properly used CISG interpretive methodology. An example is the Greek *Bullet-proof vests case*, which observed that:

The interpretation of the CISG by national courts, by order of the provision of Article 7(1) of the CISG, must be made "autonomously," through its uniqueness and originality thereof as a text, i.e., through the system of its provisions and general principles and free of any ethnocentric approaches, "unique" terms of domestic law, and [free] of methods that usually follow for the interpretation of domestic provisions, since otherwise that may result in the application of institutions and provisions of domestic laws and furthermore, in undesired lack of uniformity in its application.[12]

---

[8] See also Michael G. Bridge, "The Bifocal World of International Sales: Vienna and Non-Vienna," in *Making Commercial Law: Essays in Honour of Roy Goode* (ed. Ross Cranston) (Oxford: Clarendon Press, 1997), 277, 288; Franco Ferrari, "Have the Dragons of Uniform Sales Law Been Tamed? Ruminations on the CISG's Autonomous Interpretation by Courts," in *Sharing International Commercial Law across National Boundaries, Festschrift for Albert H. Kritzer on the Occasion of His Eightieth Birthday* (ed. Camilla B. Andersen and Ulrich G. Schroeter) (London: Wildy, Simmonds & Hill Publishing, 2008), 134, 139–46.

[9] See *American Mint LLC v. GOSoftware, Inc.*, January 6, 2006, No. 05-CV-650, 2006 WL 42090 (M.D. Pa. 2006), available at http://cisgw3.law.pace.edu/cases/060106u1.html; Oberlandesgericht Karlsruhe, Germany, June 25, 1997, available at http://cisgw3.law.pace.edu/cisg/text/draft/970625case.html; Bundesgerichtshof, Germany, April 3, 1996, available at http://cisgw3.law.pace.edu/cases/960403g1.html; Richteramt Laufen, Switzerland, May 7, 1993, available at http://cisgw3.law.pace.edu/cases/930507s1.html.

[10] See *Schmitz-Werke GmbH & Co. v. Rockland Industries, Inc.*, 37 Fed. Appx. 687 (4th Cir. 2003), available at http://www.cisg.law.pace.edu/cases/020621u1.html; *Delchi Carrier, S.p.A. v. Rotorex Corp.*, 71 F.3d 1024 (2d Cir. 1995), available at http://cisgw3.law.pace.edu/cases/940909u1.html; Djakhongir Saidov, "Cases on CISG Decided in the Russian Federation," 7 *Vindobona J. of International Commercial Law & Arbitration* 1, 14 (2003).

[11] See, e.g., Serbian FTCA Award No. T-6/10, November 30, 2010 (invoking Article 54 CISG and Articles 516 and 518 LCT when deciding that the buyer is obliged to pay the price), available at http://cisgw3.law.pace.edu/cases/101130sb.html; Serbian FTCA Award No. T-12/09, November 1, 2010 (buyer is obliged to pay for the unpaid portion of the price), available at http://cisgw3.law.pace.edu/cases/101101sb.html; Appellate Court of Montenegro in Podgorica, Montenegro, Mal. Br 118/04, February 20, 2007 (Article 262 LCT as the basis for granting the seller's claim for purchase price while at the same time recognizing the CISG application by invoking the Article 31(a) CISG while explaining when seller's obligation to deliver the goods is to be deemed performed), available at http://cisgw3.law.pace.edu/cases/070220mo.html; Court of Appeals of Thessalonika 2923/2006, Greece (Dionysios P. Flambouras, ed.) (Article 516 of the Greek Civil Code in support of buyer's right to damages after thorough examination of the CISG provision), available at http://cisgw3.law.pace.edu/cases/070001gr.html; Higher Court in Ljubljana, 1 Cpg 1305/2003, Slovenia, December 14, 2005 (Article 81 CISG provides for the same consequences as Article 132 of the Slovenian Obligations Act regarding the avoidance of contract), available at http://cisgw3.law.pace.edu/cases/051214sv.html; Bulgarian Chamber of Commerce and Industry, Arbitral award, Case No. 14/98, November 30, 1998 (citing provisions of Article 55 CISG and Article 326(2) of the Bulgarian Trade Law when upholding the contract where the price was not clearly defined), available at http://cisgw3.law.pace.edu/cases/981130bu.html.

[12] See Multi-Member Court of First Instance of Athens Decision 4505/2009, Greece (Dionysios P. Flambouras, ed.), available at http://cisgw3.law.pace.edu/cases/094505gr.html.

An example of the use of an improper interpetive methodology is a decision of an arbitral tribunal in Bulgaria where the arbitrators did not award the seller interest on sums owed by the buyer from the date the debt was due.[13] In the opinion of the tribunal, a formal notice for payment by the seller is necessary to obtain interest under the CISG. Since the seller did not make formal request for payment, the tribunal ruled that it could not obtain interest for delay of payment for the period of four years. Although such notice is required under Bulgarian law, the right to interest under the CISG does not depend on formal notice to the debtor.[14]

B. *Uniformity of Application*

Diverging from the approach of autonomous interpretation reduces the likelihood of uniformity of application due to the creation of variant, national law-biased interpretations.[15] Article 7(1) of the CISG is designed to ensure uniform application of the CISG and foster legal certainty for parties involved in sales transactions. The practice of courts and arbitral tribunals of looking at CISG case law, including foreign court decisions, is one gauge in determining a court or tribunal's use of an existing consensus when rendering a decision.[16]

---

[13] Bulgarian Chamber of Commerce and Industry, Arbitral award, Case No. 11/1996, February 12, 1998, available at http://cisgw3.law.pace.edu/cases/980212bu.html.

[14] See Klaus Bacher in *Commentary on the UN Convention on the International Sale of Goods (CISG)*, 3rd ed. (ed. P. Schlechtriem and Ingebrog Schwenzer) (New York: Oxford University Press, 2010), Article 78, 1053; John Gotanda in *UN Convention on Contracts for the International Sale of Goods (CISG) Commentary* (ed. Stefan Kröll, Loukas Mistelis, and Pilar Perales Viscasillas) (Munich: C.H. Beck/Hart/Nomos, 2011), Article 78, 1047. Unlike the Bulgarian tribunal, Greek courts have properly noted that under the CISG the period when interest accrues does not depend on a notice being served to the promisor of the monetary obligation. Therefore, the interest is due regardless of any damage sustained by the promisee of the monetary obligation. See Multi-Member Court of First Instance of Athens Decision 4505/2009, Greece (Dionysios P. Flambouras, ed.), available at http://cisgw3.law.pace.edu/cases/094505gr.html; Single-Member Court of First Instance of Thessalonika 43945/2007, Greece (Dionysios P. Flambouras, ed.), available at http://cisgw3.law.pace.edu/cases/080002gr.html.

[15] See Camilla B. Andersen, *Uniform Application of the International Sales Law. Understanding Uniformity, the Global Jurisconsultorium and Examination and Notification Provisions of the CISG* (AH Alphen aan den Rijn: Kluwer Law International, 2007), 47; Michael G. Bridge, "A Commentary on Articles 1–13 and 78," in *The Draft UNCITRAL Digest and Beyond: Cases, Analysis and Unresolved Issues in the U.N. Sales Convention* (ed. Franco Ferrari, Harry Flechtner, and Ronald A. Brand) (Munich: Sellier ELP, 2004), 235, 250; Franco Ferrari, "Have the Dragons of Uniform Sales Law Been Tamed? Ruminations on the CISG's Autonomous Interpretation by Courts," in Andersen and Schroeter, *Festschrift Kritzer*, 149–50; Peter Schlechtriem *Commentary on the UN Convention on the International Sale of Goods (CISG)*, 2nd ed. (ed. Peter Schlechtriem and Ingeborg Schwenzer) (Oxford: Oxford University Press: Oxford 2005), Article 7, 96–102; Harry Flechtner, "The Several Texts of the CISG in a Decentralized System: Observations on Translations, Reservations and Other Challenges to the Uniformity Principle in Article 7(1)," 17 *J. of Law & Commerce* 187 (1998); John Honnold, "The Sales Convention in Action – Uniform International Words: Uniform Application?," 8 *J. of Law & Commerce* 207, 208 (1988); Susanne Cook, "The Need for Uniform Interpretation of the 1980 United Nations Convention on Contracts for the International Sale of Goods," 50 *U. of Pittsburgh L. Rev.* 197 (1988).

[16] For the most elaborate analyses of foreign case law, see Tribunale di Vigevano, Italy, July 12, 2000, available at http://cisgw3.law.pace.edu/cases/000712i3.html (citing forty foreign decisions regarding Article 7(1) of the CISG). See also Tribunale di Padova, Italy, February 25, 2004, available at http://cisgw3.law.pace.edu/cases/040225i3.html; Tribunale di Rimini, Italy, November 11, 2002, available at http://cisgw3.law.pace.edu/cases/021126i3.html.

Although invoking foreign case law and doctrine is rare in Southeastern Europe,[17] the practice of the Serbian FTCA contains several awards in which reference was made to foreign court decisions and arbitral awards. In the *Mineral water and wooden pallets case*, the sole arbitrator used one Hungarian and two German court decisions to support the position that the CISG is not applicable to distribution contracts, but only to the individual sales transactions concluded within the framework of a distribution.[18] This position was reaffirmed in the *Medicaments case*, invoking decisions from the same jurisdictions on the same issue.[19]

The *Medicaments case* quoted eight foreign decisions and arbitral awards from five different countries. It is an example of the Serbian FTCA tribunals' adherence to the mandate of Article 7(1). Tribunal was faced with a number issues, including CISG's applicability to distribution contracts, a choice of law clause, and deciding on the appropriate interest rate to calculate damages. In doing so, the arbitrator noted that foreign judicial and arbitral cases needed to be taken into account "for the purpose of achieving uniform application of the CISG, pursuant to Article 7(1) of the CISG."[20] In the *Milk packaging equipment case*, the arbitrator referred to an Australian court decision when deciding on the effect of a *pactum reservati dominii* clause found in a leasing contract.[21] The *Timber case* undertook an assessment of "widely accepted comparative practice" in determining the proper form of the notice of avoidance (filing of the claim was sufficient notice of avoidance).[22] However, in this case, unlike the previously quoted cases, an explicit reference to particular foreign decisions was omitted. Instead, the tribunal only noted that comparative practice is to be consulted in accordance with Article 7(1) of the CISG.[23]

The tribunal in the *Mobile Shear Baler case* expressly quoted not only the Serbian arbitral award in the *Timber case*, but also the Australian court decision *Roder v. Rosedown* when holding that the notice of avoidance requirement (Article 26 CISG) can be satisfied through the wording of the statement of claim.[24] The same tribunal relied on an ICC award when holding that the CISG does not govern the enforceability of penalty clauses.[25] Finally, the *Agricultural products and cereals case* makes reference to the UNCITRAL Digest and cases from the Pace CISG Database when concluding that the choice of law of a contracting state does not amount to exclusion of the CISG.[26] In addition, the award

---

[17] Marko Baretić and Saša Nikšić, "Croatia," in *The CISG and Its Impact on National Legal Systems* (ed. Franco Ferrari) (Munich: Sellier ELP, 2008), 102; Eleni Zervogianni, "Greece," in id., 167.

[18] Serbian FTCA Award No. T-25/06, November 13, 2007, available at http://cisgw3.law.pace.edu/cases/071113sb.html.

[19] Serbian FTCA award No. T-8/08, January 28, 2009, available at http://cisgw3.law.pace.edu/cases/090128sb.html.

[20] Id.

[21] Serbian FTCA Award No. T-4/05, July 15, 2008, available at http://cisgw3.law.pace.edu/cases/080715sb.html.

[22] Serbian FTCA Award No. T-08/06, October 1, 2007, available at http://cisgw3.law.pace.edu/cases/071001sb.html.

[23] Id.

[24] Serbian FTCA Award No. T-10/09, May 31, 2010, available at http://cisgw3.law.pace.edu/cases/100531sb.html.

[25] Id.

[26] Serbian FTCA Award No. T-5/09, May 6, 2010, available at http://cisgw3.law.pace.edu/cases/100506sb.html.

makes reference to foreign case law on the issue of applicable interest rates. In explaining the reasons for his decision, the arbitrator stated:

> Since the objective of the Vienna Convention, stated in the preamble, is the adoption of uniform rules which govern contracts for the international sale of goods and removal of the legal obstacles in international trade and promotion and development of international trade, Article 7 paragraph 2 offers the basis to determine the interest rate "autonomously, in accordance with the general principles the Convention is based on."
>
> Although the Convention does not [expressly] determine such [all its] general principles, it is understood in contemporary legal theory and practice that they can be deduced from the aims and analysis of the individual provisions of the CISG and their place in the system established by the Convention.[27]

C. *Good Faith*

Article 7(1) imposes an obligation on tribunals and courts to promote the observance of good faith in international trade. The correct application of this mandate of the CISG has been the subject of debate – whether the duty of good faith solely relates to the interpretation of the CISG or whether it can be extended to the conduct of the parties.[28] The judges and arbitrators in Southeast Europe have, in at least five decisions, adhered to the latter view.

In the *White crystal sugar case*, the tribunal examined the conduct of the seller and noted that the seller (who delivered the goods of non-Yugoslav origin, contrary to the contractual requirement, and submitted to the buyer flawed EUR 1 certificate) "has not acted in accordance with the good faith principle, which represents a cornerstone of the entire corpus of modern legislation, especially the legislative instruments which the tribunal has identified as applicable rules in this case (CISG, Law on Contracts and Torts, UNIDROIT Principles on International Commercial Contracts and European Principles of Contract Law)."[29] In the *Siemens Telephone Booths case*, the tribunal also qualified the party's behavior during the performance of the contract as contrary to the principle of good faith, where the buyer knew that the seller delivered the goods at a place different than the one contractually stipulated, and undertook certain actions in regard to such goods (concluded contracts for reexport of goods), yet at the time the dispute arose, it contested that the misdelivery constituted a fundamental breach of the contract.[30]

---

[27] Id. The same reasoning was provided in the Serbian FTCA Award No. T-6/08, October 19, 2009, available at http://cisgw3.law.pace.edu/cases/091019sb.html.

[28] See Troy Keily, "Good Faith and the Vienna Convention on Contracts for the International Sale of Goods (CISG)," 3 *Vindobona Journal of International Commercial Law & Arbitration* 15, 15–40 (1999); Paul J. Powers, "Defining the Undefinable: Good Faith and the United Nations Convention on Contracts for the International Sale of Goods," 18 *J. of Law & Commerce* 332 passim (1999); Benedict C. Sheehy, "Good Faith in the CISG: Interpretation Problems in Article 7" (Bepress Legal Series, Working Paper, 339, 2004); Disa Sim, "The Scope and Application of Good Faith in the Vienna Convention on Contracts for the International Sale of Goods," in *Review of the Convention on Contracts for the International Sale of Goods* (ed. Michael Maggi) (The Hague: Kluwer Law International, 2004), 19.

[29] Serbian FTCA Award No. T-9/07, January 23, 2008, available at http://cisgw3.law.pace.edu/cases/080123sb.html.

[30] Serbian FTCA Award No. T-15/06, January 28, 2008, available at http://cisgw3.law.pace.edu/cases/080128sb.html.

Similarly, in the *Mobile Shear Baler case*, the tribunal found that the seller's failure to deliver the agreed machine to the buyer, while at the same time continuously promising delivery and requesting further extensions, constituted behavior contrary to the principle of good faith, as it was obvious from the seller's behavior that it never had honest intentions to perform.[31] Finally, in a Greek case the importance of good faith principle was strongly emphasized, as the court held that this principle "ought to govern international trade,"[32] and a Serbian case held that the parties have a duty of cooperation stemming from the principle of diligence and good faith.[33]

It has to be stressed that despite the occasional references to the good faith principle that "obliges" the parties to act in a certain way, in no case examined was the nonobservance of the general principle of good faith sufficient in itself to trigger a remedy for breach of contract. Rather, remedies for not adhering to this "general principle" were available only if prescribed by specific rule contained elsewhere in the CISG.

D. *Gap Filling*

Article 7(2) of the CISG sets out a basic methodology for filling the gaps in the CISG. The first step is to determine whether the underlying issue falls within the *lacuna praeter legem*, issues to which the CISG applies but which it does not expressly resolve, or *lacuna intra legem*, issues not governed by the CISG.[34] If the gap is *intra legem*, the recourse is to be made to the law to which the private international law points.[35] If the gap is *praeter legem*, the CISG requires judges and arbitrators first to examine whether there are general principles underlying the CISG that could resolve the issue.[36] The resort to domestic law via means of private international law is to be regarded as *ultima ratio*.

Decisions from Southeastern Europe have routinely avoided solution through the implication of general (implied) principles in cases of *lacuna praeter legem* and instead have gone prematurely to domestic law provisions. This has been the case in determing interest rates[37] and the form of the notice of nonconformity (Article 39(1) CISG).

---

[31] Serbian FTCA Award No. T-10/09, May 31, 2010, available at http://cisgw3.law.pace.edu/cases/100531sb.html. See also Serbian FTCA Award No. T-6/10, Nov. 30, 2010, available at http://cisgw3.law.pace.edu/cases/101130sb.html.

[32] Single-Member Court of First Instance Larissa 165/2005, Greece, excerpt from Eleni Zervogianni, "Greece," in Ferrari, *CISG Impact*, 172–4, available at http://cisgw3.law.pace.edu/cases/050165gr.html.

[33] Serbian FTCA Award No. T-3/92, July 12, 1994, available at http://cisgw3.law.pace.edu/cases/940712sb.html.

[34] See Camilla Andersen, "General Principles of the CISG – Generally Impenetrable?," in Andersen and Schroeter, *Festschrift Kritzer*, 13; Franco Ferrari, "Interpretation of the Convention and Gap-Filling: Article 7," in Ferrari et al., *Draft Digest*, 157–71; Anthony J. McMahon, "Differentiating between Internal and External Gaps in the U.N. Convention on Contracts for the International Sale of Goods: A Proposed Method for Determining 'Governed by' in the Context of Article 7(2)," 44 *Columbia J. of Transnational L.* 992 *passim* (2006).

[35] CISG, Articles 4 and 5, list some examples of matters not governed by the CISG.

[36] CISG, Article 7(2). See also Ulrich Magnus, "Die allgemeinen Grundsätze im UN-Kaufrecht," 59 *Rabels Zeitschrift* 492–3 (1995) (containing the most extensive list of CISG general principles), translated at http://www.cisg.law.pace.edu/cisg/text/magnus.html.

[37] There are several examples where Article 7(2) has been invoked with regard to determination of applicable interest rates, but the issue was finally resolved under the law applicable by virtue of private international law. For example, in the protective steel fence case the tribunal noted that the applicable interest rate is a "well known" legal gap within the CISG that should be resolved, as Article 7(2) stipulates, either with recourse to general principles or, in their absence, in accordance with the law applicable by virtue

Similarly, the principle of "no formality" (no writing) requirement of Articles 11 and 29 has been neglected in at least one award.[38] Finally, in a case decided by a Bulgarian arbitral tribunal, the issue of contributory negligence was said to be an issue governed but not expressly settled in the CISG and that the issue should be settled in accordance with the otherwise applicable law.[39]

In sum, nine Serbian awards made express reference to the methodology suggested by Article 7(2) of the CISG. Eight of them did so when dealing with the issue of the determination of interest rates.[40] However, invoking Article 7(2) methodology did not always result in preventing recourse to readily available domestic solutions. For instance, in the *Aluminum case*, the award correctly starts by listing (express and implied) general principles of the CISG, such as good faith, party autonomy, foreseeability, and exchange of information and cooperation.[41] Yet the arbitrator then invoked relevant provisions of Serbian law. In contrast, a more recent award noted that "the matter of interest rate is governed but not settled under the CISG" and that, consequently, "there is no need to examine [Seller]'s request in the light of any national law, but rather examine whether it is within the checks provided in Article 7 of the CISG."[42] The arbitrator invoked the principle of full compensation, which resulted in the application of an "interest rate, which is regularly used for savings, such as short-term deposits in the first class banks at the place of payment (Serbia), as this represents rate on a relatively riskless investment."[43] The need for autonomous determination of interest rates by application of CISG general principles was also underlined in the *Agricultural products and cereals case*.[44] The general principle relating to the obligation to pay the purchase price and failure to comply with such an obligation is, according to this award, based on the implied general principle of

---

of international private law rules. The tribunal made recourse to the otherwise applicable domestic law. See Serbian FTCA, Award No. T-8/10, March 2, 2011 (unpublished). See also Higher Court in Ljubljana, 1 Cpg 1305/2003, Slovenia, December 14, 2005, available at http://cisgw3.law.pace.edu/cases/051214sv.html; High Commercial Court XXVIII Pž-2728/4–3, Croatia, July 26, 2005, abstract by Davor Babić, available at http://cisgw3.law.pace.edu/cases/050726cr.html; High Commercial Court XXVIII Pž-5580/03–3, Croatia, September 26, 2006, abstract by Davor Babić, available at http://cisgw3.law.pace.edu/cases/060926cr.html; High Commercial Court Pž-7602/03–3, Croatia, October 24, 2006, abstract by Davor Babić, available at http://cisgw3.law.pace.edu/cases/061024cr.html; Bulgarian Chamber of Commerce and Industry, Arbitral award, Case No. 33/98, March 12, 2001, available at http://cisgw3.law.pace.edu/cases/010312bu.html.

[38] See Serbian FTCA Award No. T-2/00, December 9 2002, available at http://cisgw3.law.pace.edu/cases/021209sb.html. See infra Part III.

[39] Bulgarian Chamber of Commerce and Industry, Arbitral award, Case No. 56/1995, April 24, 1996, available at http://cisgw3.law.pace.edu/cases/960424bu.html.

[40] Unlike these cases, the majority of the Serbian FTCA awards take the stance that the issue of interest rate is not governed by the CISG, or that it is to be determined on the basis of *lex mercatoria*. See Pavić and Djordjević, "CISG in Serbia," 51–8.

[41] This is the same award where the principle of lack of form was ignored. See Serbian FTCA Award No. T-2/00, December 9 2002, available at http://cisgw3.law.pace.edu/cases/021209sb.html

[42] Serbian FTCA Award No. T-08/08, January 28, 2009, available at http://cisgw3.law.pace.edu/cases/090128sb.html.

[43] Id.

[44] Serbian FTCA Award No. T-5/09, May 6, 2010, available at http://cisgw3.law.pace.edu/cases/100506sb.html. The same line of reasoning was provided in Serbian FTCA Award No. T-23/08 November 10, 2009, available at http://cisgw3.law.pace.edu/cases/091110sb.html; Serbian FTCA Award No. T-6/08, October 19, 2009, available at http://cisgw3.law.pace.edu/cases/091019sb.html. See also Serbian FTCA Award No. T-23/06–13, September 15, 2008, available at http://cisgw3.law.pace.edu/cases/080915sb.html.

full compensation. The principle of full compensation regarding the determination of relevant interest rates was also invoked in two other cases.[45]

The Greek courts have split on the issue of determining and applying relevant interest rates. Some courts resolved the issue under the law applicable by virtue of private international law,[46] another two attempted to solve it on the basis of the general principles of the CISG.[47] One of the courts noted that: "A basic principle of the CISG is its uniform interpretation. In order to achieve this result, the issue in question should be decided on the basis of an independent criterion."[48] The court found such a criterion in the principle of good faith, and on this basis decided that the relevant interest rate is the rate in the country of the creditor (it was the buyer who claimed damages).[49]

A newer method of interpreting the CISG, found in the case law, is the use of the UNIDROIT Principles for International Commercial Contracts (PICC) as a means for interpreting the CISG or filling gaps in the CISG. In the *White crystal sugar case*, the arbitral tribunal applied the CISG, but also used the PICC and the Principles of European Contract Law (PECL) as "part of *lex mercatoria*."[50] The tribunal emphasized that these "general rules for international commercial contracts may be used for interpretation and gap-filling of uniform international rules . . . and provisions of national law."[51] Invoking PECL and PICC was not only erroneous[52] but also unnecessary, given that the disputed issue – assessment of damages – is expressly dealt with in the CISG.[53]

---

[45] Serbian FTCA Award No. T-11/09, July 9, 2010, available at http://cisgw3.law.pace.edu/cases/100709sb. html; Serbian FTCA Award No. T-7/07, August 19, 2008, available at http://cisgw3.law.pace.edu/cases/ 080819sb.html.

[46] See Single-Member Court of First Instance of Thessaloniki 43945/2007, Greece (Dionysios P. Flambouras, ed.), available at http://cisgw3.law.pace.edu/cases/080002gr.html; Multi-Member Court of First Instance of Thessaloniki 22513/2003, Greece, excerpt by Eleni Zervogianni, "Greece," in Ferrari, *CISG Impact*, 172–4, available at http://cisgw3.law.pace.edu/cases/030513gr.html.

[47] See Single-Member Court of First Instance Larissa 165/2005, Greece, excerpt by Zervogianni, "Greece," in Ferrari, *CISG Impact*, 172–4; Single-Member Court of First Instance Athens 1314/2000, Greece (Dionysios P. Flambouras, ed.), available at http://cisgw3.law.pace.edu/cases/000308gr.html.

[48] See Single-Member Court of First Instance Larissa 165/2005, Greece, excerpt by Zervogianni, "Greece," in Ferrari, *CISG Impact*, 172–4.

[49] Id.

[50] Serbian FTCA Award No. T-9/07, January 23, 2008, available at http://cisgw3.law.pace.edu/cases/ 080123sb.html.

[51] Id.

[52] It is important to emphasize that the application of the PICC in arbitral practice worldwide has occurred only in one of the following situations: (1) when the parties have specifically called for their application (white crystal sugar case); (2) when the parties have otherwise called for the application of transnational commercial law; (3) when the PICC offers a solution to an issue that cannot be resolved under the applicable law; and (4) when international uniform law instruments contain gaps that the PICC can fill or ambiguities that they can clarify. See Charles Brower and Jeremy Sharpe, "The Creeping Codification of Transnational Commercial Law: An Arbitrator's Perspective," 45 *Vanderbilt Journal Int'l L.* 199, 204 (2004). A different survey of arbitral cases reported more than 30 awards that made reference to the PICC between May 1994 and December 2000. The PICC were applied when the arbitral clauses mentioned: (1) generally accepted principles of international commercial law; (2) general standards and rules of international contracts; (3) international practices; (4) natural justice, rules of natural justice, and laws of natural justice; (5) general principles of equity; and (6) Anglo-Saxon principles of law, and not the specific choice of a national law. See Nathan O'Malley and Lisa Bench Nieuwveld, "The UNIDROIT Principles: Are They Law?," 11 *Vindobona J. of Int'l Commercial Law & Arbitration* 299–304 (2007).

[53] Both the timing of these documents and the drafting process make it difficult to sustain that PICC and PECL are the principles on which the CISG is based. Namely, both PICC and PECL were drafted more than a decade after the adoption of the CISG. The scope of the CISG's application is limited

E. *Interpretation of the Parties' Statements and Conduct*

Given that the provisions of the CISG are a body of default rules and that party autonomy reigns supreme,[54] finding out what the parties *actually* agreed upon is of crucial importance. The application of the reasonable person standard has a major role in this regard, according to Article 8. In using the reasonable person standard, due regard is given to the negotiations between the parties and to the subsequent conduct of the parties. In the *Timber case*, the tribunal referred to Article 8 when interpreting the correspondence between the parties following the conclusion of the contract and found that seller had no intention of performing any of the contracted deliveries.[55]

Another example of the operation of Article 8 in Serbian arbitral practice is found in the *Berries case*, where the buyer had resold nonconforming goods although the seller objected to such an action and expressed, upon buyer's notice of nonconformity, his willingness to take the goods back and reimburse buyer's storage cost.[56] Applying Article 8(2), the arbitrator concluded that the buyer's action amounted to an implied acceptance

to certain issues arising out of contracts for sale, whereas PICC and PECL regulate some issues not governed by the CISG, such as validity of contract and other types of contracts. PECL, as its name suggests, reflects the development of *European* principles of contract law; the CISG is designed as a *global* instrument. See James Fawcett, Jonathan Harris, and Michael Bridge, *International Sale of Goods in the Conflict of Laws* (New York: Oxford University Press, 2005), 932–5; John Gotanda, "Using the Unidroit Principles to Fill Gaps in the CISG," in *Contract Damages: Domestic and International Perspectives* (ed. D. Saidov and R. Cunnington) (Oxford: Hart Publishing, 2008), 116 *et seq.*; Stefan Vogenauer, "Introduction," in *Commentary on the UNIDROIT Principles of International Commercial Contracts (PICC)* (ed. Stefan Vogenauer and Jan Kleinheisterkamp) (New York: Oxford University Press, 2009), 10 *et seq.* There are a number of scholars who advocate the use of PICC to fill in the gaps in the CISG. See Jurgen Basedow, "Uniform Law Conventions and the UNIDROIT Principles of International Commercial Contracts," 5 *Uniform L. Rev.* 129, 136–7 (2000); Klaus Peter Berger, "International Arbitral Practice and the UNIDROIT Principles of International Commercial Contracts," 46 *American J. of Comparative Law* 129, 133–5 (1998); Michael Joachim Bonell, "The UNIDROIT Principles of International Commercial Contracts and CISG – Alternative or Complementary Instruments?," 26 *Uniform L. Rev.* 26, 36, and 37 (1996); Alejandro M. Garro, "The Gap-Filling Role of the UNIDROIT Principles in the International Sales Law: Some Comments on the Interplay Between the Principles and the CISG," 69 *Tulane L. Rev.* 1149, 1152 (1995); Ulrich Magnus, "Die Allgemeinen Grundsatze im UN-Kaufrecht," 59 *Rabels Zeitschrift* 492 (1995), translation available at http://www.cisg.law.pace.edu/cisg/text/magnus.html; Pilar Perales Viscasillas, "The Role of the UNIDROIT Principles and the PECL in the Interpretation and Gap-Filling of CISG," in *CISG Methodology* (ed. Andre Janssen and Olaf Meyer) (Munich: Sellier ELP, 2009), 303–7. In the period from 1994 to date there are only 272 reported cases where the PICC was referenced (113 court decisions and 159 arbitral awards). According to ICC statistics for the period of 1996–2000, only 3 percent of the ICC awards referred to the PICC. See Pierre Mayer, "The Role of the UNIDROIT Principles in ICC Arbitration Practice," in *UNIDROIT Principles of International Commercial Contracts: Reflections on Their Use in International Arbitration*, Special Supplement, ICC International Court of Arbitration Bulletin (ed. ICC/UNIDROIT) (Paris, 2002), 106. Obviously, this number represents only a small portion of the yearly cases of the ICC and other important arbitral institutions.

[54] See Bulgarian Chamber of Commerce and Industry, Arbitral award, Case No. 20/1997, February 2, 1998, available at http://cisgw3.law.pace.edu/cases/980202bu.html. See also Multi-Member Court of First Instance of Athens Decision 4505/2009, Greece (Dionysios P. Flambouras, ed.), available at http://cisgw3.law.pace.edu/cases/094505gr.html.

[55] Serbian FTCA Award No. T-8/06, October 1, 2007, available at http://cisgw3.law.pace.edu/cases/071001sb.html. See also Serbian FTCA Award No.T-15/06, January 28, 2008, available at http://cisgw3.law.pace.edu/cases/080128sb.html

[56] Serbian FTCA Award No. T-15/01, May 25, 2001, available at http://cisgw3.law.pace.edu/cases/010525sb.html.

of the goods. Arbitrator noted that the buyer's indication that "an agreement has been reached to sell goods at the best price" was in direct contravention with the seller's express instructions to either return the goods or pay for them in full.[57] In the *Mushroom case*, the buyer contended that the parties had not entered into a contract. The arbitrator found that such an assertion contravened the behavior of the buyer, which included taking over the goods, allegedly objecting to their quality, reselling the goods, and partially paying against the seller's invoice.[58] The arbitrator concluded that the entirety of such behavior indicates that the parties had entered into a contract. Finally, the interpretation of the party's statements and conduct in the light of Article 8 played an essential role in the *Milk packaging equipment case* regarding the decision on the appropriate date of contract avoidance.[59]

F. *Role of Usages and Business Practices*

Although trade usages and established business practices play a major role in CISG interpretive methodology,[60] the Balkan case law offers only one example where the role of business practices was observed.[61] On the other hand, the role of usages was predominantly, although not exclusively, examined in the context of determining appropriate interest rates. In that regard, provisions of 1992 UNCITRAL Model Law on International Credit Transfers were applied as evidence of international trade usage under Article 9(2) in the view of several arbitral tribunals.[62] Another tribunal held that the parties "knew or ought to have known, as professional traders and business partners, of a widely accepted

---

[57] Id.

[58] Serbian FTCA Award No. T-18/01, November 27, 2002, available at http://cisgw3.law.pace.edu/cases/021127sb.html.

[59] Serbian FTCA Award No. T-4/05, July 15, 2008, available at http://cisgw3.law.pace.edu/cases/080715sb.html.

[60] See Michael Bridge, A Commentary on Articles 1–13 and 78, in Ferrari et al., *Draft Digest*, 235, 255; Aleksandar Goldstajn, "Usages of Trade and Other Autonomous Rules of International Trade According to the UN Sales Convention," in *International Sale of Goods, Dubrovnik Lectures* (ed. Paul Volken and Petar Sarcevic) (New York: Oceana Publications, 1986), 55, 95–110; John O. Honnold, *Uniform Law for International Sales under the 1980 United Nations Convention*, 3rd ed. (The Hague: Kluwer Law International, 1999), 124; Martin Schmidt-Kessel in Schlechtriem and Schwenzer, *Commentary* (2005), Article 9, 141–53.

[61] In the Production of automobiles case, the arbitrator held that "the stipulations of the written contract prevail over the established contractual practice between the same parties." Bulgarian Chamber of Commerce and Industry, Arbitral award, Case No. 14/98, November 30, 1998, available at http://cisgw3.law.pace.edu/cases/981130bu.html.

[62] For example, see Serbian FTCA Award No T-17/06, September 10, 2007 (unpublished): "These international commercial usages, codified in the Model Law, represent a common practice which has been harmonized and widely applied in international trade, and is repeatedly used and found applicable in cases where parties have not agreed otherwise. Parties, who are both traders, knew or ought to have known of such usages. Payment of interest in the case of default represents a regular and very widely observed practice in the business environment." See also Serbian FTCA Award No. T-6/10, November 30, 2010, available at http://cisgw3.law.pace.edu/cases/101130sb.html; Serbian FTCA Award No.T-5/10, November 4, 2010, available at http://cisgw3.law.pace.edu/cases/101104sb.html; Serbian FTCA Award No. T-09/07, January 23, 2008, available at http://cisgw3.law.pace.edu/cases/080123sb.html; Serbian FTCA, Award No. T-08/05, March 28, 2006 (unpublished); Serbian FTCA Award No. T-03/06, September 14, 2006 (unpublished); Serbian FTCA Award No. T-16/04, July 18, 2005 (unpublished); Serbian FTCA Award No. T-09/02, March 24, 2003 (unpublished).

principle of commercial practice that a defaulting debtor has to pay interest," and went on to apply the Federal Funds Rate on a dollar-denominated debt.[63]

The PECL and PICC were applied as *lex mercatoria* (usages) in the *White crystal sugar case*.[64] Justifying its position, the tribunal stated that it:

> [P]aid due regard to the widely known fact that from the end of the 20th and the beginning of the 21st Century there could be noted a development and harmonization of a new international commercial practice and trade usages which was "codified" in the form of the UNIDROIT Principles, UML on International Credit Transfers and Ole Lando Principles [PECL]. They became available to everyone who performs international business transactions as well as to those who arbitrate disputes in the field of international commerce. Respectable Arbitral Tribunals in the world (especially the ICC Court of Arbitration) have long since made awards pursuant to these Principles and arbitrated disputes between Parties by applying these principles as *lex mercatoria*. Considering that there is no reason for this Court of Arbitration to keep avoiding their application, the Arbitral Tribunal has decided to interpret these principles in regard to the present dispute, to apply them and to arbitrate in accordance with their contents and aims.[65]

However, the application of the PICC as general principles on which the CISG is based is problematic, and even more so is its application via Article 9(2) CISG.[66] As aptly stated by the ICC tribunal, a "recourse to the [UNIDROIT] Principles is not purely and simply the same as recourse to an actually existing international commercial usage."[67] In other words, because "there is no empirical study showing that UNIDROIT Principles are practiced as trade customs or usages by business people [they are] not a compilation of world trade customs,"[68] and thus, cannot be applied as usages within the meaning of Article 9(2) CISG.

III. Formation and Modification of Contracts

There are only a few Southeastern European cases that have dealt with the formation or modification of contracts under the CISG. In a case decided by a Slovenian court, the Slovenian buyer contested the existence of a contract with the German seller, claiming

---

[63] Serbian FTCA Award No. T-5/05, April 4, 2007 (unpublished).

[64] Serbian FTCA Award No. T-9/07, January 23, 2008, available at http://cisgw3.law.pace.edu/cases/080123sb.html.

[65] Id.

[66] See Michael Bridge, "A Commentary on Articles 1–13 and 78," in Ferrari et al., *Draft Digest*, 235, 255; Emmanuel Gaillard, "La Distinction des Principes Généraux du Droit et des Usages du Commerce International," in *Etudes offertes à Pierre Bellet* (Paris: Litec, 1991), 203–17; Fawcett et al., *International Sale of Goods in the Conflict of Laws*, 935–6; John Gotanda, "Using the Unidroit Principles to Fill Gaps in the CISG," in Saidov and Cunnington, *Contract Damages*, 120 et seq.; Pilar Perales Viscasillas, "The Role of the UNIDROIT Principles and the PECL in the Interpretation and Gap-Filling of CISG," in Janssen and Meyer, *CISG Methodology*, 309–14; U.N. Conference on Trade and Development, Dispute Settlement: International Commercial Arbitration: Law Governing the Merits of the Dispute, 25–6, UNCTAD/EDM/Misc.232/Add.40 (2005) (prepared by Jean-Michel Jacquet), available at http://www.unctad.org/en/docs/edmmisc232add40_en.pdf.

[67] ICC Arbitration Case No. 9029, March 1998, available at www.unilex.info/case.cfm?id=660. See also ICC Arbitration Case No. 8873, July 1997, available at www.unilex.info/case.cfm?id=641.

[68] ICC Arbitration Case No. 12446, 2004, available at http://www.unilex.info/case.cfm?id=1424.

that he duly revoked his purchase order.[69] However, the facts of this case show that the seller accepted the offer by notice to the buyer and also dispatched the goods. The buyer's revocation of the offer followed the seller's dispatch of acceptance. Consequently, the court was correct in finding that "[s]ince the [seller] received the revocation of the offer after he dispatched his acceptance, the statement of the [buyer] that he revoked his order could not produce any legal effect."[70] In another case, decided by a Bulgarian arbitral tribunal, the seller contested the existence of a contract due to the fact that the parties never expressly agreed upon a price.[71] However, relying on the correspondence and conduct of the parties the tribunal found that under Article 55 CISG:

> [There was] a contract for the international commercial sale of goods which, according to the provisions of article 55 of the CISG, is valid even if the contractual price is not expressly or implicitly defined on condition that the parties rely on "the price generally charged at the time of the conclusion of the contract for such goods sold under comparable circumstances in the trade concerned."[72]

The *Aluminum case*, decided by the Serbian FTCA,[73] involved in a written contract and each page of the contract was signed with each page stamped by the parties. One party alleged that the contract was subsequently amended orally, and submitted as evidence a telefax message in which the other party confirmed the oral modification. A witness challenged the authenticity of the telefax message and noted that it would be unusual to amend important provisions of an international commercial contract by telefax. Although Article 29 provides as a general rule that oral modifications are permitted, the sole arbitrator held that when parties enter a formal, written contract attesting to each page is an indication of the importance of the "evidentiary value" of the written form. The arbitrator held that "when a contract is concluded and certified in this manner, parties may agree on a contract modification, but only in the manner and in a form in which it was done in the original contract."[74] This conclusion mirrors the prevailing view under the Serbian Law on Contracts and Torts and is clearly erroneous in that it lacks the support of the text of the CISG and relevant (international) trade usages.

In the *Wheat flour case*,[75] a buyer alleged that it made partial payment directly to the seller but could not provide written proof of such payment. The arbitrator deemed that because the contract stipulated that payments were to be made through bank transfers, the buyer's assertion was denied. Furthermore, the arbitrator dismissed buyer's request for hearing of witnesses because direct, undocumented payments were "not contractually stipulated and [the buyer] did not offer any *written* proof of such payment."[76] The arbitrator's ruling is questionable because Article 29(1) CISG allows for modifications

---

[69] Higher Court in Ljubljana, 1 Cpg 951/2006, Slovenia, April 9, 2008 (Matjaz Tratnik, ed.), available at http://cisgw3.law.pace.edu/cases/080409sv.html.

[70] Id.

[71] Bulgarian Chamber of Commerce and Industry, Arbitral award, Case No. 14/98, November 30, 1998, available at http://cisgw3.law.pace.edu/cases/981130bu.html.

[72] Id.

[73] See Serbian FTCA Award No. T-2/00, December 9, 2002, available at http://cisgw3.law.pace.edu/cases/021209sb.html

[74] Id.

[75] Serbian FTCA Award No. T-12/09, November 1, 2010, available at http://cisgw3.law.pace.edu/cases/101101sb.html.

[76] Id.

of the contract *by mere agreement of the parties* and Article 11 CISG provides that a contract of sale and subsequent performance may be proved by any means, including witness testimony.

IV. Nonconformity of Goods

This part examines the often disputed issue of the appropriateness of the notice of nonconformity given by the buyer. The first section briefly analyzes the concept of nonconforming or defective goods. The second section focuses upon the notice requirements of the CISG, including the issues of the form of the notice, content of the notice, the timeliness of the notice, and, finally, the impact of the seller's knowledge of the nonconformity.

A. *Concept of Nonconformity*

Seller's obligation to deliver conforming goods and conditions for buyer's exercise of the rights in the case of nonconformity are embodied in Articles 35–44 CISG. The proper understanding of these provisions of the CISG is crucial given that more than fifty percent of all cases that have been litigated and decided under the CISG have dealt with the issue of nonconforming goods.[77]

The definition of nonconformity has been widely accepted in Southeastern European CISG jurisprudence. Discrepancies in terms of both quality and quantity of the delivered goods have regularly been found to satisfy the nonconformity test. Examples of nonconformities in the case law include: delivery of doorjambs of different colors;[78] delivery of goods of non-Yugoslav origin, where such origin was agreed upon;[79] delivery of leather of II, III, and IV quality where the contract required delivery of I, II, and III class of leather;[80] and discrepancies in the packaging labels of the goods, where such labels were nonconforming to the labeling requirements of the country of import.[81] The same principle was applied with respect to delivery of nonconforming documents[82] and to delivery of a smaller quantity of goods than agreed upon.[83] The time for determining the existence of a nonconformity has been held to be at the time when the risk passes to the buyer, as provided by Article 36(1) CISG.[84] Finally, where the buyer was aware

[77] Ingeborg Schwenzer, "Buyer's Remedies in the Case of Non-Conforming Goods: Some Problems in a Core Area of the CISG," 101 *American Society of International Law Proceedings* 416, 416 (2007).
[78] Higher Court in Ljubljana, 1 Cpg 1305/2003, Slovenia, December 14, 2005, available at http://cisgw3.law.pace.edu/cases/051214sv.html.
[79] Serbian FTCA Award No. T-9/07, January 23, 2008, available at http://cisgw3.law.pace.edu/cases/080123sb.html. See also Commercial Court in Čačak, Case No. P 33/06, Serbia, June 28, 2006, available at http://cisgw3.law.pace.edu/cases/060628sb.html.
[80] Serbian FTCA Award No. T-16/99, February 12, 2001, available at http://cisgw3.law.pace.edu/cases/010212sb.html.
[81] Serbian FTCA Award No. T-10/04, November 6, 2005, available at http://cisgw3.law.pace.edu/cases/051106sb.html.
[82] Serbian FTCA, Award No. T-9/07, January 23, 2009 (unpublished).
[83] Serbian FTCA Award No. T-13/05, January 5, 2007, available at http://cisgw3.law.pace.edu/cases/070105sb.html.
[84] This has been confirmed in one Romanian case: "The [buyer] cannot claim apparent defects after the goods were loaded in the container provided by the [buyer] and the goods were delivered to the first shipper [especially where] the representative of the [buyer] declared the quantity and quality of the accepted goods in conformity with the agreement, according to invoice no. . . . According to Article 36 of the CISG, the seller is responsible for any lack in conformity that exists at the moment when the risks of damages are

of the nonconformity at the time of the conclusion of the contract, the seller will not be held liable under Article 35(2)(b).[85]

B. *Notice of Nonconformity*

Under the CISG, the buyer may claim remedies for nonconforming goods[86] only when the buyer examines the goods as soon as practicable and notifies the seller of the nonconformity within a reasonable time, specifying the nature of the lack of conformity.[87] The absolute time limit for notifying the seller of nonconformity is set at two years, unless inconsistent with a contractual period of guarantee (Article 39(2)). However, the seller will be precluded from enforcing "the rigorous limitations on inspection and notice"[88] if the lack of conformity relates to facts of which the seller knew or could not have been unaware and which it did not disclose to the buyer (Article 40). Finally, the buyer may preserve his rights to damages (except for loss of profit) and price reduction even if he failed to give the required notice if he has a reasonable excuse for such a failure, as provided by Article 44.[89]

1. Form of Notice

The CISG does not explicitly prescribe formal requirements for the notice of nonconformity. Pursuant to Article 7(2) and the general principle of freedom of contract,

---

transferred to the buyer, even if this deficiency does not appear until later." See High Court of Cassation and Justice, Romania, No. 2957/2003 (Dossier no. 945/2002), June 6, 2003, available at http://cisgw3.law .pace.edu/cases/030606ro.html. See also Serbian FTCA Award No. T-21/06, August 29, 2008, available at http://cisgw3.law.pace.edu/cases/080829sb.html.

[85] See Serbian FTCA Award No. T-15/01, May 25, 2001, available at http://cisgw3.law.pace.edu/cases/ 010525sb.html.

[86] This has been confirmed in Southeast European case law as well. See Single-Member Court of First Instance of Athens Decision 8161/2009, Greece (Dionysios P. Flambouras, ed.), available at http://cisgw3 .law.pace.edu/cases/090000gr.html; Multi-Member Court of First Instance of Athens Decision 4505/2009, Greece (Dionysios P. Flambouras, ed.), available at http://cisgw3.law.pace.edu/cases/094505gr.html; High Commercial Court XXVIII Pž-7365/04–3, Croatia, July 11, 2007, abstract by Davor Babić, available at http://cisgw3.law.pace.edu/cases/070711cr.html; High Court of Cassation and Justice, Romania, No. 2957/2003 (Dossier no. 945/2002), June 6, 2003, available at http://cisgw3.law.pace.edu/cases/030606ro .html; Serbian FTCA Award No. T-18/01, November 27, 2002, available at http://cisgw3.law.pace.edu/ cases/021127sb.html; Serbian FTCA Award No. T-16/99, February 12, 2001, available at http://cisgw3 .law.pace.edu/cases/010212sb.html; Serbian FTCA Award No. T-3/92, July 12, 1994, available at http:// cisgw3.law.pace.edu/cases/940712sb.html. See also Commercial Court in Čačak, Case No. P 33/06, Serbia, June 28, 2006, available at http://cisgw3.law.pace.edu/cases/060628sb.html; although the court was wrong in applying the CISG in this case, it correctly underlined the importance of Articles 39 (notice) and 38 (inspection).

[87] This is prescribed by Articles 38 and 39 CISG, but could be overridden to some extent if the requirements of Articles 40 or 44 are met. In any event, the examination of the goods is not, per se, relevant for the buyer's exercise of remedies for nonconformity. However, it is an important step to be taken by the buyer within the prescribed time period as it may impact the calculation of the "reasonable time" for giving notice of nonconformity under Article 39.

[88] Richard Hyland, "Commentary on ICC Arbitration Case No. 5713 of 1989," February 1994, available at http://www.cisg.law.pace.edu/cases/895713i1.html.

[89] This has been confirmed in Southeast European case law. See Serbian FTCA Award No. T-15/04, February 21, 2005, available at http://cisgw3.law.pace.edu/cases/050221sb.html; Serbian FTCA Award No. T-3/92, July 12, 1994, available at http://cisgw3.law.pace.edu/cases/940712sb.html.

on which the CISG is based,[90] one can easily discern that no particular form is required for such notice and that oral notice is sufficient to meet the requirements of Article 39.[91] However, Yugoslav (Serbo-Croatian) official translation of this provision of the CISG suggests that the notice must be in writing. The requirement of Article 39 that a buyer has to "give notice" has been translated to be "sent" ("*pošalje obaveštenje*" in Serbo-Croatian). To a Serbo-Croatian reader, this suggests that notification has to be conducted in a manner and through a medium, which allows for "sending" in a written form.[92] This was reflected in several awards. In the *Gray cast iron case*, the tribunal held that:

> The CISG does not specify the form of the notice, but from the fact that it needs to be sent and from its contents, the most logical is the written form. It is a standard in contracts of foreign trade that objections are stated in the written form, or that notices made in verbal communication are without delay reiterated in written form. According to the Law on Contracts and Torts (of the Former Yugoslavia),which pursuant to the Law on Resolution of Conflict of Laws is to be applied to fill in the gaps of the CISG, notice of non-conformity, which contains the description of the non-conformity has to be sent via registered letter, telegram, or in another reliable way.[93]

A similar result was reached in the *Mushrom case*, where the sole arbitrator concluded that written form of notice was necessary.[94]

2. Content of Notice

According to Article 39(1) CISG, notice must "specify the nature of the lack of conformity." In light of the relevant case law and CISG-AC Opinion No. 2, the level of specificity should not be particularly high. It is not always necessary to describe the nature and cause of the problem – pointing out the "symptoms" may be sufficient.[95] However, general, vague notices such as "bad quality,"[96] "[the goods] caused some problems,"[97]

---

[90] See CISG Articles 11 and 29.

[91] Stefan Kröll in Kröll et al., *UN Convention on Contracts*, Article 39, 601, 602; Ingeborg Schwenzer in Schlechtriem and Schwenzer, *Commentary* (2005), Article 39, 465. See also CISG-AC Opinion No. 2, Examination of the Goods and Notice of Non-Conformity: Articles 38 and 39, June 7, 2004, available at http://www.cisg.law.pace.edu/cisg/CISG-AC-op2.html.

[92] See Pavić and Djordjević, CISG in Serbia, 38–9.

[93] Despite the fact that the panel's analysis of the form requirements under CISG Article 39 was erroneous, this did not impact the tribunal's finding because the written form of the notice was required by the contract and the buyer complied with such a requirement. See Serbian FTCA Award No. T-09/01, February 23, 2004, available at http://cisgw3.law.pace.edu/cases/040223sb.html.

[94] Serbian FTCA Award No. T-18/01, November 27, 2002, available at http://cisgw3.law.pace.edu/cases/021127sb.html; see also Serbian FTCA Award No. T-10/04, November 6, 2005, available at http://cisgw3.law.pace.edu/cases/051106sb.html.

[95] CISG-AC Opinion No. 2, Examination of the Goods and Notice of Non-Conformity: Articles 38 and 39, June 7, 2004, at cmt. 4 (Rapporteur: Professor Eric E. Bergsten), available at http://www.cisg.law.pace.edu/cisg/CISG-AC-op2.html.

[96] See Rechtbank van Koophandel, Kortrijk, Belgium, December 16, 1996, available at http://www.unilex.info/case.cfm?pid=1&do=case&id=340&step=FullText.

[97] Tribinule di Vigevano, Italy, July 12, 2000, available at http://cisgw3.law.pace.edu/cases/000712i3.html.

or "[the goods] were not labeled according to the schedule of items"[98] are deemed insufficient. This is because the purpose of the notice is to allow the seller to cure the defect, collect and secure evidence regarding the conformity of goods, and perform other activities in order to preserve its rights against his suppliers or other third parties.[99]

Serbian tribunals have understood the specificity requirement as prescribed here. The notice must contain a description of the lack of conformity,[100] but it need not be overtly specific. A tribunal held that notice of nonconformity of chickens – stating that the delivered chickens were nonconforming because of the belated laying of eggs, decreased egg-laying capacity, and higher mortality rate – was sufficiently precise.[101] In another case, notice that significant portions of delivered leather pieces were discarded during production was deemed inadequate.[102]

3. Timeliness of Notice

Article 39(1) CISG provides that notice has to be made within a "reasonable time" after a defect is discovered or ought to have been discovered.[103] This standard was fiercely debated during the CISG drafting process[104] and still represents one of the most disputed issues in court and arbitral practice.[105] CISG-AC Opinion No. 2 holds that a reasonable time to give notice is determined on a case-to-case basis, taking into account all the circumstances, and should not be linked to any fixed periods prescribed by national laws.[106] Relevant circumstances include the nature of the goods, the nature of the defect,

---

[98] Landesgericht Köln, Germany, November 30, 1999, available at http://cisgw3.law.pace.edu/cases/991130g1.html.

[99] Harry Flechtner, "Buyer's Obligation to Give Notice of Non-Conformity," in Ferrari, et al., *Draft Digest*, 384–8; Schwenzer in Schlechtriem and Schwenzer, *Commentary* 2005), Article 39, 462.

[100] Serbian FTCA Award No. T-18/01, November 27, 2002, available at http://cisgw3.law.pace.edu/cases/021127sb.html.

[101] Serbian FTCA Award No. T-15/04, February 21, 2005, available at http://cisgw3.law.pace.edu/cases/050221sb.html.

[102] It would have been proper to explain that the goods delivered were of classes II, III, and IV, instead of the contracted classes I, II, and III, as the buyer had done later in the proceedings. See Serbian FTCA Award No. T-16/99, February 12, 2001, available at http://cisgw3.law.pace.edu/cases/010212sb.html.

[103] The time period for giving notification under Article 39 was erroneously paraphrased to "without delay" in one case and "quickly upon examination" in another case. See Serbian FTCA Award No. T-10/04, November 6, 2005, available at http://cisgw3.law.pace.edu/cases/051106sb.html; Serbian FTCA Award No. T-15/04, February 21, 2005, available at http://cisgw3.law.pace.edu/cases/050221sb.html.

[104] See Vienna Diplomatic Conference, Summary Records, 1st comm., 16th mtg., A/Conf.97/19 (March 20, 1980).

[105] CISG-AC Opinion No. 2, Examination of the Goods and Notice of Non-Conformity: Articles 38 and 39, June 7, 2004, available at http://www.cisgac.com/default.php?ipkCat=128&ifkCat=144&sid=144 (discussing the disparate periods which have been regarded as noncompliant with the reasonableness requirement).

[106] CISG-AC Opinion no 2, Examination of the Goods and Notice of Non-Conformity: Articles 38 and 39, June 7, 2004, cmt. 3, available at http://www.cisg.law.pace.edu/cisg/CISG-AC-op2.html. See also John Honnold and Harry Flechtner, *Uniform Law for International Sales under the 1980 United Nations Convention*, 4th ed. (AH Alphen aan den Rijn: Wolters Kluwer, 2009), 369; Peter Huber and Alastair Mullis, *The CISG: A New Textbook for Students and Practitioners* (Munich: Sellier ELP, 2007), 159; Kröll in Kröll et al., *UN Convention on Contracts*, Article 39, 609; Sonja Kruisinga, *(Non)conformity in the 1980 UN Convention on Contracts for the International Sale of Goods: A Uniform Concept?* (Antwerp: Intersentia, 2004), 76; Schwenzer in Schlechtriem and Schwenzer, *Commentary* (2005), Article 39, 467.

the situation of the parties, relevant trade usages, and practices established between the parties.[107] In that respect, a Greek court correctly observed that:

> [T]he reasonableness of a notice period for the purposes of CISG art. 39(1) is based on the particular circumstances of each examined case and mainly on the nature of the goods (e.g., for consumables the reasonable period corresponds to a few days or sometimes even a few hours), the fraudulent character of the counter-contractual behavior (which normally extends the time limits), but also the nature of the remedy that the buyer is going to exercise (therefore, when the buyer intends to declare the contract avoided (see CISG art. 49(1)(a)) or to request the replacement of the goods (see CISG art. 46(2), the notice for the lack of conformity must be served in a short time; it is possible however that the same does not apply when the buyer intends to keep the goods and claim damages (see CISG art. 45(1)(b)) or reduction of price (see CISG art. 50).[108]

The court held that notice given two and a half months after delivery of the goods was reasonable. The buyer found out about the nonconformity only after his clients returned the goods. The case excerpt states that the buyer's customers returned the goods "immediately," which suggests that the conditions of Article 38(3) were met. In any event, given the nature of the nonconformity[109] and the available case law, allowing more than two months for giving notice of nonconformity seems exceptionally long.

Other cases held buyers to stricter standards, precluding them from relying on notices given after three months (*Young chickens case*),[110] one month (*Hisex Hen case*),[111] or 16 days (*Mushroom case*).[112] In the *Mushroom case*, the arbitrator noted that such period might have been reasonable under different circumstances, but the perishable nature of the goods (fresh mushrooms) meant that notice had to be made at an earlier point in time. In the *Baby beef hide case*, a period of twenty days was not considered reasonable:[113] "The deficiencies of the goods invoked by [Buyer] were not hidden but apparent, [the] [Buyer] ought to have given notice of such lack of conformity 'without delay'. The rules on short time-limits are dictated by the trade needs and established in order to eliminate uncertainty."[114]

Articles 38 and 39 are interrelated – the time taken to inspect the goods under Article 38 CISG, plays an important role in determining whether the notice of nonconformity

---

[107] Many German courts regard a one-month period as reasonable. See Bundesgerichtshof, Germany, March 8, 1995, available at http://www.cisg.law.pace.edu/cases/950308g3.html; Bundesgerichtshof, Germany, November 3, 1999, available at http://www.cisg.law.pace.edu/cases/991103g1.html; Obrelandesgericht Stuttgart, Germany, August 21, 1995, available at http://www.cisg.law.pace.edu/cases/950821g1.html.

[108] Single-Member Court of First Instance of Thessaloniki 14953/2003, Greece (Dionysios P. Flambouras, ed.), available at http://cisgw3.law.pace.edu/cases/030001gr.html.

[109] Nonconformity: boxes titled "front AUDI automobile shock absorbers" but contained back PASSAT automobile shock absorbers; delivery of front or back GOLF automobile shock absorbers but not of full sets. Id.

[110] Serbian FTCA Award No. T-15/04, February 21, 2005, available at http://cisgw3.law.pace.edu/cases/050221sb.html.

[111] Serbian FTCA Award No. T-21/06, August 29, 2008, available at http://cisgw3.law.pace.edu/cases/080829sb.html.

[112] Serbian FTCA Award No. T-18/01, November 27, 2002, available at http://cisgw3.law.pace.edu/cases/021127sb.html.

[113] Serbian FTCA Award No. T-3/92, July 12, 1994, available at http://cisgw3.law.pace.edu/cases/940712sb.html.

[114] Id.

was timely. For example, it has been held that where a simple investigation would have revealed the defect, the time for giving a notice of nonconformity is rather short.[115] In the *Terracotta stoves case*, the buyer lost the right to rely on nonconformity because he did not conduct a timely inspection upon arrival of the goods and consequently failed to send a timely notice.[116]

The absolute time limit or prescription period for notifying the seller of nonconformity is two years, unless inconsistent with a contractual period of guarantee.[117] However, where the buyer does not indicate the contractual period of guarantee and does not furnish proof to the court that he has indeed given the seller a notice of nonconformity in a timely manner, the buyer cannot bring a claim even if within the two-year period.[118] Furthermore, the notice has to be addressed to the seller and not to a third party.[119]

4. Seller's Knowledge of Nonconformity

Article 40 of the CISG precludes the seller from relying on Articles 38 and 39 if the seller fails to disclose to the buyer facts related to a nonconformity in the goods. It has been seen as an expression of the good faith principle.[120] However, given the importance of the buyer's duties in Articles 38 and 39, and the difficulties in proving seller's knowledge of nonconformity, this article has been applied only in exceptional circumstances.[121]

Only two cases relating to application of Article 40 were found in a survey of Southeastern European case law. One, before the Bulgarian arbitration tribunal, where the seller, who disclosed the nonconformity to the buyer, did not lose the right to rely on Articles 38 and 39;[122] and the other, decided by a Slovenian court, where the seller was prevented from relying on the provisions of Article 39 by operation of Article 40.[123] Unfortunately,

---

[115] According to the court, where the nonconformity related to the origin of the goods, and the delivered bags all had a label clearly specifying the (nonconforming) origin of the goods, the buyer could have noted the nonconformity by simple visual examination and should have sent notice of nonconformity instantly. See Commercial Court in Čačak, Case No. P 33/06, Serbia, June 28, 2006, available at http://cisgw3.law.pace.edu/cases/060628sb.html.

[116] High Court of Cassation and Justice, Romania, No. 2957/2003 (Dossier no. 945/2002), June 6, 2003, available at http://cisgw3.law.pace.edu/cases/030606ro.html.

[117] A Greek court ruled that the period provided for in Article 554 of the Greek CC starts running after the buyer has notified the seller pursuant to Article 39 CISG. See Single-Member Court of First Instance Larissa 165/2005, Greece, excerpt from Zervogianni, Zervogianni, "Greece," in Ferrari, *CISG Impact*, 172–4.

[118] Higher Court in Ljubljana, 1 Cpg 577/98, Slovenia, October 13, 1999, available at http://cisgw3.law.pace.edu/cases/991013sv.html.

[119] See Serbian FTCA, Award No.T-10/04, November 6, 2005, available at http://cisgw3.law.pace.edu/cases/051106sb.html.

[120] Alejandro Garro, "The Buyer's 'Safety Valve' under Article 40: What Is the Seller Supposed to Know and When?," 25 *J. of Law & Commerce* 253, 253; *Beijing Light Automobile Co., Ltd v. Connell Limited Partnership*, Arbitration Institute of the Stockholm Chamber of Commerce, Sweden, June 5, 1998, available at http://www.cisg.law.pace.edu/cases/980605s5.htm.

[121] Id.

[122] See Bulgarian Chamber of Commerce and Industry, Arbitral award, Case No. 56/1995, April 24, 1996, available at http://cisgw3.law.pace.edu/cases/960424bu.html.

[123] Higher Court in Ljubljana, 1 Cpg 1305/2003, Slovenia, December 14, 2005, available at http://cisgw3.law.pace.edu/cases/051214sv.html.

the available facts of the latter case were inconclusive as to whether it was a true Article 40 case or just a misunderstanding between the parties.[124]

V. Remedies

It has often been said that, unlike many national laws, the CISG's remedial system is based on the concept of no-fault liability.[125] The court in the *Bulletproof vest case* stated:

> "[I]n order for liability to arise, it is not important if fault exists or not, i.e., the liability of the obligor is "objective" and it is connected only to the (objective) fact of the contractual breach. Therefore, pursuant to the CISG, the reason for the generation of liability is the breach of the contractual obligation itself and not the fault of the breaching party... Therefore, the promisor is liable also for all fortuitous events, in the strict sense of the term for which he is not liable under the Civil Code, and is released only in the cases of force majeure, which is understood based on the objective theory.[126]

This view of CISG remedies has been widely accepted in Southeast European case law.[127] The remedies most often discussed are requests for performance of the contract by means of payment of the price, avoidance of contract, and damages.

A. *Avoidance*

According to Articles 45 and 61 of the CISG, in case of breach of contract, the aggrieved party may, inter alia, avoid the contract. CISG rules for avoidance of contract, as well as the manner of exercising the right to avoid the contract, depart significantly from solutions codified in Southeast European national laws.

1. Basis of Avoidance

The two major grounds of contract avoidance under the CISG are fundamental breach and nonperformance within the additional period of time fixed by the other party in accordance with Articles 47(1) and 63(1) CISG (*Nachfrist* notice). However, the aggrieved party is free to choose among the remedies available under Articles 45 and 61 CISG.[128]

---

[124] Since the lower court applied the Slovenian Law on Obligations, it remains unclear whether the Higher Court under the CISG had all the relevant facts.

[125] See John O. Honnold, *Uniform Law for International Sales Under the 1980 United Nations Convention* (New York: Kluwer Law and Taxation Publishers, 1982), 297; Huber and Mullis, *The CISG*, 256; Joseph M. Lookofsky, "Fault and No-Fault in Danish, American and International Sales Law: The Reception of the United Nations Sales Convention," 27 *Scandinavian Studies in Law* 109, 130 (1983); Stoll and Gruber in Schlechtriem and Schwenzer, *Commentary* (2005), Article 74, 750.

[126] See Multi-Member Court of First Instance of Athens Decision 4505/2009, Greece (Dionysios P. Flambouras, ed.), available at http://cisgw3.law.pace.edu/cases/094505gr.html.

[127] For example, in one award, the arbitrator explicitly rejected the relevance of the buyer's fault when nonperforming the contract (payment of the price). See Serbian FTCA Award No. T-14/07, May 23, 2008, available at http://cisgw3.law.pace.edu/cases/080523sb.html. See also Single-Member Court of First Instance of Athens Decision 8161/2009, Greece (Dionysios P. Flambouras, ed.), available at http://cisgw3.law.pace.edu/cases/090000gr.html.

[128] This rule has been emphasized in a number of cases: "[I]n case of non-performance of the buyer's obligations, and in particular with regard to non-payment of the price for the received goods, the seller

a. *Fundamental breach*

Fundamental breach represents a pivotal concept in the CISG remedial structure as it represents both a basis for avoidance of contract[129] and a precondition for the exercise of the buyer's right to substitute goods.[130] Unfortunately, current CISG case law and scholarly commentaries have not yet succeeded in providing sufficiently clear criteria for determining when a breach is fundamental.[131]

There are seven Serbian cases that deal with the issue of fundamental breach. In one case, a breach was found to be fundamental despite the amount of goods involved being only a fraction of the agreed volume.[132] Likewise, in another case, the quantity of the goods delivered was smaller than the quantity corresponding to the amount of advance payment; this was found to justify partial avoidance of contract for the quantities of the goods not delivered.[133] A subsequent refusal to deliver the goods was deemed to constitute a fundamental breach,[134] as well as the final refusal to accept further deliveries of the goods.[135] However, the delivery to a place not designated in the contract was not deemed as fundamental breach, as the buyer was notified and was capable of taking possession of the goods.[136] Similarly, in another case, the delivery of nonconforming

---

may, above all, request performance of the contract, i.e. payment – Art. 62 CISG, and only if it does not exercise this right, it is entitled to request avoidance of the contract – Art. 65 CISG. Accordingly, it is obvious that the choice amongst these two remedies available remains with the seller, i.e. it is not obliged to, in case of any breach of contractual obligations, request avoidance of the contract." See Serbian FTCA Award No. T-5/10, November 4, 2010, available at http://cisgw3.law.pace.edu/cases/101104sb.html.

[129] See CISG Articles 49(1)(a), 51(2), 64(1)(a), 72(1), 73.

[130] CISG Article 46(2).

[131] See Andrea Björklund in Kröll et al., *UN Convention on Contracts*, Article 25, 337; Leonardo Graffi, "Divergences in the Interpretation of the CISG: The Concept of 'Fundamental Breach,'" in *The 1980 Uniform Sales Law: Old Issues Revisited in the Light of Recent Experiences. Verona Conference 2003* (ed. Franco Ferrari) (Munich: Sellier ELP, 2003), 305–23; Robert Koch, "The Concept of Fundamental Breach of Contract under the United Nations Convention on Contracts for the International Sale of Goods (CISG)," in *Review of the Convention on Contracts for the International Sale of Goods (CISG)* 177, 177–354 (ed. Pace Int'l Law Rev.) (New York: Kluwer Law International, 1999), available at http://www.cisg.law.pace.edu/cisg/biblio/koch.html; Peter Schlechtriem in Schlechtriem and Schwenzer, *Commentary* (2005), Article 25, 281–98.

[132] In this case, the claimant sold artificial fishing baits to the respondent pursuant to their agreement on business cooperation: during the year 2000 only 45,816 baits were taken over and paid out of the contracted quantity of 300,000. This amounted to roughly 15% of the contracted figure. In the next year, orders were even slower, falling to less than 2% of the agreed volume. Hence, the arbitrator concluded that the breach was fundamental and that the claimant was entitled to avoid the contract. Although the contract at hand could have called for application of Serbian LCT instead of the CISG as the disputed issue regarded the avoidance of the distributorship contract as a whole, and not any of the installments made under such contract, the case is illustrative with respect to the proportionality and the seriousness of the breach, which makes it fundamental in the eyes of the Serbian FTCA arbitrators. See Serbian FTCA, Award No. T-17/02, October 2, 2006 (unpublished).

[133] Serbian FTCA Award No. T-4/01, May 10, 2002, available at http://cisgw3.law.pace.edu/cases/020510sb.html.

[134] Serbian FTCA Award No. T-8/06, October 1, 2007, available at http://cisgw3.law.pace.edu/cases/071001sb.html.

[135] Serbian FTCA Award No. T-8/09, June 15, 2010, available at http://cisgw3.law.pace.edu/cases/100615sb.html.

[136] Serbian FTCA Award No. T-15/06, January 28, 2008, available at http://cisgw3.law.pace.edu/cases/080128sb.html.

goods representing 18 percent of the delivered goods was held to be a nonfundamental breach.[137]

In one case, a Slovenian court applied Article 25 in finding a fundamental breach.[138] The court stated that

> [it] regards the breach of the sales contract in this case as a fundamental breach of contract in the meaning of Article 25 of the CISG. [Buyer] has proved that it needed the goods paid for with the advance payment for the composition of "commissions" that would be resold to the [buyer]'s customer and that this could not have been done from the goods that were actually delivered. [Buyer] did not get what it was entitled to expect under its contract with the [seller]. Therefore, the [buyer] had a right to avoid the contract in accordance with Article 49(1)(a) of the CISG. Since it was ascertained that [seller] was acquainted with the needs for which [buyer] has purchased the goods, [seller] is not entitled to rely on [buyer]'s duty to notify the [seller] of lack of conformity (Article 40 of the CISG). Therefore, assertions in the [seller]'s appeal along these lines cannot be taken into account. [Seller] was aware that the delivered goods were not in conformity with the contractual determined goods. [Seller]'s position that timely fulfillment was not a material part of the contract is correct. However, [seller]'s assertions in that direction are not significant, since the Higher Court has ascertained that other grounds for the avoidance of the contract exist.[139]

Again, the unavailability of the full text of the decision does not allow for a more detailed commentary. However, one may question the persuasiveness of the decision against the generally endorsed high threshold for fundamental breach. It can be argued that, absent special circumstances, it might have been possible for the seller to cure the defect by delivering missing doors that would have enabled the buyer to perform the contracts with its clients and prevent avoidance of the contract.

A Greek court found the existence of fundamental breach where, due to lack of conformity, the buyer was not able to resell the goods.[140] The buyer's customers returned the defective shock absorbers. The court found that:

> [T]his fact deprived the Buyer of what the Buyer was entitled to expect from the specific sale contract, i.e., to resell the goods purchased for a profit (the shock absorbers that could not be installed in the specific types of vehicles of the Buyer's customers); therefore, the first criterion of CISG Article 25 [the breach is fundamental "if it results in such

---

[137] In this case the expert report showed that certain characteristics of the goods did not conform to the contractually agreed top-class quality. Yet, the goods were approved. See Serbian FTCA Award No. T-13/05, January 5, 2007, available at http://cisgw3.law.pace.edu/cases/070105sb.html.

[138] The seller argued that the buyer did not concretize the goods to which the advance payment referred and that, consequently, the seller had a right to choose the goods that were delivered to the buyer in the value of the advance payment from stocks that the seller had already produced. In justifying its position the seller referred to the amount of advance payment by the buyer, which did not correspond to the value of the goods ordered. However, the court rejected the seller's position as unfounded. The court stated: "Considering the goods specified in pro forma invoice and the fact that [seller] knew that [buyer] needed the same number of doors and door jambs, the [court of first instance] has correctly estimated that the goods delivered by the [Seller] on 13 June 2001 do not represent a correct fulfillment of the contract, since the consignment contained 22 doors and 174 door jambs. The Higher Court regards this as grounds for the avoidance of the contract." (Id.)

[139] Id.

[140] Single-Member Court of First Instance of Thessaloniki 14953/2003, Greece (Dionysios P. Flambouras, ed.), available at http://cisgw3.law.pace.edu/cases/030001gr.html.

detriment to the other party as substantially to deprive him of what he is entitled to expect under the contract"] was met and, since, in the court's opinion, there was a fundamental breach of contract by Seller, the Buyer was entitled to declare the contract avoided.[141]

The court, however, did not consider the second requirement – the foreseeability requirement – when deciding on the issue of fundamental breach.

b. Nachfirst *period*

Unlike the concept of fundamental breach, fixing an additional period of time for contract performance and avoiding the contract upon expiration of the period is a well-established principle in the contract law of the region. However, its importance and effect differ from the provisions of the CISG.[142]

The avoidance of contract on the basis of *Nachfrist* notice was addressed in only one of the analyzed decisions. In the *Milk packaging equipment case*, the buyer issued a statement in which it promised to pay the price by January 31, 2006.[143] The arbitral tribunal considered the statement to be an effective *Nachfrist* notice within the meaning of Article 63(1). However, the seller's statement of September 15, 2006, that he would postpone enforcement of a provisional measure entitling him to repossession of the goods from the buyer for two weeks was also construed as *Nachfrist* notice, as this statement contained all the necessary contents required – both specificity of the time period, serious intentions as to the avoidance, and the reasonableness of the length of the set period for performance.[144]

2. Declaration of Avoidance

Unlike the 1978 Yugoslav Law on Contracts and Torts, that is still effectively the law in force in most of the ex-Yugoslav states, and which recognizes ipso facto rescission in certain cases,[145] the CISG requires avoidance to be effectuated by means of a declaration of avoidance (notice) under Article 26. The determination of the time of contract avoidance often affects the rights and obligations of the parties. For example, the calculation of damages on the basis of a cover transaction under Article 75 is contingent on the giving of notice of avoidance of contract. Also, damages are calculated based on the market price at the time of contract avoidance (CISG Article 76).

The declaration of avoidance may be express or implied. A Serbian arbitral decision noted that the declaration of avoidance can be made not only expressly but tacitly: "It is essential that the [breaching party] is clearly informed about the [aggrieved party]'s intention of not wanting to be bound any longer by the contract for the sale of goods,

---

[141] Id.

[142] See Pavić and Djordjević, "CISG in Serbia," 42–3.

[143] Serbian FTCA Award No. T-04/05, July 15, 2008, available at http://cisgw3.law.pace.edu/cases/080715sb.html

[144] Avoidance on the basis of *Nachfrist* notice may have been triggered in another case where the court found the contract avoided upon the expiration of the additional period of time of approximately four months given to the buyer to perform its payment obligations. See Court of Appeals of Athens 4861/2006, Greece (Dionysios P. Flambouras, ed.), available at http://cisgw3.law.pace.edu/cases/060000gr.html.

[145] See Yugoslav LCT Art. 125(1) (involving cases of fixed-time contracts); LCT Art. 126(3) (involving cases of nonperformance within an additional period of time for performance).

which the [other party] has breached."[146] Implied notice is deduced from the conduct of the nonbreaching party,[147] such as a demand for a return of goods or payment. The essential requirement is that the notice unambiguously manifests that the nonbreaching party does not wish to be further bound by the contract.[148] Issues of avoidance of a contract and the form of declaration of avoidance were raised in several cases. For example, the seller's notice that, due to the buyer's failure to remit final payment, "you are obliged to return the catalysts to GAT by 4 October 2002," was deemed sufficient to satisfy the requirements for a valid notice of avoidance.[149]

In the *Timber case*, dealing with a contract concluded between Serbian and Romanian companies, the buyer wrote to Romanian government offices asking them to urge the seller to return the sums he received as advance payments.[150] No explicit statement was at that time directed to the seller; hence, such conduct was not deemed sufficient to constitute a valid declaration of avoidance. However, taking into account comparative judicial and arbitral practice on Article 26 of the CISG, the tribunal concluded that filing a claim before an arbitration was sufficient to constitute a proper declaration of avoidance because the statement of claim contained a declaration that the claimant considered the contract to be terminated. The tribunal found such language sufficiently clear and unambiguous to meet the requirements of Article 26.[151]

In the *Milk packaging equipment case*,[152] an arbitrator recognized the moment of avoidance subsequent to the filing of a claim. Despite the claim, the seller and buyer remained in settlement negotiations. Therefore, there remained the possibility that the contract could still be saved from termination. However, when the seller sought a court order of repossession of the delivered equipment, the arbitrator concluded that such conduct amounted to effective notice of avoidance.

3. Effects of Avoidance

According to Article 81 CISG, the avoidance of a contract releases both parties from their obligations, subject to reciprocal restitution, whereby both parties are obligated to return concurrently what they have received pursuant to contract performance. When the buyer cannot return the goods substantially in the condition in which he received

[146] Serbian FTCA Award No. T-8/06, October 1, 2007, available at http://cisgw3.law.pace.edu/cases/071001sb.html. See also Serbian FTCA Award No. T-10/09, May 31, 2010, available at http://cisgw3.law.pace.edu/cases/100531sb.html.
[147] Andrea Björklund in Kröll et al., *UN Convention on Contracts*, Article 26, 355; Christiana Fountoulakis in Schlechtriem and Schwenzer, *Commentary* (2010), Article 26, 440; Rainer Hornung in Schlechtriem and Schwenzer, *Commentary* (2005), Article 26, 302–3.
[148] See Landgericht Frankfurt, Germany, September 16, 1991, available at http://www.cisg.law.pace.edu/cases/910916g1.html.
[149] Court of Appeals of Athens 4861/2006, Greece (automobile catalyst case) (Dionysios P. Flambouras, ed.), available at http://cisgw3.law.pace.edu/cases/060000gr.html.
[150] Serbian FTCA Award No. T-8/06, October 1, 2007, available at http://cisgw3.law.pace.edu/cases/071001sb.html.
[151] Filing of a statement of claim was considered as a declaration of avoidance in other cases. See Appellate Commercial Court, Serbia, Pž. 10784/2010, July 6, 2011, available at http://cisgw3.law.pace.edu/cases/110706sb.html; Serbian FTCA Award No. T-10/09, May 31, 2010, available at http://cisgw3.law.pace.edu/cases/100531sb.html.
[152] Serbian FTCA Award No. T-4/05, July 15, 2008, available at http://cisgw3.law.pace.edu/cases/080715sb.html.

them, he loses the right to avoid the contract or to require the seller to deliver substitute goods, and his obligation to pay the price for the goods remains intact.[153]

Unfortunately, in the *Trolleybus case*, the tribunal erred in applying its domestic law of restitution.[154] The tribunal wrongly stated that:

> Since the contract was terminated and [buyer] partially paid the price and [seller] failed to deliver the trolleybuses to [buyer], the Tribunal found that [buyer] has the right to demand the reimbursement of the price, along with interest (Article 214 of the Yugoslav Law of Contracts and Torts). The Tribunal holds that, in such circumstances, the rules on restitution should be applied, rather than the rules on contractual liability, since the legal grounds for payment (sales contract) ceased to exist.[155]

In addition, the court allowed only one-sided restitution based on procedural grounds. The seller formally requested the return of the supplied equipment, and the buyer failed to make a request for the restitution of monies paid. The arbitrator reasoned that his jurisdiction was limited only, the requests and to go outside of that jurisdiction would render the award partially unemforceable (*non ultra petita*). This position is supported by the wording of Article 81(2) CISG, which prescribes that either party "may claim" restitution from the other party, implying that a claim for restitution has to be made. On the other hand, one could argue that the duty of restitution follows *ex lege* as an inevitable consequence of the avoidance of the contract and, therefore, ordering mutual restitution would not have been *ultra petita*.

The obligation of the seller after the avoidance of the contract to return the price and interest on it from the date on which the price was paid was correctly emphasized in one Serbian case.[156] The appellate court reversed the lower court's ruling that interest was only to be paid from the date of the notice of avoidance.

B. *Damages*

The right to claim damages for breach of contract is an essential right of both the seller and buyer under CISG Articles 45 and 61. It is available as an independent remedy and concurrently with other remedies, such as avoidance.[157] The basic preconditions for its exercise are contained in Article 74 of the CISG,[158] whereas alternative methods of calculating damages are found in Articles 75 and 76. Article 77 contains a limitation

---

[153] Serbian FTCA Award No. T-3/01, September 24, 2001, available at http://cisgw3.law.pace.edu/cases/010924sb.html.

[154] Serbian FTCA Award No. T-22/05, October 30, 2006, available at http://cisgw3.law.pace.edu/cases/061030sb.html.

[155] Id.

[156] Appellate Commercial Court, Serbia, Pž. 10784/2010, July 6, 2011, available at http://cisgw3.law.pace.edu/cases/110706sb.html.

[157] This was emphasized in three Greek decisions. See Single-Member Court of First Instance of Athens Decision 8161/2009, Greece (Dionysios P. Flambouras, ed.), available at http://cisgw3.law.pace.edu/cases/090000gr.html; Court of Appeals of Athens 4861/2006, Greece (Dionysios P. Flambouras, ed.), available at http://cisgw3.law.pace.edu/cases/060000gr.html; Multi-Member Court of First Instance of Athens Decision 4505/2009, Greece (Dionysios P. Flambouras, ed.), available at http://cisgw3.law.pace.edu/cases/094505gr.html.

[158] The basic principle of the damages provisions of the CISG is to fully compensate the aggrieved party. See Court of Appeals of Athens 4861/2006, Greece (Dionysios P. Flambouras, ed.), available at http://cisgw3.law.pace.edu/cases/060000gr.html.

of damages, namely, a breaching party may claim a reduction in the damages in the amount by which the loss should have been mitigated by the aggrieved party. Finally, Article 79 provides the breaching party an exemption from the obligation to pay damages under certain conditions.

1. Types of Recoverable Loss

Article 74 states that damages for breach of contract shall consist of "a sum equal to the loss, including loss of profit, suffered by the other party as a consequence of the breach." Thus, the CISG remedial scheme includes recovery for "actual damages" (*damnum emergens*) and "lost profit" (*lucrum cessans*). The relevant case law has recognized the following types of recoverable losses: expectation loss;[159] costs of repair of the defective goods and loss of profits;[160] costs of sorting and repackaging the nonconforming goods;[161] travel expenses of buyer's employees in connection with the conclusion and performance of the sales contract;[162] interest payable for a bank loan obtained in order to make the advance payment of the price;[163] customs, VAT, and other expenses incurred as a result of seller's breach of contract;[164] administrative penalties;[165] costs of obtaining a letter of credit;[166] bank fees;[167] storage costs;[168] demurrage costs;[169] costs for unreturned packaging material;[170] and penalties paid by the seller to its supplier.[171] The issue of awarding attorneys' fees and dispute resolution costs as damages[172] has not been addressed

[159] Bulgarian Chamber of Commerce and Industry, Arbitral award, Case No. 26/99, February 28, 2002, available at http://cisgw3.law.pace.edu/cases/020228bu.html.
[160] Multi-Member Court of First Instance of Thessaloniki 22513/2003, Greece, excerpt from Zervogianni, "Greece," in Ferrari, *CISG Impact*, 174–5, available at http://cisgw3.law.pace.edu/cases/030513gr.html.
[161] Serbian FTCA Award No. T-13/05, January 5, 2007, available at http://cisgw3.law.pace.edu/cases/070105sb.html.
[162] Serbian FTCA Award No. T-08/06, October 1, 2007, available at http://cisgw3.law.pace.edu/cases/071001sb.html.
[163] Id.
[164] Serbian FTCA Award No. T-09/07, January 23, 2008, available at http://cisgw3.law.pace.edu/cases/080123sb.html.
[165] Serbian FTCA, Award No. T-10/06, November 27, 2006 (unpublished).
[166] Serbian FTCA Award No. T-22/05, October 30, 2006, available at http://cisgw3.law.pace.edu/cases/061030sb.html.
[167] Bulgarian Chamber of Commerce and Industry, Arbitral award, Case No. 26/99, February 28, 2002, available at http://cisgw3.law.pace.edu/cases/020228bu.html.
[168] Higher Court in Ljubljana, 1 Cpg 1305/2003, Slovenia, December 14, 2005, available at http://cisgw3.law.pace.edu/cases/051214sv.html.
[169] Bulgarian Chamber of Commerce and Industry, Arbitral award, Case No. 26/99, February 28, 2002, available at http://cisgw3.law.pace.edu/cases/020228bu.html.
[170] Serbian FTCA Award No. T-6/08, October 19, 2009, available at http://cisgw3.law.pace.edu/cases/091019sb.html.
[171] Serbian FTCA Award No. T-8/09, June 15, 2010, available at http://cisgw3.law.pace.edu/cases/100615sb.html.
[172] See John Felemegas, "An Interpretation of Article 74 CISG by the U.S. Circuit Court of Appeals," 15 *Pace International L. Rev.* 91, 91–147 (2003) (supporting the award of attorney's fees as damages). But see Joseph Lookofsky, "Commentary: *Zapata Hermanos v. Hearthside Baking*," 6 *Vindobona Journal of International Commercial Law & Arbitration* 27, 27–9 (2002); Harry M. Flechtner, "Recovering Attorneys' Fees as Damages under the U.N. Sales Convention (CISG): The Role of Case Law in the New International Commercial Practice, with Comments on *Zappa Hermanos v. Hearthside Banking*," 22 *Northwestern J. of Int'l Law & Business* 121, 12–159 (2002).

in any Southeast European cases. However, the costs of legal representation and the costs of proceedings incurred before government agencies, such as tax authorities, have been awarded as damages.[173] A Greek court broadly applied the foreseeability requirement for damage recovery in denying damages for "non-material" harm, including harm to reputation and loss of clientele.[174] This view is not in accord with contemporary CISG jurisprudence on the topic.[175]

2. Proof of Loss

The claimant has the burdern of proving with certainty the actual damages incurred.[176] However, the issue of burden of proof and standard of proof under the CISG has rarely been discussed in the Southeast European case law.[177] Nevertheless, the issue of proof of loss was addressed in several decisions and recovery of damages was denied in all cases where claimants were not able to prove the loss.[178] A buyer's request for recovery

---

[173] Serbian FTCA Award No. T-09/07, January 23, 2008, available at http://cisgw3.law.pace.edu/cases/080123sb.html.

[174] Multi-Member Court of First Instance of Athens Decision 4505/2009, Greece (Dionysios P. Flambouras, ed.), available at http://cisgw3.law.pace.edu/cases/094505gr.html. The seller requested 500,000 EUR for its nonmaterial loss suffered as a consequence of the buyer's slanderous talks about him (action in tort – rejected as vague) and another 500,000 EUR as compensation for the loss to its international reputation due to the buyer's avoidance of the contract with the seller and conclusion of a contract with a competitor of the seller's. At the same time, the buyer requested 300,000 EUR due to moral damage it sustained by the damage to its reputation caused by the seller, the disturbance of its commercial relationships with main and privileged customers, the Ministry of Defense and the Greek Police, and the harm to prestige and credibility of its goods to them. Id.

[175] Although the CISG Advisory Council supports the view that nonmaterial loss is not per se reimbursable under the CISG, it also finds that pecuniary damages caused by a loss of good can, as a matter of principle, be compensated under Article 74 CISG. See CISG-AC Opinion No. 6, Calculation of Damages under CISG Article 74 (Rapporteur: Professor John Y. Gotanda), Cmt. 7, available at http://www.cisg.law.pace.edu/cisg/CISG-AC-op6.html. See also John Gotanda in Kröll et al., *UN Convention on Contracts*, Article 74, 1001; Djakhongir Saidov, *The Law of Damages in International Sales, the CISG and Other International Instruments* (Oxford and Portland: Hart Publishing, 2008), 257–62; Peter Schlechtriem, "Non-material Damages – Recovery under the CISG?," 19 *Pace Int'l L. Rev.* 89, 95–8 (2007); Stoll and Gruber in Schlechtriem and Schwenzer, *Commentary* (2005), Article 74, 752, 753. On the other hand, Professor Schwenzer is of the opinion that the CISG does not expressly exclude liability for nonpecuniary loss, and that, consequently, "damages which are purely non-pecuniary may be recoverable where the intangible purpose of performance became part of the contract, rendering the loss incurred a typical consequence of non-performance." See Schwenzer in Schlechtriem and Schwenzer, *Commentary* (2010), Article 74, 1015. However, Professors Huber and Mullis accord with the view that damages for loss of reputation should not be recoverable unless the buyer had highlighted the risks to the seller before the conclusion of the contract. See Huber and Mullis, *The CISG*, 280.

[176] See CISG-AC Opinion no. 6, Calculation of Damages under CISG Article 74 (Rapporteur: Professor John Y. Gotanda), Cmt. 2.2, available at http://www.cisg.law.pace.edu/cisg/CISG-AC-op6.html.

[177] In only one examined case the reference to the CISG was made when deciding on the burden of proof. See Multi-Member Court of First Instance of Athens Decision 4505/2009, Greece (Dionysios P. Flambouras, ed.) available at http://cisgw3.law.pace.edu/cases/094505gr.html.

[178] For example, in the milk packaging equipment case, the claimant-seller requested avoidance of the contract, repossession of the goods, and compensation for respondent-buyer's use of the goods for several years, claiming lost profits and amortization. Claimant's request for damages was rejected on the grounds that claimant did not prove such damages. See Serbian FTCA Award No. T-4/05, July 15, 2008, available at http://cisgw3.law.pace.edu/cases/080715sb.html. See also Serbian FTCA Award No. T-8/09, June 15, 2010, available at http://cisgw3.law.pace.edu/cases/100615sb.html; Serbian FTCA Award No. T-9/07,

of interest paid on a loan from a bank for securing funds to make an advance payment under the sales contract was only partially granted.[179]

3. Foreseeability Requirement

Similar to many national contract laws,[180] the CISG requires damages arising out of a contractual relationship to be foreseeable, either subjectively or objectively, in order to be recoverable.[181]

> In order to judge if there is subjective foreseeability of the promisor, subjective factors are taken into account, such as his knowledge at the time the contract was concluded of the relative risk that caused the damage, the specialized skills or knowledge he has for the specific type of trade, any information in connection with the existence of the risk provided by the promisee. If it is not concluded that the promisor had foreseen the damage, then it is examined if he ought to have foreseen the damage. The criterion for the affirmation of subjective foreseeability is the ability to foresee of the "ideal promisor," i.e., of the prudent and "reasonable" representative of the circle of transactions in which the breaching promisor belongs, also in the light of the purpose of the specific sales contract. The object of the foreseeability is the nature and extent of the damage as a possible consequence of the contractual breach, but not the contractual breach itself. Therefore, the breaching promisor is not liable for just any damage, instead his liability under CISG is limited to the foreseeable damage, even if the promisor has intentionally breached his contractual obligations.[182]

In the *Timber case*, the buyer's claim for actual damages had two components – the costs of daily allowances and transportation costs that the buyer incurred in relation to business visits to the seller, and the interest the buyer had to pay in order to service the bank loan taken out to pay the advance payment on the contract price. The tribunal found that both types of damages were foreseeable. As to the first portion of the damages awarded, the tribunal noted that it is foreseeable that a buyer would travel to negotiate over the subsequent performance of the contract in case of nondelivery, especially when the seller had suggested to the buyer that he would subsequently perform.

With respect to the second portion of the damages award, the tribunal found that: "[The seller] at the time of conclusion of the contract could have presumed that [buyer] would obtain a loan from a bank for securing the necessary funds for the advance payment

---

January 23, 2008, available at http://cisgw3.law.pace.edu/cases/080123sb.html; Serbian FTCA Award No. T-13/05, January 5, 2007, available at http://cisgw3.law.pace.edu/cases/070105sb.html.

[179] Serbian FTCA Award No. T-8/06, October 1, 2007, available at http://cisgw3.law.pace.edu/cases/071001sb.html.

[180] See Franco Ferrari, "Comparative Ruminations on the Foreseeability of Damages in Contract Law," 53 *Louisiana L. Rev.* 1257, 1257–69 (1993); Djakhongir Saidov, "Methods of Limiting Damages under the Vienna Sales Convention on the International Sale of Goods" (2001), available at http://www.cisg.law.pace.edu/cisg/biblio/saidov.html; Stoll and Gruber in Schlechtriem and Schwenzer, *Commentary* (2005), Article 74, 763–9.

[181] See Multi-Member Court of First Instance of Athens Decision 4505/2009, Greece (Dionysios P. Flambouras, ed.), available at http://cisgw3.law.pace.edu/cases/094505gr.html; Serbian FTCA Award No. T-8/06, October 1, 2007, available at http://cisgw3.law.pace.edu/cases/071001sb.html; Serbian FTCA Award No. T-22/05, October 30, 2006, available at http://cisgw3.law.pace.edu/cases/061030sb.html.

[182] Id.

under the sales contract. . . . Consequently, [seller] is obliged to compensate [buyer] for the damage suffered."[183]

In addition, the buyer was awarded lost profits because the seller "could have foreseen that [buyer] was purchasing the poplars for the purpose of their processing and reselling, and that [buyer] had contracted for the resale of the quantity for which the advance payment was made."[184] However, since the buyer failed to submit any evidence of future lost profits, the tribunal denied the buyer's claim for such losses. This reasoning is flawed because the court could have applied the "abstract calculation" of damages under Article 76 based on the market price of the goods, which does not require any proof of loss. But, the aggrieved party never requested such a calculation of damages.[185]

In another case, the seller delivered goods of an origin other than the one required under the contract. The seller was held to be liable for the higher customs duty paid by the seller due to the different origin of the goods.[186] Finally, in the *Euro Diesel case*, the tribunal correctly noted that the seller's loss comprising penalties paid to its supplier was foreseeable to the buyer. Agreeing to penalties in such a transaction was a common practice in the type of transactions that the buyer, as a professional trader, undertook.[187]

4. Damages on the Basis of Substitute Transaction

Article 75 CISG provides means for calculating the amount of damages when a contract is avoided and a substitute transaction is concluded. The amount of damages corresponds to the difference between the price of the substitute transactions and the original contract, along with any other damages recoverable under Article 74 CISG. In the *Sunflower seed case*, the buyer, upon the seller's refusal to deliver the goods, undertook a substitute transaction at a price above the contract price.[188] The court, in this instance, neither applied the methodology suggested by Article 75 nor inquired or commented on the question of avoidance of the contract. Instead, the court followed the foreseeability requirement from Article 74 and its own damages calculation methodology. The Article 75 formula was not applied because such amount of damages was said to exceed the loss "which the breaching party foresaw or ought to have foreseen as possible in view of the facts and conditions of which it was aware or should have been aware."[189] Instead, the court, on the basis of this calculation, granted the damages to the buyer in an amount that represented the difference between "the price which, someone should pay as an average in order to purchase sunflower seeds from various suppliers in September 2001" (the time when the seller refused delivery) and the contract price, because, according to the court "this was the amount which the seller could have foreseen as a possible

---

[183] Id.

[184] Id.

[185] John Gotanda in Kröll et al., *UN Convention on Contracts*, Article 76, 1024.

[186] Serbian FTCA Award No. T-09/07, January 23, 2008, available at http://cisgw3.law.pace.edu/cases/080123sb.html (affirming that, had the goods been conforming, the buyer would have been exempt from paying custom duty in accordance with the then applicable EU preferential treatment for sugar of Yugoslav origin).

[187] Serbian FTCA, Award No. T-8/09, June 15, 2010, available at http://cisgw3.law.pace.edu/cases/100615sb.html.

[188] Court of Appeals of Lamia 63/2006, Greece (Dionysios P. Flambouras, ed.), available at http://cisgw3.law.pace.edu/cases/060001gr.html.

[189] Id.

consequence of its breach at the time the contract was concluded."[190] The methodology employed by the tribunal did not conform to the calculation of damages prescribed by the CISG.[191]

5. Mitigation

In the *Steel ropes case*,[192] the tribunal found that the buyer's request to be compensated for expenses it incurred in "mitigating the loss" resulting from the delivery of the goods it "rejected" was not justified because the seller was not in breach of the contract. Additionally, the contract itself provided that such expenses were to be borne by the buyer.[193]

6. Exemption from Liability to Pay Damages

Article 79 of the CISG provides that the debtor has the right to claim an exemption from payment of damages if he proves that the failure to perform is due to an impediment beyond his control and that he could not reasonably be expected to have taken the impediment into account at the time of the conclusion of the contract, and could not have avoided or overcome it or its consequences. Given the imposition of economic sanctions on trade with Yugoslavia (Serbia and Montenegro) in the 1990s, it was not surprising to find debtors invoking this article in defense of claims for damages for nonperformance. However, in three out of five cases where a *vis major* defense was invoked, the tribunals erred in determining the appropriate substantive law and applied the provisions of domestic law instead of the CISG.[194]

The *Euro Diesel case* confirms the view that circumstances existing at the time of the conclusion of the contract (global economic crisis) cannot serve as a *vis maior* defense.[195] In addition, the arbitrators found that the buyer's difficulties in providing sufficient storage place for the contracted goods did not excuse the buyer from liability for rejecting further deliveries.[196] Although the holding of the tribunal can be considered in line with the provisions of Article 79 CISG, the analysis relied on the contract's *force majeure* clause.

A number of Bulgarian arbitration cases dealt with claims of excuse from liability. In one case, the Ukrainian seller was not relieved from liability for its delivery of coal to a Bulgarian buyer, as the alleged impediment to performance occurred before the

---

[190] Id.

[191] See also Dionysios P. Flambouras, "Case Law of Greek Courts for the Vienna Convention (1980) for International Sale of Goods," *Nordic J. of Commercial Law* 24–5 (February 2009), available at http://www.cisg.law.pace.edu/cisg/biblio/flambouras3.html.

[192] Bulgarian Chamber of Commerce and Industry, Arbitral Award, Case No. 11/1996, February 12, 1998, available at http://cisgw3.law.pace.edu/cases/980212bu.html.

[193] See Multi-Member Court of First Instance of Athens Decision 4505/2009, Greece (Dionysios P. Flambouras, ed.), available at http://cisgw3.law.pace.edu/cases/094505gr.html.

[194] See Serbian FTCA, Award No. T-07/01, February 21, 2002 (unpublished); Serbian FTCA Award No. T-66/99, October 15, 2001 (unpublished); Serbian FTCA Award No. T-01/00, December 7, 2000 (unpublished).

[195] Serbian FTCA Award No. T-8/09, June 15, 2010, available at http://cisgw3.law.pace.edu/cases/100615sb.html.

[196] Id.

conclusion of the contract and, thus, could have been taken into account.[197] In another case, the alleged impediments – change of market conditions, buyer's distribution and storage problems, a downturn in the construction business – were not found to comply with the requirements of Article 79.[198] The arbitrators denied the buyer an excuse from liability because none of the alleged impediments made it "objectively impossibile [for the buyer] to accept the delivered goods." Furthermore, none of the events were unexpected.[199]

The *Sunflower seed case* offers an elaborate analysis of Article 79 CISG.[200] The Bulgarian seller refused to deliver the agreed quantity of seeds to the Greek buyer. The seller pleaded that its failure was due to:

> Prolonged dryness, which resulted [in] the destruction of a large quantity of the current harvest of sunflower seeds in Bulgaria and consequently a reduction of production and availability; and the lowering of the level of the river Danube; thus the seller was unable to load the goods on a ship in a river port which was located on its premises and furthermore it was obliged to use a port located in the Black Sea; however, the necessity to load the goods at a sea port entailed increased transportation costs for the seller to that port, a fact that rendered the initially agreed price highly inexpedient for the seller.[201]

The court rejected the arguments of the seller since the alleged impediment was neither unforeseeable (seller knew that the sunflower seed harvest would be limited due to dryness; also, the lowering of the river Danube was a foreseeable event as it had done so several years earlier) nor uncontrollable because the seller could have negotiated a term that would have increased the price if an alternative port was necessitated. The court also pointed out that the CISG does not provide for an equivalent of a *rebus sic stantibus* or hardship provision.

7. Liquidated Damages

There are several awards from Southeastern Europe that deal with the question of liquidated damages or penalty clauses.[202] The legal nature of these clauses, as understood within the Balkans, is elaborated in the *Trolleybus case*:

> When deciding on [buyer]'s claim for contractual penalty, the Tribunal took into consideration that the purpose of this penalty is to give an advance assessment of the amount of the damages for breach of contract. In other words, the creditor does not

---

[197] Bulgarian Chamber of Commerce and Industry, Arbitral award, Case No. 56/1995, April 24, 1996, available at http://cisgw3.law.pace.edu/cases/960424bu.html.

[198] Bulgarian Chamber of Commerce and Industry, Arbitral award, Case No. 11/1996, February 12, 1998, available at http://cisgw3.law.pace.edu/cases/980212bu.html.

[199] Id.

[200] Court of Appeals of Lamia 63/2006, Greece, edited by Dionysios P. Flambouras, available at http://cisgw3.law.pace.edu/cases/060001gr.html.

[201] Id.

[202] For comparative research on liquidated damages and contractual penalties, as understood in the common law and civil law systems, constructive criticism of the two approaches and suggestions for drafting such clauses in international commercial contracts, see Larry DiMatteo, "Enforcement of Penalty Clauses: A Civil –Common Law Comparison," *Internationales Handelsrecht (IHR)* 193 *et seq.* (May 2010); Pascal Hachem, *Agreed Sums Payable upon Breach of an Obligation: Rethinking Penalty and Liquidated Damages Clauses* (The Hague: Eleven Publishing, 2011).

have to prove the existence of loss and its amount but only that the debtor failed to fulfill its obligation – it is on debtor to prove that it was not liable for the breach (this is the underlying idea of Article 275 paragraph 1 of the Yugoslav Law on Contracts and Torts).

The Tribunal is of the opinion that the contract clause providing for different amounts of contractual penalty for the period of delay is allowed by the Law. Likewise, the Tribunal is of the opinion that the legal nature of the clause on contractual penalty is not changed by the use of the word "penal" or by the language employed in the contract specifying the buyer's right for price reduction in case of delay in delivery. Given that the contractual penalty represents an advance assessment of the parties of the amount of damages that may be suffered as a consequence of the breach of contract, in this case, regardless of the terms used, the contents of this premise are clearly expressed in the Contract.[203]

The analysis of the Balkan case law confirms the view that recovery of the amount specified in the liquidated damages (penalty) clauses is permissible under the CISG and subject only to limitations of the applicable national law.[204] As stated in the *Milk packaging equipment case*:

[The CISG] does not deal with the question of validity of the provision on liquidated damages, which are requested by the [seller]; however, in accordance with the principle of party autonomy (CISG Article 6), it is undisputed that the Convention allows the parties to freely determine the amount of compensation to be paid by the debtor to the creditor in case of non-performance or untimely performance of a contractual obligation. The validity of such a clause is not affected by the application of the Serbian Law on Contracts and Torts, which is based on the same principle and this provision could not be held contrary to the imperative norms, public policy or customs.[205]

Two cases before the Serbian FTCA related to the parties' stipulations regarding "penalties" for late payments. Although the cases had the same outcomes, the arbitrators' reasonings were different. In the *Copper wire rod case*, a provision calling for 13% annual interest on unpaid price (also called "penalties") was interpreted as an agreement on an applicable interest rate for delay in payment.[206] The tribunal held that under the

---

[203] See Serbian FTCA Award No. T-22/05, October 30, 2006, available at http://cisgw3.law.pace.edu/cases/061030sb.html.

[204] See Changwei Liu, *Remedies In International Sales – Perspectives From CISG, UNIDROIT Principles And PECL* (M.S. Newman, ed.) (New York: Juris Net, LLC, 2007), 540 *et seq.* (hereafter referred to as Liu, Remedies); Pascal Hachem, "Agreed Sums in CISG Contracts," 3 *Annals of the Faculty of Law in Belgrade – Belgrade L. Rev.* 140, 144–5 (2011); Stoll and Gruber in Schlechtriem and Schwenzer, *Commentary* (2005), Article 74, 769–70. See also Milena Djordjevic in Kröll et al., *UN Convention on Contracts*, Article 4, 75, n. 68.

[205] Serbian FTCA Award No. T-4/05, July 15, 2008, available at http://cisgw3.law.pace.edu/cases/080715sb.html. See also Serbian FTCA Award No. T-10/09, May 31, 2010, available at http://cisgw3.law.pace.edu/cases/100531sb.html.

[206] Serbian FTCA Award No. T-14/10, July 27, 2010, available at http://cisgw3.law.pace.edu/cases/110727sb.html. Given the difficulties in determining the applicable interest rate, parties are advised to fix the interest rate in their contracts. See Volker Behr, "The Sales Convention in Europe: From Problems in Drafting to Problems in Practice," 17 *J. of Law and Commerce* 263, 290 n. 156 (1998); Fritz Enderlein and Dietrich Maskow, *International Sales Law, United Nations Convention on Contracts for the International Sale of Goods: Convention on the Limitation Period in the International Sale of Goods: Commentary* (New York: Oceana, 1992), 312; Huber and Mullis, *The CISG*, 361; Liu, "Remedies," 635; Christian Thiele, "Interest on Damages and Rate of Interest Under Article 78 of the U.N. Convention on Contracts for the International Sale of Goods," 2 *Vindobona J. of Int'l Commercial Law & Arbitration* 3, 35 (1998); Peter

CISG the principle of party autonomy allows the parties to contractually agree on the applicable interest rate for late payment.[207] On the other hand, in the *Australian wool case*, the arbitrator invoked Article 74 of the CISG to uphold a similar provision.[208]

In the end, despite the divergent rules in the common and civil laws on the enforceability of penalty clauses (such clauses are unenforceable in the common law unless judged to be purely compensatory liquidated damages), none of the examined cases involved clauses whose purpose was to punish the breaching party. Quite the contrary, it is evident from the rationales of these awards that agreeing to contractual penalties provisions had the sole purpose of estimating future damages and that the tribunals showed willingness to uphold such clauses where this was the case.

VI. Preservation of Goods

Article 86 CISG requires the buyer, who has received goods and subsequently exercises a right of rejection, to take reasonable steps to preserve the goods under the circumstances.[209] However, where there is no breach of contract by the seller, a buyer is not entitled to reimbursement for the expenses incurred in storing the goods.[210]

Article 88 of the CISG has been invoked twice in the available case law. It has been clarified in these cases that the right of sale under Article 88 is available to the buyer only in situations where the seller unreasonably delays in repossessing the goods or paying the storage expenses.[211] It has also been stated that reasonable resale requires that a buyer acts "with the diligence of a good manager" and to sell the goods for a "reasonable purchase price."[212]

VII. Conclusion

The number of CISG cases reported from Southeastern Europe is not insignificant. However, a majority of the cases come from one jurisdiction (Serbia). Somewhat lackluster reporting of the court decisions and confidentiality restrictions in arbitration proceedings may explain why the number of reported cases (currently at 111) is not higher. Still, one may expect that the number of reported decisions will grow in the future, for at least three reasons. First, new generations of lawyers are being exposed to the CISG through

---

Winship, "Changing Contract Practices in the Light of the United Nations Sales Convention: A Guide for Practitioners," 29 *International L. J.* 525, 553 (1995).

[207] Serbian FTCA Award No. T-14/10, July 27, 2010, available at http://cisgw3.law.pace.edu/cases/110727sb.html.

[208] Serbian FTCA Award No. T-12/04, January 24, 2006, available at http://cisgw3.law.pace.edu/cases/060124sb.html. Although the contractual clause was entitled "penalties," the arbitrator interpreted such clause to mean the preestimated amount of damages for late payment, which, according to the award, was permissible under the CISG.

[209] See Serbian FTCA, Award No. T-15/01, May 25, 2001, available at http://cisgw3.law.pace.edu/cases/010525sb.html.

[210] Bulgarian Chamber of Commerce and Industry, Arbitral award, Case No. 11/1996, February 12, 1998, available at http://cisgw3.law.pace.edu/cases/980212bu.html.

[211] Serbian FTCA Award No. T-15/01, May 25, 2001, available at http://cisgw3.law.pace.edu/cases/010525sb.html.

[212] See Higher Court in Ljubljana, 1 Cpg 1305/2003, Slovenia, December 14, 2005, available at http://cisgw3.law.pace.edu/cases/051214sv.html.

the Willem C. Vis Moot Competition.[213] Second, the Queen Mary and Pace University Translation Program has increased the accessibility of CISG case law and scholarly commentary. Third, the dissolution of Yugoslavia has converted what would have been domestic disputes to international ones governed by the CISG. Despite evidence of homeward trend bias in Southeast European CISG case law, a considerable number of cases, especially in arbitration cases, have correctly applied the CISG.

---

[213] The universities from all of the Southeast European countries, except for Albania and Bulgaria, have participated at the Willem C. Vis International Commercial Arbitration Moot. Moreover, teams from the region regularly take part at the Belgrade Open Pre-Moot, which is annually held at the University of Belgrade Faculty of Law (Serbia). See http://www.cisg.law.pace.edu/cisg/moot/mootlist.html#18 and http://www.ius.bg.ac.rs/moot/premoot.htm.

27 Spain

Pilar Perales Viscasillas and Javier Solana Álvarez

I. Introduction

Spain ratified the 1980 Vienna Convention on Contracts for the International Sale of Goods (CISG) on July 17, 1990; the text of the CISG was published in the Spanish Official Journal on January 30, 1991. Spain is one of the top ten countries in providing CISG-related decisions.[1] Knowledge of the CISG among Spanish judges and scholars has constantly grown and domestic interpretations of the CISG have mostly been abandoned. However, there are still cases where the CISG has been used as a gap filler, but some Spanish courts seem to be unaware of the existence of legal literature or cases on the CISG. Other Spanish courts have referred to both the rules of the Spanish Commercial Code or the Civil Code along with those of the CISG (use of parallel citations). And, there remain a few cases where the CISG is interpreted at the light of domestic law (domestic trend).

As mentioned, one of the most noticeable developments in the judicial application of the CISG has been its role as a gap filler to domestic contracts, either as an aid in interpretation or as a comparative reference. This has been the case not only for the CISG but also for other international law instruments, such as the UNIDROIT Principles of International Commercial Contracts (UPIC),[2] the European Principles of Contract Law (PECL),[3] the Principles of European Tort Law (PETL), as well as the Draft Common Frame of Reference (DCFR).[4]

---

[1] See http://www.cisg.law.pace.edu/cisg/text/casecit.html for CLOUT (www.uncitral.org).

[2] International Institute for the Unification of Private Law, Rome. See Michael Joachim Bonell, *An International Restatement of Contract Law: The Unidroit Principles of International Commercial Contracts*, 3rd ed. (Transnational Publishers, 2005), 264. See also Michael Joachim Bonell, *The Unidroit Principles in Practice*, 2nd ed. (Transnational Publishers, 2006). Case law on UNIDROIT Principles is available at http://www.unilex.info.

[3] Drafted by the Commission on European Contract Law (Lando Commission). See Principles of European Contract Law, Parts 1 and 2 (ed. Ole Lando and Hugh Beale) (Kluwer Law International, 2000). Parts 1 and 2, published in 1999, deal with formation of contract, validity, performance, nonperformance, and remedies. Part 3, published in 2002, deals with assignment, assumption of debts, set-off, prescriptions, and conditions. The European Principles are similar to the UPIC closely follows the CISG and the UPIC. It covers civil and commercial contracts within the EU. See http://frontpage.cbs.dk/law/commission_on_european_contract_law/index.html.

[4] Christian von Bar, Eric Clive, and Hans Schulte-Nolke, *Principles, Definitions and Model Rules of European Private Law: Draft Common Frame of Reference (DCFR)*, Prepared by the Study Group on a European Civil Code and the Research Group on EC Private Law (Acquis Group) (Sellier, 2009), available at http://www.law-net.eu.

Particularly interesting is the position of the High Supreme Court of Spain that has recognized the value of using the CISG's fundamental rules and principles to interpret and fill gaps within the Spanish Civil and the Commercial Codes.[5] Spanish courts have also used the CISG as a comparative tool, as well as other soft law instruments such as those noted earlier.[6] However, there are no decisions yet on the role that the UNIDROIT Principles or other international instruments might have in regard to the interpretation and supplementation of the CISG.[7] The Spanish scholars have also considered the use of the CISG, and other international instruments, in the application of Spanish law favorably.[8]

II. Principle of Good Faith

A Spanish court applied the principle of good faith under CISG Article 7(1) to render a choice of forum clause invalid on the grounds of a lack of consent by the buyer.[9]

---

[5] Other countries are also following this tendency; see, e.g., Colombia: Jorge Oviedo Alban, "La Convención sobre compraventa internacional de mercaderías: antecedentes y desarrollos alternativos" 29 *Foro de Derecho Mercantil* 37–63 (2010).

[6] See STS, April 5, 2006, confirmed by several decisions of the Supreme Court, such as December 22, 2006, and January 5, 2007, dealing with the interpretation of Article 1124 of the Civil Code, which requires a severe nonperformance: "This interpretation is coherent with the modern doctrine about the breach of the contract contained in Article 25 CISG, rule that ought to be used to supplement Article 1124; in a similar fashion, see Article 8:103 PECL." This reasoning was followed by numerous appellate court decisions, such as, SAP Islas Baleares, November 9, 2006 (RA 2007/90656); SAP Madrid, June 4, 2007 (RA 1226); SAP Madrid, June 19, 2007 (RA 1843); STSJ Navarra, July 5, 2007 (RA 8234); SAP Madrid, July 9, 2007; SAP Madrid, July 11, 2007 (RA 336743); SAP Madrid, July 30, 2007 (RA 355576); SAP Madrid, October 1, 2007 (RA 363163); SAP Madrid, November 5, 2007 (RA 2008/40434); SAP Valencia, November 12, 2007 (2008/85083); SAP Madrid, November 26, 2007 (2008/84397); SAP Madrid, February 18, 2008 (RA 2008/136291); SAP Madrid, February 18, 2008 (RA 2008/136216); SAP Madrid, April 8, 2008 (RA 189148). See also STS October 31, 2006, considering also indirectly that CISG and PECL ought to be used to supplement Article 1124 CC in accordance with the interpretation of the rules in accordance with the social reality in which are to be applied. For a mere doctrinal reference of the CISG, see STS, December 3, 2008 (RA 2009/525); SAP Murcia, October 7, 2010 (RA 391604); SAP Valencia, October 15, 2010 (2011/65976); SAP Córdoba, December 7, 2010 (RA 2011/379875); SAP Valencia, February 3, 2011 (RA 321927) and JPI, no. 2 Santiago de Compostela, May 31, 2011 (RA 322187).

[7] Pilar Perales Viscasillas, "The Role of the UNIDROIT Principles and the PECL in the Interpretation and Gap-filling of CISG" in *CISG Methodology* (ed. André Janssen and Olaf Meyer) (2009), 287.

[8] See Pilar Perales Viscasillas, "La aplicación jurisprudencial en España de la Convención de Viena de 1980 sobre compraventa internacional, los Principios de UNIDROIT y los Principios del Derecho Contractual Europeo: de la mera referencia a la integración de lagunas" *La Ley* 1 (May 31, 2007); id., "Aplicación Jurisprudencial de los Principios de Derecho Contractual Europeo," in *Derecho Privado Europeo: Estado actual y perspectivas de futuro. Jornadas en la Universidad Autónoma de Madrid* 13 (December 14, 2007) (Madrid, 2008), 453–92; A. Vendrell, "The Application of the Principles of European Contract Law by Spanish Courts" 3 *Zeitschrift für Europäisches Privatrecht* 534–48 (2008); Antonio Manuel Morales *Moreno, La Modernización del Derecho de Obligaciones* (Civitas: Madrid, 2006); Beatriz Fernández Gregoraci, "El moderno derecho de obligaciones y contratos en la jurisprudencia del Tribunal Supremo Español" 2 *Revista Jurídica de Catalunya* 171 (2009); Encarnación Roca Trías and Beatriz Fernández Gregoraci, "The Modern Law of Obligations in the Spanish High Court" 5 *European Rev. Contract L.* 45 (2009); M. Eugenia Rodríguez Martínez, "El proceso de unificación del Derecho Privado Europeo: alcance, aplicación a contratos internos y confrontación con los derechos estatales" *La Ley* 1 (7331) (January 29, 2010); Nieves Fenoy Picón, "La entidad del incumplimiento en la resolución del contrato: Análisis comparativo del artículo 1124 CC y del artículo 121 del Texto Refundido de Consumidores" *Tomo I Anuario de Derecho Civil 2009* 156 (2009).

[9] Audiencia Provincial of Navarra, December 27, 2007 (CLOUT 1039), available at http://cisgws.law.pace .edu/cases071227s4.html (good faith principle in CISG Article 7(1) extends its application to arbitration

Although the extent to which arbitration clauses or forum clauses are governed by the CISG is contentious, the authors agree with the possibility of an extended application of the CISG to issues outside of its scope,[10] more so in regard to arbitration clauses included within a contract governed by the CISG.[11]

III. Contract Formation

Issues of contract formation under the CISG normally involve questions relating to the conclusion of the contract, as well determining and interpreting the exact terms contained therein. In these cases, interpretation of the parties' intent is the main criterion.[12] One case involved a dispute over the price agreed upon between a seller and buyer in a contract for the sale of rubber. The court applied Article 8 to conclude that the seller could not have ignored the intention of the buyer to purchase thirty rubber rolls at a price of 20.57 EUR per roll and not per meter and concluded that the buyer's intention prevailed.[13]

In another case, the court had to determine whether there had existed a contract between a seller and buyer for the sale of cranes.[14] The seller alleged that the offer presented was subject to a specific condition that the contract would only be valid if the buyer was the first, among other potential buyers, to pay the purchase price. However, the negotiations between the parties led to different interpretations of the offer. The Audiencia Provincial of Murcia acknowledged the possibility of a contract of sale being subject to a certain condition under the CISG, but concluded that the offer presented by the seller gave preference to the buyer as long as the former paid the purchase price before a certain deadline. The buyer proceeded with the payment but the seller rejected it on the grounds that a third person had already made the payment. The court determined that the seller had made a valid and binding offer (subsequently accepted by the seller), which the seller had failed to comply with when rejecting the buyer's timely payment. The court also concluded that, according to the negotiations between the two parties, a contract of sale had been concluded and that the seller had breached her obligations.

IV. Conformity of Goods: Inspection and Notice

The majority of cases rendered by Spanish courts between 2007 and 2011 dealt with issues concerning the interpretation of time limits under Articles 38 (buyer's duty of

---

clauses and helps the courts to determine the content of the contract in accordance with the expectation of the parties). See also Audiencia Provincial de Navarra (Spain) September 22, 2003.

[10] See Pilar Perales Viscasillas, "Articles 7, 9, 11 CISG" in *UN Convention on Contracts for the International Sale of Goods (CISG): Commentary* (ed. S. Kröll, L.A. Mistelis, and P. Perales Viscasillas) (C.H. Beck-Hart-Nomos, 2011).

[11] Pilar Perales Viscasillas and David Ramos Muñoz, "CISG and Arbitration" in *Festschrift für Ingeborg Schwenzer zum 60* (Geburstag Stämpfli Verlag AG Bern and Intersentia Publishers, 2011), Band 2, 1355.

[12] For the formation of the contract under CISG, among the Spanish scholars, see Pilar Perales Viscasillas, *La Formacion del Contrato de Compraventa Internacional* (Tirant lo Blanch: Valencia, 1996).

[13] Audiencia Provincial of Cáceres, July 14, 2010 (CLOUT 1034). Application of Article 8 CISG to interpret the intention of the parties in regard to contract formation is a common feature both by scholars and case law. See Schmidt-Kessel in *Commentary on the UN Convention on the International Sale of Goods* (ed. P. Schlechtriem and I. Schwenzer) (Oxford, 2005), Article 8; Alberto Zuppi in Kröll et al., *UN Convention on Contracts*, Article 8, p. 142; *UNCITRAL Digest*, Article 14, available at www.uncitral.org.

[14] Audiencia Provincial of Murcia, July 15, 2010, available at www.cisgspanish.com.

inspection) and 39 (buyer's duty to give notice of nonconformity).[15] Article 39 is the most litigated Article in the CISG. Under Article 39, the buyer must notify the seller specifying any lack of conformity that the goods may have within a reasonable time after they have been inspected. In cases where no notice is made, the buyer is prevented from exercising any remedy under the CISG.[16]

In one case, the seller filed suit against a buyer for the lack of payment of the purchase price under their contract of sale. The buyer alleged that the machine delivered was unusable and thus, it lawfully refused to pay the purchase price. Although it was very difficult to determine the state of the machine at the time of performance under those circumstances,[17] the court focused on two other factors in concluding that the machine was in conformance to the contract at the time of delivery. First, the buyer did not inform the seller of any lack of conformity until more than one year after delivery, a period that the court considered unreasonable pursuant to Article 39(1). Second, the third party who purchased the machine from the buyer had paid its full price and had not raised any complaints regarding the state of the machine.

Another case involved a dispute relating to a sale of cattle.[18] The buyer alleged that seventeen out of sixty-four heads of cattle were in a "bad state" unfit for human consumption. The buyer destroyed the allegedly nonconforming ones without examination and refused to pay part of the purchase price. The court concluded that the buyer had failed to provide any evidence of the alleged nonconformity and further ruled that a mere statement from the buyer to an intermediary announcing its intention to pursue future actions against the seller for lack of conformity did not qualify as a notification under Article 39(1).

A decision rendered by the Audiencia Provincial of Pontevedra provided a thoughtful and thorough good analysis of the buyer's obligations under Articles 38 and 39,[19] namely the duty to examine the goods "within as short a period as is practicable"[20] and to "give notice to the seller specifying the nature of the lack of conformity within a reasonable time

---

[15] Also previous decisions; see *inter alia*: SAP Cuenca, January 31, 2005; SAP Barcelona, June 20, 1997; SAP Barcelona, September 12, 2001; SAP Navarra, March 27, 2000; SAP La Coruña, June 21, 2002; SAP Castellón, June 21, 2000.

[16] See "CISG-AC Opinion no. 2, Examination of the Goods and Notice of Non-Conformity: Articles 38 and 39" (June 7, 2004, Rapporteur: Professor Eric E. Bergsten), available at http://www.cisg.law.pace.edu/cisg/CISG-AC-op1.html; Elisabeth Opie, "Bergsten's Mark on the Law's International Reasonable Person," in *Liber Amicorum Eric Bergsten, International Arbitration and International Commercial Law: Synergy, Convergence and Evolution* (Wolters Kluwer 2011), 677–84. See also Camilla Andersen, "Reasonable Time in Article 39(1) of the CISG – Is Article 39(1) Truly a Uniform Provision?" *Rev. Convention on Contracts for the Int'l Sale of Goods (CISG)* (2008), 63; and David Ramos Munoz, "The Rules on Communication of Defects in the CISG: Static Rules and Dynamic Environments. Different Scenarios for a Single Player" (2006), available at http://www.cisg.law.pace.edu/cisg/biblio/munoz.html#2.

[17] Audiencia Provincial de Barcelona, in a decision rendered on March 24, 2009 (CLOUT 1037), also dealt with a case where the circumstances made it difficult to determine the alleged lack of conformity at the time the risk was passed to the buyer. In this case, part of the goods had been destroyed by the authorities upon arrival at the port of destination but the seller managed to provide the court with the sanitary certificates issued before delivery. The court concluded that the buyer had failed to provide the court with enough evidence to determine that there had been a lack of conformity.

[18] Juzgado de Primera Instancia (Court of First Instance) of La Laguna, October 23, 2007, available at www.cisgspanish.com.

[19] Audiencia Provincial of Pontevedra, December 19, 2007, available at www.cisgspanish.com.

[20] CISG, Article 38(1).

after he has discovered it or ought to have discovered it."[21] The case involved a dispute over frozen crabs and cockles. The court of first instance ruled that the examination of the goods and notification of lack of conformity had been carried out diligently by the buyer despite the fact that five months had lapsed since delivery. The seller appealed and the Audiencia Provincial of Pontevedra[22] ruled that the examination and notification carried out by the buyer had not complied with the requirements set forth under Articles 38 and 39 for the following reasons:

- The perishable nature, together with the fact that the goods were to be used for human consumption, requires an even more diligent care and examination.
- There were three deliveries and more than four months, two months, and fifty days had lapsed respectively before the defects in the goods were discovered and still another month passed before the seller was informed of the lack of conformity.
- A proper examination could have been undertaken easily and quickly; the goods were individually packed and evident features such as color and smell could have easily indicated the state of the goods.
- In previous cases of nonconformity, the buyer had examined the goods within a few days after delivery and the consequent claims had been settled amicably with the corresponding party.

The court reasoned for the requirement of providing notice of nonconformity within a "reasonable time" under Article 39 provides greater certainty to the performance of the contract. Too long a period would place business relationships in an indefinite situation that would likely increase the damages suffered by the parties. For all these reasons, the court concluded that the buyer did not comply with its obligations under Articles 38 and 39. The court considered that a reasonable time would have spanned no more than a few weeks, whereas in the case at bar more than five months had lapsed in relation to some of the deliveries. Therefore, the buyer's performance should be regarded as inconsistent with its obligations under Articles 38 and 39.

After making a deep analysis of the regulation of breaches of contract due to a lack of conformity of the goods under the CISG, the High Supreme Court[23] concluded that certain defects in the goods sold did not constitute a lack of conformity because the buyer had acknowledged that their previous use might have caused several damages in the cars, such as scratches. Moreover, the court noted that a representative of the buyer had examined the cars at the place of origin and had not raised any complaints as to nonconformity of the goods. In another decision,[24] the High Supreme Court confirmed a lower court decision[25] and based its nonconformity finding on a reference to CISG Article 33. The buyer and the seller concluded a contract for the sale of grape juice. The

[21] CISG, Article 39(1).
[22] Audiencia Provincial of Pontevedra, available at www.cisgspanish.com.
[23] January 17, 2008 (CLOUT 802), available at http://cisgw3.law.pace.edu/cases/080117s4.html; Nieves Fenoy Picón, "Comentario de la STS de 17 de enero de 2008: Compraventa internacional de vehículos automóviles de segunda mano: aplicación de la Convención de Viena de 11 de abril de 1980; no hay falta de conformidad; no denuncia en plazo de la falta de conformidad [comparación con la denuncia del TRLGDCU y otros modelos de Derecho privado europeo]; desestimación de la indemnización solicitada por el comprador; descripción del sistema de la Convención de Viena de la falta de conformidad de la mercadería" 78 Cuadernos Civitas de Jurisprudencia Civil 1299 (2008).
[24] Tribunal Supremo, December 9, 2008, available at www.cisgspanish.com.
[25] Audiencia Provincial of Valencia, June 7, 2003 (CLOUT 549).

parties agreed that there had been a breach of contract because the red color of the juice had faded, but differed on who would be responsible for the bad state of the juice. The buyer argued that the color had faded due to a flaw in production. The seller, however, claimed that the buyer's mismanagement of the transport had caused the color to fade.

The court held pursuant to Article 33(b), once the goods were at the buyer's disposal, the latter determined when to take charge of the goods. Being aware of the circumstances, the buyer decided to delay the transport of the juice and did not choose the appropriate means of transport (flexitanks instead of cooling containers). Furthermore, the buyer was aware of the features of the juice and knew the effect that the lapse of time would have on the juice's color. Moreover, the parties had included an "Ex Factory" clause according to which the risk of loss passed to the buyer once the goods were at its disposal. After examining the evidence presented by the parties, the court concluded that the seller had not breached the contract. The juice was in a state of conformity when placed at the buyer's disposal and the change of color had been caused by the buyer's delay in taking charge of the juice and the subsequent inappropriate transport.

Yet the buyer further alleged that the lower court had incorrectly applied Article 39 because, pursuant to Article 40, "[t]he seller is not entitled to rely on the provisions of Articles 38 and 39 if the lack of conformity relates to facts of which he knew or could not have been unaware and which he did not disclose to the buyer." However, the High Supreme Court concluded that the issue was irrelevant given that the buyer had not met its burden of proof that the goods were nonconforming at the time of delivery. The buyer should have examined the juice when it took possession and should not have waited until the juice arrived at its final destination, especially as the buyer knew or could not have been unaware of the effect of time and transport in the color of the juice.

The decision Audiencia Provincial of Zaragoza, March 31, 2009 (CLOUT 1036), dealt with an interesting dispute over a contract for sale of cured ham between a Belgian seller and a Spanish buyer. The seller filed suit against the buyer for the payment of the last purchase order, which the buyer had denied alleging an evident lack of conformity. The seller argued that the buyer had examined the goods upon receipt and failed to inform of any lack of conformity specifying the nature of the defect. On the other hand, the buyer claimed that the seller could not rely on Articles 38 and 39 CISG because she knew or could not have been unaware of the alleged lack of conformity (Article 40).

The buyer justified its denial for payment of the last purchase order, alleging that some of the hams did not meet the specific requirements of size (more than 7 kilograms for each piece) and fat levels. However, the court found that the motivation did not refer to the last installment delivered but to pieces of previous installments that had already been incorporated into the production process and pointed at inappropriate fat levels, a requirement that had not been specified in the corresponding purchase orders.

Moreover, the court affirmed that notifications of hams being undersized and having inappropriate fat levels did not meet the specificity requirement under Article 39 and only referred to potential reduction in case the mentioned defects did not halt. The court stated that the buyer's payment of the previous installments and their incorporation into the production process seven months before the last payment's denial amounted to an acceptance of the goods. Thus, given the buyer's own acknowledgement of the defects, the court rejected the application of Article 40 and confirmed the appealed decision condemning the buyer's breach of contract.

The issue of how the promptness of the required examination of the goods is affected by the "circumstances" under Article 38(1) was illustrated in a case involving a sale of 198,000 Portuguese flags with specific features, such as the signatures of Portugal's national soccer team.[26] The buyer then delivered the flags to a Portuguese client to be used as promotional gifts for a publication relating to the upcoming soccer World Cup. The flags delivered contained several defects including unclear patterns and badly made cuts. The Portuguese client noticed these defects. As a consequence, the original buyer refused to pay the seller for the final installments. The court of first instance held in favor of the seller, and ordered the buyer to make payment. It concluded that a two-month period of time for inspection and notice of nonconformity was unreasonable under the circumstances.

The experts' reports presented by both the buyer and seller agreed on the existence of the alleged defects, but differed on their consequences for the Portuguese client. The Audiencia Provincial cited a decision by the High Supreme Court[27] to differentiate between a fundamental breach of contract (Article 25) and a mere breach of contract under Article 35. If the latter, the court correctly reasoned that the appropriate remedy would be reparation, compensation, or price reduction. The court concluded that the seller had breached the contract pursuant to Article 35 and proceeded to examine whether the buyer had complied with its obligations under Articles 38 and 39. The court held that the postponement of the examination due to the transportation of the goods from the buyer to its client was reasonable. Therefore, the buyer had complied with its obligations to undertake an inspection within as a short period of time as practical given the circumstances. Further, the notice of nonconformity given two months after delivery of the goods to the buyer was reasonable.

The Audiencia Provincial Court stated that even though the goods were not perishable, the proximity of the World Cup called for an urgent action on the buyer's side. Nonetheless, it concluded that informing the seller two months after the receipt of the first delivery was sufficiently prompt notice and reasonable under the circumstances. The court cited another Spanish case that affirmed that a five-month period for informing the seller of defects was not a reasonable period of time under Article 39.[28]

The court's reasoning in this case was flawed. It referenced a previous decision that held a five-month period for notice as unreasonable, but failed to reference another case that held a fifty-day period was unreasonable as well. Given the proximity of the World Cup, inspection and notice under Articles 38 and 39 should have been interpreted to reach the conclusion that the two-month period was unreasonable. The lower court had made the proper interpretation when it concluded that the promotional purpose of the goods and their low price could not lead to the conclusion that there had been a breach of an essential obligation, as required under Article 25, but of a mere accessory obligation under Article 35.

In a case involving the sale of anchovies, a lower court ruled that the goods delivered did not meet the specifications agreed upon and that the buyer had provided notice of the lack of conformity within the time limits provided for under the CISG. Particularly, the court considered that the anchovies delivered were undersized rendering them unusable.

[26] Audiencia Provincial of Madrid, July 14, 2009, available at www.cisgspanish.com.
[27] Tribunal Supremo, January 17, 2008 (CLOUT 802).
[28] Audiencia Provincial of Pontevedra, December 19, 2007 (CLOUT 849).

On appeal, the seller based its claim on Article 336 of the Spanish Commercial Code instead of CISG Articles 35 and 39.[29] The Audiencia Provincial Court agreed with the lower court that the notice four months after delivery complied with its obligations under Article 39. It argued that the four-month period before notification was reasonable because anchovies were a perishable good and were packed in brine; hence, opening all the barrels would have put the anchovies at risk.

Another decision held that a fifty-day period before giving notice was unreasonable.[30] In the latter case the goods sold were also sea products (crabs and cockles). The difference lay in the preservation method and the defects in the goods. The crabs and cockles were frozen and individually packed. Some of them presented clear signs of putrefaction and a deep examination of their state would not have put the rest of the goods delivered at risk. However, in the anchovies' case the goods were not packed individually and the examination of one barrel could have ruined all the anchovies in that barrel. Moreover, the defect in that case (undersized anchovies) was not as obvious as the putrefaction of the crabs and cockles. For this reason, a four-month period was deemed reasonable in the anchovies' case whereas in the crabs and cockles' case a fifty-day period was held to be unreasonable.[31]

Finally, another case involved the sale of steel bars to be used in the manufacturing of industrial vehicles, trucks, and buses as components of high security.[32] It was shown that the seller was aware of the intended use and the high standards of quality control expected by the buyer. The seller alleged that the buyer did not comply with its obligations under Article 39 because the notice of the lack of conformity was not provided until two months and seven days after the delivery. The court rejected the seller's claim because the steel bars had both patent and latent defects. The latent defects consisted of hidden cracks that actually caused the defects that appeared during the manufacturing process. Given the special circumstances in the case, the court concluded that the two-month period was reasonable because it was only through use of the bars that the magnitude of the underlying defects was discoverable. In addition, the court noted that discovery of the hidden defects was necessary to conform to the specificity requirement of Article 39. Consequently, the court considered the time lapsed to be reasonable given the difficulty in determining the cause of the defect and the time needed to conduct various technical analyses.

V. Avoidance

Spanish cases on avoidance during the period from 2007 to 2011 reveal that the courts are becoming more sensitive to the need to interpret the CISG in the light of its international character and, as a result, there are fewer domestic law-biased decisions.[33]

---

[29] Audiencia Provincial of Asturias, September 29, 2010, available at www.cisgspanish.com.

[30] Audiencia Provincial of Pontevedra, December 19, 2007, available at www.cisgspanish.com.

[31] See also, Provincial of Valencia, April 8, 2008 (CLOUT 1038) (18-month period after delivery of machine held to be unreasonable); Audiencia Provincial of Valencia, May 12, 2008 (GPS radio equipment; 18 months deemed unreasonable). See also Tribunal Supremo on May 16, 2007 (CLOUT 800).

[32] Audiencia Provincial of Navarra, July 30, 2010, available at www.cisgspanish.com.

[33] See, e.g., SAP Palencia, September 26, 2005, available at www.cisgspanish.com.

In one case,[34] the court concluded – taking into account the negotiations between the parties and the purpose of the contract (energy production) – that the quality requirements agreed upon constituted an essential obligation.[35] The excessive percentages of humidity rendered the goods unusable for their original purpose and, therefore, constituted a fundamental breach. The result was the nonconforming goods produced a burdensome result for the buyer that justified an avoidance of the contract.

The often-cited 2008 decision of the High Supreme Court[36] provided a framework of understanding avoidance under the CISG. The court affirmed that Article 25 encompassed a system of objective contractual liabilities lessened by certain exemptions (fortuitous events and force majeure under Spanish Law) and reasonableness criteria.[37] A recent case citing this decision involved a contract of sale of aluminum tins.[38] The seller concluded a supply contract for aluminum tins to be sent directly to the buyer. The buyer inspected the goods upon receipt and immediately informed the seller that the tins received were not "clean" as required by the sales contract by showing traces of other metals. The court, citing the High Supreme Court decision, concluded that the alleged lack of conformity amounted to a fundamental breach under Article 25 and, thus, entitled the buyer to avoid the contract under Article 49(1)(a). The court based its decision on three grounds – a literal interpretation of the term "clean" in the sales contract, the expert's report that demonstrated that the traces in the tins delivered prevented them from being used due to potential risk of damaging the buyer's processing machines, and the seller's awareness of the commercial activity of the seller.

A 2010 case, noted in the previous section, cited the 2008 High Supreme Court decision as establishing the basic distinction between a fundamental breach and a mere breach of contract.[39] The case undertook an analysis of the object of the sales contract (steel bars) and their purpose (manufacture of industrial vehicles, trucks, and buses). The evidence presented demonstrated that the hidden defects in the steel bars impeded their use in the manufacturing process of the vehicles. Provided the high quality standards required in the automotive sector due to strict security regulations, the court concluded that the seller had breached the contract by delivering defective steel bars that, consequently, could not be used for their designated purpose.[40] This lack of conformity frustrated the buyer's expectations and, for that reason, the court ruled that the seller's breach of contract was fundamental and the buyer was entitled to avoid the contract.

---

[34] Audiencia Provincial of Madrid, February 20, 2007 (CLOUT 850), available at http://cisgw3.law.pace.edu/cases/070220s4.html.

[35] Audiencia Provincial of Navarra, December 27, 2007 (CLOUT 1039), available at http://cisgw3.law.pace.edu/cases/071227s4.html) (fundamental breach under Article 25 CISG requires that the breach be related to an essential purpose; a breach of an accessory obligation or a complementary did not undermine the purpose of the contract).

[36] Tribunal Supremo, January 17, 2008 (CLOUT 802).

[37] See Anselmo Martínez Canellas, *El Incumplimiento esencial en la Compraventa Internacional de Mercancías* (2006).

[38] Court of First Instance of Elche, July 6, 2009, available at www.cisgspanish.com.

[39] Audiencia Provincial of Navarra, available at www.cisgspanish.com.

[40] In this regard, the decision rendered by the Audiencia Provincial of Barcelona on January 27, 2010 (CLOUT 1035) pointed at the ordinary use and the particular use of the goods sold as good parameters when examining the conformity of the goods under Article 35 CISG.

VI. Remedies: Price Reduction and Damages

A. *Awarding Damages*

In a 2009 case,[41] the seller acknowledged that its wine contained ascorbic acid, but an examination carried out by the buyer disclosed that the wine also included benzoic acid, which is regarded as an unauthorized oenological practice. The buyer claimed damages under Article 74. The court analyzed three different issues relating to damages. First, it concluded that the cost for transportation of the wine to the seller's premises was not refundable because the buyer's decision to transport the wine was unilateral and, moreover, there was no evidence supporting the usefulness or the necessity of such a decision. Second, the court understood that the cost of the examination of the wine arose straight from the seller's breach of contract and it was the only means to confirm the defective quality of the wine and the potential harm to its consumers. The third issue was the loss of profit derived from the inability to sell the wine purchased. The court concluded that the seller "foresaw or ought to have foreseen" the alleged loss at the time of the conclusion of the contract pursuant to Articles 74 and 76. The seller was aware that the buyer was a trader in the wine market and was also aware that wine delivered containing benzoic acid was not resalable, and, thus, ought to be aware that the sale of a defective wine would result in a loss of profit for the buyer.

In another case, the court held that the seller had to compensate the buyer for the loss of profit calculated as the difference between the resale price and the contract price plus the transport expenses.[42] The court further affirmed that Articles 74, 75, and 77 were not applicable because the seller failed to provide any evidence on the damages exceeding "the loss which the party in breach foresaw or ought to have foreseen at the time of the conclusion of the contract" (Article 74), nor the feasibility of a substitute transaction (Article 75), or to claim that the buyer had not adopted reasonable measures to mitigate the loss in the light of the circumstances (Article 77).

In the area of incidental damages, a 2009 case dealt with a damages claim relating to the management of extrajudicial claims through a specialized company (Creditors Protection Association in Austria) and the hiring of a law firm by the aggrieved seller.[43] The Audiencia Provincial Court concluded that the expenses incurred were refundable under Article 74. The buyer was aware of the seller's management of such claims mainly because the general conditions in the sales contract expressly allowed the seller to make recourse to the aforementioned company in case of a buyer's default.

A case involved a FOB contract for sale of grated coconut where customs officials denied entry of the goods because they were not fit for human consumption.[44] The seller informed the buyer that the expiration dates placed on the goods were mistaken. There had been a mistake in the labeling of the goods and the seller attached two certifications for confirmation. The goods were returned to the seller who then only refunded a part of the purchase price. The buyer sought damages arising out of the avoidance of the contract. Due to the lack of a limitation period in the CISG, the court applied the general

---

[41] Audiencia Provincial of Madrid, March 10, 2009, available at www.cisgspanish.com.
[42] Audiencia Provincial of Murcia, July 15, 2010, available at www.cisgspanish.com.
[43] Audiencia Provincial of Alicante, April 24, 2009, available at www.cisgspanish.com.
[44] Audiencia Provincial of Valencia, March 13, 2007, available at www.cisgspanish.com.

limitation period of fifteen years fixed in Article 1964 Spanish Civil Code. The court further concluded that the buyer was not entitled to damages on the grounds that a "simple" breach of contract does not necessarily entail compensation if the creditor has not provided sufficient evidence of such damages.

B. *Enforceability of Penalty Clauses*

The Audiencia Provincial Court of Madrid[45] dealt with the applicability of a penalty clause included in a sales contract. The original contract provided for the delivery of the goods by ship but was later modified to include air transport at the seller's expense due to a delay of the marine shipment. The buyer refused to pay several invoices, alleging the application of a penalty clause included in the contract according to which a 1 percent discount would be applied for every day the goods were delivered late. The Audiencia Provincial held that Articles 48 and 74 were not applicable as purported by the buyer. The court concluded that seller's right to cure under Article 48 was not applicable because it related to "ordinary" breaches and the penalty clause is an autonomous obligation over certain relation to breaches of contract. In the case, the parties had freely consented to the penalty clause and intended it to apply from the very first day of default. In the court's opinion, Article 74 did not apply either because the penalty clause substituted for Article 74 damages.

Despite considering the penalty cause applicable in the case, the court reduced the final amount payable as damages by 50 percent under the sales contract for two reasons – the goods were effectively received by the buyer and there was no evidence of the late delivery having caused any damages, and the seller's manifest will to comply with its obligations under the contract offering alternative air transport at its expense.

The question of the enforceability of penalty clauses under the CISG is a contentious one. The majority of CISG case law holds that the issue is not covered by the CISG.[46] One scholarly view considers the function of the clause. If the intention is exclusively to punish the breaching party, the validity issue is to be determined under domestic law, or, alternatively, that such clauses are void under Article 4(a). If considered valid under domestic law, the clause might be analyzed within the CISG's general principles. This interpretation is certainly more in line with the uniformity principle as compared with the solution that entirely excludes such clauses from the scope of the CISG irrespective of the function of the clause. The authors' view is that the issue is entirely governed by the CISG even if the clause is a true penalty because the CISG intends to govern all remedies for the breach of contract. If, as is ordinarily the case, the function of the clause is to compensate (damage function), then there is no issue of validity because the matter of

---

[45] Audiencia Provincial Court of Madrid, October 18, 2007, available at www.cisgspanish.com.
[46] Arbitral Award, ICC 7197/1992, CISG-Online 36 (Pace), Tribunale di Padova (Italy) February 25, 2004, CISG-Online 819 (Pace) (*obiter dicta*), and Arbitral Award, Tribunal of International Commercial Arbitration at the Russian Federation Chamber of Commerce and Industry, March 1, 2006 (Pace). Indifferent as to the same result would be derived applying domestic law: Oberlandesgericht Hamburg (Germany) January 25, 2008, CISG-Online 1681 (Pace). The CISG does not regulate the question of whether the penalty the parties agreed upon can be moderated: Gerechtshof Arnhem (Netherlands) August 22, 1995, CISG-Online 317 (Pace). Contrary, Michael Bridge, *The International Sale of Goods: Law and Practice* (Oxford University Press: Oxford, 2007), para. 11.38 (penalty clauses are governed by the CISG; general principle derived from Article 74 implies that penalties should be disallowed because they are supracompensatory).

damages is governed by the CISG (penalty clause acts to displace Article 74).[47] The issue of adjusting or reforming the penalty amount should also be governed by the CISG. Such adjustments should only be made if the amount grossly exceeds the general principle of full compensation under the CISG. In any case, the PICC (Article 7.4.13 and Article 7.4.14) offer a useful interpretative guide to consider in conjunction with the CISG. Finally, the general principle of full compensation applies to the interpretation of the penalty clause, as well as other damages available to the aggrieved party.

C. *Interest Damages*

In the area of interest damages, a court acknowledged that Article 78 did not fix the "dies a quo."[48] However, it also argued that pursuant to Article 7(2) "questions concerning matters governed by this Convention which are not expressly settled in it are to be settled in conformity with the general principles on which it is based or, in the absence of such principles, in conformity with the law applicable by virtue of the rules of private international law." In the absence of general principles[49] the court applied Spanish law to determine the "dies a quo" under Article 63(1) of the Spanish Commercial Code. According to this provision, the effects of default over obligations of a commercial nature included in a contract with a specific date for performance will begin on the next day after the due date. The court further concluded that the interest rate applicable would be determined in the light of Spanish Insolvency Law. A similar conclusion was reached in a decision rendered by the Court of First Instance of La Laguna, October 23, 2007.

VII. Substitute Transactions

One case involved several breaches of a stock purchase agreement.[50] The dispute focused on the determination of damages deriving from those breaches. The breaching party argued that Article 75 was not applied and, further, that a substitute transaction was equivalent to a loss of profit. In relation to these two questions, the High Supreme Court stated that "in cases of breach of contract by the seller, a substitute transaction allows the buyer to purchase similar goods (of the same quality and quantity) from an alternative source as long as she behaves in good faith and, consequently, allows her to claim the possible difference in price." In this regard, the court considered that Article 75 was not applicable because Article 2(d) excludes the application of the CISG to sales of stocks or shares.

Regarding the second question, the court considered that Article 75, which regulates substitute transactions, could not be applied to cases of loss of profit. It cited the grape juice case,[51] which stated that "if the buyer purchases new sets of grape juice to hedge against the consequences of a breach of contract at a higher price this would be a consequential damage that has nothing to do with a loss of profit, which actually refers to expectations of income by the resale of the goods acquired." Furthermore, the court

[47] Although considering domestic law for its moderation was deemed for appropriate in SAP Madrid, October 18, 2007, available at www.cisgspanish.com.
[48] Audiencia Provincial of Valencia, April 8, 2008 (CLOUT 1038).
[49] Cf. John Gotanda in Kröll et al., *UN Convention on Contracts*, Article 78 CISG, nos. 16–20.
[50] Tribunal Supremo on September 3, 2010, available at: www.cisgspanish.com.
[51] STS, May 14, 2003.

considered that the decisions quoted could not be applied in the case examined because the facts differ greatly from the case of a stock purchase agreement that had been sold at a lower price. The court held that the case at bar did not warrant a substitute transaction.

VIII. Mitigation and Preservation

In a decision involving the issues of the buyer's duties of mitigation and preservation, the court considered that the buyer was aware of the alleged defect of the hams purchased from the seller and concluded that the former had breached the contract by denying payment of the last installment delivered.[52] In spite of this finding, the court examined the buyer's claim for damages and concluded that the buyer had not complied with its obligation to mitigate under Article 77. The buyer received all the goods and incorporated them into the production process. The court affirmed that, although the buyer had made clear its intention to exercise its rights under the CISG, it had failed to take reasonable measures to preserve the hams as required by Article 86. The court also rejected the buyer's assertion that it did not possess the means to preserve the hams, noting that the buyer never rejected the goods, deposited them in a warehouse of a third person (Article 87), nor attempted to resell them (Article 88).

---

[52] Audiencia Provincial of Zaragoza, March 31, 2009 (CLOUT 1036).

28 Switzerland

Corinne Widmer Lüchinger

I. History of the CISG in Switzerland

In supporting the adoption of the CISG, the Swiss government referred to the "decade-old dream of a universal lex mercatoria."[1] However, what made the CISG truly attractive for Switzerland was of a more pragmatic nature. Switzerland is a small country, and cross-border transactions play a central part in the country's economy.[2] Accordingly, the number of international sales contracts is very high. Also, due to its geographic location and political stability, Switzerland is an important center for international commercial arbitration.[3] As such, arbitral tribunals and state courts in Switzerland often deal with international sales contracts.

Before the CISG entered into force in Switzerland, the law governing international sales contracts was determined under domestic principles of conflict of laws. The resulting uncertainty in the application of law was partially overcome by the Hague Convention on the Law Applicable to International Sales of Goods of June 15, 1955, which entered into force in Switzerland in 1972. The Hague Convention provides uniform rules on conflict of laws, thus ensuring greater predictability. However, because the convention seeks only to harmonize conflict of laws rules, international sales contracts continued to be governed by domestic laws, which vary in substance. As a result, two substantive law conventions were produced – the Hague Convention relating to a Uniform Law on the Formation of Contracts for the International Sale of Goods (ULF) and the Hague Convention relating to a Uniform Law on the International Sale of Goods (ULIS), both concluded in 1964. However, only nine states adopted these conventions, and Switzerland was not one of them.[4] Despite the Hague Conventions' lack of success, they are seen as predecessor instruments to the CISG, which was adopted in Vienna in 1980.

---

[1] See "Message of the Swiss Federal Council Concerning the United Nations Convention on Contracts for the International Sale of Goods," *Bundesblatt* 1989 I 745, 748 (hereafter referred to as "Message of the Swiss Federal Council").

[2] See Eugen Bucher, "Überblick über die Neuerungen des Wiener Kaufrechts; dessen Verhältnis zur Kaufrechtstradition und zum nationalen Recht," in *Wiener Kaufrecht, Berner Tage für die juristische Praxis* (ed. E. Bucher) (Bern: Staempfli, 1991), 13–14.

[3] See, e.g., Marc Blessing, *Introduction to Arbitration: Swiss and International Perspectives* (Basel: Helbing & Lichtenhahn, 1999).

[4] See "Message of the Swiss Federal Council," 750; Ingeborg Schwenzer in *Commentary on the UN Convention on the International Sale of Goods (CISG)*, 3rd ed. (ed. I. Schwenzer) (Oxford: Oxford University Press, 2010) (hereafter referred to as *Commentary*), Introduction, 1–2 (impact of the 1964 Hague Conventions).

It is characteristic of the Swiss legislative process that prior to the government's report to the parliament and before the beginning of parliamentary debate, interested parties (Swiss chambers of commerce, the Swiss Bar Association, political parties, academics, and so forth) are invited to comment on the proposed legislation. The purpose of this consultation process (*Vernehmlassung, consultation*, or *consultazione*) is to ensure that possible concerns and suggestions for improvement are addressed. The consultation process with respect to the CISG showed support for its adoption on the condition that Switzerland's major trading partners would also be party to the CISG.[5] A minority of stakeholders, including the Swiss Bar Association, were in favor of issuing a declaration under CISG Article 95, in order to ensure that Article 1(1)(b) would not bind Switzerland. However, the Swiss government wisely rejected this suggestion. It considered that a declaration under Article 95 would only complicate matters and would also contradict the goal of finding uniform solutions for issues of international sales law.[6]

The decision to adopt the CISG in Switzerland was facilitated by its adoption in France, Germany, Italy, and the United States.[7] A further decisive element was the fact that the CISG regulated its sphere of application autonomously (CISG Article 1(1)(a)), so that the role of domestic rules on conflict of laws with all their perceived difficulties and disadvantages was diminished.[8] The Swiss government recognized the commercial need for clear and transparent rules in international sales, a need that could better be met by a set of substantive rules designed specifically for international transactions rather than by domestic rules. As a case in point, the government cited the seller's duty to deliver substitute goods or remedy the lack of conformity by repair, a duty far more limited under the CISG than under domestic law.[9] Finally, the Swiss government was persuaded that parties would more readily agree on a choice of law clause if a "neutral" law, such as the CISG, were available.[10] Despite some reservations about the CISG's coexistence with the Swiss Code of Obligations[11] (CO),[12] the two chambers of parliament with only brief discussion approved the CISG. When the CISG entered into force in Switzerland on March 1, 1991, its adoption was welcomed as a good and sensible step.[13] The opinion

---

[5] Cf. *Amtliches Bulletin* (AB) 1989 III 229; AB 1989 IV 1658.

[6] AB 1989 III 229; AB 1989 IV 1658.

[7] See Corinne Widmer and Pascal Hachem, "The CISG in Switzerland," in *The CISG and Its Impact on National Contract Law* (ed. F. Ferrari) (Munich: Sellier, 2008), 281–2; cf. "Message of the Swiss Federal Council," 838–9.

[8] Cf. also Gerold Herrmann, "Anwendungsbereich des Wiener Kaufrechts," in Bucher, *Wiener Kaufrecht, Berner Tage*, 83, 98–9.

[9] But see Heinrich Honsell, "Commentary on Article 205 OR," in *Basler Kommentar: Obligationenrecht I, Art. 1–529 OR*, 4th ed. (ed. H. Honsell, N.P. Vogt, and W. Wiegand) (Basel: Helbing Lichtenhahn, 2007), para. 5 (it is unsettled whether the buyer actually has a right to demand repair under the Swiss Code of Obligations).

[10] See "Message of the Swiss Federal Council," 838.

[11] Bundesgesetz vom 30. März 1911 betreffend die Ergänzung des Schweizerischen Zivilgesetzbuches (Fünfter Teil: Obligationenrecht); Loi fédérale du 30 mars 1911 complétant le code civil suisse (Livre cinquième: Droit des obligations); Legge federale del 30 marzo 1911 di complemento del Codice civile svizzero (Libro quinto: Diritto delle obbligazioni), SR 220.

[12] See Swiss Council of States (Ständerat, Conseil des Etats, or Consiglio degli Stati), session of June 7, 1989, AB 1989 III 229, and the session of the Swiss National Council (Nationalrat, Conseil National, or Consiglio Nazionale) of October 5, 1989, AB 1989 IV 1658, available at http://www.parlament.ch/ab/frameset/d/index.htm (accessed 30 March 2013).

[13] See, e.g., Ingeborg Schwenzer, "Das UN-Abkommen zum internationalen Warenkauf (CISG)," *recht* 113 (1991).

was even voiced that the CISG's impact in Switzerland would be far greater than in other countries, due to Switzerland's small size and the importance of cross-border transactions.[14]

More than twenty years after the CISG entered into force in Switzerland, the CISG-online database lists a total of 196 Swiss court decisions on the CISG.[15] Given the importance of cross-border transactions in Switzerland, this figure appears comparatively modest (albeit less so when compared to other countries). There are two possible explanations. First, a majority of international commercial contracts provide for arbitration, which is typically private and confidential. Second, many lawyers continue to exclude the application of the CISG in their clients' contracts. Two surveys conducted in Switzerland a few years ago[16] showed that Swiss lawyers continue to exclude the application of the CISG when drawing up contracts.[17] One reason given by participants for excluding the CISG was that it did not provide enough legal certainty.[18] Other participants noted that due to the CISG's limited scope, domestic law continued to play an important role in international sales disputes. Rather than having two distinct, and possibly conflicting, sets of rules apply, they preferred to exclude the CISG and choose a domestic law to govern all sales law issues.[19]

II. Principle of Good Faith

The principle of good faith is a concept with which Swiss lawyers are more than familiar. Under domestic Swiss law, parties to a contract are under a general duty to act in good faith (Article 2 of the Swiss Civil Code (CC)[20]). In particular, good faith can give rise to additional obligations between the parties.[21]

In contrast, under the CISG, the principle of good faith is of limited importance. The CISG's express reference to good faith in Article 7(1) limits its use to recognizing the "observance of good faith in international trade" in the interpretation of the CISG. CISG Article 8 makes no reference to good faith in the interpretation and supplementation of the parties' statements and conduct. The drafting history of the CISG[22] shows that the omission of a reference to good faith in Article 8 was not an oversight. Thus, the majority

---

[14] See Bucher, "Überblick über die Neuerungen des Wiener Kaufrechts," 13–14.

[15] See http://www.cisg-online.ch (as per March 30, 2013).

[16] See Widmer and Hachem, "The CISG in Switzerland," 282–8; Justus Meyer, "UN-Kaufrecht in der schweizerischen Anwaltspraxis," *Schweizerische Juristenzeitung* (*SJZ*) 421 (2008).

[17] Percentage of participating attorneys stating they opt out of the CISG was 40.8%. Id., 425. In Widmer and Hachem, "The CISG in Switzerland," 62% of participating attorneys stated that they routinely exclude the CISG (285, 287).

[18] This reason was given by more than 41% of attorneys, id., 285; 48% of attorneys, Meyer, "UN-Kaufrecht," 426. See also Lisa Spagnolo, "The Last Outpost: Automatic CISG Opt Outs, Misapplications and the Costs of Ignoring the Vienna Sales Convention for Australian Lawyers," *Melbourne J. Int'l L.* 10 (2009), available at http://www.austlii.edu.au/au/journals/MelbJIL/2009/10.html (accessed March 30, 2013).

[19] Widmer and Hachem, "The CISG in Switzerland," 285; Meyer, "UN-Kaufrecht", 426.

[20] Schweizerisches Zivilgesetzbuch vom 10. Dezember 1907; Code civil suisse du 10 décembre 1907; Codice civile svizzero del 10 dicembre 1907, SR 210.

[21] See, e.g., Heinrich Honsell, "Commentary on Article 2 ZGB," in *Basler Kommentar: Zivilgesetzbuch I, Art. 1–456 ZGB*, 4th ed. (ed. H. Honsell, N.P. Vogt, and T. Geiser) (Basel: Helbing Lichtenhahn, 2010), para. 16.

[22] Cf. Ingeborg Schwenzer and Pascal Hachem, "Commentary on Article 7 CISG," in *Commentary*, para. 17.

view is that good faith applies only with respect to the interpretation of the convention.[23] Nonetheless, courts whose domestic legal systems recognize a general duty of good faith in contracting have interpreted the good faith principle as an independent source of rules for contract interpretation or as a source of ancillary duties between the parties when deciding CISG cases. This "temptation" or homeward trend bias has been particularly strong in German[24] and, to a lesser extent, Swiss courts.[25]

References to good faith in Swiss CISG case law are often very general and supplemental in nature. Good faith is rarely given as the main rationale for the outcome of a given case. In one case,[26] for example, the parties to a contract for the delivery of diesel oil with a maximum sulfur content of 0.5 percent had included a clause concerning the inspection of the oil by an independent inspector. The parties' dispute centered on the number of inspectors and samples allowed under the contract clause's inspection requirement. The court held that the clause was ambiguous and that no practices between the parties or trade usages had been established. Therefore, the parties' subsequent conduct was decisive in the interpretation of the clause. As the seller had not, at the time, objected when a second inspector took additional samples, the court decided that the parties had not limited testing to one sample to be taken by one inspector. Instead of solely basing its decision on the parties' intent pursuant to Article 8, the court further stated that taking the parties' conduct into account was consistent with "the general principle of good faith." This reference to the duty of good faith was superfluous[27] and did not change the case outcome.

Under the CISG, silence can only give rise to a contract if such a means of acceptance corresponds to the usages agreed upon by the parties or practices established between them under Article 9(1) or in case of an international trade usage under Article 9(2).[28] Article 18(1) provides that silence or inactivity does not in itself amount to acceptance. In contrast, under domestic Swiss law, failure to object to a commercial confirmation letter within a reasonable time may result in a binding contract.[29] This outcome is generally derived from the principle of good faith.[30] In a 2005 decision,[31] the Swiss Federal Supreme Court appeared to apply this principle also under the CISG. The decision involved a case in which a seller had failed to object to the terms in the buyer's "purchasing

---

[23] Id., para. 18; Martin Schmidt-Kessel, "Commentary on Article 8 CISG," in *Commentary*, para. 31; contra, Christoph Brunner, "Commentary on Article 7 CISG," in *UN-Kaufrecht – CISG: Kommentar zum Übereinkommen der Vereinten Nationen über Verträge über den internationalen Warenkauf von 1980* (ed. C. Brunner) (Bern: Staempfli, 2004), para. 4.

[24] See Schwenzer and Hachem, "Commentary on Article 7 CISG," para. 17.

[25] See, e.g., Court of Appeal Thurgau (Obergericht des Kantons Thurgau), December 12, 2006, CISG-online 1566 (*obiter*) (principle of good faith, although not explicitly referred to in the CISG, is a guiding principle for contract interpretation under the CISG).

[26] Court of Appeal Zug (Obergericht des Kantons Zug), July 5, 2005, CISG-online 1155.

[27] Cf. Schmidt-Kessel, "Commentary on Article 8 CISG," in *Commentary*, para. 31, n. 157.

[28] Cf. Ulrich G. Schroeter, "Introduction to Arts. 14–24 CISG," in *Commentary*, para. 30. Cf. also Commercial Court Aargau (Handelsgericht des Kantons Aargau), February 5, 2008, CISG-online 1740.

[29] See Swiss Federal Supreme Court (Schweizerisches Bundesgericht), BGE 114 II 250, October 27, 1988, available at http://www.bger.ch (accessed March 30, 2013). Cf. also Schroeter, "Introduction to Arts. 14–24 CISG," para. 28 (on German law).

[30] See, e.g., Swiss Federal Supreme Court (Schweizerisches Bundesgericht), August 4, 2003, CISG-online 804.

[31] Decision 4C.474/2004, April 5, 2005, CISG-online 1012, reversing the decision of the Court of Appeal Fribourg (Kantonsgericht Fribourg), October 11, 2004, CISG-online 964.

confirmation," which were materially different to those in the seller's original offer. The court stated that in such a situation, the seller was under "a good faith duty to object" if it did not wish to be bound by the terms of the confirmation. However, an analysis of the case shows that the court's decision was not based on the defendant's failure to object. Rather, the court held that a reasonable person would have understood the seller's subsequent *conduct* – namely, explicit references to the buyer's "purchasing confirmation," delivery of documents requested by the buyer – as an acceptance of the confirmation's terms under Article 8(2). Thus, although the court's additional reference to good faith was out of place in this context, it had no actual impact on the outcome of the case.

Other courts in Switzerland[32] have referred to the good faith principle when applying the reasonable person standard of Article 8(2). The principles set forth in Article 8(2) correspond to the "objective test" standard under domestic Swiss law.[33] In domestic Swiss law, the "objective test" follows from the good faith principle,[34] so references to good faith in CISG cases may be a matter of habit. Although these references to good faith may not be supported by the CISG,[35] they do not, as a rule, have any impact on the outcome of the case.

III. Contract Formation

Several Swiss cases have dealt with formation issues, such as the parties' intention to be bound,[36] the qualification of parties' declarations and conduct as offer and acceptance,[37] the conclusion of a contract despite the parties' failure to fix or make provision for determining the price,[38] the burden of proof with respect to contract formation,[39] and the effect of commercial letters of confirmation.[40] This last issue merits particular attention.

---

[32] Court of Appeal Thurgau (Obergericht des Kantons Thurgau), December 19, 1995, CISG-online 496; Commercial Court Aargau (Handelsgericht des Kantons Aargau), November 26, 2008, CISG-online 1739; Commercial Court Aargau, February 5, 2008, CISG-online 1740.

[33] See Swiss Federal Supreme Court (Schweizerisches Bundesgericht), April 5, 2005, CISG-online 1012.

[34] See, e.g., Ernst Kramer, "Commentary on Article 1," in *Berner Kommentar zum schweizerischen Privatrecht, Band VI, 1. Abteilung, 1. Teilband, Art. 1–18 OR* (Bern: Staempfli, 1986), para. 37.

[35] See Martin Schmidt-Kessel, "Commentary on Article 8 CISG," in *Commentary*, para. 31, with explicit reference to these cases in n. 157.

[36] See Cantonal Court Zug (Kantonsgericht Zug), December 2, 2004, CISG-online 1194; District Court St. Gallen (Bezirksgericht St. Gallen), July 3, 1997, CISG-online 336. In the latter case, the defendant had agreed to produce 30 to 35 items of clothing out of cloth from claimant's stock, on the basis of which the parties were to decide on a possible future collaboration. After the clothes had been produced, the defendant informed the claimant that she was not interested in any further collaboration, and requested that claimant "charge for the material." Based on CISG Article 8(2), the court held that this request evidenced the defendant's intention to be bound to a sales contract with claimant for the material from claimant's stock.

[37] Commercial Court St. Gallen (Handelsgericht des Kantons St. Gallen), April 29, 2004, CISG-online 962; Cantonal Court Zug (Kantonsgericht Zug), December 2, 2004, CISG-online 1194; Swiss Federal Supreme Court (Schweizerisches Bundesgericht), April 5, 2005, CISG-online 1012; Swiss Federal Supreme Court, August 4, 2003, CISG-online 804; District Court Arbon (Bezirksgericht Arbon), December 19, 1995, CISG-online 376.

[38] District Court St. Gallen (Bezirksgericht St. Gallen), July 3, 1997, CISG-online 336 (on this case, see also *supra* note 36).

[39] Cantonal Court Zug (Kantonsgericht Zug), December 2, 2004, CISG-online 1194.

[40] Swiss Federal Supreme Court (Schweizerisches Bundesgericht), April 5, 2005, CISG-online 1012, reversing the decision of Court of Appeal Fribourg (Kantonsgericht Fribourg), October 11, 2004, CISG-online

A. *Commercial Letters of Confirmation*

As noted in the previous section, failure to object to commercial letters of confirmation within a reasonable time can result in a binding contract under domestic Swiss law. Under the CISG, silence or mere inactivity on receipt of a letter of confirmation only constitutes acceptance of the letter's terms if there is an international trade usage to that effect or a practice established by the parties. Although in the case discussed earlier,[41] the Swiss Federal Supreme Court appeared to recognize a duty to object to letters of confirmation under the CISG, its finding was actually based on the defendant's conduct, and not on mere inactivity or silence. Nonetheless, in the future it would be best if Swiss courts omitted unnecessary references to concepts of domestic Swiss law.

In two other cases dealing with letters of confirmation,[42] Swiss courts held that failure to object to a commercial letter of confirmation within a reasonable time may result in a binding contract under the CISG if both parties had their places of business in states whose domestic law recognized such a duty. Only one of the courts specifically referred to Article 9(2) in its decision,[43] but the other court also implicitly recognized an "international trade usage."[44] The key issue is whether a trade usage invoked by a party is "international" in scope as required under Article 9(2). Local trade usages can suffice,[45] but the usage must relate to international, as opposed to purely domestic, trade.[46] If the usage is only established with respect to purely domestic transactions, this will not suffice for the purposes of Article 9(2).[47] Accordingly, a party invoking an international trade usage is required to show that the local or domestic usage applies to international transactions.[48] Moreover, the party claiming the usage must show that the parties knew or ought to have known of the usage and that such usage is widely known to, and regularly

---

964; Commercial Court Aargau (Handelsgericht des Kantons Aargau), February 5, 2008, CISG-online 1740.

[41] Decision 4C.474/2004, April 5, 2005, CISG-online 1012; see *supra* II.

[42] Commercial Court Aargau (Handelsgericht des Kantons Aargau), February 5, 2008, CISG-online 1740. See also Civil Court Basel-Stadt (Zivilgericht Basel-Stadt), December 21, 1992, CISG-online 55; Ernst Kramer, "Neues aus Gesetzgebung, Praxis und Lehre zum Vertragsschluss," *Basler Juristische Mitteilungen (BJM)* 1, 8–9 (1995).

[43] See Civil Court Basel-Stadt (Zivilgericht Basel-Stadt), December 21, 1992, CISG-online 55; the court based its decision on CISG Article 9(1) and (2).

[44] Commercial Court Aargau (Handelsgericht des Kantons Aargau), February 5, 2008, CISG-online 1740. Trade usages are rules of commerce regularly observed by members of a particular trade. E. Allan Farnsworth, "Commentary on Article 9 CISG," in *Commentary on the International Sales Law* (ed. C.M. Bianca and M.J. Bonell) (Milan: Giuffrè, 1987), n. 3.2; Martin Schmidt-Kessel, "Commentary on Article 9 CISG," in *Commentary*, para. 11; Christoph Brunner, "Vorbemerkungen zu Art. 14–24 CISG," in Brunner, *UN-Kaufrecht – CISG*, para. 6.

[45] See, e.g., Schmidt-Kessel, "Commentary on Article 9 CISG," in *Commentary*, para. 18.

[46] See Civil Court Basel-Stadt (Zivilgericht Basel-Stadt), December 21, 1992, CISG-online 55.

[47] Domestic rules are generally developed with domestic transactions in mind. See Corinne Widmer, "Kollisionsrecht, Einheitsrecht und die 'internationale Auslegung' von nationalem Sachrecht," in *La loi fédérale de droit international privé: vingt ans après* (ed. A. Bonomi and E. Cashin Ritaine) (Zurich: Schulthess, 2009), 195, 207–212.

[48] According to the Civil Court Basel-Stadt (Zivilgericht Basel-Stadt), December 21, 1992, CISG-online 55, if both domestic laws acknowledge a duty to object to letters of confirmation in certain circumstances, it is "unlikely that different rules might apply to international commerce between these countries." The court's decision is problematic in that its interpretation of Swiss and Austrian law was in fact erroneous; see Kramer, "Neues aus Gesetzgebung, " 9–10; see also Brunner, "Vorbemerkungen zu Art. 14–24 CISG," in Brunner, *UN-Kaufrecht – CISG*, para. 6, n. 442.

observed by, members of the particular trade. Only then should a court recognize a trade usage under Article 9(2).[49]

The party claiming the applicability of a trade usage has the burden of meeting the requirements of Article 9(2). Several Swiss cases have dealt with the question of burden of proof, both generally and with respect to contract formation in particular.[50] In these cases, the courts held that the burden of proof is a matter governed by the CISG.[51]

B. *Battle of the Forms*

Attempts at the Vienna conference to include a specific provision on conflicting standard terms were not successful.[52] Nonetheless, the general view is that the CISG covers the topic of the battle of the forms.[53] However, the practical relevance of such "battles" appears to be less pronounced than academic attention might suggest.[54] This is certainly true for Switzerland, where there is only one decision on conflicting standard terms under the CISG.[55] In this case, the Cantonal Court of Zug was called upon to decide whether it had jurisdiction over the parties' dispute under, inter alia, Article 5(1) of the former Lugano Convention of 1988,[56] which gave jurisdiction to the court at the place of performance.[57] Under Article 5(1), the place of performance was determined in accordance with the law applicable to the disputed contract.[58] Moreover, the place of performance was not determined for the entire contract, but rather only for the specific obligation in dispute.[59] Hoping to establish the jurisdiction of its domestic court, the buyer invoked the conditions of its delivery order, which provided for delivery "free domicile" and stated that the delivery address was the buyer's domicile. Referencing

---

[49] See also Schroeter, "Introduction to Arts. 14–24 CISG," para. 33.

[50] See Cantonal Court Zug (Kantonsgericht Zug), December 2, 2004, CISG-online 1194; Commercial Court Zurich (Handelsgericht des Kantons Zürich), December 22, 2005, CISG-online 1195.

[51] See Swiss Federal Supreme Court (Schweizerisches Bundesgericht), BGE 138 III 601, July 16, 2012, CISG-online 2371; Swiss Federal Supreme Court, BGE 130 III 258, November 13, 2003, CISG-online 840; Swiss Federal Supreme Court, July 7, 2004, CISG-online 848; see also Ingeborg Schwenzer and Pascal Hachem, "Commentary on Article 4 CISG," in *Commentary*, para. 25. Older decisions considered the burden of proof not to be governed by the CISG; see District Court Saane (Bezirksgericht der Saane), February 20, 1997, CISG-online 426.

[52] See, e.g., Ulrich G. Schroeter, "Commentary on Article 19 CISG," in *Commentary*, para. 33.

[53] See, e.g., id.; Ingeborg Schwenzer and Florian Mohs, "Old Habits Die Hard: Traditional Contract Formation in a Modern World," *Internationales Handelsrecht (IHR)* 239, 241 (2006).

[54] See Schroeter, "Commentary on Article 19 CISG," para. 34.

[55] Cantonal Court Zug (Kantonsgericht Zug), December 11, 2003, CISG-online 958.

[56] Lugano Convention of 16 September 1988 on Jurisdiction and the Enforcement of Judgments in Civil and Commercial Matters. The amended Lugano Convention of October 30, 2007, entered into force in Switzerland on January 1, 2011.

[57] On the relationship between the CISG and Article 5(1) of the 1988 Lugano Convention, see generally Corinne Widmer, "Commentary on Article 31 CISG," in *Commentary*, para. 87 et seq. For the situation under the new Convention of 2007, see, e.g., Dieter A. Hoffmann and Oliver M. Kunz, "Commentary on Article 5 Lugano Convention," in *Basler Kommentar: Lugano Übereinkommen* (ed. C. Oetiker and T. Weibel) (Basel: Helbing Lichtenhahn, 2011), para. 223 et seq.

[58] See the leading case of the European Court of Justice (ECJ), October 6, 1976, ECR 1976, 1473 (*Tessili/Dunlop*), on Article 5(1) of the Brussels Convention; see also Widmer, "Commentary on Article 31 CISG," in *Commentary*, para. 89.

[59] See European Court of Justice (ECJ), October 6, 1976, ECR 1976, 1497 (*de Bloos/Bouyer*); see also Widmer, "Commentary on Article 31 CISG," in *Commentary*, para. 89.

the CISG, the court concluded that this term had not become part of the contract. The court reasoned that, upon receipt of the order, the seller had sent the buyer an "acknowledgement of order" which included an explicit reference to the seller's standard terms and conditions. Although the seller had failed to send the buyer a copy of the terms, the court held that the seller, by making reference to its standard terms, had clearly indicated that it would not accept any buyer terms and conditions that deviated from its own. Therefore, the buyer was not entitled to interpret seller's "acknowledgement of order" as an acceptance of its offer under CISG Article 8.

The court reasoned, however, that the seller's terms and conditions, including a provision on the place of performance, also had not become part of the contract. The buyer's failure to object to the seller's terms included on the back of the shipping invoice that accompanied the first delivery did not constitute an implied acceptance of the seller's terms. As the parties had not agreed on the place of performance, the court applied CISG Article 31 and concluded that the place of performance was at the seller's domicile.[60] In doing so, the court implicitly rejected the so-called last-shot rule. Under the last-shot rule, the terms of that party that last referred to its terms and conditions become part of the contract unless the other party objects.[61] Courts in several jurisdictions have applied this rule when faced with conflicting standard terms under the CISG.[62] However, the more modern – and certainly more balanced – approach is the so-called knock-out rule, according to which conflicting terms do not become part of the contract.[63]

IV. Conformity of Goods: Inspection and Notice

Rights and duties relating to the delivery of nonconforming goods have been dealt with in several Swiss cases.

A. *Lack of Conformity*

In domestic Swiss law, a distinction is drawn between the "ordinary characteristics" that the goods should possess, on the one hand, and express warranties by the seller that the goods possess particular characteristics, on the other.[64] In contrast, the CISG applies a uniform concept of lack of conformity.[65] This important difference between domestic law and the CISG was acknowledged by the Swiss Federal Supreme Court in

---

[60] The court's discussion on standard terms was superfluous with respect to jurisdiction, as clauses such as "free domicile" were in any case not sufficient to establish jurisdiction under Article 5(1) of the 1988 Lugano Convention. The court recognized this itself: Cantonal Court Zug, December 11, 2003, CISG-online 958, at [2.3]. For a general discussion of this issue, see Widmer, "Commentary on Article 31 CISG," in *Commentary*, para. 92. See also Christiana Fountoulakis, "Anmerkung zum Beschluss des Kantonsgerichts Zug vom 11.11.2003," *Internationales Handelsrecht* 119, 123 (2005).

[61] See, e.g., Schroeter, "Commentary on Art. 19 CISG," para. 35.

[62] See, e.g., *Norfolk Southern Railway Company v. Power Source Supply, Inc.*, U.S. District Court, W.D. of Pennsylvania, July 25, 2008, CISG-online 1776; see also Schroeter, "Commentary on Art. 19 CISG," para. 3, n. 119.

[63] See German Federal Court of Justice (Bundesgerichtshof), January 9, 2002, CISG-online 651; French Court of Cassation (Cour de Cassation), 1st Civil Chamber (Cass civ 1er), July 16, 1998, CISG-online 344.

[64] See Article 197(1) of the Swiss Code of Obligations.

[65] See, e.g., Ingeborg Schwenzer, "Commentary on Article 35 CISG," in *Commentary*, para. 4.

a case in which the buyer, a textile machine trader, had refused to take delivery of the seller's used machines due to an alleged lack of conformity.[66] According to the buyer, the seller had specifically represented that the machines were equipped for a repeat range of 641–1,018 mm, whereas in actual fact, they were only equipped for a repeat of 641 mm. The court stated that under the CISG, the seller was generally liable if and when the goods' characteristics did not conform to the contract. Applying the rules set forth in Article 8(2),[67] however, the court held that the contractually agreed upon repeat range was nothing more than a technical specification of the range of possible repeat lengths. Given the buyer's professional expertise, the court concluded that the seller had been entitled to assume that the buyer was aware of the used machines' equipment and technical features when the contract was concluded.[68]

B. *"Reasonable" Period of Time*

Under CISG Article 39(1), the buyer must notify the seller of any nonconformity of goods within a "reasonable time." Unlike Article 39(1) CISG, Article 201(1) of the Swiss Code of Obligations[69] requires that notice be given to the seller "immediately" after the buyer has or ought to have discovered the lack of conformity. Despite the mandate of uniform, autonomous interpretations under CISG Article 7(1), the restrictive approach of domestic Swiss law has negatively influenced Swiss court decisions applying the CISG in this area. Like their German and Austrian counterparts, Swiss courts have interpreted – and sometimes continue to interpret – the "reasonable period" under Article 39(1) very strictly.[70] The Austrian Supreme Court has repeatedly insisted on an overall period for examination and notification (CISG Articles 38 and 39) of not more than fourteen days,[71] a position supported by several scholarly commentaries,[72] as well as a number of Swiss courts.[73] Courts in other jurisdictions tend to grant considerably longer periods.[74]

---

[66] Swiss Federal Supreme Court, December 22, 2000, CISG-online 628.
[67] Cf. also Schwenzer, "Commentary on Article 35 CISG," para. 7.
[68] Swiss Federal Supreme Court, December 22, 2000, CISG-online 628, at [4].
[69] See *supra* note 11.
[70] See Commercial Court Zurich (Handelsgericht des Kantons Zürich), September 21, 1995, CISG-online 246 (Floatarium: 24 days considered too late); Commercial Court Zurich (Handelsgericht des Kantons Zürich), November 30, 1998, CISG-online 415 (lambskin jackets: notice after more than 14 days considered too late).
[71] Supreme Court of Austria (Oberster Gerichtshof), October 15, 1998, CISG-online 380; Supreme Court of Austria, August 27, 1999, CISG-online 485; Supreme Court of Austria, January 14, 2002, CISG-online 643.
[72] Ulrich Magnus, "Commentary on Article 39," in *Kommentar zum Bürgerlichen Gesetzbuch mit Einführungsgesetzen und Nebengesetzen, Wiener UN-Kaufrecht (CISG)*, 13th ed. (ed. J. Staudinger) (Berlin: Sellier de Gruyter, 2005), para. 49; Ernst A. Kramer, "Rechtzeitige Untersuchung und Mängelanzeige bei Sachmängeln nach Article 38 und 39 UN-Kaufrecht – eine Zwischenbilanz," in *Festschrift Koppensteiner* (ed. E.A. Kramer and W. Schuhmacher) (Vienna: Orac, 2001), 617–28.
[73] See District Court Appenzell Ausserrhoden (Kantonsgericht Appenzell Ausserrhoden), March 9, 2006, CISG-online 1375 ("one week generally considered to be the appropriate period for notice"; but see *infra* note 76 for a more generous interpretation by the same court); District Court Schaffhausen (Kantonsgericht Schaffhausen), January 27, 2004, CISG-online 960 ("average of one week generally considered appropriate"); Commercial Court St. Gallen (Handelsgericht des Kantons St. Gallen), February 11, 2003, CISG-online 900 ("a few days at most").
[74] See, e.g., *Shuttle Packaging Systems, L.L.C. v. Jacob Tsonakis, INA S. A. and INA Plastics Corporation*, U. S. Dist. Ct. (W. D. Mich.), December 17, 2001, CISG-online 773; *TeeVee Toons, Inc. (d/b/a TVT*

In order to achieve uniform interpretation of the CISG, it has been suggested that a one-month period be recognized as constituting a reasonable average notification period for defects in durable goods (the "noble month").[75] Several Swiss courts have applied the one-month benchmark.[76]

C. *Requirements as to Specificity*

CISG Article 39 not only requires that the notice of nonconformity be given within a reasonable time, but also that the content of the notice be specific in nature. The question of specificity was addressed by the Swiss Federal Supreme Court a few years ago.[77] The court was called upon to decide whether a buyer had given sufficiently specific notice of a machine's lack of conformity. The buyer had twice notified the seller that the machine was defective. After the first notice, the seller's representative inspected the machine in order to prepare a report. The buyer then issued a more detailed notice in which it informed the seller that the delivered machine was "defective," enumerated individual malfunctions, and requested that the seller repair the defects. In fact, the machine was completely inoperative, as it did not conform to prototype standards.

The court held that under CISG Article 39, the buyer was required to specify the nature of the lack of conformity, for example by informing the seller that a machine or its parts were defective and by indicating the symptoms. In contrast, the buyer was not required to name the reasons for the malfunctions.[78] In the opinion of the court, the buyer had not given notice of the machine's general lack of operability. By enumerating individual malfunctions and requesting the seller to repair these defects, the buyer had shown that it considered the machine to be defective, but nonetheless operable. The buyer was therefore precluded from relying on the machine's failure to meet the required prototype standard. The court's reasoning is problematic insofar as the seller's representative had examined the machine after the buyer had first given notice of the lack of conformity. By reason of this inspection, the seller was in a position to assess the nature of the lack of conformity, which is the very purpose of the notice requirement.[79]

Records) & Steve Gottlieb, Inc. (d/b/a Biobox) v. Gerhard Schubert GmbH, U.S. Dist. Ct. (S.D.N.Y.), August 23, 2006, CISG-online 1272; CIETAC, June 3, 2003, CISG-online 1451; Court of Appeal Colmar (Cour d'appel de Colmar) (France), October 24, 2000, CISG-online 578; see also Widmer and Hachem, "The CISG in Switzerland," 294–5.

[75] Ingeborg Schwenzer, "Commentary on Article 39 CISG," in *Commentary*, para. 17; id., "The Noble Month (Articles 38, 39 CISG) – The Story behind the Scenery," 7 *European J. L. Reform* 353 (2005).

[76] Cf. Court of Appeal Lucerne (*Obergericht des Kantons Luzern*), May 12, 2003, CISG-online 846; Court of Appeal Lucerne, January 8, 1997, CISG-online 228; Court of Appeal Zug (Obergericht des Kantons Zug), December 19, 2006, CISG-online 1427; District Court Appenzell Ausserrhoden (Kantonsgericht Appenzell Ausserrhoden), September 6, 2007, CISG-online 1781 (affirmed by Court of Appeal Appenzell Ausserrhoden (Obergericht des Kantons Appenzell Ausserrhoden), August 18, 2008, CISG-online 1838).

[77] Swiss Federal Supreme Court (*Schweizerisches Bundesgericht*), BGE 130 III 258, November 13, 2003, CISG-online 840.

[78] Cf. also Schwenzer, "Commentary on Article 39 CISG," in *Commentary*, para. 5; Hans-Josef Vogel, *Die Untersuchungs- und Rügepflicht im UN-Kaufrecht* (Bonn 2000), 98–9.

[79] Cf. Schwenzer, "Commentary on Article 39 CISG," para. 6; for a critique of this aspect of the decision, see Florian Mohs, "Anmerkung zu BGer, 13.11.2003, CISG-online 840 = BGE 130 III 258," *Internationales Handelsrecht* 219 (2004); see also Cantonal Court Zug (Kantonsgericht Zug), August 30, 2007, CISG-online 1722 (purpose of notice requirement).

This same case is also interesting with respect to the issue of burden of proof. As noted earlier, Swiss courts consider the burden of proof a matter governed by the CISG. Based on an analysis of foreign case law and scholarly writings, the Swiss Federal Supreme Court held that in general, each party has to prove the factual requirements of those provisions that support its claim. However, where a party is much "closer" to certain facts, then such party will bear the burden of proof with respect to those facts.[80] Applying these principles, the court concluded that the buyer who alleges lack of conformity must prove such lack once it has taken possession of the goods.[81]

D. CISG Article 39(2) and the Statute of Limitations

Switzerland is not party to the UN Convention on the Limitation Period in the International Sale of Goods of June 14, 1974. Therefore, in order to determine the law applicable to limitation periods for bringing warranty claims under the CISG, recourse must be made to private international law. Until recently, domestic Swiss law provided for a one-year limitation period (Article 210(1) of the Swiss Code of Obligations[82]). This period was shorter than the two-year time limit for giving notice under CISG Article 39(2). Thus, a warranty claim could become time-barred under Article 210(1) while the period for giving notice under Article 39(2) was still running. Although it was generally recognized in Switzerland that the limitation period must be adapted so as not to conflict with Article 39(2), there were different opinions on precisely how the conflict should be resolved.[83] Some courts extended the one-year prescription period under Article 210(1) to two years,[84] whereas others postponed the start of the prescription period until notice of the lack of conformity had been given.[85] Some scholars also suggested that instead of Article 210(1), the general ten-year prescription period under Article 127 of the Swiss Code of Obligations should apply.[86]

---

[80] Swiss Federal Supreme Court (Schweizerisches Bundesgericht), BGE 130 III 258, November 13, 2003, CISG-online 840; see also Swiss Federal Supreme Court, July 7, 2004, CISG-online 848; Schwenzer and Hachem, "Commentary on Article 4 CISG," para. 25.

[81] Swiss Federal Supreme Court (Schweizerisches Bundesgericht), BGE 130 III 258, November 13, 2003, CISG-online 840; see also Mohs, "Anmerkung zu BGer, 13.11.2003," 219–20; Michael Stalder, "Die Beweislast und wichtige Rügemodalitäten bei vertragswidriger Warenlieferung nach UN-Kaufrecht (CISG)," *Allgemeine Juristische Praxis (AJP)* 1472, 1475 (2004).

[82] See *supra* note 11.

[83] See, e.g., Felix Dasser, "Commentary on Article 148 IPRG", in *Basler Kommentar: Internationales Privatrecht*, 2nd ed. (ed. H. Honsell, N.P. Vogt, A.K. Schnyder, and S.V. Berti) (Basel: Helbing Lichtenhahn, 2007), para. 3; Christoph Brunner, "Commentary on Article 4 CISG," in Brunner, *UN-Kaufrecht – CISG*, para. 25; Michael R. Will, "Meine Grossmutter in der Schweiz . . . : Zum Konflikt von Verjährung und Rügefrist nach UN-Kaufrecht," in *Festschrift Werner Lorenz* 623 (ed. T. Rauscher and H.-P. Mansel) (Munich: Sellier, 2001), 623; Schwenzer, "Commentary on Article 39 CISG," para. 29.

[84] Court of Justice Geneva (Cour de Justice de Genève), October 10, 1997, CISG-online 295; for a critique of this decision, see Claude Witz, *Dalloz (D.)* 1998 *Somm* 316; Will, "Meine Grossmutter," 638.

[85] Commercial Court Bern (Handelsgericht des Kantons Bern), October 30, 2001, CISG-online 956; Commercial Court Bern, January 17, 2002, CISG-online 725.

[86] See, e.g., Heinrich Honsell, "Das Übereinkommen über den internationalen Warenkauf (Wiener Kaufrecht)," *Plädoyer* 38, 44 (1990); see also Schwenzer, "Commentary on Article 39 CISG," para. 29. This view was also endorsed by the Court of First Instance Geneva (Tribunal de Genève), March 14, 1997, CISG-online 898; on appeal, however, the higher court opted for an application, albeit modified, of Article 210(1) CO; see *supra* note 84.

The Swiss Federal Supreme Court[87] held that warranty claims arising under the CISG could not be time-barred under Article 210(1) before the two-year notice of Article 39(2) had expired. However, the court did not have to decide whether the two-year or ten-year period should apply, as the limitation period had been interrupted and the claim was not time-barred under any of the solutions endorsed by cantonal courts and scholars.

In the meantime, Article 210(1) of the Swiss Code of Obligations has been amended. It now provides for a limitation period of two years.[88] This amendment was, in part, motivated by the desire to harmonize domestic law with the CISG.[89]

V. Fundamental Breach and *Nachfrist* Notice

Swiss courts have held that the concept of fundamental breach under CISG Article 25 is restrictive and that in case of doubt, a breach will not be considered fundamental.[90] This view is in keeping with the general understanding that avoidance of contract, under the CISG, should only be available as a last resort (*ultima ratio*).[91]

A. *Delivery of Nonconforming Goods*

The question of fundamental breach is often raised in cases involving delivery of non-conforming goods.[92] The breach will not be considered fundamental if the defect can be remedied through a price reduction or delivery of substitute goods.[93] Nor will a breach be considered fundamental if the buyer can reasonably be expected to make use of the goods, for example by reselling them[94] or by using them for the production of other goods.[95] Thus, in a case in which the seller had delivered meat with too high a fat content, as well as excess blood and wetness, the Swiss Federal Supreme Court held that the buyer could reasonably be expected to process the meat and sell it at a lower price. It was established that the only effect of the meat's inferior quality during processing was a loss in weight.[96]

---

[87] May 18, 2009, CISG-online 1900, affirming the decision of the Court of Appeal Basel-Stadt (Appellationsgericht Basel-Stadt), September 26, 2008, CISG-online 1732. For a discussion of this decision, see Pascal Hachem and Florian Mohs, "Verjährung von Ansprüchen des Käufers wegen Nichtlieferung und Lieferung vertragswidriger Ware aus CISG nach internem Schweizer Recht – Zugleich eine Urteilsanmerkung zum Entscheid des Bundesgerichts vom 18. Mai 2009, CISG-online 1900," *Allgemeine Juristische Praxis (AJP)* 1541 (2009).

[88] Amendment of March 16, 2012, in force since January 1, 2013.

[89] See "Parliamentary Initiative: Better Protection for Consumers. Amendment of Art. 210: Opinion of the Swiss Federal Council," *Bundesblatt* 2011 3903, 3905.

[90] See, e.g., Swiss Federal Supreme Court (Schweizerisches Bundesgericht), May 18, 2009, CISG-online 1900; October 28, 1998, CISG-online 413; September 15, 2000, CISG-online 770; Commercial Court Aargau (Handelsgericht des Kantons Aargau), November 5, 2002, CISG-online 715.

[91] See, e.g., Ulrich G. Schroeter, "Commentary on Article 25 CISG," in *Commentary*, para. 1.

[92] See, e.g., Swiss Federal Supreme Court (Schweizerisches Bundesgericht), May 18, 2009, CISG-online 1900.

[93] Commercial Court Aargau (Handelsgericht des Kantons Aargau), November 5, 2002, CISG-online 715.

[94] Swiss Federal Supreme Court (*Schweizerisches Bundesgericht*), October 28, 1998, CISG-online 413; see generally Schroeter, "Commentary on Article 25 CISG," para. 52.

[95] Cantonal Court Zug (Kantonsgericht Zug), August 30, 2007, CISG-online 1722 (buyer of GMS modules for installation in mobile phones was able to install nonconforming modules in less sophisticated mobile phones, which could be sold at a lower price: no fundamental breach).

[96] Swiss Federal Supreme Court (Schweizerisches Bundesgericht), October 28, 1998, CISG-online 413.

The "reasonable use" of nonconforming goods depends on whether the buyer is a retailer, producer, or ultimate consumer. The type of goods involved is also an important factor. Thus, in a dispute over a piece of machinery, the Swiss Federal Supreme Court held that the buyer could not reasonably be expected to resell the machine to a third party as the machinery had been specially manufactured to the buyer's specifications. As the average performance of the machine was fifty-two vials per minute instead of the contractually agreed one-hundred eighty vials per minute, the court affirmed the lower court's finding that the seller had committed a fundamental breach. The court rightly concluded that the buyer had been substantially deprived of what it was entitled to expect under the contract, as the actual performance of the machine was only 29 percent of what the contract had specified.[97]

B. *Failure to Deliver Goods in a Timely Manner*

In another case, the Swiss Federal Supreme Court was called upon to decide whether timely delivery was of fundamental importance for the purposes of CISG Article 25. In their contract, the parties had specified a period of time for delivery of the goods. As the contract was for raw material that the buyer intended to sell to its customers, the delivery date was of fundamental importance to the buyer. The court also pointed out that the goods in question were subject to significant and sudden price fluctuations, which gave additional importance to timely delivery. The buyer was therefore entitled to avoid the contract under CISG Article 49(1)(a) without having to fix an additional period of time (*Nachfrist*) for delivery by the seller.[98] The court held that *Nachfrist* notice is unnecessary if nondelivery by a certain date is in itself a fundamental breach.[99]

VI. Remedies: Price Reduction, Damages, and Avoidance

This section reviews the basic elements of the CISG's remedial scheme.

A. *Price Reduction*

Price reduction claims have been at issue in comparatively few Swiss cases.[100] In several of these cases, the courts held that the amount by which the price should be reduced under CISG Article 50 is not equal to the cost of repair. Rather, the reduced price should bear the same relation to the contract price as the actual value of the goods bears to the value that conforming goods would have had at the time the contract was concluded.[101]

[97] Swiss Federal Supreme Court (Schweizerisches Bundesgericht), May 18, 2009, CISG-online 1900, affirming the decision of the Court of Appeal Basel-Stadt (Appellationsgericht Basel-Stadt), September 26, 2008, CISG-online 1732.
[98] Swiss Federal Supreme Court (Schweizerisches Bundesgericht), September 15, 2000, CISG-online 770.
[99] See Schroeter, "Commentary on Article 25 CISG," para. 10.
[100] See District Court Lucerne Country (Amtsgericht Luzern-Land), September 21, 2004, CISG-online 963; Court of Justice Geneva (Cour de Justice de Genève), November 15, 2002, CISG-online 853; Commercial Court Zurich (Handelsgericht des Kantons Zürich), February 10, 1999, CISG-online 488; Commercial Court Zurich, September 21, 1998, CISG-online 416; Court of First Instance Locarno-Campagna (Pretore della giurisdizione di Locarno-Campagna), April 27, 1992, CISG-online 68.
[101] See Court of First Instance Locarno-Campagna (Pretore della giurisdizione di Locarno-Campagna), April 27, 1992, CISG-online 68; Court of Justice Geneva (Cour de Justice de Genève), November 15, 2002,

The buyer does not have to specify the precise amount by which the price is to be reduced when declaring a price reduction under Article 50.[102] However, the amount will generally need to be quantified once court proceedings are underway, although the precise moment will depend on the law governing the procedure.[103] The remedy of price reduction can be raised concurrently with a claim for damages.[104]

B. *Damages*

Not surprisingly, damages claims are of far greater practical importance in Swiss case law than price reduction claims. Under CISG Article 74, a party is entitled to full compensation for losses suffered as a consequence of the other party's breach. It is generally recognized that Article 74 protects the promisee's expectation interest. In contrast, where recoverability of a party's reliance interest is concerned, views differ. Some Swiss courts have held that a party's reliance interest cannot be recovered under Article 74, whereas others have affirmed recoverability.[105]

Another important issue in damages claims is Article 74's requirement of foreseeability.[106] Thus, in the meat case discussed above,[107] the court held that it was foreseeable to the seller that delivery of nonconforming goods might result in a loss of buyer's customers, as the seller had known that the buyer was a wholesaler. The question of foreseeability can also arise when damages are claimed for attorney fees. Several Swiss courts[108] have been called on to decide whether such fees are recoverable as damages under the CISG.[109] A distinction is usually drawn between attorney fees arising out of litigation and attorney fees arising outside of litigation. Recovery of litigation-related costs is determined as a

---

CISG-online 853; Commercial Court Zurich (Handelsgericht des Kantons Zürich), September 21, 1998, CISG-online 416; Commercial Court Zurich, February 10, 1999, CISG-online 488 (a price reduction was denied because of the buyer's failure to substantiate his claim). On this method of "proportional calculation" see, e.g., Markus Müller-Chen, "Commentary on Article 50 CISG," in *Commentary*, para. 8.

[102] Court of Justice Geneva (Cour de Justice de Genève), November 15, 2002, CISG-online 853. See also Müller-Chen, "Commentary on Article 50 CISG," para. 4.

[103] See Court of Justice Geneva (Cour de Justice de Genève), November 15, 2002, CISG-online 853, in which a price reduction was denied as the buyer (defendant) had failed to quantify the pertinent amount; see also Commercial Court Zurich (Handelsgericht des Kantons Zürich), September 21, 1998, CISG-online 416, in which a price reduction was denied for similar reasons ("lack of even a very basic quantification by the buyer" and "lack of any basis for determining the reduced value of the goods").

[104] See District Court Lucerne Country (Amtsgericht Luzern-Land), September 21, 2004, CISG-online 963; Swiss Federal Supreme Court (Schweizerisches Bundesgericht), October 28, 1998, CISG-online 413; see also Müller-Chen, "Commentary on Article 50 CISG," para. 18.

[105] Recoverability denied in Court of Justice Geneva (Cour de Justice de Genève), November 15, 2002, CISG-online 1839; recoverability affirmed in Cantonal Court Zug (*Kantonsgericht Zug*), December 14, 2009, CISG-online2026;in support of recoverability Ingeborg Schwenzer, "Commentary on Article 74 CISG," in *Commentary*, para. 3; cf. Wolfgang Witz, "Commentary on Article 74 CISG," in *Internationales Einheitliches Kaufrecht* (ed. Wolfgang Witz, Hanns-Christian Salger, and Manuel Lorenz) (Heidelberg: Recht und Wirtschaft, 2000), para. 12.

[106] See Schwenzer, "Commentary on Article 74 CISG," para. 45 et seq.

[107] Swiss Federal Supreme Court (Schweizerisches Bundesgericht), October 28, 1998, CISG-online 413; see *supra* V.A.

[108] See District Court Willisau (Amtsgericht Willisau), March 12, 2004, CISG-online 961; Cantonal Court Valais (Tribunal Cantonal du Valais), May 23, 2006, CISG-online 1532; Commercial Court Zurich (Handelsgericht des Kantons Zürich), November 22, 2010, CISG-online 2160.

[109] See Schwenzer, "Commentary on Article 74 CISG," para. 28 et seq.

matter of procedural law and does not fall under Article 74.[110] Under the CISG, the controversy centers on the second type of costs, with some courts and scholars holding that such costs are recoverable under Article 74 if they were foreseeable,[111] and others denying the right to recover altogether.[112]

In case of late payment, the seller may suffer additional losses due to currency devaluations or changes in exchange rates.[113] It is controversial whether such losses are recoverable under Article 74.[114] The prevailing view is that such losses are recoverable; however, the conditions and extent of recoverability remain in question.[115] In a case before the Commercial Court of Zurich, the court held that exchange rate losses are recoverable.[116] Nonetheless, the damage claim failed as payment had not yet been made. The court held that until payment has been made, the actual exchange rate loss cannot be calculated.

A different question is whether the currency of compensation must always correspond to the currency of the purchase price.[117] In a recent case,[118] the Commercial Court of Aargau held that in light of the purpose of Article 74 CISG, damages should generally be calculated in the currency in which the party suffered its loss or the currency of the party's lost profits.[119]

Another issue in damages claims is whether the standard of proof is a matter governed by the CISG. According to the majority view,[120] the standard of proof must be determined by reference to the law of the forum state (*lex fori*) or, in case of arbitration, the *lex arbitrii*.[121] A different and more recent view is that, like the question of burden of proof,

---

[110] See, e.g., Ingeborg Schwenzer, "Rechtsverfolgungskosten als Schaden?," in *Festschrift Tercier* (ed. P. Gauch, F. Werro, and P. Pichonnaz) (Geneva: Schulthess, 2008), 417–26; Christoph Brunner, "Commentary on Article 74 CISG," in Brunner, *UN-Kaufrecht – CISG*, para. 31; AAA Interim Award, October 23, 2007, CISG-online 1645; unclear District Court Willisau (Amtsgericht Willisau), March 12, 2004, CISG-online 961 (recoverability of attorney fees affirmed, but nature of these fees not specified); Schwenzer, "Commentary on Article 74 CISG," para. 29.

[111] For Swiss cases in which recoverability was affirmed, see Cantonal Court Valais (Tribunal Cantonal du Valais), May 23, 2006, CISG-online 1532; Cantonal Court Zug (Kantonsgericht Zug), November 27, 2008, CISG-online 2024; unclear District Court Willisau (Amtsgericht Willisau), March 12, 2004, CISG-online 961. For examples from German case law, see, e.g., OLG Munich (Oberlandesgericht München), March 5, 2008, CISG-online 1686; see also Schwenzer, "Commentary on Article 74 CISG," para. 30.

[112] See, in particular, Schwenzer, "Commentary on Article 74 CISG," para. 30; in a decision of the Commercial Court Zurich (Handelsgericht des Kantons Zürich), November 22, 2010, CISG-online 2160, the court held that recoverability of attorney fees incurred prior to, but in preparation of, litigation was a matter governed by the applicable procedural law, and not by the CISG.

[113] Schwenzer, "Commentary on Article 74 CISG," para. 26.

[114] Contra, John P. McMahon, "Is a Post-Breach Decline in the Value of Currency an Article 74 CISG 'Loss'?," in *Festschrift Kritzer* (ed. C.B. Andersen and U.G. Schroeter) (London: Wildy, Simmons & Hill, 2008), 347.

[115] See Schwenzer, "Commentary on Article 74 CISG," para. 26.

[116] Commercial Court Zurich (Handelsgericht des Kantons Zürich), February 5, 1997, CISG-online 327.

[117] See Schwenzer, "Commentary on Article 74 CISG," para. 63.

[118] Commercial Court Aargau (Handelsgericht des Kantons Aargau), March 10, 2010, CISG-online 2176.

[119] The court followed the opinion supported by Schwenzer, "Commentary on Article 74 CISG," para. 63.

[120] Cf. Florian Mohs, "Bemerkungen zu BGE 136 III 56," *Allgemeine Juristische Praxis* (AJP) 425, 426 (2011).

[121] See CISG Advisory Council, "Opinion para. 6, Calculation of Damages under CISG Article 74," Rapporteur: John Y. Gotanda, available at http://www.cisgac.com/default.php?ipkCat=128&ifkCat=148&sid=148 (accessed March 30, 2013); Schwenzer and Hachem, "Commentary on Article 4 CISG," para. 26; Mohs, "Bemerkungen zu BGE 136 III 56," 426–7.

the standard of proof is a matter governed by the CISG. The Swiss Federal Supreme Court recently left the question open.[122]

C. *Avoidance*

The remedy of avoidance is only available under the CISG in cases of fundamental breach.[123] However, the party claiming avoidance must give timely notice in proper form. The next two sections review the requirements of declaration and timely notice.

1. Timely Declaration of Avoidance

The timeliness of a declaration of avoidance is determined under CISG Article 49(2)(b). In a case previously discussed,[124] after repeated attempts to remedy the lack of conformity, the seller declared that it was impossible to increase the machine's performance to the contractually agreed rate. After this declaration, there was further correspondence between the parties as well as a meeting, and finally, more than two months afterwards, the seller made a suggestion for a compromise. A little more than a month after receiving the seller's compromise proposal, the buyer avoided the contract. The seller argued that the declaration of avoidance was untimely. According to the seller, its declaration that performance could not be increased started the notice period under Article 49(2)(b). The court, however, rejected this argument. It stated that in general, a period of one to two months is reasonable under Article 49(2)(b), although this will vary depending on the circumstances of the case, in particular the type of product, the nature of the defect, and the seller's conduct upon being notified of the lack of conformity. The court reasoned that the period to give notice commences when the buyer knew or ought to have known of the breach and knew or ought to have known the extent and importance of the nonconformity.[125] The court concluded that in the case at hand, the buyer had only become aware that it would be substantially deprived of what it was entitled to expect under the contract (Article 25) when it received the seller's compromise proposal, as it was only then that the buyer learned that the machine's performance would remain far inferior to what the parties had agreed in their contract. Given the fact that the seller had already informed the buyer two months earlier that it would be impossible to achieve a performance rate as provided in the contract, this conclusion is far from obvious.

2. Requirements of Declaration of Avoidance

A different issue concerns the requirements of a declaration of avoidance under CISG Article 26. In one case, the parties had concluded two separate contracts for cotton.[126]

---

[122] Swiss Federal Supreme Court (Schweizerisches Bundesgericht), BGE 136 III 56, December 17, 2009, CISG-online 2022; see Mohs, "Bemerkungen zu BGE 136 III 56," 426.

[123] See, e.g., Schroeter, "Commentary on Article 25 CISG," para. 6.

[124] Swiss Federal Supreme Court (Schweizerisches Bundesgericht), May 18, 2009, CISG-online 1900, affirming the decision of the Court of Appeal Basel-Stadt (Appellationsgericht Basel-Stadt), September 26, 2008, CISG-online 1732. See *supra* V.A.

[125] Cf. also Markus Müller-Chen, "Commentary on Article 49 CISG," in *Commentary*, para. 34.

[126] Swiss Federal Supreme Court (Schweizerisches Bundesgericht), September 15, 2000, CISG-online 770. This case is also discussed *supra* V.B.

With respect to the first contract, the buyer had informed the seller that due to seller's failure to deliver the goods by the agreed date, it had to buy substitute goods in order to be able to fulfill its contractual obligations toward its own customers. Soon after, however, the buyer was informed that the seller would be able to deliver the cotton within the next month. The buyer then informed the seller that it could not accept the delivery of cotton with respect to the first contract as it had already bought substitute goods, but that it would accept delivery of cotton relating to the second contract. It was undisputed that the buyer had thereby avoided the first contract; however, the situation was less clear with respect to the second contract.

The seller did indeed ship cotton to a port, but according to the decision, the cotton corresponded to the parties' contract "only to a very limited extent." Neither party attended to the goods after they were unloaded. In its decision, the Swiss Federal Supreme Court held that as a general matter, a declaration of avoidance can also be implicit. However, the court concluded that in this case, the "prolonged inactivity" of both parties constituted a "reciprocal manifestation of a tacit will to renounce performance of the contract." The fact that this inactivity was deemed to amount to a "mutual renouncement of performance by both parties" indicates that the court felt uncomfortable finding that the buyer had made a declaration of avoidance under CISG Article 26. Another option would have been to hold that in such a situation, a declaration of avoidance was unnecessary, as neither party expected performance.[127]

VII. Mitigation and Preservation

This section briefly examines the buyer's duty to mitigate damages under CISG Article 77, as well as the parties' duties to preserve the goods.

A. *Mitigation*

The buyer's duty to mitigate its loss under Article 77 was at issue in a recent decision of the Swiss Federal Supreme Court.[128] The seller failed to deliver a certain number of watches under the parties' contract because the seller had entered into a distributorship agreement with one of the buyer's competitors, a retailer whose shop was located only a hundred meters away from the buyer. The buyer sued the manufacturer for damages for nondelivery of the goods and claimed the difference between the contractually agreed price and the price for which it would have been able to sell the watches to its customers (loss of profit). The court rejected this abstract calculation of the buyer's loss and held that under Article 77, the buyer was under a duty to enter into a substitute transaction for the watches in order to mitigate the loss caused by the seller's breach. Specifically, the court held that the buyer could have bought the watches from the very competitor with whom the seller had entered into a distributorship agreement. This decision has been criticized as "asking too much" of the buyer.[129] It is indeed doubtful that entering into

---

[127] See Christiana Fountoulakis, "Commentary on Article 26 CISG," in *Commentary*, para. 8.
[128] BGE 136 III 56, December 17, 2009, CISG-online 2022; for a discussion of this case, see Mohs, "Bemerkungen zu BGE 136 III 56," 426.
[129] Mohs, "Bemerkungen zu BGE 136 III 56," 427–9.

a substitute transaction with the very person who caused the manufacturer to breach its contractual obligations can be considered an "appropriate" measure under Article 77.[130]

B. *Preservation*

The single Swiss case on the duty to preserve the goods is exceptional in that it concerns provisional measures ordered by a district court in summary proceedings.[131] The dispute related to a contract for the sale of a machine. The court ordered the seller to advance the costs of storage of the goods for the duration of the proceedings. The seller argued that under CISG Article 87, it could deposit the goods with a third person at the buyer's expense. The court rejected this argument by reasoning that the CISG did not prevent the court from reaching different solutions where only provisional measures were at issue. For the same reason, the court also rejected the seller's claim that it was entitled to sell the goods under Article 88(1). Because the buyer was required to give security for the payment of damages that the seller might sustain, the court considered the seller's interests to be sufficiently protected. Given the summary nature of the proceedings, the court left unanswered the question of whether the Swiss Code of Obligations or the CISG applied to the dispute.

VIII. Excuse (Impediment)

To date, the question of a party's exemption under Article 79 CISG has been raised in only a few Swiss cases.[132] There is only one in which a promisor invoking an exemption under CISG Article 79 was successful.[133] However, the rarity of the granting of Article 79 exemptions is a general phenomenon in CISG jurisprudence.[134]

The Swiss decision granting an Article 79 exemption involved a seller's claim assigned to a factoring company.[135] A third company that had a claim against the seller obtained an order from a German court prohibiting the buyer from performing its obligations.

---

[130] Id., 428–9; on the duty to enter into substitute transactions in general, see Ingeborg Schwenzer, "Commentary on Article 77 CISG," in *Commentary*, para. 10 with further references. For other cases in which Article 77 CISG was discussed, see Commercial Court St. Gallen (Handelsgericht des Kantons St. Gallen), December 3, 2002, CISG-online 727; Cantonal Court Vaud (Tribunal Cantonal Vaud), December 8, 2000, CISG-online 1841; Court of Appeal Zug (Obergericht des Kantons Zug), March 24, 1998, CISG-online 897; Commercial Court Aargau (Handelsgericht des Kantons Aargau), March 10, 2010, CISG-online 2176.

[131] Cantonal Court Vaud (Tribunal Cantonal Vaud), May 17, 1994, CISG-online 122.

[132] See Swiss Federal Supreme Court (Schweizerisches Bundesgericht), June 12, 2006, CISG-online 1516; Swiss Federal Supreme Court, September 15, 2000, CISG-online 770 ("facts show no circumstance whatsoever that might constitute an unforeseeable or unavoidable impediment" under Article 79 CISG); Swiss Federal Supreme Court, April 5, 2005, CISG-online 1012 (case remanded to court of lower instance; the lower court's subsequent decision was brought before the Federal Supreme Court again and resulted in its decision of June 12, 2006, CISG-online 1516); Commercial Court Zurich (Handelsgericht des Kantons Zürich), November 22, 2010, CISG-online 2160; Civil Court Vaud (Tribunal Cantonal Vaud), December 8, 2000, CISG-online 1841 (German buyer was unable to prove that use of seller's cardboard coffins was prohibited in Germany; objection based on Article 79 CISG failed for lack of proof); for a merely hypothetical discussion of Article 79 CISG, see Court of Appeal Ticino (Tribunale d'appello Ticino), October 29, 2003, CISG-online 912.

[133] District Court Willisau (Amtsgericht Willisau), March 12, 2004, CISG-online 961.

[134] See Ingeborg Schwenzer, "Commentary on Article 79 CISG," in *Commentary*, para. 1.

[135] District Court Willisau (Amtsgericht Willisau), March 12, 2004, CISG-online 961.

The factor and the third party both claimed that they were entitled to the money owed by the buyer. The Swiss court considered that the conflicting claims constituted an impediment beyond the buyer's control, and that therefore, the buyer was exempt from liability for damages under Article 79. The assignment of the claim and the order issued by the German court could not be attributed to the buyer's sphere of control.[136] The buyer could not reasonably be expected to overcome these impediments. However, the court correctly held that claims for interest under CISG Article 78 are not subject to exemption under Article 79. Article 79(5) provides that an exemption from liability does not prevent a party from exercising any other right allowed under the CISG.[137]

The Swiss Federal Supreme Court, in another case, followed the prevailing view[138] that upstream suppliers do not qualify as third parties under CISG Article 79(2).[139] The court held that the seller bears the risk of a supplier's failure to deliver. Consequently, the seller will, as a rule, not be exempt from liability under Article 79 if a supplier fails to deliver or delivers nonconforming goods. According to the court, if a seller does not wish to bear the risk of impediments caused by a supplier, it must include an exemption clause in the contract exonerating it from liability for such an event.[140]

IX. Summary

The number of Swiss cases decided over the past twenty years is perhaps lower than one would expect in an export- and import-oriented country. Nonetheless, an analysis of these cases shows that Swiss courts are generally able to properly apply the CISG. Courts applying the CISG face a two-fold challenge. First, they must strive to resist the temptation to apply concepts of domestic law in interpreting the CISG. In Switzerland, this temptation has been particularly strong in determining the reasonable period for giving notice under CISG Article 39(1). "Domestic law leanings" can also be recognized in other areas, such as when courts habitually refer to the principle of good faith in cases involving contract interpretation. Here, however, domestic preconceptions have not had any recognizable impact on the outcome of the cases. In numerous decisions, Swiss courts have explicitly distinguished domestic law concepts from those applicable under the CISG. Decisions dealing with potential conflicts between Article 39(2) and the former Swiss statute of limitations show the courts' willingness to seek flexible and appropriate solutions and promote, rather than hinder, the uniform application of the CISG.

---

[136] See Schwenzer, "Commentary on Article 79 CISG," para. 18 (requirement that the impediment not be attributable to the promisor's sphere).

[137] See also id., para. 56.

[138] Id., para. 37 with further references.

[139] Swiss Federal Supreme Court (Schweizerisches Bundesgericht), June 12, 2006, CISG-online 1516. But see Commercial Court Zurich (Handelsgericht des Kantons Zürich), November 22, 2010, CISG-online 2160 (court held that if an upstream supplier failed to deliver goods to the seller, an exemption was available "under the narrow conditions of Article 79(1) and (2)(a) and (b) CISG"; however, the defendant seller admitted that delivery problems in case of textiles from the Far East were notorious and indeed quite common, therefore, the court held that the impediment had in any case been foreseeable).

[140] Swiss Federal Supreme Court (Schweizerisches Bundesgericht), June 12, 2006, CISG-online 1516 (seller failed to prove that parties had agreed to share the risk).

The second challenge, linked to the first, is to seek to apply, and persist in applying, a comparative law approach for interpreting the CISG.[141] Swiss courts, in particular the Swiss Federal Supreme Court, are accustomed to looking at the law of other jurisdictions even when deciding cases under domestic Swiss law. References to foreign cases and legal doctrine are common in Swiss decisions, especially in contested or new areas of law. Thus, the comparative law approach is a method with which Swiss judges are perhaps better acquainted than many of their colleagues in other countries. However, be it due to tradition or habit, comparative references in Swiss cases are mostly to German and Austrian CISG case law. A truly comparative approach to interpretation still needs to be developed in Swiss court decisions in order to promote uniformity in the CISG's application.

---

[141] On the importance of this approach under the CISG, see Schwenzer and Hachem, "Commentary on Article 7 CISG," para. 24.

29 The Netherlands

Sonja A. Kruisinga

I. Introduction

International trade has always played an important role in the Netherlands. In the seventeenth century, the Dutch East India Company – the VOC in Dutch – was established as the first multinational corporation in the world.[1] For a long time, the East India Company was the largest trading company doing business in Asia. International trade is still very important for the Netherlands. However, when the UN Convention on Contracts for the International Sale of Goods (CISG) entered into force in the Netherlands in 1992 it was largely disregarded because practitioners were focused on the New Dutch Civil Code that entered into force at the same time.[2]

However, today, the CISG plays an important role in the Netherlands for a number of reasons. First, the central role of international trade in the Dutch economy makes international sales an appealing instrument to consider. Second, the CISG has been influential in the development of the domestic law of obligations, including sales law, in the Netherlands. Third, the number of Dutch cases applying the CISG has rapidly increased, however, only a few CISG cases have reached the Dutch Supreme Court.

This chapter will examine the role of the CISG in the Netherlands. Part II reviews the history of the CISG in the Netherlands. Part III introduces the recent case law applying the CISG. The rest of the chapter analyzes Dutch case law applying the CISG in different substantive areas: contract formation and standard terms (Part IV); conformity, inspection, and notice nonconformity of goods (Part V); place of delivery and Brussels I (Part VI); avoidance (Part VII); interest and the right to suspend performance (Part VIII); and exemptions (Part IX).[3] The final two parts hypothesize on the future of the CISG in the Netherlands relative to European initiatives concerning contracts for the sale of goods (Part X) and provide some concluding remarks (Part XI).

---

[1] P. Van Schilfgaarde and J. Winter, *Van de bv en de nv* (Deventer: Kluwer, 2009), 31.

[2] Tractatenblad 1981, 184; Tractatenblad 1986, 61.

[3] For earlier overviews of Dutch cases applying the CISG see D. Dokter and S.A. Kruisinga, "The application of the CISG in the Netherlands: a Dutch treat for the CISG?," *Internationales Handelsrecht* 105–15 (2003), and A. Janssen, "The Application of the CISG in Dutch Courts," in *Quo Vadis CISG?: Celebrating the 25th Anniversary of the United Nations Convention on Contracts for the International Sale of Goods* (ed. F. Ferrari) (Munich: Sellier European Law Publishers, 2005), 129–65.

II. History of the CISG in The Netherlands

The Netherlands has a strong connection with the development of the CISG. Under the auspices of the UNIDROIT Institute for the Unification of Private Law, two sales law conventions were drafted. The drafts of these conventions were discussed at a diplomatic conference sponsored by the Dutch government in The Hague in November 1951.[4] The result was the adoption of the Convention Relating to a Uniform Law on the International Sale of Goods (ULIS) and the Convention Relating to a Uniform Law on the Formation of Contracts (ULF). The Netherlands ratified both conventions, which came into force in 1964. Unfortunately, only nine states ratified the conventions.[5] Shortly thereafter, UNCITRAL undertook a new initiative to draft a new convention based on ULIS and ULF. This new initiative became the CISG.

ULIS and ULF had an important influence on the development of the law of obligations in the Netherlands. In 1992, a new Civil Code – including sales law – was enacted in the Netherlands, the Burgerlijk Wetboek (BW). As Roeland Bertrams noted, there are only two material differences between the ULIS and the provisions on sales law found in the Dutch Civil Code.[6] First, the concept of "fundamental breach" needed for avoidance in ULIS, also incorporated in CISG Articles 25 and 49, was not adopted in the Dutch Civil Code. Second, Article 19(1) of the ULIS provides that delivery consists of the handing over of goods that are in conformity with the contract. This rule was not incorporated into the Dutch Civil Code or the CISG.

III. Application of the CISG in The Netherlands

The structure of the Dutch court system includes ten District Courts (Rechtbanken). In the case of summary proceedings at a District Court, the judge is referred to as the *voorzieningenrechter* (*Vzr*) (judge in interlocutory proceedings). There are four Courts of Appeal (Gerechtshoven) in Amsterdam, The Hague, Arnhem-Leeuwarden, and 's-Hertogenbosch.[7] The Supreme Court (Hoge Raad) is located in The Hague. The Hoge Raad only decides questions of law. The *Procureur-Generaal* (Procurator General) plays an advisory role at the Hoge Raad. The *Procureur-Generaal* at the Hoge Raad is an independent officer who is not subject to the supervision of the Minister of Justice. The *Procureur-Generaal* or his deputies the *Advocaten-Generaal* (Advocates General) prepare advisory opinions (*Conclusie*) in all civil cases decided by the Hoge Raad. These advisory opinions play an important role in the development of Dutch case law.[8]

---

[4] E. Rabel, "The Hague Conference on the Unification of Sales Law," 1 *American J. Comparative L.* 58 (1952).

[5] See http://www.unidroit.org/dynasite.cfm?dsmid=84211.

[6] R.I.V.F. Bertrams, *Enige Aspecten van het Weens Koopverdrag, Preadvies Voor de Vereniging Voor Burgerlijk Recht* 2 (Lelystad: Koninklijke Vermande, 1995).

[7] As of 2013, the court system has been adjusted. The former nineteen District Courts were merged to eleven new District Courts. The number of Courts of Appeal changed from five to four: the Courts of Appeal of Arnhem and Leeuwarden were merged. See www.rechtspraak.nl/recht-in-nederland/themadossiers/herziening-gerechtelijke-kaart-nederland/pages/default.aspx.

[8] A.F.M. Brenninkmeijer, "Judicial Organization," in *Introduction to Dutch Law* (ed. J. Chorus) (New York: Kluwer Law International, 2006), 53–61.

A number of cases, decided by the District Courts, Courts of Appeal, or the Supreme Court, are published on the Web site of the Dutch judiciary.[9] This Web site does not, however, publish all cases. In addition, the Netherlands Journal of Private International Law (*Nederlands Internationaal Privaatrecht*) publishes summaries of decisions concerning the CISG. Important decisions are published in the journal *Nederlandse Jurisprudentie (NJ)*.

A. *Uniform Application of the CISG*

In the interpretation of the CISG, the courts have to take into account its international character and the need to promote uniformity in its application (Article 7(1) CISG). In a few cases, Dutch courts have referred to foreign case law. Moreover, the CISG Advisory Council, a private initiative, promotes uniform interpretations of the CISG.[10] It does so by issuing opinions relating to the interpretation and application of the CISG. Dutch case law has referenced one of the CISG Advisory Council's opinions.[11]

B. *Scope of Application of the CISG*

The CISG applies to contracts for the sale of goods between parties whose places of business are in different States, when both these states are contracting states or when the rules of private international law lead to the application of the law of a Contracting State (Article 1(1) CISG). The CISG does not, however, define the concept of a "sale." In a case decided by the Court of Appeal of 's-Hertogenbosch,[12] the court considered this issue. The case involved a sale and barter transaction. The buyer contended that the CISG was not applicable as the contract in question was not a sales contract, but a barter contract. However, the court held that the CISG was applicable to the contract. The court held that the concept of "sale" had to be interpreted autonomously under CISG interpretive methodology. The court concluded on the basis of Articles 30 and 53 CISG that a contract of sale is a contract on the basis of which a party is bound to deliver goods and pass title and the other party is bound to pay the purchase price. In this case, the payment of the purchase price consisted of, for the largest part, an amount of money to be paid and, for a notable smaller part, the delivery of a generator. The element of a sale was more important than the element of barter. Therefore, the court concluded, the contract was not a barter contract, but was a sales contract.

C. *Excluding the CISG*

Contracting parties may exclude the application of the convention or derogate from any of its provisions (Article 6 CISG). The question may arise whether a choice of law clause, referring to the law of a contracting state, implies an exclusion of the CISG. The courts in the Netherlands generally assume that a choice of law clause that refers to

---

[9] See www.rechtspraak.nl (cases are referred to by LJN number).
[10] See www.cisgac.com.
[11] Cf. Gerechtshof Arnhem March 9, 2010, LJN: BL7399.
[12] Gerechtshof 's-Hertogenbosch, January 18, 2011, LJN: BP1861, *Nederlands Internationaal Privaatrecht* (2011), 201.

the law of a contracting state will lead to the application of the CISG.[13] This is in line with the dominant opinion in the literature and the case law.[14] In 2007, the Court of Appeal of 's-Hertogenbosch[15] was asked to interpret the following clause: "[t]o all legal relations . . . Netherlands law is exclusively applicable." The court held that the clause excluded the application of the CISG on the basis of Article 6 CISG. The court reasoned that the use of the word "exclusively" implied that the party who drafted the clause meant to apply the Dutch Civil Code. This approach is not consistent with the majority view that a choice of law clause referring to the law of a contracting state is not regarded as an exclusion of the CISG.

The parties may agree to exclude the application of the CISG at any stage. For example, on appeal, the parties may still agree to exclude the CISG.[16] Even in pending proceedings, the parties can (implicitly) agree that the CISG is not applicable.[17] In one case, the contracting parties had not specified an applicable law.[18] The Court of Appeal of 's-Hertogenbosch held that even though a choice by the parties for the application of Dutch law may also entail a choice for the CISG, the way in which the parties had addressed their rights, obligations, and remedies indicated that they intended to apply Dutch national law.[19]

IV. Contract Formation and Standard Terms

Both the CISG and the Dutch Civil Code provide that a contract comes into existence through an exchange of offer and acceptance (Article 23 CISG; Article 6:217 BW). The provisions in the Dutch Civil Code and the CISG are very similar in this respect. Part II of the CISG, however, contains some provisions that are more specific than those in the Dutch Civil Code.[20] For example, the Dutch Civil Code does not define the concepts of "offer" and "acceptance," whereas CISG Articles 14 and 18 define the elements of valid offers and acceptances. In this respect, the District Court of Utrecht[21] applied the CISG in the interpretation of Dutch law. As the Dutch Civil Code does not contain

---

[13] Cf. R.I.V.F. Bertrams and S.A. Kruisinga, *Overeenkomsten in het Internationaal Privaatrecht en het Weens Koopverdrag* (Kluwer: Deventer 2010), 180–1; Gerechtshof Arnhem, May 7, 1996, *Nederlands Internationaal Privaatrecht* 1996, 397; Gerechtshof Leeuwarden, June 5, 1996, *Nederlands Internationaal Privaatrecht* 1996, 404; Rechtbank Rotterdam, January 25, 2001, *Nederlands Internationaal Privaatrecht* 2001, 147; Rechtbank Arnhem, December 12, 2002, *Nederlands Internationaal Privaatrecht* 2003, 265; Rechtbank Arnhem, June 28, 2006, LJN: AY4692; Rechtbank Middelburg, April 2, 2008, *Nederlands Internationaal Privaatrecht* 2008, 183; Voorzieningenrechter Rechtbank Arnhem, January 31, 2008, LJN: BC4029.

[14] Cf., I. Schwenzer and P. Hachem in *Commentary on the UN Convention on the International Sale of Goods (CISG)* (ed. Peter Schlechtriem and Ingeborg Schwenzer) (Oxford: Oxford University Press, 2010), Article 6, paras. 14–17, pp. 108–11: L. Mistelis in *UN Convention on Contracts for the International Sale of Goods (CISG): Commentary* (ed. S. Kröll et al.) (Munich: C.H. Beck, 2011), Article 6, paras. 16–21, 104–6.

[15] Gerechtshof 's-Hertogenbosch, November 13, 2007, LJN: BB7736.

[16] Cf. Bertrams and Kruisinga, *Overeenkomsten in het Internationaal Privaatrecht en het Weens Koopverdrag*, 181; Gerechtshof 's-Hertogenbosch, January 2, 2007, LJN: AZ6352. See also I. Schwenzer and P. Hachem, in Schlechtriem and Schwenzer, *Commentary*, Article 6 para. 21, pp. 113–14.

[17] Rb. Dordrecht, February 16, 2011, LJN: BP4993, *Nederlands Internationaal Privaatrecht* 2011, 209, and Rb. Zutphen, February 2, 2011, LJN: BP5014, *Nederlands Internationaal Privaatrecht* 2011, 219.

[18] Gerechtshof 's-Hertogenbosch, May 22, 2001, *Nederlands Internationaal Privaatrecht* 2001, 266.

[19] See also Rechtbank Zutphen, January 11, 2006, *Nederlands Internationaal Privaatrecht* 2006, 122.

[20] Bertrams, *Enige Aspecten van het Weens Koopverdrag*, 7.

[21] Rb. Utrecht, August 1, 2001, *Nederlandse Jurisprudentie* 2002, 157.

any definition of an offer, the court provided a definition analogous to CISG Article 14. The court held that an offer is a proposal for concluding a contract addressed to one or more specific persons. Silence or inactivity does not in itself amount to an acceptance, as provided in CISG Article 18(1).[22] Another court noted that the question whether a person has concluded a contract in his or her own name (*pro se*) or in the name of another person or a company is governed by CISG Article 8.[23]

The CISG does not contain special rules regarding the inclusion of standard terms and conditions in a contract. A proposal to expressly regulate the incorporation of general terms and conditions was rejected during the drafting of the CISG. However, the incorporation of standard terms is within the scope of the CISG because the CISG contains rules for the interpretation of contracts.[24] This has also been the prevailing position in the case law and literature.[25]

In the early case law, Dutch courts held that there is a gap in the CISG with regard to standard terms, so questions concerning standard terms were the domain of national law.[26] In 2005, the Dutch Supreme Court[27] held that the CISG is applicable to questions concerning standard terms. The Court reasoned that the question of whether a party has consented to the formation of a contract and the incorporation of general terms and conditions is governed by the CISG. The Supreme Court explicitly referred to Article 7(2) CISG and concluded that whether a party has consented to general conditions is governed by the CISG.

Dutch courts have followed the Supreme Court in recognizing that the question of whether a party has consented to the use of standard terms is governed by the CISG.[28] The related CISG provisions used to make this determination include its provisions dealing with contract formation and contract interpretation. The general framework for determining whether standard terms have been incorporated in a sales contract includes: (1) whether the standard terms were part of the offer, which was subsequently accepted by the offeree (Article 14 CISG); (2) if a reasonable person of the same kind as the offeree would have understood that the offeror intended to incorporate its general terms and conditions in the contract (Article 8(2) CISG);[29] and (3) whether the recipient

---

[22] U.G. Schroeter in Schlechtriem and Schwenzer, *Commentary*, Article 18, para. 19, p. 323; Rechtbank Arnhem, November 5, 2008, LJN: BG5194.

[23] Cf. Gerechtshof Arnhem, March 9, 2010, LJN: BL7399, *Nederlands Internationaal Privaatrecht 2010*, 311.

[24] See YB IX (1978) at 81, No. 278 and U.G. Schroeter in Schlechtriem and Schwenzer, *Commentary*, Article 14, para. 33, 275–6.

[25] Schroeter, in Schlechtriem and Schwenzer, *Commentary*, Article 14, para. 33, 275–6; German Supreme Court (Bundesgerichtshof), October 31, 2001, *Internationales Handelsrecht 2002/1* at 14–16, the French Supreme Court (Cour de Cassation), of July 16, 1998, CLOUT No. 242 and, for example, the decision by the U.S. Court of Appeals for the Ninth Circuit, May 5, 2003, 328 F.3d 528, 6 *Internationales Handelsrecht* 295–6 (2003).

[26] Bertrams and Kruisinga, *Overeenkomsten in het Internationaal Privaatrecht en het Weens Koopverdrag*, 205–6.

[27] Hoge Raad, January 28, 2005, *Nederlandse Jurisprudentie 2006*, 517.

[28] See, e.g., Rechtbank Rotterdam, September 29, 2010, LJN: BO2404. The Netherlands has a civil law system and therefore does not recognize the concept of *stare decisis*. Decisions of the Supreme Court are therefore persuasive, but do not form a precedent.

[29] See e.g., Rechtbank Rotterdam, December 29, 2010, LJN: BP1037, *Nederlands Internationaal Privaatrecht 2011*, 217.

of such an offer expressly agreed to the application of the standard terms (Article 18 CISG).[30]

A. *Duty to Transmit Conditions*

Is a mere reference to standard terms sufficient to incorporate such terms or is it necessary to transmit the text of the standard terms to the offeree prior to the formation of the contract? The German Supreme Court (Bundesgerichtshof) held that the recipient of an offer must be given the possibility to become aware of the standard terms in a reasonable manner.[31] The Bundesgerichtshof explicitly held that, according to the CISG, the offeror is required to transmit the text of the conditions to the offeree or to make the text of the conditions available in another way. It placed the burden of making the standard terms and conditions available on the party attempting to incorporate them into the contract, as the recipient may not be familiar with the standard terms used in other countries and it is reasonably easy for the offeror to attach the terms to its offer.

Some commentators have agreed with the approach taken by the Bundesgerichtshof.[32] Other scholars, however, disagree and argue that a general duty to transmit the text of standard terms should be rejected.[33] According to these scholars, a reference to standard terms is sufficient for their incorporation. This approach reasons that the decisive factors are whether the other party could reasonably be expected to be aware of the standard terms and the offeror's intent to include them in the contract. To achieve this, it would be sufficient that the required reference to the standard terms is clear and understandable for a reasonable person within the meaning of Article 8(2) CISG. Moreover, upon inquiry, it must be possible to become aware of the terms in a reasonable manner. If the contracting parties have established a longstanding business relationship, it would indeed be useless to require that the text of the standard terms should be transmitted for every new contract (see also the following section).

---

[30] Cf. Gerechtshof 's-Hertogenbosch, June 22, 2010, LJN: BM9531, and Gerechtshof Leeuwarden, September 20, 2011, LJN: BT2102.

[31] Bundesgerichtshof (October 31, 2001), *Internationales Handelsrecht* 2002/1 at 14–16.

[32] Cf., e.g., U. Magnus, "Incorporation of Standard Contract Terms under the CISG," in *Sharing International Commercial Law across National Boundaries, Festschrift for Albert H. Kritzer on the Occasion of His Eightieth Birthday* (ed. C.B. Andersen and U.G. Schroeter) (London: Wildy, Simmonds and Hill, 2008), 318; U.G. Schroeter in Schlechtriem and Schwenzer, *Commentary*, Article 14, paras. 36–43, pp. 277–82; P. Mankowski in *Internationales Vertragsrecht* 276–7 (ed. F. Ferrari) (Munich: C.H. Beck, 2007); B. Piltz, "AGB in UN-Kaufverträgen," 4 *Internationales Handelsrecht* 133–8 (2004); S.A. Kruisinga, "Reactie op T.H.M. van Wechem and J.H.M. Spanjaard, De toepasselijkheid van algemene voorwaarden onder het Weens Koopverdrag: nieuwe trend in de Nederlandse (lagere) rechtspraak?," 3 *Contracteren* 107–11 (2010).

[33] Cf., e.g., K.P. Berger, "Die Einbeziehung von AGB in internationale Kaufverträge," in *Private and Commercial Law in a European and Global Context, Festschrift fur Norbert Horn Zum 70. Geburtstag* (ed. K.P. Berger et al.) (Berlin: De Gruyter Recht, 2006), 3–20; T.H.M. Van Wechem, *Toepasselijkheid van Algemene Voorwaarden* (Deventer: Kluwer, 2007), 111–23; M. Schmidt-Kessel and L. Meyer, "Allgemeine Geschäftsbedingungen und UN-Kaufrecht," 5 *Internationales Handelsrecht* 177ff. (2008), M. Schmidt-Kessel in Schlechtriem and Schwenzer, *Commentary*, Article 8, para. 57, 174–5; T.H.M. van Wechem and J.H.M. Spanjaard, "De toepasselijkheid van algemene voorwaarden onder het Weens Koopverdrag: nieuwe trend in de Nederlandse (lagere) rechtspraak?," 1 *Contracteren* 34–8 (2010).

The reasoning of the German Supreme Court was explicitly followed by a number of different courts in the Netherlands.[34] From the perspective of a uniform interpretation of the CISG, it is interesting to note that in a large number of these decisions the courts explicitly referred to the German Supreme Court's findings. This was one of the first occasions when courts in the Netherlands explicitly referred to foreign case law while applying the CISG. Moreover, courts have also held that, in general, standard terms have to be handed over to the other party.[35] The fact that so many courts in the Netherlands followed the approach enunciated in the 2001 Bundesgerichtshof decision gave rise to a debate among Dutch scholars.[36]

Some Dutch courts in the interpretation of the CISG have used the UNIDROIT Principles of International Commercial Contracts and the Principles of European Contract Law (PECL).[37] These cases all concerned parties having their places of business in different European states. The UNIDROIT Principles of International Commercial Contracts do not provide whether the text of the standard terms has to be transmitted to the other party. The Official Comments state that standard terms contained in a contract document itself are binding upon the signature of the contract, unless they are on the reverse side and are not referenced on the front of the contract document. Standard terms in a separate document have to be expressly referenced.[38] Article 2:104(1) of the PECL, however, states that standard terms may only be invoked against a party that did not have knowledge thereof if the party using the conditions "took reasonable steps to bring them to the other party's attention before or when the contract was concluded." PECL states that standard terms are not appropriately brought to a party's attention by a mere reference to them in a contract document.[39] In the aforementioned case law, it was held that, according to this provision in the PECL, a mere reference to general conditions does not suffice to incorporate standard terms in a sales contract governed by the CISG. The general conditions should be attached to the contract, or made available to the offeree in another way.

---

[34] Cf. Rechtbank Zutphen, January 14, 2009, NJF 2009 No. 244; Rechtbank Utrecht, January 21, 2009, LJN: BH0723, *Nederlands Internationaal Privaatrecht* 2010, 189; Rechtbank Rotterdam, February 25, 2009, *Jurisprudentie Ondernemingsrecht* 2009, No. 175; Rechtbank Amsterdam, June 3, 2009; LJN: BK0976, *Nederlands Internationaal Privaatrecht* 2009, 301; Rb. 's-Hertogenbosch, January 26, 2011, LJN: BP3102, *Nederlands Internationaal Privaatrecht* 2011, 244; Rechtbank Breda, June 29, 2011, *LJN*: BQ9897 and Rechtbank 's-Hertogenbosch, September 7, 2011, LJN: BR6948. Differently: Rb. Arnhem, February 10, 2010, LJN: BL4484.

[35] Gerechtshof 's-Hertogenbosch, June 22, 2010, *LJN*: BQ5298 (interim judgment); Gerechtshof 's-Hertogenbosch, May 17, 2011, *LJN*: BQ5300 (final decision). Rechtbank Arnhem, December 16, 2009; LJN: BK8904.

[36] van Wechem and Spanjaard, "De toepasselijkheid van algemene voorwaarden onder het Weens Koopverdrag: nieuwe trend in de Nederlandse (lagere) rechtspraak?," 1 *Contracteren* 34–8 (2010)," 34–8; S.A. Kruisinga, "Reactie op T.H.M. van Wechem and J.H.M. Spanjaard, De toepasselijkheid van algemene voorwaarden onder het Weens Koopverdrag: nieuwe trend in de Nederlandse (lagere) rechtspraak?," and 3 Contracteren 107–11 (2010); T.H.M. van Wechem and J.H.M. Spanjaard, Naschrift, 3 *Contracteren* 112–15 (2010).

[37] Gerechtshof 's-Hertogenbosch, October 116, 2002, *Nederlands Internationaal Privaatrecht* 2003 No. 192; rechtbank Amsterdam, June 3, 2009, LJN: BK0976, *Nederlands Internationaal Privaatrecht* 2009, 301 and the Netherlands Arbitration Institute, February 10, 2005, *Tijdschrift voor Arbitrage* 2006, No. 31.

[38] See the Official Comments to Article 2.1.19 UNIDROIT Principles of International Commercial Contracts at www.unidroit.org.

[39] PECL, Article 2:104(2).

B. *Standard Terms in Long-Term Relationships*

Contracting parties often establish a longstanding business relationship. The reference to standard terms or the attachment of such terms in a longstanding relationship may be recognized as a usage in which one party will be deemed to have implicitly accepted the other party's standard terms.[40] Ultimately, for reasons of legal certainty, consistent requirements need to be developed, pursuant to CISG Article 9.[41] In this respect, different courts in the Netherlands have taken different approaches.

In 2010, the District Court of Rotterdam[42] held that the fact that parties have a longstanding business relationship does not, by itself, mean the standard terms will be applicable. The court concluded that the application of the standard terms of the seller had not become part of the offer or the acceptance under CISG Articles 14, 18, and 19. The seller contended that its general terms and conditions applied because of a reference to these conditions on its invoices. The invoices were generally sent after the conclusion of the contract, but in the contract in question other invoices had been sent prior to the conclusion of the contract. However, the text of the conditions had not been sent to the buyer and the buyer had not been able to take note of these conditions. Therefore, the court held that it was not clear to the buyer that the seller intended to include its standard terms in the contract. Similarly, the Court of Appeal of 's-Hertogenbosch[43] held that even though the contracting parties had a longstanding business relationship, there was no usage concerning the application of the standard terms, as there was only a reference to these standard terms on the invoices.[44]

In an award rendered by the Netherlands Arbitration Institute (NAI),[45] a slightly different approach was taken. In the first contract, the standard terms of the seller were printed on the reverse side of the confirmation. The NAI held that with respect to the first contract, because the standard terms were not attached to the contract, they did not become a part of the contract. For contracts that were concluded thereafter, the NAI held that the buyer knew or could not have been unaware of the intent of the seller to apply its standard terms to the contracts. The seller repeatedly referenced its standard terms on each confirmation and provided the text of the standard terms to the buyer. In such a case, by failing to express its disagreement with the standard terms in the subsequent contracts, the buyer implicitly accepted them. A reasonable person acting in international trade would have understood that the intention of the seller was to incorporate the standard terms into the contracts.

Another 2010 District Court case[46] involved parties with a business relationship of more than twenty years, where the buyer knew that the seller used standard terms. The buyer disputed that the seller's standard terms would apply to the contract, as it had

---

[40] Cf. Rechtbank Arnhem, January 17, 2007, LJN: AZ9279 and Rechtbank Breda, February 27, 2008, LJN: BC6704.

[41] Cf. M. Schmidt-Kessel and L. Meyer, "Allgemeine Geschäftsbedingungen und UN-Kaufrecht (CISG)," 5 *Internationales Handelsrecht* 177ff. (2008).

[42] Rechtbank Rotterdam, September 29, 2010, LJN: BO2404.

[43] Gerechtshof 's-Hertogenbosch, May 29, 2007, LJN: BA6976.

[44] See also Rechtbank Rotterdam, February 25, 2009, LJN: BH6416, *Jurisprudentie Ondernemingsrecht* 2009, 175.

[45] Netherlands Arbitration Institute, February 10, 2005 (interim award), 3 *Tijdschrift voor Arbitrage* 86 (2006), and *Yearbook Comm. Arb'n XXXII* (ed. Albert Jan van den Berg) (Kluwer, 2007), 93–106.

[46] Rechtbank Arnhem, December 1, 2010, LJN: BO7905, *Nederlands Internationaal Privaatrecht* 2011, 206.

never received original invoices that included the standard terms. The court held that the standard terms applied because of the length of the business relationship.[47] Similarly, the District Court of The Hague[48] held that CISG Article 8 did not require the handing over of the standard terms in some instances. The incorporating party need only prove that the offeree reasonably knew of its wishes to incorporate the standard terms into the contract. The offeror showed that its offer contained a reference to the standard terms. In this case, there was a longstanding business relationship and the offeree had never previously protested the incorporation of the terms. The reference to the standard terms was used numerous times through the course of the relationship. The application of the standard terms had been proposed in a sufficiently clear manner by the offeror and had been accepted by the offeree. Again, in a similar case, the District Court of Rotterdam[49] concluded that the seller's standard terms were applicable to the contract on the basis of CISG Article 9(1), as the buyer had accepted the usage concerning the application of the seller's standard terms.

C. Standard Terms and Choice of Law Clause

Very often, general terms and conditions contain a choice of law clause. There has been some uncertainty in the Netherlands with regard to the question of which law applies if both contracting parties use general conditions, which contain a choice of law clause explicitly excluding the application of the CISG. The District Court of Leeuwarden did not find any reason to apply the CISG.[50] However, the Court of Appeal of 's-Hertogenbosch[51] correctly held that if at the time of concluding the contract both contracting parties had their places of business in different states that were both parties to the CISG, their contract would, in principle, be governed by the CISG. The court reasoned that before determining the effectiveness of the exclusion, it had to be determined whether the contracting parties had agreed to the application of the standard terms in the first place. The fact that both contracting parties had made a choice of law, excluding the CISG in their standard terms, did not change the fact that it first had to be ascertained whether the standard terms had been incorporated into the contract under the CISG.[52]

V. Conformity of the Goods

An important question in determining the conformity of goods is whether the seller is required to know, and comply with, the public law requirements for such goods in the buyer's country or in the country of ultimate destination. It follows from CISG case

---

[47] See also Rechtbank Breda, February 27, 2008, *Nederlands Internationaal Privaatrecht* 2008, 97.
[48] Rechtbank 's-Gravenhage, July 7, 2010, LJN: BN0572, *Nederlands Internationaal Privaatrecht* 2010, 444.
[49] Rechtbank Rotterdam, March 31, 2010, LJN: BN2112, *Nederlands Internationaal Privaatrecht* 2010, 448.
[50] Rechtbank Leeuwarden, September 3, 2008, LJN: BF0362; see also Rechtbank Utrecht, April 15, 2009, LJN: BI1182.
[51] Gerechtshof 's-Hertogenbosch, June 22, 2010, LJN: BQ5298, *Nederlands Internationaal Privaatrecht* 2011, 97, and Gerechtshof 's-Hertogenbosch, June 22, 2010, LJN: BM9531.
[52] See also Rechtbank Rotterdam, February 25, 2009, *Jurisprudentie Ondernemingsrecht* 2009, 175, and Netherlands Arbitration Institute, February 10, 2005 (interim award), 3 *Tijdschrift voor Arbitrage* 86 (2006), and van den Berg, *Yearbook Comm. Arb'n XXXII*, 93–106. Differently: Rechtbank Rotterdam, October 13, 2010, *LJN*: BO4037, *Nederlands Internationaal Privaatrecht* 2011, 126.

law[53] that the mere fact that the buyer informed the seller of the place where the goods will be used is not sufficient to place an obligation on the seller to conform the goods to the public law requirements of that country. In general the seller is not obliged to take into account any public law requirements in the buyer's country, unless the seller knew, or must have known, of these requirements.

The District Court of Zwolle[54] held that according to CISG Article 35(2), the seller has to take into account any regulation that applies in both the seller's and the buyer's country. If the requirements in the buyer's country are more stringent than those in the seller's country, it is the duty of the buyer to inform the seller of the requirements. The mere fact that the buyer informed the seller of the place where the goods will be used is not sufficient to place an obligation on the seller, to assume the costs of knowing and complying with the public law requirements of that country. In the case at hand, the goods delivered did not comply with a particular Dutch standard, but only with the more general European standard. The Dutch standard was more stringent than its European equivalent. As the buyer did not inform the seller, before the conclusion of the contract, that the Dutch standard was higher than the European standard, the court concluded that there was no lack of conformity within the meaning of Article 35 CISG.

A. Concurrent Claims

Some uncertainty exists on whether the CISG excludes the use of national remedies or whether CISG and national remedies are cumulative in nature. The CISG's drafters intended to provide a balanced and complete remedial system for the extent of a seller's liability for delivery of defective goods. Thus, the CISG precludes the use of national remedies in this area. The alternative interpretation would subvert a uniform application of the CISG.[55] According to Müller-Chen,[56] a concurrent claim by the buyer that is based on domestic law should only be allowed if three requirements are met. First, the ground on which the remedy is based does not fall within the scope of CISG rules. Second, the remedy may not be contrary to the aims of uniform sales law. Third, the applicable national law allows for the concurrence of remedies. This means that any remedy based on national law for the buyer's mistake as to the specific characteristics of the goods would be precluded by the CISG.[57] The Court of Appeal of 's-Hertogenbosch[58] correctly held that both the literature and case law assert that in the case of a lack of conformity, there is generally no room for a claim based on error or misrepresentation,

---

[53] See also Bundesgerichtshof, March 8, 1995, *Recht der Internationalen Wirtschaft* 595 (1995) (New Zealand Mussels case); U.S. District Court of Louisiana, May 17, 1999 (Medical Marketing), and Oberster Gerichtshof, January 25, 2006, *Internationales Handelsrecht* 110–12 (2006).

[54] Rb. Zwolle, December 9, 2009, LJN: BL0104; see also Rb. Rotterdam, October 15, 2008, LJN: BG2022.

[55] P. Huber, "UN-Kaufrecht und Irrtumsanfechtung: die Anwendung nationalen rechts bei einem Eigenschaftsirrtum des Käufers," *Zeitschrift für Europäisches Privatrecht* 602 (1994); P. Huber, *Irrtumsanfechtung and Sachmangelhaftung: Eine Studie zur Konkurrenzfragd vor dem Hintergrund der Internationalen Vereinheitlichung des Vertragsrecht* (Tübingen: Mohr Siebeck, 2001), 283–4.

[56] M. Müller-Chen, in Schlechtriem and Schwenzer, *Commentary*, Article 45, para. 32, 701–2.

[57] See also J.W. Bitter and M. Bijl, "Dwaling en het Weens Koopverdrag," 9 *Maandblad voor Vermogensrecht* 2007, 195–200, and S.A. Kruisinga, *(Non-)Conformity in the 1980 UN Convention on Contracts for the International Sale of Goods: A Uniform Concept?* (Mortsel: Intersentia, 2004), 187.

[58] Gerechtshof 's-Hertogenbosch, January 18, 2011, LJN: BP1861, *Nederlands Internationaal Privaatrecht* 2011, 201.

under Dutch national law.[59] The court reasoned that the Dutch remedy was not available because the CISG contains conclusive rules for the seller's liability when there is a lack of conformity.

B. *Notification and Time Limits*

Article 39(1) CISG provides that the "buyer loses the right to rely on a lack of conformity of the goods if he does not give notice to the seller specifying the nature of the lack of conformity within a reasonable time after he has discovered or ought to have discovered [the nonconformity]." Article 38(1) CISG requires the buyer to "examine the goods, or cause them to be examined, within as short a period as is practicable in the circumstances." In determining the length of these time periods, all the circumstances of the case are relevant. For example, the nature of the goods sold is relevant. In the case of a sale of perishable goods, this period of time will generally be rather short.[60]

The Court of Appeal of Arnhem[61] held that twelve days was not a reasonable period of time within the meaning of Article 39(1) CISG, as the goods sold were perishable goods (lemons and mandarins) and the defect in quality was easy to identify. The District Court of The Hague[62] had to decide a dispute concerning the sale of mangoes, in which the buyer complained, after seven days, about hidden defects in the mangoes, in particular internal rotting. The court held that this complaint had been made too late. The court noted that the buyer did not inspect the mangoes upon delivery. The court held that in this case the reasonable period of time lapsed upon delivery.

In general, courts have noted that the time requirements provided in CISG Articles 38 and 39 are rather short in the case of the delivery of perishable goods.[63] In addition, if the delivered goods will be used or mixed in such a way that it will thereafter no longer be possible to identify the goods, the buyer will have to inspect the goods immediately after receiving them.[64] In general, it has been held that a period of time of more than a month after the defect was discovered, or ought to have been discovered, will not be considered as a reasonable period within the meaning of Article 39(1) CISG in cases concerning nonperishable goods.[65]

In *Bronnenberg v. Belvédère*,[66] the Supreme Court held that the buyer had lost its right to rely on a lack of conformity relating to the sale of floor tiles. The buyer had resold the goods to another purchaser. This purchaser complained about the quality of the floor tiles in July 1991. The court held that the buyer was not allowed, as it did, to

---

[59] Dutch Civil Code, Article 6:228.
[60] See Advisory Council, "Opinion No. 2, Examination of the Goods and Notice of Non-Conformity: Articles 38 and 39," by E.E. Bergsten. Available at www.cisg.law.pace.edu/cisg/CISG-AC-op2.html. See also Gerechtshof Arnhem, March 9, 2010, LJN: BL7399.
[61] Gerechtshof Arnhem, January 19, 2010, LJN: BL0932.
[62] Rechtbank 's-Gravenhage, July 8, 2009; LJN: BJ3228.
[63] Rb. Zutphen, February 27, 2008, *Nederlands Internationaal Privaatrecht* 2008, 287, Vzr. Rb. Breda, January 16, 2009, LJN: BH1776; see also K. Dadi, *Non-conformiteit en klachtplicht onder het Weens Koopverdrag*; *Rechtbank Breda 16 januari 2009, LJN BH 1776*, 4 Juridisch up to Date 2009, 24–8, Rb. Arnhem, February 11, 2009, LJN: BH3520, Rechtbank 's-Gravenhage, July 8, 2009, LJN: BJ3228.
[64] Gerechtshof 's-Hertogenbosch, January 2, 2007, LJN: ZA6352.
[65] Gerechtshof Arnhem, June 17, 1997, *Nederlands Internationaal Privaatrecht* 1997, 341. See also the Conclusion by the Advocate General in Hoge Raad, February 4, 2005, LJN: AR6187.
[66] Hoge Raad, February 20, 1998, *Nederlandse Jurisprudentie* 1998, 489.

delay the inspection of the floor tiles until August 1991. It reasoned that the buyer should have investigated the complaints immediately and should have inspected the floor tiles earlier, and should have informed the seller of the complaints earlier. It concluded that the notice that was sent to the seller in November 1991 was not sent within a reasonable period of time, as was required by CISG Article 39(1).

VI. Place of Delivery and Brussels I

The Brussels Convention provides in Article 5(1) that a person domiciled in a contracting state may be sued in the courts of the place of performance if located in another contracting state. In 2000, the Brussels Convention became the Brussels I Regulation.[67] When the Brussels I Regulation was introduced, Article 5 was amended. Article 5(1)(b) provides that in the case of the sale of goods, the place of performance of the obligation in question shall be the place in a member state where, under the contract, the goods were delivered or should have been delivered.[68] This means that jurisdiction for all disputes concerning the contractual obligations of both seller and buyer is granted to the court of the place of delivery.

For contracts governed by the CISG, if no place of delivery had been agreed upon, the place of delivery would have to be determined under Article 31. However, the European Court of Justice[69] rejected the application of CISG Article 31 and held that Article 5(1)(b) must be interpreted as meaning that:

> [I]n the case of a sale involving carriage of goods, the place where, under the contract, the goods sold were delivered or should have been delivered must be determined on the basis of the provisions of that contract. Where it is impossible to determine the place of delivery on that basis, without reference to the substantive law applicable to the contract, that place is the place where the *physical transfer* [emphasis added] of the goods took place, as a result of which the purchaser obtained, or should have obtained, actual power of disposal over those goods at the final destination of the sales transaction.

In a 2011 decision, the European Court of Justice reasoned that in order to determine the place of delivery on the basis of the provisions of the contract within the meaning of Article 5 Brussels I, the court must take into account all the relevant terms and clauses in that contract, including "terms and clauses generally recognized and applied in international commercial usage, such as Incoterms, in so far as they enable that place to be clearly identified."[70] The court added that where a contract contains such terms or clauses, "it may be necessary to examine whether they are stipulations which merely lay down the conditions relating to the allocation of the risks connected to the carriage of

---

[67] Council Regulation (EC) No 44/2001 of December 22, 2000 on jurisdiction and the recognition and enforcement of judgments in civil and commercial matters (OJ 2000 L 12, p. 1).

[68] See also Gerechtshof Amsterdam, January 13, 2009, *Nederlands Internationaal Privaatrecht* 2009, 135.

[69] European Court of Justice, February 25, 2010, no. C-381/08, PbEU 2010, C 100/5, LJN: BK0529, Nederlands Internationaal Privaatrecht 2010, 194, *Nederlandse Jurisprudentie* 2010, 521 (Car Trim).

[70] European Court of Justice, June 9, 2011, Case C-87/10 (Electrosteel). See also Rechtbank 's-Hertogenbosch, July 21, 2010, LJN: BN2826, *Nederlands Internationaal Privaatrecht* 2010, 483, with regard to the Incoterm DDP Eindhoven and Rechtbank Rotterdam, December 23, 2009, LJN: BL1476 concerning the Incoterm DDU Hellevoetsluis. Compare also Gerechtshof 's-Hertogenbosch, July 26, 2011, LJN: BR4219, which held that it appeared from the contract itself that the seller had to deliver the goods in Vitry or Dieppe in France, because of the following clause in the contract: "prix franco Vitry ou Dieppe."

the goods or the division of costs between the contracting parties, or whether they also identify the place of delivery of the goods."

VII. Avoidance

Under the CISG, a contract may, in principle, only be avoided in case of a fundamental breach (Article 49(1)(a)). Even though Article 25 CISG defines the concept of fundamental breach, in practice it is not always clear whether a breach of contract is in fact fundamental. In one case, a buyer complained to the seller soon after the delivery of the goods that a number of the products' original packaging and the origin of the well-known manufacturers were missing.[71] In its offer, the seller stated that it would deliver the goods in the original packaging. The seller argued that the buyer was not entitled to avoid the contract in its entirety on the basis of Article 51(2) CISG, as some of the delivered components were in conformity with the contract. According to Article 51(2) CISG, the buyer may only avoid the contract in its entirety if the failure to make delivery completely or in conformity with the contract amounts to a fundamental breach. In this case, some of the goods delivered were not in the original packaging and the seller had failed to deliver the certificate from which the origin of the goods could be deduced. The seller was aware that the buyer had bought its products for a subpurchaser to use in a certain project. In order to use the goods for that purpose, knowing the origin of the components to be delivered by the seller was essential.

The Court of Appeal found that the fact that the original packaging and the promised certificates were missing in the given circumstances amounted to a fundamental breach within the meaning of Article 49(1)(a), as the buyer informed the seller in due time that all components had to be used jointly in the project, which required original packaging and certificates of origin. Therefore, the buyer's interest in the delivery of the goods could only be satisfied if all the goods were in compliance; the resale of part of the goods was not possible. Therefore, the court found that the delivery of goods that were not in compliance with the contract amounted to a fundamental breach within the meaning of Article 51(2) CISG, which entitled the buyer to avoid the contract in its entirety.

A decision of the District Court of Amsterdam provides another example of a finding of fundamental beach.[72] This case concerned a contract between a distributor and a buyer dealing with the sale of clothing. The contracting parties had agreed that the buyer would receive an exclusive right with regard to the sale of the clothing in the center of Amsterdam. The court held that the buyer had made it sufficiently clear that a violation of this exclusivity agreement amounted to a fundamental breach. It concluded that a violation of the exclusivity provision will amount to a fundamental breach.

VIII. Interest and the Right to Suspend Performance

Under CISG Article 78, the seller has a claim for interest when the buyer is late in paying. This provision does not state, however, the interest rate to be charged. Generally, courts in the Netherlands have held that the interest rate will have to be determined on

---

[71] Gerechtshof Leeuwarden, November 9, 2010, LJN: BO3784.
[72] Rechtbank Amsterdam, August 19, 2009: LJN: BJ7584.

the basis of the law applicable on the basis of conflicts of law rules pursuant to CISG Article 7(2).[73]

The CISG does not contain a general right to withhold performance in case the other party fails to perform its contractual obligations. According to the literature and the case law, such a general right to withhold performance can, however, be derived from CISG Articles 58 and 71.[74] Article 71(1) CISG provides that a party may suspend the performance of its obligations if, after the conclusion of the contract, it becomes apparent that the other party will not perform a substantial part of its obligations. National law does not apply, as CISG Articles 58 and 71 bring the issue within the scope of the CISG.[75]

IX. Exemptions

In a 2009 case, decided by the Belgian Supreme Court (Hof van Cassatie), a party claimed an exemption under Article 79(1) CISG.[76] This case involved the sale of steel tubes. Between the conclusion of the contract and the delivery, the price of steel had risen by 70 percent. The contract did not contain a price escalation or adjustment clause. The Supreme Court referred to Article 79(1) CISG, which provides that a party is not liable for a failure to perform if it proves that the failure was due to an impediment beyond its control and that it could not reasonably have foreseen such impediment. The Supreme Court held that the dramatic price increase of steel was not reasonably foreseeable at the time of the conclusion of the contract. As a result of the price increase, the nature of the contract changed in a disproportionate manner, justifying the granting of an impediment under Article 79(1) CISG.

The Supreme Court held that pursuant to CISG Article 7, gaps in the CISG are to be filled using express or implied general principles that govern the law of international trade. The court reasoned that principles found in the law of international trade in general, including UNIDROIT Principles of International Commercial Contracts, can be referenced. Under the UNIDROIT Principles, the party that invokes changed circumstances that fundamentally disturb the contractual balance is also entitled to request a renegotiation of the contract. In sum, the court explicitly referred to the UNIDROIT Principles in applying the CISG. The appropriateness of the use of the UNIDROIT Principles is questionable because CISG Article 7 directs the interpreter to only use the "general principles on which it [CISG] is based" in arriving at autonomous interpretations in matters that are not settled in the convention.

X. Future of the CISG in The Netherlands

The future position of the CISG in the Netherlands may be influenced by European developments in the field of contract law.[77] It is the position of the European Commission

---

[73] See also Rechtbank Rotterdam, March 17, 2010, LJN: BM0814; Rechtbank Dordrecht, April 21, 2010, LJN: BM2484; Rechtbank Utrecht, December 29, 2010, LJN: BO8098.

[74] M. Müller-Chen in Schlechtriem and Schwenzer, *Commentary*, Article 45, para. 22, 698; cf. Vzr. Rb. Arnhem, January 31, 2008, *Nederlands Internationaal Privaatrecht* 2008, 95.

[75] See also Rechtbank Zutphen, February 1, 2001, *Nederlands Internationaal Privaatrecht* 2001, 126.

[76] Hof van Cassatie, June 19, 2009, case no. C.07.0289.N.

[77] Communication from the Commission to the Council and the European Parliament on European Contract Law, COM (2001) 398 final, July 11, 2001.

that divergences between national contract laws constitute an obstacle to cross-border transactions and impede the functioning of the internal market.[78] Therefore, the European Commission has taken the initiative to examine several options as to how to ease legal obstructions to cross-border transactions by making contract law more coherent across the European Union. Between 2005 and 2009, a network of European contract law experts developed a Draft Common Frame of Reference (DCFR) on the basis of extensive comparative law research.

In April 2010, the European Commission established an expert group in the area of European contract law. The expert group's task was to assist the commission by undertaking a feasibility study of a possible future European contract law instrument that could be applicable to both business-to-consumer and business-to-business contracts.[79] The expert group was asked to focus on an instrument covering sales contracts and related service contracts and to select those parts of the DCFR directly related to contract law and to simplify, restructure, update, and supplement the selected content. On May 3, 2011, the expert group published a first draft of its feasibility study on a future initiative on European contract law.[80]

On the basis of this study, the European Commission published a proposal for an EU Regulation on a Common European Sales Law (CESL).[81] This draft regulation introduces an optional system of sales law that the parties to a contract can choose to apply. If the contracting parties choose to apply the CESL, then new questions will arise relating to the relative jurisdictions of the CESL and the CISG. However, it is reasonable to assume in such a case that the parties, by choosing the CESL, have implicitly excluded the application of the CISG.[82] It does not seem reasonable, however, that a choice of the CESL would imply a complete exclusion of the CISG. It is possible that a particular issue will not be covered under the CESL, leaving the CISG as the default law. From the perspective of legal certainty, this is certainly not desirable.

XI. Conclusion

The influence of the CISG in the law of obligations in the Netherlands is extensive. The Civil Code, enacted in 1992, is based on the text of the ULIS, one of the predecessors of the CISG. Thus, the codified sales law in the Netherlands and the CISG come from the same instrument. The CISG has rightfully been used as a source of inspiration for the interpretation of the Dutch Civil Code. This chapter analyzed the developments in the application of the CISG by the courts in the Netherlands. The Dutch courts have reviewed foreign case law when applying the CISG. The issue of incorporating standard terms into CISG contracts remains unsettled.

---

[78] See http://ec.europa.eu/justice/contract/.
[79] Commission Decision of April 26, 2010 setting up the Expert Group on a Common Frame of Reference in the area of European contract law (2010/233/EU); 27.4.2010 Official Journal of the European Union L 105/109.
[80] See http://ec.europa.eu/justice/contract/files/feasibility_study_final.pdf.
[81] Proposal for a Regulation of the European Parliament and of the Council on a Common European Sales Law, October 11, 2011, COM(2011) 635 final.
[82] See also M. Hesselink, "How to Opt into the Common European Sales Law?," European Rev. Private L. 195–212 (2012).

In the future, the CISG may have to compete with the Common European Sales Law. The CESL will have the advantage that the European Court of Justice will safeguard its uniform interpretation. The CISG has the advantage of automatically applying to sales contracts between parties from different contracting states, whereas businesses will have to expressly opt into the Common European Sales Law.

Part VI *A World View of the CISG*

30 The CISG in Islamic Countries: The Case of Egypt

Hossam A. El-Saghir

I. Introduction

A uniform set of rules to govern contracts for the international sale of goods was realized, after half a century of work, with the publication of the United Nations Convention for the International Sale of Goods in 1980 (CISG).[1,2] The CISG entered into force on January 1, 1988.[3] The ultimate goal of the CISG is to achieve uniformity in its application. Toward this end, Article 7 of the CISG mandates an autonomous interpretation of its rules.

The Egyptian legal system is a meld of Islamic law (Shari'a) and civil law traditions. It was one of the first ten countries to adhere to the CISG. The Egyptian legal system is considered the leading prototype in the Arab World. Under the influence of the Egyptian legal system, most Arab countries share comprehensive codes that combine elements of Islamic and French civil laws. This chapter reviews the implementation of the CISG in Egypt. Most of the CISG scholarship in the Arab world has come from Egypt. Considering that charging or assessing interest is prohibited under Islamic law, the chapter will address Article 78 of the CISG, which allows the assessment of interest as part of contract damages. This analysis of the payment of interest is undertaken in the context of Egypt's most recent constitution, which provides in its Article 2 that Islamic law is the principal source of law.

Part II provides an overview of Islamic law. It covers its sources, main principles, the prohibition of Riba (usury) under Islamic law, and the influence of Islamic law on the Egyptian legal system. Part III outlines the autonomous rules of interpretation set out in CISG Article 7. It also explores how the enactment of the New Egyptian Commercial Code affects the application of CISG gap filling rules. Part IV deals with the obstacles that impede the uniform application of the CISG in the Arab world. Part V provides a case study exploring the law of Egypt and the role of the CISG within it. It explains the

---

[1] This chapter is an adaptation of the author's article, entitled: "The Interpretation of the CISG in the Arab World," originally published in *CISG Methodology* (ed. Andre Janssen and Olaf Mayer) (Munich: Sellier European Law Publishers, 2008).

[2] The CISG replaced two treaties that date back to 1964: the Uniform Law for the International Sale of Goods (ULIS) and the Uniform Law on the Formation of Contracts for the International Sale of Goods (ULIF). These two conventions achieved little success, as they were only ratified by a limited number of states.

[3] CISG, Article 99.

implementation of Article 78 of the CISG in Egypt and reviews the CISG cases disputes brought before the Egyptian Court of Cassation and arbitral tribunals. This part also explores the position that Egyptian commentators have taken on issues relating to the construction of the CISG. Finally, an analysis is provided of the influence that the CISG has had on the drafting of Egypt's New Commercial Code.

II. Overview of Islamic Law

Islam is the last divine religion brought fourteen centuries ago by Messenger and Prophet Mohammed (peace be upon him) to mankind. The Arab word Islam means "submission." It derives from a word meaning "peace." In a religious context, it means complete submission to the will of God. Islamic law does not only deal with the relationship between man and God, but also deals with the treatment of man toward others. All behavior and transactions are covered by Shari'a as the Holy Qur'an and the Holy Sunnah of the Prophet Mohamed have laid down broad principles, in the light of which the scholars of every time have deduced specific answers to the new situations arising in their age.[4]

A. *Sources of Islamic Law*

The compilation of a number of sources that make up Islamic law is called the Shari'a. Besides the core scared document – the Qur'an – there are a number of secondary sources, including Ijma or consensus and Qiyas or analogy.

1. Primary Sources

The sources of Islamic law (Shari'a) are divided into primary sources and secondary sources. Primary sources are composed of two components in the following order of importance. (1) The Qur'an is the principal source of all forms of Islamic thoughts and behavior. The text of the Qur'an consists of over 6,000 verses, divided into 114 sourah (chapters). Muslims believe that the Qur'an is the last holy book that God has revealed through the last Messenger and Prophet Mohammed (peace be upon him) over a period of 22 years until his death in 632 C.E. Because the Qur'an is the principal source of Shari'a law, any rule that is derived from Qur'an prevails over rules derived from other sources of Shari'a law. (2) The second source of importance in Islamic law is the Sunnah. It is the compilation of Prophet Mohammed's practices as expressed in his sayings "Hadith," actions "fe'al," and/or approval "taqrir." The Sunnah derives its authenticity directly from the Qur'an. It clarifies and complements the Qur'an in respect to many matters that the Qur'an is silent about. Sunnah plays an important role in interpreting the Qur'an but it cannot conflict or amend the rules provided in the Qur'an.

2. Secondary Sources

After the death of the Prophet Mohammed, supplementary sources of Islamic law were developed to apply whenever the two primary sources of Shari'a were silent or appeared to be ambiguous or inconsistent. There are two categories of secondary sources. The first

---

[4] Mahmoud A. El-Gammal, "'Interest' and the Paradox of Contemporary Islamic Law and Finance," available at www.ruf.rice.edu/~elgamal/files/interest.pdf.

category includes materials that have been agreed on unanimously by Islamic scholars; the first is Ijma (consensus), which is based on Prophet Mohammed's saying: "My nation will never agree on something wrong"; accordingly, whenever the Islamic scholars agree on a certain issue unanimously that issue becomes settled law. Another source of law is Qiyas (analogy). When there is no rule found in the primary sources or in the Ijma, such as in the case of a novel situation, Qiyas is applied. The second category includes debatable sources that have not been agreed on by all of the Islamic scholars; it includes among others Maslaha Mursala, Al Estehsan, Sadd al Zara'e, and Al Urf (custom).

B. *Contracts under Islamic Law*

The general principle that governs contracts in Islamic law is the principle of freedom to contract. It is based on the Qur'anic order to Muslims: "O you who believe! Fulfill (your) obligations,"[5] and the Prophet Mohamed's Hadith: "Muslims are bound by their obligations or stipulations, except a stipulation which makes lawful what is unlawful or which makes unlawful what is lawful." Therefore, Muslims are free to contract and are bound by their stipulations but there are some activities that are prohibited by the Qur'an or other sources, including, among others, usury or interest – "whereas Allah has permitted trading and forbidden Riba."[6]

The contract is considered valid under Islamic law whenever certain requirements are fulfilled. The requirements for a sale or purchase contract include mutual consent between the parties and agreement on the type of goods, as well a contract price. The offer is known in the Islamic Law as Ijab and the acceptance is known as Qoboul. The mutual consent is referred to as sourat: "O you who believe! Eat not up your property among yourselves unjustly except it be a trade amongst you, by mutual consent."[7] Under Islamic Law, no formal requirements are needed for the contract to be concluded.

C. *Prohibition of Riba or Usury in Islamic Law*

The word "Riba" in the Arabic language means an increase or addition. The Qur'an prohibits Riba, although permitting trade: "O you who believe! Be afraid of Allah and give up what remains (due to you) from Riba (usury) (from now onward), if you are (real believers). And if you do not do it, then take a notice of war from Allah and His Messenger but if you repent, you shall have your capital sums. Deal not unjustly (by asking more than your capital sums), and you shall not be dealt with unjustly (by receiving less than your capital sums)."[8]

The Sunnah clarifies the meaning of Riba. According to the Prophet Mohammed's Holy Hadith, every loan that leads to an extra interest (when repaid) is considered Riba. However, the trader may make profit in other cases as in case of business profit, dividends, and partnership income; such profit is not prohibited: "whereas Allah has permitted trade and forbidden usury."[9] Although the Shari'a has prohibited the Riba, it has developed

---

[5] Quran, 5:1, King Fahd Glorious Quran Printing Complex, The Noble Quran: English Translation of the Meanings and Commentary, 1431 A.H.

[6] Quran, 2:275

[7] Quran, 3:29.

[8] Quran, 2:278 and 279.

[9] Quran, 2:275.

other forms of transactions, including the Mudarabah. In the Mudarabah, one party provides the necessary financial capital and the other provides the human capital needed for a specific economic activity. In addition, where the creditor suffers loss due to the delay of payment by the wealthy debtor who fails intentionally to pay on time, the creditor is entitled to compensation for such loss.

D. *Influence of Islamic Law (Shari'a) in the Egyptian Legal System*

The origin of the current Egyptian legal system can be traced back to the Ottoman legal reforms of the nineteenth century. The Ottoman government had a strong interest in the administration of justice, and judges, appointed by the empire or its local representatives, decided cases based on a combination of Shari'a and state law that was also heavily based on the Shari'a. A series of centralizing reforms resulted in several attempts to codify the law. The Majallah code was issued between 1869 and 1877 and was the culmination of the Ottoman codification effort.[10] Simply stated, it consisted of Islamic law in content but was based in form on the Napoleon Code.[11]

Today, the Egyptian legal system consists of a codified set of rules representing a blend of the Islamic and civil law traditions. Egypt's most recent constitution was approved in 1971 and has been amended in 1980, 2005, and 2007. Prior to the 1980 Amendment, Islamic law (Shari'a) was only one source among other sources of legislative rules. After the 1980 Amendment, Article 2 of the constitution recognized the Shari'a as the principal source of legislative rules. This means that any law may not contradict Shari'a law.[12] In strengthening Article 2 of the Constitution, the Egyptian Constitutional Court ruled that:

> It is therefore not permitted that a legislative text contradicts those rules of Shari'a whose origin and interpretation are definitive, since these rules are the only ones regarding which new interpretive effort (ijtihad) is impossible, as they represent, in Islamic Shari'a, the supreme principles and fixed foundations that admit neither allegorical interpretation, nor modification. In addition, we should not contemplate that their meaning would change with changes in time and place, from which it follows that they are impermeable to any amendment, and that it is not permitted to go beyond them or change their meaning. The authority of the High Constitutional Court in this regard is limited to safeguarding their implementation and overruling any other legal rule that contradicts them.[13]

On February 11, 2011, Former Egyptian President Hosni Mubarak was removed from office and temporarily replaced by the Supreme Council of the Armed Forces

---

[10] In the area of finance, the Islamic sources of transactions law continue to rely heavily on Majallat al-Ahkam al-Adliyyah, the latest available codification of Islamic jurisprudence, commissioned and imposed by the Ottoman Empire in its final days 1869–1926 c.e., and based on Hanafi jurisprudence. El-Gammal, "'Interest' and the Paradox."

[11] Nathan J. Brown, *The Rule of Law in the Arab World* (Cambridge Middle East Studies), 2.

[12] However, the Constitutional Court has ruled that the 1980 amendment of Article 2 limits the discretion of the legislative authority only for the legislations subsequent to this amendment. See Constitutional Court, Case No. 20, for the judicial year 1, May 4, 1985.

It is to be noted that penal law rules, as codified in the Penal Code, are entirely western, nonreligious-oriented rules whether they were ratified before or after the 1980 amendment. Egypt has also enacted a number of new statutes to respond to contemporary standards of global economic and business reform, including investment law, anti-money laundering law, intellectual property rights law, competition law, consumer protection law, electronic signatures law, banking law, taxation law, and others.

[13] As quoted in El-Gammal, "'Interest' and the Paradox."

(SCAF). The 1971 Constitution was suspended and the people's assembly and the Shura Council were dissolved following a referendum on some amended articles of the 1971 constitution. This has not influenced the stipulation that Islamic law is the main source of legislation, as per the wording of Article 2 of the suspended constitution, as confirmed by a subsequent declaration.

III. Achieving Uniformity: Autonomous Interpretation of the CISG

CISG interpretive rules (Article 7) encourage autonomous interpretations of its rules free of influence from domestic laws. A brief review is undertaken here in order to better analyze the relationship between the CISG and Egyptian domestic law.

According to Article 7(1), in interpreting the CISG, regard is to be had to its international character, the aim of promoting uniformity in its application, and the observance of good faith in international trade. The international character of the CISG means that national courts should not resort to interpreting CISG rules from the perspective of national legal systems and laws. This is implied by the fact that the CISG's primary purpose is the harmonization of international sales law.[14]

To better ensure uniformity of application of the CISG, the interpreter should take into consideration rulings on the same or similar interpretive issues made by foreign courts or arbitral tribunals. Although such decisions are not binding, they can play a significant role in promoting uniformity in the application of the CISG. Existing online databases and other compilations allow judges all over the world to review decisions made in other legal systems.[15] These readily accessible sources include UNCITRAL's CLOUT reporting system,[16] the CISG Database at the University of Pace Law School's Institute of International Commercial Law,[17] and UNILEX.[18] In the Arab world, the Middle East Center for International Commercial Law[19] was established in 1998 in cooperation with the Institute of International Commercial Law at Pace University for the purpose of disseminating information on the CISG to Arabic language countries.

The role that the principle of good faith plays in the CISG is a debated issue.[20] The inclusion of good faith in the CISG came as a result of disagreement among negotiating states. As a compromise, good faith was included as a matter of interpretation, not as a provision imposing a duty on parties to act in good faith.

It is worth mentioning that the rules of interpretation of public international law found in the Vienna Convention on the Law of Treaties, 1969 (VCLT), are not suitable to interpreting the CISG. The VCLT is more concerned with treaties that impose obligations

---

[14] One method of interpreting a vague provision of the CISG without resort to national legal concepts is the use of its legislative history. See Mohsen Shafik, *Ittifaqiyat al-Umam al-Muttahidah bi-sha'n al-Bay' al-Dawli lil-Bada'i': Dirasah fi qanun al-tijarah al-dawli (The UN Convention on Contracts for the International Sale of Goods: A Study in International Commercial Law)* (Cairo, 1988), 79.

[15] Hossam El-Saghir, *Tafsīr Ittifaqiyat al-Umam al-Muttahidah bi-sha'n or qūd al-Bay' al-Dawli lil-Bada'i' (The Interpretation of the United Nations Convention on Contracts for the International Sale of Goods)* (Cairo, 2001), 79.

[16] UNCITRAL publishes CISG case abstracts under its Case Law on UNCITRAL Texts or CLOUT. The system is explained in the UN document A/CN.9/SER.C/GUIDE/1/Rev.1.

[17] The leading CISG database is the Institute of International Commercial Law, School of Law, Pace University, available at http://www.cisg.law.pace.edu/.

[18] *UNILEX: International Case Law and Bibliography on the UN Convention on Contracts for the International Sale of Goods* (ed. Michael Joachim Bonell et al.).

[19] See http://www.cisg.law.pace.edu/cisgarabic/middleast/index.html.

[20] For more details about the position of Arab commentators on good faith, see *infra* Section C. III (1).

on contracting states. Its rules also emphasize the intentions of contracting states that are bound by such treaties. Unlike such treaties, the first three parts of the CISG address matters relating to contract law (obligations of buyers and sellers).[21] However, the applicability of individual principles of interpretation under public international law to the CISG is not completely excluded. For example, public international law's interpretive rules may be useful in interpreting the fourth part of the CISG entitled "Final Provisions" relating to the obligations of contracting states. In addition, some principles of interpretation under public international law such as those concerning the interpretation of conventions drafted in several languages can also be applied to the CISG.[22]

The second rule of interpretation is the gap-filling provision incorporated in Article 7(2) of the CISG. It deals with questions concerning matters not expressly settled by the CISG, although falling within its scope. These questions are to be settled in conformity with the general principles on which the CISG is based. This means that where the CISG does not provide a solution to the issue at stake, resort has to be made to the general principles. Only when the general principles, express or implied, fail to provide an answer should an interpreter reference the national law applicable by virtue of conflict of laws rules. This gap-filling provision aims at furthering the ability of the CISG to resolve issues that fall within its scope and to avoid recourse to national laws.

The enactment of the New Egyptian Commercial Code somehow altered the way in which Article 7(2) operates in practice. The Code regulates commercial sales transactions for the first time. As far as international sales contracts are concerned, Article 88(2) states that the Code is subject to international conventions in force in Egypt, as well as to international commercial usage. It prioritizes international trade usage over national law. It also subjects such contracts to international commercial terms compiled and adopted by international commercial organizations, such as the ICC's Incoterms.

As noted above, Egyptian legislation incorporates international trade usage by reference. It recognizes *lex mercatoria* at the legislative level. In cases where the Egyptian law governs an issue by virtue of Article 7(2) of the CISG, *lex mercatoria* prevails over national law. The substantive rules of the Code only apply where the *lex mercatoria* fails to resolve the issue at hand. This also creates an important guideline concerning the CISG's interpretation. The wording of Article 88 implies that *lex mercatoria* may be treated on equal footing with the international conventions governing the international sales of goods.

IV. Obstacles to the Uniform Application of the CISG in the Arab World

The legal community in the Arab world is largely unaware of the existence of the CISG. Paradoxically, Egypt and Syria were among the first ten countries that adhered to the CISG.[23] Law professors, jurists, and judges in the Arab world know little, if anything, about the CISG. Only five Arab countries – Egypt, Iraq, Mauritania, Syria, and

---

[21] The CISG is divided into four parts: Part I: Sphere of Application and General Provisions; Part II: Formation of Contract; Part III: Sale of Goods; Part IV: Final Provisions.

[22] *Commentary on the UN Convention on the International Sale of Goods* (CISG), 2nd ed. (ed. P. Schlechtriem and I. Schwenzer) (Oxford University Press, 2005), 97.

[23] By December 11, 1986, the instruments of adherence, ratification, or accession had been deposited with the UN Secretary General by eleven states: Argentina, China, Egypt, France, Hungary, Italy, Lesotho, Syrian Arab Republic, United States, Yugoslavia, and Zambia.

Lebanon – have adopted the CISG. No Egyptian university offers a course in the CISG at the undergraduate level. Moreover, the number of universities that offer courses covering the CISG at the graduate level is limited.[24] None of the universities in any of the four countries mentioned offer CISG-related courses. Moreover, the scholarly writings and court decisions on the CISG are extremely scarce. The scarcity of published decisions can be partially attributed to the fact that Egypt only publishes opinions rendered by the Court of Cassation and the Constitutional Court. Therefore, even assuming that lower courts apply the CISG, their opinions are inaccessible.

In 2006, the Egyptian Court of Cassation issued its only decision applying the CISG.[25] The case remains unpublished and a 2000 CISG international case law digest[26] failed to list a single court or arbitral decision in the Arab world.[27] It is worth mentioning that the delay in publishing the CISG in the Official Gazette in Egypt created a constitutional obstacle to its application by the judiciary. The CISG was not published in the Official Gazette until January 30, 1997, almost a decade after its entry into force.[28] Article 151 of the Egyptian Constitution requires publishing international conventions in the Official Gazette in order for them to come into force under national law.

A. *Official Texts of the CISG: Errors in the Arabic Version*

The CISG was issued as a single original instrument with publication in six official languages. In theory, the texts of the six versions of the CISG have the same meaning. However, this is not the case. For instance, Shafik, an eminent Egyptian scholar who represented Egypt at UNCITRAL, noted a difference between Article 1 of the English and Arabic versions of the CISG on the one hand and the corresponding Article of the French version. In the English and Arabic versions, it is crucial for the "place of business" of the seller and the buyer to be located in different states in order for the CISG to apply. The discrepancy lies in the French version's use of the term *éstablishment* instead of "place of business," which thus adopts a physical approach to determining whether the CISG applies. Shafik argues that the terminology *éstablishment* used in the French version is more accurate than the corresponding term of the English and Arabic versions. He contends that the CISG is not concerned with the place where the parties conduct their business, but is concerned with the physical location of their establishments.

The comparison between the Arabic version of the CISG and its English counterpart shows numerous divergences. This has led judges from different countries to attach different meanings to CISG provisions depending on the version on which they rely. Unfortunately, Egypt has adopted the Arabic version of the CISG and published it in the Official Gazette without any review. It became part of the national law without a proper review of the translation and contains numerous inaccuracies. The Middle East Center for International Commercial Law lobbied the UNCITRAL General Secretary about

---

[24] However, as of 1997, the author of this chapter has taught the CISG in three Egyptian universities at the post-graduate level; Menoufia, Cairo, and Helwan universities.

[25] Court of Cassation, Civil and Commercial Circuit, April 11, 2006, Case No. 979 Judicial Year 73.

[26] *Twenty Years of International Sales Law under the CISG: International Bibliography and Case Law Digest* (ed. Michael R. Will) (1980–2000).

[27] Id.

[28] 5 *Official Gazette* (January 30, 1997).

correcting the errors in the Arabic translation.[29] In 2001, an amended Arabic version was issued to correct the errors. However, the errors were not completely cured. The 2001 Arabic version still contains errors in Articles 25 and 36.

Article 25 in the English version stipulates that "[a] breach of contract committed by one of the parties is fundamental if it results in such detriment to the other party as substantially to deprive him of what he is entitled to expect under the contract, unless the party in beach did *not foresee* and the reasonable person of the same kind in the same circumstances would *not have foreseen* such a result" (emphasis added). However, the Arabic version omits the negation in the second phrase. According to the Arabic version, a breach is not fundamental if the breaching party *foresees* such breach, and if a reasonable person in the same circumstances would *have foreseen* its occurrence.

The Arabic and English versions of Article 36 make different presumptions. The English version deals with lack of conformity that does not exist at the time when the passing of the risk of loss is shifted to the buyer. It provides that the seller is liable for any lack of conformity that *occurs* after the passing of risk and that is due to a breach of any of the seller's obligations. However, the Arabic version of the same article uses the term *appears* instead of *occurs*. This discrepancy is likely to have some implications. The term *appears* used in the Arabic version implies that the seller is liable whether the nonconformity comes into existence before or after the time of passing of risk. The result of this translation error is that one of the incidents (Arabic version) of Article 36(2) covers an incident already governed by paragraph (1) of the same Article (seller's liability for the lack of conformity that exists at the time of passing of risk).

Ironically, the 2001 Arabic version contains an error that did not exist in the original version. Article 35(2)(b) of the amended Arabic version contradicts the English version. Article 35(2)(b) in the current Arabic version omits the negation concerning the buyer's reliance on the seller's skill and judgment. In other words, according to the Arabic version, the goods conform with the contract if they are fit for the particular purpose known to the seller except where the circumstances show that the buyer *relies* on the seller's skill and judgment. The Article should have stipulated that the goods conform if they are fit for their particular purpose known to the seller except in the cases where the circumstances show that the buyer *did not rely* on the seller's skill and judgment. In January 2011, UNICTRAL issued a new Arabic version correcting the errors in Articles 35(2)(b) and 36(2). However, it did not correct the error in Article 25.

V. Implementation of CISG Article 78 in Egypt

Article 78 of the CISG establishes the obligation of a party to pay interest if and insofar as he or she fails to pay the price on time or any other sum that is in arrears. However, it does not fix the interest rate. There are incompatible approaches to the question of interest based not only on different economic and political approaches but also on philosophical and even religious views, as Muslim states forbid interest.[30]

During the preparation of the draft of the CISG, some Arab countries' delegations raised objections against any provision that deals with interest. It was suggested that

---

[29] Depository Notification CN. 862 1998 Treaties – 5 of February 19, 1999, Process-Verbal of Rectification the Authentic Arabic Text.

[30] Schlechtriem and Schwenzer, *Commentary*, 794.

the CISG omit any reference to interest or at least to provide for a reservation to enable countries to opt out of the application of the interest provision. However these suggestions were not accepted and the final text encompasses Article 78, which obliges the party who delays payment to pay interest.[31] Notwithstanding the traditional prohibition of interest in Islam, Article 226 of the Egyptian Civil Code provides that where the object of an obligation is the payment of a sum of money of which the amount is known at the time when the claim is made, the debtor shall be bound, in case of delay in payment, to pay to the creditor, as compensation for the delay, interest at the rate of 4 percent in civil matters and 5 percent in commercial matters. Such interest shall run from the date of the claim in court, unless the contract or commercial usage fixes another date.

Under Article 227 of the Egyptian Civil Code, the parties may agree on another rate of interest either in the event of delay in effecting payment or in any other case in which interest has been stipulated, provided that it does not exceed 7 percent. Article 231 establishes that a creditor may demand damages in addition to interest if it proves that the loss in excess of interest damages was due to bad faith on the part of the debtor. Thus, we see here express provisions of the Egyptian Civil Code, allowing interest in contradiction with the principle of prohibition of interest under Islamic law. This contradiction was brought before the Constitutional Court. The rector of Al Azhar University filed a case against the president and others, claiming that Article 226 of the Egyptian Civil Code contradicts Article 2 of the Egyptian Constitution. The court held that charging interest is prohibited by Shari'a, but Article 2 of the Constitution has no retroactive effect. Article 2 of the Constitution as amended in 1980 obliges the legislator to apply Shari'a law in respect of any future enactment. Therefore, Article 226 of the Egyptian Civil Code remains enforceable though contrary to Shari'a law. The decision has been widely criticized.[32] In the end, the court implied that it is the duty of the legislature to amend prior laws to bring them into conformity with Islamic Law. Instead, a subsequent legislative amendment allows the Central Bank to stipulate the legal rate of interest rate.[33] It is expected that the enforceability of CISG Article 78 will face future challenges.

VI. Influence of National Laws in Arab Countries on the Interpretation of the CISG

Judges in the Egyptian courts tend to resort to national legal concepts to articulate their understanding of international agreements. However, this tendency is difficult to confirm in the matter of the CISG, as there is only a single Court of Cassation case applying it. That case involved an Italian seller of marble and an Egyptian buyer. The buyer paid part of the price and refused to pay the rest of it. The seller brought a case before the First Instance Court, seeking the payment of the amount due.[34] The seller presented two invoices showing the quantity of goods and the price. The First Instance Court applied Egyptian law to the dispute without paying any attention to the CISG. It ruled in favor

---

[31] United Nation Conference on Contracts for International Sale of Goods, Vienna, March 10–April 11, 1981, codified records UN, New York, 1980. Summary records of the First Committee, 34th meeting, April 3, 1980, nos. 10, 20, pp. 416, 418.

[32] Saleh Majid and Faris Lenzen, "Interest and Islamic Banking, Finance and Banking worldwide," March 2011, available at http://www.mondaq.com/article.asp?articleid=53350.

[33] Article 51, paras. 2 and 3, Commercial Code No. 17 of 1999. See also Article 64.

[34] South Cairo First Instance Court, Commercial Circuit 14, December 24, 2002 (unpublished decision, on file with author).

of the seller and ordered the buyer to pay the price due. The buyer appealed to the Court of Appeals, and subsequently to the Court of Cassation, arguing that the seller failed to meet the burden of proving that the buyer took delivery of the goods.[35] The Court of Cassation found that the lower court erred in applying domestic law to the dispute. It ruled that the CISG should govern the dispute and remanded the case to the appellate court to that effect.[36] It emphasized the international nature of the CISG and the role that good faith plays in its application. It also emphasized that regard should be paid to the evidentiary rules of the CISG before resorting to the national law. The case, and the lack of subsequent CISG cases, illustrates that the parties and most Egyptian courts lack adequate knowledge of the CISG. To a great extent, this decision cautioned the lower courts to apply the CISG whenever applicable.

UNILEX cites two arbitral awards of the Cairo Regional Center for International Commercial Arbitration (CRCICA) that applied the CISG.[37] The first dispute concerned a C&F contract for the sale of grains concluded between an Asian seller and an Egyptian buyer.[38] When inspected at the port of destination, the Egyptian Agricultural Quarantine Department found the grain to be infested with insects. The buyer initiated arbitration proceedings.

The arbitral panel reasoned that under C&F contracts, the risk passes to the buyer at the time the goods are loaded at the port of shipment and that the buyer had failed to prove that the defect existed at that time. The panel referred to CISG Article 36, but based its decision on the application of Incoterms. It did so without inquiring as to the applicability of the CISG to the dispute. Why the panel mentioned Article 36 and the extent to which it based its decision on its application is ambiguous.

The second arbitral award concerned a dispute between an Egyptian seller and a U.S. buyer for the sale of a certain amount of apparatuses.[39] The contract provided that all issues are to be interpreted according to the conditions of the contract, the CISG, and Egyptian law. A dispute arose concerning the conformity of some of the supplied units and the seller's nonperformance of his duty to obtain a bank guarantee. The buyer thus initiated arbitration, seeking damages. The arbitrator deviated from the autonomous interpretation rules of Article 7 of the CISG by applying the CISG in parallel with Egyptian law. He cited Article 45 of the CISG, but concluded that it did not differ from Egyptian law. As such, the arbitrator applied Egyptian rules concerning contractual liability and cited a decision rendered by the Egyptian Court of Cassation applying Egyptian law.

There are two other unpublished awards referencing the CISG.[40] In the first case, again, the panel incorrectly applied the CISG. The panel reasoned that: "the provisions of the CISG [did] not apply to the exclusion of Egyptian national law but in addition to it." The panel then noted that this was a nonissue because both texts coincided and

---

[35] Cairo Court of Appeals, Commercial Circuit 50, August 24, 2003.
[36] The case is still under review before the Court of Appeals.
[37] Bonell, *UNILEX*.
[38] Cairo Regional Center for International Commercial Arbitration (CRCICA), Cairo, Award No. 19/1990, April 13, 1991, published in *Arbitral Awards for the Cairo Regional Center for International Commercial Arbitration* (ed. Mohie Eldin and I. Alam Eldin) (Kluwer Law International, 2000), 23–7.
[39] Cairo Regional Center for International Commercial Arbitration (CRCICA), Cairo, Award No. 50/1994, October 3, 1995.
[40] Alexandria Center for International and Commercial Arbitration, case no. 6 for 2003.

consequently applied the Egyptian Civil Code (ECC) and the CISG "simultaneously." The panel failed to provide the reasons why the seller's act of reselling the goods was justified. Nothing in the award confirmed whether the seller properly exercised his right to avoid the contract under CISG Article 49, adequately performed his duty to preserve the goods as required under CISG Article 85, or fulfilled CISG Article 88's requirement to notify the buyer of intent to sell the goods.

The second arbitral award involved a dispute between an Austrian supplier and an Egyptian buyer for the sale of electronic scales and spare parts.[41] The contract neither contained a choice of law clause, nor expressly excluded the CISG. The panel failed to apply the CISG to the dispute, although it was applicable. The panel applied the Egyptian Civil Code instead. These arbitration decisions again demonstrate the extent to which the legal communities in Arab countries are unaware of the CISG and its rules.

VII. Scholarly Writings

In interpreting the CISG, scholars in the Arab world have been influenced by their culture and national legal systems. This part will look at the scholarship on the principle of good faith and barter contracts as examples of this influence.

A. *Good Faith*

Commentators disagree as to whether CISG Article 7(1)'s "observance of good faith in international trade" is a principle of interpretation and a rule of conduct. Some commentators argue for a narrow view of Article 7(1) as only applying to the interpretation of the CISG. The broader, majority view holds that good faith as a general principle of the CISG that imposes on contracting parties a general duty to act in good faith.

Influenced by their national legal systems, Egyptian scholars tend to adopt a broad interpretation of Article 7(1). They argue that good faith under the CISG addresses interpretive and regulatory issues.[42] The Egyptian legal system is a combination of codified civil law rules and Islamic law. Good faith in both is broad in reach. Under the Egyptian Law, good faith is not considered a principle of interpretation of the law. It is rather an obligation that contracting parties have to fulfill pursuant to Article 148 of the Egyptian Civil Code.

Despite the fact that Islamic law does not use the term "good faith," the concept is even broader in Islamic law. Good faith in Islamic law includes a duty to act altruistically. This is a natural approach because Islamic law does not sharply distinguish between law, morality, and religion. Private law addresses society's interests, as well as those of the contracting parties. Islamic law goes beyond the narrow interests of contracting parties. For example, traders should pay due regard to the public interest, such as making products available to consumers at reasonable prices.

Islamic law imposes a general duty to act in good faith in all transactions. It requires parties to act in good faith during negotiations, contract formation, and performance.

---

[41] Decision issued September 18, 2006, ad hoc arbitration held at the premises of Egyptian National Committee for International Chambers of Commerce (Cairo).

[42] *Shafik*, Ittifaqiyat al-Umam al-Muttahidah bi-sha'n al-Bay' al-Dawli lil-Bada'i: dirasah fi qanun al-tijarah al-dawli (*The UN Convention on Contracts for the International Sale of Goods: A Study in International Commercial Law – in Arabic*), Cairo 1988, p. 30.

For example, a party that enters into contract negotiations in order to gain access to another's confidential information violates the Islamic law duty to act in good faith. In addition, a creditor bears a duty to give his or her debtor a grace period if he or she is unable to pay the debt.[43] The broad scope that good faith has in both the civil law and Islamic law induces Egyptian commentators to attach a broad interpretation to CISG Article 7(1).

B. *Barter Contracts*

The question whether the CISG governs barter contracts is a matter of interpretation. John Honnold took the view that the exchange of goods is governed by the CISG.[44] Egyptian commentators, interpreting the CISG against the background of their own legal culture, argue that the CISG does not apply to barter transactions.[45] This argument is based on the distinction made in the Egyptian Civil and Commercial Codes between barter and sales contracts. Under Article 418 of the Egyptian Civil Code barter contracts are not considered sales.[46] In addition, Article 88 of the Egyptian Commercial Code requires the consideration to be monetary in nature in order for the transaction to qualify as a sales contract. It provides that in cases where part of the consideration is nonmonetary, the contract is considered a sale if the value of the nonmonetary portion of the consideration does not exceed the monetary portion. With this background, Egyptian commentators assert that the CISG only applies to contracts where there is a monetary payment.

VIII. Influence of the CISG on Egyptian Law

Although the CISG has limited judicial application in Arab countries, it significantly influenced the drafting of the New Egyptian Commercial Code (Code), Law No. 17 of 1997. The repealed Commercial Code, enacted in 1883, did not contain any provisions regulating commercial sales. The civil law governed all sales contracts – consumer and commercial sales. Chapter II of the Code regulates commercial contracts. Chapter II is divided into seven sections preceded by a set of general principles. The general provisions provide a set of rules that apply to all types of commercial obligations.[47] One section regulates commercial contracts, including commercial sales. The Code regulates commercial sales in a way that significantly differs from the way the Civil Code regulates noncommercial contracts. However, the Commercial Code is not all inclusive. In other words, the Civil Code applies in the absence of a governing rule in the Commercial Code.[48]

---

[43] For more examples, see Fatima Akaddaf, "Application of the United Nations Convention on Contracts for the International Sale of Goods (CISG) to Arab Islamic Countries: Is the CISG Compatible with Islamic Law Principles?," 13 *Pace International Law Review* 1 (2001).

[44] John Honnold, *Uniform Law for International Sales Under the 1980 United Nations Convention*, 2nd ed. (1991), 102.

[45] *Shafik*, n. 42, p. 47.

[46] Article 418 of the Egyptian Civil Code defines sale as "a contract whereby the seller undertakes to transfer to the buyer the ownership of a thing or any other proprietary right in consideration of a price in money."

[47] Articles 47–71, Commercial Code.

[48] The Egyptian Commercial Code is divided into five chapters. Chapter 1 lays the general provisions on which the code is based; chapter 2 deals with commercial obligations and contracts; chapter 3 regulates banking transactions; chapter 4 provides for the rules governing negotiable instruments; Chapter 5 deals with bankruptcy.

Therefore, the enactment of the New Egyptian Commercial Code created a distinction between two kinds of sales transactions, commercial and noncommercial sales. The former is primarily governed by Commercial Code rules. The Civil Code exclusively governs noncommercial sales. The New Egyptian Commercial Code incorporated many of the CISG concepts and rules. The preparatory memorandum explicitly mentions the CISG as one of the international instruments that the legislature used in the drafting of the Code.[49]

IX. Conclusion

This chapter shows that the Egyptian legal system is a blend of Islamic law and civil law traditions. Article 2 of the Egyptian Constitution, as amended in 1980, provides that the Islamic law is the principal source of legislation. However, the legal system allows for charging interest despite of its prohibition by Islamic law. Therefore, Article 78 of the CISG, interest obligation, is currently enforceable in Egypt, but that may change. On the whole, Egypt has achieved little success in applying the CISG in a way that achieves uniformity of application. The few court decisions and arbitral awards applying the CISG mostly avoided autonomous interpretations of the CISG.

The sole decision of the Egyptian Court of Cassation and four arbitral awards reviewed in this chapter failed to observe the rules of applying the CISG in an autonomous manner and instead they applied "parallel" provisions of national law. At other times, they ignored the applicability of the CISG altogether. However, there has been surprisingly substantial interaction between the CISG and the Egyptian legal system. On the one hand, the legal culture of Egyptian commentators affects their interpretation of the CISG. On the other hand, the New (Egyptian) Commercial Code adopted a number of CISG rules, concepts, and principles.

---

[49] For further details and examples, see Hossam El Saghir, "The Interpretation of the CISG in the Arab World," in *CISG Methodology* (ed. Andre Janssen and Olaf Mayer) (Munich: Sellier European Law Publishers, 2008), 371.

31 Israel

Yehuda Adar

I. Introduction

Israel adopted the CISG on October 25, 1999.[1] Israel officially became a contracting state on February 1, 2003. The adopting statute also repealed[2] the two 1964 Hague coventions on the International Sale of Goods. The late adoption of the CISG is one of the factors responsible for the relatively small body of Israeli case law relying directly on the CISG.[3] Another, arguably more significant, factor concerns the lack of awareness on the part of many practicing lawyers of the existence or relevance of the CISG. The paucity of Israeli scholarly commentary on the CISG[4] poses an additional obstacle to Israeli lawyers' and law students' understanding of the CISG. Finally, as in other jurisdictions, the low level of reliance on the CISG might be explained to a considerable extent by practicing lawyers electing to opt out of the application of the CISG.

Despite the scarcity of Israeli case law, the case law that does exist is generally of high quality. First, in a number of Israeli Supreme Court cases, a rather comprehensive

---

[1] It is noteworthy that Part IV (Articles 89–101) was completely omitted from the Israeli version of the CISG (with the exception of Article 96), which was included.

[2] Id., §5.

[3] This survey includes cases in which the CISG was either relied on directly, or as a source of comparison and inspiration, as well as cases decided on the basis of ULIS, but which have been deemed to have a considerable guiding force with respect to issues arising under the CISG. The relevant cases include, inter alia: CC (BS) 3246/09 *Iskur Pipes & Profilers Ltd. v. Eclipse Magnetics Ltd.* (03.01.2010) Nevo Legal Database (Isr.); CA 465/80 *S. Solondz Ltd. v. Hatehof Iron Industry Ltd.* [1984] IsrSC 38(3) 630; CA 366/89 *Pine Aluminum Ltd. v. D. Metal A.G Foreign Company* [1991] IsrSC 45(5) 850; CA 339/86 *Earl Orient Shipping Company v. O.T.C Oil Trading Company* [1988] IsrSC 42(1) 506; CA 741/79 *Kalanit HaSharon v. Horwitz* [1981] IsrSC 35(3) 533; CC (Jer) 618/95 *Banita Trade and Investment Ltd. v. Tiemme Raccorderie s.r.l* (22.10.2008) Nevo Legal Database (Isr.)

[4] See Arie Reich, "The Uniform Law of International Sales: A Need for Revision," 14(1) *Bar Ilan L. Studies* 127 (1997) (Hebrew). An English abstract of the article is available at: http://www.biu.ac.il/law/cisg/cisgArtEng.htm; Eyal Zamir, "European Tradition, the CISGs on International Sales and Israeli Contract Law," in *European Legal Traditions and Israel* (ed. A.M. Rabello) (Jerusalem: The Harry and Michael Sacher Institute for Legislative Research and Comparative Law, The Hebrew University of Jerusalem, 1994); Gabriela Shalev, "International Sale of Goods between Europe and Israel," in *Essays on European Law and Israel* (ed. A. Rabello) (Jerusalem: The Harry and Michael Sacher Institute for Legislative Research and Comparative Law, The Hebrew University of Jerusalem, 1996), 1113; For more recent writings relating to the CISG, see, e.g., Jonathan Yovel, "Contract Law in the Third Millennium: Neo-Classical and Relational Contract Theories in the New Israeli Civil Code," 4 *L. & Business J.* 241 (2006); Nir Bar, "Contract Validity and the CISG – Closing the Loophole" (2007), available at http://www.israelbar.org.il/uploadFiles/Contract_Validity_and_the_CISG.pdf.; Arie Reich, "Globalization and Law: The Future Impact of International Law on Israel's Commercial Law," 17(1) *Bar Ilan Law Studies* 17 (2001).

analysis is offered by the court. Some of these cases discuss not only the appropriate interpretation of relevant provisions, but also the underlying policies and principles that the judiciary should apply in resolving international sales disputes. Second, some of the cases that involve transactions that were concluded prior to 2003 and thus are officially based on the Uniform Law on the International Sale of Goods (ULIS), which was adopted at The Hague on July 1, 1964, offer insights into issues that today are raised by parallel provisions in the CISG. All cases explicitly referencing the CISG, even those decided under the ULIS, have been included in this chapter.

II. Scope of Application: Expansion of CISG Jurisdiction

One of the unique characteristics of the Israeli approach to the CISG concerns its scope of application. Although most jurisdictions have incorporated the general provisions of the CISG (Articles 1–13) "as is," the Israeli legislature expressly deviated by extending its application as follows: "In addition to what is provided by Article 1 of the CISG, its provisions will apply in the case where a party to the contract operates its business in a non-contracting state." Hence, under Israeli law, assuming an Israeli Court has jurisdiction over the dispute, *it is sufficient that either the seller or the buyer operates a business in a contracting state for the convention to apply*. There is no need to show that the rules of private international law lead to the application of the law of a contracting state.[5] This also means that the CISG would apply even if an Israeli seller or buyer operates his or her business in a noncontracting state. Moreover, a literal interpretation of the Israeli provision may enable a court to apply the CISG even if both parties operate their businesses in noncontracting states.

According to the explanatory notes to the Israeli statute, this deviation from the general norm of the CISG was deemed justified on three grounds. First, it was believed that such an arrangement would minimize uncertainties and controversies over the choice of law, especially when one party operates in a contracting state and the other party does not. Secondly, it was argued that a wide application of the CISG would introduce more coherence and consistency into the legal system. Finally, such an expansion was deemed normatively desirable, for it would enhance reliance on the CISG, which was considered by the Ministry of Justice a more sophisticated, complete and up-to-date legal regime compared with most national sales laws.[6]

Notwithstanding these advantages, the expansive approach is subject to serious criticism.[7] The deviation from the rule of application provided in the CISG, though intended to enhance consistency and reliance on the CISG, will increase uncertainty within the general business community. Thus, there is a case for reconsidering the Israeli position.

III. Concurrent Grounds of Liability

One of the most intriguing questions relating to the CISG – and one of substantial practical importance – is the question of whether, in a dispute over the performance of a transaction to which the CISG applies, the aggrieved party should be allowed to rely on

---

[5] See, respectively, CISG §§1(1)(a), 1(1)(b).
[6] Draft Bill of the Sales (International Sale of Goods) Law, 1997, HH, 432, 434.
[7] See Reich, "The Uniform Law of International Sales," 176–7.

a noncontractual cause of action (tort or in unjust enrichment). The question has been debated in the legal literature.[8] In 2009, the Israeli Supreme Court weighed in on this issue in *Pamesa v. Mendelson*.[9]

The case before the court concerned a contract for the sale of tiles between Pamesa Ceramica, a Spanish manufacturer (seller), and Mendelson Engineering, an Israeli importing company (buyer). The tiles were purchased from the seller in 1996, and were sold by the buyer to an Israeli construction company (builder) who installed them in one of its buildings. The tiles proved to be defective and had to be removed and replaced. The builder brought an action against the buyer alleging nonconformity and demanded compensation for the full cost of their replacement, as well as for loss of reputation. The buyer then sent a third party notice to the seller.

The court of first instance accepted both the claim and the third party notice.[10] The court refused to accept the seller's defense that the buyer's claim against it was barred under Article 39(a) of the ULIS (CISG). The reason given by the court for rejecting the seller's defense was two-fold. First, there was evidence that the seller had been aware of defects in its products, and thus was not allowed to rely on Article 39.[11] Second, even assuming that the contractual cause of action was barred, recovery could still be given under a theory of negligence.[12]

On appeal to the Supreme Court, the seller asserted that the contractual claim of the buyer against it was barred and further, the buyer should not be allowed to rely on an extracontractual cause of action. The issue here is whether a buyer suffering from a nonconformity of goods should be allowed to seek a tort remedy, even when his or her contractual remedies are barred under the prescription rules of the ULIS or the CISG. The court held that the nonconformity claim was time barred.[13] The court emphasized that even though the case was formally resolved according to ULIS, the same decision would apply to the CISG.[14] The court extensively referenced CISG literature in rendering its decision.

In analyzing the concurrent liability issue, the Supreme Court adopted an interpretive approach that viewed the resolution of the issue as depending first and foremost on an internal interpretation of the CISG, rather than on domestic law.[15] This decision reflected

---

[8] See, e.g., the debate between Honnold and Schlechtriem on products liability: John O. Honnold, *Uniform Law for International Sales under the 1980 United Nations CISG*, 3rd ed. (The Hague: Kluwer Law International, 1999), 74–6 (arguing that allowing concurrent liability would decrease uniformity, would ruin the balance of justice designed by the CISG, and might encourage judges to use domestic law); and compare Peter Schlechtriem, "The Borderland of Tort and Contract – Opening a New Frontier?," 21 *Cornell International L.J.* 467, 473–6 (1988) (arguing tort actions should be barred only when they are brought to protect an "economic interest," as opposed to "property interests," existing independently of any contractual relationship).

[9] CA 7833/06 *Pamesa Ceramica v. Yisrael Mendelson Engineering Technical Supply Ltd.* (17.03.2009) Nevo Legal Database (Isr.) (hereinafter the Pamesa case), available at http://cisgw3.law.pace.edu/cases/090317i5.html.

[10] CC (Hi) 137/01 *Yaakov and Tovi Eisenberger Building and Public Works Co. Ltd. v. Yisrael Mendelson Engineering Technical Supply Ltd.* (20.08.2006) Nevo Legal Database (by subscription) (Isr.).

[11] See ULIS, §40.

[12] *Eisenberger v. Mendelson*, at para. 18.

[13] See *infra*, VI.C.

[14] Pamesa case, paras. 17–18, 23.

[15] The court cited with approval Schlechtriem's view that "The question whether the ground of liability in question falls within the scope of the CISG must be clarified by interpretation and, since the CISG defines

an important, if subtle, policy choice by the court. It testifies to the courts' preference to allow the CISG to determine its own applicability. It is not at all obvious, from a legalistic point of view, that the CISG should be given priority over domestic sources of law in the area of noncontractual liability.

The second step in the courts' analysis was to analyze the relevant CISG provisions. The court referenced CISG Article 4. It noted that Article 4 made it clear that the CISG would apply, under its own terms, only to rights and obligations *arising from the contract* of sale. Legal issues arising not from the agreement but from other facts and events were to be decided according to domestic law.[16] At first blush, this analysis argues that the CISG does not apply to any obligations arising from tortuous conduct. The court, however, reasoned that such a literal interpretation would mean that the CISG would be completely ignored in any tort action. Such a sweeping approach would circumvent and frustrate the goals of the CISG, at least in those cases where the tortuous conduct is based on issues that are regulated under the CISG.[17] However, because there is no consensus in the cases or CISG commentary, the court resorted to domestic law on the general issue of competing causes of action.[18] However, Israeli case law did not provide a definitive answer. In S. *Solondz Ltd. v. Hatehof Iron*,[19] the Supreme Court explicitly rejected the buyer's attempt to recover on an alternative tort theory, reasoning that by denying recovery in contract on the basis of nonconformity, the domestic sales law barred a tort action based on the same nonconformity.[20]

The Supreme Court in *Pamesa* referenced academic criticism of the *Solondz* case and demonstrated that in practice this position was not always implemented.[21] According to the court, in these circumstances, and in light of the importance of harmonizing the Israeli position with those of other jurisdictions, adherence to the restrictive view adopted in the *Solondz* case was not absolute.[22]

In light of the indeterminacy of domestic law on the issue at stake, the court then considered the issue on its merits. It offered a general *analytic distinction between contractual and noncontractual interests*. Under this "interests" approach, the court considered whether and to what extent the interests protected by the extracontractual cause of

---

its own scope, it is the CISG itself which must be interpreted." Id., para. 53, quoting Peter Schlechtriem, *Commentary on the UN CISG on the International Sale of Goods (CISG)* (1998).

[16] Pamesa case, para. 53.

[17] Id., para. 54. The court goes on to cite Honnold's position that "Domestic rules that turn on substantially the same facts as the rules of the CISG must be displaced by the CISG; any other result would destroy the CISG's basic function to establish uniform rules" (quoting John O. Honnold, *Uniform Law for International Sales under the 1980 United Nations CISG*, 2nd ed. (Deventer: Kluwer Law & Taxation, 1991), 122).

[18] Id., para. 58.

[19] CA 465/80 S. *Solondz Ltd. v. Hatehof Iron Industry Ltd.* [1984] IsrSC 38(3) 630 (hereafter referred to as the Solondz case).

[20] Id., 636–7.

[21] The vast majority of these cases concerned disputes over nonconformity of apartments, which in Israel are regulated mainly by the Sale (Housing) Law, 5733–1973, 27 LSI 213 (1972–73) (Isr.) rather than the Sale Law, 5728–1968, 22 LSI 107 (1967–68) (Isr.) (hereafter referred to as the sales statute). Arguably, this enabled some of the courts to distinguish their case from the *Solondz* case.

[22] *Pamesa* case, para. 69. The court's assertion that "domestic law does not contain a clearer determination than the one that exists in international law" is unconvincing. Under the Israeli legal system, a ruling of the Supreme Court is a binding source of law, regardless of any deviations from it by some lower courts. It would have been better if the court either distinguished the *Pamesa* case from the *Solondz* case or expressly rejected *Solondz*.

action are identical to those protected by the contractual one. The court reasoned that this could be done in two ways. First, on the abstract level, the interests created by the agreement itself must be distinguished from those that are typically protected under the law of tort.[23]

Second, in the context of a negligence claim against a manufacturer, a distinction must be drawn between the latter's role as seller and as manufacturer. Negligence in the performance of any particular contractual obligation made by the manufacturer to a specific buyer is within the domain of the CISG. In contrast, a manufacturer also owes a duty of care towards, the public in general, which should be viewed as an independent source of obligation. Therefore, the breach of such obligations would not be subject to the specific limitations and conditions imposed by the CISG.

In implementing these distinctions, the court allowed the buyer to claim and litigate an alternative cause of action in negligence against the manufacturer:

> In the case before us, the claim is that Pamesa was negligent in manufacturing the tiles and it shipped a product that a reasonable manufacturer would not have marketed. If Pamesa was indeed negligent in this way, this is not a negligent performance of an obligation under the contract, but a negligent performance of a general duty of care of manufacturers that does not derive from the agreement between the parties.[24]

Therefore, a cause of action based on negligence is not barred a priori because a parallel contractual cause of action was barred under the CISG.[25]

In two subsequent Supreme Court cases, the analysis in the *Pamesa* was noted. In *Harel Insurance Co. Ltd. v. BTR Environmental Ltd.*,[26] the court implemented and reinforced the rule it laid down in *Pamesa*. In *Harel*, a buyer of an oil filter claimed damages for the financial loss resulting when the filter exploded. The buyer sued the seller, who was not the manufacturer of the filter. The buyer's claim was dismissed in the court of first instance, based on an alleged distinction under the CISG between sellers and manufacturers, held that a supplier (seller) is not liable for defective goods produced by the manufacturer.

The distinction between manufacturer and downstream seller of goods was rejected by the Supreme Court as unsound and inconsistent with the CISG. The court held that even if the contractual claim was barred under the CISG, the trial court erred in failing to explore the possibility of buyer's claim on an alternative cause of action in negligence against the supplier and the manufacturer. Under the *Pamesa* analysis, a tort claim founded on negligence in manufacturing was distinguishable from a claim founded on a negligent performance of a purely contractual duty; the barring of the latter kind of claim should not necessarily impede the seller's concurrent liability in tort.[27]

---

[23] For example, a buyer's interest in compensation for a tangible consequential loss (either a property loss or a personal injury) caused by a defective product would be considered a "tort interest." On the other hand, the interest of the same buyer in being compensated for the direct economic loss embodied in the defect itself should generally be regarded as a purely economic and thus a "contractual interest."

[24] Id., para. 71.

[25] However, the Supreme Court was not convinced that there had been sufficient evidence to maintain the negligence claim. Therefore, in the end, the buyer's claim against the seller was dismissed. See id., paras. 78–80.

[26] CA 9422/06 *Harel Insurance Company Ltd. v. BTR Environmental Ltd.* (17.01.2010) Nevo Legal Database (by subscription) (Isr.) (hereafter referred to as the Harel case).

[27] Id., paras. 17–19.

In the seminal case of *Adras Building Materials Ltd. v. Harlow and Jones*,[28] an importer of steel brought suit against the seller for having sold part of the contracted steel to a third party. In a very detailed and controversial judgment, the court held that the existence of a contractual cause of action (or any other kind of action, for that matter) should not, as a general rule, be regarded as sufficient reason to prevent a plaintiff from relying alternatively on a cause of action in unjust enrichment. The next issue addressed was whether the buyer was entitled to disgorgement damages based on the seller's gain from breaching the contract (rather than compensatory damages based on the buyer's loss). Answering the question in the affirmative, the majority ordered the seller to restore to the buyer, under a theory of unjust enrichment, the net profit it gained by selling the steel to a third party for a price higher than the original contract price.

Apart from setting a precedent by recognizing the general availability of disgorgement damages as a remedy for breach of contract, the *Adras* case is also illuminating in that the court ignored the international context of the transaction. The court failed to address the fundamental questions of whether and to what extent its approach could be justified under the ULIS or CISG or the potential effect of its judgment on the ability to promote uniformity and harmony in international sales law.[29]

One answer can be drawn by analogy from the *Pamesa* case. The *Pamesa* approach is based on the distinction between a pure failure to perform a contractual obligation and conduct containing additional "tort" elements. Arguably, under the same logic, one could propose a distinction between a mere failure to deliver goods under an international sales contract and a failure followed by a further malfeasance, such as the unlawful reselling of the goods to a third party. In the *Adras* case, the subsequent action is clearly separable from the breach itself. Therefore, under a *Pamesa* analysis, the CISG could be interpreted as not barring a cause of action in unjust enrichment.[30]

IV. Principle of Good Faith

The role of good faith in the application of the CISG has been thoroughly discussed and debated by numerous scholars.[31] This part will review the role of good faith in Israeli law.

---

[28] FH 20/82 *Adras Building Materials Ltd. v. Harlow and Jones G.M.B.H* [1988] IsrSC 42(1) 221 (hereafter referred to as the *Adras* case). See Peter Schlechtriem, "Uniform Sales Law – The Experience with Uniform Sales Law in the Federal Republic of Germany," *Juridisk Tidskrift* 12–13 (1991/2); Daniel Friedmann, "Restitution of Profits Gained by Party in Breach of Contract," 104 *L. Quarterly Rev.* 384–6 (1988), Itzhak England, "The Preying Eagle's Wings: On the Law of Unjust Enrichment," in *Essays in Memory of Professor Guido Tedeschi* 37 (ed. Aharon Barak et al.) (Jerusalem: The Harry and Michael Sacher Institute for Legislative Research and Comparative Law, Faculty of Law, The Hebrew University of Jerusalem, 1995), 37; The judgment was translated to English and appears at 3 *Restitution L. Rev.* 235 (1995).

[29] For this the court has been heavily criticized by both Israeli and foreign scholars. See, e.g., Arie Reich, "Headnote," available at http://www.biu.ac.il/law/cisg/adresVsHarlowEng.htm; England, "The Preying Eagle's Wings," 47–8; and cf. Schlechtriem, *Uniform Sales Law*.

[30] A number of courts have ruled that the CISG does not apply to claims in unjust enrichment. This view was adopted by the Supreme Court of Switzerland (Swiss Federal Court, July 7, 2004, 4C.144/2004/1ma) and by the Greek Courts (see Dionysios P. Flambouras, "Case Law of Greek Courts for the Vienna CISG (1980) for International Sale of Goods," 2 *Nordic Journal of Commercial Law* 39 (2009)). See also Schlechtriem, *Commentary*, 453.

[31] See, e.g., Troy Keily, "Good Faith and the Vienna CISG on Contracts for the International Sale of Goods (CISG)," 3(1) *Vindobona J. of International Commercial L. & Arbitration* 15 (1990); *UN Convention on Contracts for the International Sale of Goods (CISG) Commentary* 111–141 (ed. Stefan Kröll, Loukas

It will then analyze the use of the good faith principle by the Israeli Supreme Court in the case of *Eximin v. Itel Style Ferarri Textile (Eximin)*.[32] In *Eximin*, the Supreme Court implemented a wholly new legal doctrine, based primarily on the principle of good faith.

A. *Good Faith in Israeli Law*

Good faith is one the Israeli legal system's most important principles of contract law. The reason for the dominant role of good faith is found in the fact that Israel is a "mixed jurisdiction" that has been deeply influenced by the law and jurisprudence of both the Anglo-American and Continental legal cultures.[33] This dual influence is clearly evident in private law and is most salient with respect to contract law. However, contract law is mostly regulated by statutory law. Thus, foreign sources of law (mainly English common law), which influenced Israeli contract law in the past, no longer play a role in contract law cases.[34]

The Israeli contract law statutes contain general rules and principles applicable to all contracts. Together, they form the basic structure of the Israeli law of contracts. The Contracts (Remedies for Breach of Contract) Law provides the remedies available for breach of contract.[35] The General Contracts Law is a comprehensive contract law code.[36] It imposes on contracting parties a duty to act "in a customary manner and in good faith" not only in the exercise and performance of a contractual right or duty,[37] but also in precontractual negotiations.[38] A violation of the obligation to act in good faith in the precontractual stage entitles the aggrieved party to compensation for any loss

---

Mistelis, and Pilar Perales Viscasilas) (C.H. Beck Publishing, 2011); Lisa Spagnolo, "Opening Pandora's Box: Good Faith and Precontractual Liability in the CISG," 21(2) *Temple International & Comparative L. J.* 261 (2007); John Klein and Carla Bachechi, "Precontractual Liability and the Duty of Good Faith Negotiation in International Transactions," 17 *Houston J. of International L.* 1 (1994).

[32] CA 3912/90 *Eximin SA v. Itel Style Ferarri Textile and Shoes Ltd.* [1993] IsrSC 47(4) 64. English text available at http://cisgw3.law.pace.edu/cases/930822i5.html (hereafter referred to as the Eximin case).

[33] For discussions of the Israeli system as a mixed jurisdiction, see, e.g., Gad Tedeschi and Yaacov S. Zemach, "Codification and Case Law in Israel," in *The Role of Judicial Decisions and Doctrine in Civil Law and Mixed Jurisdictions* (ed. Joseph Dainow) (Baton Rouge: Louisiana State University Press, 1974), 273; Gabriela Shalev and Shael Herman, "A Source Study of Israel's Contract Codification," 35 *Louisiana L. Rev.* 1091 (1975).

[34] An official draft of such a civil code was first published in 2004, and, after a revision, presented to the Knesset in 2006. Ever since, the draft has been awaiting its approval. For commentary on the Israeli process of codification, see, e.g., Aharon Barak, "The Codification of Civil Law," 3 *Iyunei Mishpat (Tel Aviv Un. L. Rev.)* 5 (1973) (Hebrew); Uri Yadin, "Towards the Codification of the Civil Law in Israel," 6 *Iyunei Mishpat (Tel Aviv U. L. Rev.)* 506 (1979) (Hebrew); Aharon Barak, "The Codification of Civil Law and the Law of Torts," 24 *Isr. L. Rev.* 628 (1990). More recently, with regard to the Draft Civil Code promulgated in 2006, see Alfredo M. Rabello and Pablo Lerner, "The Project of the Israeli Civil Code: The Dilemma of Enacting A Code in A Mixed Jurisdiction," in *Liber Amicorum Guido Alpa – Private Law Beyond the National Systems* (ed. Mads Andenas et al.) (London: British Institute of International and Comparative Law Publishing, 2007), 771.

[35] Contracts (Remedies for Breach of Contract) Law, 5731–1970, 25 LSI 11 (1970–1) (Isr.). On the special characteristics of this statute, which to an extent are common to the Israeli civil legislation in general, see Yehuda Adar, "Legal Engineering in Israeli law: Codification and Unification of the Law of Remedies," in *Publications of the Swiss Institute of Comparative Law* (Zurich: Schulthess, 2010), 69, 75–80.

[36] Contracts (General Part) Law, 5733–1973, 27 LSI 117 (1972–3) (Isr.). For a survey of the scope of this statute, see Gabriela Shalev, "General Comments on Contracts (General Part) Law, 1973," 9 *Israel L. Rev.* 274 (1974).

[37] Contracts (General Part) Law, Article 39.

[38] Contracts (General Part) Law, Article 12(a).

it had incurred following the negotiations or following the formation of the contract.[39] Article 39, on the other hand, is silent regarding the remedy or sanction to be imposed for bad faith in the performance stage. These sanctions vary widely, depending on the circumstances.[40] The most frequently used remedies include the judicial broadening of a party's contractual duties or, alternatively, in limiting the party's exercise of a contractual right.[41] The good faith provisions of the General Contract Statute have become important tools for enforcing norms of decency, fairness, and social solidarity between contracting parties.[42] In *Eximin*, the Supreme Court used the good faith principle to make a major change in contract doctrine.

B. *Good Faith in International Trade*: Eximin *Case and the Birth of Comparative Negligence in Israeli Contract Law*

The case concerned a contract between an Israeli manufacturer (hereinafter "seller") and a Belgian importer (hereinafter "buyer"). The buyer ordered the manufacturing and supply of three thousand pairs of boots of a special design in order to export them to its customer, an American supplier. The required boots were made of jean material and had the sign "V" sewn into them, a symbol which at the time was a protected trademark of Levi's Jeans. The goods were supplied and shipped, as against the full payment, to the American customer. However, upon arriving at the United States, the goods were detained by the American customs authorities, due to trademark infringement. The Belgian buyer then brought suit against the Israeli seller, demanding restitution of the full price. A compromise was reached between the parties in which the symbol was removed and the boots resold to the American customer at a reduced price. The issue facing the court was limited to whether the buyer was entitled to compensation for the balance between the actual sale price and the contract price of the original contract with the American company. The trial court held that the buyer was responsible for ignoring the problem that led to the failure of the original transaction.

As a first step in the analysis, the Supreme Court accepted the buyer's claim that the dispute was to be resolved (by way of analogy) under the rules of the CISG.[43] A further reason to give weight to the CISG, even though it had not yet become effective in Israel, the court reasoned, was the need to promote uniformity and harmony in the field of international trade.[44]

---

[39] Contracts (General Part) Law, §12(b). Breach of the duty of good faith negotiations may lead in exceptional cases to the awarding of expectation damages or specific enforcement. See, CA 6370/00 *Kal Binyan Ltd. v. A.R.M Ra'anana Building and Leasing Ltd.* [2002] IsrSC 56(3) 289; CA 986/93 *Klemer v. Guy* [1996] IsrSC 50(1) 185.

[40] HCJ 59/80 *Public Transportation Services in Be'er Sheva Ltd. v. the National Labour Court in Jerusalem* [1980] IsrSC 35(1) 828, 837–8.

[41] For a detailed illustration of this pattern of operation of the principle at the performance stage, see Menachem Mautner, "Good Faith and Implied Terms," in *Contracts* (ed. D. Friedmann and N. Cohen) (Tel Aviv: Aviram, 2003), Vol. 3, pp. 313, 360–4.

[42] There seems to be a wide consensus that the "good faith" principle has been much more predominant and influential than the "freedom of contract" principle. See, e.g., Gabriela Shalev. "The Wild Horse – Where To? Or: What Happened to Public Policy?," 2 *Kiryat Ha-Mishpat (Ono Academic College L. Rev.)* 21 (2002).

[43] *Eximin* case, para. 3(a).

[44] Id., para. 3(e). The court cited FH 36/84 *Teichner v. Air France Airlines* [1987] IsrSC 41(1) 589 (where the need to unify the international laws of trade and transport was also emphasized).

Using CISG Article 42(a) by analogy in interpreting ULIS Article 52(a), the court held that the seller's obligation to transfer goods free from any right or claim of a third party included intellectual property rights, such as trademark infringement claims. Thus, the boots delivered by the seller were nonconforming goods. However, the court recognized that the CISG explicitly excludes the seller's liability if at the time of formation "the buyer knew or could not have been unaware of the right or claim [of the third party]"[45] or if that right "results from the seller's compliance with . . . specifications furnished by the buyer."[46] Applying these provisions to the circumstances of the case, the court concluded that both the seller and the buyer could not reasonably claim to have been unaware of the Levis trademark.[47] Furthermore, the buyer had been active in deciding on the exact design of the boots. It was, therefore, reasonable for the seller to regard the buyer as having assumed, at least in part, the risk of the goods not being in conformity with U.S. law.

Nevertheless, the court refused to follow the lower courts' conclusion that under the circumstances the seller was allowed to *completely* rely on the buyer in this respect. As an experienced manufacturer, the seller should have been aware of possible trademark issues and "should have ascertained whether the importer acted properly, or, at least, should have raised the question."[48]

The conclusion of the court as to the question of liability of the seller therefore comprised two seemingly contradictory statements. On the one hand, as the buyer knew or had to know about the problem, his attempt to present the seller as being responsible for the whole loss originating from that problem must fail. On the other hand, given that both parties behaved unreasonably in ignoring the problem, imposing the whole responsibility for the loss on the buyer would also seem inappropriate. The appropriate solution, according to the Court, would therefore be to apportion the responsibility and liability for the loss between both parties.[49] The Court explained:

> The parties' behaviour shows that they did not trouble to cooperate with one another . . . [E]ach of them acted, apparently, as he saw fit, ignoring the damage that was likely to be caused and assuming that the other party would be liable for it. Each of the parties, in fact, foresaw the damage but did not trouble to clarify the risk of its happening to the other party, nor did it trouble to disclose it to the other and prevent the damage, even though it was clearly able to do so. To be sure, the lack of cooperation (or lack of disclosure) of the type that existed here does not exempt the party who must carry out an action from its duty, but the question is whether it is not sufficient to grant that party a partial defence.

Having identified the apportioning of the loss as the just result under the circumstances, the challenge facing the court was to offer a legal basis for such an allocation. In rejecting the buyer's claim for full compensation, the court reasoned that it was inconsistent with a reasonable interpretation of the parties' intention and the explicit defense provided by CISG Article 42(2). However, justifying the decision to nevertheless impose liability on

---

[45] CISG §42(2)(a).
[46] CISG §42(2)(b).
[47] *Eximin* case, para. 3(f).
[48] Id., para. 3(g). The court noted that its conclusions did not depend on whether the transaction was a C.I.F or a F.O.B. transaction. Id., para. 3(h).
[49] Id., para. 4(a).

the seller for *part of the loss* sustained by the buyer was clearly a much more challenging task for the court.

In order to justify that part of its decision, the court engaged in a thorough and lengthy analysis of the nature and content of the duty of good faith, both in contract law generally, and in the special context of an international contract for the sale of goods. The following is a summary of the court's analysis:

- The duty to act in good faith in the performance of a contract is a legal norm that is aimed at securing to each of the parties the realization of their reasonable expectations of the contractual relationship, *even where such expectations are not perfectly protected by the concrete legal norms* that govern that relationship.[50]
- On a practical level, each of the parties is under an obligation to take into account the other party's expectation under the contract. Thus, a party should refrain as far as possible from acting in a way that might frustrate that expectation. Moreover, under certain circumstances, *a party may be expected to take active steps in order to avoid unnecessary prejudice to the other party*.
- More concretely, if a party can *effectively and without undue burden or cost prevent a substantial risk* to the other party from being realized (such as by bringing a matter to its attention), but nevertheless fails to take such steps, this may be deemed a violation of the obligation to act in good faith.[51]
- In the context of an international sales contract between an exporter and an importer of goods, applying the good faith principle would mean, *inter alia*, that *the exporter, being aware of a problem that might jeopardize the importer's ability to sell the goods, must warn the latter* of the problem. This is *especially so if the exporter can assume that his or her own liability toward the importer would be excluded* (as was the case in Eximin).[52]
- A violation of the duty of good faith in the performance of a contract *amounts to a breach of the contract itself,* and thus entitles the other party to remedies, including compensation for any foreseeable loss that is attributable to the breach.[53]
- In addition, a violation of the obligation of good faith might bar a party from exercising his or her right to a remedy against the other party for breaching the contract. For example, when the bad faith conduct of one party (buyer) prevented the other party (seller) from fulfilling its obligations under the contract, the former may not be allowed to rely on the nonperformance and thus may not be entitled to any remedy whatsoever.[54]
- Although most often the effect of bad faith would be of an absolute nature, that is, it would lead to the complete denial of a right or remedy; some cases may call for only a partial denial, or a reduction in the size of the violator's remedy.[55]

[50] See id., paras. 4(b) and 4(j).
[51] Id., para. 4(h).
[52] Id., para. 4(b).
[53] Id.
[54] Or, at the least, would lose the right to a particular remedy (e.g., specific performance, rescission, etc.), the awarding of which would turn out to be unjust given that party's bad faith. In the court's own words: "[T]he courts tend to attribute unequivocal and absolute implications to a lack of good faith. Thus, a party's lack of good faith may deprive him of a remedy or confer a remedy on the other party." Id., para. 4(e).
[55] Id., para. 4(d). ("[I]f it is possible to deny a remedy completely in cases like the aforesaid, then a partial denial of damages is even more possible, and as I shall show below, it is also desirable.")

- For example, when a party fails, in bad faith, to prevent the occurrence of a breach by the other party, the courts should be allowed, instead of completely releasing the latter from liability in damages, to apportion the loss caused by the breach between the parties. Indeed, a party's fault in failing to prevent its own loss should be taken into account not only when it takes place after breach (where it is regarded as a failure to mitigate damages), but also when it precedes the breach or coincides with it.[56]
- Such apportionment should be carried out by the court taking into account and comparing both the degree of bad faith manifested in the conduct of each party, as well as the causal contribution of each party to the occurrence of the loss suffered by the plaintiff.[57]

Applying these principles to the case at hand, Chief Justice Shamgar and Justice Ya'acov Malz reached the conclusion that the buyer's appeal should be allowed in part, so as to allow the latter to recover fifty percent of the loss it had incurred.

The dissenting opinion of Justice Eliezer Goldberg accepted the majority's factual determination that both parties could not have been unaware of the risk involved if the problem of trademark infringement would not be taken care of by the buyer or its customer. However, Justice Goldberg wondered how, under that assumption, the failure of the seller to warn the buyer about a problem of which he could not have been unaware could be regarded as failure to act in good faith. In the minority view, under the circumstances the seller did not violate the duty of good faith.[58]

Furthermore, the seller was not liable, under the minority view, because it had not breached the contract. Under the ULIS Article 52, the buyer is entitled to receive goods that are free from third party rights *only if buyer did not agree to receive them subject to such rights*. Given that the buyer ordered certain changes in the design of the boots, the buyer must be held to have accepted any risk of the goods supplied being in violation of a registered trademark. In other words, the buyer had implicitly agreed to receive the goods in the state in which they were actually supplied. Therefore, there was no legal cause on which to base the seller's liability in damages toward the buyer.[59] It is worth noting, however, that the minority judge did not express any reservation against the introduction of a general doctrine of comparative fault into contract law, either generally or in the particular context of international sales.

C. *Interrelationship of International Sales Law and Domestic Law*: Eximin *as a Test Case*

The *Eximin* decision not only significantly contributed to the elucidation of the duty of good faith in performance, it also stands as the precedent for establishing the defense of comparative negligence into Israeli contract law. What is most interesting, however, is that the case involved a dispute that supposedly was decided according under the ULIS and the CISG. Are there any lessons to be learned about the interrelationship between the CISG and domestic law? The following analysis will offer a few of the lessons that may be learned from the *Eximin* litigation.

---

[56] Id., para. 4(d). In this context the court referred to CISG §77 (and to ULIS §88), which deal with the duty to mitigate loss.

[57] Id., para. 4(q).

[58] Id. (Goldberg, J., dissenting).

[59] Id.

On the one hand, if a question ever arose as to the relevance and significance of the CISG to Israeli law, this question was clearly settled by the *Eximin* case. The case demonstrates the Supreme Court's willingness to implement international sales law in resolving international sales disputes. First, the court in *Eximin* embraced the opportunity to apply international sales law. Second, and more importantly, the court gave considerable weight to what it perceived as apparent changes in the international law of sales. It did not limit itself to the analysis of the pertinent ULIS provisions. The court gave more weight to the CISG than to ULIS because it viewed the CISG as a more modern sales law. This testifies to the court's approval of international efforts to advance uniformity in international trade, and its willingness to promote and assist such efforts. The same sympathetic approach toward the CISG was applied in subsequent cases.[60]

On the other hand, the *Eximin* case raises serious questions as to the level of commitment of the Israeli domestic courts to the legal regime set forth in the CISG. This issue first becomes apparent through the manner in which the Supreme Court applied the principle of good faith. Given the international nature of the transaction, one could have expected the court, prior to beginning its elaborate good faith analysis, to discuss a preliminary question, namely, to what extent, if at all, the principle of good faith in general, and the duty of good faith as understood under the Israeli law of contract in particular, is relevant and applicable to an international sales transaction. Instead the court moved directly to a general moralistic analysis of the parties' conduct in terms of fairness and good faith. Moreover, the only sentence that shows the court's awareness of its authority to perform a good faith analysis is problematic. The court stated that "the provisions of the [Israeli] Contracts Law [General Contract Statute Articles 12 and 39] also apply to the case before us, if not directly, then by virtue of Article 61(b) of the Contracts Statute."[61] Instead of trying to base its authority to impose a duty of good faith in the CISG, it looked for the answer "under the lamp-post," that is, within the boundaries of domestic law.[62]

Professor Reich has argued that had the court applied the CISG to the issue of good faith it would not have been able to reach the same result. First, under Article CISG 7(a), good faith is merely a principle of interpretation rather than a rule imposing a duty of good faith on the contracting parties.[63] Second, even assuming such a general obligation of good faith existed, applying it under the circumstances of the case would have brought it into conflict with the specific excuse given the seller under Article CISG 42. A specific provision must be given priority over general notions of fairness and good faith or any other domestic norms. General principles and norms can only be relied on to supplement the concrete rules and to fill internal gaps in the CISG.[64]

One can argue against Professor Reich's assertion that the use of good faith in *Eximin* contradicts the express rule of Article 42. Even under the assumption that good faith

---

[60] See, e.g., the *Pamesa* case, in which the court relied heavily not only on ULIS but on the CISG as well, emphasizing its impression that "No one can deny the importance of the approach embodied in these CISGs, which increases with the spread of globalization." *Pamesa* case, para. 20.

[61] Id., para. 4(b). Article 61(b) of the Contracts Statute reads as follows: "The provisions of this Law shall, as far as appropriate and *mutatis mutandis*, apply also to legal acts other than contracts and to obligations not arising out of a contract." This provision was used by the judiciary to apply notions of good faith outside the field of contract law. However, it is questionable whether it can serve as a solid basis to import domestic concepts into the international context.

[62] For a similar critique of the court, see Reich, "The Uniform Law of International Sales," 166–8.

[63] Id.

[64] Id.

notions should be used only in the interpretation of CISG's provisions, it is submitted that a "good faith-oriented" interpretation of Article 42 CISG could justify the majority ruling in *Eximin*. The desired result could be achieved in two alternative ways. First, the court could have offered a reading of the exemption granted the seller under Article 42(2) as including an implied term under which that excuse would not apply if the seller possessed actual knowledge of third party rights in the goods. Such an interpretation would exempt the seller from liability only in cases where the latter had constructive knowledge of the problem ("could not have been unaware" of the right), but not in those cases such as *Eximin* where the seller seems to have possessed actual knowledge.[65]

Second, the court could have reasoned that CISG Article 42 regulates the scope of the seller's duties on formation and is silent as regards duties *after formation*. As such, the judicial recognition of such additional duties does not contradict, but rather complements Article 42.[66]

Admittedly, however, the court did not devote much effort to reconcile its good faith analysis with the explicit wording of either the CISG or the ULIS. Rather, as mentioned earlier, the court simply assumed that the domestic duty of good faith applied to the case before it. Similarly, it devoted little effort to explaining how its finding of seller liability for not informing the buyer of a problem, of which the latter must have been aware, did not contradict the express provisions of the CISG to which the court alluded to earlier.[67]

V. Contract Formation

It is an undisputed historical fact that the primary sources of Israeli contract law, that is, the General Contracts Statute and the Remedies Statute,[68] were greatly influenced, in terms of both structure and content, not only by civilian and common law concepts, but also in particular by the 1964 Hague Conventions on the Sale of Goods.[69] This influence is most evident with respect to the rules governing formation. Indeed, the formation rules included in chapter 1 of the Israeli General Contract Statute are almost identical to those set forth in Annex I of the Convention relating to a Uniform Law on the Formation of

---

[65] An interpretive technique similar to that offered in the text was adopted by the Supreme Court in CA 2299/99 *Shfayer v. Diyur Laoleh Ltd.* [2001] IsrSC 55(4) 213. There, based on notions of good faith, the court narrowed the scope of a buyer's duty, under the domestic law of sales, to inform a seller of any nonconformity immediately upon discovering it. Contrary to the literal interpretation of the provision, the court ruled that no such duty exists if the seller possessed actual knowledge of the defect.

[66] The court might have hinted in this direction in paragraph 4(k), where it states that the imposition of an additional duty on a party to take simple acts to prevent problems arising after formation: "does not affect the basic allocation of risks between the parties. The International Sale of Goods Law does not anticipate a situation where both parties can efficiently and cheaply avoid a difficulty that arose subsequently. A risk of this kind is not defined in the law, and consequently there is no initial allocation for it. A subsequent allocation, in accordance with the lack of good faith of each of the two parties, does not therefore conflict with the initial allocation."

[67] The court did express the view that the duties of the parties to inform each other of apparent risks "are admittedly not stated expressly in the said articles, but they undoubtedly arise from them . . . " Id., para. 4(b). However, the court failed to explain or justify this assertion.

[68] See *supra* notes 35 and 36.

[69] See Uri Yadin, "The Use of Comparative Law by the Legislator," in *Israeli Reports to the XI International Congress of Comparative Law* (ed. Steve Goldstein) (Jerusalem: H. Sacher Institute for Legislative Research and Comparative Law, 1982), 10, 13. See also Shalev and Herman, "A Source Study of Israel's Contract Codification," 1103.

Contracts for the International Sale of Goods (ULF).[70] As most of the ULF rules on formation were carried on to the CISG,[71] there is a great deal of commonality between the Israeli law and the CISG rules on contract formation.

The *Aderet Shomron* case,[72] decided in 1990 by the Israeli Supreme Court, concerned a "battle of the forms" scenario.[73] A German manufacturer (seller) sold sewing equipment to an Israeli manufacturer of thread (buyer). In a subsequent contract, the buyer placed an order for spare parts, as well as obtaining professional advice in order to overcome an apparent defect in the equipment. The price, quantity, and other details concerning the second deal were communicated between the parties via a number of telex messages, following which the seller sent to the buyer an order confirmation. The seller attached its "general conditions of delivery and payment" to the confirmation. That form contained, inter alia, a jurisdiction clause granting the German courts exclusive jurisdiction over any dispute arising from the transaction. The spare parts were installed as against full payment, but the buyer alleged that they were defective and were negligently installed by the seller's representative, resulting in loss of profit to the buyer. The buyer then brought suit before an Israeli court, which summarily dismissed it on the basis of the jurisdiction clause.

The buyer appealed, claiming that the order confirmation – and the jurisdiction clause attached to it – though arriving at buyer's premises, was never actually accepted by him. Therefore, it could not form a part of the agreement between the parties. According to the buyer, the contract was formed prior to the confirmation reaching his premises.

The Supreme Court rejected the buyer's claim based on the following observations. First, given the preliminary nature of the communications preceding the order confirmation, the contract could not have been concluded prior to its arrival. Second, because the confirmation did not completely conform to the buyer's previous communication, the confirmation could not form an acceptance of the buyer's offer. Rather, the confirmation was counteroffer made by the German seller to the Israeli buyer. As such, the decisive question was whether there was enough evidence of a subsequent acceptance on the part of the buyer.

The court held that a contract was formed under Articles 5 and 6 of the General Contracts Statute. Article 5 requires conveyance of a "notice of acceptance" to the offeror, and such a notice was apparently not given by the buyer. However, Article 6 provides an exception, according to which an *act or other conduct* manifesting the offeree's implicit consent may be considered a valid acceptance. The court reasoned that although mere silence would not generally qualify as conduct amounting to acceptance, silence on the part of an offeree could be so construed, *if it was accompanied by other conduct that gave it such meaning.* Such was the case at hand. The buyer remained silent

---

[70] July 1, 1964, available at http://www.unidroit.org/english/conventions/c-ulf.htm. The domestic chapter, however, is more concise, containing only 15 provisions in 11 Articles, while the ULF includes 25 provisions in 13 Articles. The substantial affinity between the two sources is pointed out by Zamir, "European Tradition," 502–3, and by Shalev, "International Sale of Goods," 110–11.

[71] Helpful comparisons of CISG provisions with those of the Hague CISGs are available at http://www.cisg. law.pace.edu/cisg/text/cisg-toc.html. For further analysis and comparative case law discussion, see Larry A. DiMatteo et al., "The Interpretive Turn in International Sales Law: An Analysis of Fifteen Years of CISG Jurisprudence," 24 *Northwestern J. of International Law & Business* 299, Part III (2003–4).

[72] CA 65/88 *Aderet Shomron v. Hollingsworth G.M.B.H* [1990] IsrSC 44(3) 600 (hereafter referred to as the Aderet Shomron case).

[73] See generally Maria del Pilar Perales Viscasillas, "'Battle of the Forms' under the 1980 United Nations CISG on Contracts for the International Sale of Goods: A Comparison with Section 2–207 UCC and the UNIDROIT Principles," 10 *Pace International L. Rev.* 97 (1998).

in face of the order confirmation, but went forward with the transaction. In doing so, the buyer signaled that his failing to approve the confirmation was not mere silence, but a "thundering silence" that could have reasonably been understood by the seller as a manifestation of the buyer's consent to its "general conditions."[74]

Although the judgment did not include any direct reference to the CISG, it reveals the close affinity between the international and the Israeli domestic rules on formation. If the issue were decided on the basis of the ULF, or if it were to be decided today, on the basis of the CISG, the same result would have been reached, using similar reasoning. The first parallel is to be drawn between Article 11 of the General Contracts Statute and CISG Article 19(1) CISG. The latter provision states that: "A reply to an offer which purports to be an acceptance but contains additions, limitations or other modifications is a rejection of the offer and constitutes a counter-offer." The parallel domestic rule provides that: "Acceptance involving an addition to or a limitation or some other variation of the offer is tantamount to a new offer." Thus under both provisions, given the substantial modifications it included, the order confirmation would not be considered a valid acceptance but only a counteroffer.[75]

The second parallel to be drawn concerns the question of whether there had been a valid acceptance of the seller's counteroffer. On this issue, CISG Article 18(1) reads as follows: "A statement made by or other conduct of the offeree indicating assent to an offer is an acceptance. Silence or inactivity does not in itself amount to acceptance." Article 6(a) of the General Contracts Statute states that: "Acceptance may be by an act in implementation of the contract or by some other conduct if these modes of acceptance are implied in the offer."

Notwithstanding these similarities, there is also a clear difference between the two laws. The domestic norm does not expressly reject pure silence as acceptance, as does the CISG. However, as the *Aderet Shomron* case demonstrates, under Israeli contract law sheer silence would not be sufficient to constitute acceptance. The silence may amount to "acceptance by way of conduct" only when it is accompanied by an independent act or when the circumstances make it clear that the silence of the offeree is not neutral. A silence is not neutral when the surrounding circumstances (conduct, prior understandings, and trade usages) would reasonably allow the offeror to understand the silence as signaling acceptance.

VI. Conformity of Goods: Inspection and Notice

Conformity of goods is a major issue in sales law.[76] The seller's primary obligation is to deliver to the buyer goods that, in terms of both quality and quantity, conform to what

---

[74] *Aderet Shomron* case, 610.

[75] CISG Article 19(2) CISG makes a distinction between material and nonmaterial additions to the offer, a distinction which is not found in Article 11 of the General Contract Statute. Under the CISG §19(2) a modification of an offer may nevertheless constitute valid acceptance, if it does not materially alter it, and if the offeror does not object to the modifications introduced. This means that under the CISG pure silence on the part of an offeree can be considered valid acceptance, although under the Israeli provision it cannot. It is likely, however, that in cases where the modifications in the offer are minor, sheer silence on the part of the original offeror may – even under Israeli law – be considered as concluding the contract.

[76] See generally Eyal Zamir, *The Conformity Rule in the Performance of Contracts* (Jerusalem: The Harry Sacher Institute for Legislative Research and Comparative Law, 1990) (Hebrew); Eyal Zamir, "Towards a General Concept of Conformity in the Performance of Contracts," 52 *Louisiana L. Rev.* 4 (1990); see also Honnold, *Uniform Law*, 275–86; DiMatteo et al., "The Interpretive Turn," Part IV.

was promised. Much less obvious, however, are the limits imposed by the law of sales on a buyer's right to rely on nonconformity in order to seek legal remedies. These limits, frequently described as "duties" or "obligations" of the buyer, are, in fact, legal defenses that the seller is allowed to raise in order to bar the buyer's claim.

The main defense, both under the CISG and the Israeli Sales Statute,[77] turns upon issues of inspection and notice. Although regulated under separate provisions, the burden of inspection and that of giving a prompt notice to the buyer are intimately linked to each other. Indeed, arguably, the first of the two burdens is subordinate to the second, in the sense that failure to inspect the goods in a reasonable time period will partially determine the buyer's execution of its primary duty to give a timely notice of nonconformity.

The following survey outlines the manner in which the burdens of inspection and notice are interpreted by Israeli courts. In light of the similarity between the CISG and ULIS provisions on the issues of inspection and notice,[78] cases decided on the basis of the older ULIS will also be reviewed. As emphasized elsewhere in this chapter, these cases, though formally decided under the ULIS, constitute valuable points of reference for Israeli courts interpreting the parallel CISG provisions.

A. *Inspection and Notice Requirements: Scope and Content*

The main Israeli case on the burden of inspection is *Datalab Management Pty. Ltd. v. Polak*.[79] Decided in 1989 by the Supreme Court, that case concerned a contract for the sale of sterile gauze pads between an Israeli producer (seller) and an Australian importer of medical equipment (buyer). An initial contract was concluded in 1976, following which the seller began delivery. The buyer paid the full consideration, only to discover that the first two shipments contained numerous defective units. Following the buyer's complaints, a second agreement was reached between the parties. According to that agreement, the whole merchandise was to be shipped back to Israel for reexamination and repair by the seller. The agreement also declared that no more than 1% of the reshipped merchandise could be defective.

In January 1978 a first consignment, containing about 10% of the total quantity paid for under the contract, was redelivered to the seller. Four months later, the buyer informed the seller that 17 percent of the remaining merchandise was found to be defective. After a few failed attempts to bridge the gap between the parties, the buyer resold the pads to a local hospital for the full contract price. The buyer then sued the seller, claiming full restitution of the purchase price as well as compensation for other consequential losses.

The trial court dismissed the buyer's claim based on ULIS Article 38(1). The court held that the buyer had failed to execute its duty to "examine the goods, or cause them to be examined, promptly." As a result, in accordance with Article 39(1), the buyer had also lost his right to any remedy for the alleged nonconformity.

The key question before the Supreme Court turned on the appropriateness of buyer's inspection under the circumstances. The buyer claimed that it could not have been reasonably expected to carry out the examination of approximately 10,000 packs (each containing 5 gauze pads) on their delivery, because the end user of the pads was an

---

[77] *Supra* note 21.

[78] This obvious similarity was recognized by the Supreme Court in the *Pamesa* case, para. 23.

[79] CA 306/85 *Datalab Management Pty. Ltd. v. Pollak International Ltd.* [1989] IsrSC 43(2) 309 (hereafter referred to as the *Datalab* case).

Australian hospital, which only by gradual and ongoing use became aware of the magnitude of the problem. The Court held that under the circumstances both the inspection and the notice were carried out "within as short a period as possible, in the circumstances, from the moment when the act could reasonably be performed."[80]

While accepting the claim that an intermediate buyer would not be required to carry out the inspection by itself if such an inspection might entail the impairment of the goods, the court nevertheless rejected the buyer's claim. When, as in the case at hand, an intermediate buyer is well aware of the existence of a previous defect, and where both parties made clear that the transaction would be dependent on an inspection of the goods by the buyer, the latter must make every effort to perform the inspection immediately upon delivery. The court noted that this burden could have been carried out by a sample check of the pads, either by the buyer itself or by its customer. As a direct consequence of this failure to undertake a reasonably timely inspection, the buyer failed to notify the seller "promptly after he . . . ought to have discovered [the nonconformity]."[81]

However, contrary to the lower court, and notwithstanding the buyer's failure to inspect in a timely manner, the court did not regard the buyer's failure a sufficient reason to bar his right to restitution. Although the buyer was indeed barred from seeking any remedy (including restitution) for the defective goods that were actually delivered to him, he was not so barred with respect to the merchandise that remained with the seller. Examining that question, the court reasoned that in reselling the remainder of the merchandise in response to the buyer's refusal to accept it, the seller implicitly expressed his willingness to terminate the contract. Following such mutual termination, the seller was obliged to restore that part of the consideration that reflected the value of the undelivered merchandise.[82]

It is worth noting that apart from implementing the "prompt inspection" requirement, the court also interpreted it to be a stringent requirement. The court opined that:

> [It] is intended to give more stability to commercial relationships and to minimize the losses which might accrue from too long a postponement of the giving of a notice . . . This way, the seller can go on with its economic activity, free from the worry that, with no time limit, the buyer might complain of a defect in the merchandise.[83]

It should be noted that although the CISG replaced the requirement of a "prompt" notice with the requirement that a notice be given "within a reasonable time,"[84] there was no substantial change with regard to the nature of the required inspection itself, and the need to carry it out "within as short a period as is practicable in the circumstances."[85] Arguably, therefore, the distinctions set forth in the *Datalab* case with regard to the nature of a reasonable and timely inspection are still relevant today as guidelines for courts dealing with the duty of inspection under the CISG.[86]

---

[80] This being the definition of the term "promptly" under §11 ULIS.
[81] ULIS §39(1).
[82] *Datalab* case, paras. 5–7.
[83] Id., para. 4, citing with approval Justice Ben-Porat in the *Solondz* case, 637. This policy analysis gained recent support in the *Pamesa* case, para. 25.
[84] CISG §39(1).
[85] CISG §38. In our view this definition is not substantially different from the one adopted by ULIS §38.
[86] Indeed, in the *Pamesa* case, the seller tried to rely on the conservative approach in *Datalab* in order to reinforce his position that the buyer's claim should be barred. However, as we saw, the court did not adhere

There were two other occasions on which Israeli courts dealt with the issue of the burden of inspection. In *Harel Insurance Co. Ltd. v. BTR Environmental Ltd.*,[87] a foreign supplier of fuel filters was sued by a local energy producer for the losses caused by a defect in one of the filters supplied to it, which caused an explosion.[88] On appeal, the Supreme Court dealt, inter alia, with the question of whether a notice was given "promptly" enough. The court answered the question in the affirmative, taking into account the fact that given the size of the defect and its nature (a mere 50 mm welding defect), the non-conformity was undiscoverable by inspection at the time of delivery.[89] Hence, the buyer had not failed to inspect the filter upon its arrival. Consequently, in informing the seller soon after discovering the defect, the buyer carried out its "duty" to inform the seller "promptly" (ULIS Article 38) and hence also within a reasonable time after he has discovered it or ought to have discovered it under CISG Article 38.[90]

Another case, decided by the Tel-Aviv Magistrate Court,[91] involved a dispute between two Israeli businesses. The court, nevertheless, resorted to the CISG, in order to determine whether the buyer's claim had been barred due to the latter's failure to notify the seller, promptly upon delivery, that the quantity of aluminum delivered exceeded the contract amount. As the merchandise was directly shipped to the buyer's customer in the United States, the buyer became aware of the extra quantity only at a later stage, hence the belated notice to the seller.

Citing first the relevant provision in the domestic sales statute that required inspection (and hence also notice) "promptly" upon delivery, the court then turned to CISG Article 38(3), which allows the buyer to postpone inspection of the goods until their arrival at their final destination. Given the international context of the transaction, and the need to ship the goods out of the country, the judge found it not only helpful, but also legally permissible to rely on the CISG to fill a perceived gap in the domestic law.

B. *Seller's Power to Bar Buyer's Claim: Nature and Limits*

As discussed earlier, Israeli case law has justified the strict burdens of inspection and notice, and the harsh consequences of failing to discharge them, by referencing the goal of protecting two main interests – the international seller's interest in certainty and finality and the societal interest in preventing avoidable injuries and losses.[92]

However, given the harsh consequences of a belated notice to the seller, international sales law imposes limits on the seller's power to reject a buyer's claims through the defense of belated notice. The main limitation is found in CISG Article 40, which reads as follows: "The seller is not entitled to rely on the provisions of Articles 38 and 39 if the lack of conformity relates to facts of which [the seller] knew or could not have been

to the ULIS and was willing to consider also the concepts and rules of the CISG which, on the issue of notice, are more lenient.
[87] *Supra* note 26.
[88] The case was discussed earlier in the context of the issue of concurrent liability.
[89] *Datalab* case, para. 20.
[90] As noted earlier, the court of first instance applied the CISG, but the Supreme Court made clear that the transaction was still governed by ULIS. However, from the court's reasoning it is clear that the result would have been the same under the CISG.
[91] CC (TA) 11082/05 *Kalil Industries v. Rollteck Aluminum Yedidya Ltd.* (07.10.2008) Nevo Legal Database (by subscription) (Isr).
[92] See *supra*, text accompanying note 83.

unaware and which he did not disclose to the buyer."[93] The most elaborate judicial analysis of this provision to date was undertaken by the Israeli Supreme Court in the case of *Pamesa v. Mendelson*.[94] The case, the facts of which were presented earlier in this chapter,[95] involved a damage claim brought against a Spanish manufacturer of tiles (seller) by an Israeli importer (buyer). The buyer demanded compensation for consequential losses resulting from alleged defects in the tiles supplied by it to a local builder, which had sued the buyer for the costs of replacing the defective tiles.

Examining the contractual cause of action against the seller, the court first discussed the seller's claim under both the CISG and ULIS. It determined that under both laws the buyer's claim had to fail. This was apparently so, first of all, because the buyer had not informed the seller of the defects on their discovery, and secondly, because more than two years had expired from delivery, so that in any event the claim was barred under either ULIS Article 39(1) or CISG Article 39(2).

As a first step in the analysis, the court rationalized that prescription periods were not motivated merely by evidentiary considerations concerning the seller's ability to refute allegations, but mainly by substantive policy reasons. As a result, the limitations on a buyer's nonconformity claim were not procedural bars, but rather restrictions on the buyer's substantive right to sue. Citing with approval a previous decision of the court that interpreted the one-year prescription period set forth in ULIS Article 49,[96] the court stated:

> The determination of a prescription period [in the CISG] . . . is not required for the main reason that usually underlies prescription, which is the keeping of evidence, but for a quick determination of the legal position between the parties to the transaction. In order to achieve this purpose, this provision should be regarded as reflecting prescription as causing the actual right to expire.[97]

Because it was clear that the buyer had failed to notify the seller either promptly on discovery or within the two-year prescription period, the buyer in *Pamesa* was apparently barred from presenting any claim based on the nonconformity of the tiles supplied by the seller.[98] However, this could not settle the issue, as under CISG Article 40, which was cited, along with ULIS Article 40, the seller's defense did not apply if the seller knew or must have known of the facts giving rise to the alleged nonconformity. More concretely, the challenge facing the court was to decide if the seller's awareness of defects in tiles sold to other Israeli importers was sufficient for Article 40 to apply.

---

[93] Cf. the almost identical formulation of ULIS Article 40: "The seller shall not be entitled to rely on the provisions of Articles 38 and 39 if the lack of conformity relates to facts of which he knew, or of which he could not have been unaware, and which he did not disclose." For analyses of foreign case law interpreting Article 40 see, e.g., Fritz Enderlein and Dietrich Masko, *International Sales Law: United Nations Convention on Contracts for the International Sale of Goods* (New York: Oceana Publications, 1992), commentary 164; R.H. Graveson et al., *The Uniform Laws on International Sales Act 1967: A Commentary* 77 (London: Butterworths, 1968), 77; Schlechtriem, *Commentary*, 321–2; Alejandro M. Garro, "The Buyer's 'Safety Valve' under Article 40: What Is the Seller Supposed to Know and When?," 25 *J. of L. & Commerce* 253 (2005).

[94] *Supra* note 9.

[95] *Supra* text accompanying notes 9–14.

[96] CA 132/85 *Ameropa AG v. H.S.Y. HaMegader Steel Industries Ltd.* [1987] IsrSC 41(4) 477.

[97] *Pamesa* case, para. 25.

[98] Id., para. 24.

The court emphasized the close theoretical linkage between Article 40 and the principle of good faith. Based on the analysis of both legal scholarship and Continental case law interpreting that provision, the court reached the conclusion that: "[I]t is therefore clear that Article 40 was intended for cases of bad faith . . . [I]t is clear that the Article was not intended for cases where the seller did not disclose defects of which he was unaware in good faith."[99]

A further rationale advanced by the court for limiting the seller's immunity under the convention was based on a more concrete and pragmatic argument. The main goal of barring buyers' claims is to protect the sellers' legitimate interest in being assured that, after the lapse of a two-year period, its liability for defects was terminated.[100] However, such a rationale did not rationally apply if, during that period, the seller already became aware of an alleged defect in the goods it delivered to the buyer.[101] Hence, this exception to the seller's immunity from liability was explained not only by reference to the principle of good faith, but also on the independent ground that under the circumstances set forth in Article 40, granting such an immunity would be superfluous, in terms of achieving its concrete social goals.[102]

The second interpretive move of the court was to assert that in light of its being an exception to the "basic and fundamental" duty of buyers to examine and inform sellers of defects as soon as possible,[103] the exception to that duty must be narrowly construed. The buyer's right to resort to Article 40, especially in cases where the buyer's notice was seriously delayed, is therefore limited. For example, in the case at hand, the buyer had notified the seller three years after becoming aware of the alleged defect, and only following a legal suit brought against it by the builder. In this context, the court referred to Article 16 of the domestic sales statute. Under that provision, even where the seller knew (or should have known) of the facts out of which the nonconformity arose, the buyer still owes a duty to inform him *immediately* after becoming aware of it.[104]

In the specific circumstances of the case before it, the court reached the conclusion that Article 40 did not apply. First, the seller had no reason to suspect that such defects existed, especially since the tiles were examined upon their arrival by the Israeli Institution of Standards and were found to be conforming.

Second, and most importantly in the court's eyes, although the seller was aware of some defects in other shipments of the same kind of merchandise, it was clearly not aware of any alleged defect in the tiles which it sold to the buyer. In the court's

---

[99] Id., para. 30.

[100] The issue of concurrent tort liability was examined in Part III.

[101] The question of when the seller's awareness is examined is rather complex, and it was not discussed in the case, as deciding it was deemed unnecessary. This was so, for the seller's awareness was not proven at any point prior to its being informed by the buyer. Pamesa case, para. 44, citing Garro, "The Buyer's 'Safety Valve,'" 256; Peter Schlechtriem, *Commentary on the UN Convention on the International Sale of Goods (CISG)*, 2nd ed. (2005), 479–80.

[102] *Pamesa* case, paras. 31–3.

[103] In this the court relied on a 1998 judgment of the Stockholm Chamber of Commerce and on a scholarly article, in which a restricted approach to the interpretation of article 40 was taken, limiting it to "special" or "exceptional" circumstances. See id., para. 34.

[104] Article 16 states: "Where the nonconformity arises out of facts which the seller knew or ought to have known at the time the contract was concluded and which he did not disclose to the buyer, the buyer shall be entitled to rely on it notwithstanding the provisions of section 14 or 15 or of any agreement, *provided that he gives notice of it to the seller immediately upon discovering it*" (emphasis added).

view, proof of such an amorphous awareness was clearly insufficient for Article 40 to apply:

> [I]n order to succeed in an argument based on Article 40 the buyer must at least prove that in the past the seller discovered defects of the kind being alleged . . . [G]iving a general notice about "problems" in goods does not satisfy the requirement of giving notice in Article 39 . . . It would appear to follow a fortiori that a general awareness of "problems" that were discovered in the past, without any specific notice being given by a buyer with regard to specific goods, does not satisfy the requirements of Article 40.[105]

Finally, the buyer himself behaved improperly in failing to notify the seller within a reasonable period of time after becoming aware of the defects. Just as the seller should not be allowed to conduct itself in bad faith (not notifying the buyer of known defects), the court reasoned, so should be the case with the buyer. There is a need to encourage buyers to act diligently in informing sellers of nonconformities once they become aware of a nonconformity.

In *Intermas Nets v. Zilkha*,[106] the court showed reluctance, under certain circumstances, to allow a seller to rely on Article 39 to bar a buyer's otherwise justified claim. The case involved a complex dispute between a Spanish manufacturer of nets and an Israeli importer and supplier of nets. The buyer brought suit before the Magistrate Court of Tel-Aviv. The court was presented with the issue of whether the buyer, who held the defective merchandise for a period of time without notifying the seller, could still make a claim of nonconformity. Given that both Spain and Israel had adopted the CISG, the court applied the CISG.[107] It held that even if the notice was not given "within a reasonable time" according to Article 39, the buyer's claim was not barred. This was due to the fact that at a later stage the seller expressed its willingness to consider the buyer's claim and sent its representative to examine the allegedly defective merchandise. Furthermore, at another time the seller had offered the buyer compensation. Under these circumstances, even if the buyer's claim had been barred under Article 39, the seller must be taken to have forfeited its right to raise such an argument.[108]

VII. Conclusion

This chapter reviewed the status of the CISG in the Israeli legal system. As this survey revealed, the attitude of the Israeli courts toward international sales laws has in the past been rather ambivalent. At times the courts have ignored the CISG without a sufficiently clear reason. On the other hand, most Israeli cases applying the CISG reflect a sympathetic approach toward the idea of a uniform law of sales. On the last occasion in which the CISG was relied on by the Supreme Court, its analysis reflected a serious effort at implementing it correctly. In the *Pamesa* case, the Israeli Supreme Court signaled its commitment to the principles of international sales law.

---

[105] *Pamesa* case, para. 45.
[106] CC (TA) 176684/02 *Intermas Nets s.a v. Zilkha Aharon* (15.08.2007) Nevo Legal Database (by subscription) (Isr.).
[107] Id., para. 39.
[108] Id., para. 42.

32 New Zealand

*Petra Butler**

I. Introduction

The United Nations Convention on the International Sale of Goods (the CISG) came into force in New Zealand "without reservation" by way of the Sale of Goods (United Nations Convention) Act 1994 (hereafter referred to as the Act).[1] The Act is not applicable to domestic sales contracts in New Zealand, which are still covered by the Sale of Goods Act 1908. Unfortunately, there has not been any attempt to align the 1994 and 1908 Acts.[2]

The CISG is a modern code that is adaptable to modern-day businesses and international trade. New Zealand is an export-driven economy, with exports accounting for approximately 30 percent of total GDP.[3] The CISG would and should therefore be the obvious choice for traders and businesses, especially because New Zealand's most prominent bilateral trading partner – Australia – is also a CISG member state. Nevertheless, the CISG has largely been ignored in practice and in academia, notwithstanding its incorporation into New Zealand law more than 18 years ago. One possible explanation for its neglect in New Zealand is that the judicial system provides a relatively fast, efficient, and relatively cheap way to resolve disputes involving the sale of goods through application of domestic law containing accepted common law doctrine. It was therefore only recently that the CISG was "discovered" and used as an interpretive aid to provide additional arguments for the development of domestic contract law. Discovering the CISG in this manner has also led to a shift away from the initial hesitancy on the part of the New Zealand judiciary in applying the CISG to contractual disputes in favor of directly applying it as part of the domestic law of New Zealand.

* Associate Professor, Victoria University of Wellington. My sincere gratitude to Cheyne Cudby for all her help in finalizing this chapter.
[1] New Zealand Law Commission, The United Nations Convention on Contracts for the International Sale of Goods: New Zealand's Proposed Acceptance (NZLC R23, Wellington, June 1992).
[2] There is little scholarship on the synergy and/or divergence of the two acts. An exception is Nicholas Whittington, "Reconsidering Domestic Sale of Goods Remedies in Light of the CISG," 37 *VUWLR* 421 (2006).
[3] World Bank national accounts data, and OECD National Accounts data files, "Exports of goods and services (% of GDP)," World Bank, available at www.data.worldbank.org (accessed February 7, 2013).

II. The CISG's Impact on Practicing Lawyers, Legal Scholars, and Legislators

There has been a general failure on the part of New Zealand companies and the legal community to utilize the CISG as a choice of law.[4] Discussions with members of the New Zealand legal profession have indicated that lawyers are not aware of the CISG, or have only become aware of it because it was the applicable law in a dispute with a foreign party. The fact the New Zealand Law Society has not conducted any seminars on the CISG may have further exacerbated the general lack of awareness of the CISG by members of the legal profession.

New Zealand scholars have produced a limited amount of CISG scholarship.[5] Similarly, the extent to which the CISG is taught in New Zealand law schools is dependent on the individual lecturer. The CISG is taught only briefly in private international law or international commercial law courses. For this reason, it was encouraging to see that the judges in the recent decision of *RJ & AM Smallmon v. Transport Sales Limited* relied on scholarly interpretation of the CISG to discern the application of Article 35(2) of the CISG.[6] The use of academic commentary in such cases will hopefully encourage further research into the CISG and its role in the international sale of goods.

With the exception of law reform concerning certain aspects of contractual negotiations,[7] the CISG has not influenced any major reformation of domestic contract law in New Zealand. As previously mentioned, there has also not been any attempt to align the domestic sales law of New Zealand with the CISG. Furthermore, New Zealand has no immediate plans to ratify the supplementary United Nations Convention on the Use of Electronic Communications in International Contracts (2005). Rather, the New Zealand government seems to have refocused on establishing bilateral or multilateral trade agreements as a means of enhancing international trade.

III. Review of New Zealand Case Law Relating to the CISG

Despite a general lack of understanding and application of the CISG in New Zealand, the CISG has nevertheless been considered by the New Zealand courts in several decisions concerning the international sale of goods. It was only in these recent cases that the

---

[4] In 2005 Victoria University held a symposium that celebrated the tenth anniversary of the CISG in New Zealand's domestic law, as well as the 25th anniversary of the CISG itself. "The aim of the Wellington Symposium was to refamiliarise New Zealand's legal community with a part of contract law which seems to have been forgotten or, even worse, which had never gotten into the conscience of New Zealand's legal profession. However, despite having world famous CISG experts present papers at the Symposium, there was little interest sparked outside academia and a few enlightened practitioners." Petra Butler, "Celebrating Anniversaries," 36 *Victoria University of Wellington Law Review* 775, 775 (2005).

[5] Exceptions are: Nicholas Whittington, "Reconsidering Domestic Sale of Goods Remedies in Light of the CISG," 37 VUWLR 421 (2006); Katrina Winsor, "Commentary on the UN Convention on the International Sale of Goods (CISG)," *New Zealand Law Journal* 371 (2010); Katrina Winsor, "What Is the CISG?," *New Zealand Law Journal* 31 (2011); Katrina Winsor, "CISG and Commodities," *New Zealand Law Journal* 157 (2011). Scholarship that comes out of New Zealand: Peter Schlechtriem and Petra Butler, *UN Law on International Sales* (Springer, 2009); Petra Butler, "Arts 53 to 60 CISG," in *UN Convention on Contracts for the International Sale of Goods (CISG)* (ed. Kröll, Mistelis, Perales Viscasillas (Beck/Hart, 2011); Petra Butler, "The Use of the CISG in Domestic Law," *Journal of Legal and Social Science, University of Belgrade* 7 (2011), and other articles.

[6] *RJ & AM Smallmon v. Transport Sales Limited* CA545/2010 (2011) NZCA 340 at 40.

[7] See Petra Butler, "The Use of the CISG in Domestic Law," 15(1) VJ 15, 16–17 (2011).

The CISG has been used as an interpretive aid in its own right in order to develop domestic contract law. The first section of this part, A, provides a chronological overview of cases in which the CISG was used tangentially, or by analogy, as a means of influencing the common law of contracts. The second section, B, will then analyze the High Court and Court of Appeal decisions in *RJ & AM Smallmon v. Transport Sales Ltd.*,[8] in which both courts fully embraced the CISG as the substantive law governing the dispute.

A. Analogical Use of the CISG

The following case summaries provide an analysis of the various ways in which the CISG has been adopted by the New Zealand Courts as an interpretive aid in determining contractual disputes.

- *Crump v. Wala*[9] – During the course of his judgment, Justice Hammond referred to the uncertainty in New Zealand law of a buyer's rights of rejection under a sales contract. His Honor pointed to other jurisdictions and mentioned the CISG in passing, using it to support the proposition that a buyer may only avoid a contract of sale where the seller has fundamentally breached his or her contractual obligations.[10]
- *Attorney-General v. Dreux Holdings Ltd.*[11] – A key issue for the Court of Appeal in this case was whether or not the subsequent conduct of the parties could be used as an aid to interpreting the contract governing their relations. The case itself involved an agreement for the sale of a large number of parcels of land. Counsel for Dreux urged the Court that, when construing the contract, consideration must be had to the parties' subsequent conduct in performing the contract at issue. Although the Court of Appeal did not express a final view as to whether or not the parties' subsequent conduct can be used as an interpretive aid, the Court of Appeal did point out that Article 8(3) of the CISG allows the use of the negotiations and practices between the parties to construe the terms of the contract, and that it specifically allows the use of subsequent conduct as an aid to interpretation. In the end, the majority of the court interpreted the contract without considering the parties' subsequent conduct. However, the majority also noted that New Zealand's domestic contract law should ideally be consistent with international practice. Conversely, Justice Thomas, in his dissenting judgment, acknowledged Article 8(3) of the CISG, stating that it was permissible to use subsequent conduct as an interpretive aid. Justice Thomas further noted that "in a global economy the need for harmonisation in the law is self-evident."[12]
- *Tri-Star Customs and Forwarding Ltd. v. Denning*[13] – In this case, the respondents had entered into a written agreement with the appellant whereby a lease of a commercial building was granted to the appellant with an option to purchase the building. There were various offers and counter-offers made by the parties before a final agreement was reached. The majority of the offers and the final agreement stated the rental was

---

[8] *RJ & AM Smallmon v. Transport Sales Limited* (July 30, 2010) HC Christchurch, CIV-2009–409–000363). The decision on appeal was rendered in 2011.

[9] [1994] 2 NZLR 331.

[10] At 339.

[11] *Attorney-General v. Dreux Holdings Ltd* (1996) 7 TCLR 617.

[12] Id. at 642.

[13] *Tri-Star Customs and Forwarding Ltd v. Denning* [1999] 1 NZLR 33.

to be "plus GST." However, the provision concerning price contained no reference to GST. The issue that arose was whether the respondents' understanding of the benefit they would receive from the transaction was the purchase price *plus* GST, or whether this was a unilateral mistake in accordance with section 6(1)(a)(i) of the Contractual Mistakes Act 1977[14] and the domestic sales law of New Zealand.

To determine this issue, the Court had to decide whether the appellant had to have had *actual* knowledge of the respondents' mistake, or whether *constructive* knowledge was sufficient. The Court of Appeal ultimately held that Section 6(1)(a)(i) of the Contractual Mistakes Act required actual knowledge, and that constructive knowledge was insufficient for the purposes of that section. While the Court recognized that "the concept of 'knew or ought to have known' is frequently captured in legislation," it is usually done so by use of those express words. In support of this, the court referred to several provisions of domestic legislation, including the CISG, which use those express words.[15] As section 6(1)(a)(i) of the Contractual Mistakes Act 1977 did not expressly contain the words "knew or ought to have known," the court held that constructive knowledge was insufficient for the purposes of establishing unilateral mistake in accordance with section 6(1)(a)(i).

- *Integrity Cars (Wholesale) Ltd. v. Chief Executive of New Zealand Customs Services*[16] – The issue in this case was whether the value for tariff purposes of certain goods imported into New Zealand included the export and inspection charges paid by the New Zealand importer to a Japanese company. The CISG was thought to apply to the contract. However, at the time of the case, Japan had not yet ratified the CISG. In addition, the court was asked to resolve the issue of whether an agency existed between Integrity Cars and the Japanese exporter. Although no argument was addressed to the applicability of the CISG, the court showed interest in it, stating that the contract "may have been subject to the United Nations Convention on Contracts for the International Sale of Goods to which both Japan and New Zealand are party."[17] The most likely explanation for the parties' failure to address the CISG in their arguments is because agency contracts are not covered by the CISG. The *Integrity Cars* decision nevertheless shows a willingness on the part of the judiciary to consider the CISG as a source of contract law governing disputes that are international in nature.
- *Yoshimoto v. Canterbury Golf International Ltd.*[18] – The *Yoshimoto* case concerns the interpretation of a clause in a commercial contract. The judge at first instance held that the particular clause at issue had a plain meaning and ought to be interpreted in accordance with that meaning. On appeal, however, Justice Thomas stated that the

---

[14] Contractual Mistakes Act 1977, s 6(1)(a)(i): Relief may be granted where mistake by one party is known to opposing party or is common or mutual

    (1) A court may in the course of any proceedings or on application made for the purpose grant relief under section 7 to any party to a contract –
        (a) if in entering into that contract –
            (i) that party was influenced in his decision to enter into the contract by a mistake that was material to him, and the existence of the mistake was known to the other party or 1 or more of the other parties to the contract (not being a party or parties having substantially the same interest under the contract as the party seeking relief)

[15] Id., 37.
[16] *Integrity Cars (Wholesale) Ltd v. Chief Executive of New Zealand* [2001] NZCA 86.
[17] Id., 19.
[18] *Yoshimoto v. Canterbury Golf International Ltd* [2001] 1 NZLR 523.

context in which the contract was formed, the commercial objective of the contract, and the contractual matrix all pointed away from the plain meaning of the clause.[19] Furthermore, extrinsic evidence confirmed that the "plain meaning" of the clause was not the meaning that the parties had actually intended. To determine the parties' true intentions, the court was required to examine the contract as a whole, as well as its commercial objective. As a further tool for interpreting the parties' intentions, Justice Thomas referred to Article 8 of the CISG. Although Justice Thomas believed it would be open to the court to depart from the law of England and apply the CISG's liberal provisions for the interpretation of international sales contracts,[20] the fact that the Privy Council was the final court of appeal at the time prevented him from doing so as "England has not yet adopted the [CISG]."[21] Given that the Privy Council is no longer New Zealand's final court of appeal, it is likely the outcome of this decision would have been different had it been decided post-2005.

- *Bobux Marketing Ltd. v. Raynor Marketing Ltd.*[22] – The Court of Appeal in this case questioned whether the express wording of the contract precluded the implication of another term. In dissent, Justice Thomas referred to Article 7 of the CISG and the obligation to observe good faith in international trade in order to justify the implication of a contractual term in place of the express wording and give effect to the parties' intentions.[23]

- *Thompson v. Cameron*[24] – This case involved the interpretation of a bankruptcy settlement agreement and how far precontractual negotiations and postcontractual conduct can be taken into account to determine the meaning of the terms of the settlement. In his decision, Justice Chambers cited the majority in *Attorney-General v. Dreux Holdings* for its recognition of the CISG, noting that the CISG is now part of New Zealand law by virtue of the Sales of Goods Act 1994. Justice Chambers observed that Article 8(3) of the CISG allows for the use of the parties' subsequent conduct as an aid to contract interpretation. However, the court ultimately found that the state of the law concerning the use of precontractual negotiations and postcontractual conduct as an aid to contract interpretation is still uncertain.[25] As such, the court decided to determine the matter in line with the traditional view that precontractual negotiations and postcontractual conduct are inadmissible as evidence of the meaning of the contract.

- *Ka (Newmarket) Ltd. v. Hart*[26] – The issue in this case was whether the price of materials was to be calculated on a per-roll or per-meter basis. The court found that the claim between businesses situated in different countries ought not to be brought under the Sale of Goods Act 1908, but rather under the Sale of Goods Act of 1994 (CISG).[27]

---

[19] Id., [1].
[20] Id., [88].
[21] Id., [90].
[22] *Bobux Marketing Ltd v. Raynor Marketing Ltd* [2002] 1 NZLR 506.
[23] Id., [39].
[24] *Thompson v. Cameron* HC Auckland (March 27, 2002) AP117/SW99.
[25] Id., 22.
[26] *KA (Newmarket) Ltd v. Hart* HC Auckland (May 10, 2002) CP 467-SD01.
[27] Id., [68].

- *International Housewares (NZ) Ltd. v. SEB S.A.*[28] – The case involved a distribution agreement between the parties for electrical appliances and Tefal nonstick cookware in New Zealand. One of the issues before the court was whether there can be an implied term as to merchantable quality. Master Lang did not rule on this issue, but commented that the CISG demonstrated international recognition of the desirability of implying terms as to merchantable quality into sales contracts:[29]

> The insertion of an implied term as to merchantable quality could hardly be described as radical. Contracts for the supply of goods have for many years had such a term implied into them by statute in many jurisdictions. The desirability of such a term is also recognized internationally by the United Nations Convention, which forms the basis for one of the plaintiff's claims in this proceeding.

The foregoing analysis reflects a judicial hesitancy to place too great a reliance on the CISG in matters involving sales contracts, whether international or national in nature. The decision of *RJ & AM Smallmon v. Transport Sales Ltd.*,[30] however, represents a major departure from that position. The following section will discuss the *Smallmon* decision and its impact on the relationship between the CISG and New Zealand contract law.

B. RJ & AM Smallmon v. Transport Sales Limited

The High Court decision of *RJ & AM Smallmon v. Transport Sales Ltd.*[31] was the first New Zealand judgment to apply the CISG as the substantive law of the case. The case was appealed, and the judgment of the Court of Appeal rendered in 2011.[32] The Court of Appeal's decision reflects a dramatic shift in the perceived role of the CISG as it relates to New Zealand businesses and commercial traders.

Smallmon involved the purchase of trucks by an Australian company from a New Zealand company. The buyer argued that because the trucks were not registerable at the point of sale and could never be fully registered, they could not be driven and were therefore not fit for the ordinary purpose for which they were purchased, which was said to be an implied term of the contract as derived from Article 35 of the CISG.[33] The issue before the court was therefore whether or not there was a breach of Article 35 of the CISG.

At first instance, Justice French observed that "[t]here is no question that the Convention applied to the transaction between [the parties],"[34] as "[b]oth Australia and New Zealand have adopted the Convention as part of their law."[35] In determining nonconformity with Article 35 of the CISG, the court had regard to various international authorities from which it derived several principles,[36] including that:[37]

---

[28] *International Housewares (NZ) Ltd v SEB S.A.* (March 31, 2003) HC Auckland, CP395-SD01.
[29] Id. at 59.
[30] *RJ & AM Smallmon v Transport Sales Limited* (July 30, 2010) HC Christchurch, CIV-2009–409–000363). The decision on appeal was rendered in 2011.
[31] Id.
[32] *Smallmon v. Transport Sales Ltd* [2011] NZCA 340.
[33] Id., [75–6].
[34] Id., [63].
[35] Id., [62].
[36] Id., [82].
[37] Id., [83].

As a general rule, the seller is not responsible for compliance with the regulatory provisions or standards of the importing country...unless:...(c) the seller knew or should have known of the requirements because of special circumstances.

Although the parties sought to rely on domestic authorities, Justice French justified her reliance on international authorities on the basis that recourse to domestic law is prohibited by Article 7 of the CISG.[38] Article 7(1) of the CISG requires regard to be had "to the international character of the convention and to the need to promote uniformity in its application." Justice French interpreted Article 7 as requiring that the convention be interpreted "exclusively on its own terms," but that regard may be had to "the principles of the Convention and Convention-related decisions in overseas jurisdictions."[39] The court dismissed the Smallmons' claim for lost profits due because there was no express contractual warranty as to the ability to register the trucks upon arrival in Australia, and because there was no breach of Article 35(2) of the CISG.

The Smallmons appealed from the High Court decision.[40] The central issue on appeal concerned the application of Article 35 of the CISG to the sale of the trucks. As there was no express provision regarding the ability to register the trucks in Queensland, the court had to determine whether or not it was an implied contractual term that the trucks had to be registerable in Queensland when the seller was in New Zealand. To imply such a contractual term into the contract, the court relied on Article 35(2) of the CISG.

The court noted that the general principle under Article 35(2) of the CISG is that "the seller is not responsible for compliance with the regulatory provisions or standards of the buyer's country."[41] Therefore, unless the Smallmons could show that there were particular circumstances demonstrating that the respondent knew or ought to have known of those regulatory provisions, the claim under Article 35(2) would fail. Such circumstances could include whether the seller had previously exported trucks to Australia.

Applying the CISG, the Court of Appeal stated that, in determining a claim under the CISG, consideration of domestic authorities was not permissible.[42] Rather, the court ought interpret the CISG exclusively on its own terms and by applying international authorities which are related to the CISG. After analyzing various decisions from overseas jurisdictions, the court concluded that[43]

[t]he international authorities support the proposition that the seller will not be liable for goods that do not conform to the regulatory provisions or standards of the buyer's country unless the seller knew or ought to have known of the requirements because of special circumstances.

As there were no such circumstances present, the buyer's claim was rejected based on the general principle of the CISG that the seller is not liable for any nonconformity with the regulatory provisions of the buyer's country. Furthermore, the court considered that the buyers did not rely, or that it was unreasonable for them to rely, on the seller's skill and judgment.[44] In any event, the court held that Article 35 was not even engaged

[38] Id., [86].
[39] Id., [88].
[40] *Smallmon v. Transport Sales Ltd* [2011] NZCA 340.
[41] Id., [60].
[42] Id., [39].
[43] Id., [46].
[44] Id., [71–2].

as the parties had agreed that conformity with the regulatory provisions of the buyer's country was the buyer's responsibility.[45]

The *Smallmon* decision of 2011 is a landmark decision in relation to the application of the CISG by New Zealand courts. Not only was it the first decision in which the CISG was applied directly as the substantive law of the case, it was also the first decision to embrace an autonomous interpretation of Article 35 of the CISG. Although the CISG demands an autonomous interpretation, it is something that has often been overlooked. The Court of Appeal, however, resisted the homeward-trend bias reasoning in favor of a comparative analysis of overseas jurisdictions. Furthermore, *Smallmon* reflects the fact that, despite New Zealand courts having little experience with the CISG, they are nevertheless willing to render decisions encapsulating the spirit of the convention.

IV. Conclusion

Since 1995, nine judgments have mentioned and used the CISG to clarify domestic legal principles. Often, however, the CISG has been ignored or neglected, even in cases in which it was the applicable law. It was not until recently in the *Smallmon* decisions of 2010 and 2011 that the courts fully embraced the CISG.[46] The *Smallmon* decisions are the first New Zealand cases to be based on a correct application of the CISG as the substantive law governing the dispute and have shown there is potential for the CISG to emerge as a useful tool of international commercial law. The 2011 decision has further emphasized the fact that contracts concerning the sale of goods between Australia and New Zealand are governed by the CISG.

Evidence shows that the CISG has had a greater influence on New Zealand law when it has been used by analogy in the interpretation and application of domestic sales law, rather than as a stand-alone and mandatory substantive law. The use of the CISG as an interpretive aid has influenced a shift in New Zealand's contract interpretation law; it can now be said that the courts are allowed, if not required, to undertake an analysis of Article 8 of the CISG when interpreting all types of contracts.[47] As the survey of cases indicates, New Zealand judges, in particular Justice Thomas, have used Article 8 of the CISG to advance the use of pre- and postcontractual conduct as an aid to contract interpretation. The CISG has also been used by Professor David McLauchlan to support his thesis that subsequent conduct can be used as an interpretive aid.[48]

New Zealand is an example of how some countries, especially common law ones, have avoided applying the CISG despite its incorporation into domestic law. One possible explanation for its lack of recognition may be due to a relative bias of common law lawyers against the adoption or application of an international legislative framework regulating

[45] Id., [76].
[46] It has to be noted, however, that there is no statistical evidence available to indicate how many cases involving the CISG are settled. The author was called upon as an expert witness in a case involving the CISG. The parties settled after both sides had filed submissions. The author's impression was that the uncomfortableness/unfamiliarity with the application of the CISG "helped" the settlement process.
[47] See David McLauchlan, "Common Intention and Contract Interpretation," *Lloyd's Maritime and Commercial Law Quarterly* 30 (2011).
[48] For example, David McLauchlan, "The Plain Meaning Rule of Contract Interpretation," (1995) 2 *NZBLQ* 80; "Subsequent Conduct as an Aid to Interpretation," (1996) 2 *NZBLQ* 237.

the law of contract.[49] The lack of attention given to the CISG also illustrates that a country's adoption of the CISG is not necessarily reflective of its success in harmonizing international law. The success of the CISG is ultimately determined by its acceptance in the legal and business communities. In New Zealand, there are factors to indicate that the CISG is gaining increasing recognition in the legal and business communities. For example, the CISG Advisory Council Meeting held in Wellington in 2012 provided an opportunity for members of both communities to come together to discuss the CISG and its many advantages. Conferences such as that of the Advisory Council help to increase local awareness of the CISG and thereby enhance its practical value.

In line with the *Smallmon* decision, it is likely that the recent free trade agreement between New Zealand and the People's Republic of China might also increase the use and study of the CISG in New Zealand. Promoting the development of trade is one of the underlying objectives of the CISG. In order to maximize the potential benefits from our free trade agreements it is therefore essential that the CISG be understood by the business and legal community alike.

[49] It should be noted that the United Kingdom still has not ratified the CISG and that the situation in regard to the knowledge about and use of the CISG in Canada and Australia is similar to New Zealand. In regard to Australia, see Lisa Spagnolo, "The Last Outpost: Automatic CISG Opt Outs, Misapplications and the Costs of Ignoring the Vienna Sales Convention for Australian Lawyers," 10 (1) *Melbourne Journal of International Law* 141; for Canada, Peter Mazzacano, "Reflections on the Plight of the CISG in Canada: A Comparative Approach" (October 1, 2009), available at http://ssrn.com/abstract=1433609.

33 People's Republic of China

Li Wei

I. Introduction

China's position as one of the original CISG contracting states, and as an economic world power, makes its acceptance and application of the CISG an important event. Remarkably, it has actively applied the CISG, generating the most CISG cases of any legal system other than Germany. China's International Economic and Trade Arbitration Commission (CIETAC), one of the world's busiest arbitral venues, regularly applies the CISG.[1] Furthermore, CIETAC has had little difficulty in interpreting and applying CISG provisions in advancing the CISG's purpose of creating a uniform sales law. The recognition and active use of the CISG in China bodes well for its continued development as a uniform international sales law.

The key question when China adopted the CISG was how well it would be able to assimilate what was essentially an amalgamation of Western common and civil laws. China underwent a historic shift to a market economy resulting in a critical shortage of business law in 1980s. In fact, the CISG strategically aided China's entry into world trade and has been used to supplement Chinese national law governing business transactions with parties from foreign countries. Generally, Chinese lawyers do not advise their clients to directly exclude the CISG in their contracts, but indirectly exclude it by applying the Contract Law of the People's Republic of China (China Contract Law, CCL).[2] So it is important to assess the similarities and differences between the CCL and the CISG.

Part I reviews the history leading to China's adoption of the CISG, and its influence on Chinese contract law in general. Part II compares the CISG with the CCL; it concludes that the CCL suffers a severe defect in not recognizing damages for differential prices (contract price versus market price; contract price versus cover price), which may ultimately undermine the damages system of the CCL. Part III examines the problems of the Chinese language version of the CISG and it reviews the state of applying the CISG in China. Part IV analyzes the *Indian iron sand case*, which illustrates how CIETAC resolved the issue of awarding damages based on a price differential.

---

[1] From 1995 to 2005 CIETAC has heard 6634 arbitral cases involving parties from foreign countries. See CIETAC, *The Compilation of Arbitral Awards on China International Economy and Trade (2003–2006)* (Beijing, 2008), preface.

[2] China's adopted its first contract law, the Economic Contract Law of People's Republic of China (PRC), in 1981. This was followed by enactment of the Foreign-Related Economic Contract Law in 1985. These laws were replaced by the passage of the Contract Law of the People's Republic of China in 1999. In 1986, China enacted the General Principles of the Civil Law.

II. History of China's Economic Transition and the CISG

China sent a delegation to the 1980 Vienna Diplomatic Conference,[3] but it did not participate in the preparation of the Draft Convention, as did its Asian partners – Japan, India, and South Korea.[4] China did not participate in the publication of the official Chinese language version of the text. The CISG was translated into Chinese by scholars outside of China. A few reasons can be given for China's passive approach to the negotiation and drafting of the CISG. Mao's ideology and domestic policies still influenced Chinese policy, which included reservations about Western legal systems. As a result, China did not actively participate in events and projects sponsored by UNCITRAL. Second, China lacked existing market-focused private laws or experience in Western-style contract law that would have allowed it to contribute to the CISG proceedings.

The new economic and political situation China faced in the 1970s and 1980s created the context for China's adoption of the CISG. In 1978, at the Third Plenary Session of the 11th Central Committee (Communist Party), the Party made the historical decision to shift the country's focus to economic modernization, which marked the start of China's open-door policies and economic reform. This shift to a socialist market economy and the development of international trade relations required China to modernize its business laws. The deficiency of law in China governing business transactions was enormous. China's previous planned economic regime had no need for private business law. Almost all goods, products, assets were allocated by the government's mandatory planning apparatus.

The publication of the CISG came at an opportune time for the Chinese authorities, which needed a ready-made international contract law. The true nature of China's open door policy was the opening of economic relations with Western countries and the CISG provided a Western-style law to conduct those relations. Accepting the CISG showed that China possessed the confidence to transact business under rules developed by Western legal systems. China sped up its adoption of the CISG by using an administrative approval process and avoiding the lengthier legislative process. Though Article 67 of China's Constitution (1982) rules that the Standing Committee of the National People's Congress has the power to decide on the ratification or abrogation of treaties and important agreements concluded with foreign states, the CISG was determined not to be the type of treaty that needed to go through the legislative process.[5] No domestic legislation on implementation of CISG was introduced in China. On December 4, 1987, the Ministry of Foreign Trade and Economic Cooperation issued an official document, *Some Noteworthy Issues on Implementation of CISG*. This paper provided guidance to China's state-owned enterprises on how to apply the CISG when engaging in foreign trade. The joint action of China and the United States to deposit their instruments of ratification of the CISG with the United Nations Secretary General was a watershed event in China's progress to becoming an international economic power.

---

[3] China's delegation consisted of trade officers from the Ministry of Foreign Trade, China Council for the Promotion of International Trade, but no legal experts.

[4] The CISG did not enter into force in South Korea until 2005 and Japan in 2009.

[5] See Article 7, the Law of the People's Republic of China on the Procedure of the Conclusion of Treaties (1990).

However, when filing its ratification of the CISG, China declared that it would make reservations under Article 92 (opting out of Part III), Article 95 (opting out of Article 1(1)(b) jurisdiction), and Article 96 (opting out of Article 11). Chinese academics warned against the opting out of Part III (seller's and buyer's obligation; remedies).[6] Ultimately, China withdrew its intent to opt out of Part III, meaning that it adopted all of the substantive provisions of the CISG. In November 1986, the United States and China agreed to a joint approval. On December 11, 1986, China, the United States, and Italy jointly deposited their instruments of ratification.[7] More recently, China recently declared that it was rescinding its Article 96 reservation, meaning no writing will be required for an enforceable contract under the CISG in China.

China entered into the CISG without any domestic tradition of business law, which made its adoption different from that of the other original contracting states of the CISG. Because of this lack of a business law tradition, the adoption of the CISG had far-reaching influence on Chinese law in general. Adoption of the CISG, along with the enactment of the Foreign-Related Economic Contract Law of PRC (China-FRECL) in 1985, filled the void of not having a functioning contract law for international business transactions. Second, China integrated the CISG into domestic law first in the China-FRECL, and more fully in the 1999 CCL.[8] Third, the adoption of the CISG symbolized China's intent to play an important role in the promotion of a global uniform business law. China's early ratification of the CISG influenced subsequent adoptions by South Korea (2005) and Japan (2009) – China is now Japan and South Korea's leading international trading partner.

III. China's Contract Law and the CISG

On October 1, 1999, the CCL entered into force. Its forerunners – The Economic Contract Law of PRC, China-FRECL, and the Law of PRC on Technology Contracts – were simultaneously annulled. They were replaced by the CCL and, more recently (January 1, 2012), the China's Supreme Court issued *The Interpretation of Supreme People's Court on Issues Concerning the Application of Law for the Trial of Dispute over Sale Contracts*. The judicial interpretation contains 46 articles, which specify how to address the issues of the CCL applicable to sales contracts. CCL is a comprehensive contract code that governs fifteen categories of contracts with a total of 428 provisions. The CCL's underlying principle is freedom of contract and it makes no distinction between merchants' and consumers' (civil and commercial) contracts. Experts and scholars who were influenced by the CISG used the CISG and UNIDROIT Principles in the process of drafting CCL. Scholars and lawyers familiar with those sources will find numerous similarities between them and the CCL.[9] CCL is the forum law in cases before CIETAC, unless CISG 1(1)(a) jurisdiction is present.

---

[6] Professors Ri Mu, of Peking University; Guo Shoukang, of People's University; and Shi Jiuyong, Law Counselor of Department of Foreign Affairs, helped persuade the Chinese Government to withdraw its reservation relating to Part III.

[7] China's collaboration with United States on the CISG was called the "International Joint Venture." Zhang Yuqing (former Director of Treaty and Law Department of Ministry of Foreign Trade), the 30th Anniversary of the CISG: Retrospect and prospect. See Shanghai Institute of Foreign Trade, "Paper Collection of International Symposium on the Thirtieth Anniversary of CISG," 14 (November 6, 2010).

[8] See Appendix A, "Comparative Analysis: CISG and CCL."

[9] Id.

As in any comprehensive code or law, CCL is not without flaws. This comprehensive contract law governs contracts broader than the CISG, but a number of traditional areas of contract law are missing from the CCL. CCL contains the counterpart of Article 74 CISG,[10] but has no rules equivalent to CISG Articles 75 and 76. Article 74 provides the general principle of full compensation, as well as for the calculation of damages caused by breach of contract. Articles 75 and 76 are particularized applications of Article 74 and deal respectively with two familiar methods of measuring the aggrieved party's damages after a contract has been avoided. Under Article 75, the aggrieved party is entitled to recover damages based on the difference between the contract price and the price of a substitute transaction. Article 76 adopts the "abstract method" of calculating damages, the aggrieved party is entitled to recover the difference between the contract price and the current market price at the time the contract is avoided. The two damage formulas, along with other provisions set out in Part III, Chapter V of the CISG, as well as the corresponding interpreting tools developed by UNCITRAL and the CISG-AC,[11] frame an integrated remedial (damages) system.

The two damage formulas are crucial to a modern contract system. First, they respond to the fundamental principle of full compensation and the compensatory nature of recovering damages in contract law, which seeks to place the aggrieved party in the position that it would have been in had the contract been performed. Second, the damage formulas allow the aggrieved party to avoid the higher burden of proof required by Article 74. Conversely, Article 74's burden of proof increases the uncertainty and lack of predictability of recovering damages. Article 74 requires the claiming party to disclose its internal calculations and customer pricing to prove the amount of loss profits. Articles 75 and 76 do not require such disclosures in order to recover damages. Third, the two damage formulas offer a clear and foreseeable guide to damage recovery that allows the aggrieved party to take reasonable measures to mitigate loss through substitute transactions, or directly to recover the contract–market price differential. Additionally, the breaching party can foresee the cost it has to pay for its nonperformance. It can then balance the advantages and disadvantages of canceling a contract.

The damage regime of CCL consists of only the general compensation principle, found in Article 113, and the principle of mitigation in Article 119. The lack of more concrete damage rules, as found in CISG Articles 75 and 76, makes the CCL an incomplete damages regime.[12] In practice, some Chinese courts have allowed the plaintiff to recover the difference between the contract price and the current price in disputes involving the sale of houses. However, the scarcity of these cases indicates that they are a result of individual acts of judicial discretion under the CCL Article 113 and not a broad recognition of any particular rules. In these cases, courts imposed a heavy burden on plaintiffs. Because of the generality of Article 113, there remains

---

[10] CCL Article 113 provides that: "If a party fails to perform its obligations under the contract . . . and thus causes losses to the other party, the compensation for the loss shall be equivalent to the loss actually caused by the breach of contract and shall include the profit obtainable after the performance of the contract, but not exceed the sum of the loss that might be caused by a breach of contract [that] ha[d] been anticipated or ought to [have been] anticipated by the party in breach at the time of conclusion of the contract."

[11] See UNCITRAL Digest of Case Law on the United Nations Convention on Contracts for the International Sale of Goods, Articles 74–7; CISG Advisory Council Opinions Nos. 6 and 8.

[12] Comparatively, CISG contains four articles on damages; Principles of European Contract Law (PECL) has 10 articles; Unidroit Principles (2004) has 13 articles.

considerable uncertainty over the aggrieved parties, ability to recover reasonable damages. Such uncertainty is also attributed to the "negligence principle" that Chinese legal practitioners apply to recovery for breach of contract.[13] For example, tribunals often differentiate between "intentional" nondelivery of goods, such as opportunistically seeking a higher price from another party, and other objective causes of nonperformance. As a result of such uncertainty, injured parties often fail in their claims for full compensatory damages.

In one case, a state-owned company sued an American company for breach of contract.[14] Due to a surge in the price of the goods, the American seller refused to perform a contract for the delivery of forty thousand tons of sugar. The buyer sued for damages, which included the expense of obtaining a letter of credit and a penalty of five dollars per ton that the buyer had to pay domestic sub-buyers (totaling seven hundred thousand dollars). Attorney Yang Liangyi argued that the buyer was entitled to ten million dollars – the difference between the contract price and the market price. Nevertheless, the Chinese buyer maintained its claim for only seven hundred thousand dollars of damages. The very pleased seller immediately paid the damage claim.[15]

While the CCL adopted many CISG rules about formation of contract, some notable differences remain. First, CCL rules require that an acceptance shall be made in form of notice, whereas the CISG allows an acceptance by notice or conduct. Second, CISG contains no specific rules governing standard business terms. The issue of the "battle of forms" is governed by the general rules on formation in CISG Part II, which fails to provide any specific rules on the incorporation of standard term into contracts. The CCL provides specific rules (CCL Articles 39–41) in which the party providing standard clauses must make the other party aware of the standard clauses that may be disadvantageous to that party. Third, the CCL contains a rule governing the interpretation of contracts, but fails to provide any rules governing the interpretation of the statements or conduct of the parties in the negotiation and performance of a contract

In *LeaTai Textile Co. v. Manning Fabrics, Inc.*, the parties admitted that a contract existed, but disagreed on the enforceability of the arbitration clauses found in each other's forms – the American buyer's form provided for arbitration of disputes in New York under American Arbitration Association rules and the Chinese seller's form provided for arbitration in Hong Kong.[16]

The buyer's form was the offer and the seller's form was the purported acceptance. The seller's arbitration provisions constituted a material modification to the buyer's offer. The American court held that the buyer was bound by the seller's arbitration provision under the "last-shot" rule.[17] Under CCL Article 40, the result would be different. Article 40 states that a "standard clause shall become invalid . . . if the party that provides the standard clause exempts itself from the liability, imposes heavier liability on the other party, or precludes the other party [of] its main rights." This provision makes the enforceability

---

[13] The CISG rejects the negligence principle because of its unclear and outdated nature. Under CISG Articles 45 and 61, the breaching party's nonperformance is sufficient for the aggrieved party to exercise its right to remedy the breach.

[14] See Yang Liangyi, *The International Sale of Goods* (China University of Political Science and Law Press, 1999), 429–30; "Expectation Loss and Reliance Loss," 1 *Annual of China Maritime Law* 17–18 (2011).

[15] "Expectation Loss," 18.

[16] See *Lea Tai Textile C.V. Manning Fabrics, Inc.*, 411 F. Supp. 1404 (S.D.N.Y. 1975).

[17] However, there are current cases where the courts elected to apply the knock-out rule.

of the arbitration clause an issue of validity, which is outside the scope of the CISG pursuant to CISG Article 4.[18] Therefore, Article 36 of the CCL would be the applicable law, which would recognize the buyer's arbitration provision as binding the seller.[19] In essence, Chinese law adopts the "first-shot" rule in "battle of the forms" scenario. However, if the seller had called the buyer's attention to its arbitration provision, or the arbitration provision was handwritten and the buyer failed to object, then the seller's arbitration clause would have been incorporated into the contract under the CISG and the CCL.

IV. Applying the CISG in China

The major objective of the CISG is to promote uniformity in international sales law. Uniform law is a unique state of legal order for addressing international business disputes. It begins with the adoption of a uniform text and hopefully is fulfilled by a relative uniformity of application. The CISG's uniformity of text is somewhat compromised because it has been issued in six equally authentic languages. The original Chinese version is consistent with its English counterpart.[20] However, some inconsistencies do exist due to the inherent problems of translation. For example, the word "substantially" is found in CISG Articles 25 and 82(1).[21] "Substantially" was translated in Chinese as "实际上," which means "actually" in English. "Actually" is far from the correct meaning of the expression "substantially." Regarding Article 25's definition or criteria for determining fundamental breach, to deprive something substantially means to do it to a great extent, not to do it actually. For example, if the seller delivers 950 units of a product, but the contract was for the delivery of 1,000 units, then it can be said that the seller had not "actually" performed on the contract. However, the seller's delivery of 950 units would not be considered a fundamental breach of contract because the missing fifty units do not "substantially" deprive the buyer of "what he is entitled to expect under the contract." Under Article 82(1), if the seller commits a fundamental breach the buyer has the right to avoid the contract if the buyer can "make restitution of the goods *substantially* in the condition in which he received them." An "insubstantial" deterioration in the condition of goods does not prevent the buyer from exercising its right to avoid the contract. Furthermore, Article 51(2) states that: "the buyer may declare the contract avoided in its entirety only if the failure to make delivery completely or in

---

[18] Not all arbitration clauses in standard contract are invalid. According to CCL Articles 39 and 41, if the party that provided the standard term brings it to the attention of the other party in a reasonable manner or the arbitration clause is not a "standard term," then the term is enforceable.

[19] CCL Article 36 states: "Where the parties fail to make a contract in written form as provided for by laws or administrative regulations or as agreed by the parties, but a party has already performed the major obligations and the other party has accepted the performance, the contract shall be considered as formed."

[20] In case of discrepancies between the various language versions of the text, the English version is generally preferred because English was the language used by the drafting committee. See Rolf Herber in Peter Schlechtriem, *Commentary on the UN Convention on the International Sale of Goods* (Oxford: Clarendon Press, 1998), 64.

[21] CISG Article 25 states that "a breach of contract committed by one party is fundamental if it esults in such detriment to the other party as substantially to deprive him of what he is entitled to expect under the contract." CISG Article 82(1) provides that "the buyer loses the right to declare the contract avoided or to require the seller to deliver substitute goods if it is impossible for him to make restitution of the goods substantially in the condition in which he received them."

conformity with the contract amounts to a fundamental breach." In the Chinese version "only if failure to make delivery completely" was interpreted as "买方只有在(卖方)完全不交付货物." The Chinese expression's English meaning is the buyer can avoid a contract "only if seller makes no delivery completely," which is an obvious error in translation.[22]

These imprecise translations have not led to as many difficulties as one would expect. English and Chinese commentaries and scholarly articles are available to Chinese lawyers, judges, and arbitrators to enable them to better understand the meaning of CISG provisions, even those provisions that have not been well translated. Also, most college-educated Chinese lawyers know English and can refer to the deep English law literature on the CISG. Generally, Chinese, legal practitioners accept reasonable interpretations of the CISG, especially those interpretations put forward by UNCITRAL and well-known CISG experts. No specifically or uniquely "Chinese" approach to interpreting the CISG has been developed. This is encouraging for purposes of the uniform application of the CISG.

For this purpose, law practitioners should apply the CISG based on a review of CISG jurisprudence and related international private law rules. A review of the arbitral decisions of CIETAC is one way of assessing the state of the CISG in China. Most contractual disputes over international sale of goods involving Chinese parties are settled through arbitration. CIETAC has published four volumes[23] of compilations of arbitral awards. The four books collected include 419 arbitral awards in the period from 1960 to 2006. Among them, 201 were cases relating to the international sales of goods made after 1988, or after the CISG had entered into force in China.

A survey of these 201 arbitral awards, 103 of them contained no formal opinion on the application of law. Of the 128 arbitral awards made before 1993, only twelve awards included discussion of the application of law. This illustrates the informal, chaotic nature of the arbitral awards during this earlier time period. The tribunals did not focus on applying the formal rules of law, but, instead, focused on arbitrarily determining a compromise award of the parties' claims. Since the primary target was to reach a compromise, the formal rules of law were viewed as a hindrance to that objective and were mostly ignored.

The content of a Chinese arbitral award consists of three parts: finding of facts, the opinion, and the decision. As noted above, most opinions contain inadequate juridical analysis and reasoning. The tribunal simply determines whether a party had performed its obligations; whether there was a lack of conformity, and the appropriateness of the claims.

---

[22] Other obvious translation errors are found in Article 25, the Chinese words "以致于" should be changed to "以至于"; Article 3(1), "保证供应这种制造或生产" should be changed to "保证供应制造或生产这种货物"; Article 1(2), "情报" should be substituted for "信息"; Article 81(2), "局部" should be substituted for "部分".

[23] CIETAC, 1963–88, *Compilation of Arbitral Awards on China International Economy and Trade, 1963–1988* (Chinese People's University Press, 1993); CIETAC, *Compilation of Arbitral Awards on China International Economy and Trade, 1989–1995* (China Foreign Economy and Trade Press, 1997); CIETAC, *Compilation of Arbitral Awards on China International Economy and Trade, 1995–2002* (Law Press, 2002); CIETAC, *Compilation of Arbitral Awards on China International Economy and Trade, 2002–2006* (Law Press, 2009).

In the 142 arbitral awards made after 1990, at least in 6 the tribunals wrongly decided the issue of the applicability of the CISG. The 6 cases were *Shanghai Company v. U.S. Company*[24] (*TV set case*);[25] *U.S. Ltd. v. China Shanxi Import & Export Company* (*Carborundum case*);[26] *Chinese-Foreign Joint Venture Electronic Ltd. v. U.S. Technology & Industry Company* (*Plated circuit equipment case*);[27] *U.S. Company v. China Medical Company* (*Chondroitin sulfate case*);[28] *China Company v. German Company* (*Vitamin C case*);[29] and *China Breeding Stock Company v. U.S. Company* (*Imported breeding cows case*).[30] All the parties in these international sale cases had their places of business in CISG contracting states, and none of the contracts contained a choice of law clause excluding the application of the CISG. The CISG by virtue of its Article 1(1) was the applicable law in these cases. Some of the tribunals did not recognize its applicability, and in some cases the tribunals ignored the application of any law. However, in the *Vitamin C case*, the tribunal applied domestic Chinese law under the principle of it having the closest connection to the case and to the forum tribunal.

However, in *China Ltd. v. Hong Kong Company* (*Raincoat case*),[31] the parties agreed that the CISG governed their contract. Hong Kong is not a contracting party of CISG and yet, the tribunal held that the parties' choice of the CISG was a manifestation of the principle of party autonomy, and did not violate Chinese law.

Arbitral awards improved in quality and law application during the period from 2002 to 2006. Only five awards out of forty-one selected failed to reference law in their decisions. The selected arbitral decisions indicate a trend in which tribunals have recognized the CISG as governing law, as well as an increase in well-reasoned awards. There were fourteen cases or 34 percent in which the tribunal applied the CISG. Whereas the number of cases that applied the CISG from 1995 to 2002 numbered fifteen cases out of sixty-four cases or 23 percent. CIETAC's neutrality is supported by the fact that of the cases reviewed twenty-four favored the foreign parties, and only four favored the Chinese parties.

The CIETAC tribunals have correctly applied the CISG under its Article 1(1)(a) jurisdiction. In the *U.S. cotton case*,[32] a U.S. seller of cotton argued that the Rules of the Liverpool Cotton Exchange, rather than the CISG, was applicable law. The tribunal found no explicit agreement to apply the Liverpool Rules and, therefore, the parties had not opted out of the CISG. So the CISG governs the contract by virtue of Article 1(a). The tribunal affirmed buyer's claim for damages as a result of seller's delivery of defective cotton. The damages covered labor expenses for picking the defective goods, loss of import tariff paid for the portion of cotton not delivered, and the difference between the value of conforming and defective goods. But the tribunal denied the applicant's claim

[24] In Chinese arbitral awards, the published cases do not disclose the real names of the parties.
[25] CIETAC, *Compilation of Arbitral Awards on China International Economy and Trade, 1989–1995*, 492–6.
[26] CIETAC, *Compilation of Arbitral Awards on China International Economy and Trade, 1995–2002* (Law Press, 2002), 20–4.
[27] Id., 148–60.
[28] Id., 181–90.
[29] Id., 192–5.
[30] CIETAC, *Compilation of Arbitral Awards on China International Economy and Trade, 2003–2006*, 382–96.
[31] CIETAC, *Compilation of Arbitral Awards on China International Economy and Trade, 1995–2002*, 136–48.
[32] CIETAC, *Compilation of Arbitral Awards on China International Economy and Trade, 2003–2006*, 286–7.

for damages based on loss arising out of purchasing replacement goods. The tribunal held that the buyer's acceptance of the defected goods and claim for a price reduction (based upon the differential in value between conforming-defective goods) precluded it from also recovering on the loss attributed to the substitute transaction.

In the *Wool case*,[33] the tribunal confirmed that the buyer of wool, Chinese H Company, authorized a Hong Kong agent to sign three order confirmations sent by Australian DAP Company. The special clauses in the confirmations stated that all other terms and conditions are as per Chinatex's General Terms and Conditions Governing Purchase of Wool". Because the contracts contained no provisions about governing law, the CISG was the governing law. The tribunal denied the buyer's excuse for not opening a letter of credit and failing to obtain an import license. It held in favor of the seller's claim for damages based on the difference between the contract price and the market price pursuant to CISG Article 76. But the tribunal denied the applicant's claim for interest damages.

Twenty-two of the forty-one (54 percent) CIETAC cases from 2002 to 2006 applied the CCL as applicable law. This large percentage of cases reflects the fact that many of the contesting parties had places of business in noncontracting states (or areas), such as Hong Kong,[34] Taiwan, and Japan. Because China filed a reservation opting out of CISG Article 1(1)(b), the tribunal was prevented from using international private law rules in order to apply the CISG.

The modest number of CISG cases relative to the total number of international sales law cases heard in China is due to a lack of knowledge and a misunderstanding of CISG and its applicability as uniform law. The best way to ensure the use of the CISG as applicable law, especially in cases where one of the parties is from a noncontracting state, is through an express choice of law. Even an agreement to use the CISG (where one of the parties is from a noncontracting state) has been challenged by Chinese law practitioners as a validity issue to be determined under domestic law. The majority view is that such a choice of law is invalid because it violates China's reservation relating to Article 1(1)(b). In addition, the CISG does not apply, under Article 1(1)(b), when one of the parties is from an area of a contracting state that itself is not considered as a party to the CISG. In the case of China, Hong Kong, Macau, and Taiwan would be excluded under the Article (1)(b) reservation.

Article 1(1)(b) does not always prevent the application of the CISG if one or two parties to a contract are from noncontracting states. The rules of private international law generally apply the law of the country with the closest and most real connection to the contract or transaction. This may result in the application of the national law of a contracting state consisting of domestic law or the CISG, or both. For example, parties to a contract from Brazil (noncontracting state) and Germany have agreed that German law is to apply to their contract. Under Article 1(1)(b), the CISG and German domestic law are together applicable. If Germany had made a reservation opting out of Article 1(1)(b),

---

[33] Id., 313–22.

[34] Ulrich G. Schroeter has argued that Hong Kong became a contracting state of the CISG upon its transfer from British to Chinese control. See Ulrich G. Schroeter, "The Status of Hong Kong and Macao under the United Nations Convention on Contracts for the International Sale of Goods," 16 *Pace Int'l L. Rev.* 13 (2004). Chinese scholars regard Hong Kong as a noncontracting party to the CISG. This opinion is also supported by a French Supreme Court decision of April 2, 2008, available at http://cisgw3.law.pace.edu/cases/080402f1.html ("CISG is not applicable to the special administrative region of Hong Kong").

then German domestic law (BGB) would have been applicable. However, Article 1(1)(b) does not control, despite the views of some Chinese scholars, if the Brazilian and German parties expressly chose the CISG as applicable law. The principle of private autonomy underlying the CISG preempts the application of the Article 1(1)(b) reservation in such cases.

V. Case Study: *Indian Iron Sand Case*

The buyer, a Chinese company, agreed to purchase Indian iron sand from a Hong Kong company.[35] The contract provided that the seller was to deliver twenty thousand tons of sand containing a minimum iron content of 63.5%. The sand was to be delivered in July 2005 at the price of 58.40 USD per ton CFR Shandong Rizhao port. On July 15, 2005, the date specified in the contract, the buyer opened a letter of credit in favor of seller. The letter of credit set the deadline for the shipment of the goods as August 5, 2005. In the meantime, the market price of the sand increased to 65.60 USD per ton. The seller did not ship the goods by the stated deadline. The buyer gave a notice to the seller requesting a clarification by August 31 of the seller's intent to perform on the contract. The seller replied that the sand had been delivered to an Indian port, but was delayed because of extraordinary port congestion. The buyer informed the seller of avoidance of the contract on September 12. On that date, the price of Indian iron sand had risen to 72 USD per ton. In December 2005, the buyer submitted a written request for CIETAC arbitration. The buyer, referencing CISG Article 76 and Article 7.4.6 of the UNIDROIT Principles, made a claim of 322,000 USD as damages. This sum included lost profit based on the differential between the contract price (58.40 USD per ton) and the market price (72 USD) at the time of the contract avoidance. It also requested damages related to the costs of obtaining the letter of credit.

A. *Application of Law*

The tribunal recognized Hong Kong as the seller's place of business, making it an "international" transaction. The contract did not contain a choice of law clause. According to CCL Article 126, the state law most closely connected with the contract is the applicable law. Because China is the state having the closest connection with the contract (place of settlement of the dispute and buyer's place of business), Chinese law was recognized as the applicable law.[36] The tribunal denied the buyer's request to apply the CISG and

---

[35] CIETAC, *The Compilation of Arbitral Awards on China International Economy and Trade, 2003–2006*, 555–68.

[36] Chinese scholar Guo Wen-li examined 757 judicial decisions of the Chinese Intermediate People's Courts involving foreign-related disputes, published through September 10, 2009. He concluded that Chinese courts have the propensity to apply the law of the place of the court in settling foreign-related disputes. Cases in which the courts applied domestic Chinese law totaled 689 out of the 757 judicial decisions. There were only eight cases in which the courts applied foreign law and that included cases applying Hong Kong or Macau law. The CISG was applied in only five cases. In one case, heard by Shan Dong Higher People's Court in 2002, the parties were from China and France respectively. The place of performance (handing over the goods) was in Russia. The Court simply ignored the CISG and applied Chinese domestic contract law. The propensity to apply the law of the forum is also seen in CIETAC arbitrations. See Guo Wen-li, "Empirical Analysis on the Problems in the Foreign-involved Civil and Commercial Trial in China: According to 757 Judgments," 5 *Present Day Law Science* 17 (2010).

UNIDROIT Principles to the case. Chinese domestic law applied because Hong Kong was a noncontracting state of the CISG and China had opted out of Article 1(1)(b) jurisdiction. However, as argued by the buyer, the CCL contains no provisions comparable to CISG Article 76 and Article 7.4.6 of the UNIDROIT Principles. Therefore, the tribunal was free to use these more particularized rules for calculating damage, as they did not conflict with the general provisions of the CCL. The buyer argued that the two articles could be recognized as international business usage or as a supplementary source for interpreting the CCL. The tribunal did not agree. It reasoned that Article 142 of China's Principles of Civil Law allows the application of international usages in the absence of express provisions of Chinese law, but that Article 113 CCL (the equivalent to CISG Article 74) was sufficient for determining the damages owed.

B. *Damages*

The tribunal found the seller was in breach of the contract. It noted the buyer's request for belated delivery on two occasions and its attempt to arrange carriage of the goods despite the contract containing a CFR term. Further, the seller failed to reply to buyer's notice of avoidance, nor did it successfully negotiate a settlement of the dispute. The tribunal held that the contract was successfully avoided on September 12, 2005, pursuant to CCL Article 96.[37] However, the tribunal denied the buyer's claim to recover the difference between the contract price and the market price at the time of avoidance (13.60 USD per ton). Instead, it granted damages based on the difference between the contract price and the resale price of the goods to a domestic buyer or 2.50 USD per ton. The tribunal reasoned that:

> [Buyer's] requirement for recovering the [difference] between contract price and the current price is based on a wrong application of law. Parties to the contract did not foresee, and had no reason to foresee when the contract was formed that the price of Indian iron sand would sharply increase to 72 USD/ton within one or two months. They would have not concluded the contract if they had foreseen such an increase in price. [Buyer] has no ground for recovering the differential price as damages because of the unforeseeable [nature of the price increase], and such damage is unfair to [the breaching] party.

Thus, the tribunal did not expressly rule out the use of the contract price versus market price (at avoidance) means of determining damages, but it held that in this particular case that calculation would have amounted to damages not foreseeable at the time of contracting.

C. *Discussion*

CCL Article 113, like CISG Article 74, recognizes that damage recovery is restricted by the principle of foreseeability: The amount of damages the injured party is entitled to "shall not exceed the loss caused by breach of contract, and that the [breaching] party

---

[37] CCL Article 96 requires the avoiding party to notify the other party of its dissolution of the contract due to breach. The contract is dissolved when the notice reaches the other party. The other party may object to the dissolution by applying for relief from a court or arbitral institution within three months of receiving the notice of dissolution.

foresaw or ought to have foreseen at the time of conclusion of the contract." However, the tribunal's application of the foreseeability principle in the *Indian Iron Sands* case was misplaced. It failed to discuss what distinguished a foreseeable from an unforeseeable increase in the market price. It simply stated that the "parties would have not concluded the contract if they had foreseen such [an] increase in price." In fact, market prices for such commodities are characterized by a high degree of volatility. The tribunal placed the risk of such increases on the nonbreaching party. Given the facts of this case, the decision undermines the principle of good faith. The facts show that the seller acted in bad faith in failing to respond to the buyer in a timely manner and indicating that the goods would be forthcoming, but were delayed at the port. During this period the market price continued to increase. The seller should have been held liable for the price differential for the price increase under the principle of good faith. The seller should not have received the benefit of a lack of foreseeability when its subsequent bad faith conduct caused injury to the buyer.

The majority of scholarly commentary on the foreseeability requirement "define" it as that which may reasonably be supposed to have been in the contemplation of the breaching party at the time of making the contract that the damages being claimed would have been the probable result of the breach of contract.[38] According to this approach, damages caused by a fluctuation in the market price of a good or a component part is almost always a foreseeable occurrence. Thus, the differential price formulas found in CISG Articles 75 and 76 are appropriate means of determining foreseeable damages. The impact of market fluctuations in relation to the contract price provides a useful surrogate in determining the damages suffered by the nonbreaching party. Foreseeability relates to the nature or type of loss but not the amount of the loss,[39] which is best measured using the differential price formulas. The exception would be when a party claims a hardship due to a fluctuating market that fundamentally alters the equilibrium of the contract.[40] Calculating damages based on contract price–market price or contract price–substituted price differentials capture reasonable and foreseeable damages as mandated by the general principle of full compensation.

Some practitioners argue that loss calculated by using price differentials is best described as "expected" damages, not actual damages. For this reason, Chinese courts often do not endorse the methods of damage calculation provided in CISG Articles 75 and 76.[41] As a result, the Chinese contract damages system sets a high threshold for the burden of proving damages, making the recovery of lost profits problematic, which is contrary to the general principle of full compensation found in CISG Article 74. The Chinese view of recoverable damages provides greater incentive for parties to breach their contracts.

---

[38] *Hadley v. Baxendale* (1854) 9 Ex. 341.

[39] See, UNIDROIT Principles (2010), Article 7.4.4, official comment.

[40] The China Contract Law contains no provision relating to hardship, but Articles 117 and 118 deal with the issue of *force majeure*.

[41] Wan Exiang, the Vice President of the China Supreme Court, pointed out the difference between CCL Article 113 and CISG Article 74. He stated at an academic salon held by the International Law Faculty, China University of Political Science and Law (December 4, 2010), that "not full loss of profit[s] can be recovered. Chinese judicial institutions are apt to take the probable business risks into account when they calculate expected loss of profit[s]. The injured party is entitled to damages for breach of contract equal to the reasonable loss, not the full loss." See http://www.cuplfil.com/jiangzuo_detail.aspinfoid=89.

Under the principle of full compensation, the aggrieved party to provide proof of loss of profits with reasonable certainty. Reasonable proof is established on the probabilities of occurrence. Reasonable proof is construed as the claimant proving by a preponderance of the evidence (more than a fifty percent probability of loss profits) that it had incurred the given loss. Alternatively stated, a degree of uncertainty as to the correctness of the amount of the damages claimed is acceptable. The breaching party should not escape liability if the claimant is unable to prove damages with absolute certainty (because the breaching party's wrongful act is partially the cause of the difficulty of proof problem). The CISG Advisory Council's opinion on the "Calculation of Damages" states that: "Courts impose the risk of uncertainty on the breaking party whose breach gave rise to the uncertainty."[42] As long as the damages being claimed are not purely speculative, then the benefit of the doubt should favor the nonbreaching party.

VI. Conclusion

China's adoption of the CISG reflected its need to create a Western-style business law as it transitioned from a planned economic regime to a socialist market economy. The importance of adopting the CISG is symbolic, and symptomatic, of China's rise as an import–export power. The early adoption of the CISG and consolidation of Chinese contract law in the CCL (China Contract Law) was due to China's decision to open its country to the existing world trade regime. In sum, it needed a national business law that would be suitable for international transactions. The twenty-three year existence of the CISG in China has had a dramatic affect on Chinese legal practice. Today, it has become a familiar legal instrument for Chinese lawyers. The CISG has also substantially influenced Chinese domestic legislation. A total of forty-seven CISG Articles were incorporated into the CCL. It has been interesting to witness the blending of a Western-style law into a socialist legal system.

However, the absence of provisions in the CCL on the recovery of damages based on differential pricing (contract–market; contract–substituted goods) reveals a severe defect in the CCL's remedy scheme.[43] The CCL should be changed or interpreted to embrace the CISG's principle of full compensation. This failure to provide full compensatory damages in Chinese national contract law is likely the reason for the high rate of breach in Chinese contracting practice. Because the breaching party is not made to pay full compensatory damages, it incentivizes breach when there is even a modest change in market prices. The problem is exacerbated by the courts' deficiency in applying the good faith duty in business transactions.[44] For the purpose of recovering full damages, applying the CISG is more beneficial to the aggrieved party than the CCL. Damages aside, the CISG and the CCL are creating uniform results in China.

---

[42] CISG-AC Opinion 6, "Calculation of Damages under CISG Article 74," comment, para. 2.4.

[43] Recovery of damages based on price differentials is recognized in the CISG (Articles 75 and 76); "Principle of European Contract Law" (Articles 9-506 and 9-507); and by the UNIDROIT Principles of International Commercial Contracts (Articles 7.4.5 and 7.4.6).

[44] For statistics on the value the contracts in dispute and performance rates, see China Administrative Bureau for Industry and Commerce at http://www.caijing.com.cn/2008–03–10/100051613.html. ("Withholding payment is a frequent tactic used in China to force price negotiations. A contract is not an unchangeable bible for Chinese companies. Contracts are not viewed in China with the same sort of legal sanctity that they receive in most developed countries."). See Andrew Galbraith and Jason Dean, "In China, Some Firms Defy Business Norms," *Wall Street Journal* (September 6, 2011).

Appendix. Comparative Analysis: The CISG and CCL

CISG Articles	Contents of Articles	CCL Articles
Part 1	General provisions	None
Article 11	No formality requirements	Article 10
Article 13	Definition of written statement	Article 11
Part II	Formation of contract	Chapter 2
Article 14	Definition of offer	Article 14 & 15
Article 15	Effectiveness, withdrawal of offer	Article 16(1) & 17
Article 16	Revocation of offer	Article 18 & 19
Article 17	Rejection of offer	Article 20(1)
Article 18(2)	Acceptance of offer	Article 23 & 26
Article 18(3)	Acceptance by an act	Article 22 & 26
Article 19(1) & 19(3)	Modified acceptance	Article 30
Article 19(2)	Alteration of offer not materially	Article 31
Article 20(1)	Computation of time	Article 24
Article 21	Late acceptance	Article 28 & 29
Article 23	Time of conclusion of contract	Article 25
Part III	Sale of goods	None
Article 25	Fundamental nonperformance	Article 94(4)
Article 26	Notice of termination	Article 96(1)
Article 28	Right to specific performance	Article 110
Article 29(1)	Modification and termination	Article 93(1) & 77(1)
Article 30	Obligations of seller	Article 135
Article 31	Place of performance	Article 141
Article 33	Time of performance	Article 138 & 139
Article 35	Conformity of goods	Article 153, 154, 61, & 62(1)
Article 36	Time of conformity of the goods	None
Article 38	Examination of goods	Article 157 & 158
Article 39	Notice for nonconformity of goods	Article 158(2)
Article 41	Warranty (third-party claims)	Article 132, 150, & 151
Article 45 & 61(1)	Remedies for breach of contract	Article 107, 111, & 112
Article 46(1) & 62	Specific performance	Article 110
Article 46(2) & 46(3)	Remedies for nonconformity	Article 148 & 111
Article 47(1) & 63	Fixing additional period for performance	Article 94(3)
Article 50	Price reduction	Article 111(2)
Article 51	Partial delivery	Article 165
Article 52(1)	Early performance	None
Article 52(2)	Delivery of additional goods	Article 162
Article 55	Determination of price	Article 62(2)
Article 53 & 57	Place of payment	Article 159 & 160
Article 58(1) & 59	Time of payment	Article 161
Article 67	Passing of risk (goods handed over to first carrier)	Article 145
Article 68	Passing of risk (goods sold in transit)	Article 144
Article 69	Passing of risk (goods are handed over)	Article 143
Article 70	Passing of risk (seller's breach)	Article 148(2) & 149
Article 71 & 72	Anticipatory breach	Article 68, 69, & 94(2)
Article 73	Delivery of goods by installments	Article 166
Article 74	Damages	Article 113(1)
Article 75	Damages: substitute transaction	None
Article 76	Damages: no substitute transaction	None
Article 77	Duty of mitigation	Article 119
Article 78	Interest	Chapter 12
Article 79	Excuse (impediment)	Article 117 & 118
Article 80	"Unclean hands" rule	Article 67
Article 81	Effect of termination	Article 97 & 98
Article 85–88	Preservation of goods	Article 101–103

34 The United States and Canada

Robert W. Emerson and Ann M. Olazábal

The United States deposited its instrument of ratification of the CISG at the United Nations Headquarters in New York on December 11, 1986. The convention officially entered into force on January 1, 1988.[1] In ratifying the CISG, the United States has made an Article 95 declaration that the CISG would not apply to contracts between a U.S. party and a party whose place of business is in a state that has not yet adopted the CISG, unless otherwise expressly agreed by the parties.[2] The provisions of the CISG constitute federal law. Under the supremacy clause of the U.S. Constitution, the provisions of the CISG will trump any state law in conflict with it, such as the provisions of the Uniform Commercial Code (UCC).[3] Since its adoption, however, the implementation of the CISG in the United States has been generally seen as inconsistent and relatively rare. One reason advanced for this underperformance of the CISG and its lack of consistency in application by the courts is that judges routinely revert to domestic law in interpreting and applying the CISG.[4]

Canada acceded to the CISG in 1991, and the following year it came into force.[5] Unlike that of the United States, the Canadian Constitution does not give the federal government authority to implement treaties in areas of jurisdiction belonging to the provinces.[6] However, every province and territory in Canada has incorporated the CISG into its sales laws.[7]

---

[1] See Preface of the United Nations Convention on Contracts for the International Sale of Goods, April 11, 1980, S. Treaty Doc. No. 98–9 (1983), 1489 U.N.T.S. 3, 19 I.L.M. 668 (1980).

[2] CISG, Article 95, provides: "Any State may declare at the time of the deposit of its instrument of ratification, acceptance, approval or accession that it will not be bound by subparagraph (1)(b) of article 1 of this Convention." For a judicial application of this principle, see *Princesse D'Isenbourg et Cie Ltd. v. Kinder Caviar, Inc.*, No. 3: 09–29-DCR, 2011 U.S. Dist. LEXIS 17281 (E.D. Ky. February 22, 2011), available at http://cisgw3.law.pace.edu/cases/110222u1.html (holding CISG inapplicable to dispute between caviar producer in the United States and a U.K. purveyor of gourmet foods because the United Kingdom has not acceded to the treaty).

[3] See U.S. Constitution, Article VI, cl. 2.

[4] The CISG's Article 7(2) allows for courts to turn to their own domestic laws in interpreting the CISG if the other methods of interpretation in Article 7 do not produce answers. For in-depth discussion on this interpretive challenge, see Patrick C. Leyens, "CISG and Mistake: Uniform Law vs. Domestic Law" [mistake as an interpretive challenge under the "validity loophole" of Article 4(a) of the Vienna Convention of 1980] (2003), available at http://www.cisg.law.pace.edu/cisg/biblio/leyens.html.

[5] Canada acceded to the CISG pursuant to the International Sale of Goods Contracts Convention Act. See International Sale of Goods Contracts Convention Act RS C 1991 c C13.

[6] *See* Government of Canada, Department of External Affairs, *Federalism and International Relations*, 1968, 11–33.

[7] See, e.g., Ontario: S.O. 1988, ch. 45; Prince Edward Island: S.P.E.I. 1988, Chapter 33.

Similar to the U.S. courts, the Canadian courts have been slow to implement the CISG, preferring to apply their own domestic law.[8] For example, in Canada's first CISG case decided, in 1998, *Nova Tool and Mould Inc. v. London Industries Inc.*,[9] the court mentioned the applicable provisions of the CISG but applied domestic Canadian sales law even though the litigants were from countries that were both parties to the CISG. However, a year later, in the case of *La San Giuseppe v. Forti Moulding Ltd.*,[10] a Canadian court correctly applied the provisions of the CISG. Regardless, the Canadian courts, like the U.S. courts, have not developed a consistent jurisprudence nor have they consistently applied the interpretive methodology found in the CISG.

I. Analysis of the CISG: American and Canadian Case Law

This part examines a number of substantive areas of the CISG that have been discussed in Canadian and American case law, including: contract formation; battle of the forms; notice of nonconformity; nonconformity of goods; *Nachfrist* notice; fundamental breach; remedies of avoidance, price reduction, and damages; mitigation; and excuse.

A. *Contract Formation*

Over the years, a significant amount of case law has developed in American courts relating to the issue of contract formation under the CISG. The convention sets out a clear regime for analyzing the formation of international contracts for the sale of goods: (1) Article 11 states that: "A contract of sale need not be concluded in or evidenced by writing and is not subject to any other requirement as to form." (2) Article 14 explains that a proposal is an offer if it is sufficiently definite such that it "indicates the goods and expressly or implicitly fixes or makes provision for determining the quantity and the price," and it demonstrates an intention by the offeror to be bound if the proposal is accepted. (3) In turn, Article 18 provides that an offer is accepted if the offeree makes a "statement . . . or other conduct . . . indicating assent to an offer." (4) Article 23 states that: "A contract is concluded at the moment when an acceptance of an offer becomes effective." A review of the case law indicates that courts often find that a binding contract exists when the parties sufficiently agree to the goods, the quantity, and the price of the goods.

The court in *Chateau des Charmes Wines Ltd. v. Sabaté USA, Sabaté S.A.*[11] found that when an oral agreement did not contain a forum selection clause, one party's attempt to include such a provision in subsequent invoices did not alter the contract. Because the contract had already been formed, any new terms were merely offers requiring the

---

[8] In the first ten years after Canada's adoption of the CISG, only two Canadian decisions even referred to the CISG: *Nova Tool & Mold Inc. v. London Industries Inc.*, [1998] O.J. No. 5381 (QL), 84 A.C.W.S. (3d) 1089 (Sup. Ct. J.) and *La San Giuseppe v. Forti Moulding Ltd.*, [1999] O.J. No. 3352 (Sup.Ct. J.) (QL).

[9] *Nova Tool & Mold Inc. v. London Industries Inc.*, [1998] O.J. No. 5381 (QL), 84 A.C.W.S. (3d) 1089 (Sup. Ct. J.), available at http://cisgw3.law.pace.edu/cisg/wais/db/cases2/000126c4.html.

[10] *La San Giuseppe*, [1999] O.J. No. 3352, Court File No. 98-CV-142493CM (ON S.C.), available at http:// cisgw3.law.pace.edu/cases/990831c4.html.

[11] *Chateau des Charmes Wines Ltd. v. Sabaté USA, Sabaté S.A.*, 328 F.3d 528, 531 (9th Cir. 2003), available at http://cisgw3.law.pace.edu/cases/030505u1.html.

other party's express assent; the latter had no obligation to reject the term, or else be bound.[12]

A 2010 U.S. court decision dealt with the issue of acceptance by conduct as allowed under CISG Article 18(3). In *Golden Valley Grape Juice & Wine, LLC v. Centrisys Corp.*,[13] affirmed the proposition that a party's conduct can signify acceptance, as contemplated by the CISG.[14] In that case, an Australian seller of centrifuges transmitted an email message to the U.S. buyer, Centrisys, containing a sales quote that identified the goods, the quantity, and the offering price.[15] This the court found to be sufficient under the CISG to constitute an offer.[16] Attached to the same email message was the seller's general conditions document, which contained a clause identifying Victoria, Australia, as the chosen forum for litigation of any disputes.[17]

Though Centrisys never formally communicated acceptance of the offer to the seller, Centrisys did incorporate the seller's quote into a subsequent offer to sell the centrifuges.[18] The seller delivered the centrifuges directly to Golden Valley.[19] Citing Chateau de Charmes precedents, Centrisys argued that a mere receipt of the seller's general conditions was not enough to incorporate those terms into the contract.[20] The court distinguished both of the earlier U.S. decisions, noting that the document containing the Australian forum selection was not imposed unilaterally after formation of the contract, but instead was made a part of the seller's offer, which had been accepted by the buyer.[21]

B. *Battle of the Forms*

Article 19 of the CISG addresses the issue of the battle of the forms. Specifically, Article 19 provides that a purported acceptance with additional terms or limitations constitutes a rejection and subsequent counteroffer.[22] However, unless the offeror objects, a purported acceptance that adds nonmaterial terms is an acceptance, and those new terms

---

[12] The court noted that the mere performance of obligations under the oral contract did not indicate assent to what would be additional material terms under Article 19(3). As stated in Larry A. DiMatteo et al., "The Interpretive Turn in International Sales Law: An Analysis of Fifteen Years of CISG Jurisprudence," 34 *Northwestern Journal of International Law and Business* 299, 357 (2004), available at http://cisgw3. law.pace.edu/cisg/biblio/dimatteo3.html, Article 19 "is limited to issues of contract formation and not to modifications of contract. Thus, it is universally accepted that where a contract has been validly concluded, one party may not change a material term in the contract without the acceptance of the other party."

[13] No. CV F 09–1424, 2010 U.S. Dist. LEXIS 11884 (E.D. Cal. January 21, 2010), available at http://cisgw3. law.pace.edu/cases/100121u1.html.

[14] CISG, Article 18(1), (3).

[15] *Golden Valley*, 2010 U.S. Dist. LEXIS 11884, at *10.

[16] Id.

[17] Id., 10–11.

[18] Id., 11.

[19] Id.

[20] Id., 12.

[21] *Golden Valley*, 2010 U.S. Dist. LEXIS 11884, at 12–16. ("[T]he General Conditions accompanied the sales quote. [They] were attached, contemporaneously, with the sales quote and with other sale information, such as warranty information and banking information, which were included in the email . . . The General Conditions were part of the offer . . . By adopting the terms of the sales quote, Centrisys accepted the terms upon which the centrifuge had been offered, including the General Conditions.")

[22] CISG, Article 19(1). As noted by the court in *Travelers Prop. Cas. Co. of Am. v. St.-Gobain Tech. Fabrics Can., Ltd.*, 474 F. Supp. 2d 1075, 1082 (D. Minn. 2007), *available at* http://cisgw3.law.pace.edu/cases/070131u1.html, Article 19(1) of the CISG constitutes a "mirror image rule."

will govern.[23] In *Filanto, S.p.A. v. Chilewich International Corp.*,[24] an Italian footwear manufacturer was held to have accepted an arbitration provision as part of the sales agreement because it failed to object in a timely manner and commenced performance by opening a letter of credit. Although the manufacturer repeatedly objected during negotiations to the incorporation of an arbitration clause, the court noted that "a litigant may not blow hot and cold in a lawsuit," and had at times apparently accepted the disputed form that was the basis of the defendant's contentions.[25]

More recently, in *Magellan International Corp. v. Salzgitter Handel GmbH*,[26] a buyer sent specifications regarding the purchase of steel bars to the seller. The seller's response included a price increase, which the buyer later accepted and memorialized in written purchase orders.[27] The seller replied by sending "pro forma order confirmations" with slightly different terms than those included in the purchase orders.[28] After buyer rejected seller's subsequent requests to amend the agreement,[29] it brought suit when the seller failed to perform without an agreement to the proposed terms. The buyer claimed that a valid agreement existed and that seller's actions constituted a breach of contract.[30] In its order denying a motion to dismiss, the court noted that a reasonable jury could find the existence of a contract.[31] Relying on CISG Article 19(1), the court reasoned that the seller's confirmations did propose price changes. Hence that response can be seen as a counteroffer, which justified the buyer's belief that its acceptance of those new prices would form a contract."[32]

In *Miami Valley Paper, LLC v. Lebbing Engineering & Consulting GmbH*,[33] the buyer drafted a purchase order for paper winding equipment, mistakenly including a shaftless design specification. The seller confirmed the order, including the shaftless design, but responded that the equipment at issue differed in three respects from that outlined in the order.[34] In its response to the confirmation, the buyer agreed to remit payment and also

---

[23] CISG, Article 19(2).

[24] 789 F. Supp. 1229 (S.D.N.Y. 1992), available at http://cisgw3.law.pace.edu/cases/920414u1.html.

[25] Id., 1240. For a more clear-cut case of a party's objection and its consequences, see *Belcher-Robinson, LLC v. Linamar Corp.*, 699 F. Supp. 2d 1329 (M.D. Ala. 2010), available at http://cisgw3.law.pace.edu/cases/100331u1.html, in which the court gave alternative reasoning for its decision. Either the purported acceptance was objected to by the offeror, or its objectionable forum selection clause was material, in which case the "acceptance" was in fact a rejection. Regardless of the view taken, the forum selection clause was held not to be a part of the parties' agreement. Id., 1337–8.

[26] 76 F. Supp. 2d 919, 920 (N.D. Ill. 1999), available at http://cisgw3.law.pace.edu/cases/991207u1.html.

[27] Id., 920–1.

[28] Id., 921.

[29] The change would have altered the letter of credit that Magellan had issued naming Salzgitter as beneficiary.

[30] Id.

[31] Id., 925.

[32] Id. Indeed, although the goods have been delivered, a court may hold that it cannot find a valid contract had been concluded when the parties differed on the terms of delivery. In *Calzaturificio Claudia S.n.c. v. Olivieri Footwear Ltd.*, No. 96 CIV. 8052, 1998 U.S. Dist. LEXIS 4586, at (S.D.N.Y. April 6, 1998), available at http://cisgw3.law.pace.edu/cases/980406u1.html, the court considered an alleged oral agreement with terms allegedly proven later through invoices. The court referred to CISG Article 19 only in a footnote, and it apparently found a material modification of the offer – thus a counteroffer – when the parties' prior course of dealings (thirteen transactions) indicated they had not always used the same delivery term. Id., 25–8.

[33] *Miami Valley Paper, LLC v. Lebbing Eng'g & Consulting GmbH*, 2009 U.S. Dist. LEXIS 25201 (S.D. Ohio March 26, 2009), available at http://cisgw3.law.pace.edu/cases/090326u1.html.

[34] Id., 4.

asked whether the seller was interested in buying a crane.[35] This exchange of letters and faxes ultimately led to the parties' disagreement as to the date the contract was formed and to its actual terms. Specifically, the parties disagreed as to whether the contract was for a shafted or shaftless winder and whether the contract included only a winder or also additional items, such as the aforementioned crane. The court found that genuine issues of material fact existed as to the date of formation and terms of the contract; accordingly, it denied the motions to find a breach of contract.[36]

In *CSS Antenna, Inc. v. Amphenol-Tuchel Electronics, GmbH*,[37] a seller's confirmation of a purchase order included a number of additional terms related to dispute resolution. The goods were shipped and were paid for by the buyer. Applying CISG Article 19, which defines terms relating to "settlement of disputes" as material,[38] the court deemed the confirmation form to be a rejection and a counteroffer.[39] In the usual case, the subsequent conduct in accepting and paying for the goods would serve as an acceptance of the confirmation. But, the court instead resorted to CISG Article 8(1), noting that the confirmation made only ambiguous reference to the seller's general terms and conditions, which included the disputed forum selection clause. The confirmation suggested that the buyer view the seller's general conditions on the seller's Web site. The court held that a mere suggestion did not constitute an intention to incorporate the terms into the contract. Alternatively stated, the court was unwilling to find that the buyer "knew or could not have been unaware" that the seller intended its forum selection clause to apply to the parties' contract.[40]

C. *Notice of Nonconformity Requirements*

In a Canadian case regarding notice issues, a seller of Italian picture frame moldings brought suit against the buyer for failure to satisfy payment deadlines.[41] The buyer, in turn, alleged a lack of conformity due to alleged defects in some of the moldings. The Ontario Superior Court of Justice rejected the buyer's counterclaim, reasoning inter alia that the buyer had failed to provide timely notice to the seller. Specifically, the court noted that the buyer did not complain in writing, despite a history of so doing when defective goods were received. Consequently, the court found the buyer's counterclaim for damages to be barred.[42] Had the buyer provided the seller with written notice before the suit was filed, the buyer might have prevailed on its claim.

In U.S. courts, the issue of the reasonableness of the timing of the buyer's notice of nonconformity is generally a question of fact requiring a jury determination. The court in *Miami Valley Paper, LLC v. Lebbing Eng'g & Consulting GmbH*[43] noted: "The question of whether it was reasonable for the Plaintiff to wait approximately two months before tendering notice to Defendant of the alleged non-conformity must be fully

---

[35] Id., 5.

[36] Id., 20, 35.

[37] 764 F. Supp. 2d 745 (D. Md. 2011), available at http://cisgw3.law.pace.edu/cases/110208u1.html.

[38] CISG, Article 19(3).

[39] 764 F. Supp. 2d at 752.

[40] Id., 754.

[41] *La San Giuseppe v. Forti Moulding Ltd.*, 1999 O.T.C. LEXIS 2163, para. 1 (Ont. Sup. C.J. 1999), available at http://cisgw3.law.pace.edu/cases/990831c4.html.

[42] Id., para. 39.

[43] No. 1:05-CV-00702, 2009 U.S. Dist. LEXIS 25201, at 21 (S.D. Ohio March 26, 2009), available at http://cisgw3.law.pace.edu/cases/090326u1.html.

examined by a jury, in light of all circumstances of this specific case."[44] The U.S. courts have occasionally held particular intervals between the discovery of the defect(s) and notice of nonconformity to be timely as a matter of law. In *Shuttle Packaging Systems v. Tsonakis*,[45] the seller alleged that the plaintiff's complaint about the defect in performance of the equipment was not timely under CISG Article 39.[46] In its "likelihood of success" analysis required for issuance of an injunction, the court noted that the CISG does not require the buyer to provide notice immediately or within weeks because that is not always possible.[47] The court held that buyer was likely to prove that its "delayed notice" was reasonable because "[t]he [purchased equipment] was complicated, unique, delivered in installments and subject to training and on-going repairs."[48] Additionally, the court reasoned that the buyer's employees did not have the requisite knowledge or skills to perform a proper inspection of the equipment in a more timely fashion.[49]

An issue related to the question of the timeliness of a notice of nonconformity is the required content of such notice. In *Sky Cast, Inc. v. Global Direct Distrib., LLC*,[50] a seller demanded full payment of price, and the buyer claimed that no further money was owed due to seller's failure to deliver the goods in a timely fashion and in accordance with the parties' agreement.[51] The court noted that the notice requirement of CISG Article 39 does not set forth specific guidelines for the delivery of notice, other than establishing a limitation period. Thus, the buyer's counterclaim, in this case, serves as notice just as a letter would and was within the two-year time period provided in Article 39(2).[52] The court, however, failed to make a determination whether the notice was within a "reasonable time" period as specified under Article 39(1).[53]

D. *Conformity of Goods*

The CISG requires the seller to "deliver goods which are of the quantity, quality and description required by the contract and which are contained or packaged in the manner

---

[44] Id. See also *Chi. Prime Packers, Inc. v. Northam Food Trading Co.*, 320 F. Supp. 2d 702, 712 (N.D. Ill. 2004), available at http://www.cisg.law.pace.edu/cases/040521u1.html. ("The determination of what period of time is 'practicable' is a factual one and depends on the circumstances of the case.")

[45] *Shuttle Packaging Sys. v. Tsonakis*, 2001 U.S. Dist. LEXIS 21630 (W.D. Mich. December 17, 2001), available at http://cisgw3.law.pace.edu/cases/011217u1.html.

[46] Id., 25–6.

[47] Id., 27.

[48] Id., 26.

[49] Id. See also *TeeVee Toons, Inc. v. Gerhard Schubert GmbH*, 00Civ. 5189, 2006 U.S. Dist. LEXIS 59455, at 20 (S.D. N.Y. August 22, 2006), available at http://cisgw3.law.pace.edu/cases/020329u1.html (holding to be reasonable a notice of nonconformity delivered in October after an August delivery of goods).

[50] Sky Cast, Inc. v. Global Direct Distrib., LLC, 2008 U.S. Dist. LEXIS 21121, at *1 (E.D. Ky. March 18, 2008), available at http://www.cisg.law.pace.edu/cisg/wais/db/cases2/080318u1.html.

[51] Id., 2, 6–7. In an interrogatory, Sky Cast explained that the delayed delivery of the light posts was caused by a partial plant shutdown for vacations, a gas leak at the plant, and inexperienced employees on duty. Id., 6 n. 4.

[52] A 2004 decision notes that notice need not be given at all when the seller knows it has delivered nonconforming goods. *In re Siskiyou Evergreens, Inc.*, CV no. 02–66975-fra11, 2004 Bankr. LEXIS 1044 (D. Ore. Mar. 29, 2004), available at http://cisgw3.law.pace.edu/cases/040329u2.html.

[53] Id., 16. Importantly, however, the court noted that "even though Global's notice to Sky Cast that there was a problem with its goods, in the sense that Global considered the late delivery of the goods to have violated the terms of their contract, was timely, such notice does not mean that Global will or should prevail on its counterclaim for breach of contract." Id., 16–17.

required by the contract."[54] Unless otherwise stipulated by the parties, the goods shall be fit for their ordinary purpose, such a purpose "made known to the seller at the time of the conclusion of the contract," or of the same quality as any models shown to the buyer, and they shall be packaged adequately.[55] Article 36 of the CISG further notes that the seller shall be liable for any lack of conformity in the goods "which exists at the time when the risk passes to the buyer"[56] or which results from the seller's breach of the contract.[57] However, Article 35 further states that a lack of conformity is not a viable argument if the buyer knew or should have known of its existence.[58]

1. Canada

When sued for payment, the buyer in *La San Giuseppe v. Forti Moulding Ltd.*[59] counterclaimed for damages,[60] alleging a lack of conformity arising from problems with cross-grain and curly grain, dents, mismatched colors, and warping.[61] The Ontario Superior Court of Justice found the buyer's testimony unconvincing, noting that the buyer had failed to give notice of the defects, that the small amount of defective merchandise introduced in evidence revealed only minor imperfections, and that the buyer had admitted other suppliers' goods were often defective "in the range of five to eight percent."[62] Consequently, the court rejected the buyer's claim based on a lack of conformity.[63]

In *Mansonville Plastics v. Kurtz*,[64] the buyer, a producer of Styrofoam blocks, alleged that the seller failed to produce the goods ("equipment used for the production of [Styrofoam] products") in conformity with the parties' contract. After the delivery of the equipment, the buyer complained to the seller of "problems with the fusion in the blocks."[65] In response, the seller sent two representatives and a technician to the buyer's plant to review and "fix the problems."[66] The issues with the equipment were addressed, though the buyer indicated that this was a temporary solution. Communications between the parties continued after the initial repair to the equipment, and the seller's representatives returned to the buyer's plant to further work on the equipment problems.[67] In June 1998, the seller sent a letter to the buyer indicating that the equipment was now mechanically sound. The buyer did not reply to this correspondence. Referring to CISG

---

[54] CISG, Article 35(1); see also *Ajax Tool Works v. Can-Eng Mfg.*, 2003 U.S. Dist. LEXIS 1306, at 10–11 (N.D. Ill. January 29, 2003), available at http://cisgw3.law.pace.edu/cases/030129u1.html.

[55] CISG, Article 35(2).

[56] CISG, Article 36(1).

[57] Id., (2).

[58] Id., (3). Additionally, pursuant to Article 39, a party may not rely on a lack of conformity claim if he fails to provide the seller with proper notice. See *supra* Part I.C.

[59] 1999 O.T.C. LEXIS 2163, para. 13 (Ont. Sup. C.J. 1999), available at http://cisgw3.law.pace.edu/cases/990831c4.html.

[60] The buyer sought damages for costs incurred from the alleged defects, including repairs, storage costs, labor and travel, and credits for overshipments. Id., para. 11.

[61] Id., para. 13.

[62] Id., paras. 34, 35, 37.

[63] Id., para. 39.

[64] *Mansonville Plastics (B.C.) Ltd. v. Kurtz GmbH*, [2003] B.C.J. No. 1958, paras. 2–3 (B.C. S.C. 2003), available at http://cisgw3.law.pace.edu/cases/030821c4.html.

[65] Id., para. 39.

[66] Id., paras. 40–1.

[67] Id., paras. 42–52.

Article 35 and local case law, the court found that the equipment satisfied the conformity requirement because it eventually fulfilled its purpose without further repairs.[68] Thus, despite initial equipment failures, the seller's efforts to repair and ultimately resolve the issues saved it from a claim of lack of conformity.

The conformity of goods case *Dunn Paving Ltd. v. Aerco Trading Inc.*[69] involved a contract for the sale of scrap metal from a seller's recycling business. The buyer complained that the scrap metal was contaminated with sand, and the parties negotiated over the issue. The seller filed suit for the alleged amount owed by the buyer for the scrap metal. In response to the buyer's argument that the contract should be interpreted under the Sale of Goods Act rather than the CISG, the court stated:

> The two acts are not dissimilar when they speak of sale by sample. In any event I find that even if this was a sale by sample, [the buyer] had ample time to inspect the goods when they arrived at the MAC scales and exercised any right of rejection by claiming the adjustment for "fines" as they arose. They were then given [a] credit . . . and adjustments [were] made.[70]

Additionally, the court noted that the buyer acquiesced to the method used to make the adjustments. In the end, the court found in favor of the seller, ordering the buyer to remit payment.

In response to the seller's suit for payment, in *Nova Tool & Mold Inc. v. London Industries Inc.*,[71] the buyer argued that the goods failed to conform. According to the terms of the contract, the molds were to be "free from defects" and "in full conformity with [the] specification, drawings, and data, and with [the] samples, labels and advertisements."[72] Testing revealed numerous problems with one of the molds. After the seller attempted to correct the problems, the mold still did not function properly and delayed the production process. In analyzing the breach of warranty claim, the court found that the buyer had not been able to build a supply of parts in order to send the mold for repair. The court granted recovery to the buyer for the amount of the costs of repair.

2. United States

In *Schmitz-Werke GmbH & Co. v. Rockland Indus., Inc.*,[73] an American seller of drapery fabric assured the German buyer that the fabric was suitable for transfer printing. The court concluded that the seller's representations regarding transfer printing constituted

---

[68] Id., paras. 83–8. "The equipment ultimately produced suitable EPS blocks but for some unidentified cause it could not do so for a period of time following its delivery. As a matter of law, the failure of the equipment to produce suitable EPS blocks does not establish that it was not reasonably fit for that purpose. As a matter of fact, I infer from the ability of the equipment to ultimately produce suitable EPS blocks without any repairs or alterations to its mechanical functioning that it was fit for its intended purpose at the time of its delivery. Hence, Kurtz did not breach the statutory warranty of fitness under either the Convention or the B.C. statute." Id., para. 88.

[69] *Dunn Paving Ltd. v. Aerco Trading Inc.*, 2001 O.T.C. LEXIS 295, para. 1 (O.T.C. 2001), available at http://cisgw3.law.pace.edu/cases/010501c4.html.

[70] Id., paras. 9–10.

[71] *Nova Tool & Mold Inc. v. London Indus. Inc.*, 1998 O.T.C. LEXIS 2176, para. 1 (O.T.C. 1998), available at http://cisgw3.law.pace.edu/cases/981216c4.html.

[72] Id., para. 51.

[73] *Schmitz-Werke GmbH & Co. v. Rockland Indus., Inc.*, 37 Fed. Appx. 687, 689 (4th Cir. 2002), available at http://cisgw3.law.pace.edu/cases/020621u1.html.

a "warranty of fitness for a particular purpose," and the fabric did not conform to that warranty.[74] The court did not demand that Schmitz-Werke "prove the exact mechanism of the defect"; rather, the court was satisfied with evidence that the printing process was "ordinary and competent."[75]

In *Chicago Prime Packers, Inc. v. Northam Food Trading Co.*,[76] the buyer refused to pay for pork back ribs purchased from the seller on the basis that they were delivered in an "off condition."[77] The court found that the buyer had the burden of proving the lack of conformity of the goods at the time of the transfer. It reasoned that although the CISG is unclear on this issue, *a comparison with the UCC* indicates that the burden should rest with the buyer.[78] The court then held that the buyer did not satisfy its burden because it "offered no credited evidence showing that the ribs were spoiled at the time of transfer or excluding the possibility that the ribs became spoiled after the transfer."[79]

Another court addressed the issue of nonconformity in *Medical Marketing v. Internazionale Medico Scientifica*,[80] in the context of exclusive sales rights to mammography equipment. Plaintiff filed suit after the U.S. Food and Drug Administration (FDA) seized the equipment based on a lack of compliance with administrative procedures. The issue in the case was which party was responsible for ensuring compliance with FDA's regulations. The court upheld the arbitration panel's ruling in favor of the buyer, agreeing that the seller "was, or should have been, aware of" the regulations. Notably, the court explained that the case at bar fit the exception to the rule that a "seller is generally not obligated to supply goods that conform to public laws and regulations enforced at the buyer's place of business."[81] The court pointed to a number of exceptions:

(1) if the public laws and regulations of the buyer's state are identical to those enforced in the seller's state; (2) if the buyer informed the seller about those regulations; or (3) if due to "special circumstances," such as the existence of a seller's branch office in the buyer's state, the seller knew or should have known about the regulations at issue.[82]

[74] Id. For a case that turned out the other way, see *Travelers Prop. Cas. Co. of Amer. v. Saint-Gobain Tech. Fabrics Canada Ltd.*, 474 F. Supp. 2d 1075, 1085 (D. Minn. 2007) available at http://cisgw3.law.pace.edu/cases/070131u1.html (denying a warranty of fitness for a particular purpose because there was no evidence that the seller "had reason to know that its [product, a type of mesh,] would be used for [the buyer's] particular purpose" by being incorporated into exterior walls at Denver's Pepsi Center arena).

[75] Id., 690–1.

[76] *Chi. Prime Packers, Inc. v. Northam Food Trading Co.*, 408F.3d 894, 895 (7th Cir. 2005), available at http://www.cisg.law.pace.edu/cisg/wais/db/cases2/050523u1.html.

[77] Id., 895.

[78] Id., 898.

[79] Id., 900. The buyer may also have to prove that the nonconformity was the proximate cause of the alleged damage. See *Barbara Berry, S.A. de C.V. v. Ken M. Spooner Farms, Inc.*, No. C05–5538, 2009 U.S. Dist. LEXIS 28377, at 18–19 (W.D. Wash. April 2, 2009), available at http://cisgw3.law.pace.edu/cases/090403u1.html (denying summary judgment and holding that a buyer claiming nonconformity of root plants must demonstrate not only that the defect existed in the plants at the time of delivery, but also that the defect was the proximate cause of the buyer's damages resulting from "malformed" and "crumbly" fruit).

[80] *Medical Mktg. Int'l, Inc. v. Internazionale Medico Scientifica, S.R.L.*, 1999 U.S. Dist. LEXIS 7380, at 1–2 (E.D. La. May 17, 1999), available at http://cisgw3.law.pace.edu/cases/990517u1.html.

[81] Id., 5–6 (citing Entscheidunger des Bundersgerichtshofs in Zivilsachen (BGHZ) 129, 75 (1995)).

[82] Id., 6. See also *In re Siskiyou Evergreens, Inc.*, CV no. 02–66975-fra11, 2004 Bankr. LEXIS 1044 (D. Ore. March 29, 2004), available at http://cisgw3.law.pace.edu/cases/040329u2.html (holding U.S. seller liable to Mexican buyer for nonconformity of Christmas trees, despite seller's argument that its Grade 3 trees were of better quality than some Grade 1 trees, where parties' contract called for sale of Grade 1 trees).

The seller in *Miami Valley Paper, LLC v. Lebbing Engineering & Consulting GmbH*[83] responded to buyer's claim of breach of warranty by arguing that the buyer "was aware of any alleged non-conformity at the time the parties concluded the contract."[84] Pursuant to CISG Article 35(3), the seller argued that the fact that the buyer's employees participated in the contract negotiations constituted the buyer's knowledge that the winder was equipped with a shaft. The buyer contended the evidence established "that it was not aware that the Winder was shafted and duplex."[85] Finding that substantial evidence supported the buyer's lack of knowledge of the nonconformity and other "genuine issues of material fact," the court declined to grant the seller's motion for summary judgment on the breach of warranty claim.[86]

The court in *Alpha Prime Development Corporation v. Holland Loader Company*[87] also found material issues of genuine fact when analyzing the parties' claims under CISG Articles 35 and 36. In this case, the buyer and seller disputed when and where the good at issue (coal mining equipment) was to be refurbished. There was contradictory evidence as to whether the parties agreed it would be refurbished in Mexico. The court further noted that there was some question regarding whether the parties agreed that the equipment was to be refurbished on delivery to Mexico. The court noted that this question was important because it determines whether risk had passed to the buyer under CISG Articles 36 and 69:

> Article 69(2) of the CISG governs the passage of risk "if the buyer is bound to take over the goods at a place other than a place of business of the seller." It provides that "the risk passes [to the buyer] when delivery is due and the buyer is aware of the fact that the goods are placed at his disposal at that place." . . . I find that there are genuine issues of material fact as to where APDC was bound to "take over" the [equipment], *i.e.*, at its point of origin in Montana or in Monclova, Mexico, and when it was required to "take over" the [equipment], *i.e.*, before or after it was refurbished.[88]

The court denied the portion of the motion for summary judgment, relying on Article 36, because it found genuine issues of material fact about whether or not the risk actually had transferred to the buyer.[89]

E. Nachfrist *Notice*

The German law concept of *Nachfrist*, or "[p]roviding an automatic extension of time for the parties to a commercial contract to fulfill their obligations,"[90] is incorporated in

---

[83] *Miami Valley Paper, LLC v. Lebbing Eng'g & Consulting GMBH*, 2009 U.S. Dist. LEXIS 25201, at 28–29 (S.D. Ohio March 26, 2009), available at http://cisgw3.law.pace.edu/cases/990517u1.html (the parties disputed whether the paper winder was to be shafted or shaftless).

[84] Id.

[85] Id.

[86] Id., 29–30.

[87] *Alpha Prime Dev. Corp. v. Holland Loader Co., LLC*, 2010 U.S. Dist. LEXIS 67591, at 15–17 (D. Colo. July 6, 2010), available at http://cisgw3.law.pace.edu/cases/100706u1.html.

[88] Id., 17.

[89] Id.

[90] Maryellen DiPalma, "Nachfrist Under National Law, the CISG, and the UNIDROIT, and European Principles: A Comparison," 5 *International Contract Adviser* 28–38 (Winter 1999), available at http://www.cisg.law.pace.edu/cisg/biblio/DiPalma.html.

CISG Articles 47 (Buyer's Notice Fixing Additional Final Period for Performance) and 63 (Seller's Notice Fixing Additional Final Period for Performance). However, as Maryellen DiPalma notes, the CISG's concept of *Nachfrist* is nonmandatory, distinguishing it from the principle existing in German law.[91] Thus, Articles 47 and 63 provide that the buyer and seller may allow the other party more time to fulfill their contractual obligations.

In a recent U.S. decision, *Valero Marketing & Supply Company v. Greeni Trading Oy*,[92] the buyer entered an agreement with the seller for the purchase of naphtha, a liquid component of gasoline. The contract provided that the buyer had the right to approve the shipping vessel used for delivery. Despite this provision, the seller shipped the naphtha on a vessel of which the buyer had disapproved. Thereafter, the parties entered into a new agreement for offloading of the naphtha by barge and for an extension of time for delivery in exchange for a price reduction.[93] Article 47 states that "the buyer may not, during that period, resort to any remedy for breach of contract."[94] Based on this language, the lower court held that the second agreement was ineffective because the buyer could not require the seller to enter into the new contract.[95] The appellate court, however, reversed and held that the subsequent agreement was a "permissible contract modification under Article 29, rather than an extension of time for performance under Article 47 of the CISG."[96] The higher court's reasoning highlighted the fact that the seller did not claim duress; rather, the seller agreed to the new contract.[97]

F. *Fundamental Breach*

Article 25 of the CISG defines "fundamental breach" as a breach that "results in such detriment to the other party as substantially to deprive him of what he is entitled to expect under the contract, unless the party in breach did not foresee and a reasonable person of the same kind in the same circumstances would not have foreseen such a result."[98] As discussed in the following, this definition has been the subject of much interpretive debate in the courts.

1. Canada

Diversitel Communications Inc. v. Glacier Bay Inc.[99] involved a claim for a breach of contract regarding the sale of vacuum panel insulation. Although the contract set forth a specific delivery schedule, the seller failed to meet it due to issues with its own supplier.[100] The buyer terminated the contract and filed suit for monies paid; the seller counterclaimed for breach of contract. In particular, the buyer alleged that the seller's

[91] Id.

[92] *Valero Mktg. & Supply Co. v. Greeni Oy*, 242 Fed. Appx. 840, 841 (3d Cir. 2007), available at http://cisgw3.law.pace.edu/cases/070719u2.html.

[93] Id.

[94] CISG, Article 47.

[95] *Valero Mktg.*, 242 Fed. Appx. at 843–44.

[96] Id., 845.

[97] Id.

[98] CISG, Article 25.

[99] *Diversitel Commc'ns Inc. v. Glacier Bay Inc.*, [2003] O.J. No. 4025, paras. 1, 5 (Ont. Sup. C.J. 2003), abstract available at http://cisgw3.law.pace.edu/cases/031006c4.html.

[100] Id., para. 6.

failure to comply with the delivery schedule was a fundamental breach under Article 25.[101] Furthermore, the buyer argued that its position was supported by Article 33's delivery requirement.[102] The court was not persuaded by the buyer's contention that the CISG establishes a "lower threshold for the proof of fundamental breach than that required by the common law."[103] Nevertheless, the court found that the failure to deliver on time did constitute a fundamental breach even under common law, as the parties had made time of the essence in the contract's performance.[104]

2. United States

In *Magellan International v. Salzgitter Handel*,[105] the court explained that the "plain language" of Articles 25 and 72 indicate that a party claiming anticipatory repudiation "need simply allege that the defendant intended to breach the contract before the contract's performance date and that such breach was fundamental." In *Magellan* the buyer demanded an amendment to the bill of lading required in the contract. The seller took this unilateral demand as the buyer's intent to breach the contract if the stipulated, nonamended bill of lading was delivered. The seller contended that the bill of lading was "an essential part of the parties' bargain."[106] The court agreed, holding that the buyer's insistence on the amendment constituted a fundamental breach.[107]

In *Shuttle Packaging Systems v. Tsonakis*,[108] the buyer made numerous complaints about defects in the goods during delivery and training. The equipment eventually operated as promised by the seller. However, the court concluded that these complaints tended to be "opportunistic and not genuine in character."[109] Thus, any "non-conformities" with the equipment did not amount to a fundamental breach. Accordingly, it was the buyer's failure to pay, in light of the nature of its complaints, that constituted a fundamental breach.

Doolim Corp. v. R. Doll, LLC[110] involved a set of contracts for the sale of women's clothing items made to the buyer's specifications, including the branding of the buyer's trademark. Although it had received several of the ordered garments, the buyer paid only a portion of the total amount due to the seller. The parties eventually agreed that the buyer would pay in installments and provide the seller with a letter of credit to secure the remaining shipments. When the buyer failed to meet the terms of this new agreement, the seller withheld shipment of the garments. Given the trademarked nature of the goods,

[101] Id., para. 27.
[102] Id.
[103] Id.
[104] Id., paras. 34–6.
[105] *Magellan Int'l Corp. v. Salzgitter Handel GmbH*, 76 F. Supp. 2d 919, 925–926 (N.D. Ill. 1999), available at http://cisgw3.law.pace.edu/cases/991207u1.html.
[106] Id.
[107] It should be noted that in a civil jury trial, as is found in the American legal system, the issue of fundamental breach may be an issue of fact to be decided by a jury. Such was the case in *Miami Valley Paper, LLC v. Lebbing Engineering & Consulting GmbH.*: *Miami Valley Paper, LLC v. Lebbing Eng'g & Consulting GMBH*, 2009 U.S. Dist. LEXIS 25201 (S.D. Ohio March 26, 2009), available at http://cisgw3.law.pace.edu/cases/090326u1.html.
[108] *Shuttle Packaging Sys. v. Tsonakis*, 2001 U.S. Dist. LEXIS 21630, at 28 (W.D. Mich. December 17, 2001), available at http://cisgw3.law.pace.edu/cases/011217u1.html.
[109] Id.
[110] 2009 WL 1514913 (S.D.N.Y. May 29, 2009), available at http://cisgw3.law.pace.edu/cases/090529u1.html.

the seller was not able to resell the goods. The seller was thus liable for the full contract price.[111]

G. *Price Reduction Remedy*

If the goods received fail to conform to the contract specifications, CISG Article 50 allows the buyer to "reduce the price in the same proportion as the value that the goods actually delivered had at the time of the delivery bears to the value that conforming goods would have had at that time." This is true regardless of whether the buyer has already paid for the goods. Importantly, however, the CISG also states that the buyer may not reduce the price for the goods if the seller remedies the goods or if he or she refuses to accept the seller's remedy.

A reason for a seller to reject a buyer's price reduction is that the documents were non-conforming but the goods received and accepted were conforming. One U.S. court reasoned that "[t]he Vienna Convention may permit a proportionate reduction in price for non-conforming goods, but [seller] stipulated here that the goods delivered to [buyer] were conforming. Accordingly, [buyer] had no legal justification for withholding payment."[112] As to the amount of the buyer's unilateral price reduction, another U.S. court held that the resale price of nonconforming goods was probative evidence of the reasonableness of the price reduction.[113] In that regard, the court held that "it is well settled that the price obtained for defective goods on resale is probative of the value of the goods as actually received."[114]

H. *Remedies: Avoidance and Damages*

Taking account of many of the usual issues involved with contract disputes, the CISG provides some guidance for analyzing avoidance and damages claims. In particular, Article 49 provides a buyer with a right to avoid a contract if the seller fundamentally breaches the agreement.[115] The buyer may also avoid the contract if the seller fails to deliver the goods in accordance with Article 47. Notably, Article 49 limits the buyer's right of avoidance if the goods have already been delivered unless he or she does so within a reasonable amount of time. Article 64 provides the seller with an opportunity

---

[111] Id., 6. The fundamental nature of the breach in other cases may not be so clear. So, in *Banks Hardwoods Florida LLC v. Maderas Iglesias, S.A.*, No. 08–23497-CIV, 2009 U.S. Dist. LEXIS 101452 (S.D. Fla. October 29, 2009), available at http://cisgw3.law.pace.edu/cases/091029u1.html, the court denied summary judgment due to issues of fact surrounding whether the nonconformity of the Spanish seller's lumber was "slight" or whether it was sufficiently fundamental to allow the buyer to avoid the contract. Id., 4–5.

[112] *S.V. Braun, Inc. v. Alitalia-Linee Aeree Italiane, S.p.A*, 1994 U.S. Dist. LEXIS 4114, at 1, 1–2 (S.D.N.Y. April 6, 1994), available at http://cisgw3.law.pace.edu/cases/940406u1.html.

[113] *Interag Co. v. Stafford Phase Corp.*, 1990 U.S. Dist. LEXIS 6134 (S.D.N.Y. May 22, 1990), available at http://cisgw3.law.pace.edu/cases/900522u1.html.

[114] Id., 12 (citing *Lackawanna Leather Co. v. Martin & Stewart, Ltd.*, 730 F.2d 1197, 1203 (8th Cir. 1984), available at http://openjurist.org/730/f2d/1197/lackawanna-leather-company-v-martin-and-stewart-ltd.).

[115] CISG, Article 49(1)(a); Article 49 is generally analyzed in conjunction with CISG, Article 25, which defines "fundamental breach." See, e.g., *Miami Valley Paper, LLC v. Lebbing Eng'g & Consulting GmbH*, 2009 U.S. Dist. LEXIS 25201, at 16–17 (S.D. Ohio Mar. 26, 2009), available at http://cisgw3.law.pace.edu/cases/090326u1.html; *Medical Mktg. Int'l, Inc. v. Internazionale Medico Scientifica, S.R.L.*, 1999 U.S. Dist. LEXIS 7380, at 5–7 (E.D. La. May 17, 1999), available at http://cisgw3.law.pace.edu/cases/990517u1.html (upholding an arbitral decision that avoidance of the contract was proper due to a fundamental breach).

to avoid the contract if the buyer fails to perform its obligations. Additionally, Article 72 allows for avoidance based on anticipatory breach of contract. Finally, as one court put it, Articles 71 through 73 "afford both buyer and seller the right to suspend or avoid an installment contract due to fundamental breach."[116]

Article 74 sets forth the foreseeability standard for calculating damages.[117] Article 74 states that: "Such damages may not exceed the loss which the party in breach foresaw or ought to have foreseen at the time of the conclusion of the contract, in the light of the facts and matters of which he then knew or ought to have known, as a possible consequence of the breach of contract." Article 74 "is 'designed to place the aggrieved party in as good a position as if the other party had properly performed the contract.'"[118]

The 1995 case *Delchi Carrier Spa v. Rotorex Corporation*[119] remains the clearest statement of the scope of damages under the CISG, viewed from a U.S. perspective. There, the buyer complained of defects with the first of three scheduled shipments of air conditioning compressors. Specifically, the buyer notified the seller that a majority of the compressors from the first shipment did not comply with the sample compressor and specifications. After the seller declined to replace the goods, the buyer terminated the agreement. The seller disputed the buyer's claim for lost profits and contended that its own acts did not constitute a breach of the contract. The court found that the defects in the compressors constituted a fundamental breach under the CISG. The court awarded lost profits because the nonconformity forced the buyer to shut down its plant, which resulted in the loss of existing sales contracts. Finally, reasoning that lost profits would not make the buyer whole for all expenses incurred, the court found that the additional costs for expedited shipping of replacement goods, for customs, and for labor to repair the nonconforming goods were all recoverable.[120]

---

[116] *Shuttle Packaging Sys. v. Tsonakis*, 2001 U.S. Dist. LEXIS 21630, at 27 (W.D. Mich. December 17, 2001), available at http://cisgw3.law.pace.edu/cases/011217u1.html.

[117] CISG, Article 74. Courts have also stressed the importance of a party demonstrating the foreseeability of damages. See, e.g., *Al Hewar Environmental & Public Health Establishment v. Southeast Ranch LLC*, No. 10–80851-CV-Hurley/Hopkins, 2011 U.S. Dist. LEXIS 128723 (S.D. Fla. Nov. 7, 2011), available at http://cisgw3.law.pace.edu/cases/111107u1.html; *Ajax Tool Works v. Can-Eng Mfg.*, 2003 U.S. Dist. LEXIS 1306 (N.D. Ill. Jan. 29, 2003), available at http://cisgw3.law.pace.edu/cases/030129u1.html. As the *Ajax* court stated: "It is undisputed that the parties' agreement states that 'CAN-ENG shall not be liable for consequential damages.' As discussed above, such limited liability provision is enforceable under the CISG. Further, although Article 74 of the CISG provides for consequential damages, 'such damages may not exceed the loss which the party in breach foresaw or ought to have foreseen at the time of the conclusion of the contract, in the light of the facts and matters of which he then knew or ought to have known, as a possible consequence of the breach of contract ... Because Ajax did not address this point in its response memorandum, as best this court can tell, Ajax has not introduced any evidence that the consequential damages sought were foreseeable to Can-Eng. For these reasons and because there are no facts disputed, summary judgment is granted as to consequential damages." Id., 19–20 (internal citations omitted).

[118] *Delchi Carrier Spa v. Rotorex Corp.*, 71 F.3d 1024, 1029 (2d Cir. 1995), available at http://cisgw3.law.pace.edu/cases/951206u1.html (quoting *Uniform Law for International Sales under the 1980 United Nations Convention*, 2nd ed. (ed. John Honnold) (Deventer and Boston: Kluwer, 1991), 503).

[119] *Delchi Carrier Spa*, 71 F.3d at 1026–7.

[120] Id., 1030–1. The court, however, remanded for further proceedings in the lower court the question of whether or not the labor costs were variable or fixed. Id., 1031. For another recent judicial discussion of damages under the CISG, see *TeeVee Toons, Inc. v. Gerhard Schubert GmbH*, 00Civ. 5189, 2006 U.S. Dist. LEXIS 59455, at *32 (S.D. N.Y. August 22, 2006), available at http://cisgw3.law.pace.edu/cases/020329u1.html (granting summary judgment on various claims for damages).

In a related vein, several courts have reviewed the issue of whether or not attorneys' fees for a breach of contract claim are allowable in damage claims governed by the CISG. In the case of *Chicago Prime Packers, Inc. v. Northam Food Trading Co.*,[121] the prevailing party requested an award of attorneys' fees in addition to damages for breach of contract. The court denied the request because such fees do not constitute a "loss" in the context of Article 74.[122] Additionally, the court explained that "A claim for attorney's fees is a procedural matter governed by the law of the forum" rather than by the CISG.[123]

In the area of avoidance, nonpayment and nondelivery are quintessential cases of fundamental breach. In *Shuttle Packaging Systems v. Tsonakis*,[124] the court found that the buyer's failure to pay – despite its complaints of nonconformity, which the court found to be not genuine – constituted a fundamental breach. More particularly, the court stated that Article 64 indicates that a failure to pay is "the most significant form of a fundamental breach by a buyer," and, as a result, it demands "no additional notifications . . . for avoidance of the contract."[125] In *Doolim Corp. v. R Doll LLC*,[126] the seller canceled the contract because of the buyer's persistent failure, in respect of previous installments, to pay the agreed-upon price. As stated in CISG Article 72, "If prior to the date for performance of the contract it is clear that one of the parties will commit a fundamental breach of contract, the other party may declare the contract avoided." In *Doolim Corp.*, the buyer failed to secure a required letter of credit for subsequent shipments. Consequently, the court held that the seller was entitled to choose one of two remedies under CISG Articles 75–76: (1) resell the goods within a reasonable time and in a reasonable manner and recover the difference between the resale price and the contract price (in addition to any foreseeable consequential losses) or (2) recover the difference between the current price and the contract price as damages, with the current price defined as the price at

---

[121] *Chi. Prime Packers, Inc. v. Northam Food Trading Co.*, 320 F. Supp. 2d 702, 715 (N.D. Ill. 2004), available at http://www.cisg.law.pace.edu/cases/040521u1.html, *aff'd*, 408 F.3d 894 (7th Cir. 2005).

[122] Id., 716–17 (citing *Zapata Hermanos Sucesores, S.A. v. Hearthside Baking Co., Inc.*, 313 F.3d 385, 389 (7th Cir. 2002), available at http://cisgw3.law.pace.edu/cases/021119u1.html).

[123] Id., 717 (citing *Ajax Tool Works v. Can-Eng Mfg.*, 2003 U.S. Dist. LEXIS 1306, at 20–21 (N.D. Ill. Jan. 29, 2003), available at http://cisgw3.law.pace.edu/cases/030129u1.html). See also *In re San Lucio*, 2009 U.S. Dist. LEXIS 31681, at 4, 10–11 (D.N.J. April 15, 2009), available at http://cisgw3.law.pace.edu/cases/090415u1.html (applying U.S. law to the issue of attorneys' fees because the CISG is "silent" about them); *ECEM European Chemical Mktg. B.V. v. Purolite Co.*, No. 05–3078, 2010 U.S. Dist. LEXIS 109893 (E.D. Pa. October 14, 2010), available at http://cisgw3.law.pace.edu/cases/100129u1.html (holding that an award of attorneys' fees, in a dispute governed by the CISG, was proper where called for by a written agreement of the parties).

U.S. courts have similarly awarded prejudgment interest to the prevailing party in CISG-governed disputes, using a variety of rationales. See *Zeeco, Inc. v. Sivec SRL*, No. 10-CV-143-JHP, 2012 U.S. Dist. LEXIS 2557 5–6 (E.D. Okla. January 12, 2012), available at http://cisgw3.law.pace.edu/cases/120109u1.html (awarding prejudgment interest under the auspices of CISG, Article 78); *ECEM European Chemical Mktg. B.V. v. Purolite Co.*, 451 Fed. Appx. 73 (3d Cir. 2011), available at http://cisgw3.law.pace.edu/cases/111109u1.html (affirming award of prejudgment interest and finding, alternatively, that if Pennsylvania law applies award was mandatory or that if CISG applies the award was within the trial court's broad discretion); *Waterside Ocean Navigation Co., Inc. v. Int'l Navigation Ltd.*, 737 F.2d 150, 153–4 (2d Cir. 1984) (confirming award of prejudgment interest on arbitration award in case governed by the CISG, noting inter alia that the CISG is silent on the issue).

[124] *Shuttle Packaging Sys. v. Tsonakis*, 2001 U.S. Dist. LEXIS 21630, at 27–28 (W.D. Mich. December 17, 2001), available at http://cisgw3.law.pace.edu/cases/011217u1.html.

[125] Id.

[126] 2009 WL 1514913 (S.D.N.Y. May 29, 2009), available at http://cisgw3.law.pace.edu/cases/090529u1.html.

the place of delivery. An interesting sidebar is that the court allowed the seller to sell the goods in its possession even though they included the buyer's trademark.

The case of *Usinor Industeel v. Leeco Steel Products*[127] broached the issue of third-party rights. The seller sold steel to a buyer, which in turn resold the steel to other parties. The parties' contract stipulated that the seller retained rights to the goods until it received complete payment from the buyer. When the buyer failed to remit full payment, the seller sought replevin or, in the alternative, avoidance of the contract. Reasoning that the CISG applies only to the buyer and seller of the contract, the court denied the seller's motion.[128] More particularly, the court stated that, "The Convention will not override the rights of creditors, purchasers and other third persons granted by domestic law; under Article 4."[129] Thus, because the third-party bank retained a valid interest in the steel, the seller could not recover the goods.

I. *Mitigation*

When a buyer rejects goods on the basis of lack of conformity or for other reasons, the CISG requires the buyer to take steps to limit its losses and to preserve any goods in its possession.[130] If a rejecting buyer fails to mitigate its damages, the nonbreaching seller may reduce the damages owed by the amount of damages that could have been mitigated by the buyer.[131] Thus, where a buyer repaired a defective mold, the Canadian court held it to be a proper act of mitigation in light of the seller's inability to keep the production on schedule and numerous problems with two of the seller's molds.[132] A U.S. court also deemed the use of the nonconforming goods for other purposes a proper act of mitigation in a case involving breach of the warranty of fitness for a particular purpose.[133]

The reselling of goods either by the buyer (nonconformity) or by seller (failure to pay) is generally considered a reasonable act of mitigation. However, the means or process of the resale may be scrutinized by the courts. In one case, a buyer challenged the appropriateness of the seller's resale of goods after the buyer breached the contract.[134] The court determined that the mitigation efforts were reasonable because the seller sold the goods for the "highest possible prices" only seventeen days after receiving notice of

---

[127] *Usinor Industeel v. Leeco Steel Prods.*, 209 F. Supp. 2d 880, 881–82 (N.D. Ill. 2002), available at http://cisgw3.law.pace.edu/cases/020328u1.html.

[128] Id., 885–6, 889. Where third party rights are involved, the CISG may not even apply. See *Cedar Petrochemical v. Dongbu Hannong Chemical Co. Ltd.*, No. 06 Civ. 3972, 2007 U.S. Dist. LEXIS 51802 (S.D.N.Y. July 19, 2007), available at http://cisgw3.law.pace.edu/cases/070719u1.html, in which the court held the CISG inapplicable to determination of the rights of a Spanish buyer of phenol, despite the fact the CISG governed the underlying breach of contract claim between the U.S. seller and its supplier in South Korea.

[129] *Usinor Steel*, 209 F. Supp. 2d. at 885.

[130] CISG, Articles 77, 86–7.

[131] CISG, Article 77.

[132] *Nova Tool & Mold Inc. v. London Indus. Inc.*, 1998 O.T.C. LEXIS 2176 (O.T.C. 1998), available at http://cisgw3.law.pace.edu/cases/981216c4.html; see also *supra* Part I.D.1. Please note that the court opinions only mention the CISG with respect to the sections cited by the buyer. The opinions cite only Canadian cases and doctrine.

[133] *Schmitz-Werke GmbH & Co. v. Rockland Indus., Inc.*, 37 Fed. Appx. 687 (4th Cir. 2002), available at http://cisgw3.law.pace.edu/cases/020621u1.html; see also discussion at Part I.D.2.

[134] *Treibacher Industrie, A.G. v. Allegheny Technologies, Inc.*, 464 F.3d 1235, 1236 (11th Cir. 2006), *available at* http://cisgw3.law.pace.edu/cases/060912u1.html.

avoidance from the buyer.[135] Furthermore, the buyer did not prove that the seller's acts were unreasonable.

J. Excuse (Impediment)

CISG Article 79 excuses a party from liability if he or she provides the other party timely notice[136] of his or her inability to perform, and if he or she proves the failure to perform "was due to an impediment beyond his control and that he could not reasonably been expected to have taken into account at the time of the conclusion of the contract or to have avoided or overcome it, or its consequences."[137] There is no existing case law in Canada applying Article 79, but there are a number of cases from the United States. In *Macromex Srl. v. Globex International, Inc.*,[138] the court found that the alleged impediment actually could have been reasonably avoided or overcome. In that case, which involved an installment contract, the seller was notified that the goods could not be imported into the buyer's country without certification from the buyer's government as of a certain date. When installments remained undelivered after the effective date of the new certification requirements, the seller claimed the new certification requirements were an impediment that excused it from the contract. In arbitration, the seller argued that its delays in shipment were within the industry's informal standard of flexibility, and that the government's ban was a *force majeure* event. The arbitrator found that the delay in shipment itself was not a fundamental breach, but he did rule that the ban on shipment of forty-two containers could have been overcome by a substituted performance (delivery to a bordering country) as had been requested by the buyer. The arbitrator noted that other U.S. suppliers had done exactly that to avoid the import ban and also that the seller's refusal to do so enabled it to take advantage of a contemporaneous jump in the market price of the goods. Thus, the seller's claim of excuse was rejected.

II. Summary

The relative paucity of CISG case law in the Canada and the United States,[139] together with a reluctance to look outside national jurisprudence, often makes it difficult to predict a court's particular interpretation of the CISG. Combined there were only six cases referencing the principle of good faith (all from the United States); four cases on

---

[135] Id., 1239–40.

[136] CISG, Article 79(4).

[137] CISG, Article 79(1).

[138] 08 Civ. 114, 2008 WL 1752530 (S.D.N.Y., April 16, 2008), available at http://cisgw3.law.pace.edu/cases/080416u1.html. See also *Hilaturas Miel, S.L. v. Republic of Iraq*, 573 F. Supp. 2d 781 (S.D.N.Y. 2008), available at http://cisgw3.law.pace.edu/cases/080820u1.html (a contract between a Spanish seller and the Iraqi government as a buyer of 500,000 metric tons of acrylic yarn; finding an excuse when the contract required inspections of the goods, and that became impossible due to the outbreak of war in Iraq in March 2003); *Raw Materials Inc. v. Manfred Forberich GmbH & Co., KG*, No. 03 C 1154 (N.D. Ill. July 6, 2004), available at http://cisgw3.law.pace.edu/cases/040706u1.html (ruling that in a dispute concerning the freezing over of the St. Petersburg, Russia, port from which a German firm was to deliver 15,000–18,000 metric tons of used railroad rail, factual issues as to the German firm's defense of *force majeure* were presented, so the Illinois purchaser's summary judgment motion for a finding of breach of contract was denied).

[139] As of October 5, 2013, there were 161 cases for the United States and 20 for Canada in the CISG Pace database, available at http://www.cisg.law.pace.edu/cisg/text/casecit.html.

impediment (all from the United States); and two cases on mitigation and preservation. The areas where there is a larger body of case law include contract formation (23 U.S., 2 Canada); battle of the forms (21 U.S., 3 Canada); conformity of goods, inspection, and notice under CISG Articles 38–40 (12 U.S., 3 Canada); fundamental breach and *Nachfrist* notice (16 U.S., 3 Canada); damages and remedies (40 U.S., 5 Canada); and avoidance (13 U.S., 3 Canada). In Canada, more cases may be proceeding to litigation, but perhaps not: the numbers are too small to be at all certain. From one CISG case reaching its final, reported court opinion in 1999, to two in 2000, and to one each in 2001 and 2002, the numbers rose to three cases in 2003, four each in 2004 and 2005, and then down to just one in 2007, one in 2009, and two in 2011. If one allows for a time lag in cases getting into the Pace database, perhaps the downturn after 2005 is not remarkable.

To generalize about the particulars of CISG jurisprudence in these countries is difficult because the number of cases on any topic remains small. At some point U.S. courts will need to stop simply relying on provisions of the Uniform Commercial Code by analogy instead of the CISG case law.[140] And notably, the U.S. courts have routinely failed to study or apply precedents in other countries interpreting the CISG. So, for instance, the court in *Raw Materials Inc. v. Manfred Forberich GmbH & Co., KG*[141] stated that "no American court has specifically interpreted or applied Article 79 of the CISG" and ignored the case law on CISG Article 79 created by the courts of Austria, Belgium, Bulgaria, China, Finland, France, Germany, Hungary, Israel, Italy, Netherlands, Russia, and Switzerland, as well as by International Chamber of Commerce arbitrators.[142]

There is still hope that the Canada and the United States will move away from homeward trend-biased decisions and embrace CISG Article 7's call for autonomous interpretations based on the international character of the convention and the need for uniformity of application. There have been a number of well-reasoned Canadian and American cases that followed that path. For example, in *MCC-Marble Ceramic Center Inc. v. Ceramica Nuova D'Agostino Spa*,[143] a U.S. federal appeals court set aside the domestic law application of the parol evidence rule in favor of the CISG's lack of a such a rule. Going forward, familiarity with the CISG – in the courts and for the bar – is on the rise. That, in turn, should lead to increased confidence about the CISG and its contribution to unifying international sales law.

---

[140] See, e.g., *Raw Materials Inc. v. Manfred Forberich GmbH & Co., KG*, No. 03 C 1154, 2004 U.S. Dist. LEXIS 12510 (N.D. Ill. July 6, 2004), available at http://cisgw3.law.pace.edu/cases/040706u1.html (finding no U.S. precedent on CISG Article 79 and turning then to case law interpreting the UCC's provision on excuse, UCC §2–615).

[141] No. 03 C 1154 (N.D. Ill. July 6, 2004), available at http://cisgw3.law.pace.edu/cases/040706u1.html.

[142] See http://cisgw3.law.pace.edu/cisg/text/anno-art-79.html; see also Albert H. Kritzer, Comments on *Raw Materials Inc. v. Manfred Forberich*, U.S. District Court [Illinois], July 6, 2004 (2005), available at http:// www.cisg.law.pace.edu/cisg/biblio/kritzer3.html (February 2005) ("Relevant to such case law is the rule recited by the Solicitor General of the United States. He quotes the U.S. Supreme Court as follows in his brief in the case of *Zapata Hermanos v. Hearthside Baking*, available at http://cisgw3.law.pace.edu/cisg/ biblio/zapata4.html ('[J]udicial decisions from other countries interpreting a treaty term are "entitled to considerable weight."' *El Al Israel Airlines Ltd. v. Tsui Yan Tseng*, 525 U.S. 155, 176 (1999) (quoting *Air France v. Saks*, 470 U.S. 392, 404 (1985))".

[143] 144 F.3d 1384, 1389 (11th Cir. 1998), available at http://cisgw3.law.pace.edu/cases/980629u1.html.

35 Central and South America

Virginia G. Maurer

I. Introduction

The major economies of Central and South America are, or soon will be, signatories to the CISG.[1] However, most of the CISG case law is found in Argentina and Mexico. The case commentaries in this chapter are organized by country and within countries by relevant topics. After almost twenty years, Professor Garro's observation that the "Latin American experience in the unification of private substantive law... has not been very significant"[2] still holds. Further, for the most part, the CISG cases coming from these countries do not reference foreign CISG case law. This is despite a deep legal literature on the importance of following CISG interpretive methodology in order to achieve the harmonizing goal of uniformity of application,[3] as well as a history of unification of law efforts in Central and South America.[4]

II. Argentina

Argentina's early experience with the CISG was marked by a pair of cases in which the CISG was acknowledged as the law of Argentina. In both cases the issue was validity of a forum clause. Validity of terms is outside the scope of the CISG, pursuant to CISG

---

[1] The CISG entered into effect in central and south American countries in the following years: Argentina (1988), Chile (1991), Colombia (2002), Cuba (1995), Dominican Republic (July 2011), Ecuador (1993), El Salvador (2007), Honduras (2003), Mexico (1989), Paraguay (2007), Peru (2000), and Uruguay (2000). Brazil is expected to adopt the CISG in 2013.

[2] Alejandro M. Garro, "Unification and Harmonization of Private Law in Latin America," 40 *American J. Comparative L.* 587–616, 587 (1992).

[3] See, e.g., Jorge Oviedo Alban, Liza Urbina Galiano, and Nunez Laura Posada, "The Formation of the Contract on the UNIDROIT Principle for International Commercial Contracts (Compared with Colombian regulations)," J. Universitas No. 96 of the Pontifical Javeriana University (June 1999), available at http://cisg.law.pace.edu/cisg/biblio/oviedoalban1.html; Maximiliano Rodriguez Fernandez, "Concept and Scope of the Duty to Mitigate Harm in International Law of Contracts, Private Law Journal No. 15," External U. of Colombia 95 (2008), available at http://cisg.law.pace.edu/cisg/biblio/rodriguez-fernandez. html; Alberto L. Zuppi, "A Comparison of Buyer's Remedies under the CISG with the Latin American Legal Tradition, *Pace Review of the Convention on Contracts for the International Sale of Goods* (1999)," available at http://www.cisg.law.pace.edu/cisg/biblio/zuppi/html.

[4] See Antonio Boggiano, "The Experience of Latin American States," in *International Uniform Law in Practice, Acts and Proceedings of the 3rd Congress on Private Law* (Oxford University Press, 1987), 28–47.

Article 4.[5] In the *Elastar Sacifia v. Bettcher Industries*,[6] the court used domestic gap filling under Article 7(2)[7] and the application of trade usage under Article 9(1)[8] to uphold the seller's right to payment of interest. Again, in *Aguila Refractarios v. Conc. Preventivo*,[9] the court used international trade usage pursuant to Article 9(1) to fill in a gap in the contract.[10]

A. *Contract Formation*

In *Quilmes Combustibles S.A. v. Vigan S.A. (Quilmes)*[11] and *Inta v. Officina Meccanica (Inta)*,[12] the courts addressed the issue of the enforceability of forum selection clauses. More specifically, the issue was whether the clause was incorporated into the contract as a standard term. In *Quilmes*, an Argentine buyer claimed damages against a French seller because the goods were delayed and nonconforming. On the back of its invoice form, the French seller included a choice of forum clause specifying jurisdiction of French courts. The Argentine buyer sought to void the clause under Argentine law. The court held that the buyer's acceptance of the seller's standard form was the basis of the contract. The buyer also argued that for the clause to be enforceable, the buyer had to agree specifically, in writing, to the incorporation of the forum selection clause into the contract. The court disagreed and dismissed the case due to lack of jurisdiction.[13]

In *Inta*, the choice of forum clause arose again in the context of an Argentine buyer and an Italian seller, which had included in its invoice a choice of forum clause specifying the court of Bergamo, Italy. On appeal, the buyer raised, for the first time, the applicability of the CISG. The court accepted that the CISG was inapplicable on the issue the validity of the contract. Nonetheless, the buyer's endorsement of the invoice, made to

---

[5] October 20, 1989, Juzgado Nacional de Primera Instancia en lo Commercial Buenos Aires, *Quilmes Combustibles v. Vigan*, available at http://cisgw3.law.pace.edu/cases/89102a1.html; March 15, 1991, Appellate Court, available at http://cisgw3.law.pace.edu/cases/910315a1.html. See Larry A. DiMatteo et al., "The Interpretive Turn in International Sales Law: An Analysis of Fifteen Years of CISG Jurisprudence," 34 *Northwestern J. of Int'l L. & Business* 229–440, n. 295.

[6] May 20, 1991, Juzgado Nacional de Primera Instancia en lo Commercial, available at http://cisgw3.law.pace.edu/cases/910520a1.html.

[7] Article 7(2) states: "Questions concerning matters governed by this Convention which are not expressly settled in it are to be settled in conformity with the general principles on which it is based or, in the absence of such principles, in conformity with the law applicable by virtue of the rules of private international law."

[8] Article 9 states: "(1) The parties are bound by any usage to which they have agreed and by any practices which they have established between themselves; (2) The parties are considered, under otherwise agreed, to have impliedly made applicable to their contract or its formation a usage of which the parties knew or ought to have known and which in international trade is widely known to, and regularly observed by, parties to contracts of the type involved in the particular trade concerned."

[9] October 23, 1991, Juzgado Comercial de Primera Instancia en lo Comercial, *Aguila Refractarios v. Conc. Preventivo*, available at http://cisgw3.law.pace.edu/cases/911023a1.html.

[10] See also October 6, 1994, Juzgado Comercial de Primera Instancia en lo Comercial, *Bermatex v. Valentin Rius*, available at http://cisgw3.law.pace.edu/cases/941006a1.html (same).

[11] March 15, 1991, Camara Nacional de Apelaciones en lo Comercial, Division C, *Quilmes Combustibles S.A. v. Vigan S.A.*, available at http://cisgw3.law.pace.edu/cases/910315a1.html.

[12] 14–15 October 1993, Camara Nacional de Apelaciones en lo Comercial, *Inta v. Officina Meccanica*, available at http://cisgw3.law.pace.edu/cases/931014a1.html.

[13] A more complete and nuanced analysis was made by Professor Alejandro M. Garro, "The U.N. Sales Convention in the Americas: Recent Developments," 17 *J. L. & Commerce* 219, 222–34 (1998).

obtain financing of the transaction, together with it having paid for the goods, constituted performance of an act sufficient to signify acceptance, which would have been the case under CISG Article 18(3). The court upheld the lower court ruling and dismissed the case for lack of jurisdiction.[14]

B. *Conformity of Goods: Inspection and Notice*

In 2007, the Court of Commercial Appeals heard an appeal from the buyer seeking to avoid paying for goods on the ground of nonconformity.[15] The Chilean seller shipped almonds to the Argentine buyer through a third party carrier. The buyer claimed that the almonds were not of the size required by the contract. The buyer resold the almonds without notifying the seller of the nonconformity and then refused to pay for the almonds. The seller brought suit in Argentina. The lower court incorrectly reasoned that because the CISG did not provide criteria for determining conformity, rules of private international law, pursuant to Article 7(2), controlled. The court resorted to Argentine sales law, which requires a buyer to make a timely objection to the goods. The court held that the buyer did not meet its obligation under CISG Articles 38 and 39 to examine the goods and notify the seller of nonconformity within a reasonable time.

C. *Cases Involving Other CISG Articles*

Despite the CISG not being in effect, an Argentine appellate relied heavily upon the CISG in rendering a decision involving a documentary transaction.[16] The goods involved dried mushrooms that arrived in such condition that they were deemed as unfit for human consumption by Argentine health authorities. The Argentinian buyer had paid for the goods by letter of credit. Buyer then sued to recover the price of the goods. Because the buyer did not challenge the seller's certificates of quality at the time the goods were delivered to the carrier, and because there was no evidence of an act or omission of the seller, the buyer was unable to establish nonconformity under CISG Article 36. Thus, the damage to the goods was deemed to have occurred after the risk of loss passed to the buyer pursuant to both Article 36 and local law.[17]

In a series of cases beginning in 2003 with *Arbatax S.A. Reorganization Proceeding*,[18] the commercial court of Buenos Aires applied Article 9(1) to resolve questions of trade usage necessary to resolve a claim filed by a Uruguayan creditor in bankruptcy court. In the contract the parties specified the shipping term "FOB Montevideo Clause," which included the rules for interpretation of trade terms of the Paris International Chamber of Commerce (INCOTERMS). The court observed that CISG Article 9 establishes the parties' obligations under terms and usage to which they have agreed or have established between themselves. Similarly, in *Wacker-Polymer Systems GmbH v. Quiesbra v. Glaube*

---

[14] Id., 234–7. See also DiMatteo et al., "The Interpretive Turn in International Sales Law," 295.

[15] May 31, 2007, Camara Nacional de Apelaciones en lo Comercial de Buenos Aires, Sr. *Carlos Manuel del Corazon de Jesus Bravo Barros v. Salvador Martinez Gares*, available at http://cisgw3.law.pace.edu/cases/070531a1.html.

[16] October 31, 1995, Camara Nacional de Apelaciones en lo Comercial, *Bedial v. Muggenburg*, available at http://cisgw3.law.pace.edu/cases/940318a1.html.

[17] See Alejandro Garro, "The U.N. Sales Convention," 237–43.

[18] July 2, 2003, Juzgado Comercial de Primera Instancia Buenos Aires, available at http://cisgw3.law.pace.edu/cases/030702a1.html.

S.A.[19] et al. and in *Autoservicio Mayorista La Loma S.A. v. Quiesbra v. Incidente de Verificacion (Cosvega SL),*[20] the Argentine courts noted the role of Article 9 in imposing customary shipping terms of which the parties would be aware. In *Autoservicio* and *Wacker-Polymer,* the parties had in fact specified INCOTERMS, so the court's reference to CISG simply reinforced the binding nature of these terms.

In *Mayer Alejandro v. Hofferle GmbH & Co.,*[21] the court addressed the manner in which a buyer must prove that goods are not fit for the purpose known to the seller at the time of the contract, as defined in Article 35 (2)(b). The German buyer failed to prove nonconformity of a shipment of charcoal to be used for cooking purposes.[22] Two years later the court of commercial appeals decided *Cerveseria y Malteria Paysandu S.A. v. Cerveceria Argentina S.A.,*[23] in which the court again reviewed a nonconformity claim, this time in a dispute between a Uruguayan seller and an Argentine buyer. The court found that the CISG applied through Article 1(1)(b), as Uruguay was not a contracting state at the time of the contract. Again, the court noted that proof of nonconformity remained a matter of Argentine law, as the CISG was silent on the issue of proof. Because the buyer did not meet the standard of Argentine law, the seller was entitled to the purchase price plus interest, pursuant to CISG Articles 62 and 78 respectively.

In 2010, the National Commercial Court of Appeals reviewed the issue of calculating damages under CISG Articles 74 and 78 in *Ecotune (India) Private Ltd. v. Cencosud S.A.*[24] India, the home state of the seller, was not a contracting party to CISG at the time of the contract; the court applied private international law pursuant to CISG Article 1(1)(b), with the result that the CISG applied as a matter of Argentine law. Both the trial and appellate courts awarded interest to the seller for buyer's delayed payment pursuant to Article 78.

III. Brazil, Chile, and Colombia

Although Brazil is not yet a signatory of the CISG, its courts have applied provisions of the treaty that were determined to be consistent with Brazilian contract law as interpreted by the Brazilian Restatement of Law. Eduardo Grebler notes the failure of Brazil to adopt the CISG is likely due to its discomfort with certain CISG provisions relating to contract formation, fundamental breach, *Nachfrist,* and price reduction.[25] Nonetheless, the CISG appears in Brazilian cases. For example, in 2007, in the gas station fuel

[19] March 17, 2003, Juzgado Comercial de Primera Instancia Buenos Aires, available at http://cisgw3.law.pace.edu/cases/030317a1.html.
[20] April 2003, Juzgado Comercial de Primera Instancia Buenos Aires, available at http://cisgw3.law.pace.edu/cases/030400a1.html.
[21] April 24, 2000, Camara Nacional de Apelaciones en lo Comercial de Buenos Aires, available at http://cisgw3.law.pace.edu/cases/000424a1.html.
[22] See also December 30, 2009, Camara Nacional de Apelaciones en lo Comercial de Buenos Aires, *Amaravathi Textiles v. Censosud S.A. s ordinario,* available at http://turan.uc3m.es/uc3m/dpto/PR/dppr03/dargen19.html;http://cisgw3.law.pace.edu/cases/091230a1.html.
[23] July 21, 2002, Camara Nacional de Apelaciones en lo Comercial de Buenos Aires, available at http://cisgw3.law.pace.edu/cases/020721a1.html.
[24] October 7, 2010, Camara Nacional de Apelaciones en lo Comercial de Buenos Aires, available at http://cisgw3.law.pace.edu/cases/101007a1.html.
[25] Eduardo Grebler, "The Convention on the International Sale of Goods and Brazilian Law: Are Difference Irreconcilable?," 25 *J. L. & Commerce* 467–76 (2005–6).

case,[26] the court invoked CISG Article 77, and the in the 2008 mortgage loan case,[27] an appellate court used the reasoning of CISG Article 72(1), which embodies the concept of anticipatory breach, consistent with the Roman law doctrine of *exception non adimpleti contractus*. And in the 2009 case of electro-erosion machine,[28] the Tribunal de Justicia Rio Grande do Sol invoked Article 77, holding that buyer failed to mitigate its damages by taking reasonable measures to avoid loss.

Chile was an early adopter of the CISG, but there are few reported cases. In September 2008, however, the Supreme Court[29] rather dramatically failed to apply the CISG in a case involving an Argentine buyer and a Chilean seller of hides. The buyer claimed damages for seller's failure to supply the quantity of hides promised in a timely fashion. Article 145 of the Argentine Code would permit such a claim, although the Chilean Civil Code requires that such claims for damages must be made in conjunction with an action for a declaratory judgment to enforce or to cancel the contract. The Supreme Court failed to apply the CISG even though both countries were signatories of the CISG. The original pleadings of the parties did not invoke the CISG, but the buyer asserted on appeal that the CISG was the applicable law in Chile. The court disregarded the buyer's assertion, reasoning that failure to assert application of CISG in the original pleadings constituted a tacit agreement to exclude the CISG in accordance with CISG Article 6. Professor Jorge Oviedo-Alban rightly criticized the decision, arguing that the parties must affirmatively opt out; failure to invoke its applicability at the pleadings stage does not effectively exclude the convention. The Chilean Civil Code was the wrong law to apply in the first place.

Colombia, too, has produced little CISG case law. After affirming the consistency of the newly adopted CISG with the Colombian Constitution, the Constitutional Court declared the CISG as the law of the land.[30] In addition, the Supreme Court used Article 77 as an example of the broader principle (than Columbian domestic law) requiring the injured party to mitigate damages.[31] The case did not involve the interpretation of the CISG, but it reaffirmed that the judiciary fully recognizes the CISG as an integral part of Colombian commercial law.

IV. Mexico

Mexico has a more robust case law applying the CISG. However, as recently as 2007, Mexican courts have struggled with applying the CISG. In *Georgia Pacific Resins, Inc. v. Grupo Bajaplay, S.A. de C.V.*,[32] an appellate court reversed a case in which the parties

[26] July 3, 2007, Appellate Court of Sao Paulo, 16th Civil Division, available at http://cisgw3.law.pace.edu/cases/070703b5.html.

[27] April 24, 2008, Appellate Court of Sao Paulo, 4th Civil Division, available at http://cisgw3.law.pace.edu/cases/080424b5.html.

[28] May 20, 2009, Tribunal de Justicia Rio Grande do Sul, available at http://cisgw3/law/pace.edu/cases/090520b5.html.

[29] September 22, 2008 Supreme Court of Chile, *Jorge Plaza Oviedo v. Sociedad Agricola Sector Limitada*, available at http://cisgw3.law.pace.edu/cases/080922ch.html.

[30] May 10, 2000, Corte Constitucional, available at http://cisgw3.law.pace.edu/cases/000510c7.html. Professor DiMatteo observes the emphasis the Colombian court places on the role of the good faith principle in the CISG. DiMatteo et al., "The Interpretive Turn in International Sales Law," 319.

[31] December 16, 2010, Corte Suprema de Justicia, *Dicalcium phosphate*, available at http://cisgw3.law.pace.edu/cases/101216c7.html.

[32] August 9, 2007, Baja California, Fourth Panel, available at http://cisgw3.law.pace.edu/cases/070809m1.html.

had not invoked the CISG but where it clearly applied. The court reasoned that CISG was part of Mexico's domestic law. Therefore, CISG is not a foreign law that needs to be proved by the parties, said the court, but a part of the law the judge brings to any case. The reversal is an example of the fact that most Mexican courts have applied the CISG in cases where it is applicable.

A. *Principle of Good Faith*

A 1998 arbitration case[33] involved a Korean buyer who delayed performance in order to take advantage of the Mexican seller's economic vulnerability, apparently with the goal of obtaining price concessions. Among other things, buyer took out a letter of credit in favor of the seller, but included conditions in the letter of credit that were different from those required by the contract, rendering the shipping documents nonconforming and precluding payment on the letter of credit. The arbitral commission, applying CISG Article 7, found a failure to act in good faith and fair dealing on the part of the buyer. Further, the commission observed that "[t]o limit or exclude [good faith and fair dealing from the law] would be equal to a failure to acknowledge the axis that regulates international trade, as understood in international trade, unbound from the meaning given to it in Mexican law."[34] In the end, it held that the buyer acted in bad faith by forcing the seller into a breach by manipulation. A party acting in good faith must cooperate with the other party, or at least not obstruct the other party from performing.

B. *Contract Formation*

A 1993 arbitration case[35] involving a Mexican seller and a U.S. buyer dealt with the issue of nonpayment. One of the buyer's checks was returned for insufficient funds, and four other checks could not be cashed because the account they were drawn upon had been closed. The Mexican Commission for the Protection of Foreign Commerce ascertained that the CISG applied. The buyer argued that there was no enforceable contract detailing the terms of the alleged agreement. The commission held that the lack of a written agreement did not defeat the existence of a contract. Consistent with Article 11, documentation of the transaction itself, including the bounced checks, permitted the inference of a contractual agreement. As a consequence, under Article 62 the seller was entitled to full payment for the goods according to the contract.[36]

In the *Kolmar* case,[37] a U.S. buyer sued a Mexican seller for damages for seller's failure to fulfill a contract for the sale of a petrochemical product. The legal issue was whether a contract had been formed. The buyer alleged a contract based on telephone conversations and emails, including an email confirmation. The seller argued that the

---

[33] November 30, 1998, Compromex Arbitration Proceeding, *Dulces Luisi v. Seoul International*, available at http://cisgw3.law.pace.edu/cases/981130m1.html

[34] As translated in Alejandro Osuna Gonzalez, "Dictamen relative a la quja promovida por *Dulces Luisi, S.A., d C.V. en contra de Seoul International Co., Ltd. u Seoulia Confectionery Co.*," available at http://cisgw3.law.pace.edu/cases/981130m1.html.

[35] May 1993, Compromex Arbitration Proceeding M/66/72, *Jose Luis Morales v. Nez Marketing*, available at http://cisgw3.law.pace.edu/cases/930504.html.

[36] See Garro, "Unification and Harmonization of Private Law," 220–2.

[37] March 10, 2005, Primer Tribunal Colegiado en Materia Civil del Primer Circuito, *Kolmar Petrochemicals Americas, Inc. v. Idesa Petroquimica S.A. de C.V.*, available at http://cisgw3.law.pace.edu/cases/050310m1.html.

parties never agreed on the essential terms of a contract, specifically the time and place of delivery. In one email, the seller acknowledged the buyer's order but added that he lacked information about the feasibility of shipping the product from a certain tank terminal. Pressed to commit to a carrier identified by the buyer, the seller indicated that the price would increase depending on the carrier designation, but noted, "I am fully aware that I am not upholding our original agreement." Thus, the seller appeared to acknowledge the existence of an agreement. CISG Articles 19 (1) and (2), however, treat such a reply as insufficient to constitute an acceptance if it contains additions, limitations or other modifications that materially alter the terms of the offer. Article 19 (3) identifies place and time of delivery as terms that materially alter the terms of an offer. The appellate court held that there was no contract pursuant to Article 19.

CISG's rules of interpretation provided in Articles 7, 8, and 9 arguably support the buyer's claim that the parties demonstrated an intent to be bound by a contract, as the precise time and place of shipment is an operational detail rather than a material term. The time and place of delivery had been narrowed to a small range of ports and dates. The buyer argued that the real reason for the seller's nonperformance was the seller's realization that it should have received a higher price; it sought to increase the price, arguably in bad faith. Also, from a reasonable person perspective, the seller knew that the buyer interpreted the seller's communication as an acceptance. These factors, as well as evidence of trade usages, leads to a conclusion that a contract had been formed. Inevitably, the court decision turned on a very close reading of the evidence of intent and materiality. Ultimately, its decision rested on the rationalization that Article 19's purpose was to provide certainty in international transactions. In this case, however, the decision seems to have had the opposite effect.

C. Conformity of Goods: Inspection and Notice

The case of *Barcel S.A. de C.V., v. Steve Kliff* dealt with the issues of the requirements for proper notice and notice of nonconformity under CISG Articles 38 and 39.[38] In the case, a U.S. seller sought payment of the contract price for the sale of foil cards. The buyer refused to pay on the ground that the cards emitted a foul odor and were not fit to use in food packaging. Seller claimed that it was not given timely notice of the nonconformity pursuant to CISG Articles 38 and 39. The court, according to one commentator,[39] stumbled on the applicability of the CISG, but observed that, in any event, a similar result would be obtained under Mexican law. Two additional appellate courts upheld this decision,[40] but none of the three courts directly applied the CISG as the law of the case; they simply rationalized that Mexican law was consistent with CISG Articles 38 and 39.

---

[38] October 3, 2006, Juzgado Primero Civil de Primera Instancia de Lerma de Villade, *Barcel S.A. de C.V., v. Steve Kliff*, available at http://cisgw3.law.pace.edu/cases/061003m1.html.

[39] Tunon Muria Arnau, "Case Comment: *Barcel Sociedad Anonima de Capital Variable v. Steve Kliff*. The International Wine Judgment Lerma," available at http://cisgw3.law.pace.edu/cases/061003m1.html.

[40] March 13, 2007, Second Panel for Civil Matters of the Second Federal Circuit Court, *Steve Kliff v. Second Regional Camber of the Superior Court of Justice for the State of Mexico*, available at http://cisgw3.law.pace.edu/cases/070313m1.html; March 22, 2007, Superior Court of Justice, Toluca, *Barcel S.A. de C.V. v. Steve Kliff*, available at http://cisgw3.law.pace.edu/cases/070322m1.html.

D. *Cases Involving Other CISG Articles*

In *Conservas La Costena*,[41] an arbitration panel was confronted with multiple issues of contract formation and nonconformity.[42] This case involved a sale of canned fruit by an Argentine seller to a Mexican importer. The buyer claimed that the cans arrived in a damaged condition, and that, in addition, the goods did not conform in quality and content to the samples provided by the seller. Moreover, the buyer claimed that the shipping documents were nonconforming, thus negating the buyer's risk of loss. The seller challenged the formation of the contract due to the absence of a written contract. It argued that the writing formalities of Argentine domestic sales law applied because of Argentina's reservation pursuant to CISG Articles 12 and 96. As Professor Garro observes,[43] the panel did not appear to research Argentine law on formal contracts, but instead found a writing requirement satisfied by the many the documents and admissions of the seller establishing the essential terms of a contractual relationship. The seller did not argue that the buyer failed to notify it of the alleged nonconformity pursuant to Articles 38 and 39, but challenged the buyer's proof that the goods received did not conform to the samples previously provided by the seller. Professor Garro observes as well that the arbitral decision apparently failed to consider the decisions of courts of other nations applying the CISG or scholarly commentary on the CISG.

In *Banks Hardwoods California LP v. Jorge Angel Kyriakidez Garcia* (wood case),[44] the issue was at what point in time interest damages should be calculated on the unpaid price of goods. The court referenced CISG Article 58(1), identifying the time when "the seller places either the goods or documents controlling their disposition at the buyer's disposal in accordance with the contract."[45] In a subsequent case[46] involving the same parties but in a different matter, the same court held that the payment of interest provided in the contract ran from the time of the events specified in Article 58(1). Interestingly, the court drew on a decision of the Mexican Supreme Court discussing the hierarchy of Mexican law, placing treaties in a position below the Constitution and Fundamental Law, but above federal statutes. Thus, in any conflict between federal statutes on sales law and the CISG, the CISG would prevail.[47]

---

[41] April 29, 1996, Compromex Arbitration Proceeding, Conservas La Costena v. Lanin, available at http://cisgw3.law.pace.edu/cases/960429m1.html.

[42] See Alejandro M. Garro, "The U.N. Sales Convention," 244; DiMatteo et al., "The Interpretive Turn in International Sales Law," 299–440, n. 133.

[43] Garro, "The U.N. Sales Convention," 226–7.

[44] July 14, 2000, City of Tijuana, State of Baja California, Sixth Civil Court of First Instance, available at http://cisgw3.law.pace.edu/cases/000714m1.html.

[45] CISG, Article 58(1).

[46] August 30, 2005, City of Tijuana, State of Baja California, Sixth Civil Court of First instance, *Banks Hardwoods California LP v. Jorge Angel Kyriakidez Garcia*, available at http://cisgw3.law.pace.edu/cases/050830m1.html.

[47] See March 24, 2006, Superior Court of Baja California, *Banks Hardwoods California LP v. Jorge Angel Kyriakidez Garcia*, available at http://cisgw3.law.pace.edu/cases/06324m1.html.

36 The CISG across National Legal Systems

Larry A. DiMatteo

I. Introduction

This chapter summarizes the findings of the country analyses presented in the previous chapters. It will note a number of problems in CISG jurisprudence, such as the problem of scarcity of case law in certain areas or what Olaf Meyer refers to as "quiet areas,"[1] as well as the problem of national law-biased decisions. The chapter will then provide an analysis of some of the substantive findings of the country analyses. The review shows two conflated phenomena in CISG jurisprudence: unevenness and convergence. The topical areas covered include good faith (principle versus duty); contract formation; incorporation of standard terms; nonconformity, inspection, and notice of nonconformity; fundamental breach; *Nachfrist* time extension; price reduction remedy; payment of interest; and a number of "surprises." The chapter also examines the influence of the German courts, both in quantity and quality, on CISG jurisprudence. It raises an issue for debate: Is the CISG, in application and in practice, a European civil code? Finally, the chapter will briefly note the important influences the CISG has had on national contract and sales laws. It examines the distinction between the role of the CISG in harmonizing law through autonomous interpretations and the bottom-up phenomenon of CISG's use as a template for the revision of domestic contract laws. The more this CISG qua template trend continues, the more purely national-specific laws will converge.

II. Problem of Scarcity

Despite the Institute of International Commercial Law's CISG Database statement that, as of 15 October 2013, there are 2,920 cases listed in its database involving the CISG, many countries that are contracting states of the CISG have failed to develop a robust body of case law relating to its application. Many of the cases are concentrated in a handful of countries, lead undoubtedly by Germany. In addition, a significant number of the cases are decisions of arbitral panels. The application of the CISG by arbitral tribunals is, of course, a positive thing, but most such decisions are not reported or do not provide reasoned opinions. They, therefore, do not add to the corpus of CISG jurisprudence as do lengthier, well-reasoned judicial decisions.

---

[1] See Olaf Meyer, "CISG: Divergences between Success–Scarcity and Theory–Practice," Chapter 3 in this book.

Another problem that has reduced the number of CISG decisions is the disregard of the CISG by parties and courts when it is the applicable law of the case. Professor Virginia Maurer noted a 2008 Chilean Supreme Court case in which the court failed to recognize the CISG as applicable law.[2] On appeal, the buyer asserted the status of the CISG as the applicable law in Chile. The court disregarded the buyer's, arguably late assertion of the CISG, reasoning that failure to assert application of CISG in the original pleadings constituted a tacit agreement to exclude the CISG in accordance with Article 6 of the CISG. In contrast, a Mexican appellate court, in *Georgia Pacific Resins, Inc. v. Grupo Bajaplay, S.A. de C.V.*,[3] reversed a lower court decision because the parties had not invoked the CISG, even though it clearly applied. The court held that the "CISG was not foreign law to be proved but was part of the law the judge brings to any case."[4] Professor Jan Ramberg notes that the scarcity of reported case decisions in the Scandinavian countries can be explained by the facts that (1) disputes under international contracts generally are resolved by arbitration and (2) the countries opted out of Part II (contract formation) through an Article 92 Reservation.[5]

III. Problem of National Law Bias

The first section of this part will briefly review the persistence of homeward trend or national law bias in the application of the CISG. The second section looks at the technique of using parallel citations.

A. *Persistence of Homeward Trend Bias*

The use of domestic legal concepts in the interpretation of the CISG remains a problem. However, the number of well-reasoned opinions that use foreign legal sources in the attempt to fulfill the CISG mandate for autonomous interpretations is on the rise. On the surface, national law bias is observed by the lack of citations to foreign court decisions and scholarly commentary and by references to purely national sources of law. However, this does not mean that the actual decision fails to provide a reasonable interpretation and application of the CISG. This issue is addressed in the next section's discussion of parallel citations. The issue here is the case where a national court fails to look to other sources other than case law interpreting purely nation-specific laws. Professors Emerson and Olazábal note that U.S. courts will need to stop simply relying on perhaps similar, but certainly not identical, provisions of the Uniform Commercial Code instead of the CISG case law.[6] The court in *Raw Materials Inc. v. Manfred Forberich GmbH & Co., KG*[7] stated that "no American court has specifically interpreted or applied Article 79 of the CISG," neglecting to cite the case law on CISG Article 79 created by the courts

---

[2] See Virginia G. Maurer, "Central and South America," Chapter 35 in this book; *Jorge Plaza Oviedo v. Sociedad Agricola Sector Limitada*, September 22, 2008, Supreme Court of Chile, available at http://cisgw3.law.pace.edu/cases/080922ch.html.

[3] Id., citing, August 9, 2007, Baja California, Fourth Panel, available at http://cisgw3.law.pace.edu/cases/070809m1.html.

[4] Maurer, "Central and South America."

[5] See Jan Ramberg, "The Nordic Countries," Chapter 25 in this book.

[6] See Robert W. Emerson and Ann M. Olazábal, "United States and Canada," Chapter 34 in this book.

[7] *Raw Materials Inc. v. Manfred Forberich GmbH & Co., KG* No. 03 C 1154 (N.D. Ill. July 6, 2004), available at http://cisgw3.law.pace.edu/cases/040706u1.html.

of so many countries, including Austria, Belgium, Bulgaria, China, Finland, France, Germany, Hungary, Israel, Italy, the Netherlands, Russia, and Switzerland, as well as by International Chamber of Commerce arbitral panels.[8]

The application of the principle of good faith has been broadly applied by many civilian courts. This can be seen as an example of legal tradition bias. Edoardo Ferrante notes that an Italian court in *Scatolificio La Perla vs. M. Frischdienst* invoked the prohibition of *venire contra factum proprium*, as a fundamental principle of the CISG. This is a "prohibition which is evidently close to the continental principle of good faith; there is nevertheless some 'homeward trend' in referring this prohibition to the 'principles of the Convention' without specifying where the principle in question is identified [or supported] in the Convention; it is as if the experience gained in dealing with domestic law had made that research superfluous."[9]

On a more positive note, Professor Faber notes that because Austrian courts "regularly seek guidance in German literature, [this] arguably results in a relatively high standard of predictability of Austrian court decisions."[10] Again, Edoardo Ferrante in his review of Italian case law states: "If on one hand, the amount of cases is on the whole small, on the other, the quality of the decisions interpreting and applying substantive provisions of the treaty can be considered high. First of all there is a good use of autonomous interpretation, in accordance with the principles established by Article 7 CISG.[11] As far as [interpretive] method[s are] concerned, the importance of [using] foreign case-law [in interpreting the CISG] . . . is an irreplaceable means for ensuring uniformity; this is a point worth emphasising, as foreign precedents are not only considered but also applied in deciding real cases."[12]

Tidas Kilmas offers an interesting analysis of why some countries – especially those from the former Soviet Union – have ignored the CISG despite its adoption into their countries' law: "What may very well be happening in these countries is that the decisions are informed by the state or condition of law in general in those jurisdictions. If indeed the idea that damages should be limited to those which are foreseeable, or the idea of fundamental non-performance, is alien and even considered unnecessary, it is hardly to be expected that lawyers and judges in such territories would be equipped, intellectually and morally, to bring such arguments to bear in CISG cases in their jurisdictions, or even to recognize when such arguments would be applicable."[13]

B. *Parallel Citation Approach*

A common approach to trying to serve two masters – an autonomous interpretation of the CISG and national legal tradition – is the use of parallel citations to the CISG and

---

[8] See http://cisgw3.law.pace.edu/cisg/text/anno-art-79.html; see also Albert H. Kritzer, Comments on *Raw Materials Inc. v. Manfred Forberich*, U.S. District Court [Illinois], July 6, 2004 (2005), available at http://cisgw3.law.pace.edu/cases/040706u1.html#cx (February 2005).

[9] Tribunale di Padova, March 31, 2004; see also Tribunale di Vigevano, July 12, 2000, Giurisprudenza italiana 280 (2001), available at http://cisgw3.law.pace.edu/cases/000712i3.html; "Tribunale di Vigevano: Specific Aspects of the CISG Uniformly Dealt With," *J. of L. & Commerce* 225 (2001).

[10] See Wolfgang Faber, "CISG in Austria," Chapter 19 in this book.

[11] See Edoardo Ferrante, "Italy," Chapter 24 in this book. See, e.g., Tribunale di Modena, December 9, 2005, available at http://www.cisg-online.ch/cisg/urteile/1398.pdf.

[12] Id. See also Tribunale di Cuneo, January 31, 1996, *Diritto del commercio internazionale* 653 (1996), available at http://cisgw3.law.pace.edu/cases/960131i3.html.

[13] See Tidas Klimas, "Baltic States, Belarus, and Ukraine," Chapter 20 in this book.

national law in the support of an interpretation. Tidas Klimas in his review states that "often both local law and the CISG are applied, when the CISG should govern." Milena Djordjević and Vladimir Pavić noted that some cases from Serbia and other Southeastern European countries cite not only the provisions of the CISG, but also the provisions of the relevant national law where the CISG is the applicable law.[14] It is common in American judicial opinions to refer to the U.S. Uniform Commercial Code when interpreting the CISG. In the end, if courts stay true to CISG interpretive methodology and provide autonomous interpretations, despite referencing national sources, then the substance of the decision advances the cause of uniformity. The impact of parallel citations becomes more of a stylistic distraction that can be dismissed as simply providing comfort to the judicial decision maker and his or her domestic audience.

IV. Unevenness and Convergence of Jurisprudence

Certain issues and articles of the CISG have received significant attention in the case law. The most commonly discussed issues include the role of the principle of good faith in the interpretation and enforcement of contracts, contract formation issues, incorporation of standard terms, determining nonconformity, buyers' duties to inspect and give proper notice of nonconformity, and the payment of interest. However, other issues and articles have not created a critical mass of jurisprudence to support a consensus or provide adequate guidance to future application of those articles.

A. *Principle of Good Faith versus Duty of Good Faith*

The principle of good faith as enunciated in Article 7(1) restricts its use to the interpretation of the CISG itself. Despite this restriction, the majority view is that a duty of good faith in the performance and enforcement of contracts is implied by the CISG. The history of this provision in the CISG shows that the restriction of good faith to the interpretation of CISG rules was not an accident of poor drafting, but represented a compromise in which a general obligation of good faith was rejected. A number of rationales can be discerned regarding why the duty of good faith has played such a major role in CISG jurisprudence despite its limited scope in Article 7(1). First, scholars have argued that the duty of good faith can be implied through other provisions in the CISG, namely, the use of the reasonableness standard throughout the CISG. Second, Article 7(1) is actually ambiguous – possibly, intentionally so – as to the role of good faith. Even though the introductory phrase – "in the interpretation of this Convention" – restricts the use to good faith for purposes of interpreting the CISG, it later states that "regard is to be had to . . . the observance of good faith in international trade." If good faith is observed in international trade, then it is understandable why the good faith principle has been used in the application of the CISG. Finally, the overwhelming majority of CISG jurisprudence has been produced by courts in civil law systems where the principle of good faith plays a more central role in contract law than it does in the common law tradition.

The duty of good faith has been used in the interpretation of numerous CISG Articles. For example, it has generally been recognized that a seller is not obligated to know the standards of the country of the buyer or of downstream buyers in other countries.

---

[14] See, Milena Djordjević and Vladimir Pavić, "CISG in Southeastern Europe," Chapter 26 in this book.

However, the Israeli Supreme Court held that a seller has a good faith duty to protect the buyer if it is aware that the goods would infringe on a trademark if sold in the country of import.[15] The court held both parties liable for the damages caused by the trademark infringement. Of course, there is no such rule allowing the allocation of fault in the CISG. The court based the idea of comparative negligence or comparative breach on the principle of good faith: "In the context of an international sales contract between an exporter and an importer of goods, applying the good faith principle would mean, *inter alia*, that the exporter, being aware of a problem that might jeopardize the importer's ability to sell the goods, must warn the latter of the problem. This is especially so, if the exporter can assume that his own liability towards the importer would be excluded."[16]

The central role of good faith in the conceptual mindset of European judges and arbitrators was made clear by a Serbian arbitral panel:

> The contracting party has not acted in accordance with the good faith principle, which represents a cornerstone of the entire corpus of modern legislation, especially the legislative instruments which the tribunal has identified as applicable rules in this case (CISG, Law on Contracts and Torts, UNIDROIT Principles on International Commercial Contracts and European Principles of Contract Law).[17]

Professor El-Saghir noted that "Egyptian scholars tend to adopt a broad interpretation of Article 7(1) concerning the 'observance of good faith in international trade.' They tend to consider good faith one of the principles on which the Convention is based, not only to be used as a matter of interpretation. It is plausible to state that good faith is more broadly construed in the Egyptian Civil Code and under Islamic law than it is in the CISG. Good faith in Islamic Law includes a duty to act altruistically." This Islamic concept of good faith is likely to have influenced Egyptian scholars in broadly interpreting the good faith principle in the CISG.[18]

The principle of good faith has been seen as an autonomous source of distinct and additional obligations implied into the CISG under German law: "Additional information duties have been the primary field of application of the principle. For example, courts have deduced from the principle of good faith an obligation of a party to send a copy of its standard terms to the other party,[19] as well as "the obligation to provide the standard terms in a language which is the contract language or a language that is understood by the other party."[20]

Another area in which the principle of good faith has played a role is the loss of rights pursuant to prior conduct of the party claiming the rights, such as failing to provide a notice of avoidance within a reasonable time period. In practice, given the

---

[15] CA 3912/90 *Eximin SA v. Itel Style Ferarri Textile & Shoes Ltd.* [1993] IsrSC 47(4) 64, available at http://cisgw3.law.pace.edu/cases/930822i5.html.

[16] Id., para. 4(b). See Yehuda Adar, "CISG in Israel, Chapter 31 in this book.

[17] Serbian FTCA, Award No. T-9/07, January 23, 2008, available at http://cisgw3.law.pace.edu/cases/080123sb.html.

[18] See Hossam A. El-Saghir, "CISG in Islamic Countries: The Case of Egypt," Chapter 30 in this book.

[19] Landgericht Neubrandenburg, August 2, 2005, 10 O 74/04, 2006 *Internationales Handelsrecht* 26, 28.

[20] See Stefan Kröll, "Germany Country Analysis: Good Faith, Formation, and Conformity of Goods," Chapter 22 in this book, citing Oberlandesgericht Düsseldorf, April 21, 2004, I-15 U 88/03, 2004 *Internationales Handelsrecht* 108, 112; 2005 *Internationales Handelsrecht* 24, 28, CISG-Online No. 915.

vagueness of the principle of good faith,[21] courts base their decisions often not directly on the principle of good faith, but on narrower and more specific principles, such as the prohibition of contradictory behavior or *non-venire contra factum proprium*.[22] These more specific principles are merely concretized versions of the principle of good faith.[23] The most dramatic proclamation of the foundational nature of good faith comes from a 1998 arbitration in Mexico that states "[t]o limit or exclude [good faith and fair dealing] would be equal to a failure to acknowledge the axis that regulates international trade."[24]

B. *Contract Formation and Contract Modification*

CISG Article 29 has generated a fair amount of attention regarding the requirement of a written instrument in a contract to modify a contract, despite Article 29's clear language that contracts may be modified by "mere agreement."[25] Yet a Serbian arbitrator concluded that a "written" modification contract may be implied:

> When parties fail to explicitly agree on a certain form for conclusion of the contract, while at the same time respecting the strict written form with the appropriate attestation of every page of the contract while concluding it, then it is evident that the purpose of such verification is in the will of parties to give to such certified contract a complete evidentiary value and that only those terms of the contract which are found on pages so verified should produce legal effect, i.e. that those contract terms are the will of the parties and that they cannot in any other way be disputed.... When a contract is concluded and certified in this manner, parties may agree on contract modification, but only in the manner and in form in which it was done in the original contract."[26]

This conclusion is clearly wrong, given that there are no such requirements in the CISG and the arbitrator failed to cite evidence of any trade usages or to an express provision in the contract that required modifications to be in written form.[27] Professor Stefan Kröll states that the "rules on formation are not only applied to the original formation of the contract, but also to all other changes to its content based on an agreement by the parties, such as modifications or joint terminations."[28]

The power of the written confirmation remains strong in CISG jurisprudence, although it is not expressly dealt with under the CISG. The Swiss Federal Court of Justice asserted that it is a matter of good faith that a party receiving a confirmation must object in order not to be bound by its terms, despite Article 18(1)'s assertion that silence

---

[21] Contra Ulrich Magnus, 59 *Rabels Zeitschrift für ausländisches und internationales Privatrecht* 469, 480 (1989).

[22] Oberlandesgericht München, September 15, 2004, 7 U 2959/04, 2005 *Internationales Handelsrecht* 72, CISG-Online No. 1013, Clout No. 595.

[23] See Stefan Kröll, "Germany Country Analysis: Good Faith, Formation, and Conformity of Goods," Chapter 22 in this book.

[24] See Virginia G. Maurer, "Central and South America," Chapter 35 in this book, citing *S.A., d C.V. en contra de Seoul International Co., Ltd. v. Seoulia Confectionery Co.*, available at http://cisgw3.law.pace .edu/cases/981130m1.html.

[25] See CISG, Article 29(1).

[26] See Milena Djordjević and Vladimir Pavić, "CISG in Southeastern Europe," Chapter 26 in this book.

[27] See CISG, Article 29(2).

[28] See Stefan Kröll, "Germany Country Analysis: Good Faith, Formation, and Conformity of Goods," Chapter 22 in this book.

or inactivity in itself cannot be grounds of an acceptance.[29] Professor Widmer Lüchinger states this inconsistency is likely due to the fact that, "under domestic Swiss law, failure to object to a commercial letter of confirmation within a reasonable time can, in certain circumstances, result in a binding contract, and this effect is generally derived from the principle of good faith."[30] Thus, when the Swiss Federal Court of Justice spoke of a "good faith duty to object" under the CISG, it was embracing a domestic law concept.[31]

The German courts have dealt with this inconsistency by focusing on the Article 18(1) phrase "in itself" and determining that the obligation to object to terms in a written confirmation is a recognized trade usage. Professor Stefan Kröll states that the "prevailing view" is that if the duty to object exists in the law of both parties, then it justifies "the existence of a usage without further investigating whether the foreign doctrine had the same scope as the German doctrine."[32] But this can be questioned because a common usage between parties from two countries does not satisfy CISG Article 9(2)'s requirement that the usage be one "which in international trade is widely known."

C. Incorporation of Standard Terms

In Tribunal of Rovereto in *Euroflash vs. Arconvert*,[33] the court held that a seller's standard terms did not become a part of the contract despite the fact the all the standard terms were written at the bottom of the seller's confirmation order. Edoardo Ferrante criticizes the decision for a number of reasons: First, if "actual" acceptance is required then the distinction between unilateral clauses and negotiated clauses should fade. Second, "if the opinion is reliable, the Tribunal should have drawn the conclusion that not only the forum selection clause, but the whole agreement was void under Article 19(1) and (3)."[34]

A Lithuanian court asserted that standard terms are generally not inferior to negotiated terms. The court in *Veka AG vs. Omnetus UAB*[35] addressed the problem where a party's standard terms conflicted with the choice of law provisions in the main contract. "The court held that the standard terms are not as a matter of law to be considered inferior to the provisions of the main contract. *It must be noted*, however, that the standard terms referred to here were appended physically to the contract at the time of its formation and therefore no issue of surprise or unfairness arose as to them."[36]

Case law in the Netherlands generally requires (1) whether, according to the understanding of a reasonable person of the same kind as the offeree, it was clear that the offeror intended to incorporate its general terms and conditions and (2) whether the recipient of such an offer expressly agrees to them. A large number of Dutch courts explicitly referred

---

[29] See Corrine Widmer Lüchinger, "Switzerland," Chapter 28 in this book, citing Decision 4C.474/2004, April 5, 2005, CISG-online 1012.

[30] Id., citing Swiss Federal Court of Justice, BGE 114 II 250, October 27, 1988, available at http://www.bger.ch; Swiss Federal Court of Justice, August 4, 2003, CISG-online 804.

[31] Id.

[32] See Stefan Kröll and Rudolph Hennecke, "Kaufmännische Bestätigungsschreiben beim internationalen Warenkauf," *Rabels Zeitschrift für ausländisches und internationales Privatrecht* 478 (2003).

[33] Tribunale di Rovereto, August 24, 2006, available at http://www.unilex.info/case.cfm?id=1147.

[34] See Edoardo Ferrante, "Italy," Chapter 24 in this book.

[35] *Veka AG v. Omnetus UAB*, Lietuvos apeliacinis teismas, Nr. 2–567/2007 (Appellate Court of Lithuania, 2007).

[36] See Tadas Klimas, "Baltic States, Belarus, and Ukraine," Chapter 20 in this book.

to the German Supreme Court's findings.[37] However, German law currently does not require express agreement.

Germany, however, has a long tradition of policing the use of standard terms. Stefan Kröll notes that it is "common ground in Germany that the CISG's provisions on the formation of contract also govern the inclusion of standard terms into the contract.'[38] The German Supreme Court provided the means by which standard terms can be properly incorporated into a contract: "It is required that the recipient of a contract offer that is supposed to be based on general terms and conditions have the possibility to become aware of them in a reasonable manner."[39] The decision requires two findings. The first requirement is that a reasonable party would have recognized the incorporating party's intent to have the terms incorporated into the contract. The second requirement is that the incorporating party must transmit the standard terms so that the other party could not be unaware of their existence and content. Professor Kröll notes that this is not necessarily a homeward trend decision because under German law the nonincorporating party has the obligation of requesting a copy of the standard terms. Finally, the burden of proving that the general terms and conditions were made available is placed on the party using or sending the standard terms.

D. *Conformity, Inspection, and Notice of Nonconformity*

National courts have disagreed on what time frames satisfy the timely inspection and reasonable notice requirements of Articles 38 and 39. Article 38 dictates that an inspection of the goods must be performed "within as short a period as is practicable."[40] Article 39 requires the buyer to give notice of nonconformity "within a reasonable time."[41] The interrelationship between these two buyer obligations has been noted: "For example, it has been held that where a simple investigation would have revealed the defect, the time for giving a notice of non-conformity is rather short."[42] An Italian court also noted the relationship between timely notice and specificity of notice. In *Expoplast vs. Reg Mac*,[43] the Tribunal of Busto Arsizio asserted:

> Relationship between timeliness of notice and specificity of notice: the judgment tends to mediate between two opposing needs: on one hand, the need not to worsen excessively the buyer's position, by requiring notice with detailed and motivated content similar to expert evidence; on the other, the need to prevent the seller from being at the mercy of

---

[37] See Sonja A. Kruisinga, "The Netherlands," Chapter 29 in this book.

[38] Bundesgerichtshof, October 31, 2001, VIII ZR 60/01, 2002 *Internationales Handelsrecht* 2002, CISG-Online No. 617; Oberlandesgericht München, January 14, 2009, 20 U 3863/08, 9 *Internationales Handelsrecht* 201 et seq. (5/2009), CISG-Online No. 2011; see also Burghard Piltz, *Internationales Kaufrecht*, 2nd ed. (Munich: C.H. Beck, 2008), paras. 3–8, 3–80.

[39] See Stefan Kröll, "Germany Country Analysis: Good Faith, Formation, and Conformity of Goods," Chapter 22 in this book, citing Bundesgerichtshof, October 31, 2001, VIII ZR 60/01.

[40] CISG, Article 38(1).

[41] CISG, Article 39(1).

[42] See Milena Djordjević and Vladimir Pavić, "CISG in Southeastern Europe," Chapter 26 in this book. See Commercial Court in Čačak, Case No. P 33/06, Serbia, June 28, 2006, available at http://cisgw3.law.pace.edu/cases/060628sb.html (delivered bags all had a label clearly specifying the nonconforming origin of the goods; the buyer could have noted the nonconformity by simple visual examination and should have sent notice of nonconformity immediately).

[43] *Expoplast v. Reg Mac*, Tribunale di Busto Arsizio, December 13, 2001.

the buyer's complaints and to give him the opportunity to amend the lack of conformity depending on specifically identified defects.[44]

National bias was shown in a case involving the proper form of the notice of nonconformity. The CISG does not require the notice of nonconformity to be in any specific form. Yet, the Serbian Foreign-Trade Court of Arbitration interpreted Article 39 to require that the notice be "in writing as required by common practice or if given orally to be followed by a confirmation."[45] This is clearly against the spirit of Article 11 and the CISG's general rejection of formality requirements. Relating to the issue of the specificity of the notice of nonconformity, Serbian tribunals have required that the content of notice to be "devoid of any doubts," but "it need not be overtly specific."[46]

Professor Kröll notes that in "the early years of the CISG's application in Germany, the courts tended to adopt a fairly strict approach to both requirements."[47] These decisions were criticized as being influenced by the strict requirements found in German law. However, the German Supreme Court has intimated the need for a more lenient approach to the requirements of timely notice and specificity of notice. The prevailing view is based on the tissue machine case.[48] That case led to the benchmark of the "noble month" as a reasonable time for giving notice. The Netherlands has similarly noted the importance of the one-month threshold for giving notice in the sale of nonperishable goods.[49]

E. Fundamental Breach

Professor Wolfgang Faber has noted that, in the area of fundamental breach, Austrian court practice is "surprisingly poor." He notes a Court of Appeal decision as the best Austrian case on the subject.[50] In it, the court held that "the fact that the defects cannot be cured, or at least the fact that they have not been cured for an unreasonably long time could, alone, constitute a fundamental breach." Faber comments that this is inconsistent with German case law and the broad view found in German commentaries.[51]

French case law has used both subjective and objective approaches to determining fundamental breach. A party's knowledge of the importance of a term (to the other party) subject to the nonperformance is a fundamental breach. This is the case even though it would not be considered a fundamental breach under an objective standard.[52] Other cases have taken an objective approach by focusing on the merchantability of the goods. Professor Sylvaine Poillot-Peruzzetto notes that the Court of Cassation, in *Sacovini/M*

---

[44] See Edoardo Ferrante, "Italy," Chapter 24 in this book.
[45] See Milena Djordjević and Vladimir Pavić, "CISG in Southeastern Europe," Chapter 26 in this book.
[46] Id.
[47] See Stefan Kröll, "Germany Country Analysis: Good Faith, Formation, and Conformity of Goods," Chapter 22 in this book.
[48] Bundesgerichtshof, November 3, 1999, VIII ZR 287/98, CISG-Online No. 475.
[49] See Sonja A. Kruisinga, "The Netherlands," Chapter 29 in this book, citing Gerechtshof Arnhem (June 17, 1997), *Nederlands Internationaal Privaatrecht* 1997, 341.
[50] See Wolfgang Faber, "CISG in Austria," Chapter 19 in this book, citing OLG Linz, January 23, 6 R 160/05z, CISG-online 1377 (auto case), available at http://cisgw3.law.pace.edu/cases/060123a3.html.
[51] See BGH, April 3, 1996, VIII ZR 51/95, CISG-online 135 = BGHZ 132, 290 (cobalt sulphate case), English translation available at http://cisgw3.law.pace.edu/cases/960403g1.html; Ulrich Schroeter in *Commentary*, 3rd ed. (ed. P. Schlechtriem and I. Schwenzer) (2010), Article 25, para. 50.
[52] *BRI Production "Bonaventure" v. Pan African Export*, Court of Appeal of Grenoble, February 22, 1995, no. 93/3275, available at http://www.cisg.law.pace.edu/cases/950222f1.html.

Marrazza v. Les fils de Henri Ramel,[53] held that a fundamental breach occurs in cases involving the nonmerchantability of the goods.[54]

F. Nachfrist *Notice*

The concept of a right to a time extension for performance or *Nachfrist* notice is foreign to the common law. Thus, its meaning is dependent on interpreting the term in the shadow of the civil law from which it comes. Key issues, assuming the buyer or seller has no commercially viable reason not to grant an extension, are when the time extension begins and how the parties and the courts determine the reasonableness of the time of extension. The answer to the reasonableness of the duration of the extension requested or fixed can only be done on a case-by-case basis. However, the German courts have looked to a number of factors in making the reasonableness determination. Such factors include the buyer's interest in speedy delivery was made apparent at the time of formation,[55] as well as the available means for transport.[56] In the case of an unreasonably short time extension, the majority view is that, although not ineffective, it "initiates a reasonable period."[57]

G. *Price Reduction Remedy*

Professor Faber discusses the interesting proposition of whether the price reduction remedy can reduce the price owed to zero. His analysis of Austrian court decisions showed that the answer is in the affirmative:[58]

> The Supreme Court refers to the diverging opinions on the matter of "price reduction to zero" in the literature and opts for the predominant view that such reduction is possible. In the second case, decided by a Court of First Instance, a price reduction to zero is also held to be compatible with CISG rules. However, in the particular case the buyer's argument that the price should be reduced to zero "because there is no market for poppy seed of the delivered quality in Austria, and the market in Eastern Europe is of no interest to the buyer" is rejected because it disregards the possibilities of either selling the goods to Eastern Europe from Austria or cleaning the contaminated seed and subsequently selling it on the Austrian market. Applying the calculation method established in Article 50, the price was reduced by ten percent.[59]

In a Bulgarian arbitration case, a Bulgarian buyer reduced the price of coal it had purchased from a seller located in the Ukraine by 10 percent.[60] The problem before the

---

[53] *Sacovini/M Marrazza v. Les fils de Henri Ramel*, Court of Cassation, January 23, 1996, n 93–16.542, available at http://cisgw3.law.pace.edu/cases/960123f1.html.

[54] See Sylvaine Poillot-Peruzzetto, "French Perspective of the CISG," Chapter 21 in this book.

[55] Sörren Kiene, "Germany Country Analysis: Part II," Chapter 23 in this book, citing OLG Naumburg, April 27, 1999, 9 U 146/98, CISG-online no. 512.

[56] Id., citing OLG Celle, May 24, 1995, 20 U 76/94, CISG-online no. 152.

[57] Id., citing OLG Naumburg, April 27, 1999, 9 U 146/98, CISG-online no. 512; OLG Celle, May 24, 1995, 20 U 76/94, CISG-online no. 152; OLG Karlsruhe, February 14, 2008, 9 U 46/07, CISG-online no. 1649.

[58] See Wolfgang Faber, "CISG in Austria," Chapter 19 in this book.

[59] Id., citing HG Wien, May 3, 2007, 43 Cg 34/05f, CISG-online 1783 (poppy seed case), available at http://cisgw3.law.pace.edu/cases/070503a3.html.

[60] See Tidas Kilmas, "Baltic States, Belarus, and Ukraine," Chapter 20 in this book.

arbitrator was that, whereas the seller was informed of the nonconformity by the buyer within the time frame required by Article 39, apparently this was not done in the manner required by the contract, which involved an expert review. For this reason, the arbitrator applied Bulgarian law, reducing the amount payable by half based on its finding that both parties were at fault.[61]

H. *Payment of Interest*

An interesting decision from Egypt analyzes the conflict between Shari'a law's prohibition on the charging of interest and CISG Articles 78 and 84. Professor El-Saghir states that:

> Notwithstanding the traditional prohibition of interest in Islam, Article 226 of the Egyptian Civil Code provides as compensation for the delay, interest at the rate of four percent in civil matters and five percent in commercial matters. The Egyptian Constitutional Court held that charging interest is prohibited by Shari'a, but Article 2 of the Constitution [which came into force after the adoption of the Civil Code] has no retroactive effect. Therefore, Article 226 of the Civil Code remains enforceable though contrary to Shari'a.[62]

The issue of whether a party has to make a specific demand for interest was addressed by a Bulgarian arbitration panel.[63] It held that a party must specifically demand payment of interest. Also, Article 78 of the CISG does not provide the means for determining the interest rate to be charged, so recourse must be to national law. Professor Kiene states that: "German courts mainly refer to the statutory interest rate which is applicable according to the national law that has been determined via private international law.[64] Some courts, however, apply the rate of interest that is applicable at the creditor's place of business,[65] the debtor's place of business,[66] or on the currency in which the purchase price is to be paid."[67]

I. *Surprises*

One interesting outlier is Israel's expansion of the scope of CISG jurisdiction. The Israeli legislature in adopting the CISG extended its application by incorporating the following provision: "In addition to what is provided by Article 1 of the convention, its provisions will apply in the case where a party to the contract operates its business in a non-contracting state."[68] Article 1(1)(b) of the CISG states that if only one of the contracting parties is from a member state, the use of rules of private international law (conflict of law rules)

---

[61] Id., citing Unknown Parties, Arbitration Tribunal of the Bulgarian Chamber of Commerce and Industry (Case No. 56/1995) (April 24, 1996), available at http://cisgw3.law.pace.edu/cases/960424bu.html.

[62] See Hossam A. El-Saghir, "CISG in Islamic Countries: The Case of Egypt," Chapter 30 in this book.

[63] Unknown Parties, Arbitration Tribunal of the Bulgarian Chamber of Commerce and Industry (Case No. 11/1996) (February 12, 1998), available at http://cisgw3.law.pace.edu/cases/980212bu.html.

[64] See Sörren Kiene, "Germany Country Analysis: Part II," Chapter 23 in this book, citing LG Coburg, December 12, 2006, 22 O 38/06, CISG-online no. 1447; OLG Düsseldorf, July 22, 2004, I-6 U 210/03, CISG-online no. 916.

[65] Id., citing LG Heidelberg, November 2, 2005, 3 O 169/04, CISG-online no. 1416; LG Bamberg, April 13, 2005, 2 O 340/00, CISG-online no. 1402.

[66] Id., citing LG Frankfurt a.M., September 16, 1991, 3/11 O 3/91, CISG-online no. 26.

[67] Id., citing OLG Rostock, October 10, 2001, 6 U 126/00, CISG-online no. 671.

[68] See Yehuda Adar, "Israel," Chapter 31 in this book.

are to be applied and the CISG applies if the rules point to the CISG country. However, under Israeli law, if either party is from a CISG country, then Israeli courts are instructed to apply the CISG even in cases where the rules of private international law would direct the court to the law of the nonmember country.[69]

The Israeli Supreme Court also crafted an interesting theory of liability for nonconforming goods not directly related to the CISG.[70] In the case, a claim of nonconformity was not sustainable under the CISG because of the lapsing of the prescription period. The court allowed an action in negligence for the defective manufacture of the goods. It enunciated an "interest theory" that distinguished contractual from noncontractual interests stemming from the fact pattern. The plaintiff-buyer could sue for breach of the specific obligations under the contract (which were time barred) or sue for breach of the general duty not to manufacture defective products under tort law.[71]

Tadas Klimas notes a Ukrainian case, the *Metal Production Goods* case that applied Russian substantive law, as well as the CISG.[72] The arbitrator found that the fines paid by the claimant to the government could have been mitigated, under CISG Article 77, had the claimant "initiated arbitration proceedings within ninety days of the events in question. Ostensibly, the arbitrator believed that the plaintiff would have received payment within those ninety days and therefore would have been able to return certain money to the government, thus not incurring the fines."[73] The timing of the initiation of an arbitral proceeding is a strange event to base the duty to mitigate.

V. Influence of German Courts

It is not a controversial statement to state that the predominate force in shaping and interpreting the CISG has been the German court system. The sheer number of cases applying the CISG in Germany relative to other countries is substantial. The question is: What are the positive and negative consequences of this dominance?

A. *Quantity and Quality*

The role of German courts in the interpretive process will be illustrated through a sampling of CISG articles and surrounding case law. For example, there are about 336 cases in Pace's CISG Database relating to the buyer's duty to inspect. German courts rendered 107 of the 336 decisions, or 32 percent. A further look shows that a large portion of the German cases occurred during the formative years of CISG jurisprudence. From 1998 through 2000 there were 146 cases relating to Article 38. Sixty-nine, or 47 percent, of all the cases came from the German court system. Taking it one step further, looking at just the first 50 cases reported in the Database, 27, or 54 percent, were German cases.

---

[69] Id.
[70] Id., citing CA 7833/06 *Pamesa Ceramica v. Yisrael Mendelson Engineering Technical Supply Ltd.* (17.03.2009) (defective tiles case), available at http://cisgw3.law.pace.edu/cases/090317i5.html.
[71] Id.
[72] See Tadas Klimas, "Baltic States, Belarus, and Ukraine," Chapter 20 in this book, citing Unknown Parties, Tribunal of International Commercial Arbitration at Ukraine Chamber of Commerce and Trade (1999), available at http://cisgw3.law.pace.edu/cases/990709u5.html]; 22 Am Jur 2d Damages §335 (regarding mitigation of damages in general).
[73] Id.

However, if we fast forward to more recent cases, there is a much greater diversity of countries rendering decisions. Of the 50 most recently reported cases on Article 38,[74] only six, or 12 percent, were German cases. Furthermore, the cases came from 18 different countries. Despite the recent diversity of case origins, does there remain a continuing influence of German CISG jurisprudence on non-German case decisions? Of the 50 reported cases, only 35 were translated into English. By subtracting the six German cases, the remaining 29 cases showed a number of interesting facts. First, the review showed that 18 of the cases cited no external sources of law – foreign legal cases or commentary. Many of these cases, mostly from civil law countries, simply cited the CISG. A number of cases cited domestic commentaries on the CISG. For example, two Greek cases cited what seems to be a deep Greek literature relating to the CISG. Of the remaining 14 non-German cases, seven of the cases cited German scholarship (4), German case law (2), or both (1). One Swiss case in determining the promptness of a notice of nonconformity noted that "according to German jurisprudence, a time for notification of one month is reasonable in these cases"[75] This demonstrates a continuing influence of the German literature and jurisprudence on the interpretation and application of the CISG outside of Germany, but this influence is primarily confined to the European continent.

B. *The CISG as a European Code?*

The Pace Database's "Country Case Schedule" of court and arbitral decisions provides some cursory insight into the overwhelming influence of the civil law countries in the interpretation of the CISG. Of the 2,718 reported cases (as of October 15, 2011), 1,364 of the cases came from eight European countries: Germany (477), the Netherlands (203), Switzerland (182), Belgium (142), Austria (128), France (100), Spain (83), and Italy (49). As important as the quantity of cases is the fact that a majority of the cases were substantively reasoned judicial opinions.

In contrast, the common law countries yielded only 200 cases: the United States (151), Australia (19), Canada (16), New Zealand (11), and the United Kingdom (3). These numbers are inflated given the fact that a good number of the early American cases were instances where the CISG was excluded as inapplicable law. In two of the United Kingdom cases, the CISG was used as soft law. Regrettably, Lord Hoffman used the CISG as an example of how different it is, like French law, from English law: "Both the Unidroit Principles of International Commercial Contracts and the Principles of European Contract law . . . [as well as] the United Nations Convention on Contract for the International Sale of Goods . . . reflect French philosophy of contractual interpretation, which is altogether different from that of English law."[76]

The civil law–common law divide, and the differences in the degrees of application of the CISG among civil law countries, is again reflected by the number of cases that reach the highest court in the respective judicial systems. There were 241 cases that reached countries' supreme courts. CISG-related cases reached the Austrian Supreme

---

[74] These cases covered the period between January 5, 2007 and August 19, 2010.
[75] Switzerland. September 6, 2007, Kantonsgericht [District Court] Appenzel Ausserhoden (Clothing case), available at http://cisgw3.law.pace.edu/cases/070906s1.html.
[76] *Chartbrook Ltd. v. Persimmon Homes Ltd.*, United Kingdom, July 1, 2009, House of Lords, available at http://cisgw3.law.pace.edu/cases/090701uk.html.

Court (*Oberster Gerichtshof*) an astonishing 78 times, or 32 percent of all Supreme Court cases worldwide. Germany was next with 35, followed by France (27), Switzerland (26), Italy (21), Spain (13), and the Netherlands (11). In contrast, there are no cases applying the CISG as applicable law to reach a supreme court of a common law country. Eighteen cases have reached the Federal Circuit Court level in the United States.

In some countries, the primary means for the application of the CISG has been in arbitration proceedings. The CISG has been commonly used by arbitral tribunals in the Russian Federation (285) and the People's Republic of China (424). Of the 424 Chinese cases, 335 were decided by China's International Economic and Trade Arbitration Commission (CIETAC). Of the 285 arbitral cases from the Russian Federation, a majority came from the Tribunal of International Arbitration at the Russian Federation Chamber of Commerce and Industry (MKAC Arbitral Tribunal). In Serbia, 60 of the 70 case decisions came from the Foreign Trade Court of Arbitration attached to the Yugoslav Chamber of Commerce.

VI. Influence of the CISG

The first section of this part recognizes that it may take a generation of new lawyers and judges before the CISG can be universally recognized and applied. The second section looks at the influence the CISG has already had in changing national laws.

A. *Generational Lag*

The general response to the acknowledgment of the CISG as domestic law has been by practicing lawyers opting out of its application. Dr. Yehuda Adar notes that "the common practice (in Israel) is to explicitly exclude the application of the CISG, or at least to explicitly set the domestic law governing; to minimize uncertainty and to rely on familiar domestic law."[77] This is the reason often given for the scarcity of CISG cases in many contracting countries.

The hope is that, even in countries where the CISG has been ignored, the next generation of lawyers, judges, and arbitrators will have an adequate knowledge of the CISG and its benefits as a harmonizing law. In the United States, there is an effort at many law schools to at least introduce the CISG to students either through the first-year contracts course or through an upper-level sales law or international business law seminar.

B. *Vehicle for Harmonization of National Laws*

The CISG's purpose was to provide a single set of rules that would be adopted by contracting countries in order to harmonize international sales law. A somewhat unintended consequence has been the use of the CISG as a template, or more minimally as a source, in the revisions of national sales and contract laws. This has been the case, subject to debate, in Germany (BGB, 2002), the People's Republic of China, New Dutch Civil Code, and in the current revision processes for a new French Civil Code and Japanese Civil Code. Professor Sonja Kruisinga acknowledges the influence of the CISG on the

---

[77] See Yehuda Adar, "Israel," Chapter 31 in this book.

law of obligations in the New Dutch Civil Code or Burgerlijk Wetboek (BW): "It is difficult to underestimate the influence of the CISG on national sales law."[78]

Professor Stefan Kröll states that since the enactment of the revised German law of obligations, the instances of opting out of the CISG has been in the decline.[79] He notes that the increased commonality, due to the revision of the BGB, between the CISG and German domestic law has resulted in practicing lawyers becoming more familiar with CISG's concepts, and more willing to use the CISG.[80] Professor Sörren Kiene notes that "as in the laws of many other countries,[81] the reformed German Civil Code is now consciously based on UN Sales."[82]

Professor Li Wei asserts that the CISG has served to supplement Chinese law and also served a symbolic purpose. First, the General Principles of the Civil Law of People's Republic of China and the Common Contract Law (CCL) were enacted on October 1, 1999. The CCL contains many provisions similar to the rules found in the CISG and UNIDROIT Principles. The new laws symbolized the "switch from a planned economic regime to a socialist market economy." Furthermore, Li Wei notes that the CISG "deeply affects Chinese legal practice" as it has become a "familiar business instrument of the Chinese law practitioner."[83]

Another use of the CISG in harmonizing domestic law was provided by the Italian Constitutional Court. The Italian Constitutional Court was asked to interpret a provision of the Italian Civil Code that establishes the rule according to which "the seller is discharged from the obligation to deliver when he hands the goods to the carrier."[84] The court confirmed that the rule was consistent with the Constitution because it is consistent with CISG Articles 31 and 67.[85] Edoardo Ferrante notes that such rulings contribute to ensuring the conformity of the Italian Civil Code with the Constitution, "by expressing common internationally-recognized values and principles."[86]

---

[78] See Sonja A. Kruisinga, "The Netherlands," Chapter 29 in this book.
[79] See Stefan Kröll, "Germany Country Analysis: Good Faith, Formation, and Conformity of Goods," Chapter 22 in this book.
[80] Id. Kröll notes that in the official statement accompanying the proposal for the revision of the German law, it was explicitly stated that the law should be oriented on the principles of the CISG. See Bundestags-Drucksache 14/6040, p. 86.
[81] See, e.g., Dutch Burgerlijk Wetboek, the 1999 Chinese Common Contract Law, and Scandinavian sales law have been based on the CISG. See Sörren Claas Kiene, *Vertragsaufhebung und Rücktritt im UN-Kaufrecht und BGB* (Baden-Baden: Nomos Verlag, 2010), 23.
[82] See Sörren Kiene, "Germany Country Analysis: Part II," Chapter 23 in this book.
[83] See Li Wei, "People's Republic of China," Chapter 33 in this book.
[84] Italian Civil Code, Article 1510.
[85] See Edoardo Ferrante, "Italy," Chapter 24 in this book, citing Corte Costituzionale, November 19, 1992, no. 465, *Giurisprudenza costituzionale* 4191 (1992); *Foro italiano* 3201 (1992); *Giustizia civile* 314 (1994); *Diritto del commercio internazionale* 446 (1995), available at http://cisgw3.law.pace.edu/cases/921119i3.html.
[86] See Edoardo Ferrante, "Italy," Chapter 24 in this book.

Part VII *Theoretical Insights*

37 Problems of Uniform Laws

Jan M. Smits

I. Introduction

It is widely acknowledged that the United Nations Convention on Contracts for the International Sale of Goods (CISG)[1] is the best example of the unification of private law at the global level. With eighty contracting states, and more likely to join,[2] the CISG represents the greatest legislative achievement in the field of uniform private law at the international level.[3] Its success would not only include its widespread adoption, but also lie in its use as a model for other texts, including the UNIDROIT Principles of International Commercial Contracts (PICC),[4] the Principles of European Contract Law (PECL),[5] Draft Common Frame of Reference (DCFR),[6] the OHADA Acte uniforme portant sur le droit commercial général (AUDCG),[7] the Principios Generales del Derecho de Contratos,[8] the European Directive on Sale of Consumer Goods,[9] as well its influence on a number of national law revisions of contract law, such as the 1988 uniform Nordic Sale of Goods Act, 1999 Contract Law of the People's Republic of China, and the new German Law of Obligations of 2002.[10]

To summarize, the success of the CISG is seen as three-fold in nature. First, the original contracting states were able to draft and adopt a common text that can be seen as a codification of commercial contract practice. Second, the CISG has been adopted widely at a brisk pace. Third, the CISG has served as an important model for revisions of national laws and for other international texts. Interestingly, all three achievements are almost exclusively based on how *states* (and scholars) perceive the importance of

---

[1] Adopted in Vienna on April 11, 1980, and entered into force in 1988, 1489 UNTS 3, available at www.cisg.law.pace.edu.

[2] Brazil became the 79th country to adopt the CISG, followed by Bahrain (both in 2013).

[3] Cf. Joseph Lookofsky, "Loose Ends and Contorts in International Sales: Problems in the Harmonization of Private Law Rules," 39 *American J. of Comparative Law* 403 (1991).

[4] UNIDROIT, *Principles of International Commercial Contracts* (Rome, 2010; first edition, 1999).

[5] *Principles of European Contract Law, Parts I and II*, (ed. Ole Lando and Hugh Beale) (The Hague, 2000), and *Principles of European Contract Law, Part III* (ed. Ole Lando et al.) (The Hague, 2003).

[6] *Principles, Definitions and Model Rules of European Private Law: Draft Common Frame of Reference*, 6 vols. (ed. Christian Von Bar and Eric Clive) (Munich, 2009).

[7] Adopted in 2010; *Journal Officiel OHADA* 15 (2011), No. 23, available at www.droit-afrique.com.

[8] See www.fundacionfueyo.udp.cl/archivos/catedra_der_cont_informe_chile.pdf.

[9] European Directive 1999/44 on sale of consumer goods, *OJ* L 171/12.

[10] Cf. Ingeborg Schwenzer and Pascal Hachem, "The CISG: Successes and Pitfalls," 57 *American J. of Comparative Law* 457–78 (2009).

the CISG. The question becomes whether the same is true for other actors involved in the legal process, such as commercial parties, attorneys, courts, and arbitral tribunals. Unfortunately, much of the abundant literature on the CISG does not adequately deal with its use by these other actors,[11] especially in view of the evidence that parties often exclude its applicability.

This chapter will pursue a more critical perspective and discuss several problems related to uniform laws. This is not to downplay the importance of efforts to create more legal uniformity – the other contributions to this volume show that these efforts can be very valuable – but to obtain a better picture of their drawbacks and investigate ways minimize such negative results.

II. Problematic Relationship between Cross-Border Trade and Uniform Laws

Before I discuss several specific problems related to the CISG, it is useful to devote some attention to the more general relationship between cross-border trade and uniform law. The preamble to the CISG states that the convention serves to "promote the development of international trade."[12] This is usually seen as the main aim of unifying laws, based on the assumption that if laws among countries differ, parties may refrain from doing business abroad (or will in any event incur additional costs when selling goods or doing business internationally). Along with international conventions, the European legislature frequently uses the argument that when it takes harmonizing measures in the field of contract law it is lowering barriers to trade within the common market.[13]

Despite this conceptual reasoning, there is no empirical proof that there is a direct causal relationship between unification of laws and an increase in cross-border trade.[14] If there is a positive relationship, it may not be as statistically significant as one would surmise. First, parties, when making the decision (not) to contract, are usually influenced by other factors than law. If they are restrained from entering into a cross-border transaction, this may be due more due to factors such as distance and differences in language or culture than to differences in the law. And insofar as law does play a role in making decisions about whether or not to contract,[15] it is likely that fields such as procedural law or tax law form greater barriers to trade than differences in contract law, which consists largely of nonmandatory rules. The impact of the unification of contract law on international transactions is likely overestimated by those promoting such unification; decisions to contract, in reality, are influenced by various motives.

---

[11] See, however, Arthur Rosett, "Critical Reflections on the United Nations Convention on Contracts for the International Sale of Goods," 45 *Ohio State L. J.* 265ff. (1984); Paul B. Stephan, "The Futility of Unification and Harmonization in International Commercial Law," 39 *Virginia J. of Int'l L.* 743ff. (1999), Clayton P. Gillette and Robert E. Scott, "The Political Economy of International Sales Law," 25 *International Rev. of Law & Economics* 446 (2005).

[12] Also see the "Schmitthoff-report" (Report of the Secretary-General, A/6396, para. 204).

[13] An overview is provided in Jan M. Smits, "Convergence of private law in Europe: towards a new ius commune?," in *Comparative Law: A Handbook* (ed. Esin Örücü and David Nelken) (Oxford, 2007), 219–40.

[14] See the special issue of the *European Journal of Law & Economics* 2011 (see contributions by Smits, Low, O'Hara, Gomez and Ganuza, and Wagner), available at http://www.springerlink.com/content/261142tm11514620.

[15] See Gary Low, "The Ir(relevance) of Harmonisation and Legal Diversity to European Contract Law: A Perspective from Psychology," 17 *European Rev. of Private L.* 28ff. (2010).

The second point is more fundamental – commercial parties do not necessarily have an interest in international law unification. Their concerns are likely to be more general in nature – to have *some* legal system applicable to their contract, rather than one that is uniform across borders. This is important to emphasize because insofar as commercial parties have a *choice* between various legal systems that can be applicable to their contract, they are likely to choose the legal system they know best, or that (in their view) provides them with the most legal certainty. True, in an ideal world they would probably prefer to have one law applicable to all their transactions, no matter where they take place. But, in reality, they are unlikely to give it much thought. One reason they don't give it much thought is that uniform laws are never a truly self-standing legal regime that completely excludes the applicability of national law. In this sense, the creation of a uniform sales regime can complicate matters. The parties are no longer governed by one law, but by fragments consisting of national rules and the rules of the CISG. These general considerations reveal that if parties have the choice between a uniform international sales regime and a domestic system, they do not necessarily prefer the former.

III. Problems with the CISG

Scholars often identify three problems of the CISG: the unevenness of its application by national and arbitral courts in the contracting states, its regular exclusion by parties, and its incompleteness.[16] This part analyzes these three problems and suggests that all of them are a part of one overall problem with uniform laws.

A. *Uniform Application of the CISG by Courts*

Much has been written about the question of whether uniformity of application under the CISG exists[17] or whether it is likely to ever exist.[18] There is unanimity on the point that the answer is completely dependent on what one understands uniformity to be.[19] If this means an identical interpretation of every provision, such uniformity is problematic even within a single legal system. This is well captured by Lord Wilberforce, who wrote that "to plead for complete uniformity may be to cry for the moon."[20] The general opinion is that something less then complete uniformity should be the standard. Suggestions include some form of "consistent" interpretation,[21] "varying degrees of similar

---

[16] Other problems often mentioned relate to the substantive rules of the CISG, including its supposed one-sidedness (favoring the interests of the seller).

[17] See, e.g., Philip Hackney, "Is the United Nations Convention on the International Sale of Goods Achieving Uniformity?," 61 *Louisiana L. Rev.* 473 (2001); Daniela de Lukowicz, *Divergenzen in der Rechtsprechung zum CISG: Auf dem Weg zu einer einheitlichen Auslegung und Anwendung?* (Bern, 2001); *The 1980 Uniform Sales Law: Old Issues Revisited in the Light of Recent Experiences* (ed. Franco Ferrari) (Munich, 2003) (various contributions).

[18] The fundamental contribution in this respect is R.J.C. Munday, "The Uniform Interpretation of International Conventions," 27 *Int'l & Comparative L. Quarterly* 450ff. (1978).

[19] On what is uniformity, see Camilla Baasch Andersen, "Defining Uniformity in Law," 12 *Uniform L. Rev.* 5 (2007); Robert E. Scott, "The Uniformity Norm in Commercial Law," in *The Jurisprudential Foundations of Corporate and Commercial Law* (ed. Jody S. Kraus and Steven D. Walt) (Cambridge, 2000), 149ff.

[20] *Photo Production Ltd v. Securicor Transport Ltd.* [1980] 1 *All ER* 556, at 562.

[21] Eric Bergsten, "Methodological Problems in the Drafting of the CISG," in *CISG Methodology* (ed. Janssen and Meyer) (Munich, 2009), 31.

effects,"[22] or the achievement of "a standard of common discourse,"[23] or "relative uniformity"[24] is enough to meet the threshold of uniformity of application for the CISG.

This implies that, viewed from the perspective of the drafter and signatory of the CISG, a relatively low standard of uniformity suffices. This is well reflected in the open-ended provision of CISG Article 7(1), stating that in the interpretation of the CISG, "regard is to be had to its international character and to the need to promote uniformity in its application."[25] It is also reflected in the fact that the CISG is seen as a success despite the absence of a court of final appeal that deals with disputes on the CISG, or of an official administrative body that provides guidelines on how to interpret its provisions.[26]

The methods that are used in interpreting the CISG are in line with this not too ambitious desire for relative uniformity. The court is not allowed to rely on national law, but should engage in a truly autonomous interpretation.[27] This duty includes the need to take into account foreign court decisions on the interpretation of CISG provisions,[28] even though it is disputed how to undertake such a comparative analysis. Clearly, without the presence of an international appellate court, foreign case law cannot be considered to be binding precedent.[29] Various databases (access to foreign case law)[30] and soft law principles (interpretive guidance)[31] can help courts reach some level of convergence. Despite these developments, the question remains to what extent can homeward trend bias be avoided.[32] The CISG's use of open-ended terms[33] increases the likelihood of

---

[22] Camilla Baasch Andersen, "Macro-Systematic Interpretation of Uniform Commercial Law: The Interrelation of the CISG and Other Uniform Sources," in Janssen and Meyer, *CISG Methodology*, 212.

[23] Larry A. DiMatteo et al., *International Sales Law: A Critical Analysis of CISG Jurisprudence* (Cambridge, 2005), 2. See also John Honnold, "The Sales Convention in Action – Uniform International Words: Uniform Application?," 8 *J. of Law & Commerce* 207 (1988).

[24] Peter J. Mazzacano, "Harmonizing Values, Not Laws: The CISG and the Benefits of a Neo-Realist Perspective," 1 *Nordic J. of Commercial Law* (2008) (the aim is not harmonization of laws, but of values regarding the conduct of international trade in goods).

[25] Similar provisions can be found in Article 4 of UNIDROIT Convention on International Factoring and in Article 6 of UNIDROIT Convention on International Financial Leasing.

[26] However, the informal CISG Advisory Council does provide nonbinding opinions on debated interpretations. See www.cisgac.org.

[27] See *Commentary on the International Sales Law* (ed. Bianca and Bonell) (Milan, 1987), Article 7 (Bonell), 72; *Kommentar zum einheitlichen UN-Kaufrecht*, 4th ed. (ed. P. Schlechtriem and I. Schwenzer) (Munich, 2004), Article 7 (Ferrari); Sieg Eiselen, "Literal Interpretation: The Meaning of the Words," in Janssen and Meyer, *CISG Methodology*, 61–89 (pointing at the prevailing literal approach in interpreting the CISG).

[28] See Ulrich Magnus, "Tracing Methodology in the CISG: Dogmatic Foundations," in Janssen and Meyer, *CISG Methodology*, 41.

[29] Bianca and Bonell in *Commentary*, Article 7. See also Larry A. DiMatteo, "Case Law Precedent and Legal Writing," in Janssen and Meyer, *CISG Methodology*, 114 (rightly characterizing this as mere "persuasive authority").

[30] CLOUT (Case Law on Uncitral Texts), providing summaries of case law in six languages, available at www.uncitral.org/uncitral.en/case_law/digests/cisg.html; UNILEX, available at www.unilex.info; CISG Database at Pace University, available at www.cisg.law.pace.edu.

[31] In particular, the UNIDROIT Principles of International Commercial Contracts provides context to the CISG-provisions.

[32] See Franco Ferrari, "Homeward Trend: What, Why and Why Not," in Janssen and Meyer, *CISG Methodology*, 171.

[33] Not only does it contain concepts that leave much discretion to the court (such as "reasonable time" in Article 39(1) CISG), it also lacks some essential definitions (such as what is actually a contract of sale of goods).

divergent interpretations across national legal systems and legal traditions. In the end, the importance of the question to what extent the CISG can indeed be uniformly applied is of relatively little usefulness. The ultimate test is not whether the CISG creates a uniform regime, but whether it promotes the development of international trade. As previously noted, the relationship between uniform law and the promotion of trade is unclear.

B. *Exclusion by Contracting Parties*

A second perceived problem of the CISG is that parties often exclude its application in their contracts. A survey by Martin Koehler shows that 70.8 percent of parties in the United States and 72.2 percent of parties in Germany routinely exclude the applicability of the CISG.[34] The general conditions of numerous industry organizations, such as the Federation of Oils, Seeds, and Fats Associations (FOSFA) and the Grain and Feed Trade Association (GAFTA), contain provisions to the same effect. An older survey among large companies in the Netherlands demonstrated that most of them exclude the applicability of the CISG. This same survey showed that smaller Dutch companies often do not exclude the CISG, unless legal advice was obtained prior to the formation of the contract.[35] Reasons for opting out include that the parties (more likely their attorneys) are aware of the substantive rules of the CISG and fear that it leaves too much room for varying interpretations. Or, the parties are aware of the existence of the CISG, but are reluctant to invest the time and money to study its contents or to tailor (derogate) the CISG to their particular needs.

A conscious opting out of the CISG is not a bad thing. The CISG creates a uniform regime that does not *replace* existing national regimes on sale of goods, but only provides an extra option for parties that feel their interests are better served by a uniform sales regime. To the contrary, in every case in which a party is aware of the existence of the CISG and its potential applicability to the contract, there is an empirical test of its usefulness.[36] The recurrent theme is apparently that we should not confuse the goal of uniformity with the interests of parties.

C. *Incompleteness of the CISG*

The third problem is the incompleteness of the legal regime created by the CISG. This incompleteness manifests itself in different ways. The CISG governs only the formation of the contract of sale and the rights and obligations of the parties, including contractual remedies. CISG Article 4 delegates questions of validity and the effect of the contract on property issues to national law. An additional problem of the CISG is that it does

---

[34] Martin F. Koehler, "Survey Regarding the Relevance of the United Nations Convention for the International Sale of Goods (CISG) in Legal Practice and the Exclusion of Its Application (2006)," available at www.cisg.law.pace.edu/cisg/biblio/koehler.html. For an extensive analysis of the CISG's exclusion in practice, see Ulrich G. Schroeter, "Empirical Evidence of Courts and Counsels' Approach to the CISG (with Some Remarks on Professional Liability)," Chapter 40 in this book.

[35] R.I.V.F. Bertrams, *Enige aspecten van het Weens Koopverdrag* (Deventer, 1995), 72.

[36] One wonders whether it would therefore not be better to have parties explicitly *opt in* to the uniform regime, as was also proposed in the recent proposal of the European Commission for a Regulation on a Common European Sales Law, COM (2011) 635.

not exclude concurrent remedies in domestic tort laws, which means that under some jurisdictions the creditor may have extra rights.

The problem, therefore, is that the CISG regime includes numerous gaps that must be filled by the domestic law that is applicable by way of conflict of law rules; the very method of determining applicable law that the CISG was created to preempt. This is a strong reason for parties to exclude the CISG. The imperfection of one national jurisdiction may be preferred over a legal regime where rights and obligations are governed by a mixture of international and national laws, no matter the quality of the fragments.[37]

D. *Background Problem: The CISG Is Not a "Jurisdiction"*

The three problems identified in the preceding sections all deal with a specific aspect of the CISG – lack of uniform application, widespread exclusion of it by contracting parties, and the incompleteness of its coverage. All three aspects are related to an important characteristic of all uniform legal regimes created by international conventions. The uniform law does do not create a full-fledged and self-standing jurisdiction. For the moment, the CISG provides primarily a *text* without a developed system of case law, without a uniform appellate court system, and without being a part of a system of uniform laws in related areas.

This does not downplay the importance of the CISG from the viewpoint of states interested in creating a harmonized system of contract rules. However, it does suggest that the CISG is problematic from the viewpoint of commercial parties. These parties are primarily interested in legal certainty that allows them to calculate the costs of a certain transaction. If parties can choose between a national jurisdiction and the CISG, and have full information about the substantive rules in each of these regimes, they are likely to choose the former. An example of legal uncertainty relating to the CISG is given by Erich Schanze:[38] "For the case of non-delivery of marketable goods in kind, which is probably the most relevant case in international sales, German law answers: 'specific performance,' English law: 'money damages,' [and] the CISG 'maybe either.'"

The case law on the CISG is also telling in that many of the so-called "CISG cases" are about the very applicability of the CISG. Questions such as whether the CISG was excluded or not, whether there was a contract of sale, and whether the contract could be qualified as an international and commercial one remain major areas of dispute. This is proof that there is no shared conviction in the business world that the CISG is the best available law for international contracting.

Two important consequences follow from this analysis. The first is an optimistic one – the more case law is produced by the courts, the more legal certainty the CISG may be able to provide.[39] This will lead to an increase in the number of parties electing not to opt out of the CISG. We already see some signs of this "network effect."[40] Viewed

---

[37] For the status quo bias and "stickiness" of laws, see Gary Low, *European Contract Law between the Single Market and the Law Market: A Behavioural Perspective* (2011), 195ff.

[38] Erich Schanze, "Dispute resolution in the shadow of uniform contract law?," in *International Dispute Resolution*, vol. 2: *Dialogue between Courts in Times of Globalization and Regionalization* (ed. Carl Baudenbacher) (2010), 153ff.

[39] See also Hackney, "Is the United Nations Convention on the International Sale of Goods Achieving Uniformity?," 486.

[40] Cf. Schroeter, Chapter 40 of this book.

this way, it could just be a matter of time before the CISG provides the uniformity and certainty that it was intended to achieve.

The second consequence is that as long as the CISG is an optional set of rules, it will have to compete with national alternatives that, for many commercial parties, provide greater legal certainty. Unless that changes, the CISG will remain a secondary option. For example, it can be used as a compromise "neutral law" in cases where the contracting parties cannot agree to an applicable national law.

IV. Conclusion

The problems identified in this analysis are problems that beset all uniform laws. However, these are only problems if one considers the establishment of a uniform law as the only possible way in which international trade can be promoted. This is, however, not the case. If this analysis is right, it would be much more important to allow parties to make the national jurisdiction of their choice applicable to the contract. The great value of the CISG may be that it provides commercial parties with a common frame of reference in which they are able to compare the solutions provided by the CISG with various national jurisdictions. In this way, provisions of the CISG can be used to derogate from specific rules of the national law chosen by the parties.

38 The CISG as Bridge between Common and Civil Law

Sieg Eiselen

I. Introduction

The purpose of all harmonizing legislation is to replace current diverse laws in various jurisdictions with an overarching unifying or harmonizing legal regime. This can be done in a number of ways and by way of different types of instruments. The United Nations Commission for International Trade Law (UNCITRAL) was founded by the United Nations for the very purpose of harmonizing international trade law. UNCITRAL uses two types of instruments – international conventions and model laws – in order to carry out its mission.[1] Multilateral international conventions are used to introduce a single legal solution within the various jurisdictions of the member states that elect to adopt the convention. Model laws are utilized to provide a template, which may be used by different states, but there is no legal obligation to apply model laws, as is the case with multilateral conventions. The harmonizing effect of model laws is dependent on the degree to which states change their laws to conform to the model. The European Union uses a third instrument, binding directives, which require member states to change their laws to adhere to the directive's core principals, but the member states are not required to copy the directive, as long as their laws conform to the core principles of the directive.

In international trade there are two major legal traditions that usually inform any efforts to unify or harmonize law, namely the common and civil laws. The common law has its roots in the developments of English law, from where it spread to its former possessions – Australia, Canada, New Zealand, and the United States.[2] It also made its presence felt in other former colonies such as India, South Africa, Botswana, Kenya, Zambia and Zimbabwe.[3] The civil law by contrast has its origins in continental Europe and is based on Roman law. It spread throughout Europe during the late Middle Ages and the Enlightenment. The *ius commune* (general legal principles of the civil law) formed the basis for the dominant European codes, such as the French Code Civil, the German Bürgerliches Gesetzbuch and the Dutch Burgerlijk Wetboek.[4] It has also influenced the legal systems of South America, Japan, and the former socialist countries of Eastern Europe.[5]

---

[1] See UNCITRAL Web site at http://www.uncitral.org/uncitral/en/uncitral_texts.html.

[2] K. Zweigert and H. Kötz, *An Introduction to Comparative Law*, 3rd ed. (Oxford: Oxford University Press, 1998), 218ff.

[3] P. De Cruz, *Comparative Law*, 2nd ed. (London: Cavendish, 1999), 34–5.

[4] Zweigert and Kötz, *Comparative Law* 79, 132ff.; De Cruz, *Comparative Law*, 55–8; David R. Brierley, *Major Legal Systems in the World Today*, 2nd ed. (London: Stevens: London 1968), 28ff.

[5] Zweigert and Kötz, *Comparative Law*, 154–5.

The common and the civil laws are based on very different histories and influences and have developed as two very distinct legal cultures each with their very own underlying philosophies, sources, methods, and ideas. It is therefore no surprise that in fora where legal harmonization is discussed, such as UNCITRAL or the European Union, much of the discussion is often centered on these differences. Although the common law–civil law divide is sometimes exaggerated, there remain real differences between the two systems.[6] Any efforts at forming a harmonizing law must necessarily take note of these differences and deal with them in a manner that will transcend the divergences in the two legal systems.

The Vienna Convention for the International Sale of Goods (CISG) is one of the most successful instruments in the harmonization of international trade law with its adoption by eighty countries – and growing.[7] The true measure, however, of the success of a harmonizing instrument is the extent to which it is interpreted and applied in practice. A convention cannot be regarded as a successful harmonizing instrument if its interpretation varies among member countries due to homeward trend bias (application of national legal concepts).[8] The focus of this chapter is the question of whether the CISG has managed to build a bridge between the common and civil laws of sales. The first part of the discussion will be directed at highlighting the differences between the common and civil legal traditions. The next part will be devoted to identifying a number of key areas within the CISG where the common law or the civil law made a distinct contribution to the adopted rules. The final part of the discussion will be devoted to analyzing the way in which the CISG has been interpreted and applied and whether it has resulted in real harmonization in practice – that is, whether it has substantially bridged the common law–civil law divide.

II. Common Law–Civil Law Divide

The divisions and distinctions between common law and civil law are a widely held perception amongst lawyers around the world. It has long been a subject amongst comparativist scholars.[9] It is a distinction that is based on the idea that certain legal systems may be grouped together as legal families based on their common history, distinctive modes of legal thinking, common legal institutions, sources of law, and ideology.[10] The distinction has been useful as a starting point for lawyers wishing to conduct comparative research to obtain a sense of the nature and characteristics of different legal systems. It is inevitable that this analysis will be based on generalizations, which do not hold true in all circumstances.[11]

---

[6] M. Vranken, *Fundamentals of European Civil Law*, 2nd ed. (Annandale: Federation, 2010) para. [1002] ff.

[7] P. Schlechtriem and I. Schwenzer, *Commentary on the UN Convention on the International Sale of Goods*, 3rd ed. (ed. P. Schlechtriem and I. Schwenzer) (Oxford: Oxford University Press, 2010), 1–2.

[8] Franco Ferrari, "CISG Case Law: A New Challenge for Interpreters?," 17 *J. of L. & Commerce* 245–61 (1999); Ryan, "The Convention on Contracts for the International Sale of Goods: Divergent Interpretations," 4 *Tul. J. Int'l & Comp. L.* 99, 101 (1995). See also, J. Lookofsky, "Consequential Damages in Comparative Context," 19 *Pace Intl L. Rev.* 294 (2007).

[9] Zweigert and Kötz, *Comparative Law*, 63ff.; De Cruz, *Comparative Law*, 33; Brierley, *Major Legal Systems*, 11–13.

[10] Zweigert and Kötz, *Comparative Law*, 68–9; De Cruz, *Comparative Law*, 33–4.

[11] Zweigert and Kötz, *Comparative Law*, 67.

The common law–civil law paradigm is founded to a large extent on the comparativists' research of comparative private law.[12] Very different distinctions may be drawn depending on the subject matter. In the end, the distinction between legal families is only valuable if it contributes to an understanding of foreign law and foreign legal systems. Sales law, as a private law discipline, falls within the classic paradigm.[13] In the following discussion, the classical approach and criteria used in distinguishing common and civil law systems will be followed.

A. *Characteristics of the Common Law*

The development of the English Common Law is characterized to a large extent by how it developed in isolation, free from the influences that shaped the continental legal systems. To a very large measure it developed as judge-made law, with the local Anglo-Saxon rules being displaced by the law made by royal judges and the chancellor.[14] This centrally developed common law obviated the need for a codification of the law as happened on the continent. From early on the procedures in the royal courts were centred on writs.[15] A litigant was not able to bring a case unless an appropriate writ existed under which the claim could be subsumed. Thus, English law was based on procedural thinking – practitioners were thinking in terms of writs or actions rather than in terms of rights.[16] The very formalistic nature of the writ system in time led to a parallel procedure being adopted by the chancellor to hear cases based on a contravention of morals and good conscience. This led to the development of a new branch of law called "equity" with its own rules and remedies, which augmented the common law.[17] The law was further developed by ad hoc pieces of legislation issued by Parliament.[18] In sum, the common law is characterized as judge-made law, accounting for the importance of case law, procedural law, and the *stare decisis* principle.[19]

The training of lawyers strengthened the case-based creation of law.[20] During most of the history of English law, lawyers had little or no contact with academics and universities but were practically trained by other lawyers. Strongly organized professional bodies monopolized legal education. Leading lawyers were always practitioners and judges did not come from the ranks of professors or public officials. This further contributed to the fact that Roman law never obtained the influence in England that it did on the continent.[21] The practitioners' self-interests were in maintaining the common law system of which they were the experts.[22] Judges were and still are appointed mainly from the ranks of leading practitioners.

---

[12] Id., 65.
[13] See Zweigert and Kötz, *Comparative Law*, 63ff.; Brierley, *Major Legal Systems*, 9ff.; De Cruz, *Comparative Law*, 34ff.
[14] Zweigert and Kötz, *Comparative Law*, 181ff.; Brierley, *Major Legal Systems*, 258ff.
[15] Brierley, *Major Legal Systems*, 265; Zweigert and Kötz, *Comparative Law*, 184ff.
[16] Zweigert and Kötz, *Comparative Law*, 186; Brierley, *Major Legal Systems*, 271.
[17] Zweigert and Kötz, *Comparative Law*, 188; Brierley, *Major Legal Systems*, 273ff.
[18] Zweigert and Kötz, *Comparative Law*, 185; Brierley, *Major Legal Systems*, 279.
[19] De Cruz, *Comparative Law*, 103.
[20] Zweigert and Kötz, *Comparative Law*, 191ff.; Brierley, *Major Legal Systems*, 286.
[21] Zweigert and Kötz, *Comparative Law*, 194; Brierley, *Major Legal Systems*, 286.
[22] Zweigert and Kötz, *Comparative Law*, 193.

The common law and equity systems, in the eighteenth and nineteenth centuries, were fused into one legal and court system, replacing the numerous independent benches within one Supreme Court of Judicature.[23] The nineteenth century also saw the rise in the importance of legislation including various codifications of the common law.[24] Sales law was codified with the passage of the Sale of Goods Act 1893. The twentieth century witnessed a proliferation of statutory law in England. The Sale of Goods Act of 1893 was replaced by the Sale of Goods Act 1979, which modernized the law and consolidated aspects of sale found in other statutes.[25]

Against this background, the techniques and methods of legal thinking developed were attuned to a precedent-based, case law system.[26] Roscoe Pound described this approach as follows:[27]

> Behind the characteristic doctrines and ideas and techniques of the common law lawyer there is a significant frame of mind. It is a frame of mind, which habitually looks at things in the concrete, not in the abstract; which puts faith in experience rather than in abstractions. It is a frame of mind which prefers to go forward cautiously on the basis of experience from this case or that case to the next, as justice in each case seems to require, instead of seeking to refer everything back to supposed universals . . . The civilian naturally reasons from principles to instances, the common lawyer from instances to principles. The civilian lawyer puts his faith in syllogisms, the common lawyer in precedents; the first silently asking himself "What should we do this time?" and the second asking aloud in the same situation, "What did we do last time?"

Although there is a lot of truth in this assessment of the differences in approach, there is a much narrower gap in the way of thinking between common and civil lawyers in the twenty-first century than this quote suggests.[28] Common lawyers now generally obtain a legal education at a university before entering practice. This early training lends itself to a much more abstract approach to the law, much like that followed by their continental counterparts. Conversely, continental lawyers pay much more emphasis to case law and the practical application of the law than is often perceived. The greater contact with common lawyers and common law techniques has no doubt played a role in this process.

The core principle of the common law system is the doctrine of precedents (*stare decisis*). According to this doctrine, courts lower down in the hierarchy are absolutely bound to the decisions of courts higher up in the hierarchy. The law of precedents also pertains to the interpretation of statutes. The decisions of the higher courts act as a unifying mechanism for resolving differences in the lower courts.[29] The common lawyer must be capable of finding relevant case law, and accurately interpreting it and distinguishing cases. The importance of case law and recognizing operative facts is reflected in the reasoning provided in judicial decisions. Common law decisions are much more detailed in discussing facts than is found in civil law reports.

---

[23] Zweigert and Kötz, *Comparative Law*, 199; Brierley, *Major Legal Systems*, 279ff.; De Cruz, *Comparative Law*, 100.

[24] Zweigert and Kötz, *Comparative Law*, 200–1; Brierley, *Major Legal Systems*, 323.

[25] J.N. Adams and Hector Macqueen, *Atiyah's Sale of Goods*, 12th ed. (Pearson Harlow, 2010), 3.

[26] Zweigert and Kötz, *Comparative Law*, 258–9; Brierley, *Major Legal Systems*, 302–3.

[27] Roscoe Pound, "What Is Common Law?," in *The Future of the Common Law* (Gloucester: Smith, 1937), 18–19.

[28] Zweigert and Kötz, *Comparative Law*, 259.

[29] Id., 259ff.; De Cruz, *Comparative Law*, 103.

Judge-made law is most prevalent in the common law in the private law areas of contract, torts, and real property. However, legislation became a major source of law during the twentieth century. These statutes mostly focus on specific ad hoc problems and not the codification of entire areas of the law. The exceptions include England's Sale of Good Act of 1893 and then again the Sale of Goods Act of 1979.[30] In the United States, the law of sales has been codified in Article 2 of the Uniform Commercial Code, which is in forty-nine of the fifty states.[31]

There are important differences in the drafting of legislature between the common and civil law systems. In the common law systems, legislative drafting is aimed at laying down legal rules, which are as precise and detailed as possible in order to limit creative interpretation by the courts.[32] It is a common conception that courts essentially have the task of finding and applying the law, not making it. In civil law systems, statutory law is written at a much larger level of abstraction, often providing legal principles rather than legal rules. Civil law courts are not seen as making law, but are seen simply applying the law as found in the codes to concrete situations. Therefore, there is a fundamental difference in the way in which common lawyers and civilian lawyers perceive legal rules.[33] Common lawyers perceive legal rules as specific rules applicable to specific circumstances. Deduction from general principles is of lesser importance than it is in civil law where abstraction leads to the formulation of general principles, not to legal rules. Civilian lawyers see the high-level abstractions as the legal rule, and their application in specific instances merely as a manifestation of the rule in a specific instance.[34]

B. *Characteristics of the Civil Law*

The civil law systems of continental Europe consist of two distinctive legal traditions – the French Code Civil (Romanistic legal family) and the German Bürgerliches Gesetzbuch (BGB) (Germanic legal family).[35] The formative influences during the eighteenth and nineteenth centuries were quite different. The Romanistic legal family was strongly influenced by the political events in France, whereas the Germanic family remained largely uninfluenced by these events. In contrast, the Germanic legal tradition was highly influenced by the Pandectists of the nineteenth century. It consisted of a formal legal technique and clear general concepts, which formed the basis of the BGB and other codifications, but had virtually no influence in the Romanistic systems.[36]

1. Romanistic Legal Family

The Romanistic legal family is characterized by the influence of the French Revolution, which sought to replace feudal institutions with the natural law values of private

---

[30] Adams and Macqueen, *Atiyah's Sale of Goods*, 3.
[31] H. Gabriel, *Contracts for the Sale of Goods: A Comparison of Domestic and International Law* (Dobbs Ferry: Oceana, 2004), 5–7.
[32] Zweigert and Kötz, *Comparative Law*, 267–8.
[33] Id., 258–9; Brierley, *Major Legal Systems*, 74–6, 302, and 303.
[34] Brierley, *Major Legal Systems*, 73ff. and 302ff.
[35] Zweigert and Kötz, *Comparative Law*, 69; Brierley, *Major Legal Systems*, 14–15; De Cruz, *Comparative Law*, 33–4.
[36] De Cruz, *Comparative Law*, 57–9, 63–4, and 82–8; Zweigert and Kötz, *Comparative Law*, 68–9, 82–4, and 138–41.

property, freedom of contract, and family inheritance. The Code Civil is a careful blend of the historical legal influences of the Roman law and Germanic-Frankish customary law.[37] Much of this law had been recorded in accordance with a royal mandate. The draftsmen of the eventual Code Civil were further influenced by a number of eminent jurists. Pothier influenced, among others, the fields contract and sales with a number of writings of extreme lucidity and conceptual accuracy.[38] The law of contract and sales was based largely on Roman law and had little influence from customary law. Although initially influenced by the revolution, the revolutionary ideas lost significance as the value of historical continuity quickly regained its predominant influence.[39]

The Code Civil was drafted in a general style, leaving it up to the judges to apply the law in specific situations. The code remains in force, but it has been changed a great deal in its application under the influence of case law. The code provides courts with the opportunity to interpret and develop its terms, which are often inexact, incomplete, or ambiguous.[40] This is very different from the level of exactness obtained in the German BGB. In the course of time, academic commentary has become an important influence on the interpretation and application of the code. This allowed courts to interpret the code creatively according to the needs of society and the requirements of a modern economy.[41] The French Code was eventually implemented in Belgium, the Netherlands, and has been influential in Italy, Spain, and Portugal. During the era of colonization this influence spread to large parts of Africa. It also spread to Latin America.

Unlike the common law, there is a clear distinction between the legal profession and judicial practice. In France, the judiciary is made up of career judges who are appointed after completing a number of state examinations following their university legal education.

Courts of first instance provide findings of facts and law, whereas courts of appeal are restricted to addressing issues of law. French decisions are written in a dense fashion with only brief references or synopses of the facts.[42] This makes the interpretation very difficult for non-civilian lawyers to understand. This is especially the case for decisions of the Court of Cassation.[43] Even though there is no principle of *stare decisis*, lower courts generally follow the decisions of higher courts.[44] In this way the courts have concretized the broad and general statements of the Code Civil.[45] Unlike their German counterparts, French lawyers aim at clarity and brevity of expression, eloquence of style, and form, and have little time for theoretical (academic) debate.[46]

2. Germanic Legal Family

Modern German law began with the reception of Roman law from the mid-fifteenth century. It involved the widespread acceptance of the institutions and concepts of Roman

---

[37] De Cruz, *Comparative Law*, 63.
[38] Zweigert and Kötz, *Comparative Law*, 79.
[39] Id., 87–8.
[40] Id., 90.
[41] Id., 91.
[42] Id., 120–2.
[43] Id., 124.
[44] De Cruz, *Comparative Law*, 68.
[45] Id., 68–9; Zweigert and Kötz, *Comparative Law*, 91–2.
[46] Zweigert and Kötz, *Comparative Law*, 129ff.; Brierley, *Major Legal Systems*, 31; De Cruz, *Comparative Law*, 81.

law as well as intensive study and systematization of the Roman law. There was no strong centralized court system as there was in England, therefore, the shortcomings of Germanic law were filled by the ready-made Roman law. Roman law was also the law of Holy Roman Empire, providing further authority for its reception. Jurists of the time were trained in the universities of Italy and, later, Germany, where Roman law was extensively taught.[47]

During the Enlightenment, a movement to comprehensively codify law based on human reason and natural law developed. The leading lawyers of the time developed a deductive method, deducing particular legal rules from broad principles. This rational way of thinking became the dominant mode of teaching in the universities. This method was also applied to the study of and commentary on Roman law. In this way German law became the law of professors, abstract, rigorously organized, and sometimes widely removed from the reality or the needs of the time.

The period immediately preceding the German codification of the law saw the rise and influence of the Historical School with Von Savigny as its most famous proponent. This school saw law as a historically determined product of a civilization. Ironically, instead of intensifying the study and influence of Germanic law, Von Savigny and his followers turned to ancient Roman law as captured in Justinian's *Corpus Iuris Civilis*. Von Savigny believed that Roman law embodied a higher and more eternal law, which transcended local Germanic law.[48] This led to the development of the Pandectist School, which aimed at a dogmatic and systematic study of Roman law. They created a clear set of concepts integrated into a systematic exposition of the law.[49] The BGB grew from these forces, which ultimately determined its character as a logical and highly systematized body of rules and concepts. However, its historical-conservative roots did not embody the great social changes taking place at the time.[50] Other Germanic codes of the time are somewhat different, with the Austrian code described as imbued with simple common sense and the Swiss code containing a clear and popular style.[51]

In the BGB, the law of sales is contained in Book II, the Law of Obligations. This book deals with obligations arising from contracts generally and then, inter alia, from sales more specifically. Freedom of contract, premised on the beliefs that parties to a contract are free and equal partners at the point of formation, is the basic classical contract paradigm. The duty to respect contractual obligations follows naturally from this premise. This basic model of contracts did not take into account the realities of unequal bargaining positions, unfair contract terms, and oppressive contracts. Specifically targeted statutes, such as labor regulations, have intervened to provide protections. In other instances, the courts have checked these abuses by systematically developing controls based on general principles, such as the good faith requirement found in §242. This section has been extensively used to adapt the rigorous rules of the law of contract and their strict application to rectify the abuse of contracts and to meet the changing social and moral attitudes of society.[52]

[47] Zweigert and Kötz, *Comparative Law*, 133–8; Brierley, *Major Legal Systems*, 37–45; De Cruz, *Comparative Law*, 79–81.
[48] Zweigert and Kötz, *Comparative Law*, 138–41; Brierley, *Major Legal Systems*, 43.
[49] Zweigert and Kötz, *Comparative Law*, 136–7.
[50] Id., 143–4.
[51] Id., 144.
[52] Id., 149–50.

The BGB has strongly influenced the laws of China and Japan in modernizing their legal systems. This is also true of many Eastern European countries after the demise of communism.[53]

German lawyers resort first and foremost to the BGB itself, but authoritative academic commentaries have had a profound influence on the development of the law. German judges and lawyers have looked to scholarly commentaries – that reference court decisions and other scholarly writings – when interpreting and applying the BGB.[54] In Germany, like France, lawyers are trained first and foremost at universities. Judges are also career judges, similar to those in France. German judges' academic training makes them open to the use of academic writings in their decisions.

It is a common misperception that court decisions do not have an important influence in civil law legal systems. The decisions of German courts are well reported and are extensively used and discussed in academic writings. Although there is no formal *stare decisis* principle in operation, lower courts follow the decisions of higher courts, especially those of the Bundesgerichtshof (the highest civil court in Germany).[55] German court decisions tend to be briefer than their counterparts in the common law, but are less terse and better reasoned than French court decisions. Courts will usually provide a concise synopsis of the key facts of the case before a fairly comprehensive discussion of the law. The discussion of the law will refer to academic writings as well as other court decisions.

Court decisions have had a profound influence in many areas of contract law, developing new concepts and rules for situations not properly provided for in the BGB, such as novel fact patterns or the development of new transaction types. For example, the courts developed an extensive system of controls, based on the principle of good faith, regulating the use of unfair standard contract terms. These rules were eventually codified in the Allgemeine Geschäftsbedingungen Gesetz of 1977. This act has now been subsumed into the 2002 revision of BGB in §§305 to 311.[56]

C. *Characteristics of the Common and Civil Laws of Contract*

This section compares the two legal systems' laws of contract in six areas: role of codification, principles of freedom of contract and good faith, interpretation and the use of parol evidence, consideration and the binding force of offers, and specific performance and damages.

1. Codification

In the civil law countries, the law of contract as well as the law of sales has been comprehensively codified – German BGB, French Code Civil, Dutch Burgerlijk Wetboek and the Italian Codice Civile. In the common law countries, the law of contract has generally not been codified. However, in the United States, courts will, at times, cite

---

[53] Id., 154.

[54] Brierley, *Major Legal Systems*, 86–88, 112–13; Zweigert and Kötz, *Comparative Law*, 1.

[55] Brierley, *Major Legal Systems*, 110.

[56] P. Bassenge et al., *Palandt Bürgerliches Gesetzbuch Überblick*, 71st ed. (Munich: Beck,2012), §305 Rn 3–6; F.J. Säcker and R. Rixecker, *Münchener Kommentar zum Bürgerlichen Gesetzbuch* (Munich: Beck, 2007), Band 2 Vor §305 Rn 1–17.

a scholarly treatise – Restatement (Second) of the Law of Contract.[57] The law of sales has been codified in England since 1893 and in the United States since the adoption of the Uniform Commercial Code in the mid-1960s. In common law countries, sales law provides specialized rules, but remains embedded within the general law of contracts. The courts look to sales law for solutions, but if no solutions are found, they resort to the general law of contracts. Dealing with a codifying text like the CISG is therefore no more foreign to a common law lawyer than it is to a civil law lawyer. In its style, however, the CISG is more closely aligned with the civil codes than common law codes.

2. Freedom of Contract

Both the common law and civil law of contracts are strongly grounded in the principles of freedom of contract and party autonomy.[58] It is a principle that is also found in Article 6 of the CISG. The parties are free to structure their agreements as they see fit, only subject to the restrictions of public policy. In the common law, these restrictions are narrowly framed and applied with circumspection. The validity of contract terms falls outside the scope of the CISG and is accordingly determined by national law.[59]

3. Principle of Good Faith

It is characteristic of civil law systems that the negotiation, conclusion, and enforcement of contracts are subject to the principle of good faith. Although the principle is widely stated in the different codes, such as BGB §242,[60] the courts have established more specific rules. It has had a pervasive influence on the law of contract.[61] The incorporation of good faith as a general clause in the BGB has allowed the courts to use it as a gap-filler and in the general development of German contract law.[62] It has been functional in giving new meanings to old concepts and institutions and has formed the justification for the development of new remedies.[63]

In the common law system, good faith has played a much more modest role. As late as 1992, Sir Roy Goode noted the difficulty English law has had in adopting a general concept of good faith.[64] Section 61 of the Sale of Goods Act 1979 states: "A thing is deemed to be done in good faith within the meaning of this act when it is in fact done honestly, whether it is done negligently or not." Thus, good faith is only required in particular situations, rather than as a general requirement for the conduct of the parties. In English law the importance of legal certainty takes precedence over the harshness a particular rule may cause in individual circumstances.[65]

---

[57] Zweigert and Kötz, *Comparative Law*, 270.

[58] Id., 324ff.

[59] See Article 4.

[60] Section 242. Performance in good faith. An obligor has a duty to perform according to the requirements of good faith, taking customary practice into consideration. See Bassenge et al., *Palandt Bürgerliches Gesetzbuch Überblick*, §242 Rn 1–7; Säcker and Rixecker, *Münchener Kommentar*, § Rn 1–6.

[61] Schlechtriem, "Good Faith in German Law and in International Uniform Laws," in *Conferenze e Seminari* 10 (ed. P. Saggi) (Rome, 1992), 24, available at http://cisgw3.law.pace.edu/cisg/biblio/schlechtriem16.html.

[62] Id., 24.

[63] Id.

[64] Id.

[65] Roy Goode, "The Concept of 'Good Faith' in English Law," in Saggi, *Conferenze e Seminari* 10.

The position in American law is somewhat different.[66] Both the UCC and the Restatement Second impose an obligation of good faith on the parties. Section 1–203 of the UCC provides that "every contract or duty within this Act imposes an obligation of good faith in its performance or enforcement." Likewise, Section 205 of the Restatement states that: "Every contract imposes upon each party a duty of good faith and fair dealing in its performance and enforcement." The duty of good faith is not extended to the negotiations stage. However, even here there are specific rules that cater for certain situations that would be dealt with under the principle of in good faith in civil law systems.[67] As a result, the acceptance of good faith as a general underlying principle is more palatable and easier to deal with for American lawyers than it is for English lawyers.

4. Interpretation of Contracts and Parol Evidence

In the common law, courts apply the parol evidence rule to exclude evidence (negotiations, prior dealings, trade usage, business custom) that contradicts a written contract. The rule is based on the common law's objective theory of contract formation and aimed at preserving the integrity of the written instrument. In general terms the law of contract is not concerned with the subjective intent of parties, but with the outward manifestation of that intent.[68] Although there are exceptions to the rule,[69] the common law prefers form over substance to preserve legal certainty instead of searching for the true intention of the parties.

In English law, the parol evidence rule involves a rebuttable presumption that the writing was intended to include all the terms of the contract. English courts first examine the writing to determine whether it was meant to serve as a true record of the contract. Thus, under English law, the party relying on a writing has the benefit that, when the writing appears to be complete, it is presumed to represent the complete contract, subject to the other party's right of rebuttal.[70]

In U.S. law, the parol evidence rule operates in two steps. A U.S. court asks first whether the writing was "integrated," meaning whether the writing was intended to represent the final expression of the parties' agreement. If the writing is determined to be a complete integration, then parol evidence may not be introduced either to contradict the written terms.[71]

The civil law proceeds from a subjective approach to the formation of contract, searching for the true intention of the parties. There are, therefore, no formal restrictions

---

[66] E. Allan Farnsworth, "Good Faith Performance and Commercial Reasonableness Under the Uniform Commercial Code," 30 *U. Chicago L. Rev.* 666, 679 (1963); Robert S. Summers, "'Good Faith' in General Contract Law and the Sales Provisions of the Uniform Commercial Code," 54 *Virginia L. Rev.* 195, 200, 232–3 (1968); Steven Burton, "Breach of Contract and the Common Law Duty to Perform in Good Faith," 94 *Harv. L. Rev.* 369, 369, 372–3 (1980); E. Allan Farnsworth, "The Concept of Good Faith in American Law," in Saggi, *Conferenze e Seminari 10.*

[67] E. Allan Farnsworth, "Good Faith Performance and Commercial Reasonableness Under the Uniform Commercial Code," 30 *U. Chicago L. Rev.* 666, 679 (1963).

[68] Bruno Zeller, "The Parol Evidence Rule and the CISG: A Comparative Analysis," 36 *Comparative and International L.J. of Southern Africa* (2003); *Investors Compensation Scheme Limited v. West Bromwich Building Society* [1998] 1 WLR 896.

[69] Zweigert and Kötz, *Comparative Law,* 407.

[70] CISG-AC Opinion No. 3, "Parol Evidence Rule, Plain Meaning Rule, Contractual Merger Clause and the CISG" (October 23, 2004) (CISG-AC Opinion No. 3), Richard Hyland, Rapporteur, available at http://www.cisgac.com/default.php?ipkCat=128&ifkCat=145&sid=145.

[71] Id.

on the proof that parties may put forward and the content of the contract may be proven by
any means, including the testimony of witnesses relating to the prior negotiations, even
if the contract has been reduced to writing.[72] However, the admissibility of evidence
is not without restrictions. In German law, for instance, there is a presumption that
the document accurately reflects the totality of the agreement, but that presumption
is rebuttable by any evidence denying the contract. Article 1341 of the French Code
Civil lays down a rule similar to the parol evidence rule, but the rule is subject to
many exceptions. One of the exceptions is that this rule does not apply to commercial
transactions.[73]

5. Consideration and the Binding Force of Offers

It is a common feature of most legal systems that the contract formation process is
analyzed as consisting of an offer and an acceptance. In the common law, an offer is not
binding on the offeror and may be revoked at any time before acceptance by the offeree.
It lapses at the time set in the offer or within a reasonable time where no time is set, or
when it is revoked.[74] It is therefore nonbinding and there are no consequences attached
to the revocation, even at a very late stage in the proceedings and even though the offeree
may have changed its position or incurred certain expenses.[75]

The reason for the nonbinding nature of offers is found in the doctrine of consideration, which requires that each agreement must be supported by consideration.
Consideration may consist of payment in money or kind or in a returned promise. In
most instances the offeree provides no counterpromise or consideration, consequently
no binding agreement arises.[76]

In the Romanistic legal system, an offer has a stronger legal effect. Where an offer has
been made, the offer needs to be respected for a reasonable period of time. Where the
offer is revoked during this period, the offeror is liable for any provable damages incurred
by the offeree. The liability is viewed as either arising from tort or from the breach of a
preliminary contract.[77]

In the Germanic legal system, an offer remains binding for the period stated in the offer
or where no period is stated for a reasonable period of time unless the offeror has clearly
indicated that the offer is not binding.[78] Any attempted revocation is simply ineffective
and may be ignored by the offeree. The offeree is entitled to accept the offeror within
the stated time or within a reasonable time where no time limit is stated. Acceptance
within such a time results in a valid and binding contract. Where the binding nature of
the offer is excluded in the offer, it is not treated as an offer but as an invitation to make
an offer.[79]

---

[72] Zweigert and Kötz, *Comparative Law*, 407; see also CISG-AC Opinion No. 3.
[73] Zweigert and Kötz, *Comparative Law*, 369–70; 407.
[74] Id., 357–9.
[75] Id., 357–9.
[76] Id., 357.
[77] Id., 359–61.
[78] Bassenge et al., *Palandt Bürgerliches Gesetzbuch Überblick*, §145 Rn 1 ff.; Säcker and Rixecker, *Münchener Kommentar*, §45 Rn 1.
[79] Zweigert and Kötz, *Comparative Law*, 361–2; Bassenge et al., *Palandt Bürgerliches Gesetzbuch Überblick*, §145 Rn 1–5 ff.; Säcker and Rixecker, *Münchener Kommentar*, §145 Rn 1–7.

6. Specific Performance and Damages

The remedy of specific performance is treated differently in common law and civil law systems.[80] In the civil law a party is entitled to have the agreement enforced under the principle of *pacta sunt servanda* – the contract must be performed.[81] In principle it does not matter what the nature of the performance is – whether it is the payment of money, delivery of goods, or performance of a service or a specific act.[82] BGB §241 of the BGB stipulates that the creditor is entitled to demand performance from the debtor. The principle is subject to a number or exceptions such as impossibility and hardship.

In the Anglo-American legal system, the creditor only has a right to specific enforcement in actions of debt. In all other cases, the nonbreaching is only entitled to damages.[83] However, in cases where a claim for damages would be inadequate to properly compensate the non-breaching party, such as when the item is unique, an order of specific performance is made available.[84] Justice Oliver Wendell Holmes captured the American preference for damages in case of breach in a famous law review comment: "The only universal consequence of a legally binding promise is that the law makes the promissor pay damages if the promised event does not come to pass. In every case it leaves him free from interference until the time for fulfilment has gone by, and therefore, is free to break the contract if he chooses."[85]

Ingeborg Schwenzer correctly states that even though the approaches taken in these legal systems are quite different, the differences in practice are smaller than one would expect. In both systems the general rules are subject to certain exceptions, which render their practical application quite similar. In the Germanic legal system, the right to specific performance under substantive law is undermined by procedural law, which fails to provide effective coercive means to enforce performances. Schwenzer also notes that the necessities of commercial trade make the costly and time-consuming action for specific enforcement impracticable if substituted purchase or sale is available. Specific performance becomes relevant where only the specific debtor can render the performance. In such cases, the Anglo-American legal system also grants specific performance.[86]

III. The CISG as Bridge

This section examines the six areas discussed in the foregoing comparison in the context of CISG rules.

[80] Ole Lando in *Commentary on the International Sales Law* (ed. Bianca and Bonell) (Milan: Giuffrè, 1997), 232–9. Ingeborg Schwenzer, "Specific Performance and Damages According to the 1994 UNIDROIT Principles of International Commercial Contracts," 1 *European J. of L. Reform* 289 (1999).
[81] Zweigert and Kötz, Comparative Law, 472–73; Shael Herman, "Specific Performance: A Comparative Analysis," 7 *Edinburgh L. Rev.* 194ff. (2003); Ole Lando in Bianca and Bonell, *Commentary on the International Sales Law*, 232–9.
[82] Spanish law is similar. See Shael Herman, Specific Performance," 194 ff.
[83] Schwenzer, "Specific Performance."
[84] Mindy Chen-Wishart, *Contract*, 3rd ed. (Oxford: Oxford University Press, 2005), 589–90. Lando in Bianca and Bonell, *Commentary on the International Sales Law*, 232–39.
[85] Oliver Wendell Holmes, *The Common Law* (1881), 236. See also Oliver Wendell Holmes, "Path of the Law," 10 *Harv. L. Rev.* 457, 469 (1897).
[86] Schwenzer, "Specific Performance."

A. Freedom of Contract and Party Autonomy

The CISG recognizes the principle of freedom of contract and party autonomy in Article 6, which allows parties to change any of the provisions of the CISG or even to exclude it in its entirety. However, abuse of freedom of contract is primarily dealt with outside the CISG due to Article 4's delegation of validity issues to domestic law.[87]

B. Principle of Good Faith

The inclusion of a general principle of good faith in the CISG was vigorously debated during the drafting of the CISG.[88] The Article 7 compromise only refers to good faith in the context of the interpretation of the CISG. The phrasing was agreed on only after lengthy discussions in the working group and the plenary session of the conference, and it was meant as a final rejection of more far-reaching proposals to apply the principle of good faith and fair dealing to the obligations and conduct of the parties.[89] The controversy as to the extent that the principle of good faith should be applied to the interpretation of the contract itself and the relationships between the parties still remains, but the majority view favors the wider application of good faith despite the legislative history of Article 7.[90] Schlechtriem states:

> But similar to the irresistible force of fundamental laws of nature such as the law of gravity, the principle that not only the interpretation of the Convention, but also the evaluation of the relations, rights and remedies of the parties, should be subject to the principle of good faith and fair dealing has found its way into the Convention, its understanding by the majority of legal writers and its application by the courts.[91]

It would seem, however, that the majority of case and commentators favoring the general application of good faith are from civil law jurisdictions, whereas most common law

---

[87] *MSS, Inc. v. Maser Corporation*, 2011 WL 2938424, (D.C. Md. 2011), available at http://cisgw3.law.pace.edu/cases/110718u1.html.

[88] Sieg Eiselen and Albert H. Kritzer, *International Contract Manual*, vol. 4 (Rochester: Thomson West, 2008), paras. 85–10, 9; see France, February 22, 1995, Cour d'appel [Appellate Court] Grenoble (*BRI Production "Bonaventure" v. Pan African Export*), available at http://cisgw3.law.pace.edu/cases/950222f1.html]; Mexico, March 10, 2005, Primer Tribunal Colegiado en Materia Civil del Primer Circuito [Appellate Court] (*Kolmar Petrochemicals Americas, Inc. v. Idesa Petroquímica Sociedad Anónima de Capital Variable*), available at http://cisgw3.law.pace.edu/cases/050310m1.html]; France, June 30, 2004, Cour de Cassation [Supreme Court] (*Société Romay AG v. SARL Behr France*), available at http://cisgw3.law.pace.edu/cases/040630f1.html; Russia, October 22, 2003, Arbitration proceeding 134/2001, available at http://cisgw3.law.pace.edu/cases/031022r1.html; Germany, July 25, 2003, Oberlandesgericht [Appellate Court] Düsseldorf, available at http://cisgw3.law.pace.edu/cases/030725g1.html; Germany, September 15, 2004, Oberlandesgericht [Appellate Court] München (Furniture leather case), available at http://cisgw3.law.pace.edu/cases/040915g2.html; Italy, February 25, 2004, Tribunale Padova [District Court], available at http://cisgw3.law.pace.edu/cases/040225i3.html; Netherlands, April 23, 2003, Gerechtshof Gravenhage [Appellate Court], available at http://cisgw3.law.pace.edu/cases/030423n1.html; Austria, October 22, 2001, Oberster Gerichtshof [Supreme Court] [1 Ob 49/01i], available at http://cisgw3.law.pace.edu/cases/011022a4.html; Italy, September 28, 2001, Milan Arbitration proceeding (Steel wire case), available at http://cisgw3.law.pace.edu/cases/010928i3.html; Switzerland, October 24, 2003, Handelsgericht [Commercial Court] Zürich (Mattress case), available at http://cisgw3.law.pace.edu/cases/031024s1.html.

[89] Schlechtriem, "Good Faith."

[90] Ulrich Magnus, *Staudinger's Kommentar zum Bürgerlichen Gesetzbuch UN Kaufrecht* (2005), 170 and 175.

[91] Schlechtriem, "Good Faith."

commentators have been more guarded in their approach to the principle.[92] It has not been directly applied in any common law case.[93] However, in the American Arbitration Institution decision in the Macromex case, the tribunal refers to the general good faith requirements of the CISG.[94]

Although civil and common lawyers do not seem to agree on the extent to which good faith should apply to the actions of the parties, the inclusion of good faith in Article 7 has raised the level of awareness of the potential uses of the principle. The divide on this issue is still there, but courts and commentators on the common law side hopefully will move closer to the civil law approach in light of the mandate for uniform application under Article 7.

C. *Parol Evidence*

The CISG does not contain a rule similar to the common law parol evidence rule. The CISG provides that all relevant evidence is to be considered in the interpretation of contracts. Article 11 provides that "contracts may be proven by any means, including witnesses."[95] Article 8(3) provides, when determining the intent of a party, due consideration is to be given to all relevant circumstances, including the negotiations between the parties.

The Austrian Representative opposed a Canadian proposal at the drafting conference because it "was aimed at limiting the free appreciation of evidence by the judge." To prevent a judge from reviewing all the evidence would violate a "fundamental principle of Austrian law." The amendment was rejected. There were several practical reasons for not including a parol evidence rule in the CISG: (1) most of the world's legal systems admit all relevant evidence in contract litigation; (2) the parol evidence rule, especially as it operates in the United States, is characterized by great variation and extreme complexity; and (3) it has also been the subject of constant criticism.[96]

The leading U.S. case on the application of the parol evidence rule to CISG cases is *MCC-Marble Ceramic Center, Inc. v. Ceramica Nuova D'Agostino.*[97] The trial court

---

[92] Peter Schlechtriem and Pascal Hachem in *Commentary on the UN Convention on the International Sale of Goods*, 3rd ed. (ed. I. Schwenzer) (Oxford: Oxford University Press, 2010), Article 7, paras. 16 and 17; John O. Honnold, *Uniform Law for International Sales under the 1980 United Nations Convention*, 3rd ed. (Kluwer, 1999); Eiselen and Kritzer, *International Contract Manual*, para. 85:10. Cf. Bruno Zeller, "Good Faith: The Scarlet Pimpernel of the CISG," available at http://www.cisg.law.pace.edu/cisg/biblio/zeller2.html.

[93] Cf. *MCC-Marble Ceramic Center v. Ceramica Nuova D'Agostino*, 144 F.3d 1384, 1387, (11th Cir. 1998), available at http://cisgw3.law.pace.edu/cases/980629u1.html.

[94] *Macromex Srl. v. Globex International Inc.*, American Arbitration Association (October 23, 2007), available at http://cisgw3.law.pace.edu/cases/071023a5.html.

[95] See CISG-AC Opinion No. 3.

[96] United Nations Conference on Contracts for the International Sale of Goods, Official Records, U.N. Doc. A/Conf./97/19, U.N. Sales No. E.81.IV.3, at 90 (1981).

[97] *MCC-Marble Ceramic Center v. Ceramica Nuova D'Agostino*, 144 F.3d 1384, 1387, (11th Cir. 1998), available at http://cisgw3.law.pace.edu/cases/980629u1.html. See R.N. Andreason, "MCC-Marble Ceramic Center: The Parol Evidence Rule and Other Domestic Law under the Convention on Contracts for the International Sale of Goods," 1999 *Brigham Young U. L. Rev.* 351. See also Petra Butler, "The Doctrines of Parol Evidence Rule and Consideration: A Deterrence to the Common Law Lawyer?," in *Celebrating Success: 25 Years United Nations Convention on Contracts for the International Sale of Goods* (Collation of Papers at UNCITRAL–SIAC Conference September 22–3, 2005, Singapore), 54–66.

applied the parol evidence rule and refused to allow affidavits by one of the parties on the negotiations between the parties. The Court of Appeals reversed the decision, holding that the parol evidence rule does not apply when a contract is governed by the CISG:

> Courts applying the CISG cannot, therefore, upset the parties' reliance on the Convention by substituting familiar principles of domestic law when the Convention requires a different result. We may only achieve the directives of good faith and uniformity in contracts under the CISG by interpreting and applying the plain language of article 8(3) as written and obeying its directive to consider this type of parol evidence.

The court did not find any particular difficulty in considering the affidavits provided by the buyer.

From the legislative history and the subsequent application of the CISG in common law countries, the exclusion of the parol evidence rule has not seriously undermined the legal certainty attached to written contracts and that forms the basis for the rule in the common law.[98]

D. *Consideration and Binding Force of Offers*

CISG Article 29 excludes the need for consideration in the modification of contracts.[99] It provides that a contract may be modified by the mere agreement of the parties. John Honnold explains that CISG rules reject the requirement of consideration.[100] The Secretariat Commentary specifically states that Article 29(1) of the CISG was intended to "eliminate" and "overrule" the common law requirement of consideration.[101]

The rejection of the consideration requirement also impacts the revocability of offers under Article 16. Article 16 determines when an offer will be regarded as binding and irrevocable. In common law, offers are generally regarded as nonbinding and accordingly revocable unless there is a specific agreement supported by consideration making the offer irrevocable. Similarly, in the Romanistic legal system, an offer is generally regarded as nonbinding. In the Germanic legal system, however, the offer is regarded as binding for the period stated or for a reasonable period. This difference was one of most difficult issues to resolve in the drafting of CISG Part II on contract formation.[102] In the end, a compromise was reached resulting in Article 16.

---

[98] Harry M. Flechtner, "The U.N. Sales Convention (CISG) and *MCC-Marble Ceramic Center, Inc. v. Ceramica Nuova D'Agostino, S.p.A.*: The Eleventh Circuit Weighs in on Interpretation, Subjective Intent, Procedural Limits to the Convention's Scope, and the Parol Evidence Rule," 18 *J. L. & Commerce* 259, 287 (1999). See, however, the contrary view of K.H. Cross, "Parol Evidence under the CISG: The 'Homeward Trend' Reconsidered," 68 *Ohio State L.J.* 133 (1999), who argues that the continued acceptance of the CISG in the USA will be enhanced if courts give greater leeway to interpret the CISG in the light of domestic legal traditions.

[99] Petra Butler, "The Doctrines of Parol Evidence Rule," 54–66, available at http://www.cisg.law.pace.edu/cisg/biblio/butler4.htm; Eiselen and Kritzer, *International Contract Manual*, §84:34.

[100] Honnold, *Uniform Law*, §202.

[101] UNCITRAL Yearbook VIII, A/CN.9/SER.A/1977, p. 93, para. 26; John Honnold, *Documentary History of the Uniform Law for International Sales* (Kluwer, 1989), 257.

[102] Ulrich Schroeter in Schlechtriem and Schwenzer, *Commentary*, Article 16, para. 1; Eiselen and Kritzer, *International Contract Manual*, para. 86:33.

Article 16 provides that offers are freely revocable until a contract is concluded unless it indicates that it is irrevocable by stating a fixed time or if it was reasonable for the other party to rely on the offer being irrevocable. Eörsy states succinctly:

> For a civil law jurist [the wording of Article 16(2)(a)] would lead to the … result that [an offer which stated a fixed time for acceptance] is irrevocable during the time fixed for Acceptance. On the other hand, for a common law jurist the text would mean that the offer is irrevocable only if the manner of "stating a fixed time for acceptance" indicated that the offer was irrevocable. [For a common law jurist] stating a fixed time for acceptance may not by itself mean irrevocability.[103]

During the negotiation of the CISG, the United Kingdom delegation indicated that traders in common law countries would be exposed to a trap if, under the CISG, indicating a fixed period brought about a situation where an offer was deemed to be irrevocable.[104] This is an example where the deep ideological divide between the common and civil law has proven of very little practical importance. Of the more than 2,500 reported cases, Article 16 is only mentioned in seventeen of the cases. None of them deal directly with the revocability of offers.

E. *Specific Performance*

The common–civil divide becomes apparent in the different approaches to the remedy of specific performance. Article 28 states that a contracting party is entitled to receive the performance that it bargained for. This principle represents the civil law approach to remedies, namely that the nonbreaching party is entitled to specific performance and that damages is a secondary remedy (to ensure full compensation). This approach is diametrically opposed to the common law approach where specific performance is regarded as an extraordinary remedy, which should only be granted where a claim for damages cannot fully compensate the innocent party.

Article 28 in essence does not provide a uniform solution, but resorts to the domestic law of the *lex fori* to determine whether a party will be entitled to specific performance. Despite this disharmony, there has been hardly any case law dealing with Article 28.[105] This is not surprising. In international trade, there are few instances where specific performance can serve a useful purpose except in cases of substitute performance or repair.[106] In such cases, the parties usually agree on the substitute performance informally without resort to litigation. In the U.S. *Magellan International v. Salzgitter Handel*[107] case, the court applied Article 28. The court held that the plaintiff had made a sufficient case to sustain a claim for specific performance under UCC §2–716(1). In two of the relevant cases involving Article 28, a Swiss arbitral tribunal refused specific performance.

---

[103] Eörsy in Bianca and Bonell, *Commentary*, 157–8.

[104] United Nations Conference on Contracts for the International Sale of Goods, Official Records, U.N. Doc. A/Conf./97/19, U.N. Sales No.E.81.IV.3, at 75.

[105] There are only seven reported cases where the article has been mentioned or applied.

[106] See *Soinco v. NKAP* (Switzerland, May 31, 1996), Zürich Arbitration (claim was refused), available at http://cisgw3.law.pace.edu/cases/960531s1.html.

[107] *Magellan International v. Salzgitter Handel*, 76 F.Supp.2d 919, (Ill. D.C. 1999), available at http://cisgw3.law.pace.edu/cases/991207u1.html.

Although there are fundamental ideological differences between the common and civil laws on the specific performance remedy, the differences have not translated into any practical difficulties in the application of the CISG's remedial regime. It is rare that specific performance will be claimed, and when it is it may be granted in both common law and civil laws due to the special circumstances.

F. Reliance on Foreign Case Law and Scholarly Literature

The courts are extensively making use of foreign precedent at an increasing rate as these materials have become freely available on the Internet.[108] The most impressive example to date is probably the Italian decision in the Rheinland Versicherungen case.[109] The easy access provides an ideal opportunity for lawyers from the civil and common law traditions to become acquainted with the style and approach of courts in foreign jurisdictions.

Courts across the divide are also increasingly making use of academic commentary in the interpretation and application of the CISG. Harry Flechtner remarks with reference to the MCC-Marble Ceramic decision:

> Compared to the approach taken by the court in *Delchi Carrier*, the methodology employed in *MCC-Marble* represents real progress. In addition to citing U.S. case law on the CISG the Eleventh Circuit relied heavily on scholarly commentary. This is significant not only because it incorporates an aspect of civil law methodology, but also because the commentators that the court consulted presumably are at pains to bring an international perspective to their analysis of the Convention. In this regard it is significant that the *MCC-Marble* court cited a treatise by scholars whose training encompasses more than the Anglo-American legal tradition – *Understanding the CISG in Europe* by Professors Bernstein and Lookofsky.[110]

Using foreign case law and academic commentary is an approach that should be followed, especially given the easily accessible collections of case law and academic commentary. It is, however, a fact that courts most readily resort to the materials with which they are acquainted. German courts indirectly use foreign case law due to their reliance on German commentaries, which regularly refer to case law and legal scholarship from around the world.

IV. Conclusion

The CISG has been instrumental in dealing with the divide between the common law and the civil law in two stages. During the drafting phase of the CISG the differences in the domestic legal systems on certain fundamental issues such as the binding nature of offers, parol evidence, good faith, and specific performance gave rise to intense discussions on these differences and their importance. In certain cases, the delegates were successful

---

[108] Collections of case law and other materials can be found at the Pace Law School Web site at http://www.cisg.law.pace.edu; the UNILEX Web site at http://www.unilex.info; and the UNCITRAL Web site at http://www.uncitral.org/uncitral/en/caselaw/abstracts.html.

[109] *Rheinland Versicherungen v. Atlarex* (Italy, July 12, 2000), Tribunale [District Court] Vigevano, available at http://cisgw3.law.pace.edu/cases/000712i3.html.

[110] *MCC-Marble Ceramic Center, Inc., v. Ceramica Nuova d'Agostino, S.p.A.*, 144 F.3d 1384, 1388–89 (11th Cir. 1998).

in reaching compromises as in the case of parol evidence, good faith, and the binding nature of offers. In the case of specific performance, no real compromise was reached, leaving to domestic law to determine use of the remedy.

These debates highlighted the awareness of these differences in an important international forum, providing a better understanding of the issues that divide the civil and common laws. Since the adoption of the CISG, other projects have dealt with the common–civil law divide, including the UNIDROIT Principles of International Commercial Contract Law, the Principles of European Contract Law, and the European Draft Common Frame of Reference. These projects have shown that most of these differences can be transcended, as they pertain to specific rules rather than deeply ingrained principles and legal cultures. The exceptions are the intensely different views on the role of good faith and the availability of specific performance. Surprisingly, issues have given rise to few practical difficulties in the application of the CISG.

The biggest contribution of the CISG in bridging the divide is the amazing quantity of materials that have become freely available in collections such as the UNCITRAL collection of cases and the CISG Database of the Pace Institute of International Commercial Law. These sources have stimulated debate and literature from all legal cultures. Lawyers dealing with the CISG by necessity have had to engage in a comparative analysis. This familiarity contributes to the bridging of the gap and is at the heart of all the CISG.

39 Precontractual Liability and Preliminary Agreements

Marco Torsello

I. Introduction

Two different statements often describe the extent to which the 1980 United Nations Convention on Contracts for the International Sale of Goods (CISG) may apply to the relationship between parties before they enter into a binding contract. On the one hand, there stands the well-established and prevailing opinion that the CISG does not deal with, and is therefore not applicable to, possible duties and consequent liabilities that may arise in the course of negotiations.[1] On the other hand, several commentators argue that the CISG applies to "preliminary agreements," at least to the extent that this expression describes agreements that envisage or provide for the subsequent execution of contracts for the sale of goods.[2]

The two statements appear to be contradictory, in that they imply that the CISG governs certain types of preliminary agreements, the object of which is to regulate the area of precontractual liability, which is not governed by the CISG. The CISG is primarily seen as providing for a set of international default rules, while giving the parties the freedom to write alternative tailor-made rules.[3] It is incongruent to interpret the CISG as regulating tailor-made rules drafted by the parties for a stage of their relationship, which is not covered by the CISG. A coherent approach would either maintain that the CISG governs neither precontractual liability nor preliminary agreements, or that the CISG governs both.

A more comprehensive instrument on the law of sales, the 2011 Proposal for a Regulation of the European Parliament and the Council on a Common European Sales Law (CESL),[4] expressly covers preliminary agreements and precontractual liability. Part II of the CESL, "Making a binding contract," devotes a considerable number of provisions

---

[1] Cf. E. A. Farnsworth, "Duties of Good Faith and Fair Dealing under the UNIDROIT Principles, Relevant International Conventions and National Laws," 3 *Tulane J. Int'l & Comp. L.* 47, 56–7 (1995); *contra* F. Enderlein, "Rights and Obligations of the Seller under the UN Convention on Contracts for the International Sale of Goods," in *International Sale of Goods: Dubrovnik Lectures* (ed. P. Sarcevic and P. Volken) (1986), 133, 136–7.

[2] See M. Torsello, "Preliminary Agreements and CISG Contracts," in *Drafting Contracts under the CISG* 191, 214 ff. (ed. H.M. Flechtner, R.A. Brand, and M.S. Walter) (2008).

[3] I. Ayres and R.H. Gertner, "Filling Gaps in Incomplete Contracts: An Economic Theory of Default Rules," 99 *Yale L.J.* 97 (1989); R. Craswell, "Contract Law, Default Rules, and the Philosophy of Promising," 88 *Mich. L. Rev.* 489 (1989).

[4] European Commission, Proposal for a "Regulation of the European Parliament and the Council on a Common European Sales Law," COM (2011) 635 final 2011/0284 (COD).

(Articles 13 to 29) to the issue of precontractual information and to that of remedies available in the event of breach of such duties, thus suggesting that a comprehensive law of sales covers the behavior of the parties during the negotiation stage.[5]

This chapter aims at reconsidering the issue of precontractual liability and the enforceability of preliminary agreements in relation to the CISG. Does or should the CISG apply to the parties' duties throughout the negotiation of contracts which, if concluded, would fall within its scope of application? Part II briefly reviews in comparative perspective the solutions found in domestic legal systems as to the possible duties and liabilities arising at the negotiation stage. It then analyzes the distinction between various types of duties arising at the negotiation stage and the consequent liabilities for the breach of these duties. Part III considers the applicable conflict-of-laws rules, which would apply to the negotiations stage, and the extent to which a claim under domestic law can be brought concurrently with a claim under the CISG. Part IV discusses the advantages of party-made, tailored rules to cover the precontractual relationship. Given the difficulties in the application of traditional conflict-of-laws and the complexity of using domestic rules and CISG rules concurrently, the benefits of tailor-made rules, especially in relation to preliminary agreements, becomes apparent. Part V offers concluding remarks about how best to deal with the issues of liability relating to negotiations and preliminary agreements.

II. Review of Domestic Laws on Precontractual Liability

Few legal systems have codified provisions specifically dealing with the issue of precontractual liability.[6] However, in the civil law tradition it is not uncommon for courts to award damages to claimants who suffered damages resulting from the conduct of the other party in the course of negotiating a contract.[7] In legal terms, negotiations do not need to conclude in a contract for liability to be assigned to one of the negotiating parties. The very act of entering a negotiation creates a special relationship, causing them to interact to an extent that may result in damages being recoverable by the one party from the other.[8]

Unlike the many areas of great commonality among the different legal systems, the rules in this area vary widely among the different legal systems – ranging from rules on liability for breach of contract, to rules and general principles of tortious liability, to alternative remedial rules, such as those on unjust enrichment. The national rules range from absolute *caveat emptor* (denying any obligation of one party to the other) in the

---

[5] In this respect, it should also be pointed out that the EU Proposed Sales Law deals with both business-to-business ("B2B") contracts and business-to-consumers ("B2C") contracts.

[6] One notable exception is Italian Civil Code Article 1337, which sets forth an express duty to act in good faith in the course of negotiations.

[7] See, generally, H. Beale, B. Fauvarque-Cosson, J. Rutgers, D. Tallon, and S. Vogenauer, *Cases, Materials and Text on Contract Law*, 2nd ed. (2010), 371–426ff.; J. Cartwright and M. Hesselink, *Precontractual Liability in European Private Law* (Cambridge, 2008); S. Colombo, "The Present Differences between the Civil Law and Common Law Worlds with Regard to Culpa in Contrahendo," 2 *Tilburg Foreign L. Rev.* 341 (1992–3); *Precontractual Liability* (General Report of the XIII Congress of the International Academy of Comparative Law) (ed. E.H. Hondius) (Deventer, 1991); F. Kessler and E. Fine, "Culpa in Contrahendo," 77 *Harv. L. Rev.* 401 (1964).

[8] See A. Frignani and M. Torsello, *Il contratto internazionale. Diritto comparato e prassi commerciale* (2010), 155.

course of the negotiations to extreme good faithism, leading to a general cooperative duty to protect the other party's interests in the negotiation process.[9]

Also, the nature of the rules on precontractual liability varies from actions in contract, tort, and unjust enrichment.[10] One reason for the importance of the nature of the claim is that domestic statutes of limitations grant different periods of time within which the claim can be brought. The burden of proof, on the other hand, is usually entirely placed on the damaged party in tortious claims, including proving the negligence of the party, whereas in breach of contract claims a key burden is placed on the defending party to prove that its nonperformance was due to exceptional circumstances. The liability in tort tends to be personal and subjective, whereas the one for breach of contract is strict and extends to acts of any dependents, employees, and auxiliaries. Moreover, and maybe most importantly, the amount payable in compensation in contract extends to positive or expectancy damages (*lucrum cessans*), whereas (nonpunitive) damages in tort are typically limited to negative or reliance damages (*damnum emergens*).

On a different note, the characterization of a certain claim as contractual or tortious will often affect the rules on jurisdiction and the conflict-of-law provisions to be adopted, thus leading to divergent solutions on the forum court and the applicable law when the negotiation takes place in a cross-border context.

A brief survey of domestic solutions confirms that the French system has been one of the world's most influential codified legal systems in this field.[11] Following the Revolution and the end of the Ancien Régime, the Project for a Civil Code adopted in the Year VIII (based on the *calendrier révolutionnaire français*, introduced in 1793), contained a provision which imposed a duty of good faith in the negotiation of contracts – *les conventions doivent être contractées et executes de bonne foi.*

The application of good faith to negotiations, however, was left out of the 1804 Code Civil, so that Articles 1134 and 1135 do not provide any explicit support for a claim of precontractual liability.[12] As a consequence, when scholars[13] and courts[14] perceived the need to establish some sort of liability for injury caused in the course of contractual negotiations, they grounded a tort claim in Code Civil Article 1382, which is broad enough to include precontractual liability.[15] Because the parties failed to enter into a contract, precontractual liability had to be grounded on an extracontractual basis, and was therefore conceived as an *abus de droit* occurring during the *pourparlers* between the

---

[9] Cf. J. Dietrich, "Classifying Precontractual Liability: A Comparative Analysis," 21 *Legal St.* 153 (2001).

[10] See also J. Cartwright and M. Hesselink, *Precontractual Liability in European Private Law* (Cambridge, 2008), Chapter 5.

[11] See P. Giliker, "Regulating Contracting Behaviour: The Duty to Disclose in English and French Law," 5 *Eur. Rev. Pr. L.* 621 (2005) (comparison between the French and English legal systems with respect to the duty to disclose in precontractual negotiations).

[12] Code Civil Article 1134 states: "The contract is law between the parties." The *alinéa* note 3 of Article 1134 then states that "*les conventions doivent être executées de bonne foi,*" and Article 1135 adds: "*la convention oblige à toutes suites que l'equité donne a l'obligation d'après sa nature.*"

[13] See L. Josserand, *De l'abus des droits* (1905).

[14] See, e.g., Cour de Cassation, March 20, 1972, in Bull. IV, n. 93; Cour de Cassation, January 11, 1984, in Bull., IV, n. 16.

[15] French courts require substantial deviation from precontractual reliance in order to establish a basis for liability in tort under Article 1382; see J. Schmidt, "La Période Précontractuelle en Droit Français" 42 *Revue int. dr. comparé* 544, 545ff. (1990); J. Huet, "Responsabilitè contractuelle et responsabilité délictuelle: essai de délimitation des deux ordres de responsabilité," Thesis, University of Paris II, 1978, 260ff.

parties, and consisting, either in the abusive breaking off of negotiations (*rupture abusive*), or in the failure to provide complete and accurate information (*réticence dolosive*).[16]

The French model circulated extensively and was adopted with minor variations by other countries, such as Belgium, Spain, most Latin American countries, and several North African ones, including Egypt and Tunisia. The French model was also adopted in Italy in the 1865 Civil Code. The later 1942 Italian Civil Code, however, contains a provision (Article 1337) specifically devoted to the issue of the duties arising between the parties in the course of negotiations.[17] The Italian provision, setting forth a general duty of good faith in the course of negotiations, was clearly influenced by §242 of the German BGB and it can be seen as a unique blend of the French and German legal traditions. However, notwithstanding the contractual basis for Article 1337,[18] the prevailing view is still that precontractual liability in Italy is characterized as a liability in tort.

A very different characterization of the nature of precontractual liability prevails in Germany, where the issue is still largely influenced by the well-known theory of *culpa in contrahendo* first developed by Rudolf von Jhering.[19] Interestingly, however, in its original version the BGB contained no provision specifically devoted to this issue, although a number of provisions – including §122 (which places liability on a party making an invalid declaration), §179 (liability of the apparent agent), §307 (affirming the liability of the party entering a contract, although the party knew that the contract was void), and so forth – suggest the existence of a general reliance-based type of liability. However, the pivotal provision is BGB §242, which sets forth a general duty to perform obligations in accordance with *Treu und Glabuen* (good faith). German courts have referred to that provision as early as 1911 to hold a party liable for breaking off negotiations.[20] It is often maintained that the German courts have taken over and developed the doctrine of *culpa in contrahendo* due to the shortcomings of German tort law,[21] under which pure economic loss is not recoverable unless the damage is caused intentionally.[22] Accordingly, the precontractual liability under German law has always been characterized as a

---

[16] The perceived danger is the risk of too broad judicial discretion in spite of the positivistic traditional French approach, emphasizing the role of the legislature. Cf. J. Ghestin, *La Formation du Contrat*, 3rd ed. (1993), 232.

[17] See A. Musy, "The Good Faith Principle in Contract Law and the Precontractual Duty to Disclose: Comparative Analysis of New Differences in Legal Cultures," 1 *Global Jur. Adv.* 1 (2001) (comparative overview of precontractual liability from the Italian perspective).

[18] See L. Mengoni, "Sulla natura della responsabilità precontrattuale," *Riv.dir.comm.* 361 (II-1956); F. Benatti, *La responsabilità precontrattuale* (1963); F. Galgano, *Diritto civile e commerciale* (2011). See also, e.g., Trib. Milano, January 11, 1988, in *Giur. Comm.* 582 (II, 1988). For a recent Italian Supreme Court decision significantly (and surprisingly) reaffirming the contractual basis of Article 1337 Italian Civil Code (and, more broadly, the contractual nature of precontractual liability), see Cass., December 20, 2011, n. 27648, in *Contratti* 235 (2012).

[19] R. von Jhering, "Culpa in contrahendo oder Schadensersatz bei nichtigen oder nicht zur Perfection gelangten Verträgen," in *Jaherbüche für die Dogmatik des heutigen römischen und deutschen Privatrecht*, vol. 4 (1861), 1ff.

[20] Reichtsgericht, December 7, 1911 (Linoleum case), in RGZ 78.239 (1911); for a more recent overview of the issue, reviewing and confirming previous case law, see Bundesgerichtshof, July 10, 1970, in NJW 1840 (1970).

[21] A.T. von Mehren, "The Formation of Contract," in *International Encyclopedia of Comparative Law*, vol. 7: *Contracts in General* (Tübingen, 1992), Chapter 9, para. 121.

[22] On the contrary, under the *culpa in contrahendo* doctrine, German courts are open to the possibility of granting compensation relating to the positive interest; see, e.g., Bundesgerichtshof, November 25, 1992 (Olitic stones case), in NJW 520 (1993).

liability in contract,[23] stemming from the breach of "protective duties" (*vorvertragliche Schutzpflichten*), which arise from any relationship occurring as a result of willful negotiations. This approach was confirmed in the revised BGB §311(2),[24] which unequivocally states that an obligation may come into existence as a result of "the commencement of contract negotiations."

German law heavily influenced legal development in Austria, Portugal, Greece, as well as in Japan.[25] The German theory of *culpa in contrahendo* also influenced the Dutch legal system in recent times,[26] although the latter has to a large extent developed its own peculiar model, drawing inspiration also from various legal sources, including the works of Italian scholar Gabriele Faggella,[27] that seem to have had an influence on the development of Dutch law in the twentieth century. Indeed, Faggella argued that precontractual liability should be based on a three-stage view of negotiations (initial, continuing, final) and that the legal consequence of breaking off negotiations would depend on the stage of the negotiations. This approach has also been adopted, first, by the Dutch Hoge Raad (at least since 1982),[28] and then by the New Dutch Civil Code (Neue Burgerlijk Wetboek), which relies on a general "good faith" provision, as well as on specific rules devoted to the different stages of the negotiations. The code also imposes on the parties a duty to take into due account the interests of the other party, and a duty not to abruptly break off negotiations in the light of the reasonable reliance of the other party. Dutch courts may grant damages resulting from the breach of the aforementioned duties, including expectation damages, and there have been decisions that suggest that the remedy available to a plaintiff in a precontractual liability claim can also consist of specific performance.[29]

In common law jurisdictions, the situation is as diversified as in the civil law countries. The traditional view, still prevailing in England, is that freedom of contract cannot be reconciled with a doctrine of precontractual liability based on a general duty of good faith.[30] Therefore, the possibility of precontractual liability is firmly rejected.[31] The House of Lords in *Walford v. Miles* stated that "the concept of a duty to carry

---

[23] In fact, it may be argued that this solution is coherent with the fact that under German law an offer is, by default, irrevocable, thus suggesting that any declaration produces binding effects, the more insofar as it triggers reliance on the part of the addressee of the declaration.

[24] Law of Obligations (Gesetz zur Modernisierung des Schuldrechts) of November 26, 2001. See A. Heldrich and G.M. Rehm, "Modernisation of the German Law of Obligations: Harmonisation of Civil Law and Common Law in the Recent Reform of the German Civil Code," in *Comparative Remedies for Breach of Contract* (ed. N. Cohen and E. McKendrick) (2005), 123–33.

[25] In 2009, the Japanese "Kaoru Commission" proposed an amendment of the Japanese Civil Code recognizing *culpa in contrahendo*.

[26] The 1838 Burgerlijk Wetboek (BW) was modelled after the French civil code and did not contain any rule specifically devoted to precontractual liability.

[27] G. Faggella, "Dei periodi contrattuali e della loro vera ed esatta costruzione giurica," in *Studi Giuridici in Onore di Carlo Fadda*, vol. 3 269 (Naples, 1906).

[28] Hoge Raad, June 18, 1982, in NJ 723 (1983).

[29] Cf. Gerechtshof Amsterdam, May 7, 1987, in NJ 430 (1987).

[30] There is no general positive duty of good faith imposed on the parties to a contract in modern English law. However, it is of interest to point out that the English merchant law recognized the principle until its disappearance in the 18th-century admiralty law. Cf. J.H. Baker, *An Introduction to English Legal History*, 3rd ed. (1990).

[31] See S. Banakas, "Liability for Contractual Negotiations in English Law: Looking for the Litmus Test," *InDret – Revista para El Analisis del Dercho* 1 (2009) (overview of English law).

on negotiations in good faith is inherently repugnant to the adversarial position of the parties when involved in negotiations. Each party to the negotiations is entitled to pursue his (or her) own interest, so long as he avoids making misrepresentations."[32] Although most common law jurisdictions share a similar approach as to the basic general rule of no precontractual liability,[33] they have recognized exceptions to that general rule.

The broadest exception is based on the equitable remedy of promissory estoppel.[34] This remedy, in particular, is used by courts in the United States, to impose liability in favor of the promisee that reasonably relies on an assurance given by the promissor.[35] A similar approach has been adopted by Australian courts, which have gone as far as to grant expectation damages and specific performance to the aggrieved party,[36] similar to the approach adopted by the Dutch courts. Conversely, a recent attempt by the English Court of Appeal to establish the general availability of the estoppel rule in the negotiation stage[37] was rejected by the House of Lords, which preferred the more limited remedy found in *quantum meruit* or unjust enrichment.

U.S. courts, not unlike other common law courts,[38] have at times enforced a duty to disclose information by resorting to the doctrine of misrepresentation, including misrepresentation by omission,[39] where the conduct of the one party is regarded as fraudulent.[40]

III. Cross-Border Negotiations, the Concurrence of Domestic Laws, and the CISG on Precontractual Liability

The previous part highlighted that not only are the substantive national rules on precontractual liability different as far as their contents are concerned, but that they also diverge

---

[32] *Walford v. Miles* [1992] 2 AC 128.
[33] Cf. M.G. Bridge, "Does Anglo-Canadian Contract Law Need a Doctrine of Good Faith?," 9 *Canadian Bus. L. J.* 385, 426 (1984).
[34] See *Lord Denning in Central London Property v. High Trees House Ltd.* [1947] KB 130 (promissory estoppel has turned from being a shield into being a sword).
[35] See, e.g., *Dixon v. Wells Fargo Bank*, 2011 WL 2945795 (referring to the Restatement (Second) of Contracts to support its conclusion); *Hoffman v. Red Owl Stores*, 26 Wis.2d 683, 133 N.W.2d 267 (1965) (the most cited decision in the area of promissory estoppel). In scholarly writings, see L.A. DiMatteo and R. Sacasas, "Credit and Value 'Comfort' Instruments: Crossing the Line from Assurance to Legally Significant Reliance and Toward a Theory of Enforceability," 47 *Baylor Univ. L. Rev.* 357–423 (1995).
[36] Cf. High Court of Australia, February 19, 1988, *Waltons Stores (Interstate) Ltd. v. Maher* [1988] HCA 7.
[37] *Cobbe v. Yeomans Rowe Management Limited* [2005] WHC 266 (statements made in commercial negotiations may give rise to an estoppel, if they fairly create an expectation in the mind of the claimant that he would be granted certain rights).
[38] See, e.g., India, where the federal law defines misrepresentation as a "Misconception of Fact," which is dealt with under Section 90 of the Indian Penal Code.
[39] Cf. *Associated Warehousing, Inc. v. Banterra Corp.*, 2008 WL 4180260, stating that to establish a claim for misrepresentation by omission, the plaintiff must allege facts sufficient to show that the defendant: (1) had a duty to disclose a material fact, (2) failed to disclose that fact, (3) which induced the plaintiff to act, and (4) the plaintiff suffered actual damages as a result.
[40] English courts with respect to precontractual liability have referenced the law of tort. The Israeli 1973 Contract Law seemed to indicate that *culpa in contrahendo* constituted a tertium genus, but subsequent case law has characterized the matter as a form of extracontractual (tortious) liability. In Canada, the Supreme Court in 2000 rejected a general characterization of *culpa in contrahendo* as falling under tort law.

in nature. The nature of such claims can be found in specific contract doctrines, in tort, or in a *tertium genus*, such as a claim for unjust enrichment. Such variations cause a great deal of uncertainty in cross-border negotiations. For example, the characterization of the claim is important in order to select the appropriate conflict-of-law rules to be applied in determining the proper court and the applicable law. Moreover, characterization is also essential to address the question as to whether the issue is covered by the CISG (which seems to govern at least some preliminary agreements) or by domestic law.

The complexity of determining the jurisdiction and applicable law and finding precontractual liability is illustrated by *Fonderie Officine Meccaniche Tacconi v. Heinrich Wagner Sinto Maschinenfabrik (Tacconi)*,[41] where the European Court of Justice (ECJ)[42] decided that, in circumstances relating to a precontractual dispute, which were characterized by the absence of any obligation freely entered into by the parties to negotiations and by the possible breach of rules of law, in particular a duty to negotiate in good faith, an action founded in precontractual liability was a matter relating to tort, delict, or quasi-delict for the purposes of Article 5(3) of the Brussels Convention.[43] However, the *Tacconi* decision provides a solution to the issue of jurisdiction in precontractual liability cases only within the European Union (EU). Furthermore, the decision was limited to the issue of determining jurisdiction. It did not provide guidance on how claims should be characterized in general or as to the content of the rules applicable to precontractual liability.

As far as the law applicable to precontractual liability is concerned, Article 12 of the Rome II Regulation[44] provides as a general rule that "the law applicable to a non-contractual obligation arising out of dealings prior to the conclusion of a contract, regardless of whether the contract was actually concluded or not, shall be the law that applies to the contract or that would have been applicable to it had it been entered into."[45]

---

[41] *Fonderie Officine Meccaniche Tacconi v. Heinrich Wagner Sinto Maschinenfabrik, ECJ*, September 17, 2002, case C-334/2000, ECJ Reports I-07357 (2002).

[42] On January 23, 1996, Tacconi brought an action against HWS before the District Court of Perugia for a declaration that HWS was to be held liable for damages (resulting from Tacconi having already entered into a financing agreement in view of the perspective contract with HWS) resulting from HWS's breach of its precontractual duties. In its defence, HWS pleaded, among others, that the Italian court lacked jurisdiction because Article 5(1) of the Brussels Convention (on the jurisdiction of courts in matters related to contracts) was applicable, thus leading to the jurisdiction of German courts (as the products would have been delivered in Germany under the contract).

[43] See Frignani and Torsello, *Il contratto internazionale*, 167.

[44] Regulation (EC) of June 17, 2008, no. 593/2008 of the European Parliament and of the Council on the law applicable to non-contractual obligations, O.J. L 199/40 of July 31, 2007. According to the Recitals (30) "*Culpa in contrahendo* for the purposes of this Regulation is an *autonomous concept* and should not necessarily be interpreted within the meaning of national law. It should include the *violation of the duty of disclosure* and the *breakdown of contractual negotiations*."

[45] See, generally, P. Franzina, "Il regolamento no. 864/2007/Ce sulla legge applicabile alle obbligazioni extracontrattuali (Roma II)", *Nuove leggi civ. comm.* 971 (2008); P. Hay, "Contemporary Approaches to Non-Contractual Obligations in Private International Law (Conflict of Laws) and the European Community's 'Rome II' Regulation," *Chinese Yearbook Private Int'l L. & Comparative L.* 33 (2008); T. Hartley, "Choice of Law for Non-Contractual Liability: Selected Problems under the Rome II Regulation," 57 *Int'l & Comp. L. Quarterly* 899 (2008); Joubert Corneloup, *Le règlement communautaire "Rome II" sur la loi applicable aux obligations non contractuelles* (2008); Kadner, "Le nouveau droit international privé communautaire en matière de responsabilité extracontractuelle (règlement Rome II)," *Rev. critique dr. int. privé*

Again, however, notwithstanding the great value to be attached to the harmonization of conflict-of-law rules on precontractual liability, the Rome II Regulation does not apply outside the borders of the EU, nor does it lead to harmonization as regards the characterization of the claim or to the substantive rules of conduct, the breach of which can result in liability.

It is apparent that the mere characterization of an issue as precontractual proves unsatisfactory and misleading, in that it does not provide the interpreter with the tools necessary to deal with the issues presented by party misconduct. It is also inaccurate to make any general statement as to whether the CISG governs issues of precontractual liability.[46] Indeed, the proper way to address that question is to take as a starting point the various circumstances in which a claim for precontractual liability can be brought, and then to evaluate whether the situation falls within the scope of the CISG, and only after determining otherwise to resort to domestic law.

As noted previously, the CISG does not establish rules for the precontractual stage,[47] although it expressly attaches some significance to the negotiations when it instructs the interpreter, under Article 8, to take them into account in order to interpret the parties' statements and conduct.[48] The CISG does deal with the process of contract formation,[49] which inherently or indirectly relates to the parties precontractual relationship.

It is therefore appropriate to make a distinction between at least four different situations leading to a claim for damages relating to occurrences in the course of negotiations. The four situations include:[50] (1) damages to protected assets, such as personal injury and injury to property; (2) damages due to fraudulent conduct; (3) damages related to the breaking off of contractual negotiations; and (4) damages caused by misleading information or by a failure to provide information that the other party possessed.

The first situation, personal injury and property damage, is outside the scope of the CISG, not only with respect to damages consisting of the death or personal injury of the claimant, which are explicitly excluded under CISG Article 5,[51] but also with respect to damages to other protected assets.[52] This area is dealt with under applicable domestic law and in most cases the situation will be characterized as falling under the law of torts.

(2008), 445; T. Kadner Graziano, "Das auf außervertragliche Schuldverhältnisse anzuwendende Recht nach Inkrafttreten der Rom II-Verordnung," *RabelsZ* 1 (2009); Wagner, "Die neue Rom II-Verordnung," *IPRax* 1 (2008); A. Dickinson, *The Rome II Regulation* (2008).

[46] In general terms, on the possibility of unintended contractual liability arising under the CISG, see L.A. Di Matteo, "The CISG and the Presumption of Enforceability: Unintended Contractual Liability in International Business Dealings," 22 *Yale J. Int'l L.* 111–70 (1997).

[47] See I. Schwenzer and P. Hachem in *Commentary on the UN Convention on the International Sale of Goods (CISG)*, 3rd ed. (ed. P. Schlechtriem and I. Schwenzer) (2010), Article 4, p. 81.

[48] Cf. M. Schmidt-Kessel in Schlechtriem and Schwenzer, *Commentary*, Article 8, pp. 160–3.

[49] See, generally, F. Ferrari, "Formazione del contratto," in *Commentario del Codice Civile Scialoja-Branca* (ed. F. Galgano) (2006).

[50] See also U.G. Schroeter in Schlechtriem and Schwenzer, *Commentary*, "Introduction to Articles 14–24," 248ff.

[51] Cf. J. Lookofsky, *The 1980 United Nations Convention on Contracts for the International Sale of Goods* (2000), 46.

[52] See also M.J. Bonell, "Vertragsverhandlungen und culpa in contrahendo nach dem Wiener Kaufrechtsübereinkommen," *RIW* 700 (1990).

In the area of fraudulent conduct on the part of the defendant in the course of the negotiations, two different issues arise. On the one hand, the fraudulent conduct could support a claim that the resulting contract is invalid[53] under applicable domestic law, in the light of the exclusionary provision contained in CISG Article 4. On the other hand, however, the fraudulent conduct could also be invoked as a breach of contract to claim damages under the CISG.[54] The issue that arises is whether the claimant can rely on domestic damages rules on the basis of fraud, as well as making a claim under the CISG; the crucial point, in this regard, is that the CISG does not address factual situations involving fraud.[55] If the claim is based in fraud, then the damage claim falls outside the scope of the CISG.[56]

A claim for precontractual liability connected to the formation of a contract to fall under the CISG must be treated in a way other than the breaking off of contractual negotiations.[57] Because CISG Articles 15 and 16 deal with the issue of revocability of an offer it implies that the issue is covered by the CISG without providing for damages as a possible result of the revocation. The point is that under the CISG, if an offer is irrevocable the remedy available to the offeree is that, notwithstanding the revocation, he or she can accept the offer and conclude the contract. However, the revocation does not allow for a claim for damages.[58] Therefore, to the extent that a potential contract falls within the scope of the CISG, the application of concurrent domestic rules setting forth liability for breaking off negotiations is precluded.

In practical cases, however, it is difficult to conclude whether the contract under discussion will be of a kind governed by the CISG. Consider, for instance, the situation where it is unclear whether the contract will be performed by the seller through its place of business located in a noncontracting state, or by a place of business located in a contracting state. In the former case, the CISG would likely not apply, whereas it would apply in the latter. Moreover, claims relating to a future contract for sale of goods, coupled with a sale of services, will be excluded under Article 3 CISG, insofar as the preponderant part of the obligation is the supply of services, an aspect of the transaction that may be unclear at the stage of negotiations.[59]

In the aforementioned case scenarios, it is unclear whether the CISG is applicable law. If not, then recourse may be made under applicable domestic law on liability for the breaking off of negotiations. If this is the case, the question then arises as to how to determine the domestic law applicable to the matter. Within the member states of the EU, the solution is provided by Article of 12 of the Rome II Regulation.[60] In cases involving non-EU parties, the predictability of the outcome of the conflict-of-law analysis

---

[53] Schwenzer and Hachem in Schlechtriem and Schwenzer, *Commentary*, 90.

[54] Cf. *Miami Valley Paper, LLC v. Lebbing Engineering & Consulting GmbH*, WL 2924779 (S.D. Ohio 2006).

[55] See Schroeter in Schlechtriem and Schwenzer, *Commentary*, 249.

[56] Cf. J. Honnold, *Uniform Law for International Sales under the 1980 United Nations Convention* (1999), Article 4, para. 65.

[57] Cf. U. Magnus in *Julius von Staudinger Kommentar zum Bürgerlichen Gesetzbuch mit Einführungsgesetz und Nebengesetzen*, 12th ed. (ed. J. von Staudinger) (1993), Article 4, para. 14.

[58] See F. Ferrari in *Kommentar zum Einheitlichen UN-Kaufrecht – CISG*, 5th ed. (ed. P. Schlechtriem and I. Schwenzer) (2009), Article 5, para. 46.

[59] See Torsello, "Preliminary Agreements," 191.

[60] See *supra* note 42 and accompanying text.

decreases significantly partly because of the uncertainties as to how to characterize the claim in question.[61]

Finally, the analysis may differ in the situation where damages are suffered due to misleading information provided by a party during the negotiations, or by a failure to provide material information. Insofar as the misleading information is provided fraudulently, the remedy would be provided under domestic law. Some domestic courts – in particular in the United States[62] – provide remedies also where the information was provided negligently.[63] However, whenever the misleading information relates to the goods, the situation falls within the scope of CISG Article 35 CISG, so that the application of concurrent domestic rules should be precluded.[64] A similar analysis applies to the situation where the claim for damages is brought under domestic law on the basis of an alleged breach of a precontractual duty to disclose information. The claim under domestic law may concur with an action brought under the CISG only insofar as the duty to disclose pertains to matters outside the scope of the CISG. Again, to the extent that the concurrent application of the CISG and of domestic remedies proves possible, the puzzling problem arises as to what domestic law is to be applied, as the duty to disclose information cannot easily be traced back to a contractual one and, in fact, it is in most cases established by law.[65]

IV. Assessing Precontractual Liability: Contents and Purposes of Preliminary Agreements

The analysis presented in the previous section suggests that parties entering a cross-border negotiation should agree rules to regulate the course of their negotiations. The optimal solution to the uncertainty of precontractual liability is that the parties enter into a "preliminary agreement," determining by contract the rules of conduct and duties of the parties during their negotiations.

Commercial experience shows that operators entering a commercial relationship are inclined, at some point before the final contract is concluded, to agree to the framework for their future agreement.[66] Commercial contractors are inclined to conclude preliminary agreements due to their use as negotiating strategies, as well as to their responding to certain behavioral and cognitive needs. These behavioral and cognitive needs result in legal and economic implications. The relationship between the uses of preliminary

---

[61] For a decision dealing with the conflict-of-law analysis in promissory estoppel cases relating to negotiations, see, e.g., *Executone of Columbus, Inc. v. Inter-Tel, Inc.*, Ohio, 665 F.Supp.2d 899 (2009) ("a promissory estoppel cause of action is governed by the law of the state that has the most significant relationship to the dispute").

[62] *Sky Cast, Inc. v. Global Direct Distribution LLC*, WL 754734 (E.D. Ky. 2008).

[63] Cf. M. Bridge, "A Comment on 'Towards a Universal Doctrine of Breach: The Impact of the CISG,' by Jürgen Basedow," 25 *Int'l Rev. L. & Econ.* 510 (2005). Cf. Schroeter, in Schlechtriem and Schwenzer, *Commentary*, 251 (critical of common law approach because it does not consider to which facts the alleged misrepresentation pertains).

[64] The situation is, of course, different if the misleading information relates to an issue not covered by the CISG.

[65] For instance, European Commission, Proposal for a "Regulation of the European Parliament and the Council on a Common European Sales Law," contains several provisions devoted to the parties' duties to disclose information in the course of negotiations.

[66] See A. Schwartz and J.C. Watson, "The Law and Economics of Costly Contracting," 20 *J. L. Econ. & Org.* 2 (2004).

agreements to meet these needs has not been fully explored in scholarly writings,[67] notwithstanding their growing practical importance.[68]

Evidence of the need for further research is the uncertainty that characterizes the legal significance of instruments such as preliminary agreements, letters of intent, memorandum of understandings, heads of agreements, protocols, and others that are used interchangeably, thus leading to a great deal of confusion. Of course, the label used (*nomen juris*) does not in itself bear any legal consequences. The enforceability of such instruments is dependent on their contents and the intention of the parties.

The purposes for using such instruments vary. First, the parties may simply want to memorialize the state of their negotiations, without any further commitment. In many circumstances, however, the parties may want to create some sort of reciprocal obligations, not necessarily legal ones. The bases of nonlegal obligations include the bonding effects of commercial reputation, the parties making relation-specific investments, or the disclosure of confidential information. If done reciprocally, the parties create a "mutual hostage" situation that aligns their interests in continuing the negotiation. At a more advanced stage of the negotiations, the parties may want to bind themselves to concluding a future contract, some marginal aspects of which have not yet been agreed upon, or to the conclusion of a fully agreed-upon future contract that only needs to be formalized.[69]

An English court described a preliminary agreement entitled a "Gentlemen's Agreement" as "an agreement which is not an agreement, made between two persons, neither of whom is a gentleman, whereby each expects the other to be strictly bound without himself being bound at all."[70] This sarcastic definition captures the kind of agreements

---

[67] See, e.g., D. Henrich, *Vorvertrag, Optionvertrag, Vorrechtsvertrag: Eine Dogmatisch-Systematische Untersuchung der Vertrag-Lichen Bindungen vor und zu einem Vertragschluss* (1965); R. Rascio, *Il Contratto Preliminare* (1967); C.L. Knapp, "Enforcing the Contract to Bargain," 44 N.Y.U. L. Rev. 673 (1969); J.M. Mousseron, "La Durée dans la formation des contrats," in *Etudes offertes à Alfred Jouffret* (1974), 509ff.; A.M. Dugdale and N.V. Lowe, "Contracts to Contract and Contracts to Negotiate," *J. Bus. L.* 28 (1976); M. Fontaine, "Les Lettres d'intention dans la négociation des contrats internationaux," 3 *Dr. Pr. Comm. Int.* 73 (1977); C.F. Trower, "Enforceability of Letters of Intent and Other Preliminary Agreements," 24 *Rocky Mtn. Min. L. Inst.* 347 (1978); M. Lutter, *Der Letter of Intent* (Cologne, 1983); E.A. Farnsworth, "Precontractual Liability and Preliminary Agreements: Fair Dealing and Failed Negotiations," 87 *Colum. L. Rev.* 217, 249ff. (1987); A. Chianale, "Contratto preliminare in diritto comparato," in *Digesto Sez. Civ.*, vol. 5, pp. 290ff. (1989) (comparative overview); *Precontractual Liability: Reports to the XIIIth Congress of the International Academy of Comparative Law* (ed. E.H. Hondius) (1991); A. Schwartz and R.E. Scott, "The Law and Economics of Preliminary Agreements," 120 *Harv. L. Rev.* 661 (2007) (law and economics perspective).

[68] See also J. Schmidt, "Preliminary Agreements in International Contract Negotiation," 6 *Houston J. Int'l L.* 37 (1983–1984).

[69] See also E.A. Farnsworth, "Precontractual Liability and Preliminary Agreements: Fair Dealing and Failed Negotiations," 87 *Colum. L. Rev.* 217, 249–50 (1987) (broad notion of preliminary agreements). Farnsworth notes: "Parties that wish to avoid some of the uncertainties of the regime of negotiation without moving immediately to the regime of ultimate agreement often make preliminary agreements. I shall use the term 'preliminary agreement' to refer to any agreement, whether or not legally enforceable, that is made during negotiations in anticipation of some later agreement that will be the culmination of the negotiations. Such agreements are particularly common in situations in which the investment of at least one party becomes substantial in relation to the deal as a whole and cannot be spread over other similar deals, and yet the parties cannot escape from the regime of negotiation by moving to that of ultimate agreement. They appear under a variety of names, including 'letters of intent,' 'commitment letters,' 'binders,' 'agreements in principle,' 'memoranda of understandings,' and 'heads of agreement.'"

[70] *Bloom v. Kinder* [1958] T.R. 91, quoted in D.K. Allen, "England," in *Precontractual Liability: Reports to the XIIIth Congress of the International Academy of Comparative Law* (ed. E.H. Hondius) (Deventer, 1991), 125, 138.

that are considered in this chapter, although no negative implications are involved here that are at times attached to the notion of gentlemen's agreements.[71] Under such instruments the parties are not contractually bound to each other; instead, they merely want to memorialize the points that have been agreed upon and those still unsettled or unaddressed. The instrument used for this purpose is commonly called a "Memorandum of Understanding." At the most, the parties may merely intend to bind each other on the nonlegal basis of reputation,[72] which, in fact, is often effective in preventing a party from stepping out of the negotiations.[73]

The lack of legally binding effects, at least under contract law, makes it clear that these types of agreements are non-contractual,[74] hence, the application of the CISG is precluded. Nor can such agreements be interpreted as an offer directed from one party to the other. This conclusion can be drawn on the basis of the language of CISG Article 14, which requires an offer to take the form of a proposal whereby the offeror indicates, among other things, his intention "to be bound in case of acceptance." It is safe to assume that the binding effect referred to in Article 14 requires a legal intent to be bound.[75] Therefore, these nonlegal instruments may result in liability in domestic law under the theory of *culpa in contrahendo*.[76]

In practice, however, letters of intent and similar documents generate great uncertainty and concern as to whether or not enforceable obligations have been formed.[77] The intent of the parties governs the situation and the CISG has a role to play in this respect. Indeed, whether or not a *contract* exists is often to be assessed on the basis of the CISG, in particular by resort to the rules on contract formation in Articles 14 to 24,[78] and the

---

[71] The pejorative meaning of the term "Gentlemen's Agreement" in the United States is pointed out by H. Bernstein and J. Zekoll, "The Gentlemen's Agreement in Legal Theory and in Modern Practice: United States," 46 *Am. J. Comp. L.* 87, 87 (1998).

[72] See L. Bernstein, "Merchant Law in a Merchant Court: Rethinking the Code's Search for Business Norms," 144 *U. Pa. L. Rev.* 1765, 1789 (1996) (strength of reputation in commercial agreements).

[73] In practice, businesspersons often undertake legally binding contractual obligations by signing preliminary documents named without being fully aware of their enforceability. Cf. R.G. Shell, "Opportunism and Trust in the Negotiation of Commercial Contracts: Toward a New Cause of Action," 44 *Van. L. Rev.* 221, 221ff. (1991). This is particularly the case with respect to Letters of Intent, which in commercial practice are used not only to indicate nonlegally binding agreements, but also to indicate agreements that create binding obligations to be discussed later in this chapter. See R.B. Lake and U. Draetta, *Letters of Intent and Other Precontractual Documents: Comparative Analysis and Forms* (Salem, 1994), 221ff. Nonetheless, the focus here shall be on the contents, rather than the names, of the agreements. Cf. W.H. Holmes, "The Freedom Not to Contract," 60 *Tulane L. Rev.* 751, 752ff. (1963).

[74] See Bernstein and Zekoll, "Gentlemen's Agreement," 88 (use the expression "deliberate no-law").

[75] See Bundesgericht, Switzerland, April 5, 2005 (IHR 204 (2005), available at http://cisgw3.law.pace.edu/cases/050405s1.html; Oberlandesgericht Hamburg, Germany, July 4, 1997, available at http://cisgw3.law.pace.edu/cases/970704g1.html; Landgericht München, Germany, February 8, 1995, available at http://cisgw3.law.pace.edu/cases/950208g4.html (buyer unsuccessfully made an attempt to hold that the parties' declarations merely indicated details of a contract to be concluded at a later time, without expressing the intention to be legally bound).

[76] See G.A. Pietrafesa, "The Law Governing Letters of Intent and Other Preliminary Agreements," 225 *Dec N.J. Lawyer* 35, 35ff. (2003).

[77] See also L.A. Bebchuk and O. Ben-Shahar, "Precontractual Reliance," 30 *J. Legal St.* 423 (2001).

[78] See, e.g., G. Eörsi, "Problems of Unifying the Law on the Formation of Contracts for the International Sale of Goods," 27 *Am. J. Comp. L.* 311, 311ff. (1979); G. Eörsi, "Formation of Contract," in *Schweizerisches Institut für Rechtsvergleichung, Wiener übereinkommen von 1980 über den internationalen Warenkauf. Lausanner Kolloquium* (Lausanne, 1985), 43ff.; J. Lookofsky, "Alive and Well in Scandinavia: CISG Part II," 18 *J. L. & Comm.* 289, 289ff. (1999); M. Perales Viscasillas, "Comments on the Draft Digest Relating to Articles 14–24 and 66–70," in *The Draft UNCITRAL Digest and Beyond: Cases, Analysis and Unresolved*

interpretation of the parties' intent and conduct under CISG Article 8,[79] which prevail over any domestic rules dealing with those issues.[80]

Under a different scheme, in the course of the negotiations the parties may decide to enter a legally binding agreement in order to prevent one of the other parties from stepping out of the negotiation.[81] This proves to be of particular importance when either one or both of the parties are required to make relation-specific investments.[82] The parties thus bind themselves to conduct negotiations over a certain period of time, under an "agreement to negotiate."

The rationale for entering a binding agreement is to lock in parties to negotiate (in good faith) because the common economic benefits of a final contract are still uncertain.[83] However, the parties do not want to be subject to liability in the event the venture proves not to be profitable. In many agreements of the kind in question, the parties set a timetable for the negotiations.

The legally binding nature of these agreements is undisputed in most civil law jurisdictions,[84] whereas it has proved to be somewhat problematic in common law legal systems.[85] As a result, the choice of the competent forum and of the applicable law play an important role in determining the enforceability of the agreements. The best interpretation of these agreements is that they are not governed by the CISG, although one may argue to the contrary on the basis of the fact that the agreement in question constitutes a preparatory act in view of a final contract falling within the scope of the CISG. This *ex post* analysis should be rejected on the basis that the core concept of *sale* under the CISG, which requires an exchange (of goods for money), is not established in such agreements. The preliminary agreement only binds the parties to negotiate; this

---

Issues in the U.N. Sales Convention (ed. F. Ferrari, H.M. Flechtner, and R.A. Brand) (2004), 259, 259ff.; M. Perales Viscasillas, "Contract Conclusion under CISG," 16 *J. L. & Commerce* 315, 315ff. (1997); E.A. Farnsworth, "Formation of Contract," in *International Sales: The United Nations Convention on Contracts for the International Sale of Goods* (ed. N.M. Glaston and H. Smit) (New York, 1984), 3, 3.1ff.; S. Patti, "Silenzio, inerzia e comportamento concludente nella Convenzione di Vienna sui contratti di vendita internazionale di beni mobili," 1991 *Riv. Dir. Comm. Dir. Gen. Obbl.* 135, 135ff. (1991); F. Ferrari, "A Comparative Overview of Offer and Acceptance Inter Absentes," 10 *Boston U. Int'l L. J.* 171, 171ff. (1992) (comparative overview).

[79] See M.P. van Alstine, "Consensus, Dissensus, and Contractual Obligation through the Prism of Uniform International Sales Law," 37 *Va. J. Int'l L.* 58, 58ff. (1996); F. Ferrari, "Interpretation of Statements: Article 8," in Ferrari et al., *The Draft UNCITRAL*, 172, 172 ff.; A. Lüderitz and A. Fenge, "Article 8 CISG," in *Bürgerliches Gesetzbuch mit Einführungsgesetzen und Nebengesetzen*, vol. 13: *Übereinkommen der Vereinten Nationen über Verträge über den internationalen Warenkauf (CISG)* (2000); A. Kaczorowska, "Règles uniformes d'interprétation d'un contrat international," *Rev. Dr. Int. Dr. Comp.* 297, 297ff. (1991); A.E. Farnsworth in *Commentary on the International Sales Law: The 1980 Vienna Sales Convention* (ed. C.M. Bianca and M.J. Bonell) (1987), Article 8, pp. 95, 95ff.

[80] See Landgericht Hamburg, Germany, September 26, 1990, available at http://cisgw3.law.pace.edu/cases/900926g1.html.

[81] Cf. Farnsworth, "Precontractual Liability," 250; Knapp, "Enforcing the Contract," 673 ff.

[82] See A.W. Katz, "When Should an Offer Stick? The Economics of Promissory Estoppel in Preliminary Negotiations," 105 *Yale L. J.* 1249, 1249ff. (1996).

[83] Cf. Schmidt, "Preliminary Agreements," 39, according to which, "when parties think it useful to obligate themselves to negotiate a future contract, it is generally because they wish in this way to increase the chances of concluding the contract."

[84] See also id., 40.

[85] See Lord Denning in *Courtney & Fairbairn Ltd. v. Tolaini Brothers (Hotels) Ltd.*, 1 W.L.R. 297 (1975) (under the English common law these kinds of preliminary agreements have often been considered unenforceable).

does not ensure the future conclusion of the contract for the sale of goods. The preliminary agreement only relates to the conduct of the parties at the negotiation stage, which is clearly beyond the CISG's sphere of application.

The preliminary agreement to negotiate establishes mutual or unilateral obligations regulating the course of the negotiations. These obligations often include "preparatory expenses-sharing," "confidentiality," "standstill," and "exclusivity" provisions. They all share the common character of governing the parties' conducts during the time preceding the conclusion of the final contract.[86]

Preparatory expenses-sharing provisions allocate the costs jointly or severally borne by the parties in the course of the negotiations. Agreements of this kind are particularly relevant in that they directly set forth rules of conduct in the precontractual stage, precluding the application of alternative rules set under domestic law.[87] Confidentiality provisions are of paramount importance whenever in the course of the negotiations a party discloses valuable information.[88] Unlike the other obligations established by preliminary agreements, confidentiality agreements create obligations that typically do not expire when the negotiations or final contract are concluded.[89] As a consequence, when the final contract is concluded the confidentiality agreement may continue as part of the final sales contract.[90]

The standstill and exclusivity provisions[91] will be considered together here because of the meaning attached to them. The standstill prohibits a party, during the negotiations, to acquire interest or control in another entity, or to actively solicit or enter negotiations for the conclusion of contracts of the kind being negotiated between the negotiating parties. Similarly, an exclusivity provision or agreement (also referred to as a lock-out agreement) requires one or both parties to cease any existing negotiations with third parties for comparable business opportunities and often also to disclose any offers received by third

---

[86] See Lake and Draetta, *Letters of Intent*, 124ff.

[87] See Yeon-Koo Che and D.B. Hausch, "Cooperative Investments and the Value of Contracting," 89 *Am. Econ. Rev.* 125, 125ff. (1999) (economic efficiency of this kind of agreement).

[88] See Farnsworth, "Precontractual Liability," 278–7.

[89] See J.-M. Deleuze, *Le Contrat de Transfert de Processus Technologique* (Paris 1976), 31ff.

[90] Difficult questions thus arise, which the parties should address when drafting their contract. In particular, if, in the course of the performance of the final contract subsequently concluded, Party A breaches the confidentiality duties undertaken in the preliminary agreement, can party B resort to the remedies for breach of contract available under the CISG, leading, in particular, to the avoidance of the entire contract on the basis of a fundamental breach? It is maintained here that the answer to that question ought to be positive, as the very function of the confidentiality agreement and the unitary economic goal pursued in the transaction should induce the interpreter to conclude that the obligations stemming from the preliminary agreement are incorporated into the final contract, if concluded. However, it is here suggested that the parties would be better off making that conclusion clear by means of an explicit clause, or by providing for the incorporation of the confidentiality provision into the final contract at the earlier stage of the preliminary agreement. For a court decision dealing with a CISG contract in conjunction with a confidentiality agreement (although not of a preliminary character), see *Geneva Pharmaceuticals Technology Corp. v. Barr Laboratories, Inc.*, 201 F.Supp. 2d 236 (S.D.N.Y. 2002), available at http://cisgw3.law.pace.edu/cases/020821u1.html; see also *TeeVee Toons Records and Steve Gottlieb Inc. v. Gerhard Schubert GmbH*, 2002 WL 498627 (S.D.N.Y. 2002), available at http://cisgw3.law.pace.edu/cases/020329u1.html.

[91] On these preliminary agreements, see Farnsworth, "Precontractual Liability," 279, observing that "'Exclusive negotiation' provisions are not . . . unusual in preliminary agreements arising out of ordinary contract negotiations, where they may be assented to by a party who will not grant a right of first refusal. A typical exclusive-negotiation clause obligates one party to refrain from negotiating with others for a stated period of time."

parties in the course of the negotiations.[92] As an aside, these types of agreements are subject to competition law due to their anticompetitive nature.[93]

An alternative to the standstill or exclusivity provisions is the grant of a "right of preference."[94] This provision grants to the beneficiary a preference over any third party to conclude a contract, under the same conditions as proposed by the third party.[95] Exclusivity agreements and agreements granting a right of preference should be kept distinct from firm offers, such as those recognized under CISG Article 16(2), as well as from option contracts.[96] In firm offers and option contracts the promissor has already manifested its consent to be bound contingent on the acceptance of the other party.[97] This is not the case with respect to exclusivity agreements and agreements granting a right of preference. In these agreements, the party granting the exclusivity or preference, although limiting his or her her own possibility of entering alternative contracts, still reserves the right not to enter into the contract under consideration, despite the beneficiary of the provision's willingness to do so.[98]

A slightly contrasting variation to the foregoing types of agreements occurs when the negotiating parties decide to enter a preliminary agreement binding them to conclude a contract at a later date.[99] These types of agreements are most appropriately used where the parties have already agreed on all aspects of the final transaction but still decide not to conclude the final contract immediately. However, commercial practice confirms that there are many cases where the parties enter binding *agreements to agree*, although they still need to negotiate additional terms. In this sense these agreements can better be described as *incomplete preliminary agreements to agree*. They may still bind the parties to conclude on the basis of terms already agreed upon, irrespective of the content of the provisions not yet discussed. Of course, the more the parties are required to make relation-specific investments in the course of the negotiation, the more they are inclined to accept binding obligations, provided that they are mutual.[100] Most importantly, each

---

[92] Cf. Lake and Draetta, *Letters of Intent*, 250 (these agreements are also referred to as "no-shop" agreements in the United States).

[93] It should be noted that under several domestic jurisdictions the agreement may be considered void or unenforceable on those grounds, and parties should therefore carefully draft the agreement in light of the competent forum and applicable law.

[94] See Schmidt, "Preliminary Agreements," 44 (observing that "this type of obligation existed under Roman law, and is presently a part of most civil law systems"); see also G. Vettori, *Efficacia ed opponibilità del patto di preferenza* (Milan, 1988).

[95] See, generally, A.S. Balbaa, "La Préemtion en droit comparé," Thesis, University of Dijon, 1938); P. Gallo, *Introduzione al diritto comparato*, vol. 2: *Istituti giuridici* (Turin, 1998), 177–8.

[96] See also Schmidt, "Preliminary Agreements," 45; for papers on option contracts, see, e.g., A.W. Katz, "The Efficient Design of Option Contracts," working paper, March 2004; O. Bar-Gill, "Pricing Legal Options: A Behavioral Perspective," 1 *Rev. L. & Econ.* (2005); E. Cesaro, *Il contratto e l'opzione* (Naples 1965).

[97] Moreover, option contracts, unlike firm offers, are assignable. See G. Gorla, "Problemi sulla cedibilità dell'offerta contrattuale (di scambio), dell'opzione e del contratto preliminare," *Riv. Dir. Comm.* 23, 23ff. (1963); this character also suggests the distinction to be made between option contracts (which are final contracts conditional upon the beneficiary's declaration) and "unilateral preliminary contracts," which are final contracts that bind only one party, but require a new contract to be concluded; see F. Galgano, *Diritto civile e commerciale* (Padua, 2004), II, 1, 222.

[98] O. Ben-Shahar, "'Agreeing to Disagree': Filling Gaps in Deliberately Incomplete Contracts," 2004 *Wis. L. Rev.* 389, 406ff. (2004) (highlighting the benefits of bonding in the course of negotiation).

[99] Cf. Knapp, "Enforcing the Contract," 677.

[100] Cf. A. Schwartz and R.E. Scott, "Contract Theory and the Limits of Contract Law," 113 *Yale L. J.* 611ff. (2003).

party wants to hold the other party to the bargain, and believes the preliminary agreement performs that function.[101] In the absence of the parties' intention to that effect, however, the agreement cannot be treated as a definitive contract.[102]

Given the various roles or functions played by agreements discussed here, the parties (especially in complex transactions) may enter a series of these agreements mirroring the different steps in the negotiations ("point-by-point negotiation").[103] The subsequent agreements not only reflect the point-by-point progress of the negotiations, but also have different increasingly bonding legal consequences, in accordance with the parties' intent and confidence in the feasibility of the transaction. During the early part of the negotiations, the parties' intention is likely to only memorialize the ongoing discussion, whereas the closer the negotiations comes to a conclusion, the more likely the parties are to accept obligations to conclude a final contract.[104]

It is debatable whether the agreement "to formalize and sign the Final Contract" can be interpreted as an unconditional obligation to conclude the final contract, whatever the case. In fact, different answers would be given under different domestic legal systems.[105] Parties willing to enter a binding preliminary agreement to conclude the final contract should include language to make it clear that the preliminary agreement is intended "to bind the parties to conclude the final contract."[106]

As far as the applicability of the CISG is concerned, one may argue that preliminary agreements to conclude a future contract are beyond the scope of the CISG on the basis of the different nature and structure of the obligations undertaken by the parties. Indeed, the obligation to conclude a contract is radically different from the obligation to transfer property or to pay a purchase price. This argument, however, is too formalistic. Focus on the nature and structure of the obligation (or on the object of the contract)[107] should not prevail over the economic substance of the agreement. Accordingly, the CISG is arguably applicable to some types of preliminary agreements. For example, the commercial practice of the parties may view the preliminary agreement as sealing the deal and view the outstanding points as marginal issues, most likely to be provided by

---

[101] Ben-Shahar, "'Agreeing to Disagree,'" 406ff. (economic benefits of legal bonding in the course of contract formation).

[102] This conclusion may also be argued under the CISG, primarily on the basis of the language of Article 14, which requires the "intention to be bound" by the final contract: for a recent court decision finding that the parties intended to create a definitive CISG contract, thus rejecting arguments to the contrary brought by a buyer who sought to demonstrate that the parties did not intend to enter a binding agreement, see Kantogericht Freiburg, Switzerland, October 11, 2004 IHR 72 (2005), available at http://cisgw3.law.pace.edu/cases/041011s1.html.

[103] See also Schmidt, "Preliminary Agreements," 51, where the author points out that "facilitating the conclusion may be realized by two different techniques: either the negotiation of the future contract is divided, or it is unified for a whole series of future contracts."

[104] See A. Schwartz and J.C. Watson, "The Law and Economics of Costly Contracting," 20 *J. L. Econ. & Org.* 2 (2004) (economic explanation of the dynamics of contracting and related investments).

[105] See also Schmidt, "Preliminary Agreements," 58ff.

[106] It should be noted, however, that under some legal systems the enforceability of an agreement to conclude a contract may be denied notwithstanding the clear language used by the parties; for instance, for an analysis of the difficulties to enforce the agreement under the English common law, see Dugdale and Lowe, "Contracts," 31ff. (criticize the "so-called principle that the law does not recognize a contract to enter into a contract").

[107] Cf. G. Gorla, "The Theory of Contract Object in Civil Law: A Critical Analysis by means of the Comparative Method," 28 *Tulane L. Rev.* 442, 447ff. (1953–4).

their lawyers. Most importantly, the parties may intend the obligations stemming from the agreement to be the substantive obligations of the final contract, which is to become effective at a later stage.

From a normative perspective, the threshold of enforceability is that the likelihood of concluding a final contract is reasonably high and comparable to that of a final contract. This situation occurs when the basic elements of the future contract are already agreed upon; in this respect, the applicability of the CISG is to be determined on the basis of whether the preliminary agreement is considered to consist of sales-type obligations that are sufficiently definite.[108] In such cases, the applicability of the CISG is fully justified[109] and the breaking off of negotiations is to be treated as a breach of contract triggering the remedies available under the CISG.

V. Closing Remarks

This chapter shows that the applicability of the CISG to issues of precontractual liability should not rest upon the labeling of an agreement as "precontractual," which in fact describes different factual situations, which may or may not have legal consequences under different domestic laws or implicate the use of the CISG. As to the area of domestic remedies, a comparative analysis was undertaken. It showed that different jurisdictions provide different rules of conduct to be observed in the negotiation phase. These differences include different qualifications of the claim, which may be treated as falling under the law of contract, of tort, or under alternative doctrines such as unjust enrichment.

The foregoing leads to a great degree of uncertainty when negotiations take place in a cross-border setting. Characterization of the issue is, indeed, essential for a proper conflict-of-laws analysis to determine the competent court and the applicable law; but characterization is also essential to address the question as to whether the issue at hand is covered by the CISG.

A review of the different factual situations that may lead to claims for damages of the kind often referred to as precontractual liability has led to the conclusion that in many cases the resort to domestic rules is precluded because the preliminary agreement is within the scope of the CISG. In the end, the rules of the CISG may not recognize the claim and fail to award damages. Therefore, prudent parties negotiating a prospective cross-border sale should consider "contractualizing" the duties owed to each other throughout the negotiations, reducing the uncertainties as to the rules of conduct that must be observed and the legal consequences for nonobservance.

---

[108] Of utmost relevance, in this respect, is the rule under CISG Article 14, stating that a proposal (which in turn appears to be extendable to the contract as a whole) "is sufficiently definite if it indicates the goods and expressly or implicitly fixes or makes provision for determining the quantity and the price."

[109] See also F. Ferrari, "Vendita internazionale di beni mobile – Art. 1–13 (Ambito di applicazione. Disposizioni generali)," *Commentario del Codice Civile Scialoja-Branca* (Bologna and Rome, 1994).

Part VIII   *Practitioner's Perspective*

40 Empirical Evidence of Courts' and Counsels' Approach to the CISG (with Some Remarks on Professional Liability)

Ulrich G. Schroeter

I. Introduction

Attempts to describe the importance of the United Nations Convention on Contracts for the International Sale of Goods (CISG) – currently, the law of eighty countries – have characterized it as the law applicable to 75% of the world's exports and imports,[1] with fifteen among the twenty leading exporters in world trade having adopted the CISG.[2] These facts do not mean that three-fourths of all world trade is governed by the CISG, as the CISG's applicability to a given sales contract depends on the requirements of Article 1(1)(a) or (b) being fulfilled. A more important factor affecting the CISG's role in commercial practice is its lack of acceptance by business parties, legal advisers, and courts. According to Article 6 CISG, the parties may exclude the application of the CISG (opting out). It has been claimed that parties "regularly" or "routinely," at the suggestion of counsel,[3] do just that[4] – a claim typically made without any empirical support being cited.

This chapter collects and organizes the increasing empirical evidence on how the CISG is excluded, ignored, or actively used in practice, thereby measuring rumors against reality. The second part reviews the existing empirical, as well as anecdotal, evidence on the CISG's role in practice. It analyzes the evidence relating to its use by the courts, attorneys, and the parties to international sales contracts. The third part outlines the possible risks that legal practitioners face when they ignore the CISG, potentially exposing them to claims of professional malpractice.

---

[1] World Trade Organization, "Leading Exporters and Importers in World Merchandise Trade (2009)," in *International Trade Statistics 2010* (World Trade Organization: Geneva 2010).

[2] The non-CISG contracting states among the 20 leading exporters of the world are the United Kingdom, the United Arab Emirates, Chinese Taipeh (Taiwan), and Saudi Arabia, although the legal status of Hong Kong (the world's 11th largest exporter) under the CISG is a matter of dispute. Cf. Ulrich G. Schroeter, "The Status of Hong Kong and Macao under the United Nations Convention on Contracts for the International Sale of Goods," 16 *Pace Int'l L. Rev.* 307 (2004). For the purpose of the calculations presented in this chapter, Hong Kong has been treated as a non-contracting state.

[3] See Ulrich G. Schroeter, "Schaffung und Akzeptanz einheitlichen Privatrechts in Europa: Lehren aus der Anwendung des UN-Kaufrechts für ein Europäisches Vertragsrecht," 14 *Jahresheft der Internationalen Juristenvereinigung Osnabrück* 35, 47 (2007).

[4] Cf. inter alia Reinhard Fischer, *Vor- und Nachteile des Ausschlusses des UN-Kaufrechts aus Sicht des deutschen Exporteurs* (Hamburg: Verlag Dr. Kovač, 2008), 2–3; Christopher Sheaffer, "The Failure of the United Nations Convention on Contracts for the International Sale of Goods and a Proposal for a New Uniform Global Code in International Sales Law," 15 *Cardozo J. Int'l & Comp. L.* 461, 469–70 (2007).

II. Empirical Evidence on the Use of the CISG

A. *The CISG in Practice: Existing Surveys*

Empirical evidence on the CISG's role as law in practice essentially comes in two forms – (1) the number of court decisions and arbitral awards applying the CISG, and (2) surveys among lawyers. A number of CISG-related surveys have been conducted over the years. They followed a similar design in that questionnaires were sent to members of the targeted group. The first such survey was conducted by Michael Gordon of the University of Florida in 1997 and targeted faculty teaching at law schools in Florida, 124 practitioners specializing in transactional international law, as well as judges at state courts in Florida.[5] In 2004, Justus Meyer surveyed German attorneys specializing in international sales matters, with a sample size of 479.[6] In 2007, he duplicated the survey using Austrian attorneys with a sample size of 319,[7] and among 396 Swiss attorneys.[8] At the same time, a combined survey using identical questionnaires in three countries was conducted by Martin Koehler and Guo Yujun, with Koehler targeting practicing attorneys in Germany and the United States (in 2004–5) and Guo targeting attorneys in the People's Republic of China.[9] Unfortunately, small sample sizes – 50 responses from U.S. lawyers, 33 from German lawyers, and 27 from Chinese lawyers – limit the statistical power of the Koehler–Guo surveys.[10] In 2006–7, Peter Fitzgerald collected a total of 236 responses, primarily from California, Florida, Hawaii, Montana, and New York.[11] Two additional surveys were conducted in 2007: George Philippopoulos collected a data set from 46 commercial litigation attorneys whose practices dealt with international transactions,[12] and in Switzerland Corinne Widmer and Pascal Hachem targeted registered lawyers practicing in the field of commercial law and conflict of laws, receiving 170 usable replies.[13] Finally, in late 2009, Ingeborg Schwenzer and

---

[5] Michael Wallace Gordon, "Some Thoughts on the Receptiveness of Contract Rules in the CISG and UNIDROIT Principles as Reflected in One State's (Florida) Experience of (1) Law School Faculty, (2) Members of the Bar with an International Practice, and (3) Judges," 46 *Am. J. Comp. L.* (Suppl.) 361 (1998).

[6] Justus Meyer, "UN-Kaufrecht in der deutschen Anwaltspraxis," 69 *Rabel J. Comp. & International Private L.* 457, 468 (2005).

[7] Justus Meyer, "UN-Kaufrecht in der österreichischen Anwaltspraxis," *Österreichische Juristenzeitung* 792, 794 (2008).

[8] Justus Meyer, "UN-Kaufrecht in der schweizerischen Anwaltspraxis," *Schweizerische Juristenzeitung* 421, 423 (2008).

[9] Martin F. Koehler and Guo Yujun, "The Acceptance of the Unified Sales Law (CISG) in Different Legal Systems," 20 *Pace Int'l L. Rev.* 45, 47 (2008).

[10] The small number of replies can hardly be regarded as "an early indication of poor acceptance of the CISG," as Koehler and Guo, "Acceptance of the Unified Sales Law," 46–7, boldly claim – it is no more than an indication of the poor acceptance of the request to participate in their survey (and may have even be caused by the fact that many of the practitioners addressed had no time for a participation, as they were busy applying the CISG in real cases).

[11] Peter L. Fitzgerald, "The International Contracting Practices Survey Project: An Empirical Study of the Value and Utility of the United Nations Convention on Contracts for the International Sale of Goods (CISG) and the UNIDROIT Principles of International Commercial Contracts to Practitioners, Jurists, and Legal Academics in the United States," 27 *J. L. & Com.* 1, 4–6 (2008).

[12] George V. Philippopoulos, "Awareness of the CISG among American Attorneys," 40 *Uniform Commercial Code L. J.* 357 (2008).

[13] Corinne Widmer and Pascal Hachem, "Switzerland," in *The CISG and Its Impact on National Legal Systems* (ed. F. Ferrari) (Munich: Sellier European Law Publishers, 2008), 281, 282.

Table 40.1. *CISG Cases: 1989–2010*

Year	1989	1990	1991	1992	1993	1994	1995	1996	1997	1998	1999
Cases	18	18	28	66	69	120	146	181	184	153	140
Year	2000	2001	2002	2003	2004	2005	2006	2007	2008	2009	2010
Cases	123	111	190	169	171	156	187	142	135	97	58

her "Global Sales Law" research team at the University of Basel conducted the most comprehensive survey to date. The data set consisted of 640 responses from 66 countries.[14] While most of the surveys mentioned focused on practicing attorneys, the Global Sales Law survey encompassed four target groups, namely practicing lawyers (347 responses), arbitrators (98 responses), businesses engaged in trade (60 responses), and law schools (135 responses).

In summary, all existing CISG surveys combined yielded usable responses from a total of 2,227 practicing attorneys, with a focus on five CISG contracting states: Switzerland, Germany, the United States, Austria, and China.[15] However, as noted earlier, a number of these surveys lacked statistical power.

B. *Courts' Approach to the CISG*

1. Empirical Evidence

The number of cases applying the CISG by the courts and arbitral tribunals has steadily increased since 1988. The Albert H. Kritzer CISG Database run by the Institute of International Commercial Law at Pace Law School[16] lists a total of 2,697 court decisions and arbitral awards that, in one way or another, addressed the CISG.[17] Table 40.1 shows the development of CISG case law over the years.

The use of the numbers displayed in Table 40.1 above as empirical evidence on the CISG's practical relevance[18] meets with some caveats. First, and maybe most importantly, the CISG database does not cover all CISG decisions that have been made, but only the CISG decisions that have been published. The real number of CISG decisions in practice could be considerably higher.[19] Second, experience shows that court decisions in many jurisdictions are only published with a significant delay, sometimes years after they

---

[14] Ingeborg Schwenzer and Christopher Kee, "Global Sales Law – Theory and Practice," in *Towards Uniformity: The 2nd Annual MAA Schlechtriem CISG Conference* (ed. I. Schwenzer and Lisa Spagnolo) (The Hague: Eleven International Publishing, 2011), 155, 156. The same survey's results are reported in Ingeborg Schwenzer and Christopher Kee, "International Sales Law: The Actual Practice," 29 *Penn St. Int'l L. Rev.* 425 (2011).

[15] Switzerland: 566; Germany: 512; United States: 456; Austria: 319; China: 27. (It is unclear how many lawyers participated in more than one of the surveys.)

[16] *MCC-Marble Ceramic Center, Inc. v. Ceramica Nuova D'Agostina, S.p.A.*, June 29, 1998, 144 F.3d 1384, 1389 footnote 14 (11th Cir. 1998) refers to the database as "a promising source" for "persuasive authority from courts of other States Party to the CISG."

[17] The case count was as of October 10, 2011.

[18] Harm Peter Westermann, "Das UN-Kaufrecht im Aufschwung?," *in Privatrecht und Methode: Festschrift für Ernst A. Kramer* (ed. H. Honsell et al.) (Basel: Helbing & Lichtenhahn, 2004), 717, 719.

[19] Peter Schlechtriem, "Requirements of Application and Sphere of Applicability of the CISG," 36 *Victoria U. Wellington L. Rev.* 781 (2005); Schwenzer and Kee, "International Sales Law," 157.

were handed down ("publication lag").[20] Third, although the Kritzer Database reports a number of arbitral awards, the vast majority of arbitral awards remain unpublished.[21] Fourth, the numbers listed in the table are overstated because they count the same dispute as a separate case at each stage of the appellate process. And fifth, they also include cases in which the CISG's applicability was denied.

Surveys – potentially another source for empirical evidence on the courts' approach to the CISG – have only rarely addressed the judiciary. The two surveys that tackled this task[22] received so small a number of replies that they can hardly been seen as an indication of the judiciary's attitude in general.[23]

2. Anecdotal Evidence

Because there is currently only limited empirical evidence on CISG-related matters, the present chapter will try to supplement it with "anecdotal" evidence on the CISG's role in practice. Under this heading, it will present evidence of actions by the courts (and, in the respective following sections, by the parties and counsel), which, in the author's subjective opinion, is indicative of general trends in the CISG's application.

a. *Pretending that there is "virtually no" CISG case law: The* Filanto *dictum and its progeny*

In 1992, the United States District Court for the Southern District of New York rendered its decision in *Filanto, S.p.A. v. Chilewich Intern. Corp.*[24] It was the first U.S. decision to address the CISG in a substantive way, and accordingly attracted significant attention among academic scholars.[25] Its influence on the developing U.S. case law on the CISG, however, was not primarily due to its application of the CISG, but rather by its introductory dictum: "Although there is as yet virtually no U.S. case law interpreting the Sale of Goods Convention, ..."[26] This factual statement – certainly accurate at the time it was made, as there had merely been one earlier CISG decision by a U.S. court[27] – was soon quoted by other U.S. courts, first in *Beijing Metals & Minerals Import/Export Corp. v. American Business Center, Inc.*[28] and then in *Delchi Carrier SpA v. Rotorex Corp.*,

---

[20] The effect of the publication lag is clearly visible in the case numbers for 2009 and 2010 listed in Table 40.1.

[21] Klaus Peter Berger, *The Creeping Codification of the Lex Mercatoria* (The Hague: Kluwer Law International, 1999), 65; Schwenzer and Kee, "International Sales Law," 157 (hypothesizing that approximately 5,000 arbitrations concerning sales of goods must have been conducted between 2004 and 2008).

[22] Namely, the surveys conducted by Gordon, "Some Thoughts," and by Fitzgerald, "International Contracting Practices Survey Project."

[23] This point is also noted by Fitzgerald, "International Contracting Practices Survey Project."

[24] *Filanto, S.p.A. v. Chilewich Intern. Corp.*, 789 F. Supp. 1229, 1237 (S.D.N.Y. 1992).

[25] Cf. Ronald A. Brand and Harry M. Flechtner, "Arbitration and Contract Formation in International Trade: First Interpretations of the U.N. Sales Convention," 12 *J. L. & Commerce* 239 (1993); Peter Winship, "The U.N. Sales Convention and the Emerging Caselaw," in *Emptio-Venditio Inter Nationes* (ed. F. Majoros) (Basel: Recht und Gesellschaft, 1997), 227.

[26] *Filanto, S.p.A. v. Chilewich Intern. Corp.*, 789 F. Supp. 1229, 1237 (S.D.N.Y. 1992), appeal dismissed, 984 F.2d 58 (2nd Cir. 1993).

[27] *Interag Ltd v. Stafford Phase*, May 22, 1990, 1990 WL 71478 (S.D.N.Y.); see also, *Orbisphere v. U.S.*, October 24, 1989, 726 F.Supp. 1344 (Ct. Int'l Trade 1989) (court had made an obiter reference to the CISG without interpreting or applying any of its provisions).

[28] *Beijing Metals & Minerals Import/Export Corp. v. American Business Center, Inc.*, June 15, 1993, 993 F.2d 1178, 1183 (5th Cir. 1993).

where the court (unintentionally?) expanded the assessment's international scope by claiming that "there is virtually no case law under the Convention."[29] In doing so, the court in *Delchi Carrier* overlooked that there already was an ever-increasing number of CISG judgments from other CISG contracting states. Thus firmly rooted in U.S. case law, the *Filanto* dictum became a steady staple in American CISG jurisprudence[30] – somewhat surprisingly, as it explicitly dealt with the situation at one specific point in time (in early 1992). Even sixteen years and some 2,000 published CISG cases later, two U.S. decisions issued in 2008 still proclaimed that there is "virtually no case law under the Convention," citing the *Filanto* dictum in support.[31] This is especially troubling because the full statement found in *Filanto* stated that: "Although there is as yet virtually no U.S. case law interpreting the Sale of Goods CISG . . . , it may safely be predicted that this will change: absent a choice-of-law provision, and with certain exclusions not here relevant, the CISG governs *all* contracts between parties with places of business in different nations, so long as both nations are signatories to the CISG."[32] Since then, the court's prediction has become reality with a steadily growing body of CISG case law, both from the U.S. and from other countries.

b. *Raising the hurdles for the CISG's exclusion by party agreement under Article 6*

Courts, including those in the United States, have taken a strict view of how to properly opt out of the CISG as allowed under CISG Article 6. Interpretation of choice-of-law clauses, as with any contract term, is governed by Article 8 CISG,[33] focusing primarily on the parties' intent where the respective other party knew or could not have been unaware of the other party's intent.[34] The second order rule, when the other party's intent is not known, is the meaning affixed by a "reasonable person" under the same circumstances.[35]

In applying these standards, the search for the parties' "true" intent is the ultimate goal, and not an interpretation in accordance with the intent of some "standard" party. The courts in most CISG contracting states, however, have developed a general approach that – largely detached from the contracting parties concerned – attaches one and the same interpretation to typical contract clauses, and thereby uniformly determines whether a given clause results in an exclusion of the CISG's application (rarely) or not (usually). From a methodological perspective, this neglect of party intent in favor of standardized meanings is an inappropriate application of Article 8's interpretive methodology.

The most common type of choice-of-law clauses in international sales contracts are those that call for the application of the law of a CISG contracting state ("This contract

---

[29] *Delchi Carrier SpA v. Rotorex Corp.*, December 6, 1995, 71 F.3d 1024, 1028 (2nd Cir. 1995).

[30] See the references to the respective statements from either Filanto or Delchi Carrier in, e.g., *Claudia v. Olivieri Footware Ltd.*, April 7, 1998, 1998 WL 164824 (S.D.N.Y.); *MCC-Marble Ceramic Center, Inc., v. Ceramica Nuova d'Agostino, S.p.A.*, June 29, 1998, 144 F.3d 1384, 1389 (11th Cir. 1998); *TeeVee Toons, Inc. v. Gerhard Schubert GmbH*, August 23, 2006, 2006 WL 2463537 (S.D.N.Y.).

[31] *Hilaturas Miel, S.L. v. Republic of Iraq*, August 20, 2008, 573 F.Supp.2d 781, 799 (S.D.N.Y. 2008); *Macromex Srl. v. Globex International, Inc.*, April 16, 2008, 2008 WL 1752530 (S.D.N.Y.).

[32] *Filanto, S.p.A. v. Chilewich Intern. Corp.*, 789 F. Supp. 1229, 1237 (S.D.N.Y. 1992).

[33] Martin Schmidt-Kessel in *Commentary on the UN Convention on the International Sale of Goods (CISG)*, 3rd ed. (ed. P. Schlechtriem and I. Schwenzer) (Oxford: Oxford University Press, 2010), Article 8, paras. 1, 61.

[34] CISG, Article 8(1).

[35] Id., Article 8(2).

is governed by Danish law"). These types of clauses have generally been interpreted as *not* indicating intent to exclude the CISG's application, as the CISG is part of the law of each contracting state.[36] Although, theoretically, evidence is admissible to prove a different intent – a possibility that can hardly be neglected in cases in which neither the parties nor their legal advisers were even aware of the CISG – such proof almost never succeeds in practice.[37] Additionally, a choice-of-law clause excluding the application of the 1964 Hague Sales Laws, the predecessor to the CISG, does not exclude the CISG.[38] Some courts (primarily from the U.S.) have gone even further by making an "explicit" exclusion of the CISG a requirement for opting out[39] – an approach that has been criticized for not being in harmony with the purpose and legislative history of Article 6 CISG, which both do not generally rule out implicit exclusions of the convention.[40]

Due to lack of knowledge, attorneys for the seller and buyer both have in some cases pleaded their clients' cases based on domestic law despite the CISG being the applicable law. Such action could theoretically qualify as an implicit exclusion of the CISG under Article 6. The behavior of counsel as legal representatives of their clients could be viewed as "subsequent conduct" under CISG Article 8(3) indicating the parties' intent to exclude the CISG at the time of formation or as an implicit party exclusion of the CISG at the trial stage of the dispute.[41] The majority of courts, however, regard any implicit CISG exclusion through counsels' mutual reliance on domestic law with great skepticism, demanding a clear indication that the parties knew of the CISG's existence before finding an implicit exclusion.[42] They accordingly require more than action by counsel which, when viewed in isolation, would be deemed to sufficiently indicate that domestic law is the law under which both seller and buyer want their dispute to be decided. CISG's exclusion under Article 6 is therefore subject to stricter requirements

[36] See Ingeborg Schwenzer and Pascal Hachem in Schlechtriem and Schwenzer, *Commentary*, Article 6. See also ICC Arbitral Award, Case No 12365, CISG-online 2143; Hof van Beroep Gent, October 20, 2004, CISG-online 983 (original clause in German stated, das für Inländer in der Bundesrepublik Deutschland maßgebende Recht); *Asante Technologies v. PMC-Sierra*, July 27, 2001, 164 F. Supp. 2d 1142, 1150 (N.D.C al. 2001) (choice a national law of another CISG country results in the application of the CISG).

[37] Stefan Kröll, Loukas Mistelis, and Pilar Perales Viscasillas, "Introduction to the CISG," in *UN Convention on Contracts for the International Sale of Goods (CISG) – Commentary* (ed. S. Kröll, L. Mistelis, and P. Perales Viscasillas) (Munich: C.H. Beck, Hart, Nomos, 2011), para. 42; Lisa Spagnolo, "Iura Novit Curia and the CISG: Resolution of the Faux Procedural Black Hole," in *Towards Uniformity: The 2nd Annual MAA Schlechtriem CISG Conference* (ed. I. Schwenzer and L. Spagnolo) (The Hague: Eleven International Publishing, 2011), 181, 209.

[38] Oberlandesgericht München, October 19, 2006, *Internationales Handelsrecht* 30 (2007).

[39] See Schwenzer and Hachem in Schlechtriem and Schwenzer, *Commentary*, para. 3.

[40] Id., para. 3.

[41] Cf. id., para. 21.

[42] Oberlandesgericht Linz, January 23, 2006, CISG-online 1377; Tribunale di Padova, February 25, 2004, *Internationales Handelsrecht* 31 (2005); Oberlandesgericht Zweibrücken, February 2, 2004, CISG-online 877; Oberlandesgericht Rostock, October 10, 2001, CISG-online 671; Tribunale di Vigevano, July 12, 2000, CISG-online 493; Oberlandesgericht Dresden, December 27, 1999, CISG-online 511; Kantonsgericht Nidwalden, December 3, 1997, CISG-online 331; Landgericht Bamberg, October 23, 2006, CISG-online 1400; International Court of the Russian Chamber of Commerce and Industry, Arbitral Award of June 6, 2000, CISG-online 1249. Concurring, Peter Schlechtriem, *Internationales UN-Kaufrecht*, 4th ed. (Tübingen: Mohr Siebeck, 2007), para. 21. But see Corte Suprema, September 22, 2008, CISG-online 1787; Cour de Cassation, October 25, 2005, CISG-online 1098.

than an implicit choice of law governed by private international law rules, where reliance by both attorneys on the same domestic law is often considered a valid choice of the law.[43] The majority view on implicit exclusion of the CISG views counsels' unawareness of the CISG as insufficient party intent to exclude its application.[44]

In summary, the present CISG case law from various countries serves as anecdotal evidence for an increasing pro-convention bias by courts, which have raised the hurdles for the convention's exclusion by party agreement so high that many attempted exclusions fail in practice.

c. *Judges' refusals to apply the CISG*

Only very rarely have situations been reported that demonstrate an intentional rejection of the CISG by a judge. Anecdotal evidence of this kind is not found in written court decisions, but rather in other reports. In Florida, one state court judge who participated in Michael Gordon's 1997 survey reported to have rejected the CISG as applicable law in one case because he was "strongly opposed to world government," making clear his determination not to apply "foreign" law in "his" state court.[45] In Germany, Burghard Piltz reported two similar incidences. In 1992, a German judge stated that "UN law does not apply in Germany."[46] And even in a 2010 proceeding, another judge opened the hearing by informing counsel that although one of the parties had relied on the CISG in their brief, "this court" was not familiar with the provisions of the CISG. He strongly suggested that the parties reach a settlement of the case.[47] A refusal to apply the CISG to sales contracts that fall into its sphere of application constitutes judicial impropriety or misconduct.[48] But, as Michael Gordon has correctly remarked: Failure to apply the applicable law at the trial stage is one reason we have appellate courts.[49]

3. Evidence Explained

a. *Case numbers*

Unfortunately, simply counting cases does not provide an adequate picture of the CISG's practical use. First, the CISG database is not sufficiently granulated to determine

---

[43] See inter alia Oberlandesgericht Hamm, June 9, 1995, *Recht der Internationalen Wirtschaft* 689 (1996), where the court held that litigation exclusively based on the provisions of the German Civil Code constituted a positive choice of German law under the German conflict of laws rules, and accordingly the CISG – as part of German law so chosen – was to be applied.

[44] Some commentators, however, view the case law on this subject differently; see Spagnolo, "Iura Novit Curi," 189: "current outcomes are unpredictable and diverse."

[45] Gordon, "Some Thoughts," 361, 369, and 371. The judge added that he had no final comments that could be printed; id., 369, n. 30.

[46] Reported by Burghard Piltz, *Internationales Kaufrecht* (Munich: C.H. Beck, 1993), 10.

[47] Burghard Piltz, "Neue Entwicklungen im UN-Kaufrecht," *Neue Juristische Wochenschrift* 2261, 2262 n. 9 (2011).

[48] Ronald A. Brand, "Uni-State Lawyers and Multinational Practice: Dealing with International, Transnational, and Foreign Law," 34 *Vanderbilt J. Transnat'l L.* 1135, 1162 (2001); Burghard Piltz, *Internationales Kaufrecht*, 2nd ed. (Munich: C.H. Beck, 2008), paras. 1–36. Cf. also *Hilton v. Guyot*, 159 U.S. 113, 163 (1895) stressing that "International Law . . . is part of our law, and *must* be ascertained and administered by the courts of justice, as often as such questions are presented in litigation between man and man, duly submitted to their determination" (emphasis added).

[49] See Gordon, "Some Thoughts," 371.

Table 40.2. *CISG Cases Decided by the German Supreme Court*

Year	1991	1992	1993	1994	1995	1996	1997	1998	1999	2000
Cases		1			2	4	4	2	2	
Year	2001	2002	2003	2004	2005	2006	2007	2008	2009	2010
Cases	2	2	1	3	1	1	2	1		2

statistical significance. The inclusion of cases in which the CISG is mentioned, but not applied, skewers the total count.

Second, as already outlined, the total number of published CISG decisions represents only a portion of such decisions due to the existence of unreported cases, especially of arbitral proceedings. Counting cases does not capture contracts covered by the CISG that did not result in legal disputes. Therefore, if there is a decrease in the number of cases it may conceivably be due to the fact that interpretative issues under the CISG have become established. In addition, in a given jurisdiction, the publication of lower court decisions depends on the novelty of the issues in the case. Thus, the publication rate is likely to decrease once the CISG loses its novelty in a court system. Germany has the highest number of reported cases (477 as of October 10, 2011), but recently lower court decisions have been published less frequently. This development should not be mistaken as a sign of the decreasing importance of the CISG in German court practice, as can be see in the consistent pattern of CISG cases decided by the German Federal Supreme Court (Bundesgerichtshof) (Table 40.2).[50]

Furthermore, the number of cases published across and between legal systems is uneven. Thus, a lower reporting rate in a jurisdiction cannot be equated to low practical use of the CISG.[51] Differences among the court systems and the case publication systems may in particular affect the number of available CISG decisions by lower courts, as a comparison between CISG case statistics for Austria and Germany shows. Although Austria boasts 79 CISG decisions by its Supreme Court (Oberster Gerichtshof) out of a total of 128 CISG decisions, the German *Bundesgerichtshof* has decided only 30 cases out of the total of 477 German CISG decisions.[52] In the end, the number of court decisions on the CISG therefore says little about the CISG's role in practice. Better and more comprehensive data on the CISG's practical use are needed.

b. *Assumed lack of CISG case law as excuse for recourse to UCC*

The reason behind some U.S. courts' ongoing reliance on the *Filanto* dictum (discussed earlier) becomes clear when viewed in the context in which the courts since *Delchi Carrier* have employed the dictum: That court, and many courts afterwards, used the "virtually no case law under the Convention" statement as an argumentative "door opener," and then added: "Caselaw interpreting analogous provisions of Article 2 of the Uniform Commercial Code (UCC) may also inform a court where the language of the

---

[50] The CISG entered into force for the Federal Republic of Germany on January 1, 1991.

[51] Cf. the calculation presented (albeit in a slightly different context) by Lisa Spagnolo, "A Glimpse through the Kaleidoscope: Choices of Law and the CISG (Kaleidoscope Part I)," 13 *Vindobona J. Int'l Comm. L. & Arb*. 135, 145 (2009).

[52] All case numbers as reported by the Albert H. Kritzer CISG Database on October 10, 2011.

relevant CISG provisions tracks that of the UCC. However, UCC case law 'is not per se applicable.'"[53] The assumed lack of CISG case law accordingly serves as an excuse for an interpretative recourse to UCC case law, an approach that has rightly been criticized by many authors for being incompatible with CISG Article 7(1).[54] No matter whether there is case law under the convention on a given subject or not, and whether the language of a relevant CISG provision "tracks" that of a domestic provision (and how this alleged "tracking" is to be determined), case law on domestic law may *never* inform a court when interpreting the CISG, neither "per se" nor otherwise.

The ongoing reliance on the *Filanto* dictum can therefore also be viewed as an indication of some U.S. courts' continuing lack of familiarity with the CISG. This explanation is in line with assessments by some legal authors, who as recently as 2008 suggested that a North Carolina superior court judge, "or even a federal district court judge for that matter," would have little or no experience with the CISG.[55] Other recent U.S. court decisions, however, increasingly indicate a more open-minded approach, as notably demonstrated by the decision in *David S. Taub v. Marchesi Di Barolo*. In these proceedings – which concerned the U.S. court's jurisdiction, and not a sales law matter as such – counsel for the Italian defendant Marchesi went on

> at some length to convince the Court that the United Nations Convention on Contracts for the International Sale of Goods ("CISG"), and not New York law, will govern the parties' dispute. The apparent implication of this discussion is that the "foreign law" factor counsels in favor of deferring to the Italian court because this Court will have some difficulty in interpreting and applying the CISG. However, even if the Court assumes for the purposes of this motion that the CISG governs the instant dispute and further assumes that the CISG can be properly characterized as foreign law, Marchesi's argument is still unpersuasive. Federal courts, including this Court, have had little difficulty in interpreting and applying the CISG. [Case law citations omitted.] As such, the Court does not share Marchesi's apparent concern about the potential difficulties in applying the CISG.[56]

Cases such as Marchesi are therefore fortunate signs that courts in the U.S. are getting more and more accustomed to the convention. There is reason to hope that they may soon admit that there already *is* a significant amount of case law on the CISG (both domestic and foreign), making a recourse to UCC cases not only inappropriate – as it always has been – but simply unnecessary.

[53] *Delchi Carrier SpA v. Rotorex Corp.*, 71 F.3d 1024, 1028 (2nd Cir. 1995), citing *Orbisphere Corp. v. U.S.*, 726 F. Supp. 1344, 1355 (Ct. Int'l Trade 1989). The now (in)famous reference to UCC case law has often been repeated by U.S. courts, most recently in *Dingxi Longhai Dairy, Ltd. v. Becwood Technology Group L.L.C.*, 635 F.3d 1106 (8th Cir. 2011).

[54] See Susanne Cook, "The U.N. Convention on Contracts for the International Sale of Goods: a Mandate to Abandon Legal Ethnocentricity," 16 *J. L. & Com.* 257 (1997); Joanne M. Darkey, "U.S. Court's Interpretation of Damage Provisions Under the U.N. Convention on Contracts for the International Sale of Goods: A Preliminary Step Towards an International Jurisprudence of CISG or a Missed Opportunity?," 15 *J. L. & Com.* 139 (1995).

[55] Alicia Jurney Whitlock and Boris S. Abbey, "Who's Afraid of the CISG? Why North Carolina Practitioners Should Learn a Thing or Two about the 1980 United Nations Convention on Contracts for the International Sale of Goods," 30 *Campbell L. Rev.* 275, 290 (2008).

[56] *David S. Taub et al. v. Marchesi Di Barolo S.p.A.*, December 10, 2009, 2009 U.S. Dist LEXIS 115565.

c. *CISG as preferable to foreign domestic sales law*

The increasing pro-CISG bias demonstrated by most courts when interpreting party agreements potentially aimed at excluding the CISG's application under Article 6 CISG can be explained by different factors. First, there are policy reasons. The court in *Travelers Property Casualty Company of America v. Saint-Gobain* reasoned that "an affirmative opt-out requirement promotes uniformity and the observance of good faith in international trade, two principles that guide interpretation of the CISG,"[57] and another U.S. court in *St. Paul Guardian Insurance v. Neuromed* held that the contractual choice of the law of a CISG contracting state did not amount to an exclusion of the CISG. The court reasoned that "[t]o hold otherwise would undermine the objectives of the CISG."[58]

A second reason may be the courts' realization that the alternative to the CISG's application may not be the application of the *lex fori*, but the application of foreign domestic sales law. Peter Schlechtriem has explained this point as follows:

> When the great scholar John Honnold defended the CISG before the sub-committee of the United States Senate which was in charge of preparing the decision of the Senate on the CISG's ratification, he remarked something along the following lines: in evaluating the CISG, you should not compare it with the Uniform Commercial Code (UCC) and should not ask, whether it is better than or inferior to the UCC. Certainly, the UCC is better for American parties and their counsel and lawyers. But you should ask, whether the CISG is better and easier to apply than, for example, the sales law of Mongolia or China. For we cannot expect that the UCC will always apply to international sales and that foreign parties will always submit to American law.[59]

A practical illustration of the issue of applying foreign sales law was provided in *Italdecor v. Yiu's Industries (H.K.)*, which involved a claim by an Italian buyer against a seller from Hong Kong.[60] Although the Court of Appeal in Milan, applying Italian conflict of laws rules, came to the conclusion that the sales law of Hong Kong properly governed the buyer's claim, it chose to apply the CISG (as part of Italian law) because it "had not been able to ascertain" the content of Hong Kong law.[61] The courts' incentive to avoid the application of foreign law may therefore explain the rather strict standards often used in interpreting whether a choice-of-law clause works as an opting out of the CISG.

The explanation presented here explains why courts interpret choice-of-law clauses in favor of a *foreign* sales law in a particularly strict manner, although a similar incentive for the court would not exist where choice-of-law clause favors the sales law *of the forum*. The available CISG case law, however, shows no distinction between these two categories, which may mean that the strict interpretative standards for CISG "opt out" clauses, once

---

[57] *Travelers Property Casualty Company of America v. Saint-Gobain Technical Fabrics Canada Ltd.*, January 31, 2007, 2007 WL 313591.
[58] *St. Paul Guardian Insurance Company and Travelers Insurance Company v. Neuromed Medical Systems & Support GmbH*, March 26, 2002, 2002 U.S. Dist. Lexis 5096 (S.D.N.Y.).
[59] Peter Schlechtriem, "Requirements of Application," 793.
[60] At the time the contract concerned had been entered into and performed (in 1990–1), Hong Kong was still a British crown colony, so that Article 1(1)(a) CISG did not apply. As to the dispute about Hong Kong's status under the CISG since July 1, 1997 (the date of the "hand-over" resulting in Hong Kong being part of the People's Republic of China), see Schroeter, "The Status of Hong Kong and Macao."
[61] *Italdecor s.a.s v. Yiu's Industries (H.K.) Limited*, Corte di Appello di Milano, March 20, 1998, *Diritto del commercio internazionale* 455 (1999).

developed, are now indiscriminately applied to all party agreements aimed at excluding the CISG.

In a 2010 decision by the German Federal Supreme Court,[62] counsel for both parties had agreed on "the application of German law to the current dispute" and had subsequently submitted their legal arguments based on the German Civil Code (BGB) and the German Commercial Code (HGB). Both the court of first instance and subsequently the Court of Appeals had decided the dispute applying these two sources of German law. The Supreme Court reversed and remanded the case, admonishing the Court of Appeals for having treated the agreement on "German law" as an exclusion of the CISG, and directing it to investigate whether the parties had really intended to choose the BGB and HGB. This is remarkable, as both counsels had explicitly agreed on the applicable law. In cases such as this, the court may be actively trying to protect the parties involved from their own counsels' tendency to exclude the CISG, which may or may not be in the clients' best interest.[63]

C. Sellers, Buyers, and the CISG

Although counsels' actions when representing their clients are legally those of the clients, this legal categorization is not helpful for the purposes of the present chapter, which investigates how and on what basis decisions affecting the CISG's application are reached. This part is based on the common sense assumption that the attorney, especially in drafting standard terms, is the decision maker and the client is not.[64]

1. Empirical Evidence

Empirical evidence on the knowledge and use of the CISG by merchants is limited. The Global Sales Law survey conducted in 2009 was the only one that surveyed companies. Based on responses from 60 companies,[65] the survey found that 45 percent of the businesses where somewhat familiar with the CISG. However, 63 percent of the businesses located in CISG contracting states were somewhat familiar with the CISG.[66] Other surveys asked practicing lawyers whether they had in the past excluded the CISG during contract drafting upon their clients' request, and 41.3 percent of the German lawyers,[67] 34.1 percent of the Austrian lawyers,[68] and 32.6 percent of the Swiss lawyers[69] answered in the affirmative. Another survey adopted the reverse approach by asking practicing lawyers whether they had excluded the CISG at the contract drafting stage because their clients' *business partner* insisted on the application of his or her national

---

[62] Bundesgerichtshof, May 11, 2010, *Internationales Handelsrecht* 216 (2010). See commentary Ulrich G. Schroeter, *Entscheidungen zum Wirtschaftsrecht* (2011), 149.

[63] See in more detail below.

[64] The latter is often not true when standard terms addressing the performance of contractual obligations are concerned, but choice-of-law clauses as well as arbitration and forum selection clauses are in practice often of little interest to the client himself.

[65] Schwenzer and Kee, "Global Sales Law," 156. The survey results published do not specify in which countries the responding businesses were based.

[66] Id., 159.

[67] Meyer, "UN-Kaufrecht in der deutschen Anwaltspraxis," 476.

[68] Meyer, "UN-Kaufrecht in der österreichischen Anwaltspraxis," 796.

[69] Meyer, "UN-Kaufrecht in der schweizerischen Anwaltspraxis," 426.

law – 39.4 percent of the German, 37 percent of the Chinese, and 27.1 percent of U.S. practitioners answered in the affirmative.[70]

Another source of evidence of the merchant community's approach toward the CISG is found in the standard contract terms published by general business associations, such as the German Chambers of Industry and Commerce (DIHK). The standard terms of business associations are written from a broader perspective than those used by individual companies.[71] This justifies the assumption that choices made in their standard contracts and comparable documents are generally reflective of the business community's interest and unaffected by interests of a particular drafting attorney.[72] Neither the ICC Model International Sales Contract for Manufactured Goods[73] nor the DIHK Model Sales Contract[74] excludes the application of the CISG. Moreover, these standard forms were developed with the CISG's rules in mind. However, model contracts designed for use in particular trade sectors often include a clause excluding the CISG's application in favor of a domestic legal system (usually English law).

Anecdotal evidence on contracting parties' opinions about the CISG primarily exists in form of individually drafted contracts addressing the application (or non-application) of the CISG. Cases adjudicated by European courts surprisingly often involve international sales contracts that explicitly call for the application of the CISG.[75] It is also common that explicit agreements between businesses from the People's Republic of China and the European Union expressly choose the CISG as applicable law.

2. Evidence Explained

The evidence does not support the conclusion that the CISG is shunned or even rejected by merchants. Instead, businesspersons seem more open to the CISG's use than their legal advisers. The degree of familiarity of the CISG among merchants (63%) may be around the rate of familiarity with their own domestic sales law.

In the rare situations in which merchants themselves are personally deciding upon the law applicable to their contracts – when drafting individual contracts, or when developing model contracts through their representatives in business associations – there does not seem to be a strict preference in favor of "home law." The CISG is seen as an acceptable compromise law since it is viewed as a "neutral set of rules."[76]

---

[70] Koehler and Guo, "Acceptance of the Unified Sales Law," 50. Yet other U.S. attorneys reported no difficulties in convincing the opposing party to opt out of the CISG during negotiations; cf. Philippopoulos, "Awareness of the CISG," Article 4.

[71] Cf. Article 1(2) Constitution of the International Chamber of Commerce (June 2011).

[72] Cf. Berger, *Creeping Codification*, 108–10.

[73] The ICC Model International Sales Contract – Manufactured goods intended for resale, ICC Publications No 556 (1997). Cf. Kröll et al., "Introduction to the CISG," para. 56, who refer to the ICC Model Sales Contract as "the most prominent example" for contract forms developed on the basis of the CISG.

[74] Deutscher Industrie- und Handelskammertag, Schuldrechtsreform – Auswirkungen für den Außenhandel 24 (2003); cf. Rolf Herber, Editorial, *Internationales Handelsrecht* 1 (2002).

[75] See Oberlandesgericht Koblenz, April 22, 2010, *Internationales Handelsrecht* 255 (2010); Oberlandesgericht Saarbrücken, May 30, 2011, *Neue Juristische Online-Zeitung* 1363 (2011).

[76] The advantage of the CISG being a "neutral law" was reported by 33.8% among the German lawyers, 21.6% among the Austrian lawyers, and 21.1% among the Swiss lawyers; see Meyer, "UN-Kaufrecht in der deutschen Anwaltspraxis," 480; Meyer, "UN-Kaufrecht in der österreichischen Anwaltspraxis," 798; and Meyer, "UN-Kaufrecht in der schweizerischen Anwaltspraxis," 427.

D. *Counsels' Approach to the CISG*

In commercial practice, the law applicable to the contract will, in the vast majority of cases, be a matter handled by legal counsel, either during contract negotiations, during the drafting of standard terms, or during legal proceedings in front of courts or arbitral tribunals. The approach of counsel toward the CISG is accordingly the most important influence on the use of the CISG in international sales transactions. It is therefore no surprise that most of the empirical surveys dealing with the CISG have primarily targeted practicing lawyers.

1. Empirical Evidence

When asked about their awareness of the CISG,[77] the rate of awareness was at 92.3 percent for Swiss practitioners,[78] but it was only 30 percent for practicing lawyers in the United States.[79] In the Global Sales Law survey conducted in 2009, on the contrary, 78 percent of the lawyers reported being familiar or somewhat familiar with the CISG[80] – a promising tendency, although all numbers mentioned have to be read with the knowledge that the practitioners who responded were specialized in international trade law or neighboring fields, which means that the average CISG awareness among all lawyers is likely to be much lower.[81]

A point addressed by almost every CISG survey[82] is the degree to which counsel are preponderantly excluding the CISG's applicability in contracts or standard terms drafted for their clients. The "opting-out quota" reported varied among jurisdictions, as well as between different surveys covering the same jurisdiction. In alphabetical order, the empirical results are: Austria: 55.2 percent;[83] China: 44.4 percent;[84] Germany: 42.17 percent;[85] Switzerland: 40.8 percent[86] and 62.1 percent;[87] and the United States: 70.8 percent,[88] 55 percent (in 2006–7),[89] and 54 percent (in 2009).[90] The Global Sales Law survey (from 2009) again provides the most recent statistics, which are also the most CISG friendly: 13 percent of lawyers always and 32 percent sometimes exclude the CISG, but the majority (55%) rarely or never does.[91]

---

[77] Spagnolo, "A Glimpse through the Kaleidoscope," 137–8, helpfully lists numerous anecdotal descriptions of the CISG familiarity among attorneys from a range of jurisdictions.

[78] Widmer and Hachem, "Switzerland," 284. The number mentioned includes the 55.29% who reported a "basic" knowledge and the 37.05% who claimed "good" knowledge of the CISG.

[79] Fitzgerald, "International Contracting Practices Survey Project," 7; Gordon, "Some Thoughts," 368.

[80] Schwenzer and Kee, "Global Sales Law," 159.

[81] William S. Dodge, "Teaching the CISG in Contracts," 50 *J. Legal Educ.* 72, 75 (March 2000); see also Koehler and Guo, "Acceptance of the Unified Sales Law," 57.

[82] An exception was the 1997 Florida survey by Gordon, "Some Thoughts."

[83] Meyer, "UN-Kaufrecht in der österreichischen Anwaltspraxis," 795.

[84] Koehler & Guo, "Acceptance of the Unified Sales Law," 48.

[85] Meyer, "UN-Kaufrecht in der deutschen Anwaltspraxis," 471.

[86] Meyer, "UN-Kaufrecht in der schweizerischen Anwaltspraxis," 425.

[87] Widmer and Hachem, "Switzerland," 285.

[88] Koehler and Guo, "Acceptance of the Unified Sales Law," 48.

[89] Fitzgerald, "International Contracting Practices Survey Project,"14.

[90] Schwenzer and Kee, "Global Sales Law," 160.

[91] Id.

Anecdotally, the not infrequent claim by some attorneys to "regularly exclude" the CISG, however, is not necessarily a reflection of the CISG's real importance in practice.[92] This is due to the fact that practitioners with a preference for CISG exclusion are often practitioners with little or no knowledge of CISG's rules – an unfortunate (and risky) combination, which frequently results in the attempted exclusion not being recognized under CISG Article 6.

a. *Excluding the CISG at the contract drafting stage*

A decision by counsel to exclude the CISG's application in his or her client's contracts or standard terms may not be enough to meet the standard imposed by some courts for Article 6 exclusion. The exclusion clause (which usually forms part of a choice-of-law clause) must not only comply with Article 6, but also needs to be included in the contract in accordance with the requirements of Articles 14–24 CISG.[93] Thus, counsel attempting to exclude the CISG needs to be aware of the extensive CISG case law on both exclusion clauses and the incorporation of an exclusion clause as standard contract term.[94]

The careful drafting of contractual CISG exclusion clauses is therefore of paramount importance. A case in point focused on the use of a comma in a choice-of-law clause. The Austrian Supreme Court interpreted the following clause: "All our disputes are exclusively subject to Austrian law, excluding private international law, and the CISG."[95] Whether the CISG had been excluded by this clause was not clear, as the clause could be read in two different ways: (1) as an exclusion of merely private international law (because the phrase "and the CISG" had been separated by a comma), or (2) as an exclusion of private international law and the CISG (which required disregarding the comma). The Austrian Supreme Court adopted the latter reading, but acknowledged that "from a strict grammatical and lexical point of view the 'excluding private international law' within the standard terms can be seen as a mere insertion and thus even an explicit agreement on the application of the CISG due to the allegedly mistakenly entered comma."[96]

b. *Excluding the CISG during court proceedings*

A phenomenon not infrequently encountered during the first years of the CISG was attempts by counsel to exclude the CISG during court proceedings, usually after first finding out about its existence. Although opposing counsel may sometimes even be willing to agree to the CISG's exclusion, many courts, as noted previously, do not look favorably on counsel attempting to avoid the CISG. Any CISG exclusion at the trial stage furthermore triggers a significant professional liability risk, to be discussed in more detail in the following.

---

[92] Walter A. Stoffel, "20 Jahre Wiener Kaufrecht: Entsteht ein CISG-geprägtes Muster des transnationalen rechtlichen Diskurses?," *Zeitschrift für Europarecht* 2, 3 (2002).
[93] Schwenzer and Hachem in Schlechtriem and Schwenzer, *Commentary*, para. 24.
[94] See Schroeter in Schlechtriem and Schwenzer, *Commentary*, Article 14, paras. 32–76.
[95] Oberster Gerichtshof, April 2, 2009, *Internationales Handelsrecht* 246 (2009). The original clause in German: "Für alle unsere Streitigkeiten gilt ausschließlich österreichisches Recht, ausgenommen IPR, und UN-Kaufrecht."
[96] Oberster Gerichtshof, April 2, 2009, *Internationales Handelsrecht* 246, 247 (2009).

2. Evidence Explained

a. *Reasons for contractual exclusion of the CISG*

The early surveys showed that the CISG "is generally not widely known." In contrast, unfamiliarity was a point only rarely cited in the larger Global Sales Law survey in 2009.[97] The uncertainty in the CISG's application (due to vague legal wording and a lack of uniform interpretation) was given as a reason by 58.1 percent of the practitioners from Austria,[98] as well as 48.1 percent of the Swiss[99] and 43.2 percent of the German practitioners.[100] In a subsequent survey, the lack of sufficient CISG case law was raised as an issue by fewer attorneys – 33.3 percent in the U.S., 29.6 percent in China, and just 6.1 percent in Germany.[101]

Among those attorneys who did *not* advocate a contractual exclusion of the CISG, it was frequently argued that the CISG is easier to apply than a combination of conflict of laws rules and foreign sales laws. This advantage of the CISG was mentioned by 25.3 percent of Austrian attorneys,[102] 35 percent of the German attorneys as a whole, and 69.2 percent of international transactional attorneys in Germany.[103]

b. *Counsels' preferred ignorance of the CISG*

There is an understandable incentive for counsel avoid the CISG, as studying the CISG – a sales law with 101 articles and an ever-increasing body of international case law – requires a substantial investment of time and money.[104] Therefore, it seems that the driving force is not the parties' skepticism towards or rejection of the CISG, but rather some counsels' unwillingness to invest the time and effort necessary to learn the CISG.

III. Professional Liability

The indications that some attorneys exclude the CISG in their own interest, namely, in order to escape the need to deal with its unfamiliar rules, raises the question of professional liability. The relationship between client and counsel is a matter governed by domestic law, and the legal standard are accordingly not internationally uniform.[105] The following discussion of counsels' professional liability in CISG cases focuses on German law[106] and U.S. law.[107]

---

[97] Schwenzer and Kee, "Global Sales Law," 160.

[98] Meyer, "UN-Kaufrecht in der österreichischen Anwaltspraxis," 796.

[99] Meyer, "UN-Kaufrecht in der schweizerischen Anwaltspraxis," 426.

[100] Meyer, "UN-Kaufrecht in der deutschen Anwaltspraxis," 474.

[101] Koehler and Guo, "Acceptance of the Unified Sales Law," 50.

[102] Meyer, "UN-Kaufrecht in der österreichischen Anwaltspraxis," 797.

[103] Meyer, "UN-Kaufrecht in der deutschen Anwaltspraxis," 479.

[104] Cf. Clayton P. Gillette and Robert E. Scott, "The Political Economy of International Sales Law," 25 *Int'l Rev. L. & Econ.* 446, 478 (2005).

[105] For an overview of attorney liability in fourteen jurisdictions, see *Professional Liability of Lawyers* (ed. Dennis Campbell and Christian Campbell) (London: Lloyd's of London Press, 1995).

[106] See Thomas Lindemann, "Germany," in id., 113–126.

[107] See Michael R. Goldman and Scott A. Semenek, "United States," id., 263–305; J. Benjamin Lambert, "Professional Liability and International Lawyering: An Overview," 77 *Defense Counsel J.* 69, 73 (2010).

A. *Ignoring the CISG*

As a starting point, it is necessary to clarify whether it is legal or unethical for counsel to simply ignore the CISG. Not surprisingly, there is widespread agreement among authors from both the U.S.[108] and Germany[109] that attorneys who accept cases involving an international sales contract potentially governed by the CISG are under a legal obligation to know the CISG.

In the United States, the duty of competence is found in Rule 1.1 of the American Bar Association's Model Rules of Professional Conduct.[110] Rule 1.1 states that an attorney has the duty to possess "the legal knowledge, skill, thoroughness and preparation reasonably necessary" for competent representation. In Germany, the obligation to know the law is regarded as an implied term of the contract between lawyer and client, requiring the lawyer to know *all* domestic laws that could potentially be relevant to the client's case.[111] There are no exceptions for laws that are rarely applied in practice or beyond the experience of the attorney concerned.[112] Attorneys who accept engagements with cross-border implications are under an implied contractual obligation to know the CISG as thoroughly as other German laws and regulations.[113]

B. *The CISG as Domestic (Not Foreign) Law*

Counsel's obligation to know *foreign* law, on the contrary, is subject to less stringent conditions in some jurisdictions.[114] In the United States, however, case law has stressed

---

[108] Ronald A. Brand, "Professional Responsibility in a Transnational Transactions Practice," 17 *J. L. & Com.* 301, 336–7 (1998); Brand, "Uni-State Lawyers and Multinational Practice," 1163; Dodge, "Teaching the CISG in Contracts," 73, n. 5; Fitzgerald, "The International Contracting Practices Survey Project," 32; Tom McNamara, "U.N. Sale of Goods Convention: Finally Coming of Age?," 32 *Colorado Lawyer* 11, 21 (February 2003); Joseph F. Morrissey and Jack M. Graves, *International Sales Law and Arbitration: Problems, Cases and Commentary* (Alphen aan den Rijn: Kluwer Law International, 2008), 48.

[109] Martin Henssler, "Haftungsrisiken anwaltlicher Tätigkeit," *Juristenzeitung* 178, 185 (1994); André Janssen, "Ausschluss des UN-Kaufrechts als Haftungsfalle," *Außenwirtschaftliche Praxis* 347 (2003); Christoph Louven, "Die Haftung des deutschen Rechtsanwalts im internationalen Mandat," *Versicherungsrecht* 1050, 1051 (1997); Gottfried Raiser, "Die Haftung des deutschen Rechtsanwalts bei grenzüberschreitender Tätigkeit," *Neue Juristische Wochenschrift* 2049, 2051 (1991); Franz-Josef Rinsche, *Die Haftung des Rechtsanwalts und des Notars*, 6th ed. (Cologne: Heymann,1998), 42; Ulrich G. Schroeter, *UN-Kaufrecht und Europäisches Gemeinschaftsrecht: Verhältnis und Wechselwirkungen* (Munich: Sellier European Law Publishers, 2005), 521; Dimitri Slobodenjuk, "Vertragliche Anwaltspflichten – überspanntes Haftungsrisiko?," *Neue Juristische Wochenschrift* 113, 115 (2006); Horst Zugehör, *Handbuch der Anwaltshaftung* (Herne: ZAP-Verlag, 1999), para. 570; similarly, with respect to the 1964 Hague Sales Laws, Franz Tepper, "Anwaltshaftung und EuGVÜ," *Praxis des Internationalen Privat- und Verfahrensrechts* 98, 99 (1991).

[110] Brand, "Professional Responsibility," 337; Fitzgerald, "The International Contracting Practices Survey Project," 32; Morrissey and Graves, *International Sales Law and Arbitration*, 48.

[111] Bundesgerichtshof, April 20, 1959, *Versicherungsrecht* 638 (1959).

[112] Bundesgerichtshof, September 22, 2005, *Neue Juristische Wochenschrift* 501, 502 (2006), stressing counsel's obligation to know one Verordnung über die Herstellung und den Vertrieb von Medaillen und Marken of December 13, 1974, in a case involving the sale of metal chips.

[113] Joachim Gruber, "Anwaltshaftung bei grenzüberschreitenden Sachverhalten," *Monatsschrift für Deutsches Recht* 1399, 1400 (1998); Henssler, "Haftungsrisiken anwaltlicher Tätigkeit," 185; Louven, "Die Haftung," 1052; Peter Mankowski, "Anwaltsvertrag," in *Internationales Vertragsrecht*, 6th ed. (ed. C. Reithmann and D. Martiny) (Cologne: Verlag Dr. Otto Schmidt, 2004), para. 2166; Raiser, "Die Haftung," 2051.

[114] The early U.S. decision in *Fenaille & Despeaux v. Coudert*, 44 N.J.L. 286 (1882), is often said to be an example; cf. Mark Weston Janis, "The Lawyer's Responsibility for Foreign Law and Foreign Lawyers," 16 *Int'l Lawyer* 693, 694 (1982): "*Fenaille* might be said to represent the 'ignorance is bliss' theory of responsibility for foreign law."

that counsel "are responsible to the client for the proper conduct of the matter, and may not claim that they are not required to know the law of the foreign State."[115] German courts have adopted a similar approach, expecting an attorney who accepts a case involving the application of foreign law to obtain the necessary knowledge about that law.[116]

It is even more clear that the attorney's knowledge base must include the CISG because it is not foreign law, but part of domestic law. Despite its character as an international treaty, it becomes part of the domestic legal order of every CISG contracting state once it has entered into force.

In 1989, the Oberlandesgericht Koblenz (a German court of appeals) decided a professional liability case involving the 1964 Hague Sales Laws, the predecessors to the CISG. In this case, a German seller who was party to an international sales contract with a Dutch buyer sued his attorney for professional malpractice, because the attorney had unsuccessfully filed a claim for the outstanding contract price relying on the German Civil Code. Before the attorney had discovered that uniform law applied to the contract, the buyer was declared insolvent.[117] The court held that knowledge of the 1964 Hague Sales Laws (ULF and ULIS) and the 1968 Brussels Convention on Jurisdiction[118] could "without any doubt" be expected from the German attorney.[119] Ignorance of the CISG is accordingly not an option for counsel, as it constitutes a violation of her or his legal obligation to know the law.

C. *Exclusion of the CISG as Professional Malpractice*

Sheer unawareness of the CISG qualifies as professional malpractice,[120] but is not the only form of malpractice in CISG cases, such as in the decision to exclude the CISG. Any recommendation to exclude the CISG's application in a contract must be made in the client's best interest.[121] In this respect, some of the arguments routinely advanced by members of the legal profession – that the CISG's interpretation is uncertain, the body

---

[115] *In re Roel*, July 3, 1957, 3 N.Y.2d 224, 232 (1957) relying on *Degen v. Steinbrink*, July 14, 1922, 195 N.Y.S. 8110 (App. Div. 1922); *Rekeweg v. Federal Mutual Insurance Co.*, February 24, 1961, 27 F.R.D. 431 (N.D. Ind. 1961); Robert W. Hillman, "Providing Effective Legal Representation in International Business Transactions," 19 *Int'l Lawyer* 3, 12 (1985); Janis, "The Lawyer's Responsibility," 696.

[116] See Bundesgerichtshof, February 22, 1972, *Neue Juristische Wochenschrift* 1044 (1972): knowledge of Portuguese law; Oberlandesgericht Hamm, March 14, 1995, *Deutsche Zeitschrift für Wirtschaftsrecht* 460 (1997) (knowledge of Italian law); Friedrich Graf von Westphalen, "Einige international-rechtliche Aspekte bei grenzüberschreitender Tätigkeit von Anwälten," in *Einheit und Vielfalt des Rechts: Festschrift für Reinhold Geimer* (ed. R.A. Schütze) (Munich: C.H. Beck, 2002), 1485, 1488–90.

[117] Counsel could have successfully based the German court's jurisdiction for the contract price claim on Article 5 No. 1 Brussels Convention in conjunction with Article 59(1) ULIS, but was apparently unaware of both legal provisions.

[118] Brussels Convention on Jurisdiction and the Enforcement of Judgments in Civil and Commercial Matters of September 27, 1968.

[119] Oberlandesgericht Koblenz, June 9, 1989, *Neue Juristische Wochenschrift* 2699 (1989).

[120] Brand, "Professional Responsibility," 336–7; Dodge, "Teaching the CISG in Contracts," 73, n. 5; Fitzgerald, "International Contracting Practices Survey Project," 32; Spagnolo, "A Glimpse through the Kaleidoscope," 139.

[121] Fitzgerald, "International Contracting Practices Survey Project,"32; Spagnolo, "A Glimpse through the Kaleidoscope," 139. On the attorney's duty of loyalty under U.S. law, see Lambert, "Professional Liability," 81. See also Klaus Esser, "Anwalt, Mandant oder Formularbuch – wer gestaltet den Vertrag?," in *Gedächtnisschrift für Michael Gruson* (ed. S. Hutter and T. Baums) (Berlin: De Gruyter Recht, 2009), 125, 126–7.

of CISG case law is small, the courts' experience insufficient – by now ring increasingly hollow. There is a body of more than 2,900 easily accessible cases, along with a deep secondary literature including excellent, comprehensive commentaries; practice-focused materials; and a well-developed body of law journal articles.

Accordingly, more substantive reasons are required in order to support the CISG's contractual exclusion. Put simply, the attorney must obtain a competent level of skill and knowledge of the CISG and each of its substantive provisions before opting out. This knowledge allows the drafting attorney to see if there are CISG rules that favor the best interests of the client. Alternatively, the attorney should consider analyzing whether the CISG provides a preferential choice of law if customized – instead of excluding the CISG as a whole, tailoring some of its rules (under Article 6) on behalf of his or her client. It is therefore submitted that a presumption speaks in favor of the CISG providing the preferable set of rules for cross-border transactions, unless specific circumstances of a case indicate the opposite. Attorneys who advise their clients to contractually exclude the CISG's application in its entirety should accordingly bear the burden of explaining and proving the reasons for doing so. In situations in which a contractual exclusion of the CISG is in the client's best interest, counsel needs to draft a contract clause that properly excludes CISG. In situations in which an attempted CISG exclusion fails, counsel furthermore faces the unfortunate situation of having thereby provided evidence of his or her insufficient knowledge of the CISG's rules, which may be viewed as an indication that he or she cannot possibly have advised the client properly about the advantages and disadvantages of the CISG.

The situation is even more dangerous for counsel when he or she first becomes aware of the applicability of the CISG during litigation or arbitration proceedings. At this stage, it is almost impossible to imagine an exclusion scenario that does not involve professional malpractice from at least one of the parties' attorneys. This situation is clear when counsel for one or both parties exclusively presents arguments based on domestic sales law because he or she is unaware of the convention's applicability. As already discussed above, the prevailing opinion among international courts does not regard such behavior as an exclusion of the CISG, but it obviously constitutes a breach of counsel's obligation to know the Sales Convention and therefore renders him or her liable for the client's loss of time and for legal expenses incurred. In case both counsel know about the CISG's applicability and still decide to agree on its exclusion, such a decision will almost necessarily violate the interest of one of the parties because the change in the applicable law with usually affect the outcome of the case, thereby improving one party's position and worsening that of the other party. As the facts of the case are at this stage already clear, counsel for the latter party cannot agree to the convention's exclusion without violating his or her client's interest, thereby committing malpractice. If, on the contrary, an exclusion of the CISG should be without any effect for the outcome of the case, such exclusion is in neither party's interest, as they both can expect their counsel to represent the respective positions based on the convention's rules, which both counsel are under an obligation to know.

D. *Failure to Plead Foreign Persuasive Precedents as Professional Malpractice*

A final question concerns counsel's obligation to know the available case law on the CISG and to use it to his or her client's advantage. This is most obvious in the area of common law, where case law is the primary source of law. As counsel's duty of competence covers the CISG as much as it covers purely domestic areas of law, counsel's knowledge also of CISG case law is required.[122]

Article 7(1) CISG requires that "regard is to be had" to the CISG's international character when interpreting it. This requirement is commonly read as calling for the evaluation not only of domestic case law on the CISG, but also of CISG cases from other jurisdictions.[123] Foreign CISG case law, although not binding precedent, can be used as persuasive precedent, especially in cases of well-reasoned foreign decisions.[124] It seems both necessary and appropriate to require knowledge of foreign CISG case law,[125] but only as far as the foreign case law is reasonably accessible to counsel and has been translated into the attorney's language.

Whether counsel is obliged to actively plead foreign persuasive precedents that are favorable to his or her client's case, or whether he or she may rely on the court to discover and evaluate foreign case law on the CISG, essentially depends on the relationship between court and counsel under the applicable procedural law of the forum. The question becomes relevant in practice whenever a foreign CISG precedent would have served the client's interest better than either a domestic precedent or the interpretation reached by the court without knowledge of the foreign cases. The German approach makes it the attorneys' professional liability to inform the court of the relevant law.[126] According to this standard, counsel's failure to be aware of domestic and foreign CISG case law relating to issues of the case that benefits the client qualifies as professional malpractice.

IV. Conclusion

In summarizing the empirical and anecdotal evidence on the CISG's importance in practice, some general trends can be identified. The claim that the CISG is "generally being excluded" in practice, although still often heard and read, is not supported by empirical evidence. The courts in many CISG contracting states are increasingly adopting a positive position toward the CISG (pro-CISG bias). Its practical effect is that agreements between the parties to exclude the CISG under Article 6 CISG are subjected to strict standards, therefore frequently failing to effectively exclude the CISG's application. The approach of buyers and sellers toward the CISG is more difficult to determine,

---

[122] Brand, "Uni-State Lawyers and Multinational Practice," 1163; Harry M. Flechtner, "Another CISG Case in the U.S. Courts: Pitfalls for the Practitioner and the Potential for Regionalized Interpretations," 15 *J. L. & Com.* 127, 132 (1995).

[123] Camilla Baasch Andersen, "The Uniform International Sales Law and the Global Jurisconsultorium," 24 *J. L. & Com.* 159, 116 (2005); Schwenzer and Hachem in Schlechtriem and Schwenzer, *Commentary*, Article 7, para. 15.

[124] Tribunale di Vigevano, July 12, 2000, *Giurisprudenza italiana* 280 (2000); Gary F. Bell, "Uniformity through Persuasive International Authorities: Does Stare Decisis Really Hinder the Uniform Interpretation of the CISG?," in *Sharing International Commercial Law across National Boundaries: Festschrift for Albert H. Kritzer on the Occasion of His Eightieth Birthday* (ed. C.B. Andersen and U.G. Schroeter) (London: Wildy, Simmonds & Hill, 2008), 35, 47; Pilar Perales Viscasillas in Kröll et al., *UN Convention*, Article 7, Commentary at para. 41.

[125] Brand, "Uni-State Lawyers and Multinational Practice," 1163.

[126] Bundesgerichtshof, June 25, 1974, *Neue Juristische Wochenschrift* 1865, 1866 (1974); see also Klaus Fahrendorf, "Vertragliche Anwaltspflichten – überspanntes Haftungsrisiko?," *Neue Juristische Wochenschrift* 1911, 1914–15 (2006); Slobodenjuk, "Vertragliche Anwaltspflichten," 117.

as empirical and anecdotal evidence is hard to find. The evidence that exists indicates openness toward the CISG as applicable law. The most anti-CISG bias comes from practicing attorneys unwilling to expend the investment of time and money necessary to familiarize themselves with its rules. An attorney's ignorance of the CISG exposes him or her to the risks of professional liability, given the deep and easily accessible body of case law and scholarship on the CISG.

41 The CISG and English Sales Law: An Unfair Competition

Qi Zhou

I. Introduction

It has been more than thirty years since the adoption of the United Nations Convention on Contracts for the International Sale of Goods (CISG). It is also widely claimed in academic literature that the CISG is one of the most successful harmonization projects in the field of international commercial law.[1] As of 2012, the CISG has been adopted by eighty countries.[2] It is increasingly being applied both by national courts and by arbitration tribunals.[3]

Despite its widespread adoption, there are a number of shortcomings to its claim of success. First, some major trading countries, such as the United Kingdom and India, have not ratified the CISG. Ironically, the United Kingdom played an influential role in drafting the CISG, but subsequently has refused to ratify it as UK law. British politicians and lawyers are worried that ratification of the CISG would undermine the dominant position of English commercial law in international trade.[4] The mainstream scholarly

---

[1] Joseph M. Lookofsky, "Loose Ends and Contorts in International Sales: Problems in the Harmonisation of Private Law Rules," 39 *Am. J. Comp. L.* 403 (1991); Kazuaki Sono, "The Rise of Anational Contract Law in the Age of Globalisation," 75 *Tulane L. Rev.* 1185 (2001); Stacey A. Davis, "Unifying the Final Frontier: Space Industry Financing Reform," 106 *Com. L. J.* 455, 477 (2001); Michael Joachim Bonell, "Do We Need a Global Commercial Code?," 106 *Dick. L. Rev.* 87, 88 (2001); Petar Sarcevic, "The CISG and Regional Unification," in *The 1980 Uniform Sale Law. Old Issues Revisited in the Light of Recent Experiences* (ed. Franco Ferrari) (Sellier European Law Publisher, 2001), 3, 15; Sandeep Gopalan, "The Creation of International Commercial Law: Sovereignty Felled?," 5 *San Diego Int'l L. J.* 267, 289 (2004).

[2] Jon C. Kleefeld, "Rethinking 'Like a lawyer': An Instrumentalist's Proposal for First-Year Curriculum Reform," 53 *J. Leg. Ed.* 254, 262 (2003).

[3] See Larry A. DiMatteo et al., *International Sale Law: A Critical Analysis of CISG Jurisprudence* (Cambridge: Cambridge University Press, 2001); Bruno Zeller, *CISG and the Unification of International Trade Law* (Sydney: Cavendish, 2009); Peter Huber and Alastair Mullis, *CISG: A New Textbook for Students and Practitioners* (Berlin: Sellier European Law Publishers, 2007); *Commentary on the UN Convention on the International Sale of Goods* (CISG), 3rd ed. (ed. Peter Schlechtriem and Ingeborg Schwenzer) (Oxford: Oxford University Press, 2010).

[4] Sally Moss, "Why the United Kingdom Has Not Ratified the CISG," 2 *J. of L. & Commercex* 483, (2005–6); Angele Fort, "The United Nations Convention on Contracts for the International Sale of Goods: Reason or Unreason in the United Kingdom," 26 *Baltimore. L. Rev.* 51 (1997); Nathalie Hofmann, "Interpretation Rules and Good Faith as Obstacles to the UK's Ratification of the CISG and to the Harmonisation of Contract Law in Europe," 22 *Pace Int'l L. Rev.* 141 (2010); Barry Nicholas, "The Vienna Convention on Contracts for the International Sale of Goods," 105 *L. Quarterly Rev.* 201 (1989); Robert G. Lee, "The UN Convention on Contracts for the International Sale of Goods: OK for the UK?," *J. Bus. L.* 131 (1993).

literature has argued that the proliferation of international trade and economic global-ization makes a globally uniform contract law or sales law an imperative.

Second, although many states have adopted the CISG, a large number of businesses have opted to exclude the application of the CISG. Oftentimes, they choose English law, instead of the CISG, as applicable law. For example, some commodity associations, such as the Grain and Feed Trade Association (GAFTA); Federation of Oils, Seeds, and Fats Association (FOSFA); Refined Sugar Association (RSA); as well as Shell and British Petroleum (BP), expressly exclude the CISG in their standard form contracts. All of them prefer English law to the CISG.[5] Apart from these big international commodity trade associations, many non-British merchants also prefer English law over the CISG, even though their countries are member states of the CISG. As a result, English Sales Law is a competitor with the CISG as a suitable international sales law.

Why do so many international traders prefer English Sales Law to the CISG? This chapter aims to provide an answer. It is argued that English Sales Law has a number of competitive advantages, which make it more attractive than the CISG. Through a comparison of the CISG and English Sales Law, this chapter articulates the major competitive disadvantages of the CISG, and then suggests certain improvements for future reform.

The discussion proceeds as follows. Part II sets the historical context by briefly review-ing the histories of the CISG and English Sales Law. Part II will show that English Sales Law had been widely used by non-English commercial parties and established a dominant position in international sales law long before the enactment of the CISG. Part III addresses the fragmentary nature of the CISG. Due to the need to reach compro-mises between common and civil law representatives, the result is a fragmentary body of legal rules. The problems of ambiguity in the CISG and conflicting interpretations produced by its member states are evaluated in Parts IV and V. Finally, Part VI concludes the discussion by offering some suggestions for future reform of the CISG.

II. Histories of English Sales Law and the CISG

To fully understand why many international traders choose English Sales Law instead of the CISG, one has to conduct a comparative study of their developing histories. By the time the CISG was enacted, international traders had used English Sales Law for many years. Therefore, English Sales Law was already in the leading position at the time of the adoption of the CISG.

When examining the history of English Sales Law, one could easily make the mistake of starting with the Sale of Goods Act 1979 or its predecessor, the Sale of Goods Act of 1893. In fact, the history of English Sales Law is inherently linked with the development of English commercial law, which can be traced much further back in time. It is more appropriate to begin the discussion in the seventeenth century.[6] But English law, in general, was not then sufficiently developed to accommodate the needs of a growing commercial marketplace. Merchants had their own laws, such as commercial customs,

[5] Michael Bridge, *International Sale of Goods Law and Practice*, 2nd ed. (Oxford: Oxford University Press, 2007), 509.
[6] William Bernstein, *A Splendid Exchange* (London: Atlantic Books, 2008), 198–214 (international trade had become more widespread before the seventeenth century).

usages, and *lex mercatoria* to govern their commercial transactions; they established their own merchant courts to settle disputes arising from their commercial transactions.[7]

All of this began to change in the early seventeenth century, when the courts of common law displaced the merchant courts under the direction of Chief Justice Coke. Judges at common law courts did not adopt *lex mercatoria* as a source of law. Though borrowing certain rules from *lex mercatoria*, they primarily applied the principles of common law to solve commercial disputes. This change was clearly a misfortune for medieval merchants. Nonetheless, it was a critical legal development in English commercial law in general, and sales law in particular. It established the jurisdiction of common law courts over commercial disputes.[8]

Gradually, judges adjusted traditional common law principles to meet the needs of merchants. The significant development in English commercial law took place when Lord Mansfield was appointed as Lord Chief Justice of the King's Bench. He is regarded as the founder of English commercial law.[9] During his tenure, Lord Mansfield consolidated a vast body of case law on commercial disputes relating to sales, agency, bailment, and negotiable instruments. By the time of his retirement, English commercial law was much more advanced than the commercial laws in other countries. Lord Mansfield had laid a solid foundation for the Sale of Goods Act of 1893, enacted almost a century after his retirement.

Sir Mackenzie Chalmers[10] drafted the Sale of Goods Act of 1893.[11] In 1888, he was commissioned to prepare a bill for the codification of legal rules relating to sale of goods contracts. It was enacted in 1894 as the Sale of Goods Act of 1893. It remained entirely unchanged until 1954, when Section 4 of the Act was repealed. Later, several significant amendments were made by the Misrepresentation Act 1967, the Criminal Law Act 1967, and the Theft Act 1968. More critical textual changes were made by the Supply of Goods (Implied Terms) Act 1973, Consumer Credit Act 1974, and the Unfair Contract Terms Act 1977. Subsequently, the Sale of Goods Act 1979 consolidated all of these amendments and replaced the Sale of Goods Act of 1893. After 1979, further changes were made in 1994, 1995, and 2002.[12]

It can be seen from this brief review that English Sales Law was considered an advanced body of rules beginning in the nineteenth century. It was a sales law that aimed

---

[7] Frederic Sanborn, *Origins of the Early English Maritime and Commercial Law* (London: Century Co., 1930); Leon Trakman, *The Law Merchant: The Evolution of Commercial Law* (New York: Fred B Rothman & Co., 1983).

[8] One of the absurd developments made by common law courts is the maxim of caveat emptor, which was not the rule in either the *lex mercatoria* or Roman law. See Walton H. Hamilton, "The Ancient Maxim Caveat Emptor," 50 *Yale L. J.* 133 (1931).

[9] Ewan Mckendrick, *Goode on Commercial Law*, 4th ed. (London: Penguin Books, 2010), 7.

[10] Sir Mackenzie Chalmers (1847–1927) was a celebrated statutory draftsman. He was also the drafter of a number of key commercial law statutes, such as the Bills of Exchange 1882 and the Marine Insurance Act 1906.

[11] See Roy Goode, *Commercial Law*, 2nd ed. (London: Penguin Books, 1995), 187–95; Michael Bridge, "The Evolution of Modern Sales Law," *LMCLQ* 52 (1991).

[12] In 1994, the Sale of Goods (Amendment) Act 1994, ss1, 3(2) repealed the market overt exception to the *nemo dat* rule; the Sale and Supply of Goods Act 1994 revised the implied term of quality and the rules as to deemed acceptance. In 1995, the Sale of Goods (Amendment) Act 1995 made the prepaying buyer of an individual part of a bulk a co-owner of the bulk. In 2002 the Sale and Supply of Goods to Consumer regulation 2002 implemented the 1999 EC Consumer Sales Directive.

at meeting commercial needs. To that end, it was constantly revised to accommodate new developments in international trade.

In addition, the dominant position of English Sales Law is also largely attributable to the dominant status of the UK in international trade in the eighteenth and early nineteenth centuries. Within this period, through the expansion of overseas trade, the UK gradually established a leading role in international trade. British merchants, with stronger bargaining power, naturally preferred English Sales law and chose it as the governing law for their international transactions. This enhanced the dominance of English Sales Law in two ways. As parties from other countries became more familiar with its contents, more international traders chose English law to govern their transactions. English courts became the preferred forum to settle international disputes. On the other hand, it created more opportunities for judges to improve English law through their exposure to novel fact patterns. As a result, English law became more advanced than commercial law in other jurisdictions, which, in turn, encouraged more international traders to choose English law.

The central role played by the city of London in international trade also aided the competitive advantage of English Sales Law. London had been an international trading center from Anglo-Saxon times, having a world reputation for its highly developed speciality markets in commodities, financial transactions, and transport and insurance services.[13] This attracted merchants from around the world to do business in London. They employed English barristers and solicitors to represent them in their business transactions. Consequently, English Sales Law became firmly entrenched as the favored law for international transactions.

The British political, business, and legal communities have recognized this competitive advantage. At a meeting convened by the British government in 2004 to discuss whether the UK should ratify the CISG, the major concern was the impact that the CISG would have on English commercial law's leading position in international trade, as well as London's standing in international arbitration and litigation.[14] Although certain leading academic lawyers argued in favor of the need to harmonize international private law,[15] the majority of legal practitioners and judges did not share this view.[16]

The CISG's development was not exposed to the advantages enjoyed by English Sales Law. In 1928 Ernst Rabel, a law professor, suggested to the newly established UNIDROIT Institute that the unification of international sales law should be given the highest priority. In 1930, UNIDROIT set up a committee to produce a uniform international sales law. The Governing Council of UNIDROIT adopted a revised version in 1939. However, the

---

[13] Pamela Nightingale, *A Medieval Mercantile Community: The Grocers' Company and the Politics and Trade of London* (New Haven: Yale University Press, 1995), 1000–483.

[14] Sally Moss, "Why the United Kingdom Has Not Ratified the CISG," 25 *J. L. & Commerce* 483, 485 (2005–6); John Hobhouse, "International Conventions and Commercial Law: The Pursuit of Uniformity," 106 *L. Quarterly Rev.* 530 (1990); Roy Goode, "Insularity or Leadership?: The Role of the United Kingdom in the Harmonisation of Commercial Law," 50 *Int'l & Comp. L. Q.* 751 (2001).

[15] Goode, "Insularity or Leadership?."

[16] See House of Lords, European Contract Law: the Draft Common Frame of Reference Report with Evidence (2009), available at http://www.publications.parliament.uk/pa/ld200809/ldselect/ldeucom/95/95.pdf.

project was interrupted by World War II. It was not until 1951 that the government of The Netherlands convened a conference in The Hague in which a special Sales Committee was appointed to finish the sales law project. The committee produced two drafts – the Convention relating to a Uniform Law of International Sales (ULIS) and the Convention Relating to a Uniform Law on the Formation of Contracts for the International Sale of Goods. These two drafts were adopted at the 1964 Diplomatic Conference in Hague and came into force in 1972. Unfortunately, the two conventions were ratified by only a handful of countries.[17]

In 1966, the United Nations Commission on International Trade Law (UNCITRAL) was established. UNCITRAL established a working group in charge of modifying the Hague Sales Conventions or producing a new text. In 1978 the working group submitted a Draft Sales Convention (New York Draft). A Diplomatic Conference in Vienna was convened to discuss the draft in 1980. The draft was adopted, becoming the CISG.

This comparison of the histories of the CISG and English sales law shows that the latter developed over a considerably longer period of time. Moreover, the CISG did not have the geographical advantage enjoyed by English sales law. The long history of English sales law's use in international trade has positioned it as a strong alternative to the CISG.

III. Problem of Fragmentary Law

From the perspective of a legal practitioner, there are many areas of law, besides the law of sales, governing an international sale of goods transaction, including property, insurance, carriage of goods, and payment law. When choosing the applicable law, the practitioner has to take account of all of the relevant laws governing the transaction. If he or she chooses English law as the applicable law, he or she chooses not only English sales law, but also the whole system of English law. In contrast, the CISG's narrow scope requires the practitioner to select another national law to govern the legal issues not covered by the CISG.

Moreover, even as a sales law, the CISG does not cover all of the legal issues relating to sale of goods. The CISG was not intended as a comprehensive law of sales. It is inherently a fragmentary body of legal rules. Its fragmentary feature is one of its major disadvantages in comparison with English sales law. A cursory review of CISG text shows the limited scope of its rules taken as a whole. First, numerous areas of law relating to sales of goods are expressly excluded. CISG Article 4 states that:

> This convention governs only the formation of the contract of sale and the rights and obligations of the seller and the buyer arising from such a contract. In particular, except as otherwise expressly provided in this convention, it is not concerned with:
>
> (a) the validity of the contract or of any of its provisions or of any usage;
> (b) the effect which the contract may have on the property in the goods sold.

[17] Peter Schlechtriem, "Introduction," in Schlechtriem and Schwenzer, *Commentary.*

Article 4 delegates to national law the enforceability of numerous common contract terms, such as retention of title,[18] assignment of contract,[19] set off,[20] penalties,[21] and choice of forum clauses,[22] as well as settlement agreements.[23]

One of the main purposes for the unification of international sales law is to reduce transaction costs associated with international trade. If the parties to a transaction are located in different countries where their national contract laws differ, they have to determine the applicable law to govern their transactions through negotiations. Diverse national contract laws generate unnecessary negotiation costs for the parties in a cross-border transaction. Whichever national contract law is adopted as the applicable law, it will inevitably be unfamiliar to one of the parties, who would have to expend considerable costs in learning the foreign law. Consequently, diverse national contract laws not only generate unnecessary learning costs, but also produce a disincentive to engage in cross-border transactions. A uniform sales law reduces the transactions costs of negotiating and learning an applicable law.[24]

Unfortunately, the CISG fails to achieve the goal of reducing transaction costs relating to international trade.[25] Even when parties choose the CISG as the applicable law, they still need to choose a national law to fill in the "external gaps" in the CISG. So, the savings in negotiation costs by selecting the CISG are negligible. If there were no CISG, the parties would only need to agree on a single body of (national) law. It would be unnecessary for them to choose contract law of one jurisdiction and property law of another. Now with the CISG, the parties first need to decide whether they want the CISG to govern their transaction. If they decide to do so, they have to make a further decision on the question of which national law should be chosen to fill the gaps left by the CISG.

Unlike the CISG, the Sale of Goods Act of 1979 provides a comprehensive body of legal rules. It covers all of the key legal aspects in relation to international sale contracts. In the event of a gap, recourse would be made to general common law of contract. Accordingly, transaction costs associated with the use of English Sales Law are lower than those associated with the CISG.

A further complication in applying the CISG is that it provides a number of reservations that allow countries to opt out of certain parts of the CISG's coverage. These include not being bound by Part II (formation) or Part III (obligations of sellers and buyers) under Article 92; not applying the CISG to certain "territorial units" under Article 93; nonapplication to transactions between countries "which have the same or closely

---

[18] See *Roder Zelt-und Hallenkonstruktione GmbH v. Rosedown Park Pty Ltd and Reginald R Eustace*, Federal Court, South Australian District, Adelaide, April 28, 1995, available at http://www.unilex.info/case.cfm?pid=1&do=case&id=197&step=FullText.

[19] See Oberster Gerichtshof, April 24, 1997, Zeitschrift für Rechtsvergleichung 89 (1997).

[20] See Oberster Gerichtshof, October 22, 2001, available at http://cisgw3.law.pace.edu/cisg/wais/db/cases2/011022a4.html; Tribunale di Vigevano, July 12, 2000, in 20 *J. L. & Commerce* 209 (2001).

[21] See Rechtbank van Koohandel Hasselt, June 17, 1998, available at http://www.law.kuleuven.ac.be/int/tradelaw/WK1998–06–17.htm.

[22] See Camara Nacional de los Apelaciones en lo Comercial, October 14, 1993, available at http://www.uc3m.es/uc3m/dpto/PR/dpp03/cisg/sargen6.htm.

[23] See LG Aachen, May 14, 1993, *Recht der internationalen Wirtschaft* 760 (1993).

[24] Karl Llewellyn, "Why We Need the Uniform Commercial Code," 10 *U. Florida L. Rev.* 367, 369 (1957).

[25] Arthur Rosett, "Critical Reflections on the United Nations Convention on Contract for the International Sale of Goods," 45 *Ohio St. L. J.* 265, 266–7 (1984).

related legal rules" under Article 94; nonapplication in cases covered by Article 1(1)(b) jurisdiction (Article 95); and the ability to opt out of the "no writing" requirements of Articles 11 and 29 (Article 96). For example, the Scandinavian countries have made declarations to opt out of CISG Part II (rules governing the formation of the contract). The United States, China, the Czech Republic, Singapore, St. Vincent, the Grenadines, and Slovakia have made declarations against the application Article 1(1)(b) jurisdiction.[26]

These reservation options were inserted into the CISG as compromises and to make it attractive to as many countries as possible.[27] For example, developed countries in general prefer strict rules on the need for written documents and the necessary time for the inspection of goods because their traders have high levels of literacy and technological sophistication. On the contrary, developing countries favor more liberal rules on these issues. For example, significant debates took place at the diplomatic conference on the rule governing the time periods within which the buyer must give notice of nonconforming goods. Many Eastern European and Asian states were not prepared to adopt the principles of contractual autonomy and the primacy of customs and trade practices that are customary in the developed countries.[28] The incorporation of reservations was needed to reach a compromise. As a consequence, the CISG inevitably became a fragmentary body of legal rules due to the reservations and declarations made by its member states.[29]

The fragmentary feature of the CISG significantly undermines its attractiveness to commercial parties. From a commercial party's point of view, it would be better to exclude the application of the CISG in favor of a national law. This is one of the key reasons why many commercial parties and leading international commodity trade associations expressly opt out of the CISG and choose English law to govern their transactions.

IV. Ambiguities in the CISG

Another disadvantage of the CISG is that the CISG contains numerous general principles and abstract legal terms. This makes it very difficult for commercial parties to foresee how a rule will be applied in practice. Uncertainty in the application of law is a risk that businesses hope to avoid.

The CISG prefers general principles and abstract terms to specific rules and clear standards. For example, there are more than thirty instances in which the CISG measures the parties' conduct, defines rights or obligations, or requires certain actions or notices by referencing "a reasonable person, reasonableness, or unreasonableness."[30] Another

---

[26] For general discussion of the conflict of law problems, see Franco Ferrari, "What Sources of Law for Contracts for the International Sale of Goods? Why One Has to look beyond the CISG," 25 *Int'l Rev. L. & Economics* 314 (2005); James J. Fawcett, Jonathan M. Harris, and Michael Bridge, *International Sale of Goods in the Conflict of Laws* (Oxford: Oxford University Press, 2005), 981–4.

[27] Clayton P. Gillette and Robert E. Scott, "The Political Economy of International Sales Law," 25 *Int'l Rev. L. & Economics* 446, 460–2 (2005).

[28] CISG Advisory Council, "Opinion No. 2, Examination of the Goods and Notice of Non-Conformity, Articles 38 and 39," available at http://cisgw3.law.pace.edu/cisg/CISG-AC-op2.html.

[29] Gyula Eörsi, "A Propos the 1980 Vienna Convention on Contracts for the International Sale of Goods," *Am. J. Comp. L.* 333, 349–50 (1983).

[30] Michael Van Alstine, "Dynamic Treaty Interpretation," 146 *U. Penn. L. Rev.* 687, 751–2 (1998); Gillette and Scott, "The Political Economy of International Sales Law," 474.

example is the definition of fundamental breach, which permits a party to terminate a contract and claim damages. Considering the seriousness of contract avoidance, a clear definition or criteria should be provided for making the determination of fundamental breach. Instead, it is defined ambiguously in Article 25:

> A breach of contract committed by one of the parties is fundamental if it results in such detriment to the other party as *substantially* to deprive him of what he is entitled to expect under the contract, unless the party in breach did not foresee and a *reasonable* person of this same kind in the same circumstances would not have foreseen such a result. (Emphasis added.)

The "precise meaning of the terms substantially and reasonable is unclear. The official explanatory note by UNCITRAL is tautological and very confusing, just reproducing Article 25 with no clear, practical guidance."[31]

Why did the drafters of the CISG prefer general principles to specific rules? A number of reasons can be put forward: general principles and vague standards were needed to reach compromise; general principles allowed for flexible application across national legal traditions; and the drafters were mostly academics and government officials, and not representatives from international trade associations.[32] Some commentators have suggested that the drafters may have pursued (national) self-interests at the expense of the primary users of the uniform law.[33] Consequently, the drafters of the CISG preferred a general principle to specific rules, vague terms to clear standards, ambiguous jargon to intelligible language, because compromise on more specific rules was not possible. General principles and vague terms can be interpreted in many, even contradictory, ways. Therefore, each state could and some have interpreted the CISG to conform to their own national legal systems. These factors help explain the dissonance between the widespread adoption of the CISG at the government level and the widespread rejection of the CISG at business-to-business level.

As a consequence, the CISG is drafted in abstract language, containing more general and vague principles than clear and specific rules. For international traders, general principles and abstract terms generate a high level of uncertainty in the application of the CISG, which makes it very difficult for them to manage potential legal risks associated with the transaction. So, the best way to solve this legal uncertainty is to exclude the application of the CISG.

In contrast, the Sale of Goods Act 1979 was developed by the interaction between judges and merchants over hundreds of years. Merchants have played a significant

---

[31] A buyer can require the delivery of substitute goods only if the goods delivered were not in conformity with the contract and the lack of conformity constituted a fundamental breach of contract. The existence of a fundamental breach is one of the two circumstances that justifies a declaration of avoidance of a contract by the aggrieved party; the other circumstance being that, in the case of nondelivery of the goods by the seller or nonpayment of the price or failure to take delivery by the buyer, the party in breach fails to perform within a reasonable period of time fixed by the aggrieved party. UNCITRAL, *United Nations Convention on Contracts for the International Sale of Goods* (Austria: United Nations Publication, 2010) 40.

[32] For general discussions of the history of the CISG, see Peter Huber, "Comparative Sales Law," in *The Oxford Handbook of Comparative Law* (ed. M. Reimann and R. Zimmermann) (Oxford: Oxford University Press, 2008), 937.

[33] Alan Schwartz and Robert E. Scott, "The Political Economy of Private Legislatures," 143, *U. Penn. L. Rev.* 595, 597 (1995); Gillette and Scott, "The Political Economy of International Sales Law," 666–70.

role in shaping English Sales Law. The Sale of Goods Act 1893, and its successor, the Sale of Goods Act 1979, are largely a codification of the legal rules found in case law. Not only do many common law features remain in the Act, but also case law continually plays a crucial role in legal development and keeps the law responsive to real world change. Common law is developed incrementally. Furthermore, this type of incremental change always starts with a dispute between the contracting parties. In other words, legal changes are initiated by private litigation. As parties' disputes are often related to the legal issues, which are of practical significance, they ensure that the development of English sales law always keeps up with commercial needs. The common law continuously produces or adjusts rules facilitating rather than hindering commercial transactions.[34]

It would be misleading to claim that the Sale of Goods Act 1979 is drafted in plain language, using no general principles or abstract legal jargon. In fact, it is also a piece of ambiguous legislation. But at least it relies less on general principles and ambiguous legal terms than the CISG. For example, the Sale of Goods Act 1979 does not use the concept of fundamental breach. Though the terms "reasonable person," "reasonableness," and "unreasonableness" appear twenty-one times in the act, it should be noted that the text of the Sale of Goods Act is much longer than the CISG.

In addition, when vague terms are used, the Sale of Goods Act provides guidance on how they should be interpreted. Section 14(2) provides an illustration: "Where the seller sells goods in the course of a business, there is an implied term that the goods supplied under the contract are of *satisfactory quality*." The term "satisfactory quality" is indeed an ambiguous legal jargon. But guidance on how to define satisfactory quality is given in Section 14(2)(A) and (2)(B). Section 14 (2)(A) provides: "For the purposes of this Act, goods are of satisfactory quality if they meet the standard that a reasonable person would regard as satisfactory, taking account of any description of the goods, the price (if relevant) and all the other relevant circumstances." A listing of specific criteria for determining "satisfactory quality" is provided in Section 14(2)(B):

> For the purposes of this Act, the quality of goods includes their state and condition and the following (among others) are in appropriate cases aspects of the quality of goods:
>
> (a) fitness for all the purposes for which goods of the kind in question are commonly supplied,
> (b) appearance and finish,
> (c) freedom from minor defects,
> (d) safety, and
> (e) durability.

Unlike the CISG, which offers no practical guidance for applying many of its abstract legal terms, the Sale of Goods Act does provide instructions when a vague legal term is used. More importantly, ambiguous rules and vague legal jargon in the English sales law have been gradually clarified through the long-term development of case law.

---

[34] George L. Priest, "The Common Law Process and the Selection of Efficient Rules," 6 *J. Legal Studies* 65 (1977).

V. Divergent Legal Interpretations

Legal ambiguities are inevitable. One of the advantages of English sales law is that legal ambiguities can be gradually clarified by case law. When a dispute on the interpretation of an ambiguous legal rule in English Sales Law arises, it can be solved by courts. Where the parties argue for different legal interpretations, the court can decide which version of the interpretations should prevail. Once the case is decided, it becomes the law, having a binding effect on future transactions. Consequently, the legal ambiguity is clarified.

Nonetheless, it is likely that with the growth in case law, a legal rule may be interpreted differently or perhaps even contradictorily by courts at the same level. Not only has the legal ambiguity not been solved, but also new confusions in relation to the same rule arise. However, when given issues are addressed by the Supreme Court, the inconsistences among lower court interpretations are harmonized and ambiguities in the law are removed.

Conversely, ambiguities in the CISG have to be solved by judicial interpretations of national courts of its member states. At times, national courts of the member states have made conflicting interpretations of the same rule.[35] The problem of divergent interpretations is illustrated by the various interpretations of CISG Article 9. Article 9 provides:

(1) the parties are bound by any usage to which they have agreed and by any practices which they have established between themselves.

(2) the parties are considered, unless otherwise agreed, to have implicitly made applicable to their contract or its formation a usage of which the parties knew or ought to have known and which in international trade is widely known to, and regularly observed by, parties to contracts of the type involved in the particular trade concerned.

The meaning of these provisions has differed between developed countries and developing countries. Developed countries prefer flexibility of contracts, with the use of custom and usage as a means of increasing commercial flexibility and economic efficiency.[36] Their courts have broadly construed these provisions. For example, in the United States, the express terms of an agreement and a usage of trade are construed, whenever reasonable, to be consistent with each other.[37] Conversely, developing countries see this broad approach to the interpretation of Article 9 as too uncertain. They prefer to solely rely on the written rules and expressed agreements of the parties. This is largely because merchants in developing countries have had little influence in the development of trade usages.[38] Therefore, most developing countries take a very narrow approach to the

---

[35] Lisa M. Ryan, "The Convention on Contracts for the International Sale of Goods: Divergent Interpretations," 4 *Tulane J. Int'l & Comp. L.* 99 (1995–6).

[36] Sara G. Zwart, "The New International Law of Sales: A Marriage between Socialist Third World, Common, and Civil Law Principles," 13 *No. Carolina J. Int'l. & Commercial Regulation* 109, 117 (1988).

[37] Lisa M. Ryan, "The Convention on Contracts for the International Sale of Goods: Divergent Interpretations," 4 *Tulane J. Int'l & Comp. L.* 99, 103 (1995–6).

[38] Stephen Bainbridge, "Trade Usages in International Sale of Goods: An Analysis of the 1964 and 1980 Sale Conventions," 24 *Virginia J. Int'l. L.* 619, 641 (1984); Amy H. Kastely, "Symposium: Reflections on the International Unification of Sales Law: Convention," 8 *Nw. J. Int'l L. & Business* 574, 610.

interpretation of Article 9. They do not give effect to trade usages unless explicitly agreed by the parties and provided the usages are not in conflict with statutory provisions.[39]

This is just one of many examples of conflicting interpretations among the member states of the CISG. Apart from the interpretation of Article 9, developing and developed countries also differ in their interpretations of Articles 11, 29, 55, and 79.[40] These conflicting legal interpretations have generated a high level of uncertainty in the application of the CISG.

Moreover, this problem is further exacerbated by the fact that no reliable legal institution exists to solve these conflicting interpretations. There is no international supreme commercial court to resolve conflicts and inconsistencies in legal interpretations. Accordingly, there is no uniform interpretation of the CISG. The question of how the CISG is interpreted mostly depends on which member state's court hears the dispute. Undoubtedly, this poses a great level of uncertainty in practice. When deciding whether the CIGS should be chosen as the applicable law, the parties or their lawyers must have sufficient knowledge of differences in legal interpretation among the member states and then choose the one that they favor. This is a very demanding task. These problems make the CISG less attractive to commercial parties than English sales law.

In support of the CISG, national courts can and should reference judicial decisions in other member states. Furthermore, a vast amount of academic literature has been produced that provides some valuable guidance for interpreting and applying the CISG.[41] But it does not necessarily follow that the availability of these sources solves the problem of contradictory interpretations. The fact remains that CISG case law provides alternative interpretations that a court may choose. The problem of conflicting legal interpretations still remains a problem.

The lack of a uniform judicial institution to support the CISG means that it remains a static instrument. The current version of the CISG was enacted in 1980; no revisions have been made. The commercial world has changed dramatically; new technologies, such as the use of electrical documents and signatures and the growth of e-commerce, have had a great impact on international trade. The CISG is unable to meet new developments in the commercial world.[42]

Because the CISG is an international treaty, any amendment and revision must comply with the strict procedures required by international law. No amendment can be made unless it is agreed unanimously by all of the member states. Due to its international law status, its revision is extremely difficult. This makes it almost impossible for the CISG to be updated to reflect developments in commercial practice.[43] If the CISG is not revised in the near future to meet the new needs in the commercial world, then it will increasingly become obsolete.

---

[39] E. Allan Farnsworth, "Developing International Trade Law," 9 *California Western Int'l L. J.* 461, 465–6 (1979).

[40] Ryan, "The Convention on Contracts."

[41] See http://www.cisg.law.pace.edu/cisg/text/caseschedule.html.

[42] Jennifer E. Hill, "The Future of Electronic Contracts in International Sales; Gaps and Natural Remedies under the United Nations Convention on Contracts for the International Sale of Goods," 2 *Nw. J. Tech. & Intell. Prop.* 1 (2003).

[43] For general discussion of difficulties with international law making, see Francesco Parasi and Vincy Fon, *The Economics of Lawmaking* (Oxford: Oxford University Press, 2009), 207–70.

In contrast, English sales law has been gradually improved and developed through case law. Though it happens in an incremental way, the legal development and amendments to the Sale of Goods Act are constantly made in order to meet the needs of the commercial world. This is one of the reasons why commercial parties prefer English sales law to the CISG.

VI. Suggestions for Future Reform

Discussions in this chapter show that English sales law has four competitive advantages over the CISG. First, English sales law developed earlier than the CISG. It was well established as the leading international sales law when the CISG was enacted. Second, English sales law is a comprehensive legal system, whereas the CISG is a noncomprehensive law. When commercial parties choose the CISG they have to make a separate selection of a national law to be applied to fill the gaps in the CISG. Third, there are more ambiguities in the CISG than in the Sale of Goods Act 1979. This makes the application of the CISG more uncertain. Fourth, legal ambiguities and conflicting legal interpretations in English sales law are solved through the development of case law. There is no equivalent institution to resolve inconsistencies and conflicts in legal interpretations of the CISG produced by national courts. In order for the CISG to compete with English sales law in the future, the four disadvantages outlined here must be overcome. In this concluding section, three suggestions are offered for improving the CISG.

First, if the CISG intends to attract wide adoption by commercial parties, it is imperative that its primary users, international traders, play a leading role in the revision of the CISG. As previously discussed, the main driving forces behind the unification of international sales law are government officials, law professors, and legal practitioners. The flaw in the drafting of the CISG was a lack of sufficient input from international traders. Consequently, although the CISG has been adopted by many states, international traders have deliberately excluded its application. This is simply because the CISG does not reflect their interests. To solve this problem, more involvement of commercial parties in the future reform of the CISG is necessary. They are the primary users of the CISG; accordingly, the CISG should be sensitive to their interests.

The experience of the Uniform Customs and Practice for Documentary Credits (UCP) provides valuable insights. Unlike the CISG, the driving force behind the UCP was not a working group of politicians, law professors, and legal practitioners, but its primary users, the banking industry. It was drafted by the International Chamber of Commerce. The latest version is the UCP 600, which came into effect on July 1, 2007. From a practical perspective, the UCP 600 is more successful than the CISG. Arguably, it is the most successful harmonization of international commercial law ever made.[44] The fact that representatives of banks drafted the UCP 600 has contributed significantly to its success. Banks' interests are common in nature; namely, codified customs and practices should ensure that banks are not exposed to excessive risks.[45] Bank interests are reflected throughout – from the general principle of the autonomy to specify duties to the exercise of due care in reviewing documents against payment. The UCP 600 is not strictly a "hard

---

[44] Roy Goode, Herbert Kronke, and Ewan McKendrick, *Transnational Commercial Law, Text Cases and Materials* (Oxford: Oxford University Press, 2007), 352.

[45] Id., 350.

law," but it has been universally adopted by bankers and commercial parties throughout the world. The success of the UCP 600 illustrates the importance of the participation of primary users in the unification of international commercial law, which the CISG drafting process failed to do.

Commercial law possesses a unique feature – by nature, it is private law, meaning the parties have the freedom to decide whether they would like to choose a national sales law or an international commercial law, such as the CISG, to govern their transactions. Generally, much of commercial law, especially sales law, is voluntary in nature (default rules), with few mandatory rules. Framing this problem from an economic perspective, it can be seen that the CISG's targeted audiences was nation sates and not commercial traders. As a result, the CISG is widely adopted by states, but less often used in international trade. Therefore, to correct this mistake, the primary users of the CISG, commercial traders, should be invited to play a significant role in the future reform of the CISG.

Second, the hard law status of the CISG should be changed. As it stands now, the CISG is an international treaty, making it unable to meet new developments in the commercial world. The hard law status of the CISG undermines its ability to compete with English sales law. Sales law, in nature, is a part of a general law of contract. The nonmandatory nature of sales law, as noted earlier, is reflected in CISG Article 6, which provides that: "The parties may exclude the application of this Convention or subject to article 12, derogate from or vary the effect of any of its provisions."[46]

If the CISG becomes a soft law, it will be easier for it to be revised or amended by the drafters to meet the new needs in the commercial world. The question of whether it would be used more widely by commercial parties depends on its quality. If it does better in serving commercial needs than English sales law, it will be used more often. On the other hand, if its default rules were considered to be inefficient, then it would be rejected as a viable alternative law by commercial parties. However, if the CISG is revised and drafted by commercial parties it would be reasonable to expect that significant improvements could be made. This is because commercial parties are experts on commercial practice and the problem of conflicting national interests between the drafters and the primary users will largely be abated. In addition, this change in its status in turn creates incentives for the drafters to produce more efficient and commercially suitable default rules if they want the CISG to be widely used by commercial parties.

Third, a system of international commercial courts should be established. One of the biggest disadvantages of the CISG is that there is no solution for competing or divergent interpretations. The only solution to this problem is to create an international commercial court that is empowered to provide the ultimate authoritative interpretation of the CISG. When there is a difference in the interpretations of a particular article by the member states, the case could be referred to the international commercial court for clarification. This would reduce uncertainty in the application of the CISG and, thereby, make it more attractive to commercial parties.

---

[46] Article 12 provides that any provision of Article 11, Article 29, or Part II of this convention that allows a contract of sale or its modification or termination by agreement or any offer, acceptance, or other indication of intention to be made in any form other than in writing does not apply where any party has his place of business in a contracting state that has made a declaration under Article 96 of this CISG. These parties may not derogate from or vary this effect of this article.

Currently, there is no way to solve these competing interpretations of the CISG made by national courts of the member states. It is true that law professors play a very important role in solving this problem. A vast amount of academic literature has been produced to clarify the different interpretations of the CISG. Nonetheless, national courts of the member states are under no legal duty to use academic literature. Further, academic debates over the correctness of various interpretations cause additional confusion and uncertainty for the application of the CISG. If the establishment of an appellate institution proves impossible, then the CISG is unlikely to win the competition with the English sales law as the most viable body of sales rules.

From a practical perspective, the commercial parties are concerned with two matters. First, does the sales law provide a body of default rules that are deemed to be practical and efficient? Second, does the court apply and interpret the law consistently? In the end, the CISG, as currently constituted, fails to satisfy both of these fundamental concerns. Because of this, it has not sufficiently harmonized international sales law as claimed by legal academics. English sales law still enjoys the dominant position in the field of international commercial law.

42 The CISG in Context of Complementary Texts

*Luca G. Castellani**

I. The CISG as a Work in Progress

The United Nations Commission on International Trade Law (UNCITRAL) is the core body in the United Nations system for the modernization and harmonization of international trade law.[1] For more than forty years UNCITRAL has been active as a law-making body, preparing texts covering many areas relevant to international trade.

The United Nations Convention on Contracts for the International Sale of Goods, 1980,[2] (CISG) is the most successful treaty in terms of states' participation among those prepared by UNCITRAL.[3] Like all treaties effectively implemented, the CISG represents a work in progress. In fact, a treaty is not a piece of legislation insensitive to the changes taking place in the world. On the contrary, several aspects of a treaty are in constant evolution: the level of participation of states, the trends in judicial interpretation, and its scope of application when it may be varied by lodging declarations.[4] The UNCITRAL Secretariat is engaged in furthering the evolution of the CISG in line with its guiding principles with respect to all the aforementioned aspects – increasing the number of adopting countries, disseminating information on its application by courts and arbitral bodies, and limiting the number of declarations when possible.

The UNCITRAL Secretariat is actively engaged in promoting the adoption of the CISG by states, in the broader framework of the implementation of the action points

---

* Luca Castellani is a legal officer with the UNCITRAL Secretariat, Vienna, Austria. The views expressed herein are those of the author and do not necessarily reflect the views of the United Nations.

[1] United Nations General Assembly, Resolution 2205 (XXI) of December 17, 1966, "Establishment of the United Nations Commission on International Trade Law."

[2] United Nations, *Treaty Series*, vol. 1489, p. 3.

[3] The Convention on the Recognition and Enforcement of Foreign Arbitral Awards, 1958 (United Nations, *Treaty Series*, vol. 330, p. 38): the "New York Convention" is a treaty falling under the mandate of UNCITRAL and has more state parties than the CISG. However, it was concluded prior to the establishment of the Commission.

[4] International trade law treaties usually use the term "declarations" when referring to statements lodged by states and other parties to the treaty and purporting to modify the scope of application of that treaty. Those statements are often referred to as "reservations" in international agreements referring to other fields of international law. (In general on reservation to treaties, see International Law Commission, Guide to Practice on Reservations to Treaties, forthcoming in *Yearbook of the International Law Commission, 2011,* vol. 2, part 2, and related guide.) This difference in terminology seems related to the fact that a variation in the scope of application of an international trade law treaty has an impact primarily on relations among private citizens, and not states or other public international law entities.

defined in its strategic framework for technical cooperation.[5] Those action points high-light the potential of the CISG as an enabler of regional trade agreements. In addition, the action points stress the special contribution of the CISG in building a modern and efficient legislative framework in developing countries, while simultaneously catering to the specific needs of small- and medium-sized enterprises.[6]

The UNCITRAL Secretariat also promotes the uniform interpretation of the CISG, as mandated by Article 7(1) of the CISG. This is done, in particular, by collecting and publishing relevant abstracts for the Case Law on UNCITRAL Texts (CLOUT) collection,[7] and by preparing complementary tools such as the UNCITRAL Digest of Case Law on the United Nations Convention on the International Sales of Goods.[8]

Finally, although certain declarations are permitted under the CISG, those declarations may introduce unjustified complexity in the CISG's scope and application. There-fore, the UNCITRAL Secretariat encourages countries to review periodically whether the reasons for lodging such declarations are still valid and, if that is not the case, to consider their withdrawal.

II. Reconsideration of CISG Declarations

The process of reconsidering declarations under the CISG has been initiated by Nordic countries. In fact, on becoming a party to the treaty, Denmark, Finland, Norway and Sweden declared, in accordance with Article 92 CISG, that they would not be bound by Part II of the Convention ("Formation of the Contract"). Moreover, Denmark, Finland, Iceland, Norway, and Sweden declared, pursuant to Article 94 CISG, that the CISG would not apply to contracts of sale where the parties have their places of business in Denmark, Finland, Iceland, Norway, or Sweden.[9] Recently, the decision was made to withdraw the Article 92 declarations and extend the Article 94 declarations to the formation of the contract so as to preserve the application of a uniform Nordic law of contracts to parties with places of business in the Nordic countries.[10]

Two more types of CISG declarations may undergo such review processes. First, some states may reconsider their declaration under Articles 12 and 96 CISG, requiring the contract to be in written form. This issue is particularly relevant for economies in transition. In fact, the written form declaration was originally introduced to address concerns about the correct implementation of central plans in socialist economies. Countries such as Hungary and Lithuania have now changed their economic systems

---

[5] UN doc. A/66/17, Report of the United Nations Commission on International Trade Law on its forty-fourth session (June 27–July 8, 2011), paras. 253–5.

[6] For more information on the strategy of the UNCITRAL secretariat in promoting the CISG, see Luca Castellani, "Promoting the Adoption of the CISG," 13 *Vindobona Journal of International Commercial Law and Arbitration* 241 (2009).

[7] Available at http://www.uncitral.org/uncitral/en/case_law.html.

[8] The most recent edition, published in 2012, is available at http://www.uncitral.org/uncitral/en/case_law/digests.html.

[9] Iceland's declaration under article 94 CISG extends as well to the formation of contracts of sale, as Iceland did not exclude the application of Part II of the CISG.

[10] Denmark, Finland, and Sweden have already done so. In Norway, a public consultation has supported a similar decision, but additional work is needed, inter alia, due to the peculiar technique of adoption by incorporation of the CISG in that country. See also *CISG Part II Conference: Stockholm, September 4–5, 2008* (ed. J. Kleineman) (Stockholm: Jure Bokhandel, 2009).

and have become European Union members. Because the CISG is in force in twenty-four of the twenty-eight member states of the European Union, the written form requirement may hinder cross-border trade within the European Union. This outcome is contrary to the explicit desire to enable a European common market. Those states should therefore consider withdrawing their "written form" declaration, as has been done by Estonia and, more recently, Latvia. Outside the European Union, the People's Republic of China has also recently withdrawn its "written form" declaration, thus aligning the application of the CISG with the formal requirements for the contract of sale of goods set forth in domestic law.

Similar arguments may apply to those declarations lodged under Article 95 CISG, relating to the exclusion of the application of the CISG under its Article 1(1)(b), which allows the application of the CISG where only one party to a contract is from a CISG country and that country's laws apply by virtue of private international law rules. This reservation was entered into by several States, including the Czech Republic, the People's Republic of China, Singapore, Slovakia, and the United States. One reason for opting for this declaration was the desire to ensure the application of special legislation for foreign trade enacted in socialist countries, whereas reciprocity may have influenced the adoption of the declaration in non-socialist countries.[11] However, such special legislation for foreign trade has been repealed, for instance, in the Czech Republic, in the People's Republic of China, and in Slovakia. The same considerations expressed earlier on the desirability to expand the reach of the CISG should lead countries to withdraw their Article 95 declarations.[12]

In addition, the CISG dynamically interacts with certain other international texts that together form a "CISG system." The CISG is complemented by the Convention on the Limitation Period in the International Sale of Goods (Limitation Convention),[13] the United Nations Convention on the Use of Electronic Communications in International Contracts (Electronic Communications Convention),[14] and the Uniform Rules on Contract Clauses for an Agreed Sum Due upon Failure of Performance (Uniform Rules).[15] These complementary texts are therefore directly relevant to thoroughly appreciate the operation of the CISG.

---

[11] Gary F. Bell, "Why Singapore Should Withdraw Its Reservation to the United Nations Convention on Contracts for the International Sale of Goods (CISG)," 9 *Singapore Year Book of International Law* 55 (2005).

   The following declaration lodged by Germany may also be relevant: "The Government of the Federal Republic of Germany holds the view that Parties to the Convention that have made a declaration under article 95 of the Convention are not considered Contracting States within the meaning of subparagraph (1) (b) of article 1 of the Convention. Accordingly, there is no obligation to apply – and the Federal Republic of Germany assumes no obligation to apply – this provision when the rules of private international law lead to the application of the law of a Party that has made a declaration to the effect that it will not be bound by subparagraph (1) (b) of article 1 of the Convention. Subject to this observation the Government of the Federal Republic of Germany makes no declaration under article 95 of the Convention."

[12] A recommendation in this sense was adopted by the New York State Bar Association (NYSBA) in the Final Report of its Task Force on New York Law in International Matters (June 25, 2011), p. 82. The goal of the NYSBA is to promote the use of New York law, including the CISG, and the choice of New York as place for dispute resolution.

[13] Concluded in 1974 and amended in 1980: United Nations, *Treaty Series*, vol. 1511, p. 3.

[14] UN Sales No. E.07.V.2 (treaty under registration; entered into force on March 1, 2013).

[15] UNCITRAL, *Yearbook*, vol. 14: 1983, part 3, II, A (p. 272).

III. Convention on the Limitation Period in the International Sale of Goods

In the area of the international sale of goods, UNCITRAL started its work in its early days by capitalizing on the extensive preparatory studies carried out in the previous decades as well as on the conventions finalized shortly before the establishment of the Commission, namely, the Convention relating to a Uniform Law on the Formation of Contracts for the International Sale of Goods, 1964, (ULF)[16] and the Convention relating to a Uniform Law on the International Sale of Goods, 1964 (ULIS).[17] The first outcome of the work of UNCITRAL was the Limitation Convention, which intended to consolidate a limited but complex area of the law of sale of goods. The Limitation Convention functionally forms a part of the CISG, but was finalized and adopted in 1974 as a separate treaty due to the uncertainty surrounding the timing of the finalization of the text of the CISG. When a sudden acceleration in the drafting process led to the adoption of the CISG in 1980, the Limitation Convention was amended by a Protocol so as to harmonize its text with that of the CISG, in particular with regard to scope of application and admissible declarations.

The Limitation Convention establishes uniform rules governing the period of time within which a party under a contract for the international sale of goods must commence legal proceedings against another party to assert a claim arising from the contract, or relating to its breach, termination, or validity. By doing so, it brings clarity and predictability to an aspect of great importance for the adjudication of the claim.

In fact, most legal systems limit or prescribe a claim from being asserted after the lapse of a specified period of time. This is due to the likelihood that, after the specified time period has passed, the evidence relating to the claim is likely to be unreliable or lost, and to the desire to protect against the uncertainty resulting from the exposure of a party to unasserted claims for an extensive period of time. However, numerous disparities exist among legal systems with respect to the conceptual basis of limitation, resulting in significant variations in the length of the limitation period and in the rules governing the claims after that period. For instance, divergent views exist on the substantive or procedural nature of provisions relating to limitation. Those differences may create difficulties in the enforcement of claims arising from international sales transactions. The Limitation Convention aims at preventing those difficulties.

The Limitation Convention applies to contracts for the sale of goods between parties whose places of business are in different states if both of those states are contracting states or, but only in its amended version, when the rules of private international law lead to the application to the contract of sale of goods of the law of a contracting state. It may also apply by virtue of the parties' choice if so allowed under applicable law.

The Limitation Convention sets the limitation period at four years (Article 8).[18] Subject to certain conditions, that period may be extended to a maximum of ten years (Article 23). Furthermore, the Limitation Convention regulates certain questions pertaining to the effect of commencing proceedings in a contracting state.

The Limitation Convention sets forth rules on the cessation and extension of the limitation period. That period ceases when the claimant commences judicial or arbitral

---

[16] United Nations, *Treaty Series*, vol. 834, p. 169.

[17] Id., p. 107.

[18] Article numbers refer to the consolidated text of the amended version of the Limitation Convention.

proceedings or when it asserts claims in an existing process. If the proceedings end without a binding decision on the merits, it is deemed that the limitation period continued to run during the proceedings. However, if the period has expired during the proceedings or has less than one year to run, the claimant is granted an additional year to commence new proceedings (Article 17).

Under the Limitation Convention, no claim shall be recognized or enforced in legal proceedings commenced after the expiration of the limitation period (Article 25(1)). Such expiration is not to be taken into consideration unless invoked by the parties (Article 24); however, states may lodge a declaration allowing for courts to take the expiration into account on their own initiative (Article 36). The only exception to the rule barring recognition and enforcement of the claim after the expiration of the limitation period occurs when the party raises its claim as a defense to, or set off against, a claim asserted by the other party (Article 25(2)).

Despite clear complementarities between the two treaties, the CISG has been significantly more successful in terms of adoption by states than the Limitation Convention. Several reasons may explain this: lack of resources, including parliamentary time, for international trade law reform may have worked to prioritize the adoption of the CISG over that of the Limitation Convention;[19] in certain jurisdictions prescription is associated with public policy issues, and the legislative actors are therefore more hesitant to adopt supranational uniform texts in this field; and finally, at the outset the Limitation Convention was perceived as a product of the interests of socialist countries and as such was received with caution in Western and Central Europe. Unfortunately, the adoption of the Limitation Convention in capitalist countries, including the United States, did not affect this view enough to influence the pattern of its adoption.[20]

Nevertheless, the Limitation Convention did not disappear from the international arena. Scholars kept this treaty in due consideration in light of its remarkable technical content.[21] Furthermore, states interested in creating a comprehensive legal framework for contracts for the international sale of goods are adopting the convention. In addition, the Limitation Convention is particularly relevant in regions such as North and Central America, where early adoption by the United States and Mexico are complemented with accessions by more states in the broader framework of the creation of an enabling environment for regional trade, including with a view to better implementing the CAFTA-DR agreement.[22] The Limitation Convention has also been widely adopted and is regularly applied in Eastern Europe.

---

[19] Kazuaki Sono, "The Limitation Convention: the Forerunner to Establish UNCITRAL Credibility," available at http://cisgw3.law.pace.edu/cisg/biblio/sono3.html.

[20] The United States ratified the Limitation Convention on May 5, 1994, i.e., twenty years after the conclusion of the treaty.

[21] Selected articles discussing the Limitation Convention include: Katharina Boele-Woelki, "The Limitation of Rights and Actions in the International Sale of Goods," 4 *Uniform Law Review/Revue de droit uniforme* 621 (1999); Anita F. Hill, "A Comparative Study of the United Nations Convention on the Limitation Period in the International Sale of Goods and Section 2–725 of the Uniform Commercial Code," 25 *Texas International Law Journal* 1 (1990). See also Reinhard Zimmermann, *Comparative Foundations of a European Law of Set-off and Prescription* (Cambridge and New York: Cambridge University Press, 2002). Moreover, the provisions of the Limitation Convention are commented on in *Commentary on the UN Convention on the International Sale of Goods (CISG)*, 3rd ed. (ed. P. Schlechtriem and I. Schwenzer) (Oxford: Oxford University Press: Oxford 2010), 1215–70.

[22] In Canada, the Uniform Law Commission prepared in 2000 an Uniform International Sales Conventions Act meant to deal with multiple conventions relevant in the field. However, this act, available at http://www.ulcc.ca/en/us/index.cfm?sec=1&sub=1u6, has not yet been adopted by any Canadian jurisdiction.

The limited amount of case law readily available in international databases is another factor affecting the broader use of the Limitation Convention. However, this seems related more to the difficulty of accessing existing decisions than to the lack thereof. This situation is changing as abstracts relating to the Limitation Convention are being published in the CLOUT collection.[23] Such cases highlight the practical importance of the Limitation Convention and provide useful guidance on its application. Easier availability of case law is likely, on the one hand, to raise the awareness of practitioners on the Limitation Convention, thus leading to its wider application, and, on the other hand, to highlight the importance of reporting existing cases, thus paving the way to the collection of further material.

The Limitation Convention is now receiving renewed interest in light of a global trend that sees legislative reform toward a reduction of the time period necessary for limitation and, at the same time, increased difficulty in ascertaining the applicable law in case of cross-border exchanges, in part due to that legislative reform activity.[24] An interesting aspect of the interaction between uniform supranational models and national law reforms relates to the current trend of adopting in national legislation two limitation periods, one "objective," that is, running from a moment in time that can be identified in light of objective parameters (e.g., delivery of goods), and one "subjective," that is, running from a moment in time relating to an event that only the claimant may be aware of (e.g., discovery of lack of conformity of the good). The drafters of the Limitation Convention had already extensively discussed this approach, framed as a discussion on "patent" and "latent" defects in conjunction with the beginning of the limitation period, and decided to discard the "subjective" approach relating to "latent" defects in light of the uncertainties that this might create in long-distance business relations, and of the overall length of the limitation period, deemed sufficient to cover all needs arising from purely commercial transactions.[25] The matter is relevant to Article 39(2) CISG.

IV. Uniform Rules on Contract Clauses for an Agreed Sum Due upon Failure of Performance

After the conclusion of the CISG, work on sale of goods continued for some time, leading to the preparation of the Uniform Rules on Contract Clauses for an Agreed Sum Due

---

[23] CLOUT contains cases applying the Limitation Convention from Croatia, Cuba, Hungary, Montenegro, Poland, Serbia, and Ukraine. The first case from the United States discussing (though not applying) the Limitation Convention has also been published: CLOUT case no. 1186, District Court for the Northern District of Illinois, Eastern Division, No. 10 C 1174, *Maxxsonics USA, Inc. v. Fengshun Peiying Electro Acoustic Company, Ltd.* (March 21, 2012). More cases are emerging from other repositories and include: Foreign Trade Court attached to the Serbian Chamber of Commerce, Award No. T-13/05 (frozen plums and raspberries case), January 5, 2007, available at http://cisgw3.law.pace.edu/cases/070105sb.html. For an analysis of the case law on the Limitation Convention, see Luca G. Castellani, "An Assessment of the Convention on the Limitation Period in the International Sale of Goods through Case Law," 58 *Villanova Law Review* 645 (2013).

[24] Yasutomo Sugiura, "Japan after Acceding to the CISG – Should We Consider Ratifying the Limitation Convention Next?," in *Towards Uniformity: The 2nd Annual MAA Schlechtriem CISG Conference* (ed. I. Schwenzer and L. Spagnolo) (The Hague: Eleven/Boom Publishers, 2011), 223.

[25] United Nations Conference on Prescription (Limitation) in the International Sale of Goods, New York, May 20–June 14, 1974, *Official Records*, United Nations, New York, 1975 (UN doc. A/CONF.63/16), p. 61 (reproducing UN doc. A/CONF.63/9 and Add. 1–8), para. 72. See also the discussion under Article 10 in the *travaux préparatoires* of the Limitation Convention, available at http://www.uncitral.org/uncitral/en/uncitral_texts/sale_goods/1974Convention_travaux.html.

upon Failure of Performance (the Uniform Rules).[26] The Uniform Rules seek to unify the treatment, particularly as to validity and application, of clauses that provide for the payment by a party of a specified sum of money as damages, or as a penalty in the event of failure of the party to perform its contractual obligations in an international commercial transaction.[27]

The Uniform Rules failed to obtain broad acceptance in business practice for reasons not related to their content. In fact, this complex issue had been raised at a late stage during CISG negotiations, and its discussion was therefore postponed until after the conclusion of the CISG, thus necessarily leading to the adoption of separate provisions. In addition, the working group dealing with the matter was increasingly involved in work in other fields, such as arbitration and transport law.[28] Finally, this was an early example of UNCITRAL text not intended for formal treaty adoption, but to be used as a legislative model and for contractual incorporation. Although such texts became more common later and are now widely accepted in the context of "soft" legal codification, it may have been more difficult at the time to fully appreciate their value.

Though their use does not seem widespread, the Uniform Rules constitute an important intellectual achievement as they suggest a viable compromise between liquidated damages clauses, which are acceptable in many jurisdictions, and penalty clauses, which may, on the contrary, find more difficulties in being recognized by courts in legal systems belonging to the civil law tradition.[29] Moreover, by limiting the power of judicial intervention to cases when the sum agreed "is substantially disproportionate in relation to the loss that has been suffered,"[30] the Uniform Rules anticipated, and may further support, the trend toward the mitigation of such clauses when excessive.

It seems therefore important to give the Uniform Rules due consideration when discussing codification projects in the field of contract law.[31]

V. UN Convention on the Use of Electronic Communications in International Contracts

The CISG is further complemented by the United Nations Convention on the Use of Electronic Communications in International Contracts, 2005.[32] The Electronic Communications Convention was prepared as a contribution to clarifying the legal value of electronic communications exchanged in the context of international contracts,

---

[26] UNCITRAL, *Yearbook*, vol. 14: 1983, part 3, II, A (p. 272).

[27] On the Uniform Rules, see Alexander Komarov, "The Limitation of Contract Damages in Domestic Legal Systems and International Instruments," in *Contract Damages: Domestic and International Perspectives* (ed. D. Saidov and R. Cunnington) (Oxford and Portland, OR: Hart Publishing, 2008), 245; Pascal Hachem, *Agreed Sums Payable upon Breach of an Obligation: Rethinking Penalty and Liquidated Damages Clauses* (The Hague: Eleven/Boom Publishers, 2011).

[28] The area of work of that working group was generically identified as "International Contract Practices"; related documents are available at http://www.uncitral.org/uncitral/en/commission/working_groups/2Contract_Practices.html.

[29] However, the Uniform Rules may find application only in presence of liability for failure to perform: Uniform Rules, Article 5.

[30] Uniform Rules, Article 8.

[31] This will be the case for the forthcoming CISG Advisory Council Opinion on "Scope of the CISG under Article 4 – Fixed Sums."

[32] The Convention was adopted with United Nations General Assembly Resolution 60/21 of December 9, 2005 (A/RES/60/21).

including those falling under the regime of other international trade law treaties such as the CISG and the Limitation Convention.

The rapid diffusion of information and communication technologies is a prominent feature of globalization. In particular, the use of electronic means in the context of trade offers significant benefits in terms of speed, reliability, and effectiveness of communication. Moreover, the mobility of electronic devices is creating a borderless, permanently connected world in which traditional legal notions, including some typical of private international law, do not find easy application. In light of this, it is not surprising that the Electronic Communications Convention has attracted significant political support, academic interest, and general praise for its content.[33]

The Electronic Communications Convention fulfills four main purposes: (1) facilitating the use of electronic commerce in international trade, including in connection with the application of treaties concluded before the widespread use of electronic communications; (2) reinforcing the level of uniformity in the enactment of the UNCITRAL Model Law on Electronic Commerce (MLEC)[34] and of the UNCITRAL Model Law on Electronic Signatures (MLES);[35] (3) updating certain provisions of the MLEC and of the MLES and complementing them with new rules arising from recent practice; and (4) providing modern and uniform core electronic commerce legislation to countries missing or having incomplete law in this area. Thus, although the convention is a piece of "hard" international law, having a treaty nature, it may also operate as a soft law instrument, in a manner akin to that of model legislation.

The overarching purpose of the Electronic Communications Convention is to facilitate the use of electronic communications in international trade. In general, this goal may be achieved through the widespread adoption of uniform legislation at the national level. However, certain issues may require additional, specific solutions. One such issue relates to the possibility of employing electronic communications in contracts falling under the scope of treaties that do not foresee the use of those communications. For instance, the CISG embraces freedom of form for the contract of sale of goods, except when a state lodges a declaration under articles 11, 12, and 96 CISG requiring the contract to be in written form. This is the only provision in the CISG that the parties to the contract

[33] A bibliography on UNCITRAL texts relating to electronic commerce, including the Electronic Communications Convention, is regularly compiled by the UNCITRAL Secretariat and available on the UNCITRAL website at http://www.uncitral.org/uncitral/en/publications/bibliography.html. For further substantive information, see *The United Nations Convention on the Use of Electronic Communications in International Contracts: An In-depth Guide and Sourcebook* (ed. A. Boss and W. Kilian) (Aalphen aan den Rijn: Kluwer Law International, 2008); Luca Castellani, "The United Nations Electronic Communications Convention: Policy Goals and Potential Benefits," 19 *Korean Journal of International Trade & Business Law* 1 (2010); Kah Wei Chong and Joyce Chao Suling, "United Nations Convention on the Use of Electronic Communications in International Contracts: a New Global Standard," 18 *Singapore Academy of Law Journal* 116 (2006) (available at http://www.sal.org.sg/digitallibrary/Lists/SAL%20Journal/Attachments/390/2006–18-SAcLJ-116-Chong.pdf); Sieg Eiselen, "The UNECIC: International Trade in the Digital Era," 2 *Potchefstroom Electronic Law Journal* 1 (2007), available at http://www.puk.ac.za/opencms/export/PUK/html/fakulteite/regte/per/issuepages/2007volume10no2/2007x2x_Eiselen_art.pdf; Henry D. Gabriel, "The United Nations Convention on the Use of Electronic Communications in International Contracts: An Overview and Analysis," 11 *Uniform Law Review/Revue de droit uniforme* 285 (2006).

[34] UNCITRAL, Model Law on Electronic Commerce with Guide to Enactment, 1996, with additional article 5 bis as adopted in 1998, New York, 1999 (United Nations Publication Sales No. E.99.V.4).

[35] UNCITRAL, Model Law on Electronic Signatures with Guide to Enactment, 2001, New York, 2002 (United Nations Publication Sales No. E.02.V.8).

may not vary; it must therefore have mandatory application when one of the parties to the contract of sales has its place of business in a state that has lodged the declaration.[36] Because this is a strict formal requirement, it is doubtful whether equivalence between electronic and written form under the CISG could be achieved through the application of domestic law on electronic communications.

Two approaches are possible to make those older treaties compatible with the use of new technologies. The first approach requires the formal amendment of the treaty, typically through a protocol, and the formal adoption of the amended text. The amending procedure would need to be repeated for each treaty both at the international and at the domestic level. Completing such procedures may require a long period of time, creating, meanwhile, a dual legal regime in the application of the concerned treaty that could lead to uncertainty and disparity of treatment. Finally, the decision to adopt a formal amendment to the text in order to ensure the use of electronic communications might be construed as denying the possibility of a liberal interpretation under the original language.[37]

The second approach aims at establishing general rules of functional equivalence for electronic and paper-based requirements, in line with the method adopted in UNCITRAL texts. This approach does not demand amending each treaty, but relies on the adoption of a new text complementing all other relevant international instruments with respect to electronic communications. This is the solution embraced by the Electronic Communications Convention.

Moreover, the MLEC and the MLES have been adopted in a number of jurisdictions in every region of the world, and their principles have inspired even more legislators.[38] However, the nonbinding nature of those model laws gives legislators the possibility to vary their provisions at the time of their enactment. Such variations may significantly affect legal predictability in the cross-border use of electronic communications. Therefore, it was deemed desirable to reinforce the level of uniformity in electronic commerce legislation by providing a common statutory core through the adoption of the Electronic Communications Convention.[39]

Furthermore, the MLEC and the MLES were prepared at a time when certain technological models, such as electronic data interchange (EDI), were prevalent and others had yet to appear. Thus, on the occasion of the preparation of the Electronic Communications Convention it was deemed appropriate to review certain provisions of those model laws in light of recent technological developments and the experience in their enactment, as well as to introduce new provisions suggested by recent commercial practice. Such updated or new provisions deal with: location of parties (Article 6(4) and (5));

---

[36] A similar case could occur when the states have lodged no declaration, but the parties have agreed to exchange written communications without mentioning explicitly the admissibility of electronic means.

[37] UN doc. A/CN.9/485, Report of the Working Group on Arbitration on the work of its thirty-third session (Vienna, November 20–December 1, 2000), paras. 62–9. A liberal interpretation of formal requirements is not unusual, especially in common law jurisdictions.

[38] The status of adoption of MLEC and MLES are available on the UNCITRAL website respectively at http://www.uncitral.org/uncitral/en/uncitral_texts/electronic_commerce/1996Model_status.html and http://www.uncitral.org/uncitral/en/uncitral_texts/electronic_commerce/2001Model_status.html. However, that status information may be incomplete due to the fact that enacting jurisdictions do not always communicate the adoption of texts to the UNCITRAL Secretariat. Thus, more jurisdictions may have adopted those model laws than those listed on the website.

[39] Nevertheless, the parties may modify the convention's provisions by virtue of freedom of contract.

the notion of "intention" (as opposed to "approval") in the definition of functional equivalence for electronic signatures (Article 9(3)(a)); the principle of nonrepudiation of electronic signatures that have in fact established the actual identity and intention of the signatory (Article 9(3)(b)(ii)); rules on the determination of time and place of dispatch and receipt of electronic communications (Article 10); invitations to make offers (Article 11); contracts concluded by automated message systems (Article 12); and input errors made by physical persons when interacting with machines (Article 14).

Countries that have already enacted those model laws may wish to consider amending their domestic legislation when becoming a party to the Electronic Communications Convention in order to avoid complications arising from a dual electronic commerce regime for national and international transactions.[40]

Finally, another important function of the Electronic Communications Convention is to provide core legislation to countries still lacking such provisions.

The relevance of the Electronic Communications Convention is proportional to its adoption and use. During the two years in which it was open for signature, the convention received eighteen signatures.[41] The Dominican Republic, Honduras, and Singapore have already become a party to the Convention, which entered into force for those states on March 1, 2013. Other States, such as Australia and Thailand, have declared their intention of adopting the treaty. In the United States[42] and in Canada,[43] uniform legislation is being prepared for implementation at the state level.

At the same time, a number of developing countries, such as Guatemala[44] and Vietnam,[45] have adopted some, or all, of the substantive provisions of the Electronic Communications Convention without formally adhering to the treaty.[46] In such cases, the Electronic Communications Convention is being used as a model law rather than as an international agreement; it may therefore fulfill the third and the fourth function listed

---

[40] For instance, if the same provisions are applicable both domestically and internationally, the need to ascertain the domestic or international nature of the transaction in unclear cases becomes less compelling.

[41] Some European Union member states had informally indicated their interest in signing and becoming a party to the convention. However, this has not yet been possible, pending clarifications on the operation of the "disconnection clause" (Article 17(4) of the Electronic Communications Convention) in the context of intracommunity exchanges of electronic communications. The entry into force of the Electronic Communications Convention and its adoption by significant EU trading partners is likely to give decisive impulse to those discussions, thus eventually leading to a joint declaration on the distribution of competence between the European Union and its member states that is necessary to allow the participation of EU member states in the convention.

[42] Documents relating to the process are available on the Uniform Law Commission website at http://www.nccusl.org/Committee.aspx?title=UN%20E-Commerce%20Convention. See also John D. Gregory, "Implementing the Electronic Communications Convention," 18 *Business Law Today* 43 (2009), available at http://www.abanet.org/buslaw/blt/2009-01-02/gregory.shtml, and, on substantive issues, Henry D. Gabriel, "United Nations Convention on the Use of Electronic Communications in International Contracts and Compatibility with the American Domestic Law of Electronic Commerce," 7 *Loyola Law and Technology Annual* 1 (2006-7).

[43] Uniform Law Conference of Canada, *Proceedings of the Ninety-second Annual Meeting* 35 (Halifax, Nova Scotia, 2010).

[44] Decree No. 47-2008, August 19, 2008, "Ley para el reconocimiento de las comunicaciones y firmas electrónicas."

[45] Decree No. 57/2006/ND-CP of June 9, 2006, "Decree on Electronic Commerce."

[46] A list of the jurisdictions that have enacted some or all of the substantive provisions of the Electronic Communications Convention is available at http://www.uncitral.org/uncitral/en/uncitral_texts/electronic_commerce/1996Model_status.html (sub-footnote (e)).

earlier, and, to some extent, the second function, but not the first function, relating to removing obstacles to the use of electronic communications contained in older treaties.

The quick and widespread adoption of the Electronic Communications Convention at the domestic level demonstrates the relevance of this text as a global benchmark for e-commerce legislation and highlights the fact that the Electronic Communications Convention is attracting interest both from states traditionally at the forefront of electronic commerce, and from states with limited experience in this field but fully aware of the importance of enacting a modern and efficient enabling legislative framework.

43 Soft Laws as Models for the Improvement of the CISG

Ole Lando

A contract for the sale of goods is the prototype of the "general contract." Therefore, the Uniform Sales Laws, created in 1964, and CISG, created in 1980, were instrumental in creating the general principles of contract law. In 1980, a Working Group of the UNIDROIT began drafting the UNIDROIT Principles of International Commercial Contracts (PICC).[1] CISG also facilitated the work of the Commission on European Contract Law that in 1982 began to draft the Principles of European Contract Law (PECL), which also cover general principles of contract law. The two working groups worked simultaneously and inspired each other. Some of their members were participants in both groups, and PICC and PECL contain many similarities. The third and latest edition of PICC was published in 2011. PECL appeared in 1999 and 2003.[2]

The Study Group on a European Civil Code began in 1998 to prepare the Draft Common Frame of Reference (DCFR),[3] which was published in 2009. Parts of the DCFR dealing with contracts in general were based on a revised version of the PECL.

These soft law instruments – the PECL, DCFR, and PICC – adopted many CISG rules. However, on some issues, the groups drafted rules that differ from those of CISG. This chapter points out some of the issues and explains why the groups decided to deviate from CISG.

I. Good Faith

Article 7(1) of CISG provides that "in the interpretation of this Convention, regard is to be had to ... the observance of good faith in international trade." The majority of the delegates at the UN Conference were reluctant to apply the duty of good faith to contracts

---

[1] UNIDROIT, Unidroit Principles of International Commercial Contracts (Unidroit, Rome, 2010).

[2] Draft Common Frame of Reference (DCFR) Full Edition: *Principles, Definitions and Model Rules of European Private Law, Prepared by the Study Group on a European Civil Code and the Research Group on EC Private Law, Based in Part on a Revised Version of the Principles of European Contract Law,* vols. 1–6 (ed. Christian von Bar and Eric Clive) (Munich, 2009) (hereafter referred to as DCFR). See *Principles of European Contract Law: Parts I and II* (ed. Ole Lando and Hugh Beale) (The Hague, 2000) (hereafter referred to as PECL I and II); *Principles of European Contract Law, Part III* (ed. O. Lando, E. Clive, A. Prüm, and R. Zimmermann) (The Hague, 2003) (hereafter referred to as PECL III).

[3] The six-volume DCFR cover general contract law, specific contracts, noncontractual liability (torts, unjust enrichment, and negotiorum gestio), acquisition, loss of ownership of goods, security rights in movable goods, and trusts. Rules are provided for business-to-business and business-to-consumer contracts and for contracts between nonbusiness parties.

generally. They feared that when applying such a provision, national courts would be influenced by their own legal traditions, so that the provision would be interpreted differently in the different countries.

However, as has been pointed out, this narrow scope of the principle is not practicable.[4] When applying the CISG, several courts,[5] among them the German Supreme Court,[6] have, as do PICC Article 1(7) PECL Article 1(201) and DCFR III 1: 103 imposed on the parties a general duty to act in accordance with good faith and fair dealing when concluding, interpreting, performing, and enforcing the contract, and under PECL article 1: 202, PICC Article 5(1)(3), and DCFR III 1: 106 the parties have a duty to cooperate with each other for the performance of the contract.

II. Usages

CISG Article 9(2) provides "the Parties are considered, unless otherwise agreed, to have impliedly made applicable to their contract or its formation a usage of which the Parties knew or ought to have known and which in international trade is widely known to, and regularly observed by, Parties to contracts of the type involved in the Particular trade concerned."

This provision was drafted to accommodate those who consider usages as contractual terms, applicable only if there has been an express or implied intention of the parties to adopt them. It was also drafted to obviate the fear expressed by the developing countries that parties could be trapped by usages they would not understand or be aware of.[7]

Under PECL Article 1: 105(2), PICC Article 1.9, and DCFR II 1: 104(2),[8] usages are considered rules of law. The parties are bound by a usage, which would be considered generally applicable by persons in the same situation as the parties. PECL, PICC, and the DCFR cover both local and international usages. A party who is offered a contract by an offeror from a market in which he or she has not traded is not bound by the local usages of that market, but a foreign party who actively trades on a local market should be bound by the local usages of that market. That should not be based on the fiction that the party intends the usage to be applied. In addition, PECL, PICC, and DCFR exclude the application of an unreasonable usage. A rule similar to the rule in PECL, DCFR, and PICC should be provided in the revised convention. The word "impliedly" should be deleted.

---

[4] See Herber in *Commentary on the UN Convention on the International Sale of Goods*, 2nd ed. (ed. P. Schlechtriem) (Oxford, 1988), 63; Ulrich Magnus in Julius von Staudinger, *Kommentar zum Bürgerlichen Gesetzbuch mit Einführungsgesetz und Nebengesetzen. Wiener UN-Kaufrecht* (2005), Article 7, Comment no. 10, at 170.

[5] UNILEX lists courts in Australia, Germany, Belgium, Italy, and the Netherlands. See Unilex database: http://www.unilex.info.

[6] BGH, October 31, 2001, NJW 2002 370.

[7] On the other hand, usages connected with a local commodity exchange or other local institution should be included if foreigners operate at the locality. See Junge in Schlechtriem, *Commentary*, 78, and Austrian Supreme Court's decision of March 21, 2000, reported in Unilex under Article 9.

[8] PECL and DCFR: The parties are bound by a usage that would be considered generally applicable by persons in the same situation as the parties, except where the application of such usage would be unreasonable.

III. Price Term

CISG Article 14(1) provides that "a proposal for concluding a contract addressed to one or more specific persons constitutes an offer if it is sufficiently definite and indicates the intention of the offeror to be bound in case of acceptance. A proposal is sufficiently definite if it indicates the goods and expressly or implicitly fixes or makes provision for determining the quantity and the price."

Article 55 provides "Where a contract has been validly concluded but does not expressly or implicitly fix or make provision for determining the price, the Parties are considered, in the absence of any indication to the contrary, to have impliedly made reference to the price generally charged at the time of the conclusion of the contract for such goods sold under comparable circumstances in the trade concerned."

There is a glaring contradiction between Article 14(1) and Article 55. Article 14 requires the offer and, therefore, the contract, to fix or make provision for determining the price. Article 55 presupposes that a contract can been validly concluded without expressly or implicitly fixing or making a provision for determining the price.

The majority of legal systems[9] do not require the price to be fixed for the conclusion (formation) of a contract. Several systems provide rules similar to Article 55. The commentators of the CISG have attempted to suggest tenable solutions to the unsolvable antinomy.[10]

PECL Article 2(201), DCFR II 4(201), and PICC Article 2(1)(2) do not require the offer to contain a proposal to fix or make provision for determining the price. This provision should be provided in a revised convention.

IV. Revocation of Offer

Article 16(1) provides that until a contract is concluded an offer may be revoked if the revocation reaches the offeree before he or she has dispatched an acceptance. However, under paragraph 2(a), an offer cannot be revoked "if it indicates, whether by stating a fixed time for acceptance or otherwise, that it is irrevocable."

At the Diplomatic Conferee in Vienna, where CISG was adopted, the delegates from the common law countries wanted the setting of a time for acceptance to be only one factor indicating an intent to be bound. For parties in civil law countries, stating a fixed time for acceptance would make the offer irrevocable.[11] Article 16(1)(a), is subject to different interpretations. In common law countries a party who fixes a time for acceptance does not intend his or her offer to be irrevocable. A party from a common law country who offers a sales contract to a party from a country where the stating of a fixed time for acceptance makes the offer irrevocable will risk that his or her offer is considered irrevocable. As provided in Article 8(2), "statements made by and other conduct of a

---

[9] See UCC §2.204, and European laws notes to DCFR II, 4:201, vol. 1, p. 294f., and DCFR II, 9:104, p. 596f.

[10] See Schlechtriem, *Commentary*, 108; Ulrich Schroeter in *Commentary on the UN Convention on the International Sale of Goods (CISG)* (ed. P. Schlechtriem and I. Schwenzer) (Oxford, 2010), 267ff.; and Magnus in Staudinger, *Kommentar*, Article 4, Comments 27–35.

[11] See Magnus in Staudinger, *Kommentar*, Article 16, Comment 11; Schlechtriem, *Commentary*, Article 16, Comments 8–10. In his offer the offeror may of course indicate that the offer is revocable.

party are to be interpreted according to the understanding that a reasonable person of the same kind as the other Party would have had in the same circumstances."

CISG Article 16(2)(a) should be replaced by PECL Article 2: 202(3)(b) and DCFR II -4: 203(3)(b). They provide that an offer is irrevocable if it states a fixed time for its acceptance.

V. Battle of the Forms

CISG does not address the so-called battle of forms, the situation where the parties have reached agreement except that the offer and the acceptance refer to conflicting general conditions. Attempts to introduce a specific rule in the drafting process of the CISG failed.[12] CISG Articles 18(1) and 19(1) state that if the additional terms of the acceptance do not materially change the terms of the offer, the parties will form a binding contract unless the offeror objects without undue delay.[13] If the terms of the purported acceptance materially alter the terms of the offer, there is no contract, unless the offeror by his or her conduct shows that he or she accepts the terms of the counteroffer, for instance by performing the contract. In both cases the terms of the party who answers last, who "fires the last shot," will prevail.[14]

However, experience shows that even if the terms of the answer materially alter the terms of the offer, the parties still wish to have a contract. Therefore, they should be bound from the outset and before the contract has been performed. Furthermore, the "last shot" solution described previously depends on a coincidental factor. The same applies to the "first-shot solution," which seems to be applicable under the UCC §2–207, when the different terms of the answer materially alter the contract, but there still is a contract.[15]

PECL Article 2: 209, DCFR II 4: 209, and PICC Article 2.1.22 provide that a contract is concluded on the basis of the terms that are common in substance unless one party has indicated in advance and not by way of general conditions that he or she will not be bound by a contract that alters his or her terms, or if without delay he or she informs the other party that he or she will not be bound by such contract. This rule should be the commonly enforced option. In most cases, the "stop gap" rules of the law will apply to the issue(s) covered by the conflicting general conditions.[16]

VI. Written Confirmation

If professionals (merchants) have concluded a contract but have not reduced it to writing in a final document, and one sends the other a writing without delay that purports to be a confirmation of the contract but contains additional or different terms, such terms will become part of the contract, unless the terms materially alter the terms of the contract, or the addressee objects to them without delay.

---

[12] See Schlechtriem and Schwenzer, *Commentary*, 79, no. 42.

[13] See id., 346, Article 19, nos. 31–51.

[14] See id., 347ff., 350f., who prefers the "knock-out" rule.

[15] See, e.g., James White and Robert Summers, *Uniform Commercial Code*, vol. 1, 4th ed. (St. Paul, MN, 1995), 13f.; E. Allan Farnsworth, *Farnsworth on Contracts* (Boston, 1990), §3.21.

[16] A revised version of UCC §2–207 was promulgated in 2003. It provided solutions similar to those of PICC and PECL, but the revision has not yet been adopted as law by any state.

That rule is what PECL Article 2: 210 provides for; DFCR II- 4: 210 and PTCC Article 2.1.12 have similar provisions. The rule applies in Austria, Germany, Estonia, Poland, Turkey, Switzerland, Norway, Denmark, Sweden, and Finland.[17] It also applies under UCC §2–207 where an agreement has been reached orally or by informal correspondence and is followed by one of the parties sending a formal memorandum embodying the terms of the contract.[18] Under CISG, it only applies if it is a trade usage at the places of business of both parties,[19] but it should apply as in PECL, DCFR, and PICC.

VII. Specific Performance

CISG Article 46(1), PECL Article 9(102), PICC Article 7(22), and DCFR III 3(302) allow the buyer to require performance by the seller of his or her obligation. However, PECL, DCFR, and PICC do not, as does CISG Article 28, provide "that if in accordance with the provisions of this Convention, one party is entitled to require performance of any obligation by the other party, a court is not bound to enter a judgment for specific performance unless the court would do so under its own law in respect of similar contracts of sale not governed by this Convention."

On the other hand, PICC, PECL, and DCFR do not allow the aggrieved party to claim specific performance of a nonmonetary obligation where:

(a) performance would be unlawful or impossible;
(b) performance would cause the debtor unreasonable effort or expense;
(c) performance consists in the provision of services or work of a personal character or depends upon a personal relationship; or
(d) the aggrieved party may reasonably obtain performance from another source.

With these restrictions on the right to specific performance the difference between this solution and that of the UCC §2–716 are probably not significant.[20]

VIII. Specific Performance and *Force Majeure*

Article 79 is about *force majeure*. Article 79(1) provides that a "party is not liable for a failure to perform any of his obligations if he proves that the failure was due to an

---

[17] For Austria Germany, Estonia, Poland, Turkey, Denmark, Sweden, and Finland, see DCFR Vol. I, 315f.
[18] See the official comment 1 to the UCC §2–207, Farnsworth §3.21 at p 271.
[19] See Zivilgericht Basel, December 21,1992, reported in Unilex on CISG Article 19.
[20] UCC §2–716 (Buyer's Right to Specific Performance or Replevin).

(1) Specific performance may be decreed if the goods are unique or in other proper circumstances. In a contract other than a consumer contract, specific performance may be decreed if the Parties have agreed to that remedy. However, even if the Parties agree to specific performance, specific performance may not be decreed if the breaching Party's sole remaining contractual obligation is the payment of money.
(2) The decree for specific performance may include such terms and conditions as to payment of the price, damages, or other relief as the court may deem just.
(3) The buyer has a right of replevin or similar remedy for goods identified to the contract if after reasonable effort the buyer is unable to effect cover for such goods or the circumstances reasonably indicate that such effort will be unavailing or if the goods have been shipped under reservation and satisfaction of the security interest in them has been made or tendered

White and Summers sides with the law and economics advocates on specific performance who argue for granting specific performance more often than the traditional Anglo-American condition; see White and Summers, *Uniform Commercial Code*, 330f.

impediment beyond his control and that he could not reasonably be expected to have taken the impediment into account at the time of the conclusion of the contract or to have avoided or overcome it or its consequences." PECL Article 8:108, PICC Article 7.1.7, and DCFR III- 3:104 are almost identical with this provision.

Interestingly, Article 79(5) provides that "nothing in the article prevents either party from exercising any right other than to claim damages under this Convention." From this rule, one must conclude that in spite of the impediment, the creditor may claim specific performance. This has rightly been criticized,[21] and PECL, PICC, and DCFR relieve the debtor from his or her duty to perform when the nonperformance is excused; see PECL Article 8: 101, PICC Article 7.2.2(2)(2)(a) and (b), and DCFR III- 3: 301(2).

IX. Hardship

In most Western countries, the principle *pacta sunt servanda* governs. A debtor is obliged to perform his or her obligation even when performance has become more onerous for him or her than before he or she entered the contract. As mentioned earlier, the debtor is only relieved from his or her obligations if his or her failure to perform is due to an impediment beyond his or her control.

On the European Continent, *vis major (force majeure)* ends the contract. There is no room for modification of the terms and no duty for the parties to renegotiate the contract with a view to such modification.

In many business circles, the strict *pacta sunt servanda* rule is considered too severe. This rule applies to contracts of duration such as cooperation agreements, lasting construction contracts, and contracts for continuous supply of goods or services where unforeseen contingencies may make performance very onerous for one party, especially in times of depression or unrest. Hardship clauses are inserted in many contract documents, but often the parties forget or do not find enforcement necessary. It is argued that the party who is then exposed to hardship must bear the consequences. However, the hardship a party then suffers in these cases is often out of proportion to his or her forgetfulness or improvidence. Therefore, a more lenient hardship rule than the *vis major* rule is needed.

In addition to rules on *vis major*, some legal systems have relieved the debtor when performance, though not impossible, has become excessively onerous (Italy[22]) or so different that the economic basis on which the contract was made has disappeared (Germany: *Wegfall der Geschäftsgrundlage*).[23] A similar rule is found in French administrative law,[24] but not in civil and commercial law, and in Dutch,[25] Swiss,[26] Austrian,[27] Polish,[28] Spanish,[29] Portuguese,[30] Estonian,[31] and Greek[32] law.

---

[21] See Schlechtriem, *Commentary*, 623.

[22] Italian Civil Code, Article 1467.

[23] See K. Zweigert and H. Kötz, *Introduction to Comparative Law*, 3rd ed. (Oxford, 1988), 516ff.

[24] See B. Nicolas, *The French Law of Contract*, 2nd ed. (Oxford, 1992), 208.

[25] Civil code of 1992 (NBW), Article 6:258

[26] See Schwenzer, *Commentary*, 1064, note 9.

[27] By way of analogy from Austrian CC, §§936, 1052, and 1170a. See DCFR Vol. I, 217, note 6.

[28] Polish CC, Article 357 (1).

[29] DCFR Vol. 1, 716, no. 4.

[30] Portuguese CC, Article 437.

[31] Estonian Law of Obligations Act of September 26, 2001, §97.

[32] Greek CC, Article 388.

The Nordic rules on the contractual assumptions and §36 of the Nordic Contract Act lead to similar results.[33]

Some countries do not recognize hardship as a ground for relief. In civil cases, the French courts only give relief in case of *force majeure*.[34] The English doctrine of frustration is also "very reluctant to recognize an impediment of performance as a ground for relieving a Party of his obligations as to future performance."[35]

The American UCC §2–615 provides that "delay in delivery or non-delivery . . . by a seller . . . is not a breach of his duty . . . if performance as agreed has been made impracticable by the occurrence of a contingency the non-occurrence of which was a basic assumption on which the contract was made." This language could lead to the assumption that the UCC impracticability test is more lenient to a debtor than the English frustration doctrine; however, the reported cases show that the difference is not significant.[36]

The CISG has no separate provision on hardship. It has been argued that Article 79, dealing with "exemption," stands somewhere between the very tough French rule on *force majeure* governing civil contracts and the more lenient German rule on *Wegfall der Geschäftsgrundlage*.[37]

In addition to the rules on *force majeure*, PECL Article 6: 111, DCFR III- 1: 110, and PICC Chapter 6 section 2 have hardship provisions. PICC Article 6(2)(2) provides a definition:

> There is hardship where the occurrence of events fundamentally alters the equilibrium of the contract either because the cost of a Party's performance has increased or because the value of the performance a Party receives has diminished, and

> (a) the events occur or become known to the disadvantaged Party after the conclusion of the contract;
> (b) the events could not reasonably have been taken into account by the disadvantaged Party at the time of the conclusion of the contract;
> (c) the events are beyond the control of the disadvantaged Party; and
> (d) the risk of the events was not assumed by the disadvantaged Party.

Article 6.2.3 lays down the effects of hardship:

> (1) In case of hardship the disadvantaged Party is entitled to request renegotiations. The request shall be made without undue delay and shall indicate the grounds on which it is based.
> (2) The request for renegotiation does not in itself entitle the disadvantaged Party to withhold performance.

---

[33] On Danish law, see M. Bryde Andersen and J. Lookofsky, *Obligationsret* vol. 1, 3rd ed. (Copenhagen, 2010), 195f.; on Swedish law, see J. Hellner, *Spreciell Avtalsrätt*, vol. 2, 3rd ed. (Stockholm, 1996), 59ff.; on Finnish law, see T. Wilhelmsson, *Standardavtal*, 2nd ed. (Helsinki, 1984), 130f.; on Norwegian law, see V. Hagstrøm, *Obligasionsrett*, 2nd ed. (Oslo, 2011), 300f. and 318f.

[34] On French law, see Zweigert and Kötz, *Introduction to Comparative Law*, chapter 37, and Nicholas, 202ff.

[35] On English law, see Roy Goode, *Commercial Law*, 3rd ed. (London, 2004), 137f., and for a comparative survey of the laws of the EC countries, DCFR Vol. 1 p. 788 (notes to III 3:104).

[36] See the analysis of White and Summers, *Uniform Commercial Code*, 163ff.

[37] See Schlechtriem, *Commentary*, 618, n. 40.

(3) Upon failure to reach agreement within a reasonable time either Party may resort to the court.

(4) If the court finds hardship it may, if reasonable,

    (a) terminate the contract at a date and on terms to be fixed; or

    (b) adapt the contract with a view to restoring its equilibrium.

The hardship rules of PECL, PICC and DCFR differ from the *vis major* rules in the following respects:

1. Performance need "only" be excessively onerous, not impossible. Thus, there was hardship when in the 1920s, a company undertook to deliver water at a fixed price to a hospital for "times ever after," and in the 1980s the agreed price became derisory due to inflation.[38] Courts also found hardship when a gas company undertook to deliver gas in 1908 for a period of 30 years at a fixed price, and the outbreak of the First World War caused a severe shortage of coal, and gas increased its price by four times.[39]

2. The contract is not always terminated, but may be modified either by the parties renegotiating the contract or by the court. The hardship rules of PECL, DCFR, and PICC differ from those of the aforementioned countries in that they introduce a duty for the parties to renegotiate the contract in good faith. The parties may adapt the contract to the new situation, and, if adaption is pointless, terminate the contract. If the parties cannot agree the court may modify the contract or terminate it.

Like the *vis major* rule, the rule on hardship is not mandatory. When making their contract, the parties may agree how to allocate the risks.

X. Assurance of Performance

There is a need to protect a party to a contract who has reasonable grounds to believe that the other party will be unwilling or unable to perform the contract at the due date, but is reluctant to terminate for anticipated nonperformance under CISG Article 72. The other party may after all perform in spite of the doubt. The party in doubt is in a dilemma. To wait until the date of performance may cause him or her heavy losses if the other party does not perform. To terminate for nonperformance may be unjustified and may make him or her liable for nonperformance.

For these reasons, PECL Article 8: 105, PICC Article 7.3.4, and DCFR III-3: 505 give the party who has reason to be concerned about the other party's future performance a right to demand assurance of due performance, and to terminate the contract if that assurance is not given. The rule was inspired by §2–609 of the American UCC. CISG should contain a similar provision.

---

[38] See *Staffordshire Area Health Authority v. South Staffordshire Waterworks Co* [1978] 1 W.L.R. 1387 where the Court of Appeal led by Lord Denning through an "interpretation" of the words "for times ever after," which could not mean what they said, decided to raise the price. The decision has been criticized; see G. Treitel, *Frustration and Force Majeure London* (1995), 6.0.34 ff.

[39] See on the *Gaz de Bordeaux* decision of the French Conseil d'État of March 30, 1916 (Sirey 1916.3.17), and Nicolas, 208, 209. See also Nicolas, "Force Majeure and Frustration," 27 *Am. J. Comp. L.* 231 (1979).

XI. Remoteness of Damages

The rules on the remoteness of damage in CISG Article 74 and in PECL Article 9: 503 and DCFR III-3: 703 are the same in that, as PECL provides, "the non-performing party is liable for loss which it foresaw or could reasonably have foreseen at the time of the conclusion of the contract as a likely result of its non-performance."

However, under PECL and DCFR this rule does not apply when the nonperformance was intentional or grossly negligent. In this scenario, damages may be claimed for losses that were foreseeable at the time of the nonperformance.

XII. Interest

CISG Article 78 provides that if "a Party fails to pay the price or any other sum that is in arrears, the other Party is entitled to interest on it, without prejudice to any claim for damages recoverable under article 74." Article 78 says a party is neither entitled to accrued interest nor the rate of interest. DCFR III-3: 708, which is an improved edition of PECL Article 9: 508, provides:

> If payment of a sum of money is delayed, whether or not the non-performance is excused, the creditor is entitled to interest on that sum from the time when payment is due to the time of payment at the average commercial bank short-term lending rate to prime borrowers prevailing for the contractual currency of payment at the place where payment is due.

PICC Article 7.4.9 is a similar rule.

XIII. Proposal for a Common European Sales Law

In May 2011, a group of experts sponsored by the European Commission presented a Feasibility Study for an Instrument in European Contract Law (FS).[40] The FS focused on sales and services related to sales. The European Commission had used the FS as a tool box when, on October 11, 2011, it submitted a proposal for a Regulation of the European Parliament and the Council on a Common European Sales Law (CESL).[41]

The proposal provides rules that can be used for cross-border transactions for the sale of goods, for the supply of digital content, and for related services, where the parties agree to do so. The CESL makes available rules for business-to-business and business-to-consumer contracts, and covers the formation and the effects of these contracts, precontractual information, defects in consent (mistake, fraud, and coercion), unfair contract terms, and limitation periods.

On most of the aforementioned issues, the rules on business-to-business transactions of CESL follow the soft law instruments PECL, PICC, and the DCFR.[42] Article 2

---

[40] For the feasibility study, see *Towards a European Contract Law* (ed. R. Schulze and J. Stuyck) (Munich, 2011), Annex, 217ff.

[41] Brussels, October 11, 2011, COM(2011) 635 final 2011/0284(COD).

[42] The CESL does not contain the provisions in PECL Article 2(210), PICC Article 2.1.12, and DCFR II-4: 210 on a professional's written confirmation; in PECL Article 8: 105, PICC Article 7.3.4, and DCFR III-3: 305 on assurance of performance; and in PECL Article 9: 503 and DCFR III-4: 703 on the calculation of the foreseeability of the loss when the nonperformance has been intentional and grossly negligent.

establishes an overarching principle of good faith and fair dealing that in Article 3 includes a duty to cooperate. Article 31 does not require the offer to contain any reference to the price. Under Article 32, the stating of a fixed period for its acceptance will make the offer irrevocable. The rules in Article 39 on conflicting standard terms are similar to those found in the soft instruments, and so are the rules in Article 67 on usages and Article 89 on changed circumstance (hardship). Article 110 makes specific performance a right for the buyer, but he or she cannot claim it if performance is impossible or if the burden or expense would be disproportionate to the benefit that the buyer would obtain. Article 168 provides rules on the rate and accrual of interest where a buyer delays the payment of the price due.

However, like the soft laws, the CESL has taken over a great part of the CISG rules. Overall, there is a considerable concordance between the rules of CISG, the soft laws, and CESL. CISG and the soft laws have influenced recent legislation in several countries. In spite of its shortcomings, CISG deserves praise. CISG is the instrument that changed[43] and will continue to change[44] the contract laws of the world.

---

[43] On the Chinese Contract Law of 1999, see Bing Ling, *Contract Law in China* (Hong Kong, 2002), 14f.; on the German "Schuldrechtsreform" of 2001, Hans Schulte-Nölke, "The New German Law of Obligations: An Introduction," available at http://www.iuscomp.org/gla/literature/schulte-noelke.htm; on the Dutch Civil Code of 1992, A.S. Hartkamp in *New Netherlands Civil Code* (ed. P. Haanappel and E. McKaay) (Deventer, 1990), XXV; and on the Nordic Sale of Goods Act 1989–90, Lena Sisula-Tulokas, "European Harmonisation of Civil Law from a Nordic Perspective," 11 *Juridica International* 30–3 (2006). Recent reforms of the law of contracts of several of the former socialist countries of Central Europe have been influenced by CISG and the Soft Laws.

[44] On planned reform of the law of contract in France, see "Ministère de justice. Projet de réforme du droit des contrats (mai 2009)," and on the planned reform of the law of contracts of 18 African states, "The Harmonisation of Contract Law within OHADA," 13 *Uniform Law Review* 1–2 (2008).

44 Using the CISG Proactively

Helena Haapio

I. Introduction

The users of the CISG can be divided into two major groups: the legal community and the international business community. The former includes legal practitioners and scholars, law teachers, judges, and arbitrators. So far, the focus of CISG scholarship has been predominantly on the needs of the legal community.

This chapter focuses on the needs of the business community: the sellers and buyers whose contracts, rights, and obligations are impacted by the CISG. In recent years, a growing number of scholars and practitioners in Europe have called for a paradigm shift. This shift is most broadly labeled as the proactive law approach. This approach has two dimensions, both of which emphasize *ex ante*, forward-looking action: (1) a *preventive* dimension, seeking to prevent problems and disputes; and (2) a *promotive* dimension, seeking to secure the respective actors' successes in reaching their goals.

The CISG seeks to remove legal barriers in and promote the development of international trade. These sound like practical, trader-friendly, forward-looking goals. However, much of the discussion about the CISG is about applying it in court – reactively, *ex post*, after a dispute has arisen. For traders and their advisors, however, a different perspective is called for; one where the focus is on ways in which the CISG can be used proactively, *ex ante*, before a dispute arises and even before the consummation of a contract. In negotiating a contract, the goal is to navigate the business and legal landscape so that the parties reach a mutually satisfactory deal and lay the foundation for a strong supplier–buyer relationship.

International traders' primary concern is the predictability of their business transactions. They are less concerned about the predictability of a future legal dispute. For many traders, it is difficult to see the symbiotic connection between business and law, or between sales and sales law. Most contracts focus on failures and disputes and how to manage them when they happen, as if they are inevitable. Case law is formed based on failed contracts. Not much is said about success and prosperity. Businesspersons allocate to their lawyers the task of dealing in the contract with the problems that they do not want the future to bring.

Suppliers and buyers do not want to go to court or arbitration. They expect the law to give them a sound foundation on which they can build their strategies, business plans, deals, and relationships. Yet they mostly are unaware of the CISG and its ability to be used strategically to advance their interests. CISG-related information, knowledge, and skills could be used more extensively and beneficially. This is where the proactive approach can play a role.

Part II of this chapter introduces the proactive law approach. Part III discusses how it can be applied to the CISG and cross-border contracting and highlights the need to increase the trading community's awareness of and interest in the CISG. Part IV proposes an action plan that encourages the legal community to use the existing CISG case law and other resources to recognize the root causes of legal disputes in order to prevent their occurrence. Part V proposes the use of *visualization* – adding matrices, tables, or graphics to supplement text – to assist in the understanding of legal information in order to use law proactively. The chapter concludes by calling on practitioners and scholars to join in a visualization project, making the CISG work, with the goal of turning the core content of the CISG and related resources into a trader-friendly, visual format, so as to enhance communication and collaboration across borders, cultures, and disciplines.

II. Proactive Law Approach

Traditionally, the steps in providing legal care have resembled those of medical care: diagnosis, treatment, and referral – all steps that happen after a client or a patient has already incurred a problem. In the practice of medicine, the emphasis is increasingly on preventing illnesses before they occur. Even in other professions, such as quality management, prevention is assumed to be more effective than corrective action.

The idea of prevention in the practice of law – or legal foresight – is not new. The proactive approach to law has its origins in preventive law, an approach that emerged in the United States in the 1950s. Professor Louis M. Brown first introduced the concept of preventive law.[1] One of Louis Brown's fundamental premises was that in curative law, it is essential for the lawyer to predict what a *court* will do, while in preventive law, it is essential to predict what *people* will do.[2] He summarized his legal philosophy as follows: "The time to see an attorney is when you're legally healthy – certainly before the advent of litigation, and prior to the time legal trouble occurs." In his treatise *Preventive Law*, published in 1950, he notes a simple but profound truth: "It usually costs less to avoid getting into trouble than to pay for getting out of trouble."[3] His legacy is carried on through the National Center for Preventive Law[4] at the California Western School of Law in San Diego.

---

[1] Edward A. Dauer, "The Role of Culture in Legal Risk Management," in *A Proactive Approach*, Scandinavian Studies in Law, vol. 49 (ed. P. Wahlgren) (Stockholm: Stockholm Institute for Scandinavian Law, 2006), 93, 93–4, available at http://www.scandinavianlaw.se/pdf/49-6.pdf.

[2] Id. See, generally, Louis M. Brown, *Lawyering through Life: The Origin of Preventive Law* (Littleton, CO: Fred B. Rothman & Co., 1986); Louis M. Brown and Edward A. Dauer, *Planning by Lawyers: Materials on Nonadversarial Legal Process* (Mineola, NY: Foundation Press, 1978); Louis M. Brown, *Preventive Law* (New York: Prentice-Hall, 1950).

[3] Brown, *Preventive Law*, 3.

[4] National Center for Preventive Law, California Western School of Law, http://www.preventivelawyer.org. See also Thomas D. Barton, *Preventive Law and Problem Solving: Lawyering for the Future* (Lake Mary, FL: Vandeplas Publishing, 2009) (new emphasis on legal problem solving, the environment in which problems arise, and the need for lawyers to think both preventively and proactively).

A. *Proactive Law Movement*

Over the past decade, the proactive law movement has gained momentum in Europe. The Nordic School of Proactive Law defines proactive law as:

> A future-oriented approach to law placing an emphasis on legal knowledge to be applied before things go wrong. It comprises a way of legal thinking and a set of skills, practices and procedures that help to identify opportunities in time to take advantage of them – and to spot potential problems while preventive action is still possible. In addition to avoiding disputes, litigation and other hazards, Proactive Law seeks ways to use the law to create value, strengthen relationships and manage risk.[5]

The approach specifically called "proactive law" emerged in the late 1990s. The pioneers were a group of Finnish scholars, practitioners, and quality-driven business clients. The first applications, tools, and training were developed for quality and project managers who wanted to merge quality and risk management principles with forward-looking legal skills to improve the contracting processes in cross-border dealings. Proactive law was thus first applied in proactive contracting in a context where the CISG and contractual risk management plays a major part. The focus of the early development work in contracting was more on business and on quality than on legal issues, and more on practical tools and applications than on theoretical foundations.

Eventually, this led to a series of publications[6] and the first proactive law conference, held in Helsinki, Finland, in 2003.[7] This and other conferences eventually led to the formation of the Nordic School of Proactive Law,[8] a network of researchers and practitioners from Denmark, Finland, Iceland, Norway, and Sweden. The Nordic School has been instrumental in the creation of the ProActive ThinkTank, whose mission is to provide a forum for business leaders, lawyers, academics, and other professionals to discuss, develop, and promote the proactive management of relationships, contracts, and risks, and the prevention of legal uncertainties and disputes.[9] The Nordic School's conferences have led to the publication of four English language books, *A Proactive Approach*,[10] *Corporate Contracting Capabilities*,[11] *A Proactive Approach to Contracting*

---

[5] Nordic School of Proactive Law home page, available at http://www.proactivelaw.org (site is maintained under the leadership of Professor Cecilia Magnusson Sjöberg. University of Stockholm).

[6] See Helena Haapio, "Quality Improvement through Pro-Active Contracting: Contracts Are Too Important to Be Left to Lawyers!," 52 *Proceedings of the Annual Quality Congress* 243 (1998), abstract available at http://www.asq.org/qic/display-item/index.html?item=10690&item=10690. The graphical notes ("visualizations") are on file with the author. See also Helena Haapio, "Preventive Lawyering in International Sales: Using Contract Reviews to Integrate Preventive Law, Risk Management, and Quality," *Preventive Law Reporter* 16 (Winter 1997/8) (a later version of the paper).

[7] Proactive Law Conference in Helsinki in 2003 entitled "Future Law, Lawyering, and Language. Helping People and Business Succeed." Visualizations from the conference are available at http://www.lexpert.com/en/documents/ProactiveLawConference2003-VisualNotesbyAnnikaVarjonen.pdf.

[8] Nordic School of Proactive Law Web site.

[9] ProActive ThinkTank Mission Statement, available at http://www.juridicum.su.se/proactivelaw/main/thinktank/missionstatement.pdf.

[10] Wahlgren, *A Proactive Approach*.

[11] *Corporate Contracting Capabilities, Conference Proceeding and Other Writings* (ed. S. Nystén-Haarala) (Joensuu: University of Joensuu, 2008).

and Law,[12] and *Proactive Law in a Business Environment*.[13] Other books and research publications are available in Finnish or Swedish.[14]

Since the first publications, a number of research and development projects have emerged. Examples include Corporate Contracting Capabilities (CCC),[15] Proactive Contracting Processes in Public Procurement – Promoters for Partnership and Co-innovation (PRO2ACT),[16] and ProActive Management – ProActive Business Law (PAM PAL)[17] (a curriculum development project funded by the EU Commission). More recently, collaborations are ongoing between participants in the Nordic School, the ThinkTank, and legal scholars in the United States. These undertakings have explored the use of the law for competitive advantage and the interaction between law and strategy.[18] Figure 44.1 shows some of the major milestones in the trajectory of the proactive movement.

Through the aforementioned research, the meaning of proactive law has been refined and clarified. Proactive law has two dimensions, both of which emphasize an *ex ante*, forward-looking perspective: (1) a *preventive* dimension and (2) a *promotive* dimension. Using the analogy of health care, the proactive approach to law can be said to combine aspects of disease prevention with those of health promotion. The goal is to help clients, both individuals and businesses, stay in good legal health and avoid legal uncertainties, disputes, and litigation. The promotive dimension of proactive law has a positive and constructive emphasis: The goal "is to embed legal knowledge and skills in clients' strategy

---

[12] A *Proactive Approach to Contracting and Law* (ed. H. Haapio) (Turku: International Association for Contract and Commercial Management and Turku University of Applied Sciences, 2008).

[13] *Proactive Law in a Business Environment* (ed. G. Berger-Walliser and K. Østergaard) (Copenhagen: DJOF Publishing, 2012).

[14] See, e.g., *Ennakoiva sopiminen: Liiketoimien suunnittelu, toteuttaminen ja riskien hallinta* (ed. S. Pohjonen) (Helsinki: WSOY Lakitieto, 2002) (Proactive Contracting: Planning, Implementing and Managing Risk in Business Transactions); *Ex ante: Ennakoiva oikeus* (ed. S. Pohjonen) (Helsinki: Talentum Media Oy, 2005) (Ex ante: Proactive Law); Kaisa Sorsa, "Kansainvälisen kaupan arvoketjujen sääntely. Yhteiskuntavastuun ja ennakoivan oikeuden tarkastelua," Ph.D. dissertation, Annales Universitatis Turkuensis C 320, Faculty of Law, University of Turku, 2011), available at http://urn.fi/URN:ISBN:978-951-29-4777-5 (Regulation of Global Value Chains: Examining Corporate Social Responsibility and Proactive Law); Antti Tieva, "Pitkäkestoisuus kiinteistö- ja rakennusalan sopimussuhteissa," Ph.D. dissertation, Publication TKK-R-VK6, Aalto University School of Science and Technology, Department of Structural Engineering and Building Technology, Espoo, 2010, available at http://lib.tkk.fi/Diss/2010/isbn9789526033860/isbn9789526033860.pdf (Long-Term Contractual Relationships in the Field of Construction and Real Estate); Laura Kalliomaa-Puha, "Vanhoille ja sairaille sopivaa?: Omaishoitosopimus hoivan instrumenttina," Ph.D. dissertation, Faculty of Law, University of Helsinki, 2007, available at http://urn.fi/URN:ISBN:978–951–669–753–9 (Suitable for the Old and Sick? Informal Care Agreements as an Instrument for Organizing Care).

[15] See Corporate Contracting Capabilities (CCC), University of Eastern Finland, http://www.uef.fi/oikeustieteet/ccc.

[16] See PRO2ACT, Aalto University, SimLab, http://simlab.aalto.fi/en/research/pro2act/.

[17] See ProActive Management and ProActive Business Law – Lifelong Learning Programme Curriculum Development Project, Turku University of Applied Sciences.

[18] E.g., George Siedel and Helena Haapio, *Proactive Law for Managers: A Hidden Source of Competitive Advantage* (Farnham: Gower Publishing, 2011); George J. Siedel and Helena Haapio, "Using Proactive Law for Competitive Advantage," 17 *American Business Law Journal* 641 (2010); Larry DiMatteo, George Siedel, and Helena Haapio, "Strategic Contracting: Examining the Business-Legal Interface," in Berger-Walliser and Østergaard, *Proactive Law in a Business Environment*, 59.

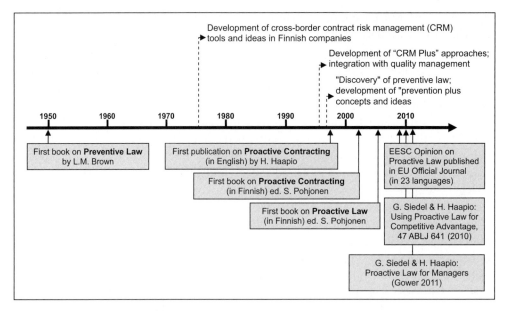

Figure 44.1. The Trajectory of the Proactive Movement.

and everyday actions to actively promote business success, ensure desired outcomes, and balance risk with reward."[19]

Louis Brown's work on preventive law was targeted toward lawyers. While influenced by his work, participants in the Nordic School and the ThinkTank have taken his work one step further by emphasizing the importance of collaboration between legal and other professionals. Soile Pohjonen, Docent at the University of Helsinki, states that: "[Preventive Law] favours the lawyer's viewpoint, i.e., the prevention of legal risks and problems. In Proactive Law, the emphasis is on achieving the desired goal in particular circumstances where legal expertise works in collaboration with the other types of expertise involved. In Proactive Law, the need for dialogue between different understandings is emphasized."[20]

B. *Opinion of the European Economic and Social Committee on Proactive Law*

The original focus of proactive law was private lawmaking, namely, contracting in the business-to-business context. Yet the proactive approach soon expanded beyond this. The Opinion of the European Economic and Social Committee (EESC)[21] explores the ways in which the proactive law approach can be applied to public lawmaking and, at the same time, serve as a means of avoiding overly detailed and unnecessary regulation.[22]

---

[19] Helena Haapio, "Introduction to Proactive Law: A Business Lawyer's View," in Wahlgren, A *Proactive Approach*, 24, available at http://www.scandinavianlaw.se/pdf/49-2.pdf.

[20] Soile Pohjonen, "Proactive Law in the Field of Law," in id., 53, 54, available at http://www.scandinavianlaw.se/pdf/49-4.pdf. See also Soile Pohjonen, "Law and Business: Successful Business Contracting, Corporate Social Responsibility and Legal Thinking," 3–4 *Tidskrift Utgiven Av Juridiska Föreningen I Finland* (*JFT*) 470, 477 (2009), available at http://www.helsinki.fi/oikeustiede/omasivu/pohjonen/Law%20and%20Business.pdf.

[21] See the European Economic and Social Committee Web site, available at http://www.eesc.europa.eu.

[22] The European Commission, the European Parliament, and the EESC have long promoted and argued for *better regulation*, *simplification*, and *communication* as main policy objectives. See also European

At its plenary session on December 3, 2008, the EESC adopted its opinion on "the proactive law approach: a further step towards better regulation at EU level."[23] In the opinion, the EESC makes reference to the work of the Nordic School of Proactive Law[24] and urges a paradigm shift in EU law making, stating:

> The time has come to give up the centuries-old reactive approach to law and to adopt a *proactive approach*. It is time to look at law in a different way: to look *forward* rather than back, to focus on *how the law is used and operates* in everyday life and how it is received in the community it seeks to regulate. While responding to and resolving problems remain important, preventing causes of problems is vital, along with serving the needs and facilitating the productive interaction of citizens and businesses.[25]

The opinion recognizes the benefits of the proactive law principle of using law as a tool to reach desired objectives, rather than focusing on legal rules and their enforcement alone. It states that "[t]o set the desired goals and to secure the most appropriate mix of means to achieve them requires involving stakeholders early, aligning objectives, creating a shared vision, and building support and guidance for successful implementation from early on."[26] This EESC approach holds true in corporate strategy and public law making. The EESC opinion further states:

> When drafting laws, the legislator should be concerned about producing operationally efficient rules that reflect real-life needs and are implemented in such a manner that the ultimate objectives of those rules are accomplished.

> The life cycle of a piece of legislation does not begin with the drafting of a proposal or end when it has been formally adopted. A piece of legislation is not the goal; its successful implementation is. Nor does implementation just mean enforcement by institutions; it also means adoption, acceptance and, where necessary, a change of behaviour on the part of the intended individuals and organisations.[27]

The EESC opinion recommends that the Commission, the Council and the European Parliament adopt the proactive law approach when planning, drawing up, revising, and implementing EU law and encourages member states also to do so wherever appropriate.[28] It asserts that the proactive law approach should be considered systematically in all lawmaking and law implementation within the EU: "The EESC strongly

---

Economic and Social Committee, Foreword of Pegado Liz, Chairman of the Single Market Observatory, available at http://www.eesc.europa.eu/?i=portal.en.self-and-co-regulation-foreword.

[23] See Opinion of the European Economic and Social Committee on "The Proactive Law Approach: A Further Step Towards Better Regulation at EU level," Official Journal of the European Union 2009/C175/05, available at http://eur-lex.europa.eu/LexUriServ/LexUriServ.do?uri=OJ:C:2009:175:0026:0033:EN:PDF (hereafter referred to as EESC Opinion). In addition to the English-language version, the EESC Opinion is also available in all other official EU languages: 23 languages altogether. The Section for the Single Market, Production and Consumption, under the leadership of Jorge Pegado Liz, was responsible for preparing EESC's work on the topic, and the author of this chapter, Helena Haapio, acted as expert in this work.

[24] Id., §§3.8 and 5.2.

[25] Id., §1.4.

[26] Id., §1.6.

[27] Id., §§2.4–2.5.

[28] Id., §2.8. See also "The proactive law approach: a novelty – For too long, the emphasis in the legal field has been on the past . . . ," Press Release CES/08/115 (December 16, 2008), European Economic and Social Committee, available at http://europa.eu/rapid/press-release_CES-08-115_en.htm.

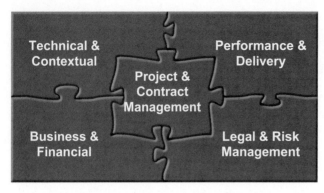

Figure 44.2. The Contract Puzzle. (See Haapio, "Innovative Contracting," 124; and Siedel and Haapio, "Using Proactive Law for Competitive Advantage," 122.)

believes that by making this approach not only part of the Better Regulation agenda, and but also a priority for legislators and administrators at the EU, national and regional levels, it would be possible to build a strong legal foundation for individuals and businesses to prosper."[29]

III. Proactive Approach: Application

The proactive approach seeks to secure the respective actors' success in reaching their goals. This part focuses on the goals of businesses, the sellers and buyers whose contract rights and obligations are impacted by the CISG. In contracts, sellers and buyers primarily want the expected performance. Sellers and buyers also want to maintain their reputation and good relationships. Securing success comes first, and preparing for failure and disputes – typical lawyers' concerns – is a secondary priority.

Instead of looking at the CISG in dispute resolution, the proactive approach looks at ways in which the CISG can be used proactively in planning and designing cross-border deals and documents. Contract law scholars often focus on issues relating to contract validity, enforceability of terms, and remedies. The proactive approach views contracts as managerial tools as well as legal tools. The goals for the contracting parties are to reach their business goals and minimize the chance of a dispute. However, to achieve these goals requires knowledgeable users of the tools that law can provide.

From a proactive point of view, Article 6, right to derogate, is the most important article of the CISG. It allows sellers and buyers to use the CISG in the way that best suits their purposes. The parties are able to tailor CISG rules to their specific needs.

A. *The Contract Puzzle: It Takes a Team!*

Today's commercial contracts can be viewed through the analogy of a jigsaw puzzle. With a complex equipment delivery project in mind, Figure 44.2 shows a contract as a puzzle of technical and contextual, performance and delivery, business and financial, and legal and risk management related parts, with project and contract management

---

[29] EESC Opinion, §1.10.

as the centerpiece. If correctly assembled, the pieces of the puzzle form a complete, synchronized picture.[30]

International sales contracts are seldom planned or crafted by one person. Teams at the seller and buyer companies produce them. In many fields, what really matters in contracts are the business and financial terms, and the input of managers and engineers is often crucial in order to construct operationally efficient contracts.[31] A wide range of people, functions, and technologies participate in the preparation of a contract. A successful contract requires communication between numerous stakeholders, often with only fragmented understanding of the issues involved.[32]

A typical corporate contracting process can be divided into three phases: (1) planning, solicitation, and bidding (precontract; preaward); (2) negotiation and execution of the contract; and (3) implementation (postcontract; postaward). For buyers and suppliers alike, the first phase is vital in creating the basis for successful contracts and relationships. Most contract information should be captured in the initial phase. At the early stages, the technical, implementation, business/financial, and legal aspects must be consistent and linked with each other.[33]

When used proactively as managerial-legal tools, contracts are planned and designed to communicate crucial information inside and between organizations; to help share, minimize, and manage cost and risk; and, in case of a dispute, to work as a record of what has been agreed and provide a means to resolve the dispute in a prompt and amicable way. Further, when used preventively, contracts communicate the deal and its terms clearly so as to avoid future disputes over meaning.[34] Good contracts provide a clear framework for successful implementation. For the parties, the contract is not the goal; successful implementation is.[35]

After negotiating and signing the contract, a divergence often occurs between the precontract sales or procurement process and postcontract implementation and management. One reason for this is that people are reluctant to read contracts.[36] Few managers

---

[30] Helena Haapio, "Innovative Contracting," in Haapio, *A Proactive Approach to Contracting and Law*, 105, 124; Siedel and Haapio, *Proactive Law for Managers*, 121–3.

[31] According to an analysis of the International Association for Contract and Commercial Management (IACCM), on average nearly 80% of the terms in business-to-business contracts are not really areas of significant legal concern – they are the business and financial terms, which include key documents such as Statements of Work, Specifications and Service Level Agreements. See IACCM, *Contracting as a Strategic Competence* (Ridgefield, CT: International Association for Contract and Commercial Management, 2003), 4, available at http://www.iaccm.com/members/library/files/contracting.pdf. See also Nicholas Argyres and Kyle J. Mayer, "Contract Design as a Firm Capability: An Integration of Learning and Transaction Cost Perspectives," 32 *Academy of Management Rev.* 1060 (2007).

[32] Martin J. Eppler, "Knowledge Communication Problems between Experts and Managers: An Analysis of Knowledge Transfer in Decision Processes," paper 1/2004, University of Lugano, Faculty of Communication Sciences, Institute for Corporate Communication, May 2004, p. 6, available at http://doc.rero.ch/lm.php?url=1000,42,6,20051020101029-UL/1_wpca0401.pdf.

[33] Haapio, "Innovative Contracting," with references.

[34] Id., at 111.

[35] Danny Ertel, "Getting Past Yes: Negotiating as if Implementation Mattered," *Harvard Business Rev.* (November 2004); and Danny Ertel and Mark Gordon, *The Point of the Deal: How to Negotiate When Yes Is Not Enough* (Boston: Harvard Business School Press, 2007).

[36] Scott. J. Burnham, "How to Read a Contract," 45 *Arizona L. Rev.* 133, 133 (2003). See also Thomas D. Barton, "Collaborative Contracting as Preventive/Proactive Law," in Berger-Walliser and Østergaard, *Proactive Law in a Business Environment*, 107 (the parties may have been trained to regard contracts "as

have formal training in *how* to read contracts or *why* they should do so.[37] Yet many people are expected to read contracts and work with them. The buyer's solicitation team and the supplier's proposal team may consist of people different from those on the contract negotiation team, none of whom may be part of the operational or delivery team. The teams just "inherit" from their predecessors the contract documents that they are expected to master and work with.

Because of the fragmented process noted earlier, delivering on the promises made in a contract may prove difficult. On the seller's side, the operational team needs to implement the supply contract, as well as pass on to subcontractors the pertinent terms of that contract. The implementation of contracts is more complicated when dealing under global umbrella or framework agreements made between group parent companies designed to be implemented in several countries with different requirements.

B. *Invisible Terms and the CISG*

Contracts and the CISG define key requirements related to the contracting parties' roles, the quality of the goods to be delivered, and many other terms that have both technical and commercial implications. They require knowledge about resources, timing, cost, and so on *before* determining the price and *before* a well-written contract can be made. If the contract is expected to work as a roadmap for the parties to follow, people involved in planning, designing, and implementing the contract need to align many – often conflicting – expectations and master a wealth of knowledge. This necessitates a fresh look at contracts and the CISG and how they interact.

Courts, arbitrators, and lawyers are not the primary readers and users of contracts. Management and operational personnel are. They use the information contained in contracts to coordinate in-house and outsourced functions and manage budget, scope, schedule, resources, and so on. Problems are often encountered not because of what the contract *says*, but because of what it *does not say* – gaps in contracts have been the basis for numerous contract disputes.[38] The concept *invisible terms*[39] has been used to refer to terms (such as implied terms, implied warranties, and statutory default rules) that do not appear in the contract but become part of it, unless they are expressly excluded or amended. A lawyer familiar with the context knows and "sees" the invisible terms, while a nonlawyer does not.

The express terms of a contract – the *visible terms* – can get quite complicated, especially in international business transactions. Sometimes the CISG becomes part of the contract, without the parties being aware of that fact or of the content of the CISG.

---

the domain of the law and lawyers, where precision of legal language and full articulation of rights and duties is deemed essential").

[37] Id.; and Gerlinde Berger-Walliser, Robert C. Bird, and Helena Haapio, "Promoting Business Success through Contract Visualisation," 17 *J. of Law, Business & Ethics* 55 (2011), available at http://ssrn.com/abstract=1744096.

[38] Helena Haapio, "Business Success and Problem Prevention through Proactive Contracting," in Wahlgren, *A Proactive Approach*, 149, 162, see esp. figure 5, "Contract – Mind the Gaps!," available at http://www.scandinavianlaw.se/pdf/49-9.pdf.

[39] See, e.g., Helena Haapio, "Invisible Terms in International Contracts and What to Do about Them," *Contract Management* (July 2004), 32 (National Contract Management Association [NCMA]), available at http://www.ncmahq.org/files/Articles/81EEB_cm_July04_32.pdf; and Helena Haapio, "Invisible Terms and Creative Silence: What You Don't See Can Help or Hurt You," *Contract Management* (September 2009), 24 (NCMA), available at http://www.ncmahq.org/files/Articles/CM0909%20-%2024-35.pdf.

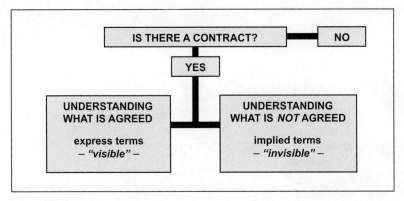

Figure 44.3. Contractual Literacy. (Adapted from Haapio, "Business Success and Problem Prevention," 170.)

Trade usage and practice may become part of the contract as well. The invisible terms may bring along requirements, liabilities, and remedies that the parties did not know existed.[40] Contractual literacy is a precondition for success in cross-border commerce. It requires an understanding of both the visible terms and the invisible terms, as illustrated by Figure 44.3.

Some contract drafters "use silence creatively," relying on the default rules of the applicable law. For example, when working for the buyer side, they may find no need to deviate from some buyer-friendly default provisions. If the supplier is not aware of these provisions, negative surprises can follow. This is not desirable for long-term business relationships, which should be built on a sound contractual foundation where both parties know the applicable requirements, rights, responsibilities, and remedies. Yet for many traders, the requirements of the CISG remain invisible – until a problem arises.

C. Improving CISG Awareness

To bridge the business–legal community divide, the prevailing reactive, litigation-focused view must change. A strategy paper by the UK Lord Chancellor's Department notes:

> Our current view of the civil justice system is litigation and court based. We believe that we should want much more than an effective court system in the future. We should want an integrated civil justice system wherein the courts are a forum of last resort.[41]

> [W]e should surely be concerned if citizens (or organisations) are not sufficiently informed to be able to know when the law might apply to them, to find out more about their legal position should they so wish, to avoid disputes where possible or resolve them using the most appropriate techniques.[42]

---

[40] Haapio, "Business Success and Problem Prevention," 171. See also Helena Haapio, "A Visual Approach to Commercial Contracts," in *Europäische Projektkultur als Beitrag zur Rationalisierung des Rechts. Tagungsband des 14. Internationalen Rechtsinformatik Symposions IRIS 2011* (ed. E. Schweighofer and F. Kummer) (Vienna: OCG Books, 2011), 559. Also published in Jusletter IT (February 24, 2011), available at http://jusletter-it.weblaw.ch/en/issues/2011/106/article_312.html.

[41] "Civil.justice.2000: A Vision of the Civil Justice System in the Information Age," Strategy Paper issued by the Lord Chancellor's Department (London, June 2000), 4, Section 1.3, available at http://www.dca.gov.uk/cj2000/cj2000fr.htm.

[42] Id., 9, Section 2.10.

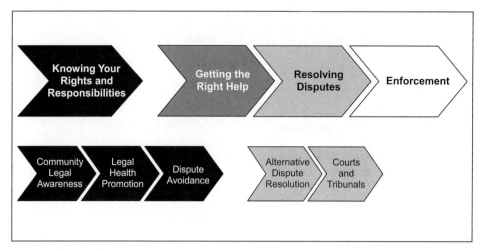

Figure 44.4. An Integrated Civil Justice System. (Adapted from Haapio, "Business Success and Problem Prevention," 4.)

When it comes to the CISG, traders are largely unaware of their legal rights and responsibilities. Knowledge of the CISG would allow them to use the CISG proactively to reach their business objectives and prevent unnecessary disputes. A vision of a CISG-aware international trading community is illustrated, using the Lord Chancellor's vision of a future civil justice system, in Figure 44.4.

IV. Action Plan: Learning from Experience

Lawyers working with international business transactions can easily list examples of contract language and terms that are often misused or misunderstood. Sharing such experience would reduce the rate of contract disputes. However, for the purposes of this chapter, more systematic ways of enabling organizational learning and knowledge sharing are needed.

A. *Learning from Case Law*

One of the methods to learn from experience, considered good practice, is to conduct a postmortem review at the end of each project. This is useful for organizational learning and knowledge sharing. If organizations do not learn from experience, how can they become better? Methods for conducting postmortems can be found in literature related to fields such as software engineering, quality engineering, risk management, and project management. Yet, in the legal field, such practices are rarely applied.

One of the early exceptions was, again, Louis M. Brown, the "father of preventive law." As early as 1955, he introduced a methodology called legal autopsy as a way to learn from past mistakes.[43] According to Brown, "the law is the only profession which records its mistakes carefully, exactly as they occurred, and yet does not identify them as mistakes."[44]

---

[43] Louis M. Brown, "Legal Autopsy," 39 *J. of the American Judicature Society* 47 (1955).
[44] Id., at 47, citing Elliott Dunlap Smith.

In his autobiography *Lawyering through Life*, Brown discusses the legal "dead body," a decided case, and how we can open it up by historical research of both sides of the dispute, so as to recreate the whole story from the earliest beginnings of the relations of the parties to the dispute.[45] "Litigation," said Louis M. Brown, is "often a symptom of legal trouble. Litigation often treats symptoms rather than underlying causes. At least, if this observation is worth testing, autopsy is the method for doing so."[46] Brown then illustrates some of the legal autopsies he and his students performed, along with their findings, and the obstacles they met on the way. Unfortunately, the American Bar Foundation and the National Science Foundation denied funding for his research. One explanation was the general lack of interest in research outside the books. Brown noted that: "It is much easier to find the law on the printed page that the law in action."[47]

Professor George J. Siedel of the University of Michigan was an early promoter of learning from case law in various contexts. In his book *Using the Law for Competitive Advantage* he presented a four-step Manager's Legal Plan™, where step three asks managers to develop business strategies and solutions to prevent legal problems, and step four is to reframe legal concerns as business concerns.[48]

The time has come to reinvent the autopsy methodology, adopt the Manager's Legal Plan, and develop them into a managerial/legal learning venture in order to avoid repeating the same disputes and to ensure the success of future deals and relationships. Another possible stream of research is offered by analyzing the deals that went right. Was it by mere luck, or by design? What were the drivers of success and what can lawyers and business managers do to strengthen those drivers?

B. *Learning from Top Negotiated Terms and Frequent Sources of Disputes*

The Internet and surveys conducted by the International Association for Contract and Commercial Management (IACCM) have revealed information relating to contract terms that was previously not accessible. In the surveys conducted by the IACCM, participants throughout the world have been asked to highlight the terms they negotiate with the greatest frequency. Although the responses cover contract negotiations generally and not just the sale of goods, the results offer valuable insights. One of the key findings of these surveys is that, year after year, two clauses have been found to be the most negotiated terms – limitation of liability and indemnification clauses.

The results of IACCM's 10th Annual Survey, "2011 Top Terms in Negotiation," are shown on the left column of Table 44.1.[49] The list of "Top Terms of Today" has been and

[45] Brown, *Lawyering through Life*, 196–203. The methodology is close to what has been more recently called legal archaeology. See, e.g., Deborah L. Threedy, "Legal Archaeology:Excavating Cases, Reconstructing Context," 80 *Tulane L. Rev.* 1197 (2006).
[46] Brown, *Lawyering through Life*, 203.
[47] Id., at 202.
[48] George J. Siedel, *Using the Law for Competitive Advantage* (San Francisco: Jossey-Bass, 2002). See also Siedel and Haapio, "Using Proactive Law for Competitive Advantage."
[49] International Association for Contract and Commercial Management (IACCM), "2011 Top Terms in Negotiation" (2011), 6, available at https://www.iaccm.com/members/library/files/top_terms_2011_1.pdf. This study of 1,123 organizations, representing more than 8,000 negotiators, was undertaken between December 2010 and April 2011 (sample included persons in the areas of procurement, legal, and sales contracting in more than 60 countries). Input typically represents large international corporations and, therefore, may not be an accurate reflection of negotiations at a local level or between smaller organizations.

Table 44.1. *IACCM 2011 Top Terms in Negotiation*

	Top Terms of Today: The terms that are negotiated with greatest frequency	Top Terms of the Future: Terms that would be more productive in supporting successful relationships
1	Limitation of liability	Change management
2	Indemnification	Scope and goals
3	Price/charge/price changes	Responsibilities of the parties
4	Intellectual property	Communications and reporting
5	Payment	Performance/guarantees/undertakings
6	Liquidated damages	Limitation of liability
7	Performance/guarantees/undertakings	Delivery/acceptance
8	Delivery/acceptance	Dispute resolution
9	Applicable law/jurisdiction	Service levels and warranties
10	Confidential information/nondisclosure	Price/charge/price changes
11	Service levels and warranties	Audits/benchmarking
12	Warranty	Indemnification
13	Insurance	Intellectual property
14	Service withdrawal or termination	Payment
15	Data protection/security	Information access and management
16	Scope and goals	Business continuity/disaster recovery
17	Responsibilities of the parties	Applicable law/jurisdiction
18	Change management	Confidential information/nondisclosure
19	Invoices/late payment	Warranty
20	Audits/benchmarking	Assignment/transfer

continues to be dominated by clauses dealing with the *consequences* of failure, claims, and disputes, rather than their *causes*. It is clearly not what the negotiators would *want* to spend their time on. In its recent surveys, IACCM has asked participants to describe not only what they spend most time negotiating today, but also where they think negotiating time should be focused in the future. The "Top Ten Terms of the Future" listed in the right column of Table 44.1 indicate that negotiators see a need to change their current negotiating agenda. They see more value in negotiating terms related to change management, scope and goals, and the parties' responsibilities than terms such as liability limitations and indemnities. The latter terms are terms of last resort in the event that the expectations of the parties become derailed.[50]

The IACCM survey conducted in 2011 also asked about the most frequent causes of contract disputes that occur during contract performance. Table 44.2 shows a summary of the core results.[51] The results show that delivery and acceptance issues constitute the most frequent source of disputes. Although empirical research is needed to confirm this, experience tells us that this is also the case in the sale and purchase of goods, especially in the sale of complex equipment. This is often due to confusion around requirements, either because of the ambiguity of contract terms or failed change management procedures. Although requirement management, change management, and acceptance criteria have been researched in other fields, they have attracted much less attention among legal scholars.

[50] IACCM, "The Top Negotiated Terms: Negotiators Admit They Are on Wrong Agenda, Contracting Excellence" (July 2009), available at http://www.iaccm.com/news/contractingexcellence/?storyid=923.
[51] "2011 Top Terms in Negotiation," 8.

Table 44.2. *Most Frequent Sources of Claim and Disputes*

	During the post-award phase of contract performance, which terms are the most frequent source of a claim or dispute?	
1	Delivery/acceptance	41%
2	Price/charge/price changes	38%
3	Change management	32%
4	Invoices/late payment	30%
5	Performance/guarantees/undertakings	27%
6	Service levels and warranties	27%
7	Payment	25%
8	Responsibilities of the parties	22%
9	Liquidated damages	22%
10	Scope and goals	21%
11	Warranty	16%
12	Limitation of liability	16%
13	Indemnification	14%
14	Service withdrawal or termination	14%
15	Intellectual property	12%
16	Audits/benchmarking	10%
17	Assignment/transfer	8%
18	Dispute resolution	8%
19	Data protection/security	7%
20	Communications and reporting	7%

The results of IACCM surveys indicate that there is a need for the legal and business communities to focus on areas such as requirements, scope and goals, and responsibilities of the parties: how these are captured and recorded and how changes are managed. Lack of attention to such areas is what the proactive approach seeks to rectify. Professor Edward A. Dauer notes this takes lawyers into somewhat unfamiliar terrain: these areas are generally considered to be the client's domain. The proactive approach rejects the view that the client designs the widgets, the corporate culture, and environmental integrity, and lawyers practice the law.[52] Success in reaching business goals and preventing problems along the way requires managerial and legal collaboration.

Experienced business lawyers know how to use the contracting process and documents to identify, articulate, and align expectations and to clarify obligations and requirements. Asking the right questions helps the parties clarify goals and task allocation, and be better prepared, not only for contingencies and legal problems, but also for successful performance. It also helps confront the issue of "invisible terms" by making the parties' rights, responsibilities, and remedies visible in the contract.

Despite the depth of CISG literature, very little of it has focused on the managerial perspective.[53] Even if CISG case law and literature are readily available technically,

---

[52] Edward A. Dauer, "Developing Preventive Law: From Lawyering to Quality," *Leadership and Management Directions Newsletter* (Summer 1998) (American Bar Association ABA, Section of Law Practice Management, Law Practice Division).

[53] Similarly, in the context of commercial law, see Petri Mäntysaari, "Commercial Law and the Theory of Management-Based Commercial Law" (September 8, 2009), available at http://ssrn.com/abstract=1473006 (noting that legal science has failed to serve the information needs of firms properly).

they may not be accessible or understandable for the business community. Experience tells us that one of the main challenges for the proactive use of law by managers is their perception of the role of contracts and the law, and what the legal profession has to offer. New approaches, tools, and techniques are needed to draw traders' attention and increase their awareness and interest in contracts and the law. One way of increasing this awareness – the use of visualization – is reviewed in the next part.

V. Visualization: Increasing Traders' Awareness

The term "visualization" is used here to describe the use of nontextual tools, such as matrices, tables, maps, or flowcharts, to convey information, organize data, promote learning, and stimulate imagination and reflection. Sometimes images stand alone, as in traffic signs or safety symbols. Often they are accompanied by text to enliven the language and make underlying concepts more comprehensible.[54]

Growing evidence in scientific literature and in organizations shows the positive impact of knowledge visualization for generating ideas, sharing knowledge, evaluating options, and planning.[55] Visualization is also increasingly used in communicating risk. Risk visualization "employs charts, conceptual diagrams, visual metaphors, and mapping techniques to improve understanding and subsequent management of risks in specialist and management teams or stakeholder groups. Risk visualization uses the power of graphics to help experts, decision makers, and laymen to better deal with risks in the areas of management, health, and security."[56]

In the German-speaking countries, the terms legal visualization (*Rechtsvisualisierung*), visual legal communication (*Visuelle Rechtskommunikation*), visual law (*Visuelles Recht*) and multisensory law (*Multisensorisches Recht*) have been used to describe this growing field of research and practice.[57] In the United States, the use of visualizations has been studied, for instance, in the context of improving the comprehension of

---

[54] See, e.g., Thomas D. Barton, Gerlinde Berger-Walliser, and Helena Haapio, "Visualization: Seeing Contracts for What They Are, and What They Could Become," in *Proceedings of the 2011 IACCM Academic Symposium for Contract and Commercial Management* (ed. R. F. Henschel) (Ridgefield, CT: International Association for Contract and Commercial Management, 2011), 19 *Journal of Law, Business & Ethics* 47, 48 (2013). See also "Visual Literacy: An E-Learning Tutorial on Visualization for Communication, Engineering and Business," available at http://www.visual-literacy.org.

[55] See Sabrina Bresciani and Martin J. Eppler, "Choosing Knowledge Visualizations to Augment Cognition: The Managers' View," in *Proceedings of the 14th International Conference on Information Visualisation, IV2010* (London, July 26–9, 2010) (ed. E. Banissi et al.) (Los Alamitos, CA: IEEE Computer Society, 2010), 355; Martin J. Eppler, "What Is an Effective Knowledge Visualization? Insights from a Review of Seminal Concepts," in *Proceedings of the 15th International Conference on Information Visualisation, IV2011* (London, July 13–15, 2011) 349 (ed. E. Banissi et al.) (Los Alamitos, CA: IEEE Computer Society, 2011).

[56] Martin J. Eppler and Markus Aeschimann, "Envisioning Risk: A Systematic Framework for Risk Visualization in Risk Management and Communication," ICA Working Paper 5/2008, Version 1.0, Università della Svizzera italiana, Faculty of Communication Sciences, Institute for Corporate Communication, September 2008, available at http://www.knowledge-communication.org/pdf/envisioning-risk.pdf.

[57] Colette R. Brunschwig, "Visualisierung von Rechtsnormen – Legal Design," Ph.D. thesis, Zürcher Studien zur Rechtsgeschichte, vol. 45 (Rechtswissenschaftliche Fakultät d. Universität Zürich, Schulthess Juristische Medien, Zürich, 2001) (Visualization of Legal Norms); Colette R. Brunschwig, "Multisensory Law and Legal Informatics – A Comparison of How these Legal Disciplines Relate to Visual Law," *Jusletter IT*, February 22, 2011, available at http://jusletter-it.weblaw.ch/en/issues/2011/104/article_324.html.

jury instructions[58] and facilitating the making of complex decisions related to dispute resolution.[59]

Visualization has also been used as a tool of persuasion in various settings, such as in the courtroom[60] and the boardroom. In law and business schools, as well as in executive education, visuals are increasingly being used to explain legal concepts. Visuals will only increase in importance in education, as students have grown up in a multimedia environment and are less receptive to black and white texts.[61]

In Sweden, a judgment of the Gothenburg Court of Appeal included two timeline images showing the chain of events leading to the alleged crime against a bank that paid monies under an export credit facility against fictitious invoices.[62] For its effort in providing clarity to a complex fact pattern, the court was recognized with the 2010 Plain Swedish Crystal Award. The award-winning ruling was praised not only for being written in a pedagogical and innovative way, having a clear structure, good paragraphing, clarifying summaries, and subheadings, but also for the fact that its clarity was enhanced by the use of bullet points and images.[63]

In Canada, recognizing the need for new ways to inspire public access to the law, the government commissioned a White Paper in 2000 proposing a new format for legislation. The White Paper,[64] written by David Berman, a communication designer, introduced a redesign which included diagrams to help describe laws, noting that this concept is "revolutionary, and likely the most innovative information design feature in

[58] Carolyn Semmler and Neil Brewer, "Using a Flow-Chart to Improve Comprehension of Jury Instructions," 9 *Psychiatry, Psychology and Law* 262 (2002); Firoz Dattu, "Illustrated Jury Instructions: A Proposal," 22 *Law & Psychology Rev.* 67 (1998).

[59] George J. Siedel, "Interdisciplinary Approaches to Alternative Dispute Resolution," 10 *Journal of Legal Studies Education* 141, 154–61 (1992); Berger-Walliser et al., "Promoting Business Success through Contract Visualisation."

[60] Neil Feigenson and Christina Spiesel, *Law on Display: The Digital Transformation of Legal Persuasion and Judgment* (New York: New York University Press, 2009); Samuel H. Solomon, "Visuals and Visualization: Penetrating the Heart and Soul of Persuasion," DOAR Litigation Consulting (October 2006), available at http://tillers.net/solomon.pdf. See also Richard K. Sherwin, *Visualizing Law in the Age of the Digital Baroque: Arabesques and Entanglements* (London: Routledge, 2011).

[61] Beyond Legal Text, a research project at the University of Edinburgh School of Law, available at http://www.law.ed.ac.uk/beyondtext, has explored visual legal education. See also Berger-Walliser et al., "Promoting Business Success through Contract Visualisation," and Eric Hilgendorf, *DTV-Atlas Recht, Band 2: Verwaltungsrecht Zivilrecht* (Munich: Deutscher Taschenbuch Verlag, 2008). See also Christa Tobler and Jacques Beglinger, *Essential EU Law in Charts*, 2nd ed., "Lisbon" ed. (Budapest: HVR-ORAC Publishing House, 2010); Frank John Doti, *Contract Law, Flowcharts and Cases: A Student's Visual Guide to Understanding Contracts*, 2nd ed. (St. Paul, MN: West, 2009); Nicole Lefton, *Kaplan PMBR: Law School Flowcharts – Detailed Topic Flowcharts for Required Law School Courses* (New York: Kaplan Publishing, 2009). In educating business management in cross-border contracts and the law, the author's firm Lexpert Ltd. has successfully used visualizations. Visualizations made by Annika Varjonen, Visual Impact Helsinki Ltd., for demonstration purposes, are available at http://www.lexpert.com/en/visualisation/index.htm.

[62] Court of Appeal for Western Sweden (Gothenburg), case number B 1534–08. See Dom i mål nr B 1534–08 (Hovrätten för Västra Sverige, Göteborg, July 15, 2009), available at http://www.domstol.se/Domstolar/vastrahovratten/Kristalldom.pdf.

[63] *Pressmeddelande: Klarspråkskristallen 2010 till CSN och Hovrätten för Västra Sverige* (Språkrådet, Stockholm, May 5, 2010), available at http://www.sprakradet.se/7121 (translated from Swedish).

[64] David Berman, "Toward a New Format for Canadian Legislation: Using Graphic Design Principles and Methods to Improve Public Access to the Law," Human Resources Development Canada and Justice Canada Project Paper, November 30, 2000, available at http://www.davidberman.com/NewFormatForCanadianLegislation.pdf.

the new design [of legislation]."[65] The new design aims at making laws more accessible to government officials and the public. In the process of creating a flow chart diagram, Berman's team discovered inconsistencies that were not accounted for in the legislation, suggesting that translating draft legislation into diagrams might substantively improve law subsequently enacted.[66]

Another example of visualizing legal information is the work of the Street Vendor Project. Candy Chang, a designer, urban planner and artist, in collaboration with the Center for Urban Pedagogy, noted that the New York City Code was "intimidating and hard to understand by anyone, let alone someone whose first language isn't English." The project published a visual Street Vendor Guide called "Vendor Power!" that makes city regulations and rights accessible and understandable. The guide features diagrams of vendors' rights and the most commonly violated rules.[67] Figure 44.5 illustrates the difference between text ("Before") and visual guidance ("After"). Although the context here is not the CISG, the outcome of the project indicates how visualizing provisions of the CISG would help increase traders' awareness, understanding, and use of its rules.

Although contracting is a core business activity, most contracts today seem to be designed for litigating lawyers rather than business users.[68] In order to reset this approach, some pioneers have already experimented with applying visualization to commercial contracting processes and documents.[69] In a case study conducted at the University of Oslo, a group of lawyers, managers, and engineers were asked to analyze the risks related to a contract proposal using a method based on graphical language and diagrams. The case study showed that the use of graphical language was helpful in communicating risk among the participants. However, the need for simplicity and usability also led

---

[65] Id., at 23.

[66] Id., at 24.

[67] Candy Chang, "Street Vendor Guide." Accessible city regulations, available at http://candychang.com/street-vendor-guide.

[68] See, e.g., Tim Cummins, the CEO of IACCM: "In addition to focusing on the wrong things, contracts are also designed for litigants, not for day-to-day users. Most contracts (especially in international transactions) are structured and written in a way that renders them almost useless to those who are charged with their implementation. We take situations where clarity of communication is key and then offer instruments that are composed by lawyers, for lawyers." Tim Cummins, "As Litigation Increases, What Should We Be Doing about It?," Commitment Matters Blog, December 5, 2011, available at http://contract-matters.com/2011/12/05/as-litigation-increases-what-should-we-be-doing-about-it/. See also Berger-Walliser et al., "Promoting Business Success through Contract Visualisation," 56; DiMatteo et al., "Strategic Contracting."

[69] For early experiments with and examples of contract visualizations, see Henry W. Jones and Michael Oswald, "Doing Deals with Flowcharts," ACCA Docket (October 2001), 94; Henry W. (Hank) Jones III, "Envisioning Visual Contracting: Why Non-textual Tools Will Improve Your Contracting," Contracting Excellence (August–September 2009), 27, available at http://www.iaccm.com/userfiles/file/CE_2_6_press_new.pdf; Katri Rekola and Helena Haapio, "Better Business through Proactive Productization and Visualization of Contracts," Contracting Excellence (June–July 2009), 17, available at http://www.iaccm.com/userfiles/file/CE_2_5_press_C2(1).pdf; Helena Haapio, "Visualising Contracts and Legal Rules for Greater Clarity," 44 The Law Teacher, 391 (2010); Barton et al., "Visualization: Seeing Contracts for What They Are, and What They Could Become"; Helena Haapio, "Communicating Contracts: When Text Alone Is Not Enough," Clarity – J. of the Int'l Association Promoting Plain Legal Language, No. 65, 33 (2011); Haapio, "A Visual Approach to Commercial Contracts"; and Helena Haapio, "Contract Clarity through Visualization – Preliminary Observations and Experiments," in Proceedings of the 15th International Conference on Information Visualisation, IV2011 (London, July 13–15, 2011), 337.

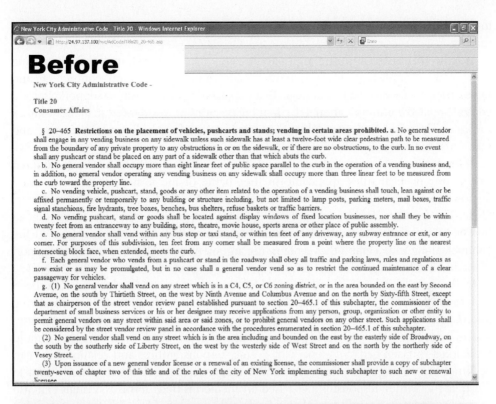

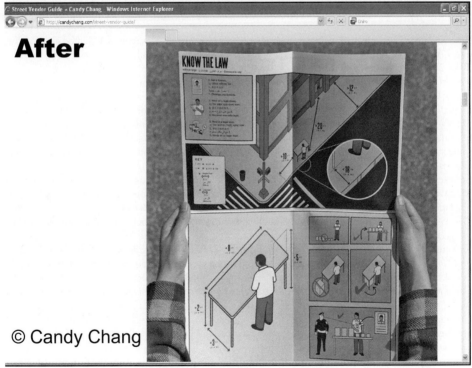

Figure 44.5. Example of Visualizing Legal Information – City Regulations Before and After. (Visualization reprinted with the permission of the Center for Urban Pedagogy and Candy Chang.)

to the use of a combination of graphical and natural language for improved decision making.[70]

At Aalto University, a multidisciplinary research project was started in 2011 seeking to develop and apply new, easier methods for cooperation, co-creation, contracting, and interaction.[71] The early results indicate that visualization offers a way to support effective contract-related communication. It helps increase awareness and interest, make complex messages clear and understandable, facilitate cross-professional communication, and make contracts more user friendly.[72]

In the Wolfram Demonstrations Project, the use of visualizations has been explored in the area of legal rules applicable in the "battle of the forms" scenario. A visual demonstration by Seth J. Chandler illustrates Article 2 of the Uniform Commercial Code. The user can choose various details, and the output shows the most likely judicial finding as to whether a contract exists and the terms that would be included in the contract, along with a graph that explains the argument that will be advanced in support of the judicial finding.[73]

As the sample illustration in Figure 44.6 shows, visualizations have already been used to illustrate CISG related issues. These examples show the potential for visualizing information related to the CISG and contracts for the international sale of goods. Pictures and drawings can be used to identify and describe the goods and how they should be marked or packaged. Sequences of events, responsibilities, and relationships can be simplified through timelines, maps, and diagrams. Several visuals already exist to illustrate the parties' responsibilities based on Incoterms trade terms.[74] Visuals can also be used to make the invisible visible by showing the impact of invisible terms,[75] helping

[70] Tobias Mahler, "Legal Risk Management: Developing and Evaluating Elements of a Method for Proactive Legal Analyses, with a Particular Focus on Contracts," Ph.D. thesis, Faculty of Law, University of Oslo, 2010, 237–62.

[71] The project studies contracting in the Finnish Metals and Engineering Competence Cluster (FIMECC) as part of User Experience and Usability in Complex Systems (UXUS), a five-year research program financed by participating companies and TEKES, the Finnish Funding Agency for Technology and Innovation. Drawing from research in proactive law, information design, user-centeredness, and other fields, the aim is to develop, prototype, and test new approaches to commercial contracts in order to increase their understandability and usability. The project looks into visualization and other possible means of creating simpler contracts.

[72] See Stefania Passera and Helena Haapio, "Facilitating Collaboration through Contract Visualization and Modularization," in *Designing Collaborative Activities. ECCE 2011 European Conference on Cognitive Ergonomics 2011 – The 29th Annual Conference of the European Association on Cognitive Ergonomics, Rostock, Germany, August 24–26, 2011* (ed. A. Dittmar and P. Forbrig) (Rostock: Universität Rostock, 2011), 57; Stefania Passera and Helena Haapio, "User-Centered Contract Design: New Directions in the Quest for Simpler Contracting," in Henschel, *Proceedings of the 2011 IACCM Academic Symposium for Contract and Commercial Management*, 80, available at http://www.iaccm.com/admin/docs/docs/HH_Paper.pdf. See also Stefania Passera and Helena Haapio, "The Quest for Clarity – How Visualization Improves the Usability and User Experience of Contracts," in *Innovative Approaches of Data Visualization and Visual Analytics (DVVA 2013)* (ed. M. Huang and W. Huang) (IGI Global, 2013); Stefania Passera, "Enhancing Contract Usability and User Experience through Visualization – An Experimental Evaluation," in *Proceedings of the 16th International Conference on Information Visualisation, IV2012 (Montpellier, France, July 11–13, 2012)* (ed. E. Banissi et al.) (Los Alamitos, CA: IEEE Computer Society, 2012), 376.

[73] Wolfram Demonstrations Project, "Visualizing Legal Rules: Battle of the Forms," available at http://demonstrations.wolfram.com/VisualizingLegalRulesBattleOfTheForms.

[74] *Incoterms® 2010 suomi-englanti*, ICC publication no. 715E-FIN (Helsinki: ICC Palvelu Oy, 2010).

[75] See Section III B, "Invisible Terms and the CISG," with references, especially notes 39 and 40. As to a business manager's and a lawyer's different ways of seeing contracts, with visualizations, see Helena

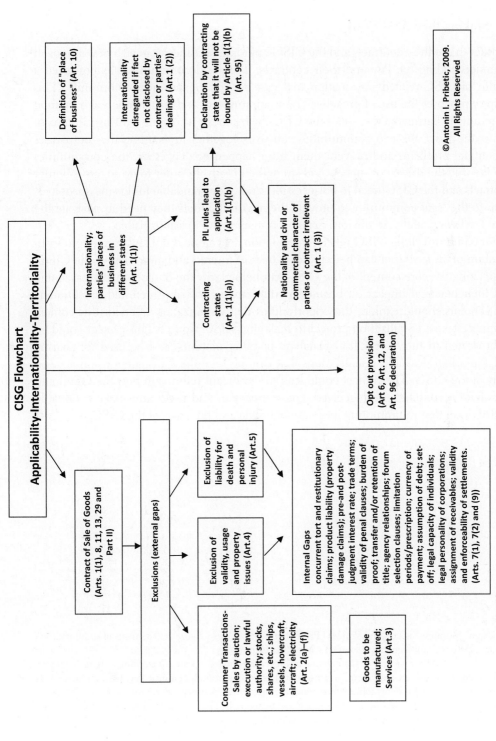

Figure 44.6. CISG Flowchart – Applicability-Internationality-Territoriality. (From Antonin I. Pribetic, "An 'Unconventional Truth': Conflict of Laws Issues Arising under the CISG," *Nordic J. of Commercial Law*, Issue 1 (2009), available at http://www.njcl.utu.fi/1_2009/article3.pdf. Figure reprinted with permission by the author and publisher.)

The flowchart content includes:

CISG Flowchart Applicability-Internationality-Territoriality

Definition of "place of business" (Art. 10)

Internationality disregarded if fact not disclosed by contract or parties' dealings (Art.1 (2))

Declaration by contracting state that it will not be bound by Article 1(1)(b) (Art. 95)

©Antonin I. Pribetic, 2009. All Rights Reserved

Internationality; parties' places of business in different states (Art. 1(1))

PIL rules lead to application (Art.1(1)(b)

Contracting states (Art. 1(1)(a))

Nationality and civil or commercial character of parties or contract irrelevant (Art. 1 (3))

Opt out provision (Art 6, Art. 12, and Art. 96 declaration)

Contract of Sale of Goods (Arts. 1(1), 8, 11, 13, 29 and Part II)

Exclusions (external gaps)

Exclusion of liability for death and personal injury (Art.5)

Exclusion of validity, usage and property issues (Art.4)

Internal Gaps
concurrent tort and restitutionary claims; product liability (property damage claims); pre-and post-judgment interest rate; trade terms; validity of penal clauses; burden of proof; transfer and/or retention of title; agency relationships; forum selection clauses; limitation periods/prescription; currency of payment; assumption of debt; set-off; legal capacity of individuals; legal personality of corporations; assignment of receivables; validity and enforceability of settlements. (Arts. 7(1), 7(2) and (9))

Consumer Transactions-Sales by auction; execution or lawful authority; stocks, shares, etc.; ships, vessels, hovercraft, aircraft; electricity (Art. 2(a)–(f))

Goods to be manufactured; Services (Art.3)

723

the parties obtain clarity about their rights and responsibilities and avoid unintended obligations and liabilities.

VI. Making the CISG Work

In order to use their contracts and the CISG optimally, businesses need a new approach to understanding the law and their contracts. The legal community has produced a wealth of CISG-related information that can benefit the business community. This chapter proposes the use of proactive law as a framework and visualization as a method for removing barriers to the use of the CISG by businesses.[76] Using existing CISG case law as the basis, the two communities can work together to examine the root causes of contract problems and prevent them from happening. Together, the communities can identify the drivers of success and strengthen them. In order to do so, cross-border contracts and the CISG need to be accessible and understandable for businesspeople. It is up to the legal community to provide them with the tools they need to navigate the legal landscape safely. An obvious first step is making the invisible visible.[77]

For communicating CISG-related information, text alone is not always enough. Visualization offers tools that can help increase traders' interest and awareness of the CISG. Visualizing the core content of the CISG can help clarify the choices that are available and their practical impact on business performance and risk. Interested practitioners and scholars should explore the opportunities that visualization offers in this context and undertake a visualization project to make the CISG work.[78] This project could be incorporated in the Pace CISG Database or other platform and be used for sharing and exploring ideas and visualizations that can advance the transparency and accessibility of the CISG. The project could lead to significant reforms in how the CISG and cross-border contracts are perceived, communicated, and used, and make a valuable contribution toward promoting international trade and the goals of the CISG.

Haapio, "Business Success and Problem Prevention," 155–63, esp. figure 2, "Elements of a Contract – A Lawyer's View," and figure 5, "Contract – Mind the Gaps!"

[76] See also Barton, "Collaborative Contracting as Preventive/Proactive Law." According to Barton, preventive/proactive law offers a different, and arguably deeper, way of understanding law, legal problems, and how lawyers can help clients achieve their goals. Barton's article focuses primarily on one recurring barrier: "an exaggerated and largely unnecessary separation between the business goals that clients seek to achieve, and the legal methods by which contractual relationships are created and managed."

[77] See Section III B, "Invisible Terms and the CISG," with references, especially at notes 39 and 40.

[78] As regards visualizing contracts, see Barton et al., "Visualization: Seeing Contracts for What They Are, and What They Could Become."

45 Future Challenges of International Sales Law

Larry A. DiMatteo

I. A Brief Look at the Past

International law harmonization can be traced to the twelfth century's *lex mercatoria*, followed by the nineteenth century's internationalist movement's search for a *uniform ius commune* and a concerted push for a uniform international sales law with the work of Ernst Rabel, which led to the establishment of the International Institute for the Unification of Private Law (UNIDROIT) in 1926.[1] Following World War II, the next major event was the publication of the Uniform Law for the International Sale of Goods (ULIS) and the Uniform Law on the Formation of Contract for the International Sale of Goods (ULF) following a 1964 Diplomatic Conference at The Hague. Unfortunately, The Hague conventions failed to attract enough support with its ratification by only nine countries.

The effort began anew with the establishment of the United Nations Commission on International Trade Law (UNCITRAL) in 1966, which began work on a new sales convention beginning in 1970, culminating with the adoption of the CISG in 1980. The CISG entered into force on January 1, 1988. The group of initial adoptees included the People's Republic of China and the United States, setting it on course to becoming the most successful international substantive law ever enacted, with its adoption by seventy-nine countries and it is likely to reach one hundred countries in the near future.

The CISG has had a major impact not only as adopted (hard) law, but also as a model (soft) law used in the revising of national contract law codes. Professor Hiroo Sono has noted that the use of the CISG as model law "is most conspicuous in legislation influenced by the CISG, such as in China, Germany, the Scandinavian countries, former socialist states such as Russia and Estonia. This process of 'legislative assimilation' is also occurring in Japan, which acceded to the CISG in 2008."[2] The CISG has also been used as a template for the 1994 revision of the Dutch Civil Code, 2002 revision of the German Civil Code (BGB), as well as the Estonian Law of Obligations Act.[3]

---

[1] See Vikki Rogers and Kaon Lai, "History of the CISG and Its Present Status," Chapter 2 in this book.

[2] Id., quoting Hiroo Sono, "The Diversity of Favor Contractus: The Impact of the CISG on Japan's Civil Code and Its Reform," in *Towards Uniformity: The 2nd Annual MAA Schlechtriem CISG Conference* (ed. I. Schwenzer and L. Spagnolo) (The Hague: Eleven International Publishing, 2011), 165.

[3] Id., citing Peter Schlechtriem, "Basic Structures and General Concepts of the CISG as Models for a Harmonization of the Law of Obligations," *Juridica Int'l*, 27–36 (2005).

II. The CISG in the Present

The information provided by the material in this book is sufficient to assess the current status of the CISG as international sales law, as it is applied by courts and arbitral tribunals, and as it is used in practice. The various chapters and country analyses show that the role of the CISG as a global sales law has been mixed and that further development is needed for it to reach its promise of uniformity.

A. CISG Jurisprudence

The CISG has produced a substantial body of court decisions. However, its greatest impact may be in its use in disputes resolved through arbitration. For example, more than four hundred published case decisions have been issued by the China International Economic and Trade Arbitration Commission (CIETAC). The facts that arbitration is the preferred method of dispute resolution and that, due to confidentiality agreements, many arbitral decisions go unreported suggest that the impact of the CISG has been much greater than the number of reported cases would indicate.[4]

The problem with the existing database of more than 2,900 decisions is the unevenness of the CISG case law across CISG Articles and rules.[5] This can be expected because certain issues in sales law are more prone to lead to litigation or arbitration. The unevenness can also be partially attributed to vaguely or poorly written provisions in the law, which invite disputes over the proper interpretation of the provisions.

But, due to the voluminous nature of CISG scholarship in numerous languages, the increase of language translations of CISG case decisions, and a trend toward better-reasoned (cross-legal traditions) interpretations, problems of the scarcity and unevenness of the case law have diminished over time. As one scholar notes: "The CISG can be credited for the decline of legal babelism that beset the private international law rules it was created to replace. There has been serious progress toward the convergence of legal systems, and the CISG has had positive influence on the reforming of a number of national contract-sales legal systems."[6] The depth of CISG case law and scholarly commentary has become more and more accessible, in multiple languages, through the creation of online databases, including the Pace CISG Database and the Queen Mary Translation Program. In the words of Albert Kritzer: "the birth of the CISG coincided with the birth of the Information Age. That has led to an explosion of material on the Internet on this law."[7] The readily available online sources include: UNCITRAL's CLOUT

---

[4] See André Janssen and Matthias Spilker, "CISG and International Arbitration," Chapter 10 in this book.

[5] See Olaf Meyer, "CISG: Divergences between Success–Scarcity and Theory–Practice," Chapter 3 in this book.

[6] See Claire Germain, "Reducing Legal Babelism: CISG Translation Issues," Chapter 5 in this book, citing Claude Witz on the "recul du babélisme juridique," in "Les vingt-cinq ans de law Convention des Nations Unies sur les contrats de vente internationale de merchandises: Bilans et perspectives" (The 25th Anniversary of the CISG: Evaluations and Perspectives), 123 *Journal du Droit Int'l* 5, 25 (2006). The Babel reference is also attributable to John Honnold, *Documentary History of the Uniform Law for International Sales* (Deventer: Kluwer, 1989), at 1 ("Babel of diverse legal systems").

[7] Albert H. Kritzer, Foreword to Camilla Andersen, Francesco Mazzotta, and Bruno Zeller, *A Practitioner's Guide to the CISG* (Huntington, NY: Juris, 2010), vii.

(Case Law on UNCITRAL texts) system; the all-encompassing Institute of International Commercial Law[8] at Pace University School of Law (Database); UNCITRAL's "Digest of Case Law on the United Nations Sales Convention" and "opinions of the CISG Advisory Council," both available through the Pace CISG Database; UNIDROIT's UNILEX database; Center for Transnational Law at the University of Cologne's TransLex database; and a variety of other commercial databases.[9]

B. *Interpreting and the Interpretation of the CISG*

The CISG provides an interpretive methodology based upon the use of general principles – international character, need to promote uniformity of application – and internationally recognized trade usage. Additionally, the CISG provides that in the interpretation of contracts the interpreter shall take into account "all relevant circumstances including the negotiations, any practices which the parties have established between themselves, usages and any subsequent conduct of the parties."[10] The contextual search for the true intent of the parties is supplemented by the default principle of implied reasonableness. If the contextual evidence directly related to the parties fails to provide the operative meaning, then the CISG directs the interpreter to find a reasonable term provided in the real world of commercial custom, usage, and practice.

The problem with the CISG interpretive methodology is that it fails to recognize traditional and nontraditional methodologies that would help guide the interpreter to the true meaning of the parties and uniform, autonomous interpretations of CISG rules.[11] Courts have implied a number of these traditional methodologies in interpreting the CISG, such as analogical or systemic reasoning within the CISG, historic interpretation (*travaux préparatoires*), and purposive interpretation. Other methodologies include analogical reasoning using CISG case law; scholarly commentary; comparative law analysis, and the use of soft law. In the future, all the different methodologies may be appropriately applied to given issues, ambiguities, and gaps in coverage presented by the CISG.

The path to uniform interpretation of the CISG has been a bit problematic. Divergent interpretations have been caused by means of process and substance. The process-produced divergences are seen in the well-documented cases of national law-biased decisions. The substantive-produced interpretations are related to the ambiguity of CISG rules, definitional shortcomings of CISG terms, and overly broad standards. Professor Zeller notes the various rules that have been used in the battle of the forms scenario.[12] Ultimately, he concludes that the voiding of conflicting standard terms (knock-out rule) is the solution that best accords with the spirit of the CISG, which primarily seeks the

---

[8] For more information about the Institute, see Marie Stefanini Newman, "Albert Kritzer: Pioneer of Open Access to International Private Law," in *Sharing International Commercial Law across National Boundaries: Festschrift for Albert H Kritzer on the Occasion of His Eightieth Birthday* (ed. C.B. Andersen and U.G. Schroeter) (London: Wildy, Simmonds & Hill Publishing, 2008), 363 n. 8.

[9] See Marie Stefanini Newman, "CISG Sources and Researching the CISG," Chapter 4 in this book.

[10] CISG, Article 8(3).

[11] See Larry DiMatteo and André Janssen, "Interpretive Methodologies in the Interpretation of the CISG," Chapter 7 in this book.

[12] See Bruno Zeller, "CISG and the Battle of the Forms," Chapter 13 in this book.

enforcement of agreements, based on mutual assent. The problems inherent in CISG language make some provisions of the CISG susceptible to divergent, reasonable interpretations. For greater uniformity to be obtained, consensus needs to be developed over the best interpretations.

Professor Morten Fogt reviews the contract formation rules found in Part II of the CISG and finds them lacking.[13] First, he argues that the fragmented nature of Part II has created numerous external and internal "gaps." Second, the formation rules fail to deal with alternative means of contract formation. Fogt argues that the only way of fully correcting the issues of CISG contract formation is by a revision of Part II. Barring such a revision, he notes that the best that can be done is to fill the gaps found in Part II "though liberal interpretation, analogies, and implied underlying principles."

Article 38 (inspection of goods) and Article 39 (notice of nonconformity of goods) are the two most disputed areas of the CISG. There have been a wide variety of interpretations as to what constitutes a reasonable time to give notice. Professor Flechtner concludes that the case law has "exaggerated [the] conception of the role and importance of the buyer's notice obligations,"[14] leading to an overly strict interpretation of the buyer's notice obligations, at the expense of diminishing the more fundamental obligation of the seller to deliver conforming goods. He suggests that the best approach is to place the burden of proof on the seller to show that the buyer failed to meet its Article 39 notice obligation.

Another unsettled substantive issue is the determination of fundamental breach. Article 25 provides a vague definition of fundamental breach as that which "substantially deprives." Professor Spaic reviews a number of approaches that have been applied in determining fundamental breach. The resulting confusion has produced a great deal of uncertainty that a single approach would eliminate.[15] Spaic proposes that that a functional definition would entail a combined approach that factors a purposive approach (whether the aggrieved party has been substantially deprived of what it expected out of the contract) and a remedy-oriented approach (whether the aggrieved party's interests can be protected through remedies short of avoidance).

On a more promising note, Professor Magnus, in an extensive review, shows that the remedies provisions incorporated in the CISG are a relatively comprehensive and functional remedial scheme.[16] Professor Davies takes note of the scarcity of cases relating to the use of Article 79's excuse of impediment.[17] His insightful analysis shows that the implicit use of the foreseeability principle that underlies most excuse doctrines is not the key requirement of Article 79: "The ultimate question under Article 79 should not be whether the impediment was foreseeable, but whether it was one that a reasonable person would have taken into account when making the contract." He provides a coherent argument as to how "taken into account" is different than foreseeability, and why it matters.

---

[13] See Morton Midtgaard Fogt, "Contract Formation under the CISG: The Need for a Reform," Chapter 12 in this book.

[14] See Harry M. Flechtner, "Conformity of Goods: Inspection and Notice," Chapter 14 in this book.

[15] See Aneta Spaic, "Interpreting Fundamental Breach," Chapter 15 in this book.

[16] See Ulrich Magnus, "Remedies: Damages, Price Reduction, Avoidance, Mitigation, and Preservation," Chapter 15 in this book.

[17] See Martin Davies, "Excuse of Impediment and Its Usefulness," Chapter 18 in this book.

The CISG does not provide rules for precontractual liability for acts of bad faith or other types of malfeasance. Professor Torsello maps the area of the precontract stage.[18] He makes the important point that the mere labeling of an exchange or an instrument as precontractual does not mean that it is not subject to the substantive rules of the CSG. It is within the scope of the CISG to make the determination on whether something is truly precontractual or whether the parties have moved into the area of binding obligations.[19] Torsello counsels that prudent parties should expressly negotiate "the duties owed to each other throughout the negotiations, and the legal consequences for non-observance."[20]

In the area of damages, a controversial issue is whether legal costs can be recovered as a matter of damages. In many legal systems, the losing party is required to pay the reasonable litigation costs of the other party. However, in the United States, parties bear the costs of their own legal expenses (American rule). Most courts, due to the CISG's failure to provide an explicit rule on litigation cost recovery, refer to national law on the matter. Professor Piltz argues that because CISG Article 74 is generally interpreted to allow for full compensation of reasonably foreseeable losses, legal costs should be recoverable as damages under the CISG.[21]

C. Country Analyses

The country analyses provided by CISG scholars from many countries and regions ferreted out the issues and debates over the proper interpretation of CISG rules. The variety and range of CISG cases among the adopting countries is broad – from the in-depth case law produced by the German court system,[22] as well as a substantial number of cases from The Netherlands,[23] Switzerland,[24] Belgium, Austria,[25] and France.[26] The CISG is also used by arbitral tribunals the reported arbitral decisions coming from the People's Republic of China indicate that the CISG may indeed play a greater role in arbitral decisions than in court decisions.[27] In comparison, some regions,[28] especially common law countries,[29] have produced a modest number of CISG cases.[30] The quality of the decisions has, also, varied greatly from cases ignoring CISG interpretive

---

[18] See Marco Torsello, "Precontractual Liability and Preliminary Agreements," Chapter 39 in this book.

[19] See Larry A. DiMatteo, "The CISG and the Presumption of Enforceability: Unintended Contractual Liability in International Business Dealings," 22 *Yale J. Int'l L.* 111 (1997).

[20] Id.

[21] See Burghard Piltz, "Litigation Costs as Reimbursable Damages," Chapter 17 in this book.

[22] See Stefan Kröll, "Germany Country Analysis: Good Faith, Formation, and Conformity of Goods," and Sörren Kiene, "Germany Country Analysis: Part II," Chapters 22 and 23 in this book.

[23] See Sonja Kruisinga, "The Netherlands," Chapter 29 in this book.

[24] See Corinne Widmer Lüchinger, "Switzerland," Chapter 28 in this book.

[25] See Wolfgang Faber, "CISG in Austria," Chapter 19 in this book.

[26] See Sylvaine Poillot-Peruzzetto, "French Perspective of the CISG," Chapter 21 in this book

[27] See Li Wei, "People's Republic of China," Chapter 33 in this book.

[28] See Jan Ramberg, "The Nordic Countries," Chapter 25; Tadas Klimas, "Baltic States, Belarus, and Ukraine," Chapter 20; Milena Djordjević and Vladimir Pavić, "CISG in Southeastern Europe," Chapter 26; and Virginia G. Maurer, "Central and South America," Chapter 35 in this book.

[29] See Petra Butler, "New Zealand," Chapter 32 in this book; Robert W. Emerson and Ann M. Olazábal, "United States and Canada," Chapter 34 in this book.

[30] See also Pilar Perales Viscasillas and Javier Solana Álvarez, "Spain," Chapter 27 in this book; Yehuda Adar, "Israel," Chapter 31 in this book.

methodology to extremely well-reasoned ones.[31] One of the studies examines the place of the CISG in an Islamic legal system with a focus on Egypt.[32] As a whole, the body of CISG case law is deep and provides the foundation for future uniform development and application.

III. Future of the CISG

The future of the CISG looks bright on a number of fronts. First, the recent adoption of the CISG by Brazil is a watershed event. It shows that the rate of adoptions continues at a brisk pace. In addition, as a BRIC country, Brazil was one of the major world trading powers that had not adopted the CISG. With the adoptions by Japan and Brazil, only two major outliers remain – India and the United Kingdom.

Second, the problem of divergent interpretations of the CISG, especially due to domestic or homeward trend-biased reasoning, persists. Professor Schwenzer notes that in the areas of inspection, notice of nonconformity, remedies, and excuse, such reasoning continues to be used and uniformity of application remains illusory.[33] However, the number of homeward trend-biased decisions is diminishing and the number of well-reasoned decisions, in which the courts and arbitral tribunals have taken an international perspective, is in the ascendancy. If these trends continue then we can begin to speak of the CISG as a global sales law.[34]

However, the problem of contracting parties opting out of the CISG as a matter of form remains a problem. This has caused a scarcity of cases on many issues and provisions of the CISG. A truly functional, supranational sales law is self-fulfilling. That is, a rich case law is not only proof of its significance but provides the substantive sources needed to render well-reasoned decisions. Professor Schwenzer points out that many of the CISG case decisions involve relatively modest amounts of money. She hypothesizes that many of the cases involving larger amounts are buried in the privacy of international commercial arbitration. If more such cases were reported, then the problem of scarcity would likely be lessened. The lack of reporting, however, will continue, because one of the features of arbitration that many parties desire is the privacy of the proceedings.

The hope, not unfounded, is that with the growing knowledge of the CISG and the diminishment of language barriers, the CISG will be more fully embraced by practicing attorneys. At the same time, as the knowledge base of future jurists improves, the use of homeward trend-biased reasoning will continue to decline. Along the same line, Lisa Spagnolo concluded that the CISG as hard law has provided the foundation for its greater acceptance by traders and lawyers in the future.[35] The current body of CISG case law provides "base-level familiarity," but the widespread use of the CISG will depend on the nature of the law as applied. To that end, Spagnolo advocates that when there are a number of possible interpretations of a CISG rule, the best interpretation is the one "which better promotes acceptability and efficiency."

---

[31] There have, for example, been a number of Italian cases that have done an exemplary job of reviewing and citing foreign CISG case law decisions. See Edoardo Ferrante, "Italy," Chapter 24 in this book.

[32] See Hossam A. El-Saghir, "CISG in Islamic Countries: The Case of Egypt," Chapter 30 in this book.

[33] See Ingeborg Schwenzer, "Divergent Interpretations: Reasons and Solutions," Chapter 8 in this book.

[34] See Camilla Andersen, "CISG in National Courts," Chapter 6 in this book.

[35] See Lisa Spagnolo, "CISG as Soft Law and Choice of Law: Gōjū Ryū?," Chapter 11 in this book.

On a more sobering note, Professor Ulrich Schroeter cautions against practicing attorneys too readily excluding the application of the CISG due to the potential for professional liability or malpractice claims.[36] The widespread use of choice of law clauses to opt out of the CISG is well known, but Schroeter asserts that there has been a more recent pro-CISG trend. More importantly, the depth of the CISG case law and scholarly commentary requires practicing attorneys to make informed decisions on whether to opt out of the CISG. Those attorneys unwilling to expend the time to familiarize themselves with its rules subject themselves to the risks of professional liability.

On an even more sobering note, Professor Jan Smits indicates that the problems associated with the CISG are the same problems that beset all uniform laws. Furthermore, in the short term, at least, these problems may be insurmountable.[37] It may be that the CISG's best use is as a guide for parties in selecting the most appropriate national law to apply to their transactions, and in derogating from specific rules found in a given national law: "The great value of the CISG may be that it provides commercial parties with a common frame of reference in which they are able to compare the solutions provided by the CISG with various national jurisdictions. In this way, provisions of the CISG can be used to derogate from specific rules of the national law chosen by the parties." Of course, it is the hope of many CISG scholars that the CISG will eventually reach a point of being perceived as a viable supranational sales law for purposes of choice of law.

IV. Marketplace for Transborder Commercial Law

The CISG is a significant achievement in the harmonization of international private law, but its ultimate impact as a global sales law is yet to be determined. The ultimate measurement of its success will be its use as the preferred default law regime in international transactions. That outcome will depend on its proving itself as the more efficient alternative to the choice of national laws or other supranational hard and soft law instruments that are available. Currently, two obstacles to the CISG ultimately reaching its intended goals of a uniform global sale law are what can be referred to as the interpretation problem and the comprehensiveness problem. In the end, merchants' foremost preference is transactional certainty, which includes a level of certainty and predictability in the law applied and how it will be applied to any future disputes. Second, merchants prefer simplicity in the chosen legal regime. The first preference goes to the interpretation problem and the send to the comprehensiveness problem. These two problems are not mutually exclusive. For example, the method and breadth of interpretation impacts the comprehensiveness or scope of the law.

One extremely important issue of interpretation is the principle of good faith. The good faith principle can be seen as an interpretive methodology in itself.[38] Good faith is a means to interpret ambiguous provisions of the CISG, to fill in the gaps within its intended scope, and to guide rule adjustments in novel cases. In the area of contract interpretation, good faith can be used to interpret contracts and recognize obligations; it can be used

---

[36] See Ulrich Schroeter, "Empirical Evidence of Courts and Counsels' Approach to the CISG (with Some Remarks on Professional Liability)," Chapter 40 in this book.

[37] Jan M. Smits, "Problems of Uniform Laws," Chapter 37 in this book.

[38] DiMatteo and Janssen, Chapter 7.

to fill in gaps in the contract and to imply terms. The heavy use of the reasonableness standard throughout the CISG provides the avenue for good faith to construct fair terms and to mark off the distinction between permissible and impermissible conduct. But, it can also be the cause of much uncertainty. Commercial parties may avoid a law that is viewed as being more concerned with substantive fairness than with freedom of contract. Francesco Mazzotta frames the issue as follows: "Situations where good faith or lack thereof requires a court's intervention is not the problem; the problem arises when, deliberately or unconsciously, good faith is used to rewrite the contractual relationship to be more just or equitable."[39] Luca Castellani asserts that some of the CISG's lack of comprehensiveness can be remedied by the use of complementary instruments.[40] The CISG is just one of a number of UNCITRAL instruments that can be used together.

Ole Lando illustrates the commonalities between the CISG and subsequently developed soft laws.[41] He notes that the PECL, DCFR, and PICC adopted many CISG rules, but, more importantly, explains why the drafters of those instruments chose to deviate from some CISG rules. In the end, what distinguishes the CISG from these other efforts is its hard law status. Its success will be achieved not just by its wide adoption, but in educating practitioners, jurists, and law students in its usefulness as an international sales law. Helena Haapio offers a framework (proactive lawyering) and a pedagogical method (visualization) that can be used to better educate these audiences.[42]

The number of instruments, some noted in the previous paragraph, attempting to provide alternative international sales or contract law regimes continues to increase. Some of these instruments have long histories, such as English sales law as international sales law, and, more recently, the proposed Common European Sales Law (CESL). Professor Qi Zhou makes a forceful argument that English sales law has long served the role of an international sales law and that in many ways it is a superior law.[43] The CESL, whether or not adopted as published in 2011, offers some additional coverage beyond the scope of the CISG, such as rules relating to the supply of digital content and trade-related services that may be mined by contract drafters and arbitrators.

In closing, it is important to note that the CISG has served as a powerful educational tool in understanding the many similarities in contract-sales law rules, as well as the significant divergences, across different national legal systems. Professor Sieg Eiselen notes how the CISG has served to help bridge the "civil–common law divide."[44] He notes that those dealing with the CISG by necessity have had to engage in a comparative analysis. This has been true for scholars teaching the CISG, students who benefit from the CISG's embrace of civil and common law rules, jurists and arbitrators who work within the CISG interpretive methodology in making well-reasoned opinions, and legal practitioners who take the time to educate themselves on the substance and benefits of utilizing the CISG in their practices.

[39] See Francesco Mazzotta, "Good Faith Principle: *Vexata Quaestio*," Chapter 9 in this book.
[40] See Luca Castellani, "CISG in Context of Complementary Texts," Chapter 42 in this book.
[41] See Ole Lando, "Soft Laws as Models for the Improvement of the CISG," Chapter 43 in this book.
[42] See Helena Haapio, "Using the CISG Proactively," Chapter 44 in this book.
[43] See Qi Zhou, "CISG and English Sales Law: An Unfair Competition," Chapter 41 in this book.
[44] See Sieg Eiselen, "CISG as Bridge between Common and Civil Law," Chapter 38 in this book.

Index